Teacher's Manual

Volume 1

Stephen Hake

A Harcourt Achieve Imprint

www.SaxonPublishers.com
1-800-284-7019

Acknowledgements

This book was made possible by the significant contributions of many individuals and the dedicated efforts of a talented team at Harcourt Achieve.

Special thanks to:

- Melody Simmons and Chris Braun for suggestions and explanations for problem solving in Courses 1-3,
- Elizabeth Rivas and Bryon Hake for their extensive contributions to lessons and practice in Course 3,
- Sue Ellen Fealko for suggested application problems in Course 3.

The long hours and technical assistance of John and James Hake on Courses 1-3, Robert Hake on Course 3, Tom Curtis on Course 3, and Roger Phan on Course 3 were invaluable in meeting publishing deadlines. The saintly patience and unwavering support of Mary is most appreciated.

– Stephen Hake

Staff Credits

Editorial: Jean Armstrong, Shelley Farrar-Coleman, Marc Connolly, Hirva Raj, Brooke Butner, Robin Adams, Roxanne Picou, Cecilia Colome, Michael Ota

Design: Alison Klassen, Joan Cunningham, Deborah Diver, Alan Klemp, Andy Hendrix, Rhonda Holcomb

Production: Mychael Ferris-Pacheco, Heather Jernt, Greg Gaspard, Donna Brawley, John-Paxton Gremillion

Manufacturing: Cathy Voltaggio

Marketing: Marilyn Trow, Kimberly Sadler

E-Learning: Layne Hedrick, Karen Stitt

ISBN 978-1-5914-1785-9
ISBN 1-5914-1785-6

8 9 0868 12 11 10
4500236978

Course 1
Content Overview

Teacher's Manual, Volume 1

Saxon Math: The Look of Results T5

Saxon Math: A Different Look T6

Saxon Math: A Different Approach T8

Saxon Math: Better Results T16

Saxon Math: Saxon Math Works T18
- Lesson structure
- Accessibility
- Assessment
- Program Resources

Table of Contents T25

Contents by Strands T37

Introduction to Problem Solving 1A

Section 1: Lessons 1–10, Investigation 1 .... 7A

Section 2: Lessons 11–20, Investigation 2 .... 58A

Section 3: Lessons 21–30, Investigation 3 .... 112A

Section 4: Lessons 31–40, Investigation 4 .... 164A

Section 5: Lessons 41–50, Investigation 5 .... 216A

Section 6: Lessons 51–60, Investigation 6 .... 268A

Glossary with Spanish Vocabulary T638

Index T646

Scope and Sequence T659

Teacher's Manual, Volume 2

Table of Contents T5

Contents by Strands T17

Section 7: Lessons 61–70, Investigation 7 .... 320A

Section 8: Lessons 71–80, Investigation 8 .... 368A

Section 9: Lessons 81–90, Investigation 9 .... 421A

Section 10: Lessons 91–100, Investigation 10 .... 474A

Section 11: Lessons 101–110, Investigation 11 .... 528A

Section 12: Lessons 111–120, Investigation 12 .... 582A

Glossary with Spanish Vocabulary T638

Index T646

Scope and Sequence T659

ABOUT THE AUTHOR

Stephen Hake has authored five books in the Saxon Math series. He writes from 17 years of classroom experience as a teacher in grades 5 through 12 and as a math specialist in El Monte, California. As a math coach, his students won honors and recognition in local, regional, and statewide competitions.

Stephen has been writing math curriculum since 1975 and for Saxon since 1985. He has also authored several math contests including Los Angeles County's first Math Field Day contest. Stephen contributed to the 1999 National Academy of Science publication on the Nature and Teaching of Algebra in the Middle Grades.

Stephen is a member of the National Council of Teachers of Mathematics and the California Mathematics Council. He earned his BA from United States International University and his MA from Chapman College.

EDUCATIONAL CONSULTANTS

Nicole Hamilton
Consultant Manager
Richardson, TX

Joquita McKibben
Consultant Manager
Pensacola, FL

John Anderson
Lowell, IN

Beckie Fulcher
Gulf Breeze, FL

Heidi Graviette
Stockton, CA

Brenda Halulka
Atlanta, GA

Marilyn Lance
East Greenbush, NY

Ann Norris
Wichita Falls, TX

Melody Simmons
Nogales, AZ

Benjamin Swagerty
Moore, OK

Kristyn Warren
Macedonia, OH

Mary Warrington
East Wenatchee, WA

SAXON MATH™

In a world where all textbooks are alike,

Saxon Math is DIFFERENT.

Saxon Math's differences make the difference in helping middle school students master the standards and obtain a foundation for algebra – with an understanding that lasts for a lifetime.

DIFFERENT LOOK

- *Distributed Units of Instruction*
- *Integrated Strands*
- *Incremental Learning*

DIFFERENT APPROACH

- *All mathematics is problem solving*
- *The meaning behind the proportion*
- *Embedded algebraic thinking*

BETTER RESULTS

- *Measurable*
- *Immediate*
- *Long-lasting*

Saxon Math
The New Look of Results in Middle School Mathematics

SAXON MATH™

Do you want students to master the standards and retain what they learn?

Saxon Math is the NEW LOOK OF RESULTS for today's standards, where mastery learning is required of all students.

Saxon Math builds depth in the standards by integrating and distributing the strands.

Distributed Units of Instruction

Mastery of standards happens at different rates for different students.

Saxon Math's distributed approach breaks apart traditional units and then distributes and integrates the concepts across the year. This creates a learning curve that provides the time most students need to master each part of every standard. With this approach, no skills or concepts get dropped and students retain what they have learned well beyond the test.

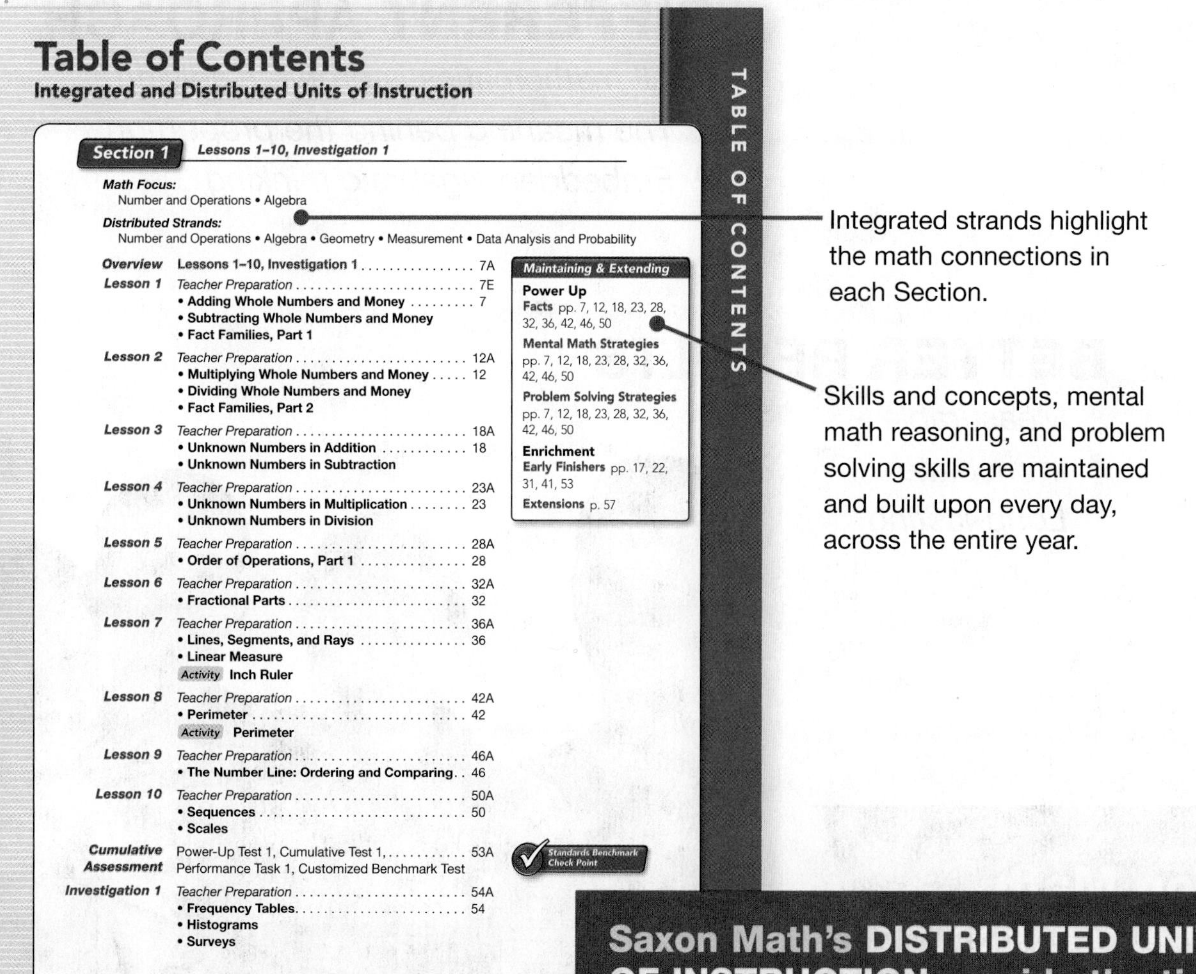

Table of Contents

Integrated and Distributed Units of Instruction

TABLE OF CONTENTS

Section 1 *Lessons 1–10, Investigation 1*

Math Focus:
Number and Operations • Algebra

Distributed Strands:
Number and Operations • Algebra • Geometry • Measurement • Data Analysis and Probability

Overview	Lessons 1–10, Investigation 1	7A
Lesson 1	*Teacher Preparation*	7E
	• Adding Whole Numbers and Money	7
	• Subtracting Whole Numbers and Money	
	• Fact Families, Part 1	
Lesson 2	*Teacher Preparation*	12A
	• Multiplying Whole Numbers and Money	12
	• Dividing Whole Numbers and Money	
	• Fact Families, Part 2	
Lesson 3	*Teacher Preparation*	18A
	• Unknown Numbers in Addition	18
	• Unknown Numbers in Subtraction	
Lesson 4	*Teacher Preparation*	23A
	• Unknown Numbers in Multiplication	23
	• Unknown Numbers in Division	
Lesson 5	*Teacher Preparation*	28A
	• Order of Operations, Part 1	28
Lesson 6	*Teacher Preparation*	32A
	• Fractional Parts	32
Lesson 7	*Teacher Preparation*	36A
	• Lines, Segments, and Rays	36
	• Linear Measure	
	Activity Inch Ruler	
Lesson 8	*Teacher Preparation*	42A
	• Perimeter	42
	Activity Perimeter	
Lesson 9	*Teacher Preparation*	46A
	• The Number Line: Ordering and Comparing	46
Lesson 10	*Teacher Preparation*	50A
	• Sequences	50
	• Scales	
Cumulative Assessment	Power-Up Test 1, Cumulative Test 1, Performance Task 1, Customized Benchmark Test	53A
Investigation 1	*Teacher Preparation*	54A
	• Frequency Tables	54
	• Histograms	
	• Surveys	

Maintaining & Extending
Power Up
Facts pp. 7, 12, 18, 23, 28, 32, 36, 42, 46, 50
Mental Math Strategies pp. 7, 12, 18, 23, 28, 32, 36, 42, 46, 50
Problem Solving Strategies pp. 7, 12, 18, 23, 28, 32, 36, 42, 46, 50
Enrichment
Early Finishers pp. 17, 22, 31, 41, 53
Extensions p. 57

Standards Benchmark Check Point

Integrated strands highlight the math connections in each Section.

Skills and concepts, mental math reasoning, and problem solving skills are maintained and built upon every day, across the entire year.

Saxon Math's DISTRIBUTED UNITS OF INSTRUCTION provide the time for every student to master the standards.

Integrated Strands

Connections are the foundation for long-term retention of learning.

Rather than separating decimals from fractions from geometry, as in a typical chapter approach, Saxon Math integrates and connects strands on a daily basis. Students see the relationships within mathematics as they develop their understanding of a concept.

In addition to its integrated instructional approach, the textbook also provides integrated review, practice and assessment throughout.

- Skills and concepts are kept alive through daily practice.
- Math connections are strengthened and made meaningful.
- Written practice sets are rich and varied – just like the state test.

Traditional Unit Structure

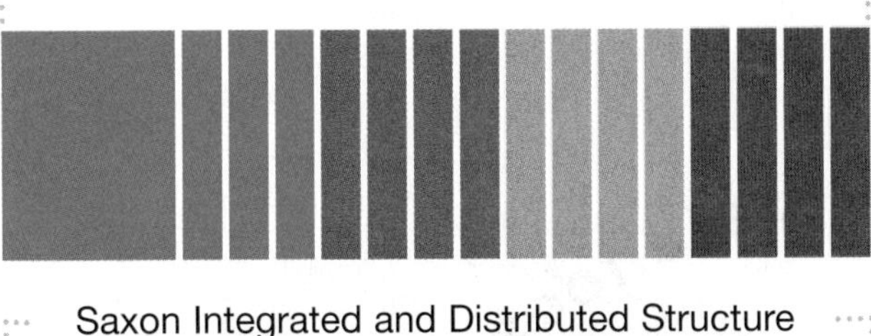

Saxon Integrated and Distributed Structure

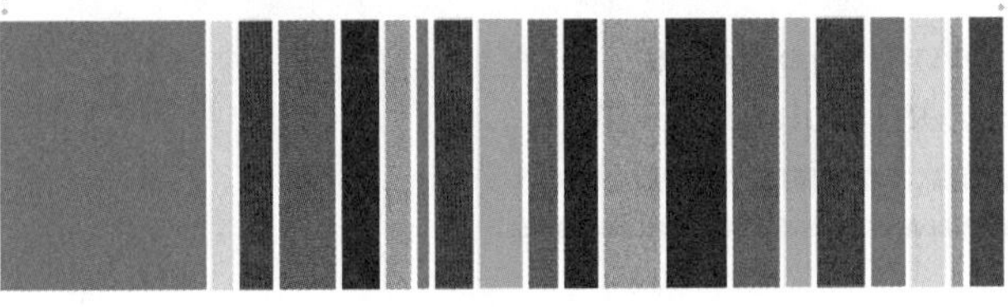

Saxon Math's INTEGRATED LEARNING results in students developing and retaining a deep understanding of mathematics.

Incremental Learning

Content is mastered through small increments followed by integrated practice and strategically-placed assessments.

Rather than learning all of a strand in a single chapter, Saxon Math instructs in smaller, more easily assimilated increments that are spread across the year. Students practice, review, and build connections to other strands every step of the way.

Before the next increment of a strand is introduced, students are assessed to check their progress. A level of mastery is reached for each increment of a strand through this consistent and integrated practice and assessment, which is distributed throughout the year.

Saxon Math's INCREMENTAL LEARNING provides a built-in system for tracking and benchmarking student mastery of every part of the standards.

Do you want students to be successful problem solvers?

Saxon Math: **The New Look of Results**

Saxon Math believes that *all* of mathematics is about PROBLEM SOLVING.

The organizing principle for the Saxon Math approach is mathematical thinking. Skills, concepts and problem solving are bridged by consistent mathematic language.

Mathematical Thinking Balances

Math Background	**Word Problems**
Relationship of Standards	**Problem Solving Skills**
Meanings of Operation	**Problem Solving Strategies**

Problem solving is more than word problems. Word problems cannot be successfully solved without an understanding of the meanings of operations and the relationship between the numbers in a problem. Teaching through mathematical thinking is the foundation for helping students become successful problem solvers.

Saxon Math's daily Problem Solving opportunities are:

- ***Guided***
- ***Embedded***
- ***Applied***

Guided Problem Solving

In addition to specific lessons on solving word problems, every lesson begins and ends with Problem Solving.

Guided problem solving instruction occurs every day and builds students' confidence as they are encouraged to use a variety of strategies to solve problems.

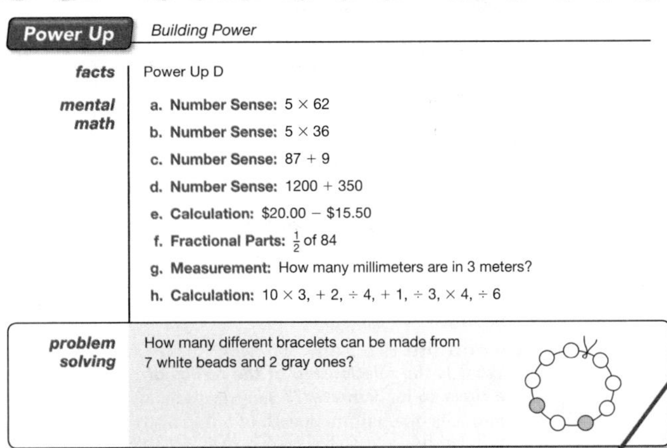

Power Up *Building Power*

facts	Power Up D
mental math	a. **Number Sense:** 5 × 62 b. **Number Sense:** 5 × 36 c. **Number Sense:** 87 + 9 d. **Number Sense:** 1200 + 350 e. **Calculation:** \$20.00 − \$15.50 f. **Fractional Parts:** $\frac{1}{2}$ of 84 g. **Measurement:** How many millimeters are in 3 meters? h. **Calculation:** 10 × 3, + 2, ÷ 4, + 1, ÷ 3, × 4, ÷ 6
problem solving	How many different bracelets can be made from 7 white beads and 2 gray ones?

Power Up Discussion *For use with Power Up, p. 123*

Problem-Solving Strategy: Use Logical Reasoning/ Draw a Diagram

Problem: How many different bracelets can be made from 7 white beads and 2 gray ones?

Understand **Understand the Problem**

"What information are we given?"

A bracelet is made of 9 beads: 7 white beads and 2 gray beads.

"What are we asked to do?"

Determine how many different bracelets can be made from 7 white beads and 2 gray beads.

"Is this a combination or permutation problem?"

It is a combination problem. Order is not important to our answer.

"What do we already know?"

We know that bracelets form a continuous circuit when clasped, which means we need to be careful not to mistakenly repeat any of our combinations.

Plan **Make a Plan**

"What problem-solving strategy will we use?"

We will *use logical reasoning* to *draw a diagram.*

"How can we modify the bracelet?"

It can be unclasped to form a string of beads, but keep in mind the bracelet will be clasped again to form a continuous circuit.

Solve **Carry out the Plan**

"What are the possible positionings for the two gray beads?"

The two gray beads can be right next to each other, or they can be separated by one, two or three beads.

"Are there bracelets with the gray beads separated by more than three beads?"

Yes, but they are the same as the bracelets above. Gray beads separated by 1 white bead are also separated by 6 white beads; by 2 white beads are also separated by 5 white beads; by 3 white beads are also separated by 4 white beads.

"So how many different bracelets can be made?"

Five.

Check **Look Back**

Verify your solutions by drawing the four combinations as clasped bracelets instead of unclasped.

123B **Saxon** *Math Course 1*

A suggested discussion guide following the four-step plan is provided in the **Teacher's Manual** to allow for a rich discussion of how and why a problem can be solved.

Extended problems in the **student text** provide students with more in-depth support for each problem solving strategy.

problem solving

What is the sum of the first ten even numbers?

Understand We are asked to find the sum of the first ten even numbers.

Plan We will begin by *making the problem simpler.* If the assignment had been to add the first *four* even numbers, we could simply add 2 + 4 + 6 + 8. However, adding columns of numbers can be time-consuming. We will try to *find a pattern* that will help add the even numbers 2–20 more quickly.

Solve We can find pairs of addends in the sequence that have the same sum and multiply by the number of pairs. We try this pairing technique on the sequence given in the problem:

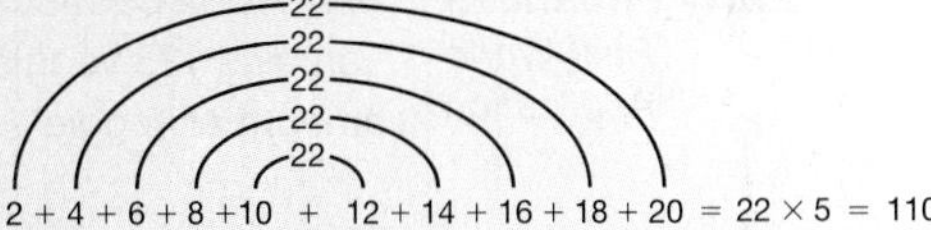

Check We found the sum of the first ten even numbers by pairing the addends and multiplying. We can verify our solution by adding the numbers one-by-one with pencil and paper or a calculator.

Embedded Problem Solving

Saxon Math develops higher-order thinking skills through the meaningful Math Conversations that occur every day in the cumulative Written Practice.

Students learn to express their understanding through these rich mathematical discussions. This is important in today's high-stakes testing, where it is not enough to compute and solve. Students have to explain their reasoning and thinking.

c. The distance from the center to the circle.

d. Explain If the diameter of a circle is 10 in., what is its radius? Describe how you know.

Written Practice *Strengthening Concepts*

1. (12) Analyze What is the product of the sum of 55 and 45 and the difference of 55 and 45?

* 2. (22) Model Potatoes are three-fourths water. If a sack of potatoes weighs 20 pounds, how many pounds of water are in the potatoes? Draw a diagram to illustrate the problem.

3. (11) Formulate There were 306 students in the cafeteria. After some went outside, there were 249 students left in the cafeteria. How many students went outside? Write an equation and solve the problem.

* 4. (27) Explain a. If the diameter of a circle is 5 in., what is the radius of the circle?

b. What is the relationship of the diameter of a circle to its radius?

5. (21) Classify Which of these numbers is divisible by both 2 and 3?
A 122 B 123 C 132

6. (16) Round 1,234,567 to the nearest ten thousand.

7. (15) Formulate If ten pounds of apples costs $12.90, what is the price per pound? Write an equation and solve the problem.

8. (6) What is the denominator of $\frac{23}{24}$?

* 9. (22) Model What number is $\frac{3}{5}$ of 65? Draw a diagram to illustrate the problem.

* 10. (22) Model How much money is $\frac{2}{3}$ of $15? Draw a diagram to illustrate the problem.

Model Use your fraction manipulatives to help answer problems 11–18.

11. (Inv. 2) $\frac{1}{6} + \frac{2}{6} + \frac{3}{6}$

12. (Inv. 2) $\frac{7}{8} - \frac{3}{8}$

13. (Inv. 2) $\frac{6}{6} - \frac{5}{6}$

14. (Inv. 2) $\frac{2}{8} + \frac{5}{8}$

15. (Inv. 2) a. How many $\frac{1}{8}$s are in 1?

b. How many $\frac{1}{8}$s are in $\frac{1}{2}$?

* 16. (26) Reduce: $\frac{4}{6}$

17. (Inv. 2) What fraction is half of $\frac{1}{4}$?

18. (Inv. 2) What fraction of a circle is 50% of a circle?

144 *Saxon Math Course 1*

3 Written Practice

Math Conversations

Discussion opportunities are provided below.

Problem 2 Model

Extend the Problem

"How can you find $\frac{3}{4}$ of 20 using mental math?" Sample: The denominator 4 means that the whole or 20 is divided into 4 equal parts, and each equal part is 20 ÷ 4 or 5. The numerator represents 3 of those equal parts, so 5 + 5 + 5 = 15.

Problem 4 Explain

Extend the Problem

"What is the relationship of the radius of a circle to its diameter?" In any circle, a radius is one-half the length of a diameter.

Problem 16 Explain

"Name the operation that is used to reduce a fraction, and explain how that operation is used." Division; divide the numerator and the denominator by a common factor of the numerator and the denominator. If the factor is the greatest common factor, the division will produce a fraction in simplest form.

Errors and Misconceptions

Problems 17

When students find one-half of a whole number, they simply divide the whole number by 2. However, when they are asked to find one-half of a unit fraction, simply dividing the denominator by 2 is a mistake. For example, $\frac{1}{2}$ of $\frac{1}{4} = \frac{1}{4 \div 2}$ is a common error.

Encourage students to use fraction manipulatives when finding a fractional part of a fraction. The manipulatives can help students see, for example, that $\frac{1}{2}$ of $\frac{1}{4}$ of a circle represents a part of the circle that is smaller than $\frac{1}{4}$.

(continued)

Teacher's Manual

Early Finishers *Real-World Application*

Mrs. Akiba bought 3 large bags of veggie sticks for her students. Each bag contains 125 veggie sticks. If $\frac{5}{6}$ of Mrs. Akiba's 30 students eat the same amount of veggie sticks, how many sticks will each student eat?

Students put it all together to solve multi-step problems in the Written Practice.

Applied Problem Solving

Saxon Math provides students with opportunities to dive more deeply into mathematics and its connections – within mathematical strands, to other subject areas, and as real-world applications.

Investigations

Every 10 Lessons

Students explore math in more depth through the Investigations. Using mathematical thinking, activities, and extensions, these Investigations allow students to develop a broader and deeper understanding of math concepts and connections.

13. Connect Form a whole circle using six of the $\frac{1}{6}$ pieces. Then remove (subtract) $\frac{1}{6}$. What fraction of the circle is left? What equation represents your model?

14. Demonstrate subtracting $\frac{1}{3}$ from 1 by forming a circle of $\frac{3}{3}$ and then removing $\frac{1}{3}$. What fraction is left?

Reading
< means
than
= means
equal to
> means
greater tha

112 Sa

INVESTIGATION 2

Focus on

• **Investigating Fractions with Manipulatives**

In this investigation you will make a set of fraction manipulatives to help you answer questions in this investigation and in future problem sets.

Activity

Using Fraction Manipulatives

Materials needed:

- Investigation Activities 2A–2F
- scissors
- envelope or zip-top bag to store fraction pieces

Preparation:

To make your own fraction manipulatives, cut out the fraction circles on the Investigation Activities. Then cut each fraction circle into its parts.

Thinking Skill
Connect
What percent is one whole circle?

Model Use your fraction manipulatives to help you with these exercises:

1. What percent of a circle is $\frac{1}{2}$ of a circle?
2. What fraction is half of $\frac{1}{2}$?
3. What fraction is half of $\frac{1}{4}$?
4. Fit three $\frac{1}{4}$ pieces together to form $\frac{3}{4}$ of a circle. Three fourths of a circle is what percent of a circle?
5. Fit four $\frac{1}{8}$ pieces together to form $\frac{4}{8}$ of a circle. Four eighths of a circle is what percent of a circle?
6. Fit three $\frac{1}{6}$ pieces together to form $\frac{3}{6}$ of a circle. Three sixths of a circle is what percent of a circle?
7. Show that $\frac{4}{8}$, $\frac{3}{6}$, and $\frac{2}{4}$ each make one half of a circle. (We say that $\frac{4}{8}$, $\frac{3}{6}$, and $\frac{2}{4}$ all *reduce* to $\frac{1}{2}$.)
8. The fraction $\frac{2}{8}$ equals which single fraction piece?
9. The fraction $\frac{6}{8}$ equals how many $\frac{1}{4}$s?
10. The fraction $\frac{2}{6}$ equals which single fraction piece?
11. The fraction $\frac{4}{6}$ equals how many $\frac{1}{3}$s?
12. The sum $\frac{1}{8} + \frac{1}{8} + \frac{1}{8}$ is $\frac{3}{8}$. If you add $\frac{3}{8}$ and $\frac{2}{8}$, what is the sum?

Investigation 2 111

Teacher Rubric

Criteria Performance	Knowledge and Skills Understanding	Communication and Representation	Process and Strategies
	The student got it! The	The student clearly	The student had an

Performance Task 3

The Four Corners States

Assign after Lesson 20 and Cumulative Test 3

Objectives

- Make a bar graph and a circle graph to display the same data.
- Formulate a question that can be answered by data.
- Communicate ideas through writing.

Materials

Name ____________________

Performance Task 3A
For use with Performance Task 3

Did you know that you could stand in four states at the same time? The boundaries of Utah, Colorado, New Mexico and Arizona—*The Four Corners States*—form a common geographic point. It is the only place in the United States where this occurs.

We can use data and graphs to gain understanding about the size and geographic characteristics of this unique area. Use the *The Four Corners States* Data Charts to complete all tasks.

1. **Make a bar graph and sketch a circle graph to display the land areas of the four states.**

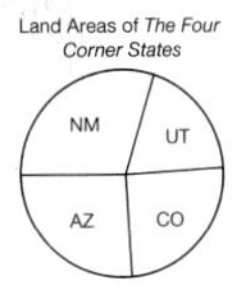

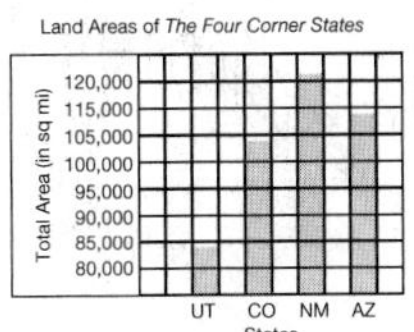

37 *Saxon Math Course 1*

Performance Tasks and Activities

Every 5 Lessons

Students apply math to real-world situations within a performance environment. Integrating problem solving with math concepts, these Tasks and Activities allow students to explore topics in the real world and to explain their thinking with open ended questions. Both teacher and student rubrics are included.

Do you want students to develop strong proportional thinking?

Saxon Math: The New Look of Results

Saxon Math focuses on how to SET UP THE PROPORTION and give meaning to the numbers in the problem.

The hardest part that students have with solving problems involving proportions is to ask themselves the right questions to set up the proportion. Students' natural inclination is to go directly to the computing!

Proportional Thinking

Proportional thinking development begins in Saxon Math with the meaning of ratio and how to solve a proportion. Then students solve simple ratio problems and build to the more complex applications of proportion.

Proportional thinking is very important to understanding mathematics because proportions are used in a variety of real-world situations and across math strands. Students use proportions to solve problems involving ratios, percents, measurement, scale drawings, and similar triangles in geometry.

The Ratio Box

The ratio box is a graphic organizer that helps students to translate the words of a problem into a proportional form.

The ratio box helps students to:

- translate the words to establish the relationship of the information,
- set up an equation or proportion to solve, and
- eliminate the chance they will make an error.

The ratio of parrots to macaws was 5 to 7 at a bird sanctuary. If there were 75 parrots, how many macaws were there?

In this problem there are two kinds of numbers: ratio numbers and actual count numbers. The ratio numbers are 5 and 7. The number 75 is an actual count of parrots. We will arrange these numbers in two columns and two rows to form the ratio box.

	Ratio	Actual Count
Parrots	5	75
Macaws	7	*m*

We were not given the actual count for macaws so we used *m* to stand for the number of macaws. The numbers in this ratio box can be used to write a proportion.

	Ratio	Actual Count
Parrots	5	75
Macaws	7	*m*

$$\frac{5}{7} = \frac{75}{m}$$

$$5m = 525$$

$$m = 105$$

There were 105 macaws.

The ratio box provides a consistent way to help students translate problems, especially application problems and more complex problems. Using the same graphic organizer for ratio, rate, proportion, and percent helps students understand, connect, and solve problems that involve proportional thinking.

Skills and Concept Trace

See the complete trace for ratios and proportional thinking in the Scope and Sequence starting on p. T659.

Do you want students to develop strong algebraic thinking?

Saxon Math: The New Look of Results

Saxon Math embeds ALGEBRAIC THINKING throughout the curriculum – not as a separate math topic.

Embedded Algebraic Thinking

There is no new math in algebra—only new language and symbolism. Without connections to arithmetic thinking, algebra has little meaning to students. Saxon Math provides that link from arithmetic to algebra.

Algebraic thinking in Saxon Math is embedded and distributed across the course in small increments, as part of every strand, not as a separate unit of instruction or topic. The distributed approach in the textbook lends itself better to providing this kind of natural integration.

Preparing for Algebra 1 Success

Although Saxon Math uses a distributed approach, all the expected algebraic topics are covered in the textbook. Patterns, relations, and functions are presented early in the student text and are reviewed and practiced throughout the year. Order of operations are applied to whole numbers, integers, rational numbers, and exponents. Students build on their understanding of variables and expressions and extend them to equations and inequalities. Students also analyze patterns and functions leading to graphing on the coordinate plane.

The development of algebraic thinking progresses from Course 1 to Course 3, building a solid foundation for students to have confidence and success in Algebra 1.

Algebraic Patterns in Problem Solving

Saxon Math provides support for helping students move from the WORDS in a problem to a non-numeric representation to writing an equation.

The Saxon Math approach to writing an equation to solve word problems:

Read → *Translate* → *Write a word equation* → *Draw a diagram* → *Write an equation* → *Solve*

The most intimidating part of algebra is word problems — translating a situation into an equation, a mathematical model.

Rather than categorize word problems, Saxon Math focuses students on the "plot." What is this story about? Are we combining or separating? Are we comparing? Are we making equal groups?

If students can identify the plot, then they can define the relationship in an equation: $a + b = c$, or $a - b = c$, or $ab = c$. When they know the plot and its corresponding relationship or formula, then students substitute, use a variable for the unknown, and solve for the unknown.

Saxon Math uses word problems to teach students how to model algebraically the commonly encountered mathematical relationships of everyday life.

Read the problem and identify the plot or pattern:

The trip odometer in Odell's car read 47 miles when he started. At the end of his trip, the odometer read 114 miles. How many miles did he travel?

Translate:

SOME + SOME MORE = TOTAL

Write a word equation and draw a diagram:

$$S + M = T$$

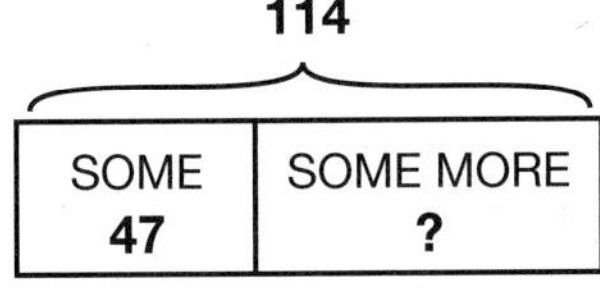

Write an equation:

$$47 + M = 114$$

Solve:

$$114 - 47 = 67$$

Odell travelled 67 miles.

Saxon Math teaches a variety of patterns or relationships that can be found in word problems.

- Addition pattern
- How many more/fewer pattern
- Larger-smaller-difference pattern
- Later-earlier-difference pattern
- Some and some more
- Subtraction pattern: Some went away

Do you want higher student achievement and increased test scores?

Saxon Math: **The New Look of Results**

Saxon Math has a long history of MEASURABLE STUDENT IMPROVEMENT – backed by years of research.

Immediate, Measurable, and Long-Lasting Results

The demands of today's state testing environment make clear the importance of selecting a math program that can deliver results. Saxon Math's look and approach have a proven track record of higher standardized test scores and subject mastery.

The evidence found on these pages is *just a selection* from the extensive body of

- independent research studies,
- case histories and
- efficacy studies

that all point to Saxon Math's power to achieve better results for students and their schools.

See how Saxon Math has built long-lasting achievement in classrooms across the nation. Saxon's results are immediate and schools show growth in one year's time. Their results are measurable quantitatively and qualitatively through test scores and customer testimonials. Saxon Math's results speak for themselves.

SEE THE RESULTS FOR YOURSELF!

For a complete report on Saxon Math Results, go to www.SaxonPublishers.com.

"Our students' test scores, math abilities and confidence have sky-rocketed."

Scott Neuman, Seventh and Eighth Grade Teacher, Humboldt Park Elementary, Milwaukee, Wisconsin

Discover What Schools Think

"The continual review and practice of concepts is very effective with my students. I also believe the mental math has developed the students to be better mathematical thinkers and has taught them how to use strategies to solve problems."

Jan Stevenson, Math Teacher, Davis County Middle School, Bloomfield, Iowa

"At a school where over 80 percent of our kids qualify for free lunch and their average grade-level equivalency upon entering fifth grade is 2.5, I have been phenomenally impressed with how well Saxon works for our kids… Saxon has helped our kids see the connections between mathematical concepts. None of the skills are taught in isolation and each new skill is woven into subsequent lessons. Our kids experience such a dramatic shift in the way they see numbers and operations that I know they are getting the foundation they need for higher-level mathematics."

Sarah Hayes, Vice Principal KIPP D.C., KEY Academy, Washington, D.C.

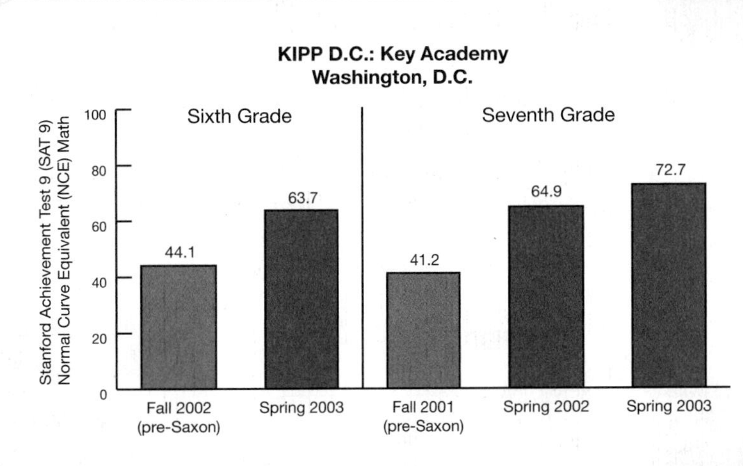

"We have been using Saxon Math for the past 13 years and have no desire to change to another series. Saxon works. Students and parents consistently express positive attitudes about Saxon and math in general. Students feel confident they can do math. Our students excel in all areas, including problem solving and computation. We have consistently scored among the top schools in the state since we started using Saxon. Teachers are confident that students understand how to use math concepts even when confronted with new problems."

David W. Schweltzer, Math Chairman, Michael Grimmer Middle School, Schererville, Indiana

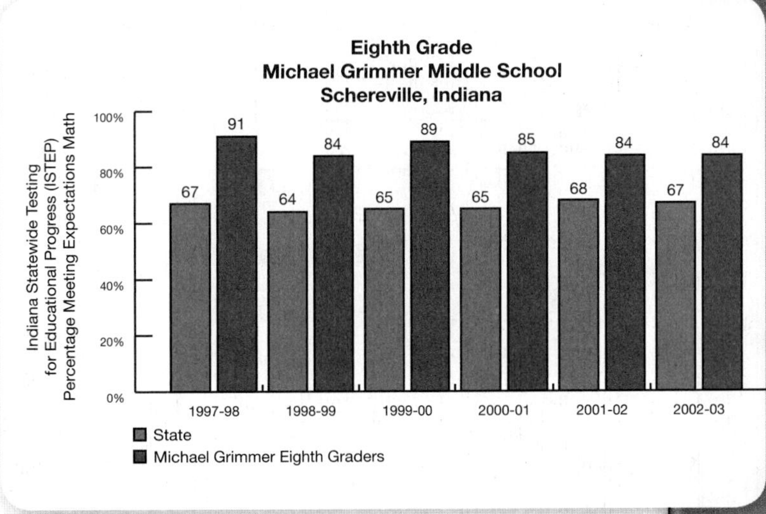

"We have found that Saxon Math eliminates the gaps in our students' achievement. Students are excited to learn. They can see a real-world connection to their learning. The fact practice ensures future success of recalling facts and ensures immediate recall… "

Dianne Tetreault, Principal, Cambridge Educational Academy, Boca Raton, Florida

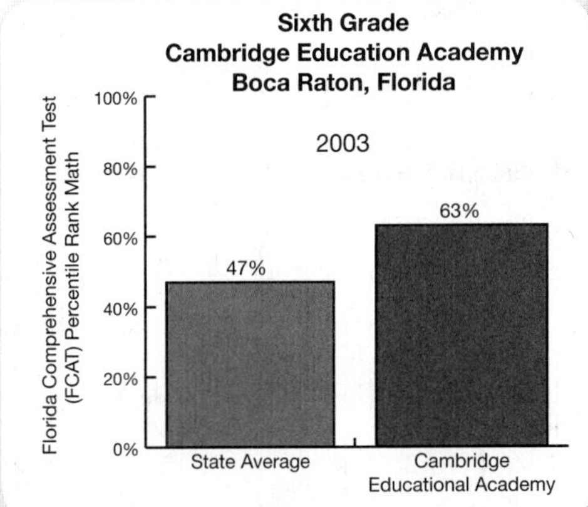

Saxon Math Works . . .

with a Consistent Lesson Structure that Enhances Success

Every lesson in Saxon Math follows the same three-part lesson plan.

This regular format allows students to become comfortable with the lessons and to know what to expect each day. By not including loud colorful photographs, Saxon Math with its predictable format lets students focus solely on the mathematics. The color and vibrancy of mathematics comes from the students' learning.

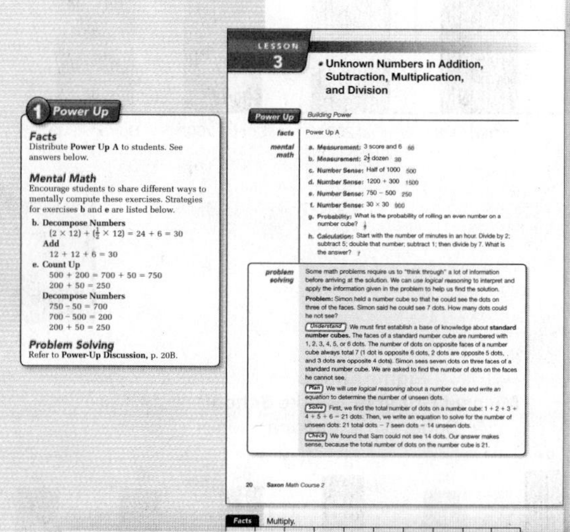

1 Power Up — Prevention Through Built-In Intervention

The **Power Up** at the beginning of every lesson provides daily reinforcement and building of:

- basic skills and concepts
- mental math
- problem solving strategies

Daily work on these problems results in automaticity of basic skills and mastery of mental math and problem solving strategies. For those students who need extra time, the Saxon approach allows for mastery gradually over time.

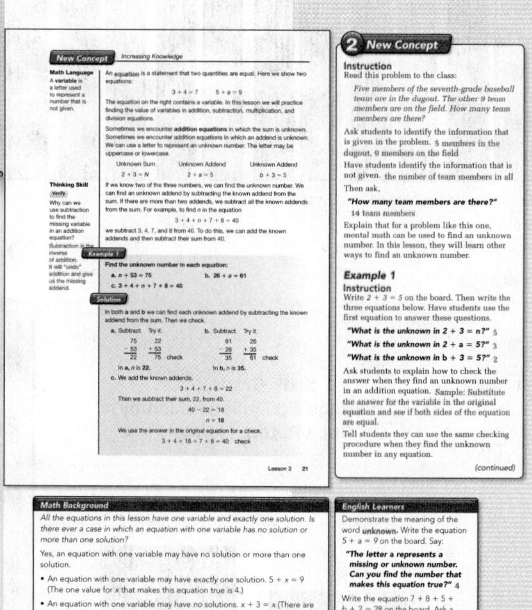

2 New Concepts — Increase Student Knowledge

Using clear explanations and a set of examples that build in depth, the **New Concepts** expand students' knowledge. Thinking skill questions, reading math hints, and math language tips help students understand how and why the math works.

Through the in-lesson **Activities**, students explore math concepts using manipulatives and other materials.

Have students work the **Practice Set** in class to see how well each student understands today's new skills and concepts.

3 Written Practice — Distributed and Integrated

Students attain a depth of understanding on a particular concept by practicing it over time and in a variety of ways. The **Written Practice** provides that depth with its integrated and distributed practice—allowing students to review, maintain, and build on concepts and skills previously taught.

To help students build their mathematical language, Saxon Math provides continual exposure to and review of **math vocabulary.**

Once a skill has been taught, students move to **higher order thinking skills** and applications of that concept. Students become confident and successful with both basic concepts and the richer, deeper mathematics that is the foundation of later math courses.

The distributed mixed practice is unpredictable and therefore challenging. It mirrors the format of state tests, giving students a **test prep** experience every day!

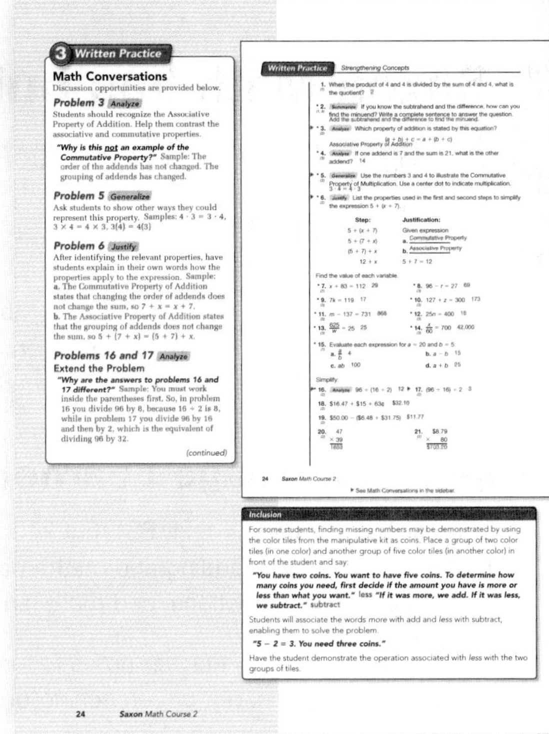

3 Written Practice

Math Conversations

Discussion opportunities are provided below.

Problem 3 Analyze

Students should recognize the Associative Property of Addition. Help them contrast the associative and commutative properties.

"Why is this not an example of the Commutative Property?" Sample: The order of the addends has not changed. The grouping of addends has changed.

Problem 5 Generalize

Ask students to show other ways they could represent this property. Samples: $4 \cdot 3 = 3 \cdot 4$, $3 \times 4 = 4 \times 3$, $3(4) = 4(3)$

Problem 6 Justify

After identifying the relevant properties, have students explain in their own words how the properties apply to the expression. Sample:
a. The Commutative Property of Addition states that changing the order of addends does not change the sum, so $7 + x = x + 7$.
b. The Associative Property of Addition states that the grouping of addends does not change the sum, so $5 + (7 + x) = (5 + 7) + x$.

Problems 16 and 17 Analyze

Extend the Problem

"Why are the answers to problems 16 and 17 different?" Sample: You must work inside the parentheses first. So, in problem 16 you divide 96 by 8, because $16 \div 2$ is 8, while in problem 17 you divide 96 by 16 and then by 2, which is the equivalent of dividing 96 by 32.

(continued)

Written Practice *Strengthening Concepts*

1. When the product of 4 and 4 is divided by the sum of 4 and 4, what is the quotient? 2

*2. Summarize If you know the subtrahend and the difference, how can you find the minuend? Write a complete sentence to answer the question. Add the subtrahend and the difference to find the minuend.

*3. Analyze Which property of addition is stated by this equation?
$(a + b) + c = a + (b + c)$
Associative Property of Addition

*4. Analyze If one addend is 7 and the sum is 21, what is the other addend? 14

*5. Generalize Use the numbers 3 and 4 to illustrate the Commutative Property of Multiplication. Use a center dot to indicate multiplication. $3 \cdot 4 = 4 \cdot 3$

*6. Justify List the properties used in the first and second steps to simplify the expression $5 + (x + 7)$.

Step:	Justification:
$5 + (x + 7)$	Given expression
$5 + (7 + x)$	a. Commutative Property
$(5 + 7) + x$	b. Associative Property
$12 + x$	$5 + 7 = 12$

Find the value of each variable.

*7. $x + 83 = 112$ 29 — *8. $96 - r = 27$ 69

*9. $7k = 119$ 17 — *10. $127 + z = 300$ 173

*11. $m - 137 = 731$ 868 — *12. $25n = 400$ 16

*13. $\frac{625}{w} = 25$ 25 — *14. $\frac{x}{60} = 700$ 42,000

*15. Evaluate each expression for $a = 20$ and $b = 5$:
a. $\frac{a}{b}$ 4 — b. $a - b$ 15
c. ab 100 — d. $a + b$ 25

Simplify:

16. Analyze $96 \div (16 \div 2)$ 12 — 17. $(96 \div 16) \div 2$ 3

18. $16.47 + $15 + 63¢ $32.10

19. $50.00 − ($6.48 + $31.75) $11.77

20. 47×39 1833 — 21. $8.79 × 80 $703.20

24 Saxon Math Course 2

▸ See Math Conversations in the sidebar.

Inclusion

For some students, finding missing numbers may be demonstrated by using the color tiles from the manipulative kit as coins. Place a group of two color tiles (in one color) and another group of five color tiles (in another color) in front of the student and say:

"You have two coins. You want to have five coins. To determine how many coins you need, first decide if the amount you have is more or less than what you want." less ***"If it was more, we add. If it was less, we subtract."*** subtract

Students will associate the words *more* with add and *less* with subtract, enabling them to solve the problem.

"5 − 2 = 3. You need three coins."

Have the student demonstrate the operation associated with *less* with the two groups of tiles.

24 Saxon Math Course 2

Recommended Daily Pacing

The Saxon distributed approach is unique in that the focus of the day is mainly on the rich depth of content in the distributed Written Practice.

In a typical 60-min class period, the author suggests you spend about half of the class period having the students complete the Written Practice problems. This allows you to have meaningful math conversations with students as they work out the problems.

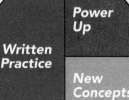

Saxon Math Works...

for All Students

Saxon Math has built-in support to help you customize and differentiate instruction.

The consistent lesson format of Saxon Math provides a predictable routine that enables all learners to be successful. By focusing on the mathematics and not the "fluff" seen in other math texts, Saxon Math makes higher-level mathematical thinking accessible for every student.

English Language Learners

Throughout the student text, ESL/ELL students will find structures to help them acquire mathematical understanding and mathematical language. Visual models, hands-on activities, mathematical conversations, and math language prompts all help students in their daily learning.

The **English Learners** teacher notes focus on language acquisition, not on reteaching or simplifying the math.

Proven Approach

- Define/Hear
- Model/Connect
- Discuss/Explain
- Apply/Use

For Spanish speakers, the **Glossary** in the student text provides a Spanish translation of each math term. The complete program is also available in Spanish.

> ***English Learners***
>
> For example 4, explain the meaning of the word **occupied.** Say:
>
> ***"The word occupied means taken up by or filled by."***
>
> Write 4.63271 on the board. Point to the seven and say:
>
> ***"The number 7 fills up this space."***
>
> Have students find the place occupied by 2, 3 and 4, answering with the phrase: "The place occupied by 3 is...", and so on.

Advanced Learners

The **Early Finishers** in the Written Practice offers the opportunity to deepen mathematical learning with problem solving, cross-curricular, and enrichment activities.

The **Extensions** in the Investigations allow students to expand their knowledge of the Investigation concepts, sharpen their higher-order thinking skills, and explore more connections.

The **Extend the Problem** suggestions in the Teacher's Manual provide even more ways to engage the advanced learner.

Special Education Students

Adaptations for Saxon Math: A Complete and Parallel Program

The flexible curriculum design of ***Adaptations for Saxon Math*** can be integrated into inclusion classrooms, pullout programs, or self-contained resource classrooms **—ensuring that Special Education students keep pace with the core curriculum.**

The unique design organizes exercises in ways that open the doors to success for students with a variety of learning disabilities, such as:

- Visual-motor integration
- Distractibility or lack of focus
- Receptive language
- Fine motor coordination
- Number reversal in reading and copy work
- Math anxiety
- Verbal explanation
- Spatial organization

Each adapted lesson begins with a **lesson summary**—an important reference tool for special education students and valuable for parents.

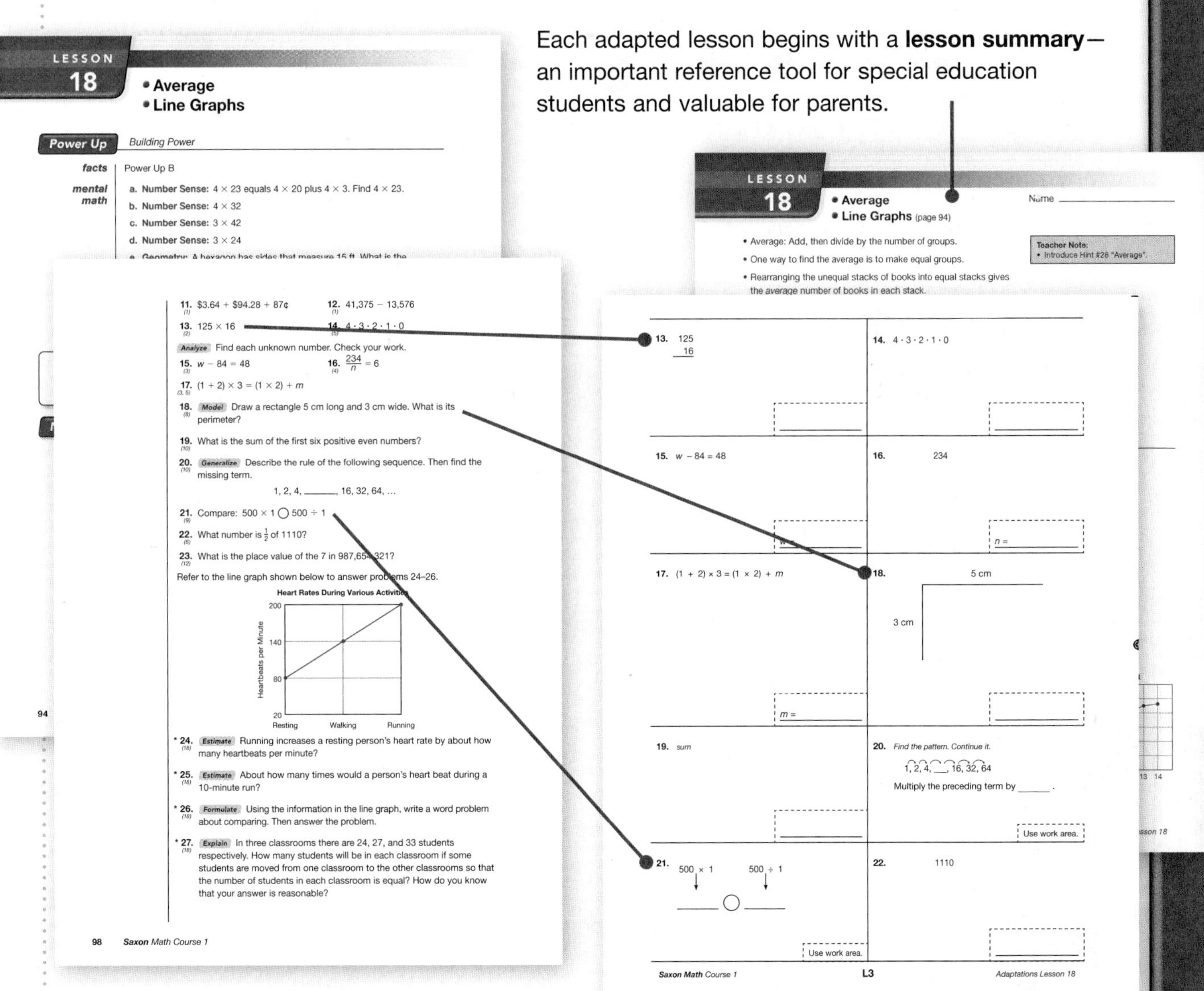

The carefully-structured layout of the **Practice exercises** helps special education students focus on mastering the concept, rather than figuring out the directions.

Saxon Math Works...

in Assessing for Learning and for Accountability

Assessments can be categorized in two ways, both of which are valuable and necessary in helping students succeed in mathematics.

Saxon Math provides opportunities for "Assessment for Learning" and for "Assessment of Learning."

Assessment *FOR* Learning	Assessment *OF* Learning
Purpose: Improvement	*Purpose:* Accountability
Assess continuously **during** teaching to influence learning.	Assess periodically **after** teaching to gather evidence of learning.
Use for immediate **feedback** to intervene, if necessary, on a particular concept.	Use **to judge** learning, usually in the form of a grade or score.

Assessment *FOR* Learning

The instructional design of Saxon Math effectively helps you to identify immediately any learning gaps and to provide intervention to keep students on track. Assessments to gauge student progress are throughout every lesson. You can use these classroom assessments and their continuous flow of information about student achievement to advance, not merely check on, student progress.

Daily Checks on New Content

Highlighted questions in the student text provide point-of-use prompts that students can use to clarify their thinking. Use the **Practice Set** each day to assess student understanding of the New Concepts.

Daily Checks on Previously-Taught Content

Because Saxon Math's **Written Practice** is distributed and integrated, you can daily assess students' retention and understanding of previously-taught content. Each problem references the lesson where the concept was first taught. By checking student homework, you can easily keep track of which concepts need reinforcement. You can remediate by reviewing the lesson again or by assigning the Reteaching Master.

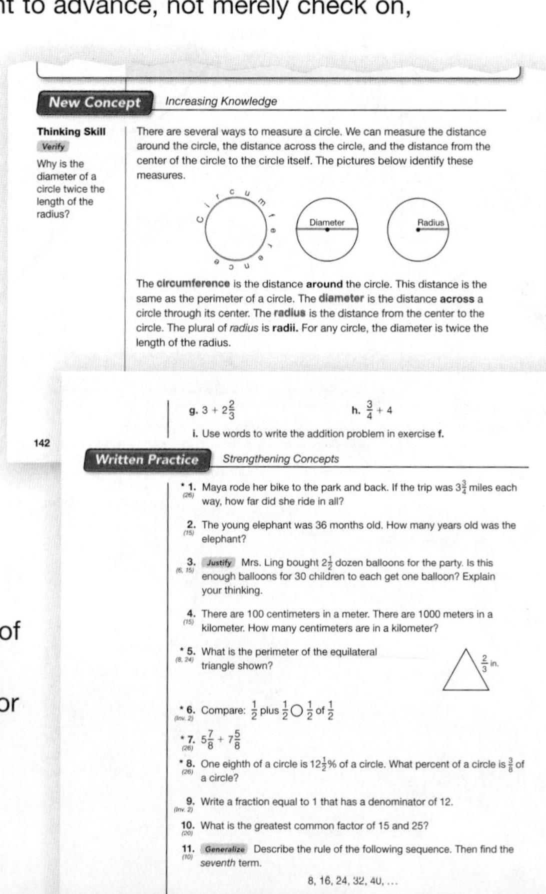

New Concept *Increasing Knowledge*

Thinking Skill *Verify* Why is the diameter of a circle twice the length of the radius?

There are several ways to measure a circle. We can measure the distance around the circle, the distance across the circle, and the distance from the center of the circle to the circle itself. The pictures below identify these measures.

The **circumference** is the distance **around** the circle. This distance is the same as the perimeter of a circle. The **diameter** is the distance **across** a circle through its center. The **radius** is the distance from the center to the circle. The plural of *radius* is **radii.** For any circle, the diameter is twice the length of the radius.

142

g. $3 + 2\frac{2}{3}$ h. $\frac{3}{4} + 4$

i. Use words to write the addition problem in exercise **f.**

Written Practice *Strengthening Concepts*

* 1. (26) Maya rode her bike to the park and back. If the trip was $3\frac{3}{4}$ miles each way, how far did she ride in all?

2. (15) The young elephant was 36 months old. How many years old was the elephant?

3. (6, 15) *Justify* Mrs. Ling bought $2\frac{1}{2}$ dozen balloons for the party. Is this enough balloons for 30 children to each get one balloon? Explain your thinking.

4. (15) There are 100 centimeters in a meter. There are 1000 meters in a kilometer. How many centimeters are in a kilometer?

* 5. (8, 24) What is the perimeter of the equilateral triangle shown? ($\frac{2}{3}$ in.)

* 6. (Inv. 2) Compare: $\frac{1}{2}$ plus $\frac{1}{2}$ ◯ $\frac{1}{2}$ of $\frac{1}{2}$

* 7. (26) $5\frac{7}{8} + 7\frac{5}{8}$

* 8. (26) One eighth of a circle is $12\frac{1}{2}$% of a circle. What percent of a circle is $\frac{3}{8}$ of a circle?

9. (Inv. 2) Write a fraction equal to 1 that has a denominator of 12.

10. (20) What is the greatest common factor of 15 and 25?

11. (10) *Generalize* Describe the rule of the following sequence. Then find the *seventh* term.

8, 16, 24, 32, 40, ...

Assessment *OF* Learning

The assessments in Saxon Math are frequent and consistently placed to offer a regular method of ongoing testing and tracking of student mastery.

Every Five Lessons

After every five lessons there is a **Power-Up Test** and a **Cumulative Test**. Use the Power-Up Test to assess basic facts and skills, as well as problem solving strategies. The Cumulative Test checks mastery of concepts from previous lessons.

Every Section (10 lessons)

Every Section also ends with a Power-Up Test and a Cumulative Test. In addition, the Teacher's Manual contains a guide for creating individualized tests.

Every Quarter

Use the **Benchmark Tests** to check student progress after lessons 30, 60 and 90. Benchmark Tests assess student knowledge of all concepts and skills up to that point in the course.

Final Test

Use the **End-of-Course Exam** to measure student progress against your beginning-of-year benchmarks.

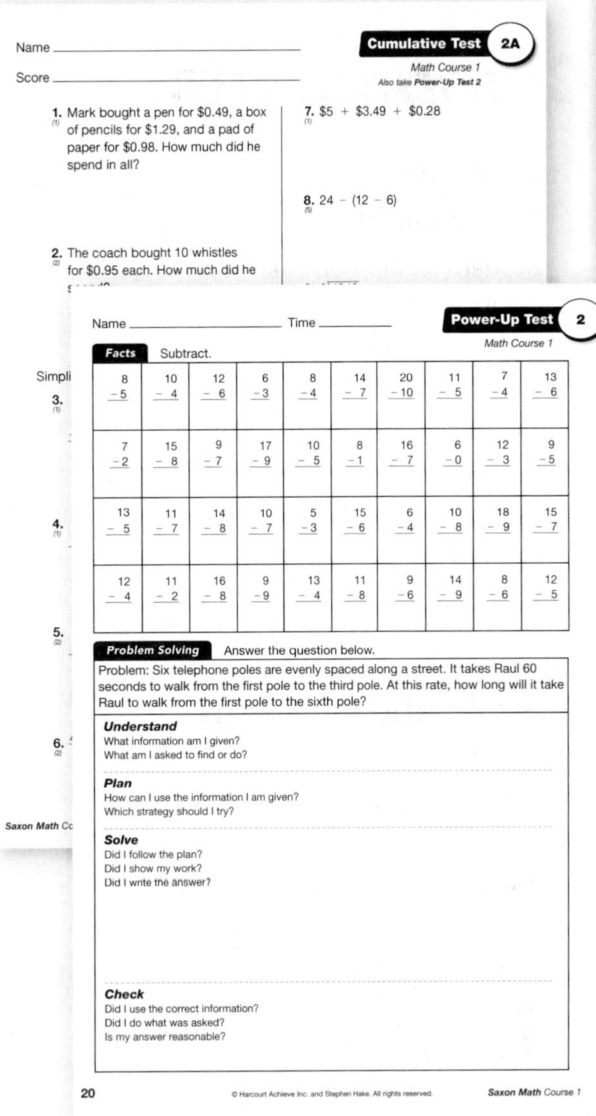

Name ____________ Score ____________

Cumulative Test 2A
Math Course 1
Also take Power-Up Test 2

1. Mark bought a pen for $0.49, a box of pencils for $1.29, and a pad of paper for $0.98. How much did he spend in all?

7. $5 + $3.49 + $0.28

8. 24 − (12 − 6)

2. The coach bought 10 whistles for $0.95 each. How much did he ...

Simpli...

3.

4.

5.

6.

Saxon Math Co...

Name ____________ Time ____________

Power-Up Test 2
Math Course 1

Facts Subtract.

8 − 5	10 − 4	12 − 6	6 − 3	8 − 4	14 − 7	20 − 10	11 − 5	7 − 4	13 − 6
7 − 2	15 − 8	9 − 7	17 − 9	10 − 5	8 − 1	16 − 7	6 − 0	12 − 3	9 − 5
13 − 5	11 − 7	14 − 8	10 − 7	5 − 3	15 − 6	6 − 4	10 − 8	18 − 9	15 − 7
12 − 4	11 − 2	16 − 8	9 − 9	13 − 4	11 − 8	9 − 6	14 − 9	8 − 6	12 − 5

Problem Solving Answer the question below.

Problem: Six telephone poles are evenly spaced along a street. It takes Raul 60 seconds to walk from the first pole to the third pole. At this rate, how long will it take Raul to walk from the first pole to the sixth pole?

Understand
What information am I given?
What am I asked to find or do?

Plan
How can I use the information I am given?
Which strategy should I try?

Solve
Did I follow the plan?
Did I show my work?
Did I write the answer?

Check
Did I use the correct information?
Did I do what was asked?
Is my answer reasonable?

20 © Harcourt Achieve Inc. and Stephen Hake. All rights reserved. *Saxon Math Course 1*

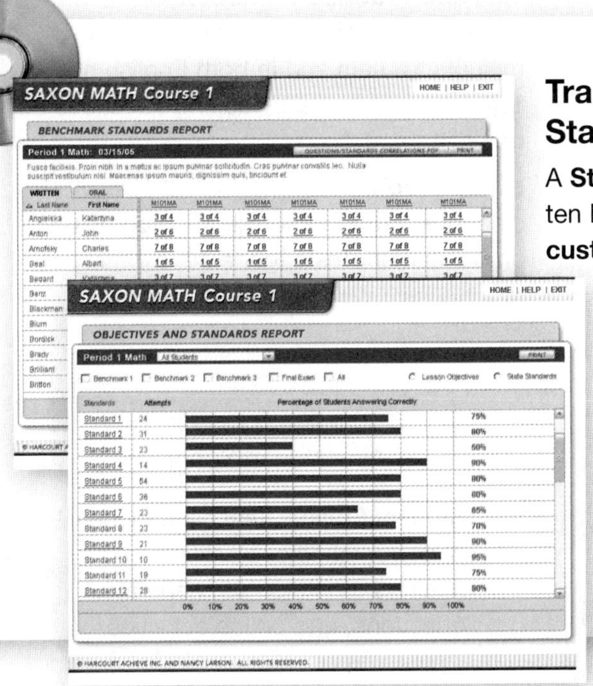

Tracking and Benchmarking the Standards

A **Standards Benchmark Checkpoint** occurs every ten lessons, at the end of each Section. Create **customized Benchmark Assessments** by using the Test and Practice Generator CD and the convenient guide in the Teacher's Manual.

If you need to create benchmark tests for a specific time frame (say, for a six-week period), you can easily use the Teacher's Manual guide for which test items on the CD to choose.

Print out **Standards Reports** to quickly track student progress against your benchmarks.

SAXON MATH™

Course 1

Course 2

Course 3

Components

Core Program

Student Edition

Student Edition eBook
complete student text on CD

Teacher's Manual
two-volume hardbound

Teacher's Manual eBook
complete teacher edition on CD

Resources and Planner CD
an electronic pacing calendar with standards, plus assessment, reteaching, and instructional masters

Meeting the Needs of All Students

Written Practice Workbook
no need to carry the textbook home

Power Up Workbook
consumable worksheets for every lesson

Reteaching Masters
one for every lesson

Manipulatives Kit
use with lesson Activities and Investigations

Adaptations for Saxon Math

A complete, parallel program for Special Education students

Classroom package,
with Teacher's Guide and CD

Title 1 Resource package
for pullout programs

Special Education Resource package
for special education or self-contained resource classrooms

Building the Depth of the Standards

Instructional Masters
performance tasks and activities, activity masters, Power-Up worksheets, recording forms, and more

Instructional Transparencies
overheads of all Instructional Masters

Graphing Calculators Activities
correlated to lessons

Instructional Posters
in English and Spanish

Answer Key CD
student answers for displaying to check homework

Online Activities – real world, graphing calculator, and exploration activities

Tracking and Benchmarking the Standards

Course Assessments
numerous assessments to check student progress, plus recording forms for easy tracking and analysis of scores

Test and Practice Generator CD
test items, correlated to standards, in multiple formats and in both English and Spanish; customize by editing questions or writing new ones

eGradebook
electronic gradebook to track progress on benchmark tests; generate a variety of reports, including standards reports

Saxon Math Works . . .
by providing a comprehensive program that is easy to plan, easy to manage, and easy to teach!

Available in Spanish

Student Edition, Teacher's Manual, plus worksheets, blackline masters, posters, test generator questions, and online activities

Table of Contents

Integrated and Distributed Units of Instruction

Section 1 *Lessons 1–10, Investigation 1*

Math Focus:
Number and Operations • Algebra

Distributed Strands:
Number and Operations • Algebra • Geometry • Measurement • Data Analysis and Probability

Overview **Lessons 1–10, Investigation 1** 7A

Lesson 1 *Teacher Preparation* 7E
- **Adding Whole Numbers and Money** 7
- **Subtracting Whole Numbers and Money**
- **Fact Families, Part 1**

Lesson 2 *Teacher Preparation* 12A
- **Multiplying Whole Numbers and Money** 12
- **Dividing Whole Numbers and Money**
- **Fact Families, Part 2**

Lesson 3 *Teacher Preparation* 18A
- **Unknown Numbers in Addition** 18
- **Unknown Numbers in Subtraction**

Lesson 4 *Teacher Preparation* 23A
- **Unknown Numbers in Multiplication** 23
- **Unknown Numbers in Division**

Lesson 5 *Teacher Preparation* 28A
- **Order of Operations, Part 1** 28

Lesson 6 *Teacher Preparation* 32A
- **Fractional Parts** 32

Lesson 7 *Teacher Preparation* 36A
- **Lines, Segments, and Rays** 36
- **Linear Measure**

Activity **Inch Ruler**

Lesson 8 *Teacher Preparation* 42A
- **Perimeter** 42

Activity **Perimeter**

Lesson 9 *Teacher Preparation* 46A
- **The Number Line: Ordering and Comparing** . . 46

Lesson 10 *Teacher Preparation* 50A
- **Sequences** 50
- **Scales**

Cumulative Assessment Power-Up Test 1, Cumulative Test 1, ... 53A
Performance Task 1, Customized Benchmark Test

Investigation 1 *Teacher Preparation* 54A
- **Frequency Tables**. 54
- **Histograms**
- **Surveys**

Maintaining & Extending

Power Up

Facts pp. 7, 12, 18, 23, 28, 32, 36, 42, 46, 50

Mental Math Strategies pp. 7, 12, 18, 23, 28, 32, 36, 42, 46, 50

Problem Solving Strategies pp. 7, 12, 18, 23, 28, 32, 36, 42, 46, 50

Enrichment

Early Finishers pp. 17, 22, 31, 41

Extensions p. 57

Section 2 Lessons 11–20, Investigation 2

Math Focus:
Number and Operations • Problem Solving

Distributed Strands:
Number and Operations • Algebra • Measurement • Data Analysis and Probability • Problem Solving

Overview	**Lessons 11–20, Investigation 2**	58A
Lesson 11	*Teacher Preparation*	58E
	• Problems About Combining	58
	• Problems About Separating	
Lesson 12	*Teacher Preparation*	63A
	• Place Value Through Trillions	63
	• Multistep Problems	
Lesson 13	*Teacher Preparation*	68A
	• Problems About Comparing	68
	• Elapsed-Time Problems	
Lesson 14	*Teacher Preparation*	73A
	• The Number Line: Negative Numbers	73
Lesson 15	*Teacher Preparation*	78A
	• Problems About Equal Groups	78
Cumulative Assessment	Power-Up Test 2, Cumulative Test 2, Performance Activity 2	81A
Lesson 16	*Teacher Preparation*	82A
	• Rounding Whole Numbers	82
	• Estimating	
Lesson 17	*Teacher Preparation*	87A
	• The Number Line: Fractions and Mixed Numbers	87
	Activity **Inch Ruler to Sixteenths**	
Lesson 18	*Teacher Preparation*	93A
	• Average	93
	• Line Graphs	
Lesson 19	*Teacher Preparation*	99A
	• Factors	99
	• Prime Numbers	
	Activity **Prime Numbers**	
Lesson 20	*Teacher Preparation*	105A
	• Greatest Common Factor (GCF)	105
Cumulative Assessment	Power-Up Test 3, Cumulative Test 3, Performance Task 3, Customized Benchmark Test	108A
Investigation 2	*Teacher Preparation*	109A
	• Investigating Fractions with Manipulatives	109
	Activity **Using Fraction Manipulatives**	

Maintaining & Extending

Power Up
Facts pp. 58, 63, 68, 73, 78, 82, 87, 93, 99, 105

Mental Math Strategies
pp. 58, 63, 68, 73, 78, 82, 87, 93, 99, 105

Problem Solving Strategies
pp. 58, 63, 68, 73, 78, 82, 87, 93, 99, 105

Enrichment
Early Finishers pp. 77, 81, 92, 98, 104, 108

Extensions p. 111

Section 3 *Lessons 21–30, Investigation 3*

Math Focus:
Number and Operations • Geometry

Distributed Strands:
Number and Operations • Geometry • Measurement • Problem Solving

Overview	Lessons 21–30, Investigation 3	112A
Lesson 21	*Teacher Preparation*	112E
	• **Divisibility**	112
Lesson 22	*Teacher Preparation*	117A
	• **"Equal Groups" Problems with Fractions**	117
Lesson 23	*Teacher Preparation*	122A
	• **Ratio**	122
	• **Rate**	
Lesson 24	*Teacher Preparation*	127A
	• **Adding and Subtracting Fractions That Have Common Denominators**	127
Lesson 25	*Teacher Preparation*	132A
	• **Writing Division Answers as Mixed Numbers**	132
	• **Multiples**	
Cumulative Assessment	Power-Up Test 4, Cumulative Test 4, Performance Activity 4	135A
Lesson 26	*Teacher Preparation*	136A
	• **Using Manipulatives to Reduce Fractions**	136
	• **Adding and Subtracting Mixed Numbers**	
Lesson 27	*Teacher Preparation*	141A
	• **Measures of a Circle**	141
	Activity **Using a Compass**	
Lesson 28	*Teacher Preparation*	145A
	• **Angles**	145
Lesson 29	*Teacher Preparation*	150A
	• **Multiplying Fractions**	150
	• **Reducing Fractions by Dividing by Common Factors**	
Lesson 30	*Teacher Preparation*	156A
	• **Least Common Multiple (LCM)**	156
	• **Reciprocals**	
Cumulative Assessment	Power-Up Test 5, Cumulative Test 5, Performance Task 5, Customized Benchmark Test	160A
Investigation 3	*Teacher Preparation*	161A
	• **Measuring and Drawing Angles with a Protractor**	161
	Activity **Measuring Angles**	

Maintaining & Extending

Power Up

Facts pp. 112, 117, 122, 127, 132, 136, 141, 145, 150, 156

Mental Math Strategies pp. 112, 117, 122, 127, 132, 136, 141, 145, 150, 156

Problem Solving Strategies pp. 112, 117, 122, 127, 132, 136, 141, 145, 150, 156

Enrichment

Early Finishers pp. 116, 126, 131, 144, 155, 160

Extensions p. 163

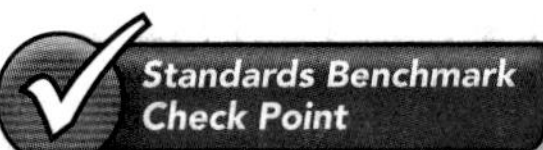

Section 4 *Lessons 31–40, Investigation 4*

Math Focus:
Number and Operations • Measurement

Distributed Strands:
Number and Operations • Geometry • Measurement • Data Analysis and Probability • Problem Solving

Overview	**Lessons 31–40, Investigation 4**	164A
Lesson 31	*Teacher Preparation*	164E
	• **Areas of Rectangles**	164
Lesson 32	*Teacher Preparation*	169A
	• **Expanded Notation**	169
	• **More on Elapsed Time**	
Lesson 33	*Teacher Preparation*	174A
	• **Writing Percents as Fractions, Part 1**	174
Lesson 34	*Teacher Preparation*	178A
	• **Decimal Place Value**	178
Lesson 35	*Teacher Preparation*	182A
	• **Writing Decimal Numbers as Fractions, Part 1**	182
	• **Reading and Writing Decimal Numbers**	
Cumulative Assessment	Power-Up Test 6, Cumulative Test 6, Performance Activity 6	186A
Lesson 36	*Teacher Preparation*	187A
	• **Subtracting Fractions and Mixed Numbers from Whole Numbers**	187
Lesson 37	*Teacher Preparation*	191A
	• **Adding and Subtracting Decimal Numbers**	191
Lesson 38	*Teacher Preparation*	195A
	• **Adding and Subtracting Decimal Numbers and Whole Numbers**	195
	• **Squares and Square Roots**	
Lesson 39	*Teacher Preparation*	200A
	• **Multiplying Decimal Numbers**	200
Lesson 40	*Teacher Preparation*	205A
	• **Using Zero as a Placeholder**	205
	• **Circle Graphs**	
Cumulative Assessment	Power-Up Test 7, Cumulative Test 7, Performance Task 7, Customized Benchmark Test	210A
Investigation 4	*Teacher Preparation*	211A
	• **Collecting, Organizing, Displaying, and Interpreting Data**	211

Maintaining & Extending

Power Up

Facts pp. 164, 169, 174, 178, 182, 187, 191, 195, 200, 205

Mental Math Strategies pp. 164, 169, 174, 178, 182, 187, 191, 195, 200, 205

Problem Solving Strategies pp. 164, 169, 174, 178, 182, 187, 191, 195, 200, 205

Enrichment

Early Finishers pp. 177, 194, 204

Extensions p. 214

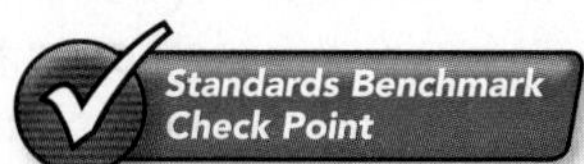

Section 5 Lessons 41–50, Investigation 5

Math Focus:
Number and Operations

Distributed Strands:
Number and Operations • Algebra • Geometry • Measurement • Data Analysis and Probability • Problem Solving

Overview	**Lessons 41–50, Investigation 5**	216A
Lesson 41	*Teacher Preparation*	216E
	• **Finding a Percent of a Number**	216
Lesson 42	*Teacher Preparation*	221A
	• **Renaming Fractions by Multiplying by 1**	221
Lesson 43	*Teacher Preparation*	225A
	• **Equivalent Division Problems**	225
	• **Finding Unknowns in Fraction and Decimal Problems**	
Lesson 44	*Teacher Preparation*	231A
	• **Simplifying Decimal Numbers**	231
	• **Comparing Decimal Numbers**	
Lesson 45	*Teacher Preparation*	235A
	• **Dividing a Decimal Number by a Whole Number**	235
Cumulative Assessment	Power-Up Test 8, Cumulative Test 8, Performance Activity 8	238A
Lesson 46	*Teacher Preparation*	239A
	• **Writing Decimal Numbers in Expanded Notation**	239
	• **Mentally Multiplying Decimal Numbers by 10 and by 100**	
Lesson 47	*Teacher Preparation*	244A
	• **Circumference**	244
	• **Pi (π)**	
	Activity **Circumference**	
Lesson 48	*Teacher Preparation*	250A
	• **Subtracting Mixed Numbers with Regrouping, Part 1**	250
Lesson 49	*Teacher Preparation*	254A
	• **Dividing by a Decimal Number**	254
Lesson 50	*Teacher Preparation*	259A
	• **Decimal Number Line (Tenths)**	259
	• **Dividing by a Fraction**	
Cumulative Assessment	Power-Up Test 9, Cumulative Test 9, Performance Task 9, Customized Benchmark Test	263A
Investigation 5	*Teacher Preparation*	264A
	• **Displaying Data**	264

Maintaining & Extending

Power Up
Facts pp. 216, 221, 225, 231, 235, 239, 244, 250, 254, 259

Mental Math Strategies
pp. 216, 221, 225, 231, 235, 239, 244, 250, 254, 259

Problem Solving Strategies
pp. 216, 221, 225, 231, 235, 239, 244, 250, 254, 259

Enrichment
Early Finishers pp. 238, 249, 253, 258, 263

Extensions p. 267

Section 6 Lessons 51–60, Investigation 6

Math Focus:
Number and Operations • Geometry

Distributed Strands:
Number and Operations • Geometry • Measurement • Data Analysis and Probability • Problem Solving

Overview	**Lessons 51–60, Investigation 6**	268A
Lesson 51	*Teacher Preparation*	268E
	• **Rounding Decimal Numbers**	268
Lesson 52	*Teacher Preparation*	272A
	• **Mentally Dividing Decimal Numbers by 10 and by 100**	272
Lesson 53	*Teacher Preparation*	276A
	• **Decimals Chart**	276
	• **Simplifying Fractions**	
Lesson 54	*Teacher Preparation*	280A
	• **Reducing by Grouping Factors Equal to 1**	280
	• **Dividing Fractions**	
Lesson 55	*Teacher Preparation*	285A
	• **Common Denominators, Part 1**	285
Cumulative Assessment	Power-Up Test 10, Cumulative Test 10, Performance Activity 10	288A
Lesson 56	*Teacher Preparation*	289A
	• **Common Denominators, Part 2**	289
Lesson 57	*Teacher Preparation*	295A
	• **Adding and Subtracting Fractions: Three Steps**	295
Lesson 58	*Teacher Preparation*	299A
	• **Probability and Chance**	299
Lesson 59	*Teacher Preparation*	306A
	• **Adding Mixed Numbers**	306
Lesson 60	*Teacher Preparation*	310A
	• **Polygons**	310
Cumulative Assessment	Power-Up Test 11, Cumulative Test 11, Performance Task 11, Customized Benchmark Test	313A
Investigation 6	*Teacher Preparation*	314A
	• **Attributes of Geometric Solids**	314
	Activity **Comparing Geometric Solids**	

Maintaining & Extending

Power Up

Facts pp. 268, 272, 276, 280, 285, 289, 295, 299, 306, 310

Mental Math Strategies
pp. 268, 272, 276, 280, 285, 289, 295, 299, 306, 310

Problem Solving Strategies
pp. 268, 272, 276, 280, 285, 289, 295, 299, 306, 310

Enrichment

Early Finishers pp. 279, 284, 294, 298, 305, 309

Extensions p. 318

Section 7 Lessons 61–70, Investigation 7

Math Focus:
Number and Operations • Geometry

Distributed Strands:
Number and Operations • Algebra • Geometry • Measurement • Problem Solving

Overview **Lessons 61–70, Investigation 7** 320A

Lesson 61 *Teacher Preparation* 320E
- **Adding Three or More Fractions** 320

Lesson 62 *Teacher Preparation* 324A
- **Writing Mixed Numbers as Improper Fractions** 324

Lesson 63 *Teacher Preparation* 329A
- **Subtracting Mixed Numbers with Regrouping, Part 2** 329

Lesson 64 *Teacher Preparation* 333A
- **Classifying Quadrilaterals** 333

Lesson 65 *Teacher Preparation* 337A
- **Prime Factorization**. 337
- **Division by Primes**
- **Factor Trees**

Cumulative Assessment Power-Up Test 12, Cumulative Test 12, Performance Activity 12 . . . . 341A

Lesson 66 *Teacher Preparation* 342A
- **Multiplying Mixed Numbers** 342

Lesson 67 *Teacher Preparation* 346A
- **Using Prime Factorization to Reduce Fractions** 346

Lesson 68 *Teacher Preparation* 349A
- **Dividing Mixed Numbers**. 349

Lesson 69 *Teacher Preparation* 353A
- **Lengths of Segments** 353
- **Complementary and Supplementary Angles**

Lesson 70 *Teacher Preparation* 358A
- **Reducing Fractions Before Multiplying**. 358

Cumulative Assessment Power-Up Test 13, Cumulative Test 13, Performance Task 13, Customized Benchmark Test 362A

Investigation 7 *Teacher Preparation* 363A
- **The Coordinate Plane** 363

Activity **Drawing on the Coordinate Plane**

Maintaining & Extending

Power Up

Facts pp. 320, 324, 329, 333, 337, 342, 346, 349, 353, 358

Mental Math Strategies pp. 320, 324, 329, 333, 337, 342, 346, 349, 353, 358

Problem Solving Strategies pp. 320, 324, 329, 333, 337, 342, 346, 349, 353, 358

Enrichment

Early Finishers pp. 323, 332, 352, 357, 362

Extensions p. 367

Section 8 — Lessons 71–80, Investigation 8

Math Focus:
Number and Operations • Geometry

Distributed Strands:
Number and Operations • Geometry • Measurement • Problem Solving

Overview **Lessons 71–80, Investigation 8** 368A

Lesson 71 *Teacher Preparation* 368E
- **Parallelograms** 368
- *Activity* **Area of a Parallelogram**

Lesson 72 *Teacher Preparation* 375A
- **Fractions Chart** 375
- **Multiplying Three Fractions**

Lesson 73 *Teacher Preparation* 380A
- **Exponents** 380
- **Writing Decimal Numbers as Fractions, Part 2**

Lesson 74 *Teacher Preparation* 385A
- **Writing Fractions as Decimal Numbers** 385
- **Writing Ratios as Decimal Numbers**

Lesson 75 *Teacher Preparation* 390A
- **Writing Fractions and Decimals as Percents, Part 1** 390

Cumulative Assessment Power-Up Test 14, Cumulative Test 14, Performance Activity 14 .... 394A

Lesson 76 *Teacher Preparation* 395A
- **Comparing Fractions by Converting to Decimal Form** 395

Lesson 77 *Teacher Preparation* 399A
- **Finding Unstated Information in Fraction Problems** 399

Lesson 78 *Teacher Preparation* 404A
- **Capacity** 404

Lesson 79 *Teacher Preparation* 408A
- **Area of a Triangle** 408
- *Activity* **Area of a Triangle**

Lesson 80 *Teacher Preparation* 413A
- **Using a Constant Factor to Solve Ratio Problems** 413

Cumulative Assessment Power-Up Test 15, Cumulative Test 15, Performance Task 15, Customized Benchmark Test 416A

Investigation 8 *Teacher Preparation* 417A
- **Geometric Construction of Bisectors** 417
- *Activity 1* **Perpendicular Bisectors**
- *Activity 2* **Angle Bisectors**
- *Activity 3* **Constructing Bisectors**

Maintaining & Extending

Power Up

Facts pp. 368, 375, 380, 385, 390, 395, 399, 404, 408, 413

Mental Math Strategies pp. 368, 375, 380, 385, 390, 395, 399, 404, 408, 413

Problem Solving Strategies pp. 368, 375, 380, 385, 390, 395, 399, 404, 408, 413

Enrichment

Early Finishers pp. 379, 384, 394, 403, 412

Extensions p. 420

Section 9 — *Lessons 81–90, Investigation 9*

Math Focus:
Algebra • Measurement

Distributed Strands:
Number and Operations • Algebra • Geometry • Measurement • Data Analysis and Probability • Problem Solving

Overview	**Lessons 81–90, Investigation 9**	421A
Lesson 81	*Teacher Preparation*	421E
	• **Arithmetic with Units of Measure**	421
Lesson 82	*Teacher Preparation*	426A
	• **Volume of a Rectangular Prism**	426
Lesson 83	*Teacher Preparation*	431A
	• **Proportions**	431
Lesson 84	*Teacher Preparation*	436A
	• **Order of Operations, Part 2**	436
Lesson 85	*Teacher Preparation*	441A
	• **Using Cross Products to Solve Proportions**	441
Cumulative Assessment	Power-Up Test 16, Cumulative Test 16, Performance Activity 16	446A
Lesson 86	*Teacher Preparation*	447A
	• **Area of a Circle**	447
Lesson 87	*Teacher Preparation*	452A
	• **Finding Unknown Factors**	452
Lesson 88	*Teacher Preparation*	456A
	• **Using Proportions to Solve Ratio Word Problems**	456
Lesson 89	*Teacher Preparation*	460A
	• **Estimating Square Roots**	460
Lesson 90	*Teacher Preparation*	465A
	• **Measuring Turns**	465
Cumulative Assessment	Power-Up Test 17, Cumulative Test 17, Performance Task 17, Customized Benchmark Test	469A
Investigation 9	*Teacher Preparation*	470A
	• **Experimental Probability**	470
	Activity **Probability Experiment**	

Maintaining & Extending

Power Up
Facts pp. 421, 426, 431, 436, 441, 447, 452, 456, 460, 465

Mental Math Strategies
pp. 421, 426, 431, 436, 441, 447, 452, 456, 460, 465

Problem Solving Strategies
pp. 421, 426, 431, 436, 441, 447, 452, 456, 460, 465

Enrichment
Early Finishers pp. 435, 440, 446, 451, 455, 469

Extensions p. 472

Section 10 *Lessons 91–100, Investigation 10*

Math Focus:
Number and Operations • Geometry

Distributed Strands:
Number and Operations • Algebra • Geometry • Measurement • Data Analysis and Probability

Overview	**Lessons 91–100, Investigation 10**	474A
Lesson 91	*Teacher Preparation*	474E
	• **Geometric Formulas**	474
Lesson 92	*Teacher Preparation*	479A
	• **Expanded Notation with Exponents**	479
	• **Order of Operations with Exponents**	
	• **Powers of Fractions**	
Lesson 93	*Teacher Preparation*	484A
	• **Classifying Triangles**	484
Lesson 94	*Teacher Preparation*	488A
	• **Writing Fractions and Decimals as Percents, Part 2**	488
Lesson 95	*Teacher Preparation*	493A
	• **Reducing Rates Before Multiplying**	493
Cumulative Assessment	Power-Up Test 18, Cumulative Test 18, Performance Activity 18	496A
Lesson 96	*Teacher Preparation*	497A
	• **Functions**	497
	• **Graphing Functions**	
Lesson 97	*Teacher Preparation*	503A
	• **Transversals**	503
Lesson 98	*Teacher Preparation*	508A
	• **Sum of the Angle Measures of Triangles. and Quadrilaterals**	508
Lesson 99	*Teacher Preparation*	513A
	• **Fraction-Decimal-Percent Equivalents**	513
Lesson 100	*Teacher Preparation*	517A
	• **Algebraic Addition of Integers**	517
Cumulative Assessment	Power-Up Test 19, Cumulative Test 19, Performance Task 19, Customized Benchmark Test	523A
Investigation 10	*Teacher Preparation*	524A
	• **Compound Experiments**	524

Maintaining & Extending

Power Up

Facts pp. 474, 479, 484, 488, 493, 497, 503, 508, 513, 517

Mental Math Strategies
pp. 474, 479, 484, 488, 493, 497, 503, 508, 513, 517

Problem Solving Strategies
pp. 474, 479, 484, 488, 493, 497, 503, 508, 513, 517

Enrichment

Early Finishers pp. 478, 483, 487, 496, 516, 523

Extensions p. 527

Section 11 *Lessons 101–110, Investigation 11*

Math Focus:
Algebra • Geometry

Distributed Strands:
Number and Operations • Algebra • Geometry • Measurement • Problem Solving

Overview	**Lessons 101–110, Investigation 11**	528A
Lesson 101	*Teacher Preparation*	528E
	• **Ratio Problems Involving Totals**	528
Lesson 102	*Teacher Preparation*	533A
	• **Mass and Weight**	533
Lesson 103	*Teacher Preparation*	538A
	• **Perimeter of Complex Shapes**	538
Lesson 104	*Teacher Preparation*	543A
	• **Algebraic Addition Activity**	543
	Activity **Sign Game**	
Lesson 105	*Teacher Preparation*	548A
	• **Using Proportions to Solve Percent Problems**	548
Cumulative Assessment	Power-Up Test 20, Cumulative Test 20, Performance Activity 20	552A
Lesson 106	*Teacher Preparation*	553A
	• **Two-Step Equations**	553
Lesson 107	*Teacher Preparation*	557A
	• **Area of Complex Shapes**	557
Lesson 108	*Teacher Preparation*	561A
	• **Transformations**	561
	Activity **Transformations**	
Lesson 109	*Teacher Preparation*	566A
	• **Corresponding Parts**	566
	• **Similar Figures**	
Lesson 110	*Teacher Preparation*	573A
	• **Symmetry**	573
Cumulative Assessment	Power-Up Test 21, Cumulative Test 21, Performance Task 21, Customized Benchmark Test	577A
Investigation 11	*Teacher Preparation*	578A
	• **Scale Factor: Scale Drawings and Models**	578

Maintaining & Extending

Power Up
Facts pp. 528, 533, 538, 548, 553, 557, 561, 566, 573
Mental Math Strategies pp. 528, 533, 538, 548, 553, 557, 561, 566, 573
Problem Solving Strategies pp. 528, 533, 538, 543, 548, 553, 557, 561, 566, 573

Enrichment
Early Finishers pp. 532, 572
Extensions p. 581

Section 12 Lessons 111–120, Investigation 12

Math Focus:
Measurement • Problem Solving

Distributed Strands:
Number and Operations • Algebra • Geometry • Measurement • Problem Solving

Overview	**Lessons 111–120, Investigation 12**	582A
Lesson 111	*Teacher Preparation*	582E
	• **Applications Using Division**	582
Lesson 112	*Teacher Preparation*	587A
	• **Multiplying and Dividing Integers**	587
Lesson 113	*Teacher Preparation*	592A
	• **Adding and Subtracting Mixed Measures**	592
	• **Multiplying by Powers of Ten**	
Lesson 114	*Teacher Preparation*	597A
	• **Unit Multipliers**	597
Lesson 115	*Teacher Preparation*	602A
	• **Writing Percents as Fractions, Part 2**	602
Cumulative Assessment	Power-Up Test 22, Cumulative Test 22, Performance Activity 22	605A
Lesson 116	*Teacher Preparation*	606A
	• **Compound Interest**	606
Lesson 117	*Teacher Preparation*	612A
	• **Finding a Whole When a Fraction Is Known**	612
Lesson 118	*Teacher Preparation*	617A
	• **Estimating Area**	617
Lesson 119	*Teacher Preparation*	621A
	• **Finding a Whole When a Percent Is Known**	621
Lesson 120	*Teacher Preparation*	626A
	• **Volume of a Cylinder**	626
Cumulative Assessment	Power-Up Test 23, Cumulative Test 23, Performance Task 23, Customized Benchmark Test	629A
Investigation 12	*Teacher Preparation*	630A
	• **Volume of Prisms, Pyramids, Cylinders and Cones**	630
	• **Surface Area of Prisms and Cylinders**	

Maintaining & Extending

Power Up

Facts pp. 582, 587, 592, 597, 602, 606, 612, 617, 621, 626

Mental Math Strategies pp. 582, 587, 592, 597, 602, 606, 612, 617, 621, 626

Problem Solving Strategies pp. 582, 587, 592, 597, 602, 606, 612, 617, 621, 626

Enrichment

Early Finishers pp. 591, 601, 605, 611, 616, 629

Extensions p. 635

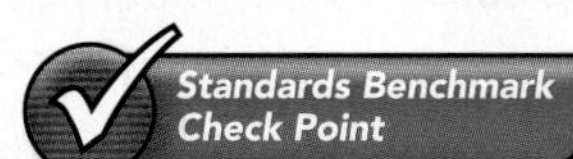

Contents by Strand

This chart gives you an overview of the instruction of math concepts by strand in *Saxon Math* Course 1. The chart shows where in the textbook each topic is taught and references the New Concepts section of a lesson or the instructional part of an Investigation.

	LESSONS
NUMBERS AND OPERATIONS	
Numeration	
digits	12, 21
read and write whole numbers and decimals	35, 46
place value to trillions	12, 32, 92
number line (integers, fractions)	9, 14, 17
expanded notation	32, 46, 92
comparison symbols (=, <, >)	9
compare and order rational numbers	9, 14, 44, 76
Basic operations	
add, subtract, multiply, and divide integers	2, 3, 5, 10, 100, 104, 112
add, subtract, multiply, and divide decimal numbers	1, 37, 45, 53
add, subtract, multiply, and divide fractions and mixed numbers	24, 25, 26, 29, 36, 50, 54, 57, 59, 61, 62, 66, 68, 70, 72
mental math strategies	1-120
regrouping in addition, subtraction, and multiplication	36, 48, 63
multiplication notations: $a \times b, a \cdot b, a(b)$	2
division notations: division box, division sign, and division bar	2
division with remainders	2, 111
Properties of numbers and operations	
even and odd integers	10, 19
factors, multiples, and divisibility	2, 19, 21, 25
prime and composite numbers	19
greatest common factor (GCF)	20
least common multiple (LCM)	30
divisibility tests (2, 3, 5, 9, 10)	21
prime factorization of whole numbers	65, 73
positive exponents of whole numbers, decimals, fractions	73, 92
square roots	38, 39
order of operations	5, 84, 92
inverse operations	1, 2, 4, 87, 106

	LESSONS
Estimation	
round whole numbers, decimals, mixed numbers	**16, 51**
estimate sums, differences, products, quotients	**16**
estimate squares and square roots	**89**
ALGEBRA	
Ratio and proportional reasoning	
fractional part of a whole, group, set, or number	**6, 22, 77, 117**
equivalent fractions	**26, 29, 55, 56**
convert between fractions, terminating decimals, and percents	**33, 35, 73, 74, 75, 99**
reciprocals of numbers	**30, 50**
identify/find percent of a whole, group, set, or number	**94, 105, 119**
percents greater than 100%	**94**
solve proportions with unknown in one term	**83, 85, 101**
find unit rates and ratios in proportional relationships	**88**
apply proportional relationships such as similarity, scaling, and rates	**23, 80; Investigation 11**
estimate and solve applications problems involving percent	**105, 119**
Patterns, relations, and functions	
use, describe, extend arithmetic sequence (with a constant rate of change)	**10**
input-output tables	**10, 82, 96**
analyze a pattern to verbalize a rule	**10, 82, 96**
Variables, expressions, and equations	
solve equations using concrete and pictorial models	**114, 116**
formulate an equation with one unknown variable given a problem situation	**11, 15, 42, 82, 87, 91, 105, 114**
solve one-step equations with whole numbers	**87**
solve two-step equations with whole numbers	**106, 116**
GEOMETRY	
Describe basic terms	
point	**7**
segment	**7**
ray	**7**
line	**7**
angle	**28, 69**
plane	**28, 69**

	LESSONS
Describe properties and relationships of lines	
parallel, perpendicular, and intersecting	**28, 71, 97**
horizontal, vertical, and oblique	**18; Investigation 7**
Describe properties and relationships of angles	
acute, obtuse, right	**28; Investigation 3**
complementary and supplementary	**69, 71, 97**
angles formed by transversals	**97**
angle bisector	**Investigation 8**
calculate to find unknown angle measures	**71, 97, 98**
Describe properties and relationships of polygons	
regular	**2, 60**
interior and exterior angles	**97, 98**
sum of angle measures	**98**
similarity and congruence	**68, 79, 108, 109**
classify triangles	**93**
classify quadrilaterals	**60, 64; Investigation 6**
3-Dimensional figures	
represent in 2-dimensional world using nets	**Investigations 6, 12**
draw 3-dimensional figures	**Investigation 6**
Coordinate geometry	
name and graph ordered pairs	**Investigation 7**
identify reflections, translations, rotations, and symmetry	**108**
graph reflections across the horizontal or vertical axes	**108**
MEASUREMENT	
Measuring physical attributes	
use customary units of length, area, volume, weight, capacity	**7, 31, 78, 82, 102**
use metric units of length, area, volume, weight, capacity	**7, 8, 82**
use temperature scales: Fahrenheit, Celsius	**10, 32**
use units of time	**13, 32**

	LESSONS
Systems of measurement	
convert in the U.S. Customary System	**78, 81, 114**
convert in the metric system	**7, 114**
convert between systems	**7**
unit multipliers	**95, 114**
Solving measurement problems	
perimeter of polygons, circles, complex figures	**8, 47, 60, 71, 103**
area of triangles, rectangles, and parallelograms	**31, 71, 79**
area of circles	**86**
area of complex figures	**107**
surface area of right prisms and cylinders	**Investigation 12**
estimate area	**86, 118**
volume of right prisms, cylinders, pyramids, and cones	**120; Investigation 12**
estimate volume	**78**
Solving problems of similarity	
scale factor	**83; Investigation 11**
scale drawings: two-dimensional	**Investigation 11**
Use appropriate measurement instruments	
ruler (U.S. customary and metric)	**7, 17**
compass	**27; Investigation 8**
protractor	**Investigation 3**
thermometer	**10, 100**
DATA ANALYSIS AND PROBABILITY	
Data collection and representation	
collect data	**Investigation 4**
display data	**Investigations 1, 4, 5**
tables and charts	**Investigation 5**
frequency tables	**Investigations 1, 9**
pictographs	**Investigation 5**
line graphs	**18**
histograms	**Investigation 1**

	LESSONS
bar graphs	Investigation 4
circle graphs	40, Investigation 5
line plots	Investigations 4, 5
stem-and-leaf plots	Investigation 5
choose an appropriate graph	Investigation 5
draw and compare different representations	40; Investigation 5
Data set characteristics	
mean, median, mode, and range	18; Investigation 5
Probability	
experimental probability	Investigations 9, 10
make predictions based on experiments	Investigations 9, 10
accuracy of predictions in experiments	Investigation 9
theoretical probability	Investigation 9
sample spaces	58
simple probability	58, 77: Investigation 9
probability of compound events	Investigation 10
probability of the complement of an event	77; Investigation 10
probability of independent events	Investigations 9, 10
PROBLEM SOLVING	
Four-step problem-solving process	1-120
Problem-solving strategies	1-120

Problem Solving

Objectives

- Use the four-step problem solving process to solve real-world problems.
- Select or develop a problem-solving strategy for different types of problems.

Lesson Preparation

Materials

- **Problem-Solving Model poster**
- **Problem-Solving Strategies poster**
- **Manipulative kit: color tiles**

Optional

- **Teacher-provided material: grid paper**

Problem-Solving Model

Understand
- ✓ What information am I given?
- ✓ What am I asked to find or do?

Plan
- ✓ How can I use the information I am given to solve the problem?
- ✓ Which strategy should I try?

Solve
- ✓ Did I follow the plan?
- ✓ Did I show my work?
- ✓ Did I write the answer?

Check
- ✓ Did I look back at the problem to see if I used the correct information?
- ✓ Did I answer the question or do what I was asked to do?
- ✓ Is my answer reasonable, does it make sense?

Problem-Solving Model

Problem-Solving Strategies

- Act It Out or Make a Model
- Use Logical Reasoning
- Draw a Picture or Diagram
- Write an Equation
- Make It Simpler
- Find a Pattern
- Make an Organized List
- Guess and Check
- Make or Use a Table, Chart, or Graph
- Work Backwards

Problem-Solving Strategies

Technology Resources

Student eBook Complete student textbook in electronic format.

Resources and Planner CD Assessment, reteaching, and instructional masters, plus a pacing calendar with standards.

Test and Practice Generator CD Create additional practice sheets and custom-made tests.

www.SaxonPublishers.com Visit for more student activities and planning materials.

Meeting Standards

National Council of Teachers of Mathematics (NCTM)

Problem Solving

PS.1a Build new mathematical knowledge through problem solving

PS.1b Solve problems that arise in mathematics and in other contexts

PS.1c Apply and adapt a variety of appropriate strategies to solve problems

PS.1d Monitor and reflect on the process of mathematical problem solving

Communication

CM.3a Organize and consolidate their mathematical thinking through communication

Connections

CN.4b Understand how mathematical ideas interconnect and build on one another to produce a coherent whole

CN.4c Recognize and apply mathematics in contexts outside of mathematics

Representation

RE.5b Select, apply, and translate among mathematical representations to solve problems

PROBLEM-SOLVING OVERVIEW

Focus on

• Problem Solving

As we study mathematics we learn how to use tools that help us solve problems. We face mathematical problems in our daily lives, in our work, and in our efforts to advance our technological society. We can become powerful problem solvers by improving our ability to use the tools we store in our minds. In this book we will practice solving problems every day.

This lesson has three parts:

Problem-Solving Process The four steps we follow when solving problems.

Problem-Solving Strategies Some strategies that can help us solve problems.

Writing and Problem Solving Describing how we solved a problem or formulating a problem.

four-step problem-solving process

Solving a problem is like arriving at a destination, so the process of solving a problem is similar to the process of taking a trip. Suppose we are on the mainland and want to reach a nearby island.

Problem-Solving Process	Taking a Trip
Step 1: Understand Know where you are and where you want to go.	We are on the mainland and want to go to the island.
Step 2: Plan Plan your route.	We might use the bridge, the boat, or swim.
Step 3: Solve Follow the plan.	Take the journey to the island.
Step 4: Check Check that you have reached the right place.	Verify that you have reached your desired destination.

Math Background

What is problem solving?

Many mathematicians would say that problem solving occurs whenever we do not know exactly how to proceed. Problem-solving abilities vary from student to student. Some students engage in problem solving while working on routine one-step problems. Other students need to be presented with more complex problems to engage in problem solving.

The goal of problem solving is to give students the tools they need to solve a wide range of problems. One tool is a process that helps them interpret and represent a problem. Another tool is a set problem-solving strategies that can be used to solve a variety of problems. In this program, problem solving is a daily experience as students encounter both routine word problems and non-routine strategy problems in every lesson.

Problem-Solving Overview

In this lesson students are reminded how to use the four-step problem-solving process, how to choose a problem-solving strategy, and how to do some writing while problem solving.

Four-Step Problem-Solving Process

Instruction

Give students the opportunity to discuss different types of problems they have encountered. Suggestions may include:

- word problems
- real-world problems
- finding a sum, difference, product, or quotient

Help students understand that uncertainty is a part of problem solving. Uncertainty gives us the opportunity to apply reasoning skills. Also explain that making errors and correcting errors is a part of the problem-solving process.

Before reading through the student page with the class, display the **Problem-Solving Model** poster. Point out that this problem-solving model is flexible and can be adapted to any problem.

(continued)

Four-Step Problem-Solving Process *(continued)*

Instruction

As you discuss the chart at the top of the student page, emphasize the importance of asking questions during the problem-solving process.

Example 1

Instruction

"How do you know that the problem requires more than one step?" If the problem asked how much money Carla needed, it would be a one-step problem. Since it asks for the number of weekends she must work to earn the amount she needs, it is a two-step problem.

Have a volunteer describe the steps of the solution.

- Subtract the amount Carla has from the amount she needs.
- Determine how many weekends she needs to work to earn an amount equal to or greater than the amount she needs.

(continued)

When we solve a problem, it helps to ask ourselves some questions along the way.

Follow the Process	Ask Yourself Questions
Step 1: Understand	What information am I given? What am I asked to find or do?
Step 2: Plan	How can I use the given information to solve the problem? What strategy can I use to solve the problem?
Step 3: Solve	Am I following the plan? Is my math correct?
Step 4: *Check* ***(Look Back)***	Does my solution answer the question that was asked? Is my answer reasonable?

Below we show how we follow these steps to solve a word problem.

Example 1

Carla wants to buy a CD player that costs $48.70 including tax. She has saved $10.50. Carla earns $10 each weekend babysitting. How many weekends does she need to babysit to earn enough money to buy the CD player?

Solution

Step 1: Understand the problem. The problem gives the following information:

- The CD player costs $48.70.
- Carla has saved $10.50.
- Carla earns $10.00 every weekend.

We are asked to find out how many weekends Carla needs to babysit to have enough money to buy the CD player.

Step 2: Make a plan. We see that we cannot get to the answer in one step. We plan how to use the given information in a manner that will lead us toward the solution. One way to solve the problem is:

- Find out how much more money Carla needs.
- Then find out how many weekends it will take to earn the needed amount.

Step 3: Solve the problem. (Follow the plan.) First we subtract $10.50 from $48.70 to find out how much more money Carla needs.

$48.70	cost
− $10.50	Carla has
$38.20	Carla needs

Carla needs $38.20 more than she has.

English Learners

Students will encounter unfamiliar words when they read word problems. Sometimes these words will be math vocabulary and other times they will be non-math words.

Use an approach that demonstrates the word by drawing or showing a picture of the word or touching an item that represents the word. The ideas provided in this program follow a similar approach.

1. Identify the word.
2. Demonstrate the word and how to use it.
3. Ask the students to use the word in a sentence or identify the word in a similar situation.

Creating a *word wall* of unfamiliar words will provide a visual reference throughout the year.

Thinking Skill

Verify

What strategy did we use to find the number of weekends? Make a Table

Now we find the number of weekends Carla needs to work. One way is to divide $38.20 by $10.00. Another way is to find the multiple of $10.00 that gives Carla enough money. We can make a table to do this.

Weekend 1	Weekend 2	Weekend 3	Weekend 4
$10	$20	$30	$40

After one weekend Carla earns $10, after two weekends $20, three weekends $30, and four weekends $40.

Carla needs an additional $38.20. She will need to work **four weekends** to have enough money to buy the CD player.

Step 4: Check your answer. (Look back.) We read the problem again to see if our solution answers the question. We decide if our answer is reasonable.

The problem asks how many weekends Carla will need to work to earn the rest of the money for the CD player. Our solution, 4 weekends, answers the question. Our solution is reasonable because $40 is just a little over the $38.20 that Carla needs.

After four weekends Carla has $10.50 + $40 = $50.50.

This is enough money to buy the CD player.

Example 2

Howard is planning to tile the top of an end table. The tabletop is 1 ft by 2 ft. He wants to show his initial "H" using the tiles. The 4-inch tiles come in black and white. How many tiles of each color does Howard need to cover the table with his initial?

Solution

Step 1: Understand the problem. The problem gives the following information:

- The table is 1 ft × 2 ft.
- The tiles are 4-inches on a side.
- The tiles are black and white.
- We need to model the letter "H".

We are asked to find how many tiles of each color we need to show the letter "H" on the tabletop.

Step 2: Make a plan. We see that we cannot get to the answer in one step. We plan how to use the given information in a manner that will lead us toward the solution.

- Change the table dimensions to inches and determine how many tiles will cover the table.
- Use tiles to model the tabletop and decide how many tiles are needed to show the letter "H".

Four-Step Problem-Solving Process *(continued)*

Example 2

Instruction

"How do you know that this problem has more than one correct answer?" The problem does not specify how the letter "H" should appear on the tabletop.

It is most efficient for students to act out this problem using **color tiles** from the Manipulative Kit. If tiles are not available, students can use grid paper.

You may wish to have several volunteers use grid paper at the overhead and share different ways that the letter "H" can be shown with 18 tiles in two colors.

(continued)

Four-Step Problem-Solving Process (continued)

Math Conversations

Discussion opportunities are provided below.

Problem 3 Connect

As students list the given information in the problem, ask a volunteer to list the information on the board. Ask the class to check that all the necessary information is included.

Problem 4 Verify

Ask another volunteer to write the goal of the problem on the board using his or her own words. Have the class verify that they agree with the goal.

Problem 7 Explain

Ask several students to work at the board and solve the problem. Have students with different approaches explain how they determined their answer and how they know it is correct.

(continued)

Step 3: Solve the problem. (Follow the plan.) There are 12 inches in 1 foot, so the table is 12 in. by 24 in.

12 in. ÷ 4 in. = 3 24 in. ÷ 4 in. = 6 $3 \times 6 = 18$

Howard needs 18 tiles to cover the table.

How can we use 18 tiles to model the letter "H"?

Here are two possibilities.

Thinking Skill *Verify*

What strategy did we use to design the tabletop? Act It Out or Make a Model

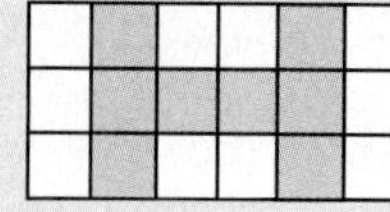

10 white tiles, 8 black tiles

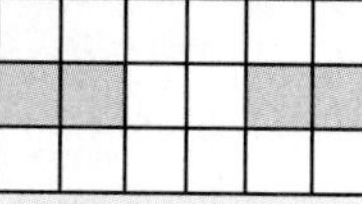

14 white tiles, 4 black tiles

Since the problem does not specify the number of each color, we can decide based on the design we choose. Howard needs 10 white tiles and 8 black tiles.

Step 4: Check your answer. (Look back.) We read the problem again to see if our solution answers the question. We decide if our answer is reasonable.

The problem asks for the number of tiles of each color Howard needs to show his initial on the tabletop. Our solution shows the letter "H" using 10 white tiles and 8 black tiles.

1. List in order the four steps in the problem-solving process. 1. Understand, 2. Plan, 3. Solve, 4. Check
2. What two questions do we answer to understand a problem? What information am I given? What am I asked to find or do to solve the problem?

Refer to the following problem to answer questions **3–8.**

Mrs. Rojas is planning to take her daughter Lena and her friend Natalie to see a movie. The movie starts at 4:30 p.m. She wants to arrive at the theater 20 minutes before the movie starts. It will take 15 minutes to drive to Natalie's house. It is 10 minutes from Natalie's house to the theater. At what time should Mrs. Rojas leave her house?

3. ▸ Connect What information are we given? Movie starts 4:30 p.m.; Get to theater 20 min before movie starts; 15 min to Natalie; 10 min to theater
4. ▸ Verify What are you asked to find? time Mrs. Rojas should leave home
5. Which step of the four-step problem-solving process did you complete when you answered questions 3 and 4? Step 1. Understand
6. Describe your plan for solving the problem. Sample: I need to work backwards from 4:30 p.m. and subtract each time from 4:30.
7. ▸ Explain Solve the problem by following your plan. Show your work. Write your solution to the problem in a way someone else will understand.
8. Check your work and your answer. Look back to the problem. Be sure you use the information correctly. Be sure you found what you were asked to find. Is your answer reasonable?

7. 4:30 movie starts
Subtract 10 min 4:20
Subtract 15 min 4:05
Subtract 20 min 3:45
Leave home: 3:45 p.m.

8. I started with 3:45 and added 20 min, then 15 min, then 10 min to get 4:30 so my answer is reasonable.

▸ See Math Conversations in the sidebar.

Inclusion

Some students may need help focusing when they read. It may be beneficial for them to use an index card while reading new concepts and word problems. Students should slide the card to uncover one line at a time to help them keep their place as they read.

Students who have difficulty transferring problems from the student page can use the "Adaptations Student Worksheets," which are specifically designed so students do not have to copy over any exercises.

problem-solving strategies

As we consider how to solve a problem we choose one or more strategies that seem to be helpful. Referring to the picture at the beginning of this lesson, we might choose to swim, to take the boat, or to cross the bridge to travel from the mainland to the island. Other strategies might not be as effective for the illustrated problem. For example, choosing to walk or bike across the water are strategies that are not reasonable for this situation.

When solving mathematical problems we also select strategies that are appropriate for the problem. Problem-solving **strategies** are types of plans we can use to solve problems. Listed below are ten strategies we will practice in this book. You may refer to these descriptions as you solve problems throughout the year.

Act it out or make a model. Moving objects or people can help us visualize the problem and lead us to the solution.

Use logical reasoning. All problems require reasoning, but for some problems we use given information to eliminate choices so that we can close in on the solution. Usually a chart, diagram, or picture can be used to organize the given information and to make the solution more apparent.

Draw a picture or diagram. Sketching a picture or a diagram can help us understand and solve problems, especially problems about graphs or maps or shapes.

Write a number sentence or equation. We can solve many word problems by fitting the given numbers into equations or number sentences and then finding the unknown numbers.

Make it simpler. We can make some complicated problems easier by using smaller numbers or fewer items. Solving the simpler problem might help us see a pattern or method that can help us solve the complex problem.

Find a pattern. Identifying a pattern that helps you to predict what will come next as the pattern continues might lead to the solution.

Make an organized list. Making a list can help us organize our thinking about a problem.

Guess and check. Guessing the answer and trying the guess in the problem might start a process that leads to the answer. If the guess is not correct, use the information from the guess to make a better guess. Continue to improve your guesses until you find the answer.

Make or use a table, chart, or graph. Arranging information in a table, chart, or graph can help us organize and keep track of data. This might reveal patterns or relationships that can help us solve the problem.

Work backwards. Finding a route through a maze is often easier by beginning at the end and tracing a path back to the start. Likewise, some problems are easier to solve by working back from information that is given toward the end of the problem to information that is unknown near the beginning of the problem.

9. Name some strategies used in this lesson. Answers will vary.

Problem-Solving Strategies

Instruction

Ten strategies are presented and practiced in this program. Use the following problems to give examples of each type.

Make a Model

While example 2 illustrates making a model to solve a problem, it also shows that sometimes there is more than one answer to a problem.

Use Logical Reasoning

Jared is older than Sarah who is younger than Enrico. Latisha is younger than Jared but older than Enrico. Who is the oldest? The youngest? Jared is the oldest; Sarah is the youngest

Draw a Diagram

A gardener is making a 24 ft^2, rectangular garden. If the measure of every side is a whole unit, how many different dimensions can the garden have?

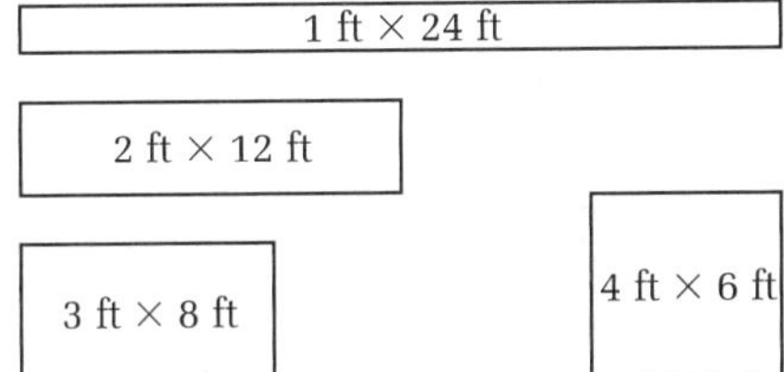

Write an Equation

There are 12 jars in each box. A crate can be filled with 36 boxes. How many jars can two crates hold? $12 \times 36 \times 2 = j$; 864 jars

Make It Simpler

One person can sit at each side of a square table. How many people can sit at 10 tables pushed together? If 2 tables were pushed together, 2 people could sit at each table and one person could sit at each end. Write an equation for this situation.

$(2 \times 2) + 2 = 6$

Use the same equation, but substitute 10 tables for 2 tables.

$(2 \times 10) + 2 = 22$

22 people can sit at 10 tables pushed together.

Find a Pattern

If you put a quarter in a coin bank on the first day and doubled the amount you put in the bank each day after that, would you save at least $15 in a week? yes, $16

Day	1	2	3	4	5	6	7
Amount	25¢	50¢	$1	$2	$4	$8	$16

(continued)

Problem-Solving Strategies *(continued)*

Instruction

You may wish to display the **Problem-Solving Strategy** concept poster throughout the year as a reference for students.

Make an Organized List

Assume you have rye bread, white bread, ham, turkey, and cheese. How many different types of sandwiches can you make with one kind of bread and one filling? 6 different sandwiches
Rye bread: ham; turkey; cheese
White bread: ham; turkey; cheese

Guess and Check

Jenna has 11 bills that total \$41 in her purse. She has \$1 bills, \$5 bills, and \$10 bills. How many of each type of bill does she have?
two \$10 bill; three \$5 bills, six \$1 bills

Make a Table

In example 1 students are shown how making a table can help them think through a routine multi-step word problem.

Work Backwards

The elapsed time problem represents a real-life situation where working backwards is required.

Writing and Problem Solving

Instruction

Point out that sometimes students will be asked to describe their thinking in words. These directions will be presented in different ways.

- Explain how you found your answer.
- Explain how you know your answer is correct.
- Explain why your answer is reasonable.

Students should write brief, accurate descriptions of their methods. Encourage them to use appropriate mathematical language.

Periodically, students will be asked to write a problem for a given situation or equation. Give students the opportunity to share the word problems they have written for problem **11.**

The chart below shows where each strategy is first introduced in this textbook.

Strategy	Lesson
Act It Out or Make a Model	Problem Solving Overview Example 2
Use Logical Reasoning	Lesson 3
Draw a Picture or Diagram	Lesson 17
Write a Number Sentence or Equation	Lesson 17
Make It Simpler	Lesson 4
Find a Pattern	Lesson 1
Make an Organized List	Lesson 8
Guess and Check	Lesson 5
Make or Use a Table, Chart, or Graph	Problem Solving Overview Example 1
Work Backwards	Lesson 84

writing and problem solving

Sometimes, a problem will ask us to explain our thinking. This helps us measure our understanding of math.

- Explain how you solved the problem.
- Explain how you know your answer is correct.
- Explain why your answer is reasonable.

For these situations, we can describe the way we followed our plan. This is a description of the way we solved example 1.

Subtract \$10.50 from \$48.70 to find out how much more money Carla needs. \$48.70 − \$10.50 = \$38.20. Make a table and count by 10s to determine that Carla needs to work 4 weekends so she can earn enough money for the CD player.

10. Write a description of how we solved the problem in example 2. Answers will vary.

Other times, we will be asked to write a problem for a given equation. Be sure to include the correct numbers and operations to represent the equation.

11. Write a word problem for the equation 32 + 32 = 64. Answers will vary.

Looking Forward

Students will use the problem-solving process and strategies in each lesson of this text. Routine and non-routine strategy problems are presented every day in the Power-Up section of each lesson. One-step, two-step, and multi-step problems are presented in the Written Practice section of every lesson.

Section 1 Overview

Lessons 1–10, Investigation 1

Lesson Planner

LESSON	NEW CONCEPTS	MATERIALS	RESOURCES
1	• Adding Whole Numbers and Money • Subtracting Whole Numbers and Money • Fact Families, Part 1	Money manipulatives or play money	**Power Up A**
2	• Multiplying Whole Numbers and Money • Dividing Whole Numbers and Money • Fact Families, Part 2	Manipulative Kit: color tiles	**Power Up A** **Multiplication/ Division Fact Families poster**
3	• Unknown Numbers in Addition • Unknown Numbers in Subtraction		**Power Up B**
4	• Unknown Numbers in Multiplication • Unknown Numbers in Division		**Power Up A**
5	• Orders of Operations, Part 1	Index cards	**Power Up B**
6	• Fractional Parts	Manipulative Kit: color tiles, overhead fraction circles	**Power Up C** **Basic Fraction Circles poster**
7	• Lines, Segments, and Rays • Linear Measure	Manipulative Kit: inch and metric rulers Narrow strips of tagboard, 6″ × 1″ (one per student)	**Power Up C**
8	• Perimeter	Manipulative Kit: inch and metric rulers	**Power Up A**
9	• The Number Line: Ordering and Comparing	Manipulative Kit: inch and metric rulers	**Power Up C**
10	• Sequences • Scales	Indoor/outdoor thermometer	**Power Up C**
Inv. 1	• Frequency Tables • Histograms • Surveys	Manipulative Kit: inch or metric rulers Grid paper	

Lesson Highlights
Lessons 1–10, Investigation 1

Problem Solving
Strategies
- **Find a Pattern** Lessons 1, 4
- **Make a Model** Lesson 10
- **Make It Simpler** Lesson 4
- **Use Logical Reasoning** Lessons 3, 5, 6, 7, 9
- **Guess and Check** Lessons 5, 6
- **Make an Organized List** Lessons 2, 8
- **Write an Equation** Lesson 3

Alternative Strategies
- **Draw a Diagram** Lessons 1, 9
- **Write an Equation** Lessons 2, 3

Real-World Applications
pp. 9, 11–13, 16, 17, 21–22, 26, 27, 30, 31, 32, 34, 37, 39, 40–44, 46, 48, 51, 52–54, 55–57

4-Step Process
Student Edition Lessons 1, 3, 4, 5, 7, 8

Teacher Edition Lessons 1–10 (Power-Up Discussions)

Connections
Math and Other Subjects
- **Math and History** pp. 52, 53
- **Math and Geography** p. 57
- **Math and Science** pp. 36, 52, 53
- **Math and Other Cultures** pp. 30, 37
- **Math and Sports** pp. 26, 41, 44, 56

Math to Math
- **Problem Solving and Measurement** Lessons 1, 2, 3, 5, 6, 7, 8, 9, 10, Inv. 1
- **Algebra and Problem Solving** Lessons 3, 4, 5
- **Fractions, Percents and Problem Solving** Lessons 1, 2, 3, 4, 5, 8, 9, Inv. 1
- **Fractions and Measurement** Lessons 6, 7, 8, 10
- **Measurement and Geometry** Lessons 8, 9, 10

Communication
Discuss
pp. 13, 14, 15, 19, 20, 24, 43, 47

Explain
pp. 11, 16, 17, 21, 22, 24, 27, 31, 33, 34, 41, 44, 45, 49, 52

Formulate a Problem
pp. 26, 35, 57

Representation
Manipulatives/Hands On
pp. 8, 13–15, 32, 33, 37, 38, 45, 48–50

Model
pp. 38, 42, 45

Represent
pp. 10, 11, 14, 16, 17, 31, 34, 35, 44, 45, 48, 49, 53, 54, 55, 57

Technology

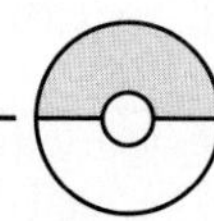

Student Resources
- **eBook**
- **Online Resources** at **www.SaxonPublishers.com/ActivitiesC1**
  - **Real-World Investigation 1** after Lesson 8
  - **Online Activities**
  - **Math Enrichment Problems**
  - **Math Stumpers**

Teacher Resources
- **Resources and Planner CD**
- **Adaptations CD** Lessons 1–10
- **Test & Practice Generator CD**
- **eGradebook**
- **Answer Key CD**

Content Highlights

Lessons 1–10, Investigation 1

In this section, students are reviewing previously learned skills. These skills involve operations and sequences.

Beginning the Year

Establish productive routines early in the school year.

Saxon Math is uniquely organized to develop and practice the various strands of mathematics concurrently. Consequently the early lessons in the book are foundational and usually seem easy to students. **If a student seems unusually challenged by early lessons, take steps to assure that the student is properly placed in the series.**

Power-Up

Each day, work through the Power-Up Section with students.

Fact practice fosters quick recall of essential knowledge and skills that allow students to focus their mental energies on problem solving. Mental Math develops facility with numbers and familiarity with commonly encountered applications of mathematics. Daily Problem Solving employs strategies that are useful for solving a wide range of real-world problems.

New Concepts

Involve students in working through each example.

Draw students' attention to new terminology. Guide student work on the Practice Set at the end of the New Concept section. These lesson practice problems should be considered part of the daily assignment. This dose of massed practice is an essential component of instruction.

Written Practice

Suggestions for Math Conversations provide support for guiding and extending problems.

Try to allow half of the class period for students to work on the Written Practice. Asterisks indicate potentially challenging problems that students should work on first, during class, where help is available. Exercises not finished in class become homework. Help students through difficult problems on the day's assignment to reduce the chance of misconceptions developing and to minimize the number of problems students might miss on homework.

Assessment

A variety of weekly assessment tools are provided.

After Lesson 10:

- Power-Up Test 1
- Cumulative Test 1
- Customized Benchmark Test
- Performance Task 1

Content Trace

Lessons 1–10, Investigation 1

LESSON	NEW CONCEPTS	PRACTICED	ASSESSED
1	• Adding Whole Numbers and Money	Lessons 1–11, 20, 72, 94	Tests 1, 2, 3
	• Subtracting Whole Numbers and Money	Lessons 1–10, 15, 16, 18, 28, 30, 37	Tests 1, 2, 3
	• Fact Families, Part 1	Lessons 1–8, 10, 15, 17, 22, 36, 42	Tests 1, 2, 3
2	• Multiplying Whole Numbers and Money	Lessons 2–13, 15–21, 23, 29, 31–33, 39, 49, 50–53, 58, 59, 72, 74	Tests 1, 2, 3
	• Dividing Whole Numbers and Money	Lessons 2–21, 23, 24, 27, 29–31, 33, 34, 35, 37, 39, 40, 42, 44, 49–53, 71, 89, 110	Tests 1, 2, 3, 4, 5, 6, 10
	• Fact Families, Part 2	Lessons 2–9, 11, 14, 19, 34, 40, 47, 53	Tests 1, 3
3	• Unknown Numbers in Addition	Lessons 3–12, 15, 17, 18, 21, 24, 29, 31, 37, 41, 67, 74, 89, 97	Tests 1, 2, 7
	• Unknown Numbers in Subtraction	Lessons 3–14, 16–24, 28, 29, 32, 33, 37, 40, 41, 54, 86	Tests 1, 3, 4, 7
4	• Unknown Numbers in Multiplication	Lessons 4–13, 15–17, 20, 23, 24, 29, 32, 34, 41	Tests 1, 2, 3, 4
	• Unknown Numbers in Division	Lessons 4–13, 15, 18, 19, 22, 24, 25, 34, 36, 47, 61, 87	Test & Practice Generator
5	• Orders of Operations, Part 1	Lessons 5–8, 11–22, 24, 25, 27–30, 34, 37, 38, 54, 56, 57, 63, 64, 66, 67, 69, 99	Tests 1, 2, 3, 6, 7, 19, 23
6	• Fractional Parts	Lessons 6–23, 26, 27, 39	Tests 2, 3, 4, 5, 19
7	• Lines, Segments, and Rays	Lessons 7–9, 11, 12, 19, 21–23, 26, 28, 36, 43, 65, 68–70, 76, 96, 99	Test 14
	• Linear Measure	Lessons 7–9, 11–15, 19, 21–23, 26, 28, 33, 35, 36, 39, 43, 52, 56, 58, 65, 68, 69, 71, 72, 76, 78, 83, 87, 96, 98, 99, 101, 105, 109–111, 113, 118, 120	Tests 2, 4
8	• Perimeter	Lessons 8–14, 16–30, 32, 33, 35–38, 40–42, 47–49, 54, 58, 63, 70, 75–77, 79, 83, 87–90, 100, 102, 103, 105, 107, 110, 116	Tests 2, 3, 4, 6, 7, 9, 11, 18
9	• The Number Line: Ordering and Comparing	Lessons 9–13, 15–24, 31, 32, 35, 38, 54, 55, 106	Test 2
10	• Sequences	Lessons 10–15, 17–21, 23, 26, 29, 31–34, 37, 47, 50, 52, 54, 57, 58, 60, 61, 63, 93, 97, 98, 108	Tests 2, 4, 6
	• Scales	Lessons 10, 11, 13, 15, 17, 18, 20, 24, 25, 28, 43, 44, 46, 57, 68, 77, 103	Test 3
Inv. 1	• Frequency Tables • Histograms • Surveys	Investigations 1, 4, 5, 9, Lessons 18, 40	Test & Practice Generator

• Adding Whole Numbers and Money
• Subtracting Whole Numbers and Money
• Fact Families, Part 1

Objectives

- Find the sum of two or more whole numbers.
- Use the Commutative and Identity Properties of Addition.
- Find the difference between two whole numbers and use addition to check the answer.
- Arrange three numbers to form a fact family made up of two addition facts and two subtraction facts.

Lesson Preparation

Materials

- **Power Up A** (in *Instructional Masters*)
- **Teacher-provided material: money manipulatives**

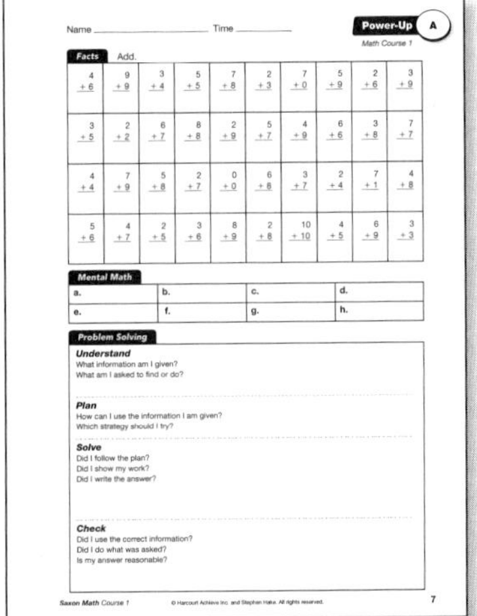

Name ____________ Time ________

Power-Up A
Math Course 1

Facts Add.

4 + 6	9 + 9	3 + 4	5 + 5	7 + 8	2 + 3	7 + 0	5 + 9	2 + 6	3 + 9
3 + 5	2 + 2	6 + 7	8 + 8	2 + 9	5 + 7	4 + 9	6 + 6	3 + 8	7 + 7
4 + 4	7 + 9	5 + 8	2 + 7	0 + 0	6 + 8	3 + 7	2 + 4	7 + 1	4 + 8
5 + 6	4 + 7	2 + 5	3 + 6	8 + 9	2 + 8	10 + 10	4 + 5	6 + 9	3 + 3

Mental Math

a.	b.	c.	d.
e.	f.	g.	h.

Problem Solving

Understand
What information am I given?
What am I asked to find or do?

Plan
How can I use the information I am given?
Which strategy should I try?

Solve
Did I follow the plan?
Did I show my work?
Did I write the answer?

Check
Did I use the correct information?
Did I do what was asked?
Is my answer reasonable?

Saxon Math Course 1 © Harcourt Achieve Inc. and Stephen Hake. All rights reserved. 7

Power Up A

Math Language

New		English Learners (ESL)
addends	Identity Property of Addition	align
Commutative Property of Addition	inverse operations	form
difference	minuend	
fact family	subtrahend	
	sum	

Technology Resources

Student eBook Complete student textbook in electronic format.

Resources and Planner CD Assessment, reteaching, and instructional masters, plus a pacing calendar with standards.

Test and Practice Generator CD Create additional practice sheets and custom-made tests.

www.SaxonPublishers.com Visit for more student activities and planning materials.

Inclusion

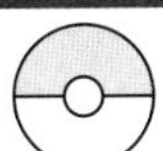

Adaptations CD Adapted lessons, investigations, practice and assessments.

Meeting Standards

National Council of Teachers of Mathematics (NCTM)

Numbers and Operations

NO.1a Work flexibly with fractions, decimals, and percents to solve problems

NO.2a Understand the meaning and effects of arithmetic operations with fractions, decimals, and integers

NO.2b Use the associative and commutative properties of addition and multiplication and the distributive property of multiplication over addition to simplify computations with integers, fractions, and decimals

NO.2c Understand and use the inverse relationships of addition and subtraction, multiplication and division, and squaring and finding square roots to simplify computations and solve problems

Power-Up Discussion *For use with Power Up, p. 7*

Problem-Solving Strategy: Find a Pattern

Sharon made three square patterns using 4 coins, 9 coins, and 16 coins. If she continues forming larger square patterns, how many coins will she need for each of the next three square patterns?

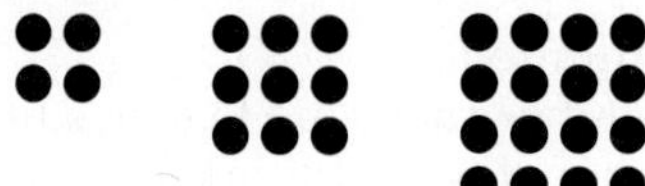

Understand We are given 4, 9, and 16 as the first four square numbers. We are asked to extend the sequence an additional three terms.

Plan We will find the pattern in the first three terms of the sequence, then use the pattern to extend the sequence an additional three terms.

Teacher Note: Ask students, "Is there only one correct strategy to use to solve this problem?" Tell students that almost any problem or challenge can be approached in a variety of ways, but that one strategy might have advantages over another. For example, drawing a diagram might make the problem easier to visualize, but it might be more time-consuming than another strategy.

Solve We see that the number of coins in each square can be found by multiplying the number of coins in each row by the number of rows: $2 \times 2 = 4$, $3 \times 3 = 9$, and $4 \times 4 = 16$. We use this rule to find the next three terms: $5 \times 5 = 25$, $6 \times 6 = 36$, and $7 \times 7 = 49$.

Teacher Note: Encourage students to look for other patterns in the sequence. Some students may recognize that each term in the sequence can be found by adding consecutive odd numbers to the previous term ($1 + 3 = 4$; $4 + 5 = 9$; $9 + 7 = 16$, etc.).

Check We found that Sharon needs 25, 36, and 49 coins to build each of the next three squares in the pattern. We can verify our answers by drawing the pictures of each of the next three terms in the pattern and counting the coins.

Alternate Approach: Draw a Diagram

Some students may have difficulty recognizing the multiplication pattern in the sequence. Instead, have these students draw the next three terms in the sequence and count the number of coins in each term.

LESSON 1

• Adding Whole Numbers and Money
• Subtracting Whole Numbers and Money
• Fact Families, Part 1

Power Up[1] *Building Power*

facts Power Up A

mental math

a. **Number Sense:** $30 + 30$ 60

b. **Number Sense:** $300 + 300$ 600

c. **Number Sense:** $80 + 40$ 120

d. **Number Sense:** $800 + 400$ 1200

e. **Number Sense:** $20 + 30 + 40$ 90

f. **Number Sense:** $200 + 300 + 400$ 900

g. **Measurement:** How many inches are in a foot? 12 in.

h. **Measurement:** How many millimeters are in a centimeter? 10 mm

problem solving

Sharon made three square patterns using 4 coins, 9 coins, and 16 coins. If she continues forming larger square patterns, how many coins will she need for each of the next three square patterns?

Understand We are given 4, 9, and 16 as the first three square numbers. We are asked to extend the sequence an additional three terms.

Plan We will *find the pattern* in the first three terms of the sequence, then use the pattern to extend the sequence an additional three terms.

Solve We see that the number of coins in each square can be found by multiplying the number of coins in each row by the number of rows: $2 \times 2 = 4$, $3 \times 3 = 9$, and $4 \times 4 = 16$. We use this rule to find the next three terms: $5 \times 5 = 25$, $6 \times 6 = 36$, and $7 \times 7 = 49$.

Check We found that Sharon needs 25, 36, and 49 coins to build each of the next three squares in the pattern. We can verify our answers by drawing pictures of each of the next three terms in the pattern and counting the coins.

[1] For instructions on how to use the Power Up, please consult the preface.

Facts Add.

4 + 6 10	9 + 9 18	3 + 4 7	5 + 5 10	7 + 8 15	2 + 3 5	7 + 0 7	5 + 9 14	2 + 6 8	3 + 9 12
3 + 5 8	2 + 2 4	6 + 7 13	8 + 8 16	2 + 9 11	5 + 7 12	4 + 9 13	6 + 6 12	3 + 8 11	7 + 7 14
4 + 4 8	7 + 9 16	5 + 8 13	2 + 7 9	0 + 0 0	6 + 8 14	3 + 7 10	2 + 4 6	7 + 1 8	4 + 8 12
5 + 6 11	4 + 7 11	2 + 5 7	3 + 6 9	8 + 9 17	2 + 8 10	10 + 10 20	4 + 5 9	6 + 9 15	3 + 3 6

1 Power Up

Facts

Distribute **Power Up A** to students. See answers below.

Mental Math

Before students begin the Mental Math exercise, do this counting exercise as a class.

Count by 10s from 10 to 100 and from 100 to 0.

Count by 100s from 100 to 1000 and from 1000 to 0.

Encourage students to share different ways to mentally compute these exercises. Strategies for exercises **c** and **e** are listed below.

c. Count on by Tens

Start with 80. Count: 90, 100, 110, 120

Add to 100

$80 + 20 = 100$; $100 + 20 = 120$

e. Add Tens

2 tens + 3 tens + 4 tens = 9 tens = 90

Count on by Tens

Start with 20. Count: 30, 40, 50

Start with 50. Count: 60, 70, 80, 90

Problem Solving

Refer to **Power-Up Discussion,** p. 7F.

2 New Concepts

Instruction

To reinforce their understanding of the Commutative Property of Addition, ask each student to name a unique example using facts. For example, 2 + 7 = 9 and 7 + 2 = 9.

Example 1

Instruction

Remind students to add from right to left, starting with the digits in the ones place. After finding the sum, invite a volunteer to explain why two regroupings were necessary.

Example 2

Instruction

Point out that $5 indicates five dollars and no cents. Explain that writing the amount as $5.00 will help students maintain correct vertical alignment of the addends.

(continued)

New Concepts *Increasing Knowledge*

adding whole numbers and money

To combine two or more numbers, we add. The numbers that are added together are called **addends.** The answer is called the **sum.** Changing the order of the addends does not change the sum. For example,

3 + 5 = 5 + 3

This property of addition is called the **Commutative Property of Addition.**

When adding numbers, we add digits that have the same place value.

Example 1

Add: 345 + 67

Solution

When we add whole numbers on paper, we write the numbers so that the place values are aligned. Then we add the digits by column.

```
   11
  345  addend
+  67  addend
  412  sum
```

Changing the order of the addends does not change the sum. One way to check an addition answer is to change the order of the addends and add again.

```
   11
   67
+ 345
  412  check
```

Example 2

Thinking Skill

Connect

$5 means five dollars and no cents. Why does writing $5 as $5.00 help when adding money amounts? Writing $5.00 helps us to align our decimals.

Add: $1.25 + $12.50 + $5

Solution

When we add money, we write the numbers so that the decimal points are aligned. We write $5 as $5.00 and add the digits in each column.

```
   $1.25
  $12.50
+  $5.00
  $18.75
```

If one of two addends is zero, the sum of the addends is identical to the nonzero addend. This property of addition is called the **Identity Property of Addition.**

5 + 0 = 5

subtracting whole numbers and money

We subtract one number from another number to find the **difference** between the two numbers. In a subtraction problem, the **subtrahend** is taken from the **minuend.**

5 − 3 = 2

In the problem above, 5 is the minuend and 3 is the subtrahend. The difference between 5 and 3 is 2.

Verify Does the Commutative Property apply to subtraction? Give an example to support your answer. No; for example, 2 − 4 does not equal 4 − 2.

8 *Saxon Math Course 1*

Manipulative Use

After completing example 2, invite students to name real-world items that represent each money amount. For example, $1.25 might represent the cost of a notebook in the school bookstore. If **money manipulatives** are available, have students use the coins and bills to model each amount, and then model the addition of the amounts.

English Learners

Write 8.99 + 17.67 on the board vertically so that the decimal points are not aligned. Say:

"Before we can add these decimal numbers, we need to align the decimal points. When we align the decimal points, we place them in a line, like this."

Rewrite the problem so the decimal points are aligned vertically. Write this problem on the board: 32.25 + 19.3. Ask a volunteer to write the problem vertically with the decimal points aligned.

Example 3

Subtract: 345 − 67

Solution

When we subtract whole numbers, we align the digits by place value. We subtract the bottom number from the top number and regroup when necessary.

$$\begin{array}{r} \overset{2}{\cancel{3}}\overset{13}{\cancel{4}}\overset{1}{}5 \\ -\ \ 67 \\ \hline \mathbf{278} \end{array} \leftarrow \text{difference}$$

Example 4

Jim spent $1.25 for a hamburger. He paid for it with a five-dollar bill. Find how much change he should get back by subtracting $1.25 from $5.

Solution

Thinking Skill
When is it necessary to line up decimals? When adding or subtracting decimals.

Order matters when we subtract. The starting amount is put on top. We write $5 as $5.00. We line up the decimal points to align the place values. Then we subtract. Jim should get back **$3.75.**

$$\begin{array}{r} \$\overset{4}{\cancel{5}}.\overset{9}{\cancel{0}}\overset{1}{}0 \\ -\ \$1.25 \\ \hline \$3.75 \end{array}$$

We can check the answer to a subtraction problem by adding. If we add the answer (difference) to the amount subtracted, the total should equal the starting amount. We do not need to rewrite the problem. We just add the two bottom numbers to see whether their sum equals the top number.

Subtract Down ↓		Add Up ↑
To find the difference	$5.00 − $1.25 $3.75	To check the answer

fact families, part 1

Addition and subtraction are called **inverse operations.** We can "undo" an addition by subtracting one addend from the sum. The three numbers that form an addition fact also form a subtraction fact. For example,

$$4 + 5 = 9 \qquad 9 - 5 = 4$$

The numbers 4, 5, and 9 are a **fact family.** They can be arranged to form the two addition facts and two subtraction facts shown below.

$$\begin{array}{r} 4 \\ +5 \\ \hline 9 \end{array} \quad \begin{array}{r} 5 \\ +4 \\ \hline 9 \end{array} \quad \begin{array}{r} 9 \\ -5 \\ \hline 4 \end{array} \quad \begin{array}{r} 9 \\ -4 \\ \hline 5 \end{array}$$

Example 5

Rearrange the numbers in this addition fact to form another addition fact and two subtraction facts.

11 + 14 = 25

2 New Concepts *(Continued)*

Example 3

Instruction

Have students note the two regroupings.

"Why are two regroupings needed when 67 is subtracted from 345?" In the subtrahend, the place values of the ones and tens are greater than the place values of the ones and tens places in the minuend.

"In any subtraction, when must you regroup?" Whenever a place value of the subtrahend is greater than the same place value of the minuend.

Example 4

Instruction

Reinforce the concept of regrouping.

"When there aren't enough hundredths to subtract, 1 tenth is regrouped as how many hundredths?" 10

"When there aren't enough tenths to subtract, 1 one is regrouped as how many tenths?" 10

"When there aren't enough ones to subtract, 1 ten is regrouped as how many ones?" 10

Example 5

Instruction

Remind students of the role of the Commutative Property in fact families.

"Reversing the addends forms another addition fact. What property of addition is demonstrated by reversing the addends?" the Commutative Property

(continued)

English Learners

In fact families, part 1, explain that the word **form** means "to make something new." Write 14 + 11 = 25 on the board and say:

"When we form a new fact from 14 + 11 = 25, we write a different fact using the same numbers."

Write 25 − 11 = 14 and say:

"I formed a new fact using the numbers 25, 11, and 14. What other addition and subtraction facts can we form using these numbers?" 11 + 14 = 25, 25 − 14 = 11

Math Background

An inverse operation is an opposite operation. Addition and subtraction are opposite operations, and generally speaking, $a + n - n = a$. In other words, adding a number, then subtracting the same number (and vice versa), produces the original number.

2 New Concepts (Continued)

Example 6

Instruction

Have students note that a fact family is made up of four related facts if the addends are not identical.

"How many addition and subtraction facts altogether are in an addition and subtraction fact family?" four

After completing the example, challenge students to use mental math to name four different fact families.

Practice Set

Problem a Error Alert

If students do not align the digits correctly, ask them to work on grid paper or lined paper turned sideways.

Problem d Error Alert

Because $5 is a whole number of dollars, there are no cents to subtract from. Remind students to write a decimal point and two placeholder zeros ($5.00) before subtracting.

Solution

We form another addition fact by reversing the addends.

14 + 11 = 25

We form two subtraction facts by making the sum, 25, the first number of each subtraction fact. Then each remaining number is subtracted from 25.

25 − 11 = 14

25 − 14 = 11

Example 6

Rearrange the numbers in this subtraction fact to form another subtraction fact and two addition facts.

$$\begin{array}{r} 11 \\ -\ 6 \\ \hline 5 \end{array}$$

Solution

The Commutative Property does not apply to subtraction, so we may not reverse the first two numbers of a subtraction problem. However, we may reverse the last two numbers.

$$\begin{array}{r} 11 \\ -\ 6 \\ \hline 5 \end{array} \quad \begin{array}{r} 11 \\ -\ 5 \\ \hline 6 \end{array}$$

For the two addition facts, 11 is the sum.

$$\begin{array}{r} 5 \\ +\ 6 \\ \hline 11 \end{array} \quad \begin{array}{r} 6 \\ +\ 5 \\ \hline 11 \end{array}$$

Practice Set Simplify:

▸ **a.** 3675 + 426 + 1357 5458 **b.** $6.25 + $8.23 + $12 $26.48

c. 5374 − 168 5206 ▸ **d.** $5 − $1.35 $3.65

e. Represent Arrange the numbers 6, 8, and 14 to form two addition facts and two subtraction facts. 6 + 8 = 14, 8 + 6 = 14, 14 − 6 = 8, 14 − 8 = 6

f. Connect Rearrange the numbers in this subtraction fact to form another subtraction fact and two addition facts. 25 − 15 = 10, 10 + 15 = 25, 15 + 10 = 25 25 − 10 = 15

Written Practice *Strengthening Concepts*

1. What is the sum of 25 and 40? 65

2. At a planetarium show, Johnny counted 137 students and 89 adults. He also counted 9 preschoolers. How many people did Johnny count in all? 235 people

▸ See Math Conversations in the sidebar.

3. **Generalize** What is the difference when 93 is subtracted from 387? 294

4. Keisha paid $5 for a movie ticket that cost $3.75. Find how much change Keisha should get back by subtracting $3.75 from $5. $1.25

5. **Explain** Tatiana had $5.22 and earned $4.15 more by taking care of her neighbor's cat. How much money did she have then? Explain how you found the answer. $9.37; Sample: I added the two amounts because I was combining what Tatiana earned with what she already had.

6. The soup cost $1.25, the fruit cost $0.70, and the drink cost $0.60. To find the total price of the lunch, add $1.25, $0.70, and $0.60. $2.55

7. $63 + 47 + 50$ = 160

8. $632 + 57 + 198$ = 887

9. $78 + 9 + 987$ = 1074

10. $432 + 579 + 3604$ = 4615

11. 345 − 67 278

12. 678 − 416 262

13. 3764 − 96 3668

14. 875 + 1086 + 980 2941

15. 10 + 156 + 8 + 27 201

16. $3.47 − $0.92 = $2.55

17. $24.15 − $1.45 = $22.70

18. $0.75 + $0.75 = $1.50

19. $0.12 + $0.46 + $0.50 = $1.08

20. What is the name for the answer when we add? sum

21. What is the name for the answer when we subtract? difference

* 22. **Represent** The numbers 5, 6, and 11 are a fact family. Form two addition facts and two subtraction facts with these three numbers. 5 + 6 = 11, 6 + 5 = 11, 11 − 6 = 5, 11 − 5 = 6

* 23. **Connect** Rearrange the numbers in this addition fact to form another addition fact and two subtraction facts.

27 + 16 = 43

16 + 27 = 43, 43 − 16 = 27, 43 − 27 = 16

* 24. **Connect** Rearrange the numbers in this subtraction fact to form another subtraction fact and two addition facts.

50 − 21 = 29

50 − 29 = 21, 29 + 21 = 50, 21 + 29 = 50

25. Describe a way to check the correctness of a subtraction answer. One way to check is to add the answer (difference) to the amount subtracted. The total should equal the starting amount.

* We encourage students to work first on the exercises on which they might want help, saving the easier exercises for last. Beginning in this lesson, we star the exercises that cover challenging or recently presented content. We suggest that these exercises be worked first.

Lesson 1 11

▶ See Math Conversations in the sidebar.

Looking Forward

Adding whole numbers and money prepares students for:

- **Lesson 3,** finding missing numbers in addition.
- **Lesson 12,** understanding place value of digits through trillions.
- **Lesson 16,** estimating the sum of two numbers.
- **Lesson 37,** adding and subtracting decimal numbers.
- **Lesson 38,** adding and subtracting decimal and whole numbers.

3 Written Practice

Math Conversations

Discussion opportunities are provided below.

Problem 3 Generalize

Challenge students to describe a variety of ways to find the difference using mental math. Sample: Subtract 100 from 387, then add back 7.

Problem 5 Explain

"Why was addition used to find the answer?" Sample: In a combining problem, the word *more* represents an increase.

Problem 22 Represent

Students should recognize that the facts within any fact family represent related equations.

"What relationship is shared by the facts in every fact family?" The facts are related equations.

Problem 23 Connect

Lead students to connect fact families to inverse operations.

"How are inverse operations a part of fact families?" The related equations are inverse operations; an operation in one equation is undone by the operation in its related equation.

Errors and Misconceptions

Problem 22

When working with fact families, students may assume that every fact family must have four related equations. To address this assumption, ask students to form an addition and subtraction fact family using the numbers 9, 9, and 18. The students will discover that the numbers only form one addition equation (9 + 9 = 18) and one subtraction equation (18 − 9 = 9). However, point out that a fact family can consist of only two related equations, and make sure that students understand that the numbers 9, 9, and 18 do form a fact family.

• Multiplying Whole Numbers and Money
• Dividing Whole Numbers and Money
• Fact Families, Part 2

Objectives

- Recognize multiplication expressions and find the product of two whole numbers.
- Multiply dollars and cents by a whole number.
- Use the Commutative Property of Multiplication to check multiplication.
- Identify and use the Identity Property of Multiplication and the Zero Property of Multiplication.
- Recognize expressions that indicate division and use division to divide whole numbers and money.
- Arrange three numbers to form a fact family made up of two multiplication facts and two division facts.

Lesson Preparation

Materials

- **Power Up A** (in *Instructional Masters*)
- **Manipulative kit: color tiles**

Optional

- **Multiplication/Division Fact Families poster**

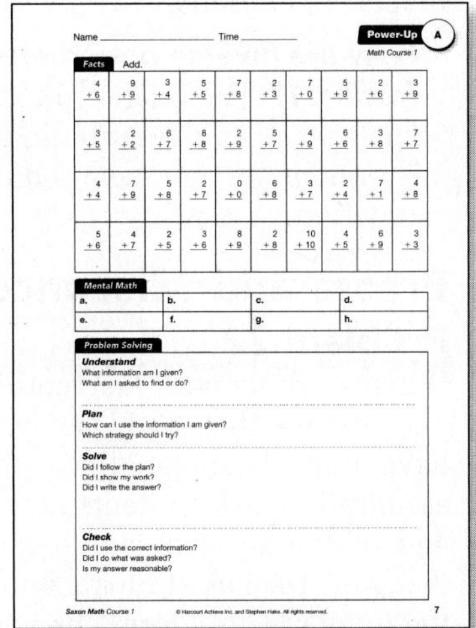

Power Up A

Math Language

New		English Learners (ESL)
Commutative Property	Identity Property of Multiplication	elevated
dividend	product	position
divisor	quotient	
factors	Zero Property of Multiplication	

Technology Resources

Student eBook Complete student textbook in electronic format.

Resources and Planner CD Assessment, reteaching, and instructional masters, plus a pacing calendar with standards.

Test and Practice Generator CD Create additional practice sheets and custom-made tests.

www.SaxonPublishers.com Visit for more student activities and planning materials.

Inclusion

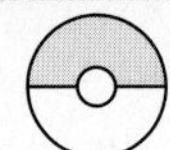

Adaptations CD Adapted lessons, investigations, practice and assessments.

Meeting Standards

National Council of Teachers of Mathematics (NCTM)

Numbers and Operations

NO.1a Work flexibly with fractions, decimals, and percents to solve problems

NO.2a Understand the meaning and effects of arithmetic operations with fractions, decimals, and integers

NO.2b Use the associative and commutative properties of addition and multiplication and the distributive property of multiplication over addition to simplify computations with integers, fractions, and decimals

NO.2c Understand and use the inverse relationships of addition and subtraction, multiplication and division, and squaring and finding square roots to simplify computations and solve problems

Power-Up Discussion *For use with Power Up, p. 12*

Problem-Solving Strategy: Make an Organized List

Sam thought of a number between ten and twenty. Then he gave a clue: You say the number when you count by twos and when you count by threes, but not when you count by fours. Of what number was Sam thinking?

Understand — *Understand the problem.*

"What information are we given?"

Sam's number is between ten and twenty.
You say the number when counting by twos.
You say the number when counting by threes.
You do not say the number when counting by fours.

Teacher Note: Tell students that when you count by a certain number, you are saying the number's multiples in order.

"What are we asked to do?"

We are asked to find Sam's number.

Plan — *Make a plan.*

"How can we use the information we know to do what we are asked to do?"

We can *make organized lists* of the numbers you say when counting by twos, threes, and fours. Then we will look for a number that satisfies the information we are given.

Solve — *Carry out the plan.*

Multiples of 2 between 10 and 20:	10	12	14		16	18	20
Multiples of 3 between 10 and 20:		12		15		18	
Multiples of 4 between 10 and 20:		12			16		20

"Which numbers do we say when counting by both twos and threes?"

12 and 18

"Which of these numbers (12 and 18) do we not say when counting by fours?"

18

Check

"Did we complete the task?"

Yes, 18 is between 10 and 20. We say it when counting by twos and threes but not when counting by fours.

Alternate Approach: Write an Equation

Some students may write equations to find the multiples of 2 and 3, 2 and 4, and 3 and 4, then compare their answers to find the solution.

1 Power Up

Facts

Distribute **Power Up A** to students. See answers below.

Mental Math

Before students begin the Mental Math exercise, do this counting exercise as a class.

Count by 5s from 5 to 100 and from 100 to 0.

Count by 2s from 2 to 20 and from 20 to 2.

Encourage students to share different ways to mentally compute these exercises. Strategies for exercises **c** and **d** are listed below.

c. Use the Associative Property

$(30 + 40) + 200 = 70 + 200 = 270$

Count on by Tens, then Add

Start with 30. Count: 40, 50, 60, 70

Add: $70 + 200 = 270$

d. Add Hundreds, then Tens

$70 + 300 + 400 = 70 + 700 = 770$

Add from Left to Right

$70 + 300 + 400 = 370 + 400 = 770$

Problem Solving

Refer to **Power Up Discussion,** p. 12B.

2 New Concepts

Instruction

The perimeter scenario helps show that multiplication is related to addition, and is a shorthand method of writing a repeated addition.

Invite volunteers to describe other real-world scenarios that involve multiplying whole numbers, or money amounts. Examples include buying more than one of the same item and hourly wages.

(continued)

LESSON **2**

• Multiplying Whole Numbers and Money
• Dividing Whole Numbers and Money
• Fact Families, Part 2

Power Up — *Building Power*

facts Power Up A

mental math

a. Number Sense: $500 + 40$ 540

b. Number Sense: $60 + 200$ 260

c. Number Sense: $30 + 200 + 40$ 270

d. Number Sense: $70 + 300 + 400$ 770

e. Number Sense: $400 + 50 + 30$ 480

f. Number Sense: $60 + 20 + 400$ 480

g. Measurement: How many inches are in 2 feet? 24 in.

h. Measurement: How many millimeters are in 2 centimeters? 20 mm

problem solving Sam thought of a number between ten and twenty. Then he gave a clue: You say the number when you count by twos and when you count by threes, but not when you count by fours. Of what number was Sam thinking? 18

New Concepts — *Increasing Knowledge*

multiplying whole numbers and money

Courtney wants to enclose a square garden to grow vegetables. How many feet of fencing does she need?

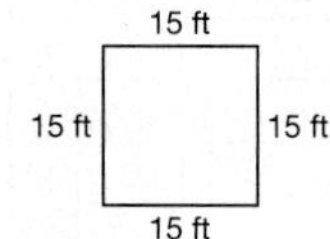

When we add the same number several times, we get a sum. We can get the same result by multiplying.

$$\underbrace{15 + 15 + 15 + 15}_{\text{Four 15s equal 60.}} = 60$$

$$4 \times 15 = 60$$

Numbers that are multiplied together are called **factors.** The answer is called the **product.**

To indicate multiplication, we can use a times sign, a dot, or write the factors side by side without a sign. Each of these expressions means that l and w are multiplied: $l \times w$ $\quad l \cdot w$ $\quad lw$

Facts Add.

4 + 6 = 10	9 + 9 = 18	3 + 4 = 7	5 + 5 = 10	7 + 8 = 15	2 + 3 = 5	7 + 0 = 7	5 + 9 = 14	2 + 6 = 8	3 + 9 = 12
3 + 5 = 8	2 + 2 = 4	6 + 7 = 13	8 + 8 = 16	2 + 9 = 11	5 + 7 = 12	4 + 9 = 13	6 + 6 = 12	3 + 8 = 11	7 + 7 = 14
4 + 4 = 8	7 + 9 = 16	5 + 8 = 13	2 + 7 = 9	0 + 0 = 0	6 + 8 = 14	3 + 7 = 10	2 + 4 = 6	7 + 1 = 8	4 + 8 = 12
5 + 6 = 11	4 + 7 = 11	2 + 5 = 7	3 + 6 = 9	8 + 9 = 17	2 + 8 = 10	10 + 10 = 20	4 + 5 = 9	6 + 9 = 15	3 + 3 = 6

Notice that in the form $l \cdot w$ the multiplication dot is elevated and is not in the position of a decimal point. The form *lw* can be used to show the multiplication of two or more letters or of a number and letters, as we show below.

$$lwh \quad 4s \quad 4st$$

The form *lw* can also be used to show the multiplication of two or more numbers. To prevent confusion, however, we use parentheses to separate the numbers in the multiplication. Each of the following is a correct use of parentheses to indicate "3 times 5," although the first form is most commonly used. Without the parentheses, we would read each of these simply as the number 35.

$$3(5) \quad (3)(5) \quad (3)5$$

Thinking Skill

Discuss

Why do we multiply 28 by 4, by 10, and then add to find the product?

We multiply by the value of the ones place and then by the value of the tens place. We add to get the total.

When we multiply by a two-digit number on paper, we multiply twice. To multiply 28 by 14, we first multiply 28 by 4. Then we multiply 28 by 10. For each multiplication we write a partial product. We add the partial products to find the final product.

```
  28   factor
× 14   factor
 112   partial product (28 × 4)
 280   partial product (28 × 10)
 392   product (14 × 28)
```

When multiplying dollars and cents by a whole number, the answer will have a dollar sign and a decimal point with two places after the decimal point.

```
  $1.35
×     6
  $8.10
```

Example 1

Find the cost of two dozen pencils at 35¢ each.

Solution

Two dozen is two 12s, which is 24. To find the cost of 24 pencils, we multiply 35¢ by 24.

```
  35¢
× 24
 140
 700
 840¢
```

The cost of two dozen pencils is 840¢, which is **$8.40.**

The **Commutative Property** applies to multiplication as well as addition, so changing the order of the factors does not change the product. For example,

$$4 \times 2 = 2 \times 4$$

2 New Concepts (Continued)

Example 1

Instruction

Another way to find the total cost is to use decimal notation.

"In the example, a cent symbol is used to show the cost of one pencil. How could decimal notation be used to show the same cost?" $0.35

Invite a volunteer to complete the computation $0.35 × 24 at the board, and ask the remainder of the class to predict the number of decimal places that should be present in the product.

(continued)

Manipulative Use

Two models for multiplication are the **rectangular array model** and **the equal groups model.** Both models may be used to illustrate the Commutative Property of Multiplication. Use **color tiles** to demonstrate both models.

- To use the rectangular array model, make four rows of two tiles to model 4 × 2, and two rows of four tiles to model 2 × 4. Then have students count the total number of tiles in each array to confirm that 4 × 2 = 2 × 4.
- To use the equal groups model, make four groups of two tiles to model 4 × 2 and two groups of four tiles to model 2 × 4. Again, have students count the total number of tiles to confirm that 4 × 2 = 2 × 4.

English Learners

Write $l \cdot w$ on the board. Point to the multiplication dot and say:

"Notice the dot between the l and w. A dot like this is a sign used for multiplication. It is elevated, or placed above, the bottom of the letters."

Draw a dotted line along the base of the equation. Write 12 and 10 on the board. Then ask a volunteer to place an elevated multiplication dot between the two numbers.

2 New Concepts (Continued)

Instruction

These sentences state the Identity Property of Multiplication and the Zero Property of Multiplication. Have students write the term Identity Property of Multiplication on their papers, and then ask them to create examples illustrating the property (for example, $365 \times 1 = 365$). Check students' work for understanding. Repeat the procedure for the Zero Property of Multiplication.

Example 2

Instruction

Have students note that the method does not produce partial products.

Instruction

When working with dividends, divisors, and quotients, students should understand that a divisor can be any number except zero.

"In a division problem, the dividend, the quotient, or the dividend and the quotient may be zero. What number can a divisor never be?" zero

(continued)

One way to check multiplication is to reverse the order of factors and multiply.

$$\begin{array}{r} 23 \\ \times\ 14 \\ \hline 92 \\ 230 \\ \hline 322 \end{array} \qquad \begin{array}{r} 14 \\ \times\ 23 \\ \hline 42 \\ 280 \\ \hline 322 \end{array} \quad \text{check}$$

The **Identity Property of Multiplication** states that if one of two factors is 1, the product equals the other factor. The **Zero Property of Multiplication** states that if zero is a factor of a multiplication, the product is zero.

Represent Give an example for each property. Examples vary. Possible examples: $23 \cdot 1 = 23$; $23 \cdot 0 = 0$

Example 2

Thinking Skill

Discuss

Why does writing trailing zeros not change the product?

Any number multiplied by 400 will have a ***dividing*** product ***whole numbers and*** that ***money*** ends with 2 zeros.

Multiply: $\begin{array}{r} 400 \\ \times\ 874 \end{array}$

Solution

To simplify the multiplication, we reverse the order of the factors and write trailing zeros so that they "hang out" to the right.

$$\begin{array}{r} {}^{2\,1} \\ 874 \\ \times\ \ 400 \\ \hline \mathbf{349{,}600} \end{array}$$

When we separate a number into a certain number of equal parts, we divide. We can indicate division with a division symbol (÷), a division box ($\overline{)\ \ }$), or a division bar (–). Each of the expressions below means "24 divided by 2":

$$24 \div 2 \qquad 2\overline{)24} \qquad \frac{24}{2}$$

The answer to a division problem is the **quotient.** The number that is divided is the **dividend.** The number by which the dividend is divided is the **divisor.**

dividend ÷ divisor = quotient
$\text{divisor}\overline{)\text{dividend}}$ with quotient above
$\frac{\text{dividend}}{\text{divisor}} = \text{quotient}$

When the dividend is zero, the quotient is zero. The divisor may not be zero. When the dividend and divisor are equal (and not zero), the quotient is 1.

Example 3

Divide: 3456 ÷ 7

Solution

On the next page, we show both the long-division and short-division methods.

Manipulative Use

Demonstrate or have students **model the division** of 24 by 2 two different times using **color tiles** from the manipulative kit.

- Show 24 tiles divided into two equal groups. How many tiles are in each group? 12 tiles
- Show 24 tiles divided into groups of two. How many groups are formed? 12 groups

Thinking Skill

Discuss

Why must the remainder always be less than the divisor?

If the remainder is equal to or greater than the divisor, it means that there is at least one more group equal to the divisor in the dividend.

Long Division	Short Division
$\begin{array}{r} 493 \text{ R } 5 \\ 7\overline{)3456} \\ \underline{28} \\ 65 \\ \underline{63} \\ 26 \\ \underline{21} \\ 5 \end{array}$	$\begin{array}{r} 4\,9\,3 \text{ R } 5 \\ 7\overline{)34{}^{6}5{}^{2}6} \end{array}$

Using the short-division method, we perform the multiplication and subtraction steps mentally, recording only the result of each subtraction.

To check our work, we multiply the quotient by the divisor. Then we add the remainder to this answer. The result should be the dividend. For this example we multiply 493 by 7. Then we add 5.

$$\begin{array}{r} {}^{62} \\ 493 \\ \times \quad 7 \\ \hline 3451 \\ + \quad 5 \\ \hline 3456 \end{array}$$

When dividing dollars and cents, cents will be included in the answer. Notice that the decimal point in the quotient is directly above the decimal point in the division box, separating the dollars from the cents.

$$\begin{array}{r} \$.90 \\ 4\overline{)\$3.60} \\ \underline{3\,6} \\ 00 \\ \underline{0} \\ 0 \end{array}$$

fact families, part 2

Multiplication and division are inverse operations, so there are multiplication and division fact families just as there are addition and subtraction fact families. The numbers 5, 6, and 30 are a fact family. We can form two multiplication facts and two division facts with these numbers.

$5 \times 6 = 30 \qquad 30 \div 5 = 6$

$6 \times 5 = 30 \qquad 30 \div 6 = 5$

Example 4

Rearrange the numbers in this multiplication fact to form another multiplication fact and two division facts.

$$\mathbf{5 \times 12 = 60}$$

Solution

By reversing the factors, we form another multiplication fact.

$$\mathbf{12 \times 5 = 60}$$

By making 60 the dividend, we can form two division facts.

$$\mathbf{60 \div 5 = 12}$$

$$\mathbf{60 \div 12 = 5}$$

2 New Concepts (Continued)

Example 3

Instruction

Remind students that multiplication is used to check division because multiplication and division are inverse operations. In this example, the multiplication check undoes the division.

Instruction

You may wish to display the **Multiplication/ Division Fact Families** concept poster as you discuss this topic with students.

Example 4

Instruction

After completing the example, ask students to write a multiplication and division fact family using 3, 7, and 21.

(continued)

Inclusion

Some students may need help remembering the multiplication and division facts. Triangular flash cards like the ones below may be helpful.

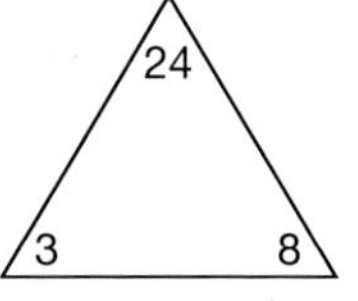

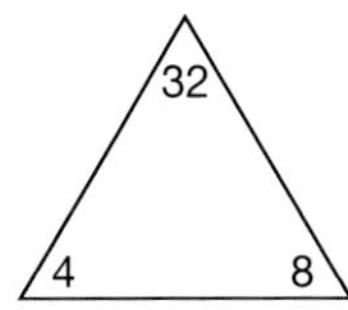

Draw the cards on the board. Then demonstrate that if you know one fact in a family, you know four facts. Have students make cards for fact families that they need to master.

Math Background

Working with fact families introduces students to inverse operations. It is essential for students to have an understanding of inverse operations because inverse operations represent the foundation, or the primary method students will use, of solving equations for unknowns.

2 New Concepts (Continued)

Practice Set

Problem a Error Alert

If students answer \$740, remind them that the cent symbol represents hundredths. Name a variety of cents such as 45¢, 8¢, and 100¢, then ask students to name the decimal equivalent for each amount (\$0.45, \$0.08, \$1.00).

Problem d Error Alert

An answer of \$168 represents a missing decimal point in the quotient. For all problems involving decimal dividends, ask students to place a decimal point in each quotient before any computations are begun.

3 Written Practice

Math Conversations

Discussion opportunities are provided below.

Problem 2 Generalize

Challenge students to describe a variety of ways to find the difference using mental math. Sample: Add 2 to 97, then subtract 2 from the difference; 99 − 79 = 20 and 20 − 2 = 18.

Problem 5 Verify

Extend the Problem

Ask students to explain how rounding can be used to help decide if the exact sum is reasonable. Sample: Round each addend to the nearest hundred, then add. Since 400 + 100 + 1700 = 2200, an exact sum that is close to 2200 is a reasonable answer.

Problem 8 Explain

When writing money amounts, some ways of writing the amount are more sensible than others.

"The cost of one energy bar is given in cents. When you write the cost of one dozen bars, you write 9 dollars. Why don't you write the cost as 900 cents?" Sample: Many people don't immediately know that \$9 and 900 cents are equivalent amounts.

Errors and Misconceptions

Problem 11

Students may regroup across one or more zeros incorrectly. Perform the computation at the board and discuss each regrouping.

Problems 19 and 20

If the answers contain zeros, the division is incorrect. Demonstrate the division and emphasize how the zeros are brought down two different times during the computation.

(continued)

Practice Set

▸ **a.** 20 × 37¢ \$7.40 **b.** 37 · 0 0 **c.** 407(37) 15,059

▸ **d.** 5)\$8.40 \$1.68 **e.** 200 ÷ 12 16 R 8 **f.** $\frac{234}{3}$ 78

g. Which numbers are the divisors in problems **d, e,** and **f?** 5; 12; 3

h. Represent Use the numbers 8, 9, and 72 to form two multiplication facts and two division facts. 8 × 9 = 72, 9 × 8 = 72, 72 ÷ 9 = 8, 72 ÷ 8 = 9

Written Practice[1] *Strengthening Concepts*

1. (2) If the factors are 7 and 11, what is the product? 77

▸ **2.** (1) Generalize What is the difference between 97 and 79? 18

3. (1) If the addends are 170 and 130, what is the sum? 300

4. (2) If 36 is the dividend and 4 is the divisor, what is the quotient? 9

▸ **5.** (1) Find the sum of 386, 98, and 1734. 2218

6. (1) Fatima spent \$2.25 for a book. She paid for it with a five-dollar bill. Find how much change she should get back by subtracting \$2.25 from \$5. \$2.75

7. (1) Luke wants to buy a \$70.00 radio for his car. He has \$47.50. Find how much more money he needs by subtracting \$47.50 from \$70.00. \$22.50

▸ **8.** (2) Explain Each energy bar costs 75¢. Find the cost of one dozen energy bars. Explain how you found your answer.

8. \$9.00; Sample: I multiplied 75¢ × 12. The answer was more than one dollar, so I wrote the answer with a dollar sign and a decimal point.

9. (1) 312 − 86 = 226

10. (1) 4106 + 1398 = 5504

▸ **11.** (1) 4000 − 1357 = 2643

12. (1) \$10.00 − \$2.83 = \$7.17

13. (2) 405(8) 3240

14. (2) 25 · 25 625

15. (2) $\frac{288}{6}$ 48

16. (2) $\frac{225}{15}$ 15

17. (2) \$1.25 × 8 \$10.00

18. (2) 400 × 50 20,000

▸ **19.** (2) 1000 ÷ 8 125

▸ **20.** (2) \$45.00 ÷ 20 \$2.25

[1] The italicized numbers within parentheses underneath each problem number are called *lesson reference numbers.* These numbers refer to the lesson(s) in which the major concept of that particular problem is introduced. If additional assistance is needed, refer to the discussion, examples, or practice problems of that lesson.

▸ See Math Conversations in the sidebar.

▶* 21. Represent Use the numbers 6, 8, and 48 to form two multiplication facts and two division facts. (2)
$6 \times 8 = 48$, $8 \times 6 = 48$, $48 \div 6 = 8$, $48 \div 8 = 6$

▶* 22. Connect Rearrange the numbers in this division fact to form another division fact and two multiplication facts. (2) $36 \div 9 = 4$, $4 \times 9 = 36$, $9 \times 4 = 36$

$$4\overline{)36} = 9$$

* 23. Connect Rearrange the numbers in this addition fact to form another addition fact and two subtraction facts. (1) $24 + 12 = 36$, $36 - 24 = 12$, $36 - 12 = 24$

$$12 + 24 = 36$$

24. a. Find the sum of 9 and 6. (1) 15

b. Find the difference between 9 and 6. 3

25. The divisor, dividend, and quotient are in these positions when we use a division sign: (2)

dividend ÷ divisor = quotient

On your paper, draw a division box and show the positions of the divisor, dividend, and quotient.

25. quotient
divisor)dividend

26. Multiply to find the answer to this addition problem: (2) $39¢ \times 6 = \$2.34$

39¢ + 39¢ + 39¢ + 39¢ + 39¢ + 39¢

27. 365×0 (2) 0 28. $0 \div 50$ (2) 0 29. $365 \div 365$ (2) 1

▶* 30. Explain How can you check the correctness of a division answer that has no remainder? (2) One way to check is to multiply the divisor by the quotient. The answer should equal the dividend.

Early Finishers *Real-World Application*

A customer at a bank deposits 2 one hundred-dollar bills, 8 twenty-dollar bills, 5 five-dollar bills, 20 one-dollar bills, 2 rolls of quarters, 25 dimes and 95 pennies. How much money will be deposited in all? Note: One roll of quarters = 40 quarters. $\$200 + \$160 + \$25 + \$20 + (80 \times \$0.25) + \$2.50 + \$0.95 = \$428.45$

▶ See Math Conversations in the sidebar.

3 Written Practice (Continued)

Math Conversations

Discussion opportunities are provided below.

Problem 21 Represent

Students should recognize that the related equations of a fact family represent inverse operations.

"How are the operations in a fact family related?" The operations are inverse operations.

Problem 22 Connect

Ask students to explain how the related equations represent inverse operations. Sample: multiplying by 4 undoes dividing by 4 and multiplying by 9 undoes dividing by 9.

Problem 30 Explain

Explanations should include the idea that multiplication is used to check a division answer because multiplication is the inverse of division.

"What operation is used to check any answer?" the inverse or opposite operation

Looking Forward

Recognizing expressions that indicate division and dividing whole numbers and money prepares students for:

- **Lesson 4,** finding missing numbers in division problems.
- **Lesson 19,** finding factors of a number.
- **Lessons 45 and 49,** dividing a decimal number by a whole number and by a decimal number.
- **Lesson 65,** mentally dividing a decimal number by 10 and by 100.
- **Lesson 111,** knowing how to write a division answer.

English Learners

Write the words *dividend, divisor,* and *quotient* on the board. Then say:

"The word position means where something is located. Watch while I change the position of one of these words."

Move *dividend* to the end of the list.

"If we write a division problem using this division symbol,), what is the position of the words divisor, dividend, and quotient?"

Ask volunteers to fill in the words in the correct positions.

• Unknown Numbers in Addition
• Unknown Numbers in Subtraction

Objectives

- Use subtraction to find an unknown addend in an addition problem.
- Check the answer to an unknown number in an addition problem by using the answer in place of the letter in the original problem.
- Find the unknown minuend in a subtraction problem by adding the subtrahend and the difference.
- Find the unknown subtrahend in a subtraction problem by subtracting the difference from the minuend.
- Check the answer for an unknown number in a subtraction problem by using the answer in place of the letter in the original problem.

Lesson Preparation

Materials

- **Power Up B** (in *Instructional Masters*)

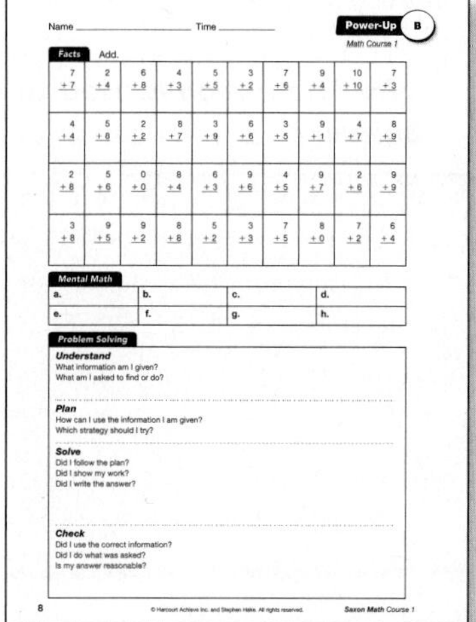

Power Up B

Math Language

New	English Learners (ESL)
equation	original
unknown	

Technology Resources

Student eBook Complete student textbook in electronic format.

Resources and Planner CD Assessment, reteaching, and instructional masters, plus a pacing calendar with standards.

Test and Practice Generator CD Create additional practice sheets and custom-made tests.

www.SaxonPublishers.com Visit for more student activities and planning materials.

Inclusion

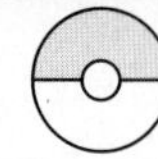

Adaptations CD Adapted lessons, investigations, practice and assessments.

Meeting Standards

National Council of Teachers of Mathematics (NCTM)

Numbers and Operations

NO.2a Understand the meaning and effects of arithmetic operations with fractions, decimals, and integers

NO.2c Understand and use the inverse relationships of addition and subtraction, multiplication and division, and squaring and finding square roots to simplify computations and solve problems

Algebra

AL.2a Develop an initial conceptual understanding of different uses of variables

Power-Up Discussion *For use with Power Up, p. 18*

Problem-Solving Strategy: Use Logical Reasoning/ Write an Equation

Tad picked up a number cube. His thumb and forefinger covered opposite faces. He counted the dots on the other four faces. How many dots did he count?

Understand We must first establish a base of knowledge about standard number cubes. The faces of a standard number cube are numbered with 1, 2, 3, 4, 5, or 6 dots. The number of dots on opposite faces of a number cube always total 7 (1 dot is opposite 6 dots, 2 dots are opposite 5 dots, and 3 dots are opposite 4 dots). Tad's thumb and forefinger covered opposite faces. We are asked to find how many dots were on the remaining four faces altogether.

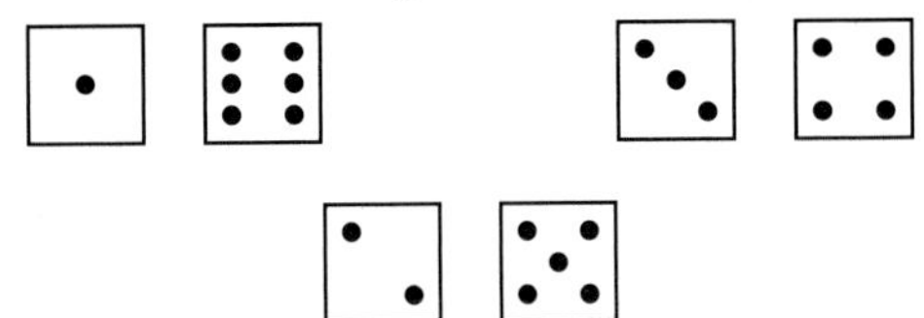

Teacher Note: You may choose to explain several additional facts.

1. *A number cube can also be referred to as a dot cube or a random number generator.*
2. *These objects are not always cubes. They can be tetrahedrons with four faces of equilateral triangles or a dodecahedron with twelve faces of regular pentagons. They may also be printed with colors, symbols, letters, or numbers higher than six.*
3. *To be used fairly, all number cubes should be perfect cubes, fairly weighted, and rolled on a smooth surface.*

Plan We will use logical reasoning about a number cube and write an equation to determine the number of dots Tad counted.

Solve Logical reasoning tells us that the four uncovered faces form two pairs of opposite faces. Each pair of opposite faces has 7 dots, so two pairs of opposite faces have 2×7, or 14 dots.

Check We determined that Tad counted 14 dots. We can check our answer by subtracting the number of dots Tad's fingers covered from the total number of dots on the number cube: $21 - 7 = 14$ dots.

Alternate Approach: Write an Equation

Students may use their knowledge of number cubes to determine all the possibilities for uncovered faces.

- If Tad is covering 1 and 6, then the dots on the uncovered faces total $2 + 3 + 4 + 5 = 14$.
- If Tad is covering 2 and 5, then the dots on the uncovered faces total $1 + 3 + 4 + 6 = 14$.
- If Tad is covering 3 and 4, then the dots on the uncovered faces total $1 + 2 + 5 + 6 = 14$.

1 Power Up

Facts

Distribute **Power Up B** to students. See answers below.

Mental Math

Before students begin the Mental Math exercise, do this counting exercise as a class.

Count by 5s from 5 to 100 and from 100 to 0.

Count by 50s from 50 to 1000 and from 1000 to 0.

Encourage students to share different ways to mentally compute these exercises. Strategies for exercises **a** and **e** are listed below.

a. Use an Addition Fact

$3 + 4 = 7$; 3 thousand + 4 thousand = 7 thousand

Count on by Thousands

Start at 3000. Count: 4000, 5000, 6000, 7000

e. Add Hundreds

$4000 + (300 + 200) = 4000 + 500 = 4500$

Count on by Hundreds

Start with 4000. Count: 4100, 4200, 4300, 4400, 4500

Problem Solving

Refer to **Power-Up Discussion,** p. 18B.

LESSON 3

• Unknown Numbers in Addition
• Unknown Numbers in Subtraction

Power Up *Building Power*

facts Power Up B

mental math

a. Number Sense: 3000 + 4000 7000

b. Number Sense: 600 + 2000 2600

c. Number Sense: 20 + 3000 3020

d. Number Sense: 600 + 300 + 20 920

e. Number Sense: 4000 + 300 + 200 4500

f. Number Sense: 70 + 300 + 4000 4370

g. Measurement: How many inches are in 3 feet? 36 in.

h. Measurement: How many millimeters are in 3 centimeters? 30 mm

problem solving

Tad picked up a number cube. His thumb and forefinger covered opposite faces. He counted the dots on the other four faces. How many dots did he count?

Understand We must first establish a base of knowledge about **standard number cubes.** The faces of a standard number cube are numbered with 1, 2, 3, 4, 5, or 6 dots. The number of dots on opposite faces of a number cube always total 7 (1 dot is opposite 6 dots, 2 dots are opposite 5 dots, and 3 dots are opposite 4 dots). Tad's thumb and forefinger covered opposite faces. We are asked to find how many dots were on the remaining four faces altogether.

Plan We will *use logical reasoning* about a number cube and *write an equation* to determine the number of dots Tad counted.

Solve Logical reasoning tells us that the four uncovered faces form two pairs of opposite faces. Each pair of opposite faces has 7 dots, so two pairs of opposite faces have 2×7, or 14 dots.

Check We determined that Tad counted 14 dots. We can check our answer by subtracting the number of dots Tad's fingers covered from the total number of dots on the number cube: $21 - 7 = 14$ dots.

New Concepts *Increasing Knowledge*

unknown numbers in addition

Below is an addition fact with three numbers. If one of the addends were missing, we could use the other addend and the sum to find the missing number.

$$\begin{array}{r} 4 \leftarrow \text{addend} \\ +\ 3 \leftarrow \text{addend} \\ \hline 7 \leftarrow \text{sum} \end{array}$$

Facts Add.

7 + 7 14	2 + 4 6	6 + 8 14	4 + 3 7	5 + 5 10	3 + 2 5	7 + 6 13	9 + 4 13	10 + 10 20	7 + 3 10
4 + 4 8	5 + 8 13	2 + 2 4	8 + 7 15	3 + 9 12	6 + 6 12	3 + 5 8	9 + 1 10	4 + 7 11	8 + 9 17
2 + 8 10	5 + 6 11	0 + 0 0	8 + 4 12	6 + 3 9	9 + 6 15	4 + 5 9	9 + 7 16	2 + 6 8	9 + 9 18
3 + 8 11	9 + 5 14	9 + 2 11	8 + 8 16	5 + 2 7	3 + 3 6	7 + 5 12	8 + 0 8	7 + 2 9	6 + 4 10

Cover the 4 with your finger. How can you use the 7 and the 3 to find that the number under your finger is 4?

Now cover the 3 instead of the 4. How can you use the other two numbers to find that the number under your finger is 3?

Notice that we can find a missing addend by subtracting the known addend from the sum. We will use a letter to stand for a missing number.

Example 1

Find the value of *m*:

$$\begin{array}{r} 12 \\ + m \\ \hline 31 \end{array}$$

Solution

One of the addends is missing. The known addend is 12. The sum is 31. If we subtract 12 from 31, we find that the missing addend is **19.** We check our answer by using 19 in place of *m* in the original problem.

$$\begin{array}{r} \overset{2}{\cancel{3}}\overset{1}{1} \\ -\ 12 \\ \hline 19 \end{array} \quad \text{Use 19 in place of } m. \rightarrow \quad \begin{array}{r} \overset{1}{1}2 \\ +\ 19 \\ \hline 31 \end{array} \text{ check}$$

Example 2

Find the value of *n*:

$$36 + 17 + 5 + n = 64$$

Solution

First we add all the known addends.

$$\underbrace{36 + 17 + 5}_{58} + n = 64$$
$$58 \quad + n = 64$$

Then we find n by subtracting 58 from 64.

$64 - 58 = 6$ So n is **6.**

We check our work by using 6 in place of n in the original problem.

$36 + 17 + 5 + 6 = 64$ The answer checks.

unknown numbers in subtraction

Discuss Cover the 8 with your finger, and describe how to use the other two numbers to find that the number under your finger is 8.

$$\begin{array}{r} 8 \leftarrow \text{minuend} \\ -\ 3 \leftarrow \text{subtrahend} \\ \hline 5 \leftarrow \text{difference} \end{array}$$

Now cover the 3 instead of the 8. Describe how to use the other two numbers to find that the covered number is 3.

As we will show below, we can find a missing minuend by adding the other two numbers. We can find a missing subtrahend by subtracting the difference from the minuend.

2 New Concepts

Instruction

Point out that any letter of the alphabet can be used to represent a missing number.

Example 1

Instruction

Have students note that subtraction is used to find the answer, and addition—the inverse or opposite operation—is used to check.

Example 2

Instruction

In this example, $n = 6$. Make sure students understand that the value of n is likely to be different in a different equation. To reinforce this concept, write the equation $10 + 7 + n = 20$ on the board, and invite students to use mental math to determine the unknown addend. Students should note that the value of n ($n = 3$) in this equation is different than the value of n in example 2.

(continued)

English Learners

Write this equation from exercise 1 on the board: $12 + m = 31$. Point to it and say:

"This is the original problem. Original means first or earlier."

Then write this equation on the board: $12 + 19 = 31$. Say:

"I rewrote the original problem with 19 in place of m."

Demonstrate this again with another pair of problems. Ask students to identify the original problem.

Math Background

The goal of the steps shown in the example 2 solution is to isolate the variable. Often when solving equations, various terms can first be combined to help simplify the equation (such as rewriting $36 + 17 + 5$ as 58). Once the terms that can be combined have been combined, one or more inverse operations are then used to isolate the variable and learn the value of the unknown number.

2 New Concepts (Continued)

Example 3

Instruction

After the example has been completed, invite students to describe another way to check the answer.

"This example shows that one way to check addition is to use subtraction. What is another way to check the answer?"
Sample: Break apart an addend, and then add.

$$16 + 24 = 16 + 4 + 20$$
$$= 20 + 20$$
$$= 40$$

Example 4

Instruction

Emphasize the "find a simpler problem" strategy. Encourage students to use this strategy whenever they are trying to solve a more complex problem. Remind them to think of a simpler problem, solve it, and then apply that method to the more complex problem.

(continued)

Example 3

Find the value of w:

$$\begin{array}{r} w \\ -\ 16 \\ \hline 24 \end{array}$$

Solution

We can find the first number of a subtraction problem by adding the other two numbers. We add 16 and 24 to get **40.** We check our answer by using 40 in place of w.

$$\begin{array}{r} \overset{1}{16} \\ +\ 24 \\ \hline 40 \end{array} \quad \xrightarrow{\text{Use 40 in place of } w.} \quad \begin{array}{r} \overset{3\,1}{\cancel{4}0} \\ -\ 16 \\ \hline 24 \end{array} \text{ check}$$

Example 4

Find the value of y:

$$236 - y = 152$$

Solution

One way to determine how to find a missing number is to think of a simpler problem that is similar. Here is a simpler subtraction fact:

$$5 - 3 = 2$$

In the problem, y is in the same position as the 3 in the simpler subtraction fact. Just as we can find 3 by subtracting 2 from 5, we can find y by subtracting 152 from 236.

$$\begin{array}{r} \overset{1\,1}{\cancel{2}36} \\ -\ 152 \\ \hline 84 \end{array}$$

We find that y is **84.** Now we check our answer by using 84 in place of y in the original problem.

$$\begin{array}{r} \overset{1\,1}{\cancel{2}36} \\ -\ 84 \\ \hline 152 \end{array} \quad \begin{array}{l} \leftarrow \text{Use 84 in place of } y. \\ \leftarrow \text{The answer checks.} \end{array}$$

Thinking Skill
Discuss
What is another way we can check the subtraction?
We can add 84 to 152.

Statements such as $12 + m = 31$ are equations. An **equation** is a mathematical sentence that uses the symbol = to show that two quantities are equal. In algebra we refer to a missing number in an equation as an **unknown.** When asked to find the unknown in the exercises that follow, look for the number represented by the letter that makes the equation true.

Inclusion

Presenting a problem in context can help students who have difficulty visualizing the process of finding a missing number in a subtraction problem. Write this equation on the board, and then read the following problem:

$$n - 3 = 2$$

"You have some books in your locker. You take out 3 books. Now there are 2 books in the locker. How many books were in the locker to start with?"

Ask:

"Were there more or less than 3 books to start with?" more

Demonstrate the solution by saying:

"From our fact families we know that 3 + 2 = 5, so the missing number n is 5, which is more than 3."

You may also refer the students to the "Missing Numbers" chart in the Student Reference Guide.

Practice Set

Math Language

We can use a lowercase or an uppercase letter as an unknown:

$a + 3 = 5$

$A + 3 = 5$

The equations have the same meaning.

▸ **Analyze** Find the unknown number in each problem. Check your work by using your answer in place of the letter in the original problem.

a. $A + 12 = 45$ 33

b. $32 + B = 60$ 28

c. $C - 15 = 24$ 39

d. $38 - D = 29$ 9

e. $e + 24 = 52$ 28

f. $29 + f = 70$ 41

g. $g - 67 = 43$ 110

h. $80 - h = 36$ 44

i. $36 + 14 + n + 8 = 75$ 17

Written Practice

Strengthening Concepts

Math Language

Remember that **factors** are multiplied together to get a **product.**

1. (2) If the two factors are 25 and 12, what is the product? 300

2. (1) If the addends are 25 and 12, what is the sum? 37

3. (1) What is the difference of 25 and 12? 13

▸ 4. (2) Each of the 31 students brought 75 aluminum cans to class for a recycling drive. Find how many cans the class collected by multiplying 31 by 75. 2325 cans

5. (2) Find the total price of one dozen pizzas at \$7.85 each by multiplying \$7.85 by 12. \$94.20

▸ 6. (1) **Explain** The basketball team scored 63 of its 102 points in the first half of the game. Find how many points the team scored in the second half. Explain how you found your answer. 39 points; Sample: I subtracted 63, the number of points in the first half of the game, from 102, the total.

7. (2) $\$3.68 \times 9$ \$33.12

8. (2) 407×80 32,560

9. (2) $28¢ \times 14$ \$3.92

10. (2) 370×140 51,800

11. (2) $100 \cdot 100$ 10,000

12. (2) $144 \div 12$ 12

13. (2) $(12)(5)$ 60

14. (1) $3627 + 598 + 4881$ 9106

▸ 15. (1) $5010 - 1376$ 3634

▸ 16. (1) $\$10.00 - \$0.26$ \$9.74

Find the unknown number in each problem.

17. (3) $A + 16 = 48$ 32

18. (3) $23 + B = 52$ 29

▸ See Math Conversations in the sidebar.

2 New Concepts (Continued)

Practice Set

Problems a–i Error Alert

Encourage students who have difficulty finding the unknown numbers to use the "find a simpler problem" strategy. For example, for problem e, ask students to write an addition fact such as $2 + 3 = 5$. Then ask, "How would you find the first number if it was unknown?" For problem h, ask students to write a subtraction fact such as $8 - 2 = 6$. Then ask,

"How would you find the second number if it was unknown?"

3 Written Practice

Math Conversations

Discussion opportunities are provided below.

Problem 4 Predict

Extend the Problem

A related problem gives students an opportunity to make a generalization.

"Suppose each of the 31 students collected 150 cans instead of 75 cans. How could you use mental math to find the total number of cans the students collected?" Sample: Since 150 is double 75, the total number will be double 2325, or 4650.

Problem 6 Explain

After completing the problem, ask,

"Why did you use subtraction to solve the problem?" Sample: The whole is made up of two parts. To find the unknown part, subtract the known part from the whole.

Problem 16 Generalize

Extend the Problem

Challenge students to describe a variety of ways to find the difference using mental math. Sample: \$10 minus a quarter gives \$9.75, and the amount is one penny less or \$9.74.

Errors and Misconceptions

Problem 15

An answer of 3734 shows that students forgot to regroup in the hundreds place of the minuend. Demonstrate on the board that 5 thousands is regrouped as 4 thousands and 10 hundreds, and then 10 hundreds is regrouped as 9 hundreds and 10 tens.

(continued)

3 Written Practice (Continued)

Math Conversations

Discussion opportunities are provided below.

Problem 25 Connect

Ask students to explain how the related equations represent inverse operations. Sample: Subtracting 48 undoes adding 48 and subtracting 24 undoes adding 24.

Problem 26 Connect

Ask students to explain how the related equations represent inverse operations. Sample: Dividing by 15 undoes multiplying by 15 and dividing by 6 undoes multiplying by 6.

Problem 28 Connect

Extend the Problem

A repeated addition can often be grouped in different ways.

"Why can you find the answer to 15 × 8 by multiplying 30 × 4?" Sample: the repeated addition can be grouped to show 4 groups of (15 + 15) or 4 groups of 30.

Work with students to generalize that when one factor is doubled and the other is halved, the product is unchanged.

19. (3) $C - 17 = 31$ 48

20. (3) $42 - D = 25$ 17

21. (3) $x + 38 = 75$ 37

22. (2) $x - 38 = 75$ 113

23. (3) $75 - y = 38$ 37

24. (3) $6 + 8 + w + 5 = 32$ 13

▸* **25.** (1) Connect Rearrange the numbers in this addition fact to form another addition fact and two subtraction facts. 48 + 24 = 72, 72 − 24 = 48, 72 − 48 = 24

24 + 48 = 72

▸* **26.** (2) Connect Rearrange the numbers in this multiplication fact to form another multiplication fact and two division facts. 15 × 6 = 90, 90 ÷ 6 = 15, 90 ÷ 15 = 6

6 × 15 = 90

Math Language
Remember the **divisor** is divided into the **dividend.** The resulting answer is the **quotient.**

27. (2) Find the quotient when the divisor is 20 and the dividend is 200. 10

▸ **28.** (2) Connect Multiply to find the answer to this addition problem:

15 + 15 + 15 + 15 + 15 + 15 + 15 + 15

15 × 8 = 120

29. (2) 144 ÷ 144 1

* **30.** (3) Explain How can you find a missing addend in an addition problem? To find a missing addend, subtract the known addend(s) from the sum.

Early Finishers
Real-World Application

Petrov's family has a compact car that gets an average of 30 miles per gallon of gasoline. The family drives an average of 15,000 miles a year.

a. Approximately how many gallons of gas do they purchase every year? 15000 miles ÷ 30 mpg = 500 gallons; Petrov's family would have to purchase 500 gallons of gasoline a year.

b. If the average price of gas is $2.89 a gallon, how much should the family expect to spend on gas in a year? 500 gallons × $2.89 per gallon = $1445

▸ See Math Conversations in the sidebar.

Looking Forward

Finding missing addends in addition problems prepares students for:

- **Lesson 4,** finding missing numbers in multiplication and division problems.
- **Lesson 11,** solving problems about combining.
- **Lesson 43,** finding missing numbers in fraction and decimal problems.
- **Lesson 98,** finding a missing angle in a triangle.
- **Lesson 103,** finding the perimeter of complex shapes with the missing length of a side.

• Unknown Numbers in Multiplication
• Unknown Numbers in Division

Objectives

- Use division to find an unknown factor in a multiplication problem.
- Find the unknown dividend in a division problem by multiplying the divisor and quotient.
- Find the unknown divisor in a division problem by dividing the dividend by the quotient.

Lesson Preparation

Materials

- **Power Up A** (in *Instructional Masters*)

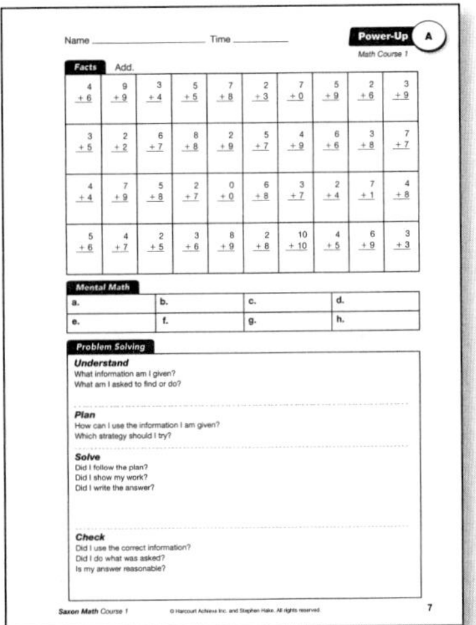

Power Up A

Math Language

Maintain	English Learners (ESL)
factor	figure out

Technology Resources

Student eBook Complete student textbook in electronic format.

Resources and Planner CD Assessment, reteaching, and instructional masters, plus a pacing calendar with standards.

Test and Practice Generator CD Create additional practice sheets and custom-made tests.

www.SaxonPublishers.com Visit for more student activities and planning materials.

Inclusion

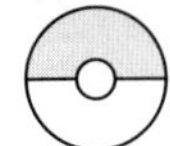

Adaptations CD Adapted lessons, investigations, practice and assessments.

Meeting Standards

National Council of Teachers of Mathematics (NCTM)

Numbers and Operations

NO.2a Understand the meaning and effects of arithmetic operations with fractions, decimals, and integers

NO.2c Understand and use the inverse relationships of addition and subtraction, multiplication and division, and squaring and finding square roots to simplify computations and solve problems

Algebra

AL.2a Develop an initial conceptual understanding of different uses of variables

Power-Up Discussion *For use with Power Up, p. 23*

Problem-Solving Strategy: Make It Simpler/Find a Pattern

The diagram below is called a *Jordan curve*. It is a simple *closed curve* (think of a clasped necklace that has been casually dropped on a table). Which letters are on the inside of the curve, and which letters are on the outside of the curve?

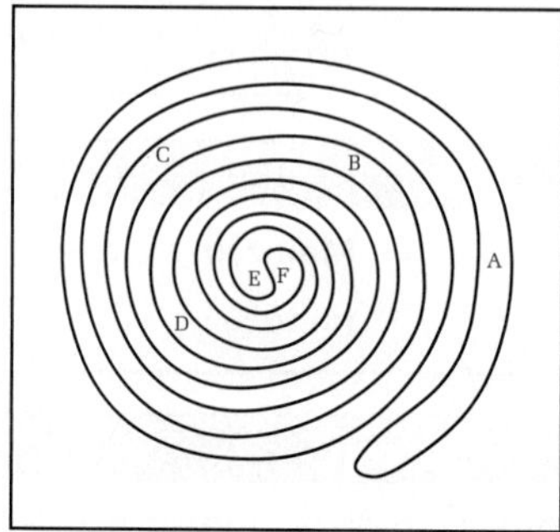

Understand We must determine if A, B, C, D, E and F are inside or outside the closed curve.

Plan We will make the problem simpler and use the simpler problems to find a pattern.

Solve We will draw less complicated closed curves, and place an X inside and a Y outside each of the closed curves.

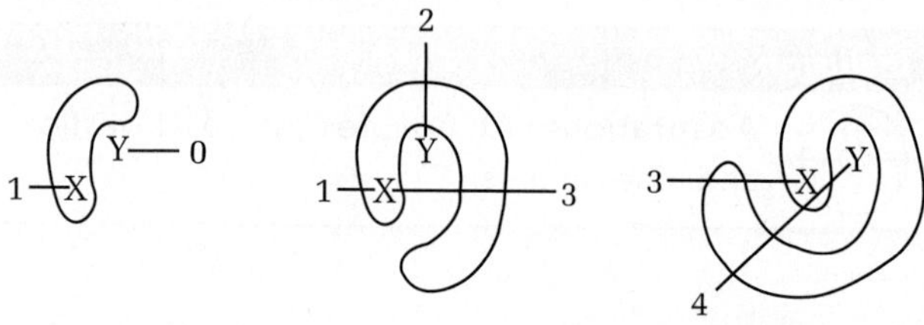

In our simpler curves, we notice that lines drawn from the outside of the curve to the X cross 1 or 3 lines. Lines drawn to the Y cross 0, 2, or 4 lines. We see this pattern: Lines drawn to letters on the inside of the curve cross an odd number of lines, and lines drawn to letters on the outside of the curve cross an even number of lines.

Teacher Note: Ask the students where the letter A is located—inside or outside the closed curve. Allow the students to discuss that the A appears to be inside the "tail" of the curve.

We look at the Jordan curve again.

- A line drawn to A crosses 1 line, so it is inside the closed curve.
- A line drawn to B crosses 4 lines, so it is outside.
- A line drawn to C crosses 3 lines, so it is inside.
- A line drawn to D crosses 5 times and is inside.
- A line drawn to E crosses 9 times and is inside.
- A line drawn to F crosses 10 times and is outside.

Check We determined that A, C, D, and E are inside the closed curve and that B and F are both outside of the closed curve. We found a pattern that can help us quickly determine whether points are on the inside or outside of a closed curve.

Teacher Note: Explain that if the closed curve is drawn on a piece of scrap paper, we could begin at A and use a highlighter to color in the closed curve to verify the solution is correct.

LESSON 4

• Unknown Numbers in Multiplication
• Unknown Numbers in Division

Power Up

Building Power

facts Power Up A

mental math

a. **Number Sense:** 600 + 2000 + 300 + 20 2920

b. **Number Sense:** 3000 + 20 + 400 + 5000 8420

c. **Number Sense:** 7000 + 200 + 40 + 500 7740

d. **Number Sense:** 700 + 2000 + 50 + 100 2850

e. **Number Sense:** 60 + 400 + 30 + 1000 1490

f. **Number Sense:** 900 + 8000 + 100 + 50 9050

g. **Measurement:** How many feet are in a yard? 3 ft

h. **Measurement:** How many centimeters are in a meter? 100 cm

problem solving

The diagram below is called a *Jordan curve.* It is a simple *closed curve* (think of a clasped necklace that has been casually dropped on a table). Which letters are on the inside of the curve, and which letters are on the outside of the curve?

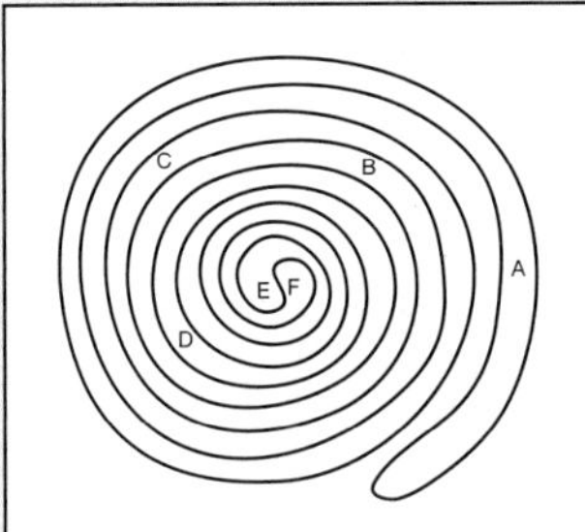

Understand We must determine if A, B, C, D, E and F are inside or outside the closed curve.

Plan We will make the problem simpler and use the simpler problems to find a pattern.

Facts Add.

4 + 6 10	9 + 9 18	3 + 4 7	5 + 5 10	7 + 8 15	2 + 3 5	7 + 0 7	5 + 9 14	2 + 6 8	3 + 9 12
3 + 5 8	2 + 2 4	6 + 7 13	8 + 8 16	2 + 9 11	5 + 7 12	4 + 9 13	6 + 6 12	3 + 8 11	7 + 7 14
4 + 4 8	7 + 9 16	5 + 8 13	2 + 7 9	0 + 0 0	6 + 8 14	3 + 7 10	2 + 4 6	7 + 1 8	4 + 8 12
5 + 6 11	4 + 7 11	2 + 5 7	3 + 6 9	8 + 9 17	2 + 8 10	10 + 10 20	4 + 5 9	6 + 9 15	3 + 3 6

1 Power Up

Facts

Distribute **Power Up A** to students. See answers below.

Mental Math

Before students begin the Mental Math exercise, do this counting exercise as a class.

Count up and down by 5s between 5 and 100.

Count up and down by 50s between 50 and 1000.

Encourage students to share different ways to mentally compute these exercises. Strategies for exercises **b** and **f** are listed below.

b. Add Thousands First

8000 + 20 + 400 = 8000 + 420 = 8420

Add the Addends from Greatest to Least

5000 + 3000 + 400 + 20 = 8420

f. Add Hundreds First

1000 + 8000 + 50 = 9050

Add the Addends from Greatest to Least

8000 + 900 + 100 + 50 = 9050

Problem Solving

Refer to **Power-Up Discussion,** p. 23B.

2 New Concepts

Instruction

To illustrate unknown numbers in multiplication, write the example

$$\begin{array}{r} 4 \\ \times\ 3 \\ \hline 12 \end{array}$$

on the board two different times. In one example, erase the 4, and in the other example, erase the 3. Ask students to explain how they could use the remaining numbers in each multiplication to find the unknown number.

(continued)

Solve We will draw less complicated closed curves, and place an X inside and a Y outside each of the closed curves.

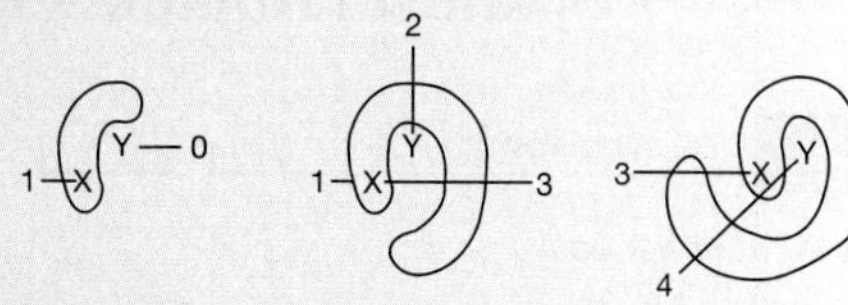

On our simpler curves, we notice that lines drawn from the outside of the curve to the X cross 1 or 3 lines. Lines drawn to the Y cross 0, 2, or 4 lines. We see this pattern: lines drawn to letters on the inside of the curve cross an odd number of lines, and lines drawn to letters on the outside of the curve cross an even number of lines.

We look at the Jordan curve again.

- A line drawn to A crosses 1 line, so it is inside the closed curve.
- A line drawn to B crosses 4 lines, so it is outside.
- A line drawn to C crosses 3 lines, so it is inside.
- A line drawn to D crosses 5 lines, so it is inside.
- A line drawn to E crosses 9 lines, so it is inside.
- A line drawn to F crosses 10 lines, so it is outside.

Check We determined that A, C, D, and E are inside the closed curve and that B and F are outside of the closed curve. We found a pattern that can help us quickly determine whether points are on the inside or outside of a closed curve.

New Concepts *Increasing Knowledge*

unknown numbers in multiplication

This multiplication fact has three numbers. If one of the **factors** were unknown, we could use the other factor and the product to figure out the unknown factor.

$$\begin{array}{r} 4 \\ \times\ 3 \\ \hline 12 \end{array}$$

Thinking Skill
Discuss
Why can we use division to find a missing factor?
Multiplication and division are inverse operations.

Explain With your finger, cover the factors in this multiplication fact one at a time. Describe how you can use the two uncovered numbers to find the covered number. Notice that we can find an unknown factor by dividing the product by the known factor.

Example 1

Find the value of A: $\begin{array}{r} A \\ \times\ 6 \\ \hline 72 \end{array}$

Math Background

In examples 1–3 in this lesson, an inverse operation is used to solve for the unknown. As you work through each example, be sure that students can identify the operation that is present, and then identify the inverse operation that will be used to solve for the unknown.

Solution

The unknown number is a factor. The product is 72. The factor that we know is 6. Dividing 72 by 6, we find that the unknown factor is **12.** We check our work by using 12 in the original problem.

$$6\overline{)7^{1}2} = 12 \longrightarrow \begin{array}{r} \overset{1}{12} \\ \times\ 6 \\ \hline 72 \end{array} \text{ check}$$

Example 2

Find the value of w: $6w = 84$

Solution

Reading Math
In this problem $6w$ means "6 times w."

We divide 84 by 6 and find that the unknown factor is **14.** We check our work by multiplying.

$$6\overline{)8^{2}4} = 14 \longrightarrow \begin{array}{r} \overset{2}{14} \\ \times\ 6 \\ \hline 84 \end{array} \text{ check}$$

unknown numbers in division

This division fact has three numbers. If one of the numbers were unknown, we could figure out the third number.

$$6\overline{)24} = 4$$

Cover each of the numbers with your finger, and describe how to use the other two numbers to find the covered number. Notice that we can find the dividend (the number inside the division box) by multiplying the other two numbers. We can find either the divisor or quotient (the numbers outside of the box) by dividing.

Example 3

Find the value of k: $\frac{k}{6} = 15$

Solution

The letter k is in the position of the dividend. If we rewrite this problem with a division box, it looks like this:

$$6\overline{)k} = 15$$

We find an unknown dividend by multiplying the divisor and quotient. We multiply 15 by 6 and find that the unknown number is **90.** Then we check our work.

$$\begin{array}{r} \overset{3}{15} \\ \times\ 6 \\ \hline 90 \end{array} \longrightarrow 6\overline{)9^{3}0} = 15 \text{ check}$$

English Learners

Explain that the phrase **figure out** means to use information to find something you do not know. Write this division on the board and ask:

$$15 \div n = 5$$

"How can we figure out what number the n represents?" divide 15 by 5

Then write the following problems with unknown numbers on the board:

$$24 \div n = 6 \qquad \frac{t}{6} = 6 \qquad 125 \div p = 25$$

For each problem, ask the students how they can figure out the value of the unknown dividend. As students respond, have them include the term in their answer. For example, a student might say, "I figured out that the answer is 4 because 24 divided by 6 equals 4."

2 New Concepts *(Continued)*

Example 2

Instruction

Have students note that an inverse operation is present twice. First, an inverse operation is used to find the unknown factor. The inverse of that operation is then used to check the computation.

Example 3

Instruction

Give students an opportunity to recall that a fraction bar represents division.

"What operation does a fraction bar represent?" division

Example 4

Instruction

Remind students frequently that checking their work is an important step in solving a problem. When solving and checking problems, students should generalize that an operation is used to solve a problem, and the inverse of that operation is used to check the problem.

(continued)

2 New Concepts (Continued)

Practice Set

Problems a–h (Error Alert)

Encourage students who have difficulty finding the unknown numbers to use the "find a simpler problem" strategy. For example, for problem a, ask students to write a multiplication fact such as $5 \times 2 = 10$. Then ask,

"How would you find the first number if it was missing?"

For problem **h,** ask students to write a division fact such as $\frac{6}{3} = 2$. Then ask,

"How would you find the numerator if it was missing?"

Problems g and h (Analyze)

"Why was division used to find the unknown number in problem g, but not used to find the unknown number in problem h?" Students should generalize that division was used when the denominator was unknown, and multiplication was used when the numerator was unknown.

Problem i (Formulate)

Invite students to share the different problems that were written to represent this equation.

Example 4

Find the value of *m*: 126 ÷ *m* = 7

Solution

The letter *m* is in the position of the divisor. If we were to rewrite the problem with a division box, it would look like this:

$$m\overline{)126}\ \text{quotient } 7$$

We can find *m* by dividing 126 by 7.

$$7\overline{)12^56}\ \text{quotient } 18$$

We find that *m* is **18.** We can check our division by multiplying as follows:

$$\begin{array}{r} \scriptstyle 5 \\ 18 \\ \times\ 7 \\ \hline 126 \end{array}$$

In the original equation we can replace the letter with our answer and test the truth of the resulting equation.

$$126 \div 18 = 7$$
$$7 = 7$$

Practice Set ▸ Analyze Find each unknown number. Check your work by using your answer in place of the letter in the original problem.

a. $\begin{array}{r} A \\ \times\ 7 \\ \hline 91 \end{array}$ 13

b. $\begin{array}{r} 20 \\ \times\ B \\ \hline 440 \end{array}$ 22

c. $7\overline{)C}$ quotient 15   105

d. $D\overline{)144}$ quotient 8   18

e. $7w = 84$ 12

f. $112 = 8m$ 14

g. $\frac{360}{x} = 30$ 12

h. $\frac{n}{5} = 60$ 300

i. Formulate Write a word problem using the equation in exercise **h.** See student work.

Written Practice *Strengthening Concepts*

1. (2) Five dozen carrot sticks are to be divided evenly among 15 children. Find how many carrot sticks each child should receive by dividing 60 by 15. 4 carrot sticks

2. (2) Matt separated 100 pennies into 4 equal piles. Find how many pennies were in each pile. Explain how you found your answer. 25 pennies; Sample: I divided 100 pennies by 4 to make four equal groups of pennies.

3. (2) Sandra put 100 pennies into stacks of 5 pennies each. Find how many stacks she formed by dividing 100 by 5. 20 stacks

4. (2) For the upcoming season, 294 players signed up for soccer. Find the number of 14-player soccer teams that can be formed by dividing 294 by 14. 21 teams

5. Angela is reading a 280-page book. She has just finished page 156. (1) Find how many pages she still has to read by subtracting 156 from 280. 124 pages

6. Each month Bill earns $0.75 per customer for delivering newspapers. (2) Find how much money he would earn in a month in which he had 42 customers by multiplying $0.75 by 42. $31.50

▶ * **Analyze** Find each unknown number. Check your work.

7. (4) $\begin{array}{r} J \\ \times\ 5 \\ \hline 60 \end{array}$ 12

8. (3) $\begin{array}{r} 27 \\ +\ K \\ \hline 72 \end{array}$ 45

9. (3) $\begin{array}{r} L \\ +\ 36 \\ \hline 37 \end{array}$ 1

10. (3) $\begin{array}{r} 64 \\ -\ M \\ \hline 46 \end{array}$ 18

11. (3) $n - 48 = 84$ 132

12. (4) $7p = 91$ 13

13. (4) $q \div 7 = 0$ 0

14. (4) $144 \div r = 6$ 24

15. (2) $6\overline{)\$12.36}$ $2.06

16. (2) $\frac{5760}{8}$ 720

▶ 17. (2) 526 ÷ 18 29 R 4

18. (1) 563 + 563 + 563 + 563 2252

19. (2) $3.75 · 16 $60.00

20. (1) $3 + $2.86 + $0.98 $6.84

21. (1) $10 − $6.43 $3.57

22. (4) If the divisor is 3 and the quotient is 12, what is the dividend? 36

23. (4) If the product is 100 and one factor is 5, what is the other factor? 20

▶* 24. (1) **Connect** Rearrange the numbers in this subtraction fact to form another subtraction fact and two addition facts.
17 − 8 = 9, 8 + 9 = 17, 9 + 8 = 17
17 − 9 = 8

▶* 25. (2) **Connect** Rearrange the numbers in this division fact to form another division fact and two multiplication facts. 72 ÷ 9 = 8, 8 × 9 = 72, 9 × 8 = 72
72 ÷ 8 = 9

26. (3) $w + 6 + 8 + 10 = 40$ 16

27. (2) Find the answer to this addition problem by multiplying:

23¢ + 23¢ + 23¢ + 23¢ + 23¢ + 23¢ + 23¢

23¢ × 7 = $1.61

28. (4) $25m = 25$ 1

29. (4) $15n = 0$ 0

▶* 30. (4) **Explain** How can you find an unknown factor in a multiplication problem? To find an unknown factor, divide the product by the known factor.

▶ See Math Conversations in the sidebar.

Looking Forward

Using division to find missing factors in a multiplication problem prepares students for:

- **Lesson 15,** finding a missing number in a problem about equal groups.
- **Lesson 43,** finding a missing number in fraction problems.
- **Lesson 83,** finding a missing term in a proportion.
- **Lessons 85, 101, and 105,** using cross products to solve proportions.
- **Lesson 87,** finding a missing factor that is a mixed number or decimal number.

3 Written Practice

Math Conversations

Discussion opportunities are provided below.

Problems 7–10 Analyze

For problem **7**, ask these questions.

"What operation is used to find the answer? What operation is used to check the answer?" multiplication; division

Ask the questions again for problems 8–10.

Problem 24 Connect

The numbers in a fact family are not limited to one- or two-digit numbers. Challenge each student to form an addition and subtraction fact family using three-digit numbers. Sample: 200 + 400 = 600; 400 + 200 = 600; 600 − 400 = 200; 600 − 200 = 400

Problem 25 Connect

Extend the Problem

Invite students to form a variety of multiplication and division fact families that include the number 100. Sample: (100, 50, 2); (100, 25, 4); (100, 20, 5); (100, 10, 10)

Problem 30 Explain

Extend the Problem

Several methods are used to find an unknown number in a division problem. Write the equation $\frac{8}{4} = 2$ on the board. Then ask,

"In this division equation, suppose the numerator was missing. What method would be used to find the missing numerator?" multiply the divisor or denominator by the quotient

"Suppose the denominator was missing. What method would be used to find the missing denominator?" divide the dividend or numerator by the quotient

"Suppose the quotient was missing. What method would be used to find the missing quotient?" divide the dividend or numerator by the divisor or denominator

Errors and Misconceptions

Problem 17

If students answer 28 R22, the division was not completed in its entirety. Explain that a division is complete when the remainder is less than the divisor. Remind students that if a remainder is greater than the divisor, or if a number can be brought down from the dividend to make the remainder greater than the divisor, they must divide again.

• Order of Operations, Part 1

Objectives

- Take steps in order from left to right in a problem with more than one addition or subtraction step.
- Take steps in order from left to right in a problem with more than one multiplication or division step.
- Do the work within parentheses first when solving a problem with more than one step.
- Identify and use the Associative Property of Addition and the Associative Property of Multiplication.
- Perform the operations above the bar and below the bar before dividing in a division problem with a bar.

Lesson Preparation

Materials

- **Power Up B** (in *Instructional Masters*)

Optional

- **Teacher-provided material: index cards**

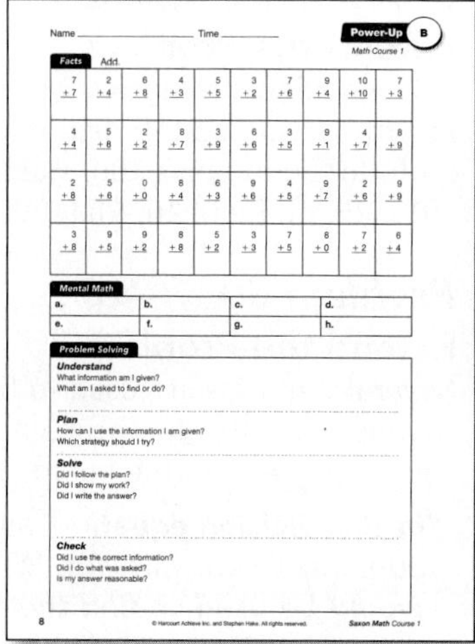

Power Up B

Math Language

New	English Learners (ESL)
Associative Property of Addition	calculation
Associative Property of Multiplication	
Order of Operations	

Technology Resources

Student eBook Complete student textbook in electronic format.

Resources and Planner CD Assessment, reteaching, and instructional masters, plus a pacing calendar with standards.

Test and Practice Generator CD Create additional practice sheets and custom-made tests.

www.SaxonPublishers.com Visit for more student activities and planning materials.

Inclusion

Adaptations CD Adapted lessons, investigations, practice and assessments.

Meeting Standards

National Council of Teachers of Mathematics (NCTM)

Numbers and Operations

NO.2a Understand the meaning and effects of arithmetic operations with fractions, decimals, and integers

Problem Solving

PS.1b Solve problems that arise in mathematics and in other contexts

Communication

CM.3b Communicate their mathematical thinking coherently and clearly to peers, teachers, and others

Power-Up Discussion *For use with Power Up, p. 28*

Problem-Solving Strategy: Guess and Check/ Use Logical Reasoning

Use the digits 5, 6, 7, and 8 to complete this addition problem. There are two possible arrangements.

$$\begin{array}{r} \_\_ \\ +\ \ 9 \\ \hline \_\_ \end{array}$$

Understand We are shown an addition problem with several digits missing. We are asked to complete the problem using the digits 5, 6, 7, and 8. Because the bottom addend is 9, we know that the ones digit of the sum will be one less than the ones digit of the top addend.

Teacher Note: Remind students when adding nine to any number, the digit in the ones place of the sum will always be one less than the digit in the ones place of the original number. Tell them to think "plus 10, minus 1."

Plan We will intelligently guess and check for the ones place in the top addend by trying the numbers in an orderly way. We will then use logical reasoning to fill in the remaining digits of the problem.

Solve We quickly eliminate 5 as a possibility for the ones digit of the top addend because we do not have a 4 to place in the sum. We try 6 for the ones digit of the top addend. Six plus 9 is 15, so we write a 5 as the ones digit of the sum. If we write 7 as the tens digit of the top addend, we get 76 + 9. We add the two numbers and get 85. Placing an 8 in the sum, we see that we have used all the digits 5, 6, 7, and 8. We have found the first of two possible arrangements.

Next, we try 7 as the ones digit of the top addend. Seven plus 9 is 16, so we place a 6 in the sum. Now we must use the digits 5 and 8 in the tens column. We try 57 + 9 = 66. That does not work, because it does not use the 8. We try 87 + 9 = 96. That also does not work, because it omits the 5.

Finally, we try 8 in the top addend and 7 in the sum. This leaves 5 and 6 for the tens column. We try 58 + 9 = 67, and find the second solution to the problem.

Check The digits 5, 6, 7, and 8 can be used to form two solutions for our missing digit problem:

$$\begin{array}{r} 76 \\ +\ \ 9 \\ \hline 85 \end{array} \qquad \begin{array}{r} 58 \\ +\ \ 9 \\ \hline 67 \end{array}$$

1 Power Up

Facts

Distribute **Power Up B** to students. See answers below.

Mental Math

Before students begin the Mental Math exercise, do this counting exercise as a class.

Count by 25s from 25 to 1000.

Encourage students to share different ways to mentally compute these exercises. Strategies for exercises **c** and **f** are listed below.

c. Count on by Thousands
Start with 5200. Count: 6200, 7200
Add Thousands First
$5000 + 200 + 2000 = 7000 + 200 = 7200$

f. Add Hundreds First
$400 + 40 + 200 = 600 + 40 = 640$
Count on by Hundreds
Start with 440. Count: 540, 640

Problem Solving

Refer to **Power-Up Discussion,** p. 28B.

LESSON 5

• Order of Operations, Part 1

Power Up

Building Power

facts Power Up B

mental math

a. **Number Sense:** 560 + 200 760

b. **Number Sense:** 840 + 30 870

c. **Number Sense:** 5200 + 2000 7200

d. **Number Sense:** 650 + 140 790

e. **Number Sense:** 3800 + 2000 5800

f. **Number Sense:** 440 + 200 640

g. **Measurement:** How many days are in a week? 7 days

h. **Measurement:** How many hours are in a day? 24 hours

problem solving

Use the digits 5, 6, 7, and 8 to complete this addition problem. There are two possible arrangements.

$$\begin{array}{r} \_\,\_ \\ +\ 9 \\ \hline \_\,\_ \end{array}$$

Understand We are shown an addition problem with several digits missing. We are asked to complete the problem using the digits 5, 6, 7, and 8. Because the bottom addend is 9, we know that the ones digit of the sum will be one less than the ones digit of the top addend.

Plan We will intelligently guess and check for the ones place in the top addend by trying the numbers in an orderly way. We will then use logical reasoning to fill in the remaining digits of the problem.

Solve We quickly eliminate 5 as a possibility for the ones digit of the top addend because we do not have a 4 to place in the sum. We try 6 for the ones digit of the top addend. Six plus 9 is 15, so we write a 5 as the ones digit of the sum. If we write 7 as the tens digit of the top addend, we get 76 + 9. We add the two numbers and get 85. Placing an 8 in the sum, we see that we have used all the digits 5, 6, 7, and 8. We have found the first of two possible arrangements.

Next, we try 7 as the ones digit of the top addend. Seven plus 9 is 16, so we place a 6 in the sum. Now we must use the digits 5 and 8 in the tens column. We try 57 + 9 = 66. That does not work, because it does not use the 8. We try 87 + 9 = 96. That also does not work, because it omits the 5.

Finally, we try 8 in the top addend and 7 in the sum. This leaves 5 and 6 for the tens column. We try 58 + 9 = 67, and find the second solution to the problem.

Check The digits 5, 6, 7, and 8 can be used to form two solutions for our missing digit problem:

$$\begin{array}{r} 76 \\ +\ 9 \\ \hline 85 \end{array} \qquad \begin{array}{r} 58 \\ +\ 9 \\ \hline 67 \end{array}$$

Facts Add.

7 + 7 14	2 + 4 6	6 + 8 14	4 + 3 7	5 + 5 10	3 + 2 5	7 + 6 13	9 + 4 13	10 + 10 20	7 + 3 10
4 + 4 8	5 + 8 13	2 + 2 4	8 + 7 15	3 + 9 12	6 + 6 12	3 + 5 8	9 + 1 10	4 + 7 11	8 + 9 17
2 + 8 10	5 + 6 11	0 + 0 0	8 + 4 12	6 + 3 9	9 + 6 15	4 + 5 9	9 + 7 16	2 + 6 8	9 + 9 18
3 + 8 11	9 + 5 14	9 + 2 11	8 + 8 16	5 + 2 7	3 + 3 6	7 + 5 12	8 + 0 8	7 + 2 9	6 + 4 10

New Concept

Increasing Knowledge

Thinking Skill

Analyze

Why is it important to have rules for the order of operations?
The rules ensure that problems requiring more than one operation have only one correct answer.

When there is more than one addition or subtraction step within a problem, we take the steps in order from left to right. In this problem we first subtract 4 from 9. Then we add 3.

$$9 - 4 + 3 = 8$$

If a different order of steps is desired, parentheses are used to show which step is taken first. In the problem below, we first add 4 and 3 to get 7. Then we subtract 7 from 9.

$$9 - (4 + 3) = 2$$

These two rules are part of the rules for the **Order of Operations** in mathematics.

Example 1

a. 18 − 6 − 3 **b. 18 − (6 − 3)**

Solution

a. We subtract in order from left to right.

$18 - 6 - 3$ First subtract 6 from 18.

$12 - 3$ Then subtract 3 from 12.

9 The answer is 9.

b. We subtract within the parentheses first.

$18 - (6 - 3)$ First subtract 3 from 6.

$18 - 3$ Then subtract 3 from 18.

15 The answer is 15.

When there is more than one multiplication or division step within a problem, we take the steps in order from left to right. In this problem we divide 24 by 6 and then multiply by 2.

$$24 \div 6 \times 2 = 8$$

If there are parentheses, then we first do the work within the parentheses. In the problem below, we first multiply 6 by 2 and get 12. Then we divide 24 by 12.

$$24 \div (6 \times 2) = 2$$

Example 2

a. 18 ÷ 6 ÷ 3 **b. 18 ÷ (6 ÷ 3)**

Solution

a. We take the steps in order from left to right.

$18 \div 6 \div 3$ First divide 18 by 6.

$3 \div 3$ Then divide 3 by 3.

1 The answer is 1.

Math Background

Since expressions often contain more than one operation, mathematics in general would have little or no value is there wasn't a *consistent* way to simplify those expressions. The *order of operations* is a set of rules that restricts the way an expression can be simplified, and ensures that everyone completes it in the same way.

In their future studies, students will expand their understanding of the order of operations when they learn to work with a wider variety of expressions, such as those containing exponents, for example.

2 New Concepts

Instruction

Introduce the lesson by writing the following problem on the board or overhead.

At a lake, 40 people are water skiing or on the beach. Nine of the 12 people on the beach decide to swim. How many people are not on the beach?

Write the equation $40 - (12 - 9) = n$ and explain how it represents the problem. After solving it to learn the number of people not on the beach ($n = 37$), point out that the same equation without parentheses has a very different answer ($40 - 12 - 3 = 25$). Explain to students that whenever they work with expressions and equations, the order in which operations are completed can be very important.

Example 1

Instruction

To emphasize the importance of parentheses, write the following statements on the board and ask students to identify if each statement is correct or incorrect.

$16 - 7 + 2 = 11$ correct

$36 \div 4 \times 3 = 27$ correct

$19 - 8 + 4 = 7$ incorrect; 15

$20 \div 5 \times 2 = 2$ incorrect; 8

Then ask volunteers to write parentheses in each incorrect statement to make the statement correct.

$19 - (8 + 4) = 7$

$20 \div (5 \times 2) = 2$

(continued)

2 New Concepts (Continued)

Example 2

Instruction

Students may think of the Associative Property as the grouping property.

Example 3

Instruction

Remind students that the numerator and/or the denominator of a fraction may consist of more than just a number.

Practice Set

Problems a–f (Error Alert)

If students get the same answer for **a** and **b**, **c** and **d**, or **e** and **f**, they are not following the order of operations. Ask these students to write the order of operations on an index card. The card can be used as a bookmark, and students can refer to it until the sequence of steps to follow is familiar.

Problem i (Connect)

Extend the Problem

Challenge students to rewrite problem g using two sets of parentheses. Sample: (6 ÷ 3) + (9 ÷ 3) or (9 ÷ 3) + (6 ÷ 3)

3 Written Practice

Math Conversations

Discussion opportunities are provided below.

Problem 2

Extend the Problem

You may wish to mention that a kilogram is a little more than 2 pounds.

After completing the problem, point out that multiplication can be used to estimate the amount of food the elephant would eat in one week.

"What numbers would you use as factors to estimate the amount of food the elephant would eat in one week? Why?" Sample: Use 7 to represent the number of days in one week and round 102 to 100 to represent the amount of food eaten in one day.

"What is a reasonable estimate of the amount of food the elephant eats in one week?" Sample: 7 × 100 or 700 kilograms

(continued)

---

b. We divide within the parentheses first.

18 ÷ (6 ÷ 3)	First divide 6 by 3.
18 ÷ 2	Then divide 18 by 2.
9	The answer is 9.

Only two numbers are involved in each step of a calculation. If three numbers are added (or multiplied), changing the two numbers selected for the first addition (or first multiplication) does not change the final sum (or product).

$$(2 + 3) + 4 = 2 + (3 + 4) \qquad (2 \times 3) \times 4 = 2 \times (3 \times 4)$$

This property applies to addition and multiplication and is called the **Associative Property.** As shown by examples 1 and 2, the Associative Property does not apply to subtraction or to division.

Example 3

$$\frac{5 + 7}{1 + 2}$$

Solution

Before dividing we perform the operations above the bar and below the bar. Then we divide 12 by 3.

$$\frac{5+7}{1+2} = \frac{12}{3} = \mathbf{4}$$

Practice Set

▸ **a.** 16 − 3 + 4 17

▸ **b.** 16 − (3 + 4) 9

▸ **c.** 24 ÷ (4 × 3) 2

▸ **d.** 24 ÷ 4 × 3 18

▸ **e.** 24 ÷ 6 ÷ 2 2

▸ **f.** 24 ÷ (6 ÷ 2) 8

g. $\frac{6 + 9}{3}$ 5

h. $\frac{12 + 8}{12 - 8}$ 5

▸ **i.** Connect Rewrite exercise **g** using parentheses instead of a bar. (6 + 9) ÷ 3

Written Practice *Strengthening Concepts*

1. (1) Jack paid $5 for a sandwich that cost $1.25 and milk that cost $0.60. How much change should he get back? $3.15

▸ **2.** (1) In one day the elephant ate 82 kilograms of hay, 8 kilograms of apples, and 12 kilograms of leaves and raw vegetables. How many kilograms of food did it eat in all? 102 kilograms

3. (1) What is the difference of 110 and 25? 85

4. (2) What is the total price of one dozen apples that cost 25¢ each? $3.00

5. (3) What number must be added to 149 to total 516? 367

▸ See Math Conversations in the sidebar.

English Learners

Write 35 ÷ 5 on the board. Say:

"When we solve this problem we perform a calculation. A calculation is the act of figuring out the solution to a problem."

We can calculate mentally, with a pencil and paper, or with a calculator. Write 35 − 12 − 3 on the board. Ask:

"Which calculation should we perform first, 35 − 12 or 12 − 3? What is the answer to this calculation?" 35 − 12; 20

6. To find the average number of pages she needs to read each day, divide: 235 pages divided by 5 days equals 47 pages a day.

▶ * 6. (2) **Explain** Judy plans to read a 235-page book in 5 days. How can you find the average number of pages she needs to read each day.

7. (5) $5 + (3 \times 4)$ 17

8. (5) $(5 + 3) \times 4$ 32

9. (5) $800 - (450 - 125)$ 475

10. (5) $600 \div (20 \div 5)$ 150

11. (5) $800 - 450 - 125$ 225

12. (5) $600 \div 20 \div 5$ 6

13. (5) $144 \div (8 \times 6)$ 3

14. (5) $144 \div 8 \times 6$ 108

15. (5) $\$5 - (\$1.25 + \$0.60)$ $3.15

* 16. (2) **Represent** Use the numbers 63, 7, and 9 to form two multiplication facts and two division facts. $7 \times 9 = 63, 9 \times 7 = 63, 63 \div 7 = 9, 63 \div 9 = 7$

17. (4) If the quotient is 12 and the dividend is 288, what is the divisor? 24

Reading Math

Read expressions such as (4)(6) as "four times six." The parentheses indicate multiplication.

▶ 18. (2) $25\overline{)\$10.00}$ $0.40

19. (2) (378)(64) 24,192

20. (2) 506×370 = 187,220

▶ 21. (1) $\$10.10 - \$9.89$ = $0.21

* **Analyze** Find each unknown number. Check your work.

22. (3) $n - 63 = 36$ 99

23. (3) $63 - p = 36$ 27

24. (3) $56 + m = 432$ 376

25. (4) $8w = 480$ 60

▶ 26. (3) $5 + 12 + 27 + y = 50$ 6

27. (4) $36 \div a = 4$ 9

28. (4) $x \div 4 = 8$ 32

▶* 29. (1) **Represent** Use the numbers 7, 11, and 18 to form two addition facts and two subtraction facts. $7 + 11 = 18, 11 + 7 = 18, 18 - 11 = 7, 18 - 7 = 11$

30. (5) $3 \cdot 4 \cdot 5$ 60

Early Finishers
Real-World Application

A painter is painting three exam rooms at a veterinarian's office. If each exam room requires 2 gallons of paint and the total cost of the paint is $270, how much does each gallon of paint cost? 6 gallons $\times N = \$270$; $45

▶ See Math Conversations in the sidebar.

3 Written Practice (Continued)

Math Conversations

Discussion opportunities are provided below.

Problem 6 Explain

After completing the problem, invite students to explain different ways to divide 235 by 5 using mental math. Sample: Break apart 235 to 200 + 35, then divide each addend by 5; 40 + 7 = 47.

Problem 26 Explain

After finding the answer, ask students to describe the steps they followed to solve the problem. Then point out that collecting the addends and rewriting their sum as 44 helps simplify the equation, which in turn helps make it simpler to find the value of *y*.

Problem 29 Represent

Extend the Problem

Ask students to decide if the numbers 10, 20, and 30 can be arranged to form an addition and subtraction fact family. yes

Errors and Misconceptions

Problem 18

An answer of $40 represents a missing decimal point in the quotient. For all division problems involving money, ask students to place a decimal point in each quotient before any computations are begun.

Problem 21

Watch for students who have difficulty regrouping. To alert those students to regrouping errors, ask them how they could check their work by counting up to $10.10 from $9.89.

Looking Forward

Learning the order of operations for more than one addition or subtraction step or more than one multiplication or division step within a problem prepares students for:

- **Lesson 9,** comparing expressions.
- **Lessons 38 and 73,** simplifying problems with exponents and one other operation.
- **Lesson 84,** performing the order of operations with more than one type of operation.
- **Lesson 92,** reviewing the order of operations and extending the steps to include exponents and roots.

• Fractional Parts

Objectives

- Use a fraction to name a part of a whole.
- Use a fraction to name a part of a group.
- Divide a number into equal parts to find a fractional part of that number.

Lesson Preparation

Materials

- **Power Up C** (in *Instructional Masters*)

Optional

- **Manipulative kit: color tiles, overhead fraction circles**
- **Basic Fraction Circles poster**

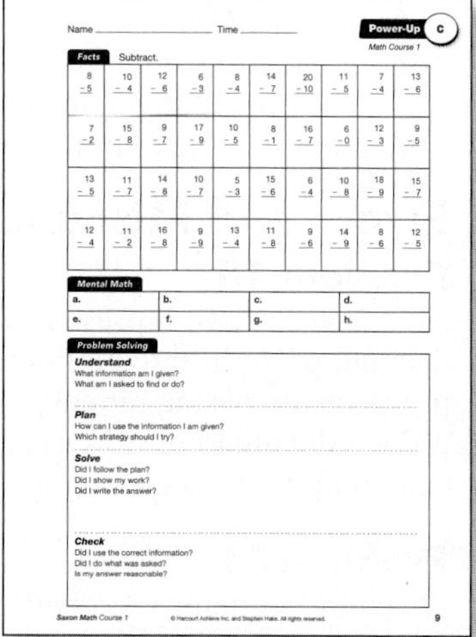

Name ____________ Time ________ **Power-Up C** *Math Course 1*

Facts Subtract.

8 − 5	10 − 4	12 − 6	6 − 3	8 − 4	14 − 7	20 − 10	11 − 5	7 − 4	13 − 6
7 − 2	15 − 8	9 − 7	17 − 9	10 − 5	8 − 1	16 − 7	6 − 0	12 − 3	9 − 5
13 − 5	11 − 7	14 − 8	10 − 7	5 − 3	15 − 6	6 − 4	10 − 8	18 − 9	15 − 7
12 − 4	11 − 2	16 − 8	9 − 9	13 − 4	11 − 8	9 − 6	14 − 9	8 − 6	12 − 5

Mental Math

a.	b.	c.	d.
e.	f.	g.	h.

Problem Solving

Understand
What information am I given?
What am I asked to find or do?

Plan
How can I use the information I am given?
Which strategy should I try?

Solve
Did I follow the plan?
Did I show my work?
Did I write the answer?

Check
Did I use the correct information?
Did I do what was asked?
Is my answer reasonable?

Saxon Math Course 1 © Harcourt Achieve Inc. and Stephen Hake. All rights reserved. 9

Power Up C

Math Language

New	English Learners (ESL)
denominator	represent
fractions	
numerator	

Technology Resources

Student eBook Complete student textbook in electronic format.

Resources and Planner CD Assessment, reteaching, and instructional masters, plus a pacing calendar with standards.

Test and Practice Generator CD Create additional practice sheets and custom-made tests.

www.SaxonPublishers.com Visit for more student activities and planning materials.

Inclusion

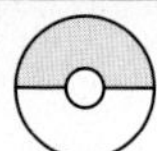

Adaptations CD Adapted lessons, investigations, practice and assessments.

Meeting Standards

National Council of Teachers of Mathematics (NCTM)

Numbers and Operations

NO.1a Work flexibly with fractions, decimals, and percents to solve problems

Geometry

GM.4d Use geometric models to represent and explain numerical and algebraic relationships

Representation

RE.5b Select, apply, and translate among mathematical representations to solve problems

Power-Up Discussion *For use with Power Up, p. 32*

Problem-Solving Strategy: Use Logical Reasoning/ Guess and Check

Carrisa's school library received a gift of 500 new reference books. The books were arranged on a bookcase as shown in the diagram below. How many books are on each shelf?

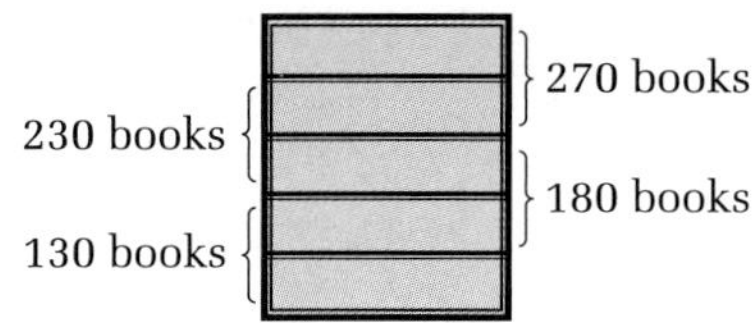

Understand ***Understand the problem.***

"What information are we given?"

There are 500 books packed into five shelves. We are given four statements about the sums of books on four different sets of two shelves.

"What are we asked to do?"

Determine how many books are on each shelf.

Plan ***Make a plan.***

"What problem-solving strategy will we use?"

We could guess the number on one shelf, then calculate the number of books on the other shelves, and then check to see if the total is 500.

"Is there another strategy we could use?"

We could use logical reasoning to find the number of books on one shelf.

"How can we find the number of books on the top shelf?"

Since there are 500 books in all, we can subtract the total number of books on the four lower shelves (230 + 130) from 500 to find the number of books on the top shelf. Once we know how many books are on the top shelf, we can calculate the number of books on each of the other shelves.

Solve ***Carry out the plan.***

"How many books are on the top shelf?"

500 − (230 + 130) = 140 books.

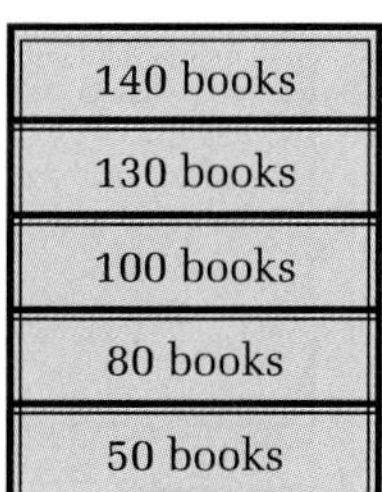

"How many books are on the second shelf?"

270 − 140 = 130 books.

"How many books are on the third shelf?"

230 − 130 = 100 books.

"How many books are on the fourth shelf?"

180 − 100 = 80 books.

"How many books are on the bottom shelf?"

130 − 80 = 50 books.

Check ***Look back.***

"How can we verify the solution is correct?"

We can add to see if the totals for each pair of shelves is correct and to see if the grand total is 500.

Teacher Note: The problem can be solved by first finding the number of books on the bottom shelf. You may wish to challenge some students to work independently to find the number of books on each shelf in reverse order. The solutions should match.

1 Power Up

Facts

Distribute **Power Up C** to students. See answers below.

Mental Math

Before students begin the Mental Math exercise, do this counting exercise as a class.

Count up and down by 25s between 25 and 1000.

Encourage students to share different ways to mentally compute these exercises. Strategies for exercises **c** and **f** are listed below.

c. Count on by Hundreds

Start with 370. Count: 470, 570, 670, 770

Add Hundreds First

$300 + 70 + 400 = 700 + 70 = 770$

f. Add 20, then Subtract 20

$480 + 20 = 500$; $500 + 2500 = 3000$; $3000 - 20 = 2980$

Decompose 480

$400 + 80 + 2500 = 2900 + 80 = 2980$

Problem Solving

Refer to **Power-Up Discussion,** p. 32B.

2 New Concepts

Instruction

Use the **overhead fraction circles** from the Manipulative Kit to model fractional parts of a whole. Using the fourths, remove 3 of the parts, leaving 1 part shaded. Point out that one fourth of the circle is shaded.

You may wish to display the **Basic Fraction Circles** concept poster as you discuss fractional parts with students.

Example 1

Instruction

To give students additional practice in naming fractional parts of a whole, draw different figures on the board, such as squares and rectangles. Divide the figures into a variety of equal parts and shade a number of parts in each figure. Ask students to identify the fraction of each figure that is shaded.

(continued)

LESSON **6**

• Fractional Parts

Power Up *Building Power*

facts Power Up C

mental math

a. **Number Sense:** 2500 + 400 2900

b. **Number Sense:** 6000 + 2400 8400

c. **Number Sense:** 370 + 400 770

d. **Number Sense:** 9500 + 240 9740

e. **Number Sense:** 360 + 1200 1560

f. **Number Sense:** 480 + 2500 2980

g. **Measurement:** How many seconds are in a minute? 60 sec.

h. **Measurement:** How many minutes are in an hour? 60 min.

problem solving Carrisa's school library received a gift of 500 new reference books. The books were arranged on a bookcase as shown in the diagram at right. How many books are on each shelf? from top to bottom: 140 books, 130 books, 100 books, 80 books, and 50 books

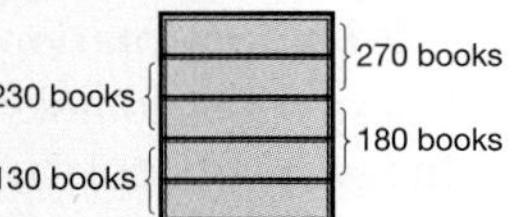

New Concept *Increasing Knowledge*

As young children we learned to count objects using whole numbers. As we grew older, we discovered that there are parts of wholes—like sections of an orange—that cannot be named with whole numbers. We can name these parts with **fractions.** A common fraction is written with two numbers and a fraction bar. The "bottom" number is the **denominator.** The denominator shows the number of equal parts in the whole. The "top" number, the **numerator,** shows the number of the parts that are being represented.

Example 1

What fraction of this circle is shaded?

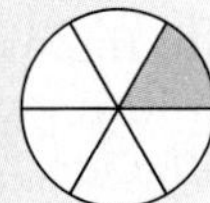

Solution

The circle has been divided into 6 equal parts. We use 6 for the bottom of the fraction. One of the parts is shaded, so we use 1 for the top of the fraction. The fraction of the circle that is shaded is one sixth, which we write as $\frac{1}{6}$.

Facts Subtract.

8 − 5 3	10 − 4 6	12 − 6 6	6 − 3 3	8 − 4 4	14 − 7 7	20 − 10 10	11 − 5 6	7 − 4 3	13 − 6 7
7 − 2 5	15 − 8 7	9 − 7 2	17 − 9 8	10 − 5 5	8 − 1 7	16 − 7 9	6 − 0 6	12 − 3 9	9 − 5 4
13 − 5 8	11 − 7 4	14 − 8 6	10 − 7 3	5 − 3 2	15 − 6 9	6 − 4 2	10 − 8 2	18 − 9 9	15 − 7 8
12 − 4 8	11 − 2 9	16 − 8 8	9 − 9 0	13 − 4 9	11 − 8 3	9 − 6 3	14 − 9 5	8 − 6 2	12 − 5 7

We can also use a fraction to name a part of a group. There are 6 members in this group. We can divide this group in half by dividing it into two equal groups with 3 in each half. We write that $\frac{1}{2}$ of 6 is 3.

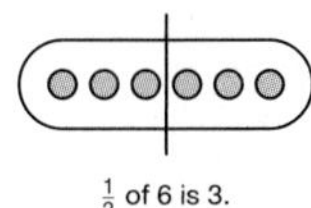

$\frac{1}{2}$ of 6 is 3.

Thinking Skill
Explain
How would we find $\frac{1}{6}$ of 6? We would divide the group into 6 equal groups. There is 1 in each group, so $\frac{1}{6}$ of 6 is 1.

We can divide this group into thirds by dividing the 6 members into three equal groups. We write that $\frac{1}{3}$ of 6 is 2.

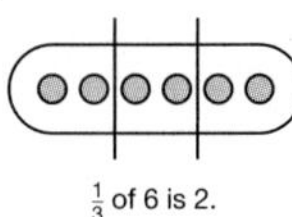

$\frac{1}{3}$ of 6 is 2.

Example 2

a. What number is $\frac{1}{2}$ of 450?

b. What number is $\frac{1}{3}$ of 450?

c. How much money is $\frac{1}{5}$ of \$4.50?

Solution

a. To find $\frac{1}{2}$ of 450, we divide 450 into two equal parts and find the amount in one of the parts. We find that $\frac{1}{2}$ of 450 is **225.**

$2\overline{)450}$ = 225 ⟶ $\frac{1}{2}$ of 450 is 225.

b. To find $\frac{1}{3}$ of 450, we divide 450 into three equal parts. Since each part is 150, we find that $\frac{1}{3}$ of 450 is **150.**

$3\overline{)450}$ = 150 ⟶ $\frac{1}{3}$ of 450 is 150.

c. To find $\frac{1}{5}$ of \$4.50, we divide \$4.50 by 5. We find that $\frac{1}{5}$ of \$4.50 is **\$0.90.**

$5\overline{)\$4.50}$ = \$0.90 ⟶ $\frac{1}{5}$ of \$4.50 is \$0.90.

Example 3

Copy the figure at right, and shade $\frac{1}{3}$ of it:

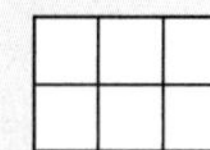

Solution

The rectangle has six parts of equal size. Since $\frac{1}{3}$ of 6 is 2, we shade any two of the parts.

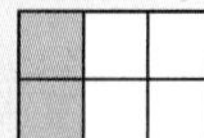

2 New Concepts *(Continued)*

Instruction

To reinforce naming parts of a group, give each student 12 **color tiles** from the Manipulative Kit. Ask students to find $\frac{1}{2}$ of 12 by dividing the tiles into two equal groups. Repeat using $\frac{1}{3}$, $\frac{1}{4}$, and $\frac{1}{6}$.

Example 2

Instruction

Suggest that students look at the denominator of each fraction to help understand the number of equal groups that must be formed. For example, two equal groups will be formed by finding $\frac{1}{2}$ of 450.

Example 3

Instruction

Because $\frac{1}{3}$ is a unit fraction, another way for students to find $\frac{1}{3}$ of 6 is to divide 6 by 3.

(continued)

Math Background

A fraction whose numerator is 1 is a unit fraction. For example, the fractions $\frac{1}{2}$, $\frac{1}{3}$, and $\frac{1}{5}$ in example 2 are unit fractions. To find a unit fraction of a whole or group, students need only to divide the whole or group by the denominator of the unit fraction.

However, this method of simply dividing by the denominator is used only with unit fractions. For other fractional parts of a whole or group (such as $\frac{2}{3}$ or $\frac{5}{8}$, for example), an additional step must be completed, or a different method must be used. Such fractions will be a part of future lessons.

English Learners

Draw a circle that represents the fraction $\frac{1}{4}$. Write $\frac{1}{4}$ next to it. Say:

"This circle is divided into 4 equal parts. The four sections show that the denominator 4 is represented, or shown. The shaded part shows that numerator 1 is represented, or shown."

Shade in two more parts and ask:

"What fraction is represented now?" $\frac{3}{4}$

Repeat the process with the fractions $\frac{1}{2}$ and $\frac{1}{3}$.

2 New Concepts (Continued)

Practice Set

Problems a–c (Error Alert)

When using a fraction to describe the number of shaded parts of a whole or of a group, remind students that the denominator of the fraction represents the number of equal parts in the whole or group, and the numerator represents the number of shaded parts.

Problem g (Explain)

After completing the problem, invite students to share the different ways they found the answer.

Problem h (Represent)

To show $\frac{1}{2}$, the figure can be shaded in a variety of ways. Challenge students to describe some of those ways.

3 Written Practice

Math Conversations

Discussion opportunities are provided below.

Problem 6 (Analyze)

Extend the Problem

Numbers that are multiples of 10, such as those in this problem, create an opportunity to practice mental math skills. Challenge students to find the answer using only mental math.

Errors and Misconceptions

Problem 6

If students have difficulty solving the problem, encourage them to solve a simpler problem. For example, dividing both amounts in the problem by 10 (which is the same as shifting both decimal points one place to the left) would change the question to "How many \$2 bills would it take to make \$100?"

Another simpler problem that could be used would be to find the number of \$20 bills in \$100, then multiply that number by 10 because \$100 is $\frac{1}{10}$ of \$1000.

(continued)

Practice Set ▸ Use both words and numbers to write the fraction that is shaded in problems **a–c.**

a. 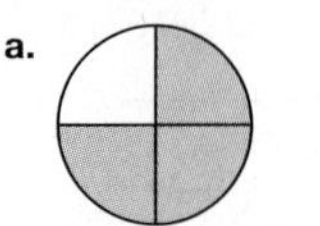

three fourths; $\frac{3}{4}$

b. 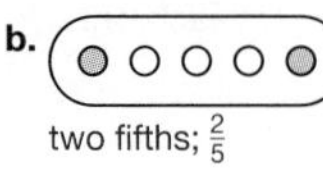

two fifths; $\frac{2}{5}$

c. 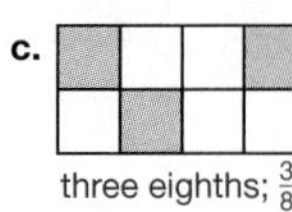

three eighths; $\frac{3}{8}$

d. What number is $\frac{1}{2}$ of 72? 36

e. What number is $\frac{1}{2}$ of 1000? 500

f. What number is $\frac{1}{3}$ of 180? 60

▸ **g.** Explain How much money is $\frac{1}{3}$ of \$3.60? One third of \$3.60 is \$1.20 because \$1.20 + \$1.20 + \$1.20 = \$3.60.

▸ **h.** Represent Copy this figure and shade one half of it.

h. Sample:

Written Practice — *Strengthening Concepts*

1. (6) What number is $\frac{1}{2}$ of 540? 270

2. (6) What number is $\frac{1}{3}$ of 540? 180

3. (1) In four days of sight-seeing the Richmonds drove 346 miles, 417 miles, 289 miles, and 360 miles. How many miles did they drive in all? 1412 miles

4. (1) Tanisha paid \$20 for a book that cost \$12.08. How much money should she get back? \$7.92

5. (2) How many days are in 52 weeks? 364 days

▸ * **6.** (2) Analyze How many \$20 bills would it take to make \$1000? 50 bills

7. (6) Use words and numbers to write the fraction of this circle that is shaded. five sixths; $\frac{5}{6}$

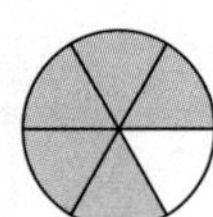

8. (1)
$$\begin{array}{r} 3604 \\ 5186 \\ +\ 7145 \\ \hline 15{,}935 \end{array}$$

9. (1)
$$\begin{array}{r} \$30.01 \\ -\ \$15.76 \\ \hline \$14.25 \end{array}$$

10. (2)
$$\begin{array}{r} 376 \\ \times\ 87 \\ \hline 32{,}712 \end{array}$$

11. (2)
$$\begin{array}{r} 470 \\ \times\ 203 \\ \hline 95{,}410 \end{array}$$

▸ See Math Conversations in the sidebar.

12. $20 − $11.98 $8.02 (1)

▸ 13. 596 − (400 − 129) 325 (5)

14. 32 ÷ (8 × 4) 1 (5)

15. $8\overline{)4016}$ 502 (2)

16. $15\overline{)6009}$ 400 R 9 (2)

17. $36\overline{)9000}$ 250 (2)

Find each unknown number. Check your work.

18. $8w = 480$ 60 (4)

19. $x - 64 = 46$ 110 (3)

20. $\frac{49}{N} = 7$ 7 (4)

21. $\frac{M}{7} = 15$ 105 (4)

22. $365 + P = 653$ 288 (3)

23. 36¢ + 25¢ + m = 99¢ 38¢ (3)

▸* 24. (6) **Conclude** The square at right was divided in half. Then each half was divided in half. What fraction of the square is shaded? $\frac{1}{4}$

25. (answer: one fourth of the figure shaded)

* 25. (6) **Represent** Copy this figure on your paper, and shade one fourth of it.

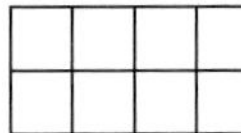

26. $6.35 · 12 $76.20 (2)

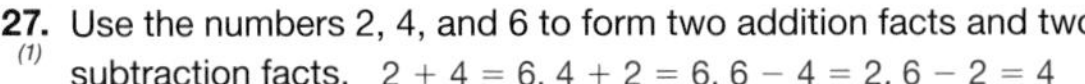

27. (1) Use the numbers 2, 4, and 6 to form two addition facts and two subtraction facts. 2 + 4 = 6, 4 + 2 = 6, 6 − 4 = 2, 6 − 2 = 4

28. (2) Write two multiplication facts and two division facts using the numbers 2, 4, and 8. 2 × 4 = 8, 4 × 2 = 8, 8 ÷ 2 = 4, 8 ÷ 4 = 2

▸* 29. (2) **Connect** Write a multiplication equation to solve this addition problem.

38 + 38 + 38 + 38 + 38 + 38 + 38 + 38 + 38 + 38

38 × 10 = 380

* 30. (6) **Formulate** Make up a fractional-part question about money, as in Example 2 part c. Then find the answer. See student work.

▸ See Math Conversations in the sidebar.

3 Written Practice (Continued)

Math Conversations

Discussion opportunities are provided below.

Problem 24 Conclude

Extend the Problem

Have students suppose that each of the four congruent squares in the figure is divided in half.

"Does the fraction of the figure that is shaded change? Explain your answer."
no; $\frac{2}{8} = \frac{1}{4}$

Problem 29 Connect

Challenge students to explain how mental math and two or more different operations could be used to find the answer. Sample: Change each addend from 38 to 40 by adding 2; 10(38 + 2) − (10 × 2) = 400 − 20 = 380.

Errors and Misconceptions

Problem 13

An answer of 67 indicates that the order of operations was not followed. Remind students that the order of operations state that all work inside parentheses must be performed first.

Looking Forward

Using fractions to name parts of a whole or group and finding a fractional part of a number prepare students for:

- **Lesson 17,** naming points on a number line with fractions or mixed numbers.
- **Investigation 2,** making and using fraction manipulatives to solve problems.
- **Lesson 29,** relating the fractional part of a number to multiplying fractions.
- **Lesson 77,** finding unstated information in fractional parts problems.
- **Lesson 117,** finding a whole when a fraction is known.

• Lines, Segments, and Rays
• Linear Measure

Objectives

- Identify lines, segments and rays.
- Use an inch ruler to measure line segments to the nearest quarter inch.
- Use a centimeter ruler to measure line segments in centimeters and millimeters.

Lesson Preparation

Materials

- **Power Up C** (in *Instructional Masters*)
- **Manipulative kit: rulers**
- **Teacher-provided material: narrow strips of tagboard,** 6 in. by 1 in.—one per student

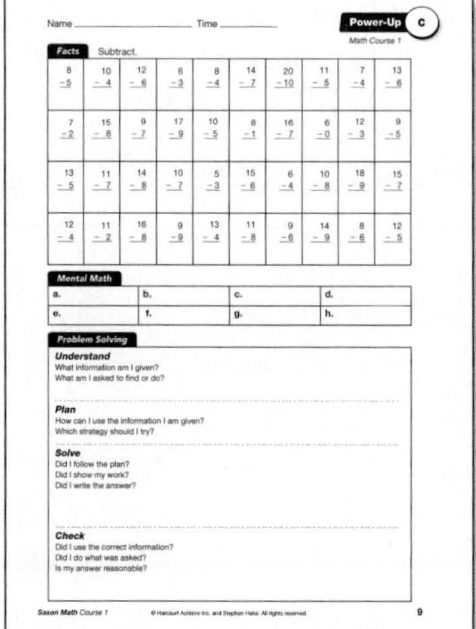

Power Up C

Math Language

New		English Learners (ESL)
endpoints	ray	length
International System	segment	
line	U.S. Customary System	
metric system		

Technology Resources

Student eBook Complete student textbook in electronic format.

Resources and Planner CD Assessment, reteaching, and instructional masters, plus a pacing calendar with standards.

Test and Practice Generator CD Create additional practice sheets and custom-made tests.

www.SaxonPublishers.com Visit for more student activities and planning materials.

Inclusion

Adaptations CD Adapted lessons, investigations, practice and assessments.

Meeting Standards

National Council of Teachers of Mathematics (NCTM)

Geometry

GM.1a Precisely describe, classify, and understand relationships among types of two- and three-dimensional objects using their defining properties

Measurement

ME.1a Understand both metric and customary systems of measurement

ME.2a Use common benchmarks to select appropriate methods for estimating measurements

Representation

RE.5b Select, apply, and translate among mathematical representations to solve problems

Power-Up Discussion

For use with Power Up, p. 36

Problem-Solving Strategy: Use Logical Reasoning

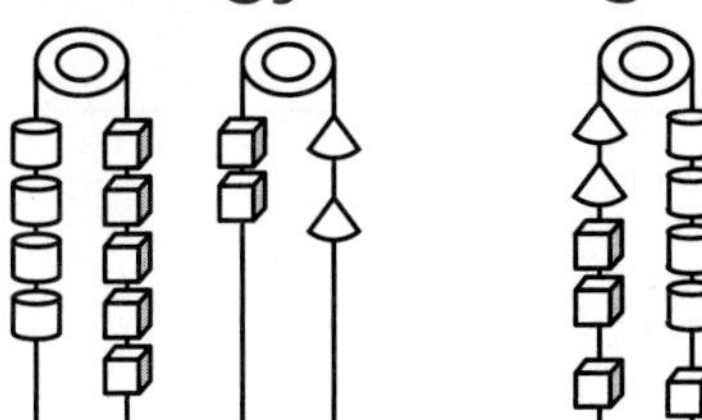

A pulley is in *equilibrium* when the total weight suspended from the left side is equal to the total weight suspended from the right side.

The two pulleys on the left are both in equilibrium. Is the pulley on the right in equilibrium, or is one side heavier than the other?

Teacher Note: To further explain the concept of equilibrium, compare a pulley to a balance scale. When one side is weighted more than the other, the scale is not in equilibrium, so it is off balance. By using a scale, the difference is noticeable visually.

Understand We are shown three pulleys on which three kinds of weights are suspended. The first two pulleys are in equilibrium. We are asked to determine if the third pulley is in equilibrium or if one side is heavier than the other.

Plan We will *use logical reasoning* to determine whether the third pulley is in equilibrium.

Solve From the first pulley we see that four cylinders are equal in weight to five cubes. This means that cylinders are heavier than cubes. The second pulley shows that two cubes weigh the same as two cones. This means that cubes and cones weigh the same.

On the third pulley, the bottom cubes on either side have the same weight. We are left with two cones and two cubes on one side and four cylinders on the other. We know that cylinders are heavier than cones, so the pulley is not in equilibrium. The right side is heavier, so the pulley will pull to the right.

Check We can confirm our conclusion by looking at the third pulley as five cubes on the left (because the two cones are equal in weight to two cubes). From the first pulley, we know that five cubes are equal in weight to four cylinders. Another cube on the right side makes the right side heavier.

Alternative Approach: Draw a Picture

For students who need a visual example, allow them to draw the weights to find the answer.

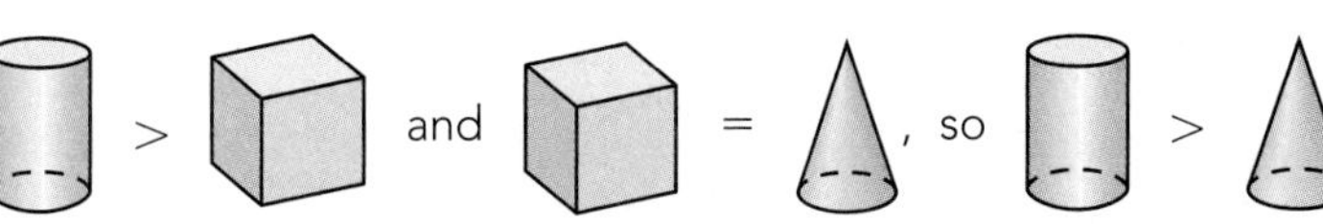

1 Power Up

Facts

Distribute **Power Up C** to students. See answers below.

Mental Math

Before students begin the Mental Math exercise, do this counting exercise as a class.

Count up and down by $\frac{1}{2}$s between $\frac{1}{2}$ and 10.

Count up and down by 2s between 2 and 40.

Encourage students to share different ways to mentally compute these exercises. Strategies for exercises **a** and **e** are listed below.

a. Use a Fact

$8 - 3 = 5$; $800 - 300 = 500$

Count Back by Hundreds

Start with 800. Count: 700, 600, 500

e. Decompose 480

$400 + 80 - 80 = 400$

Subtract Tens

4 hundreds 8 tens − 8 tens = 4 hundreds

Problem Solving

Refer to **Power-Up Discussion,** p. 36B.

LESSON 7

• Lines, Segments, and Rays
• Linear Measure

Power Up *Building Power*

facts Power Up C

mental math

a. **Number Sense:** 800 − 300 500

b. **Number Sense:** 3000 − 2000 1000

c. **Number Sense:** 450 − 100 350

d. **Number Sense:** 2500 − 300 2200

e. **Number Sense:** 480 − 80 400

f. **Number Sense:** 750 − 250 500

g. **Measurement:** How many weeks are in a year? 52 weeks

h. **Measurement:** How many days are in a year? 365 days

problem solving

A pulley is in *equilibrium* when the total weight suspended from the left side is equal to the total weight suspended from the right side.

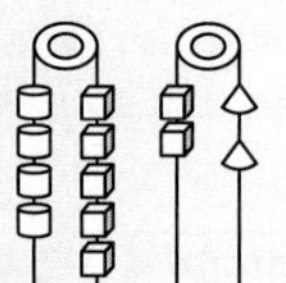

The two pulleys on the left are both in equilibrium. Is the pulley on the right in equilibrium, or is one side heavier than the other?

Understand We are shown three pulleys on which three kinds of weights are suspended. The first two pulleys are in equilibrium. We are asked to determine if the third pulley is in equilibrium or if one side is heavier than the other.

Plan We will *use logical reasoning* to determine whether the third pulley is in equilibrium.

Solve From the first pulley we see that four cylinders are equal in weight to five cubes. This means that cylinders are heavier than cubes. The second pulley shows that two cubes weigh the same as two cones. This means that cubes and cones weigh the same.

On the third pulley, the bottom cubes on either side have the same weight. We are left with two cones and two cubes on one side and four cylinders on the other. We know that cylinders are heavier than cubes and cones, so the pulley is not in equilibrium. The right side is heavier, so the pulley will pull to the right.

Check We can confirm our conclusion by looking at the third pulley as five cubes on the left (because the two cones are equal in weight to two cubes). From the first pulley, we know that five cubes are equal in weight to four cylinders. Another cube on the right side makes the right side heavier.

36 **Saxon** *Math Course 1*

Facts Subtract.

8 − 5 3	10 − 4 6	12 − 6 6	6 − 3 3	8 − 4 4	14 − 7 7	20 − 10 10	11 − 5 6	7 − 4 3	13 − 6 7
7 − 2 5	15 − 8 7	9 − 7 2	17 − 9 8	10 − 5 5	8 − 1 7	16 − 7 9	6 − 0 6	12 − 3 9	9 − 5 4
13 − 5 8	11 − 7 4	14 − 8 6	10 − 7 3	5 − 3 2	15 − 6 9	6 − 4 2	10 − 8 2	18 − 9 9	15 − 7 8
12 − 4 8	11 − 2 9	16 − 8 8	9 − 9 0	13 − 4 9	11 − 8 3	9 − 6 3	14 − 9 5	8 − 6 2	12 − 5 7

New Concepts

Increasing Knowledge

lines, segments, and rays

Thinking Skill

Conclude

If two opposite-facing rays are joined at their endpoints, what is the result? What do those endpoints become? A line. The endpoints become one point on the line.

In everyday language the following figure is often referred to as a line:

However, using mathematical terminology, we say that the figure represents a **segment,** or line segment. A segment is part of a line and has two **endpoints.** A mathematical **line** has no endpoints. To represent a line, we use arrowheads to indicate a line's unending quality.

A **ray** has one endpoint. We represent a ray with one arrowhead.

A ray is roughly represented by a beam of sunlight. The beam begins at the sun (which represents the endpoint of the ray) and continues across billions of light years of space.

linear measure

Line segments have length. In the United States we have two systems of units that we use to measure length. One system is the **U.S. Customary System.** Some of the units in this system are inches (in.), feet (ft), yards (yd), and miles (mi). The other system is the **metric system (International System).** Some of the units in the metric system are millimeters (mm), centimeters (cm), meters (m), and kilometers (km).

Some Units of Length and Benchmarks

U.S. Customary System		**Metric System**	
inch (in.)	width of thumb	millimeter (mm)	thickness of a dime
foot (ft)	length of ruler, 12 inches	centimeter (cm)	thickness of little finger tip, 10 millimeters
yard (yd)	a long step, 3 ft or 36 inches	meter (m)	a little over a yard, 100 centimeters
miles (mi)	distance walked in 20 minutes, 5280 feet	kilometer (km)	distance walked in 12 minutes, 1000 meters

In this lesson we will practice measuring line segments with an inch ruler and with a centimeter ruler, and we will select appropriate units for measuring lengths.

Activity

Inch Ruler

Materials needed:

- inch ruler
- narrow strip of tagboard about 6 inches long and 1 inch wide
- pencil

2 New Concepts

Instruction

To reinforce these figures and terms, invite volunteers to draw and label lines, line segments, and rays in a variety of orientations on the board.

Refer to the chart and invite volunteers to make a list on the board of objects or things that are typically measured using inches, feet, yards, and miles.

Elsewhere on the board, challenge other students to list objects or things that are typically measured using millimeters, centimeters, meters, and kilometers. Sample answers shown.

inches: length of a baby
feet: height of a building
yards: dimensions of a football field
miles: driving distances in the U.S.
millimeters: width of camera film
centimeters: height of a tabletop
meters: length of a swimming pool
kilometers: foreign driving distances

(continued)

Math Background

Which is used more, the metric system or the U.S. Customary System?

The metric system, also known as the International System of Units (SI), is the primary system of measurement in almost every part of the world, except the United States. Although the U.S. Customary System, which includes units such as inches, feet, gallons, and pounds, originated in Great Britain, that country now uses the metric system. The United States is the only large country in the world that still uses the Customary System as its primary system of measurement.

English Learners

Draw a horizontal line on the board and place a point at each end. Run your hand along the **length** of the line and say:

"Length is a measure of how long something is. The length of this line is from here to here. What are some units of measure we use to measure length?"

Draw another line on the board and have students trace its length with their hand. Ask students to measure the length of both lines.

2 New Concepts (Continued)

Instruction

Ask students to find zero on their rulers. On some rulers, the zero mark is the end of the ruler. On others, the zero mark is indented.

Using their strips of tagboard or rulers from the Manipulative Kit, ask students to measure, to the nearest quarter inch, the length of a pencil, the width of a sheet of paper, and the thickness of a book. Then ask students to measure each object again using the metric scale of their ruler and write the measurements in centimeters or millimeters.

Example 1

Instruction

Have students note that a length of $1\frac{1}{4}$ inches is equivalent to $\frac{5}{4}$ inches.

"The line segment is one and one-fourth inches long. How many fourths of an inch long is the segment?" five-fourths

(continued)

Model Use your pencil and ruler to draw inch marks on the strip of tagboard. Number the inch marks. When you are finished, the tagboard strip should look like this:

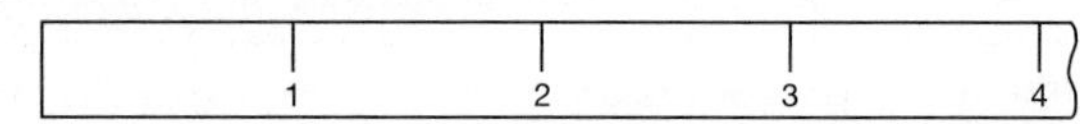

Estimate Now set aside your ruler. We will use estimation to make the rest of the marks on the tagboard strip. Estimate the halfway point between inch marks, and make the half-inch marks slightly shorter than the inch marks, as shown below.

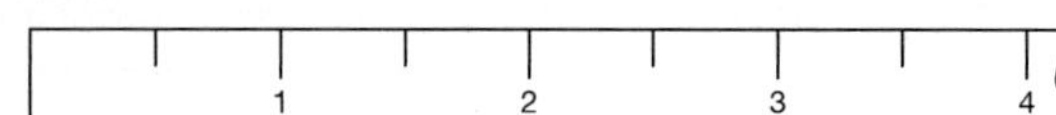

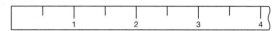

Now show every quarter inch on your tagboard ruler. To do this, estimate the halfway point between each mark on the ruler, and make the quarter-inch marks slightly shorter than the half-inch marks, as shown below.

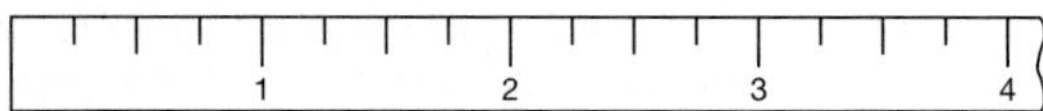

Save your tagboard ruler. We will be making more marks on it in a few days.

Connect A metric ruler is divided into centimeters. There are 100 centimeters in a meter. Each centimeter is divided into 10 millimeters. So 1 centimeter equals 10 millimeters, and 2 centimeters equals 20 millimeters.

By comparing an inch ruler with a centimeter ruler, we see that an inch is about $2\frac{1}{2}$ centimeters.

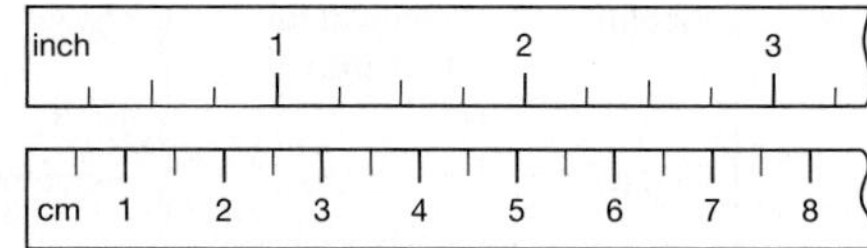

A cinnamon stick that is 3 inches long is about $7\frac{1}{2}$ cm long. A foot-long ruler is about 30 cm long.

Example 1

How long is the line segment?

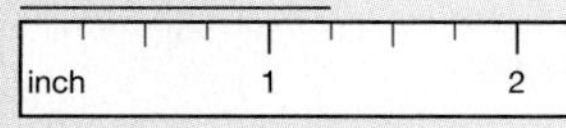

Solution

Reading Math
The abbreviation for inches (in.) ends with a period so it is not confused with the word *in*.

The line is one whole inch plus a fraction. The fraction is one fourth. So the length of the line is **$1\frac{1}{4}$ in.**

Inclusion

Materials: metric rulers

Demonstrate how to align the zero mark of a ruler with the end of the item to be measured. Then have students look at the scale of the metric ruler above example 1. Ask:

"What do the small tick marks between the numbers do?" They divide each centimeter in half.

Then have students look at the metric ruler in Practice Set b. Point out that each centimeter is divided into ten equal parts called centimeters. Ask:

"How many millimeters are in 2 centimeters?" 20 cm

"In 5 centimeters?" 50 cm

Ask students to measure several objects such as a book, a pencil, and an eraser. Have students record each measurement in millimeters.

Example 2

How long is the line segment?

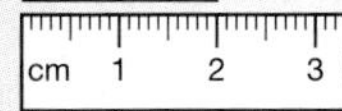

Solution

We simply read the scale to see that the line is **2 cm** long. The segment is also **20 mm** long.

Example 3

Select the appropriate unit for measuring the length of a soccer field.

A centimeters **B meters** **C kilometers**

Solution

An appropriate unit can give us a good sense of the measure of an object. Describing a soccer field as thousands of centimeters or a small fraction of a kilometer can be accurate without being appropriate. The best choice is **B meters** for measuring the length of a soccer field.

Practice Set How long is each line segment?

▸ **a.** $1\frac{3}{4}$ in.

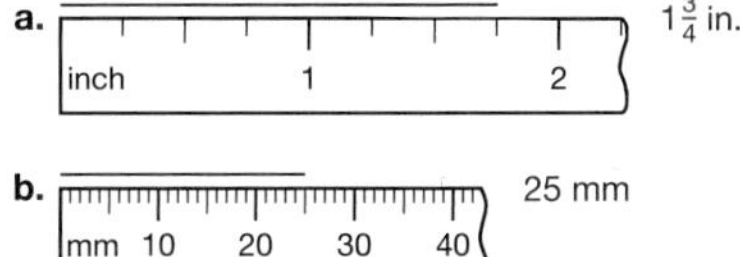

b. 25 mm

▸ **c.** Connect Measure the following segment twice, once with an inch ruler and once with a centimeter ruler. 2 in.; 5.1 cm (accept 5 cm)

Use the words *line, segment,* or *ray* to describe each of these figures:

d. ray

e. line

f. segment

g. Which of these units is most appropriate for measuring the length of a pencil? **A**

A inches **B** yards **C** miles

h. Select the appropriate unit for measuring the distance between two towns. **C**

A centimeters **B** meters **C** kilometers

▸ See Math Conversations in the sidebar.

2 New Concepts (Continued)

Example 2

Instruction

After discussing the example, write the following table on the board.

centimeters (cm)	1	2	3	4	5	6
millimeters (mm)	10	20	30	40	50	60

Explain that the table is designed to show the proportional relationship shared by centimeters and millimeters.

Ask students to complete the table, then write a rule that can be used to determine the number of millimeters for any number of centimeters. Sample: The number of millimeters is equal to the product of the number of centimeters and ten.

Example 3

Instruction

Explain that another way to help decide if a unit is appropriate is to choose a unit that creates a sensible number. A sensible number is one that, whenever possible, is not too big or not too small. In other words, the number is easy for people to understand. For example, a distance of one kilometer is best described as 1 kilometer or 1000 meters, not 1,000,000 millimeters.

Practice Set

Problem a Error Alert

To measure correctly, it is important for students to recognize that the number of tick marks between any two consecutive inches is one less than the number of equal divisions those tick marks form. For example, one tick mark is used to divide each inch into two equal parts, or halves. Three tick marks are used to divide each inch into four equal parts, or fourths.

Problem c Connect

Extend the Problem

Using the measurements that were made, ask students to estimate the number of centimeters in one inch. about $2\frac{1}{2}$

3 Written Practice

Math Conversations

Discussion opportunities are provided below.

Problem 3 Analyze

After completing the problem, ask students to name the operations they used to find the answer, and explain why those operations were used.

Problem 19 Generalize

Extend the Problem

"How would the quotient change if the divisor was doubled?" the quotient would be halved

To form the generalization, students may benefit from solving a simpler problem first. For example, in the fact $12 \div 2 = 6$, the divisor is 2. Doubling the divisor produces $12 \div 4 = 3$, or a quotient that is half the original quotient.

Errors and Misconceptions

Problem 9

Although an answer of 2072¢ is computationally correct, any number of cents greater than 100 should be expressed in a simpler way. To change 2072¢ to dollars and cents, students must place a decimal point in the product, or change the factor 28¢ to $0.28 before completing the multiplication.

(continued)

Written Practice *Strengthening Concepts*

1. (2) To earn money for gifts, Debbie sold decorated pinecones. If she sold 100 pinecones at $0.25 each, how much money did she earn? $25.00

2. (1) There are 365 days in a common year. April 1 is the 91st day. How many days are left in the year after April 1? 274 days

▶ 3. (5) The Cardaso family is planning to complete a 1890-mile trip in 3 days. If they drive 596 miles the first day and 612 miles the second day, how far must they travel the third day? (*Hint:* This is a two-step problem. First find how far they traveled the first two days.) 682 miles

4. (6) What number is $\frac{1}{2}$ of 234? 117

5. (6) How much money is $\frac{1}{3}$ of $2.34? $0.78

6. (6) Use words and digits to write the fraction of this circle that is shaded. three eighths; $\frac{3}{8}$

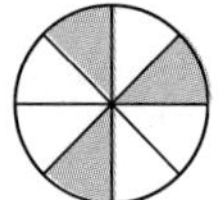

7. (1) 3654 + 2893 + 5614 = 12,161

8. (1) $41.01 − $15.76 = $25.25

▶ 9. (2) 28¢ × 74 = $20.72

10. (2) 906 × 47 = 42,582

11. (2) $6\overline{)5000}$ 833 R 2

12. (2) 800 ÷ 16 50

13. (2) $60\overline{)3174}$ 52 R 54

14. (3) 3 + 6 + 5 + w + 4 = 30 12

15. (5) 300 − 30 + 3 273

16. (5) 300 − (30 + 3) 267

17. (2) $4.32 · 20 $86.40

18. (2) 24(48¢) $11.52

▶ 19. (2) $8.75 ÷ 25 $0.35

Find each unknown number. Check your work.

20. (4) $W \div 6 = 7$ 42

21. (4) $6n = 96$ 16

22. (4) $58 + r = 213$ 155

* 23. (1) Connect Rearrange the numbers in this subtraction fact to form another subtraction fact and two addition facts.

60 − 24 = 36

23. 60 − 36 = 24, 36 + 24 = 60, 24 + 36 = 60

24. (7) How long is the line segment below? $1\frac{1}{2}$ in.

inch 1 2

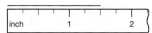

▶ See Math Conversations in the sidebar.

25. Find the length, in centimeters and in millimeters, of the line segment below. 3 cm; 30 mm
(7)

cm 1 2 3 4

▶* 26. **Connect** Use the numbers 9, 10, and 90 to form two multiplication facts and two division facts. $9 \times 10 = 90$, $10 \times 9 = 90$, $90 \div 9 = 10$, $90 \div 10 = 9$
(2)

▶* 27. **Explain** How can you find a missing dividend in a division problem?
(4) To find a missing dividend, multiply the quotient by the divisor.

28. $w - 12 = 8$ 20
(3)

29. $12 - x = 8$ 4
(3)

▶ 30. a. A meterstick is 100 centimeters long. One hundred centimeters is how many millimeters? 1000 millimeters
(7)

b. The length of which of the following would most likely be measured in meters? B

A a pencil **B** a hallway **C** a highway

Early Finishers
Real-World Application

The district championship game will be played on an artificial surface. One-fifth of the team needs new shoes for the game. There are 40 players on the team, and each pair of shoes sells for $45.

a. How many players need new shoes? 8 players

b. How much money must the booster club raise to cover the entire cost of the shoes? $360

▶ See Math Conversations in the sidebar.

3 Written Practice (Continued)

Math Conversations

Discussion opportunities are provided below.

Problem 26 Connect

Ask students to explain how the related equations represent inverse operations. Sample: Multiplying by 9 undoes dividing by 9 and multiplying by 10 undoes dividing by 10.

Problem 27 Explain

Extend the Problem

Challenge students to explain how to find a missing divisor in a division problem. Divide the dividend by the quotient.

Errors and Misconceptions

Problem 30

Shifting the decimal point to the left instead of to the right indicates that students chose to divide instead of multiply. Explain that to change centimeters to millimeters, the number of centimeters is multiplied by 10, which is the same as shifting the decimal point one place to the right.

When changing units, students should generalize:

- To change from a larger unit to a smaller unit, multiply.
- To change from a smaller unit to a larger unit, divide.

Looking Forward

Understanding the concepts of lines, segments, and rays prepares students for:

- **Lesson 28,** forming angles, naming angles, and kinds of angles.
- **Investigation 3,** measuring and drawing angles with a protractor.
- **Lesson 69,** finding the length of a line segment.
- **Investigation 8,** using a compass to bisect a line segment and angle.
- **Lesson 97,** studying the effects of a transversal intersecting parallel lines.

• Perimeter

Objectives

- Recognize that the total distance around the classroom is the perimeter of the classroom.
- Find the perimeter of a shape by adding the lengths of the shape's sides.
- Find the length of a side of a square when the perimeter of the square is known.

Lesson Preparation

Materials

- **Power Up A** (in *Instructional Masters*)
- **Manipulative kit: rulers**

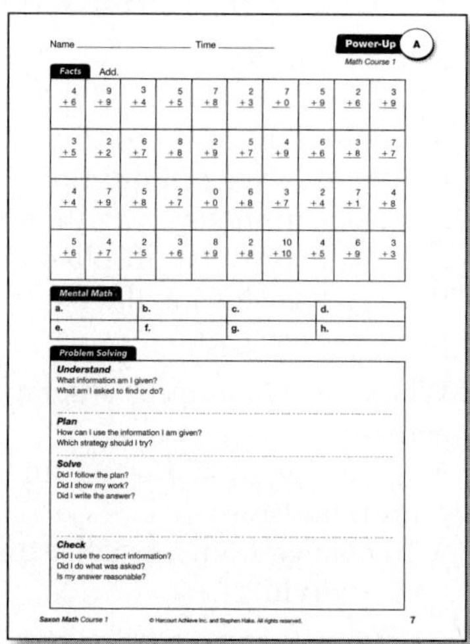
Name ________ Time ________

Power-Up A
Math Course 1

Facts Add.

4 + 6	9 + 9	3 + 4	5 + 5	7 + 8	2 + 3	7 + 0	5 + 9	2 + 6	3 + 9
3 + 5	2 + 2	6 + 7	8 + 8	2 + 9	5 + 7	4 + 9	6 + 6	3 + 8	7 + 7
4 + 4	7 + 9	5 + 8	2 + 7	0 + 0	6 + 8	3 + 7	2 + 4	7 + 1	4 + 8
5 + 6	4 + 7	2 + 5	3 + 6	8 + 9	2 + 8	10 + 10	4 + 5	6 + 9	3 + 3

Mental Math

a.	b.	c.	d.
e.	f.	g.	h.

Problem Solving

Understand
What information am I given?
What am I asked to find or do?

Plan
How can I use the information I am given?
Which strategy should I try?

Solve
Did I follow the plan?
Did I show my work?
Did I write the answer?

Check
Did I use the correct information?
Did I do what was asked?
Is my answer reasonable?

Saxon Math Course 1 © Harcourt Achieve Inc. and Stephen Hake. All rights reserved. 7

Power Up A

Math Language

New	**English Learners (ESL)**
perimeter	distance

Technology Resources

Student eBook Complete student textbook in electronic format.

Resources and Planner CD Assessment, reteaching, and instructional masters, plus a pacing calendar with standards.

Test and Practice Generator CD Create additional practice sheets and custom-made tests.

www.SaxonPublishers.com Visit for more student activities and planning materials.

Inclusion

Adaptations CD Adapted lessons, investigations, practice and assessments.

Meeting Standards

National Council of Teachers of Mathematics (NCTM)

Geometry

GM.4d Use geometric models to represent and explain numerical and algebraic relationships

GM.4e Recognize and apply geometric ideas and relationships in areas outside the mathematics classroom, such as art, science, and everyday life

Measurement

ME.1c Understand, select, and use units of appropriate size and type to measure angles, perimeter, area, surface area, and volume

ME.2a Use common benchmarks to select appropriate methods for estimating measurements

Power-Up Discussion *For use with Power Up, p. 42*

Problem-Solving Strategy: Make an Organized List

The digits 2, 4, and 6 can be arranged to form six different three-digit numbers. Each ordering is called a **permutation** of the three digits. The smallest permutation of 2, 4, and 6 is 246. What are the other five permutations? List the six numbers in order from least to greatest.

Teacher Note: Give several examples of permutations using other numbers, such as 123, 132, 213, 231.

Understand We have been asked to find five of the six permutations that exist for three digits, and then list the permutations from least to greatest.

Teacher Note: Explain to the students that being able to identify all possible permutations of a set of objects is an important skill in the study of probability.

Plan To make sure we find all permutations possible, we will make an organized list.

Solve We first write the permutations of 2, 4, and 6 that begin with 2, then those that begin with 4, then those that begin with 6: 246, 264, 426, 462, 624, 642.

Teacher Note: Emphasize to students the value of organizing a set of information (which in the future could be digits, names, letters, colors, etc.) in ascending or descending order. This helps ensure that no possibilities are inadvertently missed.

Check We found all six permutations of the digits 2, 4, and 6. Writing them in an organized way helped us ensure we did not overlook any permutations. Because we wrote the numbers from least to greatest as we went along, we did not have to re-order our list to solve the problem.

1 Power Up

Facts

Distribute **Power Up A** to students. See answers below.

Mental Math

Before students begin the Mental Math exercise, do this counting exercise as a class.

Count up by $\frac{1}{4}$s from $\frac{1}{4}$ to 10.

Encourage students to share different ways to mentally compute these exercises. Some strategies for exercises **b** and **d** are listed below.

b. Add Tens

$700 + 50 + 30 + 6 = 700 + 80 + 6 = 786$

Add 4, Then Subtract 4

$36 + 4 = 40$; $750 + 40 = 790$;
$790 - 4 = 786$

d. Subtract Tens

$900 + 80 - 60 = 900 + 20 = 920$

Count Back by Tens

Start with 980. Count: 970, 960, 950, 940, 930, 920

Problem Solving

Refer to **Power-Up Discussion,** p. 42B.

2 New Concepts

Instruction

After students understand the concept of perimeter, give them an opportunity to connect their understanding to the real world.

"When might an understanding of perimeter be useful to a homeowner?" Sample: measuring a garden prior to purchasing a fence to keep out animals

Encourage students to suggest other real-world situations and scenarios that involve perimeter.

(continued)

LESSON 8

• Perimeter

Power Up *Building Power*

facts Power Up A

mental math

a. **Number Sense:** 400 + 2400 2800

b. **Number Sense:** 750 + 36 786

c. **Number Sense:** 8400 + 520 8920

d. **Number Sense:** 980 − 60 920

e. **Number Sense:** 4400 − 2000 2400

f. **Number Sense:** 480 − 120 360

g. **Measurement:** How many feet are in 2 yards? 6 ft

h. **Measurement:** How many centimeters are in 2 meters? 200 cm

problem solving

The digits 2, 4, and 6 can be arranged to form six different three-digit numbers. Each ordering is called a **permutation** of the three digits. The smallest permutation of 2, 4, and 6 is 246. What are the other five permutations? List the six numbers in order from least to greatest.

Understand We have been asked to find five of the six permutations that exist for three digits, and then list the permutations from least to greatest.

Plan To make sure we find all permutations possible, we will make an organized list.

Solve We first write the permutations of 2, 4, and 6 that begin with 2, then those that begin with 4, then those that begin with 6: 246, 264, 426, 462, 624, 642.

Check We found all six permutations of the digits 2, 4, and 6. Writing them in an organized way helped us ensure we did not overlook any permutations. Because we wrote the numbers from least to greatest as we went along, we did not have to re-order our list to solve the problem.

New Concept *Increasing Knowledge*

The distance around a shape is its **perimeter.** The perimeter of a square is the distance around it. The perimeter of a room is the distance around the room.

Activity

Perimeter

Model Walk the perimeter of your classroom. Start at a point along a wall of the classroom, and, staying close to the walls, walk around the room until you return to your starting point. Count your steps as you travel around the room. How many of your steps is the perimeter of the room?

Facts Add.

4 + 6 10	9 + 9 18	3 + 4 7	5 + 5 10	7 + 8 15	2 + 3 5	7 + 0 7	5 + 9 14	2 + 6 8	3 + 9 12
3 + 5 8	2 + 2 4	6 + 7 13	8 + 8 16	2 + 9 11	5 + 7 12	4 + 9 13	6 + 6 12	3 + 8 11	7 + 7 14
4 + 4 8	7 + 9 16	5 + 8 13	2 + 7 9	0 + 0 0	6 + 8 14	3 + 7 10	2 + 4 6	7 + 1 8	4 + 8 12
5 + 6 11	4 + 7 11	2 + 5 7	3 + 6 9	8 + 9 17	2 + 8 10	10 + 10 20	4 + 5 9	6 + 9 15	3 + 3 6

a. Probably not. Different-size steps will result in different counts.
b. The perimeter does not change. A uniform unit of measure is needed for consistent measurements.
c. 2. Although molding does not cross doorways, it is a good physical model for the perimeter of the room.

Discuss

a. Did everyone count the same number of steps?

b. Does the perimeter depend upon who is measuring it?

c. Which of these is the best real-world example of perimeter?

1. The tile or carpet that covers the floor.

2. The molding along the base of the wall.

Here we show a rectangle that is 3 cm long and 2 cm wide.

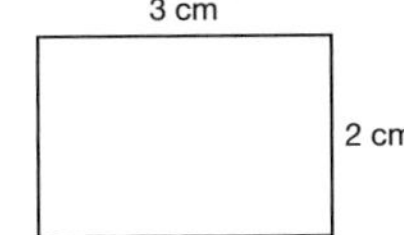

If we were to start at one corner and trace the perimeter of the rectangle, our pencil would travel 3 cm, then 2 cm, then 3 cm, and then 2 cm to get all the way around. We add these lengths to find the perimeter of the rectangle.

3 cm + 2 cm + 3 cm + 2 cm = **10 cm**

Example 1

What is the perimeter of this triangle?

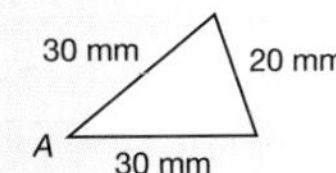

Solution

The perimeter of a shape is the distance around the shape. If we trace around the triangle from point *A*, the point of the pencil would travel 30 mm, then 20 mm, and then 30 mm. Adding these distances, we find that the perimeter is **80 mm.**

Example 2

The perimeter of a square is 20 cm. What is the length of each side?

Solution

The four sides of a square are equal in length. So we divide the perimeter by 4 to find the length of each side. We find that the length of each side is **5 cm.**

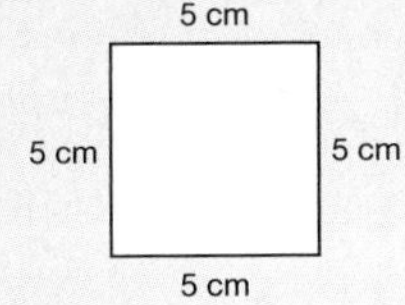

2 New Concepts (Continued)

Instruction

Invite students to use the eraser end of their pencils to trace the perimeter of the rectangle, and then explain how they know that the lengths of the unlabeled sides are 2 cm and 3 cm. Because the opposite sides of a rectangle are congruent, the opposite sides are the same length.

Example 1

Instruction

Invite a volunteer to explain how to change millimeters to centimeters, and then name the perimeter of the triangle in centimeters. 8 cm

Example 2

Instruction

Remind students of the importance of checking their work.

"Name two operations that could be used to check the answer, and explain how those operations could be used." Sample: addition and multiplication; count on by fives four times, beginning with 5 or multiply 5 by 4

(continued)

English Learners

On the board, draw a triangle like the one in example 1 and say:

"Watch while I use my hand to show the **distance** ***around this triangle."***

Use your hand to trace the distance of the perimeter of the triangle. Say:

"What is the distance around this triangle?" 80 mm

Have students draw triangles or rectangles on the board and trace the distance around them with their hand.

Math Background

Perimeter is always expressed using linear measure. Common examples of linear measurement units include inches, feet, yards, millimeters, centimeters, and meters.

2 New Concepts (Continued)

Practice Set

Problems a–e Error Alert

Remind students to include a label (such as centimeters or cm) with each answer. Explain that numbers without units do not indicate the size of the shape. For example, describing the perimeter of the square in problem a as 48 does not represent how big or how small the square really is.

Problem f Conclude

Before finding the answer, ask students to explain what they need to know about a square in order to find the answer. All of the sides of a square are congruent. Therefore, multiplication or repeated addition can be used to find the perimeter.

Problem g Error Alert

If students have difficulty knowing how to begin drawing the figures, ask them to choose a number to represent both perimeters. The students should then draw two figures that have the same shape, or different shapes. For example, both figures may be rectangles, or one figure may be a square and the other an irregular quadrilateral.

3 Written Practice

Math Conversations

Discussion opportunities are provided below.

Problem 2 Explain

More than one equation can be used to represent this problem. Challenge students to name an addition equation and a subtraction equation that represent the problem and can be used to find the answer. Variables will vary; $n + 765 = 1750$ and $1750 - 765 = n$.

(continued)

Practice Set

Thinking Skill
Verify
Why can we find the perimeter of a regular polygon when we know the length of one side?
All of the sides of a regular polygon are the same length.

▶ What is the perimeter of each shape?

a. square
b. rectangle
c. trapezoid

12 mm
48 mm

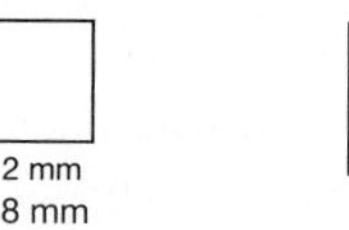

20 mm
70 mm

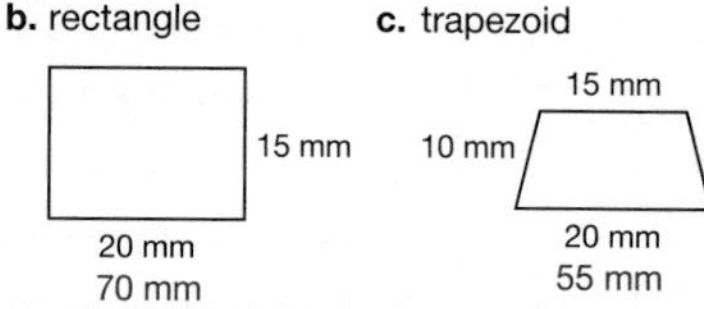

55 mm

▶ Figures **d** and **e** below are regular polygons because all of their sides are the same length and all of their angles are the same size. Find the perimeter of each shape.

d. equilateral triangle
e. pentagon

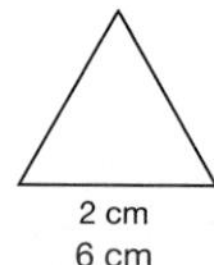
2 cm
6 cm

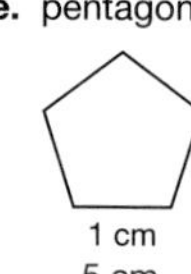
1 cm
5 cm

▶ **f.** Conclude The perimeter of a square is 60 cm. How long is each side of the square? 15 cm

▶ **g.** Represent Draw two different figures that have perimeters that are the same length. See student work.

h. Select the appropriate unit for measuring the perimeter of a classroom.
A inches **B** feet **C** miles B

Written Practice *Strengthening Concepts*

1. (2) In an auditorium there are 25 rows of chairs with 18 chairs in each row. How many chairs are in the auditorium? 450 chairs

▶ *** 2.** (1) Explain The sixth-graders collected 765 cans of food for the food pantry last year. This year they collected 1750 cans. How many fewer cans did they collect last year than this year? Explain how you found the answer. 985 fewer cans; Sample: I subtracted last year's total from this year's total.

3. (2) A basketball team is made up of 5 players. Suppose there are 140 players signed up for a tournament. How many teams will there be of 5 players per team? 28 teams

4. (8) What is the perimeter of this triangle? 60 mm

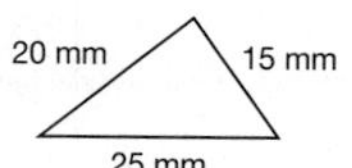

5. (6) How much money is $\frac{1}{2}$ of \$6.54? \$3.27

6. (6) What number is $\frac{1}{3}$ of 654? 218

▶ See Math Conversations in the sidebar.

▶ * 7. (6) Represent What fraction of this rectangle is shaded? $\frac{3}{10}$

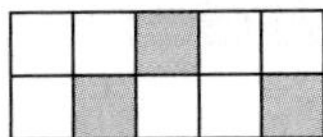

8. (2) $4\overline{)\$9.00}$ \$2.25

9. (2) $10\overline{)373}$ 37 R 3

10. (2) $12\overline{)1500}$ 125

11. (2) $39\overline{)800}$ 20 R 20

12. (5) 400 ÷ 20 ÷ 4 5

13. (5) 400 ÷ (20 ÷ 4) 80

▶* 14. (2) Connect Use the numbers 240, 20, and 12 to form two multiplication facts and two division facts.

14. 20 × 12 = 240, 12 × 20 = 240, 240 ÷ 20 = 12, 240 ÷ 12 = 20

15. (1) Rearrange the numbers in this addition fact to form another addition fact and two subtraction facts. 80 + 60 = 140, 140 − 80 = 60, 140 − 60 = 80

60 + 80 = 140

16. (8) The ceiling tiles used in many classrooms have sides that are 12 inches long. What is the perimeter of a square tile with sides 12 inches long? 48 inches

17. (1, 2) a. Find the sum of 6 and 4. 10

b. Find the product of 6 and 4. 24

18. (3) \$5 − M = \$1.48 \$3.52

19. (5) 10 × 20 × 30 6000

20. (2) 825 ÷ 8 103 R 1

Find each unknown number. Check your work.

21. (3) $w - 63 = 36$ 99

▶ 22. (3) $150 + 165 + a = 397$ 82

23. (4) $12w = 120$ 10

24. (4) If the divisor is 8 and the quotient is 24, what is the dividend? 192

▶* 25. (7) Estimate a. Measure the length of the line segment below to the nearest centimeter. about 3 centimeters

b. Measure the length of the segment in millimeters. 28 millimeters

▶* 26. (7) Model Use a ruler to draw a line segment that is $2\frac{3}{4}$ in. long. See student work.

27. (3) $w - 27 = 18$ 45

28. (3) $27 - x = 18$ 9

29. (2) Multiply to find the answer to this addition problem: 35 × 4 = 140

35 + 35 + 35 + 35

▶* 30. (8) Explain How can you calculate the perimeter of a rectangle? One way to calculate the perimeter of a rectangle is to add the lengths of the four sides.

▶ See Math Conversations in the sidebar.

Looking Forward

Finding the perimeter of a shape or using the perimeter of a square to find the length of a side prepares students for:

- **Lessons 27 and 47,** understanding the measures of a circle, finding pi, and finding the circumference of a circle.
- **Investigation 7,** finding the perimeter of a rectangle graphed on a coordinate plane.
- **Lesson 71,** finding the perimeter of a parallelogram.
- **Lesson 91,** using formulas to find the perimeters of squares, rectangles, parallelograms, and triangles.
- **Lesson 103,** finding the perimeter of complex shapes.

3 *Written Practice (Continued)*

Math Conversations

Discussion opportunities are provided below.

Problem 7 Represent

Extend the Problem

Challenge students to explain how to shade $\frac{3}{20}$ of the figure. Sample: Divide each square in two to double the number of equal parts, and delete one-half of the existing shading in each of the three shaded parts.

Problem 14 Connect

Students should recognize that the related equations of a fact family represent inverse operations.

"How are the operations in a fact family related?" The operations are inverse operations.

Problem 25 Estimate

"Which measurement is a more precise way of describing the length of the segment? Why?" Sample: 28 millimeters is more precise because the segment is closer to 28 millimeters long than to 30 millimeters long.

Problem 26 Model

Extend the Problem

Using their rulers, challenge students to name the length of a segment that is one-half as long, and name the length of a segment that is twice as long, as the given segment. $1\frac{3}{8}$ in.; $5\frac{1}{2}$ in.

Problem 30 Explain

Extend the Problem

Ask students to generalize how the perimeter of a rectangle would change if the length of each of its sides was doubled. Doubling each length will double the perimeter.

Invite volunteers to each draw two rectangles on the board to prove their generalization.

Errors and Misconceptions

Problem 22

To find the value of a, students should first simplify the equation by collecting like terms, which in this equation represents finding the sum of the addends 150 and 165.

• The Number Line: Ordering and Comparing

Objectives

- Use a number line to order numbers from least to greatest.
- Use the symbols >, <, and = to compare two numbers.
- Find the value of two expressions and compare them using the symbols >, <, or =.
- Use digits and other symbols to write comparisons that are stated in words.

Lesson Preparation

Materials

- **Power Up C** (in *Instructional Masters*)
- **Manipulative kit: rulers**

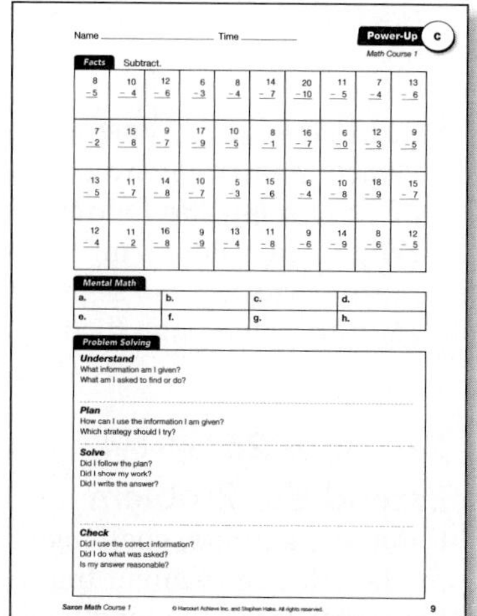

Name ______ Time ______

Power-Up C
Math Course 1

Facts Subtract.

8 − 5	10 − 4	12 − 6	6 − 3	8 − 4	14 − 7	20 − 10	11 − 5	7 − 4	13 − 6
7 − 2	15 − 8	9 − 7	17 − 9	10 − 5	8 − 1	16 − 7	6 − 0	12 − 3	9 − 5
13 − 5	11 − 7	14 − 8	10 − 7	5 − 3	15 − 6	6 − 4	10 − 8	18 − 9	15 − 7
12 − 4	11 − 2	16 − 8	9 − 9	13 − 4	11 − 8	9 − 6	14 − 9	8 − 6	12 − 5

Mental Math

a.	b.	c.	d.
e.	f.	g.	h.

Problem Solving

Understand
What information am I given?
What am I asked to find or do?

Plan
How can I use the information I am given?
Which strategy should I try?

Solve
Did I follow the plan?
Did I show my work?
Did I write the answer?

Check
Did I use the correct information?
Did I do what was asked?
Is my answer reasonable?

Saxon Math Course 1 9

Power Up C

Math Language

New	English Learners (ESL)
counting numbers	symbol
negative numbers	
number line	
whole numbers	

Technology Resources

Student eBook Complete student textbook in electronic format.

Resources and Planner CD Assessment, reteaching, and instructional masters, plus a pacing calendar with standards.

Test and Practice Generator CD Create additional practice sheets and custom-made tests.

www.SaxonPublishers.com Visit for more student activities and planning materials.

Inclusion

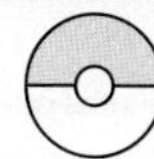

Adaptations CD Adapted lessons, investigations, practice and assessments.

Meeting Standards

National Council of Teachers of Mathematics (NCTM)

Numbers and Operations

NO.1b Compare and order fractions, decimals, and percents efficiently and find their approximate locations on a number line

NO.1g Develop meaning for integers and represent and compare quantities with them

CN.4c Recognize and apply mathematics in contexts outside of mathematics

Power-Up Discussion *For use with Power Up, p. 46*

Problem-Solving Strategy: Use Logical Reasoning

As you sit at your desk facing forward, you can describe the locations of people and objects in your classroom compared to your position. Perhaps a friend is two seats in front and one row to the left. Perhaps the door is directly to your right about 6 feet. Describe the location of your teacher's desk, the pencil sharpener, and a person or object of your choice.

Understand — *Understand the problem.*

"What information are we given?"

We can describe the locations of objects and people as compared to our own position.

"What are we asked to do?"

Describe the location of the teacher's desk, the pencil sharpener, and a person or object of our choice.

Plan — *Make a plan.*

"What problem-solving strategy will we use?"

We will *use logical and spatial reasoning* to describe the location of objects in the classroom relative to our position.

"What information do we need to solve the problem?"

We need to find our teacher's desk, the pencil sharpener, and another object or person whose location we will describe.

"To help describe, how can we specify the direction and distance?"

We can describe direction by using phrases like *to the right, to the left, in front, beside, etc.* We can describe distance by using measurement units (such as feet) or counting units (such as rows or seats).

Solve — *Carry out the plan.*

"Describe the distance to the teacher's desk. If the desk is directly in front of you, about how many (feet/meters) would you have to walk to get to it?"

Answers vary depending on individual student locations.

"If the desk is not directly in front of you (or directly to your left or right or behind you), how can you describe the distance to the desk?"

We say the desk is a number of (feet/meters/rows) in front of us (or behind us) and a number of (feet/meters/rows) to the right or left of us.
Repeat with pencil sharpener and another object.

Check — *Look back.*

"Did we complete the task?"

Yes, we described the location of people/objects by giving direction and distance.

Alternate Approach: Draw a Diagram

To help show the location of objects compared to each student's position, have each student use grid paper to draw a diagram of the classroom. Label the top of the paper "in front," the bottom "behind," and the left and right "to the left/right" respectively. Instruct the students to draw and label dots to represent the desk and other objects. The space between each grid line can be used to represent one unit of distance.

1 Power Up

Facts

Distribute **Power Up C** to students. See answers below.

Mental Math

Before students begin the Mental Math exercise, do this counting exercise as a class.

Count up and down by 25s between 25 and 1000.

Encourage students to share different ways to mentally compute these exercises. Strategies for exercises **a** and **b** are listed below.

a. Add 2, Then Subtract 2

$48 + 2 = 50; 50 + 120 = 170; 170 - 2 = 168$

Add Tens First

$40 + 8 + 100 + 20 = 60 + 8 + 100 = 168$

b. Add From Left to Right

$76 + 10 + 3 = 86 + 3 = 89$

Add Tens, Then Add Ones

$70 + 6 + 10 + 3 = 80 + 9 = 89$

Problem Solving

Refer to **Power-Up Discussion,** p. 46B.

2 New Concepts

Instruction

When working with number lines, students should generalize that from left to right, the numbers are ordered from least to greatest, and from right to left, the numbers are ordered from greatest to least.

(continued)

LESSON 9

• The Number Line: Ordering and Comparing

Power Up *Building Power*

facts Power Up C

mental math

a. **Number Sense:** 48 + 120 168

b. **Number Sense:** 76 + 10 + 3 89

c. **Number Sense:** 7400 + 320 7720

d. **Number Sense:** 860 − 50 810

e. **Number Sense:** 960 − 600 360

f. **Number Sense:** 365 − 200 165

g. **Geometry:** A square has a length of 5 inches. What is the perimeter of the square? 20 in.

h. **Measurement:** How many days are in a leap year? 366 days

problem solving

As you sit at your desk facing forward, you can describe the locations of people and objects in your classroom compared to your position. Perhaps a friend is two seats in front and one row to the left. Perhaps the door is directly to your right about 6 feet. Describe the location of your teacher's desk, the pencil sharpener, and a person or object of your choice. Answers will vary depending on students' locations.

New Concept *Increasing Knowledge*

Thinking Skill

Connect

Name some real-life situations in which we would use negative numbers. Temperature readings below zero degrees; depths below sea level; losses, decreases, or negative balances, such as −20 yards or a balance of −$125.

A **number line** is a way to show numbers in order.

−2 −1 0 1 2 3 4 5 6 7

The arrowheads show that the line continues without end and that the numbers continue without end. The small marks crossing the horizontal line are called *tick marks.* Number lines may be labeled with various types of numbers. The numbers we say when we count (1, 2, 3, 4, and so on) are called **counting numbers.** All the counting numbers along with the number zero make up the **whole numbers.**

To the left of zero on this number line are **negative numbers,** which will be described in later lessons. As we move to the right on this number line, the numbers are greater in value. As we move to the left, the numbers are lesser in value.

Example 1

Arrange these numbers in order from least to greatest:

121 112 211

Facts Subtract.

8 − 5 3	10 − 4 6	12 − 6 6	6 − 3 3	8 − 4 4	14 − 7 7	20 − 10 10	11 − 5 6	7 − 4 3	13 − 6 7
7 − 2 5	15 − 8 7	9 − 7 2	17 − 9 8	10 − 5 5	8 − 1 7	16 − 7 9	6 − 0 6	12 − 3 9	9 − 5 4
13 − 5 8	11 − 7 4	14 − 8 6	10 − 7 3	5 − 3 2	15 − 6 9	6 − 4 2	10 − 8 2	18 − 9 9	15 − 7 8
12 − 4 8	11 − 2 9	16 − 8 8	9 − 9 0	13 − 4 9	11 − 8 3	9 − 6 3	14 − 9 5	8 − 6 2	12 − 5 7

Solution

On a number line, these three numbers appear in order from least (on the left) to greatest (on the right).

112 121 211

For our answer, we write

112 121 211

Thinking Skill

Discuss

When using place value to compare two numbers, what do you need to do first? Compare the digits in each place from left to right until they differ.

When we **compare** two numbers, we decide whether the numbers are equal; if they are not equal, we determine which number is greater and which is lesser. We show a comparison with symbols. If the numbers are equal, the comparison symbol we use is the **equal sign** (=).

$$1 + 1 = 2$$

If the numbers are not equal, we use one of the **greater than/less than symbols** (> or <). When properly placed between two numbers, the small end of the symbol points to the lesser number.

Example 2

Compare: 5012 ◯ 5102

Solution

In place of the circle we should write =, >, or < to make the statement true. Since 5012 is less than 5102, we point the small end to the 5012.

$$\mathbf{5012 < 5102}$$

Example 3

Compare: 16 ÷ 8 ÷ 2 ◯ 16 ÷ (8 ÷ 2)

Solution

Reading Math

Remember to follow the order of operations. Do the work within the parentheses first. Then divide in order from left to right.

Before we compare the two expressions, we find the value of each expression.

$$\underbrace{16 \div 8 \div 2}_{1} \bigcirc \underbrace{16 \div (8 \div 2)}_{4}$$

Since 1 is less than 4, the comparison symbol points to the left.

$$\mathbf{16 \div 8 \div 2 < 16 \div (8 \div 2)}$$

Example 4

Use digits and symbols to write this comparison:

One fourth is less than one half.

2 New Concepts *(Continued)*

Instruction

The sentence that preceeds example 2 suggests one way of remembering how to choose the appropriate inequality symbol. Invite students to suggest other ways of remembering.

Example 2

Instruction

Some students may need to review the step-by-step process of comparing numbers. Write the number 5102 on the board, and below it, write the number 5012. Align the place values of the numbers, then invite a volunteer to go to the board and demonstrate how to compare the numbers, beginning with the digits in the greatest (or thousands) place. 5102 > 5012 and 5012 < 5102

Example 3

Instruction

Have students note that before an inequality symbol is chosen, each side of the inequality is simplified by following the order of operations.

(continued)

English Learners

Write these **symbols** on the board:

+ − × ÷ > <

Explain that each is a symbol that stands for a word or phrase. Say:

"In math, we use symbols to represent operations and to show relationships between numbers. For example, 2 < 8, means that 2 is less than 8."

Ask volunteers to tell what each symbol above means. Ask if there are other math symbols to add to the list. $, %, °, ∠, √

Math Background

Is zero a positive number, or is it a negative number?

When some students see an integer number line for the first time, they wonder if zero belongs to the set of positive numbers or to the set of negative numbers. The answer is that it does not belong to either set of numbers. Zero is neither positive nor negative.

2 New Concepts (Continued)

Practice Set

Problem a Analyze

"What must we do to these numbers before we compare them?" Write the numbers in the same notation; change two amounts to cents or change one amount to dollars and cents.

Problems b–c Error Alert

Prior to completing the exercises, have students note the presence of parentheses, and explain what they represent. When working on the right side of each inequality, the operation inside of the parentheses must be completed first.

Problem c Error Alert

Because multiplication and division are in the same step of the order of operations, students may think that multiplication is completed before division. Remind students that in any step of the order of operations, the operations are completed from left to right.

3 Written Practice

Math Conversations

Discussion opportunities are provided below.

Problem 2 Generalize

Extend the Problem

Challenge students to describe a variety of ways to find the number of years using mental math. Sample: 1500 is 8 more than 1492, 1600 is 100 more than 1500, and 1603 is 3 more than 1600; 8 + 100 + 3 = 111 years

Problem 3 Conclude

Some students may give an answer other than 5 trips. For example, they may say $4\frac{1}{2}$ or 9 trips. Ask these students to provide support for their conclusions.
Sample:
To and from the house: Martin walks to the house with 2 bags of groceries and returns to the car. This is 4 trips.
To the house: Martin walks to the house with 1 bag of groceries but does not return to the car. This is $\frac{1}{2}$ a trip.

Problem 4 Conclude

Extend the Problem

Invite students to explain how the perimeter of the rectangle would change if its length was doubled and its width was halved. The perimeter would increase by 50% to 9 cm.

(continued)

Solution

We write the numbers in the order stated.

$$\frac{1}{4} < \frac{1}{2}$$

Practice Set

▸ **a.** Arrange these amounts of money in order from least to greatest. 12¢, $1.20, $12
12¢ $12 $1.20

▸ **b.** Compare: 16 − 8 − 2 ⓘ< 16 − (8 − 2)

▸ **c.** Compare: 8 ÷ 4 × 2 > 8 ÷ (4 × 2)

d. 2 × 3 > 2 + 3

e. 1 × 1 × 1 < 1 + 1 + 1

f. Represent Use digits and symbols to write this comparison: $\frac{1}{2} > \frac{1}{4}$
One half is greater than one fourth.

g. Compare the lengths: 10 inches < 1 foot

Written Practice

Strengthening Concepts

1. (2) Tamara arranged 144 books into 8 equal stacks. How many books were in each stack? 18 books

▸ **2.** (1) Generalize Find how many years there were from 1492 to 1603 by subtracting 1492 from 1603. 111 years

▸ ***3.** (2) Conclude Martin is carrying groceries in from the car. If he can carry 2 bags at a time, how many trips will it take him to carry in 9 bags?
5 trips; Accept other answers if the student can provide support.

▸ ***4.** (7, 8) Conclude Use a centimeter ruler to measure the length and width of the rectangle below. Then calculate the perimeter of the rectangle.
length = 2 cm;
width = 1 cm;
perimeter = 6 cm

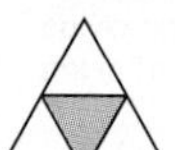

5. (6) How much money is $\frac{1}{2}$ of $5.80? $2.90

6. (6) How many cents is $\frac{1}{4}$ of a dollar? 25¢

***7.** (6) Represent Use words and digits to name the fraction of this triangle that is shaded.
one fourth; $\frac{1}{4}$

8. (7, 9) Compare:

a. 5012 < 5120

b. 1 mm < 1 cm

9. (9) Arrange these numbers in order from least to greatest: $0, \frac{1}{2}, 1$
$1, 0, \frac{1}{2}$

10. (9) Compare: 100 − 50 − 25 < 100 − (50 − 25)

▸ See Math Conversations in the sidebar.

11. (1) 478 + 3692 + 45 = 4215

12. (1) $50.00 − $31.76 = $18.24

13. (2) $4.20 × 60 = $252.00

14. (2) 78 × 36 = 2808

▶ 15. (2) $9\overline{)7227}$ 803

16. (2) $25\overline{)7600}$ 304

17. (2) $20\overline{)8014}$ 400 R 14

18. (2) 7136 ÷ 100 71 R 36

▶ 19. (2) 736 ÷ 736 1

Find each unknown number. Check your work.

20. (3) $165 + a = 300$ 135

21. (3) $b - 68 = 86$ 154

22. (4) $9c = 144$ 16

23. (4) $\frac{d}{15} = 7$ 105

▶* 24. (7) **Estimate** Use an inch ruler to draw a line segment two inches long. Then use a centimeter ruler to find the length of the segment to the nearest centimeter. See student work.; 5 cm

25. (7) Which of the figures below represents a ray? C

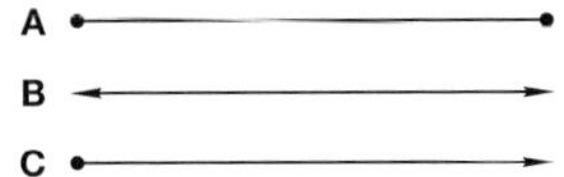

▶* 26. (9) **Represent** Use digits and symbols to write this comparison: $\frac{1}{2} > \frac{1}{3}$

One half is greater than one third.

* 27. (2) **Connect** Arrange the numbers 9, 11, and 99 to form two multiplication facts and two division facts. 9 × 11 = 99, 11 × 9 = 99, 99 ÷ 11 = 9, 99 ÷ 9 = 11

28. (9) Compare: 25 + 0 ⓖ 25 × 0

29. (3) $100 = 20 + 30 + 40 + x$ 10

▶* 30. (9) **Explain** How did you choose the positions of the small and large ends of the greater than/less than symbols that you used in problem 8? Point the small end of the symbol to the lesser number. 5012 is less than 5120, and 1 mm is less than 1 cm, which equals 10 mm.

▶ See Math Conversations in the sidebar.

Looking Forward

Ordering numbers using a number line and comparing numbers using the symbols >, <, or = prepare students for:

- **Lesson 14,** ordering, comparing, and subtracting with negative numbers.
- **Lesson 17,** locating fractions and mixed numbers on a number line and measuring a line segment with a ruler.
- **Lesson 50,** locating decimal numbers (tenths) on a number line.
- **Lesson 76,** comparing fractions by converting a fraction to a decimal.
- **Lesson 100,** using a number line to show algebraic addition of integers.

3 Written Practice *(Continued)*

Math Conversations

Discussion opportunities are provided below.

Problem 24 Estimate

Extend the Problem

Ask students to use the relationship that 2 inches is about 5 centimeters to make another estimate.

"About how many centimeters long is a 12-inch ruler? Explain your answer."

Sample: Since 2 inches is about 5 centimeters, 4 inches is about 10 centimeters, 6 inches is about 15 centimeters, and so on; a 12-inch ruler is about 30 centimeters long.

Problem 26 Represent

Extend the Problem

Write the unit fractions $\frac{1}{2}, \frac{1}{3}, \frac{1}{4}, \frac{1}{5}, \frac{1}{6}$ from left to right on the board. Ask students to compare the fractions and make a generalization about comparing unit fractions. Sample: When comparing two unit fractions, the fraction having the greater denominator is the lesser fraction and the fraction having the lesser denominator is the greater fraction.

Problem 30 Explain

Extend the Problem

Ask students to use inequality symbols and write a statement of inequality for the numbers in Problem 9. Sample: $0 < \frac{1}{2} < 1$ or $1 > \frac{1}{2} > 0$

Errors and Misconceptions

Problem 15

Use the given division, or a division such as 4935 ÷ 7 or 2015 ÷ 5, to demonstrate that if two numbers are brought down from the divisor, a zero must be written in the quotient.

Problem 19

If students write a quotient of 0, have them review the Property of 1.

• Sequences
• Scales

Objectives

- Identify addition sequences and multiplication sequences.
- Discover the rule for a sequence and use it to find missing numbers in the sequence.
- Identify even and odd numbers.
- Find the value of the marks on a scale.
- Read the number indicated on a scale.

Lesson Preparation

Materials

- **Power Up C** (in *Instructional Masters*)

Optional

- **Teacher-provided material: indoor/outdoor thermometer**

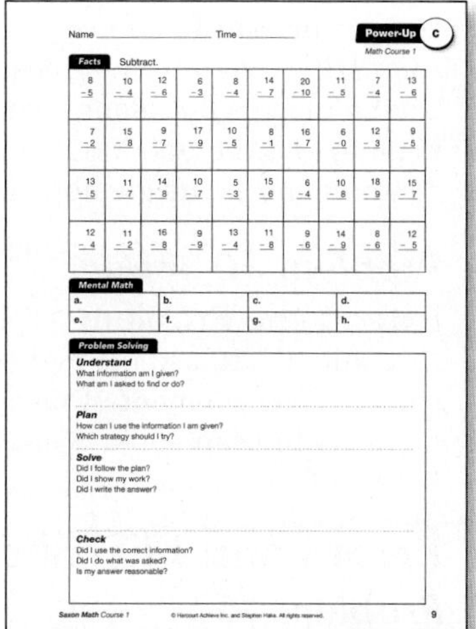

Name ______________ Time ________

Power-Up C

Math Course 1

Facts Subtract.

8 − 5	10 − 4	12 − 6	6 − 3	8 − 4	14 − 7	20 − 10	11 − 5	7 − 4	13 − 6
7 − 2	15 − 8	9 − 7	17 − 9	10 − 5	8 − 1	16 − 7	6 − 0	12 − 3	9 − 5
13 − 5	11 − 7	14 − 8	10 − 7	5 − 3	15 − 6	6 − 4	10 − 8	18 − 9	15 − 7
12 − 4	11 − 2	16 − 8	9 − 9	13 − 4	11 − 8	9 − 6	14 − 9	8 − 6	12 − 5

Mental Math

a.	b.	c.	d.
e.	f.	g.	h.

Problem Solving

Understand
What information am I given?
What am I asked to find or do?

Plan
How can I use the information I am given?
Which strategy should I try?

Solve
Did I follow the plan?
Did I show my work?
Did I write the answer?

Check
Did I use the correct information?
Did I do what was asked?
Is my answer reasonable?

Saxon Math *Course 1* © Harcourt Achieve Inc. and Stephen Hake. All rights reserved. 9

Power Up C

Math Language

New		English Learners (ESL)
Celsius scale	scale	digit
even numbers	sequence	
Fahrenheit scale	term	
odd numbers		

Technology Resources

Student eBook Complete student textbook in electronic format.

Resources and Planner CD Assessment, reteaching, and instructional masters, plus a pacing calendar with standards.

Test and Practice Generator CD Create additional practice sheets and custom-made tests.

www.SaxonPublishers.com Visit for more student activities and planning materials.

Inclusion

Adaptations CD Adapted lessons, investigations, practice and assessments.

Meeting Standards

National Council of Teachers of Mathematics (NCTM)

Numbers and Operations

NO.1f Use factors, multiples, prime factorization, and relatively prime numbers to solve problems

Algebra

AL.1a Represent, analyze, and generalize a variety of patterns with tables, graphs, words, and, when possible, symbolic rules

AL.1b Relate and compare different forms of representation for a relationship

Power-Up Discussion *For use with Power Up, p. 50*

Problem-Solving Strategy: Make a Model

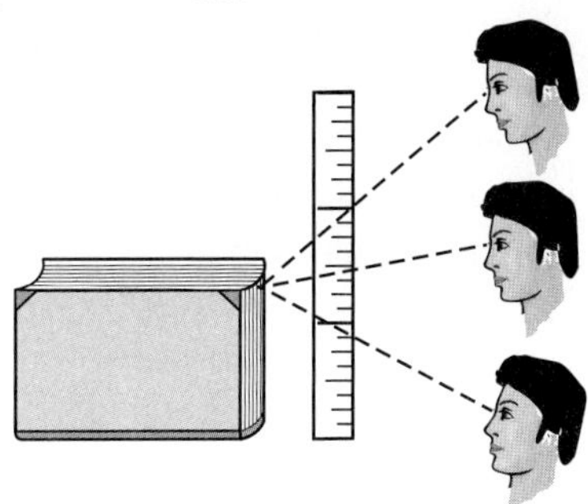

A ***parallax*** is an error that can result from an observer changing their position and not reading a measurement tool while directly in front of it.

Hold a ruler near the width of your textbook on your desk. Then read the ruler from several angles as the diagram shows. How short can you make the width of the book appear? How tall can you make it appear? What is your best measure of the width of the book?

Understand Understand the problem.

"What are some common errors when using a ruler?"

1. Measuring from the end of the ruler instead of starting at the true zero.
2. Incorrectly identifying fractions of an inch.

"What information are we given?"

A *parallax* is a measurement error that occurs when a person's eyes are not directly in front of the object they are measuring.

"What are we asked to do?"

Determine the actual width of our math book, but also see how short and tall we can make the book *appear* by changing our angle of observation.

Teacher Note: Instruct students to sit up very straight to view their book at an angle above. Then have them slide down slowly in their seats to view their book directly and continue sliding to view from an angle below.

Plan Make a plan.

"What problem-solving strategy will we use?"

We have been told to *use a model* (our textbook).

"What do we anticipate our answer to be in the range of?"

While an estimate for the actual width of the book may not present a problem, answers will vary as to the "parallaxed" widths.

Solve Carry out the plan.

"What is the range of measurements we were able to view the width of our textbook as?"

Answers will vary.

"What is the actual width of the textbook?" *Answers will vary.*

Check Look back.

"What other measuring tools may result in a parallax?"

A person standing to the extreme left or right reads the dial on a bathroom scale differently. The driver and the passenger read the speedometer in a car differently. A measuring cup may hold more or less depending on the angle it is read.

Teacher Note: Extend this lesson by exploring how the shape of an object can be distorted. Using a nickel or other flat, round object, have the students view the flat side directly, the edge, and various angles in between. The students will see a perfect circle, a narrow rectangle, and a number of ellipses of various sizes.

1 Power Up

Facts

Distribute **Power Up C** to students. See answers below.

Mental Math

Before students begin the Mental Math exercise, do this counting exercise as a class.

Count by $\frac{1}{4}$s from $\frac{1}{4}$ to 10.

Encourage students to share different ways to mentally compute these exercises. Strategies for exercises **b** and **e** are listed below.

b. Count on by Hundreds
Start with 670. Count: 770, 870
Add from Left to Right
670 + 200 = 870

e. Count Back by Tens
Start with 300. Count: 290, 280, 270, 260, 250
Count Back by 50
Start with 300. Count: 250

Problem Solving

Refer to **Power-Up Discussion,** p. 50B.

LESSON 10

• Sequences • Scales

Power Up — *Building Power*

facts Power Up C

mental math

a. **Number Sense:** 43 + 20 + 5 68
b. **Number Sense:** 670 + 200 870
c. **Number Sense:** 254 + 20 + 5 279
d. **Number Sense:** 100 − 50 50
e. **Number Sense:** 300 − 50 250
f. **Number Sense:** 3600 − 400 3200
g. **Measurement:** How many feet are in 3 yards? 9 ft
h. **Measurement:** How many centimeters are in 3 meters? 300 cm

problem solving

A ***parallax*** is an error that can result from an observer changing their position and not reading a measurement tool while directly in front of it.

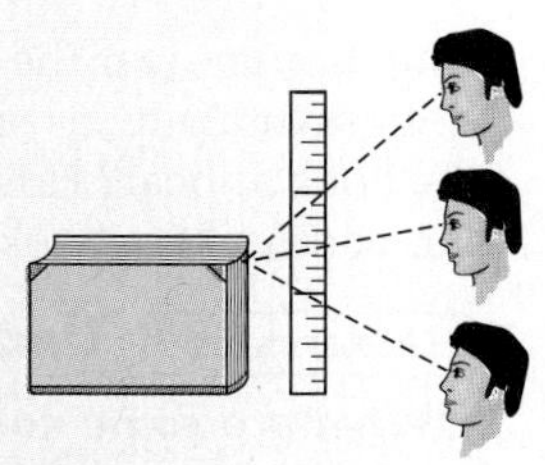

Hold a ruler near the width of your textbook on your desk. Then read the ruler from several angles as the diagram shows. How short can you make the width of the book appear? How tall can you make it appear? What is your best measure of the width of the book?

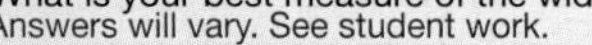
Answers will vary. See student work.

New Concepts — *Increasing Knowledge*

sequences

A **sequence** is an ordered list of numbers, called **terms,** that follows a certain rule. Here are two different sequences:

a. 5, 10, 15, 20, 25, …

b. 5, 10, 20, 40, 80, …

Sequence **a** is an **addition sequence** because the same number is added to each term of the sequence to get the next term. In this case, we add 5 to the value of a term to find the next term. Sequence **b** is a **multiplication sequence** because each term of the sequence is multiplied by the same number to get the next term. In **b** we find the value of a term by multiplying the preceding term by 2. When we are asked to find unknown numbers in a sequence, we inspect the numbers to discover the rule for the sequence. Then we use the rule to find other numbers in the sequence.

Facts Subtract.

<table>
<tr><td>8
− 5
3</td><td>10
− 4
6</td><td>12
− 6
6</td><td>6
− 3
3</td><td>8
− 4
4</td><td>14
− 7
7</td><td>20
− 10
10</td><td>11
− 5
6</td><td>7
− 4
3</td><td>13
− 6
7</td></tr>
<tr><td>7
− 2
5</td><td>15
− 8
7</td><td>9
− 7
2</td><td>17
− 9
8</td><td>10
− 5
5</td><td>8
− 1
7</td><td>16
− 7
9</td><td>6
− 0
6</td><td>12
− 3
9</td><td>9
− 5
4</td></tr>
<tr><td>13
− 5
8</td><td>11
− 7
4</td><td>14
− 8
6</td><td>10
− 7
3</td><td>5
− 3
2</td><td>15
− 6
9</td><td>6
− 4
2</td><td>10
− 8
2</td><td>18
− 9
9</td><td>15
− 7
8</td></tr>
<tr><td>12
− 4
8</td><td>11
− 2
9</td><td>16
− 8
8</td><td>9
− 9
0</td><td>13
− 4
9</td><td>11
− 8
3</td><td>9
− 6
3</td><td>14
− 9
5</td><td>8
− 6
2</td><td>12
− 5
7</td></tr>
</table>

Example 1

Generalize **Describe the following sequence as an addition sequence or a multiplication sequence. State the rule of the sequence, and find the next term.**

1, 3, 9, 27, _____, ...

Solution

The sequence is a **multiplication sequence** because **each term in the sequence can be multiplied by 3 to find the next term.** Multiplying 27 by 3, we find that the term that follows 27 in the sequence is **81.**

Thinking Skill

Generalize

Is the sum of an even number and an odd number even or odd? Give some examples to support your answer.

odd; possible examples: $2 + 3 = 5$, $4 + 5 = 9$, $4 + 3 = 7$

The numbers ..., 0, 2, 4, 6, 8, ... form a special sequence called **even numbers.** We say even numbers when we "count by twos." Notice that zero is an even number. Any whole number with a ones digit of 0, 2, 4, 6, or 8 is an even number. Whole numbers that are not even numbers are **odd numbers.** The odd numbers form the sequence ..., 1, 3, 5, 7, 9, ... An even number of objects can be divided into two equal groups. An odd number of objects cannot be divided into two equal groups.

Example 2

Think of a whole number. Double that number. Is the answer even or odd?

Solution

The answer is **even.** Doubling any whole number—odd or even—results in an even number.

scales

Numerical information is often presented to us in the form of a **scale.** A scale is a display of numbers with an indicator to show the value of a certain measure. To read a scale, we first need to discover the value of the tick marks on the scale. Marks on a scale may show whole units or divisions of a unit, such as one fourth (as with the inch ruler from Lesson 7). We study the scale to find the value of the units before we try to read the indicated number.

Two commonly used scales on thermometers are the **Fahrenheit scale** and the **Celsius scale.** A cool room may be 68°F (20°C). The temperature at which water freezes under standard conditions is 32 degrees Fahrenheit (abbreviated 32°F) and zero degrees Celsius (0°C). The boiling temperature of water is 212°F, which is 100°C. Normal body temperature is 98.6°F (37°C). The thermometer on the right shows three temperatures that are helpful to know:

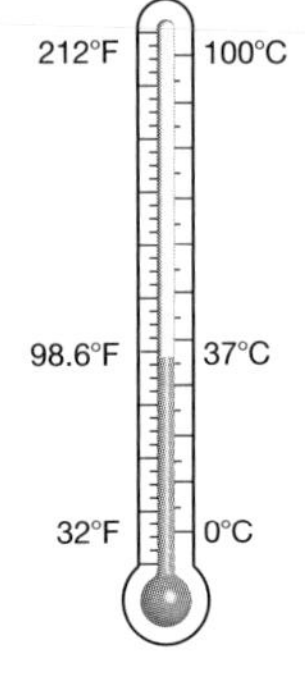

Boiling temperature of water	212°F	100°C
Normal body temperature	98.6°F	37°C
Freezing temperature of water	32°F	0°C

2 New Concepts

Example 1

Instruction

After completing example 1, you might choose to invite students to create other addition or multiplication sequences, and then challenge one or more classmates to identify the rule of each sequence.

To help students connect Fahrenheit and Celsius temperatures to the real world, give them opportunities to measure temperatures in degrees Fahrenheit and in degrees Celsius. One way to accomplish this, for example, is to have students measure and record the temperature of the classroom and the temperature outdoors, in degrees Fahrenheit and in degrees Celsius, for several days.

(continued)

Math Background

Two different types of number sequences are presented in this lesson.

- If each successive term in a sequence is obtained from the previous term by the addition of a fixed number (such as 5, 10, 15, 20, 25, ...), the sequence is an *arithmetic* sequence.
- If each successive term in a sequence is obtained from the preceding term by multiplying it by a fixed number (such as 5, 10, 20, 40, 80, ...), the sequence is a *geometric* sequence.

English Learners

Write the following on the board and say:

one = 1 two = 2 twenty-nine = 29

"A digit is a symbol used to write a number. In the numbers above, we used three digits: 1, 2, and 9."

Write 3, 4, and 5 on the board. Ask:

"What numbers can we write with these digits?"

Have volunteers write numbers such as 35 and 453, saying the number's name and the digits used to write it.

2 New Concepts (Continued)

Example 3

Instruction

Encourage students to suggest the names of various places in the United States that might experience an outdoor winter temperature of 4°F.

Practice Set

Problem c Generalize

Extend the Problem

Ask students to write generalizations for the sum of two odd numbers, the sum of two even numbers, and the sum of an odd number and an even number. The sum of two odd numbers is an even number; the sum of two even numbers is an even number; the sum of an odd and an even number is an odd number.

Problem d Estimate

The most important aspect of reading a thermometer is to first correctly identify its scale.

"On this thermometer, what does the distance between two consecutive tick marks represent?" two degrees

3 Written Practice

Math Conversations

Discussion opportunities are provided below.

Problem 1 Generalize

Extend the Problem

Write the following relationship on the board. Then ask the question that follows.

Flowers	1	2	3	4	5
Petals	8	16	24	32	40

"How could you predict the number of petals for any number of flowers? Write a rule or equation." Sample: To find the number of petals, multiply the number of flowers by eight; $p = 8f$.

(continued)

Example 3

What temperature is shown on this thermometer?

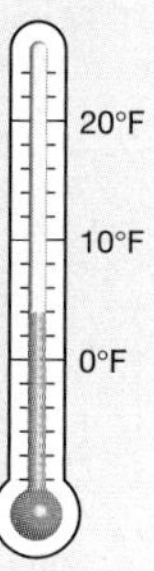

Solution

As we study the scale on this Fahrenheit thermometer, we see that the tick marks divide the distance from 0°F to 10°F into five equal sections. So the number of degrees from one tick mark to the next must be 2°F. Since the fluid in the thermometer is two marks above 0°F, the temperature shown is **4°F.**

Practice Set

a. Addition sequence. Add 9 to the value of a term to find the next term.
b. Multiplication sequence. Multiply the value of a term by 2 to find the next term.

Thinking Skill
Explain
Why is the thermometer shown with a broken scale? The lower temperature marks are omitted so the thermometer can be drawn smaller.

Generalize For the sequence in problems **a** and **b**, determine whether the sequence is an addition sequence or a multiplication sequence, state the rule of the sequence, and find the next three terms.

a. ..., 18, 27, 36, 45, 54, 63, 72, ...

b. 1, 2, 4, 8, 16, 32, 64, ...

▶ **c.** Think of a whole number. Double that number. Then add 1 to the answer. Is the final number even or odd? odd

▶ **d.** Estimate This thermometer indicates a comfortable room temperature. Find the temperature indicated on this thermometer to the nearest degree Fahrenheit and to the nearest degree Celsius. 72°F; 22°C

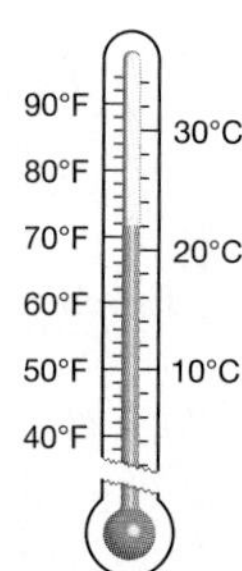

Written Practice *Strengthening Concepts*

▶ * **1.** (10) Generalize State the rule of the following sequence. Then find the next three terms.
16, 24, 32, 40, 48, 56, ...
Add 8 to the value of a term to find the next term.

2. (1) Find how many years there were from the year the Pilgrims landed in 1620 to the year the colonies declared their independence in 1776. 156 years

* **3.** (10) Explain Is the number 1492 even or odd? How can you tell?
The number 1492 is even because the last digit, 2, is even.

52 **Saxon** *Math Course 1*

▶ See Math Conversations in the sidebar.

Inclusion

Students who need help reading temperatures on thermometers or points on a number line may find it helpful to use a technique called "splitting the difference." Use example 3 to demonstrate. Ask:

"The scale shows what two numbers above and below the marked temperature?" 10 and 0

"What is the difference between these two numbers?" 10 − 0 = 10

Write the difference, 10, on the board. Then ask the students to count with you as you count the intervals between 0 and 10. Count from 1 to 5. Say:

"There are five intervals between 0 and 10. We can split the difference by dividing the difference by the number of intervals."

Write 10 ÷ 5 = 2 on the board and say:

"Now count by 2s, starting from the lower number 0 and continuing to the temperature mark on the scale: 0, 2, 4. The temperature is 4°."

4. What weight is indicated on this scale? 154 pounds
(10)

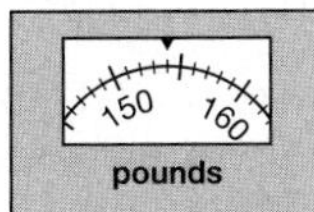

▶ * 5. Conclude If the perimeter of a square is 40 mm, how long is each side of the square? 10 mm
(8)

6. How much money is $\frac{1}{2}$ of \$6.50? \$3.25
(6)

7. Compare: $4 \times 3 + 2$ ⓞ $4 \times (3 + 2)$ <
(9)

▶ * 8. Represent Use words and digits to write the fraction of this circle that is **not** shaded. three fourths; $\frac{3}{4}$
(6)

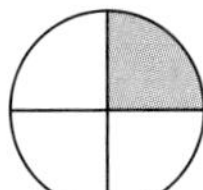

▶ 9. What is the
(1, 2)

a. product of 100 and 100? 10,000

b. sum of 100 and 100? 200

▶ 10. (2) $365 \times 100 = 36{,}500$ 11. (2) $146 \times 240 = 35{,}040$ 12. (2) $78¢ \times 48 = \$37.44$ 13. (2) $907 \times 36 = 32{,}652$

14. (2) $\frac{4260}{10}$ 426 15. (2) $\frac{4260}{20}$ 213 16. (2) $\frac{4260}{15}$ 284

17. (1) 28,347 − 9,637 18,710 18. (3) \$8 + w = \$11.49 \$3.49

19. (1) \$10 − \$0.75 \$9.25 20. (2) \$0.56 × 60 \$33.60 21. (2) \$6.20 ÷ 4 \$1.55

Find each unknown number. Check your work.

22. (3) $56 + 28 + 37 + n = 200$ 79

23. (3) $a - 67 = 49$ 116 24. (3) $67 - b = 49$ 18

25. (4) $8c = 120$ 15 26. (4) $\frac{d}{8} = 24$ 192

27. Here are three ways to write "12 divided by 4."
(2)

$4\overline{)12}$ $12 \div 4$ $\frac{12}{4}$

Show three ways to write "20 divided by 5." $5\overline{)20}$, $20 \div 5$, $\frac{20}{5}$

28. What number is one third of 36? 12
(6)

* 29. Connect Arrange the numbers 346, 463, and 809 to form two addition equations and two subtraction equations. 346 + 463 = 809, 463 + 346 = 809, 809 − 463 = 346, 809 − 346 = 463
(1)

30. At what temperature on the Fahrenheit scale does water freeze? 32°F
(10)

▶ See Math Conversations in the sidebar.

3 Written Practice (Continued)

Math Conversations

Discussion opportunities are provided below.

Problem 5 Conclude

Extend the Problem

Challenge students to write a formula that can be used to find the length of a side of a square when the perimeter of the square is known. Sample: $s = P \div 4$ where s is the length of one side of a square and P is the perimeter of the square.

Problem 8 Represent

"What fraction of the circle is shaded?" $\frac{1}{4}$

"What whole number represents the sum of the shaded and unshaded parts of the circle? Explain your answer." 1; $\frac{1}{4} + \frac{3}{4} = \frac{4}{4}$, and $\frac{4}{4}$ is the same as $4 \div 4$ or 1.

Problem 10 Generalize

Powers of 10, such as the factor 100, provide straightforward opportunities to use mental math.

"How can you use mental math to find each product?" Sample: Count zeros; the number of zeros in the factors is equal to the number of zeros in the product.

Errors and Misconceptions

Problem 9

When using the multiplication algorithm with factors that end in zero, some students lose or gain zeros during the computation. Demonstrate how such products can be checked by counting zeros.

Looking Forward

Reading a scale such as the Fahrenheit or Celsius scale prepares students for:

- **Lesson 17,** reading fractions and mixed numbers on a number line and reading an inch ruler in sixteenths.
- **Investigation 3,** reading the scale on a protractor to measure and draw angles.
- **Lesson 32,** finding elapsed time on a clock.
- **Lesson 90,** measuring turns.
- **Investigation 11,** using the legend of a scale drawing to find the actual measurements of an object.

Assessment

30–40 minutes *For use after Lesson 10*

Distribute **Cumulative Test 1** to each student. Two versions of the test are available in *Saxon Math Course 1 Course Assessments Book*. Have students complete the **Power-Up Test** first. Allow 10 minutes. Then have students work the 20 numbered items on the **Cumulative Test.** Students may use copies of the answer sheet to record their work. Track individual and class progress with the **Test Analysis** forms.

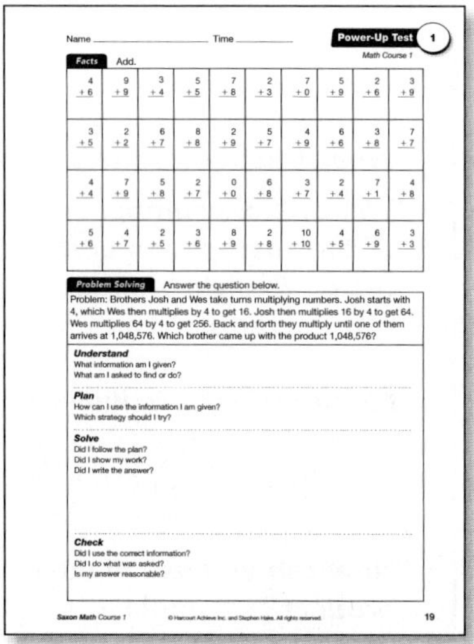

Power-Up Test 1

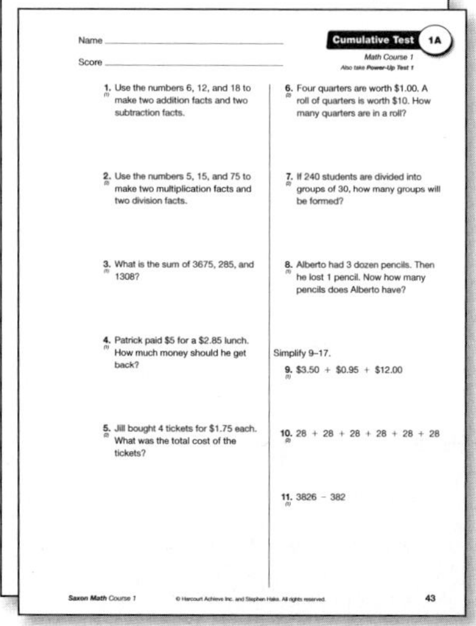

Cumulative Test 1A

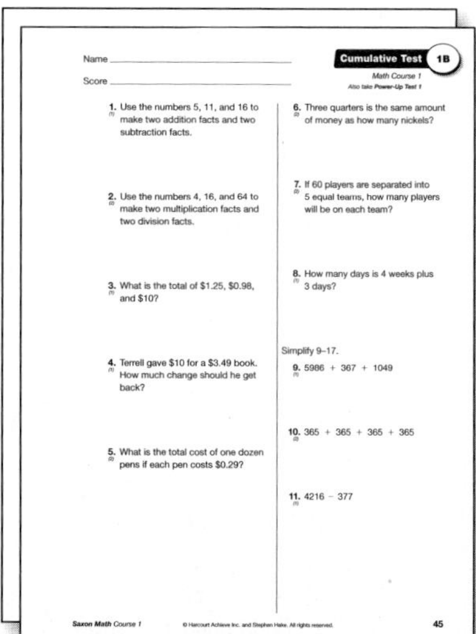

Alternative Cumulative Test 1B

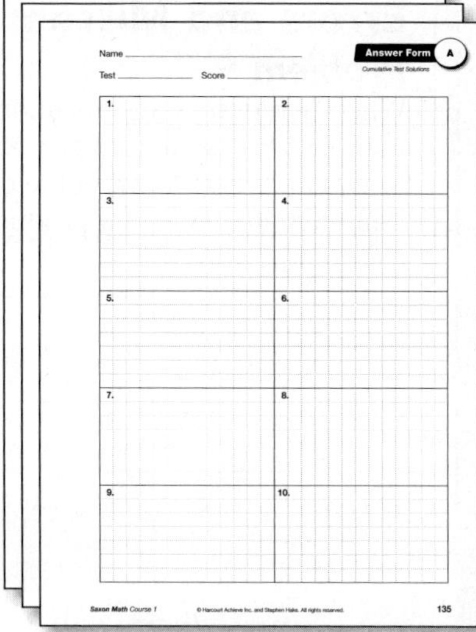

Optional Answer Forms

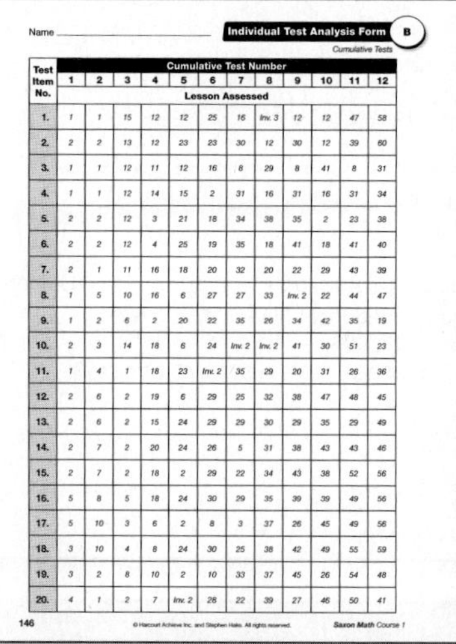

Individual Test Analysis Form

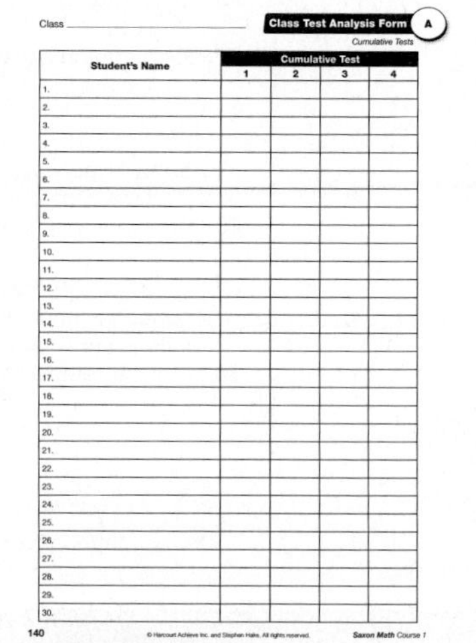

Class Test Analysis Form

Reteaching

Students who score below 80% on the assessment may be in need of reteaching. Look for the causes of student mistakes. If errors are conceptual, refer to the *Reteaching Masters* for reteaching.

Customized Benchmark Assessment

You can develop customized benchmark tests using the Test Generator located on the *Test & Practice Generator CD.*

This chart shows the lesson, the standard, and the test item question that can be found on the *Test & Practice Generator CD.*

LESSON	NEW CONCEPTS	LOCAL STANDARD	TEST ITEM ON CD
1	• Adding Whole Numbers and Money		1.1.1
	• Subtracting Whole Numbers and Money		1.1.2
	• Fact Families, Part 1		1.1.3
2	• Multiplying Whole Numbers and Money		1.2.1
	• Dividing Whole Numbers and Money		1.2.2
	• Fact Families, Part 2		1.2.3
3	• Unknown Numbers in Addition		1.3.1
	• Unknown Numbers in Subtraction		1.3.2
4	• Unknown Numbers in Multiplication		1.4.1
	• Unknown Numbers in Division		1.4.2
5	• Orders of Operations, Part 1		1.5.1
6	• Fractional Parts		1.6.1
7	• Lines, Segments, and Rays		1.7.1
	• Linear Measure		1.7.2
8	• Perimeter		1.8.1
9	• The Number Line: Ordering and Comparing		1.9.1
10	• Sequences		1.10.1
	• Scales		1.10.2

Using the Test Generator CD

- Develop tests in both English and Spanish.
- Choose from multiple-choice and free-response test items.
- Clone test items to create multiple versions of the same test.
- View and edit test items to make and save your own questions.
- Administer assessments through paper tests or over a school LAN.
- Monitor student progress through a variety of individual and class reports —for both diagnosing and assessing standards mastery.

Performance Task 1

Where the Green Grass Grows

Assign after Lesson 10 and Test 1

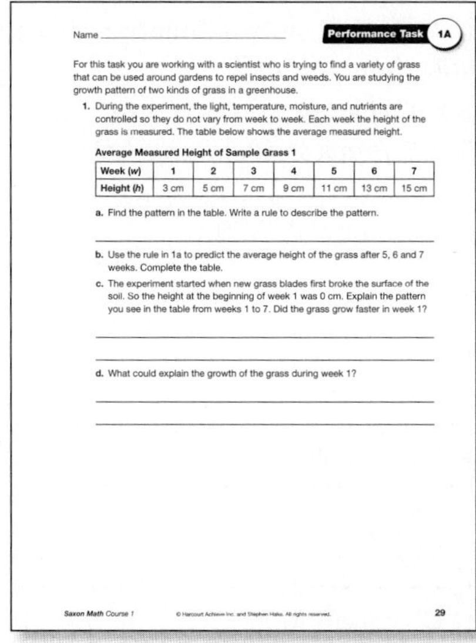

Name ______________ **Performance Task 1A**

For this task you are working with a scientist who is trying to find a variety of grass that can be used around gardens to repel insects and weeds. You are studying the growth pattern of two kinds of grass in a greenhouse.

1. During the experiment, the light, temperature, moisture, and nutrients are controlled so they do not vary from week to week. Each week the height of the grass is measured. The table below shows the average measured height.

Average Measured Height of Sample Grass 1

Week (w)	1	2	3	4	5	6	7
Height (h)	3 cm	5 cm	7 cm	9 cm	11 cm	13 cm	15 cm

a. Find the pattern in the table. Write a rule to describe the pattern.

b. Use the rule in 1a to predict the average height of the grass after 5, 6 and 7 weeks. Complete the table.

c. The experiment started when new grass blades first broke the surface of the soil. So the height at the beginning of week 1 was 0 cm. Explain the pattern you see in the table from weeks 1 to 7. Did the grass grow faster in week 1?

d. What could explain the growth of the grass during week 1?

Saxon Math Course 1 © Harcourt Achieve Inc. and Stephen Hake. All rights reserved. 29

Performance Task 1A

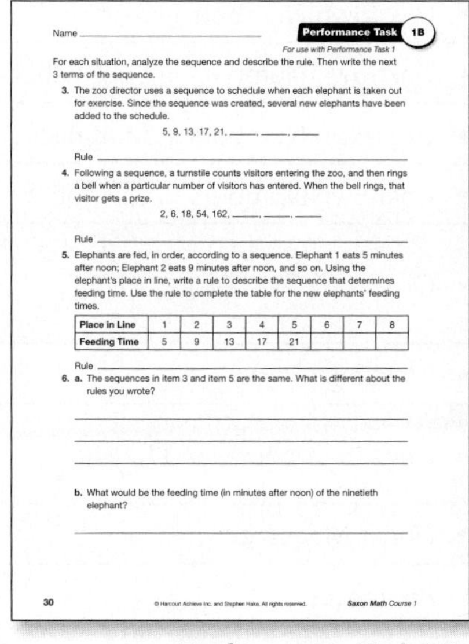

Name ______________ **Performance Task 1B**

For use with Performance Task 1

For each situation, analyze the sequence and describe the rule. Then write the next 3 terms of the sequence.

3. The zoo director uses a sequence to schedule when each elephant is taken out for exercise. Since the sequence was created, several new elephants have been added to the schedule.

5, 9, 13, 17, 21, ____, ____, ____

Rule ______________

4. Following a sequence, a turnstile counts visitors entering the zoo, and then rings a bell when a particular number of visitors has entered. When the bell rings, that visitor gets a prize.

2, 6, 18, 54, 162, ____, ____, ____

Rule ______________

5. Elephants are fed, in order, according to a sequence. Elephant 1 eats 5 minutes after noon; Elephant 2 eats 9 minutes after noon, and so on. Using the elephant's place in line, write a rule to describe the sequence that determines feeding time. Use the rule to complete the table for the new elephants' feeding times.

Place in Line	1	2	3	4	5	6	7	8
Feeding Time	5	9	13	17	21			

Rule ______________

6. a. The sequences in item 3 and item 5 are the same. What is different about the rules you wrote?

b. What would be the feeding time (in minutes after noon) of the ninetieth elephant?

30 © Harcourt Achieve Inc. and Stephen Hake. All rights reserved. *Saxon Math* Course 1

Performance Task 1B

Objectives

- Identify and use a pattern to complete a sequence.
- Write an equation to describe a rule.
- Communicate ideas through writing.

Materials

Performance Tasks 1A and **1B**

Preparation

Make copies of **Performance Tasks 1A** and **1B.** (One each per student.)

Time Requirement

20 minutes; Begin in class and complete at home.

Task

Explain to students that for this task they will be helping a scientist study the growth of two kinds of grass. They will examine data in tables to find patterns. They will also write equations to describe the rules for various sequences. They will be required to explain the rule in words and to think about how the rule applies to the experiment. Then they will compare two sequences and calculate a unit measure conversion. Point out that all of the information students need is on **Performance Tasks 1A** and **1B.**

Criteria for Evidence of Learning

- Identifies rule for a sequence and accurately uses the rule to find terms in the sequence.
- Writes valid equation for the rule for a sequence and accurately uses the equation to find terms in the sequence.
- Communicates ideas clearly through writing.

Meeting Standards

National Council of Teachers of Mathematics (NCTM)

Algebra

AL.1a Represent, analyze, and generalize a variety of patterns with tables, graphs, words, and, when possible, symbolic rules

AL.2a Develop an initial conceptual understanding of different uses of variables

AL.2c Use symbolic algebra to represent situations and to solve problems, especially those that involve linear relationships

AL.3a Model and solve contextualized problems using various representations, such as graphs, tables, and equations

Communication

CM.3a Organize and consolidate their mathematical thinking through communication

Connections

CN.4c Recognize and apply mathematics in contexts outside of mathematics

Focus on

- **Frequency Tables**
- **Histograms**
- **Surveys**

Objectives

- Interpret a frequency table.
- Count and write tally marks.
- Make a frequency table.
- Interpret a histogram.
- Make a histogram.
- Interpret survey results.
- Distinguish between a closed-option survey and an open-option survey.

Lesson Preparation

Materials

- **Manipulative kit: inch or metric rulers**
- **Teacher-provided material: grid paper**

Math Language

New

bar graph	**open-option survey**
closed-option survey	**sample**
frequency table	**survey**
histogram	

Technology Resources

Student eBook Complete student textbook in electronic format.

Resources and Planner CD Assessment, reteaching, and instructional masters, plus a pacing calendar with standards.

Test and Practice Generator CD Create additional practice sheets and custom-made tests.

www.SaxonPublishers.com Visit for more student activities and planning materials.

Inclusion

Adaptations CD Adapted lessons, investigations, practice and assessments.

Meeting Standards

National Council of Teachers of Mathematics (NCTM)

Data Analysis and Probability

DP.1a Formulate questions, design studies, and collect data about a characteristic shared by two populations or different characteristics within one population

DP.1b Select, create, and use appropriate graphical representations of data, including histograms, box plots, and scatterplots

DP.2b Discuss and understand the correspondence between data sets and their graphical representations, especially histograms, stem-and-leaf plots, box plots, and scatterplots

INVESTIGATION 1

In this investigation, students will be introduced to frequency tables and learn that frequency tables and histograms can represent the same data in different ways.

Students will also learn about surveys, and explore how the sensibility of a prediction may be related to the sample size of a survey.

Frequency Tables

Instruction

The frequency table shows a one-to-one correspondence of tally marks and the number of tests in each range of scores. To help students recognize this correspondence, ask,

"What does each tally mark in the chart represent?" a student's test

It is important for students to recognize that each interval of the table shows a range of correct answers, and that the exact number of correct answers for any test in a range is unknown.

Math Conversations

Discussion opportunities are provided below.

Problem 1 Justify

"How many tests altogether are represented in the frequency table? Explain your answer." 22; Since each tally represents one test, the sum of the tallies (or the sum of the numbers in the frequency column) represents the total number of tests that were recorded.

Problem 2 Conclude

"How many different intervals are shown in the frequency table?" Four; the intervals are 13–14, 15–16, 17–18, and 19–20.

After completing the problem, ask

"For this frequency table, Mr. Lawson chose to display the scores in four intervals. Could he have chosen a different number of intervals?" yes

INVESTIGATION 1

Focus on

- **Frequency Tables**
- **Histograms**
- **Surveys**

frequency tables

Mr. Lawson made a frequency table to record student scores on a math test. He listed the intervals of scores (bins) he wanted to tally. Then, as he graded each test, he made a tally mark for each test in the corresponding row.

Frequency Table

Number Correct	Tally	Frequency
19–20	𝍸 ||||	9
17–18	𝍸 ||	7
15–16	||||	4
13–14	||	2

When Mr. Lawson finished grading the tests, he counted the number of tally marks in each row and then recorded the count in the frequency column. For example, the table shows that nine students scored either 19 or 20 on the test. A **frequency table** is a way of pairing selected data, in this case specified test scores, with the number of times the selected data occur.

1. No. In the frequency table, the number of students who scored 20 is combined with the number who scored 19.
2. Each interval is 2 scores wide. One reason he might have arranged the scores in these intervals is to group the scores by A's, B's, C's, and D's.

▸ **1.** *Justify* Can you tell from this frequency table how many students had 20 correct answers on the test? Why or why not?

▸ **2.** *Conclude* Mr. Lawson tallied the number of scores in each interval. How wide is each interval? Suggest a reason why Mr. Lawson arranged the scores in such intervals.

3. *Represent* Show how to make a tally for 12. 𝍸 𝍸 ||

4. *Represent* As a class activity, make a frequency table of the birth months of the students in the class. Make four bins by grouping the months: Jan.–Mar., Apr.–Jun., Jul.–Sep., Oct.–Dec.

histograms

Using the information in the frequency table, Mr. Lawson created a histogram to display the results of the test.

▸ See Math Conversations in the sidebar.

Math Background

Although a histogram and a bar graph share some similarities, they also have characteristics that make them very different from each other.

- Both histograms and bar graphs use shaded rectangles to display data.
- A histogram is used to represent the frequency of data; a bar graph is usually used to compare data.
- A vertical bar in a histogram represents a range of values; a vertical (or horizontal) bar in a bar graph represents an exact value.

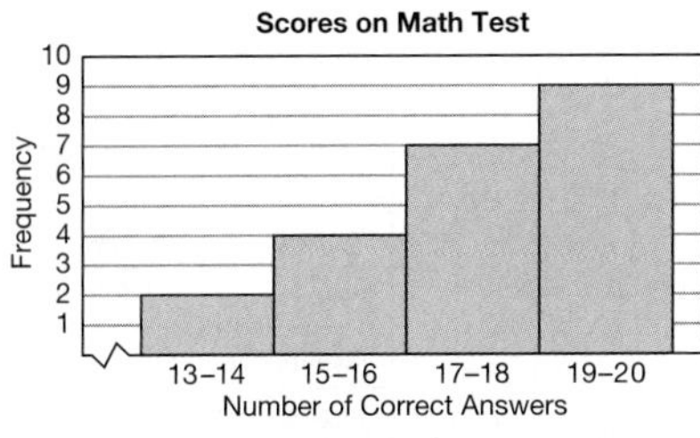

Bar graphs display numerical information with shaded rectangles (bars) of various lengths. Bar graphs are often used to show comparisons.

A **histogram** is a special type of bar graph. This histogram displays the data (test scores) in equal-size intervals (ranges of scores). There are no spaces between the bars. The break in the horizontal scale (-√-) indicates that the portion of the scale between 0 and 13 has been omitted. The height of each bar indicates the number of test scores in each interval.

Refer to the histogram to answer problems **5–7.**

5. Which interval had the lowest frequency of scores? 13–14

6. Which interval had the highest frequency of scores? 19–20

7. Which interval had exactly twice as many scores as the 13–14 interval? 15–16

8. *Represent* Make a frequency table and a histogram for the following set of test scores. (Use 50–59, 60–69, 70–79, 80–89, and 90–99 for the intervals.)

63, 75, 58, 89, 92, 84, 95, 63, 78, 88,

96, 67, 59, 70, 83, 89, 76, 85, 94, 80

surveys

8.

Frequency Table

Number Correct	Tally	Frequency
90–99	||||	4
80–89	~~||||~~ ||	7
70–79	||||	4
60–69	|||	3
50–59	||	2

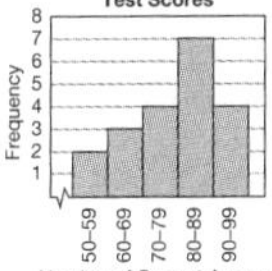

A **survey** is a way of collecting data about a population. Rather than collecting data from every member of a population, a survey might focus on only a small part of the population called a **sample.** From the sample, conclusions are formed about the entire population.

Mrs. Patterson's class conducted a survey of 100 students to determine what sport middle school students most enjoyed playing. Survey participants were given six different sports from which to choose. The surveyors displayed the results on the frequency table shown on the following page.

Histograms

Instruction

The following questions will help students make the connection that the frequency table and the histogram are two different ways of representing the same data.

"How do the intervals shown in the frequency table compare to the intervals shown in the histogram?" each shows the same intervals

"How is the frequency of each interval of the histogram related to the frequency of each interval of the table?" Sample: they are different ways of naming the same number.

Surveys

Instruction

Introduce the activity by encouraging students to share what they know about surveys. For example, a student might describe a television commercial that represents a consumer product and data from a survey. Another student might describe how voters are sometimes surveyed before a presidential election.

(continued)

Surveys *(continued)*

Math Conversations

Discussion opportunities are provided below.

Problems 11 Evaluate

Extend the Problem

The following questions provide opportunities for students to generalize how predictions may be influenced by changes in sample size.

"Suppose you ask a classmate to name his or her favorite subject, and the classmate names spelling. Would it be sensible for you to make the following prediction: **The favorite subject of the students in our school is spelling.** ***Explain why or why not."*** Answers should reflect the idea that one student's preference should not be used to predict the preference of all of the students in a school.

"Suppose you could ask some students in your school, but not all of them, to name their favorite subject. How many students would you need to ask to make a reasonable prediction about the favorite subject of the students in your school? Explain your reasoning." Answers will vary.

Frequency Table

Sport	Tally	Frequency
Basketball	𝍸 𝍸 𝍸 |	16
Bowling	𝍸 𝍸 ||	12
Football	𝍸 𝍸 𝍸	15
Softball	𝍸 𝍸 𝍸 𝍸 𝍸 |	26
Table Tennis	𝍸 𝍸 ||	12
Volleyball	𝍸 𝍸 𝍸 ||||	19

From the frequency table, Mrs. Patterson's students constructed a bar graph to display the results.

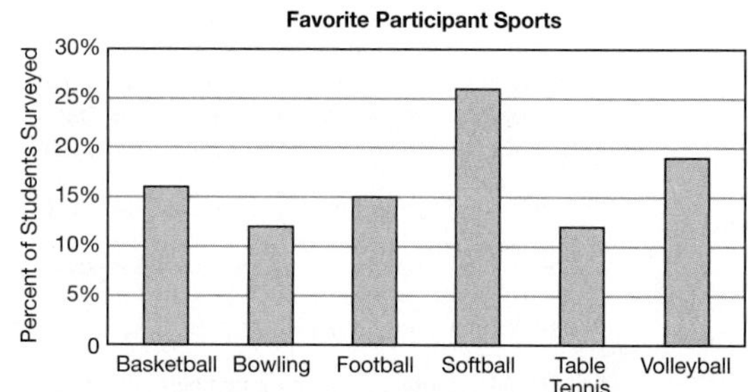

Since 16 out of 100 students selected basketball as their favorite sport to play, basketball was the choice of 16% (which means "16 out of 100") of the students surveyed. Refer to the frequency table and bar graph for this survey to answer problems **9–12.**

9. Which sport was the favorite sport of about $\frac{1}{4}$ of the students surveyed? softball

10. Which sport was the favorite sport of the girls who were surveyed? **D**

A softball **B** volleyball

C basketball **D** cannot be determined from given information

▶ **11.** Evaluate How might changing the sample group change the results of the survey? Sample: Consider only girls' responses; consider only boys' responses. Discuss.

12. How might changing the survey question—the choice of sports—change the results of the survey? Consider eliminating some choices while adding others. Discuss.

This survey was a **closed-option survey** because the responses were limited to the six choices offered. An **open-option survey** does not limit the choices. An example of an open-option survey question is "What is your favorite sport?"

▶ See Math Conversations in the sidebar.

extensions

▶ **a.** Represent Make a histogram based on the frequency table created in problem **4.** What intervals did you use? What questions can be answered by referring to the histogram?

▶ **b.** Formulate Conduct a survey of favorite foods of class members. If you choose to conduct a closed-option survey, determine which food choices will be offered. What will be the size of the sample? How will the data gathered by the survey be displayed?

▶ **c.** Analyze The table below uses negative integers to express the estimated greatest depth of each of the Great Lakes.

U.S. Great Lakes
Est. Greatest Depth (in meters)

Lake	Depth
Erie	−65 m
Huron	−230 m
Michigan	−280 m
Ontario	−245 m
Superior	−400 m

- Write the depths of the lakes in order from the deepest to shallowest. −400 m, −280 m, −245 m, −230 m, −65 m
- Is a bar graph an appropriate way to represent the data in the table? yes
- Are the data in the table displayed correctly on the bar graph below? Explain why or why not. no; The depths for Lakes Michigan and Ontario have been switched.

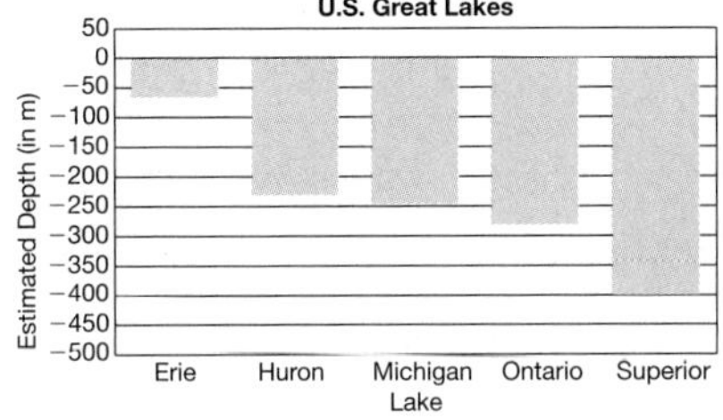

▶ **d.** Analyze Choose between mental math, paper and pencil, or estimation to answer each of the following questions. Explain your choice. Use the table in extension **c** as a reference.

- Lake Superior is how much deeper than Lake Erie? 335 m; See student work.
- Is the depth of Lake Michigan closer to the depth of Lake Ontario or Lake Huron? Lake Ontario; See student work.
- How much deeper is Lake Michigan than Lake Huron? 50 m; See student work.

▶ See Math Conversations in the sidebar.

Extensions

a. **Represent** Prior to constructing the histograms, remind students that the intervals of a histogram must be consistent. For example, if the first interval has a range of three months, all successive intervals must have a range of three months.

b. **Formulate** You might choose to have one-half of the class design and conduct a closed-option survey, and one-half design and conduct an open-option survey. Conclude the activity by asking students to share their designs, design considerations, and results with their classmates.

c. **Analyze** Lead students to conclude that a bar graph is an appropriate way to represent the depths given. Careful inspection should lead students to realize that the bar length (or the bar labels) for Lakes Michigan and Ontario have been switched. Ask students to describe other ways the data could be represented.

d. **Analyze** Students should choose whatever method of calculation works best for them. You may want to discuss the different options.

- Many students will use paper and pencil. Others will use a mental math strategy such as: $65 + 10 = 75$, $100 - 75 = 25$, $25 + 10 = 35$.
- Many students will estimate by comparing numbers: $280 > 245 > 230$.
- Many students will use mental math: $8 - 3 = 5$, so $280 - 230 = 50$.

Looking Forward

Conducting, displaying, and interpreting information from a survey prepares students for:

- **Lesson 18,** interpreting information from a line graph.
- **Lesson 40,** interpreting information from a circle graph.
- **Investigation 4,** understanding data collection and surveys.
- **Investigation 5,** looking at ways to display data.
- **Investigation 9,** interpreting and presenting data in a table to show experimental probability.

Section 2 Overview

Lessons 11–20, Investigation 2

Lesson Planner

LESSON	NEW CONCEPTS	MATERIALS	RESOURCES
11	• Problems About Combining • Problems About Separating		Power Up D
12	• Place Value Through Trillions • Multistep Problems		Power Up D Place Value poster
13	• Problems About Comparing • Elapsed-Time Problems	Manipulative Kit: inch rulers	Power Up A
14	• The Number Line: Negative Numbers	Manipulative Kit: metric rulers Calculators	Power Up D Lesson Activity 1 Transparency
15	• Problems About Equal Groups		Power Up C
16	• Rounding Whole Numbers • Estimating	Index cards or playing cards	Power Up D
17	• The Number Line: Fractions and Mixed Numbers	Student-made tag board inch rulers from Lesson 7	Power Up E
18	• Average • Line Graphs	Manipulative Kit: metric rulers, color tiles, 18 books Square pieces of paper, scissors	Power Up B Lesson Activity 2
19	• Factors • Prime Numbers	Manipulative Kit: rulers	Power Up D Lesson Activity 3 Primes and Composites poster
20	• Greatest Common Factor (GCF)	Manipulative Kit: inch rulers	Power Up C
Inv. 2	• Investigating Fractions with Manipulatives	Scissors, envelopes or zip-lock bags, colored paper	Investigation Activities 4–8 Basic Fraction Circles poster

Lesson Highlights

Lessons 11–20, Investigation 2

Problem Solving

Strategies

- **Find a Pattern** Lessons 11, 12, 16
- **Make a Table** Lessons 11, 14
- **Make It Simpler** Lesson 12
- **Use Logical Reasoning** Lessons 13, 15, 18, 19
- **Draw a Diagram** Lessons 14, 17, 20
- **Work Backwards** Lesson 15
- **Write an Equation** Lesson 17

Alternative Strategies

- **Make a Model** Lessons 11, 17
- **Act It Out** Lessons 13, 17

Real-World Applications

pp. 58, 59–62, 66, 67, 69–73, 75–77, 79, 80, 81, 83, 84, 86–88, 91–95, 98, 103, 104, 106–108

4-Step Process

Student Edition Lessons 11, 12, 13, 15, 17

Teacher Edition Lessons 11–20 (Power-Up Discussions)

Communication

Explain

pp. 67, 69, 71, 72, 79, 85, 91, 92, 97, 104, 107–108, 111

Formulate a Problem

pp. 61, 62, 67, 79–80, 86, 97, 98

Connections

Math and Other Subjects

- **Math and History** pp. 63, 69, 70, 81, 85, 91, 103
- **Math and Geography** pp. 75, 77, 84
- **Math and Science** pp. 62, 66, 71–73, 76, 77, 79, 80, 85, 97, 103, 106
- **Math and Sports** pp. 61, 86, 91, 99, 107

Math to Math

- **Problem Solving and Measurement** Lessons 11, 13, 14, 15, 16, 17, 18, 20
- **Algebra and Problem Solving** Lessons 11, 13, 15, 17, 20
- **Fractions, Percents, Decimals, and Problem Solving** Lessons 11, 12, 14, 15, 16, 17, 18, 20, Inv. 2
- **Fractions and Measurement** Lessons 16, 17, 18, 19, 20
- **Measurement and Geometry** Lessons 12, 13, 14, 16, 17, 18, 19

Representation

Manipulatives/Hands On

pp. 72, 76, 78, 82, 88–91, 94, 98, 104, 107, 109–111

Model

pp. 97, 98, 100, 104, 109, 110

Represent

pp. 62, 80–81, 86, 90, 91, 103, 106, 110

Formulate an Equation

pp. 61, 66, 70, 71, 76, 79, 80, 85

Technology

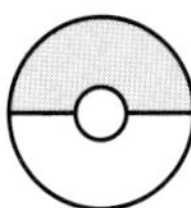

Student Resources

- **eBook**
- **Calculator** Lesson 14
- **Online Resources** at www.SaxonPublishers.com/ActivitiesC1
  - **Graphing Calculator Activities** Lessons 14, 20
  - **Real-World Investigation 2** after Lesson 18
  - **Online Activities**
  - **Math Enrichment Problems**
  - **Math Stumpers**

Teacher Resources

- **Resources and Planner CD**
- **Adaptations CD** Lessons 11–20
- **Test & Practice Generator CD**
- **eGradebook**
- **Answer Key CD**

In this section, students are writing equations for word problems and formulating word problems for equations. They extend the use of the number line to fractions and explore the concept of average.

Algebraic Thinking

Writing and solving equations are presented early in the year and are practiced throughout the year.

Writing equations to solve word problems is an extremely difficult skill for students learning algebra. Students begin acquiring this skill in Lessons 11, 13, and 15, where they learn that there are a few common plots to many word problems and that these plots can be expressed with just a few different formulas.

Factoring is useful in arithmetic and is an essential skill in algebra. Lessons 19 and 20 explain the relationship between factors and prime numbers and ask students to find the greatest common factor of two or more numbers.

The Number Line

Graphic organizers help students visualize mathematics.

The number line is one of the big ideas in mathematics that has application in measurement, statistics, algebra, and geometry. Lessons 14, 16, and 17 introduce the number line, use its visual strength to explain rounding, illustrate the order of integers, fractions and mixed numbers, and apply the number line for linear measurement.

Graphing and Statistics

Line graphs are a real-world application of number lines.

Lesson 18 provides a review of average and follows the introduction to statistics in Investigation 1 with instruction on line graphs.

Fraction Concepts

Using manipulatives helps students understand concepts.

Investigation 2 gives students hands-on experience with fraction manipulatives. Using student-made materials, students find equivalent fractions and compare fractions, relate fractions to percents, add and subtract fractions, and convert between improper fractions and mixed numbers.

Assessment

A variety of weekly assessment tools are provided.

After Lesson 15:
- Power-Up Test 2
- Cumulative Test 2
- Performance Activity 2

After Lesson 20:
- Power-Up Test 3
- Cumulative Test 3
- Customized Benchmark Test
- Performance Task 3

Content Trace

Lessons 11–20, Investigation 2

LESSON	NEW CONCEPTS	PRACTICED	ASSESSED
11	• Problems About Combining	Lessons 11, 12, 18, 19, 22, 24, 26, 37, 43, 46, 50, 51, 53, 56, 58, 61, 75, 77, 79, 85	Tests 3, 4
	• Problems About Separating	Lessons 11, 13, 14, 15, 21, 27, 28, 32, 38, 39, 40, 41, 43, 48, 52, 64, 70, 71, 72, 77, 85, 86	Tests 3, 4
12	• Place Value Through Trillions	Lessons 12, 13, 14, 15, 16, 17, 18, 19, 20, 21, 22, 23, 25, 31, 33, 34, 37, 39, 42, 52, 54, 59, 60, 65, 70, 73, 82, 89, 113, 114, 120	Tests 3, 4, 5, 8, 10
	• Multistep Problems	Lessons 12, 13, 14, 16, 17, 20, 21, 22, 27, 30, 31, 32, 33, 44, 49, 51, 57, 58, 63, 64, 68, 72, 85, 86, 89, 96, 98, 100, 103	Tests 3, 4, 5, 9, 10
13	• Problems About Comparing	Lessons 13, 15, 33, 44, 46, 48, 52, 53, 54, 66, 67, 102, 104, 106, 111	Test & Practice Generator
	• Elapsed-Time Problems	Lessons 13, 16, 17, 28, 32, 38, 40, 43, 44, 47, 48, 51, 55, 57, 59, 64, 68	Test 3
14	• The Number Line: Negative Numbers	Lessons 14, 15, 16, 18, 19, 20, 21, 22, 29, 34, 35, 37, 39, 41, 43, 46, 48, 57, 59, 62, 69, 72, 77, 85, 87, 90, 94, 98, 101, 102, 105, 118	Tests 3, 4, 22
15	• Problems About Equal Groups	Lessons 15, 16, 17, 18, 19, 21, 22, 23, 24, 25, 26, 27, 28, 29, 30, 32, 34, 36, 38, 41, 44, 45, 46, 47, 50, 55, 60, 63, 63, 64, 65, 66, 67, 68, 69, 74, 75, 76, 80, 82, 85, 111, 112	Tests 3, 4
16	• Rounding Whole Numbers	Lessons 16, 17, 18, 19, 20, 21, 22, 23, 24, 25, 26, 27, 29, 31, 33, 34, 36, 37, 38, 39, 40, 42, 43, 44, 45, 46, 48, 51, 52, 54, 56, 59, 61, 63, 68, 74, 76, 82, 115	Tests 4, 5, 6, 7, 8, 10
	• Estimating	Lessons 16, 17, 18, 21, 22, 23, 24, 24, 25, 26, 29, 30, 31, 33, 34, 36, 37, 39, 42, 45, 46, 48, 51, 54, 56, 61, 68, 74, 76, 82	Tests 4, 5, 6, 8, 10
17	• The Number Line: Fractions and Mixed Numbers	Lessons 17, 18, 19, 20, 25, 26, 28, 31, 32, 33, 37, 39, 40, 41, 43, 44, 45, 46, 47, 49, 68, 70, 74, 81, 90, 92, 93, 98, 112	Test & Practice Generator
18	• Average	Lessons 18, 19, 20, 21, 22, 25, 26, 28, 30, 32, 34, 36, 37, 39, 41, 42, 44, 45, 47, 48, 49, 50, 53, 54, 56, 58, 60, 61, 62, 66, 67, 68, 69, 70, 72, 73, 74, 79, 80, 90, 92, 93, 94, 96, 97, 100, 101, 102, 103, 104, 106, 107, 111	Tests 4, 5, 6, 8, 10
	• Line Graphs	Lessons 18, 59, 64, 70, 86	Test 4
19	• Factors	Lessons 19, 20, 21, 22, 30, 36, 38, 40, 44, 47, 49, 50, 51, 53, 55, 57, 62	Tests 4, 6, 12
	• Prime Numbers	Lessons 19, 20, 22, 23, 24, 26, 27, 28, 30, 33, 41, 42, 43, 53, 55, 56, 60, 62, 63, 64, 67, 72, 76, 91, 99, 103, 109, 114	Test 12
20	• Greatest Common Factor (GCF)	Lessons 20, 21, 22, 23, 24, 25, 26, 28, 29, 32, 36, 38, 45, 46, 66, 71, 75, 81, 83, 99, 107	Tests 4, 5, 6, 8, 9
Inv. 2	• Investigating Fractions with Manipulatives	Investigation 2, Lessons 21, 22, 23, 24, 26, 27, 28, 29, 30, 32, 33, 34, 35, 36, 37, 41, 42, 44, 45, 59, 71, 77	Tests 5, 6, 8, 9

• Problems About Combining
• Problems About Separating

Objectives

- Identify the addition pattern in word problems about combining.
- Follow the four-step method to solve word problems about combining.
- Write an equation to solve a word problem about combining.
- Identify the subtraction pattern in a word problem about separating.
- Follow the four-step method to solve word problems about separating.
- Write an equation to solve a word problem about separating.

Lesson Preparation

Materials

- **Power Up D** (in *Instructional Masters*)

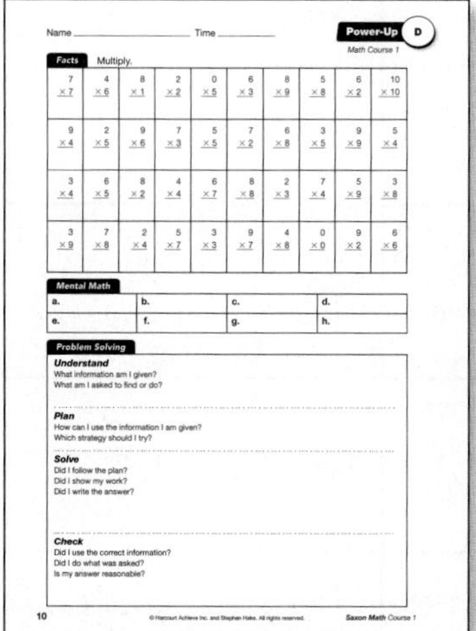

Power Up D

Math Language

English Learners (ESL)
previous
plot

Technology Resources

Student eBook Complete student textbook in electronic format.

Resources and Planner CD Assessment, reteaching, and instructional masters, plus a pacing calendar with standards.

Test and Practice Generator CD Create additional practice sheets and custom-made tests.

www.SaxonPublishers.com Visit for more student activities and planning materials.

Inclusion

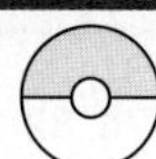

Adaptations CD Adapted lessons, investigations, practice and assessments.

Meeting Standards

National Council of Teachers of Mathematics (NCTM)

Algebra

AL.1b Relate and compare different forms of representation for a relationship

AL.2a Develop an initial conceptual understanding of different uses of variables

AL.3a Model and solve contextualized problems using various representations, such as graphs, tables, and equations

Problem Solving

PS.1b Solve problems that arise in mathematics and in other contexts

PS.1c Apply and adapt a variety of appropriate strategies to solve problems

Connections

CN.4a Recognize and use connections among mathematical ideas

Power-Up Discussion

For use with Power Up, p. 58

Problem-Solving Strategy: Find a Pattern/Use a Table

Sitha began building stair-step structures with blocks. She used one block for a one-step structure, three blocks for a two-step structure, and six blocks for a three-step structure. She wrote the information in a table. Copy the table and complete it through a ten-step structure.

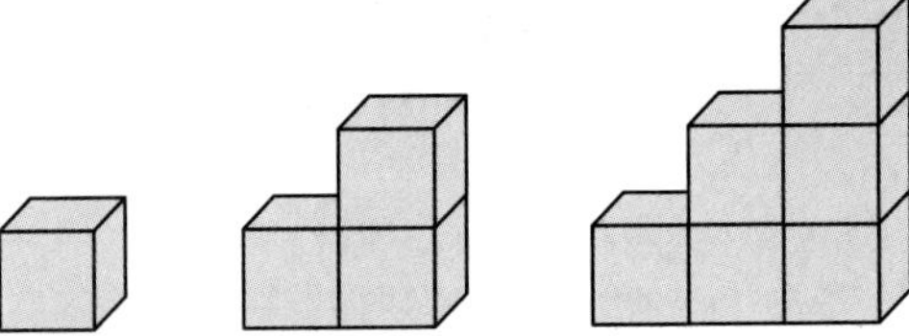

Understand **Understand the problem.**

"What information are we given?"

Sitha is building stair-step structures with blocks. She used one block for a one-step structure, three blocks for a two-step structure, and six blocks for a three-step structure.

"What are we asked to do?"

Copy the table and complete it through ten-steps.

Plan **Make a plan.**

"What problem-solving strategy have we been asked to use?"

We will *find patterns* as we fill in and *use the table* provided.

Solve **Carry out the plan.**

"What patterns emerge in the table?"

1. The steps in each structure are formed by stacks of blocks, and Sitha forms each new step by adding a new stack of blocks next to the tallest stack she already has. The number of stair-steps in the structure equals the number of additional blocks needed to build the structure.
2. The total number of blocks equals the existing number of blocks in the previous structure plus the number of additional blocks needed to build the newest structure.

Teacher Note: Discuss how the terms in this sequence can be written as sums. (1, 1 + 2, 1 + 2 + 3, 1 + 2 + 3 + 4 ...)

Check **Look back.**

"Did the table help us find patterns?"

Yes.

Teacher Note: Extend this problem by having students draw and discuss triangular numbers, which can be shown as a sequence of numbers 1, 3, 6, 10... or as a diagram of objects:

Alternative Approach: Make a Model

If blocks are readily available, make a model to represent the fourth step in the pattern.

LESSON **11**

• Problems About Combining
• Problems About Separating

Power Up — *Building Power*

facts Power Up D

mental math

a. **Number Sense:** 3 × 40 120

b. **Number Sense:** 3 × 400 1200

c. **Number Sense:** \$4.50 + \$1.25 \$5.75

d. **Number Sense:** 451 + 240 691

e. **Number Sense:** 4500 − 400 4100

f. **Number Sense:** \$5.00 − \$1.50 \$3.50

g. **Geometry:** A rectangle has a length of 3 cm and a width of 2 cm. What is the perimeter of the rectangle? 10 cm

h. **Calculation:** Start with 10. Add 2; divide by 2; add 2; divide by 2; then subtract 2. What is the answer? 2

problem solving

Sitha began building stair-step structures with blocks. She used one block for a one-step structure, three blocks for a two-step structure, and six blocks for a three-step structure. She wrote the information in a table. Copy the table and complete it through a ten-step structure.

Number of Steps	Total Number of Blocks	Blocks Added to Previous Structure
1	1	N/A
2	3	2
3	6	3

Number of Steps	Total Number of Blocks	Blocks Added to Previous Structure
1	1	N/A
2	3	2
3	6	3
4	10	4
5	15	5
6	21	6
7	28	7
8	36	8
9	45	9
10	55	10

New Concepts — *Increasing Knowledge*

Like stories in your reading books, many of the stories we analyze in mathematics have plots. We can use the plot of a word problem to write an equation for the problem. Problems with the same plot are represented by the same equation. That is why we say there are **patterns** for certain plots.

problems about combining

Many word problems are about **combining.** Here is an example:

Before he went to work, Pham had \$24.50. He earned \$12.50 more putting up a fence. Then Pham had \$37.00. (Plot: Pham had some money and then he earned some more money.)

Facts Multiply.

7 × 7 49	4 × 6 24	8 × 1 8	2 × 2 4	0 × 5 0	6 × 3 18	8 × 9 72	5 × 8 40	6 × 2 12	10 × 10 100
9 × 4 36	2 × 5 10	9 × 6 54	7 × 3 21	5 × 5 25	7 × 2 14	6 × 8 48	3 × 5 15	9 × 9 81	5 × 4 20
3 × 4 12	6 × 5 30	8 × 2 16	4 × 4 16	6 × 7 42	8 × 8 64	2 × 3 6	7 × 4 28	5 × 9 45	3 × 8 24
3 × 9 27	7 × 8 56	2 × 4 8	5 × 7 35	3 × 3 9	9 × 7 63	4 × 8 32	0 × 0 0	9 × 2 18	6 × 6 36

1 Power Up

Facts

Distribute **Power Up D** to students. See answers below.

Mental Math

Before students begin the Mental Math exercise, do this counting exercise as a class.

Count up and down by $\frac{1}{2}$s between $\frac{1}{2}$ and 12.

Encourage students to share different ways to mentally compute these exercises. Strategies for exercises **a** and **c** are listed below.

a. Use a Fact

3 × 4 = 12; 3 × 4 tens = 12 tens or 120

Count on by 40

Start with 40. Count: 80, 120

c. Count Dollars, Count Cents

\$4.00 + \$1.00 + \$0.50 + \$0.25 = \$5.00 + \$0.75 = \$5.75

Decompose \$1.25, then Add

\$4.50 + \$1.00 + 0.25 = \$5.50 + \$0.25 = \$5.75

Problem Solving

Refer to **Power-Up Discussion,** p. 58F.

2 New Concepts

Instruction

To prepare students for writing and solving equations in this lesson, review Lesson 3:

- *Unknown Numbers in Addition.*
- *Unknown Numbers in Subtraction.*

(continued)

Problems about combining have an **addition pattern.**

Some + some more = total

$s + m = t$

There are three numbers in the pattern. In a word problem one of the numbers is unknown, as in the story below.

Katya had 734 stamps in her collection. Then her uncle gave her some more stamps. Now Katya has 813 stamps. How many stamps did Katya's uncle give her?

This problem has a plot similar to the previous one. (Plot: Katya had some stamps and was given some more stamps.) In this problem, however, one of the numbers is unknown. Katya's uncle gave her some stamps, but the problem does not say how many. We use the four-step process to solve the problem.

Step 1: *Understand* Since this problem is about combining, it has an addition pattern.

Step 2: *Plan* We use the pattern to set up an equation.

Pattern: Some + some more = total

Equation: 734 stamps + m = 813 stamps

Step 3: *Solve* The answer to the question is the unknown number in the equation. Since the unknown number is an addend, we subtract 734 from 813 to find the number.

Find answer:	Check answer:
813 stamps	813 stamps
− 734 stamps	− 79 stamps
79 stamps	734 stamps

Step 4: *Check* We review the question and write the answer. Katya's uncle gave her 79 stamps.

Example 1

Thinking Skill

Connect

How is an odometer the same as a ruler? How is it different? Both measure distance. Odometers measure long distances. Rulers usually measure short distances.

Jenny rode her bike on a trip with her bicycling club. After the first day Jenny's trip odometer showed that she had traveled 86 miles. After the second day the trip odometer showed that she had traveled a total of 163 miles. How far did Jenny ride the second day?

Solution

Step 1: Jenny rode some miles and then rode some more miles. The distances from the two days combine to give a total. Since this is a problem about combining, it has an **addition pattern.**

Step 2: The trip odometer showed how far she traveled the first day and the total of the first two days. We record the information in the pattern.

Some	86 miles
+ Some more	+ m miles
Total	163 miles

2 New Concepts (Continued)

Instruction

Review the problem about Katya and her stamp collection.

Step 2: This step shows the equation:
734 stamps + m = 813 stamps.
Ask the following question to help students understand how the equation relates to the word problem.

"In the equation, what does the letter m represent?" The number of stamps Katya received from her uncle.

"The equation we used to find the answer was 734 + m = 813. What operation did that equation represent?" addition

"What operation was used to find the answer?" subtraction

Have students note that an inverse operation was used to find the answer.

"What operation was used to check the answer?" subtraction

"Addition could have been used to check the answer. Explain how." Find the sum of 734 and 79, and then compare the sum to 813; if the sum is equal to 813, the problem checks.

(continued)

English Learners

Explain that the word ***previous*** means "the one before." Say:

"When we refer to 'the previous one' we are talking about the problem just before this one."

Write Step 1, Step 2, Step 3, and Step 4 on the board. Explain that Step 1 is previous to Step 2. Ask:

"Which Step is previous to Step 3? To Step 4?" Step 2, Step 3

Ask which problem is previous to the problem about Katya. the problem about Pham

Point out that both of these problems have a **plot.** One meaning of the word *plot* is "what a story is about." Say:

"One plot is about Katya getting more stamps for her stamp collection. What is the plot of the previous problem?" Pham earning more money putting up a fence.

2 New Concepts *(Continued)*

Example 1

Instruction

Step 3: In this step of the solution, have students again note that an inverse operation is used to find the unknown number.

Step 4: After completing step 4, tell students to always show all of the steps of a solution and to write neatly. Point out that step 4 is important because it is a reminder to reread the original problem to be sure the solution answers the question that was asked and is reasonable or sensible.

(continued)

Step 3: We solve the equation by finding the unknown number. From Lesson 3 we know that we can find the missing addend by subtracting 86 miles from 163 miles. We check the answer.

Find answer:		Check answer:
163 miles		86 miles
− 86 miles	→	+ 77 miles
77 miles		163 miles

Step 4: We review the question and write the answer. Jenny rode **77 miles** on the second day of the trip.

problems about separating

Another common plot in word problems is **separating.** There is a beginning amount, then some goes away, and some remains. Problems about separating have a **subtraction pattern.**

Beginning amount − some went away = what remains

$$b - a = r$$

Here is an example:

Waverly took $37.00 to the music store. She bought headphones for $26.17. Then Waverly had $10.83. (Plot: Waverly had some money, but some of her money went away when she spent it.)

This is a problem about separating. Thus it has a subtraction pattern.

Pattern:

Beginning amount − some went away = what remains

Equation:

$37.00 − $26.17 = $10.83

Example 2

On Saturday 47 people volunteered to clean up the park. Some people chose to remove trash from the lake. The remaining 29 people left to clean up the hiking trails. How many people chose to remove trash from the lake?

Solution

Step 1: There were 47 people. Then some went away. This problem has a **subtraction pattern.**

Step 2: We use the pattern to write an equation for the given information. We show the equation written vertically.

Beginning amount	47 people
− Some went away	− *p* people
What remains	29 people

Step 3: We find the unknown number by subtracting 29 from 47. We check the answer.

Find answer:	Check answer:
47 people	47 people
− 29 people	− 18 people
18 people	29 people

Step 4: We review the question and write the answer. There were **18 people** who chose to remove trash from the lake.

Practice Set

Formulate Follow the four-step method to solve each problem. Along with each answer, include the equation you use to solve the problem.

▶ **a.** When Tim finished page 129 of a 314-page book, how many pages did he still have to read? 185 pages; $314 - 129 = P$

▶ **b.** The football team scored 19 points in the first half of the game and 42 points by the end of the game. How many points did the team score in the second half of the game? 23 points; $19 + P = 42$

▶ **c.** Formulate Write a word problem about combining. Solve the problem and write the answer. See student work.

Written Practice

Strengthening Concepts

▶ * **1.** (11) Formulate Juan ran 8 laps and rested. Then he ran some more laps. If Juan ran 21 laps in all, how many laps did he run after he rested? Write an equation and solve the problem. $8 + l = 21$; 13 laps

2. (1, 2) **a.** Find the product of 8 and 4. 32

b. Find the sum of 8 and 4. 12

3. (5) The expression below means "the product of 6 and 4 divided by the difference of 8 and 5." What is the quotient? 8

$$(6 \times 4) \div (8 - 5)$$

* **4.** (11) Marcia went to the store with $20.00 and returned home with $7.75. How much money did Marcia spend at the store? Write an equation and solve the problem. $\$20.00 - m = \$7.75$; $12.25

* **5.** (11) When Franklin got his Labrador Retriever puppy, it weighed 8 pounds. A year later, it weighed 74 pounds. How much weight did Franklin's dog gain in that year? Write the equation and solve the problem. $8 + g = 74$; 66 pounds

6. (1) $0.65 + $0.40 $1.05

▶ Analyze Find each unknown number. Check your work.

7. (3) $87 + w = 155$ 68

8. (3) $1000 - x = 386$ 614

9. (3) $y - 1000 = 386$ 1386

10. (3) $42 + 596 + m = 700$ 62

▶* **11.** (9) Compare: $1000 - (100 - 10) \; \textcircled{>} \; 1000 - 100 - 10$

▶ See Math Conversations in the sidebar.

2 New Concepts (Continued)

Example 2

Instruction

Step 4: After completing the example, challenge each student to write one word problem about combining or about separating. Invite volunteers to read the problems they wrote aloud, and have all students write, compare, and discuss equations that can be used to represent and solve the problems.

Practice Set

Problems a–b Formulate

After completing each problem, invite volunteers to say the equation they wrote and explain why addition or subtraction was used to find the answer.

Problem c Formulate

Extend the Problem

Ask students to explain how writing a word problem about combining is different from writing a word problem about comparing.

3 Written Practice

Math Conversations

Discussion opportunities are provided below.

Problem 1 Formulate

Extend the Problem

After completing the problem, ask students to look at the equation they wrote and identify the operation it represents. Then challenge students to write an equation to represent the problem that includes the inverse operation. Sample: $8 + l = 21$ and $l = 21 - 8$

Problems 7–10 Analyze

Encourage students to discuss and compare the different ways they checked their work.

Problem 11 Conclude

"Why is an inequality symbol used for the answer?" Sample: The amount on one side of the statement is not equal to the amount on the other side.

(continued)

3 Written Practice (Continued)

Math Conversations

Discussion opportunities are provided below.

Problem 17 Predict

Before completing the problem, ask students to discuss the pattern and identify its rule.

Problem 18 Generalize

Invite volunteers to describe how the Associative Property of Multiplication (sometimes called the grouping property) can be used to group the numbers to make it easier to find the product mentally. Sample: group 2 and 3 and group 4 and 5; $(2 \times 3) \times (4 \times 5) = 6 \times 20 = 120$

Problem 22 Connect

Extend the Problem

Using their rulers if necessary, ask students to decide how long the segment would be if it was twice as long. $4\frac{2}{4}$ in. or $4\frac{1}{2}$ in.

Problem 25 Generalize

Extend the Problem

Invite a volunteer to describe (or demonstrate at the board) how the numbers can be grouped in pairs having sums of 10. $(1 + 9) + (3 + 7) + 5 = 10 + 10 + 5 = 25$

Errors and Misconceptions

Problem 14

If students cannot recognize how to find the value of *W*, ask them to identify the operation that is present, and then identify the inverse of that operation. division; multiplication

Problem 23

Point out the problem contains the word "not" and remind students to always read a problem carefully.

12. (2) $8\overline{)1000}$ 125 **13.** (2) $10\overline{)987}$ 98 R 7 ▶ **14.** (4) $12\overline{)W}$ 35 420

15. (2) 600×300 180,000 **16.** (4) $365w = 365$ 1

▶* **17.** (10) Predict What are the next three numbers in the following sequence?

2, 6, 10, 14, 18, 22, ...

▶ **18.** (5) $2 \times 3 \times 4 \times 5$ 120

19. (6) What number is $\frac{1}{2}$ of 360? 180

20. (6) What number is $\frac{1}{4}$ of 360? 90

21. (2) What is the product of eight and one hundred twenty-five? 1000

▶* **22.** (7) Connect How long is the line segment below? $2\frac{1}{4}$ in.

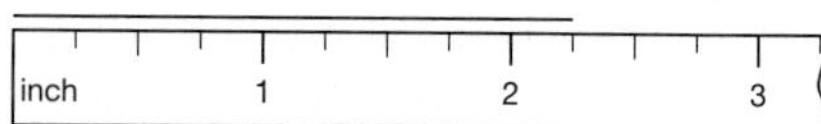

▶ **23.** (6) What fraction of the circle at right is not shaded? $\frac{5}{8}$

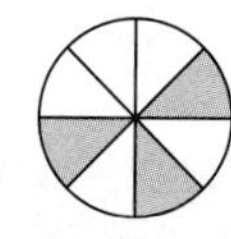

24. (6) What is the perimeter of the square shown? 36 mm

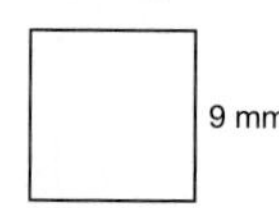

▶* **25.** (10) What is the sum of the first five odd numbers greater than zero? 25

26. (2) Here are three ways to write "24 divided by 4":

$4\overline{)24}$ $24 \div 4$ $\frac{24}{4}$

Show three ways to write "30 divided by 6." $6\overline{)30}$, $30 \div 6$, $\frac{30}{6}$

27. (6) Seventeen of the 30 students in the class are girls. So $\frac{17}{30}$ of the students in the class are girls. What fraction of the students in the class are boys? $\frac{13}{30}$

* **28.** (10) At what temperature on the Celsius scale does water freeze? 0°C

29. (2) Represent Use the numbers 24, 6, and 4 to write two multiplication facts and two division facts. $6 \times 4 = 24$, $4 \times 6 = 24$, $24 \div 4 = 6$, $24 \div 6 = 4$

* **30.** (11) Formulate In the second paragraph of this lesson there is a problem with an addition pattern. Rewrite the problem by removing one of the numbers from the problem and asking a question instead. Answers will vary. See student work.

▶ See Math Conversations in the sidebar.

Looking Forward

Writing and solving an equation for a story problem about combining prepares students for:

- **Lesson 15,** solving problems about equal groups.
- **Lesson 43,** solving missing number problems with fractions and decimals.
- **Lesson 98,** finding the sum of the angle measures of triangles and quadrilaterals.
- **Lesson 103,** finding the perimeter of a complex shape.

• Place Value Through Trillions
• Multistep Problems

Objectives

- Identify the place value through trillions of a digit in a whole number.
- Use words and digits to write numbers through trillions.
- Use addition, subtraction, multiplication, and division to solve problems with several steps.

Lesson Preparation

Materials

- **Power Up D** (in *Instructional Masters*)

Optional

- **Place Value poster**

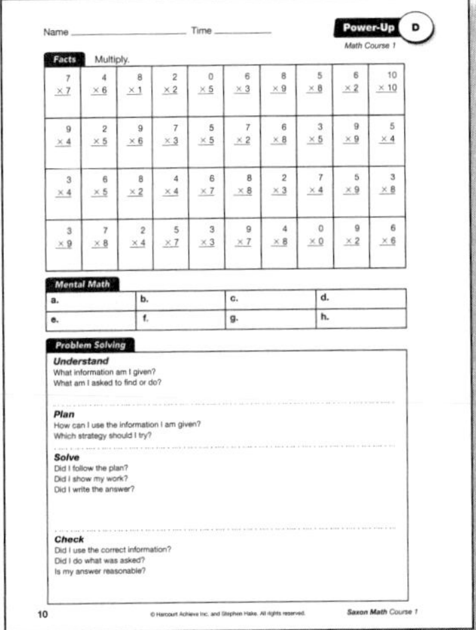

Name ______ Time ______ **Power-Up D** *Math Course 1*

Facts Multiply.

7 × 7	4 × 6	8 × 1	2 × 2	0 × 5	6 × 3	8 × 9	5 × 8	6 × 2	10 × 10
9 × 4	2 × 5	9 × 6	7 × 3	5 × 5	7 × 2	6 × 8	3 × 5	9 × 9	5 × 4
3 × 4	6 × 5	8 × 2	4 × 4	6 × 7	8 × 8	2 × 3	7 × 4	5 × 9	3 × 8
3 × 9	7 × 8	2 × 4	5 × 7	3 × 3	9 × 7	4 × 8	0 × 0	9 × 2	6 × 6

Mental Math

a.	b.	c.	d.
e.	f.	g.	h.

Problem Solving

Understand
What information am I given?
What am I asked to find or do?

Plan
How can I use the information I am given?
Which strategy should I try?

Solve
Did I follow the plan?
Did I show my work?
Did I write the answer?

Check
Did I use the correct information?
Did I do what was asked?
Is my answer reasonable?

10 © Harcourt Achieve Inc. and Stephen Hake. All rights reserved. *Saxon Math Course 1*

Power Up D

New	Maintain	English Learners (ESL)
operations of arithmetic	difference	sequence
place value	product	
	sum	

Technology Resources

Student eBook Complete student textbook in electronic format.

Resources and Planner CD Assessment, reteaching, and instructional masters, plus a pacing calendar with standards.

Test and Practice Generator CD Create additional practice sheets and custom-made tests.

www.SaxonPublishers.com Visit for more student activities and planning materials.

Inclusion

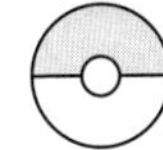

Adaptations CD Adapted lessons, investigations, practice and assessments.

Meeting Standards

National Council of Teachers of Mathematics (NCTM)

Numbers and Operations

NO.1e Develop an understanding of large numbers and recognize and appropriately use exponential, scientific, and calculator notation

NO.1g Develop meaning for integers and represent and compare quantities with them

Problem Solving

PS.1c Apply and adapt a variety of appropriate strategies to solve problems

Connections

CN.4b Understand how mathematical ideas interconnect and build on one another to produce a coherent whole

Power-Up Discussion *For use with Power Up, p. 63*

Problem-Solving Strategy: Make It Simpler/ Find a Pattern

When he was a boy, German mathematician Karl Friedrich Gauss (1777–1855) developed a method for quickly adding a sequence of numbers. Like Gauss, we can sometimes solve difficult problems by *making it simpler.*

What is the sum of the first ten natural numbers?

Understand We are asked to find the sum of the first ten natural numbers.

Plan We will begin by making the problem simpler. If the assignment had been to add the first *four* natural numbers, we could simply add 1 + 2 + 3 + 4. However, adding columns of numbers can be time consuming. We will try to find a pattern that will help add the natural numbers 1–10 more quickly.

Solve We can find pairs of addends in the sequence that have the same sum and multiply by the number of pairs. We try this pairing technique on the sequence given in the problem:

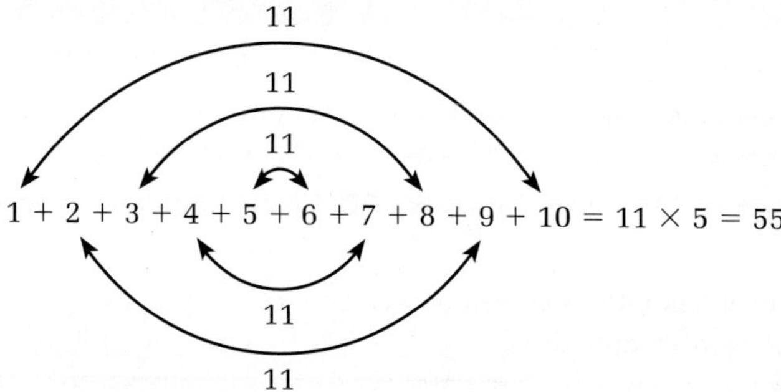

Check We found the sum of the first ten natural numbers by pairing the addends and multiplying. We can verify our solution by adding the numbers one-by-one with pencil and paper or a calculator.

Teacher Note: Extend this lesson by creating other number sequences to solve Gauss's original problem: What is the sum of the first 100 natural numbers?

LESSON 12

• Place Value Through Trillions
• Multistep Problems

Power Up

Building Power

facts Power Up D

mental math

a. **Number Sense:** 6 × 40 240

b. **Number Sense:** 6 × 400 2400

c. **Number Sense:** \$12.50 + \$5.00 \$17.50

d. **Number Sense:** 451 + 24 475

e. **Number Sense:** 7500 − 5000 2500

f. **Number Sense:** \$10.00 − \$2.50 \$7.50

g. **Measurement:** How many inches are in a yard? 36 in.

h. **Calculation:** Start with 12. Divide by 2; subtract 2; divide by 2; then subtract 2. What is the answer? 0

problem solving

When he was a boy, German mathematician Karl Friedrich Gauss (1777–1855) developed a method for quickly adding a sequence of numbers. Like Gauss, we can sometimes solve difficult problems by *making the problem simpler.*

What is the sum of the first ten natural numbers?

Understand We are asked to find the sum of the first ten natural numbers.

Plan We will begin by making the problem simpler. If the assignment had been to add the first *four* natural numbers, we could simply add 1 + 2 + 3 + 4. However, adding columns of numbers can be time consuming. We will try to find a pattern that will help add the natural numbers 1–10 more quickly.

Solve We can find pairs of addends in the sequence that have the same sum and multiply by the number of pairs. We try this pairing technique on the sequence given in the problem:

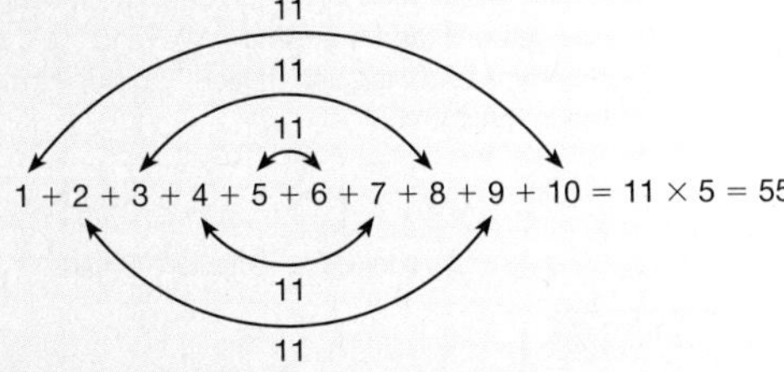

Check We found the sum of the first ten natural numbers by pairing the addends and multiplying. We can verify our solution by adding the numbers one-by-one with pencil and paper or a calculator.

Facts Multiply.

7 × 7 49	4 × 6 24	8 × 1 8	2 × 2 4	0 × 5 0	6 × 3 18	8 × 9 72	5 × 8 40	6 × 2 12	10 × 10 100
9 × 4 36	2 × 5 10	9 × 6 54	7 × 3 21	5 × 5 25	7 × 2 14	6 × 8 48	3 × 5 15	9 × 9 81	5 × 4 20
3 × 4 12	6 × 5 30	8 × 2 16	4 × 4 16	6 × 7 42	8 × 8 64	2 × 3 6	7 × 4 28	5 × 9 45	3 × 8 24
3 × 9 27	7 × 8 56	2 × 4 8	5 × 7 35	3 × 3 9	9 × 7 63	4 × 8 32	0 × 0 0	9 × 2 18	6 × 6 36

1 Power Up

Facts

Distribute **Power Up D** to students. See answers below.

Mental Math

Before students begin the Mental Math exercise, do this counting exercise as a class.

Count by $\frac{1}{4}$s from $\frac{1}{4}$ to 12.

Encourage students to share different ways to mentally compute these exercises. Strategies for exercises **b** and **d** are listed below.

b. Use a Fact

6 × 4 = 24; 6 × 4 hundreds = 24 hundreds or 2400

Count by 400

Start with 400. Count: 800, 1200, 1600, 2000, 2400

d. Subtract 1 and Add 1

451 − 1 = 450 and 24 + 1 = 25; 450 + 25 = 475

Count by Tens, then Count by Ones

Start with 451. Count: 461, 471

Start with 471. Count: 472, 473, 474, 475

Problem Solving

Refer to **Power-Up Discussion,** p. 63B.

2 New Concepts

Instruction

You may wish to display the **Place Value Chart** concept poster as you discuss this topic.

Example 1

Instruction

To reinforce examples 1 and 2, copy the Whole-Number Place Values chart from the student page on the board, and then write the numbers from the examples in the chart.

(continued)

New Concepts *Increasing Knowledge*

place value through trillions

Math Language
Our number system is based on a pattern of tens. In a place value chart, each place has a value ten times greater than the place to its right.

In our number system the value of a digit depends upon its position. The value of each position is called its **place value.**

Whole-Number Place Values

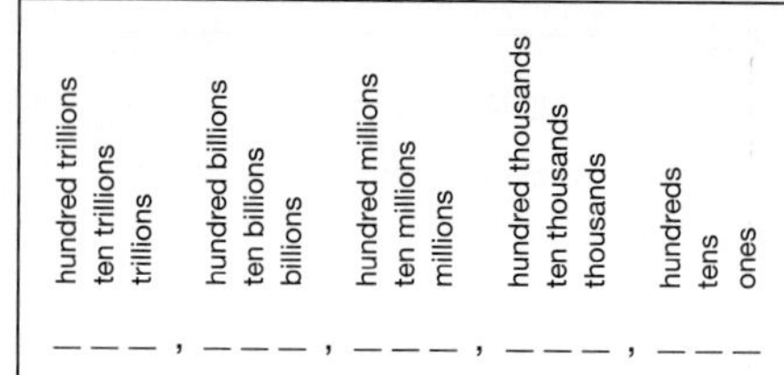

Example 1

In the number 123,456,789,000, which digit is in the ten-millions place?

Solution

Either by counting places from the right or looking at the chart, we find that the digit in the ten-millions place is **5.**

Example 2

In the number 5,764,283, what is the place value of the digit 4?

Solution

By counting places from the right or looking at the chart, we can see that the place value of 4 is **thousands.**

Thinking Skill
Connect
Make a list of real-life situations in which large number are used.
Samples:
population
money
time

Large numbers are easy to read and write if we use commas to group the digits. To place commas, we begin at the right and move to the left, writing a comma after every three digits.

Putting commas in 1234567890, we get 1,234,567,890.

Commas help us read large numbers by marking the end of the trillions, billions, millions, and thousands. We read the three-digit number in front of each comma and then say "trillion," "billion," "million," or "thousand" when we reach the comma.

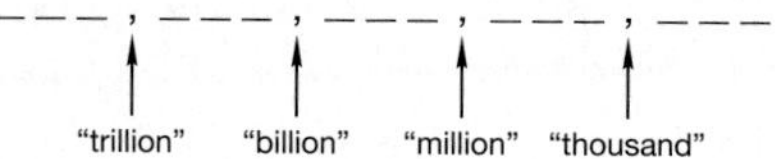

Example 3

Use words to write the number 1024305.

Inclusion

Refer students to the "Place Value" chart in the Student Reference Guide. Call attention to the commas separating each group of three digits and the name of each group. Use the following dialogue to help students write the number "fifty-two thousand, sixty-four." First write the number on the board in words.

"How many digits does fifty-two have?" 2

Draw two digit lines and write 52 on them. 5 2

"The word thousand tells you to write a comma."

Add the comma. 5 2 ,

"How many digits follow every comma?" 3

Draw three more lines. 5 2 , _ _ _

"Now fill in the digits. The number sixty-four has no hundreds, so write a zero in the hundreds place." 5 2 , 0 6 4

Solution

First we insert commas.

1,024,305

We write **one million, twenty-four thousand, three hundred five.**

Note: We write commas after the words *trillion, billion, million,* and *thousand.* We hyphenate compound numbers from 21 through 99. We do not say or write "and" when naming whole numbers.

Example 4

Use digits to write the number one trillion, two hundred fifty billion.

Solution

When writing large numbers, it may help to sketch the pattern before writing the digits.

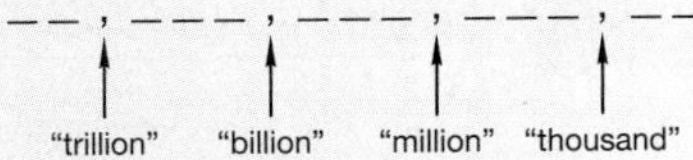

We write a 1 to the left of the trillions comma and 250 in the three places to the left of the billions comma. The remaining places are filled with zeros.

1,250,000,000,000

multistep problems

The **operations of arithmetic** are addition, subtraction, multiplication, and division. In this table we list the terms for the answers we get when we perform these operations:

Sum	the answer when we add
Difference	the answer when we subtract
Product	the answer when we multiply
Quotient	the answer when we divide

We will use these terms in problems that have several steps.

Example 5

What is the difference between the product of 6 and 4 and the sum of 6 and 4?

Solution

Math Language
Sometimes it is helpful to rewrite a question and underline the phrases that indicate operations of arithmetic.

We see the words *difference, product,* and *sum* in this question. We first look for phrases such as "the product of 6 and 4." We will rewrite the question, emphasizing these phrases.

What is the difference between the product of 6 and 4 and the sum of 6 and 4?

Math Background

In our place value system, each group of three digits is named for the value of its least significant digit. For example, the group names include ones, thousands, millions, billions, and so on. When writing numbers using our number system, it is customary to use a comma to separate groups.

However, elsewhere in the world commas can be used in other ways. For example, it is customary in some countries to use a comma instead of a decimal point, and in those countries, a number written as 25,4 represents twenty-five and four tenths.

2 New Concepts *(Continued)*

Example 3

Instruction

To provide students with more practice reading and writing large numbers, say a sequence of up to 15 digits, including zeros, while students record the digits in the order they are spoken from left to right.

Ask students to insert commas and write the number in word form, then invite a volunteer to read the number aloud.

Repeat using other sequences of digits, varying the number of digits in each sequence.

Example 4

Instruction

Use the example to help students connect large numbers to the real world.

"Where in the everyday world might you find large numbers?" Sample: In a budget such as the number of dollars a state or federal government spends each year, or in an estimate of a distance in space, such as the distance in miles the Earth moves each year in its journey around the sun.

Example 5

Instruction

The words sum, difference, product, and quotient can often be included in discussions about mathematics. Encourage students to include the words in their discussions whenever possible.

(continued)

2 New Concepts (Continued)

Practice Set

Problem d Error Alert

A typical error in problems of this nature involves an incorrect number of zeros. To help students identify the correct way to represent the number, encourage them to refer to a place value chart, and if necessary, write the number in the chart.

Problem e Analyze

Challenge students to write two different equations to represent the problem.

Sample: $(6 \times 4) \div (6 - 4) = n$ and $\frac{6 \times 4}{6 - 4} = n$.

3 Written Practice

Math Conversations

Discussion opportunities are provided below.

Problem 1 Connect

Before solving the problem, ask students to recall the operation that each of these words represents: sum; difference; product; quotient. addition; subtraction; multiplication; division

Problems 3 and 4 Formulate

After completing each problem, have students look at the equation that was used, and then write a different equation that can be used to solve the problem. Students should then solve the equation and compare the answers each equation produced.

Explain that writing and solving a second equation is a good way for students to check their work.

Problem 10 Predict

Before completing the problem, ask students to discuss the pattern and identify its rule.

(continued)

For each phrase we find one number. "The product of 6 and 4" is 24, and "the sum of 6 and 4" is 10. So we can replace the two phrases with the numbers 24 and 10 to get this question:

What is the difference between 24 and 10?

We find this answer by subtracting 10 from 24. The difference between 24 and 10 is **14.**

Practice Set

a. Which digit is in the millions place in 123,456,789? 3

b. What is the place value of the 1 in 12,453,000,000? ten billions

c. Use words to write 21,350,608. twenty-one million, three hundred fifty thousand, six hundred eight

▶ **d.** Use digits to write four billion, five hundred twenty million. 4,520,000,000

▶ **e.** Analyze When the product of 6 and 4 is divided by the difference of 6 and 4, what is the quotient? 12

Written Practice — *Strengthening Concepts*

▶ * **1.** (12) What is the difference between the product of 1, 2, and 3 and the sum of 1, 2, and 3? 0

* **2.** (12) Earth is about ninety-three million miles from the Sun. Use digits to write that distance. 93,000,000 miles

▶ * **3.** (11) Formulate Gilbert and Kadeeja cooked 342 pancakes for the pancake breakfast. If Gilbert cooked 167 pancakes, how many pancakes did Kadeeja cook? Write an equation and solve the problem. $167 + K = 342$; 175 pancakes

▶ * **4.** (11) Formulate The two teams scored a total of 102 points in the basketball game. If the winning team scored 59 points, how many points did the losing team score? Write an equation and solve the problem. $59 + l = 102$; 43 points

* **5.** (8) What is the perimeter of the rectangle at right? 56 mm

10 mm
18 mm

6. (4) $6m = 60$ 10

7. (6) **a.** What number is $\frac{1}{2}$ of 100? 50

b. What number is $\frac{1}{4}$ of 100? 25

8. (9) Compare: $300 \times 1 \; (=) \; 300 \div 1$

9. (5) $(3 \times 3) - (3 + 3)$ 3

▶ * **10.** (10) Predict What are the next three numbers in the following sequence?

1, 2, 4, 8, __16__, __32__, __64__, ...

11. (3) $1 + m + 456 = 480$ 23

12. (3) $1010 - n = 101$ 909

▶ See Math Conversations in the sidebar.

English Learners

To help students with problem 10, write 2, 3, 4, 5, ___, ___ on the board and say:

"This is a sequence of four numbers. Things that follow one another in an orderly pattern are in sequence. These numbers are the first four counting numbers. What are the next two numbers in the sequence?" 6, 7

Show this sequence of numbers and ask:

2, 4, 6, ___, ___

"This is a sequence of what type of numbers? What are the next two numbers in this sequence?" even numbers; 8, 10

Tell students that the pattern in this sequence is to "add 2" to the previous number.

13. (2) 1234 ÷ 10 123 R 4

14. (2) 1234 ÷ 12 102 R 10

▶* **15.** (10) What is the sum of the first five even numbers greater than zero? 30

▶ **16.** (7) Connect How many millimeters long is the line segment below? 32 mm

mm 10 20 30 40

▶* **17.** (12) In the number 123,456,789,000, which digit is in the ten-billions place? 2

▶* **18.** (12) In the number 5,764,283,000, what is the place value of the digit 4? millions

* **19.** (12) Which digit is in the hundred-thousands place in the number 987,654,321? 6

▶ **20.** (5) 1 × 10 × 100 × 1000 1,000,000

21. (2) $3.75 × 3 $11.25

22. (4) $22y = 0$ 0

23. (3) 100 + 200 + 300 + 400 + w = 2000 1000

24. (2) 24 × 26 624

25. (4) $m\overline{)625}$ with quotient 25   25

26. (4) If the divisor is 4 and the quotient is 8, what is the dividend? 32

27. (2) Show three ways to write "27 divided by 3." $3\overline{)27}$, 27 ÷ 3, $\frac{27}{3}$

28. (6) Explain Seven of the ten marbles in a bag are red. So $\frac{7}{10}$ of the marbles are red. What fraction of the marbles are not red? Explain why your answer is correct. $\frac{3}{10}$; If 7 of the 10 marbles are red, then 3 of the 10 are not red.

▶* **29.** (12) Use digits to write four trillion. 4,000,000,000,000

* **30.** (12) Formulate Using different numbers, make up a question similar to example 5 in this lesson. Then find the answer. Answers will vary. See student work.

▶ See Math Conversations in the sidebar.

3 Written Practice (Continued)

Math Conversations

Discussion opportunities are provided below.

Problem 15 Generalize

Extend the Problem

Invite a volunteer to describe (or demonstrate at the board) how the numbers can be grouped in pairs having sums of 10. (2 + 8) + (4 + 6) + 10 = 10 + 10 + 10 = 30

Problem 16 Connect

Challenge students to estimate the length of the segment in centimeters. Accept reasonable estimates; the segment is about 3 centimeters long.

Problem 29 Generalize

When writing large numbers without the assistance of a place value chart, it is important for students to understand and apply these generalizations:

- 1 million has six zeros
- 1 billion has nine zeros
- 1 trillion has twelve zeros

Errors and Misconceptions

Problems 17 and 18

When working with whole number place values, students must recognize that every period includes ones, tens, and hundreds, and may include up to three digits. Using a place value chart and a variety of numbers, work with students to better understand our place value system and its relationships.

Problem 20

When using the multiplication algorithm with factors that are powers of 10, some students may lose or gain zeros during the computation. Demonstrate how such products can be checked by counting zeros.

Looking Forward

Solving multistep problems prepares students for:

- **Lesson 13,** solving problems involving comparing and elapsed time.
- **Lesson 15,** solving problems about equal groups with whole numbers.
- **Lesson 18,** finding the average of two or more numbers.
- **Investigation 11,** using scale drawings and models to find actual measurements.
- **Lesson 117,** finding a whole when a fraction is known.

• Problems About Comparing
• Elapsed-Time Problems

Objectives

- Identify the subtraction pattern in a story problem about comparing.
- Write an equation to solve a story problem about comparing.
- Identify the subtraction pattern in an elapsed-time problem.
- Write an equation to solve an elapsed-time problem.

Lesson Preparation

Materials

- **Power Up A** (in *Instructional Masters*)
- **Manipulative kit: rulers**

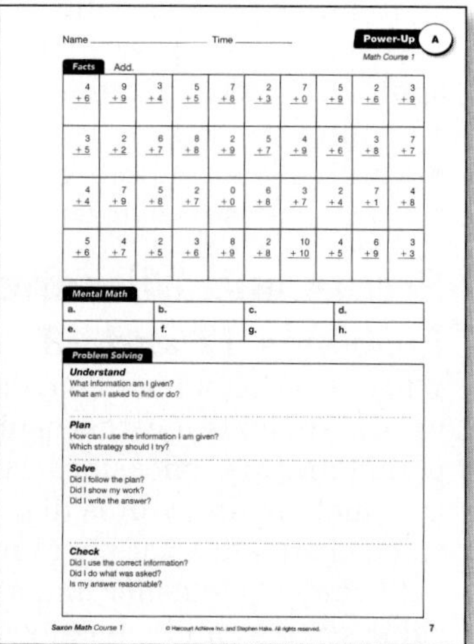

Power Up A

Math Language

English Learners (ESL)
elapsed-time

Technology Resources

Student eBook Complete student textbook in electronic format.

Resources and Planner CD Assessment, reteaching, and instructional masters, plus a pacing calendar with standards.

Test and Practice Generator CD Create additional practice sheets and custom-made tests.

www.SaxonPublishers.com Visit for more student activities and planning materials.

Inclusion

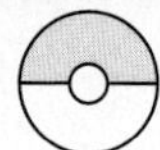

Adaptations CD Adapted lessons, investigations, practice and assessments.

Meeting Standards

National Council of Teachers of Mathematics (NCTM)

Algebra

AL.1b Relate and compare different forms of representation for a relationship

AL.2a Develop an initial conceptual understanding of different uses of variables

Problem Solving

PS.1b Solve problems that arise in mathematics and in other contexts

Connections

CN.4a Recognize and use connections among mathematical ideas

CN.4b Understand how mathematical ideas interconnect and build on one another to produce a coherent whole

Power-Up Discussion *For use with Power Up, p. 68*

Problem-Solving Strategy: Use Logical Reasoning

A pair of number cubes is tossed. The total number of dots on the two top faces is 6. What is the total of the dots on the bottom faces of the pair of number cubes?

Understand — *Understand the problem.*

"What information are we given?"

Two dot cubes are rolled, and the total number of dots on the top two faces is 6.

"What are we asked to do?"

We are asked to determine the total number of dots on the two bottom faces.

"What do we know about opposite faces of number cubes that will help us solve the problem?"

We know that the sum of the opposite faces of a dot cube always equals seven.

Plan — *Make a plan.*

"What problem-solving strategy will we use?"

We will *use logical reasoning* to determine the number of dots on the bottom two faces.

Solve — *Carry out the plan.*

"What is the total of the dots on the tops and bottoms of two number cubes?"

The dots on top and bottom of two cubes total 2×7, or 14.

"How many dots are we told can be seen on the top faces?"

We are told there are 6 dots showing on the top faces.

"How many total dots must be on the bottom two faces?"

There must be $14 - 6$, or 8 dots, on the bottom two faces.

"To solve the problem, did we need to know how many dots were showing on each of the two number cubes?"

No. The top faces could have shown combinations of 1 and 5, 2 and 4, or 3 and 3. For all three of these outcomes, the sum of the dots on the bottom faces equals 8.

Check — *Look back.*

"Did we complete the task?"

Yes. We determined the number of dots on the bottom faces of two dot cubes when the top faces total 6.

Alternate Approach: Act It Out

To help some students visualize the problem, you may wish to have dot cubes available. Students can verify the solution by recreating all three combinations of the top faces (1 and 5, 2 and 4, 3 and 3). For each combination, have students count the total dots shown on the bottom faces.

1 Power Up

Facts

Distribute **Power Up A** to students. See answers below.

Mental Math

Before students begin the Mental Math exercise, do this counting exercise as a class.

Count up and down by 25s between 25 and 1000.

Count up and down by 2s between 2 and 40.

Encourage students to share different ways to mentally compute these exercises. Strategies for exercises **b** and **e** are listed below.

b. Use a Fact
  5 × 3 = 15; 5 × 3 thousand = 15 thousand
 Count by 3000
  Start with 3000. Count: 6000, 9000, 12,000, 15,000

e. Count Back by 500
  Start with 4500. Count: 4000
 Decompose 4500
  4000 + 500 − 500 = 4000

Problem Solving

Refer to **Power-Up Discussion,** p. 68B.

2 New Concepts

Instruction

In this lesson, students use subtraction to compare two groups. In future lessons, they will study how division can be used to compare.

(continued)

LESSON 13

• Problems About Comparing
• Elapsed-Time Problems

Power Up — *Building Power*

facts Power Up A

mental math

a. **Number Sense:** 5 × 300 1500

b. **Number Sense:** 5 × 3000 15,000

c. **Number Sense:** $7.50 + $1.75 $9.25

d. **Number Sense:** 3600 + 230 3830

e. **Number Sense:** 4500 − 500 4000

f. **Number Sense:** $20.00 − $5.00 $15.00

g. **Measurement:** How many millimeters are in a meter? 1000 mm

h. **Measurement:** How many years are in a decade? 10 yrs.

problem solving A pair of number cubes is tossed. The total number of dots on the two top faces is 6. What is the total of the dots on the bottom faces of the pair of number cubes? 8

New Concepts — *Increasing Knowledge*

We practiced using patterns to solve word problems in Lesson 11. For problems about combining, we used an addition pattern. For problems about separating, we used a subtraction pattern. In this lesson we will look at two other kinds of math word problems.

problems about comparing

Some word problems are about **comparing** the size of two groups. They usually ask questions such as "How many more are in the first group" and "How many fewer are in the second group?" Comparison problems such as these have a **subtraction pattern.** We write the numbers in the equation in this order:

Greater − lesser = difference

In place of the words, we can use letters. We use the first letter of each word.

$$g - l = d$$

Example 1

There were 324 girls and 289 boys in the school. How many fewer boys than girls were there in the school?

Solution

Again we use the four-step process to solve the problem.

Facts Add.

4 + 6 10	9 + 9 18	3 + 4 7	5 + 5 10	7 + 8 15	2 + 3 5	7 + 0 7	5 + 9 14	2 + 6 8	3 + 9 12
3 + 5 8	2 + 2 4	6 + 7 13	8 + 8 16	2 + 9 11	5 + 7 12	4 + 9 13	6 + 6 12	3 + 8 11	7 + 7 14
4 + 4 8	7 + 9 16	5 + 8 13	2 + 7 9	0 + 0 0	6 + 8 14	3 + 7 10	2 + 4 6	7 + 1 8	4 + 8 12
5 + 6 11	4 + 7 11	2 + 5 7	3 + 6 9	8 + 9 17	2 + 8 10	10 + 10 20	4 + 5 9	6 + 9 15	3 + 3 6

68 *Saxon Math Course 1*

Step 1: We are asked to compare the number of boys to the number of girls. The question asks "how many fewer?" This problem has a **subtraction pattern.**

Step 2: We use the pattern to write an equation. There are more girls than boys, so the number of girls replaces "greater" and the number of boys replaces "lesser."

Pattern: Greater − lesser = difference

Equation: $324 - 289 = d$

Step 3: We find the missing number by subtracting.

324 girls
− 289 boys
35 fewer boys

Step 4: We review the question and write the answer. There were **35 fewer boys** than girls in the school. We can also state that there were 35 more girls than boys in the school.

Explain How can we check the answer? Sample: We can add 35 to the number of boys to see if the total equals the number of girls.

elapsed-time problems

Elapsed time is the length of time between two events. We illustrate this on the ray below.

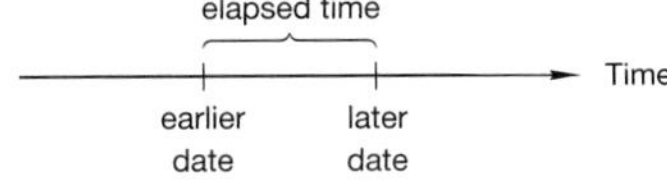

Thinking Skill

Verify

When you subtract your birth year from the current year, why don't you always get your exact age? If you have not yet had your birthday, the age calculated will be 1 year more than your actual age.

The time that has elapsed since the moment you were born until now is your age. Subtracting your birth date from today's date gives your age.

Today's date	(later)
− Your birth date	(earlier)
Your age	(difference)

Elapsed-time problems are like comparison problems. They have a **subtraction pattern.**

Later − earlier = difference

We use the first letter of each word to represent the word.

$$l - e = d$$

Example 2

How many years were there from the year Columbus landed in America in 1492 to the year the Pilgrims landed in 1620?

Solution

Step 1: This is an **elapsed-time** problem. It has a **subtraction pattern.** We use *l*, *e*, and *d* to stand for "later," "earlier," and "difference."

$$l - e = d$$

2 New Concepts (Continued)

Example 1

Instruction

Step 4: Remind students of the importance of checking their work.

"How can addition be used to check the answer?" Add 289 and 35, and then compare the sum to 324.

"How can subtraction be used to check the answer?" Subtract 35 from 324 and compare the difference to 289.

Instruction

After discussing the concept of elapsed time, challenge students to find their age in years by subtracting their birth year from the current year. For some students, this method will not give the correct age. Ask these students to explain why. If a birthday has not yet occurred this year, the method will not give the correct answer.

(continued)

Math Background

Finding elapsed time in years requires subtracting one number from another. When subtracting two numbers, the following patterns are always true.

even − even = even	even − odd = odd	odd − odd = even
6 − 2 = 4	8 − 1 = 7	9 − 3 = 6

An understanding of these patterns can give a student an expectation of the odd or even nature of a difference prior to performing a computation.

English Learners

Write the times 9:00 and 12:30 on the board. Say:

"I left my house at 9:00 and came home at 12:30. Three hours and 30 minutes elapsed, or passed, between the time I left and the time I came home."

Ask volunteers to give other examples of elapsed-time, such as time from the start of class to end of class, number of years living in one city, and so on. Sample: I lived in Houston from 1995 to 2001. During this time, six years elapsed.

2 New Concepts (Continued)

Example 3

Instruction

After completing the example, ask each student to write one story problem that involves comparing two numbers (such as example 1) or finding elapsed time (such as examples 2 and 3). Then invite volunteers to read their story problems aloud while the other students write, compare, and solve an equation for each problem.

Practice Set

Problems a and b Formulate

Remind students that one way to check an answer for reasonableness is to compare the answer to an estimate. For problems **a** and **b**, ask students to estimate each difference before solving the equations. After the equations have been solved, ask students to check their exact differences for reasonableness by comparing those differences to their estimates.

Step 2: The later year is 1620. The earlier year is 1492.

$$1620 - 1492 = d$$

Step 3: We find the missing number by subtracting. We can check the answer by adding.

$$\begin{array}{r} 1620 \\ -\ 1492 \\ \hline 128 \end{array} \quad \longrightarrow \quad \begin{array}{r} 1492 \\ +\ 128 \\ \hline 1620 \end{array}$$

Step 4: We review the question and write the answer. There were **128 years** from 1492 to 1620.

Example 3

Abraham Lincoln was born in 1809 and died in 1865. How many years did he live?

Solution

Step 1: This is an **elapsed-time** problem. It has a **subtraction pattern.** We use *l* for the later time, *e* for the earlier time, and *d* for the difference of the times.

$$l - e = d$$

Step 2: We write an equation using 1809 for the earlier year and 1865 for the later year.

$$1865 - 1809 = d$$

Step 3: We find the missing number by subtracting. We may add his age to the year of his birth to check the answer.

$$\begin{array}{r} 1865 \\ -\ 1809 \\ \hline 56 \end{array} \quad \longrightarrow \quad \begin{array}{r} 1809 \\ +\ 56 \\ \hline 1865 \end{array}$$

We also note that 56 is a reasonable age, so our computation makes sense.

Step 4: We review the question and write the answer. Abraham Lincoln lived **56 years.**

Practice Set

Formulate Follow the four-step method to solve each problem. Along with each answer, include the equation you use to solve the problem.

▶ **a.** The population of Castor is 26,290. The population of Weston is 18,962. How many more people live in Castor than live in Weston?
7328 people; 26,290 − 18,962 = *d*

▶ **b.** Two important dates in British history are the Norman Conquest in 1066 and the signing of the Magna Carta in 1215, which limited the power of the king. How many years were there from 1066 to 1215?
149 years; 1215 − 1066 = *d*

▶ See Math Conversations in the sidebar.

Written Practice *Strengthening Concepts*

* **1.** (12) When the sum of 8 and 5 is subtracted from the product of 8 and 5, what is the difference? 27

▶ * **2.** (12) The Moon is about two hundred fifty thousand miles from the Earth. Use digits to write that distance. 250,000 miles

▶ * **3.** (12) Use words to write 521,000,000,000. five hundred twenty-one billion

▶ * **4.** (12) Use digits to write five million, two hundred thousand. 5,200,000

5. (2) **Explain** Robin entered a tennis tournament when she was three-score years old. How old was Robin when she entered the tournament? How do you know your answer is correct? (Recall that one score equals 20 years.) 60 years; A score is 20, so three score is three 20s which is 60.

* **6.** (11) The auditorium at the Community Cultural Center has seats for 1000 people. For a symphony concert at the center, 487 tickets have already been sold. How many more tickets are still available? Write an equation and solve the problem. $1000 - 487 = T$; 513 tickets

▶ * **7.** (13) **Formulate** It is 405 miles from Minneapolis, Minnesota to Chicago, Illinois. It is 692 miles from Minneapolis to Cincinnati, Ohio. Cincinnati is how many miles farther from Minneapolis than Chicago? Write an equation and solve the problem. $d = 692 - 405$; 287 miles

Justify Use mental math to solve exercises **8** and **9.** Describe the mental math strategy you used for each exercise. See student work for descriptions.

8. (1) $99 + 100 + 101$ 300

9. (5) $9 \times 10 \times 11$ 990

* **10.** (12) Which digit is in the thousands place in 54,321? 4

* **11.** (12) What is the place value of the 1 in 1,234,567,890? billions

12. (8) The three sides of an equilateral triangle are equal in length. What is the perimeter of the equilateral triangle shown? 54 mm

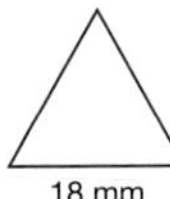

13. (2) $5432 \div 100$ 54 R 32

14. (2) $\frac{60,000}{30}$ 2000

15. (2) $1000 \div 7$ 142 R 6

16. (2) $\$4.56 \div 3$ \$1.52

17. (9) Compare: $3 + 2 + 1 + 0 \; (>) \; 3 \times 2 \times 1 \times 0$

▶* **18.** (10) **Predict** The rule for the sequence below is different from the rules for addition sequences or multiplication sequences. What is the next number in the sequence?

1, 4, 3, 6, 5, 8, __7__, ...

▶ See Math Conversations in the sidebar.

3 Written Practice

Math Conversations

Discussion opportunities are provided below.

Problem 2 Estimate

Extend the Problem

"About what fraction of one million miles is that distance?" about $\frac{1}{4}$

Problem 7 Formulate

Read the problem aloud or invite a volunteer to read the problem aloud.

"What operation is used to find the answer—addition or subtraction? Tell why." Sample: Subtraction; since distances are being compared, the lesser distance is subtracted from the greater.

Problem 18 Predict

Before completing the problem, ask students to discuss the pattern and identify its rule.

Errors and Misconceptions

Problem 3

Remind students that commas are used to separate whole numbers into periods.

Work with students to identify the periods, and the names of the periods, in the given number. If necessary, ask students to refer to a place value chart or display one for them.

Problem 4

If students struggle writing the word name in standard form, ask them to name the number of zeros in 1 million. six

Continue by asking them to write 5 million, and then write 5 million and 200,000 more. 5,000,000; 5,200,000

(continued)

3 Written Practice (Continued)

Math Conversations

Discussion opportunities are provided below.

Problem 19 Generalize

Challenge students to describe a variety of ways to divide 5280 by 2 using mental math. Sample: Divide 5200 by 2, divide 80 by 2, and then add the quotients; divide thousands, hundreds, and tens each by 2, and then add the quotients.

Problem 22 Connect

Extend the Problem

Extend the problem by asking students to measure the width of the rectangle, and then determine its perimeter by writing and solving an equation. Equations may vary; $P = 2(1\frac{3}{4}) + 2(\frac{3}{4}) = 3\frac{1}{2} + 1\frac{1}{2} = 5$ in.

Challenge students to explain how the equation $P = 2(2\frac{1}{2})$ represents the perimeter of the rectangle.

Problems 27–30 Analyze

For each problem, ask students to name an operation and describe how that operation could be used to check the answer. Sample:
Problem 27: multiply 102 by 8
Problem 28: divide 48 by 12 or by 4
Problem 29: multiply 4 by 3
Problem 30: subtract 61 or 16 from 77

▶ **19.** (6) Generalize What is $\frac{1}{2}$ of 5280? 2640

20. (4) $365 \div w = 365$ 1

21. (5) $(5 + 6 + 7) \div 3$ 6

▶ **22.** (7) Use a ruler to find the length in inches of the rectangle below. $1\frac{3}{4}$ in.

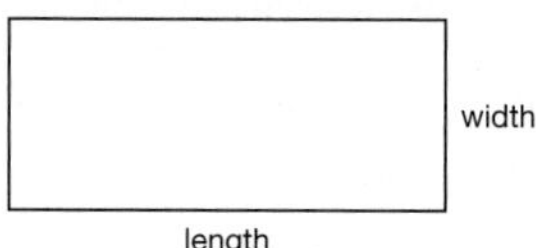

23. (8) Explain Write two ways to find the perimeter of a square: one way by adding and the other way by multiplying.

23. To find the perimeter of a square, either add the lengths of the four sides or multiply the length of one side by four.

24. (2) Multiply to find the answer to this addition problem: $125 \times 6 = 750$

125 + 125 + 125 + 125 + 125 + 125

25. (10) At what temperature on the Fahrenheit scale does water boil? 212°F

26. (2) Show three ways to write "21 divided by 7." $7\overline{)21}$, $21 \div 7$, $\frac{21}{7}$

▶ Analyze Find each unknown number. Check your work.

27. (4) $8a = 816$ 102

28. (4) $\frac{b}{4} = 12$ 48

29. (4) $\frac{12}{c} = 4$ 3

30. (3) $d - 16 = 61$ 77

▶ See Math Conversations in the sidebar.

Looking Forward

Writing and solving an equation for a story problem about comparing prepares students for:

- **Lesson 15,** solving story problems about equal groups.
- **Lesson 16,** estimating answers when reading graphs.
- **Lesson 18,** using line graphs to find measurement changes over time.
- **Lesson 36,** relating the subtraction of fractions and mixed numbers from whole numbers to a subtraction pattern.
- **Lesson 48,** relating the subtraction of mixed numbers with regrouping to a subtraction pattern.

• The Number Line: Negative Numbers

Objectives

- Use a number line to order and compare integers.
- Identify numbers that are opposites.
- Use a number line to subtract a larger number from a smaller number.

Lesson Preparation

Materials

- **Power Up D** (in *Instructional Masters*)
- **Lesson Activity 1 Transparency** (in *Instructional Masters*)
- **Manipulative kit: rulers**
- **Calculators**

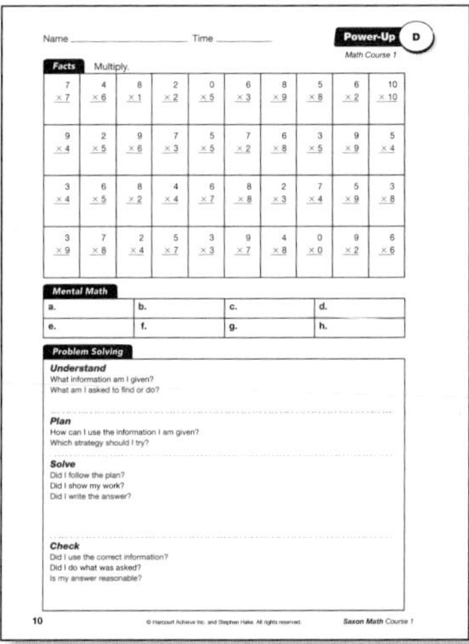

Name ____________ Time ________ **Power-Up D** *Math Course 1*

Facts Multiply.

7 × 7	4 × 6	8 × 1	2 × 2	0 × 5	6 × 3	8 × 9	5 × 8	6 × 2	10 × 10
9 × 4	2 × 5	9 × 6	7 × 3	5 × 5	7 × 2	6 × 8	3 × 5	9 × 9	5 × 4
3 × 4	6 × 5	8 × 2	4 × 4	6 × 7	8 × 8	2 × 3	7 × 4	5 × 9	3 × 8
3 × 9	7 × 8	2 × 4	5 × 7	3 × 3	9 × 7	4 × 8	0 × 0	9 × 2	6 × 6

Mental Math

a.	b.	c.	d.
e.	f.	g.	h.

Problem Solving

Understand
What information am I given?
What am I asked to find or do?

Plan
How can I use the information I am given?
Which strategy should I try?

Solve
Did I follow the plan?
Did I show my work?
Did I write the answer?

Check
Did I use the correct information?
Did I do what was asked?
Is my answer reasonable?

10 *Saxon Math Course 1*

Power Up D

Math Language

New	Maintain	English Learners (ESL)
integers	negative numbers	express
opposites		
positive numbers		

Technology Resources

Student eBook Complete student textbook in electronic format.

Resources and Planner CD Assessment, reteaching, and instructional masters, plus a pacing calendar with standards.

Test and Practice Generator CD Create additional practice sheets and custom-made tests.

www.SaxonPublishers.com Visit for more student activities and planning materials.

Inclusion

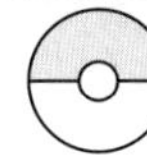

Adaptations CD Adapted lessons, investigations, practice and assessments.

Meeting Standards

National Council of Teachers of Mathematics (NCTM)

Numbers and Operations

NO.1g Develop meaning for integers and represent and compare quantities with them

NO.2a Understand the meaning and effects of arithmetic operations with fractions, decimals, and integers

Algebra

AL.1b Relate and compare different forms of representation for a relationship

Representation

RE.5b Select, apply, and translate among mathematical representations to solve problems

Power-Up Discussion *For use with Power Up, p. 73*

Problem-Solving Strategy: Draw a Diagram/ Make a Table

It takes the local hardware store 8 seconds to cut through a piece of round galvanized steel pipe. How long will it take to cut a piece of pipe in half? Into quarters? Into six pieces? (Each cut must be perpendicular to the length of the pipe.)

Understand Understand the problem.

"What information are we given?"

Each cut a local hardware store makes through a piece of pipe takes 8 seconds.

"What are we asked to do?"

We are asked to determine the time needed to cut a pipe into 2, 4, and 6 pieces.

"What prior knowledge do we bring to this problem?"

To cut something in half means to cut it into 2 pieces. To cut into quarters means to cut into four pieces.

"With the information provided, would we also be able to solve for 3 and 5 pieces?"

Yes. First we have to determine the number of cuts.

Plan Make a plan.

"What problem-solving strategies could we use?"

We will *draw a diagram* and *make a table* of the number of pieces that result and the accumulated time each time we make a "cut."

Solve Carry out the plan.

"How do we begin?"

We will draw our diagram of the pipe and set up our table.

"How do we proceed?"

By making our "cuts" and filling in the table to find the time.

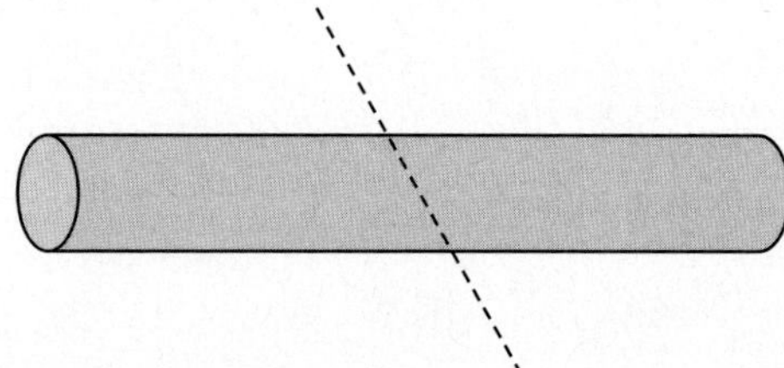

# of Cuts	# of Pieces	Time
0	1	0 sec
1	2	8 sec
2	3	16 sec
3	4	24 sec
4	5	32 sec
5	6	40 sec
6	7	48 sec

It takes one less cut than the number of pieces we need.
Therefore, for two pieces it will take 8 seconds for the 1 cut we will need.
For 4 pieces we need 3 cuts for a total of 24 seconds. For 6 pieces we need 5 cuts for 40 seconds.

Check Look back.

"Did we do what we were asked to do?"

Yes, we found the amount of time it would take to cut a piece of pipe into two, four, and six pieces.

"How could we relate this problem to the use of a ruler?"

When we measure with a ruler, we are counting *intervals*, not the lines that mark the increments.

LESSON 14

The Number Line: Negative Numbers

Power Up *Building Power*

facts Power Up D

mental math

a. **Number Sense:** 8 × 400 3200

b. **Number Sense:** 6 × 3000 18,000

c. **Number Sense:** $7.50 + $7.50 $15.00

d. **Number Sense:** 360 + 230 590

e. **Number Sense:** 1250 − 1000 250

f. **Number Sense:** $10.00 − $7.50 $2.50

g. **Measurement:** How many years are in a century? 100 yrs.

h. **Calculation:** Start with 10. Add 2; divide by 3; multiply by 4; then subtract 5. What is the answer? 11

problem solving It takes the local hardware store 8 seconds to cut through a piece of round galvanized steel pipe. How long will it take to cut a piece of pipe in half? Into quarters? Into six pieces? (Each cut must be perpendicular to the length of the pipe.) 8 seconds; 24 seconds; 40 seconds

New Concept *Increasing Knowledge*

We have seen that a number line can be used to arrange numbers in order.

−5 −4 −3 −2 −1 0 1 2 3 4 5

On the number line above, the points to the right of zero represent **positive numbers.** The points to the left of zero represent negative numbers. Zero is neither positive nor negative.

Reading Math
Negative numbers are represented by writing a minus sign before a number: −5.

Negative numbers are used in various ways. A temperature of five degrees below zero Fahrenheit may be written as −5°F. An elevation of 100 feet below sea level may be indicated as "elev. −100 ft." The change in a stock's price from $23.00 to $21.50 may be shown in a newspaper as −1.50.

Example 1

Arrange these numbers in order from least to greatest:

0, 1, −2

Facts Multiply.

7 × 7 = 49	4 × 6 = 24	8 × 1 = 8	2 × 2 = 4	0 × 5 = 0	6 × 3 = 18	8 × 9 = 72	5 × 8 = 40	6 × 2 = 12	10 × 10 = 100
9 × 4 = 36	2 × 5 = 10	9 × 6 = 54	7 × 3 = 21	5 × 5 = 25	7 × 2 = 14	6 × 8 = 48	3 × 5 = 15	9 × 9 = 81	5 × 4 = 20
3 × 4 = 12	6 × 5 = 30	8 × 2 = 16	4 × 4 = 16	6 × 7 = 42	8 × 8 = 64	2 × 3 = 6	7 × 4 = 28	5 × 9 = 45	3 × 8 = 24
3 × 9 = 27	7 × 8 = 56	2 × 4 = 8	5 × 7 = 35	3 × 3 = 9	9 × 7 = 63	4 × 8 = 32	0 × 0 = 0	9 × 2 = 18	6 × 6 = 36

1 Power Up

Facts

Distribute **Power Up D** to students. See answers below.

Mental Math

Before students begin the Mental Math exercise, do this counting exercise as a class.

Count up and down by $\frac{1}{4}$s between $\frac{1}{4}$ and 6.

Encourage students to share different ways to mentally compute these exercises. Strategies for exercises **b** and **d** are listed below.

b. Use a Fact
6 × 3 = 18; 6 × 3 thousand = 18 thousand
Count by 3000
Start with 3000. Count: 6000, 9000, 12,000, 15,000, 18,000

d. Add Hundreds, then Add Tens
300 + 60 + 200 + 30 = 500 + 90 = 590
Decompose 230
360 + 200 + 30 = 560 + 30 = 590

Problem Solving

Refer to **Power-Up Discussion,** p. 73B.

2 New Concepts

Instruction

Display the transparency of **Lesson Activity 1** Number Lines. Ask students to copy the number line from the transparency or from the first page of the lesson on a separate piece of paper. Have students refer to the number line as they complete the examples and the problems throughout this lesson.

Example 1

Instruction

Suggest that students first place the numbers on the number line.

(continued)

2 New Concepts (Continued)

Example 2

Instruction

Reinforce the solution and its explanation by asking students to use the number line they copied to compare −3 and −4.

"Place a mark on your number line at −3 and place a mark at −4. Which number is greater, −3 or −4? Why?" −3; −3 is to the right of −4, and when using a number line to compare numbers, numbers increase in value as we move from left to right, and numbers decrease in value as we move from right to left.

Instruction

Give students examples of negative numbers in the real world. Write −5°C, −2 points, −4 yards on the board.

"These are examples of negative numbers in the real world. For example, we write −5 degrees Celsius to indicate a temperature of five degrees below zero on a Celsius thermometer. A deduction of two points on a quiz can be shown as −2 points, or a loss of four yards on a football play can be shown as −4 yards. What other examples of negative numbers in the real world can you name?" Examples will vary.

(continued)

Solution

All negative numbers are less than zero. All positive numbers are greater than zero.

−2, 0, 1

Visit www.SaxonPublishers.com/ActivitiesC1 *for a graphing calculator activity.*

Example 2

Compare: −3 ◯ −4

Solution

Negative three is three less than zero, and negative four is four less than zero. So

−3 > −4

Math Language

Zero is neither positive nor negative. Zero has no opposite.

The number −5 is read "negative five." Notice that the points on the number line marked 5 and −5 are the same distance from zero but are on opposite sides of zero. We say that 5 and −5 are **opposites.** Other opposite pairs include −2 and 2, −3 and 3, and −4 and 4. The tick marks show the location of numbers called **integers.** Integers include all of the counting numbers and their opposites, as well as the number zero.

If you subtract a larger number from a smaller number (for example, 2 − 3), the answer will be a negative number. One way to find the answer to such questions is to use the number line. We start at 2 and count back (to the left) three integers. Maybe you can figure out a faster way to find the answer.

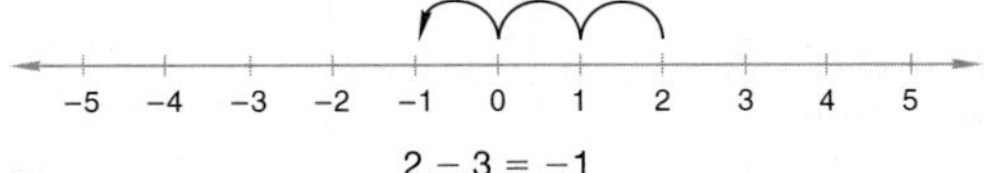

Example 3

Subtract 5 from 2.

Solution

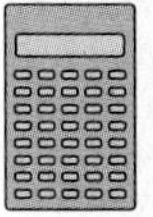

Order matters in subtraction. Start at 2 and count to the left 5 integers. You should end up at **−3.** Try this problem with a calculator by entering 2 − 5 =. What number is displayed after the = is pressed?

We see that the calculator displays -3 as the solution.

Example 4

Arrange these four numbers in order from least to greatest:

1, −2, 0, −1

Math Background

The number lines in this lesson are integer number lines. The set of integers consists of positive whole numbers and their opposites and zero. Because integers extend without end to the left and to the right of zero on the number line, the set of integers is infinite.

Solution

A number line shows numbers in order. By arranging these numbers in the order they appear on a number line, we arrange them in order from least to greatest.

−2, −1, 0, 1

Example 5

What number is 7 less than 3?

Solution

The phrase "7 less than 3" means to start with 3 and subtract 7.

3 − 7

We count to the left 7 integers from 3. The answer is **−4.**

Practice Set

▸ **a.** Compare: −8 ⊘ −6

b. Use words to write this number: −8. negative eight

c. What number is the opposite of 3? −3

▸ **d.** Arrange these numbers in order from least to greatest: −3, −1, 0, 2

0, −1, 2, −3

e. What number is 5 less than 0? −5

▸ **f.** What number is 10 less than 5? −5

g. 5 − 8 −3

h. 1 − 5 −4

▸ **i.** Verify All five of the numbers below are integers. True or false? true

−3, 0, 2, −10, 50

j. The temperature was twelve degrees below zero Fahrenheit. Use a negative number to write the temperature. −12°F

k. The desert floor was 186 feet below sea level. Use a negative number to indicate that elevation. −186 ft

l. The stock's price dropped from $18.50 to $16.25. Use a negative number to express the change in the stock's value. −2.25 or −$2.25

Written Practice *Strengthening Concepts*

▸ * **1.** (12) Connect What is the quotient when the sum of 15 and 12 is divided by the difference of 15 and 12? 9

* **2.** (12) What is the place value of the 7 in 987,654,321,000? billions

▸ See Math Conversations in the sidebar.

English Learners

Write the word ***express*** on the board. Say:

"One meaning of the word express is 'to show'."

Write the following on the board:

two and one-fifth $2\frac{1}{5}$ 2.2

"We can express the quantity two and one-fifth in these three ways."

Then say:

"How can we express the quantity '6 feet below sea level'?" −6

"In problem l, we need to express the answer as a negative number. What symbol do we use to express a negative number?" a − symbol

2 New Concepts (Continued)

Example 4

Instruction

If help is needed ordering the integers, ask students to place a mark on their number lines for each integer.

Practice Set

Problem a Error Alert

Watch for students who compare the numbers as if they are positive numbers. Have students note the negative sign that accompanies each number in the problem.

Problem d Error Alert

Ask students who struggle ordering the numbers to arrange them on a number line. Work with the students, using other examples if necessary, to generalize that on a number line, left is less and right is greater.

Problem f Explain

Invite a volunteer to draw a number line on the board or overhead and then demonstrate how to count back by ones to find the number that is 10 less than 5.

Problem i Verify

Have students define the set of integers using their own words. The set of integers consists of positive whole numbers, their opposites, and zero.

3 Written Practice

Math Conversations

Discussion opportunities are provided below.

Problem 1 Connect

Invite several students to write on the board or overhead a single expression to represent the information. Then discuss with students why the expressions are correct and/or identify the changes that must be made to make them correct. Samples: $(15 + 12) \div (15 - 12)$; $\frac{15 + 12}{15 - 12}$

(continued)

3 Written Practice (Continued)

Math Conversations

Discussion opportunities are provided below.

Problem 5 Connect

Have students who need assistance completing the problem use the number lines they drew at the beginning of the lesson. The given integers should be arranged on the number lines, and then compared.

"On a number line, how do the numbers change as you move from left to right?" the numbers increase or become bigger

"How do the numbers change as you move from right to left?" the numbers decrease or become smaller

Problem 6 Generalize

Invite a volunteer to demonstrate on a board or overhead number line how to use a combination of counting back and counting on to find the number.

Problem 12 Justify

Encourage a student who names -2 as the answer to use a number line at the board or overhead to show why -2 is correct.

Problem 20 Estimate

Extend the Problem

"One inch is about $2\frac{1}{2}$ centimeters. About how long is the nail in inches?" Accept reasonable estimates; the nail is about $1\frac{1}{2}$ inches long.

Errors and Misconceptions

Problem 18

Remind students who answer incorrectly that they can multiply by 10 last because the Associative Property of Multiplication allows the factors to be grouped in a different way.

Problem 22

Use a place value chart to remediate incorrect answers. When using the chart, remind students that every period contains ones, tens, and hundreds, and may contain up to three digits.

(continued)

* **3.** (12) Light travels at a speed of about one hundred eighty-six thousand miles per second. Use digits to write that speed. 186,000 miles per second

* **4.** (14) Connect What number is three integers to the left of 2 on the number line? -1

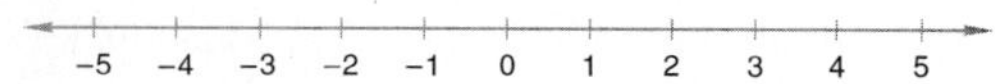

▶ * **5.** (14) Connect Arrange these numbers in order from least to greatest: $-3, -2, 0, 1, 5$

5, −3, 1, 0, −2

▶ * **6.** (14) What number is halfway between -4 and 0 on the number line? -2

* **7.** (11) Formulate There are 140 sixth-grade students in the school. Seventy-two play on school sports teams. How many are not on school sports teams? Write an equation and solve the problem.
$140 - 72 = a$; 68 students

8. (9) Compare: $1 + 2 + 3 + 4 \; ⓒ\!< \; 1 \times 2 \times 3 \times 4$

9. (8) What is the perimeter of this right triangle? 60 mm

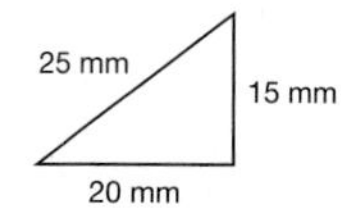

10. (10) Predict What are the next two numbers in the following sequence?

..., 16, 8, 4, __2__, __1__, ...

* **11.** (13) Formulate There are 365 days in a common year. How much less than 500 is 365? Write an equation and solve the problem.
$500 - 365 = d$;135

▶* **12.** (14) What number is 8 less than 6? -2

13. (2) $1020 \div 100$ 10 R 20

14. (2) $\frac{36{,}180}{12}$ 3015

15. (2) $18\overline{)564}$ 31 R 6

16. (1) $1234 + 567 + 89$ 1890

17. (3) $n - 310 = 186$ 496

▶ **18.** (5) $10 \cdot 11 \cdot 12$ 1320

19. (3) $\$3.05 - m = \$2.98$ $0.07

▶ **20.** (7) Estimate About how long is this nail in centimeters? Use a centimeter ruler to find its length to the nearest centimeter and to the nearest millimeter. 4 cm; 40 mm

21. (5) (100)(100)(100) 1,000,000

▶ **22.** (12) What digit in 123,456,789 is in the ten-thousands place? 5

23. (7) Verify If you know the length of an object in centimeters, how can you figure out the length of the object in millimeters without remeasuring?

24. (2) Connect Use the numbers 19, 21, and 399 to write two multiplication facts and two division facts.

23. To find the length of the object in millimeters, multiply its length in centimeters by 10.

24. $19 \times 21 = 399$, $21 \times 19 = 399$, $399 \div 19 = 21$, $399 \div 21 = 19$

▶ See Math Conversations in the sidebar.

25. Compare: $12 \div 6 \times 2 \bigcirc\!\!\!> 12 \div (6 \times 2)$
(9)

26. Show three ways to write "60 divided by 6." $6\overline{)60}$, $60 \div 6$, $\frac{60}{6}$
(2)

* 27. In January, 2005, the world's population was about six billion, four hundred million people. Use digits to write this number of people. 6,400,000,000
(12)

28. One third of the 12 eggs in the carton were cracked. How many eggs were cracked? 4 eggs
(6)

▶* 29. What number is the opposite of 10? −10
(14)

▶* 30. Arrange these numbers in order from least to greatest: $-1, 0, \frac{1}{2}, 1$
(14)
$1, 0, -1, \frac{1}{2}$

Early Finishers
Real-World Application

At dawn the temperature was 42°F. By 5:00 p.m. the temperature had risen 33°F to its highest value for the day. Between 5:00 p.m. and dusk the temperature fell 12°F.

a. What was the temperature at dusk? 63°F

b. A cold front passes through during the night causing the temperature to drop 32°F just before dawn. What is the temperature at that time? 31°F

▶ See Math Conversations in the sidebar.

3 Written Practice (Continued)

Math Conversations

Discussion opportunities are provided below.

Problem 29 Justify

Invite a volunteer who names −10 as the answer to use a number line at the board or overhead to show why −10 is correct. Sample explanation: On a number line, −10 and 10 are each the same distance from zero, but in opposite directions.

Errors and Misconceptions

Problem 30

Watch for students who assume that $\frac{1}{2}$ is less than −1 because $\frac{1}{2}$ is a fraction. To disprove this assumption, ask those students to arrange the given numbers on a number line.

Looking Forward

Using a number line to order, compare, show opposites, and subtract larger numbers from smaller numbers prepares students for:

- **Lesson 17,** finding positive and negative fractions and mixed numbers.
- **Lesson 50,** locating and identifying tenths on a decimal number line.
- **Lesson 100,** using algebraic addition to solve subtraction problems.
- **Lesson 104,** adding signed numbers.
- **Lesson 112,** multiplying and dividing.

• Problems About Equal Groups

Objectives

- Identify the pattern in a word problem about equal groups.
- Write an equation to solve a word problem about equal groups.

Lesson Preparation

Materials

- **Power Up C** (in *Instructional Masters*)

Optional

- **Teacher-provided material: grid paper**

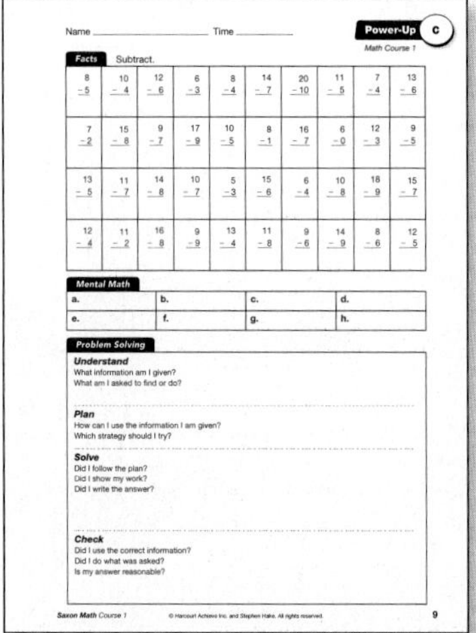

Power Up C

Math Language

Maintain	English Learners (ESL)
equation	abbreviation
factor	
unknown	

Technology Resources

Student eBook Complete student textbook in electronic format.

Resources and Planner CD Assessment, reteaching, and instructional masters, plus a pacing calendar with standards.

Test and Practice Generator CD Create additional practice sheets and custom-made tests.

www.SaxonPublishers.com Visit for more student activities and planning materials.

Inclusion

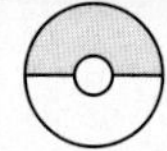

Adaptations CD Adapted lessons, investigations, practice and assessments.

Meeting Standards

National Council of Teachers of Mathematics (NCTM)

Algebra

AL.1b Relate and compare different forms of representation for a relationship

Problem Solving

PS.1c Apply and adapt a variety of appropriate strategies to solve problems

Connections

CN.4c Recognize and apply mathematics in contexts outside of mathematics

Power-Up Discussion *For use with Power Up, p. 78*

Problem-Solving Strategy: Work Backwards/ Use Logical Reasoning

Copy this subtraction problem and fill in the missing digits:

$$\begin{array}{r} 4\_7 \\ -\ \_9\_ \\ \hline 21 \end{array}$$

Understand — Understand the problem.

"What information are we given?"

We are shown a subtraction problem with missing digits in the minuend and the difference.

"What are we asked to do?"

We are asked to find the missing digits.

"What knowledge do we already have that we can use to solve this problem?"

We can use our basic addition and subtraction skills.

Plan — Make a plan.

"What problem-solving strategy will we use?"

We will *work backwards* using the information we have been given and *use logical reasoning* to determine the missing digits.

Solve — Carry out the plan.

"Basic number sense tells us that what number is in the ones place of the difference?"

The missing digit is 6 because $7 - 1 = 6$.

"How can we work backwards to find the missing digit in the tens place?"

We know 2 plus 9 equals 11. Using this information, we put a 1 in the tens place of the minuend. We understand and will remember that there was regrouping from the 4 in the hundreds place.

"What does logical reasoning tell us the missing digit in the hundreds place is?"

In the previous step, we added up in the tens column and got 11. Since we know that 2 cannot be subtracted from 1, we realize the 4 in the hundreds column must have been reduced to 3 during regrouping. The only way for the subtraction answer to have no digit in the hundreds place is for the missing hundreds digit to be 3.

$$\begin{array}{r} 417 \\ -\ 396 \\ \hline 21 \end{array}$$

Check — Look back.

"How can we verify the solution is correct?"

We can use addition (the inverse operation of substraction) to check the answer: $396 + 21 = 417$.

1 Power Up

Facts

Distribute **Power Up C** to students. See answers below.

Mental Math

Before students begin the Mental Math exercise, do this counting exercise as a class.

Count up and down by $\frac{1}{4}$s between $\frac{1}{4}$ and 10.

Encourage students to share different ways to mentally compute these exercises. Strategies for exercises **a** and **d** are listed below.

a. Use a Fact

$7 \times 4 = 28$; 7×4 thousand $= 28$ thousand

Count on by 7000

Start with 7000. Count: 14,000, 21,000, 28,000

d. Add from Left to Right

$80 + 12 = 92$

Decompose 12

$80 + 10 + 2 = 90 + 2 = 92$

Problem Solving

Refer to **Power-Up Discussion,** p. 78B.

2 New Concepts

Instruction

Students who have difficulty visualizing the arrangement of chairs may benefit from looking at a 15 by 20 rectangle drawn on grid paper, and assuming that each unit square in the rectangle represents one chair.

(continued)

LESSON 15

• Problems About Equal Groups

Power Up — *Building Power*

facts Power Up C

mental math

a. **Number Sense:** 7×4000 28,000

b. **Number Sense:** 8×300 2400

c. **Number Sense:** \$12.50 + \$12.50 \$25.00

d. **Number Sense:** $80 + 12$ 92

e. **Number Sense:** $6250 - 150$ 6100

f. **Number Sense:** \$20.00 − \$2.50 \$17.50

g. **Measurement:** How many decades are in a century? 10 decades

h. **Calculation:** Start with a dozen. Subtract 3; divide by 3; subtract 3; then multiply by 3. What is the answer? 0

problem solving

Copy this subtraction problem and fill in the missing digits:

$$\begin{array}{r} 4\_7 \\ -\ \_9\_ \\ \hline 21 \end{array} \qquad \begin{array}{r} 417 \\ -\ 396 \\ \hline 21 \end{array}$$

New Concept — *Increasing Knowledge*

We have studied several types of mathematical word problems. Problems about combining have an addition pattern. Problems about separating, comparing, and elapsed-time have subtraction patterns. Another type of mathematical problem is the **equal groups** problem. Here is an example:

In the auditorium there were 15 rows of chairs with 20 chairs in each row. Altogether, there were 300 chairs in the auditorium.

The chairs were arranged in 15 groups (rows) with 20 chairs in each group. Here is how we write the pattern:

15 rows × 20 chairs in each row = 300 chairs

Number of groups × number in group = total

$$n \times g = t$$

In a problem about equal groups, any one of the numbers might be unknown. We multiply to find the **unknown** total. We divide to find an unknown **factor.**

Facts Subtract.

8 − 5 3	10 − 4 6	12 − 6 6	6 − 3 3	8 − 4 4	14 − 7 7	20 − 10 10	11 − 5 6	7 − 4 3	13 − 6 7
7 − 2 5	15 − 8 7	9 − 7 2	17 − 9 8	10 − 5 5	8 − 1 7	16 − 7 9	6 − 0 6	12 − 3 9	9 − 5 4
13 − 5 8	11 − 7 4	14 − 8 6	10 − 7 3	5 − 3 2	15 − 6 9	6 − 4 2	10 − 8 2	18 − 9 9	15 − 7 8
12 − 4 8	11 − 2 9	16 − 8 8	9 − 9 0	13 − 4 9	11 − 8 3	9 − 6 3	14 − 9 5	8 − 6 2	12 − 5 7

Example

At Russell Middle School there were 232 seventh-grade students in 8 classrooms. If there were the same number of students in each classroom, how many students would be in each seventh-grade classroom at Russell Middle School?

Solution

Step 1: A number of students is divided into equal groups (classrooms). This is a problem about **equal groups.** The words *in each* often appear in "equal groups" problems.

Step 2: We draw the pattern and record the numbers, writing a letter in place of the unknown number.

Pattern	Equation
Number in each group	n in each classroom
× Number of groups	× 8 classrooms
Number in all groups	232 in all classrooms

Step 3: We find the unknown factor by dividing. Then we check our work.

$$8\overline{)232} = 29 \qquad \begin{array}{r} 29 \\ \times\ 8 \\ \hline 232 \end{array}$$

Step 4: We review the question and write the answer. If there were the same number of students in each classroom, there would be **29 students** in each seventh-grade classroom at Russell Middle School.

Practice Set

Reading Math
Sometimes it is helpful to write dollars and cents in cents-only form.

Formulate Follow the four-step method to solve each problem. Along with each answer, include the equation you use to solve the problem.

▶ **a.** Marcie collected $4.50 selling lemonade at 25¢ for each cup. How many cups of lemonade did Marcie sell? (*Hint:* Record $4.50 as 450¢.) 18 cups; $n \times 25¢ = 450¢$

▶ **b.** In the store parking lot there were 18 parking spaces in each row, and there were 12 rows of parking spaces. Altogether, how many parking spaces were in the parking lot? 216 parking spaces; $18 \times 12 = t$

Written Practice *Strengthening Concepts*

▶ * **1.** (15) Formulate The second paragraph of this lesson contains an "equal groups" situation. Write a word problem by removing one of the numbers in the problem and writing an "equal groups" question. Answers will vary. See student work.

* **2.** (13) Explain On the Fahrenheit scale, water freezes at 32°F and boils at 212°F. How many degrees difference is there between the freezing and boiling points of water? Write an equation and solve the problem. Explain why your answer is reasonable. $212° - 32° = d$; 180°F; See student work.

▶ See Math Conversations in the sidebar.

2 New Concepts (Continued)

Example

Instruction

Step 1: Have students note that the words such as *in each* often appear in problems about equal groups.

Step 3: Point out the connection of inverse operations to this problem.

"Why is division used to find the missing factor?" In the equation $8n = 232$, the expression $8n$ represents the product of two factors. To solve for the unknown factor, use division, the inverse operation of multiplication.

Practice Set

Problem a Formulate

Invite students to describe a variety of ways to find the answer using mental math. Sample: Every dollar earned represents 4 cups and fifty cents represents 2 cups; $4 + 4 + 4 + 4 + 2 = 18$.

Problem b Error Alert

Watch for students who multiply 12 and 18 incorrectly. Frequently remind students of the importance of checking their work.

3 Written Practice

Math Conversations

Discussion opportunities are provided below.

Problem 1 Formulate

Give students an opportunity to share the problems they wrote and their solutions with each other.

(continued)

Inclusion

A method used to solve proportion problems can also help students organize information in a problem about equal groups. Use the example in the student text to demonstrate this method. Ask:

"What two things is this problem about?" students and classrooms

Write the following on the board. Then follow the bulleted steps.

students	232	?
classrooms	8	1

- Draw a loop around the diagonal number pair: 232 and 1
- Multiply these numbers: $232 \times 1 = 232$
- Divide the product by the remaining number: $232 \div 8 = 29$

There are 29 students in each classroom.

3 Written Practice (Continued)

Math Conversations

Discussion opportunities are provided below.

Problem 3 Formulate

Read the problem aloud, or invite a volunteer to read the problem aloud.

"What operation does this problem represent? Why?" Sample: The problem represents multiplication because multiplication is used to find a whole when a fractional part of the whole is given.

Problem 6 Represent

After completing the problem, ask students to make a generalization about subtracting a larger number from a smaller number. Sample: A difference will be negative when a subtrahend is greater than the minuend.

Problem 8 Predict

Before completing the problem, ask students to discuss the pattern and identify its rule. Sample: Count back 2 from the previous term.

Problem 12 Connect

Extend the Problem

Challenge students to name the number that is halfway between 400 and 700, and then explain their thinking. 550; sample explanation: using the same number, count on from 400 and count back from 700 until you arrive at the same number.

Problems 17–21 Analyze

After completing the problems, ask students to name the operation that was used to check each problem, and explain why that operation was used.

Errors and Misconceptions

Problem 10

Watch for students who don't recognize that the symbols are different. When students recognize that the symbols are different, they must use a common notation to subtract by changing the dollars to cents or by changing the cents to dollars.

Problem 15

An answer of 48 indicates that the division was not continued because there was nothing left to divide. Remediate this error by working with students as they perform the division again, and if necessary, provide other divisions such as 1380 ÷ 6 and 2520 ÷ 7 for practice.

(continued)

▶ * **3.** (15) Formulate There are about three hundred twenty little O's of cereal in an ounce. About how many little O's are there in a one-pound box? Write an equation and solve the problem (1 pound = 16 ounces). 5120 little O's; $16 \cdot 320 = t$

* **4.** (11) There are 31 days in August. How many days are left in August after August 3? Write an equation and solve the problem. $31 - 3 = d$; 28 days

* **5.** (14) Compare: $3 - 1 \bigcirc\!\!> 1 - 3$

▶ * **6.** (14) Represent Subtract 5 from 2. Use words to write the answer. negative three

* **7.** (14) The stock's value dropped from \$28.00 to \$25.50. Use a negative number to show the change in the stock's value. −2.50 or −\$2.50

▶ * **8.** (10) Predict What are the next three numbers in the following sequence?

..., 6, 4, 2, 0, __−2__, __−4__, __−6__, ...

* **9.** (10, 14) What is the temperature reading on this thermometer? Write the answer twice, once with digits and an abbreviation and once with words. −6°F; negative six degrees Fahrenheit or six degrees below zero Fahrenheit

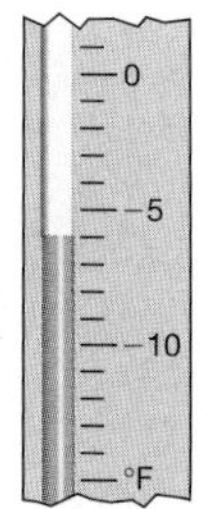

▶ **10.** (1) \$10 − 10¢ \$9.90

11. (6) How much money is $\frac{1}{2}$ of \$3.50? \$1.75

▶ **12.** (9) Connect To which hundred is 587 closest? 600

587
400 500 600 700

13. (1) 9 + 87 + 654 + 3210 3960

14. (2) 574 × 76 43,624

▶ **15.** (2) $\frac{4320}{9}$ 480

16. (2) $36\overline{)493}$ 13 R 25

▶ Analyze Find each unknown number. Check your work.

17. (4) 1200 ÷ w = 300 4

18. (4) $63w = 63$ 1

19. (4) $\frac{76}{m} = 1$ 76

20. (3) w + \$65 = \$1000 \$935

21. (3) $3 + n + 12 + 27 = 50$ 8

▶ See Math Conversations in the sidebar.

English Learners

Explain that an **abbreviation** is a shortened form of a word. Write this chart on the board.

Word	Fahrenheit	Celsius	feet	pound
Abbreviation	F	C		

Then say:

"This table shows the abbreviation for the terms Fahrenheit and Celsius. Let's add some abbreviations to the table."

Ask for a volunteer to write in the abbreviations for *feet* and *pound*. Then ask for other abbreviations that students can add to the chart.

22. There are 10 millimeters in 1 centimeter. How many millimeters long is this paper clip? 30 mm
(7)

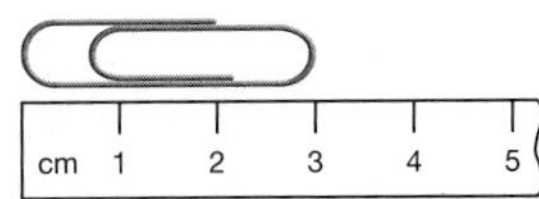

cm 1 2 3 4 5

23. (8 + 9 + 16) ÷ 3 11
(5)

24. What is the place value of the 5 in 12,345,678? thousands
(12)

25. Which digit occupies the ten-billions place in 123,456,789,000? 2
(12)

26. **Represent** Use the numbers 19, 21, and 40 to write two addition facts and two subtraction facts.
(1)
19 + 21 = 40, 21 + 19 = 40, 40 − 19 = 21, 40 − 21 = 19

▸* 27. Arrange these numbers in order from least to greatest: −3, −1, 0, 2
(14)
0, −1, 2, −3

28. Of the seventeen students in Angela's class, eight play in the school band. What fraction of the total number of students in Angela's class are in the band? $\frac{8}{17}$
(6)

▸* 29. **Analyze** Reggie sold buttons with a picture of his school's mascot for 75¢ each. If Reggie sold seven buttons, how much money did he receive? $5.25
(15)

* 30. What number is neither positive nor negative? 0
(14)

Early Finishers
Real-World Application

Franklin D. Roosevelt, the thirty-second president of the United States, was born on January 30, 1882 in Hyde Park, New York. His presidency began March 4, 1933 and ended April 12, 1945.

a. How old was Franklin D. Roosevelt when he took office? 1933 − 1882 = 51 years old

b. How many years did he serve as president? 1945 − 1933 = 12 years in office

▸ See Math Conversations in the sidebar.

Looking Forward

Using an equation to solve word problems about equal groups prepares students for:

- **Lesson 18,** finding the average of two or more numbers.
- **Lesson 22,** solving problems about equal groups with fractions.
- **Lesson 31,** finding the number of square units to cover the area of a rectangle.
- **Lesson 77,** finding unstated information in fractional-parts problems.
- **Lesson 117,** finding a whole when a fraction is known.

3 Written Practice (Continued)

Math Conversations

Discussion opportunities are provided below.

Problem 27 Represent

Encourage students who have difficulty ordering the numbers correctly to arrange the numbers on a number line.

Problem 29 Connect

Read the problem aloud, or invite a volunteer to read the problem aloud.

"What two operations could we use to solve this problem?" multiplication and repeated addition

"If you choose to use multiplication to solve this problem, explain how you know, without multiplying, the number of decimal points that will be in the answer." Sample: When multiplying cents by a whole number, there will be two decimal points in the product.

Assessment

30–40 minutes *For use after Lesson 15*

Distribute **Cumulative Test 2** to each student. Two versions of the test are available in *Saxon Math Course 1 Course Assessments Book.* Have students complete the **Power-Up Test** first. Allow 10 minutes. Then have students work the 20 numbered items on the **Cumulative Test.** Students may use copies of the answer sheet to record their work. Track individual and class progress with the **Test Analysis** forms.

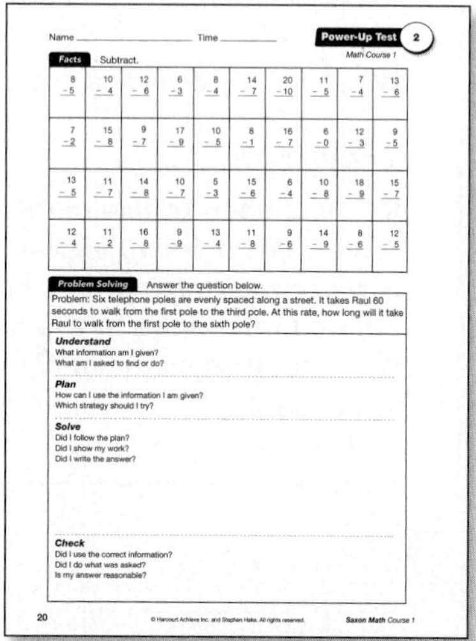
Name ______ Time ______ Power-Up Test 2
Math Course 1
Facts Subtract.
Problem Solving Answer the question below.
Problem: Six telephone poles are evenly spaced along a street. It takes Raul 60 seconds to walk from the first pole to the third pole. At this rate, how long will it take Raul to walk from the first pole to the sixth pole?
Understand
What information am I given?
What am I asked to find or do?
Plan
How can I use the information I am given?
Which strategy should I try?
Solve
Did I follow the plan?
Did I show my work?
Did I write the answer?
Check
Did I use the correct information?
Did I do what was asked?
Is my answer reasonable?

Power-Up Test 2

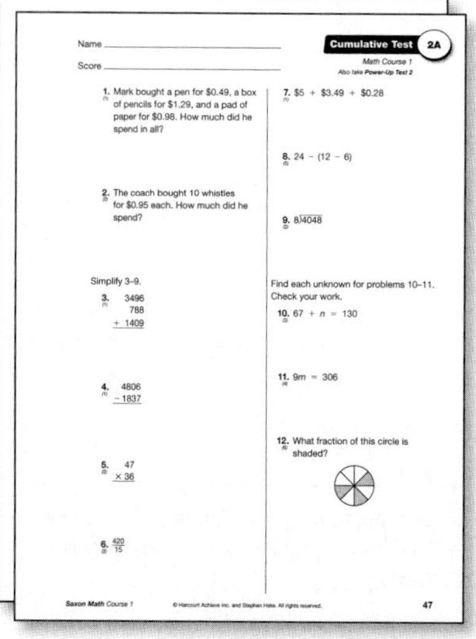
Name ______ Score ______ Cumulative Test 2A
1. Mark bought a pen for $0.49, a box of pencils for $1.29, and a pad of paper for $0.98. How much did he spend in all?
2. The coach bought 10 whistles for $0.95 each. How much did he spend?
Simplify 3–9.
3. 3496 + 788 + 1409
4. 4806 − 1837
5. 47 × 36
7. $5 + $3.49 + $0.28
8. 24 − (12 − 6)
9. 8)4048
Find each unknown for problems 10–11. Check your work.
10. 67 + n = 130
11. 9m = 306
12. What fraction of this circle is shaded?

Cumulative Test 2A

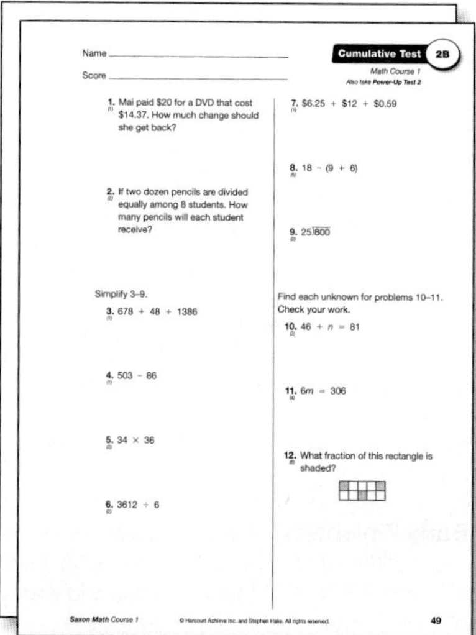
Name ______ Score ______ Cumulative Test 2B
1. Mai paid $20 for a DVD that cost $14.37. How much change should she get back?
2. If two dozen pencils are divided equally among 8 students. How many pencils will each student receive?
Simplify 3–9.
3. 678 + 48 + 1386
4. 503 − 86
5. 34 × 36
6. 3612 ÷ 6
7. $6.25 + $12 + $0.59
8. 18 − (9 + 6)
9. 25)800
Find each unknown for problems 10–11. Check your work.
10. 46 + n = 81
11. 6m = 306
12. What fraction of this rectangle is shaded?

Alternative Cumulative Test 2B

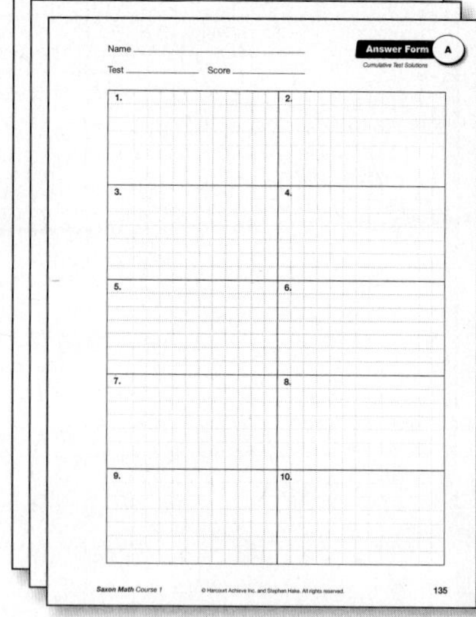
Name ______ Score ______ Answer Form A
Test ______

Optional Answer Forms

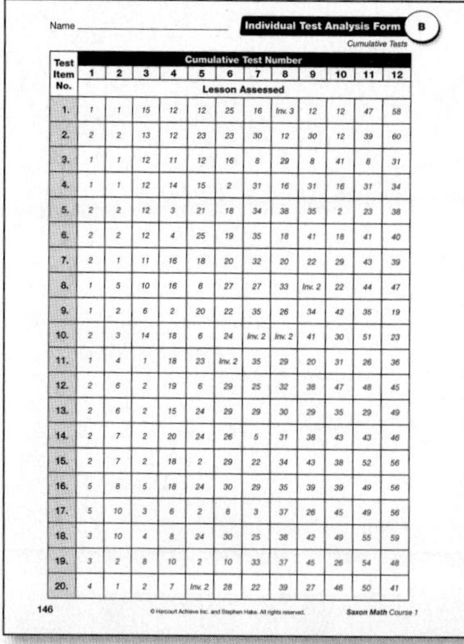
Name ______ Individual Test Analysis Form B
Cumulative Tests

Individual Test Analysis Form

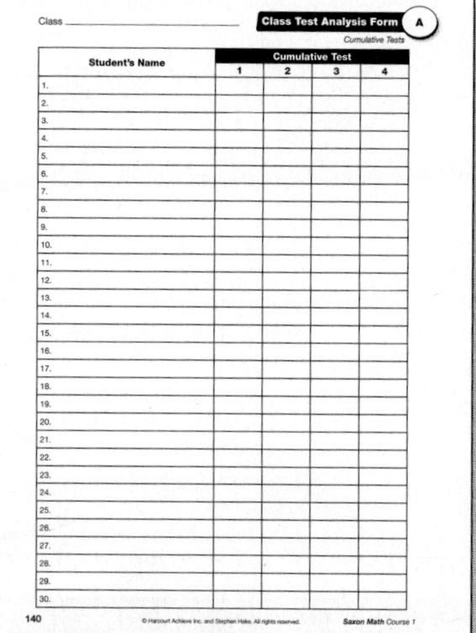
Class ______ Class Test Analysis Form A
Student's Name | Cumulative Test 1 2 3 4

Class Test Analysis Form

Reteaching

Students who score below 80% on the assessment may be in need of reteaching. Look for the causes of student mistakes. If errors are conceptual, refer to the *Reteaching Masters* for reteaching.

Performance Activity 2

Proofs and Disproofs

Assign after Lesson 15 and Test 2

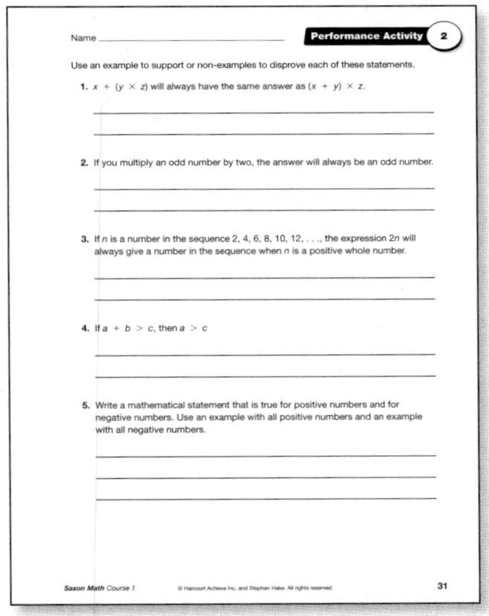

Name ____________ **Performance Activity 2**

Use an example to support or non-examples to disprove each of these statements.

1. $x + (y \times z)$ will always have the same answer as $(x + y) \times z$.

2. If you multiply an odd number by two, the answer will always be an odd number.

3. If n is a number in the sequence 2, 4, 6, 8, 10, 12, . . ., the expression $2n$ will always give a number in the sequence when n is a positive whole number.

4. If $a + b > c$, then $a > c$

5. Write a mathematical statement that is true for positive numbers and for negative numbers. Use an example with all positive numbers and an example with all negative numbers.

Saxon Math Course 1 31

Performance Activity 2

Objectives

- Use examples and non-examples to support or disprove mathematical statements.
- Communicate ideas through writing.

Materials

Performance Activity 2

Preparation

Make copies of **Performance Activity 2.** (One each per student.)

Time Requirement

15–30 minutes; Begin in class and complete at home.

Activity

Explain to students that for this activity they will use examples and non-examples to support or disprove a mathematical statement. You may want to discuss the term **non-example.** Tell students that a non-example is the opposite of an example. For example, a 7 is a non-example of an even number, and a circle is a non-example of a polygon. Discuss how non-examples can be used to prove that a statement is incorrect.

Explain that they will also write a mathematical statement that is true for both positive numbers and negative numbers. Explain that all of the information students need is on **Performance Activity 2.**

Criteria for Evidence of Learning

- Uses examples and non-examples correctly to support or disprove a mathematical statement.
- Communicates ideas clearly through writing.

Meeting Standards

National Council of Teachers of Mathematics (NCTM)

Reasoning and Proof

RP.2b Make and investigate mathematical conjectures

RP.2c Develop and evaluate mathematical arguments and proofs

Communication

CM.3a Organize and consolidate their mathematical thinking through communication

Connections

CN.4b Understand how mathematical ideas interconnect and build on one another to produce a coherent whole

• Rounding Whole Numbers
• Estimating

Objectives

- Round whole numbers to the nearest ten, hundred, and thousand.
- Use rounding to help estimate the answer to a problem.
- Use estimation skills when reading graphs.

Lesson Preparation

Materials

- **Power Up D** (in *Instructional Masters)*

Optional

- **Teacher-provided material: index cards** (labeled 1–9) or deck of cards (no face cards)

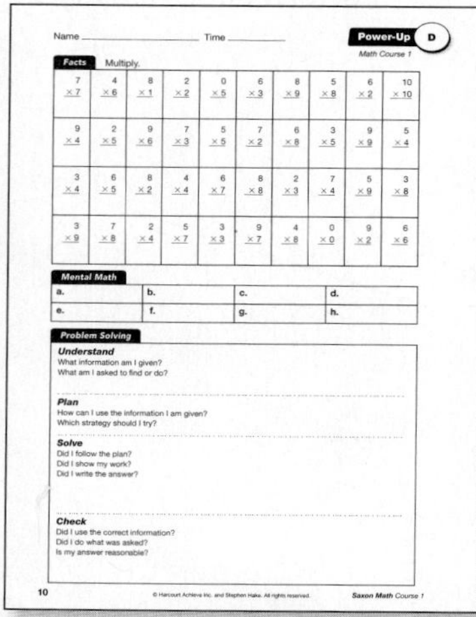

Power Up D

Math Language

New	English Learners (ESL)
estimate	reasonable
round	

Technology Resources

Student eBook Complete student textbook in electronic format.

Resources and Planner CD Assessment, reteaching, and instructional masters, plus a pacing calendar with standards.

Test and Practice Generator CD Create additional practice sheets and custom-made tests.

www.SaxonPublishers.com Visit for more student activities and planning materials.

Inclusion

Adaptations CD Adapted lessons, investigations, practice and assessments.

Meeting Standards

National Council of Teachers of Mathematics (NCTM)

Numbers and Operations

NO.1g Develop meaning for integers and represent and compare quantities with them

NO.3a Select appropriate methods and tools for computing with fractions and decimals from among mental computation, estimation, calculators or computers, and paper and pencil, depending on the situation, and apply the selected methods

NO.3c Develop and use strategies to estimate the results of rational-number computations and judge the reasonableness of the results

Problem Solving

PS.1b Solve problems that arise in mathematics and in other contexts

Power-Up Discussion *For use with Power Up, p. 82*

Problem-Solving Strategy: Find a Pattern

Find the next four numbers in this sequence:
2, 3, 5, 8, 9, 11, 14, 15, ...

Understand ***Understand the problem.***

"What information are we given?"

We are shown the sequence 2, 3, 5, 8, 9, 11, 14, 15, ...

"What are we asked to do?"

We are asked to find the next four numbers in the sequence.

"What prior knowledge do we bring to this problem?"

Sequences follow a rule or pattern.

"Does this sequence increase, decrease, or fluctuate?"

The sequence is an increasing pattern.

Plan ***Make a plan.***

"What problem-solving strategy will we use?"

We must first *find the pattern* so that we can extend the sequence.

Solve ***Carry out the plan.***

We begin by determining how much each term in the sequence increases from the previous term.

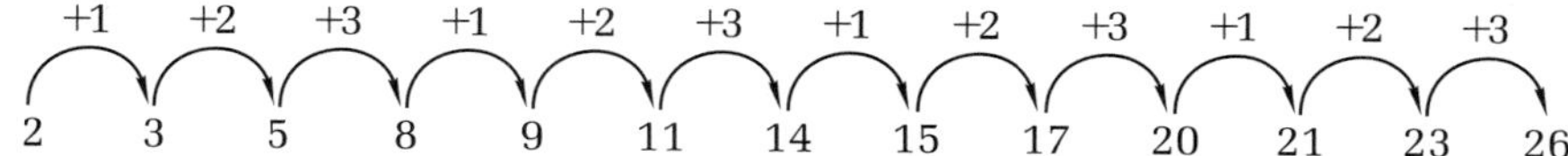

Teacher Note: You may also determine the pattern in this sequence by beginning at 14 and working backward using subtraction.

We notice that the increase from term to term forms a repeating pattern: +1, + 2, + 3, +1, + 2, + 3. If we continue this addition pattern, we can find the next 4 digits.

$15 + \mathbf{2} = 17$ $17 + \mathbf{3} = 20$ $20 + \mathbf{1} = 21$ $21 + \mathbf{2} = 23$

Check ***Look back.***

"Did we do what we were asked to do?"

Yes, we found that the next four numbers in the sequence are 17, 20, 21, and 23.

"Is our solution expected?"

Answers may vary. Students may be used to following a single operation (i.e. add 3) to extend a pattern.

"When might a sequence in real-life follow a pattern using more than a single operation?"

Some people must take different dosages of medication at different times of the day. They may take 25 mg when they wake up, 50 mg in the afternoon, and 25 mg before bed. Some people balance their diet by eating a certain number of calories at every meal, such a moderate amount of calories at breakfast, more at lunch, and the fewest at dinner.

1 Power Up

Facts

Distribute **Power Up D** to students. See answers below.

Mental Math

Before students begin the Mental Math exercise, do this counting exercise as a class.

Count by 3s from 3 to 60.

Encourage students to share different ways to mentally compute these exercises. Strategies for exercises **a** and **d** are listed below.

a. Add Partial Products

$3 \times 30 = 90$ and $3 \times 2 = 6$; $90 + 6 = 96$

Use the Distributive Property

$(3 \times 30) + (3 \times 2) = 3(30 + 2) = 3(32) = 96$

d. Add 10, then Subtract 1

$75 + 10 = 85$; $85 - 1 = 84$

Add Ones, Then Tens

$75 + 9 = 70 + 5 + 9 = 70 + 14 = 84$

Problem Solving

Refer to **Power-Up Discussion,** p. 82B.

2 New Concepts

Instruction

One way to encourage students to practice their rounding skills is to invite them to select two cards from a set of index cards labeled 1 through 9 (or from a deck of playing cards with the face cards removed—an ace counts as 1). The chosen cards are arranged face up side by side, and the number formed by the cards is read and rounded to the nearest ten.

After students are comfortable rounding to the nearest ten, encourage them to select three cards and round to the nearest hundred, and then select four cards and round to the nearest thousand.

(continued)

LESSON 16

• Rounding Whole Numbers
• Estimating

Power Up *Building Power*

facts Power Up D

mental math

a. **Number Sense:** 3×30 plus 3×2 96

b. **Number Sense:** 4×20 plus 4×3 92

c. **Number Sense:** $150 + 20$ 170

d. **Number Sense:** $75 + 9$ 84

e. **Number Sense:** $800 - 50$ 750

f. **Number Sense:** $8000 - 500$ 7500

g. **Measurement:** How many yards are in 6 feet? 2 yds.

h. **Calculation:** Start with 1. Add 2; multiply by 3; subtract 4; then divide by 5. What is the answer? 1

problem solving Find the next four numbers in this sequence: 2, 3, 5, 8, 9, 11, 14, 15, …
17, 20, 21, 23

New Concepts *Increasing Knowledge*

rounding whole numbers

When we **round** a whole number, we are finding another whole number, usually ending in zero, that is close to the number we are rounding. The number line can help us visualize rounding.

In order to round 667 to the nearest ten, we recognize that 667 is closer to 670 than it is to 660. In order to round 667 to the nearest hundred, we recognize that 667 is closer to 700 than to 600.

Example 1

Round 6789 to the nearest thousand.

Solution

The number we are rounding is between 6000 and 7000. It is closer to **7000.**

Thinking Skill
Verify
Draw a number line to verify the answer is correct. See student work.

Facts Multiply.

7 × 7 49	4 × 6 24	8 × 1 8	2 × 2 4	0 × 5 0	6 × 3 18	8 × 9 72	5 × 8 40	6 × 2 12	10 × 10 100
9 × 4 36	2 × 5 10	9 × 6 54	7 × 3 21	5 × 5 25	7 × 2 14	6 × 8 48	3 × 5 15	9 × 9 81	5 × 4 20
3 × 4 12	6 × 5 30	8 × 2 16	4 × 4 16	6 × 7 42	8 × 8 64	2 × 3 6	7 × 4 28	5 × 9 45	3 × 8 24
3 × 9 27	7 × 8 56	2 × 4 8	5 × 7 35	3 × 3 9	9 × 7 63	4 × 8 32	0 × 0 0	9 × 2 18	6 × 6 36

Example 2

Round 550 to the nearest hundred.

Solution

The number we are to round is halfway between 500 and 600. When the number we are rounding is halfway between two round numbers, we round **up.** So 550 rounds to **600.**

estimating

Rounding can help us **estimate** the answer to a problem. Estimating is a quick way to "get close" to the answer. It can also help us decide whether an answer is reasonable. In some situations an estimate is sufficient to solve a problem because an exact answer is not needed. To estimate, we round the numbers before we add, subtract, multiply, or divide.

Example 3

Estimate the sum of 467 and 312.

Solution

Estimating is a skill we can learn to do in our head. First we round each number. Since both numbers are in the hundreds, we will round each number to the nearest hundred.

467 rounds to 500

312 rounds to 300

To estimate the sum, we add the rounded numbers.

$$\begin{array}{r} 500 \\ +\ 300 \\ \hline 800 \end{array}$$

We estimate the sum of 467 and 312 to be **800.**

Example 4

Stephanie stopped at the store to pick up a few items she needs. She has a $10 bill and a couple of quarters. She needs to buy milk for $2.29, her favorite cereal for $4.78, and orange juice for $2.42. Does Stephanie have enough money to buy what she needs?

Solution

An estimate is probably good enough to solve the problem. Milk and juice are less than $2.50 each, so they total less than $5. Cereal is less than $5.00, so all three items are less than $10. If tax is not charged on food, she has enough money. Even if tax is charged she probably has enough.

2 New Concepts (Continued)

Example 2

Instruction

Emphasize this important rounding rule:

"When the number we are rounding is halfway between two round numbers, we round up. For example, when rounding 25 to the nearest ten, 25 rounds to 30 because 25 is halfway between 20 and 30."

"Now think of 24 and 26. Does 24 round to 20 or to 30? Does 26 round to 20 or to 30? Why?" 24 rounds to 20 and 26 rounds to 30; Sample explanation: 24 is closer to 20 than to 30 and 26 is closer to 30 than to 20.

Example 4

Instruction

After discussing the example and its solution, invite students to suggest other ways of rounding the amounts and using mental math to complete an estimate. Sample: Round each amount to the nearest quarter and add the amounts.

$2.29 rounds to $2.25 and $4.78 rounds to $4.75; the sum of $2.25 and $4.75 is $7.00.

$2.42 rounds to $2.50 and the sum of $7.00 and $2.50 is $9.50; Stephanie should have enough money.

(continued)

Math Background

All of the rounding in this lesson involves rounding to the lead (or first) digit of a number. For example, if the lead digit is in the hundreds place, the number is rounded to the nearest hundred.

In their future studies, students will explore rounding to other places in a number, such as rounding a number in thousands to the nearest hundred or nearest ten, as well as rounding decimal numbers to a variety of decimal places or to the nearest whole number.

English Learners

On the board, draw and label a $20 bill and then a CD that costs $17.99. Say:

"If something is reasonable then it makes good sense. Would it be reasonable to take $20 to the mall to buy a CD that costs $17.99? Why or why not?" Yes, because $17.99 is less than $20.

Write $50.00 on the board and ask:

"Is this a reasonable price for a new CD?" Most students will think that it would not make good sense to pay this price.

2 New Concepts (Continued)

Example 5

Instruction

Have students study the bar graph and the data it displays.

"Look above the graph and read the question. Which word in the question suggests that our answer should be an estimate?" about

"Other words that suggest an estimate are approximately and approximate. Look again at the graph. What was the approximate population of Ashton in 1990?" approximately 5000 people

"Why can't the question be answered with an exact answer?" Sample: The top of the data bar is between two intervals of the vertical scale, so we can only appropximate its value.

Practice Set

Problems j–n Estimate

After completing each estimate, ask students to say if they used mental math or paper and pencil to make the estimate, and explain why they made that choice.

Problem o Predict

Extend the problem by asking students to use the graph to make a reasonable prediction of when the population of Ashton will reach 10,000 people.

Invite volunteers to share their predictions, along with an explanation of how the predictions were made, with the class.

Math Language

Words such as *about* and *approximately* indicate that an estimate, not an exact answer, is needed.

Example 5

According to this graph, about how many more people lived in Ashton in 2000 than in 1980?

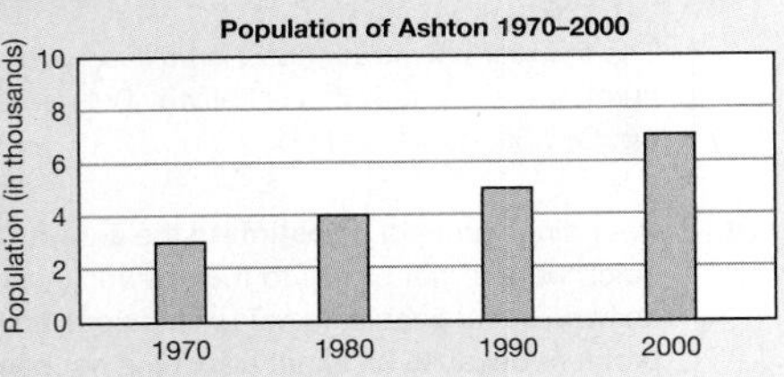

Solution

We often need to use estimation skills when reading graphs. The numbers along the left side of the graph (the vertical axis) indicate the population in thousands. The bar for the year 2000 is about halfway between the 6000 and 8000 levels, so the population was about 7000. In 1980 the population was about 4000. This problem has a subtraction pattern. We subtract and find that about **3000 more people** lived in Ashton in 2000 than in 1980.

Practice Set Round each of these numbers to the nearest ten:

a. 57 60 **b.** 63 60 **c.** 45 50

Round each of these numbers to the nearest hundred:

d. 282 300 **e.** 350 400 **f.** 426 400

Round each of these numbers to the nearest thousand:

g. 4387 4000 **h.** 7500 8000 **i.** 6750 7000

▶ Estimate Use rounded numbers to estimate each answer.

j. 397 + 206 600 **k.** 703 − 598 100

l. 29 × 31 900 **m.** $29\overline{)591}$ 20

Use the graph in example 5 to answer problems **n** and **o.**

n. Estimate About how many fewer people lived in Ashton in 1980 than in 1990? 1000 fewer people

▶ **o.** Predict The graph shows an upward trend in the population of Ashton. If the population grows the same amount from 2000 to 2010 as it did from 1990 to 2000, what would be a reasonable projection for the population in 2010? 9000 people

▶ See Math Conversations in the sidebar.

Inclusion

Students may find this strategy useful as an alternative to rounding on a number line. Use the following steps to demonstrate the strategy with the examples below.

- Identify the place value that you will be rounding to.
- Underline that digit and circle the digit to its right.
- Ask: **"Is the circled number 5 or more?"**
- If the answer is yes, add 1 to the underlined digit.
- If the answer is no, the underlined digit does not change.
- Replace the circled number and the numbers to its right with zeros.

As a class, follow the steps above to round 5447 to the nearest hundred and 4829 to the nearest thousand. 5400; 5000

Written Practice *Strengthening Concepts*

* **1.** (12) What is the difference between the product of 20 and 5 and the sum of 20 and 5? 75

▶ * **2.** (13) Walter Raleigh began exploring the coastline of North America in 1584. Lewis and Clark began exploring the interior of North America in 1803. How many years after Raleigh did Lewis and Clark begin exploring North America? Write an equation and solve the problem.
$1803 - 1584 = y$; 219 years

▶ * **3.** (15) **Explain** Jacob separated his 140 trading cards into 5 equal groups. He placed four of the groups into binders. The remaining cards he placed in a box. How many cards did he put in the box? Write an equation and solve the problem. Explain why your answer is reasonable.

4. (12) Which digit in 159,342,876 is in the hundred-thousands place? 3

5. (12) In the 2004 U.S. presidential election, 121,068,715 votes were tallied for president. Use words to write that number of votes.

6. (9) What number is halfway between 5 and 11 on the number line? 8

* **7.** (16) Round 56,789 to the nearest thousand. 57,000

* **8.** (16) Round 550 to the nearest hundred. 600

* **9.** (16) Estimate the product of 295 and 406 by rounding each number to the nearest hundred before multiplying. 120,000

10. (1) $45 + 5643 + 287$ 5975

11. (1) $40{,}312 - 14{,}908$ 25,404

▶ **12.** (2) $\frac{7308}{12}$ 609

13. (2) $100\overline{)5367}$ 53 R 67

▶ **14.** (5) $(5 + 11) \div 2$ 8

15. (6) How much money is $\frac{1}{2}$ of \$5? \$2.50

16. (6) How much money is $\frac{1}{4}$ of \$5? \$1.25

17. (2) $\$0.25 \times 10$ \$2.50

18. (5) $325(324 - 323)$ 325

19. (9) Compare: $1 + (2 + 3) \ominus (1 + 2) + 3$

▶* **20.** (14) **Explain** *Wind chill* describes the effect of temperature and wind combining to make it feel colder outside. At 3 p.m. in Minneapolis, Minnesota, the wind chill was $-10°$ Fahrenheit. At 11 p.m. the wind chill was $-3°$ Fahrenheit. At which time did it feel colder outside, 3 p.m. or 11 p.m.? Explain how you arrived at your answer.

▶* **21.** (15) **Formulate** Your heart beats about 72 times per minute. At that rate, how many times will it beat in one hour? (Write an equation and solve the problem.) 4320 times; $60 \cdot 72 = t$

3. $5 \cdot g = 140$; 28 cards; Sample: 30 is a little more than 28, and $30 \times 5 = 150$, which is a little more than 140.

5. one hundred twenty-one million, sixty-eight thousand, seven hundred fifteen votes

20. 3 p.m. Sample: The wind chill at 3 p.m. was -10°F, and the wind chill at 11 p.m. was -3°F. It felt colder at 3 p.m. because $-10 < -3$.

▶ See Math Conversations in the sidebar.

3 Written Practice

Math Conversations

Discussion opportunities are provided below.

Problem 3 Explain

Extend the Problem

Ask students to name the number of trading cards Jacob placed in binders and explain two different ways to find the answer. 112; 28×4 and $140 - 28$

Problem 14 Verify

Extend the Problem

Have students write a word problem that represents this expression.

Write $5 + 11 \div 2$ on the board and remind students of the order of operations. Then ask students to justify that the expression in the text, and not the expression at the board, has an answer of 8.

Problem 20 Explain

Extend the Problem

Write a string of integer temperatures on the board and have students compute a final temperature by using addition and subtraction to simplify the string.

For example, $-2° + 3° + 1° - 4° + 2° = 0°$.

Challenge a volunteer to demonstrate how to determine the final temperature by <u>not</u> performing the computations from left to right.

Problem 21 Formulate

Extend the Problem

Ask students to estimate the number of times their heart will beat in 10 years. To make an estimate, students should write and solve an equation, then compare their estimate to the estimates of their classmates.

Errors and Misconceptions

Problem 2

An answer of 229 represents not regrouping in the tens place correctly. Demonstrate all of the regroupings in 1803–1584 for the students. For additional practice, ask them to subtract 3137 from 3506 and 7225 from 7404.

Problem 12

When dividing a dividend that has one or more internal zeros, a common error is to not write a zero in the quotient when a second consecutive digit is brought down from the dividend. Demonstrate why 609 and not 69 is the correct quotient when dividing 7308 by 12.

(continued)

3 Written Practice (Continued)

Math Conversations

Discussion opportunities are provided below.

Problem 25 Explain

Extend the Problem

Give students an opportunity to think about how an estimate of the amount eaten in one year might be made.

"Multiplication can be used to estimate the amount eaten in one year. To make such an estimate using multiplication, which factors would you choose? Tell why." Sample: Round 420 pounds per week to 400 pounds and round 52 weeks in one year to 50 weeks; $400 \times 50 = 20{,}000$ pounds.

Problem 30 Represent

After completing the problem, you might choose to ask students to write and share two conclusions and one word problem about the graph.

22. (8) Estimate The distance between bases on a major league baseball diamond is 90 feet. A player who runs around the diamond runs about how many feet? 360 feet

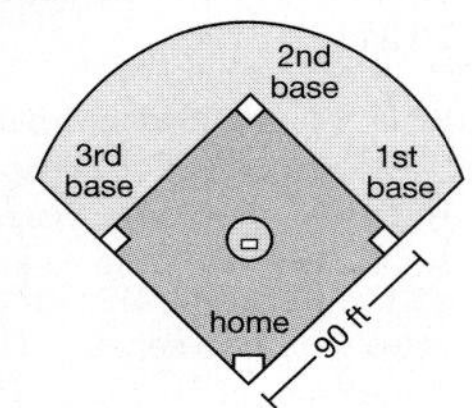

Refer to the bar graph shown below to answer problems **23–26.**

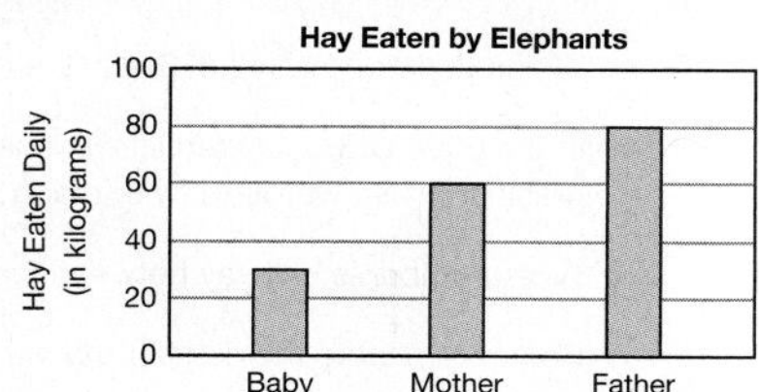

* **23.** (16) How many more kilograms of hay does the father elephant eat each day than the baby elephant? 50 more kilograms

* **24.** (16) Altogether, how many kilograms of hay do the three elephants eat each day? 170 kilograms

▶* **25.** (16) How many kilograms of hay would the mother elephant eat in one week? 420 kilograms

* **26.** (16) Formulate Using the information in this graph, write a comparison word problem. Answers will vary. See student work.

Analyze Find each unknown number. Check your work.

27. (4) $6w = 66$ 11

28. (3) $m - 60 = 37$ 97

29. (3) $60 - n = 37$ 23

▶* **30.** (Inv. 1) Represent Each day Chico, Fuji, and Rolo drink 6, 8, and 9 glasses of water respectively. Draw a bar graph to illustrate this information.

30.

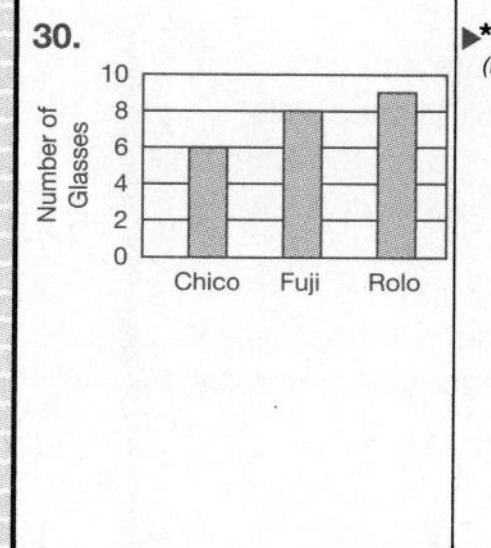

▶ See Math Conversations in the sidebar.

Looking Forward

Estimating to find a sum, difference, product, or quotient or when reading graphs prepares students for:

- **Lesson 17,** making and using a ruler divided into estimated eighths and sixteenths.
- **Lesson 47,** estimating the number of diameters in the circumference of a circle to find pi.
- **Lesson 51,** rounding decimal numbers in order to estimate their products.
- **Lesson 89,** estimating square roots.
- **Lesson 118,** estimating the area of a figure.

The Number Line: Fractions and Mixed Numbers

Objectives

- Determine which fraction or mixed number is represented by a point on a number line.
- Measure the lengths of segments to the nearest sixteenth of an inch.

Lesson Preparation

Materials

- **Power Up E** (in *Instructional Masters*)
- **Student-made tagboard inch rulers from Lesson 7**

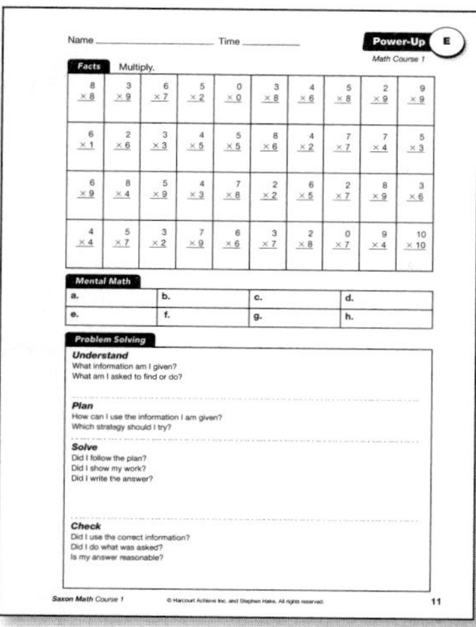

Power Up E

Math Language

New	Maintain	English Learners (ESL)
mixed numbers	integers	consecutive

Technology Resources

Student eBook Complete student textbook in electronic format.

Resources and Planner Assessment, reteaching, and instructional masters, plus a pacing calendar with standards.

Test and Practice Generator CD Create additional practice sheets and custom-made tests.

www.SaxonPublishers.com Visit for more student activities and planning materials.

Inclusion

Adaptations CD Adapted lessons, investigations, practice and assessments.

Meeting Standards

National Council of Teachers of Mathematics (NCTM)

Numbers and Operations

NO.1a Work flexibly with fractions, decimals, and percents to solve problems

NO.1b Compare and order fractions, decimals, and percents efficiently and find their approximate locations on a number line

Algebra

AL.1a Represent, analyze, and generalize a variety of patterns with tables, graphs, words, and, when possible, symbolic rules

Power-Up Discussion For use with Power Up, p. 87

Problem-Solving Strategy: Draw a Diagram/ Write an Equation

If an 8 in.-by-8 in. pan of lasagna serves four people, how many 12 in.-by-12 in. pans of lasagna should be purchased to serve 56 people? (*Hint:* You may have "leftovers.")

Understand An eight-inch-square pan of lasagna will serve four people. We are asked to find how many 12-inch-square pans of lasagna are needed to feed 56 people.

Plan We will *draw a diagram* to help us visualize the problem. Then we will *write an equation* to find the number of 12-inch-square pans of lasagna needed.

Solve First, we find the size of each serving by "cutting" the 8-inch-square pan into four pieces. Then we see how many pieces of the same size can be made from the 12-inch-square pan:

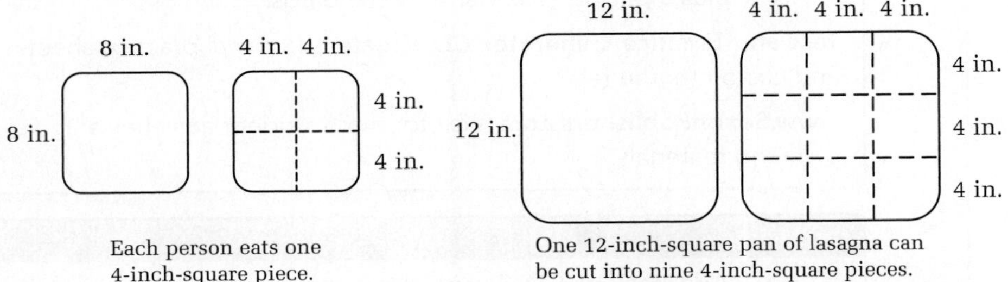

Each person eats one 4-inch-square piece.

One 12-inch-square pan of lasagna can be cut into nine 4-inch-square pieces.

One 12-inch-square pan of lasagna can serve 9 people. We use this information to write an equation: $N \times 9 = 56$. We divide to find that $N = 6$ R2. Six pans of lasagna would only provide 54 pieces, so we must buy seven pans of lasagna in order to serve 56 people.

Check We found that we need to buy seven 12-inch-square pans of lasagna to serve 56 people. It would take 14 8-inch-square pans of lasagna to feed 56 people, and one 12-inch-square pan of lasagna feeds about twice as many people as one 8-inch-square pan, so our answer is reasonable.

Teacher Note: You may wish to extend this lesson by increasing the number of people that need to eat or by increasing the size of a pan of lasagna.

Alternate Approach: Act It Out/Use a Model

If pattern blocks are available, use them to create the pans of lasagna. To check the solution, have students continue building pans of lasagna until there are 56 servings. Remind students the last servings must be part of an entire pan.

LESSON
17

• The Number Line: Fractions and Mixed Numbers

Power Up *Building Power*

facts Power Up E

mental math

a. **Number Sense:** 5 × 30 plus 5 × 4 170

b. **Number Sense:** 4 × 60 plus 4 × 4 256

c. **Number Sense:** 180 + 12 192

d. **Calculation:** 64 + 9 73

e. **Number Sense:** 3000 − 1000 − 100 1900

f. **Calculation:** $10.00 − $7.50 $2.50

g. **Measurement:** How many millimeters are in 2 meters? 2000 mm

h. **Calculation:** Start with 5. Multiply by 4; add 1; divide by 3; then subtract 2. What is the answer? 5

problem solving If an 8 in.-by-8 in. pan of lasagna serves four people, how many 12 in.-by-12 in. pans of lasagna should be purchased to serve 56 people? (*Hint:* You may have "leftovers.")

Understand An eight-inch-square pan of lasagna will serve four people. We are asked to find how many 12-inch-square pans of lasagna are needed to feed 56 people.

Plan We will *draw a diagram* to help us visualize the problem. Then we will *write an equation* to find the number of 12-inch-square pans of lasagna needed.

Solve First, we find the size of each serving by "cutting" the 8-inch-square pan into four pieces. Then we see how many pieces of the same size can be made from the 12-inch-square pan:

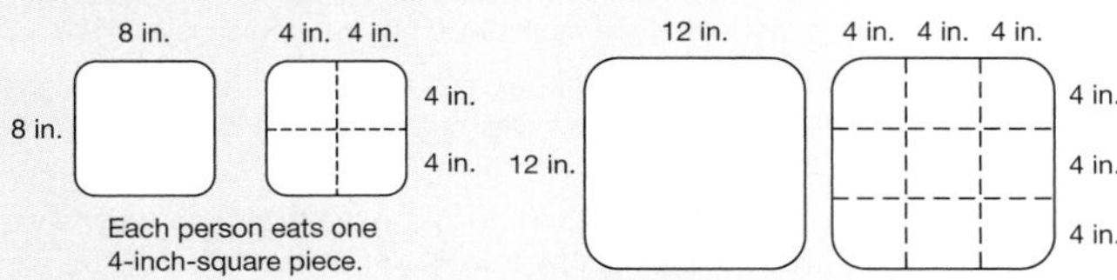

Each person eats one 4-inch-square piece.

One 12-inch-square pan of lasagna can be cut into nine 4-inch-square pieces.

One 12-inch-square pan of lasagna can serve 9 people. We use this information to write an equation: $N \times 9 = 56$. We divide to find that $N = 6$ R2. Six pans of lasagna would only provide 54 pieces, so we must buy seven pans of lasagna in order to serve 56 people.

Facts Multiply.

8 × 8 64	3 × 9 27	6 × 7 42	5 × 2 10	0 × 0 0	3 × 8 24	4 × 6 24	5 × 8 40	2 × 9 18	9 × 9 81
6 × 1 6	2 × 6 12	3 × 3 9	4 × 5 20	5 × 5 25	8 × 6 48	4 × 2 8	7 × 7 49	7 × 4 28	5 × 3 15
6 × 9 54	8 × 4 32	5 × 9 45	4 × 3 12	7 × 8 56	2 × 2 4	6 × 5 30	2 × 7 14	8 × 9 72	3 × 6 18
4 × 4 16	5 × 7 35	3 × 2 6	7 × 9 63	6 × 6 36	3 × 7 21	2 × 8 16	0 × 7 0	9 × 4 36	10 × 10 100

1 Power Up

Facts

Distribute **Power Up E** to students. See answers below.

Mental Math

Before students begin the Mental Math exercise, do this counting exercise as a class.

Count up and down by $\frac{1}{4}$s between $\frac{1}{4}$ and 12.

Encourage students to share different ways to mentally compute these exercises. Strategies for exercises **b** and **c** are listed below.

b. Add Partial Products

$4 \times 60 = 240$ and $4 \times 4 = 16$;
$240 + 16 = 256$

Use the Distributive Property

$(4 \times 60) + (4 \times 4) = 4(60 + 4) =$
$4(64) = 256$

c. Add 10, then Add 2

$180 + 10 + 2 = 190 + 2 = 192$

Add 10, then Count Up 2

$180 + 10 = 190$; Count: 191, 192

Problem Solving

Refer to **Power-Up Discussion,** p. 87B.

2 New Concepts

Instruction

Have students practice dividing consecutive integers into halves by creating a number line from -5 to 5 and marking and labeling the whole and mixed numbers from $-4\frac{1}{2}$ to $4\frac{1}{2}$.

Example 1

Instruction

Have students count the number of horizontal segments between 2 and 3. The answer is 5. If students answer 4, then they may be counting the tick marks instead of the segments. Point out that the horizontal segments are equal in length, and each represents $\frac{1}{5}$ of the distance between 2 and 3.

Instruction

The following questions will help students notice the relationship shared by fractional parts of an inch.

"Halves divide each inch of a ruler into how many equal parts?" two

"Fourths or quarters divide each inch of a ruler into how many equal parts?" four

"Eighths divide each inch of a ruler into how many equal parts?" eight

(continued)

Check We found that we need to buy seven 12-inch-square pans of lasagna to serve 56 people. It would take 14 8-inch-square pans of lasagna to feed 56 people, and one 12-inch-square lasagna feeds about twice as many people as one 8-inch-square pan, so our answer is reasonable.

New Concept *Increasing Knowledge*

Math Language
Recall that **integers** are the set of counting numbers, their opposites, and zero.

On this number line the tick marks show the location of the integers:

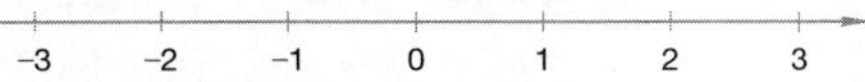

There are points on the number line between the integers that can be named with fractions or **mixed numbers.** A mixed number is a whole number plus a fraction. Halfway between 0 and 1 is $\frac{1}{2}$. Halfway between 1 and 2 is $1\frac{1}{2}$. Halfway between -1 and -2 is $-1\frac{1}{2}$.

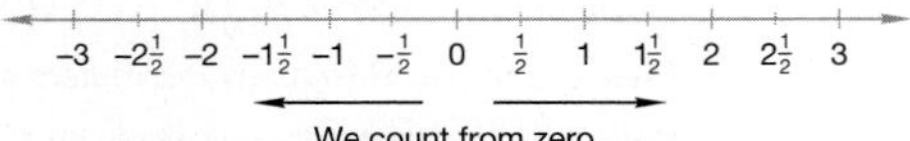

The distance between consecutive integers on a number line may be divided into halves, thirds, fourths, fifths, or any other number of equal divisions. To determine which fraction or mixed number is represented by a point on the number line, we follow the steps described in the next example.

Example 1

Point *A* represents what mixed number on this number line?

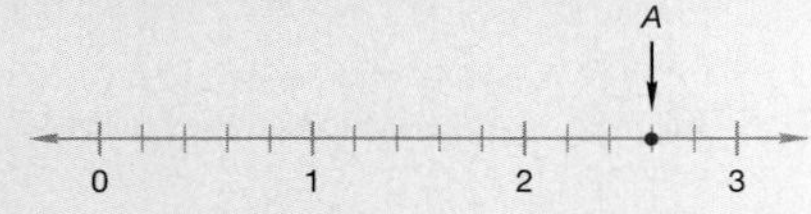

Solution

We see that point *A* represents a number greater than 2 but less than 3. So point *A* represents a mixed number, which is a whole number plus a fraction.

To find the fraction, we first notice that the segment from 2 to 3 has been divided into five smaller segments. The distance from 2 to point *A* crosses three of the five segments. Thus, point *A* represents the mixed number $\mathbf{2\frac{3}{5}}$.

Analyze Why did we focus on the number of segments on the number line and not the number of vertical tick marks?

The four vertical tick marks divide the space between the numbers 2 and 3 into five segments, just as four cuts divide a ribbon into five pieces.

English Learners

The text speaks of the distance between **consecutive** numbers on the number line. Write 1, 2, 3, 4, and 5. Say:

"These numbers are consecutive whole numbers. They are in order and follow the pattern +1."

Write 6, 9, 11, and 15 on the board and mark an X across them. Say:

"These numbers are not consecutive. They do not follow a +1 pattern and are not next to each other on a number line."

Math Background

Fractions and mixed numbers belong to the set of numbers known as the rational numbers. A *rational* number is any number that can be expressed as $\frac{a}{b}$, where a and b are integers and $b \neq 0$.

Every integer is a rational number because every integer can be written as the numerator of a fraction having a denominator of 1.

Activity

Inch Ruler to Sixteenths

Materials needed:

- inch ruler made in Lesson 7

In Lesson 7 we made an inch ruler divided into fourths. In this activity we will divide the ruler into eighths and sixteenths. First we will review what we did in Lesson 7.

We used a ruler to make one-inch divisions on a strip of tagboard.

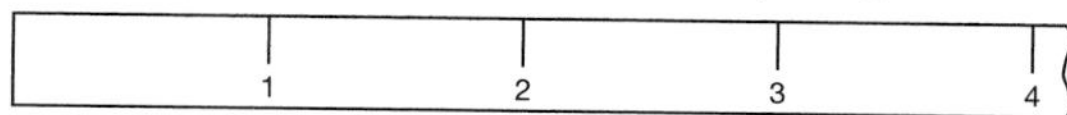

Then we estimated the halfway point between inch marks and drew new marks. The new marks were half-inch divisions. Then we estimated the halfway point between the half-inch marks and made quarter-inch divisions.

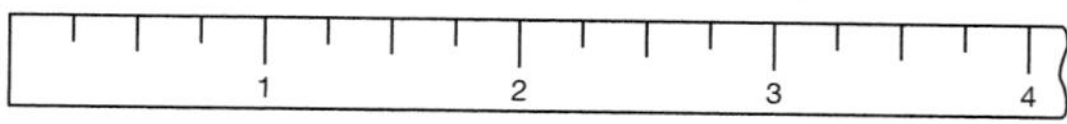

We made the half-inch marks a little shorter than the inch marks and the quarter-inch marks a little shorter than the half-inch marks.

Now divide your ruler into eighths of an inch by estimating the halfway point between the quarter-inch marks. Make these eighth-inch marks a little shorter than the quarter-inch marks.

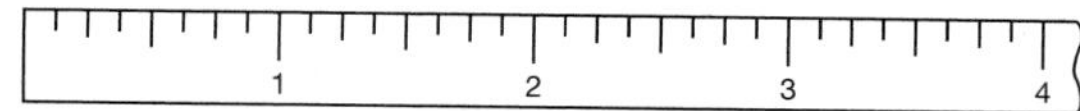

Finally, divide your ruler into sixteenths by estimating the halfway point between the eighth-inch marks. Make these marks the shortest marks on the ruler.

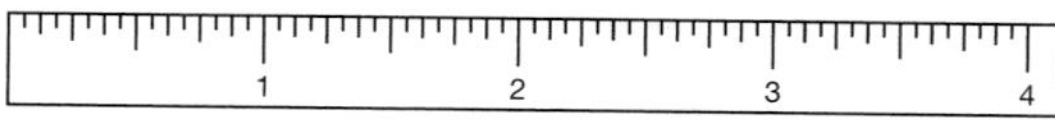

Example 2

Estimate the length of this line segment in inches. Then use your ruler to find its length to the nearest sixteenth of an inch.

Solution

The line segment is about 3 inches long. The ruler has been divided into sixteenths. We align the zero mark (or end of the ruler) with one end of the line segment. Then we find the mark on the ruler closest to the other end of the line segment and read this mark. As shown on the next page, we will enlarge a portion of a ruler to show how each mark is read.

Activity

Instruction

Remind students of the relationship shared by fractional parts of an inch.

"To create a ruler that shows eighths of an inch, each inch of the ruler is divided into eight equal parts. To create a ruler that shows sixteenths of an inch, into how many equal parts will each inch be divided?" sixteen

2 New Concepts (Continued)

Instruction

Challenge students to locate the tick mark for $2\frac{1}{2}$ inches on the magnified ruler and then give three other names for $2\frac{1}{2}$. Sample answers: $2\frac{2}{4}$ or $\frac{10}{4}$ inches, $2\frac{4}{8}$ or $\frac{20}{8}$ inches, and $2\frac{8}{16}$ or $\frac{40}{16}$ inches.

Invite students to practice measuring an assortment of everyday objects. For example, measure to the nearest sixteenth of an inch the length of a pencil, the thickness of a book, and the width of a paper clip.

Practice Set

Problem a Generalize

Before continuing the sequence, ask students to discuss the pattern and describe its rule. To find the next term in the pattern, add $\frac{1}{16}$ to the previous term.

Problem c Represent

After completing the problem, invite students to describe other ways to find the number halfway between 2 and 5. Sample: Count up from 2, and back from 5, by fourths.

Problem d Connect

It is important for students to recognize the divisions into which the number line is divided.

"On the number line, how many equal units are between 0 and 1 and between 1 and 2?" six

"What fractional part of 1 does each tick mark represent?" $\frac{1}{6}$

Thinking Skill

Connect

How is a number line like a ruler? The distance between all like units is equal. On a number line the distance between 0, 1, 2 and so on is equal. This is also true on a ruler.

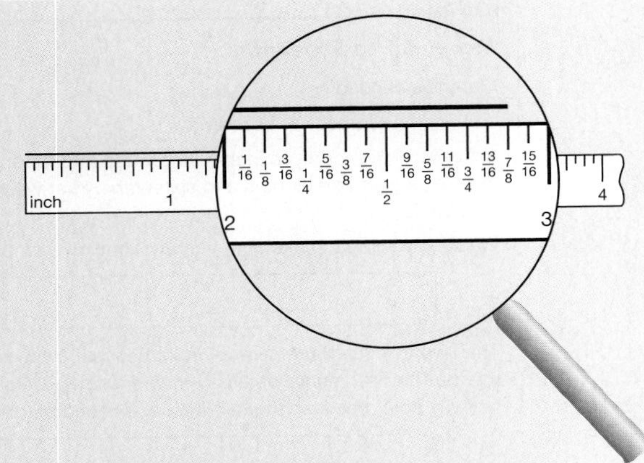

Estimate We find that the line segment is about $2\frac{7}{8}$ **inches long.** This is the nearest sixteenth because the end of the segment aligns more closely to the $\frac{7}{8}$ mark (which equals $\frac{14}{16}$) than it does to the $\frac{13}{16}$ mark or to the $\frac{15}{16}$ mark.

Practice Set

a. $\frac{9}{16}, \frac{5}{8}, \frac{11}{16}, \frac{3}{4}, \frac{13}{16}, \frac{7}{8}, \frac{15}{16}, 1, 1\frac{1}{16}, 1\frac{1}{8}, 1\frac{3}{16}, 1\frac{1}{4}, 1\frac{5}{16}, 1\frac{3}{8}, 1\frac{7}{16}, 1\frac{1}{2}$

a. Generalize Continue this sequence to $1\frac{1}{2}$:

$$\frac{1}{16}, \frac{1}{8}, \frac{3}{16}, \frac{1}{4}, \frac{5}{16}, \frac{3}{8}, \frac{7}{16}, \frac{1}{2}, \ldots$$

b. What number is halfway between −2 and −3? $-2\frac{1}{2}$

c. Represent What number is halfway between 2 and 5? Draw a number line to show the number that is halfway between 2 and 5. $3\frac{1}{2}$; See student work.

d. Connect Point *A* represents what mixed number on this number line? $1\frac{5}{6}$

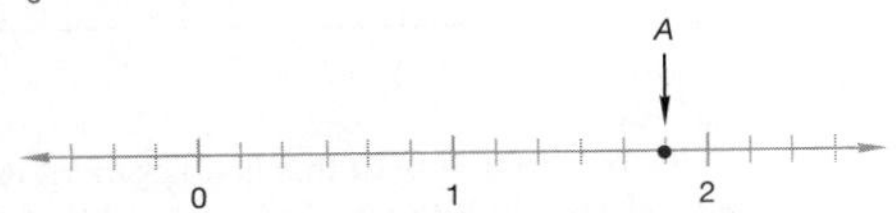

Use your ruler to find the length of each of these line segments to the nearest sixteenth of an inch:

e. ________ $\frac{13}{16}$ in.

f. ________________________ $2\frac{4}{16}$ or $2\frac{1}{4}$ in.

g. ________________________________ $3\frac{3}{16}$ in.

Written Practice *Strengthening Concepts*

1. (12) What is the sum of twelve thousand, five hundred and ten thousand, six hundred ten? 23,110

▶ See Math Conversations in the sidebar.

8. $b + a = c$, $c - a = b$, $c - b = a$; Sample: $a = 2$, $b = 3$, and $c = 5$. $b + a = c$, $3 + 2 = 5$; $c - a = b$, $5 - 2 = 3$; $c - b = a$, $5 - 3 = 2$. The equations are true so the order is correct.

10. A square has four sides of equal length. So to find the perimeter, we add (10 cm + 10 cm + 10 cm + 10 cm), or we multiply (4 × 10 cm).

2. (13) In 1903 the Wright brothers made the first powered airplane flight. In 1969 Americans first landed on the moon. How many years was it from the first powered airplane flight to the first moon landing? (Write an equation and solve the problem.) 66 years; $1969 - 1903 = d$

* 3. (15) Linda can run about 6 yards in one second. About how far can she run in 12 seconds? Write an equation and solve the problem. $12 \times 6 = 72$; 72 yards

* 4. (15) A coin collector has a collection of two dozen rare coins. If the value of each coin is $1000, what is the value of the entire collection? Write an equation and solve the problem. $24 \times \$1000 = v$; $24,000

▶ * 5. (16) **Estimate** Find the sum of 5280 and 1760 by rounding each number to the nearest thousand before adding. 7000

6. (2) $\frac{480}{3}$ 160

7. (5) $\frac{6-6}{3}$ 0

▶ 8. (1) **Represent** The letters *a*, *b*, and *c* represent three different numbers. The sum of *a* and *b* is *c*.

$$a + b = c$$

Rearrange the letters to form another addition equation and two subtraction equations. Hint: To be sure you arranged the letters in the correct order, choose numbers for *a*, *b*, and *c* that make $a + b = c$ true. Then try those numbers in place of the letters in your three equations.

9. (2) Rewrite $2 \div 3$ with a division bar, but do not divide. $\frac{2}{3}$

10. (8) **Explain** A square has sides 10 cm long. Describe how to find its perimeter.

* 11. (17) **Connect** Use a ruler to find the length of the line segment below to the nearest sixteenth of an inch. $3\frac{3}{16}$ in.

Find each unknown number. Check your work.

12. (3) $\$3 - y = \$1.75$ $1.25

13. (3) $m - 20 = 30$ 50

14. (4) $12n = 0$ 0

15. (3) $16 + 14 = 14 + w$ 16

16. (9) Compare: 19×21 ⓐ 20×20 ($<$)

17. (5) $100 - (50 - 25)$ 75

18. (2) $\frac{5280}{44}$ 120

19. (1) $365 + 4576 + 50,287$ 55,228

20. (10) What number is missing in the following sequence?

5, 10, __15__, 20, 25, ...

21. (12) Which digit in 987,654,321 is in the hundred-millions place? 9

▶ 22. (2) $250,000 \div 100$ 2500

23. (2) $\$3.75 \times 10$ $37.50

▶ See Math Conversations in the sidebar.

3 Written Practice

Math Conversations

Discussion opportunities are provided below.

Problem 5 **Estimate**

Extend the Problem

"Suppose each addend was rounded to the nearest hundred instead of to the nearest thousand. How would the estimate change when compared to the exact sum?" Students should generalize that rounding to a lesser place will produce an estimate that is closer to the exact sum.

To support the generalization, ask students to make such an estimate, then compare both estimates to the exact sum of 7040.

Problem 8 **Represent**

Extend the Problem

Write the equation $a + b = c$ on the board. Ask students to use only whole numbers and generate sums by substituting numbers for a and b.

After a number of substitutions, challenge students to write a statement of inequality that compares the sum of a and b to c for whole numbers a and b. Sample: $c \geq a + b$ or $a + b \leq c$

Errors and Misconceptions

Problem 22

Watch for students who write the division as a fraction and make a canceling error. A typical error involves canceling three zeros in the numerator because there are three digits in the denominator. This error results in an incorrect quotient of 250.

When the numerator and the denominator are each a power of 10, as they are in problem **22**, remind students that canceling zeros involves just that—canceling zeros—and does not involve canceling non-zero digits.

(continued)

3 Written Practice (Continued)

Math Conversations

Discussion opportunities are provided below.

Problem 25 Analyze

Extend the Problem

Invite a volunteer to describe (or demonstrate at the board) how the numbers can be grouped in pairs having sums of 12. $(1 + 11) + (3 + 9) + (5 + 7) = 12 + 12 + 12 = 36$.

Problem 26 Explain

After completing the problem, encourage students to explain how they found $\frac{1}{4}$ of 52. Then challenge students to demonstrate at the board other methods that may be used. Sample: Break 52 apart into 40 + 12, then divide each addend by 4.

$\frac{40}{4} + \frac{12}{4} = 10 + 3 = 13$

Problem 28 Analyze

Extend the Problem

Ask students to identify a fraction that is halfway between $\frac{1}{4}$ and $\frac{3}{8}$, and identify a fraction that is halfway between $\frac{3}{8}$ and $\frac{1}{2}$. $\frac{5}{16}$; $\frac{7}{16}$

* **24.** (15) Estimate An 8-ounce serving of 2% milk contains 26 grams of protein, fat, and carbohydrates. About half the grams are carbohydrates. About how many grams are not from carbohydrates? about 13 grams

▶ **25.** (10) Analyze What is the sum of the first six positive odd numbers? 36

▶ **26.** (6) Explain How can you find $\frac{1}{4}$ of 52? One way to find $\frac{1}{4}$ of 52 is to divide 52 by 4.

27. (6) A quarter is $\frac{1}{4}$ of a dollar.

a. How many quarters are in one dollar? 4 quarters

b. How many quarters are in three dollars? 12 quarters

▶* **28.** (17) On an inch ruler, which mark is halfway between the $\frac{1}{4}$-inch mark and the $\frac{1}{2}$-inch mark? $\frac{3}{8}$-inch mark

* **29.** (17) Point A represents what mixed number on the number line below? $4\frac{1}{6}$

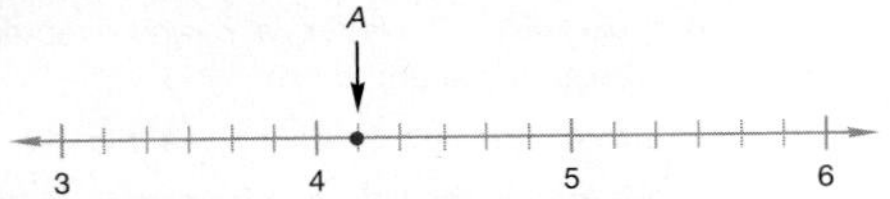

* **30.** (17) A segment that is $\frac{1}{2}$ of an inch long is how many sixteenths of an inch long? 8 sixteenths of an inch

Early Finishers *Real-World Application*

Read the problem below. Then decide whether you can use an estimate to answer the question or if you need to compute an exact answer. Explain how you find your answer.

Manny has one gallon of paint. The label states that it covers about 350–450 square feet. Manny wants to paint the living room, dining room and family room of his home. The lateral surface area of all of the rooms totals about 800 square feet. How much more paint should Manny buy? Sample: Use an estimate: 800 sq. ft ÷ 2 = 400 sq. ft. Since one gallon of paint will cover about one-half the walls Manny plans to paint, he should buy one more gallon of paint.

▶ See Math Conversations in the sidebar.

Looking Forward

Reading fractions and mixed numbers on a number line prepares students for:

- **Lesson 47,** measuring and finding the circumference and diameter of circular objects.
- **Investigation 11,** using the legend on a scale drawing to find the actual measurement of an object.

• Average
• Line Graphs

Objectives

- Make equal groups to find an average.
- Find the average of several numbers by adding the numbers and dividing the sum by the number of addends.
- Identify a number that is halfway between two numbers by finding the average of the two numbers.
- Interpret a line graph.

Lesson Preparation

Materials

- **Power Up B** (in *Instructional Masters*)
- **Lesson Activity 2** (in *Instructional Masters*)
- **Manipulative kit: rulers**
- **Teacher-provided material: square pieces of paper; scissors**

Optional

- **Manipulative kit: color tiles**
- **18 books**

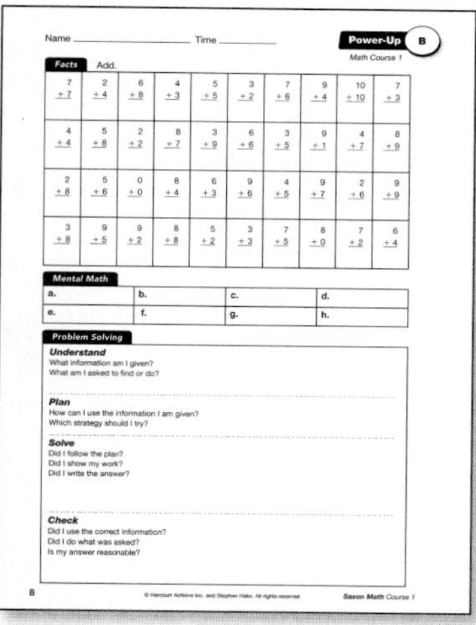
Name ____ Time ____ Power-Up B
Math Course 1
Facts Add.
Mental Math
a. b. c. d.
e. f. g. h.
Problem Solving
Understand
What information am I given?
What am I asked to find or do?
Plan
How can I use the information I am given?
Which strategy should I try?
Solve
Did I follow the plan?
Did I show my work?
Did I write the answer?
Check
Did I use the correct information?
Did I do what was asked?
Is my answer reasonable?

Power Up B

Math Language

New	Maintain	English Learners (ESL)
average	**graph**	**respectively**
line graph		
mean		

Technology Resources

Student eBook Complete student textbook in electronic format.

Resources and Planner CD Assessment, reteaching, and instructional masters, plus a pacing calendar with standards.

Test and Practice Generator CD Create additional practice sheets and custom-made tests.

www.SaxonPublishers.com Visit for more student activities and planning materials.

Inclusion

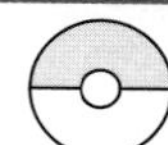

Adaptations CD Adapted lessons, investigations, practice and assessments.

Meeting Standards

National Council of Teachers of Mathematics (NCTM)

Data Analysis and Probability

DP.2a Find, use, and interpret measures of center and spread, including mean and interquartile range

Problem Solving

PS.1b Solve problems that arise in mathematics and in other contexts

CN.4c Recognize and apply mathematics in contexts outside of mathematics

Power-Up Discussion *For use with Power Up, p. 93*

Problem-Solving Strategy: Use Logical Reasoning

In his pocket Alex had seven coins totaling exactly one dollar. Name a possible combination of coins in his pocket. How many different combinations of coins are possible?

Understand **Understand the problem.**

"What information are we given?"

Alex had seven coins, and the coins totaled one dollar.

"What are we asked to do?"

1. We are asked to name a coin combination that could be in Alex's pocket.
2. We are asked to find the number of possible seven–coin combinations that make $1.

"What else do we know?"

We know the total value of coins. We also know that the coins could include the following: penny (1¢), nickel (5¢), dime (10¢), quarter (25¢), and half-dollar (50¢).

Plan **Make a Plan.**

"What problem-solving strategy will we use?"

We can *use logical reasoning* to determine the coin combinations Alex could have.

Solve **Carry out the plan.**

"Does Alex have any pennies?"

No, because to total exactly one dollar he would need at least 5 pennies. But then Alex would need two more coins that total 95¢, which is impossible.

"Can Alex have any coin combinations that do not include half-dollars or quarters?"

No. The coin with the next highest value is the dime. Even if all seven of Alex's coins were dimes, he would have only 70¢. Therefore, each combination must have at least 2 quarters or 1 half dollar.

"Can Alex have 4 quarters?"

No, because 4 quarters are equal to $1. Additional coins would make the total more than $1.

"Can Alex have 3 quarters?"

Yes, he has 75¢ and needs four other coins to total 25¢. One dime and 3 nickels is 25¢.

"Can Alex have 2 quarters (50¢)?"

Alex would need five other coins that total 50¢. Five dimes is 50¢.

"Can Alex have 1 quarter (25¢)?"

If one of the other coins is a half-dollar, then the other five coins total 25¢. Five nickels is 25¢.

"Are there other combinations that include a half-dollar?"

Yes, a half-dollar plus four dimes and 2 nickels total $1.00.

HD	Q	D	N	Total
	3	1	3	$1.00
	2	5		$1.00
1	1		5	$1.00
1		4	2	$1.00

"How many different combinations of seven coins total $1.00?" Four.

Check **Look back.**

"Did we complete the task?"

Yes. We found four different combinations of seven coins that total $1.00.

LESSON 18

• Average
• Line Graphs

Power Up — *Building Power*

facts Power Up B

mental math

a. **Number Sense:** 4 × 23 equals 4 × 20 plus 4 × 3. Find 4 × 23. 92

b. **Number Sense:** 4 × 32 128

c. **Number Sense:** 3 × 42 126

d. **Number Sense:** 3 × 24 72

e. **Geometry:** A hexagon has sides that measure 15 ft. What is the perimeter of the hexagon? 90 ft

f. **Measurement:** How many days are in 2 weeks? 14 days

g. **Measurement:** How many hours are in 2 days? 48 hours

h. **Calculation:** Start with a half dozen. Add 2; multiply by 3; divide by 4; then subtract 5.What is the answer? 1

problem solving In his pocket Alex had seven coins totaling exactly one dollar. Name a possible combination of coins in his pocket. How many different combinations of coins are possible? 4 combinations are possible: 3Q, 1D, 3N; 2Q, 5D; 1HD, 1Q, 5N; 1HD, 4D, 2N

New Concepts — *Increasing Knowledge*

average Here we show three stacks of books; the stacks contain 8 books, 7 books, and 3 books respectively. Altogether there are 18 books, but the number of books in each stack is not equal.

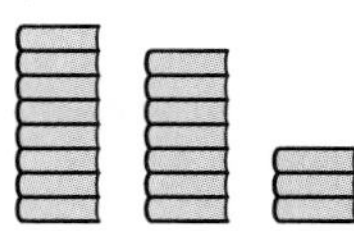

If we move some of the books from the taller stacks to the shortest stack, we can make the three stacks the same height. Then there will be 6 books in each stack.

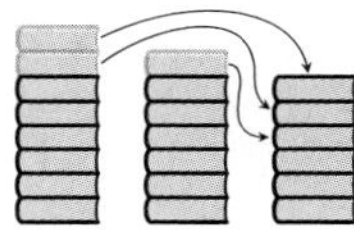

Facts Add.

7 + 7 = 14	2 + 4 = 6	6 + 8 = 14	4 + 3 = 7	5 + 5 = 10	3 + 2 = 5	7 + 6 = 13	9 + 4 = 13	10 + 10 = 20	7 + 3 = 10
4 + 4 = 8	5 + 8 = 13	2 + 2 = 4	8 + 7 = 15	3 + 9 = 12	6 + 6 = 12	3 + 5 = 8	9 + 1 = 10	4 + 7 = 11	8 + 9 = 17
2 + 8 = 10	5 + 6 = 11	0 + 0 = 0	8 + 4 = 12	6 + 3 = 9	9 + 6 = 15	4 + 5 = 9	9 + 7 = 16	2 + 6 = 8	9 + 9 = 18
3 + 8 = 11	9 + 5 = 14	9 + 2 = 11	8 + 8 = 16	5 + 2 = 7	3 + 3 = 6	7 + 5 = 12	8 + 0 = 8	7 + 2 = 9	6 + 4 = 10

1 Power Up

Facts

Distribute **Power Up B** to students. See answers below.

Mental Math

Before students begin the Mental Math exercise, do this counting exercise as a class.

Count by 3s from 3 to 60.

Encourage students to share different ways to mentally compute these exercises. Strategies for exercises **b** and **d** are listed below.

b. Add Partial Products
4 × 32 = (4 × 30) + (4 × 2) =
120 + 8 = 128

Multiply Tens and Ones, then Add
4 × 32 = 4 × 3 tens + 4 × 2 ones =
12 tens + 8 ones = 128

d. Count on by 25, then Subtract 3
Start with 25. Count: 50, 75; 75 − 3 = 72

Add Partial Products
3 × 24 = (3 × 20) + (3 × 4) =
60 + 12 = 72

Problem Solving

Refer to **Power-Up Discussion**, p. 93B.

2 New Concepts

Instruction

Preview the lesson by posing the introductory word as a problem to act out. Collect 18 books and arrange them to form a stack of 8 books, a stack of 7 books, and a stack of 3 books. Ask volunteers to model the average number of books in each stack by rearranging the books into three stacks of equal number.

(continued)

2 New Concepts (Continued)

Example 1

Instruction

After completing the example, remind students that finding an average is a two-step process that involves "combining" (using addition to find a sum) and finding "equal groups" (using division to find the number in each group).

Invite students to suggest real-world situations that involve averages, and you might choose to ask one or more volunteers to record the situations on the board.

Example 2

Instruction

To reinforce the idea of finding an average by combining and making equal groups, have students use color tiles from the Manipulative Kit or classroom items such as paper clips to model example 2 and its solution. Using groups of 3, 7, and 8 items, students first combine the items in one large pile and count the items in the pile. Then, ask students to separate the items into three equal groups and count the number in each group.

(continued)

By making the stacks equal, we have found the **average** number of books in the three stacks. Notice that the average number of books in each stack is greater than the number in the smallest stack and less than the number in the largest stack. One way we can find an average is by making equal groups.

Example 1

In four classrooms there were 28 students, 27 students, 26 students, and 31 students respectively. What was the average number of students per classroom?

Solution

The average number of students per classroom is how many students there would be in each room if we made the numbers equal. So we will take the total number of students and make four equal groups. To find the total number of students, we add the numbers in each classroom.

$$\begin{array}{r} 28 \text{ students} \\ 27 \text{ students} \\ 26 \text{ students} \\ +\ 31 \text{ students} \\ \hline 112 \text{ students in all} \end{array}$$

We make four equal groups by dividing the total number of students by four.

$$4\overline{)112 \text{ students}} = 28 \text{ students}$$

If the groups were equal, there would be 28 students in each classroom. The average number of students per classroom would be **28.**

Notice that an average problem is a "combining" problem and an "equal groups" problem. First we found the total number of students in all the classrooms ("combining" problem). Then we found the number of students that would be in each group if the groups were equal ("equal groups" problem).

Example 2

Use counters to model the average of 3, 7, and 8.

Solution

Thinking Skill

Connect

What are some other real-life situations where we might need to find the average of a set of numbers? Sample answer: sports scores, weather data, science experiments

This question does not tell us whether the numbers 3, 7, and 8 refer to books or students or coins or quiz scores. Still, we can find the average of these numbers by combining and then making equal groups. We can model the problem with counters. Since there are three numbers, there will be three groups of counters with 3, 7, and 8 counters in the groups. To find the average we make the groups equal. One way to do this is to first combine all the counters in the three groups. That gives us a total of 18 counters.

$$3 + 7 + 8 = 18$$

Then we divide the total into three equal groups.

$$18 \div 3 = 6$$

English Learners

Explain that in example 1 the word **respectively** refers to the order that information is given. Draw this illustration on the board.

Row 1: □□□

Row 2: □□

Row 3: □□□□

Ask the students how many squares are in each row. Then say:

"Rows 1, 2 and 3 have three squares, two squares, and four squares, respectively. Notice that I said the number of squares in the same order shown in the illustration on the board."

Draw a similar illustration with different numbers of squares. Have the students say with you, "There are ___, ___, and ___ squares respectively."

That gives us three groups of six counters. We find that the average of 3, 7, and 8 is **6.**

Example 3

What number is halfway between 27 and 81?

Solution

The number halfway between two numbers is also the average of the two numbers. For example, the average of 7 and 9 is 8, and 8 is halfway between 7 and 9. So the average of 27 and 81 will be the number halfway between 27 and 81. We add 27 and 81 and divide by 2.

$$\text{Average of 27 and 81} = \frac{27 + 81}{2}$$

$$= \frac{108}{2}$$

$$= 54$$

The number halfway between 27 and 81 is **54.**

The average we have talked about in this lesson is also called the **mean.** We will learn more about average and mean in later lessons.

line graphs

Line graphs display numerical information as points connected by line segments. Whereas bar graphs often display comparisons, line graphs often show how a measurement changes over time.

Example 4

Reading Math

On this line graph, the *horizontal axis* is divided into equal segments that represent years. The *vertical axis* is divided into equal segments that represent inches. The labels on the axes tell us how many years and how many inches.

This line graph shows Margie's height in inches from her eighth birthday to her fourteenth birthday. During which year did Margie grow the most?

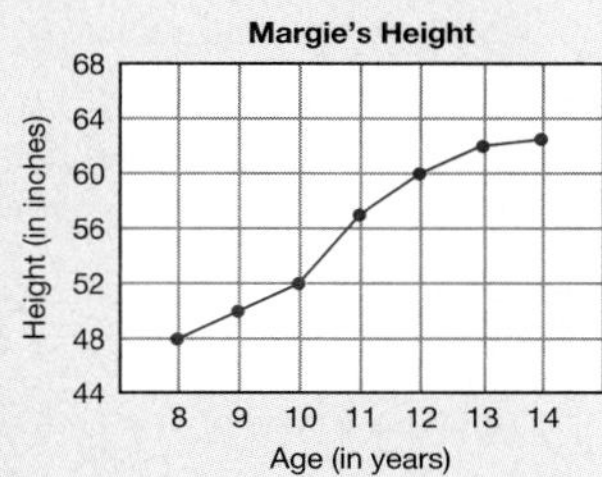

Solution

From Margie's eighth birthday to her ninth birthday, she grew about two inches. She also grew about two inches from her ninth to her tenth birthday. From her tenth to her eleventh birthday, Margie grew about five inches. Notice that this is the steepest part of the growth line. So the year Margie grew the most was **the year she was ten.**

2 New Concepts (Continued)

Example 3

Instruction

Emphasize that a number halfway between two numbers is the average of the two numbers.

Example 4

Instruction

Before working through this example, review with students how to read a line graph. For your review, you might choose to duplicate the line graph from this example on the board, or on an overhead transparency. Include as part of your review a discussion of different ways to estimate values that are between intervals.

(continued)

Math Background

There is more than one kind of average. The most commonly used average is the *arithmetic mean*, or simply *mean*, which is presented in this lesson.

In an effort to use time efficiently, students often work with data that produce a mean that is a whole number. However, it is important for students to realize that some data will produce a mean that is not a whole number.

2 New Concepts (Continued)

Practice Set

Problem a Verify

"To solve this problem, you added 26, 36, and 43, and then you divided the sum by 3. Did the order in which you added the numbers matter? Explain why or why not." No; the Associative Property of Addition states that three numbers can be added in any order.

Problem c Justify

Extend the Problem

"To solve this problem, suppose a student subtracts 2 from 82 to make 80, and adds 2 to 28 to make 30. The student then uses mental math to find the number that is halfway between 30 and 80.

Will this method produce the correct answer? Explain why or why not." Yes; the sum of 82 and 28 is the same as the sum of 80 and 30, and the quotient $(82 + 28) \div 2$ is the same as the quotient $(80 + 30) \div 2$.

Problem e Evaluate

Extend the Problem

"Suppose another number was added to the data set, and the number was 9. Would the average of the data change? Explain why or why not." No; ask students to check their explanations by comparing the two averages.

3 Written Practice

Math Conversations

Discussion opportunities are provided below.

Problem 3 Estimate

To check their answers for reasonableness, ask students to estimate the cost before finding the exact cost.

Problem 5 Evaluate

Extend the Problem

"Suppose one number in the data is changed and the new average of the data is 10. What number was changed and what new number was it changed to?" The possibilities include: 7 changed to 13; 8 changed to 14; or 9 changed to 15.

Problem 7 Analyze

"How can we tell that the answer to this problem will be a negative number?" Students should generalize that when a larger number is subtracted from a smaller number, the difference will be a negative number.

(continued)

Your teacher might ask you to keep a line graph of your math test scores. The **Lesson Activity 2** Test Scores Line Graph can be used for this purpose.

Practice Set

▶ **a.** There were 26 books on the first shelf, 36 books on the second shelf, and 43 books on the third shelf. Velma rearranged the books so that there were the same number of books on each shelf. After Velma rearranged the books, how many were on the first shelf ? 35 books

b. What is the average of 96, 44, 68, and 100? 77

▶ **c.** What number is halfway between 28 and 82? 55

d. What number is halfway between 86 and 102? 94

▶ **e.** Find the average of 3, 6, 9, 12, and 15. 9

Use the information in the graph in example 4 to answer these questions:

f. How many inches did Margie grow from her eighth to her twelfth birthday? 12 in.

g. During which year did Margie grow the least? between her thirteenth and her fourteenth birthdays

h. Predict Based on the information in the graph, would you predict that Margie will grow to be 68 inches tall? no

Written Practice *Strengthening Concepts*

1. (11) Jumbo ate two thousand, sixty-eight peanuts in the morning and three thousand, nine hundred forty in the afternoon. How many peanuts did Jumbo eat in all? What kind of pattern did you use? 6008 peanuts; addition pattern

2. (11) Jimmy counted his permanent teeth. He had 11 on the top and 12 on the bottom. An adult has 32 permanent teeth. How many more of Jimmy's teeth need to grow in? What kind of pattern did you use? 9 teeth; addition pattern

▶ ***3.** (15) Olivia bought one dozen colored pencils for an art project. Each pencil cost 53¢ each. How much did Olivia spend on pencils? What kind of pattern did you use? $6.36; multiplication pattern

***4.** (16) Estimate Find the difference of 5035 and 1987 by rounding each number to the nearest thousand before subtracting. 3000

▶ ***5.** (18) Find the average of 9, 7, and 8. 8

***6.** (18) What number is halfway between 59 and 81? 70

▶ ***7.** (14) What number is 6 less than 2? −4

8. (2) $0.35 × 100 $35

9. (2) 10,010 ÷ 10 1001

10. (2) 34,180 ÷ 17 2010 R 10

▶ See Math Conversations in the sidebar.

11. (1) $3.64 + $94.28 + 87¢ $98.79

12. (1) 41,375 − 13,576 27,799

13. (2) 125 × 16 2000

14. (5) 4 · 3 · 2 · 1 · 0 0

Analyze Find each unknown number. Check your work.

15. (3) $w - 84 = 48$ 132

16. (4) $\frac{234}{n} = 6$ 39

17. (3, 5) $(1 + 2) \times 3 = (1 \times 2) + m$ 7

▶ **18.** (8) **Model** Draw a rectangle 5 cm long and 3 cm wide. What is its perimeter? 16 cm

19. (10) What is the sum of the first six positive even numbers? 42

20. Multiply the value of a term by 2 to find the next term.

20. (10) **Generalize** Describe the rule of the following sequence. Then find the missing term.

1, 2, 4, __8__, 16, 32, 64, ...

21. (9) Compare: 500 × 1 (=) 500 ÷ 1

▶ **22.** (6) **Generalize** What number is $\frac{1}{2}$ of 1110? 555

23. (12) What is the place value of the 7 in 987,654,321? millions

Refer to the line graph shown below to answer problems **24–26.**

Heart Rates During Various Activities

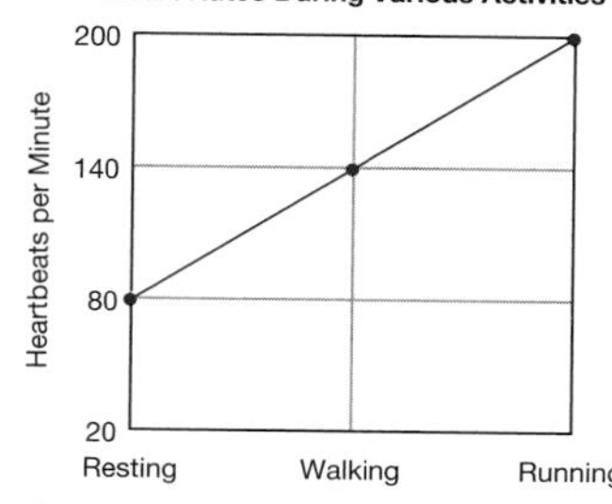

* **24.** (18) **Estimate** Running increases a resting person's heart rate by about how many heartbeats per minute? 120 heartbeats per minute

* **25.** (18) **Estimate** About how many times would a person's heart beat during a 10-minute run? 2000 times

* **26.** (18) **Formulate** Using the information in the line graph, write a word problem about comparing. Then answer the problem. Answers will vary. See student work.

* **27.** (18) **Explain** In three classrooms there are 24, 27, and 33 students respectively. How many students will be in each classroom if some students are moved from one classroom to the other classrooms so that the number of students in each classroom is equal? How do you know that your answer is reasonable? 28 students; The average should be a central number between the least and greatest numbers being averaged. Since 28 is between 24 and 33, the answer is reasonable.

▶ See Math Conversations in the sidebar.

3 Written Practice (Continued)

Math Conversations

Discussion opportunities are provided below.

Problem 18 Model

Extend the Problem

Invite students to sketch a rectangle that has a perimeter of 16 cm but a different ratio of length to width. Sample: A square having a side measure of 4 cm or a rectangle having a length of 6 cm and a width of 2 cm.

Ask students to describe their rectangles.

Problem 22 Generalize

After completing the problem, challenge students to describe different ways of finding $\frac{1}{2}$ of 1110 using mental math. Sample: Divide each place value by 2; $(1000 \div 2) + (100 \div 2) + (10 \div 2) = 500 + 50 + 5 = 555$.

Errors and Misconceptions

Problem 14

Students should recognize without computing that the product is zero. Remind students to read expressions in their entirety before simplifying or solving them.

(continued)

3 Written Practice (Continued)

Math Conversations

Discussion opportunities are provided below.

Problem 29 Model

Review the concept of perimeter by having students find the perimeter of the rectangle.

Problem 30 Formulate

Ask students to write and solve a word problem about finding an average. Students should then exchange and solve other word problems, and compare answers.

28. (6) A dime is $\frac{1}{10}$ of a dollar.

a. How many dimes are in a dollar? 10 dimes

b. How many dimes are in three dollars? 30 dimes

29.

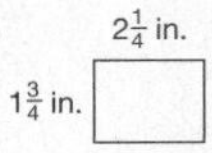

▶* **29.** (17) Model Use a ruler to draw a rectangle that is $2\frac{1}{4}$ inches long and $1\frac{3}{4}$ inches wide.

▶* **30.** (18) Formulate Word problems about finding an average include which two types of problems? (Select two)

combining separating comparing equal groups

combining, equal groups

Early Finishers
Real-World Application

The cost of one cubic foot of natural gas in my town is \$0.67. My meter reading on July 31 was 1518. On August 31 it was 1603. The meter measures natural gas in cubic feet.

a. How many cubic feet of gas did I use in the month of August (between the two meter readings)? 1603 − 1518 = 85 cubic feet

b. What was my total gas cost for the month? 85 × \$0.67 = \$56.95

98 *Saxon Math Course 1*

▶ See Math Conversations in the sidebar.

Looking Forward

Reading and interpreting information from line graphs prepares students for:

- **Lesson 40,** interpreting information on circle graphs.
- **Investigation 4,** understanding data collection and surveys.
- **Investigation 5,** looking at ways to display data such as horizontal bar graphs, pictographs, and pie charts.
- **Investigation 9,** interpreting and presenting data in a table to show experimental probability.
- **Investigation 10,** creating diagrams to show compound experiment results.

• Factors
• Prime Numbers

Objectives

- Name all the factors of a given number.
- Identify prime numbers.

Lesson Preparation

Materials

- **Power Up D** (in *Instructional Masters*)
- **Lesson Activity 3** (in *Instructional Masters*)
- **Manipulative kit: rulers**

Optional

- **Primes and Composites poster**

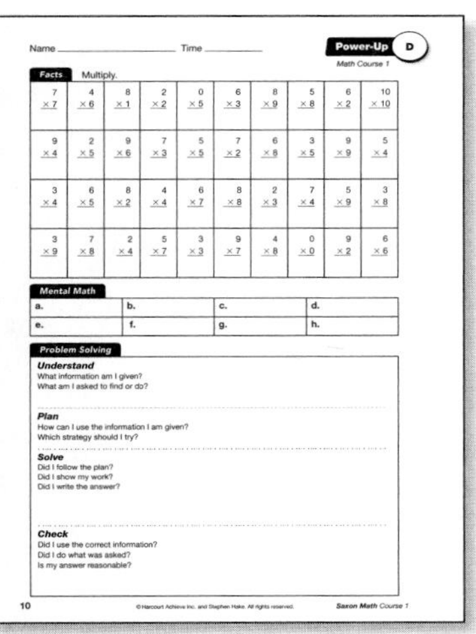

Power Up D

Math Language

New	Maintain	English Learners (ESL)
prime number	factor	shared

Technology Resources

Student eBook Complete student textbook in electronic format.

Resources and Planner CD Assessment, reteaching, and instructional masters, plus a pacing calendar with standards.

Test and Practice Generator CD Create additional practice sheets and custom-made tests.

www.SaxonPublishers.com Visit for more student activities and planning materials.

Inclusion

Adaptations CD Adapted lessons, investigations, practice and assessments.

Meeting Standards

National Council of Teachers of Mathematics (NCTM)

Numbers and Operations

NO.1f Use factors, multiples, prime factorization, and relatively prime numbers to solve problems

NO.1g Develop meaning for integers and represent and compare quantities with them

Problem Solving

PS.1b Solve problems that arise in mathematics and in other contexts

Connections

CN.4a Recognize and use connections among mathematical ideas

Power-Up Discussion *For use with Power Up, p. 99*

Problem-Solving Strategy: Use Logical Reasoning

Doubles tennis is played on a rectangular-shaped court that is 78 feet long and 36 feet wide. In the drawing of the doubles tennis court, how many rectangles can you find?

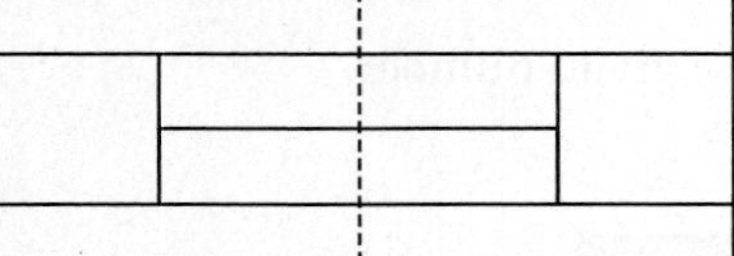

Understand Understand the problem.

"What information are we given?"

We are given a diagram and the dimensions of a doubles' tennis court.

"What are we asked to do?"

Determine how many different rectangles can be found on the tennis court.

"What do we already know about rectangles?"

A rectangle has 4 right angles and 2 pairs of parallel sides. Each pair of parallel sides is equal in length. We also know rectangles of varying sizes located side-by-side form larger, overlapping rectangles.

"We expect our answer to be in what range?"

Student answers will vary. We can immediately see the whole court as one large rectangle that is divided into ten smaller rectangles. We know our answer will be greater than 11.

Plan Make a plan.

"What problem solving strategy will we use?"

We will *use logical and spatial reasoning* to visualize rectangles of various sizes/dimensions.

Solve Carry out the plan.

"What will we need to do to "see" all the rectangles?"

We will need to divide larger rectangles into smaller rectangles, and to adjoin smaller rectangles to make larger ones.

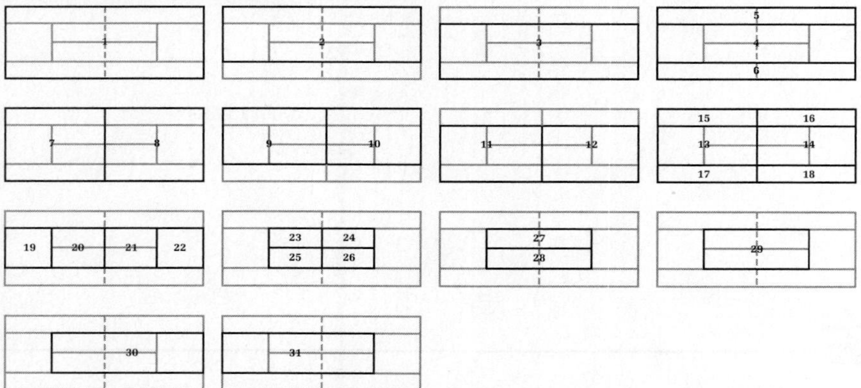

Check Look back.

Did we complete the task?

Yes. We found there are 31 different rectangles on a doubles tennis court.

LESSON 19

• Factors
• Prime Numbers

Power Up — *Building Power*

facts Power Up D

mental math

a. **Number Sense:** 3×64 192

b. **Number Sense:** 3×46 138

c. **Number Sense:** $120 + 18$ 138

d. **Calculation:** $34 + 40 + 9$ 83

e. **Calculation:** $34 + 50 - 1$ 83

f. **Calculation:** \$20.00 − \$12.50 \$7.50

g. **Measurement:** How many decades are in 2 centuries? 20 decades

h. **Calculation:** Start with 100. Divide by 2; subtract 1; divide by 7; then add 3. What is the answer? 10

problem solving Doubles tennis is played on a rectangular-shaped court that is 78 feet long and 36 feet wide. In the drawing of the doubles tennis court, how many rectangles can you find? See script for solution.

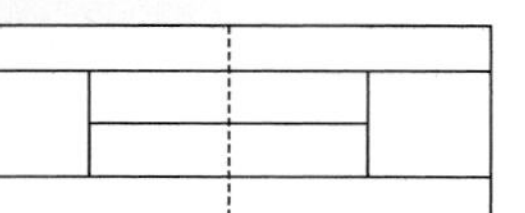

New Concepts — *Increasing Knowledge*

factors Recall from Lesson 2 that a factor is one of the numbers multiplied to form a product.

$2 \times 3 = 6$ Both 2 and 3 are factors.

$1 \times 6 = 6$ Both 1 and 6 are factors.

We see that each of the numbers 1, 2, 3, and 6 are factors of 6. Notice that when we divide 6 by 1, 2, 3, or 6, the resulting quotient has no remainder (that is, it has a remainder of zero). We say that 6 is "divisible by" 1, 2, 3, and 6.

$$1\overline{)6} = 6 \text{ r } 0 \qquad 2\overline{)6} = 3 \text{ r } 0 \qquad 3\overline{)6} = 2 \text{ r } 0 \qquad 6\overline{)6} = 1 \text{ r } 0$$

This leads us to another definition of *factor*.

> The **factors** of a given number are the whole numbers that divide the given number without a remainder.

Thinking Skill

How are the two definitions of **factor** connected? The first definition refers to multiplication; it begins with the factors and works to find the product. The second refers to division; it begins with the product and works to find the factors.

Facts Multiply.

7 × 7 = 49	4 × 6 = 24	8 × 1 = 8	2 × 2 = 4	0 × 5 = 0	6 × 3 = 18	8 × 9 = 72	5 × 8 = 40	6 × 2 = 12	10 × 10 = 100
9 × 4 = 36	2 × 5 = 10	9 × 6 = 54	7 × 3 = 21	5 × 5 = 25	7 × 2 = 14	6 × 8 = 48	3 × 5 = 15	9 × 9 = 81	5 × 4 = 20
3 × 4 = 12	6 × 5 = 30	8 × 2 = 16	4 × 4 = 16	6 × 7 = 42	8 × 8 = 64	2 × 3 = 6	7 × 4 = 28	5 × 9 = 45	3 × 8 = 24
3 × 9 = 27	7 × 8 = 56	2 × 4 = 8	5 × 7 = 35	3 × 3 = 9	9 × 7 = 63	4 × 8 = 32	0 × 0 = 0	9 × 2 = 18	6 × 6 = 36

1 Power Up

Facts
Distribute **Power Up D** to students. See answers below.

Mental Math
Before students begin the Mental Math exercise, do this counting exercise as a class.

Count up and down by $\frac{1}{4}$s between $\frac{1}{4}$ and 12.

Encourage students to share different ways to mentally compute these exercises. Strategies for exercises **c** and **e** are listed below.

c. Add 10, then Add 8

$120 + 18 = 120 + 10 + 8 = 130 + 8 = 138$

Add 20, then Subtract 2

$120 + 20 = 140;\ 140 - 2 = 138$

e. Add 50, then Subtract 1

$34 + 50 - 1 = 84 - 1 = 83$

Count by Tens, then Count Back 1

Start with 34. Count: 44, 54, 64, 74, 84

Count back 1: 83

Problem Solving
Refer to **Power-Up Discussion,** p. 99B.

2 New Concepts

Instruction
When working with factors, the phrase "divides evenly" is sometimes used to indicate that one number is divisible by another. For example: 6 can be divided evenly by 1, 2, 3, and 6.

(continued)

2 New Concepts (Continued)

Example 1

Instruction

After completing the example, make sure students generalize that the factors of a whole number always include the number itself, but a factor can never be greater than the number itself.

Example 2

Instruction

Students may be interested to learn that the proper factors of a number are all of the factors of that number except the number itself.

A number is said to be a *perfect* number if the sum of its proper factors is equal to the number, a number is said to be an *abundant* number if the sum of its proper factors is greater than the number, and a number is said to be a *deficient* number if the sum of its proper factors is less than the number.

You might choose to use these ideas if your students require extra practice in finding factors.

(continued)

We can illustrate the factors of 6 by arranging 6 tiles to form rectangles. With 6 tiles we can make a 1-by-6 rectangle. We can also make a 2-by-3 rectangle.

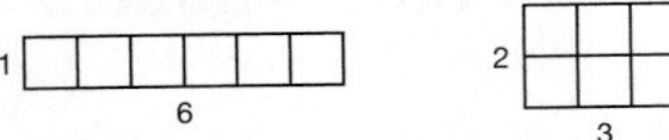

The number of tiles along the sides of these two rectangles (1, 6, 2, 3) are the four factors of 6.

Example 1

What are the factors of 10?

Solution

The factors of 10 are all the numbers that divide 10 evenly (with no remainder). They are **1, 2, 5,** and **10.**

$$\begin{array}{r}10\\1\overline{)10}\end{array} \quad \begin{array}{r}5\\2\overline{)10}\end{array} \quad \begin{array}{r}2\\5\overline{)10}\end{array} \quad \begin{array}{r}1\\10\overline{)10}\end{array}$$

We can illustrate the factors of 10 with two rectangular arrays of tiles.

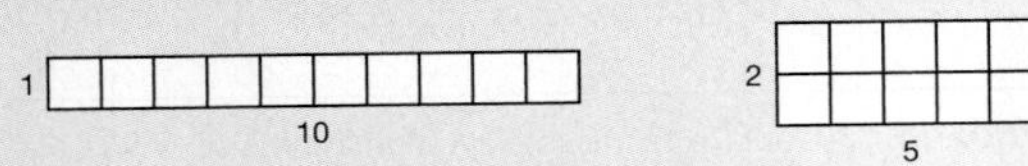

The number of tiles along the sides of the two rectangles (1, 10, 2, 5) are the factors of 10.

Example 2

How many different whole numbers are factors of 12?

Solution

Twelve can be divided evenly by 1, 2, 3, 4, 6, and 12. The question asked "How many?" Counting factors, we find that 12 has **6** different whole-number factors.

Twelve tiles can be arranged to form three different shapes of rectangles. The lengths of the sides illustrate that the six factors of 12 are 1, 12, 2, 6, 3, and 4.

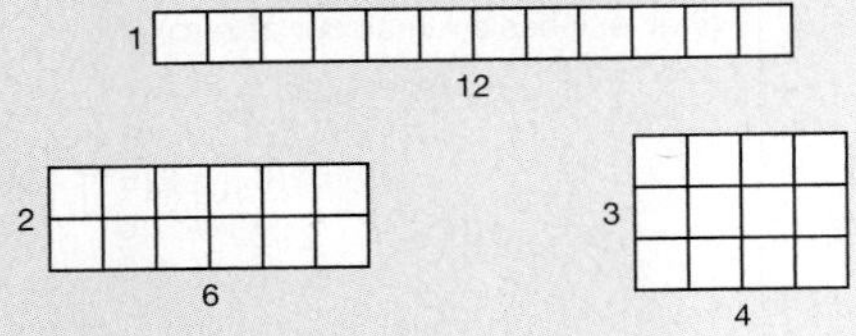

Model Draw tiles to illustrate the factors of 18. How many different shapes of rectangles can you make? Drawing should show rectangles that are: 1 × 18, 2 × 9, and 3 × 6; 3 rectangles

Inclusion

To help students find all of the factors of a number, demonstrate this strategy using 12 as an example.

- List the smallest and the largest factors, which are always 1 and the number itself:

  12: 1 12

- Use the number 2 and division facts to find the next two factors, 12 ÷ 2 = 6

  12: 1, 2, 6, 12

- Use the number 3 and division facts to find the next two factors, 12 ÷ 3 = 4

  12: 1, 2, 3, 4 6, 12

- Use the numbers 5, and 7–11 and division facts to continue. As 12 is not divisible by 5, 7, 8, 9, 10, or 11, the factors of 12 are: 1, 2, 3, 4, 6, and 12.

prime numbers

Here we list the first ten counting numbers and their factors. Which of the numbers have exactly two factors? 2, 3, 5, 7

Number	Factors
1	1
2	1, 2
3	1, 3
4	1, 2, 4
5	1, 5
6	1, 2, 3, 6
7	1, 7
8	1, 2, 4, 8
9	1, 3, 9
10	1, 2, 5, 10

Counting numbers that have exactly two factors are **prime numbers.** The first four prime numbers are 2, 3, 5, and 7. The only factors of a prime number are the number itself and 1. The number 1 is not a prime number, because it has only one factor, itself.

Therefore, to determine whether a number is prime, we may ask ourselves the question, "Is this number divisible by any number other than the number itself and 1?" If the number is divisible by any other number, the number is not prime.

Example 3

The first four prime numbers are 2, 3, 5, and 7. What are the next four prime numbers?

Solution

We will consider the next several numbers and eliminate those that are not prime.

8, 9, 10, 11, 12, 13, 14, 15, 16, 17, 18, 19, 20

All even numbers have 2 as a factor. So no even numbers greater than two are prime numbers. We can eliminate the even numbers from the list.

~~8~~, 9, ~~10~~, 11, ~~12~~, 13, ~~14~~, 15, ~~16~~, 17, ~~18~~, 19, ~~20~~

Since 9 is divisible by 3, and 15 is divisible by 3 and by 5, we can eliminate 9 and 15 from the list.

~~8~~, ~~9~~, ~~10~~, 11, ~~12~~, 13, ~~14~~, ~~15~~, ~~16~~, 17, ~~18~~, 19, ~~20~~

Each of the remaining four numbers on the list is divisible only by itself and by 1. Thus the next four prime numbers after 7 are **11, 13, 17,** and **19.**

2 New Concepts *(Continued)*

Instruction

You may wish to display the **Primes and Composites** concept poster as you discuss this topic with students.

Example 3

Instruction

Some students may ask if zero is a prime number. The answer is no because prime numbers are restricted to the set of positive integers. Aside from that, however, zero is not prime because it has an infinite number of factors—it is divisible by all other numbers except itself.

(continued)

Activity

Instruction

This activity is an example of Eratosthenes' Sieve. (See Math Background at the bottom of this page.)

To help students make sense of a sieve and the activity, you might share with them the following analogy: A sieve is like a spaghetti strainer; the water drains out and the spaghetti is left behind. Eratosthenes' Sieve is a prime number strainer; the nonprime numbers fall out and the prime numbers are left behind.

2 New Concepts (Continued)

Practice Set

Problems a–d Error Alert

When naming the factors of a number, students sometimes omit 1 and/or the number itself. Remind students that all whole numbers greater than 1 have at least two factors—the number itself, and 1.

Also when naming the factors of a number, students can look for pairs of factors. For example, the factors of 12 include 1 and 12, 2 and 6, and 3 and 4. Have students note that the product of the factor pairs is the number itself. The only exception to this rule is a number that is a perfect square (such a 4, 9, 16, 25, and so on). When naming the factors of a perfect square, one factor will be paired with itself. For example, the factors of 16 are 1 and 16, 2 and 8, and 4 (because $4 \times 4 = 16$).

Problems e–g Justify

After identifying the prime number in each group, ask students to explain why the other numbers in the group are not prime.

Activity

Prime Numbers

List the counting numbers from 1 to 100 (or use **Lesson Activity 3** Hundred Number Chart). Then follow these directions:

Step 1: Draw a line through the number 1. The number 1 is not a prime number.

Step 2: Circle the prime number 2. Draw a line through all the other multiples of 2 (4, 6, 8, etc.).

Step 3: Circle the prime number 3. Draw a line through all the other multiples of 3 (6, 9, 12, etc.).

Step 4: Circle the prime number 5. Draw a line through all the other multiples of 5 (10, 15, 20, etc.).

Step 5: Circle the prime number 7. Draw a line through all the other multiples of 7 (14, 21, 28, etc.).

Step 6: Circle all remaining numbers on your list (the numbers that do not have a line drawn through them).

When you have finished, all the prime numbers from 1 to 100 will be circled on your list.

Thinking Skill
Conclude
Why don't the directions include "Circle the number 4" and "Circle the number 6"? Four and six will be crossed out when we circle the multiples of 2.

Practice Set

▶ List the factors of the following numbers:

a. 14 1, 2, 7, 14

b. 15 1, 3, 5, 15

c. 16 1, 2, 4, 8, 16

d. 17 1, 17

▶ Justify Which number in each group is a prime number? Explain how you found your answer. See student work.

e. 21, 23, 25 23

f. 31, 32, 33 31

g. 43, 44, 45 43

Classify Which number in each group is not a prime number?

h. 41, 42, 43 42

i. 31, 41, 51 51

j. 23, 33, 43 33

Prime numbers can be multiplied to make whole numbers that are not prime. For example, $2 \cdot 2 \cdot 3$ equals 12 and $3 \cdot 5$ equals 15. (Neither 12 nor 15 are prime.) Show which prime numbers we multiply to make these products:

k. 16 $2 \cdot 2 \cdot 2 \cdot 2$

l. 18 $2 \cdot 3 \cdot 3$

▶ See Math Conversations in the sidebar.

Math Background

What is Eratosthenes' Sieve and how is it related to prime numbers?

Eratosthenes' Sieve is a method of "straining" composite (nonprime) numbers from a group of numbers so that only the prime numbers remain. It was developed by Eratosthenes of Cyrene, a Greek mathematician who lived from about 275 B.C. to 194 B.C. The activity on this page is an example of the method he devised around 200 B.C.

Written Practice *Strengthening Concepts*

Math Language
The **dividend** is the number that is to be divided.

1. (4) If two hundred fifty-two is the dividend and six is the quotient, what is the divisor? 42

*** 2.** (11, 15) In 1863, President Abraham Lincoln gave his Gettysburg Address, which began "Fourscore and seven years ago . . . ." A *score* equals twenty. What year was Lincoln referring to in his speech? Explain how you found your answer. 1776; sample: Four score and seven is $(4 \times 20) + 7 = 87$; 87 years before 1863 is 1776.

*** 3.** (14) The temperature in Barrow, Alaska was –46°F on January 22, 2002. It was 69°F on July 15, 2002. How many degrees warmer was it on July 15 than on January 22? 115° warmer

*** 4.** (15) If 203 turnips are to be shared equally among seven rabbits, how many should each receive? Write an equation and solve the problem. $7 \cdot g = 203$; 29 turnips

*** 5.** (18) What is the average of 1, 2, 4, and 9? 4

6. (10) **Predict** What is the next number in the following sequence?

1, 4, 9, 16, 25, __36__, . . .

▶ **7.** (8) A regular hexagon has six sides of equal length. If each side of a hexagon is 25 mm, what is the perimeter? 150 mm

8. (7) One centimeter equals ten millimeters. How many millimeters long is the line segment below? 30 millimeters

cm 1 2 3 4 5

*** 9.** (19) What are the whole-number factors of 20? 1, 2, 4, 5, 10, 20

*** 10.** (19) How many different whole numbers are factors of 15? 4

▶* **11.** (19) **Classify** Which of the numbers below is a prime number? C

A 25 **B** 27 **C** 29

12. (12) $250{,}000 \div 100$ 2500

13. (2) $1234 \div 60$ 20 R 34

▶* **14.** (15) $\frac{6 + 18 + 9}{3}$ 11

15. (2) $\$3.45 \times 10$ $34.50

Find each unknown number. Check your work.

16. (3) $\$10.00 - w = \$1.93$ $8.07

17. (4) $\frac{w}{3} = 4$ 12

18. (2) **Represent** The letters *a*, *b*, and *c* represent three different numbers. The product of *a* and *b* is *c*.

$$ab = c$$

Rearrange the letters to form another multiplication equation and two division equations. $ba = c$, $c \div a = b$, $c \div b = a$

▶ See Math Conversations in the sidebar.

3 Written Practice

Math Conversations

Discussion opportunities are provided below.

Problem 7 Connect

Extend the Problem

Write the following table on the board.

side length (s)	1	2	3	4	5	6
perimeter (P)	6	12	18	24	30	36

Explain that the table is designed to show the proportional relationship shared by the perimeter of a regular hexagon and the length of its sides.

Have students complete the table and write a formula to describe the relationship. $P = 6s$

Problem 11 Classify

Extend the Problem

Ask students to provide a non-example to disprove the statement, that all prime numbers are odd. Non-example to disprove: 2 is an even prime number.

Problem 14 Connect

Students are likely to simplify the expression by adding first, then dividing. Challenge students to describe how to simplify the expression by dividing first. $\frac{6}{3} + \frac{18}{3} + \frac{9}{3} = 2 + 6 + 3 = 11$

(continued)

English Learners

Explain that ***shared*** means "given out in parts or portions." Refer to problem 4 and write "203 turnips" on the board. Then draw 7 rabbits or some symbols to represent them. Say:

"If 203 turnips are shared equally with 7 rabbits, each rabbit will receive the same number of turnips. How will we find the number of turnips each rabbit will receive?" Divide 203 by 7.

As a class, work the problem on the board. Then as a class, state the answer in a complete sentence using the word *shared:* "The rabbits shared 203 turnips and each rabbit received 29 turnips."

3 Written Practice (Continued)

Math Conversations

Discussion opportunities are provided below.

Problem 22 Connect

Extend the Problem

Write 100,000,000 on the board and have students compare it to the number in problem **22**.

"If the number in Problem 22 was rounded to the number on the board, to which place was it rounded?" hundred millions

Problem 26 Classify

After identifying 2 as the prime number, ask students to name the prime factors that have a product of 22. 2×11

Problem 29 Model

Extend the Problem

"Without computing, decide if the perimeter of the square is greater than 6 inches. Explain your decision." No; Sample: $1\frac{1}{2} \times 4 = 6$, and because $1\frac{3}{8}$ is less than $1\frac{1}{2}$, the product $1\frac{3}{8} \times 4$ is less than 6.

Errors and Misconceptions

Problem 25

If students state that the answer is zero, it is likely that they changed $(51 + 49)$ to $(50 + 50)$ and $(51 - 49)$ to $(50 - 50)$ before multiplying.

Address this error by demonstrating that while you can change $(51 + 49)$ to $(50 + 50)$ because both sums are 100, you cannot change $(51 - 49)$ to $(50 - 50)$ because the difference $51 - 49$ is not the same as the difference $50 - 50$.

* **19.** (17) Arrange these numbers in order from least to greatest: $-2, 0, \frac{1}{2}, 1, 3$

$3, -2, 1, \frac{1}{2}, 0$

20. (9) Compare: $123 \div 1 \bigcirc 123 - 1$ (>)

21. (12) Which digit in 135,792,468,000 is in the ten-millions place? 9

▶* **22.** (16) Connect Round 123,456,789 to the nearest million. 123,000,000

23. (6) How much money is $\frac{1}{2}$ of \$11.00? \$5.50

24. (8) If a square has a perimeter of 48 inches, how long is each side of the square? 12 inches

▶ **25.** (5) $(51 + 49) \times (51 - 49)$ 200

▶* **26.** (19) Classify Which of the numbers below is a prime number? A

A 2 **B** 22 **C** 222

* **27.** (19) Prime numbers can be multiplied to make whole numbers that are not prime. To make 18, we perform the multiplication $2 \cdot 3 \cdot 3$. Show which prime numbers we multiply to make 20. $2 \cdot 2 \cdot 5$

* **28.** (18) The dictionaries are placed in three stacks. There are 6 dictionaries in one stack and 12 dictionaries in each of the other two stacks. How many dictionaries will be in each stack if some dictionaries are moved from the taller stacks to the shortest stack so that there are the same number of dictionaries in each stack? 10 dictionaries

▶* **29.** (17) Model Draw a square with sides that are $1\frac{3}{8}$ inches long.

* **30.** (10, 19) Explain How can you use the concepts of "even" and "odd" numbers to determine whether a number is divisible by 2.

29. [square] $1\frac{3}{8}$ in.

30. If the number is even, it is divisible by 2. All even numbers are divisible by 2. Odd numbers are not divisible by 2.

Early Finishers *Real-World Application*

The school newspaper reported that middle school students own an average of 47 CDs. Yolanda asked seven of her friends how many CDs they owned and got these results.

32, 49, 21, 59, 37, 44, 52

a. What is the average number of CDs owned by Yolanda's seven friends? $32 + 49 + 21 + 59 + 37 + 44 + 52 = 294$, $294 \div 7 = 42$; 42 CDs

b. How does this average compare to the average reported in the school newspaper? $47 - 42 = 5$. Yolanda's friends averaged 5 fewer than the reported average.

▶ See Math Conversations in the sidebar.

Looking Forward

Finding the factors of a number prepares students for:

- **Lesson 20,** identifying the greatest common factor (GCF) of two or three numbers.
- **Lesson 21,** using divisibility tests for 2, 3, 5, 9, and 10 to find the factors of a number.
- **Lesson 29,** reducing fractions by dividing by common factors.
- **Lesson 54,** reducing fractions by grouping factors equal to 1.
- **Lesson 67,** using prime factorization to reduce fractions.

• Greatest Common Factor (GCF)

Objectives

- Find the greatest common factor of two or more numbers.

Lesson Preparation

Materials

- **Power Up C** (in *Instructional Masters*)
- **Manipulative kit: rulers**

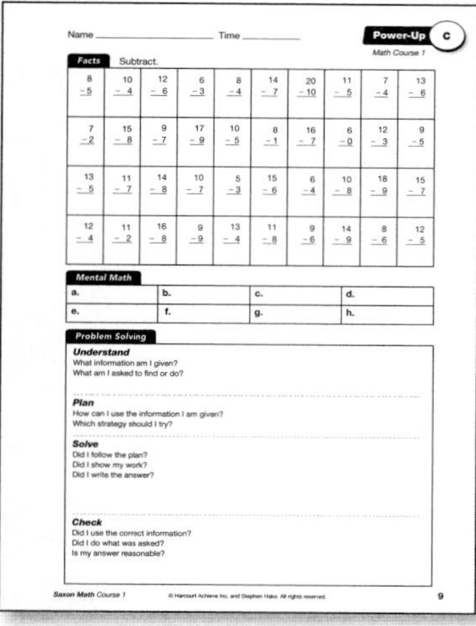

Power Up C

Math Language

New	Maintain
greatest common factor	factor

Technology Resources

Student eBook Complete student textbook in electronic format.

Resources and Planner CD Assessment, reteaching, and instructional masters, plus a pacing calendar with standards.

Test and Practice Generator CD Create additional practice sheets and custom-made tests.

www.SaxonPublishers.com Visit for more student activities and planning materials.

Inclusion

Adaptations CD Adapted lessons, investigations, practice and assessments.

Meeting Standards

National Council of Teachers of Mathematics (NCTM)

Numbers and Operations

NO.1f Use factors, multiples, prime factorization, and relatively prime numbers to solve problems

Problem Solving

PS.1b Solve problems that arise in mathematics and in other contexts

Connections

CN.4a Recognize and use connections among mathematical ideas

Power-Up Discussion For use with Power Up, p. 105

Problem-Solving Strategy: Draw a Diagram

A card with a triangle on it in the position shown is rotated 90° clockwise three times. Sketch the pattern and draw the triangles in the correct position.

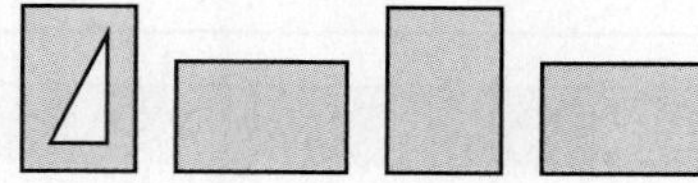

Understand ***Understand the problem.***

"What information are we given?"

A right triangle will be rotated 90° three times.

"What are we asked to do?"

Draw the three remaining terms to complete the pattern.

"What prior knowledge do we have?"

We know 90° is a right angle and four right angles equal 360°, or a full rotation. If we make four turns, we will have made a full rotation and be back at the original starting point. The term *clockwise* means to rotate to the right around a point.

Plan ***Make a plan.***

"What problem-solving strategy could we use?"

We have been asked to *draw a diagram.*

Teacher Note: Students could also make a model of the card and act it out.

Solve ***Carry out the plan.***

We sketch the card shown and three more cards. We draw the triangle on each one in the appropriate position, rotating 90° clockwise each time.

Check ***Look back.***

"How can we verify the solution?"

We can verify our solution by continuing the rotation pattern one more 90° turn to see if the card returns to its original position.

Teacher Note: In the future, students may be asked to rotate a shape around a given point on a coordinate plane.

LESSON
20 • Greatest Common Factor (GCF)

Power Up
Building Power

facts Power Up C

mental math

a. **Number Sense:** 6 × 23 138

b. **Number Sense:** 6 × 32 192

c. **Number Sense:** 640 + 1200 1840

d. **Calculation:** 63 + 20 + 9 92

e. **Calculation:** 63 + 30 − 1 92

f. **Number Sense:** $100.00 − $75.00 $25.00

g. **Measurement:** How many minutes are in 2 hours? 120 min.

h. **Calculation:** Start with 10. Multiply by 10; subtract 1; divide by 9; then add 1. What is the answer? 12

problem solving A card with a triangle on it in the position shown is rotated 90° clockwise three times. Sketch the pattern and draw the triangles in the correct positions.

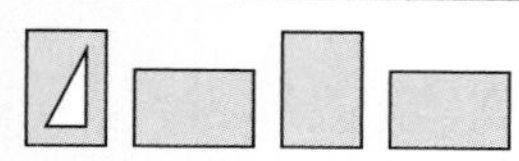

New Concept
Increasing Knowledge

The factors of 8 are

1, 2, 4, and 8

The factors of 12 are

1, 2, 3, 4, 6, and 12

Math Language
Recall that a **factor** is a whole number that divides another whole number without a remainder.

We see that 8 and 12 have some of the same factors. They have three factors in common. These common factors are 1, 2, and 4. Their **greatest common factor**—the largest factor that they both have—is 4. *Greatest common factor* is often abbreviated **GCF.**

Example 1

Find the greatest common factor of 12 and 18.

Solution

The factors of 12 are: 1, 2, 3, 4, 6, and 12.

The factors of 18 are: 1, 2, 3, 6, 9, and 18.

We see that 12 and 18 share four common factors: 1, 2, 3, and 6. The greatest of these is **6.**

Facts Subtract.

8 − 5 3	10 − 4 6	12 − 6 6	6 − 3 3	8 − 4 4	14 − 7 7	20 − 10 10	11 − 5 6	7 − 4 3	13 − 6 7
7 − 2 5	15 − 8 7	9 − 7 2	17 − 9 8	10 − 5 5	8 − 1 7	16 − 7 9	6 − 0 6	12 − 3 9	9 − 5 4
13 − 5 8	11 − 7 4	14 − 8 6	10 − 7 3	5 − 3 2	15 − 6 9	6 − 4 2	10 − 8 2	18 − 9 9	15 − 7 8
12 − 4 8	11 − 2 9	16 − 8 8	9 − 9 0	13 − 4 9	11 − 8 3	9 − 6 3	14 − 9 5	8 − 6 2	12 − 5 7

1 Power Up

Facts
Distribute **Power Up C** to students. See answers below.

Mental Math
Before students begin the Mental Math exercise, do this counting exercise as a class.

Count up and down by 3s between 3 and 60.

Encourage students to share different ways to mentally compute these exercises. Strategies for exercises **b** and **c** are listed below.

b. Use the Distributive Property
6 × 32 = (6 × 30) + (6 × 2) = 180 + 12 = 192

Count on by 30, then by 6
Start with 30. Count: 60, 90, 120, 150, 180
Start with 180. Count: 186, 192

c. Decompose 640
600 + 40 + 1200 = 1800 + 40 = 1840

Subtract 40 from 640, then Add 40
600 + 1200 = 1800; 1800 + 40 = 1840

Problem Solving
Refer to **Power-Up Discussion,** p. 105B.

2 New Concepts

Example 1
Instruction
A Venn diagram can be used to form a visual model of the common factors, and the greatest common factor, of 12 and 18. On a sheet of paper, ask students to draw two overlapping circles—one containing the factors of 12 and the other containing the factors of 18. The common factors should then be written in the intersection or overlapping portions of the circles. Students can identify the greatest common factor by comparing the numbers in the intersection and identifying the greatest number.

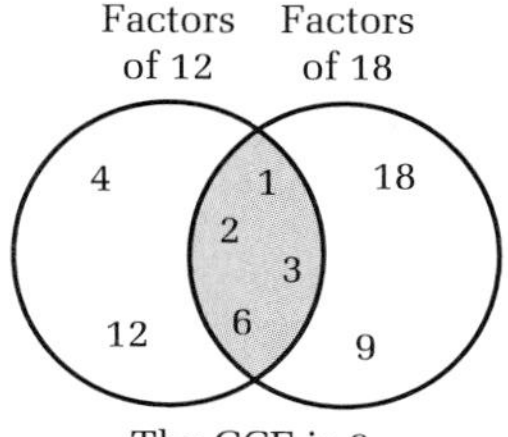

The GCF is 6.

(continued)

2 New Concepts (Continued)

Example 2

Instruction

As you discuss the solution note, remind students of the meaning of the phrase "evenly divides."

"What does the phrase evenly divides mean?" The phrase represents a quotient with no remainder or a quotient having a remainder of zero.

Practice Set

Problems a–h Error Alert

As students complete the problems, they can check their work using the generalization that the greatest common factor of two or more numbers can never be greater than the least of those numbers. For example, the greatest common factor of 4 and 60 can never be greater than 4.

3 Written Practice

Math Conversations

Discussion opportunities are provided below.

Problem 1 Represent

Extend the Problem

Ask students to write a symbolic expression to represent the problem. Sample: $12 \times 8 - (12 + 8)$

Students should conclude that parentheses must be present, because without parentheses, the expression will not simplify to 76.

Problem 4 Estimate

Extend the Problem

"How could Jill have made a better estimate?" Sample: Round the number of beads to the nearest ten; Jill has about 430 beads.

Errors and Misconceptions

Problem 2

When writing numbers in billions without the assistance of a place value chart, it is important for students to understand and apply these generalizations:

- 1 thousand has three zeros
- 1 million has six zeros
- 1 billion has nine zeros

(continued)

One; a prime number has exactly two factors, 1 and the number itself. One is the only common factor of two prime numbers, so it is the GCF.

Visit www.SaxonPublishers.com/ActivitiesC1 *for a graphing calculator activity.*

Example 2

Find the GCF of 6, 9, and 15.

Solution

The factors of 6 are: 1, 2, 3, and 6.

The factors of 9 are: 1, 3, and 9.

The factors of 15 are: 1, 3, 5, and 15.

The GCF of 6, 9, and 15 is **3.**

Note: The search for the greatest common factor of two or more numbers is a search for the **largest** number that evenly divides each of them. In this problem we can quickly determine that 3 is the largest number that evenly divides 6, 9, and 15. A complete listing of the factors might be helpful but is not required.

Generalize What is the GCF of any two prime numbers? Explain your answer.

Practice Set

Find the greatest common factor (GCF) of the following:

a. 10 and 15 5 **b.** 18 and 27 9

c. 18 and 24 6 **d.** 12, 18, and 24 6

e. 15 and 25 5 **f.** 20, 30, and 40 10

g. 12 and 15 3 **h.** 20, 40, and 60 20

i. Analyze Write a list of three numbers whose GCF is 7.

i. Answers will vary but should show a list of numbers that are all multiples of 7 and have no greater common factor.

Written Practice *Strengthening Concepts*

▸ **1.** (12) What is the difference between the product of 12 and 8 and the sum of 12 and 8? 76

▸ **2.** (12) Saturn's average distance from the Sun is one billion, four hundred twenty-nine million kilometers. Use digits to write that distance. 1,429,000,000 km

3. (12) Which digit in 497,325,186 is in the ten-millions place? 9

▸ *** 4.** (16) Estimate Jill has exactly 427 beads, but when Dwayne asked her how many beads she has, Jill rounded the amount to the nearest hundred. How many beads did Jill say she had? about 400

*** 5.** (14) The morning temperature was −3°C. By afternoon it had warmed to 8°C. How many degrees had the temperature risen? 11°C

▸ See Math Conversations in the sidebar.

Math Background

When working with factors of positive numbers, there are three important facts for students to remember:

- The least factor of every number is 1.
- The greatest factor of every number is the number itself.
- All of the other factors of the number (if any), are greater than 1 and less than the number itself.

* 6. (18) In three basketball games Allen scored 31, 52, and 40 points. What was the average number of points Allen scored per game? 41 points per game

* 7. (20) Find the greatest common factor of 12 and 20. 4

* 8. (20) Find the GCF of 9, 15, and 21. 3

9. (6) **Connect** How much money is $\frac{1}{4}$ of $3.24? $0.81

10. (2) 5432 ÷ 10 543 R 2

11. (5) $\frac{28 + 42}{14}$ 5

12. (1) 56,042 + 49,985 106,027

13. (2) 37,080 ÷ 12 3090

14. (2) $6.47 × 10 $64.70

15. (5) 5 × 4 × 3 × 2 × 1 120

Analyze Find each unknown number. Check your work.

16. (3) $w - 76 = 528$ 604

17. (3) $14{,}009 - w = 9670$ 4339

18. (4) $6w = 90$ 15

19. (3) $q - 365 = 365$ 730

20. (3) $365 - p = 365$ 0

21. (10) **Generalize** Find the missing number in the following sequence:

__4__, 10, 16, 22, 28, ...

22. (9) Compare: 50 − 1 ⊙ 49 + 1 (<)

23. (10) **Predict** The first positive odd number is 1. What is the tenth positive odd number? 19

24. (8) **Explain** The perimeter of a square is 100 cm. Describe how to find the length of each side.

24. Since the four sides of a square have equal lengths, we divide the perimeter, 100 cm, by 4 to find the length of each side.

* 25. (17) **Estimate** Estimate the length of this key to the nearest inch. Then use a ruler to find the length of the key to the nearest sixteenth of an inch. Student estimates may vary; $2\frac{4}{16}$ or $2\frac{1}{4}$ inches

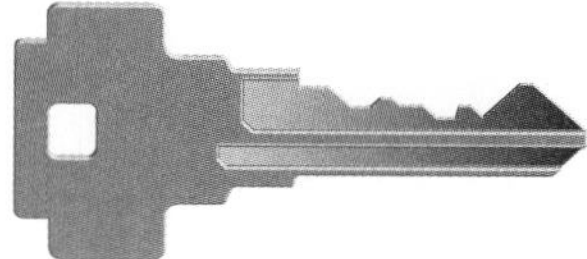

26. (6) A "bit" is $\frac{1}{8}$ of a dollar.

a. How many bits are in a dollar? 8 bits

b. How many bits are in three dollars? 24 bits

* 27. (18) In four boxes there are 12, 24, 36, and 48 golf balls respectively. If the golf balls are rearranged so that there are the same number of golf balls in each of the four boxes, how many golf balls will be in each box? 30 golf balls

▶ See Math Conversations in the sidebar.

3 Written Practice *(Continued)*

Math Conversations

Discussion opportunities are provided below.

Problem 6 Analyze

Extend the Problem

"We were told in the problem that Allen played three games. Suppose that after Allen's fourth game, his scoring average was 40 points per game. How many points did Allen score in that fourth game? Explain your answer." 37 points; if Allen's average after 4 games was 40 points per game, he scored 4 × 40 or 160 points during those games. Subtract the total number of points he scored in the first three games from 160 to find the number of points he scored in the fourth game.

Problem 9 Connect

Challenge students to describe a variety of ways to find $\frac{1}{4}$ of $3.24 using mental math. Sample: Since 32 ÷ 4 = 8, $3.20 ÷ 4 = 80¢, and the leftover 4 cents divided by 4 is 1¢. So $\frac{1}{4}$ of $3.24 is 80¢ + 1¢ or 81¢.

Problem 21 Generalize

Before completing the problem, ask students to discuss the pattern and identify its rule. Sample: To find any term in the sequence, subtract 6 from the term to its right.

Problem 25 Estimate

Encourage students to develop and use practical benchmarks to help them estimate lengths. For smaller lengths, such as the length of the key, students might use the width of a thumb to help make the estimate. For example, if the width of a thumb is known to be about $\frac{1}{2}$ inch, and the key is measured to be about five thumbs wide, a good estimate of its length is $5 \times \frac{1}{2}$ or $2\frac{1}{2}$ inches.

Invite students to discuss and describe other benchmarks they might use to estimate greater lengths, such as the length of a classroom or school hallway.

(continued)

3 Written Practice (Continued)

Math Conversations

Discussion opportunities are provided below.

Problem 28 Classify

"Why is 5 a prime number?" The number 5 has exactly two factors, 1 and itself.

Problem 30 Connect

Extend the Problem

To help students better understand large numbers, encourage them to use a calculator to help answer the following questions.

"About how many days does it take for 1 million seconds to elapse?" about 11.57 days

"About how old will you be when you have been alive for one billion seconds?" about 32 years old

If students have difficulty making these estimates, invite them to work in groups and share different strategies for answering the questions.

Errors and Misconceptions

Problem 30

Some students require extra time to become comfortable working with large numbers, such as those in billions and trillions. Encourage these students to use a place value chart when completing problem 30 and other problems like it.

▸ * **28.** (19) Classify Which of the numbers below is a prime number? A

A 5 **B** 15 **C** 25

* **29.** (19) Explain List the whole-number factors of 24. How did you find your answer? 1, 2, 3, 4, 6, 8, 12, 24; See student work.

▸ * **30.** (12) Ten billion is how much less than one trillion? 990,000,000,000

Early Finishers *Real-World Application*

Tino's parents like mathematics, especially prime numbers. So they made a plan for his allowance. They will number the weeks of the year from 1 to 52. On week 1, they will pay Tino $1. On weeks that are prime numbers, they will pay him $3. On weeks that are composite numbers, they will pay him $5.

a. How much money will Tino receive for one year? Show your work.

b. Would Tino receive more or less if his parents paid him $5 on "prime weeks" and $3 on "composite weeks"? Show your work.

a. There are 15 prime numbers from 1 to 52 (2, 3, 5, 7, 11, 13, 17, 19, 23, 29, 31, 37, 41, 43, 47). There are also 36 composite numbers.

Week 1: $1

Prime number weeks: $3 × 15 = $45

Composite number weeks: $5 × 36 = $180

$1 + $45 + $180 = $226

Tino's total for the year will be $226.

b. Tino will receive $1, plus $5 × 15, plus $3 × 36. $1 + $75 + $108 = $184. Tino would make less.

108 **Saxon** *Math Course 1*

▸ See Math Conversations in the sidebar.

Looking Forward

Finding the greatest common factor (GCF) of two or more numbers prepares students for:

- **Lesson 21,** using divisibility tests for 2, 3, 5, 9, and 10 to find the factors of a number.
- **Lesson 29,** reducing fractions by dividing by common factors.
- **Lesson 33,** writing a percent as a reduced fraction.
- **Lesson 53,** simplifying fractions.
- **Lesson 73,** writing decimal numbers as reduced fractions.

Assessment

30–40 minutes | For use after Lesson 20

Distribute **Cumulative Test 3** to each student. Two versions of the test are available in *Saxon Math Course 1 Course Assessments Book*. Have students complete the **Power-Up Test** first. Allow 10 minutes. Then have students work the 20 numbered items on the **Cumulative Test.** Students may use copies of the answer sheet to record their work. Track individual and class progress with the **Test Analysis** forms.

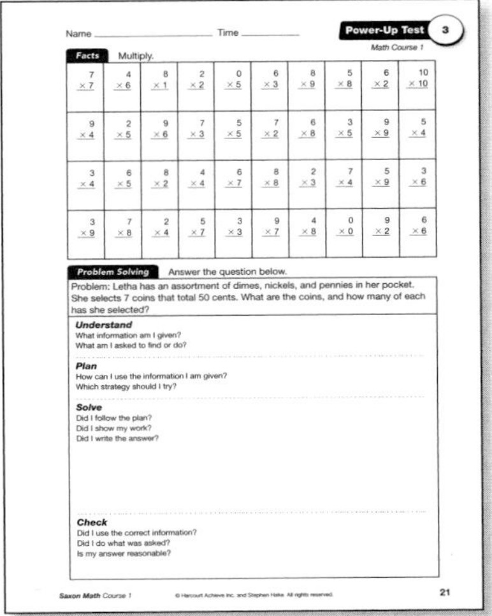

Name ______ Time ______

Power-Up Test 3
Math Course 1

Facts Multiply.

7×7	4×6	8×1	2×2	0×5	6×3	8×9	5×8	6×2	10×10
9×4	2×5	9×6	7×3	5×5	7×2	6×8	3×5	9×9	5×4
3×4	6×5	8×2	4×4	6×7	8×8	2×3	7×4	5×9	3×6
3×9	7×8	2×4	5×7	3×3	9×7	4×8	0×0	9×2	6×6

Problem Solving Answer the question below.

Problem: Letha has an assortment of dimes, nickels, and pennies in her pocket. She selects 7 coins that total 50 cents. What are the coins, and how many of each has she selected?

Understand
What information am I given?
What am I asked to find or do?

Plan
How can I use the information I am given?
Which strategy should I try?

Solve
Did I follow the plan?
Did I show my work?
Did I write the answer?

Check
Did I use the correct information?
Did I do what was asked?
Is my answer reasonable?

Saxon Math Course 1 © Harcourt Achieve Inc. and Stephen Hake. All rights reserved. 21

Power-Up Test 3

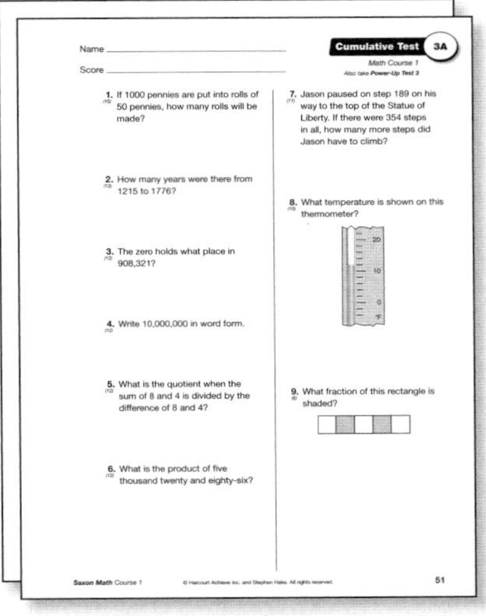

Name ______
Score ______

Cumulative Test 3A
Math Course 1
Also take **Power-Up Test 3**

1. If 1000 pennies are put into rolls of 50 pennies, how many rolls will be made?
2. How many years were there from 1215 to 1776?
3. The zero holds what place in 908,321?
4. Write 10,000,000 in word form.
5. What is the quotient when the sum of 8 and 4 is divided by the difference of 8 and 4?
6. What is the product of five thousand twenty and eighty-six?
7. Jason paused on step 189 on his way to the top of the Statue of Liberty. If there were 354 steps in all, how many more steps did Jason have to climb?
8. What temperature is shown on this thermometer?
9. What fraction of this rectangle is shaded?

Saxon Math Course 1 © Harcourt Achieve Inc. and Stephen Hake. All rights reserved. 51

Cumulative Test 3A

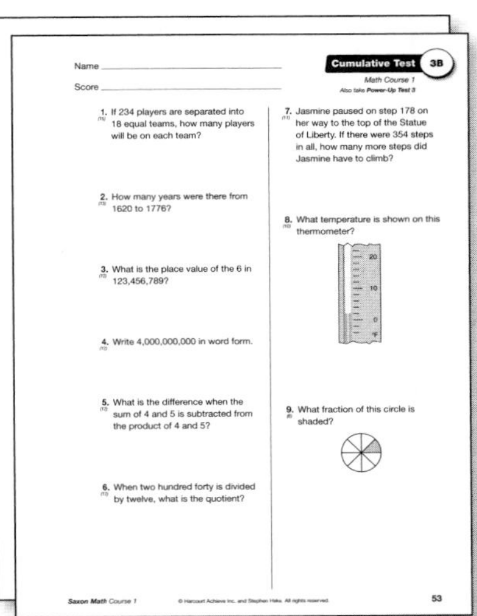

Name ______
Score ______

Cumulative Test 3B
Math Course 1
Also take **Power-Up Test 3**

1. If 234 players are separated into 18 equal teams, how many players will be on each team?
2. How many years were there from 1620 to 1776?
3. What is the place value of the 6 in 123,456,789?
4. Write 4,000,000,000 in word form.
5. What is the difference when the sum of 4 and 5 is subtracted from the product of 4 and 5?
6. When two hundred forty is divided by twelve, what is the quotient?
7. Jasmine paused on step 178 on her way to the top of the Statue of Liberty. If there were 354 steps in all, how many more steps did Jasmine have to climb?
8. What temperature is shown on this thermometer?
9. What fraction of this circle is shaded?

Saxon Math Course 1 © Harcourt Achieve Inc. and Stephen Hake. All rights reserved. 53

Alternative Cumulative Test 3B

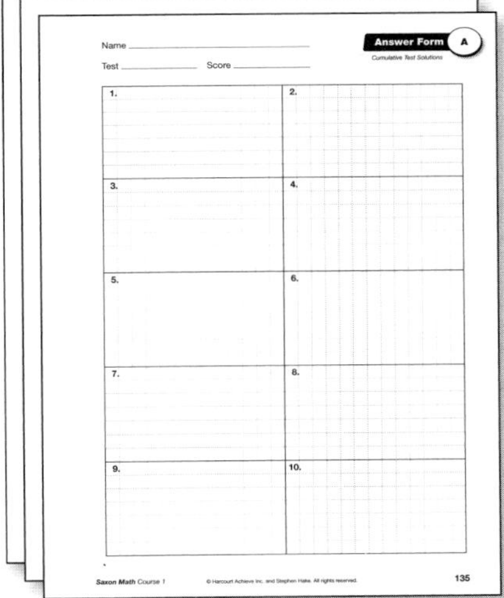

Name ______
Test ______ Score ______

Answer Form A
Cumulative Test Solutions

1. 2.
3. 4.
5. 6.
7. 8.
9. 10.

Saxon Math Course 1 © Harcourt Achieve Inc. and Stephen Hake. All rights reserved. 135

Optional Answer Forms

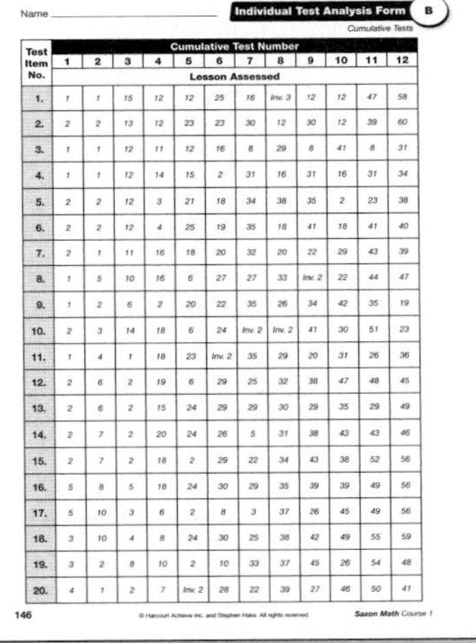

Name ______

Individual Test Analysis Form B
Cumulative Tests

Test Item No.	1	2	3	4	5	6	7	8	9	10	11	12
	Lesson Assessed											
1.	1	1	15	12	12	25	16	Inv. 3	12	12	47	58
2.	2	2	13	12	23	23	30	12	30	12	39	60
3.	1	1	12	11	12	16	8	29	8	41	8	31
4.	1	1	12	14	15	2	31	16	31	16	31	34
5.	2	2	12	3	21	18	34	38	35	2	23	38
6.	2	2	12	4	25	19	35	18	41	18	41	40
7.	2	1	11	16	18	20	32	20	22	29	43	39
8.	1	5	10	16	6	27	27	33	Inv. 2	22	44	47
9.	1	2	6	2	20	22	35	26	34	42	35	19
10.	2	3	14	18	6	24	Inv. 2	Inv. 2	41	30	51	23
11.	1	4	1	18	23	Inv. 2	35	29	20	31	26	36
12.	2	6	2	19	6	29	25	32	38	47	48	45
13.	2	6	2	15	24	29	29	30	29	35	29	49
14.	2	7	2	20	24	26	5	31	38	43	43	46
15.	2	7	2	18	2	29	22	34	43	38	52	56
16.	5	8	5	18	24	30	29	35	39	39	49	56
17.	5	10	3	6	2	8	3	37	26	45	49	56
18.	3	10	4	8	24	30	25	38	42	49	55	59
19.	3	2	8	10	2	10	33	37	45	26	54	48
20.	4	1	2	7	Inv. 2	28	22	39	27	46	50	41

(Column headings 1–12: Cumulative Test Number)

146 © Harcourt Achieve Inc. and Stephen Hake. All rights reserved. *Saxon Math Course 1*

Individual Test Analysis Form

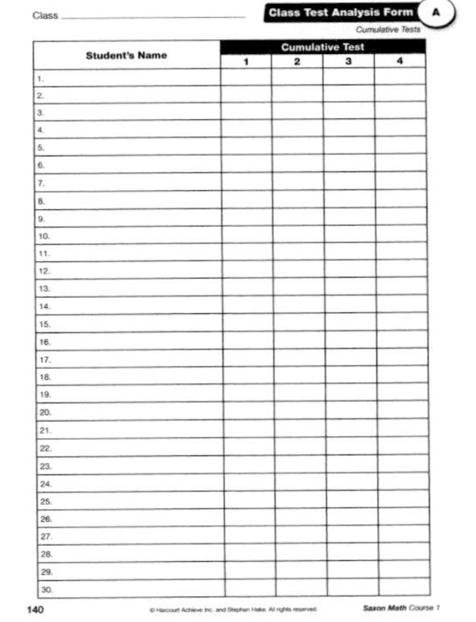

Class ______

Class Test Analysis Form A
Cumulative Tests

	Student's Name	Cumulative Test 1	2	3	4
1.					
2.					
3.					
4.					
5.					
6.					
7.					
8.					
9.					
10.					
11.					
12.					
13.					
14.					
15.					
16.					
17.					
18.					
19.					
20.					
21.					
22.					
23.					
24.					
25.					
26.					
27.					
28.					
29.					
30.					

140 © Harcourt Achieve Inc. and Stephen Hake. All rights reserved. *Saxon Math Course 1*

Class Test Analysis Form

Reteaching

Students who score below 80% on the assessment may be in need of reteaching. Look for the causes of student mistakes. If errors are conceptual, refer to the *Reteaching Masters* for reteaching.

Customized Benchmark Assessment

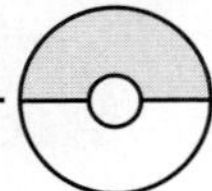

You can develop customized benchmark tests using the Test Generator located on the *Test & Practice Generator CD.*

This chart shows the lesson, the standard, and the test item question that can be found on the *Test & Practice Generator CD.*

LESSON	NEW CONCEPTS	LOCAL STANDARD	TEST ITEM ON CD
11	• Problems About Combining		2.11.1
	• Problems About Separating		2.11.2
12	• Place Value Through Trillions		2.12.1
	• Multistep Problems		2.12.2
13	• Problems About Comparing		2.13.1
	• Elapsed-Time Problems		2.13.2
14	• The Number Line: Negative Numbers		2.14.1
15	• Problems About Equal Groups		2.15.1
16	• Rounding Whole Numbers		2.16.1
	• Estimating		2.16.2
17	• The Number Line: Fractions and Mixed Numbers		2.17.1
18	• Average		2.18.1
	• Line Graphs		2.18.2
19	• Factors		2.19.1
	• Prime Numbers		2.19.2
20	• Greatest Common Factor (GCF)		2.20.1

Using the Test Generator CD

- Develop tests in both English and Spanish.
- Choose from multiple-choice and free-response test items.
- Clone test items to create multiple versions of the same test.
- View and edit test items to make and save your own questions.
- Administer assessments through paper tests or over a school LAN.
- Monitor student progress through a variety of individual and class reports —for both diagnosing and assessing standards mastery.

Performance Task 3

The Four Corners States

Assign after Lesson 20 and Test 3

Objectives

- Make a bar graph and a circle graph to display the same data.
- Formulate a question that can be answered by data.
- Communicate ideas through writing.

Materials

Performance Tasks 3A, 3B, and **3C**

Preparation

Make copies of **Performance Tasks 3A, 3B,** and **3C.** (One each per student.)

Time Requirement

30–60 minutes; Begin in class and complete at home.

Task

Explain to students that for this task they will be looking at data about *The Four Corner States*, and making graphs to represent the data. They will also write about the data and draw conclusions from it. Point out that all of the information students need is on **Performance Tasks 3A, 3B,** and **3C.**

Criteria for Evidence of Learning

- Creates an accurate bar graph and circle graph to display a set of data.
- Draws valid conclusions from the data.
- Formulates an appropriate question that can be answered by the data and correctly answers it.
- Communicates ideas clearly through writing.

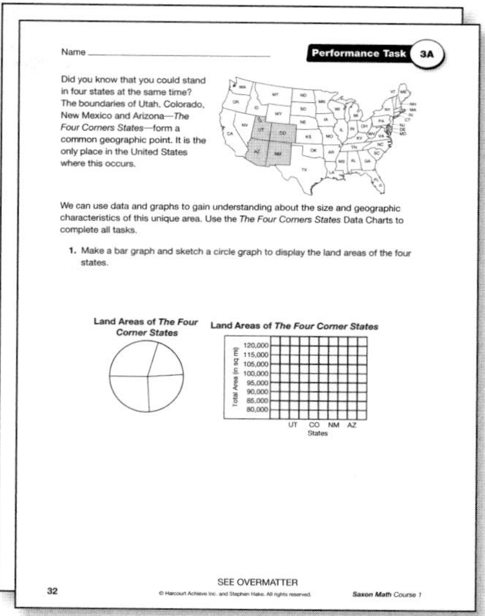

Name ______________ **Performance Task 3A**

Did you know that you could stand in four states at the same time? The boundaries of Utah, Colorado, New Mexico and Arizona—*The Four Corners States*—form a common geographic point. It is the only place in the United States where this occurs.

We can use data and graphs to gain understanding about the size and geographic characteristics of this unique area. Use the *The Four Corners States* Data Charts to complete all tasks.

1. Make a bar graph and sketch a circle graph to display the land areas of the four states.

SEE OVERMATTER

Performance Task 3A and 3B

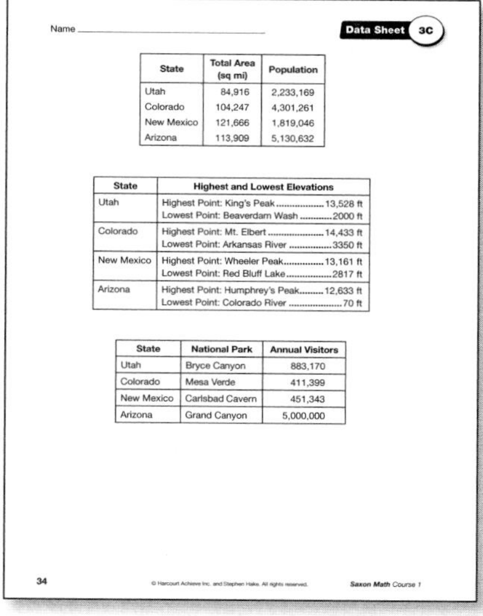

Name ______________ **Data Sheet 3C**

State	Total Area (sq mi)	Population
Utah	84,916	2,233,169
Colorado	104,247	4,301,261
New Mexico	121,666	1,819,046
Arizona	113,909	5,130,632

State	Highest and Lowest Elevations
Utah	Highest Point: King's Peak .... 13,528 ft Lowest Point: Beaverdam Wash .... 2000 ft
Colorado	Highest Point: Mt. Elbert .... 14,433 ft Lowest Point: Arkansas River .... 3350 ft
New Mexico	Highest Point: Wheeler Peak .... 13,161 ft Lowest Point: Red Bluff Lake .... 2817 ft
Arizona	Highest Point: Humphrey's Peak .... 12,633 ft Lowest Point: Colorado River .... 70 ft

State	National Park	Annual Visitors
Utah	Bryce Canyon	883,170
Colorado	Mesa Verde	411,399
New Mexico	Carlsbad Cavern	451,343
Arizona	Grand Canyon	5,000,000

Data Sheet C

Meeting Standards

National Council of Teachers of Mathematics (NCTM)

Data Analysis and Probability

DP.1b Select, create, and use appropriate graphical representations of data, including histograms, box plots, and scatterplots

Problem Solving

PS.1b Solve problems that arise in mathematics and in other contexts

Reasoning and Proof

RP.2b Make and investigate mathematical conjectures

Communication

CM.3a Organize and consolidate their mathematical thinking through communication

Representation

RE.5b Select, apply, and translate among mathematical representations to solve problems

Focus on

• Investigating Fractions with Manipulatives

Objectives

- Create and use a set of fraction circle manipulatives.
- Use fraction circles to solve problems.

Lesson Preparation

Materials

- **Investigation Activities 4–8** (in *Instructional Masters*), one copy of each activity per two students
- **Teacher-provided material: scissors, envelopes or zip-top plastic bags, colored paper**

Optional

- **Basic Fraction Circles poster**

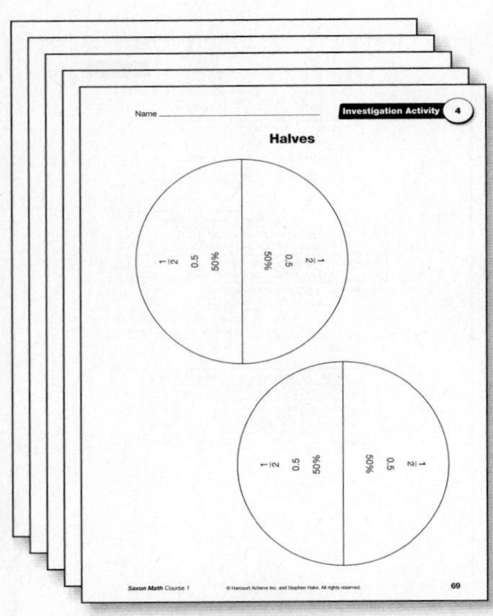

Investigation Activities 4–8

Math Language

New

improper fraction

nonexamples

Technology Resources

Student eBook Complete student textbook in electronic format.

Resources and Planner CD Assessment, reteaching, and instructional masters, plus a pacing calendar with standards.

Test and Practice Generator CD Create additional practice sheets and custom-made tests.

www.SaxonPublishers.com Visit for more student activities and planning materials.

Inclusion

Adaptations CD Adapted lessons, investigations, practice and assessments.

Meeting Standards

National Council of Teachers of Mathematics (NCTM)

Numbers and Operations

NO.1a Work flexibly with fractions, decimals, and percents to solve problems

NO.1b Compare and order fractions, decimals, and percents efficiently and find their approximate locations on a number line

NO.3a Select appropriate methods and tools for computing with fractions and decimals from among mental computation, estimation, calculators or computers, and paper and pencil, depending on the situation, and apply the selected methods

Geometry

GM.4d Use geometric models to represent and explain numerical and algebraic relationships

Problem Solving

PS.1b Solve problems that arise in mathematics and in other contexts

Representation

RE.5b Select, apply, and translate among mathematical representations to solve problems

INVESTIGATION 2

Focus on

• Investigating Fractions with Manipulatives

In this investigation you will make a set of fraction manipulatives to help you answer questions in this investigation and in future problem sets.

Activity

Using Fraction Manipulatives

Materials needed:

- Investigation Activities 4–8
- scissors
- envelope or zip-top bag to store fraction pieces

Preparation:

To make your own fraction manipulatives, cut out the fraction circles on the Investigation Activities. Then cut each fraction circle into its parts.

Thinking Skill
Connect
What percent is one whole circle? 100%

Model Use your fraction manipulatives to help you with these exercises:

1. What percent of a circle is $\frac{1}{2}$ of a circle? 50%
2. What fraction is half of $\frac{1}{2}$? $\frac{1}{4}$
3. What fraction is half of $\frac{1}{4}$? $\frac{1}{8}$
4. ▸ Fit three $\frac{1}{4}$ pieces together to form $\frac{3}{4}$ of a circle. Three fourths of a circle is what percent of a circle? 75%
5. ▸ Fit four $\frac{1}{8}$ pieces together to form $\frac{4}{8}$ of a circle. Four eighths of a circle is what percent of a circle? 50%
6. ▸ Fit three $\frac{1}{6}$ pieces together to form $\frac{3}{6}$ of a circle. Three sixths of a circle is what percent of a circle? 50%
7. ▸ Show that $\frac{4}{8}$, $\frac{3}{6}$, and $\frac{2}{4}$ each make one half of a circle. (We say that $\frac{4}{8}$, $\frac{3}{6}$, and $\frac{2}{4}$ all *reduce* to $\frac{1}{2}$.)

7. ⊕ = ⊖; ⊕ = ⊖; ⊕ = ⊖

8. The fraction $\frac{2}{8}$ equals which single fraction piece? $\frac{1}{4}$
9. The fraction $\frac{6}{8}$ equals how many $\frac{1}{4}$s? 3
10. The fraction $\frac{2}{6}$ equals which single fraction piece? $\frac{1}{3}$
11. The fraction $\frac{4}{6}$ equals how many $\frac{1}{3}$s? 2
12. The sum $\frac{1}{8}+\frac{1}{8}+\frac{1}{8}$ is $\frac{3}{8}$. If you add $\frac{3}{8}$ and $\frac{2}{8}$, what is the sum? $\frac{5}{8}$

▸ See Math Conversations in the sidebar.

Teacher Tip

Students can work in **pairs** and/or **groups** to complete this activity. Either arrangement provides many opportunities for discussion among students as well as opportunities to check and justify answers.

Manipulative Use

After the activity has been completed, have students **store their fraction manipulatives** in envelopes or zip-top plastic bags so they will be available for upcoming lessons. Remind students to write their names on the envelopes or bags before they are put away.

INVESTIGATION 2

In this investigation, students will make a set of fraction manipulatives and use them to solve problems involving fractions. Making and using manipulatives helps students form a better understanding of the relationships shared by equivalent fractions, decimals, and percents.

Preparing the Materials

Color-coding the fraction manipulatives will make it easier for students to sort and organize the materials. You can accomplish this by copying each master on different color paper, or by directing students to color each set of circles a different color.

Distribute copies of **Investigation Activities 4–8** to each pair of students. Using scissors, ask the students to cut out the circles, and then cut out the pieces of each circle. Also supply each pair of students with an envelope or zip-top plastic bag for storage of the pieces.

Activity

The five different activity masters used in this investigation each display circles showing equivalent fractions, decimals, and percents. One or more pieces of a circle will be used to model each of the given situations. For example, in problem **2,** students will use five pieces of a circle that is cut into eighths to model $\frac{5}{8}$.

You may wish to display the **Basic Fraction Circles** concept poster as you discuss this topic with students.

Math Conversations

Discussion opportunities are provided below.

Problems 4–6 Model

To solve the problems, students must find the sum of the percents. For each problem, ask

"What operation is used to find the percent of the circle?" addition

Use similar questions for problems **5** and **6.**

Problem 7 Model

Give students an opportunity to recall that equivalent fractions are different names for the same number or amount.

"Why are $\frac{4}{8}$, $\frac{3}{6}$, $\frac{2}{4}$, and $\frac{1}{2}$ equivalent fractions?" Each fraction is a different name for the same amount, $\frac{1}{2}$.

(continued)

Activity (Continued)

Math Conversations

Discussion opportunities are provided below.

Problem 13 Connect

Before $\frac{1}{6}$ of the circle is removed, ask,

"What whole number does the entire circle represent? Explain your answer."
1; $\frac{6}{6} = 6 \div 6$ and $6 \div 6 = 1$

After $\frac{1}{6}$ of the circle has been removed, ask,

"How can you check your answer?"
Sample: Count the number of $\frac{1}{6}$ pieces; $\frac{1}{6} + \frac{1}{6} + \frac{1}{6} + \frac{1}{6} + \frac{1}{6} = \frac{5}{6}$.

Problem 15 Connect

"Why are 4 one-fourths used to represent 1?" $\frac{4}{4}$ and 1 are equivalent because $\frac{4}{4} = 4 \div 4$ and $4 \div 4 = 1$

Problems 21 Represent

Extend the Problem

Have students write an inequality that compares the shaded amounts and includes a > or < symbol. $\frac{1}{5} < \frac{1}{3}$ or $\frac{1}{3} > \frac{1}{5}$

Then have students write an inequality that compares the unshaded amounts and includes a > or < symbol. $\frac{2}{3} < \frac{4}{5}$ or $\frac{4}{5} > \frac{2}{3}$

(continued)

▶ **13.** Connect Form a whole circle using six of the $\frac{1}{6}$ pieces. Then remove (subtract) $\frac{1}{6}$. What fraction of the circle is left? What equation represents your model? $\frac{5}{6}$; $1 - \frac{1}{6} = \frac{5}{6}$

14. Demonstrate subtracting $\frac{1}{3}$ from 1 by forming a circle of $\frac{3}{3}$ and then removing $\frac{1}{3}$. What fraction is left? $\frac{2}{3}$

▶ **15.** Use four $\frac{1}{4}$s to demonstrate the subtraction $1 - \frac{1}{4}$. Then write the answer. $\frac{3}{4}$

16. Eight $\frac{1}{8}$s form one circle. If $\frac{3}{8}$ of a circle is removed from one circle $(1 - \frac{3}{8})$, then what fraction of the circle remains? $\frac{5}{8}$

17. What percent of a circle is $\frac{1}{3}$ of a circle? $33\frac{1}{3}\%$

18. What percent of a circle is $\frac{1}{6}$ of a circle? $16\frac{2}{3}\%$

Fraction manipulatives can help us compare fractions. Since $\frac{1}{2}$ of a circle is larger than $\frac{1}{3}$ of a circle, we can see that

$$\frac{1}{2} > \frac{1}{3}$$

Model For problems **19** and **20,** use your fraction manipulatives to construct models of the fractions. Use the models to help you write the correct comparison for each problem.

19. Compare: $\frac{2}{3} \bigcirc \frac{3}{4}$; $\frac{2}{3} < \frac{3}{4}$

20. Compare: $\frac{2}{3} \bigcirc \frac{3}{8}$; $\frac{2}{3} > \frac{3}{8}$

Reading Math
< means *is less than;*
= means *is equal to;*
> means *is greater than.*

Represent We can also draw pictures to help us compare fractions.

▶ **21.** Draw two rectangles of the same size. Shade $\frac{1}{3}$ of one rectangle and $\frac{1}{5}$ of the other rectangle. What fraction represents the rectangle that has the larger amount shaded?

22. Draw and shade rectangles to illustrate this comparison:

$$\frac{3}{5} > \frac{3}{10}$$

21. ; $\frac{1}{3}$

22. Sample: >

Problems **23–29** involve **improper fractions.** Improper fractions are fractions that are equal to or greater than 1. In a fraction equal to 1 the numerator equals the denominator (as in $\frac{3}{3}$). In a fraction greater than 1 the numerator is greater than the denominator (as in $\frac{4}{3}$).

Work in groups of two or three students for the remaining problems.

23. Show that the improper fraction $\frac{5}{4}$ equals the mixed number $1\frac{1}{4}$ by combining four of the $\frac{1}{4}$ pieces to make a whole circle.

24. The improper fraction $\frac{7}{4}$ equals what mixed number? $1\frac{3}{4}$

25. The improper fraction $\frac{3}{2}$ equals what mixed number? $1\frac{1}{2}$

110 **Saxon** *Math Course 1*

▶ See Math Conversations in the sidebar.

Math Background

Why use manipulatives to investigate mathematical concepts?

Manipulatives involve students mentally and physically in the learning process, offering them alternative ways to explore a problem. Kinesthetic, visual, and social learners will all benefit from activities that allow them to cooperate as they learn concepts by seeing and touching representations of mathematical ideas.

- Manipulatives are especially useful for illustrating elementary concepts, but can also make complex concepts more accessible.
- Manipulatives provide the teacher with alternative ways of visiting a topic and extra practice for students in need of reinforcement.

27. 6; Sample: We put fraction pieces together to make two circles using six $\frac{1}{3}$s. Alternate: Three $\frac{1}{3}$s make one circle, so two circles use twice as many, $2 \times 3 = 6$.

26. Form $1\frac{1}{2}$ circles using only $\frac{1}{4}$s. How many $\frac{1}{4}$ pieces are needed to make $1\frac{1}{2}$? 6

▶27. **Explain** How many $\frac{1}{3}$ pieces are needed to make two whole circles? How do you know your answer is correct?

28. The improper fraction $\frac{4}{3}$ equals what mixed number? $1\frac{1}{3}$

29. Convert $\frac{11}{6}$ to a mixed number. $1\frac{5}{6}$

▶30. **Evaluate** An analog clock can serve as a visual reference for twelfths. At 1 o'clock the hands mark off $\frac{1}{12}$ of a circle; at 2 o'clock the hands mark off $\frac{2}{12}$ of a circle, and so on. How many twelfths are in each of these fractions of a circle? $\frac{6}{12}, \frac{3}{12}, \frac{4}{12}, \frac{2}{12}$

$\frac{1}{2}, \frac{1}{4}, \frac{1}{3}, \frac{1}{6}$

Hint: Try holding each fraction piece at arm's length in the direction of the clock (as an artist might extend a thumb toward a subject.)

After you have completed the exercises, gather and store your fraction manipulatives for later use.

extensions

▶ a. **Justify** Use examples and **nonexamples** to support or disprove that the Commutative Property can be applied to the addition and subtraction of two fractions. See student work.

▶ b. **Analyze** Choose between mental math or estimation and use that method to answer each of the following questions. Explain your choice.

1. One-fourth of a pizza was eaten. How much of the pizza was not eaten? mental math; $\frac{3}{4}$
2. Each of 3 students ate $\frac{1}{8}$ of a new box of cereal. What amount of cereal in the box was eaten? mental math; $\frac{3}{8}$
3. More than half of the students in the class are girls. What fraction of the students in the class are boys? estimation; less than $\frac{1}{2}$

▶ c. **Estimate** Copy this number line.

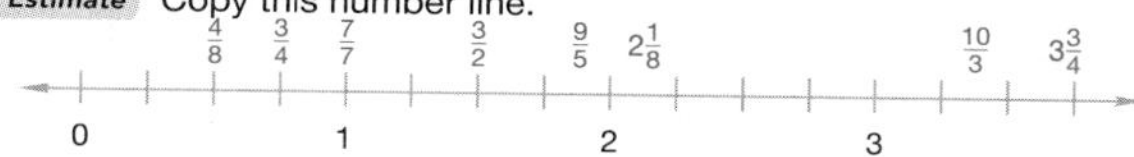

Then estimate the placement of the following fractions on the number line. Use your fraction pieces to help you if you need to.

$\frac{3}{4}$ $\frac{3}{2}$ $\frac{4}{8}$ $3\frac{3}{4}$ $\frac{9}{5}$ $\frac{10}{3}$ $2\frac{1}{8}$ $\frac{7}{7}$

▶ See Math Conversations in the sidebar.

Activity (Continued)

Math Conversations

Discussion opportunities are provided below.

Problem 27 Explain

After completing the problem, ask,

"How can you represent the 2 whole circles as a fraction?" $\frac{2}{1}$

"What kind of fraction is $\frac{2}{1}$?" an improper fraction

Problem 30 Evaluate

Extend the Problem

"What unit of time represents $\frac{1}{60}$ of a hour? Explain your answer." One hour = 60 minutes, so 1 minute is $\frac{1}{60}$ of an hour.

Extensions

a. Justify Examples should be given to illustrate that the addition of two fractions is commutative. Nonexamples should be given to prove that the subtraction of two fractions is not commutative.

b. Analyze After students answer the questions, ask them to name the method they chose, and explain why it was chosen.

c. Estimate The number line is divided into fourths. Students should easily recognize that $\frac{4}{8} = \frac{1}{2}$, $\frac{3}{2} = 1\frac{1}{2}$, $\frac{10}{3} = 3\frac{1}{3}$, and $\frac{7}{7} = 1$. Some students may recognize that $2\frac{1}{8}$ is halfway between 2 and $2\frac{1}{4}$. Most students will have to think about where to place $\frac{9}{5}$. Help them understand that $\frac{9}{5} = 1\frac{4}{5}$, which is greater than $1\frac{3}{4}$ and less than 2.

Looking Forward

Investigating fractions with manipulatives prepares students for:

- **Lesson 24,** adding and subtracting fractions with common denominators.
- **Lesson 26,** reducing fractions and adding and subtracting mixed numbers.
- **Lesson 42,** renaming fractions by multiplying by 1.
- **Lessons 55 and 56,** adding and subtracting fractions after changing them to fractions with common denominators.
- **Lessons 75 and 94,** writing fractions and decimals as percents.

Section 3 Overview

Lessons 21–30, Investigation 3

Lesson Planner

LESSON	NEW CONCEPTS	MATERIALS	RESOURCES
21	• Divisibility	Manipulative Kit: inch and metric rulers	Power Up D
22	• "Equal Groups" Problems with Fractions	Manipulative Kit: inch rulers, overhead tiles	Power Up C
23	• Ratio • Rate		Power Up D
24	• Adding and Subtracting Fractions That Have Common Denominators	Manipulative Kit: fraction circles Fraction manipulatives from Investigation 2	Power Up C
25	• Writing Division Answers as Mixed Numbers • Multiples	Manipulative Kit: inch rulers, fraction circles Fraction manipulatives from Investigation 2	Power Up F
26	• Using Manipulatives to Reduce Fractions • Adding and Subtracting Mixed Numbers	Manipulative Kit: inch rulers, fraction circles Fraction manipulatives from Investigation 2	Power Up C Basic Fraction Circles poster
27	• Measures of a Circle	Manipulative Kit: inch and metric rulers, compasses Fraction manipulatives from Investigation 2	Power Up E
28	• Angles	Manipulative Kit: inch and metric rulers Fraction manipulatives from Investigation 2	Power Up F Lesson Activity 9
29	• Multiplying Fractions • Reducing Fractions by Dividing by Common Factors	Manipulative Kit: color tiles Fraction manipulatives from Investigation 2	Power Up B
30	• Least Common Multiple (LCM) • Reciprocals		Power Up E Lesson Activity 3
Inv. 3	• Measuring and Drawing Angles with a Protractor	Manipulative Kit: protractors, rulers	Investigation Activity 10

Lesson Highlights

Lessons 21–30, Investigation 3

Problem Solving

Strategies

- **Use Logical Reasoning** Lessons 21, 23, 25, 26, 27, 28
- **Draw a Diagram** Lessons 23, 24, 29, 30
- **Write an Equation** Lesson 22
- **Guess and Check** Lesson 25
- **Make an Organized List** Lesson 26
- **Make a Model** Lesson 30

Alternative Strategies

- **Make a Model** Lesson 22
- **Act It Out** Lesson 22

Real-World Applications

pp. 114, 116, 117, 119–121, 124–126, 127, 129–131, 134, 135, 138–140, 143–145, 148–150, 153–155, 159, 160, 163

4-Step Process

Teacher Edition Lessons 21–30 (Power-Up Discussion)

Communication

Discuss

pp. 112, 113, 123, 128, 142, 151

Explain

pp. 125, 129, 143, 144, 148

Formulate a Problem

p. 140

Connections

Math and Other Subjects

- **Math and History** pp. 114, 119, 148, 154
- **Math and Geography** pp. 130, 131, 148
- **Math and Science** pp. 125, 130, 134, 154, 159
- **Math and Sports** pp. 120, 122, 126, 134, 135, 154, 155

Math to Math

- **Problem Solving and Measurement** Lessons 21, 22, 23, 24, 25, 26, 27, 28, 29, 30, Inv. 3
- **Algebra and Problem Solving** Lesson 28
- **Fractions, Percents, Decimals, and Problem Solving** Lessons 21, 22, 23, 24, 25, 26, 27, 28, 29, 30
- **Fractions and Measurement** Lessons 21, 22, 23, 24, 25, 26, 27, 28, 29, 30
- **Geometry and Measurement** Lessons 21, 22, 23, 24, 25, 26, 27, 28, 29, 30, Inv. 3

Representation

Manipulatives/Hands On

pp. 115, 121, 125–129, 136–138, 140, 142, 143, 148, 149, 151, 162, 163

Model

pp. 115, 119, 120, 121, 125, 126, 129, 135–138, 140, 143, 148, 149, 151, 159

Represent

pp. 115, 116, 121, 131, 135, 142, 147, 155, 162, 163

Formulate an Equation

pp. 114, 134, 135, 143, 148, 159

Technology

Student Resources

- **eBook**
- **Online Resources** at **www.SaxonPublishers.com/ActivitiesC1**
  - **Graphic Calculator Activity** Lesson 30
  - **Online Activities**
  - **Math Enrichment Problems**
  - **Math Stumpers**

Teacher Resources

- **Resources and Planner CD**
- **Adaptations CD** Lessons 21–30
- **Test & Practice Generator CD**
- **eGradebook**
- **Answer Key CD**

Content Highlights

Lessons 21–30, Investigation 3

In this section, students focus on concepts and skills involving fractions. The concept of ratio is introduced. After discussing the measures of a circle, the connection between lines and angles are presented.

Proportional Thinking

Fraction concepts and skills are the foundation of proportional thinking.

Following the experience with fraction manipulatives in Investigation 2, students hone in on fractions in Lessons 22–26, 29, and 30. Students find a fraction of a group, add and subtract fractions and mixed numbers, reduce fractions, find reciprocals of fractions, and write quotients of whole numbers as mixed numbers.

In Lesson 21 students learn divisibility rules that build number sense and assist in reducing fractions. Students express ratios in fraction form in Lesson 23 and prepare the foundation for the many proportion-related lessons to follow.

Spatial Thinking

Angles are introduced early in the year so they can be connected to other geometric ideas throughout the year.

Students continue the sequence of geometry lessons in Lessons 27 and 28 and in Investigation 3. In the introductory lesson on circles students use a compass which they will employ in a later investigation on geometric construction. Students are introduced to angle terminology in Lesson 28 and use a protractor to measure and draw angles in Investigation 3.

Assessment

A variety of weekly assessment tools are provided.

After Lesson 25:
- Power-Up Test 4
- Cumulative Test 4
- Performance Activity 4

After Lesson 30:
- Power-Up Test 5
- Cumulative Test 5
- Customized Benchmark Test
- Performance Task 5

Content Trace

Lessons 21–30, Investigation 3

LESSON	NEW CONCEPTS	PRACTICED	ASSESSED
21	• Divisibility	Lessons 21, 22, 23, 24, 25, 26, 27, 28, 33, 41, 50	Test 5
22	• "Equal Groups" Problems with Fractions	Lessons 22, 23, 24, 25, 26, 27, 28, 29, 30, 31, 32, 33, 34, 35, 36, 37, 42, 43, 45, 49, 52, 53, 54, 56, 57, 60, 87, 96, 116	Tests 6, 7, 9, 10, 17, 19
23	• Ratio	Lessons 23, 24, 25, 27, 28, 30, 31, 32, 34, 36, 39, 40, 41, 44, 46, 48, 52, 54, 55, 57, 79, 82, 84, 85, 87, 88, 90, 90, 91, 93, 96, 98, 100, 103, 104, 107, 109, 118	Tests 5, 11, 12, 17
	• Rate	Lessons 23, 24, 26, 27, 28, 30, 32	End of Course Exam
24	• Adding and Subtracting Fractions That Have Common Denominators	Lessons 24, 25, 26, 28, 29, 30, 30, 31, 32, 33, 34, 35, 37, 39, 89	Tests 5, 6, 7, 10
25	• Writing Division Answers as Mixed Numbers	Lessons 25, 26, 27, 28, 29, 30, 31, 34, 35, 37, 39, 43, 45, 46, 54, 61, 119	Tests 6, 7
	• Multiples	Lessons 25, 28, 30, 31, 32, 34, 36, 37, 38, 39, 40, 42, 43, 44, 45, 46, 48, 51, 52, 78	Test & Practice Generator
26	• Using Manipulatives to Reduce Fractions	Lessons 26, 27, 28, 29, 32, 33, 34, 36, 38, 40, 41, 42, 43, 44, 45, 47, 49, 50, 51, 53	Test & Practice Generator
	• Adding and Subtracting Mixed Numbers	Lessons 26, 27, 28, 29, 31, 32, 35, 36, 37, 38, 40, 41, 43, 44, 45, 47, 49, 50, 51, 53, 55	Tests 6, 7, 8, 9, 10, 11
27	• Measures of a Circle	Lessons 27, 29, 31, 36, 41, 45, 46, 47, 48, 49, 50, 51, 53, 54, 55, 56, 95, 98, 99, 100, 101, 115	Tests 6, 7, 9, 13
28	• Angles	Lessons 28, 29, 30, 31, 36, 41, 55, 67, 68, 69, 70, 76, 83, 89, 108, 109	Test 6
29	• Multiplying Fractions	Lessons 29, 30, 31, 32, 33, 34, 35, 36, 37, 38, 39, 40, 41, 42, 43, 45, 46, 47, 48, 49, 50, 51, 52, 53, 54, 55, 56, 57, 58, 59, 60, 61, 62, 63, 65, 66, 77, 88, 89, 92, 106, 107	Tests 7, 8, 9 11
	• Reducing Fractions by Dividing by Common Factors	Lessons 29, 30, 31, 32, 33, 34, 35, 36, 37, 38, 40, 44, 46, 48, 52, 53, 54, 55, 56, 57, 58, 60, 61, 63, 65, 66, 67, 69, 71, 72, 74, 77, 81, 83, 84, 99, 119	Tests 6, 7, 8, 10, 17
30	• Least Common Multiple (LCM)	Lessons 30, 32, 34, 36, 37, 38, 39, 40, 42, 43, 44, 45, 46, 48, 50, 51, 52, 53, 54, 55, 57, 71, 74, 108, 114	Tests 6, 8, 10, 15
	• Reciprocals	Lessons 30, 31, 32, 33, 35, 36, 38, 39, 41, 42, 44, 45, 46, 49, 53, 55, 56, 58, 60, 67, 69, 70, 75, 77, 78	Tests 6, 7, 9
Inv. 3	• Measuring and Drawing Angles with a Protractor	Inv. 3, Lessons 32, 34, 41, 43, 108	Test 8

• Divisibility

Objectives

- Use divisibility tests to determine whether a number is divisible by 2, 3, 5, 9, or 10.
- Use divisibility tests to determine if 2, 3, 5, 9, and 10 are factors of a number.

Lesson Preparation

Materials

- **Power Up D** (in *Instructional Masters*)
- **Manipulative kit: rulers**

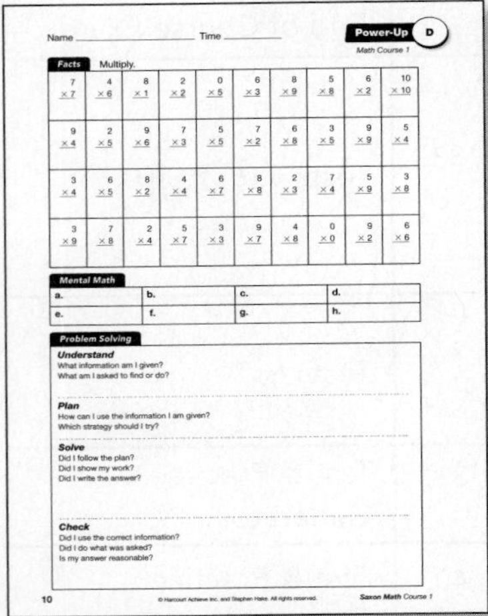

Power Up D

Math Language

English Learners (ESL)
divisible

Technology Resources

Student eBook Complete student textbook in electronic format.

Resources and Planner CD Assessment, reteaching, and instructional masters, plus a pacing calendar with standards.

Test and Practice Generator CD Create additional practice sheets and custom-made tests.

www.SaxonPublishers.com Visit for more student activities and planning materials.

Inclusion

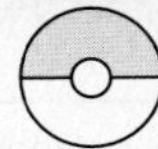

Adaptations CD Adapted lessons, investigations, practice and assessments.

Meeting Standards

National Council of Teachers of Mathematics (NCTM)

Numbers and Operations

NO.2a Understand the meaning and effects of arithmetic operations with fractions, decimals, and integers

Problem Solving

PS.1c Apply and adapt a variety of appropriate strategies to solve problems

Reasoning and Proof

RP.2b Make and investigate mathematical conjectures

Representation

RE.5b Select, apply, and translate among mathematical representations to solve problems

Power-Up Discussion For use with Power Up, p. 112

Problem-Solving Strategy: Use Logical Reasoning

Here is part of a randomly ordered multiplication table. What is the missing product?

48	30	42
32	?	28
56	35	49

Understand Understand the problem.

"What information are we given?"

We are shown a 3-by-3 portion of a multiplication table with rows and columns re-ordered. The center number is missing.

"What are we asked to do?"

We are asked to find what number is missing from the multiplication table.

Plan Make a plan.

"What problem-solving strategy will we use?"

We will *use logical reasoning* and *number sense* to determine the common factors for each row and column in the table.

Solve Carry out the plan.

Mentally break the chart into columns and rows. Use your knowledge of multiplication facts to determine common factors.

"What is a common factor in the first column?" 8

"What is a common factor in the second column?" 5

"What is a common factor in the third column?" 7

"What is a common factor in the first row?" 6

"What is a common factor in the second row?" 4

"What is a common factor in the third row?" 7

	8	**5**	**7**
6	48	30	42
4	32	**20**	28
7	56	35	49

"Using the common factor from the second column and the common factor from the second row, we multiply the two factors to get our answer. What is the missing factor?" 20

Check Look back.

"Did we complete the task?"

Yes. We identified the factors and used them to find the missing number in the multiplication table (20).

"How can we verify our answer?"

We can use our completed table and multiply the factor pairs to check that the products match those in the chart.

1 Power Up

Facts

Distribute **Power Up D** to students. See answers below.

Mental Math

Before students begin the Mental Math exercise, do this counting exercise as a class.

Count up and down by $\frac{1}{4}$s between $\frac{1}{4}$ and 12.

Encourage students to share different ways to mentally compute these exercises. Strategies for exercises **a, c, d,** and **h** are listed below.

a. Use the Distributive Property
$4 \times 42 = (4 \times 40) + (4 \times 2) = 160 + 8 = 168$

Count by 40, then Count by 2
Start with 40. Count: 80, 120, 160
Start with 160. Count: 162, 164, 166, 168

c. Add 20, then Subtract 1
$64 + 20 = 84$; $84 - 1 = 83$

d. Add 40, then Subtract 3
$450 + 40 = 490$; $490 - 3 = 487$

Decompose Numbers
$400 + 50 + 30 + 7 = 400 + 80 + 7 = 487$

h. Perform the operations within the commas.
$25 \times 2 = 50$, then $50 - 1 = 49$, then $49 \div 7 = 7$, then $7 + 1 = 8$, then $8 \div 2 = 4$.

Problem Solving

Refer to **Power-Up Discussion,** p. 112F.

2 New Concepts

Instruction

Help students make the connection that any counting number is divisible by 2, 5, and 10 if the number has a zero in its ones place. Choose numbers such as 30 and 300 and use them to demonstrate this fact.

(continued)

LESSON 21

• Divisibility

Power Up *Building Power*

facts Power Up D

mental math

a. Number Sense: 4×42 168

b. Number Sense: 3×76 228

c. Number Sense: $64 + 19$ 83

d. Number Sense: $450 + 37$ 487

e. Calculation: $10.00 − $6.50 $3.50

f. Fractional Parts: $\frac{1}{2}$ of 24 12

g. Measurement: How many months are in a year? 12 months

h. Calculation: Start with 25, × 2, − 1, ÷ 7, + 1, ÷ 2 4

problem solving Here is part of a randomly-ordered multiplication table. What is the missing product? 20

48	30	42
32	?	28
56	35	49

New Concept *Increasing Knowledge*

Thinking Skill
Discuss
Without dividing by 2, how can you tell that a number is even? A number is even if the last digit of the number is 2, 4, 6, 8, or 0.

There are ways of discovering whether some numbers are factors of other numbers without actually dividing. For instance, even numbers can be divided by 2. Therefore, 2 is a factor of every even counting number. Since even numbers are "able" to be divided by 2, we say that even numbers are "divisible" by 2.

Tests for **divisibility** can help us find the factors of a number. Here we list divisibility tests for the numbers 2, 3, 5, 9, and 10.

Last-Digit Tests

Inspect the last digit of the number. A number is divisible by ...

2 if the last digit is even.

5 if the last digit is 0 or 5.

10 if the last digit is 0.

Facts Multiply.

7 × 7 49	4 × 6 24	8 × 1 8	2 × 2 4	0 × 5 0	6 × 3 18	8 × 9 72	5 × 8 40	6 × 2 12	10 × 10 100
9 × 4 36	2 × 5 10	9 × 6 54	7 × 3 21	5 × 5 25	7 × 2 14	6 × 8 48	3 × 5 15	9 × 9 81	5 × 4 20
3 × 4 12	6 × 5 30	8 × 2 16	4 × 4 16	6 × 7 42	8 × 8 64	2 × 3 6	7 × 4 28	5 × 9 45	3 × 8 24
3 × 9 27	7 × 8 56	2 × 4 8	5 × 7 35	3 × 3 9	9 × 7 63	4 × 8 32	0 × 0 0	9 × 2 18	6 × 6 36

Sum-of-Digits Tests

Add the digits of the number and inspect the total. A number is divisible by …

3 if the sum of the digits is divisible by 3.

9 if the sum of the digits is divisible by 9.

Example 1

Which of these numbers is divisible by 2?

365 1179 1556

Solution

To determine whether a number is divisible by 2, we inspect the last digit of the number. If the last digit is an even number, then the number is divisible by 2. The last digits of these three numbers are 5, 9, and 6. Since 5 and 9 are not even numbers, neither 365 nor 1179 is divisible by 2. Since 6 is an even number, 1556 is divisible by 2. It is not necessary to perform the division to answer the question. By inspecting the last digit of each number, we see that the number that is divisible by 2 is **1556.**

Example 2

Which of these numbers is divisible by 3?

365 1179 1556

Solution

To determine whether a number is divisible by 3, we add the digits of the number and then inspect the sum. If the sum of the digits is divisible by 3, then the number is also divisible by 3.

The digits of 365 are 3, 6, and 5. The sum of these is 14.

$$3 + 6 + 5 = 14$$

We try to divide 14 by 3 and find that there is a remainder of 2. Since 14 is not divisible by 3, we know that 365 is not divisible by 3 either.

The digits of 1179 are 1, 1, 7, and 9. The sum of these digits is 18.

$$1 + 1 + 7 + 9 = 18$$

We divide 18 by 3 and get no remainder. We see that 18 is divisible by 3, so 1179 is also divisible by 3.

The sum of the digits of 1556 is 17.

$$1 + 5 + 5 + 6 = 17$$

Since 17 is not divisible by 3, the number 1556 is not divisible by 3.

By using the divisibility test for 3, we find that the number that is divisible by 3 is **1179.**

Discuss Is 9536 divisible by 2? by 3? How do you know? It ends with a 6, so it is divisible by 2. The sum of the digits is 23, so it is not divisible by 3.

2 New Concepts (Continued)

Instruction

If the sum of the digits is a number having two or more digits, those digits can also be added.

For example, the sum of the digits in the number 12,345,678 is 36, and 36 is divisible by 9. The sum of the digits in 36 $(3 + 6 = 9)$ is also divisible by 9.

Example 1

Instruction

The following question can be asked to check students' understanding of divisibility by 2.

"How many numbers from 1 to 100 are divisible by 2? Use a pattern to help find the answer." In each decade of numbers (1–10, 11–20, 21–30, and so on), five numbers are divisible by 2. Since there are ten decades altogether, 5×10 or 50 numbers are divisible by 2.

Example 2

Instruction

One way to check understanding of divisibility by 3 is to ask each student in class to name a digit. As the digits are named, write them from left to right on the board. Challenge students to use mental math and identify the sum of the digits, then decide if the number is divisible by 3. Answers will vary.

You might extend the activity by challenging students to name the number of commas that would need to be inserted in the number to make it easier to read.

(continued)

Math Background

Only the divisibility rules for 2, 3, 5, 9, and 10 are presented in this lesson. There are other rules. Some students may enjoy creating, then testing, new rules using what they already know about divisibility and their understanding of multiples.

For example, students generally know that the first four multiples of 25 are 25, 50, 75, and 100. Using that knowledge, they might predict, then test, the idea that any number having two or more digits and ending in 25, 50, 75, or 00 is divisible by 25.

Invite students who explore new rules to share their conclusions with their classmates.

English Learners

Explain that when a number is **divisible** by another number, it divides evenly with no remainder. Write these divisions on the board:

$$\begin{array}{r} 6 \\ 4\overline{)24} \\ \underline{24} \\ 0 \end{array} \qquad \begin{array}{r} 6\text{ R1} \\ 4\overline{)25} \\ \underline{24} \\ 1 \end{array}$$

Say:

"24 is divisible by 4. 25 is not divisible by 4? Why is 25 not divisible by 4?" There is a remainder of 1.

2 New Concepts (Continued)

Example 3

Instruction

You can summarize divisibility by writing the digits 0, 5, 6, and 7, and the conditions listed below, on the board. Working in pairs, ask students to arrange the digits to create a four-digit number that meets each condition.

a. Divisible by 2, 3, 5, 9, 10. Any arrangement with zero in the ones place.
b. Divisible by only 3, 5, and 9. Any arrangement with 5 in the ones place.
c. Divisible by only 2, 3, and 9. Any arrangement with 6 in the ones place.
d. Divisible by only 3 and 9. Any arrangement with 7 in ones place.

Ask students to name the numbers they formed for each condition. Write the numbers under or next to each condition as they are named. Then work with students to form a generalization about the numbers for each condition.

Practice Set

Problem b Predict

Extend the Problem

Explain that if a number is divisible by 2 and it is divisible by 3, the number is also divisible by 6. Then ask students to name the number or numbers in the problem that are divisible by 6. 3456

3 Written Practice

Math Conversations

Discussion opportunities are provided below.

Problem 3 Formulate

Extend the Problem

Ask students to write a related equation that can also be used to solve the problem.
Sample: A related equation for $16w = 240$ is $w = \frac{240}{16}$.

(continued)

Example 3

Which of the numbers 2, 3, 5, 9, and 10 are factors of 135?

Solution

First we will use the last-digit tests. The last digit of 135 is 5, so 135 is divisible by 5 but not by 2 or by 10. Next we use the sum-of-digits tests. The sum of the digits in 135 is 9 $(1 + 3 + 5 = 9)$. Since 9 is divisible by both 3 and 9, we know that 135 is also divisible by 3 and 9. So **3, 5,** and **9** are factors of 135.

Predict Will the product of any two prime factors of 135 given above also be a factor of 135? Yes

Practice Set

a. Which of these numbers is divisible by 2? 234
123 234 345

▶ **b.** Which of these numbers is divisible by 3? 3456
1234 2345 3456

Use the divisibility tests to decide which of the numbers 2, 3, 5, 9, and 10 are factors of the following numbers:

c. 120 2, 3, 5, 10 **d.** 102 2, 3

Written Practice *Strengthening Concepts*

Math Language
The word **product** is related to multiplication, the word **sum** is related to addition, and the word **difference** is related to subtraction.

1. (12) What is the product of the sum of 8 and 5 and the difference of 8 and 5? 39

2. (13) Formulate In 1787 Delaware became the first state. In 1959 Hawaii became the fiftieth state admitted to the Union. How many years were there between these two events? Write an equation and solve the problem. $1959 - 1787 = d$; 172 years

▶ *** 3.** (15) Formulate Maria figured that the bowling balls on the rack weighed a total of 240 pounds. How many 16-pound bowling balls weigh a total of 240 pounds? Write an equation and solve the problem.
$16 \cdot w = 240$; 15 bowling balls

4. (6) An apple pie was cut into four equal slices. One slice was quickly eaten. What fraction of the pie was left? $\frac{3}{4}$

5. (6) There are 17 girls in a class of 30 students. What fraction of the class is made up of girls? $\frac{17}{30}$

6. (6) Use digits to write the fraction three hundredths. $\frac{3}{100}$

7. (6) How much money is $\frac{1}{2}$ of \$2.34? \$1.17

8. (6) What is the place value of the 7 in 987,654,321? millions

▶ See Math Conversations in the sidebar.

Inclusion

Encourage students to use the tests for divisibility to help them identify the factors of numbers with two or more digits. Have students begin with these three questions:

- Is the last digit 5 or 0? If so, the number is divisible by 5.
- Is the last digit even? If so, the number is divisible by 2.
- What is the sum of the digits? If the sum is divisible by 3, the number is divisible by 3. If the sum is divisible by 9, the number is divisible by 9.

Refer students to the "Tests for Divisibility" in the Student Reference Guide for other tests that are useful in identifying factors.

Show students how to use these tests to find the factors of 120 and 102 in the Practice Set exercises *c* and *d* above.

9. (10) **Generalize** Describe the rule of the following sequence. Then find the next term.

1, 4, 16, 64, ___256___, ...

Multiply the value of a term by 4 to find the next term.

10. (9) Compare: $64 \times 1 \bigcirc 64 + 1$ <

▶* 11. (21) Which of these numbers is divisible by 9? B

A 365 B 1179 C 1556

* 12. (16) **Estimate** Find the sum of 396, 197, and 203 by rounding each number to the nearest hundred before adding. 800

* 13. (20) What is the greatest common factor (GCF) of 12 and 16? 4

14. (2) $100\overline{)4030}$ 40 R 30

15. (2) $48{,}840 \div 24$ 2035

16. (2) $\frac{678}{6}$ 113

17. (2) $\$4.75 \times 10$ $47.50

Find each unknown number. Check your work.

▶ 18. (3) $\$10 - w = 87¢$ $9.13

19. (3) $463 + 27 + m = 500$ 10

* 20. (17) Arrange these numbers in order from least to greatest: $-2, 0, \frac{1}{4}, \frac{1}{2}, 1$

$1, \frac{1}{2}, 0, -2, \frac{1}{4}$

* 21. (18) What is the average of 12, 16, and 23? 17

▶* 22. (19) List the whole numbers that are factors of 28. 1, 2, 4, 7, 14, 28

▶* 23. (19) What whole numbers are factors of both 20 and 30? 1, 2, 5, 10

24. (7) Use an inch ruler to draw a line segment four inches long. Then use a centimeter ruler to find the length to the nearest centimeter. See student work.; 10 cm

25. (5) $(12 \times 12) - (11 \times 13)$ 1

▶* 26. (Inv. 2) **Represent** To divide a circle into thirds, John first imagined the face of a clock. From the center of the "clock," he drew one segment up to the 12. Then, starting from the center, John drew two other segments. To which two numbers on the "clock" did John draw the two segments when he divided the circle into thirds? 4 and 8

▶* 27. (Inv. 2) **Model** Draw and shade rectangles to illustrate this comparison:

$\frac{2}{3} < \frac{3}{4}$

▶ See Math Conversations in the sidebar.

3 Written Practice (Continued)

Math Conversations

Discussion opportunities are provided below.

Problem 11 Verify

Extend the Problem

Ask students to use an example to prove, or a non-example to disprove, the following statement.

"If a number is divisible by 3, the number is also divisible by 9." non-examples to disprove: 3 or 6

Problem 26 Represent

Extend the Problem

Challenge students to describe where they would draw segments on the clock face to divide it into sixths. from the center to 2, 4, 6, 8, 10, and 12; six segments altogether

Problem 27 Model

Extend the Problem

Ask students to write a comparison statement about the unshaded areas. $\frac{1}{3} > \frac{1}{4}$ or $\frac{1}{4} < \frac{1}{3}$

Errors and Misconceptions

Problem 18

If students do not regroup correctly to find that the correct answer is $9.13, demonstrate how to check the answers using mental math. For example, work with students to count up from 87¢ to $1, then add the 13¢ to $9.

Encourage students to describe other ways to use mental math to check the answer.

Problem 22

Watch for students who don't include 1 and/or 28 as factors.

(continued)

3 Written Practice *(Continued)*

Math Conversations

Discussion opportunities are provided below.

Problem 29 Connect

Extend the Problem

Write the following table on the board.

Side length (s)	1	2	3	4	5	6
Perimeter (P)	8	16	24	32	40	48

Explain that the table is designed to show the proportional relationship shared by the perimeter of a regular octagon and the length of its sides.

Have students complete the table and write a formula to describe the relationship. $P = 8s$

* **28.** (6) A "bit" is $\frac{1}{8}$ of a dollar.

a. How many bits are in a dollar? 8 bits

b. How many bits are in a half-dollar? 4 bits

▶ **29.** (8) A regular octagon has eight sides of equal length. What is the perimeter of a regular octagon with sides 18 cm long? 144 cm

* **30.** (Inv. 2) **Represent** Describe a method for dividing a circle into eight equal parts that involves drawing a plus sign and a times sign. Illustrate the explanation. Draw a circle ◯. Through the center of the circle, draw a plus sign ⊕. Then draw a times sign through the center of the circle ⊛.

Early Finishers *Real-World Application*

The 22 sixth grade students at the book fair want to buy a mystery or science fiction novel. Ten of the 15 students who want a mystery book changed their minds and decided to look for a humorous book. How many sixth grade students are NOT looking for mystery books?

Write one equation and use it to solve the problem.
Sample: $22 - (15 - 10) = 17$

116 **Saxon** *Math Course 1*

▶ See Math Conversations in the sidebar.

Looking Forward

Testing a number for divisibility by 2, 3, 5, 9, or 10 and determining if 2, 3, 5, 9 or 10 are factors of a number prepare students for:

- **Lesson 29,** reducing fractions by dividing by common factors.
- **Lesson 33,** writing percents as reduced fractions.
- **Lesson 53,** simplifying fractions.
- **Lesson 65,** writing the prime factorization of a number using division by primes or factor trees.
- **Lesson 70,** reducing fractions before multiplying.

• "Equal Groups" Problems with Fractions

Objectives

- Use two steps to solve equal groups problems with fractions.
- Divide objects into equal groups and count to find a fractional part of a number.
- Divide a given number into equal groups and then multiply to find a fractional part of the number.

Lesson Preparation

Materials

- **Power Up C** (in *Instructional Masters*)
- **Manipulative kit: inch rulers, overhead tiles**

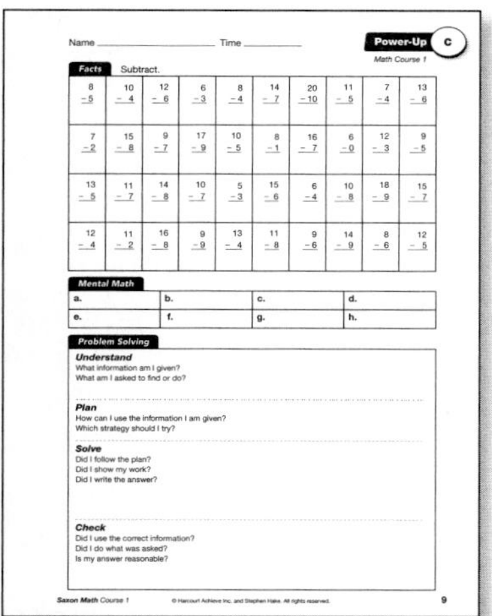

Name ______________ Time ________

Power-Up C
Math Course 1

Facts Subtract.

8 − 5	10 − 4	12 − 6	6 − 3	8 − 4	14 − 7	20 − 10	11 − 5	7 − 4	13 − 6
7 − 2	15 − 8	9 − 7	17 − 9	10 − 5	8 − 1	16 − 7	6 − 0	12 − 3	9 − 5
13 − 5	11 − 7	14 − 8	10 − 7	5 − 3	15 − 6	6 − 4	10 − 8	18 − 9	15 − 7
12 − 4	11 − 2	16 − 8	9 − 9	13 − 4	11 − 8	9 − 6	14 − 9	8 − 6	12 − 5

Mental Math

a.	b.	c.	d.
e.	f.	g.	h.

Problem Solving

Understand
What information am I given?
What am I asked to find or do?

Plan
How can I use the information I am given?
Which strategy should I try?

Solve
Did I follow the plan?
Did I show my work?
Did I write the answer?

Check
Did I use the correct information?
Did I do what was asked?
Is my answer reasonable?

Saxon Math Course 1 © Harcourt Achieve Inc. and Stephen Hake. All rights reserved. 9

Power Up C

Math Language

Maintain	English Learners (ESL)
Perimeter	diagram

Technology Resources

Student eBook Complete student textbook in electronic format.

Resources and Planner CD Assessment, reteaching, and instructional masters, plus a pacing calendar with standards.

Test and Practice Generator CD Create additional practice sheets and custom-made tests.

www.SaxonPublishers.com Visit for more student activities and planning materials.

Inclusion

Adaptations CD Adapted lessons, investigations, practice and assessments.

Meeting Standards

National Council of Teachers of Mathematics (NCTM)

Numbers and Operations

NO.1a Work flexibly with fractions, decimals, and percents to solve problems

NO.1d Understand and use ratios and proportions to represent quantitative relationships

Geometry

GM.4c Use visual tools such as networks to represent and solve problems

Problem Solving

PS.1b Solve problems that arise in mathematics and in other contexts

Power-Up Discussion *For use with Power Up, p. 117*

Problem-Solving Strategy: Write an Equation

Truston has 16 tickets, Sergio has 8 tickets, and Melina has 6 tickets. How many tickets should Truston give to Sergio and to Melina so that they all have the same number of tickets?

Understand — *Understand the problem.*

"What information are we given?"

Truston has 16 tickets, Sergio has 8 tickets, and Melina has 6 tickets.

"What are we asked to do?"

We are asked to determine how many tickets Truston should give to Sergio and Melina so that they each have the same number of tickets.

"We expect our answer to be in what range?"

Students may answer this question differently. Some may misinterpret what the question is asking. They may assume since Sergio and Melina have 14 tickets between themselves, Truston will give two of his tickets away leaving him with only 14 tickets.

"To what math concept does equal distribution relate?"

It is like finding an average or arithmetic mean.

Plan — *Make a plan.*

"What problem-solving strategies could we use?"

We will use our number sense to *write an equation* to find the number of tickets each person must give or receive.

Solve — *Carry out the plan.*

"What is the total number of tickets Truston, Sergio, and Melina have?"

Together they have 30 tickets.

"How many tickets will each have if they divide the 30 tickets evenly amongst them?"

$30 \div 3 = 10$ tickets each

"How many tickets should Truston give to Sergio so that Sergio has 10 tickets?"

$10 - 8 = 2$ tickets

"How many tickets should Truston give to Melina so that Melina has 10 tickets?"

$10 - 6 = 4$ tickets

"After he has given tickets away to Sergio and Melina, how many tickets will Truston have?"

$16 - (2 + 4) = 10$

Check — *Look back.*

"Did we complete the task?"

Yes. We found that Truston should give 2 tickets to Sergio and 4 tickets to Melina so that they will have 10 tickets each.

Alternate Approach: Act It Out/Make a Model

If a set of 30 objects is available (pencils, blocks, paper clips, etc.), allow students to arrange the objects so there are three equal groups. Studen designate each group as Sergio (8 objects), Melina (6 objects), and Trust (16 objects). Help students use the groups to determine the number of t Truston will give to each person.

LESSON 22

• "Equal Groups" Problems with Fractions

Power Up — *Building Power*

facts Power Up C

mental math

a. **Number Sense:** 4×54 216

b. **Number Sense:** 3×56 168

c. **Number Sense:** $36 + 29$ 65

d. **Calculation:** $359 - 42$ 317

e. **Calculation:** $10.00 − $3.50 $6.50

f. **Fractional Parts:** $\frac{1}{2}$ of 48 24

g. **Measurement:** How many yards are in 9 feet? 3 yds

h. **Calculation:** Start with 100, − 1, ÷ 9, + 1, ÷ 2, − 1, × 5 25

problem solving Truston has 16 tickets, Sergio has 8 tickets, and Melina has 6 tickets. How many tickets should Truston give to Sergio and to Melina so that they all have the same number of tickets? Truston should give Melina 4 tickets and Sergio 2 tickets. (Then they will each have 10.)

New Concept — *Increasing Knowledge*

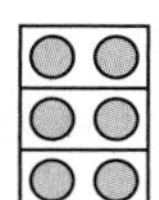

Here we show a collection of six objects. The collection is divided into three equal groups. We see that there are two objects in $\frac{1}{3}$ of the collection. We also see that there are four objects in $\frac{2}{3}$ of the collection.

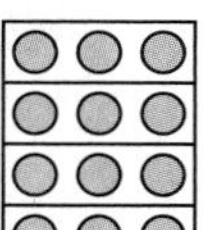

This collection of twelve objects is divided into four equal groups. There are three objects in $\frac{1}{4}$ of the collection, so there are nine objects in $\frac{3}{4}$ of the collection.

Example 1

Thinking Skill
Infer
Why do you divide the musicians by 3?
The denominator of the fraction $\frac{2}{3}$ means you divide into 3 parts.

Two thirds of the 12 musicians played guitars. How many of the musicians played guitars?

Solution

This is a two-step problem. First we divide the 12 musicians into three equal groups (thirds). Each group contains 4 musicians. Then we count the number of musicians in two of the three groups.

Facts Subtract.

8 − 5 = 3	10 − 4 = 6	12 − 6 = 6	6 − 3 = 3	8 − 4 = 4	14 − 7 = 7	20 − 10 = 10	11 − 5 = 6	7 − 4 = 3	13 − 6 = 7
7 − 2 = 5	15 − 8 = 7	9 − 7 = 2	17 − 9 = 8	10 − 5 = 5	8 − 1 = 7	16 − 7 = 9	6 − 0 = 6	12 − 3 = 9	9 − 5 = 4
13 − 5 = 8	11 − 7 = 4	14 − 8 = 6	10 − 7 = 3	5 − 3 = 2	15 − 6 = 9	6 − 4 = 2	10 − 8 = 2	18 − 9 = 9	15 − 7 = 8
12 − 4 = 8	11 − 2 = 9	16 − 8 = 8	9 − 9 = 0	13 − 4 = 9	11 − 8 = 3	9 − 6 = 3	14 − 9 = 5	8 − 6 = 2	12 − 5 = 7

1 Power Up

Facts

Distribute **Power Up C** to students. See answers below.

Mental Math

Before students begin the Mental Math exercise, do this counting exercise as a class.

Count by 2s from 2 to 40. Count by 4s from 4 to 40.

Count up and down by $\frac{1}{4}$s between $\frac{1}{4}$ and 12.

Encourage students to share different ways to mentally compute these exercises. Strategies for exercises **a, c,** and **e** are listed below.

a. Use the Distributive Property
$4 \times 54 = (4 \times 50) + (4 \times 4) =$
$200 + 16 = 216$

Count on by 50, then by 4
Start with 50. Count: 100, 150, 200
Start with 200. Count: 204, 208, 212, 216

c. Add 30, then Subtract 1
$36 + 30 = 66$; $66 - 1 = 65$

e. Count Back by Dollars, then by 50¢
Start with $10. Count: $9, $8, $7
Start with $7. Count: $6.50

Change to Cents, then Subtract
$10.00 = 1000¢ and $3.50 = 350¢
1000¢ − 350¢ = 650¢ or $6.50

Problem Solving

Refer to **Power-Up Discussion,** p. 117B.

2 New Concepts

Example 1

Instruction

To model this example using overhead tiles from the Manipulative Kit, use 12 tiles to represent the 12 musicians. Divide the tiles into three equal groups, and ask students to count the number of tiles in two of the three groups.

(continued)

2 New Concepts (Continued)

Example 2

Instruction

You might choose to place 28 **tiles** from the Manipulative Kit on the overhead, then invite one or more volunteers to go to the overhead and model the situation and its solution.

Example 3

Instruction

Ask students to describe real-world situations that involve finding a fractional part of a whole or of a money amount. Sample: An allowance, and a variety of fractions that are used to determine how that allowance can be spent.

(continued)

	12 musicians
$\frac{1}{3}$ did not play guitars.	4 musicians
$\frac{2}{3}$ played guitars.	4 musicians
	4 musicians

Since there are 4 musicians in each third, the number of musicians in two thirds is 8. We find that **8 musicians** played guitars.

Example 2

Cory has finished $\frac{3}{4}$ of the 28 problems on the assignment. How many problems has Cory finished?

Solution

First we divide the 28 problems into four equal groups (fourths). Then we find the number of problems in three of the four groups. Since 28 ÷ 4 is 7, there are 7 problems in each group (in each fourth).

	28 problems
$\frac{1}{4}$ are not finished.	7 problems
$\frac{3}{4}$ are finished.	7 problems
	7 problems
	7 problems

In each group there are 7 problems. So in two groups there are 14 problems, and in three groups there are 21 problems. We see that Cory has finished **21 problems.**

Example 3

How much money is $\frac{3}{5}$ of $3.00?

Solution

First we divide $3.00 into five equal groups. Then we find the amount of money in three of the five groups. We divide $3.00 by 5 to find the amount of money in each group.

$$5\overline{)\$3.00} = \$0.60 \text{ in each group}$$

Now we multiply $0.60 by 3 to find the amount of money in three groups.

$$\$0.60 \times 3 = \$1.80$$

	$3.00
$\frac{2}{5}$ of $3.00	$0.60
	$0.60
$\frac{3}{5}$ of $3.00	$0.60
	$0.60
	$0.60

We find that $\frac{3}{5}$ of $3.00 is **$1.80.**

Math Background

Is there a shorter method that can be used to find a fractional part of a number?

It is essential that students understand the concept of finding a fractional part of a number. In today's lesson, illustrations are used to build a foundational understanding of this concept. In an upcoming lesson, a shorter method will be presented, and students will learn in that lesson to find a fractional part of a number by finding the product of the fraction and that number.

Example 4

What number is $\frac{3}{4}$ of 100?

Solution

We divide 100 into four equal groups. Since $100 \div 4$ is 25, there are 25 in each group. We will find the total of three of the parts.

$$3 \times 25 = \mathbf{75}$$

100
$\frac{1}{4}$ of 100 { 25
$\frac{3}{4}$ of 100 { 25, 25, 25

Example 5

a. What percent of a whole circle is $\frac{1}{5}$ of a circle?

b. What percent of a whole circle is $\frac{3}{5}$ of a circle?

Solution

A whole circle is 100%. We divide 100% into five equal groups.

a. One of the five parts $\left(\frac{1}{5}\right)$ is **20%.**

b. Three of the five parts $\left(\frac{3}{5}\right)$ is $3 \times 20\%$, which equals **60%.**

100%
$\frac{2}{5}$ of 100% { 20%, 20%
$\frac{3}{5}$ of 100% { 20%, 20%, 20%

Practice Set ▶ *Model* Draw a diagram to illustrate each problem.

a. Three fourths of the 12 musicians could play the piano. How many of the musicians could play the piano? 9 musicians

b. How much money is $\frac{2}{3}$ of $4.50? $3.00

c. What number is $\frac{4}{5}$ of 60? 48

d. What number is $\frac{3}{10}$ of 80? 24

e. Five sixths of 24 is what number? 20

f. Giovanni answered $\frac{9}{10}$ of the questions correctly. What percent of the questions did Giovanni answer correctly? 90%

a.
12 musicians
$\frac{3}{4}$ could play piano. { 3 musicians, 3 musicians, 3 musicians
$\frac{1}{4}$ could not play piano. { 3 musicians

b.
$4.50
$\frac{2}{3}$ of $4.50 { $1.50, $1.50
$\frac{1}{3}$ of $4.50 { $1.50

Written Practice *Strengthening Concepts*

c.

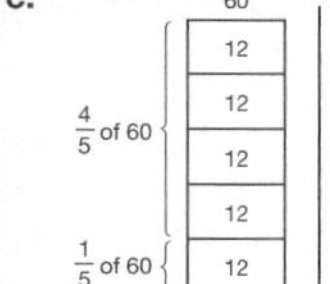

1. (12) When the sum of 15 and 12 is subtracted from the product of 15 and 12, what is the difference? 153

2. (6) There were 13 original states. There are now 50 states. What fraction of the states are the original states? $\frac{13}{50}$

▶ See Math Conversations in the sidebar.

English Learners

Explain that a **diagram** is a type of illustration used to explain something in a way that we can see rather than hear. Draw one of the diagrams from the solution to an exercise. Say:

"Let's look at this diagram. What part of the diagram shows how many equal groups are in the problem?" the number of rows in the column

"What part of the diagram shows how many are in each of the equal groups?" the words or numbers in the rows

"What does the number at the top of the rows mean?" the total number in all of the equal groups

"Why is the sum of the fractions to the left of the rows always 1?" because the fractions represent some part of the whole, which is 1

Emphasize that a diagram helps us see and understand a problem visually.

2 New Concepts (Continued)

Example 4

Instruction

Remind students that when finding a fractional part of a whole, the denominator of the fraction represents the number of equal groups the whole will be divided into.

Example 5

Instruction

Have students note that because 5 is the denominator, the whole is divided into 5 equal parts, and each of those equal parts represents $100\% \div 5$ or 20% of the whole.

Practice Set

Problems a–f (Error Alert)

Remind students of the importance of checking their work. Explain that one way to check the answers for these problems is to find both fractional parts of the whole, and then compare the sum of those parts to the whole.

In problem **a**, for example, if students believe that $\frac{3}{4}$ of 12 is 9, they should also find $\frac{1}{4}$ of 12, which is 3. If the sum of the fractional parts $(9 + 3)$ is equal to the whole (12), students can assume that their answer $(\frac{3}{4}$ of $12 = 9)$ is sensible.

3 Written Practice

Math Conversations

Discussion opportunities are provided below.

Problem 4 Model

Reinforce the concept of working with fractional parts of a whole.

"Eight apples were eaten. What number of apples were not eaten?" 12 − 8 or 4 apples

"Eight apples represent $\frac{2}{3}$ of the whole. What fraction of the whole does 4 apples represent?" $\frac{1}{3}$

Remind students that the sum of the apples (8 + 4) is equal to the whole (12 apples), and the sum of the fractions ($\frac{3}{4} + \frac{1}{4} = \frac{4}{4}$) is equal to 1 because $\frac{4}{4}$ = 4 ÷ 4 and 4 ÷ 4 = 1.

Problem 5 Model

Extend the Problem

Encourage students to describe a way to find $\frac{3}{4}$ of 16 using mental math. Sample: The denominator 4 means that the whole is divided into 4 equal parts, and each equal part is 16 ÷ 4 or 4. The numerator represents three of those equal parts, so 4 + 4 + 4 = 12.

Problem 14 Estimate

Extend the Problem

Challenge students to describe how Shannon could have made her estimate using whole numbers and fractions instead of whole numbers and decimals. Sample: Since 24¢ is about $\frac{1}{4}$ of a dollar, each of the 36 party favors costs about $1\frac{1}{4}$ dollars. Because $\frac{1}{4}$ of \$36 = \$9 and \$1 × 36 = \$36, the total cost will be about \$9 + \$36 or \$45.

Problem 21 Classify

Before completing the problem, ask a volunteer to explain what makes one number prime and another number not prime.

Problem 23 Generalize

Challenge students to describe a variety of ways to find the halfway number using mental math. Sample: Add 3 to 27 and subtract 3 from 43; the number halfway between 30 and 40 is 35.

(continued)

d. 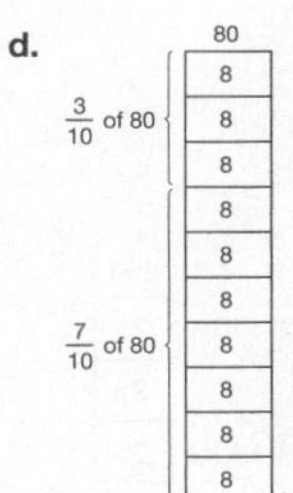

e. 24; $\frac{5}{6}$ of 24: 4, 4, 4, 4, 4; $\frac{1}{6}$ of 24: 4

f. 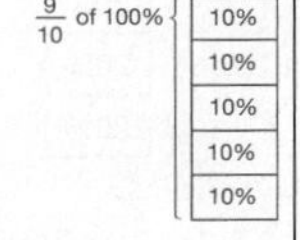

4. 12 apples; $\frac{2}{3}$ were eaten: 4 apples, 4 apples; $\frac{1}{3}$ were not eaten: 4 apples

5. 16; $\frac{3}{4}$ of 16: 4, 4, 4; $\frac{1}{4}$ of 16: 4

6. \$3.50; $\frac{3}{10}$ of \$3.50: \$0.35, \$0.35, \$0.35; $\frac{7}{10}$ of \$3.50: \$0.35, \$0.35, \$0.35, \$0.35, \$0.35, \$0.35, \$0.35

* **3.** (11, 15) A marathon race is 26 miles plus 385 yards long. A mile is 1760 yards. Altogether, how many yards long is a marathon? (First use a multiplication pattern to find the number of yards in 26 miles. Then use an addition pattern to include the 385 yards.) 46,145 yards

▶ * **4.** (22) **Model** If $\frac{2}{3}$ of the 12 apples were eaten, how many were eaten? Draw a diagram to illustrate the problem. 8 apples

▶ * **5.** (22) **Model** What number is $\frac{3}{4}$ of 16? Draw a diagram to illustrate the problem. 12

* **6.** (22) **Model** How much money is $\frac{3}{10}$ of \$3.50? Draw a diagram to illustrate the problem. \$1.05

* **7.** (14) As Shannon rode her bike out of the low desert, the elevation changed from −100 ft to 600 ft. What was the total elevation change for her ride? 700 ft

Find each unknown number. Check your work.

8. (3) $w - 15 = 8$ 23

9. (4) $\frac{w}{15} = 345$ 5175

10. (1) 36¢ + \$4.78 + \$34.09 \$39.23

11. (2) \$12.45 ÷ 3 \$4.15

12. (2) $35\overline{)1000}$ 28 R 20

13. (5) $\frac{7 + 9 + 14}{3}$ 10

▶* **14.** (16) **Estimate** Shannon bought three dozen party favors for \$1.24 each. To estimate the total cost she thought of 36 as 9 × 4, and she thought of \$1.24 as \$1.25. Then she multiplied the three numbers.

a. What was Shannon's estimate of the cost? \$45.00

b. To find the cost quickly, which two numbers should she multiply first? First multiply 4 × \$1.25 to get \$5.00. Then multiply 9 × \$5.00.

15. (12) Which digit in 375,426,198,000 is in the ten-millions place? 2

* **16.** (20) Find the greatest common factor of 12 and 15. 3

* **17.** (19) List the whole numbers that are factors of 30. 1, 2, 3, 5, 6, 10, 15, 30

* **18.** (21) The number 100 is divisible by which of these numbers: 2, 3, 5, 9, 10? 2, 5, 10

* **19.** (22) **Model** Jeb answered $\frac{4}{5}$ of the questions correctly. What percent of the questions did Jeb answer correctly? Draw a diagram to illustrate the problem. 80%

20. (9) Compare: $\frac{1}{3} \bigcirc \frac{1}{2}$ <

▶* **21.** (19) **Classify** Which of these numbers is not a prime number? C

A 19 **B** 29 **C** 39

22. (5, 14) (3 + 3) − (3 × 3) −3

▶ **23.** (18) **Generalize** Find the number halfway between 27 and 43. 35

120 **Saxon** Math Course 1

▶ See Math Conversations in the sidebar.

Math Language
Perimeter is the distance around a closed, flat shape.

24. (8) What is the perimeter of the rectangle below? 50 cm

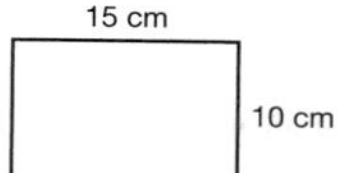

19.

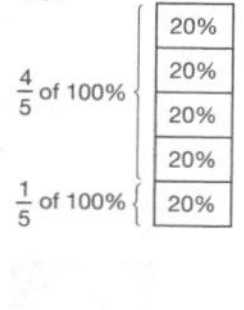

25. (7) Use an inch ruler to find the length of the line segment below. $2\frac{1}{4}$ in.

▶* **26.** (Inv. 2) **Analyze** Corn bread and wheat bread were baked in pans of equal size. The corn bread was cut into six equal slices. The wheat bread was cut into five equal slices. Which was larger, a slice of corn bread or a slice of wheat bread? a slice of wheat bread

* **27.** (Inv. 2) Compare these fractions. Draw and shade rectangles to illustrate the comparison. [shaded rectangle] < [shaded rectangle]

$$\frac{2}{4} \bigcirc \frac{3}{5}$$

(answer: $\frac{2}{4} < \frac{3}{5}$)

28.

1 year = 12 months

$\frac{1}{4}$ of a year	3 months
$\frac{3}{4}$ of a year	3 months
	3 months
	3 months

* **28.** (22) **Model** A quarter of a year is $\frac{1}{4}$ of a year. There are 12 months in a year. How many months are in a quarter of a year? Draw a diagram to illustrate the problem. 3 months

29. (6) A "bit" is one eighth of a dollar.

a. How many bits are in a dollar? 8 bits

b. How many bits are in a quarter of a dollar? 2 bits

▶* **30.** (1) **Represent** The letters *c*, *p*, and *t* represent three different numbers. When *p* is subtracted from *c*, the answer is *t*.

$$c - p = t$$

Use these letters to write another subtraction equation and two addition equations. *Hint:* To be sure you arranged the letters in the correct order, choose numbers for *c*, *p*, and *t* that make $c - p = t$ true. Then try those numbers with these letters for your three equations.
$c - t = p$, $p + t = c$, $t + p = c$

▶ See Math Conversations in the sidebar.

3 Written Practice (Continued)

Math Conversations

Discussion opportunities are provided below.

Errors and Misconceptions

Problem 26

When comparing *unit* fractions (fractions with a numerator of 1, such as $\frac{1}{2}$, $\frac{1}{3}$, $\frac{1}{4}$, $\frac{1}{5}$, and so on), encourage students to use the generalization that the fraction having the lesser denominator is the greater fraction or the fraction having the greater denominator is the lesser fraction.

"Suppose you do a favor for someone and you will be paid either $\frac{1}{4}$ of a dollar of $\frac{1}{2}$ of a dollar. Which amount would you rather be paid? Tell why." $\frac{1}{2}$ of a dollar because $\frac{1}{2} > \frac{1}{4}$

Problem 30

If students have difficulty writing the related equations, ask them to make the substitutions $c = 3$, $p = 2$, and $t = 1$ into the given equation, then rearrange the numbers to form other number facts. Students can then translate each number in the number facts to a letter.

$c - p = t \longrightarrow 3 - 2 = 1$

$3 - 1 = 2 \longrightarrow c - t = p$

$2 + 1 = 3 \longrightarrow p + t = c$

$1 + 2 = 3 \longrightarrow t + p = c$

Looking Forward

Solving story problems about equal groups with fractional parts of numbers prepares students for:

- **Lesson 77,** finding unstated information in fractional-parts problems.
- **Lesson 117,** finding a whole when a fraction is known in a fractional-parts problem.

• Ratio
• Rate

Objectives

- Use ratios to describe relationships between numbers.
- Identify ratios and write them in fraction form.

Lesson Preparation

Materials

- **Power Up D** (in *Instructional Masters*)

Optional

- **Manipulative kit: color tiles**

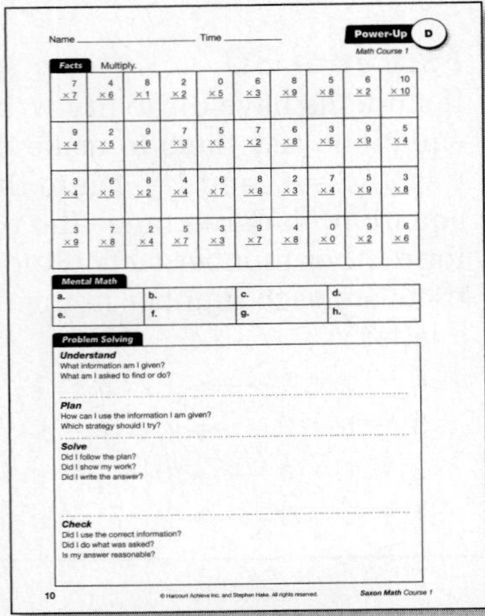

Name ________________ Time ________

Power-Up D
Math Course 1

Facts Multiply.

7 × 7	4 × 6	8 × 1	2 × 2	0 × 5	6 × 3	8 × 9	5 × 8	6 × 2	10 × 10
9 × 4	2 × 5	9 × 6	7 × 3	5 × 5	7 × 2	6 × 8	3 × 5	9 × 9	5 × 4
3 × 4	6 × 5	8 × 2	4 × 4	6 × 7	8 × 8	2 × 3	7 × 4	5 × 9	3 × 8
3 × 9	7 × 8	2 × 4	5 × 7	3 × 3	9 × 7	4 × 8	0 × 0	9 × 2	6 × 6

Mental Math

a.	b.	c.	d.
e.	f.	g.	h.

Problem Solving

Understand
What information am I given?
What am I asked to find or do?

Plan
How can I use the information I am given?
Which strategy should I try?

Solve
Did I follow the plan?
Did I show my work?
Did I write the answer?

Check
Did I use the correct information?
Did I do what was asked?
Is my answer reasonable?

10 © Harcourt Achieve Inc. and Stephen Hake. All rights reserved. *Saxon Math Course 1*

Power Up D

Math Language

New	English Learners (ESL)
ratio	win-loss
rate	

Technology Resources

Student eBook Complete student textbook in electronic format.

Resources and Planner CD Assessment, reteaching, and instructional masters, plus a pacing calendar with standards.

Test and Practice Generator CD Create additional practice sheets and custom-made tests.

www.SaxonPublishers.com Visit for more student activities and planning materials.

Inclusion

Adaptations CD Adapted lessons, investigations, practice and assessments.

Meeting Standards

National Council of Teachers of Mathematics (NCTM)

Numbers and Operations

NO.1a Work flexibly with fractions, decimals, and percents to solve problems

NO.1d Understand and use ratios and proportions to represent quantitative relationships

NO.2a Understand the meaning and effects of arithmetic operations with fractions, decimals, and integers

NO.3d Develop, analyze, and explain methods for solving problems involving proportions, such as scaling and finding equivalent ratios

Power-Up Discussion *For use with Power Up, p. 122*

Problem-Solving Strategy: Draw a Diagram/ Use Logical Reasoning

How many different bracelets can be made from 7 white beads and 2 gray ones?

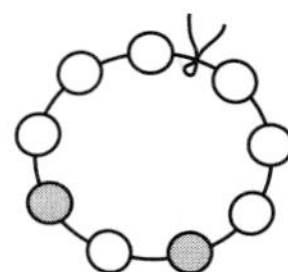

Understand ***Understand the problem.***

"What information are we given?"

A bracelet is made of 9 beads: 7 white beads and 2 gray beads.

"What are we asked to do?"

Determine how many different bracelets can be made from 7 white beads and 2 gray beads.

"What do we already know?"

We know that bracelets form a continuous circuit when clasped, which means we need to be careful not to mistakenly repeat any of our combinations.

Plan ***Make a plan.***

"What problem-solving strategy will we use?"

We will *use logical reasoning* to help us *draw a diagram*.

"How can we modify the bracelet?"

It can be unclasped to form a string of beads, but we will keep in mind the bracelet will be clasped again to form a continuous loop.

Solve ***Carry out the plan.***

"What are the possible positions for the two gray beads?"

The two gray beads can be right next to each other, or they can be separated by one, two or three beads.

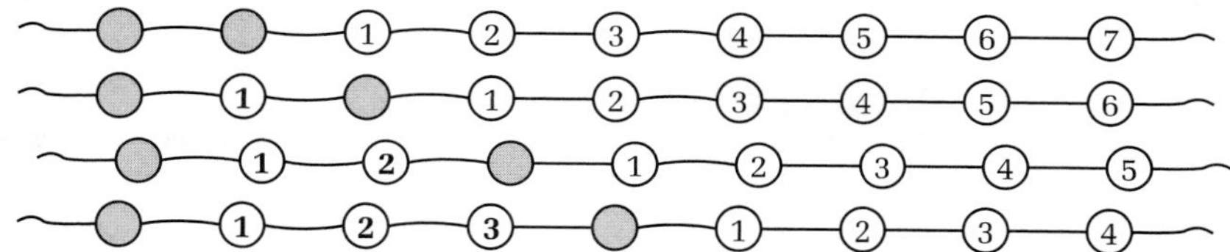

"Are there bracelets with the gray beads separated by more than three beads?"

Yes, but they are the same as the bracelets above. Gray beads separated by 1 white bead are also separated by 6 white beads; by 2 white beads are also separated by 5 white beads. The one below, separated by 4 white beads, is equivalent to the last one above once it is clasped.

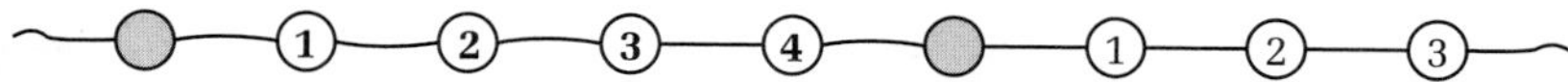

"So how many different bracelets can be made?"

four

Check ***Look back.***

"How can we verify that our answer is correct?"

We can verify our solutions by drawing the four combinations as clasped bracelets instead of unclasped.

1 Power Up

Facts

Distribute **Power Up D** to students. See answers below.

Mental Math

Before students begin the mental math exercise, do this counting exercise as a class.

Count up and down by 3s between 3 and 60.

Count up and down by $\frac{1}{4}$s between $\frac{1}{4}$ and 12.

Encourage students to share different ways to mentally compute these exercises. Strategies for exercises **d** and **f** are listed below.

d. Count by 100, then by 50

Start with 1200. Count: 1300, 1400, 1500

Start with 1500. Count: 1550

Decompose Numbers

$1000 + 200 + 300 + 50 = 1000 + 500 + 50 = 1500 + 50 = 1550$

f. Divide Tens, Then Ones

$84 = 80 + 4$; $\frac{1}{2}$ of $80 = 40$ and $\frac{1}{2}$ of $4 = 2$; $40 + 2 = 42$

Use an Addition Pattern

$40 + 40 = 80$; $41 + 41 = 82$; $42 + 42 = 84$

Problem Solving

Refer to **Power-Up Discussion,** p. 122B.

2 New Concepts

Instruction

After discussing the introductory material, you might choose to begin solving ratio problems by having students identify various ratios that are present in their lives. Examples of questions you might ask include:

- In our classroom today, what is the ratio of girls to boys? What is the ratio of students to teachers? What is the ratio of students who are not wearing sneakers to students who are wearing sneakers?
- In the spelling of your name, what is the ratio of consonants to vowels?
- In your phone number or street address, what is the ratio of even digits to odd digits? (Zero is an even digit.)

(continued)

LESSON 23

• Ratio
• Rate

Power Up *Building Power*

facts Power Up D

mental math

a. **Number Sense:** 5×62 310

b. **Number Sense:** 5×36 180

c. **Number Sense:** $87 + 9$ 96

d. **Number Sense:** $1200 + 350$ 1550

e. **Calculation:** $20.00 − $15.50 $4.50

f. **Fractional Parts:** $\frac{1}{2}$ of 84 42

g. **Measurement:** How many millimeters are in 3 meters? 3000 mm

h. **Calculation:** $10 \times 3, + 2, \div 4, + 1, \div 3, \times 4, \div 6$ 2

problem solving How many different bracelets can be made from 7 white beads and 2 gray ones? 4

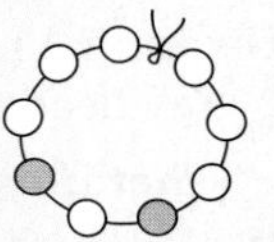

New Concepts *Increasing Knowledge*

ratio A **ratio** is a way to describe a relationship between numbers. If there are 13 boys and 15 girls in a classroom, then the ratio of boys to girls is 13 to 15. Ratios can be written in several forms. Each of these forms is a way to write the boy-girl ratio:

13 to 15   13:15 $\frac{13}{15}$

Math Language
13 and 15 are the terms of the ratio.

Each of these forms is read the same: "Thirteen to fifteen."

In this lesson we will focus on the fraction form of a ratio. When writing a ratio in fraction form, we keep the following points in mind:

1. We write the terms of the ratio in the order we are asked to give them.
2. We reduce ratios in the same manner as we reduce fractions.
3. We leave ratios in fraction form. We do not write ratios as mixed numbers.

Example 1

A team lost 3 games and won 7 games. What was the team's win-loss ratio?

Facts Multiply.

7 × 7 49	4 × 6 24	8 × 1 8	2 × 2 4	0 × 5 0	6 × 3 18	8 × 9 72	5 × 8 40	6 × 2 12	10 × 10 100
9 × 4 36	2 × 5 10	9 × 6 54	7 × 3 21	5 × 5 25	7 × 2 14	6 × 8 48	3 × 5 15	9 × 9 81	5 × 4 20
3 × 4 12	6 × 5 30	8 × 2 16	4 × 4 16	6 × 7 42	8 × 8 64	2 × 3 6	7 × 4 28	5 × 9 45	3 × 8 24
3 × 9 27	7 × 8 56	2 × 4 8	5 × 7 35	3 × 3 9	9 × 7 63	4 × 8 32	0 × 0 0	9 × 2 18	6 × 6 36

Solution

The question asks for the ratio in the order of wins, then losses. The team's win-loss ratio was 7 to 3, which we write as the fraction $\frac{7}{3}$.

$$\frac{\text{number of games won}}{\text{number of games lost}} = \frac{\mathbf{7}}{\mathbf{3}}$$

We leave the ratio in fraction form.

Discuss Is the win-loss ratio the same as the loss-win ratio? no; The loss-win ratio is $\frac{3}{7}$.

Example 2

In a class of 28 students, there are 13 boys. What is the ratio of boys to girls in the class?

Solution

To write the ratio, we need to know the number of girls. If 13 of the 28 students are boys, then 15 of the students are girls. We are asked to write the ratio in "boys to girls" order.

$$\frac{\text{number of boys}}{\text{number of girls}} = \frac{\mathbf{13}}{\mathbf{15}}$$

Model Use tiles of two colors to model this ratio. See student work.

rate A **rate** is a ratio of measures. Below are some commonly used rates. Notice that per means "for each" and substitutes for the division sign.

Common Rates

Name	Rate of Measures	Example	Alternate Form
Speed	$\frac{\text{distance}}{\text{time}}$	$\frac{\text{55 miles}}{\text{1 hour}}$	55 miles per hour
Mileage	$\frac{\text{distance}}{\text{fuel used}}$	$\frac{\text{28 miles}}{\text{1 gallon}}$	28 miles per gallon
Unit price	$\frac{\text{price}}{\text{quantity}}$	$\frac{\$2.89}{\text{1 pound}}$	\$2.89 per pound

Rate problems are a type of equal groups problem. The rate is the number in each group. The problems often involve three numbers. One number is the rate, and the other two numbers are about the measures that form the rate. The three numbers are related by multiplication or division as we show below.

Pattern: $\text{distance} = \frac{\text{distance}}{\text{time}} \times \text{time}$

Example: 165 miles = 55 miles per hour × 3 hours

In a rate problem one of the numbers is unknown. We find an unknown product by multiplying, and we find an unknown factor by dividing the product by the known factor.

2 New Concepts (Continued)

Example 1

Instruction

Emphasize that ratios are not expressed as mixed numbers.

Students can model this ratio using 10 tiles in two colors. Have students arrange the tiles in a 1 to 1 correspondence using 7 tiles of one color and 3 tiles of another color.

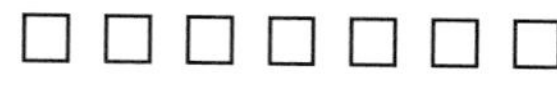

Example 2

Instruction

Have students note that when working with ratios, the idea of "order" is very important. For example, point out that the ratio of boys to girls (13 to 15) is very different than the ratio of girls to boys (15 to 13).

"Because we are asked to write the ratio of boys to girls, we must write $\frac{13}{15}$ and not write $\frac{15}{13}$."

Instruction

After discussing the examples of rates shown in the table, encourage students to name other real-world rates, or situations that involve rates. Sample:

- The speed of light and the speed of sound.
- The amount of rent a tenant pays each month.
- The interest charged against a credit card debt.

(continued)

English Learners

Example 1 talks about a **win-loss** ratio. Write the following on the board:

5 games won, 2 games lost

Then say, pointing to each term as you speak:

"A team played 7 games. They won 5 games but lost 2 games. Their win-loss ratio is 5 to 2."

Write the following on the board:

4 games won, 3 games lost

Then ask:

"What is the win-loss ratio for these 7 games?" 4 to 3

Math Background

A ratio is a comparison of two quantities by division, and can be expressed as a to b, a:b, or $\frac{a}{b}$. A ratio is in simplest form when a and b are whole numbers ($b \neq 0$), and the only common factor of a and b is 1.

2 New Concepts (Continued)

Example 3

Instruction

A related formula that incorporates the concept of rate is the distance formula $d = rt$, in which distance equals the product of rate and time.

The formula $r = \frac{d}{t}$ is used to find a rate, and the formula $t = \frac{d}{r}$ is used to find time.

Example 4

Instruction

Point out that the rate "32 miles per gallon" is an example of a unit rate. A unit rate is any ratio that has a denominator of 1. Generally speaking, expressing a rate as a unit rate is more meaningful than expressing the rate in some other way. For example, describing the fuel economy of a car as "32 miles per gallon" is more meaningful than saying "16,000 miles for 500 gallons," which is the same rate (32 miles per gallon) expressed in a different way.

Practice Set

Problem b Analyze

"What other ratio about the class is true?"

The boy-girl ratio is $\frac{17}{13}$.

Example 3

On a bike trip Jeremy rode 60 miles in 4 hours. What was his average speed in miles per hour?

Solution

We are given the distance and time. We are asked for the speed, which is distance divided by time.

$$\frac{\text{distance}}{\text{time}} \quad \frac{60 \text{ miles}}{4 \text{ hour}} = \textbf{15 miles per hour}$$

Example 4

Mr. Moscal's car averages 32 miles per gallon on the highway. Predict about how far he can expect to travel on a road trip using 10 gallons of fuel.

Solution

This is a problem about gas mileage. Notice the similar pattern.

$$\text{distance} = \frac{\text{distance}}{\text{fuel used}} \times \text{fuel used}$$

We are given the rate and the fuel used. We are asked for the distance, which is the product.

$$\text{distance} = 32 \text{ miles per gallon} \times 10 \text{ gallons}$$
$$= 320 \text{ miles}$$

Mr. Moscal can expect to travel about **320 miles** on 10 gallons of fuel.

Making a table can help us solve some rate problems. Here is the beginning of a table for example 4.

Distance Traveled at 32 Miles per Gallon

Fuel Used (gallon)	1	2	3	4	5
Distance (miles)	32	64	96	128	160

Practice Set

a. What is the ratio of dogs to cats in a neighborhood that has 19 cats and 12 dogs? $\frac{12}{19}$

▸ **b.** Analyze What is the girl-boy ratio in a class of 30 students with 17 boys? $\frac{13}{17}$

c. If the ratio of cars to trucks in the parking lot is 7 to 2, what is the ratio of trucks to cars in the parking lot? $\frac{2}{7}$

d. How long will it take a trucker to drive 400 miles at 50 miles per hour? 8 hours

e. If a four-quart container of milk costs $2.48, what is the cost per quart? $0.62 per quart

▸ See Math Conversations in the sidebar.

Written Practice *Strengthening Concepts*

2. [diagram: 30 problems; $\frac{2}{3}$ are finished: 10 problems, 10 problems; $\frac{1}{3}$ are not finished: 10 problems]

1. How many millimeters long is a ruler that is 30 cm long? 300 mm (7)

* 2. **Model** Dan has finished $\frac{2}{3}$ of the 30 problems on an assignment during class. How many problems did Dan finish during class? Draw a diagram to illustrate the problem. 20 problems (22)

3. Diego walked the length of a football field in 100 large paces. About how long was the football field? about 100 yards (7)

* 4. On the open highway the car traveled 245 miles on 7 gallons of gas. What was the car's gas mileage for the trip in miles per gallon? 35 miles per gallon (23)

5. [diagram: 25; $\frac{3}{5}$ of 25: 5, 5, 5; $\frac{2}{5}$ of 25: 5, 5]

▶ * 5. **Model** What number is $\frac{3}{5}$ of 25? Draw a diagram to illustrate the problem. 15 (22)

* 6. **Model** How much money is $\frac{7}{10}$ of \$36.00? Draw a diagram to illustrate the problem. \$25.20 (22)

6. [diagram: \$36.00; $\frac{7}{10}$ of \$36.00: \$3.60, \$3.60, \$3.60, \$3.60, \$3.60, \$3.60, \$3.60; $\frac{3}{10}$ of \$36.00: \$3.60, \$3.60, \$3.60]

Use your fraction manipulatives to help answer problems **7–9.**

▶ * 7. What is the sum of $\frac{3}{8}$ and $\frac{4}{8}$? $\frac{7}{8}$ (Inv. 2)

* 8. The improper fraction $\frac{9}{8}$ equals what mixed number? $1\frac{1}{8}$ (Inv. 2)

* 9. Two eighths of a circle is what percent of a circle? 25% (Inv. 2)

10. $\$3.75 \cdot 16$ \$60.00 (2)

11. $\dfrac{\$3.75}{25}$ \$0.15 (2)

12. What is the place value of the 6 in 36,174,591? millions (12)

▶* 13. **Explain** How can you find $\frac{2}{3}$ of a number? One way to find $\frac{2}{3}$ of a number is to first divide the number by 3; then multiply that answer by 2. (22)

Find each unknown number. Check your work.

14. $\$0.35n = \$35.00$ 100 (4)

15. $\$10.20 - m = \$3.46$ \$6.74 (3)

▶ 16. Compare: $\frac{3}{4} < 1$ (17)

* 17. **Analyze** The length of a rectangle is 20 inches. The width of the rectangle is half its length. What is the perimeter of the rectangle? 60 inches (8)

18. **Generalize** Describe the rule for the following sequence. Then, write the sixth number in the sequence. To find a number, multiply the number before it by 2. 64 (10)

2, 4, 8, 16, ...

19. Yesterday it snowed. The meteorologist on the radio said that it was 14° outside. What scale was the meteorologist reading? How do you know? (10)

19. Fahrenheit; Snow indicates a temperature at or below the freezing temperature of water, and 14° is below freezing on the Fahrenheit scale but far above freezing on the Celsius scale.

20. Compare: $12 \div 6 - 2 < 12 \div (6 - 2)$ (9)

▶* 21. What is the greatest common factor (GCF) of 24 and 32? 8 (20)

22. What is the sum of the first seven positive odd numbers? 49 (10)

▶ See Math Conversations in the sidebar.

3 Written Practice

Math Conversations

Discussion opportunities are provided below.

Problem 5 Model

Extend the Problem

Encourage students to describe a way to find $\frac{3}{5}$ of 25 using mental math. Sample: The denominator 5 means that the whole is divided into 5 equal parts, and each equal part is $25 \div 5$ or 5. The numerator 3 represents three of those equal parts, so $5 + 5 + 5 = 15$.

Problem 13 Explain

Before completing the problem, write "$\frac{2}{3}$ of 15 is 10" on the board. Then after a method of finding $\frac{2}{3}$ of a number is described, have students use the method to find $\frac{2}{3}$ of 15. Then compare the answer to the statement on the board. If a method does not give an answer of 10, encourage students to discuss ways to change the method so it produces the correct answer.

Problem 16

Extend the Problem

Students often assume that a fraction is *always* less than a whole number.

Ask students to suppose the comparison was $\frac{4}{3} \bigcirc 1$. Ask students to compare $\frac{4}{3}$ and 1 by first rewriting 1 and as equivalent fraction having a denominator of 3. Then students can compare to discover that $\frac{4}{3} > \frac{3}{3}$, and conclude that $\frac{4}{3} > 1$.

Problem 21 Generalize

Remind students of the importance of checking their work.

"How does the greatest common factor of two numbers compare to those numbers?" Students should generalize that the GCF of two numbers (or more than two numbers) can never be greater than the least of those numbers.

Errors and Misconceptions

Problem 7

The following analogy may help students who add denominators when adding like fractions.

"Think about apples whenever you add fractions that have the same denominator. For example, if you add 3 apples and 4 apples, what do you get?" 7 apples

"In the same way, when you add 3 eighths and 4 eighths, what do you get?" 7 eighths

Another strategy for reminding students to not add like denominators is to write the denominators in word form. For example, $\frac{3}{8} + \frac{4}{8} = 3$ eighths + 4 eighths.

(continued)

3 Written Practice *(Continued)*

Math Conversations

Discussion opportunities are provided below.

Problem 25 Analyze

Remind students that $\frac{4}{8}$ is not the only fraction that is equivalent to $\frac{1}{2}$.

"Four-eighths is equivalent to $\frac{1}{2}$. Is $\frac{4}{8}$ the only fraction that is equivalent to $\frac{1}{2}$?" no

"How many other fractions are equivalent to $\frac{1}{2}$?" too many to count; an infinite number

Problem 30 Connect

Extend the Problem

"Could this ratio be based on the team having played 20 games in all? Explain why or why not." No; 20 is not a multiple of 14, the number of games described by the ratio.

Model Use your fraction manipulatives to help answer problems **23–25.**

* **23.** (Inv. 2) **a.** How many $\frac{1}{4}$s are in 1? 4

b. How many $\frac{1}{4}$s are in $\frac{1}{2}$? 2

* **24.** (Inv. 2) One eighth of a circle is what percent of a circle? $12\frac{1}{2}\%$

▶* **25.** (Inv. 2) Write a fraction with a denominator of 8 that is equal to $\frac{1}{2}$. $\frac{4}{8}$

* **26.** (23) There were 16 members of the 2004–2005 men's national swim team. Five of them competed in the freestyle. What is the ratio of those who competed in the freestyle to those who did not? $\frac{5}{11}$

* **27.** (19) **Classify** Which prime numbers are greater than 20 but less than 30? 23, 29

28. (7) Which of the figures below represents a line? B

A •————•

B ←————→

C •————→

* **29.** (21) **Classify** Which of these numbers is divisible by both 2 and 5? C

A 252 **B** 525 **C** 250

▶* **30.** (23) If a team lost 9 games and won 5 games, then what is the team's win-loss ratio? $\frac{5}{9}$

Early Finishers *Real-World Application*

Mrs. Akiba bought 3 large bags of veggie sticks for her students. Each bag contains 125 veggie sticks. One sixth of Mrs. Akiba's 30 students did not eat any veggie sticks. The remaining students split the veggie sticks evenly and ate them. How many veggie sticks did each of the remaining students eat? 15 veggie sticks

▶ See Math Conversations in the sidebar.

Looking Forward

Determining a ratio and writing a ratio as a fraction prepare students for:

- **Lesson 80,** using a scale factor to solve ratio problems.
- **Lesson 83,** using two equivalent ratios to write a proportion and to find a missing number in a proportion.
- **Lesson 85,** using cross products to see if two ratios form a proportion and to solve a proportion.
- **Lesson 88,** using a proportion and a ratio box to solve ratio problems.
- **Lesson 101,** solving ratio problems involving totals with a ratio box and proportion.

Adding and Subtracting Fractions That Have Common Denominators

Objectives

- Use fraction manipulatives to model addition and subtraction of fractions that have common denominators.
- Add and subtract fractions that have common denominators.

Lesson Preparation

Materials

- **Power Up C** (in *Instructional Masters*)
- **Teacher-provided material: fraction manipulatives** from Investigation 2
- **Manipulative kit: fraction circles**

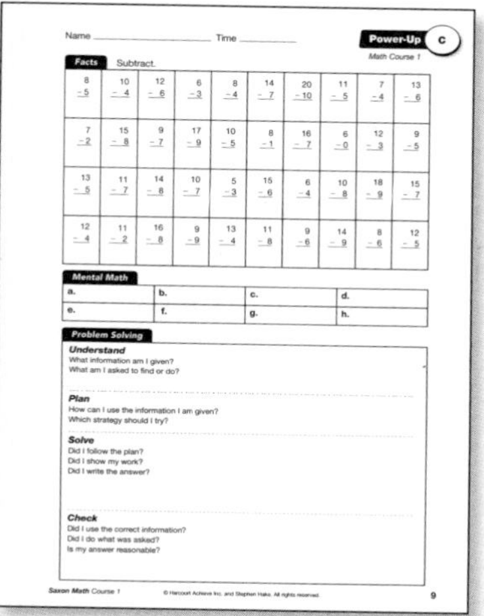

Power Up C

Math Language

Maintain	English Learners (ESL)
denominator	route

Technology Resources

Student eBook Complete student textbook in electronic format.

Resources and Planner CD Assessment, reteaching, and instructional masters, plus a pacing calendar with standards.

Test and Practice Generator CD Create additional practice sheets and custom-made tests.

www.SaxonPublishers.com Visit for more student activities and planning materials.

Inclusion

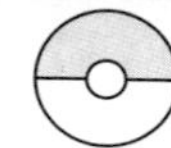

Adaptations CD Adapted lessons, investigations, practice and assessments.

Meeting Standards

National Council of Teachers of Mathematics (NCTM)

Numbers and Operations

NO.1a Work flexibly with fractions, decimals, and percents to solve problems

NO.1f Use factors, multiples, prime factorization, and relatively prime numbers to solve problems

NO.2a Understand the meaning and effects of arithmetic operations with fractions, decimals, and integers

NO.3a Select appropriate methods and tools for computing with fractions and decimals from among mental computation, estimation, calculators or computers, and paper and pencil, depending on the situation, and apply the selected methods

Power-Up Discussion

For use with Power Up, p. 127

Problem-Solving Strategy: Draw a Diagram

Tom followed the directions on the treasure map. Starting at the big tree, he walked five paces north, turned right, and walked seven more paces. He turned right again and walked nine paces, turned left, and walked three more paces. Finally, he turned left, and took four paces. In which direction was Tom facing, and how many paces was he from the big tree?

Understand — Understand the problem.

"What information are we given?"

We are given the directions and the distances Tom walked.

"What are we asked to do?"

We are asked to determine in which direction Tom is facing, and how many paces he is from the tree.

"What do we already know about directions?"

We know our four navigational directions—north, south, east, and west.

Teacher Note: Consider providing graph paper for this activity. It will provide the students with evenly spaced intervals and some students may feel it necessary to turn the paper as they draw.

Plan — Make a plan.

"What problem-solving strategies could we use?"

We will *draw a diagram* to track Tom's movements.

Solve — Carry out the plan.

"We can diagram Tom's journey step-by-step:"

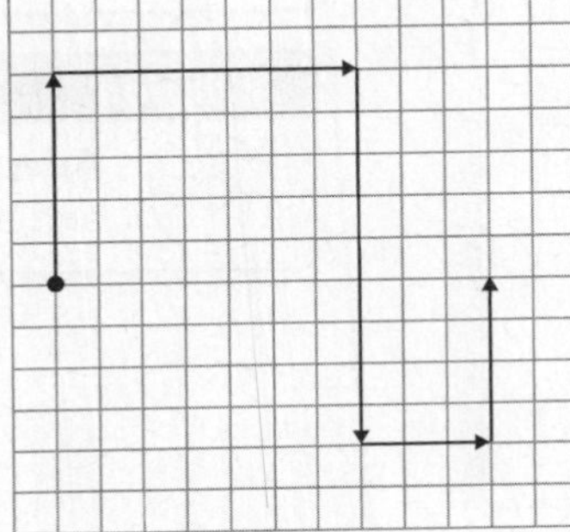

1. Walk 5 paces north.
2. Turn right, and walk 7 paces.
3. Turn right, and walk 9 paces.
4. Turn left, and walk 3 paces.
5. Turn left, and walk 4 paces.

"Where did Tom end?"

Tom ended his journey facing north and 10 paces from the tree.

Check — Look back.

"How would we retrace Tom's path?"

We would walk south 4 paces; turn right, walk 3 paces; turn right, walk 9 paces; turn left, and walk 7 paces; turn left, and walk 5 paces, ending at the big tree.

LESSON 24

• Adding and Subtracting Fractions That Have Common Denominators

Power Up — *Building Power*

facts Power Up C

mental math

a. **Number Sense:** 6 × 24 144

b. **Number Sense:** 4 × 75 300

c. **Number Sense:** 47 + 39 86

d. **Number Sense:** 1500 − 250 1250

e. **Calculation:** \$20.00 − \$14.50 \$5.50

f. **Fractional Parts:** $\frac{1}{2}$ of 68 34

g. **Measurement:** How many yards are in 12 feet? 4 yds

h. **Calculation:** 6 × 7, − 2, ÷ 5, × 2, − 1, ÷ 3 5

problem solving

Tom followed the directions on the treasure map. Starting at the big tree, he walked five paces north, turned right, and walked seven more paces. He turned right again and walked nine paces, turned left, and walked three more paces. Finally, he turned left, and took four paces. In which direction was Tom facing, and how many paces was he from the big tree? Tom was facing north. He was 10 steps away from the big tree.

New Concept — *Increasing Knowledge*

Math Language
The **denominator** tells you into how many parts the whole is divided.

Using our fraction manipulatives, we see that when we add $\frac{2}{8}$ to $\frac{3}{8}$ the sum is $\frac{5}{8}$.

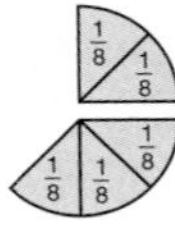

$$\frac{3}{8} + \frac{2}{8} = \frac{5}{8}$$

Three eighths plus two eighths equals five eighths.

Likewise, if we subtract $\frac{2}{8}$ from $\frac{5}{8}$, then $\frac{3}{8}$ are left.

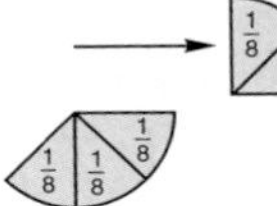

$$\frac{5}{8} - \frac{2}{8} = \frac{3}{8}$$

Five eighths minus two eighths equals three eighths.

1 Power Up

Facts

Distribute **Power Up C** to students. See answers below.

Mental Math

Before students begin the Mental Math exercise, do this counting exercise as a class.

Count by 4s from 4 to 80.

Count up and down by $\frac{1}{4}$s between $\frac{1}{4}$ and 12.

Encourage students to share different ways to mentally compute these exercises. Strategies for exercises **b** and **c** are listed below.

b. Multiply Tens and Ones, then Add
$4 \times 75 = (4 \times 70) + (4 \times 5) = 280 + 20 = 300$

Round 75 to 80, then Subtract 4 × 5
$4 \times 80 = 320; 320 - (4 \times 5) = 320 - 20 = 300$

c. Round 47 to 50, then Subtract 3
$50 + 39 = 89; 89 - 3 = 86$

Round 39 to 40, then Subtract 1
$47 + 40 = 87; 87 - 1 = 86$

Problem Solving

Refer to **Power-Up Discussion**, p. 127B.

2 New Concepts

Instruction

The overhead fraction circles from the Manipulative Kit can be used to model both problems. To have students work individually and model each problem, ask them to use their **fraction manipulatives** from Investigation 2.

(continued)

Facts Subtract.

8 − 5 3	10 − 4 6	12 − 6 6	6 − 3 3	8 − 4 4	14 − 7 7	20 − 10 10	11 − 5 6	7 − 4 3	13 − 6 7
7 − 2 5	15 − 8 7	9 − 7 2	17 − 9 8	10 − 5 5	8 − 1 7	16 − 7 9	6 − 0 6	12 − 3 9	9 − 5 4
13 − 5 8	11 − 7 4	14 − 8 6	10 − 7 3	5 − 3 2	15 − 6 9	6 − 4 2	10 − 8 2	18 − 9 9	15 − 7 8
12 − 4 8	11 − 2 9	16 − 8 8	9 − 9 0	13 − 4 9	11 − 8 3	9 − 6 3	14 − 9 5	8 − 6 2	12 − 5 7

2 New Concepts (Continued)

Example 2

Instruction

"The solution shows that the simplest form of $\frac{2}{2}$ is 1. Why is $\frac{2}{2}$ equal to 1?" A fraction bar represents division, and $\frac{2}{2}$ is the same as $2 \div 2$ or 1.

(continued)

Thinking Skill
Justify
Why does the denominator stay the same when we add fractions with the same denominator?
The number of parts in the whole does not change.

Notice that we add the numerators when we add fractions that have the same denominator, and we subtract the numerators when we subtract fractions that have the same denominator. The denominators of the fractions do not change when we add or subtract fractions that have the same denominator.

Example 1

Add: $\frac{1}{4} + \frac{1}{4} + \frac{1}{4}$

Solution

The denominators are the same. We add the numerators.

$$\frac{1}{4} + \frac{1}{4} + \frac{1}{4} = \mathbf{\frac{3}{4}}$$

Example 2

Add: $\frac{1}{2} + \frac{1}{2}$

Solution

One half plus one half is two halves, which is one whole.

$$\frac{1}{2} + \frac{1}{2} = \frac{2}{2} = \mathbf{1}$$

Example 3

Add: $\frac{3}{4} + \frac{3}{4} + \frac{3}{4} + \frac{3}{4}$

Solution

Thinking Skill
Discuss
Why can we write $\frac{12}{4}$ as 3?
$\frac{4}{4} + \frac{4}{4} + \frac{4}{4} = \frac{12}{4}$
Three groups of $\frac{4}{4}$ equals $\frac{12}{4}$

The denominators are the same. We add the numerators.

$$\frac{3}{4} + \frac{3}{4} + \frac{3}{4} + \frac{3}{4} = \frac{12}{4} = \mathbf{3}$$

Example 4

Subtract: $\frac{7}{8} - \frac{2}{8}$

Solution

The denominators are the same. We subtract the numerators.

$$\frac{7}{8} - \frac{2}{8} = \mathbf{\frac{5}{8}}$$

Manipulative Use

In this lesson, the **overhead fraction circles** from the manipulative kit can be used to model examples 1, 2, 4, and 5.

Example 5

Subtract: $\frac{1}{2} - \frac{1}{2}$

Solution

If we start with $\frac{1}{2}$ and subtract $\frac{1}{2}$, then what is left is zero.

$$\frac{1}{2} - \frac{1}{2} = \frac{0}{2} = \mathbf{0}$$

Practice Set

Find each sum or difference:

a. $\frac{3}{8} + \frac{4}{8}$ $\frac{7}{8}$

▶ b. $\frac{3}{4} + \frac{1}{4}$ 1

c. $\frac{1}{8} + \frac{1}{8} + \frac{1}{8}$ $\frac{3}{8}$

d. $\frac{4}{8} - \frac{1}{8}$ $\frac{3}{8}$

e. $\frac{3}{4} - \frac{2}{4}$ $\frac{1}{4}$

▶ f. $\frac{1}{4} - \frac{1}{4}$ 0

g. **Connect** Use words to write the subtraction problem in exercise **d.**
Four eighths minus one eighth equals three eighths.

Written Practice

Strengthening Concepts

1. $35.00; multiplication pattern (equal groups); addition pattern (combining)

2. 1 dozen eggs: $\frac{3}{4}$ used — 3 eggs, 3 eggs, 3 eggs; $\frac{1}{4}$ not used — 3 eggs

3. 1 mile = 1760 yards: $\frac{1}{8}$ of a mile — 220 yards; $\frac{7}{8}$ of a mile — 220 yards, 220 yards, 220 yards, 220 yards, 220 yards, 220 yards, 220 yards

1. (11, 15) **Analyze** Martin worked in the yard for five hours and was paid $6.00 per hour. Then he was paid $5.00 for washing the car. Altogether, how much money did Martin earn? What pattern did you use to find Martin's yard-work earnings? What pattern did you use to find his total earnings?

▶ *** 2.** (22) **Model** Juan used $\frac{3}{4}$ of a dozen eggs to make omelets for his family. How many eggs did Juan use? Draw a diagram to illustrate the problem. 9 eggs

▶ *** 3.** (22) **Explain** One mile is one thousand, seven hundred sixty yards. How many yards is $\frac{1}{8}$ of a mile? Explain how you found your answer.
220 yards; Sample: To find $\frac{1}{8}$ of 1760, I divided by 8.

▶ **Model** Use your fraction manipulatives to help with exercises **4–8.** Then choose one of the exercises to write a word problem that is solved by the exercise. See student work.

*** 4.** (24) $\frac{1}{4} + \frac{2}{4}$ $\frac{3}{4}$

*** 5.** (24) $\frac{7}{8} - \frac{4}{8}$ $\frac{3}{8}$

*** 6.** (24) $\frac{1}{2} + \frac{1}{2}$ 1

*** 7.** (24) $\frac{1}{2} - \frac{1}{2}$ 0

*** 8.** (Inv. 2) What percent of a circle is $\frac{1}{2}$ of a circle plus $\frac{1}{4}$ of a circle? 75%

*** 9.** (23) In the classroom library there were 23 nonfiction books and 41 fiction books. What was the ratio of fiction to nonfiction books in the library? $\frac{41}{23}$

10. (18) **Explain** How can you find the number halfway between 123 and 321?
Add 123 and 321 and divide by 2.

▶ See Math Conversations in the sidebar.

2 New Concepts (Continued)

Example 5

Instruction

After completing the solution, point out that the examples in this lesson described how to add or subtract halves, fourths, eighths, and sixteenths. Then invite students to name or describe real-world measurement situations that involve subtracting fractional lengths of inches, such as halves, fourths, eighths, or sixteenths.

Practice Set

Problems b and f (Error Alert)

Remind students to write their answers in simplest form.

3 Written Practice

Math Conversations

Discussion opportunities are provided below.

Problem 2 Model

Remind students that "a dozen" represents 12.

Problem 3 Explain

Extend the Problem

Challenge students to describe a way to find $\frac{1}{8}$ of 1760 using mental math. Sample: Because $16 \div 2 = 8$, break apart 1760 to $1600 + 160$, then divide; $(1600 \div 8) + (160 \div 8) = 200 + 20$ or 220.

Problems 4–7 Model

Encourage volunteers to read their word problems aloud. Ask the other students to discuss each problem and decide if it correctly represents the sum or difference of two like fractions.

(continued)

3 Written Practice (Continued)

Math Conversations

Discussion opportunities are provided below.

Problem 12 Classify

Encourage students to try and use mental math, and what they know about prime and non-prime numbers, to classify the numbers.

Problem 18 Connect

Extend the Problem

Have students suppose that when Mr. Johnson said he drove from Seattle to Portland in 4 hours, he described only the time he spent behind the wheel, and he did not count a 1 hour stop he made to eat. So Mr. Johnson spent 4 hours driving, but took 5 hours altogether, to make the trip. Then ask

"Predict how Mr. Johnson's average speed for the entire trip would be changed if he counted the additional hour? Explain your thinking." Students should generalize that increasing the divisor decreases the quotient, so his average spent in miles per hour will decrease.

Problem 21

Extend the Problem

Suppose we include 35 in the set. Is the greatest common factor still 7? Ask a volunteer to demonstrate the answer.

21: 1, 3, 7, 21

28: 1, 2, 4, 7, 14, 28

35: 1, 5, 7, 35

Yes, 7 is the GCF.

"Do we have to factor 35 to find the answer? Why or why not?" No, we only need to know that 7 is also a factor of 35. Any factor of 35 that is greater than 7 is not a common factor of 21 and 28.

Problem 22 Classify

Remind students to use the divisibility rule for 9, and not paper and pencil computations, to classify the numbers.

(continued)

11. (8) Mr. Chen wanted to fence in a square corral for his horse. Each side needed to be 25 feet long. How many feet of fence did Mr. Chen need for the corral? 100 feet

▶* **12.** (19) Classify Which of these numbers is not a prime number? A
A 21 **B** 31 **C** 41

13. (2) $9\overline{)1000}$ 111 R 1

14. (2) 22,422 ÷ 32 700 R 22

15. (2) $350.00 ÷ 100 $3.50

16. (17) Compare: $\frac{1}{2} \textcircled{>} \frac{1}{4}$

* **17.** (16) Conclude Mr. Johnson rented a moving van and will drive from Seattle, Washington, to San Francisco, California. On the way to San Francisco he will go through Portland, Oregon. The distance from Seattle to Portland is 172 miles, and the distance from Portland to San Francisco is 636 miles. The van rental company charges extra if a van is driven more than 900 miles. If Mr. Johnson stays with his planned route, will he be charged extra for the van? To solve this problem, do you need an exact answer or an estimate? Explain your thinking.

17. no; an estimate; I rounded 172 to 200 and 636 to 600; 200 + 600 = 800; 800 < 900, so Mr. Johnson will not be charged extra for the van.

▶* **18.** (23) If Mr. Johnson drives 172 miles from Seattle to Portland in 4 hours, then the average speed of the rental van for that portion of the trip is how many miles per hour? 43 miles per hour

19. (10) Connect What temperature is shown on the thermometer at right? 44°F

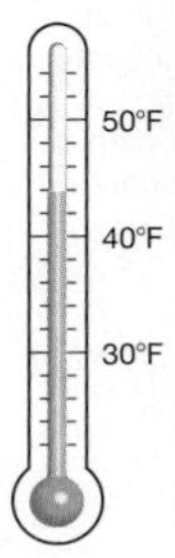

20. (16) Round 32,987,145 to the nearest million. 33,000,000

Math Language
The abbreviation GCF stands for *greatest common factor.*

▶* **21.** (20) What is the GCF of 21 and 28? 7

▶* **22.** (21) Classify Which of these numbers is divisible by 9? B
A 123 **B** 234 **C** 345

23. (Inv. 2) Write a fraction equal to 1 that has 4 as the denominator. $\frac{4}{4}$

Find each unknown number. Check your work.

24. (4) $\frac{w}{8} = 20$ 160

25. (4) $7x = 84$ 12

26. (3) $376 + w = 481$ 105

27. (3) $m - 286 = 592$ 878

130 **Saxon** *Math Course 1*

▶ See Math Conversations in the sidebar.

English Learners

To help students understand the meaning of the word **route** in problem 17, draw the north-south route from Seattle through Portland to San Francisco on the board. Say:

"A route is a planned path used to get from one place to another. What route does this map show?" the route from Seattle to San Francisco

"What city does this route pass through?" Portland

Demonstrate how to use the information in the problem to add mileages to the route: Seattle to Portland, 172 miles, and Portland to San Francisco, 636 miles.

Refer to the bar graph shown below to answer problems **28–30.**

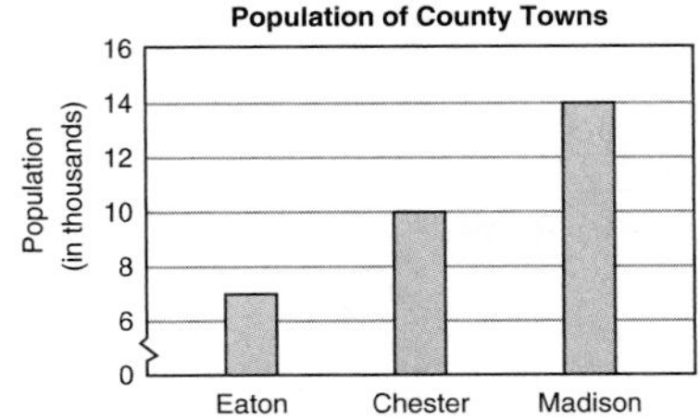

▶ **28.** (16) **Estimate** Which town has about twice the population of Eaton? Madison

▶ **29.** (16) **Estimate** About how many more people live in Madison than in Chester? about 4000 more people

30. (Inv. 1) **Represent** Copy this graph on your paper, and add a fourth town to your graph: Wilson, population 11,000.

Early Finishers *Real-World Application*

Gina's dance team is performing at a local charity event on Saturday. Some members of the team will ride in vans to the event, while others will ride in cars. Seven-eighths of the 112 members will travel to the event in vans.

a. How many members will be traveling in vans? 98 members

b. If each van can carry 11 passengers, how many vans will they need? 9 vans

30.

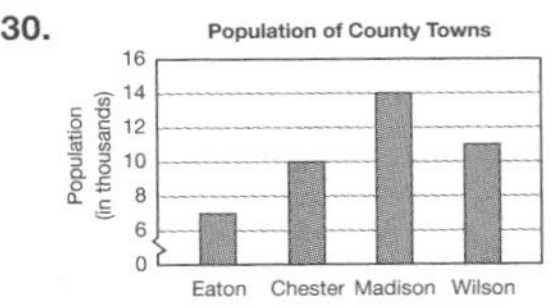

▶ See Math Conversations in the sidebar.

3 Written Practice (Continued)

Math Conversations

Discussion opportunities are provided below.

Problem 29 Estimate

Extend the Problem

These questions give students opportunities to interpret other aspects of the data.

"The populations of Chester and Madison represent estimates, not exact populations. Why don't the numbers represent exact populations?" Sample: It is very unlikely that the exact population of each city is a multiple of 1000.

"To what unit has each population on the graph been rounded to? Explain your answer." Sample: Thousands; the population of each city is a multiple of 1000.

Errors and Misconceptions

Problem 28

Some students may make the estimate by not looking at the numerical scale of the vertical axis. Instead, these students will simply compare the heights of the bars, and conclude that because the bar for Eaton is about $1\frac{1}{2}$ intervals tall, Chester is the city with about twice the population because the bar for Chester is 3 intervals tall, or about twice the number of intervals.

Explain to these students that the method does not work because the vertical axis of the graph is not linear. In other words, the first interval of the vertical axis represents 6000 people, while all other intervals represent 2000 people.

Looking Forward

Adding and subtracting fractions that have common denominators prepares students for:

- **Lessons 26 and 59,** adding and subtracting mixed numbers with common denominators and adding mixed numbers without common denominators.
- **Lesson 36,** subtracting fractions and mixed numbers from whole numbers.
- **Lessons 48 and 63,** subtracting mixed numbers with regrouping.
- **Lessons 55 and 56,** renaming one or both fractions so they have common denominators before adding or subtracting fractions.
- **Lesson 61,** adding three or more fractions or mixed numbers without common denominators.

• Writing Division Answers as Mixed Numbers
• Multiples

Objectives

- Write the answers to division problems as mixed numbers.
- Write improper fractions as mixed numbers.
- Find multiples of numbers.

Lesson Preparation

Materials

- **Power Up F** (in *Instructional Masters*)
- **Manipulative kit: inch rulers, fraction circles**
- **Teacher-provided material: fraction manipulatives** from Investigation 2

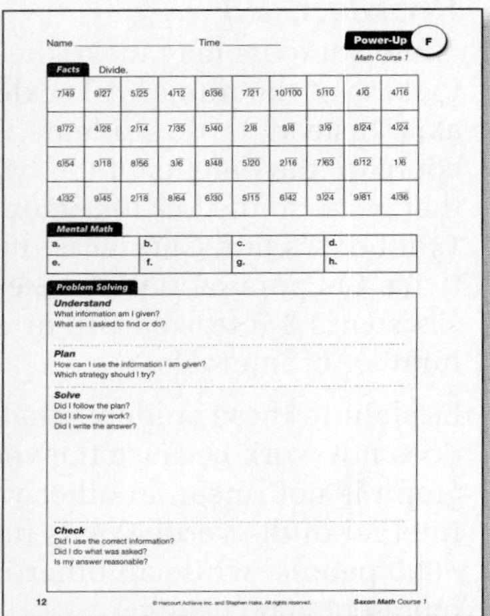

Name ______________ Time ________ **Power-Up F** *Math Course 1*

Facts Divide.

$7\overline{)49}$	$9\overline{)27}$	$5\overline{)25}$	$4\overline{)12}$	$6\overline{)36}$	$7\overline{)21}$	$10\overline{)100}$	$5\overline{)10}$	$4\overline{)0}$	$4\overline{)16}$
$8\overline{)72}$	$4\overline{)28}$	$2\overline{)14}$	$7\overline{)35}$	$5\overline{)40}$	$2\overline{)8}$	$8\overline{)8}$	$3\overline{)9}$	$8\overline{)24}$	$4\overline{)24}$
$6\overline{)54}$	$3\overline{)18}$	$8\overline{)56}$	$3\overline{)6}$	$8\overline{)48}$	$5\overline{)20}$	$2\overline{)16}$	$7\overline{)63}$	$6\overline{)12}$	$1\overline{)6}$
$4\overline{)32}$	$9\overline{)45}$	$2\overline{)18}$	$8\overline{)64}$	$6\overline{)30}$	$5\overline{)15}$	$6\overline{)42}$	$3\overline{)24}$	$9\overline{)81}$	$4\overline{)36}$

Mental Math

a.	b.	c.	d.
e.	f.	g.	h.

Problem Solving

Understand
What information am I given?
What am I asked to find or do?

Plan
How can I use the information I am given?
Which strategy should I try?

Solve
Did I follow the plan?
Did I show my work?
Did I write the answer?

Check
Did I use the correct information?
Did I do what was asked?
Is my answer reasonable?

12 © Harcourt Achieve Inc. and Stephen Hake. All rights reserved. *Saxon Math Course 1*

Power Up F

Math Language

New

multiples

Technology Resources

Student eBook Complete student textbook in electronic format.

Resources and Planner CD Assessment, reteaching, and instructional masters, plus a pacing calendar with standards.

Test and Practice Generator CD Create additional practice sheets and custom-made tests.

www.SaxonPublishers.com Visit for more student activities and planning materials.

Inclusion

Adaptations CD Adapted lessons, investigations, practice and assessments.

Meeting Standards

National Council of Teachers of Mathematics (NCTM)

Numbers and Operations

NO.1a Work flexibly with fractions, decimals, and percents to solve problems

NO.1f Use factors, multiples, prime factorization, and relatively prime numbers to solve problems

NO.2a Understand the meaning and effects of arithmetic operations with fractions, decimals, and integers

Power-Up Discussion *For use with Power Up, p. 132*

Problem-Solving Strategy: Use Logical Reasoning/ Guess and Check

The digits 1 through 9 are used in this subtraction problem. Copy the problem and fill in the missing digits.

$$\begin{array}{r} \_\_\_ \\ -\ 452 \\ \hline 3\_\_ \end{array}$$

Understand ***Understand the problem.***

"What information are we given?"

We are shown a subtraction problem where the digits 2, 3, 4, and 5 are placed, but the remaining digits are missing. We are told the digits 1 through 9 are used in the problem.

"What do we need to do?"

Fill in the missing digits with the digits 1, 6, 7, 8, and 9.

Plan ***Make a plan.***

What problem-solving strategies will we use?

We will *use logical reasoning* to *guess and check* to find the answer.

Solve ***Carry out the plan.***

"What digits could be in the hundreds place of the minuend?"

Adding up, 3 + 4 tells us the digit could be 7 or 8. (It could be 8 from regrouping.) We try 7.

"Assuming the hundreds place of the minuend is 7, can the remaining digits (1, 6, 8, 9) be placed to make the subtraction correct?"

No.

"We try 8 in the hundreds place, remembering that we will regroup in the hundreds column. Which remaining pair of digits can we write in the tens column?"

Only 1 and 6 with regrouping from the hundreds column will work.

"Will the remaining pair of digits work for the ones column?"

Yes, 9 and 7 work.

"What do we write?"

$$\begin{array}{r} 819 \\ -\ 452 \\ \hline 367 \end{array}$$

Check ***Look back.***

"Did we complete the task?"

Yes, we copied the problem and found the missing digits.

1 Power Up

Facts

Distribute **Power Up F** to students. See answers below.

Mental Math

Before students begin the Mental Math exercise, do this counting exercise as a class.

Count by $\frac{1}{8}$s from $\frac{1}{8}$ to 2.

Encourage students to share different ways to mentally compute these exercises. Strategies for exercises **b** and **c** are listed below.

b. Count on by 70, then by 5

Start with 70. Count 140, 210

Start with 210. Count 215, 220, 225

Use the Distributive Property

$3 \times 75 = (3 \times 70) + (3 \times 5) =$

$210 + 15 = 225$

c. Add 30, then Subtract 1

$57 + 30 = 87;\ 87 - 1 = 86$

Add 60, then Subtract 3

$60 + 29 = 89;\ 89 - 3 = 86$

Problem Solving

Refer to **Power-Up Discussion,** p. 132B.

2 New Concepts

Example 1

Instruction

Have students note that a mixed number consists of an integer and a fraction.

(continued)

LESSON 25

• Writing Division Answers as Mixed Numbers
• Multiples

Power Up

Building Power

facts Power Up F

mental math

a. **Number Sense:** 6×43 258

b. **Number Sense:** 3×75 225

c. **Number Sense:** $57 + 29$ 86

d. **Calculation:** $2650 - 150$ 2500

e. **Calculation:** \$10.00 − \$6.25 \$3.75

f. **Fractional Parts:** $\frac{1}{2}$ of 30 15

g. **Measurement:** Which is greater, 5 millimeters or one centimeter? one centimeter

h. **Calculation:** 10×2, $+ 1$, $\div 3$, $+ 2$, $\div 3$, $\times 4$, $\div 3$ 4

problem solving The digits 1 through 9 are used in this subtraction problem. Copy the problem and fill in the missing digits.

$$\begin{array}{r} \_\_\_ \\ -\ 452 \\ \hline 3\_\_ \end{array} \qquad \begin{array}{r} 819 \\ -\ 452 \\ \hline 367 \end{array}$$

New Concepts

Increasing Knowledge

writing division answers as mixed numbers

We have been writing division answers with remainders. However, not all questions involving division can be appropriately answered using remainders. Some word problems have answers that are mixed numbers, as we will see in the following example.

Example 1

A 15-inch length of ribbon was cut into four equal lengths. How long was each piece of ribbon?

Solution

We divide 15 by 4 and write the answer as a mixed number.

$$\begin{array}{r} 3\frac{3}{4} \\ 4\overline{)15} \\ 12 \\ \hline 3 \end{array}$$

Notice that the remainder is the numerator of the fraction, and the divisor is the denominator of the fraction. We find that the length of each piece of ribbon is $3\frac{3}{4}$ **inches.**

Facts Divide.

7 7)49	3 9)27	5 5)25	3 4)12	6 6)36	3 7)21	10 10)100	2 5)10	0 4)0	4 4)16
9 8)72	7 4)28	7 2)14	5 7)35	8 5)40	4 2)8	1 8)8	3 3)9	3 8)24	6 4)24
9 6)54	6 3)18	7 8)56	2 3)6	6 8)48	4 5)20	8 2)16	9 7)63	2 6)12	6 1)6
8 4)32	5 9)45	9 2)18	8 8)64	5 6)30	3 5)15	7 6)42	8 3)24	9 9)81	9 4)36

Example 2

A whole circle is 100% of a circle. One third of a circle is what percent of a circle?

Solution

If we divide 100% by 3, we will find the percent equivalent of $\frac{1}{3}$.

$$\begin{array}{r} 33\frac{1}{3}\% \\ 3\overline{)100\%} \\ \underline{9} \\ 10 \\ \underline{9} \\ 1 \end{array}$$

Connect One third of a circle is $\mathbf{33\frac{1}{3}\%}$ of a circle. Notice that our answer matches our fraction manipulative piece for $\frac{1}{3}$.

Example 3

Reading Math $\frac{25}{6}$ is read "25 divided by 6".

Write $\frac{25}{6}$ as a mixed number.

Solution

The fraction bar in $\frac{25}{6}$ serves as a division symbol. We divide 25 by 6 and write the remainder as the numerator of the fraction.

$$\begin{array}{r} 4\frac{1}{6} \\ 6\overline{)25} \\ \underline{24} \\ 1 \end{array}$$

We find that the improper fraction $\frac{25}{6}$ equals the mixed number $\mathbf{4\frac{1}{6}}$.

multiples

We find **multiples** of a number by multiplying the number by 1, 2, 3, 4, 5, 6, and so on.

The first six multiples of 2 are 2, 4, 6, 8, 10, and 12.

The first six multiples of 3 are 3, 6, 9, 12, 15, and 18.

The first six multiples of 4 are 4, 8, 12, 16, 20, and 24.

The first six multiples of 5 are 5, 10, 15, 20, 25, and 30.

Example 4

What are the first four multiples of 8?

Solution

Multiplying 8 by 1, 2, 3, and 4 gives the first four multiples: **8, 16, 24,** and **32.**

2 New Concepts (Continued)

Example 2

Instruction

Point out that the quotient is expressed as a mixed number, not with a remainder.

Example 3

Instruction

The fraction $\frac{25}{6}$ is an example of an improper fraction. A fraction is improper if its numerator is greater than or equal to its denominator. When working with positive numbers, students should work with the understanding that an improper fraction is either greater than 1, or equal to 1.

(continued)

Math Background

A multiple of a number is the product of that number and a counting number. For example, 20 is a multiple of 10 because $10 \times 2 = 20$.

When working with multiples, students should recognize that a multiple of a positive number is never less than the number itself. It is always equal to, or greater than, that number.

2 New Concepts (Continued)

Practice Set

Problems d and e (Error Alert)

Watch for students who name the first multiple of a number as the product of the number and 2. For example, a student incorrectly names the first multiple of 15 as 30.

Explain that the first multiple of a number is the number itself.

Problem f (Error Alert)

Help students recognize that a multiple of a number is different than a factor of a number.

"24 is the third multiple of 8 and the second multiple of 12. How are the numbers 8 and 12 related to the number 24?" 8 and 12 are factors of 24

"Can the same number ever be a factor of a number and a multiple of that number? Give an example to support your answer." Yes; sample explanation: the greatest factor of 10 is 10 and the first multiple of 10 is 10.

3 Written Practice

Math Conversations

Discussion opportunities are provided below.

Problem 1 (Represent)

Extend the Problem

Ask students to write a symbolic expression to represent the problem. Sample: $\frac{1}{2} + \frac{1}{2} - (\frac{1}{3} + \frac{1}{3})$

Students should conclude that parentheses must be a part of the expression because without them the expression will not simplify to $\frac{1}{3}$.

Problem 5 (Formulate)

Extend the Problem

Ask students to write a related equation that can also be used to solve the problem. Sample: A related equation for $4p = 30$ is $p = \frac{30}{4}$.

Errors and Misconceptions

Problem 8

To help students solve this problem, encourage them to solve a simpler problem first: What number is one-half of the number that is one-half of 100?

To solve the simpler problem, ask the students to work backward. The number that is one-half of 100 is 50, and the number that is one-half of 50 is 25.

Students should apply the same working backward strategy to problem **8**.

(continued)

Example 5

What number is the eighth multiple of 7?

Solution

The eighth multiple of 7 is 8 × 7, which is **56.**

Practice Set

a. A 28-inch long ribbon was cut into eight equal lengths. How long was each piece of ribbon? $3\frac{4}{8}$ or $3\frac{1}{2}$ in.

b. A whole circle is 100% of a circle. What percent of a circle is $\frac{1}{7}$ of a circle? $14\frac{2}{7}$%

c. Divide 467 by 10 and write the quotient as a mixed number. $46\frac{7}{10}$

▶ **d.** What are the first four multiples of 12? 12, 24, 36, 48

▶ **e.** What are the first six multiples of 8? 8, 16, 24, 32, 40, 48

▶ **f.** (Classify) What number is both the third multiple of 8 and the second multiple of 12? 24

Write each of these improper fractions as a mixed number:

g. $\frac{35}{6}$ $5\frac{5}{6}$ **h.** $\frac{49}{10}$ $4\frac{9}{10}$ **i.** $\frac{65}{12}$ $5\frac{5}{12}$

Written Practice *Strengthening Concepts*

▶ * **1.** (Inv. 2) What is the difference between the sum of $\frac{1}{2}$ and $\frac{1}{2}$ and the sum of $\frac{1}{3}$ and $\frac{1}{3}$? $\frac{1}{3}$

2. (18) In three tries Carlos punted the football 35 yards, 30 yards, and 37 yards. How can Carlos find the average distance of his punts?

2. Carlos can find the average distance of the three punts by adding 35 yards, 30 yards, and 37 yards and then dividing the sum by 3.

3. (12) Earth's average distance from the Sun is one hundred forty-nine million, six hundred thousand kilometers. Use digits to write that distance. 149,600,000 kilometers

* **4.** (8, 24) (Connect) What is the perimeter of the rectangle? 1 in.

$\frac{3}{8}$ in.

$\frac{1}{8}$ in.

▶ * **5.** (25) (Formulate) A 30-inch length of ribbon was cut into 4 equal lengths. How long was each piece of ribbon? Write an equation and solve the problem. $4 \cdot p = 30$; $7\frac{2}{4}$ or $7\frac{1}{2}$ inches

6. (Inv. 2) Two thirds of the class finished the test on time. What fraction of the class did not finish the test on time? $\frac{1}{3}$

* **7.** (22) Compare: $\frac{1}{2}$ of 12 $>$ $\frac{1}{3}$ of 12

▶ * **8.** (Inv. 2) (Evaluate) What fraction is half of the fraction that is half of $\frac{1}{2}$? $\frac{1}{8}$

* **9.** (25) A whole circle is 100% of a circle. What percent of a circle is $\frac{1}{9}$ of a circle? $11\frac{1}{9}$%

▶ See Math Conversations in the sidebar.

Math Language
What operation do the words *"are in"* tell us to perform?
division

▸* **10.** (Inv. 2) **a.** How many $\frac{1}{6}$s are in 1? 6

b. How many $\frac{1}{6}$s are in $\frac{1}{2}$? 3

* **11.** (25) What fraction of a circle is $33\frac{1}{3}\%$ of a circle? $\frac{1}{3}$

* **12.** (25) Divide 365 by 7 and write the answer as a mixed number. $52\frac{1}{7}$

* **13.** (24) $\frac{2}{3} + \frac{2}{3} + \frac{2}{3}$ 2

* **14.** (24) $\frac{6}{6} - \frac{5}{6}$ $\frac{1}{6}$

15. (5) $30 \times 40 \div 60$ 20

* **16.** (24) $\frac{5}{12} - \frac{5}{12}$ 0

* **17.** (23) A team won seven of the twenty games played and lost the rest. What was the team's win-loss ratio? $\frac{7}{13}$

▸ **18.** (15) **Formulate** Cheryl bought 10 pens for 25¢ each. How much did she pay for all 10 pens? Write an equation and solve the problem. $10 \cdot 25 = t$; $2.50

19. (20) What is the greatest common factor (GCF) of 24 and 30? 6

20. (22) What number is $\frac{1}{100}$ of 100? 1

Find each unknown number. Check your work.

21. (Inv. 2) $\frac{5}{8} + m = 1$ $\frac{3}{8}$

22. (4) $\frac{144}{n} = 12$ 12

▸ **23.** (16) **Estimate** What is the sum of 3142, 6328, and 4743 to the nearest thousand? 14,000

24.

	60 students
$\frac{2}{3}$ liked peaches.	20 students
	20 students
$\frac{1}{3}$ did not like peaches.	20 students

* **24.** (22) **Model** Two thirds of the 60 students liked peaches. How many of the students liked peaches? Draw a diagram that illustrates the problem. 40 students

▸ **25.** (17) **Estimate** Estimate the length in inches of the line segment below. Then use an inch ruler to find the length of the line segment to the nearest sixteenth of an inch. about 2 inches; $1\frac{14}{16}$ or $1\frac{7}{8}$ inches

26. Sample: Jan could draw segments from the center of the circle to the places where 12, 4, and 8 would be on a clock face.

26. (Inv. 2) **Represent** To divide a circle into thirds, Jan imagined the circle was the face of a clock. Describe how Jan could draw segments to divide the circle into thirds.

* **27.** (25) Write $\frac{15}{4}$ as a mixed number. $3\frac{3}{4}$

28. (Inv. 2) **Model** Draw and shade rectangles to illustrate and complete this comparison: <

$\frac{3}{4} \bigcirc \frac{4}{5}$

* **29.** (25) What are the first four multiples of 25? 25, 50, 75, 100

▸ **30.** (21) **Classify** Which of these numbers is divisible by both 9 and 10? How do you know?

A 910 **B** 8910 **C** 78,910

B The sum of the digits is 18 which is divisible by 9, so the number is divisible by 9, and the last digit is zero so the number is divisible by 10.

▸ See Math Conversations in the sidebar.

3 Written Practice (Continued)

Math Conversations

Discussion opportunities are provided below.

Problem 10 Verify

Remind students of the importance of checking their work.

For Problem **a**, ask,

"How can you use addition and division to check your answer?" Simplify the sum of 6 one-sixths.

For Problem **b**, ask,

"How can you use addition and division to check your answer?" Simplify the sum of 3 one-sixths.

Problem 18 Formulate

Extend the Problem

Challenge students to describe a variety of ways to find the total cost using mental math. Sample: Four pens cost $1, so eight pens cost $2. Four pens cost $1, so two pens cost 50¢. The cost of ten pens is $2 + 50¢ or $2.50.

Problem 23 Estimate

Extend the Problem

Point out that the numbers were rounded to the nearest thousand. Then ask

"Will rounding the numbers to the nearest hundred cause the estimate to be closer to, or farther away from, the exact answer? Why?" Closer; sample explanation: the numbers don't change as much when they are rounded to the nearest hundred.

Problem 25 Estimate

Extend the Problem

Remind students that 1 inch is about the same as $2\frac{1}{2}$ centimeters, then ask them to estimate the length of the segment in centimeters. about 5 cm

Problem 30 Classify

Remind students to use divisibility rules, and not paper and pencil computations, to classify the numbers.

ooking Forward

xpressing a division answer with a remainder as a mixed number and xpressing an improper fraction as a mixed number prepare students for:

Lesson 29, multiplying fractions.

Lesson 53, simplifying fractions by converting improper fractions to mixed numbers.

Lesson 62, writing mixed numbers as improper fractions.

Lesson 94, changing fractions and decimals to percents.

Lesson 111, understanding real-world applications for division problems.

Assessment

30–40 minutes *For use after Lesson 25*

Distribute **Cumulative Test 4** to each student. Two versions of the test are available in *Saxon Math Course 1 Course Assessments Book.* Have students complete the **Power-Up Test** first. Allow 10 minutes. Then have students work the 20 numbered items on the **Cumulative Test.** Students may use copies of the answer sheet to record their work. Track individual and class progress with the **Test Analysis** forms.

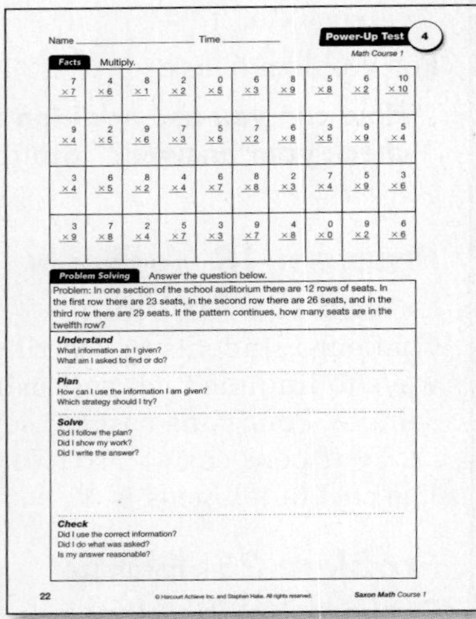

Power-Up Test 4

Name ____ Score ____

Cumulative Test 4A
Math Course 1
Also take Power-Up Test 4

1. When the sum of 9 and 3 is divided by the difference of 9 and 3, what is the quotient?
2. Which digit is in the millions place in 123,456,789?
3. Tom has read 96 pages of a 312-page book. How many pages does Tom need to read to finish the book?
4. The morning temperature was -5°. By noon the temperature was 4°. How many degrees had the temperature risen?

Find each unknown for problems 5–6. Check your work.

5. $Q - 40 = 25$
6. $3n = 87$
7. Round 37,542 to the nearest thousand.
8. Estimate the product of 51 and 48.
9. Simplify: $\frac{123}{3}$
10. What is the average of 3, 7, 9, 10, 10, and 9?
11. What number is halfway between 24 and 98?
12. List the whole-number factors of 18.

Saxon Math Course 1 © Harcourt Achieve Inc. and Stephen Hake. All rights reserved. 55

Cumulative Test 4A

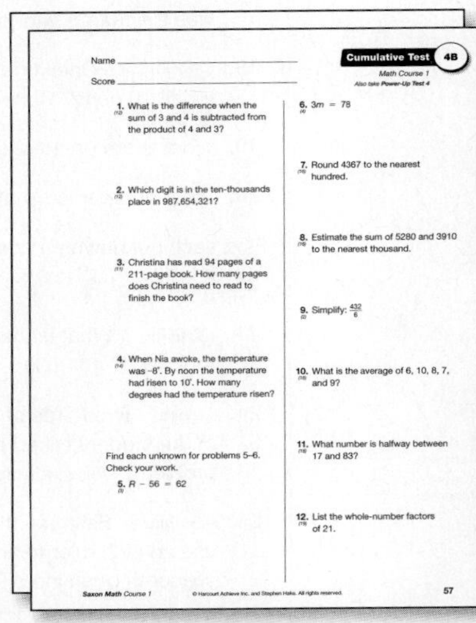

Name ____ Score ____

Cumulative Test 4B
Math Course 1
Also take Power-Up Test 4

1. What is the difference when the sum of 3 and 4 is subtracted from the product of 4 and 3?
2. Which digit is in the ten-thousands place in 987,654,321?
3. Christina has read 94 pages of a 211-page book. How many pages does Christina need to read to finish the book?
4. When Nia awoke, the temperature was -8°. By noon the temperature had risen to 10°. How many degrees had the temperature risen?

Find each unknown for problems 5–6. Check your work.

5. $R - 56 = 62$
6. $3m = 78$
7. Round 4367 to the nearest hundred.
8. Estimate the sum of 5280 and 3910 to the nearest thousand.
9. Simplify: $\frac{432}{6}$
10. What is the average of 6, 10, 8, 7, and 9?
11. What number is halfway between 17 and 83?
12. List the whole-number factors of 21.

Saxon Math Course 1 © Harcourt Achieve Inc. and Stephen Hake. All rights reserved. 57

Alternative Cumulative Test 4B

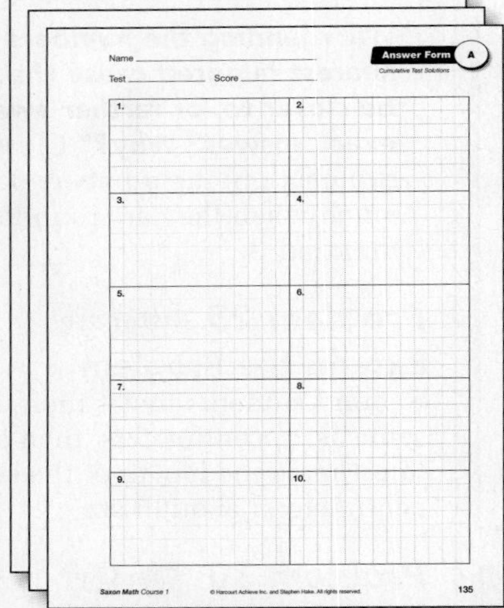

Optional Answer Forms

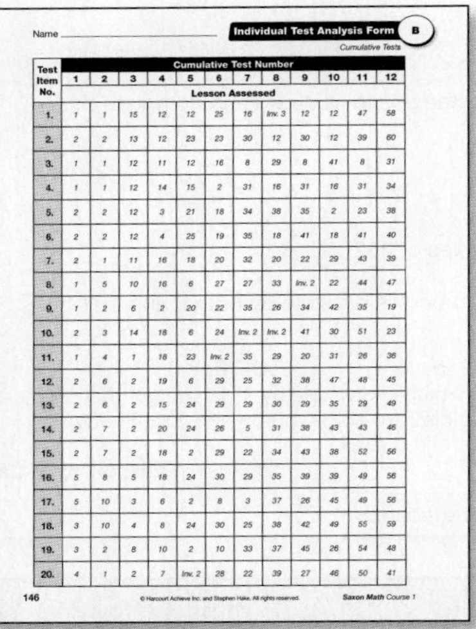

Name ____ **Individual Test Analysis Form B** Cumulative Tests

Test Item No.	Cumulative Test Number 1	2	3	4	5	6	7	8	9	10	11	12
	Lesson Assessed											
1.	1	1	15	12	12	25	16	Inv. 3	12	12	47	58
2.	2	2	13	12	23	23	30	12	30	12	39	60
3.	1	1	12	11	12	16	8	29	8	41	8	31
4.	1	1	12	14	15	2	31	16	31	16	31	34
5.	2	2	12	3	21	18	34	38	35	2	23	38
6.	2	2	12	4	25	19	35	18	41	18	41	40
7.	2	1	11	16	18	20	32	20	22	29	43	39
8.	1	5	10	16	6	27	27	33	Inv. 2	22	44	47
9.	1	2	6	2	20	22	35	26	34	42	35	19
10.	2	3	14	18	6	24	Inv. 2	Inv. 2	41	30	51	23
11.	1	4	1	18	23	Inv. 2	35	29	20	31	26	36
12.	2	6	2	19	6	29	25	32	38	47	48	45
13.	2	6	2	15	24	29	29	30	29	35	29	49
14.	2	7	2	20	24	26	5	31	38	43	43	46
15.	2	7	2	18	2	29	22	34	43	38	52	56
16.	5	8	5	18	24	30	29	35	39	39	49	56
17.	5	10	3	6	2	8	3	37	26	45	49	56
18.	3	10	4	8	24	30	25	38	42	49	55	59
19.	3	2	8	10	2	10	33	37	45	26	54	48
20.	4	1	2	7	Inv. 2	28	22	39	27	46	50	41

146 © Harcourt Achieve Inc. and Stephen Hake. All rights reserved. Saxon Math Course 1

Individual Test Analysis Form

Class Test Analysis Form

Reteaching

Students who score below 80% on the assessment may be in need of reteaching. Look for the causes of student mistakes. If errors are conceptual, refer to the *Reteaching Masters* for reteaching.

Performance Activity 4

Selecting Tools and Techniques

Assign after Lesson 25 and Test 4

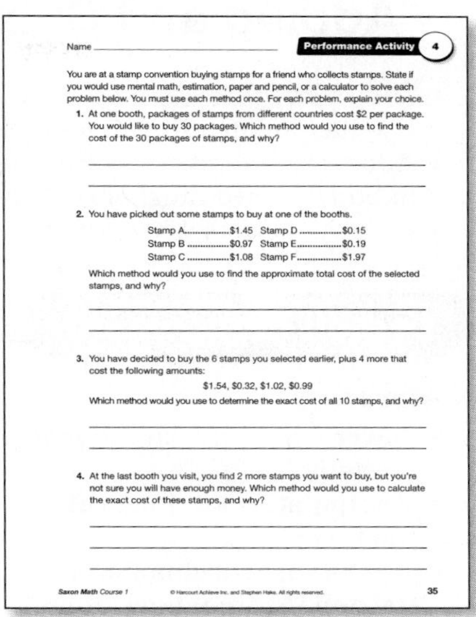

Name ____________ **Performance Activity 4**

You are at a stamp convention buying stamps for a friend who collects stamps. State if you would use mental math, estimation, paper and pencil, or a calculator to solve each problem below. You must use each method once. For each problem, explain your choice.

1. At one booth, packages of stamps from different countries cost $2 per package. You would like to buy 30 packages. Which method would you use to find the cost of the 30 packages of stamps, and why?

2. You have picked out some stamps to buy at one of the booths.

   Stamp A........$1.45 Stamp D........$0.15
   Stamp B........$0.97 Stamp E........$0.19
   Stamp C........$1.08 Stamp F........$1.97

   Which method would you use to find the approximate total cost of the selected stamps, and why?

3. You have decided to buy the 6 stamps you selected earlier, plus 4 more that cost the following amounts:

   $1.54, $0.32, $1.02, $0.99

   Which method would you use to determine the exact cost of all 10 stamps, and why?

4. At the last booth you visit, you find 2 more stamps you want to buy, but you're not sure you will have enough money. Which method would you use to calculate the exact cost of these stamps, and why?

Saxon Math Course 1 35

Performance Activity 4

Objectives

- Choose mental math, estimation, paper and pencil, or a calculator to solve a problem.
- Communicate ideas through writing.

Materials

Performance Activity 4

Preparation

Make copies of **Performance Activity 4.** (One each per student.)

Time Requirement

15–30 minutes; Begin in class and complete at home.

Activity

Explain to students that for this activity they will be buying stamps at a convention for people who collect stamps. They will choose mental math, estimation, paper and pencil, or a calculator as appropriate methods to solve different problems. They will be required to explain their choices. Explain that all of the information students need is on **Performance Activity 4.**

Criteria for Evidence of Learning

- Makes a reasonable choice for a tool or technique to solve a problem.
- Communicates ideas clearly through writing.

Meeting Standards

National Council of Teachers of Mathematics (NCTM)

Numbers and Operations

NO.2a Understand the meaning and effects of arithmetic operations with fractions, decimals, and integers

NO.3a Select appropriate methods and tools for computing with fractions and decimals from among mental computation, estimation, calculators or computers, and paper and pencil, depending on the situation, and apply the selected methods

NO.3c Develop and use strategies to estimate the results of rational-number computations and judge the reasonableness of the results

Problem Solving

PS.1c Apply and adapt a variety of appropriate strategies to solve problems

Communication

CM.3a Organize and consolidate their mathematical thinking through communication

• Using Manipulatives to Reduce Fractions
• Adding and Subtracting Mixed Numbers

Objectives

- Use fraction manipulatives to reduce fractions.
- Add mixed numbers by first adding the fraction parts and then the whole-number parts.
- Subtract mixed numbers by first subtracting the fraction parts and then the whole-number parts.
- Reduce answers when adding and subtracting mixed numbers.

Lesson Preparation

Materials

- **Power Up C** (in *Instructional Masters*)
- **Manipulative kit: inch rulers, fraction circles**
- **Teacher-provided material: fraction manipuatives** from Investigation 2
- **Basic Fraction Circles poster**

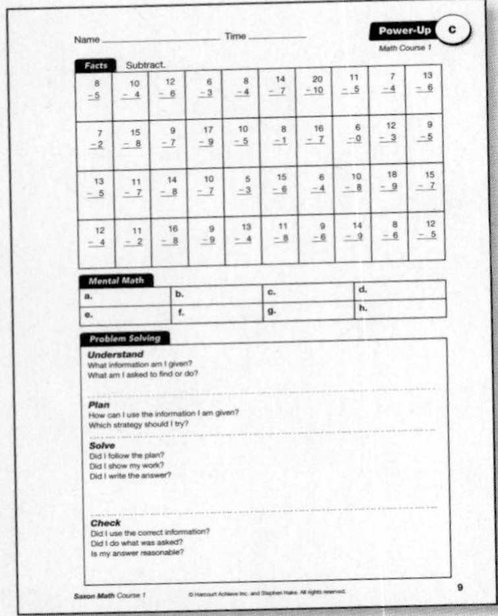

Power Up C

Math Language

New	Maintain	English Learners (ESL)
reduces	improper fraction	equivalent

Technology Resources

Student eBook Complete student textbook in electronic format.

Resources and Planner CD Assessment, reteaching, and instructional masters, plus a pacing calendar with standards.

Test and Practice Generator CD Create additional practice sheets and custom-made tests.

www.SaxonPublishers.com Visit for more student activities and planning materials.

Inclusion

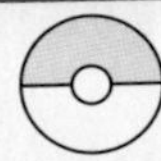

Adaptations CD Adapted lessons, investigations, practice and assessments.

Meeting Standards

National Council of Teachers of Mathematics (NCTM)

Numbers and Operations

NO.1a Work flexibly with fractions, decimals, and percents to solve problems

NO.2a Understand the meaning and effects of arithmetic operations with fractions, decimals, and integers

NO.3a Select appropriate methods and tools for computing with fractions and decimals from among mental computation, estimation, calculators or computers, and paper and pencil, depending on the situation, and apply the selected methods

Geometry

GM.4d Use geometric models to represent and explain numerical and algebraic relationships

Power-Up Discussion *For use with Power Up, p. 136*

Problem-Solving Strategy: Use Logical Reasoning/ Make an Organized List

James was thinking of a prime number between 75 and 100 that did not have 9 as one of its digits. Of what number was he thinking?

Understand ***Understand the problem.***

"What information are we given?"

Jim was thinking of a prime number between 75 and 100. The number did not have a 9 as one of its digits.

"What are we asked to do?"

We are asked to find the prime number between 75 and 100 that does not contain a 9.

"What math skills will we need to solve this problem?"

Divisibility rules will help us determine prime numbers.

"What prior knowledge do we have?"

We know that every prime number besides 2 is an odd number and is divisible only by 1 and itself. A composite number is divisible by at least one number other than 1 and itself. We know to immediately rule out all of the numbers between 90 and 99 because they all begin with 9.

Teacher Note: See Lesson 21 regarding divisibility.

Plan ***Make a plan.***

"How can we use the information we know to do what we are asked to do?"

We will *make an organized list* of numbers that are possible answers, and then we will *use logical reasoning* to cross off composite numbers until we find the prime number James was thinking of.

Solve ***Carry out the plan.***

"Let's make a list of possible answers. What numbers do we leave off our list?"

We omit all even numbers between 75 and 100, because they are divisible by 2. We also omit 79, 89, and all the 90s, because James's number does not contain a 9.

"What does our list of numbers look like?"

77, 81, 83, 85, 87

"Which numbers stand out as composite numbers?"

We cross off 85 because it is divisible by 5. We recognize 81 as a perfect square, so we cross it off.

"Which of the remaining numbers is James's number?"

We recognize that 77 is the product of 7 and 11, so it is not prime. If we apply the divisibility tests to 87, we find that it is divisible by 3. This leaves us with the number 83, which is prime.

Check ***Look back.***

"Does our answer fit the problem?"

Yes. The number 83 is divisible only by 1 and itself, and does not contain the digit 9.

1 Power Up

Facts

Distribute **Power Up C** to students. See answers below.

Mental Math

Before students begin the Mental Math exercise, do this counting exercise as a class.

Count up and down by $\frac{1}{8}$s between $\frac{1}{8}$ and 2.

Encourage students to share different ways to mentally compute these exercises. Strategies for exercises **c** and **d** are listed below.

c. Add 20, then Subtract 1
$74 + 20 = 94$; $94 - 1 = 93$
Add 4 and 19, then Add 70
$4 + 19 = 23$; $70 + 23 = 93$

d. Add 75 and 25, then Add 400 and 100
$75 + 25 = 100$ and $400 + 100 = 500$; $100 + 500 = 600$
Count on by 100, then by 25
Start with 475. Count: 575
Start with 575. Count: 600

Problem Solving

Refer to **Power-Up Discussion,** p. 136B.

2 New Concepts

Instruction

Use the overhead fraction circles from the Manipulative Kit to model these fractions for students, or have students work individually with their **fraction manipulatives.**

Instruction

Explain that when working with fractions, "simplify" and "express in lowest terms" are expressions that mean the same as "reduce".

(continued)

LESSON 26

• Using Manipulatives to Reduce Fractions
• Adding and Subtracting Mixed Numbers

Power Up *Building Power*

facts Power Up C

mental math

a. Number Sense: 7×34 238

b. Number Sense: 4×56 224

c. Number Sense: $74 + 19$ 93

d. Calculation: $475 + 125$ 600

e. Money: $5.00 − $1.75 $3.25

f. Fractional Parts: $\frac{1}{2}$ of 32 16

g. Statistics: Find the average of the following: 20, 25, 30 25

h. Calculation: 7×5, $+ 1$, $\div 6$, $\times 3$, $\div 2$, $+ 1$, $\div 5$ 2

problem solving James was thinking of a prime number between 75 and 100 that did **not** have 9 as one of its digits. Of what number was he thinking? 83

New Concepts *Increasing Knowledge*

using manipulatives to reduce fractions

You can use fraction manipulatives to model these fractions:

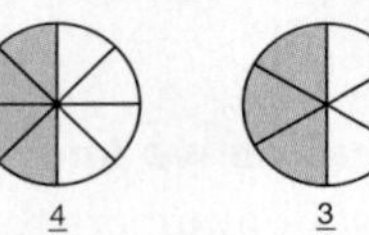

$\frac{4}{8}$ $\frac{3}{6}$

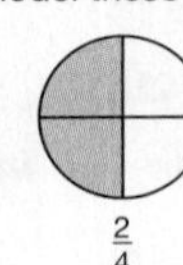

$\frac{2}{4}$

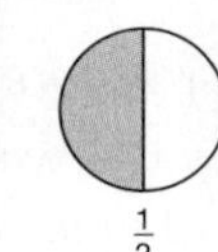

$\frac{1}{2}$

We see that each picture illustrates half of a circle. The model that uses the fewest pieces is $\frac{1}{2}$. We say that each of the other fractions **reduces** to $\frac{1}{2}$.

Thinking Skill
Verify
Why doesn't $\frac{2}{3}$ reduce to $\frac{1}{2}$?
$\frac{2}{3}$ of a whole is more than $\frac{1}{2}$.

Model We can use our fraction manipulatives to reduce a given fraction by making an equivalent model that uses fewer pieces.

136 *Saxon Math Course 1*

Facts Subtract.

8 − 5 = 3	10 − 4 = 6	12 − 6 = 6	6 − 3 = 3	8 − 4 = 4	14 − 7 = 7	20 − 10 = 10	11 − 5 = 6	7 − 4 = 3	13 − 6 = 7
7 − 2 = 5	15 − 8 = 7	9 − 7 = 2	17 − 9 = 8	10 − 5 = 5	8 − 1 = 7	16 − 7 = 9	6 − 0 = 6	12 − 3 = 9	9 − 5 = 4
13 − 5 = 8	11 − 7 = 4	14 − 8 = 6	10 − 7 = 3	5 − 3 = 2	15 − 6 = 9	6 − 4 = 2	10 − 8 = 2	18 − 9 = 9	15 − 7 = 8
12 − 4 = 8	11 − 2 = 9	16 − 8 = 8	9 − 9 = 0	13 − 4 = 9	11 − 8 = 3	9 − 6 = 3	14 − 9 = 5	8 − 6 = 2	12 − 5 = 7

Example 1

Use your fraction manipulatives to reduce $\frac{2}{6}$.

Solution

First we use our manipulatives to form $\frac{2}{6}$.

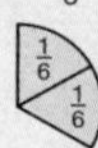

Then we search for a fraction piece equivalent to the $\frac{2}{6}$ model. We find $\frac{1}{3}$.

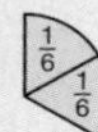

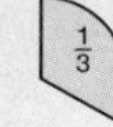

The models illustrate that $\frac{2}{6}$ reduces to $\frac{1}{3}$.

adding and subtracting mixed numbers

When adding mixed numbers, we first add the fraction parts, and then we add the whole-number parts. Likewise, when subtracting mixed numbers, we first subtract the fraction parts, and then we subtract the whole-number parts.

Example 2

Thinking Skill

Justify

Explain how to change $\frac{1}{3}$ to $33\frac{1}{3}\%$. $\frac{1}{3}$ of 100% means 100% divided by 3.

$$3\overline{)100\%} = 33\tfrac{1}{3}\%$$

Two thirds of a circle is what percent of a circle?

Solution

Model Use your fraction manipulatives to represent $\frac{1}{3} + \frac{1}{3}$.

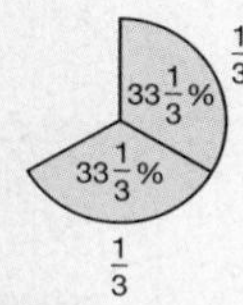

One third equals $33\frac{1}{3}\%$. So two thirds can be found by adding $33\frac{1}{3}\%$ and $33\frac{1}{3}\%$.

$$\begin{array}{r} 33\frac{1}{3}\% \\ +\ 33\frac{1}{3}\% \\ \hline \mathbf{66\frac{2}{3}\%} \end{array}$$

Example 3

Two sixths of a circle is what percent of a circle?

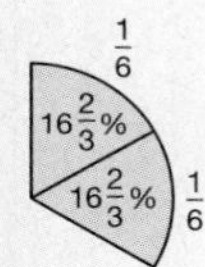

2 New Concepts (Continued)

Example 1

Instruction

You may wish to display the **Basic Fraction Circles** concept poster as you discuss examples 1–3 with students.

Example 2

Instruction

Have students recall that 100% represents the whole circle. $\frac{1}{3}$ of 100% means 100% divided by 3.

(continued)

English Learners

Explain that the term ***equivalent*** means "is equal to." On the board, sketch the two $\frac{1}{6}$ and the one $\frac{1}{3}$ manipulatives from Exercise 1. Say:

"In example 1, we found that these two are equivalent. Why are they equivalent?" The $\frac{1}{3}$ fraction piece is exactly the same size as the two $\frac{1}{6}$ fraction pieces.

Draw two $\frac{1}{4}$ fraction pieces and one fraction piece. Ask what statement we can make about them. The sketches are equivalent.

Math Background

When a fraction that is not in simplest form is changed to a fraction in simplest form, the fractions look different but they are equivalent. Equivalent fractions name the same number.

For every fraction, there is an infinite number of equivalent fractions.

2 New Concepts (Continued)

Example 3

Instruction

Demonstrate, or invite a volunteer to demonstrate how to rewrite $\frac{4}{3}$ as $1\frac{1}{3}$.

Example 4

Instruction

Emphasize the different steps that students need to complete to solve this problem. Write each step on the board or on an overhead projector.

1. Add the fraction parts.
2. Add the whole-number parts.
3. If the fraction part of the answer is an improper fraction, change it to a mixed number.
4. Reduce the mixed number if necessary.
5. Add the mixed number to the whole number to find the answer.

Example 5

Instruction

Have students note that that the fractions $\frac{2}{8}$ and $\frac{1}{4}$ are equivalent fractions.

Practice Set

Problems a and b (Error Alert)

When using division to reduce fractions, remind students to divide both the numerator and the denominator by the same number. Point out that the number can be any common factor (greater than 1) of the numerator and the denominator, but the number of divisions will be minimized if the greatest common factor is used.

(continued)

Solution

We add $16\frac{2}{3}\%$ and $16\frac{2}{3}\%$.

$$\begin{array}{r} 16\frac{2}{3}\% \\ +\ 16\frac{2}{3}\% \\ \hline 32\frac{4}{3}\% \end{array}$$

We notice that the fraction part of the answer, $\frac{4}{3}$, is an improper fraction that equals $1\frac{1}{3}$.

So $32\frac{4}{3}\%$ equals $32\% + 1\frac{1}{3}\%$, which is **$33\frac{1}{3}\%$**. This makes sense because $\frac{2}{6}$ reduces to $\frac{1}{3}$, which is the same as $33\frac{1}{3}\%$.

Math Language
Recall that an **improper fraction** is a fraction with a numerator equal to or greater than the denominator.

Example 4

Rory lives $2\frac{3}{4}$ miles from school. He rode his bike from home to school and back to home. How far did Rory ride?

Solution

This problem has an addition pattern.

$$\begin{array}{r} 2\frac{3}{4}\text{ mi} \\ +\ 2\frac{3}{4}\text{ mi} \\ \hline 4\frac{6}{4}\text{ mi} \end{array}$$

The fraction part of the answer reduces to $1\frac{1}{2}$ $\left(\frac{6}{4} = 1\frac{2}{4} = 1\frac{1}{2}\right)$. So we add $1\frac{1}{2}$ to the whole-number part of the answer and find that Rory rode his bike **$5\frac{1}{2}$ miles.**

Example 5

Subtract: $5\frac{3}{8} - 1\frac{1}{8}$

Solution

We subtract $\frac{1}{8}$ from $\frac{3}{8}$, and we subtract 1 from 5. The resulting difference is $4\frac{2}{8}$.

$$5\frac{3}{8} - 1\frac{1}{8} = 4\frac{2}{8}$$

We reduce the fraction $\frac{2}{8}$ to $\frac{1}{4}$ and write the answer as **$4\frac{1}{4}$**.

Practice Set ▶ **Model** Use your fraction manipulatives to reduce these fractions:

a. $\frac{2}{8}$ $\frac{1}{4}$

b. $\frac{6}{8}$ $\frac{3}{4}$

Add. Reduce the answer when possible.

c. $12\frac{1}{2}\% + 12\frac{1}{2}\%$ 25%

d. $16\frac{2}{3}\% + 66\frac{2}{3}\%$ $83\frac{1}{3}\%$

e. $3\frac{3}{4} + 2\frac{3}{4}$ $6\frac{1}{2}$

f. $1\frac{1}{8} + 2\frac{7}{8}$ 4

▶ See Math Conversations in the sidebar.

g. $3 + 2\frac{2}{3}$ $5\frac{2}{3}$

▸ **h.** $\frac{3}{4} + 4$ $4\frac{3}{4}$

i. Use words to write the addition problem in exercise **f.**
One and one eighth plus two and seven eighths equals four.

Written Practice *Strengthening Concepts*

* **1.** (26) Maya rode her bike to the park and back. If the trip was $3\frac{3}{4}$ miles each way, how far did she ride in all? $7\frac{1}{2}$ miles

2. (15) The young elephant was 36 months old. How many years old was the elephant? 3 years old

3. (6, 15) **Justify** Mrs. Ling bought $2\frac{1}{2}$ dozen balloons for the party. Is this enough balloons for 30 children to each get one balloon? Explain your thinking. Yes. Sample: A dozen is 12 and $12 + 12 + 6 = 30$.

4. (15) There are 100 centimeters in a meter. There are 1000 meters in a kilometer. How many centimeters are in a kilometer? 100,000 centimeters

* **5.** (8, 24) What is the perimeter of the equilateral triangle shown? 2 in.

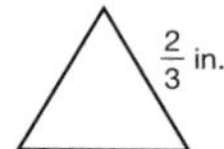

* **6.** (Inv. 2) Compare: $\frac{1}{2}$ plus $\frac{1}{2}$ ⊘ $\frac{1}{2}$ of $\frac{1}{2}$ (>)

* **7.** (26) $5\frac{7}{8} + 7\frac{5}{8}$ $13\frac{1}{2}$

* **8.** (26) One eighth of a circle is $12\frac{1}{2}$% of a circle. What percent of a circle is $\frac{3}{8}$ of a circle? $37\frac{1}{2}$%

9. (Inv. 2) Write a fraction equal to 1 that has a denominator of 12. $\frac{12}{12}$

10. (20) What is the greatest common factor of 15 and 25? 5

▸ **11.** (10) **Generalize** Describe the rule of the following sequence. Then find the *seventh* term.

8, 16, 24, 32, 40, ...

Add 8 to the value of a term to find the next term; 56

* **12.** (25) Write $\frac{14}{5}$ as a mixed number. $2\frac{4}{5}$

* **13.** (26) Add and simplify: $\frac{2}{5} + \frac{4}{5}$ $1\frac{1}{5}$

Find the unknown number. Remember to check your work.

14. (Inv. 2) $\frac{2}{3} + n = 1$ $\frac{1}{3}$

▸ **15.** (20) **Classify** What is the greatest factor of both 12 and 18? 6

16. (Inv. 2) $1 - \frac{3}{4}$ $\frac{1}{4}$

* **17.** (26) $3\frac{3}{4} + 3$ $6\frac{3}{4}$

* **18.** (26) $2\frac{1}{2} - 2\frac{1}{2}$ 0

▸ **19.** (21) **Classify** Which of the numbers below is divisible by both 2 and 3? B

A 4671 **B** 3858 **C** 6494

▸ See Math Conversations in the sidebar.

2 New Concepts (Continued)

Practice Set

Problem h (Error Alert)

Students who rewrite horizontal addends as vertical addends sometimes have difficulty maintaining correct alignment. To help align these addends correctly, students may benefit from rewriting 4 as $4\frac{0}{4}$.

3 Written Practice

Math Conversations

Discussion opportunities are provided below.

Problem 11 Generalize

Extend the Problem

Challenge students to extend the sequence.

"Explain how to find the 100th term of the sequence, and then name the 100th term." 800; sample explanation: multiply the term number by 8; $100 \times 8 = 800$.

Problem 15 Classify

Remind students that before they name the greatest factor of the numbers, it is a good idea to first find all of the common factors.

Also remind students that the greatest factor of two (or more than two) numbers is always less than or equal to the least of those numbers; it is never greater.

Problem 19 Classify

Encourage students to use divisibility rules, and not paper and pencil computations, to classify the numbers.

(continued)

3 Written Practice (Continued)

Math Conversations

Discussion opportunities are provided below.

Problem 22 Model

Extend the Problem

Challenge students to explain how division and mental math can be used to reduce the fraction. Divide the numerator and the denominator by the same number. Since $6 \div 2$ is 3 and $8 \div 2$ is 4, $\frac{6}{8} = \frac{3}{4}$.

Problem 25 Connect

Extend the Problem

"What is the length of the segment, rounded to the nearest centimeter? Explain your answer." 3 cm; sample explanation: 25 mm is closer to 30 mm than to 20 mm, and 30 mm is the same as 3 cm.

Problem 30 Formulate

Extend the Problem

Invite students to exchange the problems they wrote, solve them, and then compare answers.

Errors and Misconceptions

Problem 21

Watch for students who find an exact difference, and then round that difference to the nearest thousand. Have students note that the word "Estimate" precedes the problem, and explain that it represents an approximation, not an exact answer. To make an estimate, students should round both the minuend and the subtrahend before subtracting.

Problem 28

An answer of 120 inches represents the total rainfall for three years, not the average rainfall per year. Ask students who answer 120 inches to reread the problem more carefully and note that the problem contains the word "average."

---

20. (19) List the prime numbers between 30 and 40. 31, 37

▶ **21.** (16) **Estimate** Find the difference of 5063 and 3987 to the nearest thousand. 1000

▶* **22.** (26) **Model** Use your fraction manipulatives to reduce $\frac{6}{8}$. $\frac{3}{4}$

23. (23) At $2.39 per pound, what is the cost of four pounds of grapes? $9.56

* **24.** (22) **Model** How much money is $\frac{3}{5}$ of $30? Draw a diagram to illustrate the problem. $18

24. $30: $6, $6, $6 ($\frac{3}{5}$ of $30); $6, $6 ($\frac{2}{5}$ of $30)

▶ **25.** (7, 17) **Connect** **a.** How many millimeters long is the line segment below? 25 millimeters

mm 10 20 30

b. Use an inch ruler to find the length of the segment to the nearest sixteenth of an inch. 1 inch

26. (17) Arrange these numbers in order from least to greatest: $-1, 0, \frac{1}{2}, 1$

$\frac{1}{2}, 0, -1, 1$

Adriana began measuring rainfall when she moved to her new home. The bar graph below shows the annual rainfall near Adriana's home during her first three years there. Refer to this graph to answer problems **27–30.**

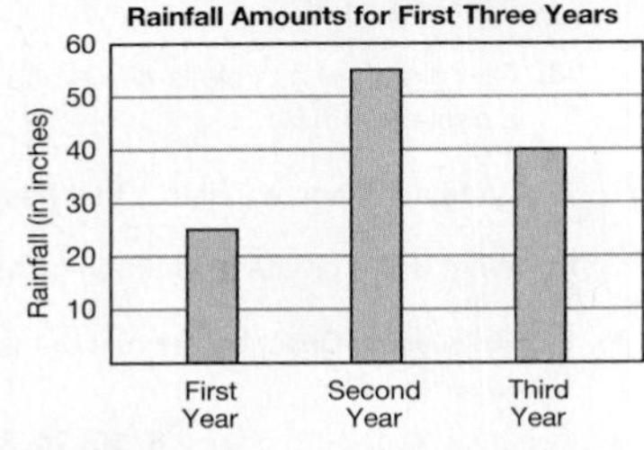

27. (16) About how many more inches of rain fell during the second year than during the first year? about 30 inches

▶ **28.** (18) What was the approximate average annual rainfall during the first three years? 40 inches

29. (18) The first year's rainfall was about how many inches below the average annual rainfall of the first three years? about 15 inches

▶ **30.** (11) **Formulate** Write a problem with an addition pattern that relates to the graph. Then answer the problem. Answers will vary. See student work.

▶ See Math Conversations in the sidebar.

Looking Forward

Adding and subtracting mixed numbers and reducing answers prepares students for:

- **Lesson 36,** subtracting a fraction or a mixed number from a whole number.
- **Lessons 48 and 63,** using regrouping to subtract mixed numbers with and without common denominators.
- **Lesson 57,** following three steps for adding and subtracting fractions.
- **Lesson 59,** adding mixed numbers without common denominators.
- **Lesson 61,** adding three or more fractions without common denominators.

• Measures of a Circle

Objectives

- Identify the circumference, diameter, and radius of a circle.
- Use a compass to draw a circle with a given radius.
- Find the diameter of a circle when the radius is known.
- Find the radius of a circle when the diameter is known.

Lesson Preparation

Materials

- **Power Up E** (in *Instructional Masters*)
- **Manipulative kit: compasses, inch and metric rulers**
- **Teacher-provided material: fraction manipulatives** from Investigation 2

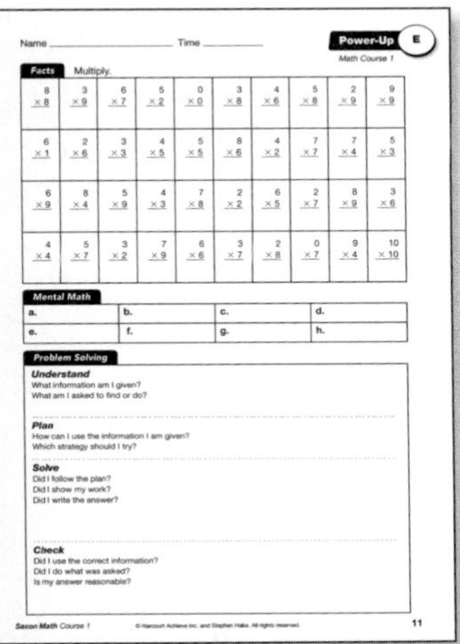

Power Up E

Math Language

New	Maintain	English Learners (ESL)
circumference	circle	concentric
compass		
concentric circles		
diameter		
radius		

Technology Resources

Student eBook Complete student textbook in electronic format.

Resources and Planner CD Assessment, reteaching, and instructional masters, plus a pacing calendar with standards.

Test and Practice Generator CD Create additional practice sheets and custom-made tests.

www.SaxonPublishers.com Visit for more student activities and planning materials.

Inclusion

Adaptations CD Adapted lessons, investigations, practice and assessments.

Meeting Standards

National Council of Teachers of Mathematics (NCTM)

Geometry

GM.1a Precisely describe, classify, and understand relationships among types of two- and three-dimensional objects using their defining properties

GM.4a Draw geometric objects with specified properties, such as side lengths or angle measures

Measurement

ME.1c Understand, select, and use units of appropriate size and type to measure angles, perimeter, area, surface area, and volume

Power-Up Discussion *For use with Power Up, p. 141*

Problem-Solving Strategy: Use Logical Reasoning

If [arrows] + [arrows] = 25, and [arrows] − [arrows] = 5,

then [arrows] × [arrows] = ?

Understand ***Understand the problem.***

"What information are we given?"

We are given two number sentences that use symbols and numbers.

"What are we asked to do?"

Complete a third number sentence.

Plan ***Make a plan.***

"What problem-solving strategy will we use?"

We will *use logical reasoning.*

"What can we speculate about the "numbers" made up of the arrows?"

A five-digit plus a three-digit number would not have a sum of 25, so each arrow represents a unique value, not a place value.

Teacher Note: It is important for the students to understand that each set of arrows represents a sum of the values of the arrows, not a product.

Solve ***Carry out the plan.***

"What does the second number sentence tell us?"

Two downward arrows and two upward arrows are subtracted from two downward arrows and three upwards arrows. We can remove the arrows of the subtrahend from the minuend which leaves a single upward arrow to equal 5.

[arrows] − [arrows] = 5

"By substituting 5 for the upward arrow in the first equation, what do we find the downward arrow is worth?"

The three upward arrows total 15. We subtract 15 from 25 which equals 10, so the five downward arrows account for 10. We divide 10 by 5 to find each downward arrow is worth 2.

Teacher Note: It may be helpful for some students to see the substituion of numbers for arrows drawn on the board as you describe the steps of the problem.

"What is the solution to the third number sentence?"

We know two upward arrows equal 10 and a downward arrow equals 2, then the first set equals 12. We know one upward arrow equals 5 and two downward arrows equals 4, then the second set equals 9. We know $12 \times 9 = 108$.

Check ***Look back.***

"How can we verify the solution is correct/valid?"

We can substitute the number 5 for all upward arrows and 2 for all downward arrows in the first two equations to confirm that the values are correct: $16 + 9 = 25$ and $19 - 14 = 5$.

LESSON 27

• Measures of a Circle

Power Up

Building Power

facts Power Up E

mental math

a. **Number Sense:** 7 × 52 364

b. **Number Sense:** 6 × 33 198

c. **Number Sense:** 63 + 19 82

d. **Number Sense:** 256 + 50 306

e. **Money:** $10.00 − $7.25 $2.75

f. **Fractional Parts:** $\frac{1}{2}$ of 86 43

g. **Geometry:** The perimeter of a square is 16 ft. What is the length of the sides of the square? 4 ft

h. **Calculation:** 8 × 8, − 1, ÷ 7, × 2, + 2, ÷ 2 10

problem solving

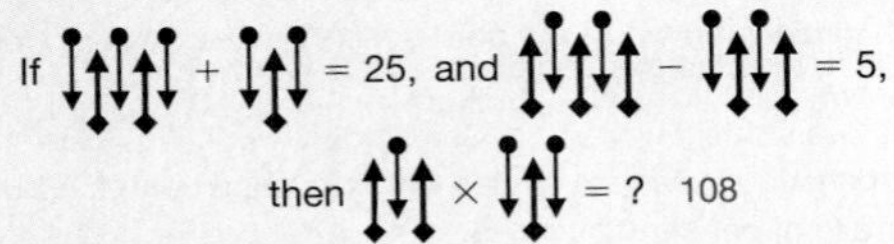

If [figure] + [figure] = 25, and [figure] − [figure] = 5, then [figure] × [figure] = ? 108

New Concept

Increasing Knowledge

Thinking Skill
Verify
Why is the diameter of a circle twice the length of the radius?
The center of a circle is the same length from any point on the circle.

There are several ways to measure a circle. We can measure the distance around the circle, the distance across the circle, and the distance from the center of the circle to the circle itself. The pictures below identify these measures.

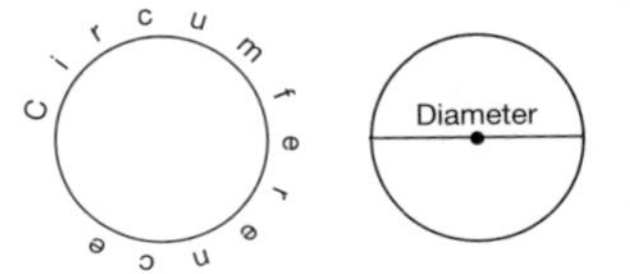

The **circumference** is the distance **around** the circle. This distance is the same as the perimeter of a circle. The **diameter** is the distance **across** a circle through its center. The **radius** is the distance from the center to the circle. The plural of *radius* is **radii.** For any circle, the diameter is twice the length of the radius.

Facts Multiply.

8 × 8 64	3 × 9 27	6 × 7 42	5 × 2 10	0 × 0 0	3 × 8 24	4 × 6 24	5 × 8 40	2 × 9 18	9 × 9 81
6 × 1 6	2 × 6 12	3 × 3 9	4 × 5 20	5 × 5 25	8 × 6 48	4 × 2 8	7 × 7 49	7 × 4 28	5 × 3 15
6 × 9 54	8 × 4 32	5 × 9 45	4 × 3 12	7 × 8 56	2 × 2 4	6 × 5 30	2 × 7 14	8 × 9 72	3 × 6 18
4 × 4 16	5 × 7 35	3 × 2 6	7 × 9 63	6 × 6 36	3 × 7 21	2 × 8 16	0 × 7 0	9 × 4 36	10 × 10 100

1 Power Up

Facts

Distribute **Power Up E** to students. See answers below.

Mental Math

Before students begin the Mental Math exercise, do this counting exercise as a class.

Count up and down by 3s between 3 and 60.

Count up and down by 6s between 6 and 60.

Encourage students to share different ways to mentally compute these exercises. Strategies for exercises **a** and **d** are listed below.

a. Multiply Tens and Multiply Ones
7 × 50 = 350 and 7 × 2 = 14;
350 + 14 = 364

Count on by 50, then by 7
Start with 50. Count: 100, 150, 200, 250, 300, 350; Start with 350. Count: 357, 364

d. Count on by 10
Start with 256. Count: 266, 276, 286, 296, 306

Subtract 6, then Add 6
256 − 6 = 250; 250 + 50 = 300;
300 + 6 = 306

Problem Solving

Refer to **Power-Up Discussion,** p. 141B.

2 New Concepts

Instruction

Discuss the circumference, radii, and diameters of circles.

"These circles show the circumference, a diameter, and a radius of a circle. A circle has only one circumference, or distance around. Does a circle also have only one diameter, or more than one?" more than one

"Does a circle have only one radius, or more than one?" more than one

"How many radii and diameters does any circle have?" an infinite number (too many to count)

(continued)

Activity

Instruction

For the activity Using a Compass on the board or overhead, draw a dot to represent the center of a circle, and then demonstrate how to use a compass to draw a circle that has a radius of 2 inches.

When drawing circles, students may sometimes find that a circle cannot be completed because the compass slipped or because the circle required a series of motions instead of one continuous motion. Explain to students that drawing a dot first will make it easier to complete a circle that is incomplete.

To reinforce the concepts of radius and diameter, ask students to use a ruler and draw a diameter on each circle they constructed in parts **a**, **b**, and **c**. Then ask students to find, without measuring, the lengths of the diameters of the circles in problems **a** (4 in.), **b** (6 cm), and **c** ($3\frac{1}{2}$ in.).

Activity

Using a Compass

Materials needed:

- compass and pencil
- plain paper

A **compass** is a tool for drawing a circle. Here we show two types:

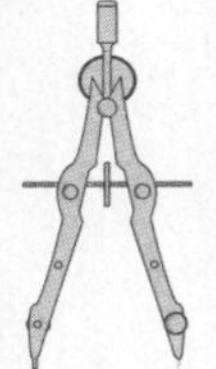

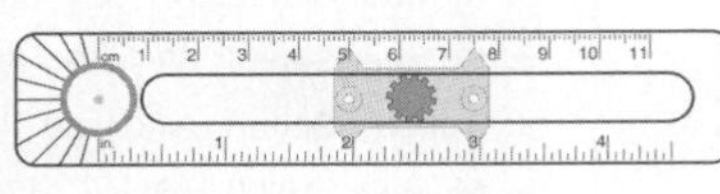

To use a compass, we select a radius and a center point for a circle. Then we rotate the compass about the center point to draw the circle. In this activity you will use a compass and paper to draw circles with given radii.

Thinking Skill
Discuss
Why do we use the length of a radius instead of a diameter to draw a circle? One part of the compass is on the center of the circle.

Represent Draw a circle with each given radius. How can you check that each circle is drawn to the correct size? Use a ruler to measure the radius, or measure the diameter and divide that length by 2.

a. 2 in. See student work. **b.** 3 cm See student work. **c.** $1\frac{3}{4}$ in. See student work.

Concentric circles are circles with the same center. A bull's-eye target is an example of concentric circles.

d. *Represent* Draw three concentric circles with radii of 4 cm, 5 cm, and 6 cm. See student work.

Example 1

What is the name for the perimeter of a circle?

Solution

The distance around a circle is its **circumference.**

Example 2

If the radius of a circle is 4 cm, what is its diameter?

Solution

The diameter of a circle is twice its radius—in this case, **8 cm.**

Practice Set In problems **a–c,** name the described measure of a circle.

a. The distance across a circle diameter

b. The distance around a circle circumference

142 *Saxon* Math Course 1

Math Background

Perimeter is a general term that applies to all closed shapes, and refers to a boundary, or to the length of a boundary. If the boundary is a circle, the length of the boundary is its circumference. Circumference is simply a special term for the perimeter of a circle.

English Learners

Explain that **concentric** circles share the same center point, but each circle has a different radius. Draw a bull's-eye with three circles on the board and say:

"These circles are concentric. Notice that they share the same center point but the radii of the circles become smaller and smaller."

Ask students to think of places in the real world where they might see concentric circles.

c. The distance from the center to the circle radius

▶ **d.** Explain If the diameter of a circle is 10 in., what is its radius? Describe how you know. 5 in.; The radius is half the diameter because two radii in opposite directions form a diameter.

Written Practice *Strengthening Concepts*

1. (12) Analyze What is the product of the sum of 55 and 45 and the difference of 55 and 45? 1000

2.
20 pounds
$\frac{3}{4}$ is water. {5 pounds, 5 pounds, 5 pounds}
$\frac{1}{4}$ is not water. {5 pounds}

▶ ***2.** (22) Potatoes are three-fourths water. If a sack of potatoes weighs 20 pounds, how many pounds of water are in the potatoes? Draw a diagram to illustrate the problem. 15 pounds

3. (11) Formulate There were 306 students in the cafeteria. After some went outside, there were 249 students left in the cafeteria. How many students went outside? Write an equation and solve the problem. $306 - 249 = d$ or $306 - a = 249$; 57 students

▶ ***4.** (27) **a.** If the diameter of a circle is 5 in., what is the radius of the circle? $2\frac{1}{2}$ in.

b. What is the relationship of the diameter of a circle to its radius? The diameter is twice the radius of a circle.

5. (21) Classify Which of these numbers is divisible by both 2 and 3? C

A 122 **B** 123 **C** 132

6. (16) Round 1,234,567 to the nearest ten thousand. 1,230,000

7. (15) Formulate If ten pounds of apples costs \$12.90, what is the price per pound? Write an equation and solve the problem. $10p = \$12.90$; \$1.29 per pound

8. (6) What is the denominator of $\frac{23}{24}$? 24

9.
65
$\frac{3}{5}$ of 65 {13, 13, 13}
$\frac{2}{5}$ of 65 {13, 13}

***9.** (22) Model What number is $\frac{3}{5}$ of 65? Draw a diagram to illustrate the problem. 39

10.
\$15
$\frac{2}{3}$ of \$15 {\$5, \$5}
$\frac{1}{3}$ of \$15 {\$5}

***10.** (22) Model How much money is $\frac{2}{3}$ of \$15? Draw a diagram to illustrate the problem. \$10

Model Use your fraction manipulatives to help answer problems **11–18.**

11. (Inv. 2) $\frac{1}{6} + \frac{2}{6} + \frac{3}{6}$ 1

12. (Inv. 2) $\frac{7}{8} - \frac{3}{8}$ $\frac{1}{2}$

13. (Inv. 2) $\frac{6}{6} - \frac{5}{6}$ $\frac{1}{6}$

14. (Inv. 2) $\frac{2}{8} + \frac{5}{8}$ $\frac{7}{8}$

15. (Inv. 2) **a.** How many $\frac{1}{8}$s are in 1? 8

b. How many $\frac{1}{8}$s are in $\frac{1}{2}$? 4

▶ ***16.** (26) Reduce: $\frac{4}{6}$ $\frac{2}{3}$

▶ **17.** (Inv. 2) What fraction is half of $\frac{1}{4}$? $\frac{1}{8}$

18. (Inv. 2) What fraction of a circle is 50% of a circle? $\frac{1}{2}$

▶ See Math Conversations in the sidebar.

2 New Concepts *(Continued)*

Practice Set

Problem d Explain

Extend the Problem

Write "radius = *r*" and "diameter = *d*" on the board. Then challenge students to write an equation for any circle that compares the length of its diameter to the length of its radius, and write an equation for any circle that compares the length of its radius to the length of its diameter. In each equation they write, have students include the variables *d* and *r*. Sample: $d = 2r$ and $r = \frac{d}{2}$

3 Written Practice

Math Conversations

Discussion opportunities are provided below.

Problem 2 Model

Extend the Problem

"How can you find $\frac{3}{4}$ of 20 using mental math?" Sample: The denominator 4 means that the whole or 20 is divided into 4 equal parts, and each equal part is $20 \div 4$ or 5. The numerator represents 3 of those equal parts, so $5 + 5 + 5 = 15$.

Problem 4 Explain

Extend the Problem

"What is the relationship of the radius of a circle to its diameter?" In any circle, a radius is one-half the length of a diameter.

Problem 16 Explain

Extend the Problem

"Name the operation that is used to reduce a fraction, and explain how that operation is used." Division; divide the numerator and the denominator by a common factor of the numerator and the denominator. If the factor is the greatest common factor, the division will produce a fraction in simplest form.

Errors and Misconceptions

Problems 17

When students find one-half of a whole number, they simply divide the whole number by 2. However, when they are asked to find one-half of a unit fraction, simply dividing the denominator by 2 is a mistake. For example, $\frac{1}{2}$ of $\frac{1}{4} = \frac{1}{4 \div 2}$ is a common error.

Encourage students to use fraction manipulatives when finding a fractional part of a fraction. The manipulatives can help students see, for example, that $\frac{1}{2}$ of $\frac{1}{4}$ of a circle represents a part of the circle that is smaller than $\frac{1}{4}$.

(continued)

3 Written Practice (Continued)

Math Conversations

Discussion opportunities are provided below.

Problem 25 Justify

Write the following four numbers on the board and point out that all of the numbers are divisible by 9.

216 5373 9342 288,450

Ask students to use each method they develop to test the four numbers for divisibility by 9. If a method finds that one or more of the numbers is not divisible by 9, the method is not reliable.

Problem 28 Explain

"Is order an important concept when writing ratios? Explain." Yes; sample explanation: a ratio of 4 to 5 is different than a ratio of 5 to 4.

19. (2) Divide 2100 by 52 and write the answer with a remainder. 40 R 20

20. (8) If a 36-inch-long string is made into the shape of a square, how long will each side be? 9 inches

* **21.** (25) Convert $\frac{7}{6}$ to a mixed number. $1\frac{1}{6}$

22. (2) $\frac{432}{18}$ 24

23. (5) $(55 + 45) \div (55 - 45)$ 10

24. (21) Classify Which of these numbers is divisible by both 2 and 5? **C**

A 502 **B** 205 **C** 250

▶ **25.** (21) Justify Describe a method for determining whether a number is divisible by 9.

25. One method is to add the digits of the number. If the sum of the digits is divisible by 9, the number is also divisible by 9.

26. (19) Which prime number is not an odd number? 2

* **27.** (27) What is the name for the perimeter of a circle? circumference

▶ **28.** (23) Explain What is the ratio of even numbers to odd numbers in the square below? Explain your thinking.

1	2	3
4	5	6
7	8	9

28. $\frac{4}{5}$; There are four even numbers (2, 4, 6, 8) and five odd numbers (1, 3, 5, 7, 9) so the ratio of even to odd is 4 to 5.

* **29.** (26) $37\frac{1}{2}\% - 12\frac{1}{2}\%$ 25%

* **30.** (26) $33\frac{1}{3}\% + 16\frac{2}{3}\%$ 50%

Early Finishers *Real-World Application*

While the neighbors are on vacation, Jason is taking care of their dogs Max, Fifi, and Tinker. Max needs $2\frac{1}{4}$ cups of food. Fifi needs $\frac{3}{4}$ cup of food, and Tinker needs $1\frac{3}{4}$ cups. How much food will Jason need to feed all three dogs? Show your work. $2\frac{1}{4} + \frac{3}{4} + 1\frac{3}{4} = 3 + \frac{7}{4} = 3 + 1\frac{3}{4} = 4\frac{3}{4}$; $4\frac{3}{4}$ cups

▶ See Math Conversations in the sidebar.

Looking Forward

Identifying measures (circumference, diameter, and radius) of a circle and using a compass to draw a circle prepares students for:

- **Lesson 47,** finding the circumference of a circle and understanding pi (the number of diameters in the circumference of circle).
- **Investigation 8,** using a compass to bisect line segments and angles.
- **Lesson 86,** finding the area of a circle by estimating (counting square units) and by using the formula for area.
- **Lesson 120,** finding the volume of a cylinder.

Angles

Objectives

- Identify parallel lines, perpendicular lines, and oblique lines.
- Name angles using one letter, three letters, or one number.
- Identify right angles, acute angles, and obtuse angles.

Lesson Preparation

Materials

- **Power Up F** (in *Instructional Masters*)
- **Manipulative kit: rulers**
- **Teacher-provided material: fraction manipulatives** from Investigation 2

Optional

- **Lesson Activity 9 Transparency** (in *Instructional Masters*)

Math Language

New		English Learners (ESL)
acute angle	parallel lines	interior
angles	perpendicular lines	
intersect	plane	
oblique lines	right angle	
ray	vertex	
obtuse angle		

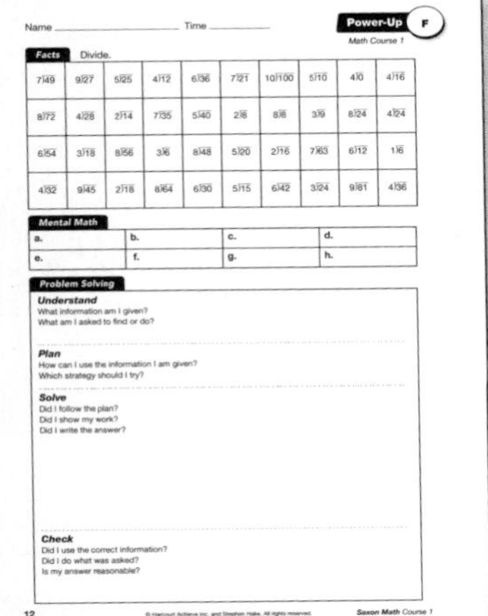

Name ____________ Time ________

Power-Up F
Math Course 1

Facts Divide.

7)49	9)27	5)25	4)12	6)36	7)21	10)100	5)10	4)0	4)16
8)72	4)28	2)14	7)35	5)40	2)8	8)8	3)9	8)24	4)24
6)54	3)18	8)56	3)6	8)48	5)20	2)16	7)63	6)12	1)6
4)32	9)45	2)18	8)64	6)30	5)15	6)42	3)24	9)81	4)36

Mental Math

a.	b.	c.	d.
e.	f.	g.	h.

Problem Solving

Understand
What information am I given?
What am I asked to find or do?

Plan
How can I use the information I am given?
Which strategy should I try?

Solve
Did I follow the plan?
Did I show my work?
Did I write the answer?

Check
Did I use the correct information?
Did I do what was asked?
Is my answer reasonable?

12 © Harcourt Achieve Inc. and Stephen Hake. All rights reserved. *Saxon Math* Course 1

Power Up F

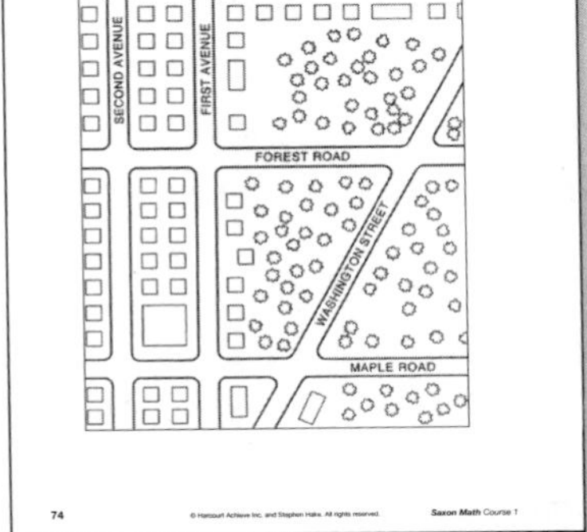

Lesson Activity 9

Technology Resources

Student eBook Complete student textbook in electronic format.

Resources and Planner CD Assessment, reteaching, and instructional masters, plus a pacing calendar with standards.

Test and Practice Generator CD Create additional practice sheets and custom-made tests.

www.SaxonPublishers.com Visit for more student activities and planning materials.

Inclusion

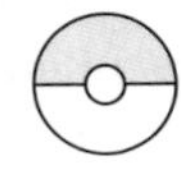

Adaptations CD Adapted lessons, investigations, practice and assessments.

Meeting Standards

National Council of Teachers of Mathematics (NCTM)

Geometry

GM.1a Precisely describe, classify, and understand relationships among types of two- and three-dimensional objects using their defining properties

GM.4a Draw geometric objects with specified properties, such as side lengths or angle measures

GM.4e Recognize and apply geometric ideas and relationships in areas outside the mathematics classroom, such as art, science, and everyday life

Measurement

ME.1c Understand, select, and use units of appropriate size and type to measure angles, perimeter, area, surface area, and volume

ME.2b Select and apply techniques and tools to accurately find length, area, volume, and angle measures to appropriate levels of precision

Power-Up Discussion *For use with Power Up, p. 145*

Problem-Solving Strategy: Use Logical Reasoning

Zuna has 2¢ stamps, 3¢ stamps, 10¢ stamps, and 37¢ stamps. She wants to mail a package that requires $1.29 postage. In order to pay the expected postage, what is the smallest number of stamps Zuna can use? What is the largest number of stamps she can use? If Zuna only has two 37¢ stamps, what is the fewest number of stamps she can use?

Understand — Understand the problem.

"What information are we given?"

We are told the denominations of stamps that Zuna has. We are told that the postage for Zuna's package is $1.29.

"What are we asked to do?"

We are asked to find the smallest and the largest number of stamps Zuna can use to pay exact postage. We are also asked to find the fewest stamps she could use if she only has two 37¢ stamps.

Plan — Make a plan.

"How can we use the information we know to do what we are asked to do?"

Logical reasoning tells us that we need fewer stamps when we use larger denominations. We will first divide to find how many 37¢ stamps Zuna can use without going over $1.29. If there is postage remaining to be paid, then we will try to make up the difference with 10¢ stamps, then 3¢ stamps, and then 2¢ stamps until we find a combination that totals $1.29. Similarly, to find the largest number of stamps, we will begin with 2¢ stamps, then use 3¢ stamps.

Solve — Carry out the plan.

"How many 37¢ stamps will Zuna use?"

Zuna will use three 37¢ stamps because $1.29 ÷ 37¢ = 3 stamps with 18¢ as the remainder.

"What other stamps will Zuna use?"

Zuna still needs 18¢ postage ($1.29 − $1.11). Zuna will use one 10¢ stamp. Zuna's remaining postage is 18¢ − 10¢, or 8¢. She can use two 3¢ stamps and one 2¢ stamp.

"What is the total number of stamps Zuna will use?"

We found that Zuna needs to use three 37¢ stamps, one 10¢ stamp, two 3¢ stamps, and one 2¢ stamp. That is a total of seven stamps.

"What is the largest number of stamps Zuna will use?"

If Zuna divides the amount of postage ($1.29) by the cost of the smallest stamp (2¢), she would need 64 of the 2¢ stamps with 1¢ of the postage left unpaid. This would only give Zuna a total of $1.28 in postage so we will reduce the number of 2¢ stamps to 63 and use one 3¢ stamp to equal $1.29. The largest number of stamps Zuna will use is 64 stamps.

"If Zuna has only two 37¢ stamps, how many stamps will she need to pay the postage?"

Two 37¢ stamps total 74¢, so Zuna needs $1.29 − $0.74 = $0.55. The fewest stamps she has that total $0.55 is five 10¢ stamps, one 3¢ stamp, and one 2¢ stamp. Zuna needs nine stamps to pay the postage.

Check — Look back.

"Did we complete the task?"

Yes, we found the smallest and largest number of stamps Zuna could use to pay $1.29 postage. We also found the minimum number of stamps she could need if she only has two 37¢ stamps.

LESSON 28

• Angles

Power Up

Building Power

facts Power Up F

mental math

a. **Number Sense:** 8 × 42 336

b. **Number Sense:** 3 × 85 255

c. **Number Sense:** 36 + 49 85

d. **Number Sense:** 1750 − 500 1250

e. **Money:** $10.00 − $8.25 $1.75

f. **Fractional Parts:** $\frac{1}{2}$ of 36 18

g. **Measurement:** Which is greater, 9 inches or one foot? one foot

h. **Calculation:** 8 × 4, + 1, ÷ 3, + 1, × 2, + 1, ÷ 5 5

problem solving

Zuna has 2¢ stamps, 3¢ stamps, 10¢ stamps, and 37¢ stamps. She wants to mail a package that requires $1.29 postage. In order to pay exactly the expected postage, what is the smallest number of stamps Zuna can use? What is the largest number of stamps she can use? If Zuna only has two 37¢ stamps, what is the fewest number of stamps she can use? 7 stamps; 64 stamps; 9 stamps

New Concept

Increasing Knowledge

In mathematics, a **plane** is a flat surface, such as a tabletop or a sheet of paper. When two lines are drawn in the same plane, they will either cross at one point or they will not cross at all. When lines do not cross but stay the same distance apart, we say that the lines are **parallel.** When lines cross, we say that they **intersect.** When they intersect and make square angles, we call the lines **perpendicular.** If lines intersect at a point but are not perpendicular, then the lines are **oblique.**

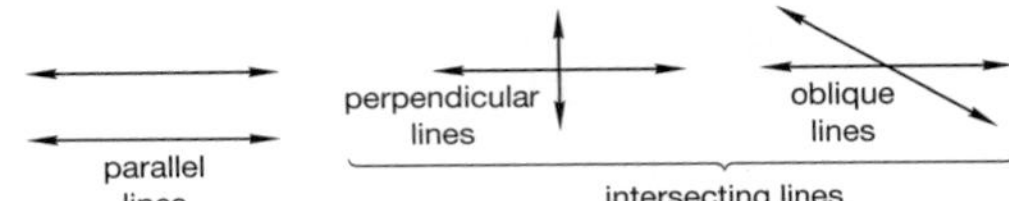

Where lines intersect, **angles** are formed. We show several angles below.

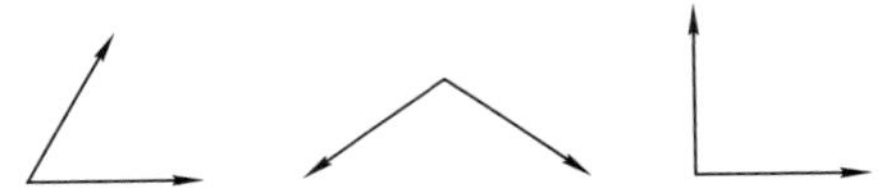

Facts Divide.

7)49 = 7	9)27 = 3	5)25 = 5	4)12 = 3	6)36 = 6	7)21 = 3	10)100 = 10	5)10 = 2	4)0 = 0	4)16 = 4
8)72 = 9	4)28 = 7	2)14 = 7	7)35 = 5	5)40 = 8	2)8 = 4	8)8 = 1	3)9 = 3	8)24 = 3	4)24 = 6
6)54 = 9	3)18 = 6	8)56 = 7	3)6 = 2	8)48 = 6	5)20 = 4	2)16 = 8	7)63 = 9	6)12 = 2	1)6 = 6
4)32 = 8	9)45 = 5	2)18 = 9	8)64 = 8	6)30 = 5	5)15 = 3	6)42 = 7	3)24 = 8	9)81 = 9	4)36 = 9

1 Power Up

Facts

Distribute **Power Up F** to students. See answers below.

Mental Math

Before students begin the Mental Math exercise, do this counting exercise as a class.

Count up and down by 3s between 3 and 60.

Count up and down by 6s between 6 and 60.

Encourage students to share different ways to mentally compute these exercises. Strategies for exercises **c** and **d** are listed below.

c. Change 49 to 50, then Subtract 1

36 + 50 = 86; 86 − 1 = 85

Count by 10, then Count Back 1

Start with 36. Count: 46, 56, 66, 76, 86

Start with 86. Count back: 85

d. Count Back by Hundreds

Start with 1750. Count: 1650, 1550, 1450, 1350, 1250

Subtract Hundreds

1700 + 50 − 500 = 1200 + 50 = 1250

Problem Solving

Refer to **Power-Up Discussion,** p. 145B.

2 New Concepts

Instruction

Distribute copies of the transparency for **Lesson Activity 9** Street Map or display it on an overhead projector. Ask students to identify examples of parallel lines, perpendicular lines, and oblique lines that are formed by the streets shown on the map. Also ask students to name angles that are formed by the intersection of streets.

(continued)

2 New Concepts (Continued)

Instruction

When letters are used to label and name angles, the letters are typically upper case or capital letters. Lower case letters are usually used in other ways, such as to represent variables.

Ask students to identify the number of right angles that are formed by the intersection of two perpendicular lines. four

(continued)

Math Language

A **ray** has one endpoint and continues in one direction without end.

Rays make up the sides of the angles. The rays of an angle originate at a point called the **vertex** of the angle.

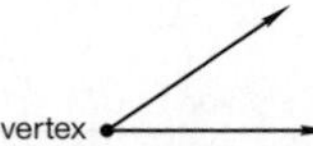

Angles are named in a variety of ways. When there is no chance of confusion, an angle may be named with only one letter: the letter of its vertex. Here is angle *B* (abbreviated $\angle B$):

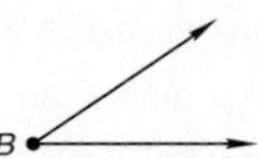

An angle may also be named with three letters, using a point from one side, the vertex, and a point from the other side. Here is angle *ABC* ($\angle ABC$):

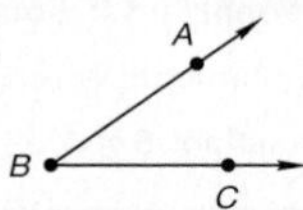

This angle may also be named angle *CBA* ($\angle CBA$). However, it may not be named $\angle BAC$, $\angle BCA$, $\angle CAB$, or $\angle ACB$. The vertex must be in the middle. Angles may also be named with a number or letter in the interior of the angle. In the figure below we see $\angle 1$ and $\angle 2$.

Thinking Skill

Analyze

What figure is created when we add the measures of $\angle 1$ and $\angle 2$? a line

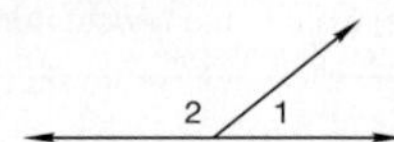

The square angles formed by perpendicular lines, rays, or segments are called **right angles.** We may mark a right angle with a small square.

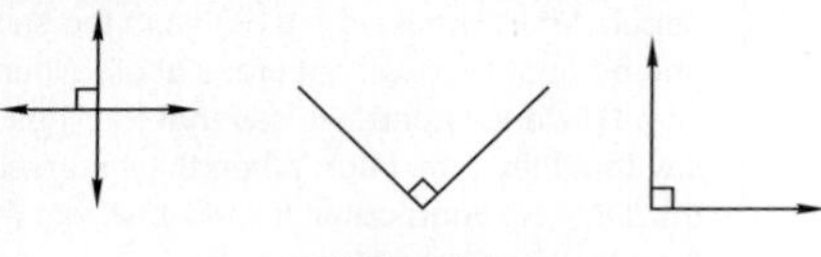

Angles that are less than right angles are **acute angles.** Angles that are greater than right angles but less than a straight line are **obtuse angles.** A pair of oblique lines forms two acute angles and two obtuse angles.

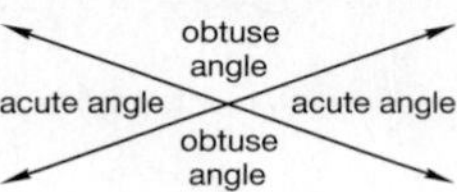

Math Background

Do the nonmathematical definitions of acute and obtuse represent the appearance of acute and obtuse angles?

Yes; the term acute can mean "ending in a sharp point" and the term obtuse can mean "not pointed" or "blunt." In a visual sense, the angle formed by the intersecting rays of an acute angle appears to be very sharp when compared to the angle formed by the rays of an obtuse angle.

English Learners

To help students understand the meaning of "the **interior** of the angle," draw this diagram on the board.

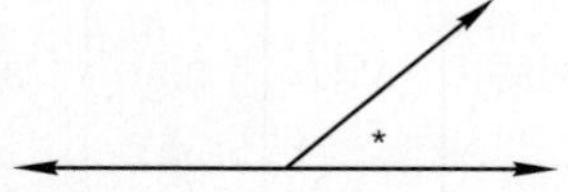

As you point to the asterisk, say:

"The interior of the angle is the space between the two rays of the angle. On this drawing, the asterisk marks the interior of one of the angles."

Ask a volunteer to point to the interior of the second angle. Then draw a horizontal line. Ask a volunteer to add a ray and to mark an interior angle formed by the ray.

Example 1

a. Name the acute angle in this figure.

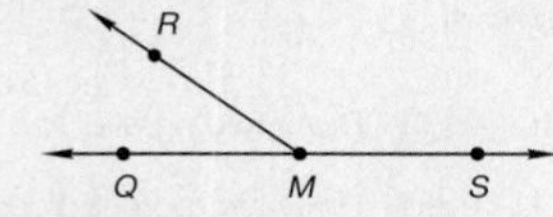

b. Name the obtuse angle in this figure.

Reading Math

When we use three letters to name an angle, the middle letter is the vertex of the angle.

Solution

To avoid confusion, we use three letters to name the angles.

a. The acute angle is **∠*QMR*** (or **∠*RMQ***).

b. The obtuse angle is **∠*RMS*** (or **∠*SMR***).

Example 2

In this figure, angle *D* is a right angle.

a. Which other angle is a right angle?

b. Which angle is acute?

c. Which angle is obtuse?

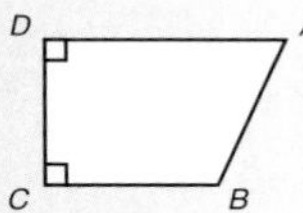

Solution

Since there is one angle at each vertex, we may use a single letter to name each angle.

a. Angle *C* is a right angle.

b. Angle *A* is acute.

c. Angle *B* is obtuse.

Practice Set

a. Represent Use two pencils to approximate an acute angle, a right angle, and an obtuse angle. Observe students.

Describe each angle below as acute, right, or obtuse.

b. **c.** **d.**

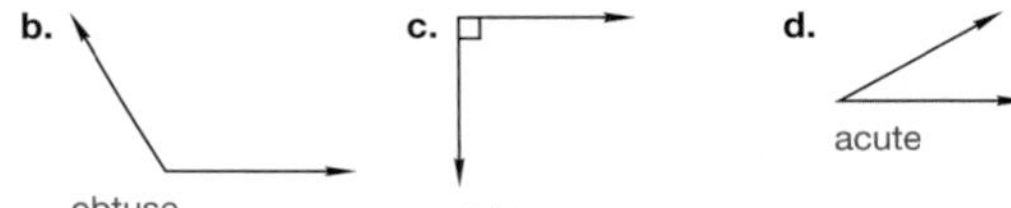

obtuse right acute

▸ **e.** Connect What type of angle is formed by the hands of a clock at 4 o'clock? obtuse angle

f. Connect What type of angle is formed at the corner of a door in your classroom? right angle

▸ See Math Conversations in the sidebar.

Inclusion

Students with special needs may have difficulty remembering the terminology used to describe lines and angles. The hands-on activities below can help.

Have students use their arms and fingers to demonstrate parallel, perpendicular, and intersecting lines. Point out the parallel *l*'s in the word *parallel* to help students distinguish parallel lines from perpendicular lines.

Show students how the corner of a rectangular piece of paper forms a right angle. Draw several examples of acute, obtuse, and right angles on the board. Tell students that an *acute angle* has an opening *smaller* than a right angle and that an *obtuse angle* has an opening *larger* than a right angle. Show students how to use the corner of a piece of paper to identify each angle on the board. Then have students draw their own examples of each angle type.

You may also refer students to the "Types of Angles" and "Types of Lines" in the Student Reference Guide.

2 New Concepts *(Continued)*

Example 1

Instruction

Ask students to explain why they should *not* use only one letter to identify the acute angle shown in example 1. The letter *M* represents the vertex of an acute angle, and it also represents the vertex of an obtuse angle. To clearly identify either or both angles, a combination of three letters is needed.

Practice Set

Problem e Connect

Extend the Problem

Challenge students to consider other whole hour times that the hands of a clock can display (1 o'clock, 2 o'clock, 3 o'clock, and so on) and name the type of angle the hands form at each time.

Sample:

1 o'clock	acute
2 o'clock	acute
3 o'clock	right
5 o'clock	obtuse
6 o'clock	straight
7 o'clock	obtuse
8 o'clock	obtuse
9 o'clock	right
10 o'clock	acute
11 o'clock	acute

(continued)

2 New Concepts (Continued)

Practice Set

Problem h Model

When drawing the perpendicular lines, remind students to draw an arrowhead at each end of each line because a line extends without end in opposite directions. Point out that without the arrowheads, the figures will represent line segments.

3 Written Practice

Math Conversations

Discussion opportunities are provided below.

Problem 5 Connect

Extend the Problem

Remind students that division is used to write an improper fraction as a mixed number, and the remainder of the division is written as the numerator of a fraction that has the divisor as its denominator.

Extend the problem by asking students to explain how to write the mixed number $7\frac{2}{3}$ as an improper fraction.

Problem 10 Model

Extend the Problem

"How can you find $\frac{2}{3}$ of \$24 using mental math?" Sample: The denominator of the fraction represents \$24 divided into three equal parts, and each equal part is \$24 ÷ 3 or \$8. The numerator represents two of those equal parts, so \$8 × 2 = \$16.

(continued)

---

g. Which two angles formed by these oblique lines are acute angles? ∠1 and ∠3

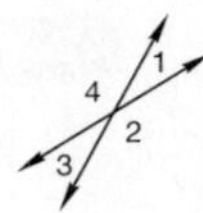

h. **Model** Draw two parallel line segments.

i. **Model** Draw two perpendicular lines.

Refer to the triangle to answer problems **j** and **k**.

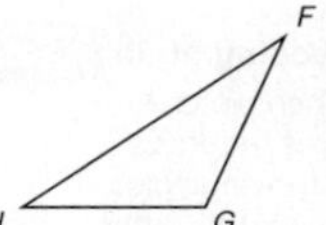

j. Angle *H* is an acute angle. Name another acute angle. ∠*F* (or ∠*HFG* or ∠*GFH*)

k. Name an obtuse angle. ∠*G* (or ∠*FGH* or ∠*HGF*)

Written Practice *Strengthening Concepts*

* 1. (24) What is the sum of $\frac{1}{3}$ and $\frac{2}{3}$ and $\frac{3}{3}$? 2

* 2. (22) **Explain** According to the 2000 census, about $\frac{2}{5}$ of the 20 million people who lived in Texas at the time were under the age of 24. About how many Texans were under 24 years old in 2000? Explain how you found your answer.

2. about 8 million; Sample: I found $\frac{1}{5}$ of 20 million by dividing 20 by 5 and got 4 million. Then to find $\frac{2}{5}$, I multiplied 4 million by 2 and got 8 million.

3. (15) **Formulate** Seven hundred sixty-eight peanuts are to be shared equally by the thirty-two children at the party. How many peanuts should each child receive? Write an equation and solve the problem. $32g = 768$; 24 peanuts

4. (13) **Formulate** The Declaration of Independence was signed in 1776. How many years ago was that? Write an equation and solve the problem. (current year) − 1776 = *d*; answer depends on current year

* 5. (25) Convert $\frac{23}{3}$ to a mixed number. $7\frac{2}{3}$

* 6. (26) $1\frac{2}{3} + 1\frac{2}{3}$ $3\frac{1}{3}$ * 7. (26) $3 + 4\frac{2}{3}$ $7\frac{2}{3}$ * 8. (26) $3\frac{5}{6} - 1\frac{4}{6}$ $2\frac{1}{6}$

* 9. (26) **Model** Use your fraction manipulatives to reduce $\frac{4}{8}$. $\frac{1}{2}$

10. (22) **Model** How much money is $\frac{2}{3}$ of \$24.00? Draw a diagram to illustrate the problem. \$16.00

10.

	\$24.00
$\frac{2}{3}$ of \$24	\$8.00
	\$8.00
$\frac{1}{3}$ of \$24	\$8.00

11. (22) a. What is $\frac{1}{10}$ of 100%? 10%

b. What is $\frac{3}{10}$ of 100%? 30%

12. (Inv. 2) Twenty-five percent of a circle is what fraction of a circle? $\frac{1}{4}$

13. (23) At 26 miles per gallon, how far can Ms. Olsen expect to drive on 11 gallons of gas? 286 miles

Find each missing number. Remember to check your work.

14. (Inv. 2) $\frac{1}{4} + m = 1$ $\frac{3}{4}$ 15. (3) $423 - w = 297$ 126

▶ See Math Conversations in the sidebar.

▶* 16. (28) **Represent** Refer to the figure below to answer **a** and **b**.

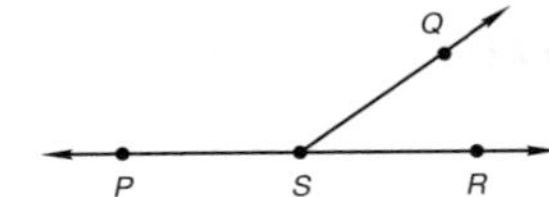

a. Name an obtuse angle. ∠PSQ or ∠QSP

b. Name an acute angle. ∠QSR or ∠RSQ

17. (18) On the last four tests the number of questions Christie answered correctly was 22, 20, 23, and 23 respectively. She averaged how many correct answers on each test? 22 correct answers

18. (8) The three sides of an equilateral triangle are of equal length. If a 36-inch-long string is formed into the shape of an equilateral triangle, how long will each side of the triangle be? 12 inches

19. (20) What is the greatest common factor (GCF) of 24, 36, and 60? 12

20. (1) 10,010 − 9909 101

21. (5) (100 × 100) − (100 × 99) 100

22. (22) **Model** If $\frac{1}{10}$ of the class was absent, what percent of the class was absent? Draw a diagram to illustrate the problem. 10%

22.

100%
10%
10%
10%
10%
10%
10%
10%
10%
10%
10%

$\frac{1}{10}$ was absent. (first 10%)
$\frac{9}{10}$ was not absent. (remaining nine 10%)

* **23.** (25) Divide 5097 by 10 and write the answer as a mixed number. $509\frac{7}{10}$

▶ **24.** (22) **Model** Three fourths of two dozen eggs is how many eggs? Draw a diagram to illustrate the problem. 18 eggs

24.

24 eggs
6 eggs
6 eggs
6 eggs
6 eggs

$\frac{3}{4}$ of 24 (first three 6 eggs)
$\frac{1}{4}$ of 24 (last 6 eggs)

* **25.** (7, 17) **a.** Use a ruler to find the length of the line segment below to the nearest sixteenth of an inch. $3\frac{3}{16}$ inches

b. Use a centimeter ruler to find the length of the line segment to the nearest centimeter. 8 centimeters

▶* **26.** (25) **Analyze** List the first five multiples of 6 and the first five multiples of 8. Circle any numbers that are multiples of both 6 and 8. 6, 12, 18, (24), 30
8, 16, (24), 32, 40

▶ **27.** (Inv. 2) **Model** Which fraction manipulative covers $\frac{1}{2}$ of $\frac{1}{3}$? $\frac{1}{6}$

28. (23) There are thirteen stripes on the United States flag. Seven of the stripes are red, and the rest of the stripes are white. What is the ratio of red stripes to white stripes on the United States flag? $\frac{7}{6}$

29. (19) Here we show 24 written as a product of prime numbers:

$$2 \cdot 2 \cdot 2 \cdot 3$$

Show how prime numbers can be multiplied to equal 27. $3 \cdot 3 \cdot 3 = 27$

30. (21) **Classify** Which of the numbers below is not divisible by 9?

A 234 **B** 345 **C** 567 B

▶ See Math Conversations in the sidebar.

3 Written Practice (Continued)

Math Conversations

Discussion opportunities are provided below.

Problem 16 a and b Represent

"Two different names can be given for each angle. What characteristic is shared by each of those names?" The vertex of the angle is always the middle letter.

"Why isn't it a good idea to name each angle using one letter, such as S?" Sample: There would be no way to know if you were referring to acute angle S or obtuse angle S.

Problem 24 Model

"How many eggs are the same as two dozen? Explain how you know." 24; since one dozen is 12, two dozen is double 12 or 24.

Problem 26 Analyze

"What name is given to the multiples that are circled?" common multiples

"How many common multiples are there for any two numbers?" an infinite number; too many to count

Problem 27 Model

"Covering $\frac{1}{2}$ of $\frac{1}{3}$ is the same as finding or naming $\frac{1}{2}$ of $\frac{1}{3}$, so $\frac{1}{2}$ of $\frac{1}{3}$ is $\frac{1}{6}$."

Errors and Misconceptions

Problem 26

When listing the multiples of a number, students sometimes forget that the first multiple of any number is the number itself. Watch for students who list the first multiple of 6 as 12 and the first multiple of 8 as 16.

Looking Forward

Identifying lines and forming, naming, and classifying angles prepare students for:

- **Investigation 3,** measuring and drawing angles with a protractor.
- **Lesson 64,** classifying quadrilaterals by the characteristics of their sides.
- **Lesson 71,** understanding the characteristics of parallelograms and finding the perimeter and the area of parallelograms.
- **Lesson 93,** classifying triangles by their angles.
- **Lesson 109,** naming corresponding angles from congruent triangles.

• Multiplying Fractions
• Reducing Fractions by Dividing by Common Factors

Objectives

- Multiply a fraction by a fraction.
- Multiply a whole number by a fraction.
- Reduce a fraction in one step by dividing the numerator and the denominator by the greatest common factor (GCF) of the two numbers.
- Reduce a fraction in two or more steps by dividing the numerator and the denominator by a common factor other than the GCF and repeating this process until the fraction is completely reduced.

Lesson Preparation

Materials

- **Power Up B** (in *Instructional Masters*)
- **Manipulative kit: color tiles**
- **Teacher-provided material: fraction manipulatives** from Investigation 2

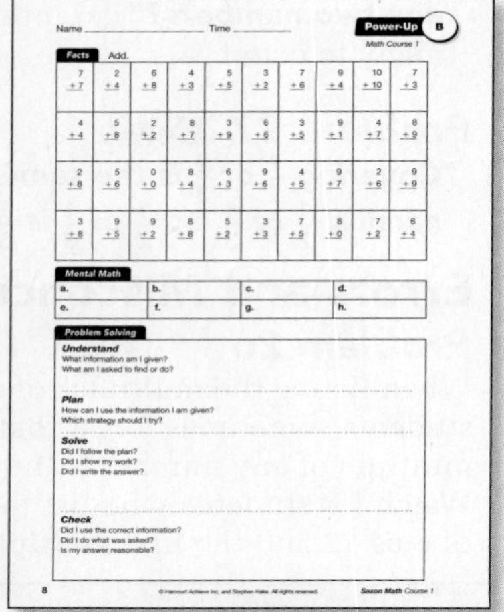

Name ______________ Time ________ **Power-Up B** *Math Course 1*

Facts Add.

7 + 7	2 + 4	6 + 8	4 + 3	5 + 5	3 + 2	7 + 6	9 + 4	10 + 10	7 + 3
4 + 4	5 + 8	2 + 2	8 + 7	3 + 9	6 + 6	3 + 5	9 + 1	4 + 7	8 + 9
2 + 8	5 + 6	0 + 0	8 + 4	6 + 3	9 + 6	4 + 5	9 + 7	2 + 6	9 + 9
3 + 8	9 + 5	9 + 2	8 + 8	5 + 2	3 + 3	7 + 5	8 + 0	7 + 2	6 + 4

Mental Math

a.	b.	c.	d.
e.	f.	g.	h.

Problem Solving

Understand
What information am I given?
What am I asked to find or do?

Plan
How can I use the information I am given?
Which strategy should I try?

Solve
Did I follow the plan?
Did I show my work?
Did I write the answer?

Check
Did I use the correct information?
Did I do what was asked?
Is my answer reasonable?

8 © Harcourt Achieve Inc. and Stephen Hake. All rights reserved. *Saxon Math Course 1*

Power Up B

Math Language

English Learners (ESL)
convert

Technology Resources

Student eBook Complete student textbook in electronic format.

Resources and Planner CD Assessment, reteaching, and instructional masters, plus a pacing calendar with standards.

Test and Practice Generator CD Create additional practice sheets and custom-made tests.

www.SaxonPublishers.com Visit for more student activities and planning materials.

Inclusion

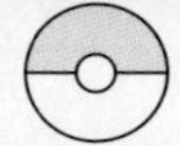

Adaptations CD Adapted lessons, investigations, practice and assessments.

Meeting Standards

National Council of Teachers of Mathematics (NCTM)

Numbers and Operations

NO.1a Work flexibly with fractions, decimals, and percents to solve problems

NO.1f Use factors, multiples, prime factorization, and relatively prime numbers to solve problems

NO.2a Understand the meaning and effects of arithmetic operations with fractions, decimals, and integers

Problem Solving

PS.1c Apply and adapt a variety of appropriate strategies to solve problems

Power-Up Discussion *For use with Power Up, p. 150*

Problem-Solving Strategy: Draw a Diagram

Vivian bought a pizza and ate one fourth of it. Then her sister ate one-third of what was left. Then their little brother ate half of what his sisters had left. What fraction of the whole pizza did Vivian's little brother eat?

Understand ***Understand the problem.***

"What information are we given?"

Vivian bought a pizza and ate one fourth of it. Then her sister ate one-third of what was left. Then their little brother ate half of what his sisters had left.

"What are we asked to do?"

We are asked to find the fraction of the whole pizza that Vivian's little brother ate.

Plan ***Make a plan.***

"How can we use the information we know to do what we are asked to do?"

We will represent the whole pizza with a circle. We will divide the circle to show the portions that each family member ate. We will find the fractions that Vivian and her sister ate, and then use that information to determine the fraction that their little brother ate.

Solve ***Carry out the plan.***

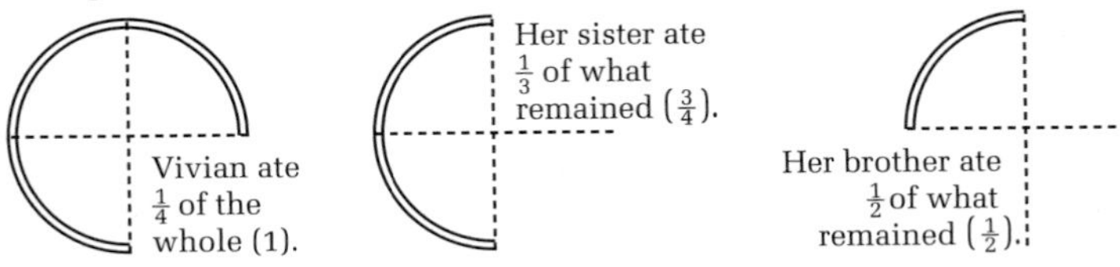
Vivian ate $\frac{1}{4}$ of the whole (1).
Her sister ate $\frac{1}{3}$ of what remained ($\frac{3}{4}$).
Her brother ate $\frac{1}{2}$ of what remained ($\frac{1}{2}$).

"How much pizza did Vivian's little brother eat?

Vivian's little brother ate half of two-fourths of the pizza, which is one fourth of the pizza.

Check ***Look back.***

"How can we verify that our answer is correct?

Vivian's $\frac{1}{4}$ + the sister's $\frac{1}{4}$ + the brother's $\frac{1}{4}$ + $\frac{1}{4}$ remaining = 1 whole pizza

"Why does the problem description make this problem seem almost like a riddle?

The problem describes fractions of fractions. For our problem, Vivian's fourth, her sister's third, and her brother's half are all equal to a fourth of the original whole.

1 Power Up

Facts

Distribute **Power Up B** to students. See answers below.

Mental Math

Before students begin the Mental Math exercise, do this counting exercise as a class.

Count up and down by $\frac{1}{8}$s between $\frac{1}{8}$ and 3.

Encourage students to share different ways to mentally compute these exercises. Strategies for exercises **c** and **f** are listed below.

c. Change 39 to 40, then Subtract 1

$53 + 40 = 93$; $93 - 1 = 92$

Count on by Tens, then Count Back 1

Start with 53. Count: 63, 73, 83, 93

Start with 93. Count: 92

f. Use Addition

What number plus itself equals 70?

$35 + 35 = 70$, so $\frac{1}{2}$ of 70 is 35

Use a Pattern

Since $\frac{1}{2}$ of 60 is 30 and $\frac{1}{2}$ of 80 is 40, $\frac{1}{2}$ of 70 is 35.

Problem Solving

Refer to **Power-Up Discussion,** p. 150B.

2 New Concepts

Instruction

If students have difficulty recognizing $\frac{1}{2}$ of $\frac{1}{2}$, ask them to:

- draw a circle.
- draw a diameter that divides the circle in half horizontally.
- draw a diameter that divides the circle in half vertically.
- fold the circle along one diameter.
- shade one part.
- unfold the circle to see that one of four equal parts is shaded.

In this activity, $\frac{1}{2}$ of $\frac{1}{2}$ is represented when students shade half of the half circle.

(continued)

LESSON 29

• Multiplying Fractions
• Reducing Fractions by Dividing by Common Factors

Power Up *Building Power*

facts Power Up B

mental math

a. **Number Sense:** 7×43 301

b. **Number Sense:** 4×64 256

c. **Number Sense:** $53 + 39$ 92

d. **Number Sense:** $325 + 50$ 375

e. **Money:** \$20.00 − \$17.25 \$2.75

f. **Fractional Parts:** $\frac{1}{2}$ of 70 35

g. **Measurement:** Which is greater, 10 millimeters or one centimeter? equal

h. **Calculation:** 4×5, $- 6$, $\div 7$, $\times 8$, $+ 9$, $\times 2$ 50

problem solving Vivian bought a pizza and ate one fourth of it. Then her sister ate one-third of what was left. Then their little brother ate half of what his sisters had left. What fraction of the whole pizza did Vivian's little brother eat? one fourth

New Concepts *Increasing Knowledge*

multiplying fractions

Below we have shaded $\frac{1}{2}$ of $\frac{1}{2}$ of a circle.

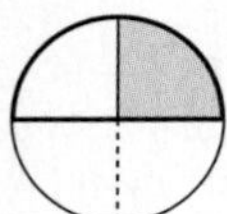

We see that $\frac{1}{2}$ of $\frac{1}{2}$ is $\frac{1}{4}$.

When we find $\frac{1}{2}$ of $\frac{1}{2}$, we are actually multiplying.

$$\frac{1}{2} \times \frac{1}{2} = \frac{1}{4}$$

Reading Math

The "of" in "$\frac{1}{2}$ of $\frac{1}{2}$" means to multiply.

When we multiply fractions, we multiply the numerators to find the numerator of the product, and we multiply the denominators to find the denominator of the product.

Facts Add.

7 + 7 = 14	2 + 4 = 6	6 + 8 = 14	4 + 3 = 7	5 + 5 = 10	3 + 2 = 5	7 + 6 = 13	9 + 4 = 13	10 + 10 = 20	7 + 3 = 10
4 + 4 = 8	5 + 8 = 13	2 + 2 = 4	8 + 7 = 15	3 + 9 = 12	6 + 6 = 12	3 + 5 = 8	9 + 1 = 10	4 + 7 = 11	8 + 9 = 17
2 + 8 = 10	5 + 6 = 11	0 + 0 = 0	8 + 4 = 12	6 + 3 = 9	9 + 6 = 15	4 + 5 = 9	9 + 7 = 16	2 + 6 = 8	9 + 9 = 18
3 + 8 = 11	9 + 5 = 14	9 + 2 = 11	8 + 8 = 16	5 + 2 = 7	3 + 3 = 6	7 + 5 = 12	8 + 0 = 8	7 + 2 = 9	6 + 4 = 10

Example 1

What fraction is $\frac{1}{2}$ of $\frac{3}{4}$?

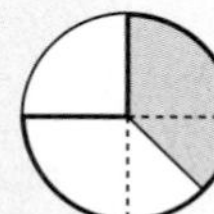

Solution

The word *of* in the question means to multiply. We multiply $\frac{1}{2}$ and $\frac{3}{4}$ to find $\frac{1}{2}$ of $\frac{3}{4}$.

$$\frac{1}{2} \times \frac{3}{4} = \frac{3}{8} \begin{array}{l} \longleftarrow (1 \times 3 = 3) \\ \longleftarrow (2 \times 4 = 8) \end{array}$$

Model We find that $\frac{1}{2}$ of $\frac{3}{4}$ is $\frac{3}{8}$. You can illustrate this with your fraction manipulatives by using three $\frac{1}{4}$s to make $\frac{3}{4}$ of a circle, then covering half of that area with three $\frac{1}{8}$s.

Example 2

Multiply: $\frac{3}{4} \times \frac{2}{3}$

Solution

By performing this multiplication, we will find $\frac{3}{4}$ of $\frac{2}{3}$. We multiply the numerators to find the numerator of the product, and we multiply the denominators to find the denominator of the product.

$$\frac{3}{4} \times \frac{2}{3} = \frac{6}{12}$$

The fraction $\frac{6}{12}$ can be reduced to $\frac{1}{2}$, as we can see in this figure:

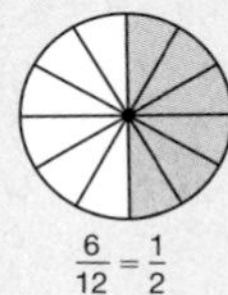

$$\frac{6}{12} = \frac{1}{2}$$

A whole number can be written as a fraction by writing the whole number as the numerator of the fraction and 1 as the denominator of the fraction. Thus, the whole number 2 can be written as the fraction $\frac{2}{1}$. Writing whole numbers as fractions is helpful when multiplying whole numbers by fractions.

Example 3

Thinking Skill

Discuss

How do you change $\frac{8}{3}$ to $2\frac{2}{3}$? Explain your thinking. $\frac{3}{3} + \frac{3}{3} + \frac{2}{3}$

Multiply: $4 \times \frac{2}{3}$

Solution

We write 4 as $\frac{4}{1}$ and multiply.

$$\frac{4}{1} \times \frac{2}{3} = \frac{8}{3}$$

2 New Concepts (Continued)

Example 1

Instruction

Another way to write the computation is $\frac{1 \times 3}{2 \times 4}$.

Example 2

Instruction

Have students note that because 6 is half of 12 and 1 is half of 2, the fractions $\frac{6}{12}$ and $\frac{1}{2}$ are equivalent fractions. Equivalent fractions name the same number.

Instruction

To help students understand why 2 can be written as $\frac{2}{1}$, remind them that a fraction bar represents division, and then write "$\frac{2}{1} = 2 \div 1$ and $2 \div 1 = 2$" on the board or overhead.

Example 3

Instruction

Encourage students to model this problem by drawing and shading parts of circles. Work at the board or on an overhead and create the following model:

Draw four congruent circles. Divide each circle into three equal parts. Shade two parts in each circle.

As you work, ask students to work on a sheet of paper and duplicate your actions. Then ask students to explain how their models show $4 \times \frac{2}{3}$. Sample: Two thirds of each of four models is shaded. If you count all of the shaded thirds, there are eight thirds altogether.

(continued)

Math Background

If both terms of a fraction cannot be divided by the same prime number, then the fraction cannot be reduced. For example, if both terms of a fraction are less than 49, we can determine if the fraction can be reduced simply by testing the divisibility of each term by 2, 3, and 5.

Consider the fraction $\frac{26}{39}$. The numerator is divisible by 2 and equals 2×13. The denominator is divisible by 3 and equals 3×13. So both 26 and 39 can be divided by the prime number 13, which reduces the fraction to $\frac{2}{3}$.

Now consider $\frac{26}{35}$. Again, the numerator 26 is divisible by 2 and equals 2×13. The denominator 35 is divisible by 5 and equals 5×7. Since the numerator and the denominator do not share a common prime factor, $\frac{26}{35}$ cannot be reduced—it is in simplest form.

2 New Concepts (Continued)

Instruction

Ask students to begin by naming all of the factors of 6 and all of the factors of 12. Write each factor on the board or on an overhead as it is named.

Factors of 6: 1, 2, 3, 6
Factors of 12: 1, 2, 3, 4, 6, 12

Ask students to identify the common factors of 6 and 12, and then identify the greatest of those common factors. common factors: 1, 2, 3, 6; GCF: 6

Example 5

Instruction

Have students compare the methods and note that Method 1 requires more divisions because the GCF was not used. Help students generalize that using the GCF ensures only one division will be required to reduce a fraction to simplest form.

Then invite volunteers to name the method they prefer and tell why.

(continued)

Then we convert the improper fraction $\frac{8}{3}$ to a mixed number.

$$\frac{8}{3} = \mathbf{2\frac{2}{3}}$$

Example 4

Three pennies are placed side by side as shown below. The diameter of one penny is $\frac{3}{4}$ inch. How long is the row of pennies?

$\frac{3}{4}$ in.

Solution

We can find the answer by adding or by multiplying. We will show both ways.

$$\text{Adding: } \frac{3}{4}\text{ in.} + \frac{3}{4}\text{ in.} + \frac{3}{4}\text{ in.} = \frac{9}{4}\text{ in.} = 2\frac{1}{4}\text{ in.}$$

$$\text{Multiplying: } \frac{3}{1} \times \frac{3}{4}\text{ in.} = \frac{9}{4}\text{ in.} = 2\frac{1}{4}\text{ in.}$$

We find that the row of pennies is **$2\frac{1}{4}$ inches** long.

reducing fractions by dividing by common factors

We can reduce fractions by dividing the numerator and the denominator by a factor of both numbers. To reduce $\frac{6}{12}$, we will divide both the numerator and the denominator by 6.

$$\frac{6 \div 6}{12 \div 6} = \frac{1}{2}$$

Math Language
$\frac{6}{12}$ and $\frac{1}{2}$ are called *equivalent fractions* or equal fractions.

We divided both the numerator and the denominator by 6 because 6 is the largest factor (the GCF) of 6 and 12. If we had divided by 2 instead of by 6, we would not have completely reduced the fraction.

$$\frac{6 \div 2}{12 \div 2} = \frac{3}{6}$$

The fraction $\frac{3}{6}$ can be reduced by dividing the numerator and the denominator by 3.

$$\frac{3 \div 3}{6 \div 3} = \frac{1}{2}$$

It takes two or more steps to reduce fractions if we do not divide by the greatest common factor in the first step.

Example 5

Reduce: $\frac{8}{12}$

152 ***Saxon** Math Course 1*

English Learners

Write $\frac{20}{6}$ on the board. Say,

"Convert means to change to a different form that expresses the same thing. Watch while I convert this improper fraction to a mixed number."

Show the division to convert $\frac{20}{6}$ to $3\frac{2}{6}$. Say,

"What do we need to do to the fraction $\frac{2}{6}$ in our answer?" reduce it to its simplest form

"To express $\frac{2}{6}$ in its simplest form, we convert it to a fraction with a denominator of three."

Ask a volunteer to convert $\frac{2}{6}$ to a fraction with a denominator of 3. $2 \div \frac{2}{6} \div 2 = \frac{1}{3}$

Solution

We will show two methods.

Method 1: Divide both numerator and denominator by 2.

$$\frac{8 \div 2}{12 \div 2} = \frac{4}{6}$$

Again divide both numerator and denominator by 2.

$$\frac{4 \div 2}{6 \div 2} = \frac{2}{3}$$

Method 2: Divide both numerator and denominator by 4.

$$\frac{8 \div 4}{12 \div 4} = \frac{2}{3}$$

Either way, we find that $\frac{8}{12}$ reduces to $\frac{2}{3}$. Since the greatest common factor of 8 and 12 is 4, we reduced $\frac{8}{12}$ in one step in Method 2 by dividing the numerator and denominator by 4.

Example 6

Multiply: $2 \times \frac{5}{12}$

Solution

We write 2 as $\frac{2}{1}$ and multiply.

$$\frac{2}{1} \times \frac{5}{12} = \frac{10}{12}$$

We can reduce $\frac{10}{12}$ because both 10 and 12 are divisible by 2.

$$\frac{10 \div 2}{12 \div 2} = \mathbf{\frac{5}{6}}$$

Example 7

There were 8 boys and 12 girls in the class. What was the ratio of boys to girls in the class?

Solution

We reduce ratios the same way we reduce fractions. The ratio 8 to 12 reduces to $\frac{2}{3}$.

$$\frac{\text{number of boys}}{\text{number of girls}} = \frac{8}{12} = \mathbf{\frac{2}{3}}$$

Practice Set ▸ Multiply; then reduce if possible.

a. $\frac{1}{2}$ of $\frac{4}{5}$ $\frac{2}{5}$ **b.** $\frac{1}{4}$ of $\frac{2}{3}$ $\frac{1}{6}$ **c.** $\frac{2}{3} \times \frac{3}{4}$ $\frac{1}{2}$

▸ Multiply; then convert each answer from an improper fraction to a whole number or to a mixed number.

d. $\frac{5}{6} \times \frac{6}{5}$ 1 **e.** $5 \times \frac{2}{3}$ $3\frac{1}{3}$ **f.** $2 \times \frac{4}{3}$ $2\frac{2}{3}$

▸ See Math Conversations in the sidebar.

nclusion

Materials: fraction bars or circles

Use fraction circles or bars to show that $\frac{6}{8}$ is equivalent to $\frac{3}{4}$. Draw the following on the board:

$\frac{1}{8}$	$\frac{1}{8}$	$\frac{1}{8}$	$\frac{1}{8}$	$\frac{1}{8}$	$\frac{1}{8}$
$\frac{1}{4}$		$\frac{1}{4}$		$\frac{1}{4}$	

Ask students to model $\frac{6}{8}$ and $\frac{3}{4}$ as shown. Point out that because the row of fraction bars have the same length (or both circles are the same size) that $\frac{6}{8} = \frac{3}{4}$, and the two fractions are equivalent.

Refer students to the "Fraction Families Equivalent Fractions" chart in the Student Reference Guide to reinforce common equivalencies. Frequently referring to the chart helps students commit these equivalencies to memory.

2 New Concepts (Continued)

Example 6

Instruction

"Why are 2 and $\frac{2}{1}$ names for the same number?" A fraction bar represents division; $\frac{2}{1}$ is the same as $2 \div 1$, and the quotient of $2 \div 1$ is 2.

Example 7

Instruction

Students can act out this ratio problem using 20 tiles in two colors. Have students arrange the tiles in a 1 to 1 correspondence, using 8 tiles of one color to represent the number of boys and 12 tiles of another color to represent the number of girls.

□□□□□□□□

■■■■■■■■■■■■

"For every 8 boys there are 12 girls. How do we write this relationship as a ratio?" $\frac{8}{12}$

"What is the greatest common factor of 8 and 12?" 4

Ask students to divide the tiles into 4 equal groups.

□□ □□ □□ □□

■■■ ■■■ ■■■ ■■■

"For every 2 boys there are 3 girls. How do we write this relationship as a ratio?" $\frac{2}{3}$

Point out that $\frac{2}{3}$ is the ratio of boys to girls in simplest form.

Practice Set

Problems a–c (Error Alert)

If students multiply the fractions incorrectly, ask them to rewrite each expression using one fraction bar. For example, problem **a** is rewritten as $\frac{1 \times 4}{2 \times 5}$.

Problems d–f (Error Alert)

Remind students that division is used to write an improper fraction as a mixed number, and the remainder of the division is written as the numerator of a fraction that has the divisor as its denominator.

3 Written Practice

Math Conversations

Discussion opportunities are provided below.

Problem 3 Analyze

Extend the Problem

Ask students to write a symbolic expression to represent the problem. Sample: $\frac{1}{2} + \frac{1}{2} - (\frac{1}{2} \times \frac{1}{2})$

Students should conclude that parentheses must be a part of the expression, because without them, the expression will not simplify to $\frac{3}{4}$.

Problem 4 Connect

Extend the Problem

"What does the ratio 4 to 3 describe?" The ratio of games lost to games won.

"Why is the idea of order important when writing ratios, such as the ratios in this problem?" Sample: In this problem, the ratio 3 to 4 describes the 14 games that have been played differently than the ratio 4 to 3 describes those games.

Problem 11 Connect

"Why is 12 the denominator of the fraction?" Sample: When a fraction is used to describe an amount, the denominator of the fraction represents the whole. Since the whole in this problem is 1 year, and we are asked to describe months, the denominator is 12 because 1 year = 12 months.

(continued)

Reduce each fraction:

g. $\frac{9}{12}$ $\frac{3}{4}$ **h.** $\frac{6}{10}$ $\frac{3}{5}$ **i.** $\frac{18}{24}$ $\frac{3}{4}$

j. In a class of 30, there were 20 girls. What was the ratio of boys to girls? $\frac{1}{2}$

Written Practice *Strengthening Concepts*

1. (15) The African elephant can weigh eight tons. A ton is two thousand pounds. How many pounds can an African elephant weigh? 16,000 pounds

2. (15) If sixteen dried beans weigh one ounce, then how many dried beans weigh one pound (1 pound = 16 ounces)? 256 dried beans

▶ ***3.** (Inv. 2, 29) Analyze If the product of $\frac{1}{2}$ and $\frac{1}{2}$ is subtracted from the sum of $\frac{1}{2}$ and $\frac{1}{2}$, what is the difference? $\frac{3}{4}$

▶ ***4.** (29) A team won 6 games and lost 8 games. What was the team's win-loss ratio? $\frac{3}{4}$

***5.** (29) Reduce: $\frac{16}{24}$ $\frac{2}{3}$ ***6.** (24, 29) $\frac{1}{8} + \frac{3}{8}$ $\frac{1}{2}$

***7.** (29) $\frac{1}{2} \times \frac{2}{3}$ $\frac{1}{3}$ ***8.** (24, 29) $\frac{7}{12} - \frac{3}{12}$ $\frac{1}{3}$

9. (22) The Nobel Prize is a famous international award that recognizes important work in physics, chemistry, medicine, economics, peacemaking, and literature. Ninety-six Nobel Prizes in Literature were awarded from 1901 to 1999. One eighth of the prizes were given to Americans. How many Nobel Prizes in Literature were awarded to Americans from 1901 to 1999? 12 prizes

10. (10) Predict Find the next three numbers in the sequence below:

1, 4, 7, 10, 13, 16, 19, ...

▶ **11.** (Inv. 2) Connect When five months have passed, what fraction of the year remains? $\frac{7}{12}$

12. (2) $3.60 × 100 $360 **13.** (2) 50,000 ÷ 100 500

***14.** (25) Convert $\frac{18}{4}$ to a mixed number. Remember to reduce the fraction part of the mixed number. $4\frac{1}{2}$

15. (14) The temperature rose from –8°F to 15°F. This was an increase of how many degrees? 23°F

Find each unknown number. Remember to check your work.

16. (3) $m + 496 + 2684 = 3217$ 37

17. (3) $1000 - n = 857$ 143 **18.** (4) $24x = 480$ 20

19. (5) $7 \cdot 11 \cdot 13$ 1001

▶ See Math Conversations in the sidebar.

20. To estimate 4963 ÷ 39, first round 4963 to 5000 and round 39 to 40. Then divide 5000 by 40.

▶ **20.** (16) **Estimate** Explain how to estimate the quotient of 4963 ÷ 39.

* **21.** (29) Compare: $\frac{2}{3} \times \frac{3}{2} \; \textcircled{=} \; 1$

22. (8) **Analyze** The perimeter of the rectangle shown is 60 mm. The width of the rectangle is 10 mm. What is its length? 20 mm

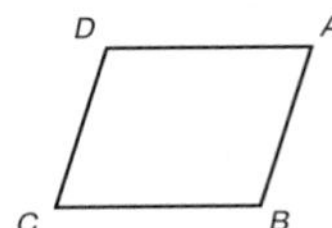

23. (14) 12 − 40 −28

▶* **24.** (29) $\left(\frac{1}{2} \times \frac{1}{2}\right) - \frac{1}{4}$ 0

* **25.** (28) **a.** Which angles in the figure at right are acute angles? ∠A and ∠C

b. Which angles are obtuse angles? ∠B and ∠D

D A C B

* **26.** (29) What fraction is $\frac{2}{3}$ of $\frac{3}{5}$? $\frac{2}{5}$

* **27.** (29) What is the product of $\frac{3}{4}$ and $\frac{4}{3}$? 1

▶* **28.** (27, 29) **Connect** If the diameter of a bicycle wheel is 24 inches, what is the ratio of the radius of the wheel to the diameter of the wheel? $\frac{1}{2}$

* **29.** (28) **Represent** What type of an angle is formed by the hands of a clock at 2 o'clock? acute angle

30. (22) What percent of a circle is $\frac{2}{5}$ of a circle? Explain why your answer is correct. 40%; Sample: A whole circle is 100%, so $\frac{1}{5}$ of a circle is 20% and $\frac{2}{5}$ is 40%.

Early Finishers *Real-World Application*

The high school basketball team has 14 players: $\frac{2}{7}$ are guards, $\frac{1}{2}$ are forwards, and the rest are centers. Find the number of players in each position on the team. Show your work. $14 \times \frac{2}{7} = 4$, 4 guards; $14 \times \frac{1}{2} = 7$, 7 forwards; 14 − 11 = 3, 3 centers

▶ See Math Conversations in the sidebar.

3 Written Practice (Continued)

Math Conversations

Discussion opportunities are provided below.

Problem 24 Infer

Extend the Problem

"The parentheses are not needed to simplify this expression correctly. Why not?" If the parentheses are not present, the order of operations states that multiplication is performed before subtraction.

Problem 28 Connect

"Why don't we need to know the diameter of the wheel to answer the question?" For every circle, the ratio of the length of a radius to the length of a diameter is $\frac{1}{2}$.

Errors and Misconceptions

Problem 20

When making estimates, students may assume that there is only one correct estimate for any exact answer. Explain to students that one measure of a good estimate is its reasonableness. For this reason, there are often a variety of numbers that can represent a good estimate for many computations.

Ask students to apply this idea and make several different estimates for the quotient.

Looking Forward

Multiplying a fraction or a whole number by a fraction prepares students for:

- **Lesson 42,** renaming fractions by multiplying by 1.
- **Lessons 50 and 54,** dividing by a fraction.
- **Lessons 66 and 68,** multiplying mixed numbers and dividing mixed numbers.
- **Lesson 70,** simplifying fraction multiplication and division problems by reducing fractions before multiplying.
- **Lesson 94,** changing fractions and decimals to percents by multiplying by 100%.

• Least Common Multiple (LCM)
• Reciprocals

Objectives

- Identify common multiples of two numbers.
- Find the least common multiple (LCM) of two numbers.
- Identify reciprocals as numbers that have a product of 1 when multiplied.
- Find the reciprocal of a given number by reversing the position of the numerator and the denominator of the number.

Lesson Preparation

Materials

- **Power Up E** (in *Instructional Masters*)
- **Lesson Activity 3** (in *Instructional Masters*)

Math Language

New	Maintain	English Learners (ESL)
least common multiple (LCM)	**multiple**	**reverse**
reciprocal		
term		

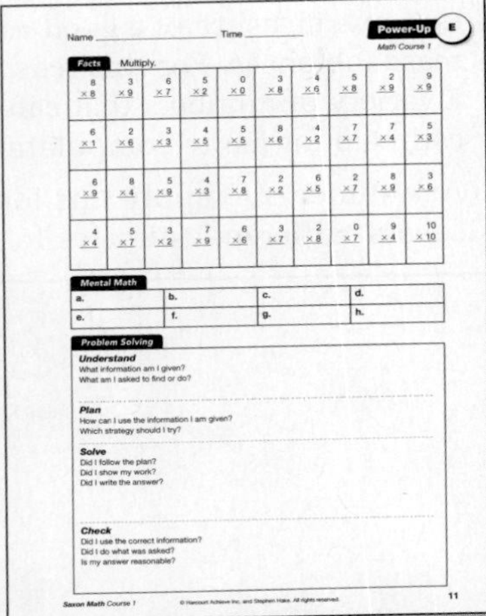

Name ______ Time ______ **Power-Up E**
Math Course 1

Facts Multiply.

8 × 8	3 × 9	6 × 7	5 × 2	0 × 0	3 × 8	4 × 6	5 × 8	2 × 9	9 × 9
6 × 1	2 × 6	3 × 3	4 × 5	5 × 5	8 × 6	4 × 2	7 × 7	7 × 4	5 × 3
6 × 9	8 × 4	5 × 9	4 × 3	7 × 8	2 × 2	6 × 5	2 × 7	8 × 9	3 × 6
4 × 4	5 × 7	3 × 2	7 × 9	6 × 6	3 × 7	2 × 8	0 × 7	9 × 4	10 × 10

Mental Math

a.	b.	c.	d.
e.	f.	g.	h.

Problem Solving

Understand
What information am I given?
What am I asked to find or do?

Plan
How can I use the information I am given?
Which strategy should I try?

Solve
Did I follow the plan?
Did I show my work?
Did I write the answer?

Check
Did I use the correct information?
Did I do what was asked?
Is my answer reasonable?

Saxon Math Course 1 © Harcourt Achieve Inc. and Stephen Hake. All rights reserved. 11

Power Up E

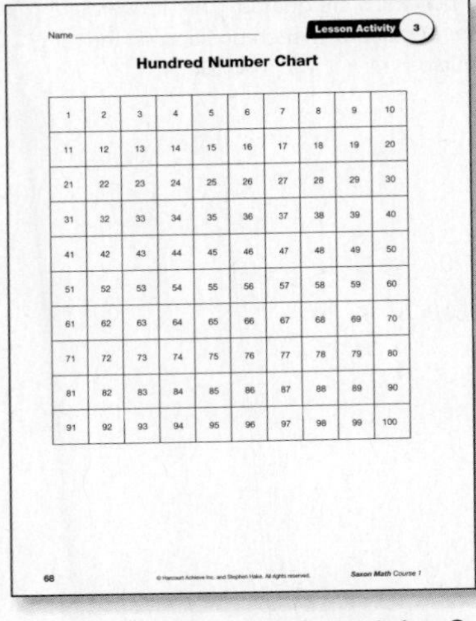

Name ______ **Lesson Activity 3**

Hundred Number Chart

1	2	3	4	5	6	7	8	9	10
11	12	13	14	15	16	17	18	19	20
21	22	23	24	25	26	27	28	29	30
31	32	33	34	35	36	37	38	39	40
41	42	43	44	45	46	47	48	49	50
51	52	53	54	55	56	57	58	59	60
61	62	63	64	65	66	67	68	69	70
71	72	73	74	75	76	77	78	79	80
81	82	83	84	85	86	87	88	89	90
91	92	93	94	95	96	97	98	99	100

68 © Harcourt Achieve Inc. and Stephen Hake. All rights reserved. *Saxon Math* Course 1

Lesson Activity 3

Technology Resources

Student eBook Complete student textbook in electronic format.

Resources and Planner CD Assessment, reteaching, and instructional masters, plus a pacing calendar with standards.

Test and Practice Generator CD Create additional practice sheets and custom-made tests.

www.SaxonPublishers.com Visit for more student activities and planning materials.

Inclusion

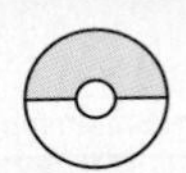

Adaptations CD Adapted lessons, investigations, practice and assessments.

Meeting Standards

National Council of Teachers of Mathematics (NCTM)

Numbers and Operations

NO.1a Work flexibly with fractions, decimals, and percents to solve problems

NO.1f Use factors, multiples, prime factorization, and relatively prime numbers to solve problems

Connections

CN.4a Recognize and use connections among mathematical ideas

Power-Up Discussion *For use with Power Up, p. 156*

oblem-Solving Strategy: Make a Model/ raw a Diagram

. *pentomino* is a geometric shape made of five equal squares joined by their dges. There are twelve different pentominos, and they are named after letters f the alphabet: F I, L, N, P, T, U, V, W, X, Y, and Z. (The rotation or reflection f a pentomino does not count as a different pentomino.) Can you create the emaining ten pentominos?

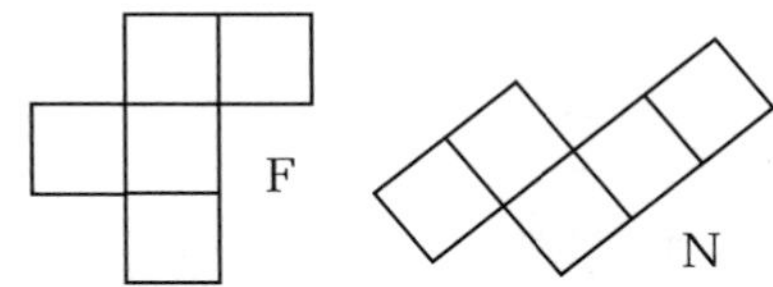

Understand ***Understand the problem.***

"What information are we given?"

'here are 12 shapes that can be made by joining 5 congruent squares at their ides. These 12 shapes are called pentominos.

"What are we asked to do?"

'ind the shapes of the remaining ten pentominos.

"What do we need to remember so that we don't repeat any pentominos?"

'hat any reflections, translations, and rotations of pentominos are repetitions.

'eacher Note: To help students understand the concept of a pentomino, compare : to a domino. A domino has two congruent squares joined at the sides. The refix pent- means five.

Plan ***Make a plan.***

"What problem-solving strategy will we use?"

Ve can *make a model* by using five square tiles, or *draw a diagram* of the entominos.

"How will we use the letter names we are given?"

'entominos are named after letters because the shape of a pentomino resembles he shape of the letter. The letters can be used as a pattern for the remaining ten entominos.

Solve ***Carry out the plan.***

'eacher Note: Graph paper might help students outline these pentominos.

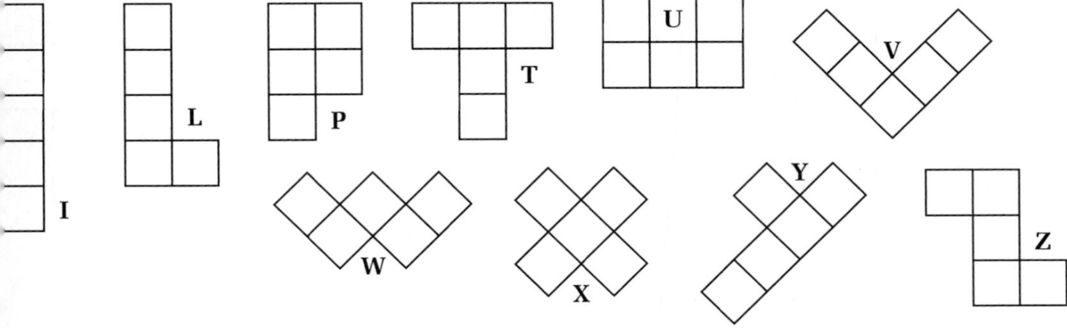

Check ***Look back.***

"Did we do what we were asked to do?"

Yes, we found the remaining 10 pentominos.

1 Power Up

Facts

Distribute **Power Up E** to students. See answers below.

Mental Math

Before students begin the Mental Math exercise, do this counting exercise as a class.

Count up and down by 3s between 3 and 30.

Count up and down by 4s between 4 and 40.

Encourage students to share different ways to mentally compute these exercises. Strategies for exercises **d** and **e** are listed below.

d. Add 100, then Subtract 1
$436 + 100 = 536$; $536 - 1 = 535$
Subtract 1 from 436 and Add 1 to 99
$435 + 100 = 535$

e. Subtract \$12.00, then Subtract \$0.75
\$20.00 − \$12.00 = \$8.00;
\$8.00 − \$0.75 = \$7.25
Subtract \$13.00, then Add \$0.25
\$20.00 − \$13.00 = \$7.00;
\$7.00 + \$0.25 = \$7.25

Problem Solving

Refer to **Power-Up Discussion,** p. 156B.

2 New Concepts

Instruction

If students are having difficulty understanding the concept of common multiples and the least common multiple (LCM), have them find multiples on a hundred number chart.

Give each student a copy of **Lesson Activity 3** Hundreds Number Chart. Ask them to circle all the multiples of 2 up to 30 and draw a square around all the multiples of 3 up to 30.

Point out that the numbers that have a circle and a square around them are common multiples of 2 and 3, and the first number with a circle and a square is the least common multiple. As students compare the various multiples of 2 and 3, remind them that the least common multiple or LCM of two numbers (or more than two numbers) is always the smallest common multiple.

(continued)

LESSON 30

• Least Common Multiple (LCM)
• Reciprocals

Power Up *Building Power*

facts Power Up E

mental math

a. **Number Sense:** 9×32 288

b. **Number Sense:** 5×42 210

c. **Number Sense:** $45 + 49$ 94

d. **Number Sense:** $436 + 99$ 535

e. **Money:** \$20.00 − \$12.75 \$7.25

f. **Fractional Parts:** $\frac{1}{2}$ of 72 36

g. **Statistics:** Find the average: 120, 99, 75 98

h. **Calculation:** 7×7, − 1, ÷ 6, × 3, + 1, × 2, − 1 49

problem solving

A *pentomino* is a geometric shape made of five equal squares joined by their edges. There are twelve different pentominos, and they are named after letters of the alphabet: F, I, L, N, P, T, U, V, W, X, Y, and Z. (The rotation or reflection of a pentomino does not count as a different pentomino.) Can you create the remaining ten pentominos? See script for remaining pentominos.

F

New Concepts *Increasing Knowledge*

least common multiple (LCM)

A number that is a multiple of two or more numbers is called a *common multiple* of those numbers. Here we show some multiples of 2 and 3. We have circled the common multiples.

Multiples of 2: 2, 4, (6), 8, 10, (12), 14, 16, (18), 20, ...

Multiples of 3: 3, (6), 9, (12), 15, (18), 21, ...

We see that 6, 12, and 18 are common multiples of 2 and 3. Since the number 6 is the least of these common multiples, it is called the **least common multiple.** The term *least common multiple* is abbreviated LCM.

Math Language
Recall that a **multiple** is the product of a counting number and another number.

Example 1

What is the least common multiple of 3 and 4?

Facts Multiply.

8 × 8 64	3 × 9 27	6 × 7 42	5 × 2 10	0 × 0 0	3 × 8 24	4 × 6 24	5 × 8 40	2 × 9 18	9 × 9 81
6 × 1 6	2 × 6 12	3 × 3 9	4 × 5 20	5 × 5 25	8 × 6 48	4 × 2 8	7 × 7 49	7 × 4 28	5 × 3 15
6 × 9 54	8 × 4 32	5 × 9 45	4 × 3 12	7 × 8 56	2 × 2 4	6 × 5 30	2 × 7 14	8 × 9 72	3 × 6 18
4 × 4 16	5 × 7 35	3 × 2 6	7 × 9 63	6 × 6 36	3 × 7 21	2 × 8 16	0 × 7 0	9 × 4 36	10 × 10 100

Visit www.SaxonPublishers.com/ActivitiesC1 *for a graphing calculator activity.*

Solution

We will list some multiples of each number and emphasize the common multiples.

Multiples of 3: 3, 6, 9, (12), 15, 18, 21, (24), ...

Multiples of 4: 4, 8, (12), 16, 20, (24), 28, ...

We see that the number 12 and 24 are in both lists. Both 12 and 24 are common multiples of 3 and 4. The least common multiple is **12.** When we list the multiples in order, the first number that is a common multiple is always the least common multiple.

Example 2

What is the LCM of 2 and 4?

Solution

We will list some multiples of 2 and 4.

Multiples of 2: 2, (4), 6, (8), 10, (12), 14, (16), ...

Multiples of 4: (4), (8), (12), (16), ...

The first number that is a common multiple of both 2 and 4 is **4.**

reciprocals

Reciprocals are two numbers whose product is 1. For example, the numbers 2 and $\frac{1}{2}$ are reciprocals because $2 \times \frac{1}{2} = 1$.

$$2 \times \frac{1}{2} = 1$$

reciprocals

We say that 2 is the reciprocal of $\frac{1}{2}$ and that $\frac{1}{2}$ is the reciprocal of 2. Sometimes we want to find the reciprocal of a certain number. One way we will practice finding the reciprocal of a number is by solving equations like this:

$$3 \times \square = 1$$

The number that goes in the box is $\frac{1}{3}$ because 3 times $\frac{1}{3}$ is 1. One third is the reciprocal of 3.

Reciprocals also answer questions like this:

How many $\frac{1}{4}$s are in 1?

The answer is the reciprocal of $\frac{1}{4}$, which is 4.

Fractions have two **terms,** the numerator and the denominator. To form the reciprocal of a fraction, we reverse the terms of the fraction.

$$\frac{3}{4} \rightleftarrows \frac{4}{3}$$

The new fraction, $\frac{4}{3}$, is the reciprocal of $\frac{3}{4}$.

If we multiply $\frac{3}{4}$ by $\frac{4}{3}$, we see that the product, $\frac{12}{12}$, equals 1.

$$\frac{3}{4} \times \frac{4}{3} = \frac{12}{12} = 1$$

2 New Concepts (Continued)

Example 2

Instruction

After completing the example, challenge students to name the least common multiple of 3, 5, and 12. 60

Instruction

Point out that $\frac{1}{2}$ and 2 are reciprocals. To write any integer as a fraction, the integer is written as the numerator of a fraction having a denominator of 1. So 2 and $\frac{2}{1}$ name the same number, and the reciprocal of $\frac{2}{1}$ is $\frac{1}{2}$.

(continued)

Math Background

Students sometimes confuse factors with multiples and multiples with factors. One way to minimize the confusion is to accustom students to working with generalizations.

When working with multiples of positive numbers, students should generalize that the least common multiple of two numbers must be greater than or equal to the greatest number.

This generalization is also true for working with more than two numbers.

2 New Concepts (Continued)

Example 3

Instruction

Remind students that multiplication can be used to check a reciprocal, and that the product of a number and its reciprocal is 1.

For example, since $\frac{2}{3} \times \frac{3}{2} = \frac{6}{6}$ and $\frac{6}{6} = 1$, $\frac{3}{2}$ is the reciprocal of $\frac{3}{2}$.

Example 5

Instruction

After completing the example, challenge students to name the reciprocal of an unknown such as x when x represents any non-zero number. $\frac{1}{x}$

Practice Set

Problems h–k Analyze

Prior to completing the problems, have students name the product in each equation. Then ask,

"What is the product of any number and its reciprocal?" 1

After completing the problems, lead students to generalize that the missing factor in each equation was the reciprocal of the given factor.

Example 3

How many $\frac{2}{3}$s are in 1?

Solution

To find the number of $\frac{2}{3}$s in 1, we need to find the reciprocal of $\frac{2}{3}$. The easiest way to find the reciprocal of $\frac{2}{3}$ is to reverse the positions of the 2 and the 3. The reciprocal of $\frac{2}{3}$ is $\frac{3}{2}$. (We may convert $\frac{3}{2}$ to $1\frac{1}{2}$, but we usually write reciprocals as fractions rather than as mixed numbers.)

Example 4

What number goes into the box to make the equation true?

$$\frac{5}{6} \times \square = 1$$

Solution

When $\frac{5}{6}$ is multiplied by its reciprocal, the product is 1. So the answer is the reciprocal of $\frac{5}{6}$, which is $\frac{6}{5}$. When we multiply $\frac{5}{6}$ by $\frac{6}{5}$, we get $\frac{30}{30}$.

$$\frac{5}{6} \times \frac{6}{5} = \frac{30}{30}$$

The fraction $\frac{30}{30}$ equals 1.

Example 5

What is the reciprocal of 5?

Solution

Recall that a whole number can be written as a fraction that has a denominator of 1. So 5 can be written as $\frac{5}{1}$. (This means "five wholes.") Reversing the positions of the 5 and the 1 gives us the reciprocal of 5, which is $\frac{1}{5}$. This makes sense because five $\frac{1}{5}$s make 1, and $\frac{1}{5}$ of 5 is 1.

Practice Set Find the least common multiple of each pair of numbers:

a. 6 and 8 24 **b.** 3 and 5 15 **c.** 5 and 10 10

Write the reciprocal of each number:

d. 6 $\frac{1}{6}$ **e.** $\frac{2}{3}$ $\frac{3}{2}$ **f.** $\frac{8}{5}$ $\frac{5}{8}$ **g.** $\frac{1}{3}$ $\frac{3}{1}$

▶ Analyze For problems **h–k,** find the number that goes into the box to make the equation true.

h. $\frac{3}{8} \times \square = 1$ $\frac{8}{3}$ **i.** $4 \times \square = 1$ $\frac{1}{4}$

j. $\square \times \frac{1}{6} = 1$ $\frac{6}{1}$ **k.** $\square \times \frac{7}{8} = 1$ $\frac{8}{7}$

l. How many $\frac{2}{5}$s are in 1? $\frac{5}{2}$

m. How many $\frac{5}{12}$s are in 1? $\frac{12}{5}$

▶ See Math Conversations in the sidebar.

English Learners

To help students understand the meaning of reverse in Example 3, explain that when we **reverse** something, we place it in the opposite order. Demonstrate that to reverse a fraction, we flip it over. List on the board:

$\frac{A}{B}$ = fraction $\frac{B}{A}$ = reverse of fraction

"We flipped the fraction $\frac{A}{B}$ to make $\frac{B}{A}$. The letters A and B are now in reverse order."

Ask volunteers to show how to reverse the positions of the numbers in these fractions: $\frac{1}{3}, \frac{9}{10}, \frac{7}{8}$. Then ask: $\frac{3}{1}, \frac{10}{9}, \frac{8}{7}$

"When we reverse the position of the numbers in a fraction what do w form?" the reciprocal of the fraction

Written Practice *Strengthening Concepts*

▶ * **1.** (12, 25) **Analyze** If the fourth multiple of 3 is subtracted from the third multiple of 4, what is the difference? 0

2\.
117 pounds
$\frac{2}{3}$ is water. 39 pounds, 39 pounds
$\frac{1}{3}$ is not water. 39 pounds

▶ **2.** (22) **Model** About $\frac{2}{3}$ of a person's body weight is water. Albert weighs 117 pounds. About how many pounds of Albert's weight is water? Draw a diagram to illustrate the problem. about 78 pounds

3. (15, 23) **Formulate** Cynthia ate 42 pieces of popcorn during the first 15 minutes of a movie. If she kept eating at the same rate, how many pieces of popcorn did she eat during the 2-hour movie? Write an equation and solve the problem. $42 \cdot 8 = p$; 336 pieces of popcorn

4. (25) What are the first four multiples of 12? 12, 24, 36, 48

* **5.** (30) What is the least common multiple (LCM) of 4 and 6? 12

$\frac{12}{48} = \frac{1}{4}$; Sample: An hour is 60 minutes, so if 12 minutes were commercials then 48 minutes are not commercials.

▶ **6.** (23) **Connect** There were 12 minutes of commercials during the one-hour program. What was the ratio of commercial to noncommercial time during the one-hour program? Explain how you found your answer.

7. (24) $\frac{2}{5} + \frac{2}{5} + \frac{2}{5}$ $1\frac{1}{5}$ **8.** (Inv. 2) $1 - \frac{1}{10}$ $\frac{9}{10}$ * **9.** (24, 29) $\frac{11}{12} - \frac{1}{12}$ $\frac{5}{6}$

* **10.** (29) $\frac{3}{4} \times \frac{4}{3}$ 1 * **11.** (29) $5 \times \frac{3}{4}$ $3\frac{3}{4}$ * **12.** (29) $\frac{5}{2} \times \frac{5}{3}$ $4\frac{1}{6}$

13. (19) The number 24 has how many different whole-number factors? 8

14. (1) \$3 + \$24 + \$6.50 \$33.50 **15.** (1) \$5 − \$1.50 \$3.50

16. (16) Estimate the product: 596 × 405 240,000

▶ * **17.** (28) Which angle of the triangle at right is an obtuse angle? angle *C*

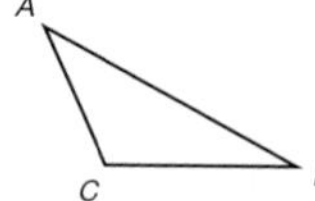

* **18.** (29) Compare: $\frac{2}{3} \times \frac{2}{3} \; (<) \; \frac{2}{3} \times 1$

▶ * **19.** (29) 500,000 ÷ 100 5000 **20.** (2) $35\overline{)8540}$ 244

* **21.** (25) $\frac{100\%}{7}$ $14\frac{2}{7}\%$ ▶ * **22.** (29) Reduce: $\frac{4}{12}$ $\frac{1}{3}$

23. (18) What is the average of 375, 632, and 571? 526

24. (8) A regular hexagon has six sides of equal length. If a regular hexagon is made from a 36-inch-long string, what is the length of each side? 6 inches

* **25.** (30) What is the product of a number and its reciprocal? 1

* **26.** (30) How many $\frac{2}{5}$s are in 1? $\frac{5}{2}$

▶ See Math Conversations in the sidebar.

3 Written Practice

Math Conversations

Discussion opportunities are provided below.

Problem 1 Analyze

"How can a list be used to help solve this problem?" List the first few multiples of 3 beginning with 3 and list the first few multiples of 4 beginning with 4. Then subtract the fourth multiple of 3 from the third multiple of 4.

Problem 2 Model

Extend the Problem

"Describe a way to make this estimate using mental math." Sample: Since 117 is about 120, find $\frac{2}{3}$ of 120. I know that $\frac{1}{3}$ of 12 is 4, so $\frac{1}{3}$ of 120 is 40, and $\frac{2}{3}$ of 120 is 40 + 40 or 80.

Problem 6 Connect

Extend the Problem

"Does the ratio $\frac{1}{4}$ describe one hour of programming? Explain." Yes; $\frac{1}{4}$ is equivalent to $\frac{12}{48}$, and the sum of 12 and 48 is 60, the number of minutes in 1 hour.

Problem 17 Represent

Extend the Problem

"Give three different names for the obtuse angle." $\angle C$; $\angle ACB$; $\angle BCA$

Problem 22

"To reduce $\frac{4}{12}$ to simplest form using only one division, what factor should we choose? Why?" 4, which is the greatest common factor of 4 and 12. If we choose to divide by a different common factor such as 2, we must divide again.

Errors and Misconceptions

Problem 19

Encourage students who divide incorrectly to complete the division by first writing it as a fraction and canceling zeros.

(continued)

3 Written Practice (Continued)

Math Conversations

Discussion opportunities are provided below.

Problem 28 Connect

"What is a prime number?" Any counting number greater than 1 that has exactly two factors—itself and 1.

Problem 30

Extend the Problem

"One reason we rewrite $\frac{12}{4}$ as 3 is because $\frac{12}{4}$ is not in simplest form. What is another reason?" Sample: $\frac{12}{4}$ inches is not a meaningful measurement; many people quickly understand what a measurement of 3 inches represents, but cannot understand what a measurement of $\frac{12}{4}$ inches represents.

Errors and Misconceptions

Problem 27

Some students may answer 1 because they believe the equation represents an example of the Identity Property of Multiplication. Remind these students that the product of every non-zero number and 1 is that number. The product is never 1 unless the non-zero number is 1.

▸* **27.** (30) Analyze What number goes into the box to make the equation true? $\frac{8}{3}$

$$\frac{3}{8} \times \square = 1$$

▸* **28.** (19, 30) Connect What is the reciprocal of the only even prime number? $\frac{1}{2}$

29. (25) Convert $\frac{45}{10}$ to a mixed number. Remember to reduce the fraction part of the mixed number. $4\frac{1}{2}$

▸* **30.** (29) Four pennies are placed side by side as shown below. The diameter of one penny is $\frac{3}{4}$ inch. What is the length of the row of pennies? 3 inches

$\vdash \frac{3}{4}$ in. $\dashv$

Early Finishers *Real-World Application*

Fernando's class is going to make cheese sandwiches for their school picnic. They want to have at least 80 sandwiches. Each package of bread contains enough slices for 10 sandwiches. Each package of cheese contains enough slices for 18 sandwiches. The class wants to buy the fewest packages of cheese and bread with no slices left over.

a. How many sandwiches should the class make? Explain how you found your answer.

b. How many packages of bread and cheese should they buy? Show your work.

a. 90 sandwiches; To find the number of sandwiches they should make, find the least common multiple of 10 and 18.
Multiples of 10: 10, 20, 30, 40, 50, 60, 70, 80, 90, 100, . . .
Multiples of 18: 18, 36, 54, 72, 90, 108, . . .
They should make 90 sandwiches to have no left over slices.

b. Divide the number of sandwiches (90) by the number of slices. $\frac{90}{10} = 9$, $\frac{90}{18} = 5$; 9 packages of bread and 5 packages of cheese

▸ See Math Conversations in the sidebar.

Looking Forward

Finding the reciprocal of a number prepares students for:

- **Lesson 50,** dividing a whole number by a fraction.
- **Lesson 54,** dividing fractions.
- **Lesson 68,** dividing mixed numbers.
- **Lesson 70,** simplifying fraction division problems by reducing fractions before multiplying.
- **Lesson 72,** using the fractions chart to explain steps for dividing fractions.

Assessment

30–40 minutes *For use after Lesson 30*

Distribute **Cumulative Test 5** to each student. Two versions of the test are available in *Saxon Math Course 1 Course Assessments Book*. Have students complete the **Power-Up Test** first. Allow 10 minutes. Then have students work the 20 numbered items on the **Cumulative Test.** Students may use copies of the answer sheet to record their work. Track individual and class progress with the **Test Analysis** forms.

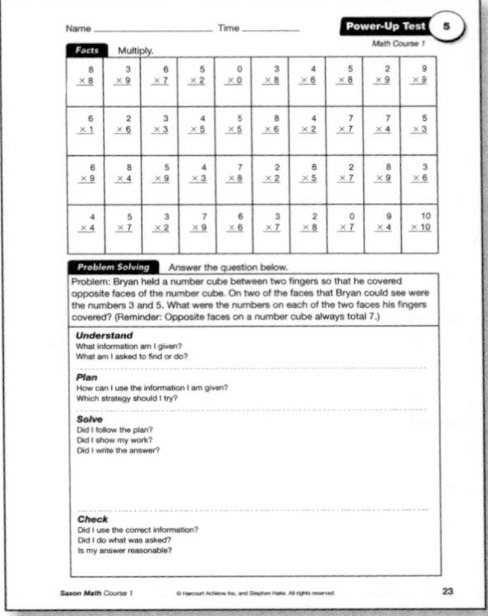

Power-Up Test 5

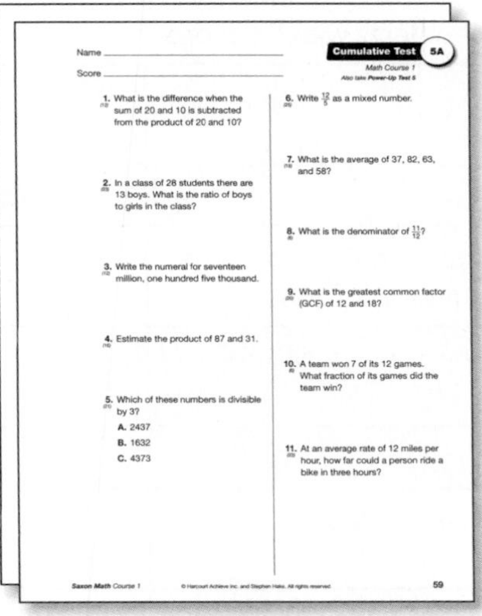

Cumulative Test 5A

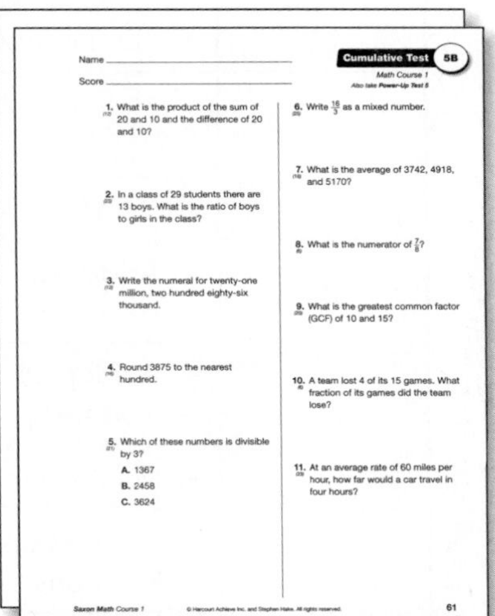

Alternative Cumulative Test 5B

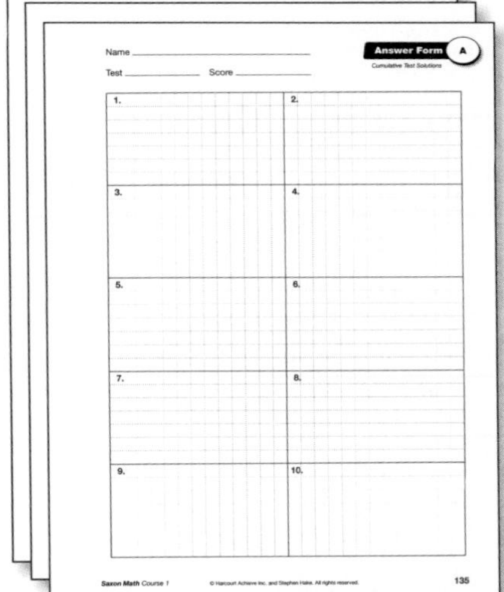

Optional Answer Forms

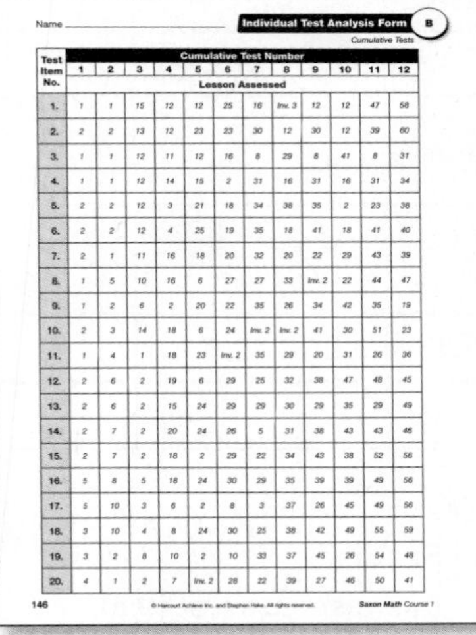

Individual Test Analysis Form

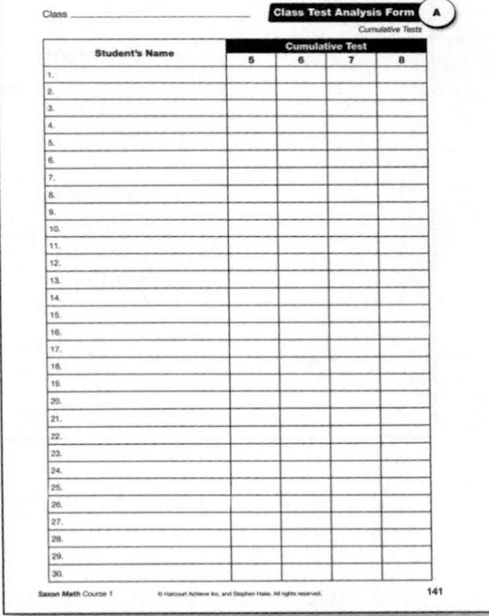

Class Test Analysis Form

Reteaching

Students who score below 80% on the assessment may be in need of reteaching. Look for the causes of student mistakes. If errors are conceptual, refer to the *Reteaching Masters* for reteaching.

Customized Benchmark Assessment

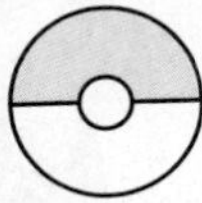

You can develop customized benchmark tests using the Test Generator located on the *Test & Practice Generator CD.*

This chart shows the lesson, the standard, and the test item question that can be found on the *Test & Practice Generator CD.*

LESSON	NEW CONCEPTS	LOCAL STANDARD	TEST ITEM ON CD
21	• Divisibility		3.21.1
22	• "Equal Groups" Problems with Fractions		3.22.1
23	• Ratio		3.23.1
	• Rate		3.23.2
24	• Adding and Subtracting Fractions That Have Common Denominators		3.24.1
25	• Writing Division Answers as Mixed Numbers		3.25.1
	• Multiples		3.25.2
26	• Using Manipulatives to Reduce Fractions		3.26.1
	• Adding and Subtracting Mixed Numbers		3.26.2
27	• Measures of a Circle		3.27.1
28	• Angles		3.28.1
29	• Multiplying Fractions		3.29.1
	• Reducing Fractions by Dividing by Common Factors		3.29.2
30	• Least Common Multiple (LCM)		3.30.1
	• Reciprocals		3.30.2

Using the Test Generator CD

- Develop tests in both English and Spanish.
- Choose from multiple-choice and free-response test items.
- Clone test items to create multiple versions of the same test.
- View and edit test items to make and save your own questions.
- Administer assessments through paper tests or over a school LAN.
- Monitor student progress through a variety of individual and class reports —for both diagnosing and assessing standards mastery.

Performance Task 5

Estimating Measurements

Assign after Lesson 30 and Test 5

Objectives

- Estimate and measure length using metric and U.S. customary systems of measurement.
- Estimate and measure the distance around a circle (circumference).
- Communicate ideas through writing.

Materials

Performance Tasks 5A and **5B**
Customary rulers/yardsticks/tape measures
Metric rulers/tape measurers

Preparation

Make a copy of **Performance Tasks 5A** and **5B.** (One each per student.)

Time Requirement

30–60 minutes; Begin in class and complete at home.

Task

Explain to students that for this task they will estimate the length of objects and then measure them to get actual measurements. They will be required to explain why they think their estimates are reasonable. They will be asked to reflect on their strategies to see if better methods of estimating could be used next time. Point out that all of the information students need is on **Performance Tasks 5A** and **5B.**

Criteria for Evidence of Learning

- Makes reasonable estimates.
- Measures the lengths of objects accurately.
- Measures distance around a circle accurately using appropriate measuring tools, such as a measuring tape.
- Communicates ideas clearly through writing.

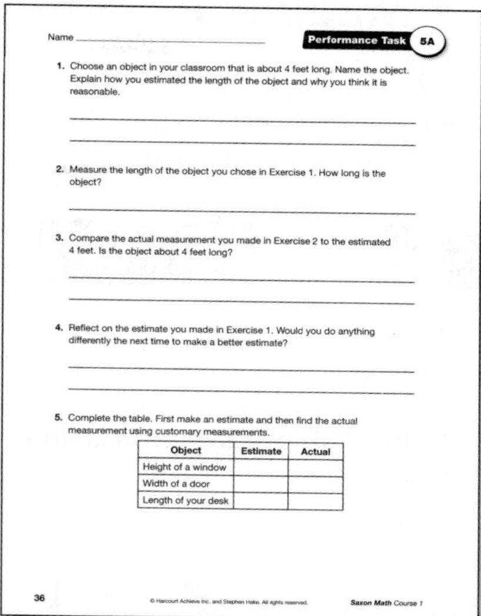

Name ______________ **Performance Task 5A**

1. Choose an object in your classroom that is about 4 feet long. Name the object. Explain how you estimated the length of the object and why you think it is reasonable.

2. Measure the length of the object you chose in Exercise 1. How long is the object?

3. Compare the actual measurement you made in Exercise 2 to the estimated 4 feet. Is the object about 4 feet long?

4. Reflect on the estimate you made in Exercise 1. Would you do anything differently the next time to make a better estimate?

5. Complete the table. First make an estimate and then find the actual measurement using customary measurements.

Object	Estimate	Actual
Height of a window		
Width of a door		
Length of your desk		

36 © Harcourt Achieve Inc. and Stephen Hake. All rights reserved. *Saxon Math* Course 1

Performance Task 5A

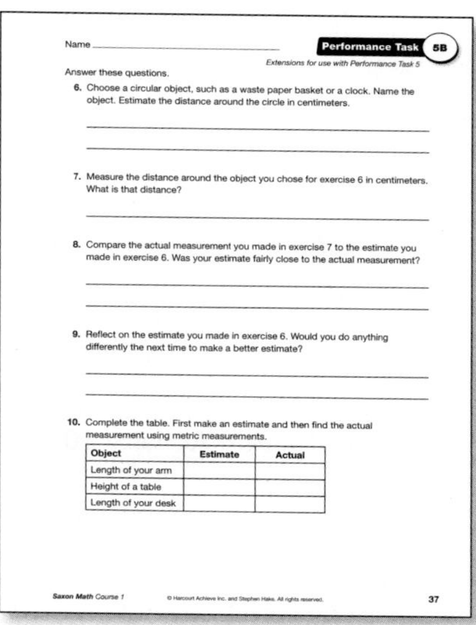

Name ______________ **Performance Task 5B**

Extensions for use with Performance Task 5

Answer these questions.

6. Choose a circular object, such as a waste paper basket or a clock. Name the object. Estimate the distance around the circle in centimeters.

7. Measure the distance around the object you chose for exercise 6 in centimeters. What is that distance?

8. Compare the actual measurement you made in exercise 7 to the estimate you made in exercise 6. Was your estimate fairly close to the actual measurement?

9. Reflect on the estimate you made in exercise 6. Would you do anything differently the next time to make a better estimate?

10. Complete the table. First make an estimate and then find the actual measurement using metric measurements.

Object	Estimate	Actual
Length of your arm		
Height of a table		
Length of your desk		

Saxon Math Course 1 © Harcourt Achieve Inc. and Stephen Hake. All rights reserved. 37

Performance Task 5B

Meeting Standards

National Council of Teachers of Mathematics (NCTM)

Numbers and Operations

NO.3c Develop and use strategies to estimate the results of rational-number computations and judge the reasonableness of the results

Measurement

ME.1a Understand both metric and customary systems of measurement

ME.1c Understand, select, and use units of appropriate size and type to measure angles, perimeter, area, surface area, and volume

Focus on

• Measuring and Drawing Angles with a Protractor

Objectives

- Use a protractor to find the measure of an angle.
- Use a protractor to draw an angle with a given measure.

Lesson Preparation

Materials

- **Investigation Activity 10** (in *Instructional Masters*)
- **Manipulative kit: protractors, rulers**

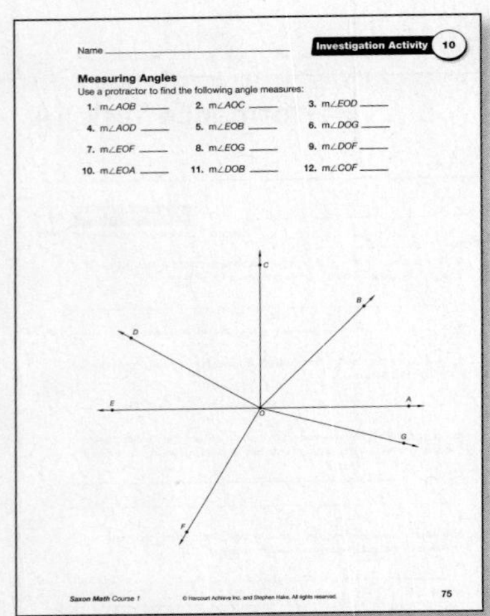

Investigation Activity 10

Math Language

New

degrees

protractor

Technology Resources

Student eBook Complete student textbook in electronic format.

Resources and Planner CD Assessment, reteaching, and instructional masters, plus a pacing calendar with standards.

Test and Practice Generator CD Create additional practice sheets and custom-made tests.

www.SaxonPublishers.com Visit for more student activities and planning materials.

Inclusion

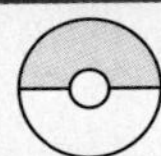

Adaptations CD Adapted lessons, investigations, practice and assessments.

Meeting Standards

National Council of Teachers of Mathematics (NCTM)

Geometry

GM.4a Draw geometric objects with specified properties, such as side lengths or angle measures

Measurement

ME.1c Understand, select, and use units of appropriate size and type to measure angles, perimeter, area, surface area, and volume

ME.2b Select and apply techniques and tools to accurately find length, area, volume, and angle measures to appropriate levels of precision

Connections

CN.4c Recognize and apply mathematics in contexts outside of mathematics

Focus on

• Measuring and Drawing Angles with a Protractor

eading Math
'e abbreviate 60 degrees as 60°.

One way to measure angles is with units called **degrees.** A full circle measures 360 degrees. A tool to help us measure angles is a **protractor.** To measure an angle, we place the center point of the protractor on the vertex of the angle, and we place one of the zero marks on one ray of the angle. Where the other ray of the angle passes through the scale, we can read the degree measure of the angle.

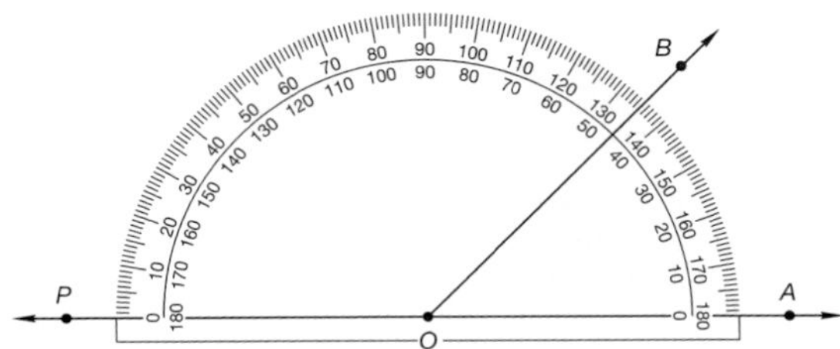

The scale on a protractor has two sets of numbers. One set is for measuring angles starting from the right side, and the other set is for measuring angles starting from the left side. The easiest way to ensure that we are reading from the correct scale is to decide whether the angle we are measuring is acute or obtuse. Looking at $\angle AOB$, we read the numbers 45° and 135°. Since the angle is less than 90° (acute), it must measure 45°, not 135°. We say that "the measure of angle *AOB* is 45°," which we may write as follows:

$$m\angle AOB = 45°$$

Classify Practice reading a protractor by finding the measures of these angles. Then tell whether each is obtuse, acute, or right.

Thinking Skill
Extend
n exercises 1 and **3,** we found $m\angle AOC$ and $m\angle AOF$. Tell how to find $m\angle COF$ without using the protractor.
We subtract $m\angle AOC$ (15°) from $m\angle AOF$ (90°) to get 75°.

▸ **1.** $\angle AOC$
15°, acute

▸ **2.** $\angle AOE$
45°, acute

▸ **3.** $\angle AOF$
90°, right

▸ **4.** $\angle AOH$
142°, obtuse

▸ **5.** $\angle IOH$
38°, acute

▸ **6.** $\angle IOE$
135°, obtuse

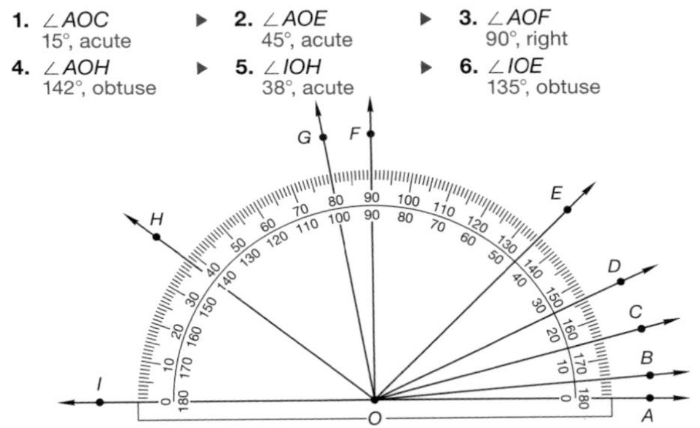

▸ See Math Conversations in the sidebar.

INVESTIGATION 3

In this investigation, students will use a protractor to measure angles and to draw angles to given measures.

Students will also use a protractor to draw a variety of triangles to given side and angle measures.

Instruction

Ask students to look at their protractors and identify the center point of the protractor, and the zero marks of the scale.

"Why does the scale of a protractor have two sets of numbers?" Sample: One set is used to measure angles that open to the right, and one set is used to measure angles that open to the left.

"What unit is used to label the measure of an angle?" degrees

Point out that the two scales of a protractor help to minimize the number of times an angle needs to be turned in order to be measured.

Math Conversations

Discussion opportunities are provided below.

Problems 1–6 Classify

Before completing the problems, ask

"In degrees, how are the measures of acute, obtuse, and right angles different?" An acute angle has a measure of less than 90°; an obtuse angle has a measure of greater than 90° and less than 180°; a right angle has a measure of exactly 90°.

(continued)

Manipulative Use

You might choose to draw several different types of angles on the board or overhead. You can then demonstrate, or invite volunteers to demonstrate, how to use a protractor to measure each angle.

Activity

Investigation Activity 10 Measuring Angles can be distributed to give students additional practice measuring angles.

Instruction

In this portion of the investigation, students will draw an angle to a given measure.

You might choose to work at the board or overhead and have students work at their desks and duplicate your actions.

"The ray we draw should be longer than half the diameter of the protractor. Why?" The ray must be long enough to reach the scale.

"After the ray is drawn we position the protractor so that it is centered on the endpoint. The ray passes through one of the 0° marks of the scale. We see two 60° marks on the scales. Which one do we use to help draw our 60° angle?" the 60° mark that makes the angle acute, and not obtuse

After students complete the drawing of the angle, ask them to label its measure as shown in the text, with a curved arrow and a degree measure.

Math Conversations

Discussion opportunities are provided below.

Problems 7–15 Represent

"What steps should we follow to draw an angle to a given measure?" Sample: Draw a ray; center the protractor; mark the degree measure with a dot; draw a second ray and label the angle.

For additional practice measuring angles, you might ask each student to correct the work of another student.

(continued)

Activity

Measuring Angles

Materials needed:

- Investigation Activity 10
- protractor

Use a protractor to find the measures of the angles.

To draw angles with a protractor, follow these steps. Begin by drawing a horizontal ray. The sketch of the ray should be longer than half the diameter of the protractor.

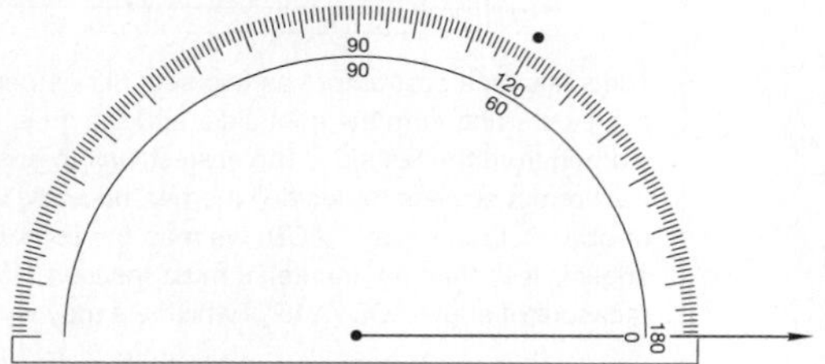

Next, position the protractor so that the center point of the protractor is on the endpoint of the ray and a zero degree mark of the protractor is on the ray.

Then, with the protractor in position, make a dot on the paper at the appropriate degree mark for the angle you intend to draw. Here we show the placement of a dot for drawing a 60° angle:

Finally, remove the protractor and draw a ray from the endpoint of the first ray through the dot you made.

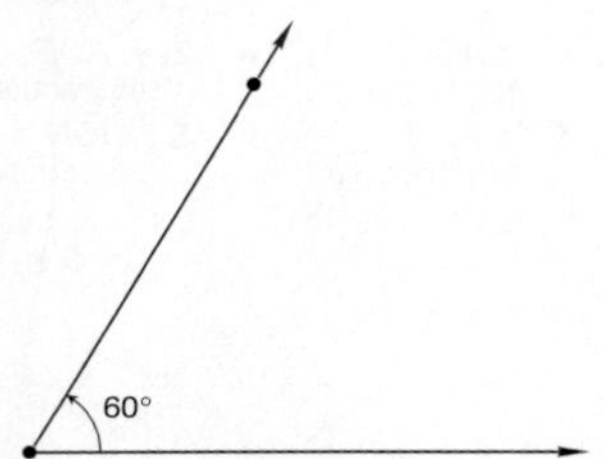

Represent Use your protractor to draw angles with these measures:

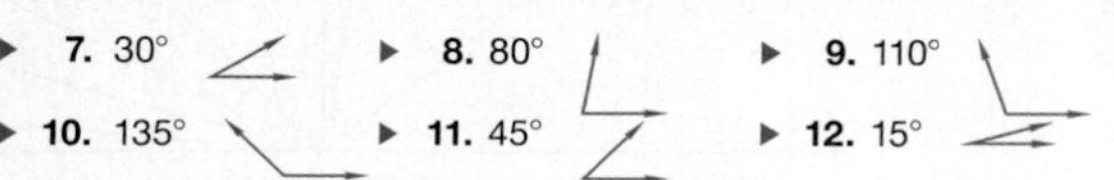

▸ See Math Conversations in the sidebar.

Math Background

The angle measure of a circle is 360°. An angle with its vertex at the center of a circle divides the 360° measure of the circle into two parts.

For example, suppose an angle with its vertex at the center of a circle has a measure of 115°. You might think of that as the "inside" measure of the angle. The "outside" measure of the angle, or in other words, measuring the angle the other way around, is 360° − 115° = 245°.

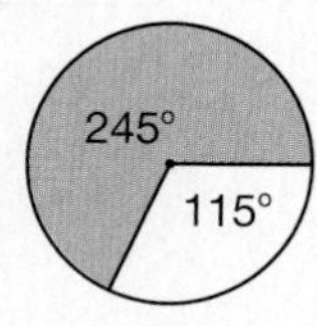

An angle whose measure is greater than 180° and less than 360° is a *reflex* angle.

▶ **13.** **Represent** Draw triangle *ABC* by first drawing segment *BC* six inches long. Then draw a 60° angle at vertex *B* and a 60° angle at vertex *C*. Extend the segments so that they intersect at point *A*. See student work.

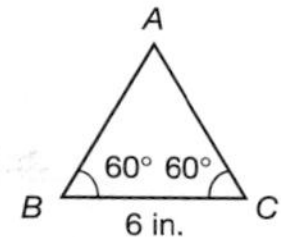

Refer to the triangle you drew in problem **13** to answer problems **14** and **15**.

▶ **14.** Use a ruler to find the lengths of segment *AB* and segment *AC* in triangle *ABC*. $AB = 6$ in.; $AC = 6$ in.

▶ **15.** Use a protractor to find the measure of angle *A* in triangle *ABC*. 60°

16. **Represent** Draw triangle *STU* by first drawing angle *S* so that angle *S* is 90° and segments *ST* and *SU* are each 10 cm long. Complete the triangle by drawing segment *TU*.
See student work.

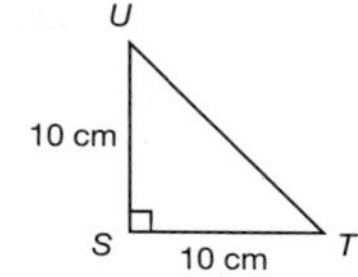

Refer to the triangle you drew in problem **16** to answer problems **17** and **18**.

17. Use a protractor to find the measures of angle *T* and angle *U*.
m $T = 45°$; m $U = 45°$

▶ **18.** **Estimate** Use a centimeter ruler to measure segment *TU* to the nearest centimeter. 14 cm

extensions

a. yes; Sample: I measured the angle of the staircase with a protractor and found that it falls within the required 30° to 35°.

b. See student work. Accept any answer that a student can support. Sample: an octagon; All of the figures in Set 1 contain at least two obtuse angles. None of the figures in Set 2 contain an obtuse angle. Since the angles in an octagon are obtuse, it fits in Set 1.

▶ **a.** **Analyze** The building code for this staircase requires that the inclination be between 30° and 35°. Does this staircase meet the building code? Explain your thinking.

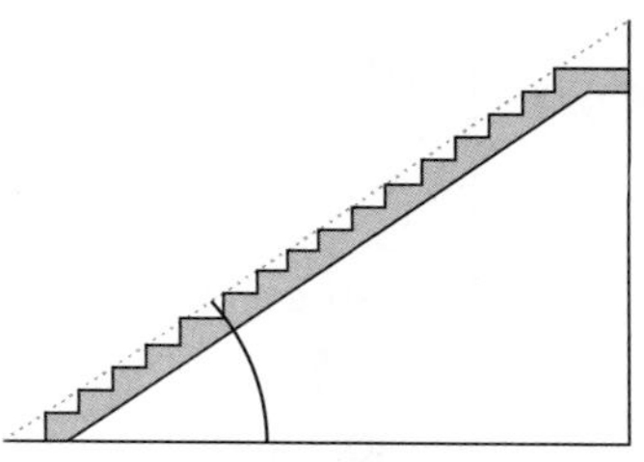

▶ **b.** **Conclude** Look at the two sets of polygons. Set 1 contains something not found in Set 2. Name another figure that would fit in Set 1. Support your choice.

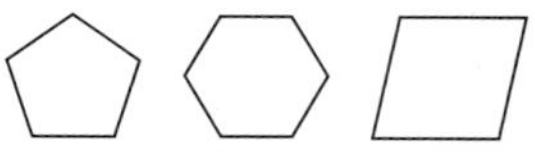

Set 1

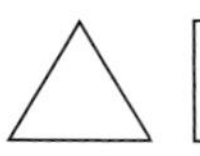
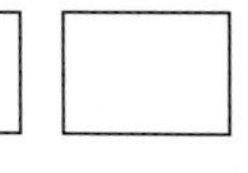

Set 2

▶ See Math Conversations in the sidebar.

Math Conversations

Discussion opportunities are provided below.

Problem 15 Represent

Extend the Problem

"What kind of triangle is triangle ABC? Explain why." Equilateral; all of the angles have the same measure and all of the sides have the same length.

Problem 18 Estimate

Extend the Problem

"What kind of triangle is triangle STU? Explain why." Right Isosceles; the triangle has a right angle and two sides the same length.

Extensions

a. **Analyze** You might choose to point out that building codes are specifications to which a building must be built. For example, a staircase that is too steep may cause injuries, so a building code will determine, among other things, the minimum and maximum rise to run ratio of a staircase. To help decide if the staircase meets the building code, students will need to measure and compare the rise to the run.

b. **Conclude** A sensible explanation must accompany each conjecture.

English Learners

Have students look at the art in **18a.** Explain that **inclination** is the degree of the angle from the floor, or base line of the drawing. Draw an angle with a greater inclination than shown in the illustration. Ask,

"Is the inclination of this angle greater or less than the angle in the student book?" greater

Looking Forward

Using a protractor to measure and draw angles prepares students for:

- **Lesson 90,** measuring turns in degrees.

Section 4 Overview

Lessons 31–40, Investigation 4

Lesson Planner

LESSON	NEW CONCEPTS	MATERIALS	RESOURCES
31	• Areas of Rectangles	Manipulative Kit: inch rulers Grid paper	**Power Up F** **Geometric Formulas poster**
32	• Expanded Notation • More on Elapsed Time	Manipulative Kit: inch rulers, protractors Demonstration analog clock	**Power Up G** **Place Value poster**
33	• Writing Percents as Fractions, Part 1	Grid paper	**Power Up G**
34	• Decimal Place Value	Manipulative Kit: inch rulers, protractors	**Power Up D** **Place Value poster**
35	• Writing Decimal Numbers as Fractions, Part 1 • Reading and Writing Decimal Numbers	Manipulative Kit: color tiles Fraction manipulatives from Investigation 2	**Power Up G** **Fraction-Decimal-Percent Equivalents poster**
36	• Subtracting Fractions and Mixed Numbers from Whole Numbers	Manipulative Kit: Overhead fraction circles Fraction manipulatives from Investigation 2	**Power Up F**
37	• Adding and Subtracting Decimal Numbers	Manipulative Kit: dot cubes Grid paper	**Power Up G**
38	• Adding and Subtracting Decimal Numbers and Whole Numbers • Squares and Square Roots	Manipulative Kit: color tiles	**Power Up A**
39	• Multiplying Decimal Numbers	Manipulative Kit: inch rulers Fraction manipulatives from Investigation 2	**Power Up G**
40	• Using Zero as a Placeholder • Circle Graphs	Fraction manipulatives from Investigation 2	**Power Up D**
Inv. 4	• Collecting, Organizing, Displaying, and Interpreting Data		

Lesson Highlights

Lessons 31–40, Investigation 4

Problem Solving

Strategies

- **Make It Simpler** Lessons 31, 36, 40
- **Use Logical Reasoning** Lessons 33, 34, 35, 37
- **Draw a Diagram** Lessons 36, 39
- **Write an Equation** Lessons 37, 40
- **Guess and Check** Lessons 31, 32, 40
- **Make an Organized List** Lessons 32, 38
- **Make a Model** Lesson 34
- **Act It Out** Lesson 38

Alternative Strategies

- **Make a Model** Lesson 39
- **Act It Out** Lesson 39

Real-World Applications

pp. 165–168, 170–173, 175–177, 180, 181, 185, 187, 189, 190, 192–195, 198, 199, 202–204, 207-211, 214, 215

4-Step Process

Teacher Edition Lessons 31–40 (Power-Up Discussions)

Communication

Discuss

pp. 165, 171, 175, 179, 188, 201, 205, 207

Explain

pp. 171, 173, 177, 194

Formulate a Problem

pp. 189, 210, 215

Connections

Math and Other Subjects

- **Math and History** pp. 172, 177, 198, 202, 208
- **Math and Geography** pp. 175, 202
- **Math and Science** pp. 167, 168, 176, 180, 189, 202
- **Math and Sports** pp. 170–173, 199, 202, 209, 211–212, 215

Math to Math

- **Problem Solving and Measurement** Lessons 31, 32, 33, 34, 35, 36, 37, 38, 39, 40, Inv. 4
- **Algebra and Problem Solving** Lessons 32, 38, 40
- **Fractions, Percents, Decimals, and Problem Solving** Lessons 31, 32, 33, 34, 35, 36, 37, 38, 39, 40, Inv. 4
- **Fractions and Measurement** Lessons 32, 33, 35, 36, 37, 39, 40
- **Measurement and Geometry** Lessons 31, 32, 33, 34, 35, 36, 37, 38, 39, 40

Representation

Manipulatives/Hands On

pp. 168, 174, 184, 188, 190, 203, 208

Model

pp. 167, 168, 172, 177, 180, 181, 185, 189, 190, 194, 208

Represent

pp. 173, 180, 181, 185, 186, 190, 192, 194, 203, 210, 212, 214

Formulate an Equation

pp. 172, 181, 186, 198, 208

Technology

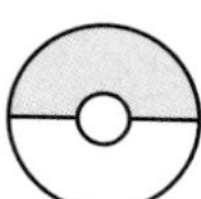

Student Resources

- **eBook**
- **Online Resources** at **www.SaxonPublishers.com/ActivitiesC1**
  - **Online Activities**
  - **Math Enrichment Problems**
  - **Math Stumpers**

Teacher Resources

- **Resources and Planner CD**
- **Adaptations CD** Lessons 31–40
- **Test & Practice Generator CD**
- **eGradebook**
- **Answer Key CD**

Content Highlights

Lessons 31–40, Investigation 4

In this section, students continue to focus on concepts and skills involving fractions. Area of rectangles, expanded notation, and elapsed time are reviewed.

Proportional Thinking

In this text, 50% of the lessons teach a concept and/or a skill involving fractions, decimals, ratios, proportions, or percents.

A major goal of middle-school mathematics is to develop within students a facility with rational numbers expressed as fractions, decimals, and percents. We emphasize the decimal form of rational numbers in this section of lessons. After a review of our base-ten number system in Lesson 32, students extend the system to decimal place value in Lesson 34, reading and writing decimal numbers in Lesson 35, and operations with decimal numbers including adding, subtracting, and multiplying in Lessons 37–40.

Equivalence

Students learn to represent numbers in a variety of forms.

Students should be able to shift easily between different forms of rational numbers. We introduce conversions from percents to fractions in Lesson 33 and decimals to fractions in Lesson 35. Converting between forms will be continued in later lessons.

Perimeter and Area

The concepts of perimeter and area are compared.

The concept of area is essential to secondary mathematics and is necessary consumer knowledge due to its real-world applications. The concept is introduced in Lesson 31. Finding the area of a rectangle is practiced throughout this section of lessons.

Data and Statistics

Students collect and organize data for a variety of situations.

Statistics is the topic in Lesson 40 and Investigation 4. Students are introduced to circle graphs and they collect quantitative and qualitative data in the investigation that they will display in the following investigation.

Assessment

A variety of weekly assessment tools are provided.

After Lesson 35:
- Power-Up Test 6
- Cumulative Test 6
- Performance Activity 6

After Lesson 40:
- Power-Up Test 7
- Cumulative Test 7
- Customized Benchmark Test
- Performance Task 7

Content Trace

Lessons 31–40, Investigation 4

LESSON	NEW CONCEPTS	PRACTICED	ASSESSED
31	• Areas of Rectangles	Lessons 31, 32, 33, 34, 35, 36, 37, 39, 40, 41, 42, 46, 48, 49, 50, 54, 57, 63, 64, 67, 68, 70, 73, 75, 77, 85, 103, 104, 105, 106, 107	Tests 7, 8, 9, 11, 12, 13, 14
32	• Expanded Notation	Lessons 32, 33, 34, 35, 36, 38, 39, 40, 44, 55, 83, 98	Test 7
	• More on Elapsed Time	Lessons 32, 33, 34, 35, 37, 39, 40, 42, 44, 48, 53, 55, 59, 61, 63, 68, 71, 75, 77, 81, 83, 84, 85, 86, 90, 91, 97	Test 8
33	• Writing Percents as Fractions, Part 1	Lessons 33, 34, 35, 36, 37, 38, 40, 43, 44, 45, 46, 47, 48, 52, 53, 54, 56, 57, 58, 63, 64, 65, 67, 68, 69, 71, 75, 81, 82, 84, 88, 100	Tests 7, 8
34	• Decimal Place Value	Lessons 34, 35, 36, 38, 39, 42, 46, 50, 53, 57, 61, 75, 84	Tests 7, 8, 9, 12, 14
35	• Writing Decimal Numbers as Fractions, Part 1	Lessons 35, 36, 37, 38, 39, 45, 51, 87, 89, 94, 105	Test 7
	• Reading and Writing Decimal Numbers	Lessons 35, 36, 37, 38, 39, 43, 44, 45, 49, 82, 87, 89, 94, 105, 117	Tests 7, 8, 9, 10, 11
36	• Subtracting Fractions and Mixed Numbers from Whole Numbers	Lessons 36, 37, 38, 39, 40, 42, 48, 54, 56, 57, 59, 68, 70, 71, 73, 74, 77, 81, 86, 87	Test 12
37	• Adding and Subtracting Decimal Numbers	Lessons 37, 38, 39, 40, 41, 42, 43, 44, 45, 46, 48, 49, 50, 51, 83, 115, 119	Tests 8, 19, 22
38	• Adding and Subtracting Decimal Numbers and Whole Numbers	Lessons 38, 39, 42, 49, 50, 53, 55, 57, 61, 63, 65, 68, 70, 73, 74, 75, 79, 83, 85, 87, 92, 95, 97, 100, 102, 107, 108, 108, 110, 120	Tests 8, 9, 10, 12, 13, 16, 23
	• Squares and Square Roots	Lessons 38, 39, 40, 41, 42, 43, 45, 46, 47, 49, 51, 52, 57, 58, 59, 60, 61, 62, 64, 65, 66, 67, 68, 69, 70, 71, 72, 76, 78, 79, 81, 82, 84, 86, 87, 95, 101, 103, 119, 120	Tests 8, 9, 11, 14, 16, 18
39	• Multiplying Decimal Numbers	Lessons 39, 40, 41, 43, 44, 45, 46, 48, 49, 50, 51, 52, 55, 56, 58, 59, 62, 63, 64, 66, 67, 70, 71, 72, 75, 76, 79, 81, 83, 85, 92, 96, 100, 101, 105, 113, 117	Tests 8, 9, 10, 11, 12, 13, 14, 15, 18
40	• Using Zero as a Placeholder	Lessons 40, 42, 43, 45, 46, 47, 48, 49, 50, 51, 53, 54, 59, 60, 62	Tests 9, 10, 12, 13, 14, 15, 17, 18, 19, 21
	• Circle Graphs	Lessons 40, 62, Investigation 4, 9	Test & Practice Generator
Inv. 4	• Collecting, Organizing, Displaying, and Interpreting Data	Investigation 4, Lessons 51, 56, 57, 62, 66, 80, 86, 89	Test & Practice Generator

• Areas of Rectangles

Objectives

- Identify square units as the units used to measure area.
- Multiply length by width to find the area of a rectangle.
- Find the side length and the perimeter of a square when the area of the square is known.

Lesson Preparation

Materials

- **Power Up F** (in *Instructional Masters*)
- **Manipulative kit: inch rulers**

Optional

- **Teacher-provided material: centimeter grid paper**
- **Geometric Formulas poster**

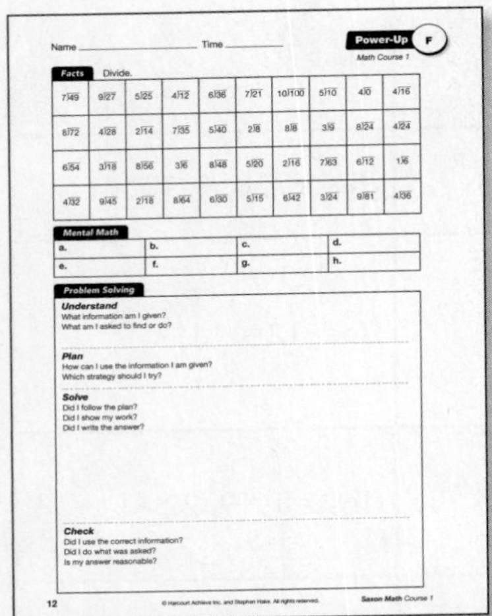

Power Up F

Math Language

New	Maintain	English Learners (ESL)
area	perimeter	mixed numbers

Technology Resources

Student eBook Complete student textbook in electronic format.

Resources and Planner CD Assessment, reteaching, and instructional masters, plus a pacing calendar with standards.

Test and Practice Generator CD Create additional practice sheets and custom-made tests.

www.SaxonPublishers.com Visit for more student activities and planning materials.

Inclusion

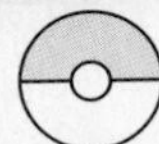

Adaptations CD Adapted lessons, investigations, practice and assessments.

Meeting Standards

National Council of Teachers of Mathematics (NCTM)

Geometry

GM.4d Use geometric models to represent and explain numerical and algebraic relationships

GM.4e Recognize and apply geometric ideas and relationships in areas outside the mathematics classroom, such as art, science, and everyday life

Measurement

ME.1c Understand, select, and use units of appropriate size and type to measure angles, perimeter, area, surface area, and volume

ME.2c Develop and use formulas to determine the circumference of circles and the area of triangles, parallelograms, trapezoids, and circles and develop strategies to find the area of more-complex shapes

Power-Up Discussion *For use with Power Up, p. 164*

Problem-Solving Strategy: Make It Simpler/ Guess and Check

Franki has 7 coins in her hand totaling 50¢. What are the coins?

Understand ***Understand the problem.***

"What information are we given?"

Franki has 7 coins. The sum of the coins is 50¢.

"What are we asked to do?"

We are asked to determine which coins are in Franki's hand.

Plan ***Make a plan.***

"What problem-solving strategy will we use?"

We will *make it simpler* and *guess and check* to find Franki's coins. We can break the problem into smaller parts by thinking of coins Franki does not have and then trying to determine the other coins that would reach the total of 50¢.

Solve ***Carry out the plan.***

"Does Franki have any half-dollars?"

No, because then she would only have one coin.

"Does she have any pennies?"

No, because she would have to have at least five pennies, which leaves only two coins to equal 45¢. No two coins total 45¢.

"Can Franki have any coin combinations that include quarters?"

No. She cannot make a 25¢ combination using 6 dimes and nickels.

"Now that we've narrowed down our coin choices to nickels and dimes, how can we begin to guess and check for the solution?"

We know a dime is worth 10¢ and a nickel is worth 5¢. Because we are trying to find a sum of 50¢, we must use an even number of nickels. If we start with two nickels, we'd need 4 dimes. We know this is not the correct answer because we are looking for 7 coins and that combination would give us only six. If we have 4 nickels, we would need 3 dimes. This combination equals 7 coins.

Check ***Look back.***

"Did we answer the question that was asked?"

Yes. We determined the combination of 3 dimes and 4 nickels equals 50¢ and 7 coins.

1 Power Up

Facts

Distribute **Power Up F** to students. See answers below.

Mental Math

Before students begin the Mental Math exercise, do this counting exercise as a class.

Count up and down by $\frac{1}{8}$s between $\frac{1}{8}$ and 2.

Encourage students to share different ways to mentally compute these exercises. Strategies for exercises **c** and **f** are listed below.

c. Change 28 to 30, then Subtract 2

$30 + 29 = 59$; $59 - 2 = 57$

Add 2 and Add 1, then Subtract 3

$28 + 2 = 30$ and $29 + 1 = 30$;

$30 + 30 - 3 = 60 - 3 = 57$

f. Shift the Decimal Points One Place

$600 \div 10 = 60 \div 1 = 60$

Cancel Zeros

$\frac{600}{10} = \frac{60\not{0}}{1\not{0}} = \frac{60}{1} = 60$

Problem Solving

Refer to **Power-Up Discussion,** p. 164F.

2 New Concepts

Instruction

Questions having real-world connections can help students understand how perimeter and area are different concepts.

"Suppose a person walks once around a city block each morning for exercise. Is the distance around the block a measure of its perimeter or a measure of its area?" perimeter

"Suppose a homeowner wants to replace the wall-to-wall carpeting in a room. Is the amount of carpeting that will be needed a measure of the perimeter of the floor or a measure of the area of the floor?" area

Encourage students to share other real-world examples of perimeter and area.

(continued)

LESSON 31

• Areas of Rectangles

Power Up *Building Power*

facts Power Up F

mental math

a. Number Sense: 4×25 100

b. Calculation: 6×37 222

c. Number Sense: $28 + 29$ 57

d. Money: $6.25 + $2.50 $8.75

e. Fractional Parts: $\frac{1}{3}$ of 63 21

f. Number Sense: $\frac{600}{10}$ 60

g. Measurement: A minute is how many seconds? 60 seconds

h. Calculation: 10×10, $- 20$, $+ 1$, $\div 9$, $\times 2$, $\div 3$, $\times 5$, $+ 2$, $\div 4$ 8

problem solving Franki has 7 coins in her hand totaling 50¢. What are the coins? 4 nickels and 3 dimes

New Concept *Increasing Knowledge*

Mr. McGregor fenced in an area for a garden.

The perimeter of a shape is the distance around it.

The number of feet of fencing he used was the perimeter of the rectangle. But how do we measure the size of the garden?

To measure the size of the garden, we measure how much surface is enclosed by the sides of a shape. When we measure the "inside" of a flat shape, we are measuring its **area.**

The area of a shape is the amount of surface enclosed by its sides.

We use a different kind of unit to measure area than we use to measure perimeter. To measure perimeter, we use units of length such as centimeters. Units of area are called **square units.** One example is a square centimeter.

This is 1 centimeter. This is 1 square centimeter.

Facts Divide.

7 7)49	3 9)27	5 5)25	3 4)12	6 6)36	3 7)21	10 10)100	2 5)10	0 4)0	4 4)16
9 8)72	7 4)28	7 2)14	5 7)35	8 5)40	4 2)8	1 8)8	3 3)9	3 8)24	6 4)24
9 6)54	6 3)18	7 8)56	2 3)6	6 8)48	4 5)20	8 2)16	9 7)63	2 6)12	6 1)6
8 4)32	5 9)45	9 2)18	8 8)64	5 6)30	3 5)15	7 6)42	8 3)24	9 9)81	9 4)36

Math Language
We use "sq." to abbreviate the word *square*.

Other common units of area are square inches, square feet, square yards, and square meters. Very large areas may be measured in square miles. We can think of units of area as floor tiles. The area of a shape is the number of "floor tiles" of a certain size that completely cover the shape.

Example 1

How many floor tiles, 1 foot on each side, are needed to cover the floor of a room that is 8 feet wide and 12 feet long?

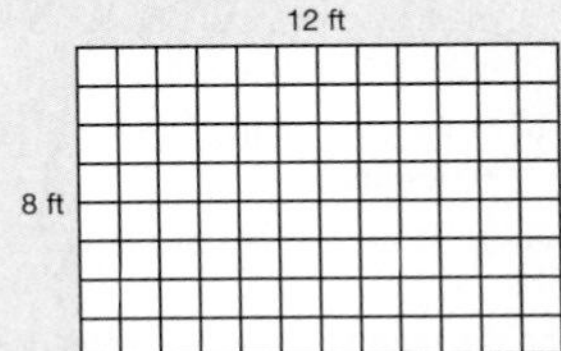

Solution

The surface of the floor is covered with tiles. By answering this question, we are finding the area of the room in square feet. We could count the tiles, but a faster way to find the number of tiles is to multiply. There are 8 rows of tiles with 12 tiles in each row.

$$\begin{array}{r} 12 \text{ tiles in each row} \\ \times \; 8 \text{ rows} \\ \hline 96 \text{ tiles} \end{array}$$

To cover the floor, **96 tiles** are needed. The area of the room is 96 sq. ft.

Discuss Why do we use square feet as the unit of measure? Each tile is one foot long on each side.

Example 2

What is the area of this rectangle?

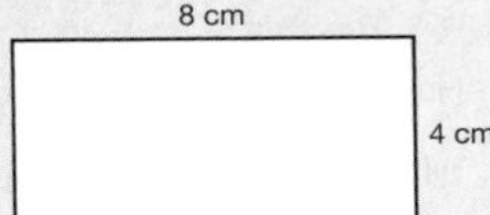

Solution

The diagram shows the length and width of the rectangle in centimeters. Therefore, we will use square centimeters to measure the area of the rectangle. We calculate the number of square-centimeter tiles needed to cover the rectangle by multiplying the length by the width.

Length × width = area

8 cm × 4 cm = **32 sq. cm**

2 New Concepts (Continued)

Example 1

Instruction

The scenario assumes there is no space between tiles.

Example 2

Instruction

To transition from example 1 to example 2, have students draw an 8 cm by 4 cm rectangle on centimeter grid paper.

As they work, remind students that each unit square has an area of one square centimeter, and each side of each unit square has a length of one centimeter.

Ask students to determine the area of the rectangle (32 square centimeters), then count the number of unit squares enclosed by the rectangle to check their answer.

(continued)

Teacher Tip

When students work with squares, a common misconception is that the **area of a square** doubles if each of its dimensions is doubled.

To explore this misconception, invite students to draw and label a square, and draw and label a square having sides twice the length. By comparing the lesser perimeter to the greater, and comparing the lesser area to the greater, students should conclude that the perimeter doubles and the area quadruples.

2 New Concepts (Continued)

Instruction

You may wish to display the **Geometric Formulas** concept poster at this time.

Example 3

After completing the example, present the following challenge.

"Describe a square whose perimeter and area are represented by the same number." A square having sides of 4 units has a perimeter of 16 units and an area of 16 square units.

Practice Set

Problem e Analyze

For problem **e**, students can check their work by answering the question.

"What number times itself is 25?" 5

Problem g Analyze

Remind students to label their answers as units or square units when solving perimeter and area problems. Point out that answers without labels have no meaning.

Problem h Analyze

Students should generalize that it is possible, but not practical, to express the area of a room in square inches or in square miles. Expressing the area in square inches typically results in a large whole number, such as one having five digits. Expressing the area in square miles results in a very small decimal number, such as one with its first significant digit in the millionths place.

Expressing the area of a room in square feet results in a number that is more easily managed and understood.

Example 3

The area of a square is 100 square inches.

a. How long is each side of the square?

b. What is the perimeter of the square?

Solution

a. The length and width of a square are equal. So we think, "What number multiplied by itself equals 100?" Since $10 \times 10 = 100$, we find that each side is **10 inches** long.

b. Since each of the four sides is 10 inches, the perimeter of the square is **40 inches.**

Justify Why can't we divide 100 by 4 to find the length of each side?

Dividing 100 by 4 would give the length of each side if the *perimeter* were 100, but then the area would be 625 (25×25). In this example, the *area* is 100, so we search for a number that results in 100 when multiplied by itself. That number is 10.

Practice Set Find the number of square units needed to cover the area of these rectangles. For reference, square units have been drawn along the length and width of each rectangle.

a.

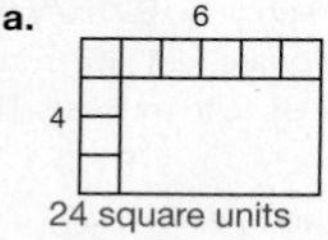

24 square units

b.

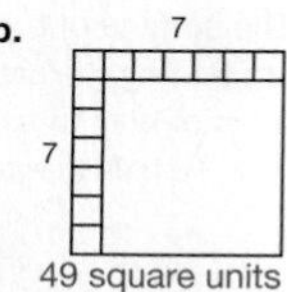

49 square units

Find the area of these rectangles:

c.

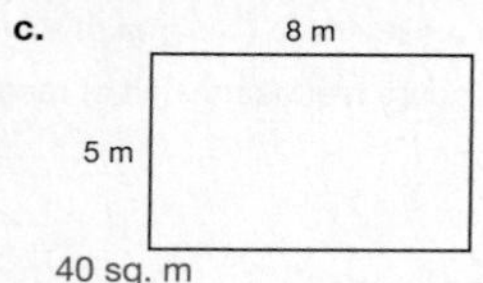

40 sq. m

d.

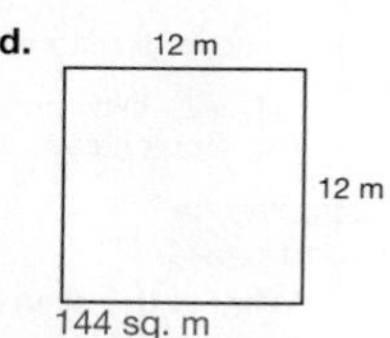

144 sq. m

Analyze The area of a square is 25 square inches.

▶ **e.** How long is each side of the square? 5 inches

f. What is the perimeter of the square? 20 inches

▶ **g.** *Analyze* Find the area of Mr. McGregor's garden described at the beginning of this lesson. 800 sq. ft

▶ **h.** *Analyze* Choose the appropriate unit for the area of a room in a home.

A square inches **B** square feet **C** square miles

B

▶ See Math Conversations in the sidebar.

Written Practice *Strengthening Concepts*

▶ 1. (12, 25) **Analyze** When the third multiple of 4 is divided by the fourth multiple of 3, what is the quotient? 1

2. (12) The distance the Earth travels around the Sun each year is about five hundred eighty million miles. Use digits to write that distance. 580,000,000 miles

3. (25) Convert $\frac{10}{3}$ to a mixed number. $3\frac{1}{3}$

▶ * 4. (31) **Generalize** How many square stickers with sides 1 centimeter long would be needed to cover the rectangle below? 8 square stickers

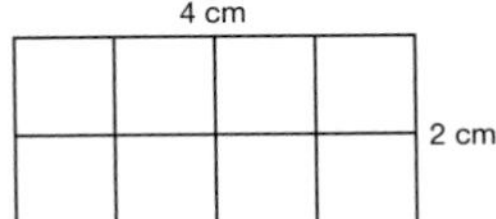

* 5. (31) How many floor tiles with sides 1 foot long would be needed to cover the square below? 100 tiles

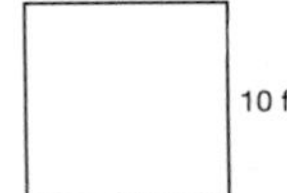

* 6. (31) What is the area of a rectangle 12 inches long and 8 inches wide? 96 square inches

▶ 7. (10) **Generalize** Describe the rule for this sequence. What is the next term?

1, 4, 9, 16, 25, 36, ...

7. Sample: 1. Add the next odd number (+3, +5, +7, +9, etc.). 2. Multiply the number of the term by itself (1 × 1, 2 × 2, 3 × 3, 4 × 4, etc.). The next term is 49.

8. (22) **Model** What number is $\frac{2}{3}$ of 24? Draw a diagram to illustrate the problem. 16

8. 24; $\frac{2}{3}$ of 24: 8, 8; $\frac{1}{3}$ of 24: 8

9. (3) Find the unknown number. Remember to check your work. 18

$$24 + f = 42$$

Write each answer in simplest form:

10. (24) $\frac{1}{8} + \frac{1}{8}$ $\frac{1}{4}$

11. (24) $\frac{5}{6} - \frac{1}{6}$ $\frac{2}{3}$

* 12. (29) $\frac{2}{3} \cdot \frac{1}{2}$ $\frac{1}{3}$

▶* 13. (29) $\frac{2}{3} \times 5$ $3\frac{1}{3}$

14. (16) Estimate the product of 387 and 514. 200,000

15. (2) \$20.00 ÷ 10 \$2.00

16. (2) (63)47¢ \$29.61

17. (2) 4623 ÷ 22 210 R 3

▶* 18. (19, 30) What is the reciprocal of the smallest odd prime number? $\frac{1}{3}$

* 19. (26) Two thirds of a circle is what percent of a circle? $66\frac{2}{3}\%$

▶ See Math Conversations in the sidebar.

English Learners

Explain that a **mixed number** is a number made up of a whole number and a fraction. Write $\frac{10}{3}$ on the board and work through the problem while you say:

"In problem number 3, you are asked to convert the fraction $\frac{10}{3}$ to a mixed number. Since the denominator lets us know how many parts a whole is made up of, we can divide the numerator (10—number of parts) by the denominator (3) and get the mixed number that $\frac{10}{3}$ represents ($3\frac{1}{3}$)."

Ask for volunteers to explain why they think we might prefer to use mixed numbers instead of improper fractions. Answers will vary.

3 Written Practice

Math Conversations

Discussion opportunities are provided below.

Problem 1 **Analyze**

"What is the first multiple of any whole number greater than 1?" the number itself

Problem 4 **Generalize**

"How can multiplication be used to find the area of any rectangle?" Multiply its length (l) by its width (w) or its base (b) by its height (h); $A = lw$ or $A = bh$.

Problem 7 **Generalize**

Extend the Problem

"How can mental math be used to find the twelfth term of this sequence?" Sample: Multiply the number of the term of the sequence by itself. For example, the fifth term is 5 × 5 or 25. The sixth term is 6 × 6 or 36, and so on. The twelfth term is 12 × 12 or 144.

Errors and Misconceptions

Problem 13

If students find the product without rewriting 5 as $\frac{5}{1}$, they must remember that 5 represents the numerator of a fraction, and the product of the numerators of the factors is 2 × 5 or 10.

Problem 18

A common error students make is to choose 1 as the smallest odd prime number. Remind students that a prime number is a counting number that is greater than 1, and whose only two factors are the number 1 and itself.

"What are the first five prime numbers?" 2, 3, 5, 7, 11

(continued)

3 Written Practice (Continued)

Math Conversations

Discussion opportunities are provided below.

Problem 20 Estimate

"What operation can be used to solve this problem? Explain." Subtraction; subtract a number from 100 or 100 from a number.

"How could a number line be used to solve this problem?" Measure a number's distance from zero by counting, then compare distances.

Problem 23 Connect

Extend the Problem

"What fraction of the players do not play outfield? Describe two different ways to find the answer." Find the fraction of 9 players that 9 − 3 or 6 players represent, or subtract $\frac{1}{3}$ from 1; $\frac{2}{3}$ of the players do not play outfield.

Problem 30 Extend

Extend the Problem

Challenge students to describe different ways to estimate the area without using formal measuring tools such as yardsticks, metersticks, or tape measures. Sample: Estimate the length of a pace and count the number of paces that are required to walk the length and the width of the room. Multiply the estimate by the number of paces for each dimension, then use that information to compute the area. If available, use the ceiling tiles visible in the room.

▶ **20.** (9) **Estimate** Which of these numbers is closest to 100? D

A 90 B 89 C 111 D 109

21. (12) For most of its orbit, Pluto is the farthest planet from the Sun in our solar system. Pluto's average distance from the Sun is about three billion, six hundred seventy million miles. Use digits to write the average distance between Pluto and the Sun. 3,670,000,000 miles

* **22.** (23, 27) The diameter of the pizza was 14 inches. What was the ratio of the radius to the diameter of the pizza? $\frac{1}{2}$

▶* **23.** (29) Three of the nine softball players play outfield. What fraction of the players play outfield? Write the answer as a reduced fraction. $\frac{1}{3}$

24. (17) Use an inch ruler to find the length of the line segment below. $2\frac{5}{8}$ in.

* **25.** (29) $\frac{3}{10} \times \frac{3}{10}$ $\frac{9}{100}$

* **26.** (30) How many $\frac{3}{4}$s are in 1? $\frac{4}{3}$

* **27.** (29) Write a fraction equal to 1 with a denominator of 8. $\frac{8}{8}$

28. (22) **Model** Five sixths of the 24 students in the class scored 80% or higher on the test. How many students scored 80% or higher? Draw a diagram to illustrate the problem. 20 students

28.

24 students
4 students
4 students
4 students
4 students
4 students
4 students

$\frac{5}{6}$ scored 80% or higher.

$\frac{1}{6}$ did not score 80% or higher.

* **29.** (28) **a.** Name an angle in the figure at right that measures less than 90°. ∠PMQ or ∠QMP

b. Name an obtuse angle in the figure at right. ∠RMQ or ∠QMR

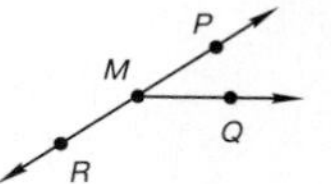

▶* **30.** (31) **Evaluate** Using a ruler, how could you calculate the floor area of your classroom? See student work. Sample: If the room is rectangular, first measure the length of the room and the width of the room. Then multiply the length by the width to calculate the floor area of the room.

▶ See Math Conversations in the sidebar.

Looking Forward

Finding the area of a rectangle in square units and finding the length of a side and the perimeter of a square when the area is known prepare students for:

- **Investigation 6,** finding the surface area of a cube and a rectangular prism.
- **Investigation 7,** using a coordinate plane to graph the vertices of a rectangle and find its perimeter and area.
- **Lessons 71 and 79,** finding the area of a parallelogram and a triangle.
- **Lesson 82,** finding the volume of a rectangular prism.
- **Lesson 107,** finding the area of complex shapes by dividing a shape into two rectangles.

• Expanded Notation
• More on Elapsed Time

Objectives

- Write a number in expanded notation.
- Use standard notation to write a number expressed in expanded notation.
- Rename units of time to solve an elapsed-time problem.
- Use mental or pencil-and-paper calculation to solve an elapsed-time problem.

Lesson Preparation

Materials

- **Power Up G** (in *Instructional Masters*)
- **Manipulative kit: inch rulers, protractors**

Optional

- **Teacher-provided material: demonstration clock**
- **Place Value poster**

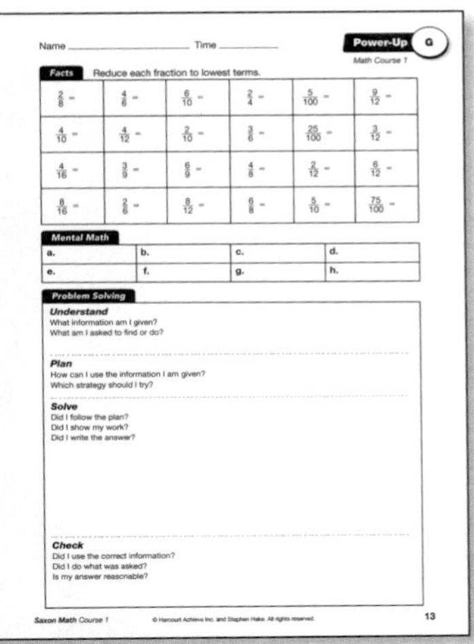

Power Up G

Math Language

New	English Learners (ESL)
a.m.	compare
expanded notation	
p.m.	

Technology Resources

Student eBook Complete student textbook in electronic format.

Resources and Planner CD Assessment, reteaching, and instructional masters, plus a pacing calendar with standards.

Test and Practice Generator CD Create additional practice sheets and custom-made tests.

www.SaxonPublishers.com Visit for more student activities and planning materials.

Inclusion

Adaptations CD Adapted lessons, investigations, practice and assessments.

Meeting Standards

National Council of Teachers of Mathematics (NCTM)

Numbers and Operations

NO.1e Develop an understanding of large numbers and recognize and appropriately use exponential, scientific, and calculator notation

Problem Solving

PS.1b Solve problems that arise in mathematics and in other contexts

Representation

RE.5a Create and use representations to organize, record, and communicate mathematical ideas

Power-Up Discussion For use with Power Up, p. 169

Problem-Solving Strategy: Guess and Check/Make an Organized List

The product of $10 \times 10 \times 10$ is 1000. Find three prime numbers whose product is 1001.

Understand **Understand the problem.**

"What information are we given?"

The product of $10 \times 10 \times 10 = 1000$.

"What are we asked to do?"

We are asked to find three prime numbers whose product is 1001.

"What do we know about prime numbers?"

A prime number is divisible only by 1 and itself.

"What can we guess about the three numbers?"

Since we know $10 \times 10 \times 10 = 1000$, we guess our numbers will be close to 10.

Plan **Make a plan.**

"What problem-solving strategies could we use?"

We will *make an organized list* of prime numbers and *guess and check* groups of three factors from the list.

Solve **Carry out the plan.**

"What are the first 10 prime numbers?"

2, 3, 5, 7, 11, 13, 17, 19, 23, 29, ...

"Which three prime numbers are closest to 10?"

7, 11, and 13

"Why are 7, 11, and 13 a good guess?"

The product of 7, 11, and 13 will have a 1 in the ones place.

"What is the product of 7, 11, and 13?"

The product of $7 \times 11 \times 13 = 1001$. The three prime numbers we are looking for are 7, 11, and 13.

Check **Look back.**

"Did we do what we were asked to do?"

Yes. We found three prime numbers whose product is 1001.

"Is our solution expected?"

Yes. We made an educated guess and our first guess worked.

LESSON 32

• Expanded Notation
• More on Elapsed Time

Power Up — *Building Power*

facts Power Up G

mental math

a. **Number Sense:** 4 × 75 300

b. **Number Sense:** 380 + 1200 1580

c. **Number Sense:** 54 + 19 73

d. **Money:** $8.00 − $1.50 $6.50

e. **Fractional Parts:** $\frac{1}{2}$ of 240 120

f. **Number Sense:** $\frac{600}{100}$ 6

g. **Geometry:** A square has a length of 4 ft. What is the area of the square? 16 square feet

h. **Calculation:** 12 × 3, − 1, ÷ 5, × 2, + 1, ÷ 3, × 2 10

problem solving The product of 10 × 10 × 10 is 1000. Find three prime numbers whose product is 1001. 7, 11, 13

New Concepts — *Increasing Knowledge*

expanded notation

The price of a new car is $27,000. The price of a house is $270,000. Which price is more, or are the prices the same? How do you know?

Recall that in our number system the location of a digit in a number has a value called its *place value.* Consider the value of the 2 in these two numbers:

27,000 270,000

In 27,000 the value of the 2 is 2 × 10,000. In 270,000 the value of the 2 is 2 × 100,000. Therefore, $270,000 is greater than $27,000.

To find a digit's value within a number, we multiply the digit by the value of the place occupied by the digit. To write a number in **expanded notation,** we write each nonzero digit times its place value.

Example 1

Write 27,000 in expanded notation.

Solution

The 2 is in the ten-thousands place, and the 7 is in the thousands place. In expanded notation we write

(2 × 10,000) + (7 × 1000)

Since zero times any number equals zero, it is not necessary to include zeros when writing numbers in expanded notation.

Facts Reduce each fraction to lowest terms.

$\frac{2}{8} = \frac{1}{4}$	$\frac{4}{6} = \frac{2}{3}$	$\frac{6}{10} = \frac{3}{5}$	$\frac{2}{4} = \frac{1}{2}$	$\frac{5}{100} = \frac{1}{20}$	$\frac{9}{12} = \frac{3}{4}$
$\frac{4}{10} = \frac{2}{5}$	$\frac{4}{12} = \frac{1}{3}$	$\frac{2}{10} = \frac{1}{5}$	$\frac{3}{6} = \frac{1}{2}$	$\frac{25}{100} = \frac{1}{4}$	$\frac{3}{12} = \frac{1}{4}$
$\frac{4}{16} = \frac{1}{4}$	$\frac{3}{9} = \frac{1}{3}$	$\frac{6}{9} = \frac{2}{3}$	$\frac{4}{8} = \frac{1}{2}$	$\frac{2}{12} = \frac{1}{6}$	$\frac{6}{12} = \frac{1}{2}$
$\frac{8}{16} = \frac{1}{2}$	$\frac{2}{6} = \frac{1}{3}$	$\frac{8}{12} = \frac{2}{3}$	$\frac{6}{8} = \frac{3}{4}$	$\frac{5}{10} = \frac{1}{2}$	$\frac{75}{100} = \frac{3}{4}$

1 Power Up

Facts

Distribute **Power Up G** to students. See answers below.

Mental Math

Before students begin the Mental Math exercise, do this counting exercise as a class.

Count up and down by 25s between 25 and 400.

Encourage students to share different ways to mentally compute these exercises. Strategies for exercises **d** and **e** are listed below.

d. Subtract $1.00, then Subtract $0.50
$8.00 − $1.00 = $7.00; $7.00 − $0.50 = $6.50
Subtract $2.00, then Add $0.50
$8.00 − $2.00 = $6.00; $6.00 + $0.50 = $6.50

e. Divide Hundreds and Tens by 2, then Add
200 ÷ 2 = 100 and 40 ÷ 2 = 20; 100 + 20 = 120
Use Addition Facts
12 + 12 = 24 and 120 + 120 = 240; $\frac{1}{2}$ of 240 = 120

Problem Solving

Refer to **Power Up Discussion,** p. 169B.

2 New Concepts

Instruction

You may wish to display the **Place Value** concept poster as you discuss expanded notation.

To compare the cost of the car to the cost of the house, students can compare the place values of the lead digits in each number, and should conclude that because 2 × 10,000 (or 20,000) is less than 2 × 100,000 (or 200,000), the cost of the car is less than the cost of the house.

If the comparison is done in the opposite way—the cost of the house is compared to the cost of the car—students should conclude that cost of the house is greater than the cost of the car.

(continued)

2 New Concepts (Continued)

Instruction

Reinforce the concept of expanded notation by asking students to explain how they would write the number 4792 using expanded notation. As they respond, write each part of the answer on the board or overhead.

(4 × 1000) + (7 × 100) + (9 × 10) + (2 × 1)

Repeat the activity using other whole numbers.

Example 2

Instruction

Point out that 5280 is the number of feet in one mile.

Instruction

For the New Concept "more on elapsed time," give students an opportunity to discuss and name everyday events that occur during a.m. or p.m. hours. Sample questions and answers are shown.

"At what time do you usually wake up each day?" 6:30 a.m.

"What other events usually happen during the a.m. hours of a day?" I travel to school. I have my first class of the day.

"What events usually happen during the p.m. hours of a day?" School is dismissed. I do my homework. I eat a meal with my family. I go to sleep.

An overhead clock or demonstration clock can be used to model the elapsed time in examples 3 and 4.

Example 3

Instruction

Encourage students to use mental math to check the answer by counting forward from the earlier time to the later time.

Start at 7:15 a.m. and count by hours (8:15, 9:15, 10:15, 11:15) to find that 11:10 a.m. is 5 minutes less than 4 hours later.

Invite volunteers to describe other ways to calculate the elapsed time using mental math.

(continued)

Example 2

Write (5 × 1000) + (2 × 100) + (8 × 10) in standard notation.

Solution

Standard notation is our usual way of writing numbers. One way to think about this number is 5000 + 200 + 80. Another way to think about this number is 5 in the thousands place, 2 in the hundreds place, and 8 in the tens place. We may assume a 0 in the ones place. Either way we think about the number, the standard form is **5280.**

Verify How would the expanded notation change if we added 20 to 5280? (5 × 1000) + (3 × 100)

more on elapsed time

The hours of the day are divided into two parts: **a.m.** and **p.m.** The 12 "a.m." hours extend from midnight (12:00 a.m.) to the moment just before noon (12:00 p.m.). The 12 "p.m." hours extend from noon to the moment just before midnight. Recall from Lesson 13 that when we calculate the amount of time between two events, we are calculating elapsed time (the amount of time that has passed). We can use the later-earlier-difference pattern to solve elapsed-time problems about hours and minutes.

Example 3

Jason started the marathon at 7:15 a.m. He finished the race at 11:10 a.m. How long did it take Jason to run the marathon?

Solution

This problem has a subtraction pattern. We find Jason's race time (elapsed time) by subtracting the earlier time from the later time.

Later	11:10 a.m.
− Earlier	− 7:15 a.m.
Difference	

Since we cannot subtract 15 minutes from 10 minutes, we rename one hour as 60 minutes. Those 60 minutes plus 10 minutes equal 70 minutes. (This means 70 minutes after 9:00, which is the same as 10:10.)

```
  10:70
  1̶1̶:1̶0̶
−  7:15
   3:55
```

We find that it took Jason **3 hours 55 minutes** to run the marathon.

Example 4

What time is two and a half hours after 10:43 a.m.?

170 Saxon Math Course 1

Math Background

Timekeeping systems can vary. For example, the U.S. military system of timekeeping uses four digits to indicate a time of day. The first two digits of a time indicate the hour and the last two digits indicate the minute.

Civilian Time	Military Time
1 minute after 12 midnight	0001
2:00 a.m.	0200
6:30 a.m.	0630
Noon	1200
6:30 p.m.	1830
midnight	2400

Solution

This is an elapsed-time problem, and it has a subtraction pattern. The elapsed time, $2\frac{1}{2}$ hours, is the difference. We write the elapsed time as 2:30. The earlier time is 10:43 a.m.

Later	Later
− Earlier	− 10:43 a.m.
Difference	2:30

We need to find the later time, so we add $2\frac{1}{2}$ hours to 10:43 a.m. We will describe two methods to do this: a mental calculation and a pencil-and-paper calculation. For the mental calculation, we could first count two hours after 10:43 a.m. One hour later is 11:43 a.m. Another hour later is 12:43 p.m. (Note the switch from a.m. to p.m.) From 12:43 p.m., we count 30 minutes (one half hour). To do this, we can count 10 minutes at a time from 12:43 p.m.: 12:53 p.m., 1:03 p.m., 1:13 p.m. We find that $2\frac{1}{2}$ hours after 10:43 a.m. is **1:13 p.m.**

Thinking Skill
Discuss
What is another way to solve this problem using mental math?
Add 3 hours and then subtract 30 minutes.

To perform a pencil-and-paper calculation, we add 2 hours 30 minutes to 10:43 a.m.

```
  10:43 a.m.
+  2:30
  12:73 p.m.
```

Notice that the time switches from a.m. to p.m. and that the sum, 12:73 p.m., is improper. Seventy-three minutes is more than an hour. We think of 73 minutes as "one hour plus 13 minutes." We add 1 to the number of hours and write 13 as the number of minutes. So $2\frac{1}{2}$ hours after 10:43 a.m. is **1:13 p.m.**

Practice Set

▶ Write each of these numbers in expanded notation:

a. 270,000 (2 × 100,000) + (7 × 10,000)

b. 1760 (1 × 1000) + (7 × 100) + (6 × 10)

c. 8050 (8 × 1000) + (5 × 10)

Write each of these numbers in standard form:

d. (6 × 1000) + (4 × 100) 6400 **e.** (7 × 100) + (5 × 1) 705

▶ **f.** **Explain** George started the marathon at 7:15 a.m. He finished the race at 11:05 a.m. How long did it take George to run the marathon? How do you know your answer is correct?

f. 3 hr 50 min; Sample: If I add 3 hours to the starting time, I get 10:15 a.m. Then if I add 50 minutes, I get 11:05 a.m., which is the finish time.

g. What time is $3\frac{1}{2}$ hours after 11:50 p.m.? 3:20 a.m.

h. **Analyze** Dakota got home from soccer practice $4\frac{1}{2}$ hours before she went to sleep. If she went to sleep at 10:00 p.m., at what time did she get home? 5:30 p.m.

▶ See Math Conversations in the sidebar.

2 New Concepts (Continued)

Example 4

Instruction

When changing 73 minutes to hours and minutes, remind students that when they add 1 hour to a time of 12:00 p.m., they are representing a time that is 1 hour past 12:00 p.m., and the time that is 1 hour past 12:00 p.m. is 1 p.m., and not 12 + 1 or 13 p.m.

Practice Set

Problems a–c (Error Alert)

After writing each number in expanded notation, ask students to check their work by simplifying the expression to standard form, and then compare the standard form of the expression to the given number.

Problem f (Explain)

Challenge students to describe a variety of ways to solve the problem or check the answer using mental math.

nclusion

o help students visualize elapsed time, demonstrate how to solve example 3 on the previous page, using a time line. Remind students how an hour breaks down into 60, 30, 15, 5, and 1-minute intervals. Demonstrate on the time line.

Show students how to mark off intervals of 60 minutes from 7:15 a.m. to 9:15 a.m. Then mark smaller intervals to count the remaining time. Demonstrate how to count the total time marked on the line from 7:15 a.m. to 10:10 a.m.

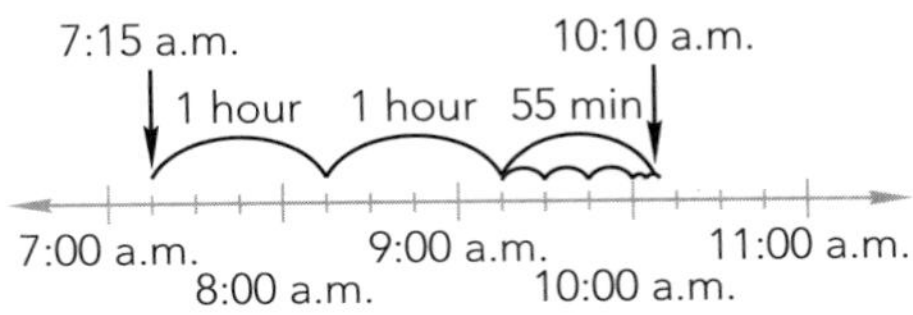

Give students additional examples to practice on their own as needed to reinforce understanding.

3 Written Practice

Math Conversations

Discussion opportunities are provided below.

Problem 2 Formulate

Extend the Problem

"The equation you wrote includes an operation. What is another equation that can be used to solve the problem that includes the opposite operation?" Sample: $1836 - 1786 = d$ and $1786 + d = 1836$

Problem 6 Analyze

Extend the Problem

"The distance between each base on a softball field is 60 feet. In simplest form, what fraction of the perimeter of a baseball field is the perimeter of a softball field?"

$\frac{60 \times 4}{90 \times 4} = \frac{240}{360} = \frac{2}{3}$

Problem 14 Analyze

Encourage students to describe a way to find $\frac{3}{4}$ of \$24 using mental math. Sample: The denominator 4 means that the whole is divided into 4 equal parts, and each equal part is \$24 ÷ 4 or \$6. The numerator represents three of those equal parts, so \$6 × 3 = 18.

Errors and Misconceptions

Problem 2

When solving elapsed-time problems that are related to a person's age, students should generalize that some answers may be approximations, even though those answers appear to be exact. For example, Davy Crockett was born on August 17, 1786, and he died at the Alamo on March 6, 1836, five months before his 50th birthday.

Problem 5

When using division to reduce a fraction, students must remember to divide the numerator *and* the denominator by the same number. Students should generalize that a common factor of the numerator and the denominator must be used, and using the greatest common factor will produce a fraction that is in simplest form.

(continued)

Written Practice *Strengthening Concepts*

1. (12) Analyze When the sum of 24 and 7 is multiplied by the difference of 18 and 6, what is the product? 372

▶ 2. (13) Formulate Davy Crockett was born in Tennessee in 1786 and died at the Alamo in 1836. How many years did he live? Write an equation and solve the problem. $1836 - 1786 = d$; 50 years

3. (15, 23) A 16-ounce box of a certain cereal costs \$2.24. What is the cost per ounce of the cereal? \$0.14 per ounce

* 4. (32) What time is 3 hours 30 minutes after 6:50 a.m.? 10:20 a.m.

▶ * 5. (29) Forty percent equals $\frac{40}{100}$. Reduce $\frac{40}{100}$. $\frac{2}{5}$

▶ * 6. (31) A baseball diamond is the square section formed by the four bases on a baseball field. On a major league field the distance between home plate and 1st base is 90 feet. What is the area of a baseball diamond? 8100 square feet

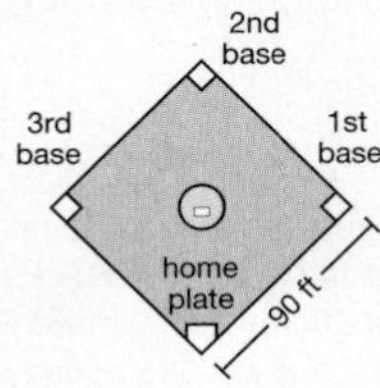

7. (8) What is the perimeter of a baseball diamond, as described in problem 6? 360 ft

8. (10) Generalize Describe the sequence below. Then find the **eighth** term.

1, 3, 5, 7, ...

8. This is a sequence of positive odd numbers. (Add 2 to the value of a term of find the next term.); 15

* 9. (32) Write 7500 in expanded notation. $(7 \times 1000) + (5 \times 100)$

10. (9) Estimate Which of these numbers is closest to 1000? C

A 990 B 909 C 1009 D 1090

11. (18) In three separate bank accounts Sumi has \$623, \$494, and \$380. What is the average amount of money she has per account? \$499

12. (2) \$0.05 × 100 \$5

* 13. (30) How many $\frac{2}{5}$s are in 1? $\frac{5}{2}$

▶ 14. (22) Model How much money is $\frac{3}{4}$ of \$24? Draw a diagram to illustrate the problem. \$18

14. \$24: $\frac{3}{4}$ of \$24 = \$6, \$6, \$6; $\frac{1}{4}$ of \$24 = \$6

Write each answer in simplest form:

15. (24) $\frac{3}{5} + \frac{3}{5}$ $1\frac{1}{5}$

16. (24) $\frac{3}{4} - \frac{1}{4}$ $\frac{1}{2}$

* 17. (29) $\frac{3}{4} \times \frac{1}{3}$ $\frac{1}{4}$

▶ See Math Conversations in the sidebar.

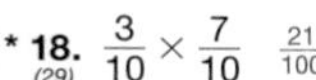

* **18.** (29) $\frac{3}{10} \times \frac{7}{10}$ $\frac{21}{100}$ * **19.** (26) $1\frac{2}{3} - 1\frac{1}{3}$ $\frac{1}{3}$

▶ **20.** (Inv. 2) **Connect** Three fourths of a circle is what percent of a circle? 75%

Find each unknown number. Remember to check your work.

21. (3) $w - 53 = 12$ 65 **22.** (4) $8q = 240$ 30

23. (23) Fifteen of the three dozen students in the science club were boys. What was the ratio of boys to girls in the club? $\frac{5}{7}$

* **24.** (30) What is the least common multiple of 4 and 6? 12

▶* **25.** (Inv. 3) **Represent** Draw triangle ABC so that $\angle C$ measures 90°, side AC measures 3 in., and side BC measures 4 in. Then draw and measure the length of side AB.

25. B, 4 in., 5 in., C, 3 in., A

* **26.** (29) If 24 of the 30 students finished the assignment in class, what fraction of the students finished in class? $\frac{4}{5}$

▶* **27.** (32) Ajani and Sharon began the hike at 6:45 a.m. and finished at 11:15 a.m. For how long did they hike? 4 hr 30 min

* **28.** (32) Compare: $(3 \times 100) + (5 \times 1)$ ⓐ 350 $<$

▶ **29.** (17) **Connect** What fraction is represented by point A on the number line below? $\frac{3}{10}$

30. (15, 23) **Explain** Some grocery stores post the price per ounce of different cereals to help customers compare costs. How can we find the cost per ounce of a box of cereal? To find the cost per ounce, divide the price of the box of cereal by the weight of the cereal in ounces.

▶ See Math Conversations in the sidebar.

3 Written Practice (Continued)

Math Conversations

Discussion opportunities are provided below.

Problem 20 Connect

Ask students to explain why 75% is the correct answer. 100% represents a whole circle, and $\frac{3}{4}$ of 100 is 75.

Problem 25 Represent

"Give two different names for the triangle. Include the word right in each name." right triangle ACB; right triangle BCA

Problem 27 Connect

Extend the Problem

"Suppose that the length of the trail Ajani and Sharon hiked was $6\frac{3}{4}$ miles. How could you find Ajani and Sharon's average hiking speed in miles per hour?" divide $6\frac{3}{4}$ by $4\frac{1}{2}$; their average speed was $1\frac{1}{2}$ or 1.5 miles per hour

Problem 29 Connect

It is important for students to recognize the divisions into which the number line is divided.

"On the number line, how many equal units are between 0 and 1?" ten

"What fractional part of 1 does each tick mark represent?" $\frac{1}{10}$

Looking Forward

Finding elapsed time by renaming hours and minutes prepares students for:

- **Lesson 81,** performing arithmetic operations with units of measure.
- **Lesson 95,** reducing units of measure before multiplying.
- **Lesson 102,** finding mass and weight by renaming pounds and ounces.
- **Lesson 114,** using unit multipliers to convert units of measure.

English Learners

Write **compare** on the board. Say:

"To compare things means to see how they are alike and different. Question number 30 states that customers compare costs of cereals. What does that mean?"

Explain that we compare things everyday. Often, we compare in math to order numbers, determine the best estimate, determine reasonableness, etc.

Writing Percents as Fractions, Part 1

Objectives

- Write a percent as a reduced fraction.

Lesson Preparation

Materials

- **Power Up G** (in *Instructional Masters*)

Optional

- **Teacher-provided material: grid paper**

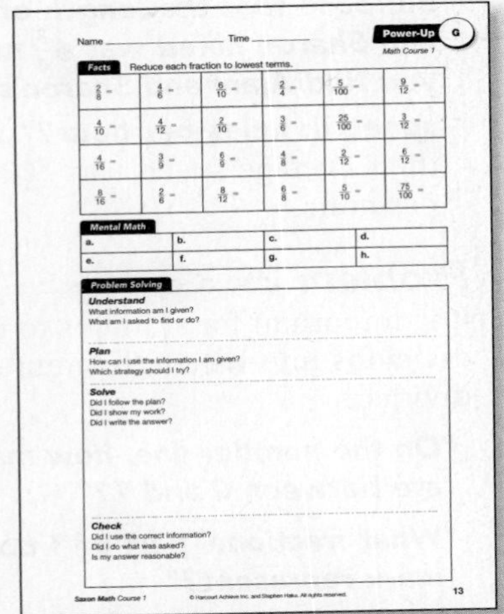

Power Up G

Math Language

New	Maintain
percent	Greatest Common Factor (GCF)

Technology Resources

Student eBook Complete student textbook in electronic format.

Resources and Planner CD Assessment, reteaching, and instructional masters, plus a pacing calendar with standards.

Test and Practice Generator CD Create additional practice sheets and custom-made tests.

www.SaxonPublishers.com Visit for more student activities and planning materials.

Inclusion

Adaptations CD Adapted lessons, investigations, practice and assessments.

Meeting Standards

National Council of Teachers of Mathematics (NCTM)

Numbers and Operations

NO.1a Work flexibly with fractions, decimals, and percents to solve problems

Communication

CM.3a Organize and consolidate their mathematical thinking through communication

CM.3d Use the language of mathematics to express mathematical ideas precisely

Representation

RE.5b Select, apply, and translate among mathematical representations to solve problems

Power-Up Discussion   For use with Power Up, p. 174

roblem-Solving Strategy: Use Logical Reasoning

Monica picked up a number cube and held it so that she could see the dots on three adjoining faces. Monica said that she could see a total of 7 dots. How many dots were on each of the faces she could see? What was the total number of dots on the three faces she could not see?

Understand *Understand the problem.*

"What information are we given?"

Monica can see a total of 7 dots on the three faces of a dot cube.

"What are we asked to do?"

We are asked to find the number of dots on each face that Monica could see. We are also asked to find the total number of dots on the faces she could not see.

"What do we know about number cubes?"

We know that the 6 sides of a cube are marked with 1, 2, 3, 4, 5, or 6 dots. We also know that the sum of dots on opposite sides will always total seven.

Teacher Note: You may wish to have number cubes available to allow students to verify their work.

Plan *Make a plan.*

"What problem-solving strategy will we use?"

We will *use logical reasoning* to determine the number of dots on the three faces Monica could see and then use our knowledge of number cubes to determine the number of dots Monica could not see.

Solve *Carry out the plan.*

"We are looking for three different numbers from 1 through 6 that total 7. What could these three numbers be?"

There is only one possibility: 1, 2, and 4. Any other set of three different numbers from 1 through 6 will result in a sum greater than 7.

"What is the total number of dots on the faces Monica could not see?"

If Monica can see the faces with 1, 2, and 4 dots, she cannot see the faces with 3, 5, and 6 dots. We add to find the total number of dots she cannot see: $3 + 5 + 6 = 14$.

Check *Look back.*

"Did we complete the task?"

Yes, we found how many dots were on each face Monica could see (1, 2, and 3 dots). We also found how many dots were on the faces she could not see (14 dots).

1 Power Up

Facts

Distribute **Power Up G** to students. See answers below.

Mental Math

Before students begin the Mental Math exercise, do this counting exercise as a class.

Count by 7s from 7 to 84.

Encourage students to share different ways to mentally compute these exercises. Strategies for exercises **c** and **e** are listed below.

c. Change 28 to 30, then Subtract 2

$56 + 30 = 86; 86 - 2 = 84$

Add Tens, then Ones

$50 + 6 + 20 + 8 = 70 + 14 = 84$

e. Double Hundreds, then Double Tens

$100 + 100 = 200$ and $20 + 20 = 40$; $200 + 40 = 240$

Use an Addition Fact

$12 + 12 = 24; 120 + 120 = 240$

Problem Solving

Refer to **Power-Up Discussion,** p. 174B.

2 New Concepts

Instruction

Percent is a ratio of a number to 100. That number can be greater than, less than, or equal to 100.

Remind students that the word "equivalent" means "names the same number." For the given grids, make sure students recognize that 50% of a grid describes the same number of shaded squares as $\frac{1}{2}$ of the grid, and 25% of a grid describes the same number of shaded squares as $\frac{1}{4}$ of the grid. The percent and the fraction for each grid are equivalent because they are different ways of naming the same number of shaded squares.

(continued)

LESSON 33

• Writing Percents as Fractions, Part 1

Power Up *Building Power*

facts Power Up G

mental math

a. Order of Operations: (4 × 100) + (4 × 25)   500

b. Number Sense: 7 × 29   203

c. Calculation: 56 + 28   84

d. Money: $5.50 + $1.75 $7.25

e. Number Sense: Double 120.   240

f. Number Sense: $\frac{120}{10}$ 12

g. Geometry: A rectangle has a length of 6 in. and a width of 3 in. What is the area of the rectangle?   18 square inches

h. Calculation: 2 × 3, + 1, × 8, + 4, ÷ 6, × 2, + 1, ÷ 3   7

problem solving

Monica picked up a number cube and held it so that she could see the dots on three adjoining faces. Monica said that she could see a total of 7 dots. How many dots were on each of the faces she could see? What was the total number of dots on the three faces she could not see?
1, 2, and 4 dots; 14 dots

New Concept *Increasing Knowledge*

Our fraction manipulatives describe parts of circles as fractions and as percents. The manipulatives show that 50% is equivalent to $\frac{1}{2}$ and that 25% is equivalent to $\frac{1}{4}$. A **percent** is actually a fraction with a denominator of 100. The word *percent* and its symbol, %, mean "per hundred."

We can use a grid with 100 squares to model percent.

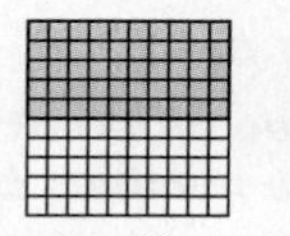

$50\% = \frac{50}{100} = \frac{1}{2}$

$25\% = \frac{25}{100} = \frac{1}{4}$

To write a percent as a fraction, we remove the percent sign and write the number as the numerator and 100 as the denominator. Then we reduce if possible.

Example 1

In Benjamin's class, 60% of the students walk to school. Write 60% as a fraction.

Facts Reduce each fraction to lowest terms.

$\frac{2}{8} = \frac{1}{4}$	$\frac{4}{6} = \frac{2}{3}$	$\frac{6}{10} = \frac{3}{5}$	$\frac{2}{4} = \frac{1}{2}$	$\frac{5}{100} = \frac{1}{20}$	$\frac{9}{12} = \frac{3}{4}$
$\frac{4}{10} = \frac{2}{5}$	$\frac{4}{12} = \frac{1}{3}$	$\frac{2}{10} = \frac{1}{5}$	$\frac{3}{6} = \frac{1}{2}$	$\frac{25}{100} = \frac{1}{4}$	$\frac{3}{12} = \frac{1}{4}$
$\frac{4}{16} = \frac{1}{4}$	$\frac{3}{9} = \frac{1}{3}$	$\frac{6}{9} = \frac{2}{3}$	$\frac{4}{8} = \frac{1}{2}$	$\frac{2}{12} = \frac{1}{6}$	$\frac{6}{12} = \frac{1}{2}$
$\frac{8}{16} = \frac{1}{2}$	$\frac{2}{6} = \frac{1}{3}$	$\frac{8}{12} = \frac{2}{3}$	$\frac{6}{8} = \frac{3}{4}$	$\frac{5}{10} = \frac{1}{2}$	$\frac{75}{100} = \frac{3}{4}$

Solution

We remove the percent sign and write 60 over 100.

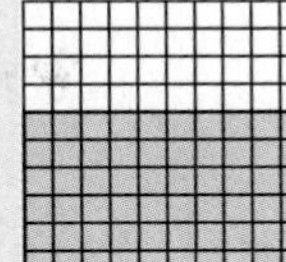

$$60\% = \frac{60}{100}$$

Reading Math
GCF stands for *greatest common factor.* The greatest common factor is the greatest number that is a factor of each of two or more numbers.

We can reduce $\frac{60}{100}$ in one step by dividing 60 and 100 by their GCF, which is 20. If we begin by dividing by a number smaller than 20, it will take more than one step to reduce the fraction.

$$\frac{60 \div 20}{100 \div 20} = \frac{3}{5}$$

We find that 60% is equivalent to the fraction $\frac{3}{5}$.

Example 2

Find the reduced fraction that equals 4%.

Solution

Thinking Skill
Discuss
How do you find the greatest common factor of two numbers? Write all the factors of each number. Circle the factors common to both numbers. Identify the greatest of the common factors.

We remove the percent sign and write 4 over 100.

$$4\% = \frac{4}{100}$$

We reduce the fraction by dividing both the numerator and denominator by 4, which is the GCF of 4 and 100.

$$\frac{4 \div 4}{100 \div 4} = \frac{1}{25}$$

We find that 4% is equivalent to the fraction $\frac{1}{25}$.

Practice Set

Write each percent as a fraction. Reduce when possible.

a. 80% $\frac{4}{5}$ **b.** 5% $\frac{1}{20}$ **c.** 25% $\frac{1}{4}$

d. 24% $\frac{6}{25}$ **e.** 23% $\frac{23}{100}$ **f.** 10% $\frac{1}{10}$

g. 20% $\frac{1}{5}$ **h.** 2% $\frac{1}{50}$ **i.** 75% $\frac{3}{4}$

▶ **j.** *Justify* Describe the steps you would take to write 40% as a reduced fraction. Sample: Write 40% as $\frac{40}{100}$ and then reduce by dividing 40 and 100 by 20 to get $\frac{2}{5}$.

Written Practice *Strengthening Concepts*

▶ **1.** (12) *Analyze* When the product of 10 and 15 is divided by the sum of 10 and 15, what is the quotient? 6

2. (13) The Nile River is 6690 kilometers long. The Mississippi River is 3792 kilometers long. How much longer is the Nile River than the Mississippi? Write an equation and solve the problem. $6690 - 3792 = d$; 2898 kilometers

▶ See Math Conversations in the sidebar.

2 New Concepts (Continued)

Example 1
Instruction
Have students recall that one way to find the greatest common factor (GCF) of two numbers is to write all of the factors of each number, circle the common factors, and then identify the greatest of those common factors.

Example 2
Instruction
Make sure students understand that 4% is written as $\frac{4}{100}$ because a percent and its symbol represent "per hundred."

Practice Set
Problem j Error Alert
To reduce the fraction, some students may choose to divide by a common factor less then 20 (such as 2, 4, 5, or 10). Remind these students that the result will be a fraction that is not in simplest form.

3 Written Practice

Math Conversations
Discussion opportunities are provided below.

Problem 1 Analyze
Extend the Problem
Ask students to write a symbolic expression to represent the problem. Sample: $10 \times 15 \div (10 + 15)$

Students should conclude that parentheses must be a part of the expression, because without them, the expression will not simplify to 6.

(continued)

clusion

ncourage students to use the tests for divisibility introduced in Lesson 21 help them identify the factors of the numerator and denominator when educing a fraction.

efer students to the "Tests for Divisibility" in the Student Reference Guide r tests that are useful in identifying when numbers are divisible by 2, 3, 4, 5, 8, 9, and 10. Show students how to use these tests to reduce the fractions ey create in the Practice Set *a–i*.

3 Written Practice (Continued)

Math Conversations

Discussion opportunities are provided below.

Problem 6 Connect

"What is another name for these two fractions?" equivalent fractions

"Why are the fractions equivalent fractions?" They are different names for the same number.

Problem 10 Classify

"What does it mean for one number to be divisible by another?" Sample: The numbers divide evenly; the division of the numbers does not produce a remainder.

Problem 19 Generalize

Extend the Problem

Challenge students to extend the sequence.

"Explain how to find the 100th term of the sequence using only mental math, and then name the 100th term. 200; sample: the first term in the sequence is 2, the second term is 4, the third term is 6, and so on. Multiply the term of the sequence by 2; $100 \times 2 = 200$.

Problem 23 Estimate

Extend the Problem

"In basketball, the rim is about 3 meters above the floor. About how many centimeters above the floor is the rim? Explain your answer?" About 300 cm; to change meters to centimeters, multiply the number of meters by 100 because 1 meter = 100 centimeters.

"Most doors are about 1 meter wide. About how many millimeters wide are those doors? Explain your answer." About 1000 mm; to change meters to millimeters, multiply the number of meters by 1000 because 1 meter = 1000 millimeters.

Errors and Misconceptions

Problem 4

The zero in the hundreds place of 3040 is called an internal zero. Internal zeros sometimes cause errors when writing the expanded notation of a number. For example, students will incorrectly write 3040 as $(3 \times 1000) + (4 \times 100)$, using the reasoning that since the first place value that is written is thousands, the next place value that is written must be hundreds.

To help prevent this error, ask students to identify the place of each non-zero digit in a number before writing that number in expanded notation.

(continued)

3. (12) Some astronomers think that the universe is about fourteen billion years old. Use digits to write that number of years. 14,000,000,000 years

▶ *** 4.** (32) Write 3040 in expanded notation. $(3 \times 1000) + (4 \times 10)$

*** 5.** (32) Write $(6 \times 100) + (2 \times 1)$ in standard notation. 602

▶ *** 6.** (29) **Connect** Write two fractions equal to 1, one with a denominator of 10 and the other with a denominator of 100. $\frac{10}{10}, \frac{100}{100}$

*** 7.** (30) By what number should $\frac{5}{3}$ be multiplied for the product to be 1? $\frac{3}{5}$

8. (8) What is the perimeter of this rectangle? 40 in.

*** 9.** (31) How many square tiles with sides 1 inch long would be needed to cover this rectangle? 96 tiles

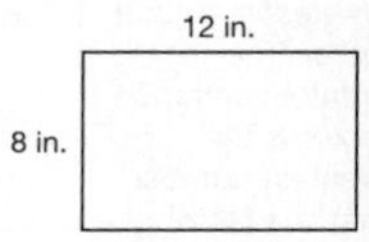

▶ **10.** (21) **Classify** Which of these numbers is divisible by both 2 and 3? D

A 56 **B** 75 **C** 83 **D** 48

11. (16) Estimate the difference of 4968 and 2099. 3000

12. (2) $\$4.30 \times 100$ \$430.00

13. (2) $\$402.00 \div 25$ \$16.08

14. (29) What is $\frac{3}{5}$ of 20? 12

Write each answer in simplest form:

15. (24) $\frac{4}{5} + \frac{4}{5}$ $1\frac{3}{5}$

16. (24) $\frac{5}{8} - \frac{1}{8}$ $\frac{1}{2}$

*** 17.** (29) $\frac{5}{2} \times \frac{3}{2}$ $3\frac{3}{4}$

*** 18.** (29) $\frac{3}{10} \times \frac{3}{100}$ $\frac{9}{1000}$

▶ **19.** (10) **Generalize** Describe the sequence below. Then find the **tenth** term.

2, 4, 6, 8, . . .

19. This is a sequence of positive even numbers. (Add 2 to the value of a term to find the next term.); 20

Find each unknown number. Remember to check your work.

20. (3) $q - 24 = 23$ 47

*** 21.** (30) $\frac{1}{2}w = 1$ 2

22. (19) Here we show 16 written as a product of prime numbers:

$2 \cdot 2 \cdot 2 \cdot 2$

Write 15 as a product of prime numbers. $3 \cdot 5$

▶ **23.** (7) **Estimate** A meter is a little longer than a yard. About how many meters tall is a door? about 2 meters

*** 24.** (29) Five of the 30 students in the class were absent. What fraction of the class was absent? Write the answer as a reduced fraction. How do you know your answer is correct?
$\frac{1}{6}$; Sample: Five over 30 reduces to $\frac{1}{6}$, and $\frac{1}{6}$ of 30 is 5.

176 *Saxon Math Course 1*

▶ See Math Conversations in the sidebar.

Math Background

In the everyday world, some fraction-percent equivalents are quite common. These include:

$\frac{1}{2} = 50\%$	$\frac{1}{3} = 33\frac{1}{3}\%$	$\frac{1}{4} = 25\%$	$\frac{3}{4} = 75\%$
$\frac{1}{5} = 20\%$	$\frac{2}{5} = 40\%$	$\frac{3}{5} = 60\%$	$\frac{4}{5} = 80\%$
$\frac{1}{10} = 10\%$	$\frac{3}{10} = 30\%$	$\frac{7}{10} = 70\%$	$\frac{9}{10} = 90\%$

27.

20 answers

$\frac{4}{5}$ were correct.	4 answers
	4 answers
	4 answers
	4 answers
$\frac{1}{5}$ were not correct.	4 answers

28. If the numerator is more than half of the denominator, the fraction is greater than $\frac{1}{2}$. If the numerator is less than half of the denominator, the fraction is less than $\frac{1}{2}$.

* **25.** (17) **Connect** To what mixed number is the arrow pointing on the number line below? $1\frac{7}{10}$

* **26.** (33) Write each percent as a reduced fraction:

a. 70% $\frac{7}{10}$ **b.** 30% $\frac{3}{10}$

▶ **27.** (22) **Model** Four fifths of Gina's 20 answers were correct. How many of Gina's answers were correct? Draw a diagram to illustrate the problem. 16 answers

▶ **28.** (Inv. 2) **Explain** By looking at the numerator and denominator of a fraction, how can you tell whether the fraction is greater than or less than $\frac{1}{2}$?

▶* **29.** (32) **Analyze** What time is $6\frac{1}{2}$ hours after 8:45 p.m.? 3:15 a.m.

30. (17) Arrange these fractions in order from least to greatest: $\frac{1}{16}, \frac{1}{8}, \frac{1}{4}, \frac{1}{2}$

$\frac{1}{8}, \frac{1}{4}, \frac{1}{16}, \frac{1}{2}$

Early Finishers
Real-World Application

The Parthenon was built in Ancient Greece over 2500 years ago. The Parthenon's base is a rectangle measuring approximately 31 meters by 70 meters.

a. What is the approximate area of the Parthenon's base? about 2170 square meters

b. What is the approximate perimeter of the Parthenon's base? about 202 meters

▶ See Math Conversations in the sidebar.

3 Written Practice (Continued)

Math Conversations

Discussion opportunities are provided below.

Problem 27 Model

Extend the Problem

"How can you find $\frac{4}{5}$ of 20 using mental math?" Sample: The denominator of the fraction represents 20 divided into five equal parts, and each equal part is $20 \div 5$ or 4. The numerator represents four of those equal parts, so $4 \times 4 = 16$.

Problem 28 Explain

On the board or overhead, ask students to write a variety of fractions to support their explanations.

Problem 29 Analyze

"To solve this problem using mental math, suppose you count ahead 7 hours from 8:45 p.m. What time would that be?" 3:45 a.m.

"How many minutes should you count back from 3:45 a.m.? Why?" 30 minutes; $7 - 6\frac{1}{2} = \frac{1}{2}$ hour, and $\frac{1}{2}$ hour is the same as 30 minutes.

Looking Forward

Writing a percent as a reduced fraction prepares students for:

- **Lesson 41,** writing a percent as a fraction or a decimal in order to find the percent of a number.
- **Lessons 75 and 94,** writing fractions and decimals as percents.
- **Lesson 99,** finding fraction-decimal-percent equivalents.
- **Lesson 115,** writing a fractional percent as a reduced fraction.
- **Lesson 119,** finding a whole when a percent is known.

• Decimal Place Value

Objectives

- Identify the value of decimal places through millionths.
- Name the digit that occupies a specific decimal place in a number.
- Name the decimal place occupied by a given digit in a number.

Lesson Preparation

Materials

- **Power Up D** (in *Instructional Masters*)
- **Manipulative kit: inch rulers, protractors**
- **Place Value poster**

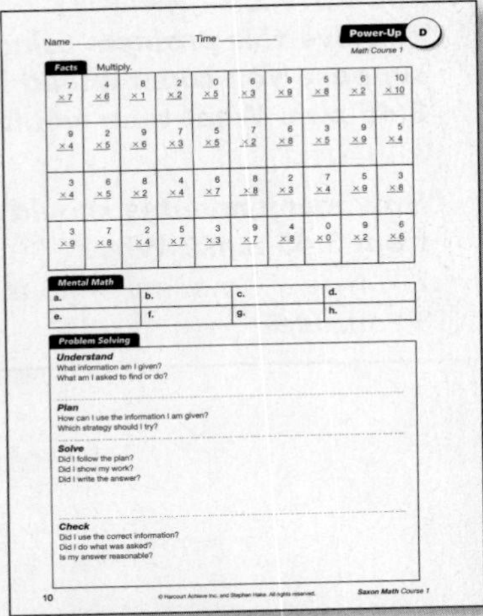

Name ______________ Time ________

Power-Up D
Math Course 1

Facts Multiply.

7×7	4×6	8×1	2×2	0×5	6×3	8×9	5×8	6×2	10×10
9×4	2×5	9×6	7×3	5×5	7×2	6×8	3×5	9×9	5×4
3×4	6×5	8×2	4×4	6×7	8×8	2×3	7×4	5×9	3×8
3×9	7×8	2×4	5×7	3×3	9×7	4×8	0×0	9×2	6×6

Mental Math

a.	b.	c.	d.
e.	f.	g.	h.

Problem Solving

Understand
What information am I given?
What am I asked to find or do?

Plan
How can I use the information I am given?
Which strategy should I try?

Solve
Did I follow the plan?
Did I show my work?
Did I write the answer?

Check
Did I use the correct information?
Did I do what was asked?
Is my answer reasonable?

10 © Harcourt Achieve Inc. and Stephen Hake. All rights reserved. *Saxon Math* Course 1

Power Up D

Math Language

New	English Learners (ESL)
decimal places	preceding
decimal point	

Technology Resources

Student eBook Complete student textbook in electronic format.

Resources and Planner CD Assessment, reteaching, and instructional masters, plus a pacing calendar with standards.

Test and Practice Generator CD Create additional practice sheets and custom-made tests.

www.SaxonPublishers.com Visit for more student activities and planning materials.

Inclusion

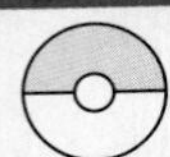

Adaptations CD Adapted lessons, investigations, practice and assessments.

Meeting Standards

National Council of Teachers of Mathematics (NCTM)

Numbers and Operations

NO.1a Work flexibly with fractions, decimals, and percents to solve problems

Connections

CN.4a Recognize and use connections among mathematical ideas

Power-Up Discussion *For use with Power Up, p. 178*

Problem-Solving Strategy: Use Logical Reasoning/ Make a Model

Jeanna folded a square piece of paper in half so that the left edge aligned with the right edge. Then she folded the paper again so that the top edge aligned with the bottom edge. With scissors, Jeanna cut off the top, left corner of the square. Which diagram will the paper look like when it is unfolded?

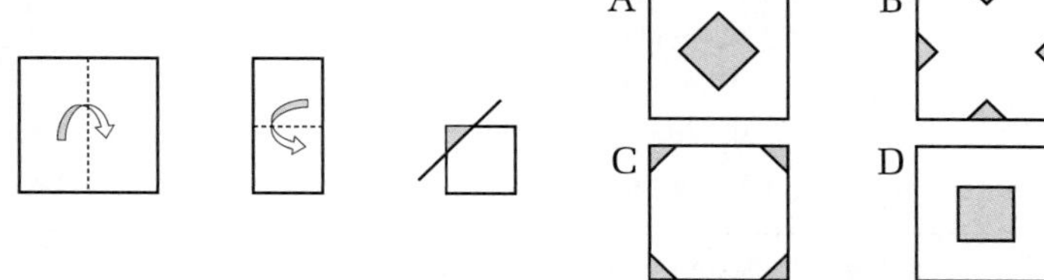

Understand ***Understand the Problem.***

"What information are we given?"

We are told how a square piece of paper is folded and are shown a diagram to help us follow the directions.

"What are we asked to do?"

We are asked to determine what the paper will look like after the directions are followed and it is unfolded.

Plan ***Make a plan.***

"How can we use the information we are given to do what we are asked to do?"

We will *use logical and spatial reasoning* to visualize the result and then *make a model* using a square piece of scrap paper.

Solve ***Carry out the plan.***

"Can we make an educated guess at which diagram is correct before making a model?"

We notice from analyzing the diagram that all four original corners of the square are at the lower right. The edges of the paper are on the bottom and right-hand sides. The center of the original square sheet is at the upper left corner. When Jeanna cuts off the upper left corner, she is cutting a hole in the middle of the square sheet because the cut does not touch any of the original edges or corners of the paper. We might be able to visualize that we cut a square hole, with each of the 4 corners placed on one of the creases. Our guess corresponds to diagram A.

Teacher Note: Lead students through the steps Jeanna followed. You may choose to have each student fold and cut a piece of paper on his or her own, or you may choose to demonstrate the steps to the class yourself.

"Now we unfold our paper. Which diagram does it look like?"

Our paper looks like diagram A, which was our original prediction.

Check ***Look back.***

"Did we answer the question that was asked?"

Yes, we determined what Jeanna's paper looked like when it was unfolded.

1 Power Up

Facts

Distribute **Power Up D** to students. See answers below.

Mental Math

Before students begin the Mental Math exercise, do this counting exercise as a class.

Count up and down by $\frac{1}{8}$s between $\frac{1}{8}$ and 2.

Encourage students to share different ways to mentally compute these exercises. Strategies for exercises **b** and **e** are listed below.

b. Subtract Hundreds, Subtract Tens

$1400 - 300 = 1100$ and $80 - 50 = 30$; $1100 + 30 = 1130$

Count Back by Hundreds, then by Tens

Start with 1480. Count: 1380, 1280, 1180

Start with 1180. Count: 1170, 1160, 1150, 1140, 1130

e. Double Hundreds and Double Tens

Double 200 is 400 and double 50 is 100; $400 + 100 = 500$

Use an Addition Fact

$25 + 25 = 50$; $250 + 250 = 500$

Problem Solving

Refer to **Power-Up Discussion,** p. 178B.

2 New Concepts

Instruction

You may wish to display the **Place Value** concept poster as you discuss decimal place value.

(continued)

LESSON 34

• Decimal Place Value

Power Up *Building Power*

facts Power Up D

mental math

a. **Order of Operations:** $(4 \times 200) + (4 \times 25)$ 900

b. **Number Sense:** $1480 - 350$ 1130

c. **Number Sense:** $45 + 18$ 63

d. **Money:** $12.00 − $2.50 $9.50

e. **Number Sense:** Double 250. 500

f. **Number Sense:** $\frac{1500}{100}$ 15

g. **Measurement:** Which is greater, 3 feet or 1 yard? equal (or neither)

h. **Calculation:** 3×3, $\times 9$, $- 1$, $\div 2$, $+ 2$, $\div 7$, $\times 2$ 12

problem solving

Jeanna folded a square piece of paper in half so that the left edge aligned with the right edge. Then she folded the paper again so that the top edge aligned with the bottom edge. With scissors, Jeanna cut off the top, left corner of the square. Which diagram will the paper look like when it is unfolded?

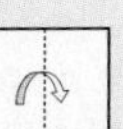

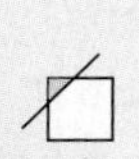

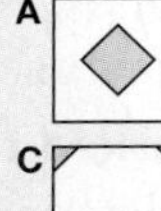

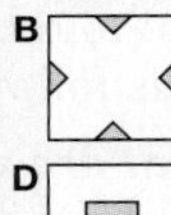

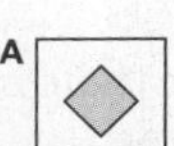

New Concept *Increasing Knowledge*

Since Lesson 12 we have studied place value from the ones place leftward to the hundred trillions place. As we move to the left, each place is ten times as large as the preceding place. If we move to the right, each place is one tenth as large as the preceding place.

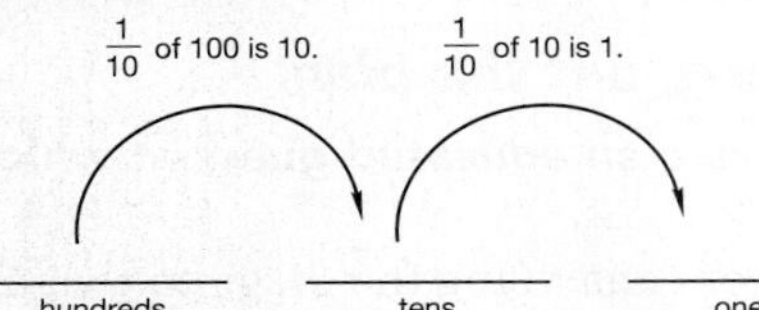

Each place to the right of the ones place also has a value one tenth the value of the place to its left. Each of these places has a value less than one (but more than zero). We use a **decimal point** to mark the separation between

Facts Multiply.

7 × 7 49	4 × 6 24	8 × 1 8	2 × 2 4	0 × 5 0	6 × 3 18	8 × 9 72	5 × 8 40	6 × 2 12	10 × 10 100
9 × 4 36	2 × 5 10	9 × 6 54	7 × 3 21	5 × 5 25	7 × 2 14	6 × 8 48	3 × 5 15	9 × 9 81	5 × 4 20
3 × 4 12	6 × 5 30	8 × 2 16	4 × 4 16	6 × 7 42	8 × 8 64	2 × 3 6	7 × 4 28	5 × 9 45	3 × 8 24
3 × 9 27	7 × 8 56	2 × 4 8	5 × 7 35	3 × 3 9	9 × 7 63	4 × 8 32	0 × 0 0	9 × 2 18	6 × 6 36

178 **Saxon** *Math Course 1*

the ones place and places with values less than one. Places to the right of a decimal point are often called **decimal places.** Here we show three decimal places:

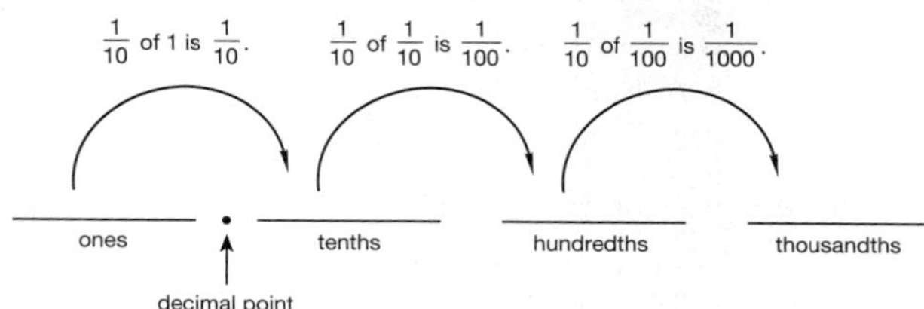

Thinking Skill

Connect

Why is thinking about money a helpful way to remember decimal place values?
Money uses the base-ten place value system. We use money almost every day.

Thinking about money is a helpful way to remember decimal place values.

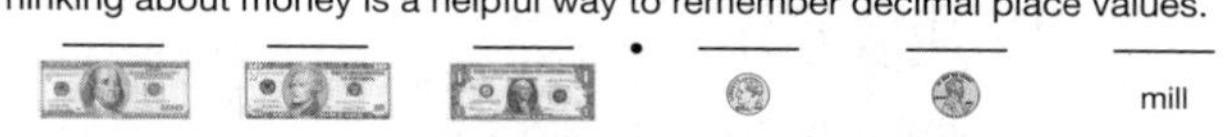

A mill is $\frac{1}{1000}$ of a dollar and $\frac{1}{10}$ of a cent. We do not have a coin for a mill. However, purchasers of gasoline are charged mills at the gas pump. A price of $\$2.29\frac{9}{10}$ per gallon is one mill less than \$2.30 and nine mills more than \$2.29.

Of course, decimal place values extend beyond the thousandths place. The chart below shows decimal place values from the millions place through the millionths place. Moving to the right, the place values get smaller and smaller; each place has one tenth the value of the place to its left.

Discuss What pattern do you see? Each place has 10 times the value of the place to its right.

Decimal Place Values

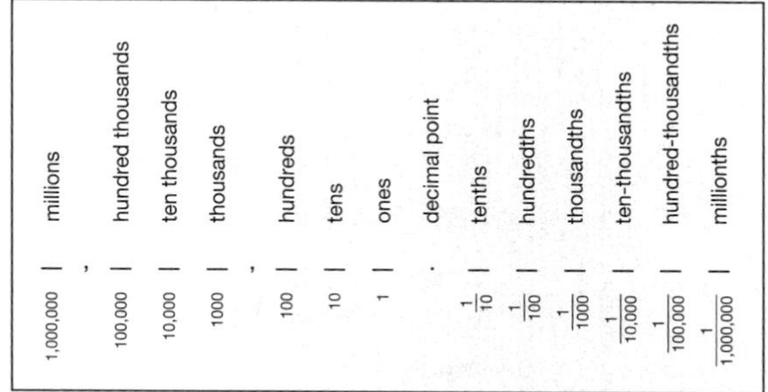

Example 1

Which digit in 123.45 is in the hundredths place?

Solution

The *-ths* ending of *hundredths* indicates that the hundredths place is to the right of the decimal point. The first place to the right of the decimal point is the tenths place. The second place is the hundredths place. The digit in the hundredths place is **5.**

2 New Concepts *(Continued)*

Instruction

Write the Decimal Place Values chart shown below on the board.

To help students complete examples 1 and 2, write the numbers from each example in the Decimal Place Values chart.

Suggest that students copy the chart and use it to help complete the Practice Set problems.

(continued)

Math Background

Our number system is a base-ten number system because 10 is the number that is raised to various powers to create our place values.

English Learners

Notice the term **preceding place** on the previous page. Explain that the word *preceding* means "directly before." Say:

"When we refer to 'the preceding place' we are referring to the place just before."

Write the 1, 2, 3, and 4 on the board. Explain that the number preceding "3" is "2."

2 New Concepts (Continued)

Example 2

Instruction

Invite students to name real world situations that involve numbers in tenths or hundredths. Samples: Automobile odometers record distance traveled in tenths of a mile and pennies represent hundredths of a dollar.

Practice Set

Problems a–c Error Alert

To give students additional practice identifying place values, ask them to identify the place value of each digit in each number.

3 Written Practice

Math Conversations

Discussion opportunities are provided below.

Problems 4a and 4b Connect

"When we write 60% or 40% as a reduced fraction, we first write a fraction that has a numerator of 60 or 40. What is the denominator of each fraction? Why?" The denominator is 100 because a percent and its symbol mean "per hundred."

"To reduce $\frac{60}{100}$ or $\frac{40}{100}$ by division, what number should we divide both the numerator and the denominator by? Explain your answer." We can divide by any common factor greater than 1. If we divide by the greatest common factor, the quotient will be a fraction that is in simplest form.

Problem 6 Analyze

"How is the order of operations used to simplify this expression?" The order of operations state that the operation(s) inside parentheses must be completed first.

Problem 9 Represent

To ensure that $\angle C$ is drawn as a right angle, you might ask students to draw the triangle on grid paper.

(continued)

Example 2

What is the place value of the 8 in 67.89?

Solution

The 8 is in the first place to the right of the decimal point, which is the **tenths** place.

Practice Set

▸ **a.** What is the place value of the 5 in 12.345? thousandths

▸ **b.** Which digit in 5.4321 is in the tenths place? 4

▸ **c.** In 0.0123, what is the digit in the thousandths place? 2

d. Connect What is the value of the place held by zero in 50.375? ones

e. What is the name for one hundredth of a dollar? cent

f. Conclude What is the name for one thousandth of a dollar? mill

Written Practice *Strengthening Concepts*

1\. 24 members: 3 members, 3 members, 3 members, 3 members, 3 members, 3 members, 3 members, 3 members; $\frac{3}{8}$ were tenors. $\frac{5}{8}$ were not tenors.

1. (22) Model Three eighths of the 24 choir members were tenors. How many tenors were in the choir? Draw a diagram to illustrate the problem. 9 tenors

2. (15) Mom wants to triple a recipe for fruit salad. If the recipe calls for 8 ounces of pineapple juice, how many ounces of pineapple juice should she use? 24 ounces

* **3.** (32) The mayfly has the shortest known adult life span of any animal on the planet. The mayfly grows underwater in a lake or stream for two or three years, but it lives for as little as an hour after it sprouts wings and becomes an adult. If a mayfly sprouts wings at 8:47 a.m. and lives for one hour and fifteen minutes, at what time does it die? 10:02 a.m.

▸ * **4.** (33) Connect Write each percent as a reduced fraction:

a. 60% $\frac{3}{5}$ **b.** 40% $\frac{2}{5}$

* **5.** (29) Compare: $\frac{100}{100} \circledequal \frac{10}{10}$

▸ * **6.** (32) Analyze Write $(6 \times 100) + (5 \times 1)$ in standard notation. 605

* **7.** (34) Which digit is in the ones place in $42,876.39? 6

* **8.** (31) If the perimeter of a square is 24 inches,

a. how long is each side of the square? 6 inches

b. what is the area of the square? 36 square inches

9\.
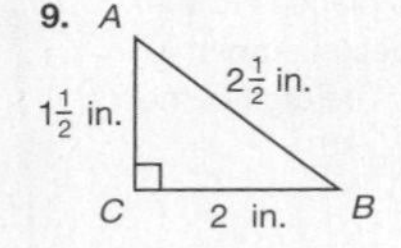

▸ * **9.** (Inv. 3) Represent Draw triangle ABC so that $\angle C$ is a right angle, side AC is $1\frac{1}{2}$ inches, and side BC is 2 inches. Then measure the length of side AB.

* **10.** (30) What is the least common multiple of 6 and 8? 24

180 **Saxon** *Math Course 1*

▸ See Math Conversations in the sidebar.

11. $5.60 ÷ 10 $0.56 (2)

12. $\frac{9}{10} \cdot \frac{9}{10}$ $\frac{81}{100}$ (29)

13. Estimate the quotient when 898 is divided by 29. 30 (16)

14. Round 36,847 to the nearest hundred. 36,800 (16)

Find each unknown number. Remember to check your work.

15. $6d = 144$ 24 (4)

16. $\frac{d}{6} = 144$ 864 (4)

▶* 17. Compare: $\frac{5}{2} + \frac{5}{2}$ (=) $2 \times \frac{5}{2}$ (29)

18. $\frac{3}{8} + \frac{3}{8}$ $\frac{3}{4}$ (24)

▶ 19. $\frac{11}{12} - \frac{1}{12}$ $\frac{5}{6}$ (24)

* 20. $\frac{5}{4} \times \frac{3}{2}$ $1\frac{7}{8}$ (29)

▶ 21. **Predict** What is the ratio of the first term to the fifth term of the sequence below? $\frac{6}{30} = \frac{1}{5}$ (10, 23)

6, 12, 18, 24, ...

22. **Formulate** The movie theater sold 88 tickets to the afternoon show for $7.50 per ticket. What was the total of the ticket sales for the show? Write an equation and solve the problem. Explain why your answer is reasonable. (15)

22. $88 \times 7.50 = t$; $660.00; Sample: At $10 each, 88 tickets would be $880. At $5 each, 88 tickets would be half as much, $440. Since $7.50 is halfway between $10 and $5 the total should be halfway between $880 and $440, which it is.

23. **Connect** To what number is the arrow pointing on the number line below? −6 (14)

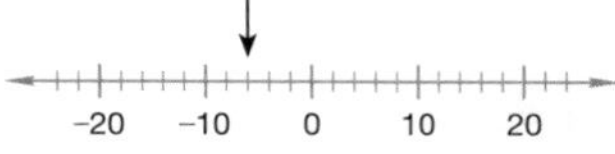

24. $(80 ÷ 40) − (8 ÷ 4)$ 0 (5)

25. Which digit in 2,345.678 is in the thousandths place? 8 (24)

▶ 26. **Model** Draw a circle and shade $\frac{2}{3}$ of it. (Inv. 2)

27. Divide 5225 by 12 and write the quotient as a mixed number. $435\frac{5}{12}$ (25)

28. **Evaluate** The first glass contained 12 ounces of water. The second glass contained 11 ounces of water. The third glass contained 7 ounces of water. If water was poured from the first and second glasses into the third glass until each glass contained the same amount, then how many ounces of water would be in each glass? 10 ounces (18)

29. **Represent** The letters *r*, *t*, and *d* represent three different numbers. The product of *r* and *t* is *d*. (2)

$$rt = d$$

Arrange the letters to form another multiplication equation and two division equations. $tr = d$, $d ÷ t = r$, $d ÷ r = t$

30. **Connect** Instead of dividing 75 by 5, Sandy mentally doubled both numbers and divided 150 by 10. Find the quotient of 75 ÷ 5 and the quotient of 150 ÷ 10. 15; 15 (2)

▶ See Math Conversations in the sidebar.

ooking Forward

dentifying and understanding decimal place value by naming the digit in specific decimal place and naming the decimal place of a specific digit repares students for:

- **Lesson 35,** writing decimal numbers as fractions, fractions as decimal numbers, and reading and writing decimal numbers.
- **Lesson 40,** using zero as a placeholder in order to write a decimal number.
- **Lesson 44,** simplifying decimal numbers by removing unnecessary zeros and comparing decimal numbers.
- **Lesson 46,** writing decimal numbers in expanded notation.
- **Lesson 51,** rounding decimal numbers to a given place value.

3 Written Practice (Continued)

Math Conversations

Discussion opportunities are provided below.

Problem 19 Analyze

"Whenever we subtract fractions that have the same denominators, we subtract only the numerators. Why is an answer of $\frac{10}{12}$ not the best answer we can give for this subtraction?" $\frac{10}{12}$ can be reduced to $\frac{5}{6}$

Problem 21 Predict

The fifth term is unknown and must be inferred from the pattern. Remind students that a ratio can be written as a fraction, and when it is, the ratio should be written in simplest form.

Problem 26 Model

To help students divide their circles into three equal parts, encourage them to think of the circle as an analog clock face, and then decide how a clock face can be divided into three equal parts. Sample: Draw these three radii from the center of the circle: to 12 o'clock; to 4 o'clock; to 8 o'clock.

Errors and Misconceptions

Problem 17

When multiplying a fraction by a whole number, a common error is to not recognize that a whole number represents the numerator of a fraction having 1 as its denominator.

Before completing the multiplication, ask students to rewrite 5 as $\frac{5}{1}$. To help remind students how to multiply the fractions, write the expression below on the board or overhead.

$$\frac{2 \times 5}{1 \times 2}$$

Point out that the expression shows that the product of the numerators is written over the product of the denominators. Complete the example by reminding students to reduce their fraction answers whenever possible.

• Writing Decimal Numbers as Fractions, Part 1
• Reading and Writing Decimal Numbers

Objectives

- Write a decimal number as a fraction.
- Write a fraction as a decimal number.
- Read and write decimal numbers in word form.
- Write the word form of a decimal number as a fraction and as a decimal.

Lesson Preparation

Materials

- **Power Up G** (in *Instructional Masters*)

Optional

- **Teacher-provided material: fraction manipulatives** from Investigation 2
- **Fraction-Decimal-Percent Equivalents poster**
- **Manipulative kit: color tiles**

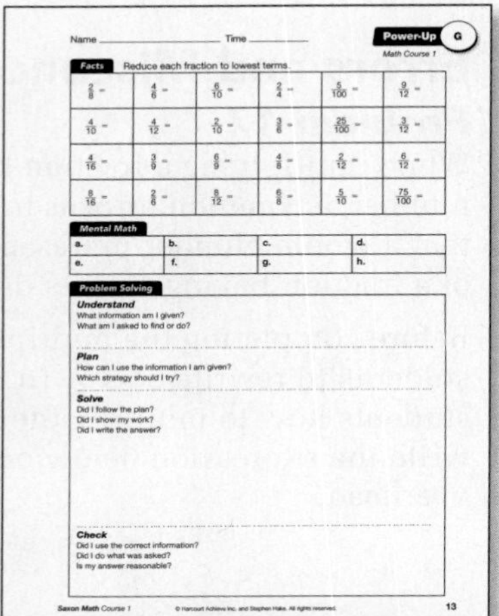

Name ______________ Time ________

Power-Up G
Math Course 1

Facts Reduce each fraction to lowest terms.

$\frac{2}{8}$ =	$\frac{4}{6}$ =	$\frac{6}{10}$ =	$\frac{2}{4}$ =	$\frac{5}{100}$ =	$\frac{9}{12}$ =
$\frac{4}{10}$ =	$\frac{4}{12}$ =	$\frac{2}{10}$ =	$\frac{3}{6}$ =	$\frac{25}{100}$ =	$\frac{3}{12}$ =
$\frac{4}{16}$ =	$\frac{3}{9}$ =	$\frac{6}{9}$ =	$\frac{4}{8}$ =	$\frac{2}{12}$ =	$\frac{6}{12}$ =
$\frac{8}{16}$ =	$\frac{2}{6}$ =	$\frac{8}{12}$ =	$\frac{6}{8}$ =	$\frac{5}{10}$ =	$\frac{75}{100}$ =

Mental Math

a.	b.	c.	d.
e.	f.	g.	h.

Problem Solving

Understand
What information am I given?
What am I asked to find or do?

Plan
How can I use the information I am given?
Which strategy should I try?

Solve
Did I follow the plan?
Did I show my work?
Did I write the answer?

Check
Did I use the correct information?
Did I do what was asked?
Is my answer reasonable?

Saxon Math *Course 1* © Harcourt Achieve Inc. and Stephen Hake. All rights reserved. 13

Power Up G

Math Language

English Learners (ESL)
product

Technology Resources

Student eBook Complete student textbook in electronic format.

Resources and Planner CD Assessment, reteaching, and instructional masters, plus a pacing calendar with standards.

Test and Practice Generator CD Create additional practice sheets and custom-made tests.

www.SaxonPublishers.com Visit for more student activities and planning materials.

Inclusion

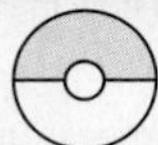

Adaptations CD Adapted lessons, investigations, practice and assessments.

Meeting Standards

National Council of Teachers of Mathematics (NCTM)

Numbers and Operations

NO.1a Work flexibly with fractions, decimals, and percents to solve problems

NO.3a Select appropriate methods and tools for computing with fractions and decimals from among mental computation, estimation, calculators or computers, and paper and pencil, depending on the situation, and apply the selected methods

Connections

CN.4b Understand how mathematical ideas interconnect and build on one another to produce a coherent whole

Power-Up Discussion *For use with Power Up, p. 182*

Problem-Solving Strategy: Use Logical Reasoning

Copy this problem and fill in the missing digits:

$$\begin{array}{r} \_\,\_\,\_ \\ \times \quad 9 \\ \hline \_\,\_\,2 \end{array}$$

Understand ***Understand the problem.***

"What information are we given?"

We are shown a multiplication problem that has several missing digits.

"What are we asked to do?"

We are asked to find the missing digits.

"What prior knowledge do we have?"

We know the multiples of 9.

Plan ***Make a plan.***

"What problem-solving strategy will we use?"

We will *use number sense and logical reasoning* to find the missing digits.

Solve ***Carry out the plan.***

"What can we infer from a three-digit factor times 9 resulting in a three-digit product?"

The top factor will be 111 or less, and the product will be 999 or less. If the top number were greater than 111, it would yield a four-digit product when multiplied by 9.

"What number times 9 gives us a product that ends in 2?"

8. $8 \times 9 = 72$, so we write an 8 in the top number.

"If the multiplicand needs to be 111 or less, what number should we try for the multiplicand?"

108

$$\begin{array}{r} 108 \\ \times \quad 9 \\ \hline 972 \end{array}$$

Check ***Look back.***

"How can we verify the solution is correct?"

We can check our answer using the inverse operation of multiplication (division): $972 \div 9 = 108$.

1 Power Up

Facts

Distribute **Power Up G** to students. See answers below.

Mental Math

Before students begin the Mental Math exercise, do this counting exercise as a class.

Count by 3s from 3 to 60. Count by 7s from 7 to 84.

Encourage students to share different ways to mentally compute these exercises. Strategies for exercises **d** and **f** are listed below.

d. Add Dollars and Add Cents

$\$7 + \$7 = \$14$ and $\$0.50 + \$0.50 = \$1.00$; $\$14 + \$1 = \$15$

Double a Mixed Number

Double $7\frac{1}{2} = 15$, so $\$7.50 + \$7.50 = \$15$

f. Cancel Zeros

$\frac{3600}{10} = \frac{360\not{0}}{1\not{0}} = \frac{360}{1} = 360$

Shift the Decimal Points One Place

$\frac{3600}{10} = \frac{360}{1} = 360$

Problem Solving

Refer to **Power-Up Discussion,** p. 182B.

2 New Concepts

Instruction

Some students may be unsure of when to write zeros in the numerator of an equivalent fraction. To help students understand if zeros are necessary, encourage them to first read the decimal number, then write the number that was read. For example:

0.7 is read "seven tenths" and the numerator of the equivalent fraction is 7.

0.06 is read "six hundredths" and the numerator of the equivalent fraction is 6.

0.409 is read "four hundred nine thousandths" and the numerator of the equivalent fraction is 409.

(continued)

LESSON **35**

• Writing Decimal Numbers as Fractions, Part 1
• Reading and Writing Decimal Numbers

Power Up

Building Power

facts Power Up G

mental math

a. Order of Operations: $(4 \times 300) + (4 \times 25)$ 1300

b. Number Sense: 8×43 344

c. Number Sense: $37 + 39$ 76

d. Money: $\$7.50 + \$7.50$ \$15.00

e. Fractional Parts: $\frac{1}{3}$ of 360 120

f. Number Sense: $\frac{3600}{10}$ 360

g. Measurement: Which is greater, 10 centimeters or 10 millimeters? 10 cm

h. Calculation: 5×5, $- 1$, $\div 3$, $\times 4$, $+ 1$, $\div 3$, $+ 1$, $\div 3$ 4

problem solving Copy this problem and fill in the missing digits:

$$\begin{array}{r} \_\_\_ \\ \times \quad 9 \\ \hline \_\_2 \end{array} \qquad \begin{array}{r} 108 \\ \times \quad 9 \\ \hline 972 \end{array}$$

New Concepts

Increasing Knowledge

writing decimal numbers as fractions, part 1

Decimal numbers are actually fractions. Their denominators come from the sequence 10, 100, 1000, ... The denominator of a decimal fraction is not written. Instead, it is indicated by the number of decimal places.

One decimal place indicates that the denominator is 10.

$$0.3 = \frac{3}{10}$$

$\frac{3}{10}$

Two decimal places indicate that the denominator is 100.

$$0.03 = \frac{3}{100}$$

$\frac{3}{100}$

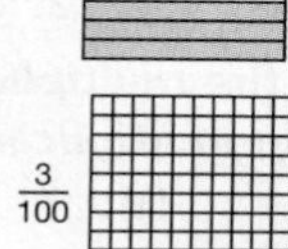

182 *Saxon* Math Course 1

Facts Reduce each fraction to lowest terms.

$\frac{2}{8} = \frac{1}{4}$	$\frac{4}{6} = \frac{2}{3}$	$\frac{6}{10} = \frac{3}{5}$	$\frac{2}{4} = \frac{1}{2}$	$\frac{5}{100} = \frac{1}{20}$	$\frac{9}{12} = \frac{3}{4}$
$\frac{4}{10} = \frac{2}{5}$	$\frac{4}{12} = \frac{1}{3}$	$\frac{2}{10} = \frac{1}{5}$	$\frac{3}{6} = \frac{1}{2}$	$\frac{25}{100} = \frac{1}{4}$	$\frac{3}{12} = \frac{1}{4}$
$\frac{4}{16} = \frac{1}{4}$	$\frac{3}{9} = \frac{1}{3}$	$\frac{6}{9} = \frac{2}{3}$	$\frac{4}{8} = \frac{1}{2}$	$\frac{2}{12} = \frac{1}{6}$	$\frac{6}{12} = \frac{1}{2}$
$\frac{8}{16} = \frac{1}{2}$	$\frac{2}{6} = \frac{1}{3}$	$\frac{8}{12} = \frac{2}{3}$	$\frac{6}{8} = \frac{3}{4}$	$\frac{5}{10} = \frac{1}{2}$	$\frac{75}{100} = \frac{3}{4}$

Three decimal places indicate that the denominator is 1000.

$$0.003 = \frac{3}{1000}$$

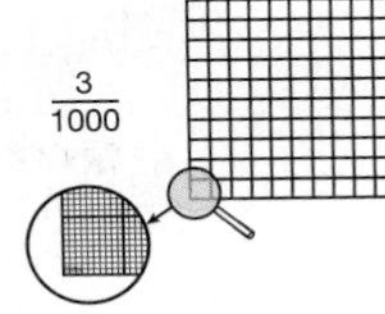

Notice that the number of zeros in the denominator equals the number of decimal places in the decimal number.

Example 1

A quart is 0.25 gallons. Write 0.25 as a fraction.

Solution

The decimal number 0.25 has two decimal places, so the denominator is 100. The numerator is 25.

$$0.25 = \mathbf{\frac{25}{100}}$$

The fraction $\frac{25}{100}$ reduces to $\frac{1}{4}$.

Example 2

A kilometer is about $\frac{6}{10}$ of a mile. Write $\frac{6}{10}$ as a decimal number.

Solution

The denominator is 10, so the decimal number has one decimal place. We write the digit 6 in this place.

$$\frac{6}{10} \longrightarrow 0.\_ \longrightarrow \mathbf{0.6}$$

reading and writing decimal numbers

We read numbers to the right of a decimal point the same way we read whole numbers, and then we say the place value of the last digit. We read 0.23 as "twenty-three hundredths" because the last digit is in the hundredths place. To read a mixed decimal number like 20.04, we read the whole number part, say "and," and then read the decimal part.

Example 3

The length of a football field is about 0.057 miles. Write 0.057 with words.

Solution

We see 57 and three decimal places. We write **fifty-seven thousandths.**

2 New Concepts (Continued)

Example 1

Instruction

You may wish to display the **Fraction-Decimal-Percent Equivalents** concept poster at this time.

When discussing the solution, ask,

"To reduce $\frac{25}{100}$, we divide by the greatest common factor. What is the greatest common factor of 25 and 100?" 25

Example 2

Instruction

After completing the example, ask

"Which distance is greater, 1 kilometer or 1 mile?" 1 mile

(continued)

Math Background

When an equivalent fraction is written for a decimal, only significant digits are written in the numerator of the fraction. For example, in the decimal number 0.04, the zeros are not significant digits. They are used simply to place the decimal point.

Three zeros would be used to place the decimal point when writing "seven thousandths" (0.007) and the numerator of its equivalent fraction ($\frac{7}{1000}$) would not display the zeros because they are not significant.

2 New Concepts (Continued)

Example 4

Instruction

Point out that 2.54 is a decimal number greater than 1, and remind students that whenever a decimal number is greater than or equal to 1, the word "and" must be used to represent the decimal point when reading the number and when writing the word form of the number. For example, 1.0 is read and written "one and zero tenths."

After completing the example, ask

"Which distance is greater, 1 inch or 1 centimeter?" 1 inch

Example 6

Instruction

After completing the example, make sure students have a general understanding that decimal numbers in tenths have one digit to the right of the decimal point, decimal numbers in hundredths have two digits to the right of the decimal point, and decimal numbers in thousandths have three digits to the right of the decimal point.

Example 4

An inch is 2.54 centimeters. Use words to write 2.54.

Solution

The decimal point separates the whole number part of the number from the decimal part of the number. We name the whole number part, write "and," and then name the decimal part.

two and fifty-four hundredths

Example 5

Write twenty-one hundredths

a. as a fraction.

b. as a decimal number.

Solution

The same words name both a fraction form and a decimal form of the number.

a. The word *hundredths* indicates that the denominator is 100.

$$\frac{21}{100}$$

b. The word *hundredths* indicates that the decimal number has two decimal places.

0.21

Example 6

Write fifteen and two tenths as a decimal number.

Solution

The whole number part is fifteen. The fractional part is two tenths, which we write in decimal form.

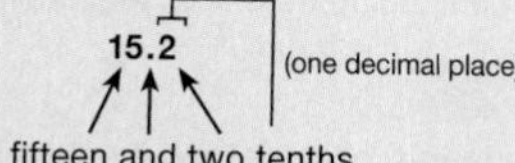

Verify How would you write 15.2 as a mixed number? $15\frac{2}{10}$ or $15\frac{1}{5}$

Practice Set Write each decimal number as a fraction:

a. 0.1 $\frac{1}{10}$ **b.** 0.31 $\frac{31}{100}$ **c.** 0.321 $\frac{321}{1000}$

Write each fraction as a decimal number:

d. $\frac{3}{10}$ 0.3 **e.** $\frac{17}{100}$ 0.17 **f.** $\frac{123}{1000}$ 0.123

Inclusion

Materials: 100 color tiles

Some students may have difficulty understanding the difference in value between a tenth and a hundredth. Arrange 100 tiles in a 10-by-10 array and remind students that one hundredth means 1 out of 100 equal parts.

Ask, ***"How many tiles are needed to represent one hundredth of the square?"*** one

"How many columns are in the square?" ten

"How many tiles are needed to represent one tenth of the square?" ten

To reinforce the fact that one tenth is greater than one hundredth, ask:

"Suppose each tile can be exchanged for one dollar. Which would you rather have, one tenth or one hundredth of the tiles?" one tenth

Challenge students to use the model to decide which is greater, 3 tenths or 5 hundredths. 3 tenths

Use words to write each number:

g. 0.05 five hundredths **h.** 0.015 fifteen thousandths ▶ **i.** 1.2 one and two tenths

Connect Write each number first as a fraction, then as a decimal number:

j. seven tenths $\frac{7}{10}$; 0.7

k. thirty-one hundredths $\frac{31}{100}$; 0.31

l. seven hundred thirty-one thousandths $\frac{731}{1000}$; 0.731

Write each number as a decimal number:

▶ **m.** five and six tenths 5.6

▶ **n.** eleven and twelve hundredths 11.12

o. one hundred twenty-five thousandths 0.125

Written Practice *Strengthening Concepts*

1. (29) What is the product of three fourths and three fifths? $\frac{9}{20}$

2. (22) **Model** Thomas planted 360 carrot seeds in his garden. Three fourths of them sprouted. How many carrot seeds sprouted? Draw a diagram to illustrate the problem. 270 carrot seeds

2.

* **3.** (32) Sakari's casserole must bake for 2 hours 15 minutes. If she put it into the oven at 11:45 a.m., at what time will it be done? 2:00 p.m.

▶ * **4.** (35) **Represent** Write twenty-three hundredths

a. as a fraction. $\frac{23}{100}$

b. as a decimal number. 0.23

▶ * **5.** (35) **Represent** Write 10.01 with words. ten and one hundredth

* **6.** (35) Write ten and five tenths as a decimal number. 10.5

▶ * **7.** (33) **Connect** Write each percent as a reduced fraction:

a. 25% $\frac{1}{4}$ **b.** 75% $\frac{3}{4}$

* **8.** (32) Write $(5 \times 1000) + (6 \times 100) + (4 \times 10)$ in standard notation. 5640

▶ * **9.** (34) **Connect** Which digit in 1.23 has the same place value as the 5 in 0.456? 3

10. (31) What is the area of the rectangle below? 200 sq. mm

11. (8) In problem **10,** what is the perimeter of the rectangle? 60 mm

▶ See Math Conversations in the sidebar.

English Learners

Explain that to answer the question in problem 1, the student must know the meaning of the word **product.** Say:

"The answer to a multiplication problem is the product of the two factors multiplied."

Ask for a volunteer to create a problem by multiplying two numbers on the board. Have them read the problem using *product* as the term for the answer to the problem.

3 Written Practice

Math Conversations

Discussion opportunities are provided below.

Practice Set

Problem i, m, and n (Error Alert)

Remind students that the word "and" is used when naming a number that has two parts: a whole number part and a fraction or a decimal part. Explain that the word "and" is not used when naming a number that has only one part, such as a whole number, a fraction, or a decimal number less than 1.

To reinforce this concept, invite volunteers to write a variety of numbers on the board or overhead. For each number, ask the remainder of the students to decide if its word name will contain the word "and."

Problem 4 Represent

"When a fraction is written to represent a decimal number in hundredths, what number is used for the denominator of the fraction?" 100

"In a decimal number, how many decimal places does hundredths represent?" two

Problem 5 Represent

"In the word name for this decimal number, what word represents the decimal point?" and

Problem 7 Connect

"What denominator is used when a percent is written as a fraction? Why?" 100; a percent and its symbol mean "per hundred."

"What operation is used to reduce a fraction?" division

Problem 9 Connect

If students need additional practice identifying place values, ask them to identify the place value of each digit in each number.

Errors and Misconceptions

Problem 4

When reading and writing decimal numbers, a common error is to incorrectly identify the number of places a word name represents. As students read and write decimal numbers, help them apply the following generalizations.

- A decimal number in tenths has one place to the right of the decimal point.
- A decimal number in hundredths has two places to the right of the decimal point.
- A decimal number in thousandths has three places to the right of the decimal point.

(continued)

3 Written Practice (Continued)

Math Conversations

Discussion opportunities are provided below.

Problem 18b Connect

"How can you use the idea of doubling to find the number of two-fifths in 2?" Double the number of two-fifths in 1.

Problem 23 Represent

Invite students who have difficulty solving this problem to use their fraction manipulatives from Investigation 2.

Problem 25 Connect

Extend the Problem

"What number is the same distance from zero as −14, but in the opposite direction from zero?" +14 or 14

Problem 27 Conclude

"Why can't the fraction $\frac{21}{100}$ be reduced?" The greatest common factor of 21 and 100 is 1.

Problem 30 Formulate

Remind students to write the remainder as the numerator of a fraction that has the divisor as its denominator.

---

12. (7) There are 100 centimeters in a meter. How many centimeters are in 10 meters? 1000 centimeters

* 13. (34) Arrange these numbers in order from least to greatest: −1, 0, 0.001, 0.01, 0.1, 1.0
0.001, 0.1, 1.0, 0.01, 0, −1

14. (7) **Estimate** A meter is about one big step. About how many meters wide is a door? about 1 meter

15. (24) $\frac{3}{5} + \frac{2}{5}$ 1 16. (24) $\frac{5}{8} - \frac{5}{8}$ 0 17. (29) $\frac{2}{3} \times \frac{3}{4}$ $\frac{1}{2}$

* 18. (30) **a.** How many $\frac{2}{5}$s are in 1? $\frac{5}{2}$

▸ **b.** **Connect** Use the answer to part **a** to find the number of $\frac{2}{5}$s in 2. $\frac{10}{2} = 5$

19. (25) Convert $\frac{20}{6}$ to a mixed number. Remember to reduce the fraction part of the number. $3\frac{1}{3}$

20. (25) $\frac{100\%}{6}$ $16\frac{2}{3}\%$ 21. (26) $3\frac{4}{4} - 1\frac{1}{4}$ $2\frac{3}{4}$

22. (29) Compare: 5 ⊜ $4\frac{4}{4}$

▸ 23. (Inv. 2) **Represent** One sixth of a circle is what percent of a circle? $16\frac{2}{3}\%$

24. (9) Compare: 3 × 18 ÷ 6 ⊜ 3 × (18 ÷ 6)

▸ 25. (14) **Connect** To what number is the arrow pointing on the number line below? −14

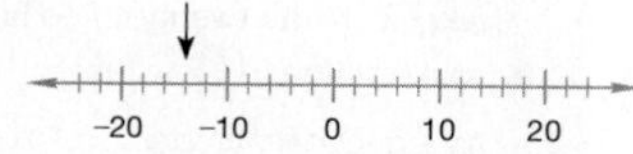

26. (2) **Conclude** Which of these division problems has the greatest quotient? D
A $\frac{6}{2}$ **B** $\frac{60}{20}$ **C** $\frac{12}{4}$ **D** $\frac{25}{8}$

▸* 27. (35) **Conclude** Write 0.3 and 0.7 as fractions. Then multiply the fractions. What is the product? $\frac{21}{100}$

* 28. (33, 35) Write 21% as a fraction. Then write the fraction as a decimal number. $\frac{21}{100}$; 0.21

29. (2) Instead of solving the division problem 400 ÷ 50, Minh doubled both numbers to form the division 800 ÷ 100. Find both quotients. 8; 8

▸ 30. (23, 25) **Formulate** A 50-inch-long ribbon was cut into four shorter ribbons of equal length. How long was each of the shorter ribbons? Write an equation and solve the problem. Explain why your answer is reasonable.
$4 \cdot r = 50$; $12\frac{1}{2}$ inches. Sample: If you cut the ribbon in half, you have two pieces 25 inches long. If you cut each piece in half you have four pieces $12\frac{1}{2}$ inches long.

▸ See Math Conversations in the sidebar.

Looking Forward

Writing a decimal number as a fraction and a fraction as a decimal number prepares students for:

- **Lesson 41,** changing percents to fractions and decimals.
- **Lesson 50,** reading a decimal number line in tenths.
- **Lesson 73,** writing decimal numbers as fractions.
- **Lesson 75,** writing fractions and decimal numbers as percents.
- **Lesson 99,** writing fraction-decimal-percent equivalents.

Assessment

30–40 minutes *For use after Lesson 35*

Distribute **Cumulative Test 6** to each student. Two versions of the test are available in *Saxon Math Course 1 Course Assessments Book.* Have students complete the **Power-Up Test** first. Allow 10 minutes. Then have students work the 20 numbered items on the **Cumulative Test.** Students may use copies of the answer sheet to record their work. Track individual and class progress with the **Test Analysis** forms.

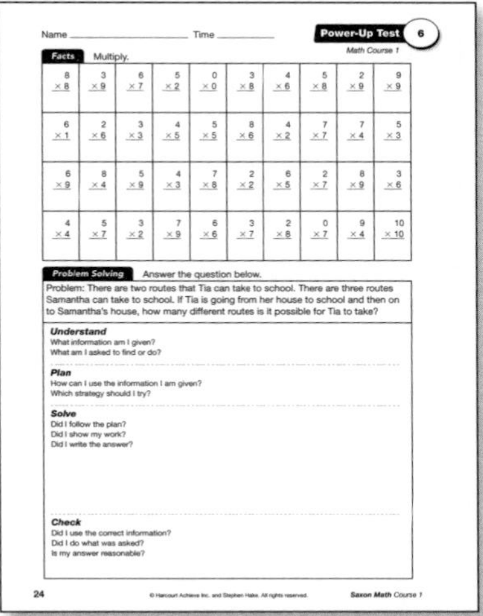

Power-Up Test 6

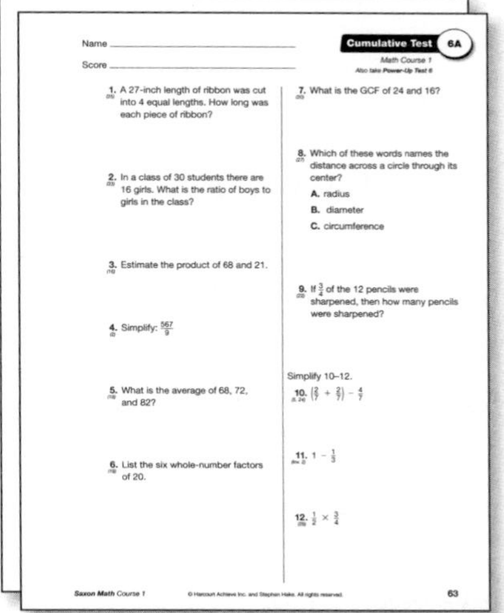

Cumulative Test 6A

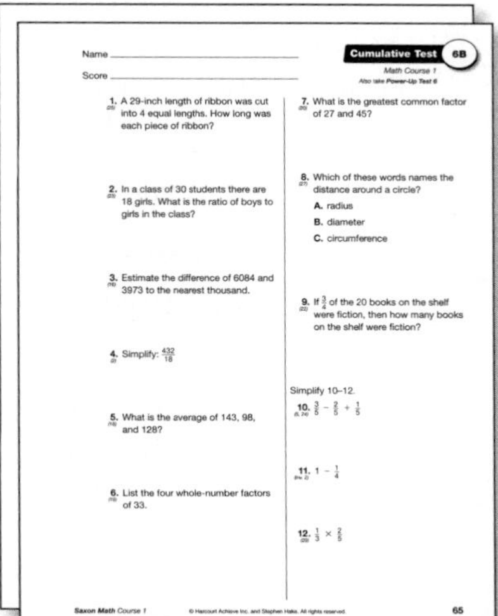

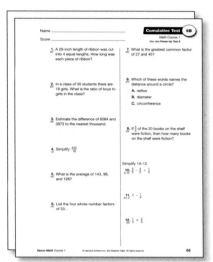

Alternative Cumulative Test 6B

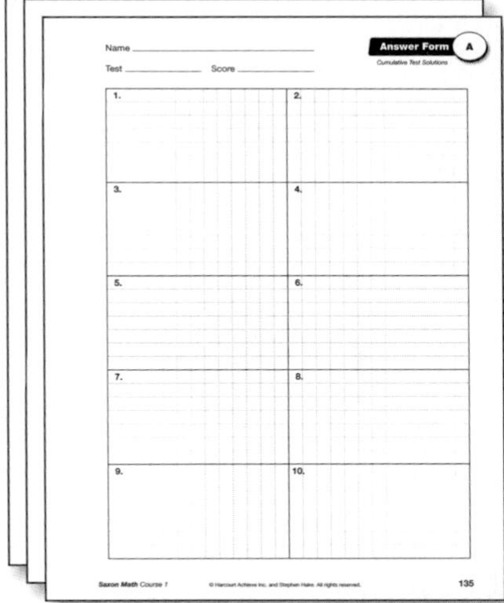

Optional Answer Forms

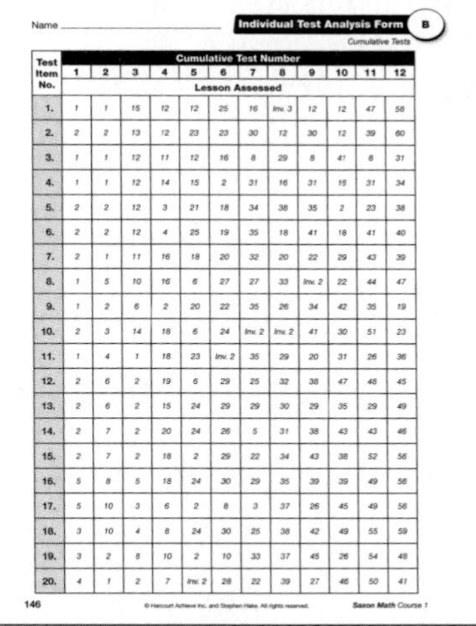

Individual Test Analysis Form

Class Test Analysis Form

Reteaching

Students who score below 80% on the assessment may be in need of reteaching. Look for the causes of student mistakes. If errors are conceptual, refer to the *Reteaching Masters* for reteaching.

Performance Activity 6

Different Ways to Represent 1000

Assign after Lesson 35 and Test 6

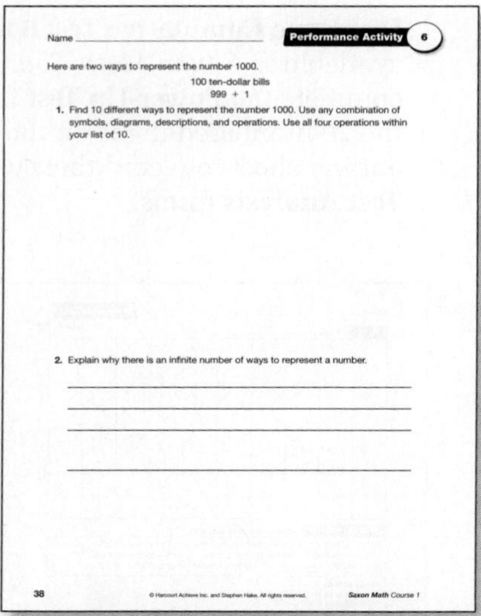

Name ____________ **Performance Activity 6**

Here are two ways to represent the number 1000.

100 ten-dollar bills
999 + 1

1. Find 10 different ways to represent the number 1000. Use any combination of symbols, diagrams, descriptions, and operations. Use all four operations within your list of 10.

2. Explain why there is an infinite number of ways to represent a number.

38 © Harcourt Achieve Inc. and Stephen Hake. All rights reserved. *Saxon Math* Course 1

Performance Activity 6

Objectives

- Represent 1000 in different ways.
- Communicate ideas through writing.

Materials

Performance Activity 6

Preparation

Make copies of **Performance Activity 6.** (One each per student.)

Time Requirement

15–30 minutes; Begin in class and complete at home.

Activity

Explain to students that for this activity they will use symbols, diagrams, descriptions, and operations to represent the number 1000 in 10 different ways. They will also be required to explain why there is an infinite number of ways to represent a number. Explain that all of the information students need is on **Performance Activity 6.**

Criteria for Evidence of Learning

- Uses correct symbols, diagrams, descriptions, and operations to represent 1000 accurately.
- Gives a correct explanation of why there is an infinite number of ways to represent a number.
- Communicates ideas clearly through writing.

Meeting Standards

National Council of Teachers of Mathematics (NCTM)

Numbers and Operations

NO.1g Develop meaning for integers and represent and compare quantities with them

Connections

CN.4a Recognize and use connections among mathematical ideas

Communication

CM.3d Use the language of mathematics to express mathematical ideas precisely

• Subtracting Fractions and Mixed Numbers from Whole Numbers

Objectives

- Subtract a fraction from a whole number.
- Subtract a mixed number from a whole number.

Lesson Preparation

Materials

- **Power Up F** (in *Instructional Masters*)
- **Teacher-provided material: fraction manipulatives** from Investigation 2

Optional

- **Manipulative kit: overhead fraction circles**

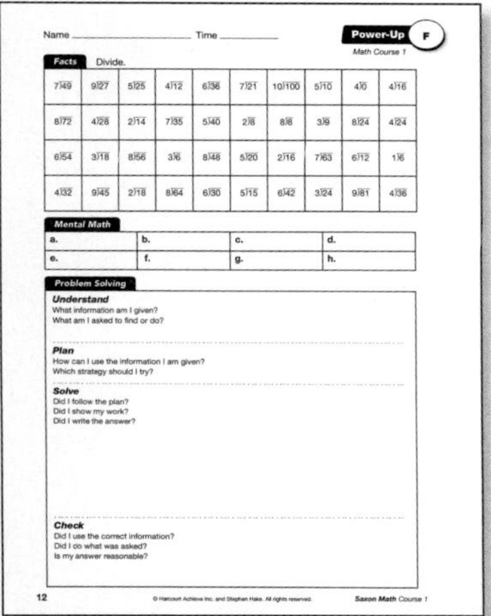

Name ____________ Time ________ **Power-Up F**

Math Course 1

Facts Divide.

7)49	9)27	5)25	4)12	6)36	7)21	10)100	5)10	4)0	4)16
8)72	4)28	2)14	7)35	5)40	2)8	8)8	3)9	8)24	4)24
6)54	3)18	8)56	3)6	8)48	5)20	2)16	7)63	6)12	1)6
4)32	9)45	2)18	8)64	6)30	5)15	6)42	3)24	9)81	4)36

Mental Math

a.	b.	c.	d.
e.	f.	g.	h.

Problem Solving

Understand
What information am I given?
What am I asked to find or do?

Plan
How can I use the information I am given?
Which strategy should I try?

Solve
Did I follow the plan?
Did I show my work?
Did I write the answer?

Check
Did I use the correct information?
Did I do what was asked?
Is my answer reasonable?

12 ***Saxon Math*** *Course 1*

Power Up F

Math Language

English Learners (ESL)
whole

Technology Resources

Student eBook Complete student textbook in electronic format.

Resources and Planner CD Assessment, reteaching, and instructional masters, plus a pacing calendar with standards.

Test and Practice Generator CD Create additional practice sheets and custom-made tests.

www.SaxonPublishers.com Visit for more student activities and planning materials.

Inclusion

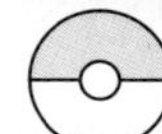

Adaptations CD Adapted lessons, investigations, practice and assessments.

Meeting Standards

National Council of Teachers of Mathematics (NCTM)

Numbers and Operations

NO.1a Work flexibly with fractions, decimals, and percents to solve problems

NO.2a Understand the meaning and effects of arithmetic operations with fractions, decimals, and integers

NO.3a Select appropriate methods and tools for computing with fractions and decimals from among mental computation, estimation, calculators or computers, and paper and pencil, depending on the situation, and apply the selected methods

Connections

CN.4a Recognize and use connections among mathematical ideas

Power-Up Discussion *For use with Power Up, p. 187*

Problem-Solving Strategy: Make It Simpler/ Draw a Diagram

The playground is filled with bicycles and wagons. If there are 24 vehicles and 80 wheels altogether, how many bicycles are on the playground? How many wagons?

Understand **Understand the problem.**

"What information are we given?"

There are a total of 24 vehicles and 80 wheels in a playground filled with bicycles and wagons.

"What are we asked to do?"

We are asked to determine how many bicycles and how many wagons are in the playground.

"What do we know about wagons and bicycles?"

Usually wagons have four wheels and bicycles have two wheels.

Plan **Make a plan.**

"What problem-solving strategy will we use?"

We can *make it simpler* by simplifying the ratio of vehicles to wheels from $\frac{24}{80}$ to $\frac{3}{10}$. Working with only 3 vehicles will allow us to *draw a diagram* to account for the vehicles and wagons.

Solve **Carry out the plan.**

"How do we begin?"

Each vehicle has at least two wheels, so our diagram will show 3 vehicles and 6 wheels.

"How many pairs of wheels must still be accounted for?"

$10 - 6 = 4$ wheels, which is 2 pairs. Now we will add one more pair of wheels to 2 of our vehicles.

"We have found that for the ratio of 3 vehicles to 10 wheels, there are 2 wagons and 1 bicycle. According to our original ratio, how many wagons are in the playground?"

16

"How many bicycles?"

8

Check **Look back.**

"How can we verify the solution is correct?"

By writing a number sentence that represents the 24 vehicles: (16 wagons $\times$ 4 wheels) + (8 bicycles $\times$ 2 wheels) = 64 wheels + 16 wheels = 80 wheels total.

Teacher Note: You may extend this lesson by using a guess and check strategy.

LESSON 36

• Subtracting Fractions and Mixed Numbers from Whole Numbers

Power Up — Building Power

facts Power Up F

mental math

a. **Order of Operations:** $(4 \times 400) + (4 \times 25)$ 1700

b. **Number Sense:** $2500 + 375$ 2875

c. **Number Sense:** $86 - 39$ 47

d. **Money:** $15.00 − $2.50 $12.50

e. **Fractional Parts:** $\frac{1}{2}$ of 320 160

f. **Number Sense:** $\frac{4800}{100}$ 48

g. **Measurement:** Which is greater, 6 months or 52 weeks? 52 weeks

h. **Calculation:** $2 \times 4, \times 5, + 10, \times 2, - 1, \div 9, \times 3, - 1, \div 4$ 8

problem solving The playground is filled with bicycles and wagons. If there are 24 vehicles and 80 wheels altogether, how many bicycles are on the playground? How many wagons? 8 bicycles; 16 wagons

New Concept — Increasing Knowledge

Read this "separating" word problem about pies.

There were four pies on the shelf. The server sliced one of the pies into sixths and took $2\frac{1}{6}$ pies from the shelf. How many pies were left on the shelf?

We can illustrate this problem with circles. There were four pies on the shelf.

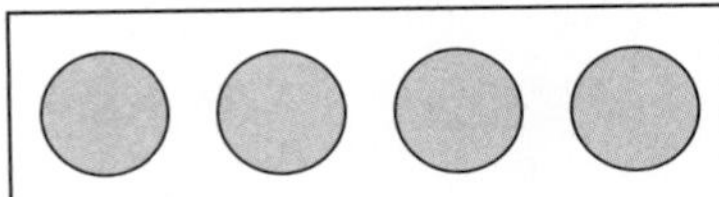

The server sliced one of the pies into sixths. (Then there were $3\frac{6}{6}$ pies, which is another name for 4 pies.)

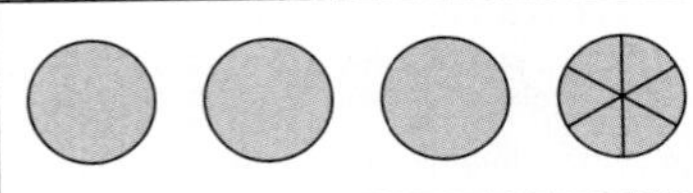

Facts Divide.

7)49 = 7	9)27 = 3	5)25 = 5	4)12 = 3	6)36 = 6	7)21 = 3	10)100 = 10	5)10 = 2	4)0 = 0	4)16 = 4
8)72 = 9	4)28 = 7	2)14 = 7	7)35 = 5	5)40 = 8	2)8 = 4	8)8 = 1	3)9 = 3	8)24 = 3	4)24 = 6
6)54 = 9	3)18 = 6	8)56 = 7	3)6 = 2	8)48 = 6	5)20 = 4	2)16 = 8	7)63 = 9	6)12 = 2	1)6 = 6
4)32 = 8	9)45 = 5	2)18 = 9	8)64 = 8	6)30 = 5	5)15 = 3	6)42 = 7	3)24 = 8	9)81 = 9	4)36 = 9

1 Power Up

Facts

Distribute **Power Up F** to students. See answers below.

Mental Math

Before students begin the Mental Math exercise, do this counting exercise as a class.

Count up and down by $\frac{1}{8}$s between $\frac{1}{8}$ and 3.

Encourage students to share different ways to mentally compute these exercises. Strategies for exercises **a** and **c** are listed below.

a. Follow the Order of Operations

$(4 \times 400) + (4 \times 25) = 1600 + 100 = 1700$

Count On by 400, then by 25

Start with 400. Count: 800, 1200, 1600

Start with 1600. Count: 1625, 1650, 1675, 1700

c. Add 3 to 86, then Subtract 3

$89 - 39 = 50$; $50 - 3 = 47$

Count Back by 10, then Add 1

Start with 86. Count: 76, 66, 56, 46

$46 + 1 = 47$

Problem Solving

Refer to **Power-Up Discussion,** p. 187B.

2 New Concepts

Instruction

Fraction circles from the Manipulative Kit can be used to model the problem. Begin by placing four whole circle manipulatives on the overhead. To represent $3\frac{6}{6}$, replace one circle with a circle showing 6 equal parts. Then model the subtraction by taking away 2 wholes and $\frac{1}{6}$ so that $1\frac{5}{6}$ remains.

(continued)

2 New Concepts (Continued)

Instruction

Have students note the vertical alignment—the whole numbers in one column and the fractions in a column to their right—throughout the computation, and remind them that neat alignment helps make the arithmetic easier to complete, and reduces the likelihood of mistakes.

Example

Instruction

After completing the example, invite volunteers to share the word problems they wrote with their classmates.

Practice Set

Problems a–f (Error Alert)

When subtracting a fraction or mixed number from a whole number, a common error is to incorrectly rename the whole number. Remind students of the importance of checking their work, then ask them to use their fraction manipulatives to check each answer.

(continued)

The server took $2\frac{1}{6}$ pies from the shelf.

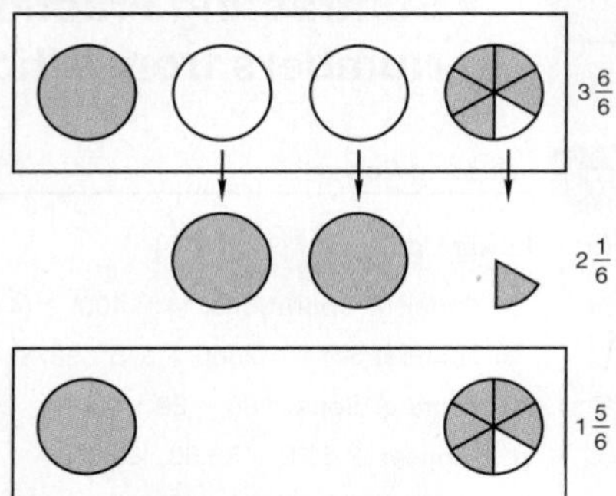

We see $1\frac{5}{6}$ pies left on the shelf.

Now we show the arithmetic for subtracting $2\frac{1}{6}$ from 4.

$$\begin{array}{r} 4 \text{ pies} \\ -\ 2\tfrac{1}{6} \text{ pies} \\ \hline \end{array}$$

The server sliced one of the pies into sixths, so we change 4 wholes into 3 wholes plus 6 sixths. Then we subtract.

$$\begin{array}{r} 4 \\ -\ 2\tfrac{1}{6} \\ \hline \end{array} \xrightarrow{3\,+\,\frac{6}{6}} \begin{array}{r} 3\tfrac{6}{6} \\ -\ 2\tfrac{1}{6} \\ \hline \mathbf{1\tfrac{5}{6}} \end{array}$$

Example

Subtract: $5 - 1\frac{2}{3}$. Then write a word problem that is solved by the subtraction.

Solution

To subtract $1\frac{2}{3}$ from 5, we first change 5 to 4 plus $\frac{3}{3}$. Then we subtract.

$$\begin{array}{r} 5 \\ -\ 1\tfrac{2}{3} \\ \hline \end{array} \xrightarrow{4\,+\,\frac{3}{3}} \begin{array}{r} 4\tfrac{3}{3} \\ -\ 1\tfrac{2}{3} \\ \hline \mathbf{3\tfrac{1}{3}} \end{array}$$

Thinking Skill

Discuss

Why do we need to change 5 to $4\frac{3}{3}$ before we subtract $1\frac{2}{3}$ from 5? We need a fraction from which to subtract $\frac{2}{3}$. This is similar to regrouping when subtracting with whole numbers.

Common subtraction word problems are about comparing or separating. Here is a sample word problem. If a clerk cuts $1\frac{2}{3}$ yards of fabric from a 5-yard length, how many yards of fabric remain?

Practice Set

▸ Show the arithmetic for each subtraction: See student work.

a. $3 - 2\frac{1}{2}$ $\frac{1}{2}$

b. $2 - \frac{1}{4}$ $1\frac{3}{4}$

c. $4 - 2\frac{1}{4}$ $1\frac{3}{4}$

d. $3 - \frac{5}{12}$ $2\frac{7}{12}$

▸ See Math Conversations in the sidebar.

Manipulative Use

Fraction circles can be used to model the subtraction in the example.

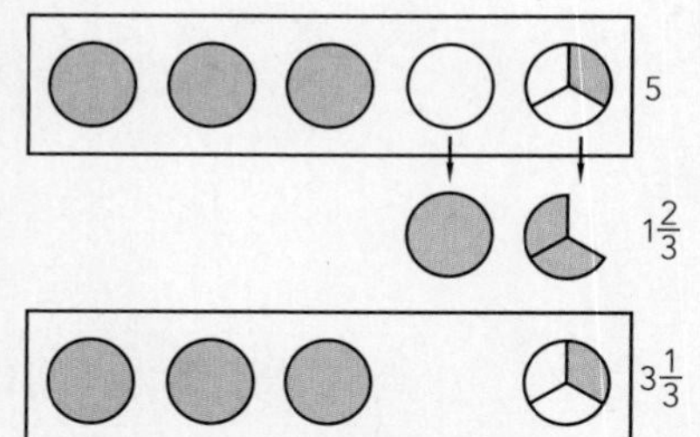

Math Background

When subtracting fractions and mixed numbers from whole numbers, the whole numbers can be renamed more than once if needed.

For example, to subtract $\frac{3}{2}$ from 9, two renamings are needed. First, 9 is renamed as $8 + \frac{2}{2}$. Then $8 + \frac{2}{2}$ is renamed as $7 + \frac{2}{2} + \frac{2}{2}$, and the arithmetic can be completed.

$$\begin{array}{r} 9 \\ -\ \tfrac{3}{2} \\ \hline \end{array} \longrightarrow \begin{array}{r} 7\tfrac{4}{2} \\ -\ \tfrac{3}{2} \\ \hline 7\tfrac{1}{2} \end{array}$$

e. $10 - 2\frac{1}{2}$ $7\frac{1}{2}$

f. $6 - 1\frac{3}{10}$ $4\frac{7}{10}$

g. Sample for exercise c:

$4 = 3\frac{4}{4}$

$-2\frac{1}{4}$

$1\frac{3}{4}$

g. **Model** Select one of the exercises to model with a drawing.

▶ h. **Formulate** Select another exercise and write a word problem that is solved by the subtraction. Sample for exercise e: Sam cut $2\frac{1}{2}$ feet from a 10-foot long board. How long is the board now?

i. There were four whole pies on the shelf. The server took $1\frac{5}{6}$ pies. How many pies were left on the shelf? $2\frac{1}{6}$ pies

j. **Formulate** Write a word problem similar to problem **i,** and then find the answer. See student work.

Written Practice

Strengthening Concepts

▶ * 1. (33) **Analyze** Twenty-five percent of the students played musical instruments. What fraction of the students played musical instruments? $\frac{1}{4}$

▶ * 2. (36) About $\frac{3}{4}$ of the Earth's surface is covered with water. What fraction of Earth's surface is not covered with water? $\frac{1}{4}$

3. (15) A mile is 5280 feet. There are 3 feet in a yard. How many yards are in a mile? 1760 yards

* 4. (34) Which digit in 23.47 has the same place value as the 6 in 516.9? 3

▶ * 5. (35) Write 1.3 with words. one and three tenths

▶ * 6. (35) Write the decimal number five hundredths. 0.05

▶ * 7. (35) Write thirty-one hundredths

a. as a fraction. $\frac{31}{100}$

b. as a decimal number. 0.31

* 8. (32) Write $(4 \times 100) + (3 \times 1)$ in standard notation. 403

▶ * 9. (34) Which digit in 4.375 is in the tenths place? 3

▶* 10. (8, 31) **Analyze** If the area of a square is 9 square inches,

a. how long is each side of the square? 3 inches

b. what is the perimeter of the square? 12 inches

11. (28) Name two obtuse angles in the figure below. $\angle AMB$ (or $\angle BMA$) and $\angle DMC$ (or $\angle CMD$)

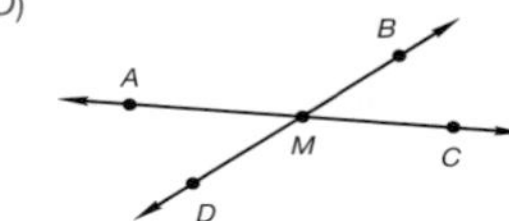

12. (26) $3\frac{1}{4} + 2\frac{1}{4}$ $5\frac{1}{2}$

* 13. (36) $3 - 1\frac{1}{4}$ $1\frac{3}{4}$

14. (26) $3\frac{1}{3} + 2\frac{2}{3}$ 6

▶ See Math Conversations in the sidebar.

English Learners

To help students with exercise **i,** draw the following illustrations on the board.

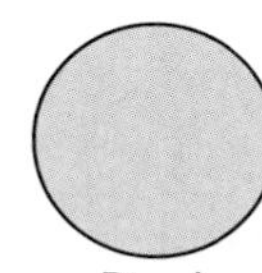

Pie A

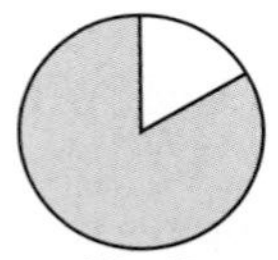

Pie B

Explain that the word **whole** means the entire thing. Point out that pie A is a whole pie, and pie B is not a whole pie. Say:

"Pie A can be cut into pieces. Those pieces will still make one whole pie. A piece has been taken from pie B, so it is no longer a whole pie."

Ask for a volunteer to provide an example of something whole/not whole in the classroom.

2 New Concepts *(Continued)*

Practice Set

Problem h Formulate

Ask students to illustrate the arithmetic in the problems they write with a sketch.

3 Written Practice

Math Conversations

Discussion opportunities are provided below.

Problem 1 Analyze

"What must we do to change a percent to a fraction?" Write the percent as the numerator of a fraction having a denominator of 100, then reduce.

Problem 2 Explain

Some students will solve this problem using mental math. Ask those students to explain the arithmetic that needs to be completed to find the answer. Subtract $\frac{3}{4}$ from 1. Rename 1 as $\frac{4}{4}$, then subtract $\frac{3}{4}$.

Problem 5 Represent

"Why must the word "and" be included in the answer?" When naming fractions or decimal numbers, we say "and" after the whole number and before the fraction. The decimal point reminds us to say or write "and" when naming decimal numbers.

Problem 7 Represent

Extend the Problem

"How many digits to the right of the decimal point does a decimal number in thousandths have?" three

"How many digits to the right of the decimal point does a decimal number in tenths have?" one

Problem 10 Analyze

"The lengths of the sides of every square share a relationship. What is that relationship?" All of the sides of a square have the same length.

Errors and Misconceptions

Problem 5, 6, 7, and 9

Encourage students who have difficulty working with decimal place values to use a decimal place value chart.

(continued)

3 Written Practice (Continued)

Math Conversations

Discussion opportunities are provided below.

Problem 28 Represent

"When we write $\frac{81}{1000}$ as a decimal number, why do we need to write a zero in the tenths place?" Sample: The fraction represents thousandths, and the zero creates three decimal places to the right of the decimal point; without a zero in the tenths place, the decimal number 0.81 would represent 81 hundredths, not 81 thousandths.

Problem 29 a and b Analyze

"Explain how multiplication and your answer from Problem a can be used to find the answer for Problem b. If the number of $\frac{3}{4}$s in 1 is $\frac{4}{3}$, then the number of $\frac{3}{4}$s in 3 must be: $\frac{4}{3} \times \frac{3}{1} = \frac{12}{3}$, which reduces to 4.

Challenge one or more volunteers to demonstrate on the overhead how fraction manipulatives can be used to check the answers to both problems.

Errors and Misconceptions

Problem 27

Watch for students who write the denominator instead of writing the product of the denominators.

---

15. (29) What is $\frac{3}{4}$ of 28? 21

16. (29) $\frac{3}{4} \times \frac{4}{6}$ $\frac{1}{2}$

17. (22) Model Chen went to the mall with \$24. He spent $\frac{5}{6}$ of his money in the music store. How much money did he spend in the music store? Draw a diagram to illustrate the problem. \$20

17.
\$24
spent $\frac{5}{6}$: \$4, \$4, \$4, \$4, \$4
did not spend $\frac{1}{6}$: \$4

18. (18) What is the average of 42, 57, and 63? 54

19. (19) The factors of 6 are 1, 2, 3, and 6. List the factors of 20. 1, 2, 4, 5, 10, 20

20. (20, 30) **a.** What is the least common multiple of 9 and 6? 18

b. What is the greatest common factor of 9 and 6? 3

Find each unknown number. Remember to check your work.

21. (4) $\frac{m}{12} = 6$ 72

22. (4) $\frac{12}{n} = 6$ 2

23. (16) Round 58,742,177 to the nearest million. 59,000,000

24. (16) Estimate the product of 823 and 680. 560,000

25. (7) How many millimeters long is the line segment shown below (1 cm = 10 mm)? 50 mm

cm 1 2 3 4 5 6 7 8

26. (Inv. 2) Model Using your fraction manipulatives, you can find that the sum of $\frac{1}{3}$ and $\frac{1}{6}$ is $\frac{1}{2}$.

$$\frac{1}{3} + \frac{1}{6} = \frac{1}{2}$$

Represent Arrange these fractions to form another addition equation and two subtraction equations. $\frac{1}{6} + \frac{1}{3} = \frac{1}{2}$, $\frac{1}{2} - \frac{1}{3} = \frac{1}{6}$, $\frac{1}{2} - \frac{1}{6} = \frac{1}{3}$

▸* **27.** (35) Write 0.9 and 0.09 as fractions. Then multiply the fractions. What is the product? $\frac{81}{1000}$

▸* **28.** (35) Represent Write $\frac{81}{1000}$ as a decimal number. (*Hint:* Write a zero in the tenths place.) 0.081

▸* **29.** (30) Analyze **a.** How many $\frac{3}{4}$s are in 1? $\frac{4}{3}$

b. Use the answer to part **a** to find the number of $\frac{3}{4}$s in 3. $\frac{12}{3} = 4$

Math Language

The **radius** is the distance from the center of a circle to a point on the circle. The **diameter** is the distance across a circle through its center.

30. (23, 27) Connect Freddy drove a stake into the ground, looped a 12-foot-long rope over it, and walked around the stake to mark off a circle. What was the ratio of the radius to the diameter of the circle? $\frac{1}{2}$

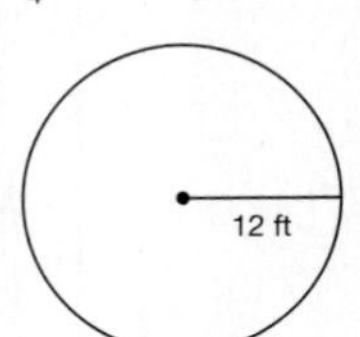

▸ See Math Conversations in the sidebar.

Looking Forward

Subtracting a fraction or a mixed number from a whole number prepares students for:

- **Lesson 42,** renaming fractions by multiplying by 1 in order to subtract the fractions.
- **Lesson 48,** using regrouping to subtract mixed numbers with common denominators.
- **Lessons 55 and 56,** finding common denominators in order to subtract fractions.
- **Lesson 57,** following three steps to add and subtract fractions.
- **Lesson 63,** using regrouping to subtract mixed numbers with unlike denominators.

190 *Saxon* Math Course 1

Adding and Subtracting Decimal Numbers

Objectives

- Add decimal numbers.
- Subtract decimal numbers.

Lesson Preparation

Materials

- **Power Up G** (in *Instructional Masters*)

Optional

- **Manipulative kit: dot cubes**
- **Teacher-provided material: grid paper**

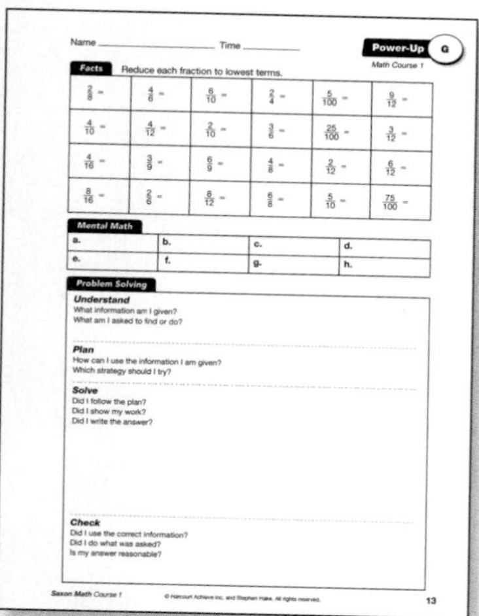

Name ______ Time ______

Power-Up G

Math Course 1

Facts Reduce each fraction to lowest terms.

$\frac{2}{8}$ =	$\frac{4}{6}$ =	$\frac{6}{10}$ =	$\frac{2}{4}$ =	$\frac{5}{100}$ =	$\frac{9}{12}$ =
$\frac{4}{10}$ =	$\frac{4}{12}$ =	$\frac{2}{10}$ =	$\frac{3}{6}$ =	$\frac{25}{100}$ =	$\frac{3}{12}$ =
$\frac{4}{16}$ =	$\frac{3}{9}$ =	$\frac{6}{9}$ =	$\frac{4}{8}$ =	$\frac{2}{12}$ =	$\frac{6}{12}$ =
$\frac{8}{16}$ =	$\frac{2}{6}$ =	$\frac{8}{12}$ =	$\frac{6}{8}$ =	$\frac{5}{10}$ =	$\frac{75}{100}$ =

Mental Math

a.	b.	c.	d.
e.	f.	g.	h.

Problem Solving

Understand
What information am I given?
What am I asked to find or do?

Plan
How can I use the information I am given?
Which strategy should I try?

Solve
Did I follow the plan?
Did I show my work?
Did I write the answer?

Check
Did I use the correct information?
Did I do what was asked?
Is my answer reasonable?

Saxon Math Course 1 © Harcourt Achieve Inc. and Stephen Hake. All rights reserved. 13

Power Up G

Math Language

English Learners (ESL)

doubled

Technology Resources

Student eBook Complete student textbook in electronic format.

Resources and Planner CD Assessment, reteaching, and instructional masters, plus a pacing calendar with standards.

Test and Practice Generator CD Create additional practice sheets and custom-made tests.

www.SaxonPublishers.com Visit for more student activities and planning materials.

Inclusion

Adaptations CD Adapted lessons, investigations, practice and assessments.

Meeting Standards

National Council of Teachers of Mathematics (NCTM)

Numbers and Operations

NO.1a Work flexibly with fractions, decimals, and percents to solve problems

NO.3a Select appropriate methods and tools for computing with fractions and decimals from among mental computation, estimation, calculators or computers, and paper and pencil, depending on the situation, and apply the selected methods

NO.3b Develop and analyze algorithms for computing with fractions, decimals, and integers and develop fluency in their use

Problem Solving

PS.1b Solve problems that arise in mathematics and in other contexts

Power-Up Discussion For use with Power Up, p. 191

Problem-Solving Strategy: Use Logical Reasoning/ Write an Equation

If a piglet weighs the same as two ducks, three piglets weigh the same as a young goat, and a young goat weighs the same as two terriers then how many of each animal weighs the same as a terrier?

Understand — Understand the problem.

"What information are we given?"

We are given the following weight relationships:

- A piglet weighs the same as two ducks.
- Three piglets weigh the same as a young goat.
- A young goat weighs the same as two terriers.

"What are we asked to do?"

We are asked to determine how many of each animal weighs the same as one terrier.

Teacher Note: Suggest to students that this problem is similar to solving problems regarding the exchange of currency: 1 dime = 2 nickels = 10 pennies.

Plan — Make a plan.

"What problem-solving strategy will we use?"

We will *use logical reasoning* and *write equations* to keep the relationships balanced.

Solve — Carry out the plan.

"How can we write the relationships between the animals' weights using variables?"

We use the first letter of each type of animal to write our equations: $P = 2D$, $3P = G$, and $G = 2T$.

"Since we are trying to find how the other animals' weights relate to a terrier, we begin with the last clue. One terrier weighs the same as how many goats?"

Since $G = 2T$, one terrier weighs the same as $\frac{1}{2}$ goat.

"From the second clue we see that three piglets equal one goat. What does this tell us about the relationship between piglets and terriers?"

Since $G = 2T$ and $G = 3P$, $2T$ and $3P$ are equal. Two terriers weigh the same as three piglets, or one terrier weighs the same as $1\frac{1}{2}$ piglets.

"How can we use this information along with the first clue to find the relationship between the weights of a duck and a terrier?"

Our first clue told us that a piglet weighs the same as two ducks, so the relationship between terriers and ducks is $2T = 3P = 6D$. If two terriers weigh the same as six ducks, then one terrier weighs the same as three ducks: $T = 3D$.

Check — Look back.

"Did we do what we were asked to do?"

Yes, we found how many of each animal weighs the same as one terrier.

LESSON 37

• Adding and Subtracting Decimal Numbers

Power Up — *Building Power*

facts Power Up G

mental math

a. **Order of Operations:** (4 × 500) + (4 × 25) 2100

b. **Number Sense:** 9 × 43 387

c. **Number Sense:** 76 − 29 47

d. **Money:** $17.50 + $2.50 $20.00

e. **Fractional Parts:** $\frac{1}{2}$ of 520 260

f. **Number Sense:** $\frac{2500}{10}$ 250

g. **Geometry:** A rectangle has a length of 10 in. and the width is $\frac{1}{2}$ as long as the length. What is the perimeter of the rectangle? 30 in.

h. **Calculation:** 6 × 8, + 1, ÷ 7, × 3, − 1, ÷ 5, + 1, ÷ 5 1

problem solving If a piglet weighs the same as two ducks, three piglets weigh the same as a young goat, and a young goat weighs the same as two terriers, then how many of each animal weighs the same as a terrier? $\frac{1}{2}$ goat; $1\frac{1}{2}$ piglets; 3 ducks

New Concept — *Increasing Knowledge*

When we add or subtract numbers using pencil and paper, it is important to align digits that have the same place value. For whole numbers this means lining up the ending digits. When we line up the ending digits (which are in the ones place) we automatically align other digits that have the same place value.

```
   23    ← Lining up the ones place
  241      automatically aligns all other
+ 317      digits by their place value.
```


Facts Reduce each fraction to lowest terms.

$\frac{2}{8}=\frac{1}{4}$	$\frac{4}{6}=\frac{2}{3}$	$\frac{6}{10}=\frac{3}{5}$	$\frac{2}{4}=\frac{1}{2}$	$\frac{5}{100}=\frac{1}{20}$	$\frac{9}{12}=\frac{3}{4}$
$\frac{4}{10}=\frac{2}{5}$	$\frac{4}{12}=\frac{1}{3}$	$\frac{2}{10}=\frac{1}{5}$	$\frac{3}{6}=\frac{1}{2}$	$\frac{25}{100}=\frac{1}{4}$	$\frac{3}{12}=\frac{1}{4}$
$\frac{4}{16}=\frac{1}{4}$	$\frac{3}{9}=\frac{1}{3}$	$\frac{6}{9}=\frac{2}{3}$	$\frac{4}{8}=\frac{1}{2}$	$\frac{2}{12}=\frac{1}{6}$	$\frac{6}{12}=\frac{1}{2}$
$\frac{8}{16}=\frac{1}{2}$	$\frac{2}{6}=\frac{1}{3}$	$\frac{8}{12}=\frac{2}{3}$	$\frac{6}{8}=\frac{3}{4}$	$\frac{5}{10}=\frac{1}{2}$	$\frac{75}{100}=\frac{3}{4}$

1 Power Up

Facts

Distribute **Power Up G** to students. See answers below.

Mental Math

Before students begin the Mental Math exercise, do this counting exercise as a class.

Count up and down by 25s between 25 and 400.

Encourage students to share different ways to mentally compute these exercises. Strategies for exercises **b** and **d** are listed below.

b. Use the Distributive Property
9 × 43 = (9 × 40) + (9 × 3) =
360 + 27 = 387

Change 9 to 10, then Subtract 43
10 × 43 = 430; 430 − 43 = 387

d. Add $0.50 and Subtract $0.50
$17.50 + $0.50 = $18 and
$2.50 − $0.50 = $2; $18 + $2 = $20

Add Dollars and Add Cents
$17 + $2 = $19 and $0.50 + $0.50 = $1;
$19 + $1 = $20

Problem Solving

Refer to **Power-Up Discussion,** p. 191B.

2 New Concepts

Instruction

After discussing whole number and decimal alignment, have students note that aligning the whole number addends by place values also aligns the addends by decimal points. This is because the decimal points in the whole number addends, although not present, are to the right of the digits in the ones place.

(continued)

2 New Concepts (Continued)

Example 1

Instruction

If any students are uneasy with the fact that the addends do not have the same number of digits, rewrite the problem on the board or overhead, using zeros as placeholders.

$$\begin{array}{r} 3.40 \\ 0.26 \\ +\ 0.30 \\ \hline 3.96 \end{array}$$

When writing extra zeros, students need to remember that the zeros must not change the value of the number. In other words, the zeros must not make the number bigger or smaller.

Example 2

Instruction

"When we subtract 2.3 from 3.78, would it be acceptable to write 2.30 instead of writing 2.3? Explain why or why not." Yes; the zero would not change the value of the number (2.3 and 2.30 are equivalent).

Practice Set

Problem h (Error Alert)

Watch for students who regroup across the zeros incorrectly. On the board or overhead, complete the computation and demonstrate how to regroup correctly. Then offer the problems shown below for additional practice.

2.00 − 0.15 1.85
6 − 3.73 2.27
3 − 2.09 0.91

3 Written Practice

Math Conversations

Discussion opportunities are provided below.

Problem 1 (Represent)

Challenge students to describe a way to solve the problem, or check the answer, using mental math. Sample: An equivalent fraction for 60% is $\frac{60}{100}$, and $\frac{60}{100}$ is the same as $\frac{6}{10}$. To reduce $\frac{6}{10}$, divide the numerator and the denominator by 2, so 60% is the same as $\frac{3}{5}$.

(continued)

Thinking Skill
Analyze

In the number 2.41, in what place is the digit 4? the digit 1? The digit 4 is the tenths place and the digit 1 is the hundredths place.

However, lining up the ending digits of decimal numbers might not properly align all the digits. We use another method for decimal numbers. **We line up decimal numbers for addition or subtraction by lining up the decimal points.** The decimal point in the answer is aligned with the other decimal points. Empty places are treated as zeros.

$$\begin{array}{r} 2.3 \\ 2.41 \\ +\ 31.7 \\ \hline . \end{array}$$

Lining up the decimal points automatically aligns digits that have the same place value.

Example 1

The rainfall over a three-day period was 3.4 inches, 0.26 inches, and 0.3 inches. Altogether, how many inches of rain fell during the three days?

Solution

We line up the decimal points and add. The decimal point in the sum is placed in line with the other decimal points. In three days **3.96 inches** of rain fell.

$$\begin{array}{r} 3.4 \\ 0.26 \\ +\ 0.3 \\ \hline 3.96 \end{array}$$

Example 2

A gallon is about 3.78 liters. If Margaret pours 2.3 liters of milk from a one-gallon bottle, how much milk remains in the bottle?

Solution

We subtract 2.3 from 3.78. We line up the decimal points to subtract and find that **1.48 liters** of milk remains in the bottle.

$$\begin{array}{r} 3.78 \\ -\ 2.3 \\ \hline 1.48 \end{array}$$

Practice Set Find each sum or difference. Remember to line up the decimal points.

a. 3.46 + 0.2 3.66
b. 8.28 − 6.1 2.18
c. 0.735 + 0.21 0.945
d. 0.543 − 0.21 0.333
e. 0.43 + 0.1 + 0.413 0.943
f. 0.30 − 0.27 0.03
g. 0.6 + 0.7 1.3
▶ **h.** 1.00 − 0.24 0.76
i. 0.9 + 0.12 1.02
j. 1.23 − 0.4 0.83

Written Practice *Strengthening Concepts*

▶ * **1.** (33) *Represent* Sixty percent of the students in the class were girls. What fraction of the students in the class were girls? $\frac{3}{5}$

2. (22) *Analyze* Penny broke 8 pencils during the math test. She broke half as many during the spelling test. How many pencils did she break in all? 12 pencils

▶ See Math Conversations in the sidebar.

Teacher Tip

Throughout this lesson, **vertical alignment by place value** of addends and minuends and subtrahends is very important. If students need practice with alignment, encourage them to use grid paper or lined paper turned sideways to complete the computations.

▶ 3. **Analyze** What number must be added to three hundred seventy-five to get the number one thousand? 625
(3)

▶ * 4. $3.4 + 0.62 + 0.3$ 4.32
(37)

* 5. $4.56 - 3.2$ 1.36
(37)

6. $\$0.37 + \$0.23 + \$0.48$ \$1.08
(1)

7. $\$5 - m = 5¢$ \$4.95
(3)

8. **Predict** What is the next number in this sequence? 10,000
(10)

1, 10, 100, 1000, ...

▶ * 9. **Connect** Harriet used 100 square floor tiles with sides 1 foot long to cover the floor of a square room.
(8, 31)

a. What was the length of each side of the room? 10 feet

b. What was the perimeter of the room? 40 feet

10. Which digit is in the ten-millions place in 1,234,567,890? 3
(12)

11. D Choices A and B are both one tenth and choice C reduces to one tenth. So $\frac{1}{10}$, 0.1, and $\frac{10}{100}$ are equal to each other but not to 0.01.

* 11. **Classify** Three of the numbers shown below are equal. Which number is not equal to the others? How do you know?
(35)

A $\frac{1}{10}$ B 0.1 C $\frac{10}{100}$ D 0.01

12. Estimate the product of 29, 42, and 39. 48,000
(16)

13. $3210 \div 3$ 1070
(2)

14. $32{,}100 \div 30$ 1070
(2)

15. $\$10{,}000 - \$345$ \$9655
(1)

16. $\frac{3}{4} + \frac{3}{4}$ $1\frac{1}{2}$
(24)

▶ * 17. **Analyze** $3 - 1\frac{3}{5}$ $1\frac{2}{5}$
(36)

▶ * 18. $\frac{3}{3} - \frac{2}{2}$ 0
(29)

19. $1\frac{1}{3} + 2\frac{1}{3} + 3\frac{1}{3}$ 7
(26)

▶ * 20. **Analyze** Compare: $\frac{1}{4} + \frac{3}{4} \textcircled{>} \frac{1}{4} \times \frac{3}{4}$
(29)

21. Convert the improper fraction $\frac{100}{7}$ to a mixed number. $14\frac{2}{7}$
(25)

22. What is the average of 90 lb, 84 lb, and 102 lb? 92 lb
(18)

23. What is the least common multiple of 4 and 5? 20
(30)

24. The stock's value dropped from \$38.50 to \$34.00. What negative number shows the change in value? −4.50
(14)

25. **Connect** To what mixed number is the arrow pointing on the number line below? $10\frac{1}{10}$
(17)

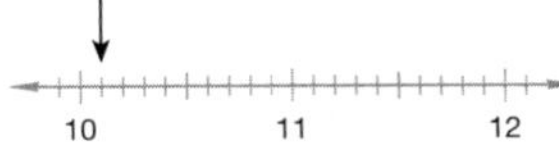

▶ See Math Conversations in the sidebar.

3 Written Practice (Continued)

Math Conversations

Discussion opportunities are provided below.

Problem 3 Analyze

"What addition equation could we use to find the answer?" Sample: $375 + n = 1000$

"What subtraction equation could we use to find the answer?" Sample: $1000 - 375 = n$

Problem 9 Connect

Remind students to assume, when solving problems of this nature, there is no space between tiles, and the tiles do not overlap. Point out that the problem will state such conditions if they exist.

Problem 17 Analyze

"In this subtraction, there aren't enough fifths to subtract $\frac{3}{5}$ from. Explain how to create more fifths." Regroup 3 as 2 and $\frac{5}{5}$.

Problem 20 Analyze

Have students note that the terms on the left side of the inequality are addends, and the terms on the right side of the inequality are factors.

Errors and Misconceptions

Problem 4

To complete the computation, students may conclude that the addends must be written in the same order as they appear in the problem. However the Associative Property of Addition states that there is more than one way to group three addends, and the Commutative Property of Addition states that changing the order of two addends does not change the sum.

Problem 18

Watch for students who subtract the numerators and subtract the denominators to produce an answer of $\frac{1}{1}$ or 1. Remind these students that a common denominator must be used to subtract fractions whose denominators are not the same.

Have students note that the key to solving the problem correctly is to follow the Order of Operations, which state that division must be performed before subtraction.

(continued)

3 Written Practice (Continued)

Math Conversations

Discussion opportunities are provided below.

Problem 26 Represent

"Explain how to multiply two fractions." Write the product of the numerators over the product of the denominators. Then use division to reduce the product, if possible.

▶ * **26.** (35) **Represent** Write 0.3 and 0.9 as fractions. Then multiply the fractions. Change the product to a decimal number. 0.27

27. (Inv. 2) **Explain** Write three different fractions equal to 1. How can you tell whether a fraction is equal to 1?

28. (2) **Justify** Instead of dividing 6 by $\frac{1}{2}$, Feodor doubled both numbers and divided 12 by 1. Do you think both quotients are the same? Write a one- or two-sentence reason for your answer.

* **29.** (32) The movie started at 2:50 p.m. and ended at 4:23 p.m. How long was the movie? 1 hr 33 min

30. (22) **Model** Three fifths of the 25 students in the class were boys. How many boys were in the class? Draw a diagram to illustrate the problem. 15 boys (See below.)

27. Fractions may vary but must include such numbers as $\frac{2}{2}$, $\frac{3}{3}$, and $\frac{4}{4}$. If the numerator and denominator of a fraction are equal (but not zero), the fraction equals 1.

Early Finishers
Real-World Application

Chamile is making a shirt and she needs to determine how many yards of fabric to buy. After calculating her measurements, Chamile determines she needs 90 inches of fabric (1 yard = 36 inches).

a. How many yards of fabric does it take to make the shirt? $\frac{36 \text{ in.}}{1 \text{ yd}} \cdot \frac{x \text{ yd}}{90 \text{ in.}} =$ 2.5 yards of fabric

b. If the fabric store only sells fabric in full yards, how much fabric will Chamile have leftover? Chamile will have to purchase 3 yards of fabric and she will have $\frac{1}{2}$ yard of fabric leftover.

28. If we multiply the dividend and divisor by the same number, the resulting problem has the same quotient as the original problem. Here the dividend and divisor were both doubled (that is, multiplied by 2), so the quotients of the two problems are the same.

30.

25 students

$\frac{3}{5}$ were boys.	5 students
	5 students
	5 students
$\frac{2}{5}$ were girls.	5 students
	5 students

▶ See Math Conversations in the sidebar.

English Learners

Explain that to be able to solve problem 28, the students must understand the word **doubled.** Say:

"When something is doubled, it is multiplied by 2, or becomes twice its original amount."

Ask for student volunteers to come to the board and double the following numbers.

$$8, 11, 14, 15, \frac{1}{4}$$

Looking Forward

Adding and subtracting decimal numbers prepares students for:

- **Lesson 38,** adding and subtracting decimal numbers and whole numbers.
- **Lesson 40,** using zero as a placeholder when subtracting.
- **Lesson 53,** using a decimal chart to summarize arithmetic rules for decimals.
- **Lesson 84,** using the order of operations to simplify problems involving decimal numbers.

• Adding and Subtracting Decimal Numbers and Whole Numbers
• Squares and Square Roots

Objectives

- Write a whole number with a decimal point.
- Add decimal numbers and whole numbers.
- Subtract whole numbers from decimal numbers.
- Square a number.
- Use the exponent 2 to indicate squaring or square units.
- Simplify an expression by applying exponents and then adding, subtracting, multiplying, or dividing.
- Find the square root of a number.

Lesson Preparation

Materials

- **Power Up A** (in *Instructional Masters*)

Optional

- **Manipulative kit: color tiles**

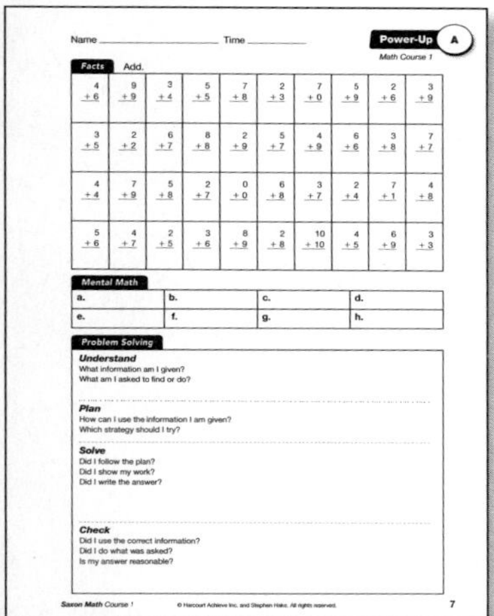

Name ____________ Time ________ **Power-Up A**

Math Course 1

Facts Add.

4 + 6	9 + 9	3 + 4	5 + 5	7 + 8	2 + 3	7 + 0	5 + 9	2 + 6	3 + 9
3 + 5	2 + 2	6 + 7	8 + 8	2 + 9	5 + 7	4 + 9	6 + 6	3 + 8	7 + 7
4 + 4	7 + 9	5 + 8	2 + 7	0 + 0	6 + 8	3 + 7	2 + 4	7 + 1	4 + 8
5 + 6	4 + 7	2 + 5	3 + 6	8 + 9	2 + 8	10 + 10	4 + 5	6 + 9	3 + 3

Mental Math

a.	b.	c.	d.
e.	f.	g.	h.

Problem Solving

Understand
What information am I given?
What am I asked to find or do?

Plan
How can I use the information I am given?
Which strategy should I try?

Solve
Did I follow the plan?
Did I show my work?
Did I write the answer?

Check
Did I use the correct information?
Did I do what was asked?
Is my answer reasonable?

Saxon Math *Course 1* © Harcourt Achieve Inc. and Stephen Hake. All rights reserved. 7

Power Up A

Math Language

New	English Learners (ESL)
base	elevated
exponent	
perfect square	
square root	

Technology Resources

Student eBook Complete student textbook in electronic format.

Resources and Planner CD Assessment, reteaching, and instructional masters, plus a pacing calendar with standards.

Test and Practice Generator CD Create additional practice sheets and custom-made tests.

www.SaxonPublishers.com Visit for more student activities and planning materials.

Inclusion

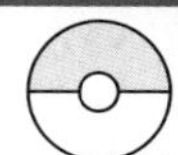

Adaptations CD Adapted lessons, investigations, practice and assessments.

Meeting Standards

National Council of Teachers of Mathematics (NCTM)

Numbers and Operations

NO.1a Work flexibly with fractions, decimals, and percents to solve problems

NO.2a Understand the meaning and effects of arithmetic operations with fractions, decimals, and integers

NO.2c Understand and use the inverse relationships of addition and subtraction, multiplication and division, and squaring and finding square roots to simplify computations and solve problems

NO.3a Select appropriate methods and tools for computing with fractions and decimals from among mental computation, estimation, calculators or computers, and paper and pencil, depending on the situation, and apply the selected methods

NO.3b Develop and analyze algorithms for computing with fractions, decimals, and integers and develop fluency in their use

Power-Up Discussion *For use with Power Up, p. 195*

Problem-Solving Strategy: Make an Organized List/ Act It Out

Andre, Robert, and Carolina stood side-by-side for a picture. Then they changed their order for another picture. Then they changed their order again. List all possible side-by-side arrangements of the three friends.

Understand ***Understand the problem.***

"What information have we been given?"

Three friends stood side-by-side for three different pictures. For each picture, they changed the order in which they were standing.

"What are we asked to do?"

We have been asked to list all the possible side-by-side arrangements that Andre, Robert, and Carolina can form.

"Is this a combination or permutation problem? Why?"

It is a permutation problem because different orders are counted.

Plan ***Make a plan.***

"We will make an organized list as we find the possible arrangements by acting out the situation. We will pick three students to portray Andre, Robert, and Carolina."

Teacher Note: Ask for three volunteers to help act out the problem by playing the parts of Andre, Robert, and Carolina.

Solve ***Carry out the plan.***

When we list the possible permutations we will refer to each of the students by their first initial. We begin by arranging the students with Andre on the left and find that there are two permutations: ARC and ACR. If Robert stands to the left there are two more permutations: RAC and RCA. Finally, we arrange the friends with Carolina to the left and find two more permutations: CAR and CRA.

Check ***Look back.***

"Did we do what we were asked to do?"

Yes, we listed six possible permutations for the three friends:

ARC ACR RAC RCA CAR CRA

Teacher Note: You may extend this lesson by increasing the number of students in the picture to four. For each of the six positions of three students, how many ways are there for the fourth student to fit into the picture? (four ways) So how many permutations are there for four students? ($4 \times 6 = 24$)

LESSON
38

• Adding and Subtracting Decimal Numbers and Whole Numbers
• Squares and Square Roots

Power Up

Building Power

facts Power Up A

mental math

a. **Order of Operations:** (4 × 600) + (4 × 25) 2500

b. **Number Sense:** 875 − 125 750

c. **Number Sense:** 56 − 19 37

d. **Money:** $10.00 − $6.25 $3.75

e. **Fractional Parts:** $\frac{1}{2}$ of 150 75

f. **Number Sense:** $\frac{\$40.00}{10}$ $4.00

g. **Geometry:** A regular octagon has sides that measure 7 cm. What is the perimeter of the octagon? 56 cm

h. **Calculation:** 10 + 10, − 2, ÷ 3, × 4, + 1, × 4, ÷ 2, + 6, ÷ 7 8

problem solving Andre, Robert, and Carolina stood side-by-side for a picture. Then they changed their order for another picture. Then they changed their order again. List all possible side-by-side arrangements of the three friends. ACR, ARC, CAR, CRA, RAC, RCA

New Concepts

Increasing Knowledge

adding and subtracting decimal numbers and whole numbers

Margie saw this sale sign in the clothing department. What is another way to write three dollars?

T-shirt close-out
$3 each

Here we show two ways to write three dollars:

$3 $3.00

We see that we may write dollar amounts with or without a decimal point. We may also write whole numbers with or without a decimal point. The decimal point follows the ones place. Here are several ways to write the whole number three:

3 3. 3.0 3.00

As we will see in the following examples, it may be helpful to write a whole number with a decimal point when adding and subtracting with decimal numbers.

Facts Add.

4 + 6 = 10	9 + 9 = 18	3 + 4 = 7	5 + 5 = 10	7 + 8 = 15	2 + 3 = 5	7 + 0 = 7	5 + 9 = 14	2 + 6 = 8	3 + 9 = 12
3 + 5 = 8	2 + 2 = 4	6 + 7 = 13	8 + 8 = 16	2 + 9 = 11	5 + 7 = 12	4 + 9 = 13	6 + 6 = 12	3 + 8 = 11	7 + 7 = 14
4 + 4 = 8	7 + 9 = 16	5 + 8 = 13	2 + 7 = 9	0 + 0 = 0	6 + 8 = 14	3 + 7 = 10	2 + 4 = 6	7 + 1 = 8	4 + 8 = 12
5 + 6 = 11	4 + 7 = 11	2 + 5 = 7	3 + 6 = 9	8 + 9 = 17	2 + 8 = 10	10 + 10 = 20	4 + 5 = 9	6 + 9 = 15	3 + 3 = 6

1 Power Up

Facts

Distribute **Power Up A** to students. See answers below.

Mental Math

Before students begin the Mental Math exercise, do this counting exercise as a class.

Count by 6s from 6 to 72. Count by 7s from 7 to 84.

Encourage students to share different ways to mentally compute these exercises. Strategies for exercises **e** and **f** are listed below.

e. Divide Hundreds and Tens by 2, then Add

100 ÷ 2 = 50 and 50 ÷ 2 = 25;
50 + 25 = 75

Use Division Facts and Multiples

$\frac{1}{2}$ of 16 is 8 and $\frac{1}{2}$ of 160 is 80; $\frac{1}{2}$ of 14 is 7 and $\frac{1}{2}$ of 140 is 70; So $\frac{1}{2}$ of 150 is 75.

f. Shift the Decimal Points One Place

$\frac{\$40.00}{10} = \frac{\$4}{1} = \$4$

Change $40.00 to $40, then Cancel Zeros

$\frac{\$40}{10} = \frac{\$4\not{0}}{1\not{0}} = \frac{\$4}{1} = \$4$

Problem Solving

Refer to **Power-Up Discussion,** p. 195B.

2 New Concepts

Instruction

Explain that writing one or more zeros to the right of the decimal point does not change the whole number 3; 3.0 and 3.00 are simply other names for 3.

(continued)

2 New Concepts (Continued)

Example 1

Instruction

Have students note that placing a decimal point to the right of a whole number is the same as placing the decimal point to the right of the ones place.

Example 3

Instruction

It is important for students to recognize that when two or more operations are present in an expression, the operations involving exponents must be completed *first*.

(continued)

Example 1

Paper used in school is often 11 inches long and 8.5 inches wide. Find the perimeter of a sheet of paper by adding the lengths of the four sides

Solution

When adding decimal numbers, we align decimal points so that we add digit with the same place values. The whole number 11 may be written with a decimal point to the right. We line up the decimal points and add. The perimeter is **39.0 inches.**

$$\begin{array}{r} 11. \\ 8.5 \\ 11. \\ +\ 8.5 \\ \hline \mathbf{39.0} \end{array}$$

Example 2

Subtract: 12.75 − 5

Solution

We write the whole number 5 with a decimal point to its right. Then we line up the decimal points and subtract.

$$\begin{array}{r} 12.75 \\ -\ \ 5.\ \ \ \\ \hline \mathbf{7.75} \end{array}$$

squares and square roots

Recall that we find the area of a square by multiplying the length of a side of the square by itself. For example, the area of a square with sides 5 cm long is 5 cm × 5 cm, which equals 25 sq. cm.

Area is 25 sq. cm

Side is 5 cm

From the model of the square comes the expression "squaring a number." We square a number by multiplying the number by itself.

"Five squared" is 5 × 5, which is 25.

To indicate squaring, we use the **exponent** 2.

$$5^2 = 25$$

"Five squared equals 25."

An exponent shows how many times the other number, the **base,** is to be used as a factor. In this case, 5 is to be used as a factor twice.

Reading Math

An exponent is elevated and written to the right of a number. Read 5^2 as "five squared."

Example 3

a. What is twelve squared?

b. Simplify: $3^2 + 4^2$

English Learners

Explain that the word, **elevated,** means "raised." Say:

"When your hand is elevated, I know you want to ask a question."

Write "6^3, 2^4, 5^1, and 8^2" on the board. Ask for student volunteers to come to the board and point to the elevated numbers.

Math Background

The perfect squares from 1 to 100 are shown in bold below.

1 × 1 = **1**	2 × 2 = **4**	3 × 3 = **9**	4 × 4 = **16**	5 × 5 = **25**
6 × 6 = **36**	7 × 7 = **49**	8 × 8 = **64**	9 × 9 = **81**	10 × 10 = **10**

Note that each perfect square is the product of its square root raised to the second power.

Solution

a. "Twelve squared" is 12 × 12, which is **144.**

b. We apply exponents before adding, subtracting, multiplying, or dividing.

$$3^2 + 4^2 = 9 + 16 = \mathbf{25}$$

Analyze What step is not shown in the solution for **b?** (3 × 3) + (4 × 4)

Example 4

What is the area of a square with sides 5 meters long?

Reading Math
We can use an exponent of 2 with a unit of length to indicate square units for measuring area. cm^2 = square centimeter

Solution

We multiply 5 meters by 5 meters. Both the units and the numbers are multiplied.

$$5 \text{ m} \cdot 5 \text{ m} = (5 \cdot 5)(\text{m} \cdot \text{m}) = \mathbf{25\ m^2}$$

We read 25 m^2 as "twenty-five square meters."

If we know the area of a square, we can find the length of each side. We do this by determining the length whose square equals the area. For example, a square whose area is 49 cm^2 has side lengths of 7 cm because 7 cm · 7 cm equals 49 cm^2.

Reading Math
The square root symbol looks like this: $\sqrt{\ }$.

Determining the length of a side of a square from the area of the square is a model for finding the principal **square root** of a number. Finding the square root of a number is the inverse of squaring a number.

6 squared is 36.

The principal square root of 36 is 6.

We read $\sqrt{100}$ as "the square root of 100." This expression means, "What positive number, when multiplied by itself, has a product of 100?" Since 10 × 10 equals 100, the principal square root of 100 is 10.

$$\sqrt{100} = 10$$

A number is a **perfect square** if it has a square root that is a whole number. Starting with 1, the first four perfect squares are 1, 4, 9, and 16, as illustrated below.

1 × 1 = 1
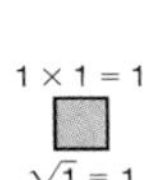
$\sqrt{1} = 1$

2 × 2 = 4
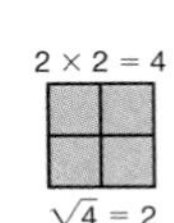
$\sqrt{4} = 2$

3 × 3 = 9
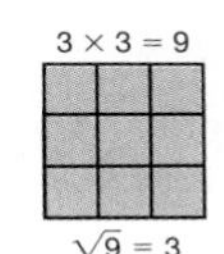
$\sqrt{9} = 3$

4 × 4 = 16
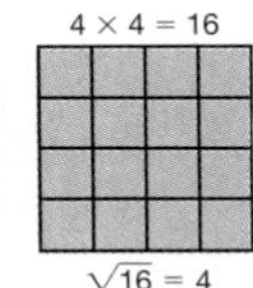
$\sqrt{16} = 4$

Generalize What is the fifth perfect square? Draw it. 25

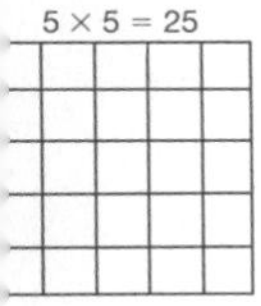

5 × 5 = 25

2 New Concepts (Continued)

Example 4

Instruction

Some students may benefit from looking at a sketch of the square drawn on the board or overhead. Write the label "5 m" on two adjacent sides of the square.

Instruction

Have students recall that when two operations are inverse operations, one operation "undoes" the other. Point out that addition and subtraction, multiplication and division, and squaring and finding square roots are all examples of inverse operations.

Invite students to use the perfect square grids as an aid for naming the next eight perfect squares. Students should continue the pattern $1^2, 2^2, 3^2, 4^2, \ldots.$ 25, 36, 49, 64, 81, 100, 121, 144

(continued)

Inclusion

Materials: color tiles

Use color tiles to reinforce the concepts of squares and square roots. Arrange tiles into a square and explain how the model shows that 16 is a perfect square. Ask:

"How many tiles are in a single row of the square?" 4

"How many rows of 4 are in the square?" 4

Explain that the square root of 16 can be found by counting the number of tiles (or length) along one side of a square with an area of 16 tiles. Ask:

"What is the square root of 16?" 4

Give each student 50 tiles. Tell students to use the tiles to find out which of the following numbers are perfect squares: 10 no, 25 yes, 36 yes, 38 no.

Have students locate each perfect square in the multiplication table in the Student Reference Guide.

2 New Concepts (Continued)

Example 5

Instruction

Remind students that finding the square root of a number and squaring a number are inverse operations. One operation undoes the other.

When working with the squares and square roots of whole numbers greater than 1, students can generalize that squaring a number makes the number bigger and square rooting a number makes the number smaller.

Practice Set

Problem l (Error Alert)

Remind students that they must find the values of the square roots before adding, subtracting, multiplying, or dividing.

Problem p (Error Alert)

If students have difficulty simplifying the expression, encourage them to first write the square root of 64, and then write the square root of m^2.

Problem q Predict

Extend the Problem

"Explain how to find the twentieth perfect square, then name it." Find the square of 20; 400.

3 Written Practice

Math Conversations

Discussion opportunities are provided below.

Problem 2 Formulate

Extend the Problem

"Suppose that Roberto only needed to save \$125 to buy the bicycle. Would it take him one fewer week, or 41 weeks altogether, to save that amount? Explain why or why not." No; it would take the same number of weeks because in 41 weeks, Roberto would save only 41 × \$3 or \$123.

Errors and Misconceptions

Problems 4, 5, and 9

Simplifying square roots is a part of the exponents step of the Order of Operations, and it is step 2. So beginning with this lesson, students must follow these steps to simplify expressions correctly:

Step 1: Parentheses
Step 2: Exponents
Step 3: Multiplication and Division
Step 4: Addition and Subtraction

(continued)

Example 5

Simplify: $\sqrt{64}$

Solution

The square root of 64 can be thought of in two ways:

1. What is the side length of a square that has an area of 64 square units?
2. What positive number multiplied by itself equals 64?

With either approach, we find that $\sqrt{64}$ equals **8.**

Practice Set Simplify:

a. $4 + 2.1$ 6.1
b. $4.3 - 2$ 2.3
c. $3 + 0.4$ 3.4
d. $43.2 - 5$ 38.2
e. $0.23 + 4 + 3.7$ 7.93
f. $6.3 - 6$ 0.3
g. $12.5 + 10$ 22.5
h. $75.25 - 25$ 50.25
i. 9^2 81
j. $\sqrt{81}$ 9
k. $6^2 + 8^2$ 100
▶ l. $\sqrt{100} - \sqrt{49}$ 3
m. 15^2 225
n. $\sqrt{144}$ 12
o. 6 ft · 6 ft 36 ft^2
▶ p. $\sqrt{64\text{ m}^2}$ 8 m
▶ q. Predict Starting with 1, the first four perfect squares are as follows:

1, 4, 9, 16

What are the next four perfect squares? Explain how you know.

q. 25, 36, 49, 64; Sample: The first four perfect squares are equal to 1^2, 2^2, 3^2, and 4^2. The next four perfect squares will be equal to 5^2, 6^2, 7^2, and 8^2.

Written Practice *Strengthening Concepts*

1. (20) What is the greatest factor of both 54 and 45? 9

▶ 2. (15) Formulate Roberto began saving \$3 each week for a bicycle, which costs \$126. How many weeks will it take him to save that amount of money? Write an equation and solve the problem.
$3 \cdot w = 126$; 42 weeks

3. (13) Formulate Gandhi was born in 1869. About how old was he when he was assassinated in 1948? Write an equation and solve the problem.
$1948 - 1869 = d$; 79 years old

▶ * 4. (38) $\sqrt{9} + 1.2$ 4.2 ▶ * 5. (38) $3.6 + \sqrt{16}$ 7.6 * 6. (37) $5.63 - 1.2$ 4.43

* 7. (37) $5.376 + 0.24$ 5.616 * 8. (37) $4.75 - 0.6$ 4.15 ▶ * 9. (38) $\sqrt{16} - \sqrt{9}$ 1

* 10. (35) Write forty-seven hundredths
a. as a fraction. $\frac{47}{100}$
b. as a decimal number. 0.47

▶ See Math Conversations in the sidebar.

11. (32) Write $(9 \times 1000) + (4 \times 10) + (3 \times 1)$ in standard notation. 9043

* 12. (34) Which digit is in the hundredths place in $123.45? 5

* 13. (8, 38) The area of a square is 81 square inches.

a. What is the length of each side? 9 inches

b. What is the perimeter of the square? 36 inches

14. (30) What is the least common multiple of 2, 3, and 4? 12

15. (26) $1\frac{2}{3} + 2\frac{2}{3}$ $4\frac{1}{3}$

* 16. (36, 38) $3^2 - 1\frac{1}{4}$ $7\frac{3}{4}$

17. (29) What is $\frac{3}{4}$ of $\frac{4}{5}$? $\frac{3}{5}$

18. (29) $\frac{7}{10} \times \frac{11}{10}$ $\frac{77}{100}$

19. (30) a. How many $\frac{2}{3}$s are in 1? $\frac{3}{2}$

b. Use the answer to part **a** to find the number of $\frac{2}{3}$s in 2. $\frac{6}{2} = 3$

20. (29) Six of the nine players got on base. What fraction of the players got on base? $\frac{2}{3}$

21. (19) List the factors of 30. 1, 2, 3, 5, 6, 10, 15, 30

* 22. (33) Write each percent as a reduced fraction:

a. 35% $\frac{7}{20}$

b. 65% $\frac{13}{20}$

23. (16) Round 186,282 to the nearest thousand. 186,000

24. (30) $\frac{1}{3}m = 1$ 3

25. (5) $\frac{22 + 23 + 24}{3}$ 23

26. (9) Compare: $24 \div 8 \,(=)\, 240 \div 80$

* 27. (35) Write 0.7 and 0.21 as fractions. Then multiply the fractions. Change the product to a decimal number. Explain why your answer is reasonable. (*Hint:* Round the original problem.) 0.147; Sample: $0.7 \times 0.20 = 0.140$. This is close to 0.147. So the answer is reasonable.

28. (15) Peter bought ten carrots for $0.80. What was the cost for each carrot? $0.08

▶* 29. (38) **Estimate** Which of these fractions is closest to 1? D

A $\frac{1}{5}$ **B** $\frac{2}{5}$ **C** $\frac{3}{5}$ **D** $\frac{4}{5}$

* 30. (36) ***Justify*** If you know the perimeter of a square, you can find the area of the square in two steps. Describe the two steps.
First divide the perimeter by 4 to find the length of each side. Then square the length of a side (multiply the length by itself) to find the area.

▶ See Math Conversations in the sidebar.

3 Written Practice (Continued)

Math Conversations

Discussion opportunities are provided below.

Problem 29 Estimate

"What fraction has a denominator of 5 and is equivalent to 1?" $\frac{5}{5}$

"Which of the given fractions is closest to $\frac{5}{5}$?" $\frac{4}{5}$

ooking Forward

quaring a number and finding the square root of a number prepare tudents for:

Lesson 39, multiplying decimals.

Lesson 40, using zero as a placeholder when subtracting, multiplying, and dividing decimals.

Lesson 73, working with exponents.

Lesson 89, estimating square roots of numbers that are not perfect squares and finding square roots of numbers larger than 100.

Lesson 92, simplifying expressions as part of the order of operations.

• Multiplying Decimal Numbers

Objectives

- Multiply a decimal number by a decimal number.
- Multiply a decimal number by a whole number.

Lesson Preparation

Materials

- **Power Up G** (in *Instructional Masters*)
- **Manipulative kit: inch rulers**

Optional

- **Teacher-provided material: fraction manipulatives** from Investigation 2

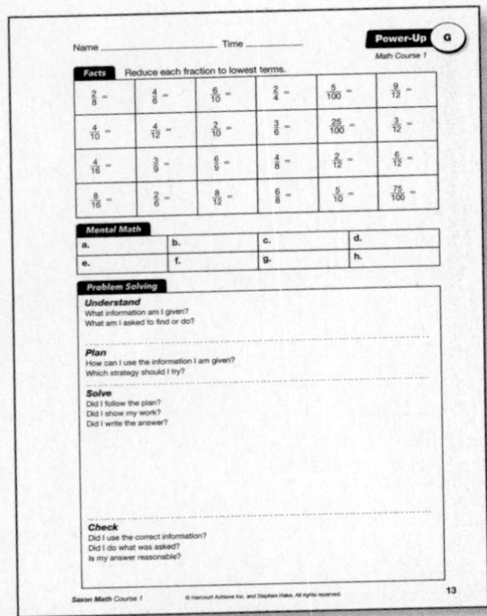

Name ______________ Time ________ **Power-Up G**

Math Course 1

Facts Reduce each fraction to lowest terms.

$\frac{2}{8}$ =	$\frac{4}{6}$ =	$\frac{6}{10}$ =	$\frac{2}{4}$ =	$\frac{5}{100}$ =	$\frac{9}{12}$ =
$\frac{4}{10}$ =	$\frac{4}{12}$ =	$\frac{2}{10}$ =	$\frac{3}{6}$ =	$\frac{25}{100}$ =	$\frac{3}{12}$ =
$\frac{4}{16}$ =	$\frac{3}{9}$ =	$\frac{6}{9}$ =	$\frac{4}{8}$ =	$\frac{2}{12}$ =	$\frac{6}{12}$ =
$\frac{8}{16}$ =	$\frac{2}{6}$ =	$\frac{8}{12}$ =	$\frac{6}{8}$ =	$\frac{5}{10}$ =	$\frac{75}{100}$ =

Mental Math

a.	b.	c.	d.
e.	f.	g.	h.

Problem Solving

Understand
What information am I given?
What am I asked to find or do?

Plan
How can I use the information I am given?
Which strategy should I try?

Solve
Did I follow the plan?
Did I show my work?
Did I write the answer?

Check
Did I use the correct information?
Did I do what was asked?
Is my answer reasonable?

Saxon Math Course 1 © Harcourt Achieve Inc. and Stephen Hake. All rights reserved. 13

Power Up G

Technology Resources

Student eBook Complete student textbook in electronic format.

Resources and Planner CD Assessment, reteaching, and instructional masters, plus a pacing calendar with standards.

Test and Practice Generator CD Create additional practice sheets and custom-made tests.

www.SaxonPublishers.com Visit for more student activities and planning materials.

Inclusion

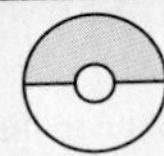

Adaptations CD Adapted lessons, investigations, practice and assessments.

Meeting Standards

National Council of Teachers of Mathematics (NCTM)

Numbers and Operations

NO.1a Work flexibly with fractions, decimals, and percents to solve problems

NO.2a Understand the meaning and effects of arithmetic operations with fractions, decimals, and integers

NO.3b Develop and analyze algorithms for computing with fractions, decimals, and integers and develop fluency in their use

NO.3c Develop and use strategies to estimate the results of rational-number computations and judge the reasonableness of the results

Measurement

ME.1b Understand relationships among units and convert from one unit to another within the same system

Power-Up Discussion *For use with Power Up, p. 200*

Problem-Solving Strategy: Draw a Diagram

Sarah used eight sugar cubes to make a larger cube. The cube she made was two cubes deep, two cubes wide, and two cubes high. How many cubes will she need to make a cube that has three smaller cubes along each edge?

Understand Understand the problem.

"What information are we given?"

Sarah used eight sugar cubes to make a larger cube that was two cubes deep, two cubes wide, and two cubes high. We are shown a picture of the larger cube.

"What are we asked to do?"

We are asked to determine how many sugar cubes Sarah will need to build a cube that has three cubes along each edge.

Plan Make a plan.

"How can we use the information we know to do what we are asked to do?"

We think about how Sarah might build the larger cube to help us *draw a diagram*. She could put down a bottom layer, then a middle layer, and then a top layer. To find how many cubes Sarah will use, we can multiply the number of cubes in each layer by the number of layers.

Solve Carry out the plan.

"How many cubes does Sarah need for the bottom layer of the larger cube?"

The layer will have three rows of three cubes each, which equals 9 cubes.

"How many layers will the cube have? How many smaller cubes are needed?"

There will be three layers: a bottom, middle, and top. If there are nine cubes in each of the three layers, there are 9×3 or 27 cubes total.

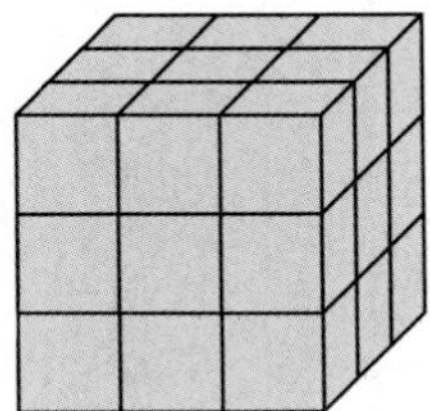

Check Look back.

"Did we complete the task?"

Yes. We found how many cubes Sarah will need to build the larger cube (27 cubes).

Teacher Note: You may extend this lesson by asking how many cubes would be needed to build a larger cube with four cubes along each edge (64 cubes) or with 5 cubes along each edge (125 cubes).

Alternative Approach: Act It Out/Make a Model

If building blocks or sugar cubes are readily available, allow students to make models of both of Sarah's cubes.

1 Power Up

Facts

Distribute **Power Up G** to students. See answers below.

Mental Math

Before students begin the Mental Math exercise, do this counting exercise as a class.

Count up and down by $\frac{1}{8}$s between $\frac{1}{8}$ and 3.

Encourage students to share different ways to mentally compute these exercises. Strategies for exercises **b** and **d** are listed below.

b. Use the Distributive Property

$6 \times 45 = (6 \times 40) + (6 \times 5) = 240 + 30 = 270$

Add 5 to 45, then Subtract 6 × 5

$6 \times 50 = 300; 300 - (6 \times 5) = 300 - 30 = 270$

d. Count on by $1, then Count Back by $0.25

Start with $8.75. Count: $9.75

Start with $9.75. Count: $9.50

Add $0.25 and Subtract $0.25

$8.75 + $0.25 = $9.00 and $0.75 − $0.25 = $0.50; $9.00 + $0.50 = $9.50

Problem Solving

Refer to **Power-Up Discussion**, p. 200B.

2 New Concepts

Have students recall that the formula for finding the area of a rectangle is $A = lw$.

(continued)

LESSON 39

• Multiplying Decimal Numbers

Power Up *Building Power*

facts Power Up G

mental math

a. **Order of Operations:** (4 × 700) + (4 × 25) 2900

b. **Number Sense:** 6 × 45 270

c. **Number Sense:** 67 − 29 38

d. **Money:** $8.75 + $0.75 $9.50

e. **Fractional Parts:** $\frac{1}{2}$ of 350 175

f. **Number Sense:** $\frac{2500}{100}$ 25

g. **Statistics:** Find the average of 68, 124, 98, and 42 83

h. **Calculation:** 8 × 5, ÷ 2, + 1, ÷ 7, × 3, + 1, ÷ 10, ÷ 2 $\frac{1}{2}$

problem solving Sarah used eight sugar cubes to make a larger cube. The cube she made was two cubes deep, two cubes wide, and two cubes high. How many cubes will she need to make a new cube that has three cubes along each edge? 27 cubes

New Concept *Increasing Knowledge*

Doris hung a stained-glass picture in front of her window to let the light shine through the design. The picture frame is 0.75 meters long and 0.5 meters wide. How much of the area of the window is covered by the stained-glass picture?

To find the area of a rectangle that is 0.75 meters long and 0.5 meters wide, we multiply 0.75 m by 0.5 m.

0.75 m

0.5 m

One way to multiply these numbers is to write each decimal number as a proper fraction and then multiply the fractions.

$$0.75 \times 0.5$$
$$\downarrow \quad \downarrow$$
$$\frac{75}{100} \times \frac{5}{10} = \frac{375}{1000}$$

The product $\frac{375}{1000}$ can be written as the decimal number 0.375. We find that the picture covers 0.375 square meters of the window area.

Facts Reduce each fraction to lowest terms.

$\frac{2}{8} = \frac{1}{4}$	$\frac{4}{6} = \frac{2}{3}$	$\frac{6}{10} = \frac{3}{5}$	$\frac{2}{4} = \frac{1}{2}$	$\frac{5}{100} = \frac{1}{20}$	$\frac{9}{12} = \frac{3}{4}$
$\frac{4}{10} = \frac{2}{5}$	$\frac{4}{12} = \frac{1}{3}$	$\frac{2}{10} = \frac{1}{5}$	$\frac{3}{6} = \frac{1}{2}$	$\frac{25}{100} = \frac{1}{4}$	$\frac{3}{12} = \frac{1}{4}$
$\frac{4}{16} = \frac{1}{4}$	$\frac{3}{9} = \frac{1}{3}$	$\frac{6}{9} = \frac{2}{3}$	$\frac{4}{8} = \frac{1}{2}$	$\frac{2}{12} = \frac{1}{6}$	$\frac{6}{12} = \frac{1}{2}$
$\frac{8}{16} = \frac{1}{2}$	$\frac{2}{6} = \frac{1}{3}$	$\frac{8}{12} = \frac{2}{3}$	$\frac{6}{8} = \frac{3}{4}$	$\frac{5}{10} = \frac{1}{2}$	$\frac{75}{100} = \frac{3}{4}$

Thinking Skill

Discuss

Why can we count the decimal places to multiply 0.75 and 0.5?

$\frac{n}{100} \times \frac{n}{10} = \frac{n \times n}{1000}$

so,

$\frac{0.75}{100} \times \frac{0.5}{100} = \frac{375}{1000}$

$\frac{375}{1000} = 0.375$

Notice that the product 0.375 has three decimal places and that three is the **total** number of decimal places in the factors, 0.75 (two) and 0.5 (one). When we multiply decimal numbers, the product has the same number of decimal places as there are in all of the factors combined. This fact allows us to multiply decimal numbers as if they were whole numbers.

After multiplying, we count the total number of decimal places in the factors. Then we place a decimal point in the product to give it the same number of decimal places as there are in the factors.

Three decimal places in the factors { 0.75 × 0.5 — We do not align decimal points. We multiply and then count decimal places.

0.375 — Three decimal places in the product

Example 1

Multiply: 0.25 × 0.7

Solution

We set up the problem as though we were multiplying whole numbers, initially ignoring the decimal points. Then we multiply.

0.25 × 0.7 } 3 places = 0.175

Next we count the digits to the right of the decimal points in the two factors. There are three, so we place a decimal point in the product three places from the right-hand end. We write .175 as **0.175.**

Predict How could we have predicted that the answer would be less than one? We multiplied 0.25 by a number that is less than one.

Example 2

Simplify: $(2.5)^2$

Solution

We square 2.5 by multiplying 2.5 by 2.5. We set up the problem as if we were multiplying whole numbers.

2.5 × 2.5 } 2 places; 125; 50; 6.25

Next we count decimal places in the factors. There are two, so we place a decimal point in the product two places from the right-hand end. We see that $(2.5)^2$ equals **6.25.**

Verify Why is 6.25 a reasonable answer?
Sample: 2.5 is between 2 and 3; $2^2 = 4$ and $3^2 = 9$; 6.25 is between 4 and 9.

2 New Concepts (Continued)

Instruction

To remind students of the relationship of the number of decimal places in the factors to the number of decimal places in the product, you might choose to write an assortment of decimal factors on the board or overhead. Then ask students to simply name the number of decimal places in each product.
For example:

0.25 × 0.73 four
18 × 0.009 three
0.602 × 5.41 five
0.34 × 16 two

Example 1

Instruction

Before completing the example, ask students to name the number of decimal places in the product.

Example 2

Instruction

When working with the product of two factors, students may believe that the only way to check an answer is to perform the arithmetic a second time. Explain that there is another way, estimating the answer prior to completing the arithmetic.

"What is a reasonable range of answers for this problem?" Sample: Since 2.5 is greater than 2 and less than 3, the square of 2.5 should be greater than the square of 2 and less than the square of 3. So a reasonable range is greater than 2^2 or 4 but less than 3^2 or 9.

After the arithmetic has been completed, remind students to check the exact answer for reasonableness by comparing it to the estimate.

(continued)

Math Background

When multiplying decimal numbers, an important generalization for students to remember is that the total number of decimal places in the factors is equal to the number of decimal places in the product.

The only time this generalization does not *seem* to be true is when a product is expressed in a simpler way. For example, the product 1.4 × 5 can be written as 7.0 or simply as 7. Writing the product as 7 *seems* to invalidate the generalization. But the generalization is still true because the product 7.0 was merely expressed in a simpler way.

2 New Concepts (Continued)

Example 3

Instruction

Prior to completing the arithmetic, ask students to estimate a reasonable range for the product and justify the estimate. Sample: Since 1.6 is greater than 1 but less than 2, the product 1.6×3 should be greater than 1×3 or 3 but less than 2×3 or 6.

Practice Set

Problems a–j (Error Alert)

When multiplying decimal numbers, errors typically involve misplaced decimal points.

Before completing the arithmetic for each problem, ask students to name the number of decimal places in each product.

Remind students that an estimate can be used to check the reasonableness of each product.

3 Written Practice

Math Conversations

Discussion opportunities are provided below.

Problem 3 Connect

"Describe two different methods that could be used to solve this problem." Sample: Find $\frac{1}{8}$ of a dollar and multiply that amount by 6; multiply $\frac{1}{8}$ by 6, then find $\frac{6}{8}$ of a dollar.

Errors and Misconceptions

Problem 7

When an expression contains more than one operation, students must simplify the expression by following the Order of Operations. When simplifying problem **7**, students should recognize that because there are no parentheses or other grouping symbols in the expression, $\sqrt{16}$ is the first term of the expression to be simplified.

(continued)

Example 3

A mile is about 1.6 kilometers. Maricruz ran a 3-mile cross-country race. About how many kilometers did she run?

Solution

We multiply as though we were multiplying whole numbers. Then we count decimal places in the factors. There is only one, so we place a decimal point in the product one place from the right-hand end. The answer is **4.8 kilometers.**

$$\begin{array}{r} 1.6 \\ \times\ 3 \\ \hline 4.8 \end{array} \quad \text{1 place}$$

Practice Set ▶ Simplify:

a. 15×0.3 4.5

b. 1.5×3 4.5

c. 1.5×0.3 0.45

d. 0.15×3 0.45

e. 1.5×1.5 2.25

f. 0.15×10 1.50 or 1.5

g. 0.25×0.5 0.125

h. 0.025×100 2.500 or 2.5

i. $(0.8)^2$ 0.64

j. $(1.2)^2$ 1.44

k. Conclude How are exercises **a–d** similar? How are they different?

k. The non-zero digits in the problem numbers are the same. The number of decimal places in the factors and products are different.

Written Practice *Strengthening Concepts*

1. (12) Mount Everest, the world's tallest mountain, rises to an elevation of twenty-nine thousand, twenty-nine feet above sea level. Use digits to write that elevation. 29,029 feet

2. (7, 25) There are three feet in a yard. About how many yards above sea level is Mount Everest's peak? $9676\frac{1}{3}$ yards

▶ ***3.** (6) Connect If you had lived in the 1800's, you may have seen a sign like this in a barber shop:

Shave and a Haircut
six bits

A bit is $\frac{1}{8}$ of a dollar. How many cents is 6 bits? 75¢

***4.** (39) 0.25×0.5 0.125

5. (2) $\$1.80 \times 10$ \$18.00

***6.** (39) 63×0.7 44.1

▶ ***7.** (38) $1.23 + \sqrt{16} + 0.5$ 5.73

***8.** (37) $12.34 - 5.6$ 6.74

***9.** (39) $(1.1)^2$ 1.21

▶ See Math Conversations in the sidebar.

▶* **10.** Write ten and three tenths
(35)
a. as a decimal number. 10.3

b. as a mixed number. $10\frac{3}{10}$

11. Evaluate Think of two different fractions that are greater than zero but less than one. Multiply the two fractions to form a third fraction. For your answer, write the three fractions in order from least to greatest. Answers will vary, but the product will be the smallest number of the three (so it will be listed first).
(17)

▶* **12.** Write the decimal number one hundred twenty-three thousandths. 0.123
(35)

13. Write $(6 \times 100) + (4 \times 10)$ in standard form. 640
(32)

▶* **14.** Connect The perimeter of a square is 40 inches. How many square tiles with sides 1 inch long are needed to cover its area? 100 tiles
(38)

15. What is the least common multiple (LCM) of 2, 3, and 6? 6
(30)

16. Convert $\frac{20}{8}$ to a mixed number. Simplify your answer. Remember to reduce the fraction part of the mixed number. $2\frac{1}{2}$
(25)

17. $\left(\frac{1}{3} + \frac{2}{3}\right) - 1$ 0 **18.** $\frac{3}{5} \times \frac{2}{3}$ $\frac{2}{5}$ **19.** $\frac{8}{9} \times \frac{9}{8}$ 1
(24) (29) (29)

▶* **20.** Represent A pie was cut into six equal slices. Two slices were eaten. What fraction of the pie was left? Write the answer as a reduced fraction. $\frac{2}{3}$
(36)

21. What time is $2\frac{1}{2}$ hours before 1 a.m.? 10:30 p.m.
(32)

22. On Hiroshi's last four assignments he had 26, 29, 28, and 25 correct answers. He averaged how many correct answers on these papers? Explain how you found your answer.
(18)

22. 27 correct answers; Sample: added 26, 29, 28, and 25 together and got 108. Then I divided 108 by 4 because there were four numbers. 108 divided by 4 equals 27. So he averaged 27 correct answers.

23. Estimate the quotient of 7987 divided by 39. 200
(16)

24. Compare: $365 - 364 \; \textcircled{>} \; 364 - 365$
(14)

▶* **25.** Which digit in 3.675 has the same place value as the 4 in 14.28? 3
(34)

26. Estimate Use an inch ruler to find the length of the segment below to the nearest sixteenth of an inch. $2\frac{3}{16}$ inches
(17)

27. **a.** How many $\frac{3}{5}$s are in 1? $\frac{5}{3}$
(30)
b. Use the answer to part **a** to find the number of $\frac{3}{5}$s in 2. $\frac{10}{3} = 3\frac{1}{3}$

28. Connect Instead of solving the division problem $390 \div 15$, Roosevelt divided both numbers by 3 to form the division $130 \div 5$. Then he multiplied both of those numbers by 2 to get $260 \div 10$. Find all three quotients. 26; 26; 26
(2)

▶ See Math Conversations in the sidebar.

3 Written Practice (Continued)

Math Conversations

Discussion opportunities are provided below.

Problem 14 Connect

Students cannot determine the number of tiles that will be needed until they know the length of a side of the square.

"The perimeter of this square is given. How can we use the perimeter to learn the length of each side of the square?" Divide the perimeter by 4 because all of the lengths are the same, and there are four lengths altogether.

"How long is each side of the square?" 10 in.

Problem 20 Represent

Invite students who have difficulty solving this problem to use their fraction manipulatives from Investigation 2.

Errors and Misconceptions

Problems 10, 12 and 25

Whenever necessary, encourage students to use the Place Value chart in the Student Reference Guide to help complete the problems.

(continued)

3 Written Practice (Continued)

Math Conversations

Discussion opportunities are provided below.

Problem 29 Analyze

Before completing the arithmetic, ask

"Why will the area of the rectangle be less than 1 square meter?" Sample: The factors 0.5 and 0.3 are each less than 1, so the product of the factors will be less than 1×1.

▶* 29. (39) Analyze Find the area of the rectangle below. 0.15 m^2

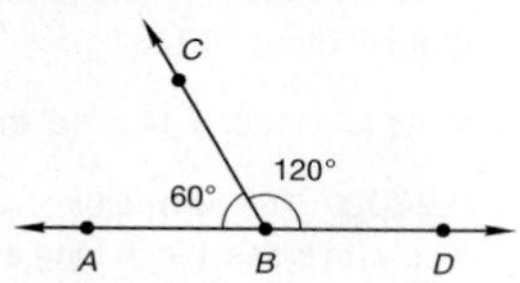

30. (23) Conclude In the figure below, what is the ratio of the measure of $\angle ABC$ to the measure of $\angle CBD$? $\frac{1}{2}$

C
60°
120°
A B D

Early Finishers
Real-World Application

On Samuel's birthday, his mother wants to cook his favorite meat, turkey. She purchased a frozen 9-pound turkey from the grocery store. The turkey takes 2 days to thaw in the refrigerator, 30 minutes to prepare and $2\frac{1}{2}$ hours to cook in the oven. If the turkey starts thawing at 9 a.m. on November 3, when will the turkey be ready to eat? Show your work. November 3 + 2 days = November 5. If the process started at 9:00 a.m. + 30 minutes to prepare + $2\frac{1}{2}$ hrs (2 hrs 30 min) of cooking time = the turkey would be ready to eat at 12:00 p.m. on November 5.

▶ See Math Conversations in the sidebar.

Looking Forward

Multiplying a decimal number by a decimal number or whole number prepares students for:

- **Lesson 40,** using zero as a placeholder when multiplying decimal numbers.
- **Lesson 44,** simplifying decimal numbers by removing extra zeros.
- **Lesson 46,** multiplying decimal numbers by 10 and by 100 mentally.
- **Lesson 84,** simplifying expressions in order of operation problems.
- **Lesson 116,** finding compound interest.

• Using Zero as a Placeholder
• Circle Graphs

Objectives

- Use zeros to fill in each empty decimal place when subtracting, multiplying, and dividing decimal numbers.
- Use zeros as placeholders as needed when writing in digits the word form of a decimal number.
- Interpret information displayed in a circle graph.
- Generalize information from a bar graph to display it in a circle graph.
- Compare how data is displayed in a bar graph and a circle graph.

Lesson Preparation

Materials

- **Power Up D** (in *Instructional Masters*)

Optional

- **Teacher-provided material: fraction manipulatives** from Investigation 2

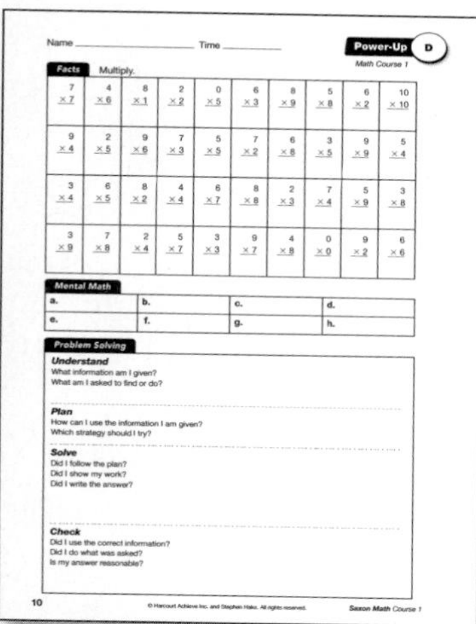

Power Up D

Math Language

New	English Learners (ESL)
circle graph	quantitative

Technology Resources

Student eBook Complete student textbook in electronic format.

Resources and Planner CD Assessment, reteaching, and instructional masters, plus a pacing calendar with standards.

Test and Practice Generator CD Create additional practice sheets and custom-made tests.

www.SaxonPublishers.com Visit for more student activities and planning materials.

Inclusion

Adaptations CD Adapted lessons, investigations, practice and assessments.

Meeting Standards

National Council of Teachers of Mathematics (NCTM)

Number and Operations

NO.2a Understand the meaning and effects of arithmetic operations with fractions, decimals, and integers

Data Analysis and Probability

DP.1b Select, create, and use appropriate graphical representations of data, including histograms, box plots, and scatterplots

DP.2b Discuss and understand the correspondence between data sets and their graphical representations, especially histograms, stem-and-leaf plots, box plots, and scatterplots

Problem Solving

PS.1c Apply and adapt a variety of appropriate strategies to solve problems

Representation

RE.5a Create and use representations to organize, record, and communicate mathematical ideas

Power-Up Discussion For use with Power Up, p. 205

Problem-Solving Strategy: Write an Equation/ Guess and Check/Make It Simpler

Using five 2s and any symbols or operations, write an expression that is equal to 5.

Understand ***Understand the problem.***

"What information are we given?"

An expression composed of five 2s will equal 5.

"What are we asked to do?"

We are asked to arrange the five 2s to equal 5.

"What operations, symbols, and procedures can we use?"

We can use addition, subtraction, multiplication, division, exponents, parentheses, brackets, and the order of operations.

Plan ***Make a plan.***

"What problem-solving strategy will we use?"

We have been asked to *write an equation*, and will *guess and check* arrangements of the five 2s. We might also want to *make simpler problems*, such as working with 5 as a 2 and a 3, or a 1 and a 4.

Teacher Note: Remind students to follow the order of operations.

Solve ***Carry out the plan.***

List a few possible answers to the questions below:

"How can we use 2s to make 1?"

$2 \div 2$

"How can we use 2s to make 2?"

2 or $(2 - 2 + 2)$

"How can we use 2s to make 3?"

$[2 + (\frac{2}{2})]$ or $[(2 \times 2) - (\frac{2}{2})]$

"How can we use 2s to make 4?"

$2 + 2$ or 2×2 or 2^2

"How can we use five 2s to make 5?"

$2^2 + 2 - (2 \div 2) = 4 + 2 - 1 = 5$

Teacher Note: There is more than one possible equation.

Check ***Look back.***

"Did we do what we were asked to do?"

Yes. We found a way to make five 2s equal 5.

"Is there only one solution?"

No.

"What are some other possible combinations?"

$2 + [(2 \times 2) - (\frac{2}{2})]$

$[(2 \times 2) - (\frac{2}{2})] + 2$

$(2 + 2 + 2) - (2 \div 2)$

Teacher Note: You may extend this lesson by asking students to find more than one answer. Discuss other possible answers with students.

LESSON **40**

• Using Zero as a Placeholder
• Circle Graphs

Power Up

Building Power

facts Power Up D

mental math

a. **Order of Operations:** $(4 \times 800) + (4 \times 25)$ 3300

b. **Number Sense:** $1500 + 750$ 2250

c. **Number Sense:** $74 - 39$ 35

d. **Money:** $8.25 − $1.50 $6.75

e. **Number Sense:** Double 240. 480

f. **Number Sense:** $\frac{480}{10}$ 48

g. **Measurement:** Convert 180 minutes into hours. 3 hours

h. **Calculation:** 4×4, -1, $\div 5$, $\times 6$, $+2$, $\times 2$, $+2$, $\div 6$ 7

problem solving Using five 2s and any symbols or operations, write an expression that is equal to 5. Sample: $2 \times 2 + 2 - \frac{2}{2}$

New Concepts

Increasing Knowledge

using zero as a placeholder

When subtracting, multiplying, and dividing decimal numbers, we often encounter empty decimal places.

$$\begin{array}{r} 0.5\_ \\ -\ 0.32 \\ \hline \end{array} \qquad \begin{array}{r} 0.2 \\ \times\ 0.3 \\ \hline \_.\_6 \end{array} \qquad 3\overline{)\$0.12}\ \text{quotient } \$0.\_4$$

When this occurs, we will fill each empty decimal place with a zero.

In order to subtract, it is sometimes necessary to attach zeros to the top number.

Example 1

Subtract: 0.5 − 0.32

Solution

We write the problem, making sure to line up the decimal points. We fill the empty place with zero and subtract.

$$\begin{array}{r} 0.5\_ \\ -\ 0.32 \\ \hline \end{array} \longrightarrow \begin{array}{r} \overset{4}{\cancel{5}}\overset{1}{0} \\ 0.50 \\ -\ 0.32 \\ \hline \mathbf{0.18} \end{array}$$

Discuss How can you check subtraction? Use addition

Facts Multiply.

7 × 7 49	4 × 6 24	8 × 1 8	2 × 2 4	0 × 5 0	6 × 3 18	8 × 9 72	5 × 8 40	6 × 2 12	10 × 10 100
9 × 4 36	2 × 5 10	9 × 6 54	7 × 3 21	5 × 5 25	7 × 2 14	6 × 8 48	3 × 5 15	9 × 9 81	5 × 4 20
3 × 4 12	6 × 5 30	8 × 2 16	4 × 4 16	6 × 7 42	8 × 8 64	2 × 3 6	7 × 4 28	5 × 9 45	3 × 8 24
3 × 9 27	7 × 8 56	2 × 4 8	5 × 7 35	3 × 3 9	9 × 7 63	4 × 8 32	0 × 0 0	9 × 2 18	6 × 6 36

1 Power Up

Facts

Distribute **Power Up D** to students. See answers below.

Mental Math

Before students begin the Mental Math exercise, do this counting exercise as a class.

Count by 8s from 8 to 96.

Encourage students to share different ways to mentally compute these exercises. Strategies for exercises **a** and **b** are listed below.

a. Use a Fact

Since $4 \times 8 = 32$, $4 \times 800 = 3200$.
$3200 + (4 \times 25) = 3200 + 100 = 3300$

Count On by 800, then by 25

Start with 800. Count: 1600, 2400, 3200
Start with 3200. Count: 3225, 3250, 3275, 3300

b. Break Apart 750

$1500 + 500 + 250 = 2000 + 250 = 2250$

Add Hundreds

$1500 + 700 + 50 = 2200 + 50 = 2250$

Problem Solving

Refer to **Power-Up Discussion,** p. 205B.

2 New Concepts

Instruction

Remind students that when zeros are written in a number, the zeros must not change the value of the number. In other words, the number cannot become bigger or smaller. Share the following examples of this concept with students.

Given the decimal number 0.5, writing a zero to the left of the digit 5 causes the number to become 0.05, which is less than 0.5. In this example, the value of the given number has changed.

It would be correct, however, to write a zero to the right of the digit 5 and change the number to 0.50. It is correct because 0.5 and 0.50 are simply different names for the same number.

(continued)

2 New Concepts (Continued)

Example 2

Instruction

Remind students to subtract in the order indicated. To subtract, the student should place the decimal point on the whole number 3 and affix a zero. Marking the decimal point is like playing "freeze tag" with the digits. The place values are "frozen" by the decimal point and do not change when zeros are affixed.

Example 3

Instruction

After completing the example, have students compare the number of decimal places in the factors to the number of decimal places in the product. Sample: There are the same number of decimal places in the factors as in the product.

(continued)

Example 2

Subtract: 3 − 0.4

Solution

We place a decimal point on the back of the whole number and line up the decimal points. We fill the empty place with zero and subtract.

$$\begin{array}{r} 3.\_ \\ -\ 0.4 \\ \hline \end{array} \longrightarrow \begin{array}{r} \overset{2}{3}.\overset{1}{0} \\ -\ 0.4 \\ \hline \mathbf{2.6} \end{array}$$

When multiplying decimal numbers, we may need to insert one or more zeros between the multiplication answer and the decimal point to hold the other digits in their proper places.

Example 3

Multiply: 0.2 × 0.3

Solution

We multiply and count two places from the right. We fill the empty place with zero, and we write a zero in the ones place.

$$\begin{array}{r} 0.2 \\ \times\ 0.3 \\ \hline \_.\_6 \end{array} \longrightarrow \begin{array}{r} 0.2 \\ \times\ 0.3 \\ \hline \mathbf{0.06} \end{array}$$

Verify Why must the product of 0.2 and 0.3 have two decimal places? tenths × tenths = hundredths; There are two decimal places in the factors.

Example 4

Use digits to write the decimal number twelve thousandths.

Solution

The word *thousandths* tells us that there are three places to the right of the decimal point.

._ _ _

We fit the two digits of twelve into the last two places.

._ 1 2

Then we fill the empty place with zero.

0.012

circle graphs **Circle graphs,** which are sometimes called **pie graphs** or **pie charts,** display quantitative information in fractions of a circle. The next example uses a circle graph to display information about students' pets.

English Learners

Explain that **quantitative** information involves measurement or numbers. On the board write, "Ronald is 20 cm taller than his sister." Say:

"This is an example of quantitative information because it involves a measurement."

On the board write, "Ronald is taller than his sister." Say:

"This is not quantitative information because a measurement or number amount is not used in this example."

Ask for a volunteer to give an example of quantitative information.

Example 5

Brett collected information from his classmates about their pets. He displayed the information about the number of pets in a circle graph.

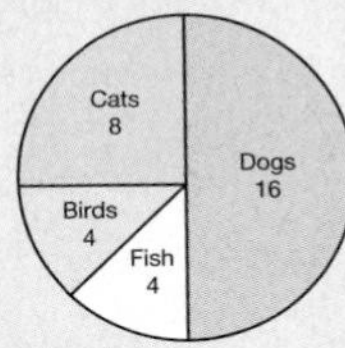

Use the graph to answer the following questions:

a. How many pets are represented in the graph?

b. What fraction of the pets are birds?

c. What percent of the pets are dogs?

Thinking Skill

Discuss

What information would we need to find the number of each kind of pet if we were given the percentages? We would need to know the total number of pets.

Solution

a. We add the number of dogs, cats, birds, and fish. The total is **32**.

b. Birds are 4 of the 32 pets. The fraction $\frac{4}{32}$ reduces to $\mathbf{\frac{1}{8}}$. (The bird portion of the circle is $\frac{1}{8}$ of the whole circle.)

c. Dogs are 16 of the 32 pets, which means that $\frac{1}{2}$ of the pets are dogs. From our fraction manipulatives we know that $\frac{1}{2}$ equals **50%**. Circle graphs often express portions in percent form. Instead of showing the number of each kind of animal, the graph could have labeled each portion with a percent.

Example 6

A newspaper polled likely voters to survey support for a local bond measure on the November ballot. Display the data shown below with a circle graph. Then compare the two graphs.

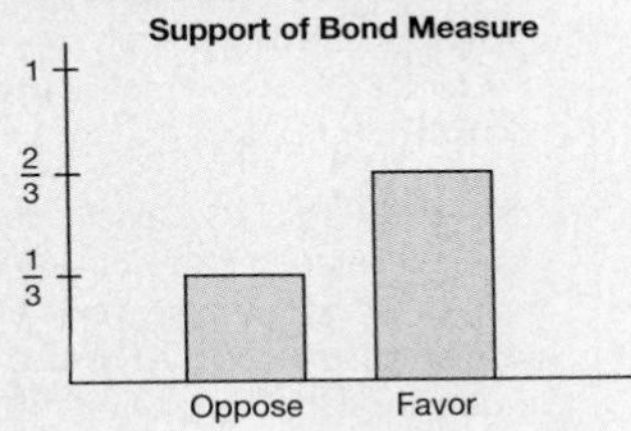

Math Background

A circle graph shows the relationship of two or more parts to a whole. The parts may be numbers, fractions, decimals, or percents. The sum of the parts is equal to the whole.

2 New Concepts (Continued)

Example 5

Instruction

As they work with circle graphs, students should understand that a circle graph represents one whole. To reinforce this understanding, ask students to sketch a copy of the circle graph after your work with the example and its solution has been completed. Then ask students to change all of the numbers on the sketches to percents.

After the changes have been made , ask students to name the sum of the percents (100) and name the whole number that is equivalent to 100% (1). Then remind students that the sum of all of the parts of a circle graph represent one whole.

Example 6

Instruction

Point out that circle graphs can be labeled with numbers, with fractions, or with percents. One way students can check a completed graph for reasonableness is to compare the sum of the data the graph displays to 1 or to 100%. For example, if a circle graph displays fractional parts, the sum of those parts, when reduced, should be 1. If a circle graph displays percents, the sum of those percents should be 100.

(continued)

2 New Concepts (Continued)

Practice Set

Problem d (Error Alert)

Students might attempt to subtract 0.4 from 0.32 because 0.32 might appear to be the greater number. Remind students that the Commutative Property does not apply to subtraction; order matters.

Problem g (Error Alert)

Some students may write the product $(0.3)^2$ as 0.9 using this reasoning: since the factor 0.3 has one decimal place, there should be one decimal place in the product.

To help demonstrate that this reasoning is not correct, write the copy shown below on the board or overhead.

$$(0.3)^2 = 0.3 \times 0.3 \text{ or } (0.3)^2 = \begin{array}{r} 0.3 \\ \times\ 0.3 \\ \hline \end{array}$$

Then ask the students to identify the number of decimal places that should be in the product. two

Problem j (Error Alert)

Ask students who have difficulty writing an equivalent percent for $\frac{8}{32}$ to first reduce the fraction to simplest form.

3 Written Practice

Math Conversations

Discussion opportunities are provided below.

Problem 3 Analyze

Tell students that the White Rabbit in this problem is a character in *Alice's Adventures in Wonderland*®, a classic children's book by Lewis Carroll. Lewis Carroll also taught mathematics at Oxford University.

Errors and Misconceptions

Problem 2 Formulate

When solving elapsed-time problems related to time in years, a misconception students sometimes have is that the elapsed time is an exact answer. To remediate this misconception, say,

"About how much time will elapse from January first of this year to December thirty-first of next year? Explain." about two years; from January to December is about 1 year, and from December of this year to December of next year is about 1 year.

Have students note that subtracting the years in the situation produces an elapsed time of 1 year.

(continued)

Solution

The bar graph shows us that $\frac{1}{3}$ of the voters oppose the bond measure and $\frac{2}{3}$ are in favor of it. Using the fraction circle manipulatives from Investigation 2, we can draw a circle and divide it into 3 sectors. We label one sector "Oppose" and two sectors "Favor." We know from our fraction manipulatives that $\frac{1}{3}$ is $33\frac{1}{3}\%$ and $\frac{2}{3}$ is $66\frac{2}{3}\%$, so we add these percentages to our labels.

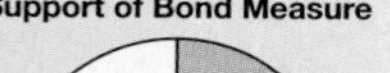

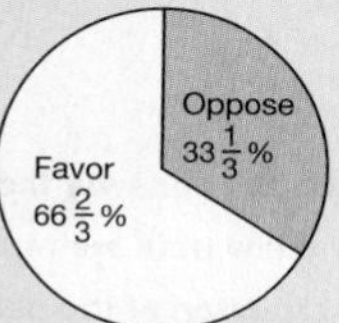

The bar graph helps us visualize the quantities relative to each other, and the circle graph helps us see their relationship to the whole.

Practice Set Simplify:

a. 0.2×0.3 0.06

b. $4.6 - 0.46$ 4.14

c. 0.1×0.01 0.001

d. $0.4 - 0.32$ 0.08

e. 0.12×0.4 0.048

f. $1 - 0.98$ 0.02

▶ **g.** $(0.3)^2$ 0.09

h. $(0.12)^2$ 0.0144

i. Write the decimal number ten and eleven thousandths. 10.011

▶ **j.** Connect In the circle graph in example 5, what percent of the pets are cats? 25%

Written Practice *Strengthening Concepts*

1. (40) Model In the circle graph in example 5, what percent of the pets are birds? (Use your fraction manipulatives to help you answer the question.) $12\frac{1}{2}\%$

▶ **2.** (13) Formulate The U.S. Constitution was ratified in 1788. In 1920 the 19th amendment to the Constitution was ratified, guaranteeing women the right to vote. How many years after the Constitution was ratified were women guaranteed the right to vote? Write an equation and solve the problem. $1920 - 1788 = d$; 132 years

▶ **3.** (32) Analyze White Rabbit is three-and-a-half-hours late for a very important date. If the time is 2:00 p.m., what was the time of his date? 10:30 a.m.

▶ See Math Conversations in the sidebar.

Answers to 4 and 5 are obviously greater than 1. The answer to exercise 9 is harder to see, so students may have difficulty predicting it.

Predict Look at problems **4–9.** Predict which of the answers to those problems will be greater than 1. Then simplify each expression and check your predictions.

* **4.** (38, 40) $\sqrt{9} - 0.3$ 2.7 * **5.** (40) $1.2 - 0.12$ 1.08 * **6.** (40) $1 - 0.1$ 0.9

* **7.** (40) 0.12×0.2 0.024 * **8.** (40) $(0.1)^2$ 0.01 * **9.** (39) 4.8×0.23 1.104

* **10.** (40) Write one and two hundredths as a decimal number. 1.02

11. (32) Write $(6 \times 10{,}000) + (8 \times 100)$ in standard form. 60,800

▶ **12.** (8, 31) **Connect** A square room has a perimeter of 32 feet. How many square floor tiles with sides 1 foot long are needed to cover the floor of the room? 64 tiles

13. (30) What is the least common multiple (LCM) of 2, 4, and 8? 8

14. (26) $6\frac{2}{3} + 4\frac{2}{3}$ $11\frac{1}{3}$ **15.** (36) $5 - 3\frac{3}{8}$ $1\frac{5}{8}$

16. (29) $\frac{5}{8} \times \frac{2}{3}$ $\frac{5}{12}$ **17.** (26) $2\frac{5}{6} + 5\frac{2}{6}$ $8\frac{1}{6}$

▶ **18.** (29) Compare: $\frac{1}{2} \times \frac{2}{2} \ominus \frac{1}{2} \times \frac{3}{3}$

19. (3) $1000 - w = 567$ 433

20. (19) **Classify** Nine whole numbers are factors of 100. Two of the factors are 1 and 100. List the other seven factors. 2, 4, 5, 10, 20, 25, 50

* **21.** (38) $9^2 + \sqrt{9}$ 84

22. (16) Round \$4167 to the nearest hundred dollars. \$4200

* **23.** (40) The circle graph below displays the favorite sports of a number of students in a recent survey. Use the graph to answer **a–c.**

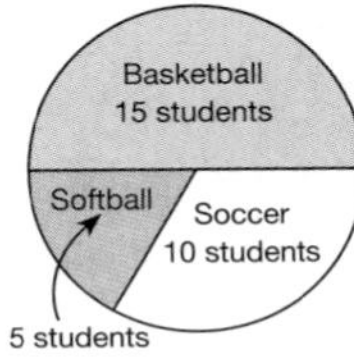

a. **Analyze** How many students responded to the survey? 30 students

b. What fraction of the students named softball as their favorite sport? $\frac{1}{6}$

c. What percent of the students named basketball as their favorite sport? 50%

24. (35) Jamal earned \$5.00 walking his neighbor's dog for one week. He was given $\frac{1}{5}$ of the \$5.00 at the beginning of the week and $\frac{1}{5}$ in the middle of the week. How much of the \$5.00 was Jamal given at the end of the week? Express your answer as a fraction and as a dollar amount. $\frac{3}{5}$; \$3.00

▶ See Math Conversations in the sidebar.

3 Written Practice (Continued)

Math Conversations

Discussion opportunities are provided below.

Problem 12 Connect

"What formula can we use to find the area of a square?" $A = s^2$ where A represents the area of a square and s represents the length of any side of the square.

Errors and Misconceptions

Problem 18

Some students may compare the products by first multiplying the factors. Remind these students that the factors $\frac{2}{2}$ and $\frac{3}{3}$ are equivalent to 1, and the product of any number and 1 is that number. These concepts can be used by students to solve the problem an alternative way—using only mental math.

$$\frac{1}{2} \times \frac{2}{2} = \frac{1}{2} \times \frac{3}{3}$$
$$\frac{1}{2} \times 1 = \frac{1}{2} \times 1$$
$$\frac{1}{2} = \frac{1}{2}$$

(continued)

3 Written Practice (Continued)

Math Conversations

Discussion opportunities are provided below.

Problem 25 Formulate

"What is a ratio?" a comparison of two quantities by division.

"What operation does a fraction bar represent?" division

"Is a fraction a comparison of two quantities by division? yes

"Is a fraction an example of a ratio?" yes

Problem 28 Analyze

"We are asked to write the ratio of girls to boys. Are there more girls, or more boys, in the class? Explain how you know." More girls; since 40% of the class are boys, 100% − 40%, or 60%, of the class are girls.

"When we write the ratio of girls to boys, will the ratio be greater than 1 or less than 1? Explain why." Greater than 1; because the number of girls in the class is greater than the number of boys, the numerator of a ratio written as a fraction will be greater than the denominator.

Remind students to always write ratios in simplest form.

▶ * **25.** (23, 40) **Formulate** Write a ratio problem that relates to the circle graph in problem **23.** Then answer the problem. Answers will vary. See student work.

* **26.** (2) **Represent** Arrange the numbers in this multiplication fact to form another multiplication fact and two division facts.

$$0.2 \times 0.3 = 0.06$$

$0.3 \times 0.2 = 0.06$, $0.06 \div 0.3 = 0.2$, $0.06 \div 0.2 = 0.3$

27. (2) **Connect** To solve the division problem 240 ÷ 15, Elianna divided both numbers by 3 to form the division 80 ÷ 5. Then she doubled 80 and 5 to get 160 ÷ 10. Find all three quotients. 16; 16; 16

▶ * **28.** (23, 33) **Analyze** Forty percent of the 25 students in the class are boys. Write 40% as a reduced fraction. Then find the ratio of girls to boys in the class. $\frac{2}{5}$, $\frac{3}{2}$

29. (17) **Connect** What mixed number is represented by point *A* on the number line below? $5\frac{9}{10}$

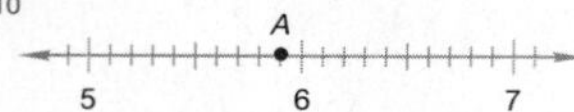

30. (40) Make a circle graph that shows the portion of a full day spent in various ways. Include activities such as sleeping, attending school, and eating. Label each sector with the activity name and its percent of the whole. Draw a circle and divide it into 24 equal sections. Use the circle below as a model. See student work.

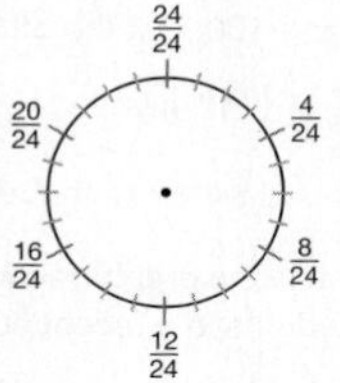

▶ See Math Conversations in the sidebar.

Looking Forward

Interpreting circle graphs prepares students for:

- **Investigation 4,** understanding data collection and surveys.
- **Investigation 5,** displaying data in graphs and finding the mean, median, mode, and range of a set of data points.
- **Investigation 9,** displaying data in a relative frequency table and finding experimental probability.
- **Investigation 10,** displaying outcomes from compound experiments and figuring the probability of the outcomes.

Assessment

30–40 minutes *For use after Lesson 40*

Distribute **Cumulative Test 7** to each student. Two versions of the test are available in *Saxon Math Course 1 Course Assessments Book*. Have students complete the **Power-Up Test** first. Allow 10 minutes. Then have students work the 20 numbered items on the **Cumulative Test.** Students may use copies of the answer sheet to record their work. Track individual and class progress with the **Test Analysis** forms.

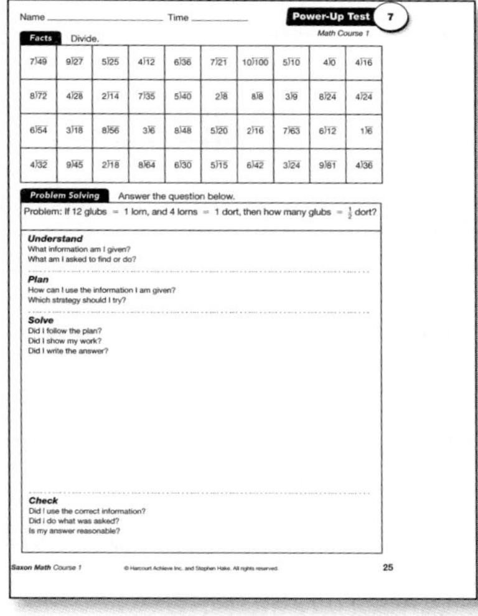
Name ______ Time ______ **Power-Up Test 7**
Math Course 1

Facts Divide.

7)49	9)27	5)25	4)12	6)36	7)21	10)100	5)10	4)0	4)16
8)72	4)28	2)14	7)35	5)40	2)8	8)8	3)9	8)24	4)24
6)54	3)18	8)56	3)6	8)48	5)20	2)16	7)63	6)12	1)6
4)32	9)45	2)18	8)64	6)30	5)15	6)42	3)24	9)81	4)36

Problem Solving Answer the question below.

Problem: If 12 glubs = 1 lorn, and 4 lorns = 1 dort, then how many glubs = $\frac{1}{2}$ dort?

Understand
What information am I given?
What am I asked to find or do?

Plan
How can I use the information I am given?
Which strategy should I try?

Solve
Did I follow the plan?
Did I show my work?
Did I write the answer?

Check
Did I use the correct information?
Did I do what was asked?
Is my answer reasonable?

Saxon Math Course 1 © Harcourt Achieve Inc. and Stephen Hake. All rights reserved. 25

Power-Up Test 7

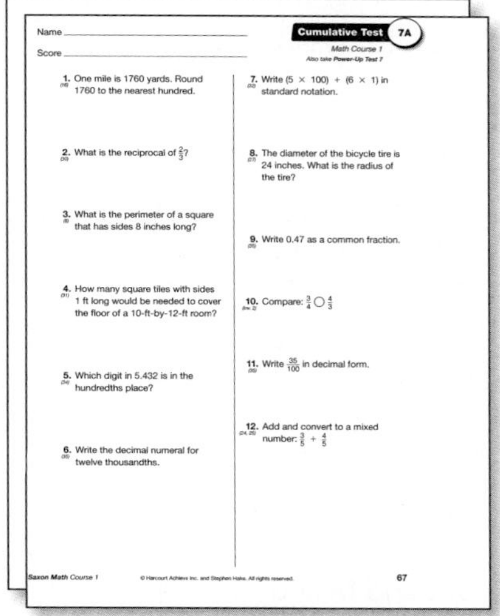
Name ______ **Cumulative Test 7A**
Score ______ *Math Course 1*
Also take ***Power-Up Test 7***

1. One mile is 1760 yards. Round 1760 to the nearest hundred.
2. What is the reciprocal of $\frac{2}{3}$?
3. What is the perimeter of a square that has sides 8 inches long?
4. How many square tiles with sides 1 ft long would be needed to cover the floor of a 10-ft-by-12-ft room?
5. Which digit in 5.432 is in the hundredths place?
6. Write the decimal numeral for twelve thousandths.
7. Write $(5 \times 100) + (6 \times 1)$ in standard notation.
8. The diameter of the bicycle tire is 24 inches. What is the radius of the tire?
9. Write 0.47 as a common fraction.
10. Compare: $\frac{3}{4} \bigcirc \frac{4}{3}$
11. Write $\frac{35}{100}$ in decimal form.
12. Add and convert to a mixed number: $\frac{3}{5} + \frac{4}{5}$

Saxon Math Course 1 © Harcourt Achieve Inc. and Stephen Hake. All rights reserved. 67

Cumulative Test 7A

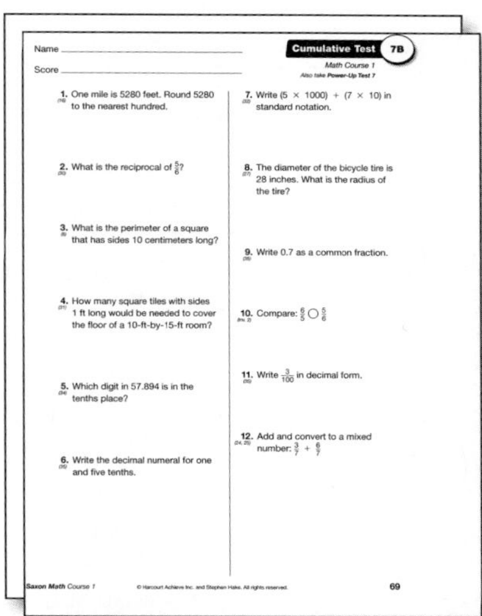
Name ______ **Cumulative Test 7B**
Score ______ *Math Course 1*
Also take ***Power-Up Test 7***

1. One mile is 5280 feet. Round 5280 to the nearest hundred.
2. What is the reciprocal of $\frac{5}{6}$?
3. What is the perimeter of a square that has sides 10 centimeters long?
4. How many square tiles with sides 1 ft long would be needed to cover the floor of a 10-ft-by-15-ft room?
5. Which digit in 57.894 is in the tenths place?
6. Write the decimal numeral for one and five tenths.
7. Write $(5 \times 1000) + (7 \times 10)$ in standard notation.
8. The diameter of the bicycle tire is 28 inches. What is the radius of the tire?
9. Write 0.7 as a common fraction.
10. Compare: $\frac{6}{5} \bigcirc \frac{5}{6}$
11. Write $\frac{3}{100}$ in decimal form.
12. Add and convert to a mixed number: $\frac{3}{7} + \frac{6}{7}$

Saxon Math Course 1 © Harcourt Achieve Inc. and Stephen Hake. All rights reserved. 69

Alternative Cumulative Test 7B

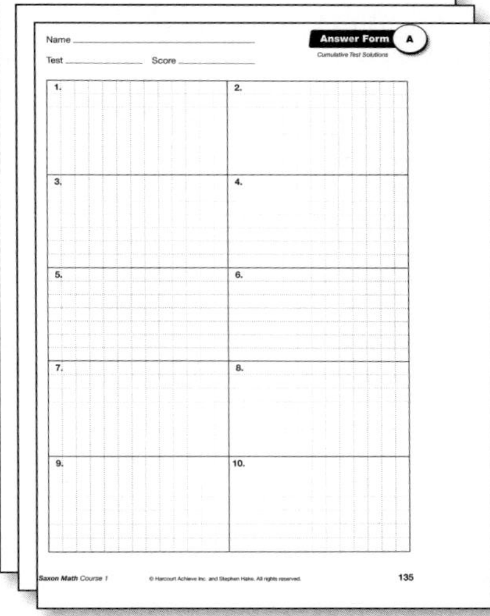
Name ______ **Answer Form A**
Test ______ Score ______ *Cumulative Test Solutions*

1. 2. 3. 4. 5. 6. 7. 8. 9. 10.

Saxon Math Course 1 © Harcourt Achieve Inc. and Stephen Hake. All rights reserved. 135

Optional Answer Forms

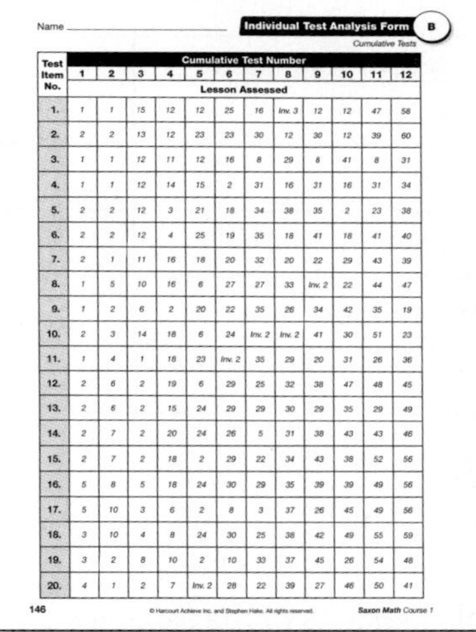
Name ______ **Individual Test Analysis Form B**
Cumulative Tests

Test Item No.	Cumulative Test Number 1	2	3	4	5	6	7	8	9	10	11	12
	Lesson Assessed											
1.	1	1	15	12	12	25	16	Inv. 3	12	12	47	58
2.	2	2	13	12	23	23	30	12	30	12	39	60
3.	1	1	12	11	12	16	8	29	8	41	8	31
4.	1	1	12	14	15	2	31	16	31	16	31	34
5.	2	2	12	3	21	18	34	38	35	2	23	38
6.	2	2	12	4	25	19	35	18	41	18	41	40
7.	2	1	11	16	18	20	32	20	22	29	43	39
8.	1	5	10	16	6	27	27	33	Inv. 2	22	44	47
9.	1	2	6	2	20	22	35	26	34	42	35	19
10.	2	3	14	18	6	24	Inv. 2	Inv. 2	41	30	51	23
11.	1	4	1	18	23	Inv. 2	35	29	20	31	26	36
12.	2	6	2	19	6	29	25	32	38	47	48	45
13.	2	6	2	15	24	29	29	30	29	35	29	49
14.	2	7	2	20	24	26	5	31	38	43	43	46
15.	2	7	2	18	2	29	22	34	43	38	52	56
16.	5	8	5	18	24	30	29	35	39	39	49	56
17.	5	10	3	6	2	8	3	37	26	45	49	56
18.	3	10	4	8	24	30	25	38	42	49	55	59
19.	3	2	8	10	2	10	33	37	45	26	54	48
20.	4	1	2	7	Inv. 2	28	22	39	27	46	50	41

146 © Harcourt Achieve Inc. and Stephen Hake. All rights reserved. *Saxon Math Course 1*

Individual Test Analysis Form

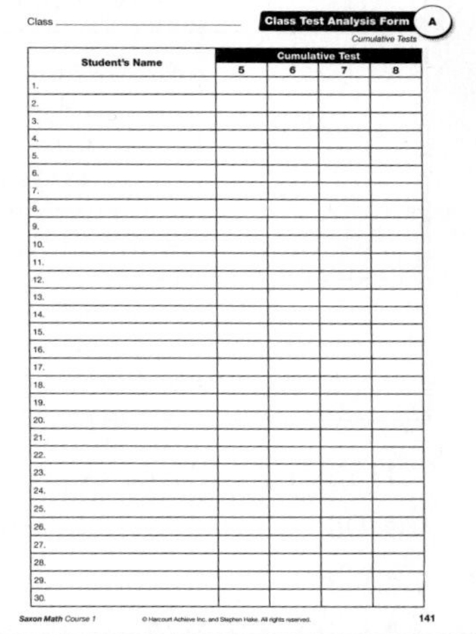
Class ______ **Class Test Analysis Form A**
Cumulative Tests

Student's Name	Cumulative Test 5	6	7	8
1.				
2.				
3.				
4.				
5.				
6.				
7.				
8.				
9.				
10.				
11.				
12.				
13.				
14.				
15.				
16.				
17.				
18.				
19.				
20.				
21.				
22.				
23.				
24.				
25.				
26.				
27.				
28.				
29.				
30.				

Saxon Math Course 1 © Harcourt Achieve Inc. and Stephen Hake. All rights reserved. 141

Class Test Analysis Form

Reteaching

Students who score below 80% on the assessment may be in need of reteaching. Look for the causes of student mistakes. If errors are conceptual, refer to the *Reteaching Masters* for reteaching.

Customized Benchmark Assessment

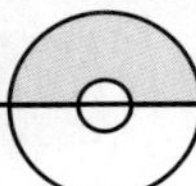

You can develop customized benchmark tests using the Test Generator located on the *Test & Practice Generator CD.*

This chart shows the lesson, the standard, and the test item question that can be found on the *Test & Practice Generator CD.*

LESSON	NEW CONCEPTS	LOCAL STANDARD	TEST ITEM ON CD
31	• Areas of Rectangles		4.31.1
32	• Expanded Notation		4.32.1
	• More on Elapsed Time		4.32.2
33	• Writing Percents as Fractions, Part 1		4.33.1
34	• Decimal Place Value		4.34.1
35	• Writing Decimal Numbers as Fractions, Part 1		4.35.1
	• Reading and Writing Decimal Numbers		4.35.2
36	• Subtracting Fractions and Mixed Numbers from Whole Numbers		4.36.1
37	• Adding and Subtracting Decimal Numbers		4.37.1
38	• Adding and Subtracting Decimal Numbers and Whole Numbers		4.38.1
	• Squares and Square Roots		4.38.2
39	• Multiplying Decimal Numbers		4.39.1
40	• Using Zero as a Placeholder		4.40.1
	• Circle Graphs		4.40.2

Using the Test Generator CD

- Develop tests in both English and Spanish.
- Choose from multiple-choice and free-response test items.
- Clone test items to create multiple versions of the same test.
- View and edit test items to make and save your own questions.
- Administer assessments through paper tests or over a school LAN.
- Monitor student progress through a variety of individual and class reports —for both diagnosing and assessing standards mastery.

Performance Task 7

Inventory at a Grocery Store

Assign after Lesson 40 and Test 7

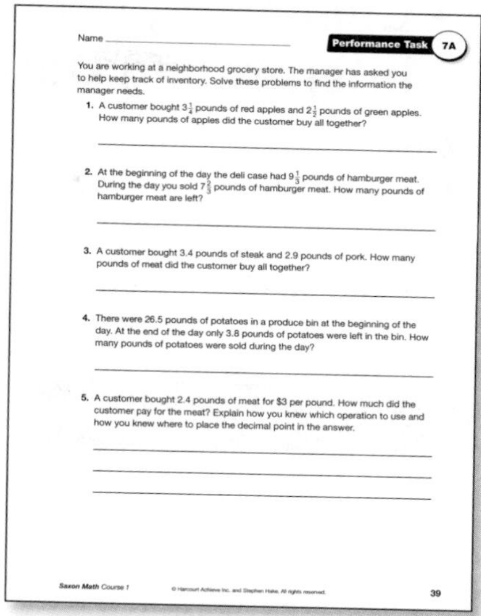

Name ____________ **Performance Task 7A**

You are working at a neighborhood grocery store. The manager has asked you to help keep track of inventory. Solve these problems to find the information the manager needs.

1. A customer bought $3\frac{1}{4}$ pounds of red apples and $2\frac{1}{2}$ pounds of green apples. How many pounds of apples did the customer buy all together?

2. At the beginning of the day the deli case had $9\frac{1}{3}$ pounds of hamburger meat. During the day you sold $7\frac{2}{3}$ pounds of hamburger meat. How many pounds of hamburger meat are left?

3. A customer bought 3.4 pounds of steak and 2.9 pounds of pork. How many pounds of meat did the customer buy all together?

4. There were 26.5 pounds of potatoes in a produce bin at the beginning of the day. At the end of the day only 3.8 pounds of potatoes were left in the bin. How many pounds of potatoes were sold during the day?

5. A customer bought 2.4 pounds of meat for $3 per pound. How much did the customer pay for the meat? Explain how you knew which operation to use and how you knew where to place the decimal point in the answer.

Saxon Math Course 1 © Harcourt Achieve Inc. and Stephen Hake. All rights reserved. 39

Performance Task 7A

Objectives

- Add and subtract fractions, mixed numbers, and decimals; multiply decimals and whole numbers.
- Write percents as fractions.
- Write ratios.
- Communicate ideas through writing.

Materials

Performance Tasks 7A and **7B**

Preparation

Make copies of **Performance Tasks 7A** and **7B.** (One each per student.)

Time Requirement

30–60 minutes; Begin in class and complete at home.

Task

Explain to students that for this task they will be helping a manager of a grocery store. They will make calculations relating to the inventory of the store. They will be required to explain their choices of mathematical operations, placements of decimal points in their answers, and how they found ratios. Point out that all of the information students need is on **Performance Tasks 7A** and **7B.**

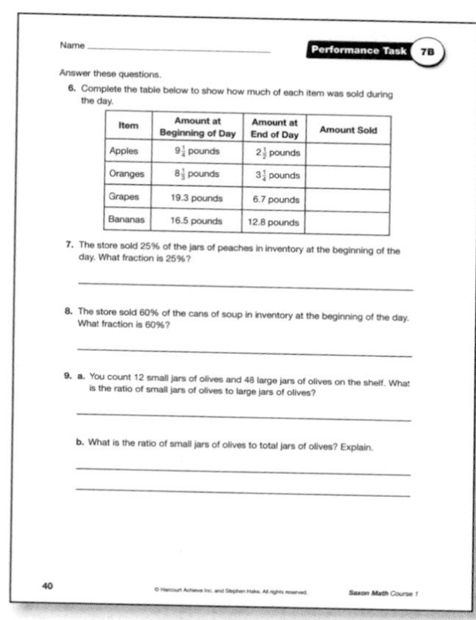

Name ____________ **Performance Task 7B**

Answer these questions.

6. Complete the table below to show how much of each item was sold during the day.

Item	Amount at Beginning of Day	Amount at End of Day	Amount Sold
Apples	$9\frac{1}{4}$ pounds	$2\frac{1}{2}$ pounds	
Oranges	$8\frac{1}{3}$ pounds	$3\frac{1}{4}$ pounds	
Grapes	19.3 pounds	6.7 pounds	
Bananas	16.5 pounds	12.8 pounds	

7. The store sold 25% of the jars of peaches in inventory at the beginning of the day. What fraction is 25%?

8. The store sold 60% of the cans of soup in inventory at the beginning of the day. What fraction is 60%?

9. a. You count 12 small jars of olives and 48 large jars of olives on the shelf. What is the ratio of small jars of olives to large jars of olives?

   b. What is the ratio of small jars of olives to total jars of olives? Explain.

40 © Harcourt Achieve Inc. and Stephen Hake. All rights reserved. *Saxon Math* Course 1

Performance Task 7B

Criteria for Evidence of Learning

- Makes accurate calculations by adding and subtracting fractions, mixed numbers and decimals; and by multiplying decimals and whole numbers.
- States ratios and a percent as a fraction correctly.
- Communicates ideas clearly through writing.

Meeting Standards

National Council of Teachers of Mathematics (NCTM)

Numbers and Operations

NO.1a Work flexibly with fractions, decimals, and percents to solve problems

NO.1d Understand and use ratios and proportions to represent quantitative relationships

NO.2a Understand the meaning and effects of arithmetic operations with fractions, decimals, and integers

Communication

CM.3b Communicate their mathematical thinking coherently and clearly to peers, teachers, and others

Focus on

• Collecting, Organizing, Displaying, and Interpreting Data

Objectives

- Describe whether data are quantitative or qualitative in nature.
- Create an open-option and a closed-option survey.
- Explain why a sample is not representative of a population.
- Identify bias in a survey.
- Conduct surveys and collect data.

Lesson Preparation

Materials

- **Teacher-provided material: graph paper**

Math Language

New	Maintain	English Learners (ESL)
data	bar graphs	record
line plot	sample	
population		
qualitative data		
quantitative data		
statistics		

Technology Resources

Student eBook Complete student textbook in electronic format.

Resources and Planner CD Assessment, reteaching, and instructional masters, plus a pacing calendar with standards.

Test and Practice Generator CD Create additional practice sheets and custom-made tests.

www.SaxonPublishers.com Visit for more student activities and planning materials.

Inclusion

Adaptations CD Adapted lessons, investigations, practice and assessments.

Meeting Standards

National Council of Teachers of Mathematics (NCTM)

Data Analysis and Probability

DP.1a Formulate questions, design studies, and collect data about a characteristic shared by two populations or different characteristics within one population

DP.1b Select, create, and use appropriate graphical representations of data, including histograms, box plots, and scatterplots

DP.2b Discuss and understand the correspondence between data sets and their graphical representations, especially histograms, stem-and-leaf plots, box plots, and scatterplots

DP.3a Use observations about differences between two or more samples to make conjectures about the populations from which the samples were taken

INVESTIGATION 4

Focus on

• Collecting, Organizing, Displaying, and Interpreting Data

Math Language
The term *data* is plural because it refers to a collection of individual figures and facts. Its singular form is *datum.*

Statistics is the science of gathering and organizing **data** (a plural word meaning information) in such a way that we can draw conclusions from the data.

For example, Patricia wondered which of three activities—team sports, dance, or walking/jogging—was most popular among her classmates. She gathered data by asking each classmate to select his or her favorite. Then she displayed the data with a **bar graph.**

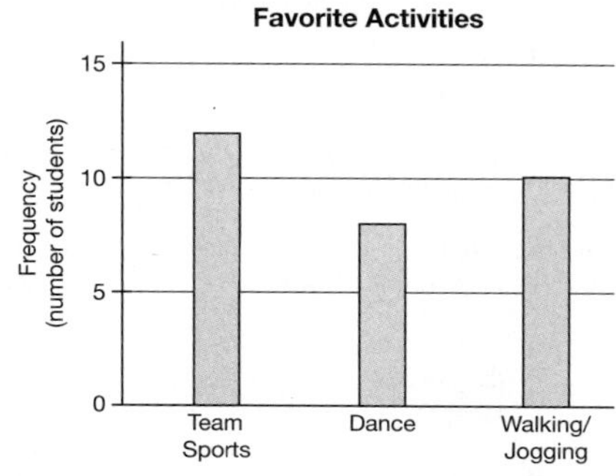

Analyze Which type of exercise is most popular among Patricia's classmates? team sports

Roger wondered how frequently the residents on his street visit the city park. He went to every third house on his street and asked, "How many times per week do you visit the city park?" Roger displayed the data he collected with a **line plot,** which shows individual data points. For each of the 16 responses, he placed an "x" above the corresponding number.

Number of Visits to the City Park per Week

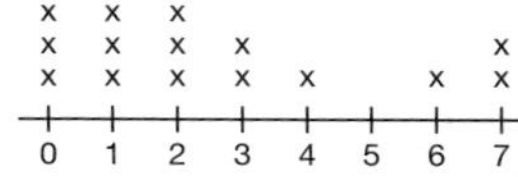

Analyze For most of the residents surveyed, the number of visits to the city park are between what numbers? between 0 and 4 visits per week

INVESTIGATION 4

In this investigation, students will learn about statistics and different ways statistics can be displayed.

Instruction

"How does a bar graph make it easy to compare data?" To compare data, compare the heights of the bars.

"One conclusion we can form from the data is that team sports was chosen by the greatest number of people. What is another conclusion we can form from the data?" Sample: Dance was chosen by the least number of people.

"How many people were surveyed? Explain how you know." 30; find the sum of the numbers that the bars represent.

Refer to the line plot in the student text.

"How does a line plot show frequency?" An 'x' represents one response; the frequency is the sum of the x's for any value.

"One conclusion we can form from the data is that 16 people altogether were surveyed. What is another conclusion we can form from the data?" Sample: Less than half the people surveyed visit the park 3 or more times per week.

(continued)

Instruction

Explain that one way students can remember how quantitative data differs from qualitative data is to connect "quantitative" with "quantity" and the idea that numbers are often used to represent quantities.

Encourage students to give other examples of quantitative and qualitative data. You might choose to ask one volunteer to record the quantitative examples, and another volunteer to record the qualitative examples, in a list at the board.

If students name more quantitative examples than qualitative examples, or vice versa, ask them to name the same number of examples of each kind.

Math Conversations

Discussion opportunities are provided below.

Problems 1–5 Classify

Explain to students that Jagdish's data are quantitative because Jagdish is recording the number of peanuts in each bag. Then ask students to explain why the data in problems **2** through **5** are either quantitative or qualitative.

Problem 6 Represent

Pair students for this exercise so that two students can work together to develop the questions.

Ask one volunteer from each pair to read their survey questions aloud. Then choose one question to ask the class, and record students' responses on the board.

Instruction

Explain that ordering the data from least to greatest (or from greatest to least) helps organize the data and makes it easier to plot.

"On the line plot of the data, what is the relationship shared by the number of people who responded to the survey question and the number of dots?" The number of people is equal to the number of dots.

Point out that the relationship of the number of people to the number of dots is a 1 to 1 relationship. Students may recall that a 1 to 1 relationship is not true for all types of graphs. For example, each symbol of a pictograph often represents more than 1.

(continued)

In this Investigation we will focus on ways in which statistical data can be collected. We also will practice collecting, organizing, displaying, and interpreting data. Data can be either quantitative or qualitative in nature. **Quantitative data** come in numbers: the population of a city, the number of pairs of shoes someone owns, or the number of hours per week someone watches television. **Qualitative data** come in categories: the month in which someone is born or a person's favorite flavor of ice cream.

Roger collected quantitative data when he asked about the number of visits to the park each week. Patricia collected qualitative data when she asked about the student's favorite sport.

Classify In problems **1–5** below, determine what information is collected. Then decide whether the data are qualitative or quantitative.

▶ **1.** Jagdish collects 50 bags of clothing for a clothing drive and counts the number of items in each bag. number of items, quantitative

▶ **2.** For one hour Carlos notes the color of each car that drives past his house. color, qualitative

▶ **3.** Sharon rides a school bus home after school. For two weeks she measures the time the bus trip takes. time of bus trip, quantitative

▶ **4.** Brigit asks each student in her class, "Which is your favorite holiday—New Year's, Thanksgiving, or Independence Day?" holiday, qualitative

▶ **5.** Marcello asks each player on his little league team, "Which major league baseball team is your favorite? Which team do you like the least?" team name, qualitative

▶ **6.** Write a survey about television viewing with two questions: one that collects quantitative data and one that collects qualitative data. Conduct the survey in your class.

Represent For question **6** above, organize your data. Then use a line plot to display the quantitative data and a bar graph to display the qualitative data. Interpret the results. See student work.

This question will give you quantitative data: "How many hours a week do you spend watching television?" We record the number of hours a person watches TV each week. Then we organize the quantitative data from least to greatest.

0 1 1 2 2 2 2 3 3 3 3 3 4 4 4 4 4 4
5 5 6 6 7 7 7 7 8 8 8 10 12 15

▶ See Math Conversations in the sidebar.

We display the data with a line plot. (We may use an "x" or dot for this.)

Number of Hours of TV Watched per Week

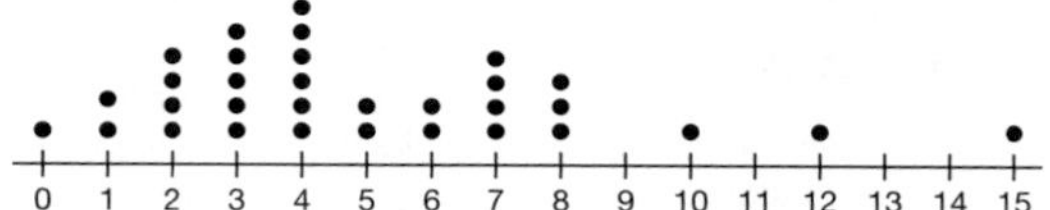

The line plot illustrates that the 32 students surveyed watch between 0 and 15 hours of TV each week. Many students watch either 2–4 or 7–8 hours each week.

This question will give you qualitative data: "Which type of TV shows do you prefer to watch–sports, news, animation, sit-coms, or movies?" We organize the qualitative data by category and tally the frequency of each category.

Category	Tally	Frequency
Sports	𝍸 𝍸 I	11
News	III	3
Animation	𝍸 I	6
Sit-coms	𝍸 IIII	9
Movies	III	3

We can display the data with a bar graph.

Types of TV Shows Preferred

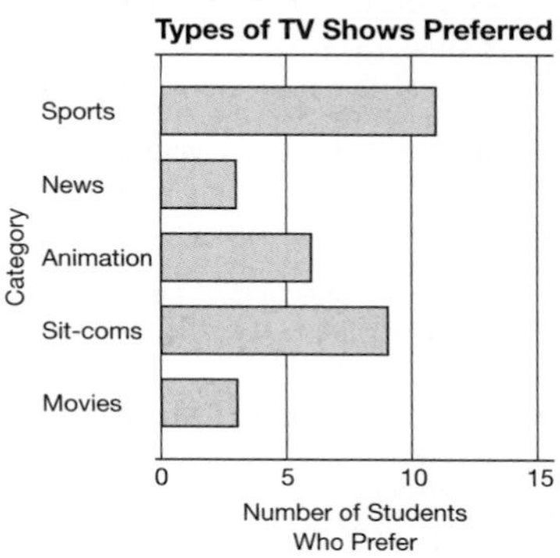

The most popular type of TV show among the students surveyed is sports.

Surveys can be designed to gather data about a certain group of people. This "target group" is called a **population.** For example, if a record company wants to know about teenagers' music preferences in the United States, it would not include senior citizens in the population it studies.

Instruction

"What does each tally in the chart represent?" the response of one person

"For any type of show, how does the number of tallies compare to the frequency?" The frequency is equal to the number of tallies.

"Does the tally chart show the number of people altogether who answered the survey question? Explain why." Yes; since each tally represents a response, the sum of the tallies, or the sum of the frequencies, represents the number of people who answered the survey question.

Refer the students to the bar graph. Ask,

"To compare data on a vertical bar graph, we compare the heights of the bars. How do we compare data on a bar graph when the bars are horizontal?" Sample: To compare two or more bars, compare their distance from the vertical axis. The bar farthest from the vertical axis represents the greater quantity.

Point out that a "population" can represent any number of people. Students should conclude that when a population is large, it is not practical to survey each member of the population.

"Suppose you wanted to learn something about the people who live in a large city, such as those who live in Houston, Texas. Would it be very easy or very difficult to survey each person who lived in Houston?" very difficult

(continued)

Instruction

Explain that when a population is large, a sample is used to predict the responses of the entire population. Students should understand that in a comparative sense, a sample of a population is usually very small when compared to the population.

"Why is it important for a sample to be representative?" Sample: A prediction that is based on a sample that is not representative is less likely to be accurate.

Ask students to give examples of biased survey questions, or examples of survey samples that are not representative because the sample group is biased in some way.

To begin the discussion, you might choose to share the situation described below with students.

"Suppose that at the end of a basketball game, a referee makes a call that changes the outcome of the game. Then after the game, fans of the winning team and fans of the losing team are surveyed and asked if the referee who made the call is a good referee. Will either group of fans give a biased answer to the question? Explain your thinking." Sample: Both groups will give a biased answer. The referee may be labeled a good referee by fans of the winning team, and probably be labeled as not a good referee by fans of the losing team.

Extensions

a–c Represent Students should work collectively to complete extensions **a** and **b**. After the data has been collected and compiled in a frequency table, students will need to determine the size of the circle graph sectors that will be needed to display the data. You might choose to point out that because the degree measure of a circle is 360 and the circle graph must show 48 responses altogether, each response will represent a $360° \div 48$ or $7.5°$ degrees of the circle.

(continued)

---

7. Pet store shoppers are more likely to own pets than people from the general population. Support for a leash law might be lower among those surveyed than among the general population.
8. Orchestra members are more likely to have a high interest in music than students in general. Thus, movies preferred by orchestra members might be more musically oriented than movies preferred by students in general.

Often it is not realistic to poll an entire population. In these cases, a small part of the population is surveyed. We call this small part a sample. Surveyors must carefully select their samples, because different samples will provide different data. It is important that the sample for a population be a *representative sample.* That is, the characteristics of the sample should be similar to those of the entire population. In order to do this, researchers often randomly select participants for a survey from the entire population.

Validate In problems **7** and **8** below, explain why each sample is not representative. How would you expect the sample's responses to differ from those of the general population?

7. To determine public opinion in the city of Miami about a proposed leash law for dogs, Sally interviews shoppers in several Miami pet stores.

8. Tamika wants to know the movie preferences of students in her middle school. Since she is in the school orchestra, she chooses to survey orchestra members.

Often the results of a survey depend on the way its questions are worded or who is asking the questions. These factors can introduce **bias** into a survey. When a survey is biased, the people surveyed might be influenced to give certain answers over other possible answers.

Verify For problems **9** and **10,** identify the bias in the survey that is described. Is a "yes" answer *more likely* or *less likely* because of the bias?

9. The researcher asked the group of adults, "If you were lost in an unfamiliar town, would you be sensible and ask for directions?" (See below.)

10. Mrs. Wong baked oatmeal bars for her daughter's fundraising sale. She asked the students who attended the sale, "Would you have preferred fruit salad to my oatmeal bars?" (See below.)

extensions

Represent For extensions **a–c,** conduct a survey and organize the data with a frequency table. Then display the results with a circle graph. Interpret the results.

Thinking Skill
Verify
Why would a good survey for **a** and **b** include data from the same number of young people and adults? Sample: Including the same number in both groups surveyed ensures that neither groups' data overly influences the results.

▸ **a.** One might guess that young people prefer different seasons than adults. *As a class,* interview exactly 24 people under the age of 15 and 24 people over the age of 20. Ask, "Which season of the year do you like most—fall, winter, spring, or summer?"

▸ **b.** One might guess that young people drink different beverages for breakfast than adults. *As a class,* interview exactly 24 people under 15 and 24 people over 20. Ask, "Which of the following beverages do you most often drink at breakfast—juice, coffee, milk, or something else?" If the choice is "something else," record the person's preferred breakfast drink.

9. People generally prefer to be considered "sensible" over being considered "not sensible." So a "yes" answer would be more likely due to the bias (the way the question is worded).

10. Discuss as a class. Politeness toward Mrs. Wong should be considered as a reason that the students might be less likely to give a "yes" answer.

▸ See Math Conversations in the sidebar.

English Learners

Explain that in extension **b.** the meaning of **record** is "to write down." Say:

"When you record something, you write down information you want to keep. If you record data, you are able to use the information later."

Explain that what you write down is in turn called a "record". Our first use of record was a verb, and this one is a noun.

c. For ten consecutive days, count the number of students in your class who wear something green (or some other color of your choosing). Count the same color all ten days.

d. **Formulate** With a friend, construct a six-question, true-false quiz on a topic that interests you both (for example, music, animals, or geography). Have your classmates take the quiz; then record the number of questions that each student answers correctly. To encourage participation, ask students not to write their names on the quiz.

e. **Analyze** Use the menu to answer the questions below.

Seafood Cafe	
Appetizers	**Main Course**
Shrimp Cocktail.................$7.00	Halibut.............................$15.75
Zucchini Fingers...............$5.00	Swordfish.........................$18.00
Soup	Flounder...........................$13.75
Seafood Gumbo...............$4.50	Crab Cakes.......................$12.50
Lobster Bisque.................$4.50	**Dessert**
	Sorbet................................$3.25

- What is the most expensive item on the menu? The least expensive? swordfish; sorbet
- What is the average price of the main course dinners? $15.00
- What is the range of prices on the menu? $14.75

f. **Evaluate** A number of bicyclists participated in a 25-mile bicycle race. The winner completed the race in 45 minutes and 27 seconds. The table below shows the times of the next four riders expressed in the number of minutes and seconds that they placed behind the winner.

Rider Number	Time Behind Winner (minutes and seconds in hundredths)
021	−1:09.02
114	−0.04.64
008	−1:29.77
065	−0:13.45

The least time in the table represents the rider who finished second. The greatest time represents the rider who finished fifth. Write the four rider numbers in the order of their finish. 114; 065; 021; 008

g. **Analyze** The average rate of speed for rider 008 was 33 miles per hour. At that rate, did this rider finish more than 1 mile or less than 1 mile behind the winner? Show your work. (Hint: Change the average rate in miles per hour to miles per minute, and round the rider number 008's time to the nearest second.)

$\frac{mi}{hr} = \frac{33\text{ mi}}{60\text{ min}} = \frac{0.55\text{ mi}}{1\text{ min}}$. .77 rounds to 1.5 0.55 × 1.5 = 0.825 1.5 min. Since mi < 1 mi, rider inished less than 1 behind the winner.

▶ See Math Conversations in the sidebar.

Extensions *(continued)*

After students complete extension **c**, ask them to share their findings with their classmates.

Extend the Problem

d. Formulate Have the students tally the frequency of each correctly answered question. Then have them display the data on a line plot graph.

Ask the students to analyze the language of each quiz question to determine if any bias exists or if clues that affect the answer were given.

e. Analyze Students are computing the average price of only the main courses. If necessary, remind students that they must subtract the lowest price from the highest price to find the range of prices.

f. Evaluate Help students understand what the times in the table mean. Explain that a time of −1:29.77 represents 1 minute + 29 seconds + $\frac{77}{100}$ of a second. This rider finished 1 minute 29 and $\frac{77}{100}$ seconds after the winner.

g. Analyze Discuss the solution to problem **f** with the students. First change the rate to miles per minute: 33 miles per hour divided by 60 minutes per hour equals 0.55 miles per minute. Then round the time to the nearest second: 1:29.77 rounds to 1:30 seconds. Since there are 60 seconds in a minute, this is equivalent to 1.5 minutes. Finally, see how far this rider cycled in 1.5 minutes: 1.5 × 0.55 miles per minute = 0.825 miles.

Looking Forward

Understanding data collection and surveys prepares students for:

- **Investigation 5,** displaying data in graphs and finding the mean, median, mode, and range of a set of data points.
- **Investigation 9,** displaying data in a relative frequency table and finding experimental probability.
- **Investigation 10,** displaying outcomes from compound experiments and figuring the probability of the outcomes.

Section 5 Overview

Lessons 41–50, Investigation 5

Lesson Planner

LESSON	NEW CONCEPTS	MATERIALS	RESOURCES
41	• Finding a Percent of a Number	Grid paper	**Power Up G** **Fraction-Decimal-Percent Equivalents poster**
42	• Renaming Fractions by Multiplying by 1	Fraction manipulatives from Investigation 2	**Power Up G**
43	• Equivalent Division Problems • Finding Unknowns in Fraction and Decimal Problems	Manipulative Kit: inch rulers Calculators	**Power Up C**
44	• Simplifying Decimal Numbers • Comparing Decimal Numbers	Calculators, grid paper	**Power Up G**
45	• Dividing a Decimal Number by a Whole Number	Manipulative Kit: inch rulers	**Power Up F**
46	• Writing Decimal Numbers in Expanded Notation • Mentally Multiplying Decimal Numbers by 10 and 100	Manipulative Kit: inch rulers	**Power Up G**
47	• Circumference • Pi (π)	Manipulative Kit: inch rulers Circular objects such as cans, lids, pie pans, etc.; string or masking tape; scissors; cloth tape measures, calculators	**Power Up E** **Lesson Activity 11** **Geometric Formulas poster**
48	• Subtracting Mixed Numbers with Regrouping, Part 1	Manipulative Kit: overhead fraction circles Fraction manipulatives from Investigation 2	**Power Up G**
49	• Dividing by a Decimal Number	Manipulative Kit: inch rulers	**Power Up H**
50	• Decimal Number Line (Tenths) • Dividing by a Fraction		**Power Up G**
Inv. 5	• Displaying Data	Manipulative Kit: compasses, protractors	

Lesson Highlights

Lessons 41–50, Investigation 5

Problem Solving

Strategies

- **Use Logical Reasoning** Lessons 43, 44, 45, 46, 47, 49
- **Draw a Diagram** Lessons 48, 50
- **Write an Equation** Lessons 41, 42, 50
- **Make an Organized List** Lesson 42

Alternative Strategies

- **Draw a Diagram** Lesson 41

Real-World Applications

pp. 216, 218–220, 229, 230, 233, 234, 236–238, 242, 243, 247–250, 252–254, 256–264, 267

4-Step Process

Teacher's Edition Lessons 41–50 (Power-Up Discussions)

Communication

Discuss

pp. 218, 250, 256

Explain

pp. 219, 223, 224, 246, 253, 258, 267

Formulate a Problem

pp. 252, 261

Connections

Math and Other Subjects

- **Math and History** p. 229
- **Math and Geography** p. 233
- **Math and Science** pp. 223, 242, 248, 267
- **Math and Sports** pp. 216, 229, 236, 243, 252

Math to Math

- **Problem Solving and Measurement** Lessons 41, 42, 43, 44, 45, 46, 47, 48, 49, 50, Inv. 5
- **Algebra and Problem Solving** Lessons 43, 45, 46, 47
- **Fractions, Percents, Decimals, and Problem Solving** Lessons 41, 42, 43, 44, 45, 46, 47, 48, 49, 50, Inv. 5
- **Fractions and Measurement** Lessons 42, 43, 44, 45, 46, 47, 48, 49, 50, Inv. 5
- **Measurement and Geometry** Lessons 41, 42, 43, 45, 46, 47, 48, 49, 50, Inv. 5

Representation

Manipulatives/Hands On

pp. 221, 230, 231, 245, 248, 251, 257, 265

Model

pp. 217, 223, 224, 230, 237, 245, 247, 252, 256, 260

Represent

pp. 222, 224, 257

Formulate an Equation

pp. 219, 229, 237, 242, 247, 252

Technology

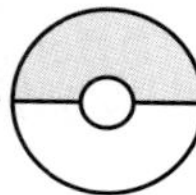

Student Resources

- **eBook**
- **Calculator** Lesson 44
- **Online Resources** at **www.SaxonPublishers.com/ActivitiesC1**
  - **Real-World Investigation 3** after Lesson 41
  - **Online Activities**
  - **Math Enrichment Problems**
  - **Math Stumpers**

Teacher Resources

- **Resources and Planner CD**
- **Adaptations CD** Lessons 41–50
- **Test & Practice Generator CD**
- **eGradebook**
- **Answer Key CD**

Content Highlights

Lessons 41–50, Investigation 5

In this section, students continue to focus on concepts and skills involving fractions and decimals.

Equivalence

Representing fraction and decimals in equivalent forms is emphasized in these lessons

The emphasis on the decimal form of rational numbers continues in this section. Students simplify and compare decimal numbers in Lesson 44, express decimal numbers in expanded notation in Lesson 46, and locate decimal numbers on the number line in Lesson 50. Students distinguish between division of a decimal number by a whole number and division by a decimal number in Lessons 45 and 49, and practice mentally multiplying decimal numbers by powers of ten in Lesson 46.

Students continue to work with fractions, finding equivalent fractions in Lesson 42, regrouping to subtract mixed numbers in Lesson 48, and dividing by fractions in Lesson 50. Students convert from a percent to a fraction or decimal to find a percent of a number in Lesson 41.

Generating a Formula

Concepts involving circles are utilized during an exploration of circumference.

Students are introduced to pi in Lesson 47, learning through a measurement activity that pi is the number of diameters in a circumference. Students will encounter pi again in later lessons on the area of a circle and the volume of a cylinder.

Data and Graphing

Students organize and display data in a variety of ways.

Students display the data collected in Investigation 4 in Investigation 5. To display qualitative data students use bar graphs and pictographs. To display quantitative data students use line plots and box-and-whisker plots. Students find the mean, median, mode, and range of a set of data.

Assessment

A variety of weekly assessment tools are provided.

After Lesson 45:
- Power-Up Test 8
- Cumulative Test 8
- Performance Activity 8

After Lesson 50:
- Power-Up Test 9
- Cumulative Test 9
- Customized Benchmark Test
- Performance Task 9

Content Trace

Lessons 41–50, Investigation 5

LESSON	NEW CONCEPTS	PRACTICED	ASSESSED
41	• Finding a Percent of a Number	Lessons 41–47, 49–53, 56, 60–63, 66, 68, 71, 73, 75, 77, 79, 81, 85, 86, 88, 93–97, 99, 104, 105, 108, 111, 112, 115, 117, 118	Tests 9, 10, 11, 12, 13, 14, 15, 16, 17, 18
42	• Renaming Fractions by Multiplying by 1	Lessons 42–55, 61, 65, 67–69, 75, 76, 78, 92, 101	Tests 9, 10, 13, 14, 16
43	• Equivalent Division Problems	Lessons 43–45, 54, 58, 60, 62, 67–70, 76, 103	Test & Practice Generator
	• Finding Unknowns in Fraction and Decimal Problems	Lessons 43–54, 56, 58–60, 62–73, 75–80, 82, 85–87, 95, 101, 103	Tests 9, 10, 11, 13, 15, 20
44	• Simplifying Decimal Numbers	Lessons 44, 45, 48, 49, 50, 52, 56, 59, 64, 66, 69, 70, 85, 92, 96, 101, 105, 113, 116, 117	Test & Practice Generator
	• Comparing Decimal Numbers	Lessons 44, 46, 48–50, 52, 57, 59, 64, 69, 73, 76, 79, 80, 92, 94, 108, 115, 116	Tests 11, 14
45	• Dividing a Decimal Number by a Whole Number	Lessons 45–51, 53, 54, 57, 59, 61–63, 65–68, 70, 73, 75, 80, 81, 85, 97, 99	Tests 9, 10, 12, 13, 14, 16, 18, 21
46	• Writing Decimal Numbers in Expanded Notation	Lessons 46–48, 51, 56, 72, 79, 95	Test & Practice Generator
	• Mentally Multiplying Decimals Numbers by 10 and 100	Lessons 47, 48, 50–52, 54–56, 58, 59, 62, 64, 66–88	Tests 10, 12, 14
47	• Circumference	Lessons 47–57, 59–63, 65, 67, 71–75, 79, 81, 83, 89, 94, 100–103, 106, 107, 109–113, 116, 120	Tests 10, 11, 12, 17, 18, 21, 23
	• Pi (π)	Lessons 47–57, 59–63, 65, 67, 71–75, 79, 81, 83, 89, 94, 100, 101–103, 106, 107, 109–113, 116, 120	Tests 10, 11, 12, 17, 18, 21, 23
48	• Subtracting Mixed Numbers with Regrouping, Part 1	Lessons 48, 51, 53, 54, 56, 57, 59, 60–63, 66–71, 73, 74, 77, 83, 84, 90, 91	Tests 11, 12
49	• Dividing by a Decimal Number	Lessons 49–52, 55–58, 60–63, 66–73, 79, 80, 82, 84, 86, 88, 90, 93, 96–99, 101–107, 109–112, 115, 116, 120	Tests 10, 11, 12, 13, 14, 15, 16, 18, 19, 21, 23
50	• Decimal Number Line (Tenths)	Lessons 50–53, 58, 59, 60, 63, 67, 69, 76, 78, 79, 92, 94, 101, 109, 115	Test 11
	• Dividing by a Fraction	Lessons 50–53, 55, 57, 59, 60, 62, 63, 66, 68, 83, 86, 88, 89, 91, 97, 98, 100, 103	Test & Practice Generator
Inv. 5	• Displaying Data	Investigation 5, Lessons 51, 56, 59, 62, 66, 89, 94, 99, 102, 107, 113–120	Test 19

Finding a Percent of a Number

Objectives

- Write a percent as a decimal.
- Find the percent of a number by changing the percent to either a fraction or a decimal and multiplying.
- Calculate the sales tax on a purchase and find the total price of the purchase including tax.

Lesson Preparation

Materials

- **Power Up G** (in *Instructional Masters*)
- **Teacher-provided material: grid paper**

Optional

- **Fraction-Decimal-Percent Equivalents poster**

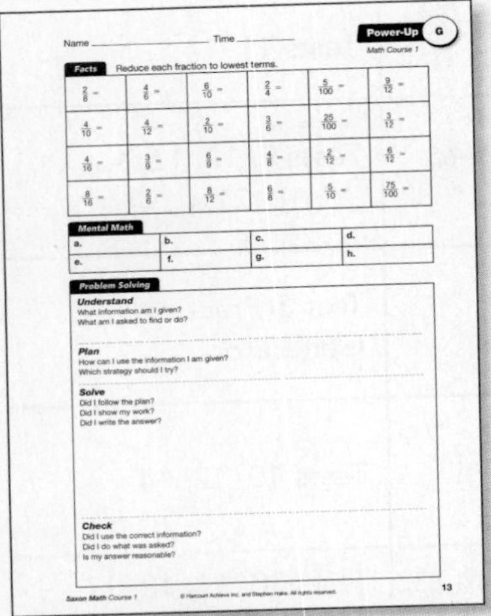

Power Up G

Math Language

New	Maintain	English Learners (ESL)
sales tax	percent	nonzero
	reduce	

Technology Resources

Student eBook Complete student textbook in electronic format.

Resources and Planner CD Assessment, reteaching, and instructional masters, plus a pacing calendar with standards.

Test and Practice Generator CD Create additional practice sheets and custom-made tests.

www.SaxonPublishers.com Visit for more student activities and planning materials.

Inclusion

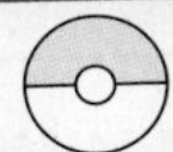

Adaptations CD Adapted lessons, investigations, practice and assessments.

Meeting Standards

National Council of Teachers of Mathematics (NCTM)

Numbers and Operations

NO.1a Work flexibly with fractions, decimals, and percents to solve problems

NO.1c Develop meaning for percents greater than 100 and less than 1

NO.3a Select appropriate methods and tools for computing with fractions and decimals from among mental computation, estimation, calculators or computers, and paper and pencil, depending on the situation, and apply the selected methods

NO.3c Develop and use strategies to estimate the results of rational-number computations and judge the reasonableness of the results

Power-Up Discussion For use with Power Up, p. 216

Problem-Solving Strategy: Write an Equation

Tennis is played on a rectangular surface that usually has two different courts drawn on it. Two players compete on a singles court, and four players (two per team) compete on a doubles court. The singles court is 78 feet long and 27 feet wide. The doubles court has the same length, but is 9 feet wider. What is the perimeter and the area of a singles tennis court? How wide is a doubles court? What is the perimeter and the area of the doubles court?

Understand — *Understand the problem.*

"What information are we given?"

Tennis courts are rectangular. A singles tennis court is $78' \times 27'$. A doubles court has the same length as a singles court but is 9 feet wider.

"What are we asked to find?"

1. The perimeter of a singles court.
2. The area of a singles court.
3. The width of a doubles court.
4. The perimeter of a doubles court.
5. The area of a doubles court.

"What prior knowledge do we have about perimeter and area?"

Perimeter is the distance around a shape measured in linear units. Area is the space within a shape measured in square units.

Teacher Note: You may wish to draw a diagram to help students visualize the tennis courts.

Plan — *Make a plan.*

"What problem-solving strategy will we use?"

We will *write an equation* using the formulas for the perimeter ($P = 2l + 2w$) and area ($A = l \times w$) of a rectangle.

Solve — *Carry out the plan.*

"What equation can we write to find the perimeter of a singles court?"

$2(78) + 2(27) = 210$ feet

"What equation can we write to find the area of a singles court?"

$78 \times 27 = 2106$ square feet

"What is the width of a doubles court?"

A doubles court is 9 feet wider than a singles court (27 feet), or 36 feet.

"What equation can we write to find the perimeter of a doubles court?"

$2(78) + 2(36) = 228$ feet

"What equation can we write to find the area of a doubles court?"

$78 \times 36 = 2808$ square feet

Check — *Look back.*

"Did we answer the questions that were asked?"

Yes. We answered all five questions.

Teacher Note: You may extend this lesson by asking:

"What fraction of the area of the doubles court is the area of the singles court?" $\frac{3}{4}$

"What fraction of the perimeter of the doubles court is the perimeter of the singles court?" $\frac{35}{38}$

Alternate Approach: Draw a Diagram

Some students may wish to draw a diagram to better visualize the two tennis courts before solving the equations.

1 Power Up

Facts

Distribute **Power Up G** to students. See answers below.

Mental Math

Before students begin the Mental Math exercise, do this counting exercise as class.

Count up and down by $\frac{1}{8}$s between $\frac{1}{8}$ and 2.

Encourage students to share different ways to mentally compute these exercises. Strategies for exercises **a** and **c** are listed below.

a. Use a Multiplication Fact
$4 \times 25 = 100$, so $4 \times 250 = 1000$
Count on by 200, then by 50
Start with 200. Count: 400, 600, 800
Start with 800. Count: 850, 900, 950, 1000

c. Change 8 to 10, then Subtract 2
$47 + 10 = 57$; $57 - 2 = 55$
Break Apart 47, then Add Ones
$47 + 8 = 40 + 7 + 8 = 40 + 15 = 55$

Problem Solving

Refer to **Power-Up Discussion**, p. 216F.

2 New Concepts

Instruction

You may wish to display the **Fraction-Decimal-Percent Equivalents** concept poster as you discuss finding percent of a number with students.

(continued)

LESSON 41

• Finding a Percent of a Number

Power Up *Building Power*

facts Power Up G

mental math

a. Number Sense: 4×250 1000

b. Number Sense: $625 + 50$ 675

c. Calculation: $47 + 8$ 55

d. Money: \$3.50 + \$1.75 \$5.25

e. Fractional Parts: $\frac{1}{2}$ of 700 350

f. Number Sense: $\frac{600}{10}$ 60

g. Measurement: How many feet are in 60 inches? 5 ft

h. Calculation: $5 \times 3, + 1, \div 2, + 1, \div 3, \times 8, \div 2$ 12

problem solving

Tennis is played on a rectangular surface that usually has two different courts drawn on it. Two players compete on a singles court, and four players (two per team) compete on a doubles court. The singles court is 78 feet long and 27 feet wide. The doubles court has the same length, but is 9 feet wider. What is the perimeter and the area of a singles tennis court? How wide is a doubles court? What is the perimeter and the area of the doubles court? Singles court: perimeter = 210 ft; area = 2106 sq. ft
Doubles court: width = 36 ft; perimeter = 228 ft; area = 2808 sq. ft

New Concept *Increasing Knowledge*

Math Language
Recall that a **percent** is really a fraction whose denominator is 100.

To describe part of a group, we often use a fraction or a percent. Here are a couple of examples:

Three fourths of the students voted for Imelda.
Tim answered 80% of the questions correctly.

We also use percents to describe financial situations.

Music CDs were on sale for 30% off the regular price.
The sales-tax rate is 7%.
The bank pays 3% interest on savings accounts.

When we are asked to find a certain percent of a number, we usually change the percent to either a fraction or a decimal before performing the calculation.

25% means $\frac{25}{100}$, which reduces to $\frac{1}{4}$.
5% means $\frac{5}{100}$, which reduces to $\frac{1}{20}$.

Facts Reduce each fraction to lowest terms.

$\frac{2}{8} = \frac{1}{4}$	$\frac{4}{6} = \frac{2}{3}$	$\frac{6}{10} = \frac{3}{5}$	$\frac{2}{4} = \frac{1}{2}$	$\frac{5}{100} = \frac{1}{20}$	$\frac{9}{12} = \frac{3}{4}$
$\frac{4}{10} = \frac{2}{5}$	$\frac{4}{12} = \frac{1}{3}$	$\frac{2}{10} = \frac{1}{5}$	$\frac{3}{6} = \frac{1}{2}$	$\frac{25}{100} = \frac{1}{4}$	$\frac{3}{12} = \frac{1}{4}$
$\frac{4}{16} = \frac{1}{4}$	$\frac{3}{9} = \frac{1}{3}$	$\frac{6}{9} = \frac{2}{3}$	$\frac{4}{8} = \frac{1}{2}$	$\frac{2}{12} = \frac{1}{6}$	$\frac{6}{12} = \frac{1}{2}$
$\frac{8}{16} = \frac{1}{2}$	$\frac{2}{6} = \frac{1}{3}$	$\frac{8}{12} = \frac{2}{3}$	$\frac{6}{8} = \frac{3}{4}$	$\frac{5}{10} = \frac{1}{2}$	$\frac{75}{100} = \frac{3}{4}$

A percent is also easily changed to a decimal number. Study the following changes from percent to fraction to decimal:

$25\% \rightarrow \frac{25}{100} \rightarrow 0.25 \qquad 5\% \rightarrow \frac{5}{100} \rightarrow 0.05$

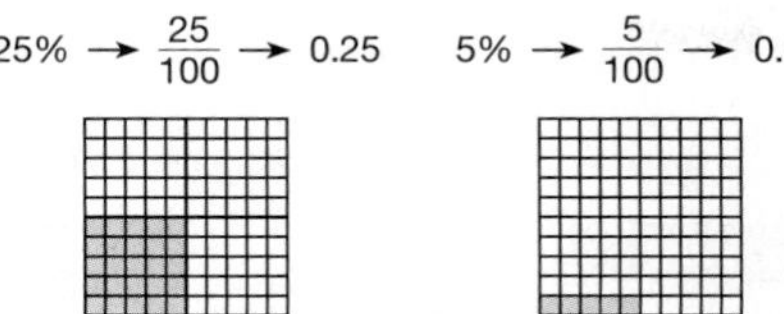

We see that the same nonzero digits are in both the decimal and percent forms of a number. In the decimal form, however, the decimal point is shifted two places to the left.

Example 1

Write 15% in decimal form.

Solution

Fifteen percent means $\frac{15}{100}$, which can be written **0.15**.

Model Use a grid to show 15%. Grid should show 15 of 100 shaded.

Example 2

Write 75% as a reduced fraction.

Solution

We write 75% as $\frac{75}{100}$ and reduce.

$$\frac{75}{100} = \mathbf{\frac{3}{4}}$$

Example 3

What number is 75% of 20?

Solution

We can translate this problem into an equation, changing the percent into either a fraction or a decimal. We use a letter for "what number," an equal sign for "is," and a multiplication sign for "of."

Percent To Fraction

What number is 75% of 20?

$n = \frac{3}{4} \times 20$

Percent To Decimal

What number is 75% of 20?

$n = 0.75 \times 20$

We show both the fraction form and the decimal form. Often, one form is easier to calculate than the other form.

2 New Concepts (Continued)

Example 1

Instruction

When grids are used to represent percents, students should recognize that the whole grid represents 100%.

"When a grid is shaded to show 15%, what percent of the grid is not shaded? Explain how you know." 85%; The whole grid represents 100%, and 100% − 15% is 85%.

Example 3

Instruction

After completing the example, challenge students to think about finding a percent of a number using only mental math.

"How could you find 50% of a number using only mental math?" Sample: Since 50% is the same as $\frac{1}{2}$, finding 50% of a number is the same as dividing that number by 2.

"How could you find 25% of 40 using only mental math?" Sample: Since 25% is the same as $\frac{1}{4}$, finding 25% of a number is the same as dividing that number by 4; 25% of 40 is the same as 40 ÷ 4 or 10.

(continued)

English Learners

Explain the term **nonzero.** Say:

"Non means not. So nonzero means not zero. What are the nonzero digits in 0.25?" 2 and 5

Write 0.05, 0.75, 0.08, and 0.36 on the board. Ask for volunteers to come to the board and identify the nonzero digits.

2 New Concepts (Continued)

Example 4

Instruction

This example shows two ways to find a percent of a number. After completing the example, tell students that both methods are helpful ways to find a percent of a number and that whichever method is best depends upon the numbers involved in the problem.

Example 5

Instruction

Challenge students to find out if their state, county, city, and/or town has a sales tax. The data that is collected should include the rate(s) as a percent and the types of purchases that are taxable.

(continued)

Thinking Skill
Conclude
Since 75% of 20 is 15, what is 25% of 20? 5

$\frac{3}{4} \times 20 = 15$ $\qquad$ $0.75 \times 20 = 15.00$

We find that 75% of 20 is **15**.

Discuss Which is easier to compute, $\frac{3}{4} \times 20$ or 0.75×20? Why? Opinions will vary. Be sure that students can support their choice.

Example 4

Jamaal correctly answered 80% of the 25 questions. How many questions did he answer correctly?

Solution

Thinking Skill
Verify
How do you change 80% to a fraction? To a decimal?
$\frac{80}{100} \div \frac{20}{20} = \frac{4}{5}$; $\frac{80}{100} = 0.80$

We want to find 80% of 25. We can change 80% to a fraction ($\frac{80}{100} = \frac{4}{5}$) or to a decimal number (80% = 0.80).

Percent To a Fraction	**Percent To a Decimal**
80% of 25	80% of 25
$\frac{4}{5} \times 25$	0.80×25

Then we calculate.

$\frac{4}{5} \times 25 = 20$ $\qquad$ $0.80 \times 25 = 20.00$

We find that Jamaal correctly answered **20 questions.**

Example 5

The sales-tax rate was 6%. Find the tax on a $12.00 purchase. Then find the total price including tax.

Solution

Math Language
Sales tax is a tax charged on the sale of an item. It is some percent of the item's purchase price.

We can change 6% to a fraction ($\frac{6}{100} = \frac{3}{50}$) or to a decimal number (6% = 0.06). It seems easier for us to multiply $12.00 by 0.06 than by $\frac{3}{50}$, so we will use the decimal form.

6% of $12.00

0.06 × $12.00 = $0.72

So the tax on the $12.00 purchase was **$0.72.** To find the total price including tax, we add $0.72 to $12.00.

```
  $12.00
+   0.72
  $12.72
```

Practice Set Write each percent in problems **a–f** as a reduced fraction:

a. 50% $\frac{1}{2}$ $\qquad$ **b.** 10% $\frac{1}{10}$ $\qquad$ **c.** 25% $\frac{1}{4}$

d. 75% $\frac{3}{4}$ $\qquad$ **e.** 20% $\frac{1}{5}$ $\qquad$ **f.** 1% $\frac{1}{100}$

Write each percent in problems **g–l** as a decimal number:

g. 65% 0.65 **h.** 7% 0.07 **i.** 30% 0.30 or 0.3

j. 8% 0.08 **k.** 60% 0.60 or 0.6 **l.** 1% 0.01

▶ **m.** Explain Mentally find 10% of 350. Describe how to perform the mental calculation. 35; 10% of 350 is $\frac{1}{10}$ of 350. Divide 350 by 10 to get 35.

n. Explain Mentally find 25% of 48. Describe how to perform the mental calculation. 12; 25% of 48 is $\frac{1}{4}$ of 48. Divide 48 by 4 to get 12.

o. How much money is 8% of $15.00? $1.20

▶ **p.** Estimate The sales-tax rate is $9\frac{1}{2}$%. Estimate the tax on a $9.98 purchase. How did you arrive at your answer?

p. $1; $9\frac{1}{2}$% rounds to 10%, and $9.98 rounds to $10. Find 10% ($\frac{1}{10}$) of $10, which is $1.

q. Erika sold 80% of her 30 baseball cards. How many baseball cards did she sell? 24 baseball cards

Written Practice *Strengthening Concepts*

*** 1.** (41) A student correctly answered 80% of the 20 questions on the test. How many questions did the student answer correctly? 16 questions

*** 2.** (41) Ramon ordered items from the menu totaling $8.50. If the sales-tax rate is 8%, how much should be added to the bill for sales tax? Explain why your answer is reasonable.

2. $0.68; Sample: An 8% sales tax means 8 cents per dollar, so the tax on $8 is 64¢ and the tax on half a dollar is 4¢. 64¢ + 4¢ = 68¢.

▶ **3.** (8) Analyze The ten-acre farm is on a square piece of land 220 yards on each side. A fence surrounds the land. How many yards of fencing surrounds the farm? 880 yards

▶ *** 4.** (41) Explain Describe how to find 20% of 30. Convert 20% to a fraction ($\frac{1}{5}$) or a decimal (0.20), and multiply that number by 30.

▶ **5.** (11) The dinner cost $9.18. Jeb paid with a $20 bill. How much money should he get back? Write an equation and solve the problem. $20.00 - 9.18 = b$; $10.82

6. (15) Formulate Two hundred eighty-eight chairs were arranged in 16 equal rows. How many chairs were in each row? Write an equation and solve the problem. $16 \cdot c = 288$; 18 chairs

7. (18) Yuki's bowling scores for three games were 126, 102, and 141. What was her average score for the three games? 123

*** 8.** (31, 39) What is the area of this rectangle? 5 m^2

2.5 m

2 m

9. (14, 17) Arrange these numbers in order from least to greatest: $-1, 0, \frac{2}{3}, \frac{3}{2}$

$\frac{3}{2}, 0, -1, \frac{2}{3}$

▶ See Math Conversations in the sidebar.

2 New Concepts (Continued)

Practice Set

Problem m Explain

Lead students to generalize that finding 10% of a number is the same as shifting the decimal point in that number one place to the left.

To reinforce the generalization, write a variety of whole and decimal numbers on the board, and then ask students to name 10% of each number.

Problem p Estimate

Explain to students that when estimating a percent of a number, it is sometimes helpful to round both the percent and the number before making the estimate.

Remind students that finding 10% of a number is the same as shifting the decimal point in that number one place to the left.

3 Written Practice

Math Conversations

Discussion opportunities are provided below.

Problem 3 Analyze

"The shape of this property is a square. How can you use multiplication to find the perimeter of a square?" Multiply the length of one side of the square by 4.

Problem 4 Explain

"How can we find the answer, or check the answer, using mental math?" Sample: 20% is the same as $\frac{1}{5}$. The denominator of the fraction represents 30 divided into five equal parts, and each equal part is 30 ÷ 5 or 6. The numerator represents one of those equal parts, so 20% of 30 is 6.

Problem 5 Formulate

Extend the Problem

Ask students to write a related equation that can also be used to solve the problem. Sample: A related equation for $16c = 288$ is $c = \frac{288}{16}$.

(continued)

3 Written Practice (Continued)

Math Conversations

Discussion opportunities are provided below.

Problem 16 Analyze

"In this expression, what number represents the base?" 2.5

"What does the exponent represent?" the number of times the base is used as a factor

Problem 30 Verify

Extend the Problem

"Explain how you could use Fran's method to estimate 28% of $32.17." Sample: Estimate 10% of $30, then multiply the estimate by 3.

Errors and Misconceptions

Problem 16

Watch for students who simplify the expression by finding the product 2.5×2.

Problem 19

Some students may generalize that when a percent is changed to a decimal number, the decimal number will *always* be in hundredths. Explain that such a generalization is not true. For example, a decimal equivalent for 20% is 0.20, but 0.2 is also a correct equivalent, and is a decimal number in tenths. Another example is a percent that is not a whole percent, such as 7.5%. The decimal equivalent for 7.5% is 0.075, a decimal number in thousandths.

10. (19) List the first eight prime numbers. 2, 3, 5, 7, 11, 13, 17, 19

11. (21) Classify By which of these numbers is 600 not divisible? D

A 2 **B** 3 **C** 5 **D** 9

12. (27) The fans were depressed, for their team had won only 15 of the first 60 games. What was the team's win-loss ratio after 60 games? $\frac{15}{45} = \frac{1}{3}$

13. (27) To loosen her shoulder, Mary swung her arm around in a big circle. If her arm was 28 inches long, what was the diameter of the circle? 56 inches

14. (28) Connect The map shows three streets in town.

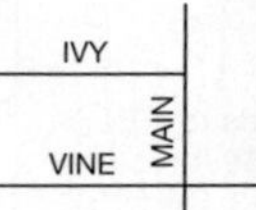

a. Name a street parallel to Vine. Ivy

b. Name a street perpendicular to Vine. Main

15. (28, Inv. 3) Rob remembers that an acute angle is "a cute little angle." Which of the following could be the measure of an acute angle? B

A 0° **B** 45° **C** 90° **D** 135°

▸* **16.** (38, 39) $(2.5)^2$ 6.25

* **17.** (38) $\sqrt{81}$ 9

* **18.** (41) Write 40% as a reduced fraction. $\frac{2}{5}$

▸* **19.** (41) Write 9% as a decimal number. Then find 9% of $10. 0.09; $0.90

20. (30) What is the reciprocal of $\frac{2}{3}$? $\frac{3}{2}$

Find each unknown number. Remember to check your work.

21. (4) $7m = 3500$ 500

22. (3) $\$6.25 + w = \$10.00$ $3.75

* **23.** (30) $\frac{2}{3}n = 1$ $\frac{3}{2}$

24. (3) $x - 37 = 76$ 113

25. (37) $6.25 + (4 - 2.5)$ 7.75

26. (26) $3\frac{3}{4} + 2\frac{3}{4}$ $6\frac{1}{2}$

27. (Inv. 2) $\frac{4}{4} - \frac{3}{3}$ 0

28. (29) $\frac{5}{6} \cdot \frac{3}{5}$ $\frac{1}{2}$

29. (29) What is $\frac{3}{4}$ of 48? 36

▸* **30.** (41) Justify Fran estimated 9% of $21.90 by first rounding 9% to 10% and rounding $21.90 to $20. She then mentally calculated 10% of $20 and got the answer $2. Use Fran's method to estimate 9% of $32.17. Describe the steps. $3; Round 9% to 10% and $32.17 to $30. Then find 10% ($\frac{1}{10}$) of $30.

220 Saxon Math Course 1

▸ See Math Conversations in the sidebar.

Looking Forward

Using a percent in fractional or decimal form to find a percent of a number and the sales tax and total price of a purchase prepares students for:

- **Lesson 51,** rounding decimal numbers to the nearest cent and other places.
- **Lesson 75,** writing fractions and decimals as percents.
- **Lesson 105,** using proportions to solve percent problems.
- **Lesson 116,** finding compound interest.
- **Lesson 119,** finding a whole when a percent is known.

• Renaming Fractions by Multiplying by 1

Objectives

- Rename fractions by multiplying them by fractions equal to 1.
- Add or subtract fractions with different denominators by renaming each fraction as an equivalent fraction with the same denominator.

Lesson Preparation

Materials

- **Power Up G** (in *Instructional Masters*)

Optional

- **Teacher-provided material: fraction manipulatives** from Investigation 2

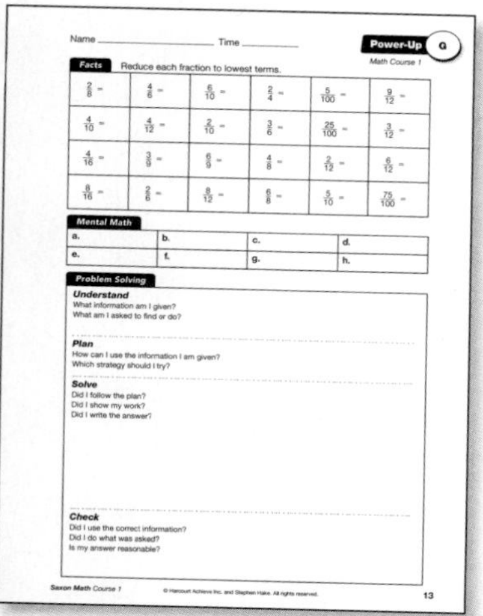
Name ______ Time ______ Power-Up G
Math Course 1
Facts Reduce each fraction to lowest terms.
Mental Math a. b. c. d. e. f. g. h.
Problem Solving
Understand
What information am I given?
What am I asked to find or do?
Plan
How can I use the information I am given?
Which strategy should I try?
Solve
Did I follow the plan?
Did I show my work?
Did I write the answer?
Check
Did I use the correct information?
Did I do what was asked?
Is my answer reasonable?
Saxon Math Course 1 13

Power Up G

Math Language

New	Maintain	English Learners (ESL)
equivalent fractions	Identity Property of Multiplication	discount

Technology Resources

Student eBook Complete student textbook in electronic format.

Resources and Planner CD Assessment, reteaching, and instructional masters, plus a pacing calendar with standards.

Test and Practice Generator CD Create additional practice sheets and custom-made tests.

www.SaxonPublishers.com Visit for more student activities and planning materials.

Inclusion

Adaptations CD Adapted lessons, investigations, practice and assessments.

Meeting Standards

National Council of Teachers of Mathematics (NCTM)

Numbers and Operations

NO.1a Work flexibly with fractions, decimals, and percents to solve problems

NO.1d Understand and use ratios and proportions to represent quantitative relationships

NO.3b Develop and analyze algorithms for computing with fractions, decimals, and integers and develop fluency in their use

Power-Up Discussion *For use with Power Up, p. 221*

Problem-Solving Strategy: Make an Organized List/ Write an Equation

Victor dropped a rubber ball and found that each bounce was half as high as the previous bounce. He dropped the ball from 8 feet, measured the height of each bounce, and recorded the results in a table. Copy this table and complete it through the fifth bounce.

Heights of Bounces

First	4 ft
Second	
Third	
Fourth	
Fifth	

Understand **Understand the problem.**

"What information are we given?"

Victor dropped a rubber ball from 8 feet and found that each bounce was half as high as the previous bounce.

"What are we asked to do?"

We are asked to fill in the table through the fifth bounce.

Plan **Make a plan.**

"What problem-solving strategy will we use?"

We will *write equations* to help us *make an organized list* of the heights.

Solve **Carry out the plan.**

"How can we find the values to fill in the table?"

If the ball is dropped from 8 feet, we know the bounce is only half as high (4 ft). We must divide the previous height by 2 to find the new height.

Bounce	Previous Height	÷ 2	= New Height
1	8 feet	÷ 2	4 feet
2	4 feet	÷ 2	2 feet
3	2 feet	÷ 2	1 foot
4	1 foot	÷ 2	6 inches
5	6 inches	÷ 2	3 inches

Teacher Note: Point out the unit conversion in the fourth bounce.

We copy the information into the given table to solve the problem.

Check **Look back.**

"Is our solution reasonable?"

Yes. If we look back at the new heights we found, we see that each one is half of the previous bounce.

Teacher Note: You may extend this lesson by increasing the height from which the ball is dropped.

LESSON 42

• Renaming Fractions by Multiplying by 1

Power Up — *Building Power*

facts Power Up G

mental math

a. **Number Sense:** 4 × 125 500

b. **Number Sense:** 825 + 50 875

c. **Calculation:** 67 + 8 75

d. **Money:** \$6.75 + \$2.50 \$9.25

e. **Fractional Parts:** $\frac{1}{2}$ of 1000 500

f. **Number Sense:** $\frac{580}{10}$ 58

g. **Measurement:** How many millimeters are in 10 centimeters? 100 mm

h. **Calculation:** 3 × 4, − 2, × 5, − 2, ÷ 6, + 1, ÷ 3 3

problem solving Victor dropped a rubber ball and found that each bounce was half as high as the previous bounce. He dropped the ball from 8 feet, measured the height of each bounce, and recorded the results in a table. Copy this table and complete it through the fifth bounce.

Heights of Bounces

First	4 ft
Second	
Third	
Fourth	
Fifth	

Heights of Bounces

First	4 ft
Second	2 ft
Third	1 ft
Fourth	$\frac{1}{2}$ ft
Fifth	$\frac{1}{4}$ ft

New Concept — *Increasing Knowledge*

With our fraction manipulatives we have seen that the same fraction can be named many different ways. Here we show six ways to name the fraction $\frac{1}{2}$:

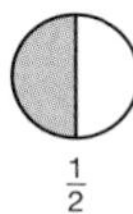
$\frac{1}{2}$

$\frac{2}{4}$

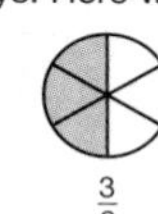
$\frac{3}{6}$

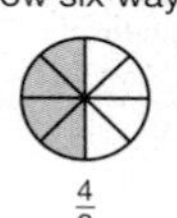
$\frac{4}{8}$

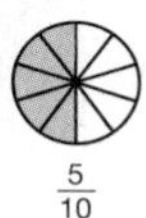
$\frac{5}{10}$

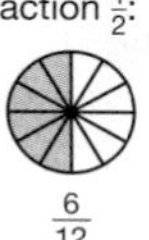
$\frac{6}{12}$

In this lesson we will practice renaming fractions by multiplying them by a fraction equal to 1. Here we show six ways to name 1 as a fraction:

$\frac{1}{1}$

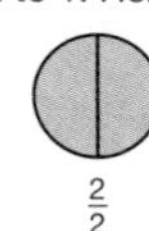
$\frac{2}{2}$

$\frac{3}{3}$

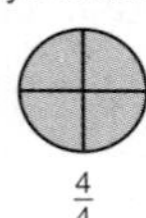
$\frac{4}{4}$

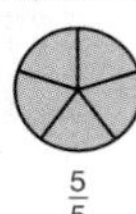
$\frac{5}{5}$

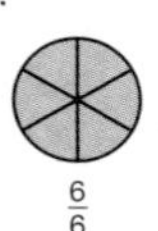
$\frac{6}{6}$

Facts Reduce each fraction to lowest terms.

$\frac{2}{8}=\frac{1}{4}$	$\frac{4}{6}=\frac{2}{3}$	$\frac{6}{10}=\frac{3}{5}$	$\frac{2}{4}=\frac{1}{2}$	$\frac{5}{100}=\frac{1}{20}$	$\frac{9}{12}=\frac{3}{4}$
$\frac{4}{10}=\frac{2}{5}$	$\frac{4}{12}=\frac{1}{3}$	$\frac{2}{10}=\frac{1}{5}$	$\frac{3}{6}=\frac{1}{2}$	$\frac{25}{100}=\frac{1}{4}$	$\frac{3}{12}=\frac{1}{4}$
$\frac{4}{16}=\frac{1}{4}$	$\frac{3}{9}=\frac{1}{3}$	$\frac{6}{9}=\frac{2}{3}$	$\frac{4}{8}=\frac{1}{2}$	$\frac{2}{12}=\frac{1}{6}$	$\frac{6}{12}=\frac{1}{2}$
$\frac{8}{16}=\frac{1}{2}$	$\frac{2}{6}=\frac{1}{3}$	$\frac{8}{12}=\frac{2}{3}$	$\frac{6}{8}=\frac{3}{4}$	$\frac{5}{10}=\frac{1}{2}$	$\frac{75}{100}=\frac{3}{4}$

1 Power Up

Facts

Distribute **Power Up G** to students. See answers below.

Mental Math

Before students begin the Mental Math exercise, do this counting exercise as a class.

Count by 12s from 12 to 96.

Encourage students to share different ways to mentally compute these exercises. Strategies for exercises **d** and **e** are listed below.

d. Count on by Dollars, then by Quarters
Start with \$6.75. Count: \$7.75, \$8.75
Start with \$8.75. Count: \$9.00, \$9.25
Add \$0.25 and Subtract \$0.25
\$6.75 + \$0.25 = \$7.00 and
\$2.50 − \$0.25 = \$2.25;
\$7.00 + \$2.25 = \$9.25

e. Use a Pattern of Halves
$\frac{1}{2}$ of 10 = 5; $\frac{1}{2}$ of 100 = 50; $\frac{1}{2}$ of 1000 = 500
Use a Repeated Addition Pattern
Since 5 + 5 = 10, 50 + 50 = 100, and 500 + 500 = 1000, $\frac{1}{2}$ of 1000 = 500.

Problem Solving

Refer to **Power-Up Discussion**, p. 221B.

2 New Concepts

Instruction

You might choose to have students use their fraction manipulatives to model the different names for $\frac{1}{2}$ and for 1.

(continued)

2 New Concepts (Continued)

Instruction

The Math Background feature at the bottom of this page contains additional background information.

Example 1

Instruction

Make sure that students understand why $\frac{1}{2}$ is multiplied by $\frac{10}{10}$.

"If we want to write an equivalent fraction for $\frac{1}{2}$ that has a denominator of 20, we need to think 'Two times what number equals 20?' We know that two times ten equals twenty, so we multiply $\frac{1}{2}$ by a fraction equal to 1 that has a denominator of 10, and so we multiply by $\frac{10}{10}$."

Example 2

Instruction

This example and the problems in the Practice Set lay the groundwork for adding and subtracting fractions in Lessons 55 and 56.

(continued)

Math Language

The **Identity Property of Multiplication** states that if one of two factors is 1, the product equals the other factor.

We know that when we multiply a number by 1, the product equals the number multiplied. So if we multiply $\frac{1}{2}$ by 1, the answer is $\frac{1}{2}$.

$$\frac{1}{2} \times 1 = \frac{1}{2}$$

However, if we multiply $\frac{1}{2}$ by fractions equal to 1, we find different names for $\frac{1}{2}$. Here we show $\frac{1}{2}$ multiplied by $\frac{2}{2}$, $\frac{3}{3}$, and $\frac{4}{4}$:

$$\frac{1}{2} \times \frac{2}{2} = \frac{2}{4} \qquad \frac{1}{2} \times \frac{3}{3} = \frac{3}{6} \qquad \frac{1}{2} \times \frac{4}{4} = \frac{4}{8}$$

Fractions with the same value but different names are called **equivalent fractions.** The fractions $\frac{2}{4}$, $\frac{3}{6}$, and $\frac{4}{8}$ are all equivalent to $\frac{1}{2}$.

Example 1

Write a fraction equal to $\frac{1}{2}$ that has a denominator of 20.

$$\frac{1}{2} = \frac{?}{20}$$

Solution

To rename a fraction, we multiply the fraction by a fraction equal to 1. The denominator of $\frac{1}{2}$ is 2. We want to make an equivalent fraction with a denominator of 20.

$$\frac{1}{2} = \frac{?}{20}$$

Since we need to multiply the denominator by 10, we multiply $\frac{1}{2}$ by $\frac{10}{10}$.

$$\frac{1}{2} \times \frac{10}{10} = \mathbf{\frac{10}{20}}$$

Example 2

Write $\frac{1}{2}$ and $\frac{1}{3}$ as fractions with denominators of 6. Then add the renamed fractions.

Solution

Thinking Skill

Represent

Draw a diagram to show that $\frac{1}{2} = \frac{3}{6}$.

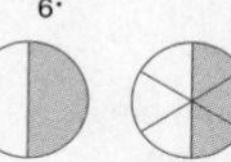

We multiply each fraction by a fraction equal to 1 to form fractions that have denominators of 6.

$$\frac{1}{2} = \frac{?}{6} \qquad \frac{1}{3} = \frac{?}{6}$$

We multiply $\frac{1}{2}$ by $\frac{3}{3}$, and we multiply $\frac{1}{3}$ by $\frac{2}{2}$.

$$\frac{1}{2} \times \frac{3}{3} = \mathbf{\frac{3}{6}} \qquad \frac{1}{3} \times \frac{2}{2} = \mathbf{\frac{2}{6}}$$

The renamed fractions are $\frac{3}{6}$ and $\frac{2}{6}$. We are told to add these fractions.

$$\frac{3}{6} + \frac{2}{6} = \mathbf{\frac{5}{6}}$$

Math Background

The pattern of multiplying $\frac{1}{2}$ by $\frac{2}{2}$, $\frac{3}{3}$, $\frac{4}{4}$, and so on, can be continued indefinitely. For this reason, there are an infinite number of equivalent fractions for $\frac{1}{2}$, and in a more general way, there are an infinite number of equivalent names for any number.

Practice Set ▶ In problems **a–d,** multiply by a fraction equal to 1 to complete each equivalent fraction.

a. $\frac{1}{3} = \frac{?}{12}$ 4 **b.** $\frac{2}{3} = \frac{?}{6}$ 4

c. $\frac{3}{4} = \frac{?}{8}$ 6 **d.** $\frac{3}{4} = \frac{?}{12}$ 9

e.

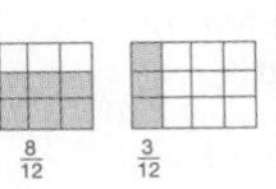

$\frac{8}{12}$ $\frac{3}{12}$

▶ **e.** Model On your paper draw two rectangles that look like this one. Shade $\frac{2}{3}$ of the squares of one rectangle and shade $\frac{1}{4}$ of the squares of the other rectangle. Then name each shaded rectangle as a fraction with a denominator of 12.

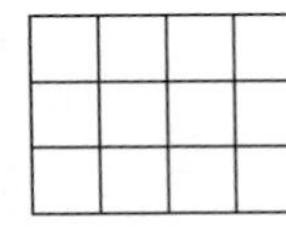

f. Write $\frac{2}{3}$ and $\frac{1}{4}$ as fractions with denominators of 12. Then add the renamed fractions. $\frac{8}{12} + \frac{3}{12} = \frac{11}{12}$

g. Describe how the rectangles you drew for exercise **e** can help you add the fractions in **f.**

g. Sample: The shaded rectangles show the number of twelfths in $\frac{2}{3}$ and $\frac{1}{4}$. I can count the total number of shaded twelfths

h. Write $\frac{1}{6}$ as a fraction with 12 as the denominator. Subtract the renamed fraction from $\frac{5}{12}$. Reduce the subtraction answer. $\frac{2}{12}$; $\frac{5}{12} - \frac{2}{12} = \frac{3}{12} = \frac{1}{4}$

Written Practice *Strengthening Concepts*

▶ * **1.** (42) Analyze Write $\frac{1}{2}$ and $\frac{2}{3}$ as fractions with denominators of 6. Then add the renamed fractions. Write the answer as a mixed number. $\frac{3}{6} + \frac{4}{6} = \frac{7}{6} = 1\frac{1}{6}$

2. (13) According to some estimates, our own galaxy, the Milky Way, contains about two hundred billion stars. Use digits to write that number of stars. 200,000,000,000 stars

▶ **3.** (31) Explain The rectangular school yard is 120 yards long and 40 yards wide. How many square yards is its area? Explain why your answer is reasonable. 4800 square yards; See student work.

▶ * **4.** (41) Analyze What number is 40% of 30? 12

In problems **5** and **6,** multiply $\frac{1}{2}$ by a fraction equal to 1 to complete each equivalent fraction.

* **5.** (42) $\frac{1}{2} = \frac{?}{8}$ 4 * **6.** (42) $\frac{1}{2} = \frac{?}{10}$ 5

* **7.** (37, 38) $4.32 + 0.6 + \sqrt{81}$ 13.92 ▶ * **8.** (37) $6.3 - 0.54$ 5.76

▶ * **9.** (38, 40) $(0.15)^2$ 0.0225

10. (30) What is the reciprocal of $\frac{6}{7}$? $\frac{7}{6}$

11. (34) Which digit in 12,345 has the same place value as the 6 in 67.89? 4

12. (30) What is the least common multiple of 3, 4, and 6? 12

▶ See Math Conversations in the sidebar.

2 New Concepts (Continued)

Practice Set

Problems a–d Error Alert

Remind students of the importance of checking their work. Then suggest that they check their answers for these problems by reducing each equivalent fraction.

Problem e Represent

For this activity, ask students to draw two congruent rectangles.

3 Written Practice

Math Conversations

Discussion opportunities are provided below.

Problem 1 Analyze

"Explain how to change $\frac{2}{3}$ to an equivalent fraction that has a denominator of 6."

Sample: To change a denominator of 3 to a denominator of 6, multiply the denominator of $\frac{2}{3}$ by 2. Complete the equivalent fraction by multiplying the numerator of $\frac{2}{3}$ by 2; $\frac{2}{3} \times \frac{2}{2} = \frac{4}{6}$.

Problem 3 Explain

"How is multiplication used to find the area of a rectangle?" Multiply the length of the rectangle by its width.

Problem 4 Analyze

Challenge students to describe a way, or a variety of ways, to solve the problem or check the answer using mental math. Sample: Finding 10% of a number is the same as shifting the decimal point in that number one place to the left. So 10% of 30 is 3, and 3 × 4 is 12.

Errors and Misconceptions

Problem 8

Some students may have difficulty completing the subtraction because the subtrahend has a greater number of digits to the right of the decimal point than the minuend. Remind these students that writing a zero in the hundredths place of the minuend does not change the value of the minuend because 6.30 and 6.3 are equivalent decimal numbers. In other words, they are different names for the same number.

Problem 9

Encourage students who have difficulty maintaining correct vertical alignment of the addends to rewrite the addends on grid paper or lined paper turned sideways.

(continued)

3 Written Practice (Continued)

Math Conversations

Discussion opportunities are provided below.

Problem 19 Represent

Extend the Problem

"Is it possible to form 10 different fractions that are equal to $\frac{1}{3}$? Explain why or why not." Yes; to form a fraction that is equal to $\frac{1}{3}$, multiply $\frac{1}{3}$ by a fraction that is equal to 1. Since there are an infinite number of fractions that are equal to 1 (such as $\frac{2}{2}$, $\frac{3}{3}$, $\frac{4}{4}$, $\frac{5}{5}$, and so on), there are an infinite number of fractions equal to $\frac{1}{3}$.

Lead students to generalize that there are an infinite number of equivalent fractions for any fraction.

13. (26) $5\frac{3}{5} + 4\frac{4}{5}$ $10\frac{2}{5}$

* **14.** (36, 38) $\sqrt{36} - 4\frac{2}{3}$ $1\frac{1}{3}$

15. (29) $\frac{8}{3} \times \frac{1}{2}$ $1\frac{1}{3}$

16. (29) $\frac{6}{5} \times 3$ $3\frac{3}{5}$

* **17.** (36) $1 - \frac{1}{4}$ $\frac{3}{4}$

18. (Inv. 2) $\frac{10}{10} - \frac{5}{5}$ 0

▶* **19.** (42) Form three different fractions that are equal to $\frac{1}{3}$. (*Hint:* Multiply $\frac{1}{3}$ by three different fraction names for 1). Sample: $\frac{2}{6}$, $\frac{3}{9}$, and $\frac{4}{12}$.

20. (19) **Analyze** The prime numbers that multiply to form 35 are 5 and 7. Which prime numbers can be multiplied to form 34? 2 and 17

21. (18) **Estimate** In three games Alma's scores were 12,143; 9870; and 14,261. Describe how to estimate her average score per game.

22. (16) **Explain** Estimate the quotient of $\frac{8176}{41}$. Describe how you performed the estimate.

23. (22) **Model** How many eggs are in $\frac{2}{3}$ of a dozen? Draw a diagram to illustrate the problem. 8 eggs

* **24.** (42) Write $\frac{3}{4}$ with a denominator of 8. Subtract the renamed fraction from $\frac{7}{8}$. $\frac{6}{8}$; $\frac{7}{8} - \frac{6}{8} = \frac{1}{8}$

25. (8) What is the perimeter of this rectangle? 1.2 m

0.4 m

0.2 m

26. (31) What is the area of this rectangle? $0.08\ m^2$

* **27.** (1) **Represent** The regular price r minus the discount d equals the sale price s.

$$r - d = s$$

Arrange these letters to form another subtraction equation and two addition equations. $r - s = d$, $s + d = r$, $d + s = r$

28. (2) Below we show the same division problem written three different ways. Identify which number is the divisor, which is the dividend, and which is the quotient. Divisor is 4; dividend is 20; quotient is 5.

$$\frac{20}{4} = 5 \qquad 4\overline{)20}^{\,5} \qquad 20 \div 4 = 5$$

29. (32) What time is $2\frac{1}{2}$ hours after 11:45 a.m.? 2:15 p.m.

* **30.** (30) **a.** How many $\frac{5}{6}$s are in 1? $\frac{6}{5}$

b. Use the answer to part **a** to find the number of $\frac{5}{6}$s in 3. $\frac{18}{5} = 3\frac{3}{5}$

21. Round the scores to 12,000; 10,000 and 14,000. Add the scores and get 36,000; then divide by 3 to find the average (12,000 points).

22. 200; Round 8176 to 8000, and round 41 to 40 then divide 8000 by 40.

23.

	12 eggs
$\frac{2}{3}$ of 12	4 eggs
	4 eggs
$\frac{1}{3}$ of 12	4 eggs

▶ See Math Conversations in the sidebar.

English Learners

Explain the meaning of **discount** by referring to shopping. Write $r - d = s$ on the board. Say:

"When something is discounted, it costs less than the regular price. For example, if a bicycle costs $100 and it has a $25 discount, the bicycle will cost $100 minus the $25 discount. The sale price of the bicycle will be $75."

Ask the students to give an example of something they have purchased that has been discounted.

Looking Forward

Renaming fractions by multiplying by 1 to form equivalent fractions and renaming fractions in order to add and subtract fractions prepares students for

- **Lessons 46 and 49,** dividing by a decimal number by multiplying by 1 to change the divisor to a whole number.
- **Lesson 53,** simplifying fractional answers after adding fractions with unlike denominators.
- **Lesson 55 and 56,** finding common denominators in order to add and subtract fractions and in order to compare fractions.
- **Lesson 83,** finding a missing term in a proportion.
- **Lesson 114,** multiplying by unit multipliers to convert from one unit of measure to another.

• Equivalent Division Problems
• Finding Unknowns in Fraction and Decimal Problems

Objectives

- Find division answers by forming equivalent division problems.
- Find the unknown number in a fraction or decimal problem.

Lesson Preparation

Materials

- **Power Up C** (in *Instructional Masters*)
- **Manipulative Kit: inch rulers**

Optional

- **Teacher-provided material: calculators**

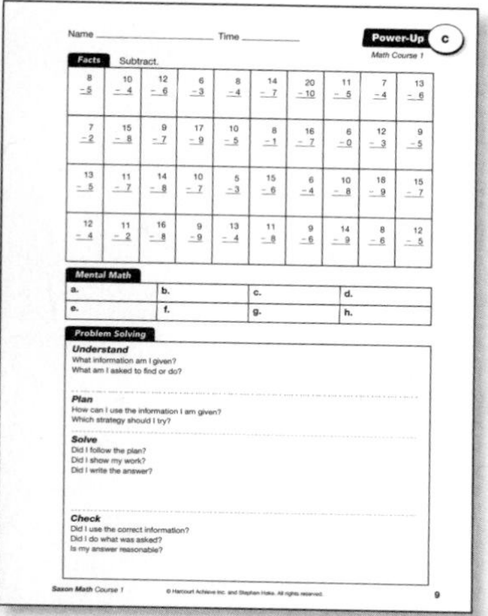

Power Up C

Math Language

	Maintain	English Learners (ESL)
	unknown	substituting

Technology Resources

Student eBook Complete student textbook in electronic format.

Resources and Planner CD Assessment, reteaching, and instructional masters, plus a pacing calendar with standards.

Test and Practice Generator CD Create additional practice sheets and custom-made tests.

www.SaxonPublishers.com Visit for more student activities and planning materials.

Inclusion

Adaptations CD Adapted lessons, investigations, practice and assessments.

Meeting Standards

National Council of Teachers of Mathematics (NCTM)

Numbers and Operations

NO.1a Work flexibly with fractions, decimals, and percents to solve problems

NO.2c Understand and use the inverse relationships of addition and subtraction, multiplication and division, and squaring and finding square roots to simplify computations and solve problems

NO.3a Select appropriate methods and tools for computing with fractions and decimals from among mental computation, estimation, calculators or computers, and paper and pencil, depending on the situation, and apply the selected methods

Connections

CN.4b Understand how mathematical ideas interconnect and build on one another to produce a coherent whole

Power-Up Discussion — For use with Power Up, p. 225

Problem-Solving Strategy: Use Logical Reasoning

Teresa wanted to paint each face of a cube so that the adjacent faces (the faces next to each other) were different colors. She wanted to use fewer than six different colors. What is the fewest number of colors she could use? Describe how the cube could be painted.

Understand — Understand the problem.

"What information are we given?"

Teresa wanted to paint each face of a cube so that the adjacent faces were different colors.

"What are we asked to do?"

We are asked to describe how the cube could be painted with the fewest colors possible.

"What do we know already know about cubes and adjacent faces?"

We know that a cube has six sides. We know that adjacent means "next to or adjoining."

Plan — Make a plan.

"How can we use the information we know to do what we are asked to do?"

We will *use logical and spatial reasoning* to mentally picture a cube and consider how Teresa could paint its faces. We will to think about opposite and adjacent faces to help us solve the problem.

Teacher Note: You may wish to have cube shapes available for students to view.

Solve — Carry out the plan.

"Mentally picture a cube, and think about the top face. What face is opposite the top face?"

The bottom face is opposite the top face.

"How many faces are adjacent to the top face?"

Four faces are adjacent to the top: the front and back faces, and the left and right faces.

"If Teresa paints the top red, what is the fewest number of colors she could use to paint the four adjacent sides?"

Two. She could paint the front and back faces the same color because they are not adjacent. Likewise, she could paint the left and right faces the same color. To help us better visualize the cube, we choose blue for the front and back faces and green for the left and right faces.

"What color could the bottom be painted?"

Red. The bottom is not adjacent to the top but is adjacent to all four of the blue and green faces.

Check — Look back.

"Did we do what we were asked to do?"

Yes, we found that the fewest number of colors Teresa could use is three.

"Are we certain Teresa cannot use fewer than three colors?"

Yes. She obviously cannot use just one color, and if she tries to use only two colors, she will always end up with some adjacent sides sharing a color.

LESSON 43

• Equivalent Division Problems
• Finding Unknowns in Fraction and Decimal Problems

Power Up — *Building Power*

facts Power Up C

mental math

a. Calculation: 4 × 225 900

b. Number Sense: 720 − 200 520

c. Number Sense: 37 + 28 65

d. Money: \$200 − \$175 \$25

e. Fractional Parts: $\frac{1}{2}$ of 1200 600

f. Number Sense: $\frac{\$70.00}{10}$ \$7.00

g. Probability: How many different three digit numbers can be made with the digits 3, 5, and 9? 6

h. Calculation: 8 × 4, − 2, × 2, + 3, ÷ 7, × 2, ÷3 6

problem solving Teresa wanted to paint each face of a cube so that the adjacent faces (the faces next to each other) were different colors. She wanted to use fewer than six different colors. What is the fewest number of colors she could use? Describe how the cube could be painted. 3 colors; Paint opposite faces the same color.

New Concepts — *Increasing Knowledge*

equivalent division problems

The following two division problems have the same quotient. We call them **equivalent division problems.** Which problem seems easier to perform mentally?

a. 700 ÷ 14

b. 350 ÷ 7

Math Language
Recall that equivalent numbers or expressions have the same value.

We can change problem **a** to problem **b** by dividing both 700 and 14 by 2.

700 ÷ 14
↓
Divide both 700 and 14 by 2.
↓
350 ÷ 7

Facts Subtract.

8 − 5 3	10 − 4 6	12 − 6 6	6 − 3 3	8 − 4 4	14 − 7 7	20 − 10 10	11 − 5 6	7 − 4 3	13 − 6 7
7 − 2 5	15 − 8 7	9 − 7 2	17 − 9 8	10 − 5 5	8 − 1 7	16 − 7 9	6 − 0 6	12 − 3 9	9 − 5 4
13 − 5 8	11 − 7 4	14 − 8 6	10 − 7 3	5 − 3 2	15 − 6 9	6 − 4 2	10 − 8 2	18 − 9 9	15 − 7 8
12 − 4 8	11 − 2 9	16 − 8 8	9 − 9 0	13 − 4 9	11 − 8 3	9 − 6 3	14 − 9 5	8 − 6 2	12 − 5 7

1 Power Up

Facts
Distribute **Power Up C** to students. See answer below.

Mental Math
Before students begin the Mental Math exercise, do this counting exercise as a class.

Count by 6s to 72. Count by 8s to 96.

Encourage students to share different ways to mentally compute these exercises. Strategies for exercises **a** and **c** are listed below.

a. Decompose 225
(4 × 200) + (4 × 25) = 800 + 100 = 900
Count on by 200, then by 25
Start with: 200. Count: 400, 600, 800
Start with: 800. Count: 825, 850, 875, 900

c. Change 28 to 30, then Subtract 2
37 + 30 = 67; 67 − 2 = 65
Change 37 to 40, then Subtract 3
40 + 28 = 68; 68 − 3 = 65

Problem Solving
Refer to **Power-Up Discussion,** p. 225B.

2 New Concepts

Instruction
One way to introduce the lesson is to present a simpler pair of equivalent division problems.

Write 18 ÷ 6 on the board and ask students to name the quotient. 3

Explain that another way to find the quotient is to divide the dividend and the divisor by a common factor (such as 2) *before* naming the quotient. Write 9 ÷ 3 on the board.

Ask students to compare the quotient 18 ÷ 6 to the quotient 9 ÷ 3, then state a conclusion about the method. Dividing a dividend and a divisor by the same number does not change the quotient.

(continued)

2 New Concepts (Continued)

Instruction

In the solutions to problems **a** and **b,** students may use calculators to confirm that 700 ÷ 14 and 350 ÷ 7 are equivalent division problems (both quotients are 50).

For problem **c** write this equation on the board:

$$\frac{7\frac{1}{2}}{\frac{1}{2}} \cdot \frac{2}{2} = \frac{15}{1}$$

Some students may not recall how to multiply a mixed number by a whole number. Review this concept with them or remind them that multiplying $7\frac{1}{2}$ by 2 is the same as adding $7\frac{1}{2} + 7\frac{1}{2}$.

Example 1

Instruction

Invite students to write other problems that are equivalent to 1200 ÷ 16 by multiplying or dividing both terms by the same number. Sample: 2400 ÷ 32, 4800 ÷ 64, 300 ÷ 4, 150 ÷ 2, and 75 ÷ 1.

Students may use calculators to confirm that the problems they wrote are equivalent to (or have the same quotient as) the example 1 solution.

(continued)

By dividing both the dividend and divisor by the same number (in this case, 2), we formed an equivalent division problem that was easier to divide mentally. This process simply reduces the terms of the division as we would reduce a fraction.

$$\frac{700}{14} = \frac{350}{7} \quad \begin{matrix}(700 \div 2 = 350)\\(14 \div 2 = 7)\end{matrix}$$

We may also form equivalent division problems by multiplying the dividend and divisor by the same number. Consider the following equivalent problems:

c. $7\frac{1}{2} \div \frac{1}{2}$

d. 15 ÷ 1

We changed problem **c** to problem **d** by doubling both $7\frac{1}{2}$ and $\frac{1}{2}$; that is, by multiplying both numbers by 2.

$7\frac{1}{2} \div \frac{1}{2}$

↓

Multiply both $7\frac{1}{2}$ and $\frac{1}{2}$ by 2.

↓

15 ÷ 1

This process forms an equivalent division problem in the same way we would form an equivalent fraction.

$$\frac{7\frac{1}{2}}{\frac{1}{2}} \cdot \frac{2}{2} = \frac{15}{1}$$

Example 1

Form an equivalent division problem for the division below. Then calculate the quotient.

1200 ÷ 16

Solution

Instead of dividing 1200 by the two-digit number 16, we can divide both the dividend and the divisor by 2 to form the equivalent division of 600 ÷ 8. We then calculate.

$$16\overline{)1200} \xrightarrow{\text{Divide both numbers by 2.}} \begin{array}{r} \mathbf{75} \\ 8\overline{)600} \\ \underline{56} \\ 40 \\ \underline{40} \\ 0 \end{array}$$

Both quotients are 75, but dividing by 8 is easier than dividing by 16.

Math Background

Forming equivalent division problems is a process commonly used to divide by fractions and divide by decimal numbers. In future lessons, students will learn that to divide by a fraction, an equivalent division problem is formed that makes the divisor 1, and to divide by a decimal number, an equivalent division problem is formed that makes the divisor a whole number.

Notice that several equivalent division problems can be formed from the original problem 1200 ÷ 16:

$$1200 \div 16 \longrightarrow 600 \div 8 \longrightarrow 300 \div 4 \longrightarrow 150 \div 2$$

All of these problems have the same quotient.

Example 2

Form an equivalent division problem for the division problem below. Then calculate the quotient.

$$7\frac{1}{2} \div 2\frac{1}{2}$$

Solution

Instead of performing the division with these mixed numbers, we will double both numbers to form a whole-number division problem.

$$7\frac{1}{2} \div 2\frac{1}{2}$$

↓

Multiply both $7\frac{1}{2}$ and $2\frac{1}{2}$ by 2.

↓

$$\mathbf{15 \div 5 = 3}$$

finding unknowns in fraction and decimal problems

Since Lessons 3 and 4 we have practiced finding **unknowns** in whole-number arithmetic problems. Beginning with this lesson we will find unknowns in fraction and decimal problems. If you are unsure how to find the solution to a problem, try making up a similar, easier problem to help you determine how to find the answer.

Example 3

Solve: $d - 5 = 3.2$

Solution

This problem is similar to the subtraction problem $d - 5 = 3$. We remember that we find the first number of a subtraction problem by adding the other two numbers. So we have the following:

$$\begin{array}{r} 5 \\ +\ 3.2 \\ \hline \mathbf{8.2} \end{array}$$

We check our work by replacing the letter with the solution and testing the result.

$$d - 5 = 3.2$$
$$8.2 - 5 = 3.2$$
$$3.2 = 3.2$$

2 New Concepts (Continued)

Example 2

Instruction

After completing the example, invite students to describe another way to use multiplication to calculate the quotient. Sample: Multiply the dividend and the divisor by 4; 30 ÷ 10 = 3.

Instruction

For the New Concept "finding unknowns in fraction and decimal problems," tell students that the steps they follow to find unknown decimal numbers and unknown fractions are the same steps they follow to find unknown whole numbers.

"Before you solve an unknown-number problem containing fractions or decimals, think of how you would solve the problem if it contained whole numbers. Then follow the same steps."

Example 3

Instruction

Point out that the equation is a subtraction problem in which the first number is unknown and the other two numbers are given.

"How do we find the unknown number?"

The unknown number is the sum of the two given numbers.

(continued)

2 New Concepts (Continued)

Example 4

Instruction

Point out that the equation is an addition problem with an unknown addend. The other addend and the sum are given.

"How do we find the unknown addend?"

Subtract the given addend from the sum.

Example 5

Instruction

Remind students that the product of any non-zero number and its reciprocal is 1.

Practice Set

Problem a Connect

After completing the problem, encourage students to describe how multiplication can be used to form another equivalent division problem. Sample: Multiply the dividend and the divisor by 6; 30 ÷ 2 = 15.

Problems c–f Error Alert

Remind students to check their answers by substituting their solutions into the original equations.

Example 4

Solve: $f + \frac{1}{5} = \frac{4}{5}$

Solution

This problem is similar to $f + 1 = 4$. We can find an unknown addend by subtracting the known addend from the sum.

$$\frac{4}{5} - \frac{1}{5} = \frac{3}{5}$$

$$f = \frac{3}{5}$$

We check the solution by substituting it into the original equation.

$$f + \frac{1}{5} = \frac{4}{5}$$

$$\frac{3}{5} + \frac{1}{5} = \frac{4}{5}$$

$$\frac{4}{5} = \frac{4}{5}$$

Example 5

Solve: $\frac{3}{5}n = 1$

Solution

In this problem two numbers are multiplied, and the product is 1. This can only happen when the two factors are reciprocals. So we want to find the reciprocal of the known factor, $\frac{3}{5}$. Switching the terms of $\frac{3}{5}$ gives us the fraction $\frac{5}{3}$. We check our answer by substituting $\frac{5}{3}$ into the original equation.

$$\frac{3}{5} \cdot \frac{5}{3} = \frac{15}{15} = 1 \quad \text{check}$$

$$n = \frac{5}{3}$$

Practice Set ▶ **a.** Connect Form an equivalent division problem for $5 \div \frac{1}{3}$ by multiplying both the dividend and divisor by 3. Then find the quotient. 15 ÷ 1 = 15

b. Connect Form an equivalent division problem for 266 ÷ 14 that has a one-digit divisor. Then find the quotient. 133 ÷ 7 = 19

▶ Solve:

c. $5 - d = 3.2$ 1.8

d. $f - \frac{1}{5} = \frac{4}{5}$ 1

e. $m + 1\frac{1}{5} = 4$ $2\frac{4}{5}$

f. $\frac{3}{8}w = 1$ $\frac{8}{3}$

▶ See Math Conversations in the sidebar.

English Learners

Write "$n + 7 = 11$" on the board. Explain the meaning of **substituting.** Say:

"Substituting means replacing one thing with another. For example, the number 4 can be substituted for the letter n in the equation."

Demonstrate substituting the number 4 for the letter n in the equation. Ask students to give other examples of substituting.

Written Practice *Strengthening Concepts*

▶ * **1.** (41) **Analyze** The bike cost \$120. The sales-tax rate was 8%. What was the total cost of the bike including sales tax? \$129.60

2. (11) **Formulate** If one hundred fifty knights could sit at the Round Table and only one hundred twenty-eight knights were seated, how many empty places were at the table? Write an equation and solve the problem. $150 - 128 = d$; 22 empty places

3. (32, 37) During the 1996 Summer Olympics in Atlanta, Georgia, the American athlete Michael Johnson set an Olympic and world record in the men's 200-meter run. He finished the race in 19.32 seconds, breaking the previous Olympic record of 19.73 seconds. By how much did Michael Johnson break the previous Olympic record? 0.41 second

In problems **4** and **5**, multiply by a fraction equal to 1 to complete each equivalent fraction.

* **4.** (42) $\frac{2}{3} = \frac{?}{6}$ 4 * **5.** (42) $\frac{1}{2} = \frac{?}{6}$ 3

Find each unknown number. Remember to check your work.

* **6.** (43) $\frac{2}{3}n = 1$ $\frac{3}{2}$ ▶ * **7.** (43) $6 - w = 1\frac{4}{5}$ $4\frac{1}{5}$

* **8.** (43) $m - 4\frac{1}{4} = 6\frac{3}{4}$ 11 * **9.** (43) $c - 2.45 = 3$ 5.45

* **10.** (43) $12 - d = 1.43$ 10.57

11. (29) $\frac{5}{8} \times \frac{1}{5}$ $\frac{1}{8}$ **12.** (29) $\frac{3}{4} \times 5$ $3\frac{3}{4}$ **13.** (26) $3\frac{7}{8} - 1\frac{3}{8}$ $2\frac{1}{2}$

14. (19) **Classify** Which of these numbers is not a prime number? B

A 23 **B** 33 **C** 43

15. (29) Compare: $\frac{2}{2} \; = \; \frac{2}{2} \times \frac{2}{2}$

16. (14) In football a loss of yardage is often expressed as a negative number. If a quarterback is sacked for a 5-yard loss, the yardage change on the play can be shown as -5. How would a 12-yard loss be shown using a negative number? -12

17. (35) Write the decimal number for nine and twelve hundredths. 9.12

18. (16) Round 67,492,384 to the nearest million. 67,000,000

▶* **19.** (38, 39) **Analyze** 0.37×10^2 37 ▶* **20.** (40) **Analyze** $0.6 \times 0.4 \times 0.2$ 0.048

21. (38) The perimeter of a square room is 80 feet. The area of the room is how many square feet? 400 square feet

22. (25) Divide 100 by 16 and write the answer as a mixed number. Reduce the fraction part of the mixed number. $6\frac{1}{4}$

▶ See Math Conversations in the sidebar.

3 Written Practice

Math Conversations

Discussion opportunities are provided below.

Problem 1 **Analyze**

Extend the Problem

"How can you use a percent that is greater than 100 to find the total cost of the bike?" The total cost is 100% + 8% or 108% of \$120; $1.08 \times \$120 = \$129.60$

Problem 19 **Analyze**

"This expression contains two operations. Name the operations." multiplication and squaring

"When an expression contains more than one operation, what must we follow to simplify the expression?" the Order of Operations

"To simplify this expression, what do we do first, multiply the factors or rewrite the exponent and its base?" rewrite the exponent and its base

Problem 20 **Analyze**

"How many decimal places will be in this product? Explain how you know." 3; When multiplying decimal numbers, the total number of decimal places in the factors is equal to the number of decimal places in the product.

Errors and Misconceptions

Problem 7

A common error when subtracting a mixed number from a whole number is to rename the whole number incorrectly. Review this concept with students by writing the following pattern of renamings on the board or overhead. Then ask students to discuss and continue the pattern.

$$6 = 5 + 1$$
$$6 = 5 + \frac{2}{2}$$
$$6 = 5 + \frac{3}{3}$$
$$6 = 5 + \frac{4}{4}$$
$$6 = 5 + \frac{5}{5}$$
$$6 = 5 + \frac{6}{6}$$

(continued)

3 Written Practice (Continued)

Math Conversations

Discussion opportunities are provided below.

Problem 23a Connect

Extend the Problem

"Sandy divided the dividend and the divisor by 4. Could Sandy have used 2 instead of 4? Explain why or why not." Yes; 100 ÷ 16 and 50 ÷ 8 have the same quotient.

"There are no other whole numbers Sandy could have used. Why not?" 2 and 4 are the only common factors of 100 and 16 that are greater than 1.

▶* **23.** (43) **Connect** **a.** Instead of dividing 100 by 16, Sandy divided the dividend and divisor by 4. What new division problem did Sandy make? What is the quotient? $25 \div 4 = 6\frac{1}{4}$

b. Form an equivalent division problem for $4\frac{1}{2} \div \frac{1}{2}$ by doubling both the dividend and divisor. Then find the quotient. $9 \div 1 = 9$

24. (30) What is the least common multiple (LCM) of 4, 6, and 8? 24

25. (17) **Predict** What are the next three numbers in this sequence?

$\frac{1}{16}, \frac{1}{8}, \frac{3}{16}, \frac{1}{4}, \frac{5}{16}, \frac{3}{8}, \frac{7}{16}$, $\frac{1}{2}$, $\frac{9}{16}$, $\frac{5}{8}$, ...

26. (17) Find the length of the segment below to the nearest eighth of an inch. $1\frac{5}{8}$ inches

27. (17) What mixed number is indicated on the number line below? $4\frac{7}{10}$

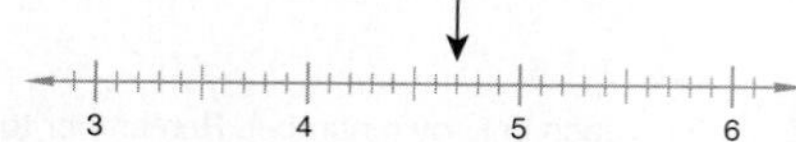

* **28.** (42) Write $\frac{1}{2}$ and $\frac{1}{5}$ as fractions with denominators of 10. Then add the renamed fractions. $\frac{5}{10} + \frac{2}{10} = \frac{7}{10}$

29.

20 seats
$\frac{2}{5}$ were occupied. 4 seats, 4 seats
$\frac{3}{5}$ were not occupied. 4 seats, 4 seats, 4 seats

29. (22, 33) **Model** Forty percent of the 20 seats on the bus were occupied. Write 40% as a reduced fraction. Then find the number of seats that were occupied. Draw a diagram to illustrate the problem. $\frac{2}{5}$; 8 seats

30. (Inv. 3) Describe each angle in the figure as acute, right, or obtuse.

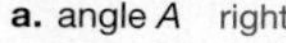

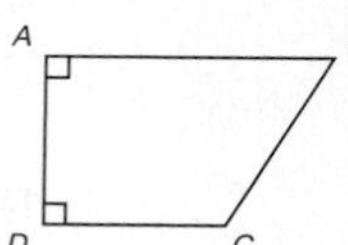

a. angle *A* right

b. angle *B* acute

c. angle *C* obtuse

d. angle *D* right

▶ See Math Conversations in the sidebar.

Looking Forward

Finding unknown numbers in equations containing fractions and decimals prepares students for:

- **Lesson 87,** finding unknown mixed numbers or decimal numbers in unknown-factor problems.
- **Lesson 98,** finding the unknown angle measure in triangles and quadrilaterals.
- **Lesson 103,** finding the unknown side and perimeter measures of complex shapes.

• Simplifying Decimal Numbers
• Comparing Decimal Numbers

Objectives

- Simplify a decimal number by removing extra zeros at the end of the number.
- Attach extra zeros to the ends of decimal numbers to help compare them.
- Order decimal numbers from least to greatest.

Lesson Preparation

Materials

- **Power Up G** (in *Instructional Masters*)
- **Teacher-provided material: calculators**

Optional

- **Teacher-provided material: grid paper**

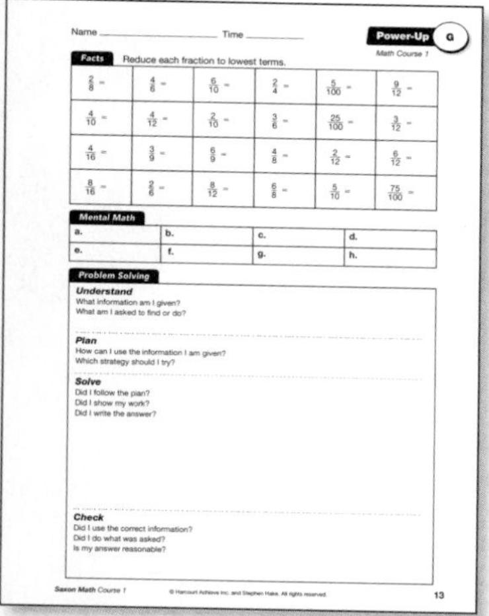

Power Up G

Math Language

English Learners (ESL)
arrange

Technology Resources

Student eBook Complete student textbook in electronic format.

Resources and Planner CD Assessment, reteaching, and instructional masters, plus a pacing calendar with standards.

Test and Practice Generator CD Create additional practice sheets and custom-made tests.

www.SaxonPublishers.com Visit for more student activities and planning materials.

Inclusion

Adaptations CD Adapted lessons, investigations, practice and assessments.

Meeting Standards

National Council of Teachers of Mathematics (NCTM)

Numbers and Operations

NO.1a Work flexibly with fractions, decimals, and percents to solve problems

NO.1b Compare and order fractions, decimals, and percents efficiently and find their approximate locations on a number line

NO.3a Select appropriate methods and tools for computing with fractions and decimals from among mental computation, estimation, calculators or computers, and paper and pencil, depending on the situation, and apply the selected methods

NO.3b Develop and analyze algorithms for computing with fractions, decimals, and integers and develop fluency in their use

Power-Up Discussion For use with Power Up, p. 231

Problem-Solving Strategy: Use Logical Reasoning

Jeanna folded a square piece of paper in half from top to bottom. Then she folded the paper in half from left to right so that the four corners were together at the lower right. Then she cut off the lower right corners as shown. Which diagram will the paper look like when it is unfolded?

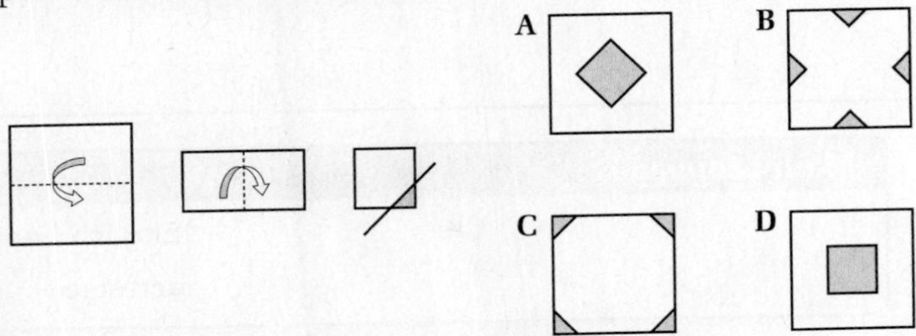

Understand ***Understand the problem.***

"What information are we given?"

We are given both written instructions and a diagram to direct us about how to fold and cut a square piece of paper.

"What are we asked to do?"

Determine what the paper will look like after the instructions are followed.

Plan ***Make a plan.***

"What problem-solving strategy will we use?"

We will *use logical and spatial reasoning* to visualize the resulting piece of paper.

Solve ***Carry out the plan.***

"What part of the original square does Jeanna cut off?"

All four original corners of the sheet are at the lower right, where Jeanna makes her cut. She cuts off the four original corners.

"What is the resulting shape when the paper is unfolded?"

It will be an octagon, like diagram C.

Check ***Look back.***

"Did we do what we were asked to do?"

Yes, we determined what Jeanna's paper will look like.

"What other problem-solving strategy could we use to verify the solution is correct?"

We could make a model and act it out with a scrap of paper.

Teacher Note: If scrap paper is available, have students follow the instructions to create the shape themselves.

LESSON 44

• Simplifying Decimal Numbers
• Comparing Decimal Numbers

Power Up — *Building Power*

facts Power Up G

mental math

a. **Calculation:** 4 × 325 1300

b. **Calculation:** 426 + 35 461

c. **Calculation:** 28 + 57 85

d. **Money:** $8.50 + $2.75 $11.25

e. **Fractional Parts:** $\frac{1}{2}$ of 1400 700

f. **Number Sense:** $\frac{\$15.00}{100}$ $0.15

g. **Probability:** How many different one-topping pizzas can be made with 2 types of crust and 4 types of toppings? 8

h. **Calculation:** 6 × 8, − 3, ÷ 5, + 1, × 6, + 3, ÷ 9 7

problem solving

Jeanna folded a square piece of paper in half from top to bottom. Then she folded the paper in half from left to right so that the four corners were together at the lower right. Then she cut off the lower right corner as shown. Which diagram will the paper look like when it is unfolded?

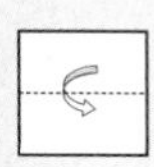
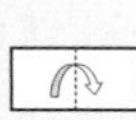

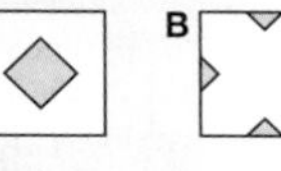
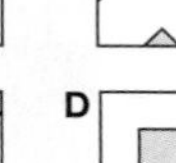

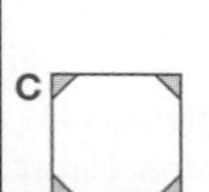

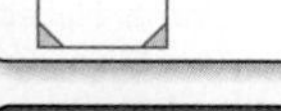

New Concepts — *Increasing Knowledge*

simplifying decimal numbers

Perform these two subtractions with a calculator. Which calculator answer differs from the printed answers below?

$$\begin{array}{r} 425 \\ -\ 125 \\ \hline 300 \end{array} \qquad \begin{array}{r} 4.25 \\ -\ 1.25 \\ \hline 3.00 \end{array}$$

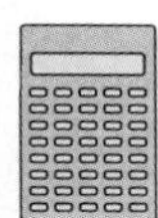

Calculators automatically simplify decimal numbers with zeros at the end by removing the extra zeros. Many calculators show a decimal point at the end of a whole number, although we usually remove the decimal point when we write the whole number. So "3.00" simplifies to "3." on a calculator. We remove the decimal point and write "3" only.

1 Power Up

Facts

Distribute **Power Up G** to students. See answers below.

Mental Math

Before students begin the Mental Math exercise, do this counting exercise as a class.

Count up and down by $\frac{1}{8}$s between $\frac{1}{8}$ and 3.

Encourage students to share different ways to mentally compute these exercises. Strategies for exercises **b** and **e** are listed below.

b. Add Tens, then Add Ones

400 + 20 + 6 + 30 + 5 = 400 + 50 + 11 = 461

Decompose Numbers

425 + 1 + 25 + 10 = 450 + 11 = 461

e. Use a Pattern of Dividing by 2

14 ÷ 2 = 7; 140 ÷ 2 = 70; 1400 ÷ 2 = 700

Divide Place Values, then Add

1000 ÷ 2 = 500 and 400 ÷ 2 = 200; 500 + 200 = 700

Problem Solving

Refer to **Power-Up Discussion,** p. 231B.

2 New Concepts

Instruction

Instruct students to use their calculators to subtract 125 from 425 and 1.25 from 4.25, then compare the calculator answers to the answers in their textbooks.

(continued)

Facts Reduce each fraction to lowest terms.

$\frac{2}{8} = \frac{1}{4}$	$\frac{4}{6} = \frac{2}{3}$	$\frac{6}{10} = \frac{3}{5}$	$\frac{2}{4} = \frac{1}{2}$	$\frac{5}{100} = \frac{1}{20}$	$\frac{9}{12} = \frac{3}{4}$
$\frac{4}{10} = \frac{2}{5}$	$\frac{4}{12} = \frac{1}{3}$	$\frac{2}{10} = \frac{1}{5}$	$\frac{3}{6} = \frac{1}{2}$	$\frac{25}{100} = \frac{1}{4}$	$\frac{3}{12} = \frac{1}{4}$
$\frac{4}{16} = \frac{1}{4}$	$\frac{3}{9} = \frac{1}{3}$	$\frac{6}{9} = \frac{2}{3}$	$\frac{4}{8} = \frac{1}{2}$	$\frac{2}{12} = \frac{1}{6}$	$\frac{6}{12} = \frac{1}{2}$
$\frac{8}{16} = \frac{1}{2}$	$\frac{2}{6} = \frac{1}{3}$	$\frac{8}{12} = \frac{2}{3}$	$\frac{6}{8} = \frac{3}{4}$	$\frac{5}{10} = \frac{1}{2}$	$\frac{75}{100} = \frac{3}{4}$

2 New Concepts (Continued)

Example 1

Instruction

Have students use a calculator and multiply 0.25 by 0.04 to confirm that the answer is displayed as 0.01. Point out that inputting the zeros to the left of the decimal points in the factors is not necessary, but students may input such zeros if they so choose.

Example 2

Instruction

To help students compare the two decimal numbers, write 0.3 and 0.303 on the board or overhead. Attach two zeros to the end of 0.3 and explain that attaching two zeros does not change the value of the number.

"To compare these numbers, we compare the digits in each place. We start at the place with the greatest value and move from left to right until we find two digits that are not equal."

Have students compare digits, starting with the digits in the ones places. When students discover that the digits are equal, have them move to the next place to the right. When they reach the thousandths place, point out that 0 is less than 3, so 0.300 is less than 0.303.

Write $0.3 < 0.303$ on the board or on an overhead.

Example 3

Instruction

Suggest that students begin by listing the numbers vertically with the decimal points aligned.

(continued)

Example 1

Multiply 0.25 by 0.04 and simplify the product.

Solution

We multiply.

$$\begin{array}{r} 0.25 \\ \times\ 0.04 \\ \hline 0.0100 \end{array}$$

Thinking Skill

Generalize

How many decimal places are in the product when each of two factors has two decimal places? 4

If we perform this multiplication on a calculator, the answer 0.01 is displayed. The calculator simplifies the answer by removing zeros at the end of the decimal number.

0.0100 simplifies to **0.01**

In this book decimal answers are printed in simplified form unless otherwise stated.

comparing decimal numbers

Zeros at the end of a decimal number do not affect the value of the decimal number. Each of these decimal numbers has the same value because the 3 is in the tenths place:

0.3 0.30 0.300

Although 0.3 is the simplified form, sometimes it is useful to attach extra zeros to a decimal number. For instance, comparing decimal numbers can be easier if the numbers being compared have the same number of decimal places.

Example 2

Compare: 0.3 ◯ 0.303

Solution

When comparing decimal numbers, it is important to pay close attention to place values. Writing both numbers with the same number of decimal places can make comparing easier. We will attach two zeros to 0.3 so that it has the same number of decimal places as 0.303.

0.3 ◯ 0.303

↓

0.300 ◯ 0.303

We see that 300 thousandths is less than 303 thousandths. We write our answer like this:

$$\mathbf{0.3 < 0.303}$$

Example 3

Arrange these numbers in order from least to greatest:

0.3 0.042 0.24 0.235

232 **Saxon** *Math Course 1*

Math Background

The result of multiplying or dividing a number by 10, 100, or 1000 is the same as shifting the decimal point in that number (left for division, right for multiplication) one, two, or three places, respectively. These concepts can be applied to compare two or more numbers.

For example, to compare 0.42, 3, and 0.705, shift the decimal point in each number three places to the right (which is the same as multiplying each number by 1000). The changed numbers (420, 3000, and 705) are then compared, and we find that 3 is the greatest and 0.42 is the least.

Solution

We write each number with three decimal places.

0.300 0.042 0.240 0.235

Then we arrange the numbers in order, omitting ending zeros.

0.042 0.235 0.24 0.3

Practice Set Write these numbers in simplified form:

a. 0.0500 0.05

▶ b. 50.00 50

c. 1.250 1.25

d. 4.000 4

▶ Compare:

e. 0.2 (>) 0.15

f. 12.5 (>) 1.25

g. 0.012 (<) 0.12

h. 0.31 (>) 0.039

i. 0.4 (=) 0.40

j. Write these numbers in order from least to greatest: 0.015, 0.12, 0.125, 0.2

0.12 0.125 0.015 0.2

Written Practice *Strengthening Concepts*

1. (12, 25) Analyze What is the sum of the third multiple of four and the third multiple of five? 27

2. (15) One mile is 5280 feet. How many feet is five miles? 26,400 feet

The summit of Mt. Everest is 29,035 feet above sea level. The summit of Mt. Whitney is 14,495 feet above sea level. Use this information to answer problems **3** and **4.**

3. (13) Mt. Everest is how many feet taller than Mt. Whitney? 14,540 feet

▶ * 4. (13) Analyze The summit of Mt. Everest is how many feet higher than 5 miles above sea level? (Refer to problem 2.) 2635 feet

Find each unknown number. Remember to check your work.

▶ * 5. (43) $5\frac{1}{3} - w = 4$ $1\frac{1}{3}$

▶ * 6. (43) $m - 6\frac{4}{5} = 1\frac{3}{5}$ $8\frac{2}{5}$

▶ * 7. (43) $6.74 + 0.285 + f = 11.025$ 4

▶ * 8. (43) $0.4 - d = 0.33$ 0.07

9. (26) Wearing shoes, Fiona stands $67\frac{3}{4}$ inches tall. If the heels of her shoes are $1\frac{1}{4}$ inches thick, then how tall does Fiona stand without shoes? $66\frac{1}{2}$ inches

* 10. (41) Form an equivalent division problem for $8\frac{1}{2} \div \frac{1}{2}$ by doubling both the dividend and divisor. Then find the quotient. $17 \div 1 = 17$

11. (35) Write thirty-two thousandths as a decimal number. 0.032

▶ See Math Conversations in the sidebar.

English Learners

Place 10 cubes of different colors on a desk or table in no order. Then say:

"In example 3 we are asked to arrange the numbers in order. When we arrange something, we put it in some kind of order. Watch how I arrange these cubes in a straight line."

Place the cubes in a straight line but do not arrange by color. Ask a volunteer to arrange the objects in some other way. Then ask the other students how the cubes are arranged by saying, "The cubes are arranged by ______."

2 New Concepts (Continued)

Practice Set

Problem b (Error Alert)

If students omit all of the zeros in 50.00 and give an answer of 5, remind them that they cannot remove zeros from whole-number places, such as the ones place, because removing the zeros will change the value of the number.

Problems e–i (Error Alert)

Encourage students who have difficulty comparing the numbers to attach one or more zeros to the right of one of the numbers, so that both numbers in each problem have the same number of decimal places.

Problem j (Error Alert)

Some students may choose to rewrite the numbers in vertical form. Invite these students to use grid paper or lined paper turned sideways to help maintain correct alignment.

3 Written Practice

Math Conversations

Discussion opportunities are provided below.

Problem 4 Analyze

"We can use several different equations to solve this problem. What addition equation could we use?"

Sample: $26{,}400 + n = 29{,}035$

"What subtraction equation could we use to solve this problem?"

Sample: $n = 29{,}035 - 26{,}400$

Write the equations on the board or overhead, and then ask students to choose an equation and use it to solve the problem.

Errors and Misconceptions

Problems 5–8

When solving equations, remind students that a good way to check their answers is to substitute them into the original equations.

If a substitution makes an equation true, students should assume that their answer is correct.

(continued)

3 Written Practice (Continued)

Math Conversations

Discussion opportunities are provided below.

Problem 15 Justify

Extend the Problem

"Finding 10% of a number is the same as shifting the decimal point in that number how many places?" one

"Does the decimal point shift one place to the left or one place to the right?" one place to the left

To practice the skill of finding 10% mentally, write a variety of whole and decimal numbers on the board or overhead. Include money amounts in the numbers you write. Then ask students to name 10% of each number without using pencil or paper.

You can extend the activity by challenging students to name or estimate 20% of each number.

12. (29) What number is $\frac{1}{6}$ of 24,042? 4007

* 13. (44) Compare:

a. 0.25 ⊘ 0.125 (>)

b. 25% ⊘ 12.5% (>)

14. (32) Write the standard numeral for $(6 \times 100) + (4 \times 1)$. 604

▸* 15. (43) Justify A $36 dress is on sale for 10% off the regular price. Mentally calculate 10% of $36. Describe the method you used to arrive at your answer.

15. $3.60; 10% of $36 is $\frac{1}{10}$ of $36. Find $\frac{1}{10}$ of $36 by dividing $36 by 10.

16. (30) a. How many $\frac{5}{8}$s are in 1? $\frac{8}{5}$

b. Use the answer to part **a** to find the number of $\frac{5}{8}$s in 3. $\frac{24}{5} = 4\frac{4}{5}$

17. (30) What is the least common multiple of 2, 3, 4, and 6? 12

18. (39) $(1.3)^2$ 1.69

19. (42) $\frac{3}{4} = \frac{?}{12}$ 9

20. (42) $\frac{2}{3} = \frac{?}{12}$ 8

21. (18) Find the average of 26, 37, 42, and 43. 37

22. (16) Round 364,857 to the nearest thousand. 365,000

23. (23, 29) Twelve of the 30 students in the classroom were girls. What was the ratio of boys to girls in the classroom? $\frac{3}{2}$

24. (19) a. List the factors of 100. 1, 2, 4, 5, 10, 20, 25, 50, 100

b. Classify Which of the factors of 100 are prime numbers? 2 and 5

25. (33, 35) Write 9% as a fraction. Then write the fraction as a decimal number. $\frac{9}{100}$; 0.09

* 26. (42) Write $\frac{3}{4}$ and $\frac{2}{3}$ as fractions with denominators of 12. Then add the renamed fractions. $\frac{9}{12} + \frac{8}{12} = \frac{17}{12} = 1\frac{5}{12}$

27. (Inv. 2) Estimate Which percent best describes the shaded portion of this rectangle? Explain why.

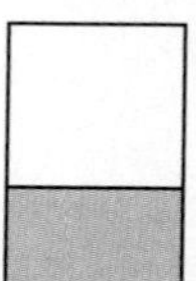

A 80%

B 40%

C 60%

D 20%

27. B Nearly half of the rectangle is shaded. Since $\frac{1}{2}$ equals 50%, the shaded part of the rectangle is close to but less than 50%.

28. (32) Shelby started working at 10:30 a.m. and finished working at 2:15 p.m. How long did Shelby work? 3 hours 45 minutes

* 29. (44) Estimate Which of these numbers is closest to 1? C

A 0.1 B 0.8 C 1.1 D 1.2

30. (17) Connect What mixed number corresponds to point X on the number line below? $10\frac{1}{10}$

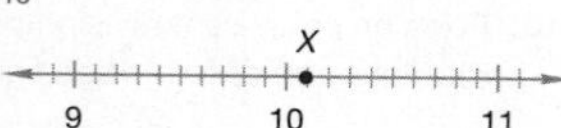

▸ See Math Conversations in the sidebar.

Looking Forward

Comparing and ordering decimal numbers prepares students for:

- **Lesson 76,** comparing fractions by converting them to decimal form.

• Dividing a Decimal Number by a Whole Number

Objectives

- Divide a decimal number by a whole number.

Lesson Preparation

Materials

- **Power Up F** (in *Instructional Masters*)
- **Manipulative Kit: inch rulers**

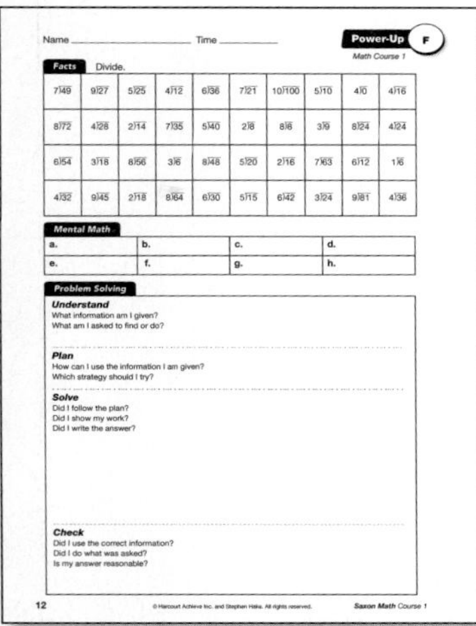

Name ______________ Time ________

Power-Up F
Math Course 1

Facts Divide.

7)49	9)27	5)25	4)12	6)36	7)21	10)100	5)10	4)0	4)16
8)72	4)28	2)14	7)35	5)40	2)8	8)8	3)9	8)24	4)24
6)54	3)18	8)56	3)6	8)48	5)20	2)16	7)63	6)12	1)6
4)32	9)45	2)18	8)64	6)30	5)15	6)42	3)24	9)81	4)36

Mental Math

a.	b.	c.	d.
e.	f.	g.	h.

Problem Solving

Understand
What information am I given?
What am I asked to find or do?

Plan
How can I use the information I am given?
Which strategy should I try?

Solve
Did I follow the plan?
Did I show my work?
Did I write the answer?

Check
Did I use the correct information?
Did I do what was asked?
Is my answer reasonable?

12 *Saxon Math* Course 1

Power Up F

Math Language

Maintain	English Learners (ESL)
dividend	scored

Technology Resources

Student eBook Complete student textbook in electronic format.

Resources and Planner CD Assessment, reteaching, and instructional masters, plus a pacing calendar with standards.

Test and Practice Generator CD Create additional practice sheets and custom-made tests.

www.SaxonPublishers.com Visit for more student activities and planning materials.

Inclusion

Adaptations CD Adapted lessons, investigations, practice and assessments.

Meeting Standards

National Council of Teachers of Mathematics (NCTM)

Numbers and Operations

NO.1a Work flexibly with fractions, decimals, and percents to solve problems

NO.3a Select appropriate methods and tools for computing with fractions and decimals from among mental computation, estimation, calculators or computers, and paper and pencil, depending on the situation, and apply the selected methods

NO.3b Develop and analyze algorithms for computing with fractions, decimals, and integers and develop fluency in their use

NO.3c Develop and use strategies to estimate the results of rational-number computations and judge the reasonableness of the results

Power-Up Discussion *For use with Power Up, p. 235*

Problem-Solving Strategy: Use Logical Reasoning

Copy this problem and fill in the missing digits:

$$\begin{array}{r} \_\_\_ \\ + \quad \_ \\ \hline \_\_\_8 \end{array}$$

Understand ***Understand the problem.***

"What information are we given?"

We are shown an addition problem that has missing digits in the four-digit sum and in the three-digit and one-digit addends.

"What are we asked to do?"

We are asked to fill in the missing digits.

Plan ***Make a plan.***

"What problem-solving strategy will we use?"

We will *use number sense and logical reasoning* to narrow our options for the two addends. Then we can make an educated guess and check our guess by adding.

Solve ***Carry out the plan.***

"How can we begin to find the missing digits?"

A three-digit number is added to a one-digit number. The sum is a four-digit number, which means it is greater than 1000. We figure that the top addend must be in the 990s because we are only adding a single digit.

We also know that the sum of the digits in the ones column is 8 or a number that ends in 8. We know it must be a two-digit number that ends in 8 because we must carry 1 to get our sum into the four-digit range. The two one-digit numbers whose sum is a two-digit number ending in 8 are 9 and 9.

$$\begin{array}{r} 999 \\ + \quad 9 \\ \hline 1008 \end{array}$$

Check ***Look back.***

"Did we complete the task?"

Yes. We filled all the missing digits of the problem.

"How can we verify the answer is correct?"

We can use the inverse operation of addition, subtraction, to verify the answer: $1008 - 9 = 999$

LESSON 45

• Dividing a Decimal Number by a Whole Number

Power Up — *Building Power*

facts Power Up F

mental math

a. **Calculation:** 4 × 425 1700

b. **Number Sense:** 375 + 500 875

c. **Calculation:** 77 + 18 95

d. **Money:** $12.00 − $1.25 $10.75

e. **Fractional Parts:** $\frac{1}{2}$ of 1500 750

f. **Money:** $\frac{\$40.00}{10}$ $4.00

g. **Geometry:** A square has a length of 9 cm. What is the area of the square? 81 square cm

h. **Calculation:** 4 × 8, − 2, ÷ 3, + 2, ÷ 3, × 5, + 1, ÷ 3 7

problem solving Copy this problem and fill in the missing digits:

$$\begin{array}{r} \_\_\_ \\ +\ \ \ \_ \\ \hline \_\_\_8 \end{array} \qquad \begin{array}{r} 999 \\ +\ \ \ 9 \\ \hline 1008 \end{array}$$

New Concept — *Increasing Knowledge*

Dividing a decimal number by a whole number is similar to dividing dollars and cents by a whole number.

$$\begin{array}{r} \$0.45 \\ 5\overline{)\$2.25} \end{array} \qquad \begin{array}{r} 0.45 \\ 5\overline{)2.25} \end{array}$$

Notice that the decimal point in the quotient is directly above the decimal point in the **dividend.**

Example 1

Divide: $3\overline{)4.2}$

Solution

The decimal point in the quotient is directly above the decimal point in the dividend.

$$\begin{array}{r} 1.4 \\ 3\overline{)4.2} \\ \underline{3} \\ 1\ 2 \\ \underline{1\ 2} \\ 0 \end{array}$$

Facts Divide.

7)49 — 7	9)27 — 3	5)25 — 5	4)12 — 3	6)36 — 6	7)21 — 3	10)100 — 10	5)10 — 2	4)0 — 0	4)16 — 4
8)72 — 9	4)28 — 7	2)14 — 7	7)35 — 5	5)40 — 8	2)8 — 4	8)8 — 1	3)9 — 3	8)24 — 3	4)24 — 6
6)54 — 9	3)18 — 6	8)56 — 7	3)6 — 2	8)48 — 6	5)20 — 4	2)16 — 8	7)63 — 9	6)12 — 2	1)6 — 6
4)32 — 8	9)45 — 5	2)18 — 9	8)64 — 8	6)30 — 5	5)15 — 3	6)42 — 7	3)24 — 8	9)81 — 9	4)36 — 9

1 Power Up

Facts

Distribute **Power Up F** to students. See answers below.

Mental Math

Before students begin the Mental Math exercise, do this counting exercise as a class.

Count up and down by 25s between 25 and 300.

Encourage students to share different ways to mentally compute these exercises. Strategies for exercises **d** and **f** are listed below.

d. Subtract $1.00, then Subtract $0.25
$12.00 − $1.00 = $11.00;
$11.00 − $0.25 = $10.75

Count Back by Quarters
Start with $12.00. Count: $11.75, $11.50, $11.25, $11.00, $10.75

f. Divide $40 by 10

$\frac{\$40.00}{10} = \frac{\$40}{10} = \$4$

Cancel Zeros

$\frac{\$40.00}{10} = \frac{\$4\not{0}}{1\not{0}} = \frac{\$4}{1} = \$4$

Problem Solving

Refer to **Power-Up Discussion,** p. 235B.

2 New Concepts

Instruction

If necessary, have students review dividing dollars and cents by a whole number (Lesson 2).

Remind students to include a dollar symbol in the quotient when dividing money.

Example 1

Instruction

Explain that the only difference when dividing a decimal dividend compared to a whole number dividend is the decimal point in the dividend and in the quotient. Aside from that, the steps involved in the division do not change.

(continued)

2 New Concepts (Continued)

Example 2

Instruction

The decimal point can be placed in the quotient before dividing, or after the division has been completed. If students wait to place the decimal point until after the division has been completed, they may forget to place it. For this reason, encourage students to place the decimal point before dividing.

Example 3

Instruction

Students should recognize that attaching a zero does not change the value of the dividend; 0.6 and 0.60 are equivalent decimal numbers.

Practice Set

Problem a (Error Alert)

Students must read the problem carefully to learn that the correct answer is one-half of the round trip distance.

Problems c–k (Error Alert)

Each dividend is a decimal dividend and each quotient will contain a decimal point. Remind students to place the decimal point in each quotient before completing the arithmetic.

3 Written Practice

Math Conversations

Discussion opportunities are provided below.

Problem 2 (Analyze)

Extend the Problem

"Another way to solve this problem is to form an equivalent division problem and solve it using mental math. Suppose we divide 20 and 1000 by 10, which is the same as shifting the decimal point in the numbers one place to the left. What will the numbers 20 and 1000 change to if each is divided by 10?" 2 and 100

"What is the quotient of 100 ÷ 2?" 50

(continued)

Example 2

Divide: $3\overline{)0.24}$

Solution

The decimal point in the quotient is directly above the decimal point in the dividend. We fill the empty place with zero.

$$\begin{array}{r} 0.08 \\ 3\overline{)0.24} \\ \underline{24} \\ 0 \end{array}$$

Decimal division answers are not written with remainders. Instead, we attac zeros to the end of the dividend and continue dividing.

Example 3

Divide: $5\overline{)0.6}$

Solution

Thinking Skill (Verify)

Why are 0.6 and 0.60 equivalent? because both decimals have 6 in the tenths place as their only value

The decimal point in the quotient is directly above the decimal point in the dividend. To complete the division, we attach a zero to 0.6, making the equivalent decimal number 0.60. Then we continue dividing.

$$\begin{array}{r} 0.12 \\ 5\overline{)0.60} \\ \underline{5} \\ 10 \\ \underline{10} \\ 0 \end{array}$$

Practice Set

▸ **a.** The distance from Margaret's house to school and back is 3.6 miles. How far does Margaret live from school? 1.8 miles

b. The perimeter of a square is 6.4 meters. How long is each side of the square? How can you check that your answer is reasonable? 1.6 meters; I can multiply 1.6 by 4 or add 1.6 + 1.6 + 1.6 + 1.6.

▸ Divide:

c. $\frac{4.5}{3}$ 1.5 **d.** 0.6 ÷ 4 0.15 **e.** $2\overline{)0.14}$ 0.07

f. 0.4 ÷ 5 0.08 **g.** $4\overline{)0.3}$ 0.075 **h.** $\frac{0.012}{6}$ 0.002

i. $10\overline{)1.4}$ 0.14 **j.** $\frac{0.7}{5}$ 0.14 **k.** 0.1 ÷ 4 0.025

Written Practice *Strengthening Concepts*

1. (30) By what fraction must $\frac{5}{3}$ be multiplied to get a product of 1? $\frac{3}{5}$

▸ **2.** (15) How many $20 bills equal one thousand dollars? 50 $20 bills

3. (29) Cindy made $\frac{2}{3}$ of her 24 shots at the basket. Each basket was worth 2 points. How many points did she score? 32 points

* **4.** (45) $3\overline{)4.5}$ 1.5 * **5.** (45) $8\overline{)0.24}$ 0.03 * **6.** (45) $5\overline{)0.8}$ 0.16

7. (30) What is the least common multiple (LCM) of 2, 4, 6, and 8? 24

▸ See Math Conversations in the sidebar.

English Learners

Explain the meaning of **score** in problem 3. Say:

"The points Cindy scored in the game are the points she made by getting the ball in the basket. She earned two points for each time she got the ball in the basket. How many points would Cindy score if she made 8 baskets?" 16 points

Ask students to give other examples of scores in sports.

Find each unknown number. Remember to check your work.

* **8.** $\sqrt{36} - m = 2\frac{3}{10}$ $3\frac{7}{10}$ *(43)*

* **9.** $g - 2\frac{2}{5} = 5\frac{4}{5}$ $8\frac{1}{5}$ *(43)*

* **10.** $m - 1.56 = 1.44$ 3 *(43)*

* **11.** $3^2 - n = 5.39$ 3.61 *(38, 43)*

12. $4\frac{3}{8} - 2\frac{1}{8}$ $2\frac{1}{4}$ *(26)*

13. $\frac{8}{3} \cdot \frac{5}{2}$ $6\frac{2}{3}$ *(29)*

14. Estimate the product of 694 and 412. 280,000 *(16)*

▶ **15.** $0.7 \times 0.6 \times 0.5$ 0.21 *(39)*

▶* **16.** 0.46×0.17 0.0782 *(40)*

▶* **17.** *(15, 45)* **Formulate** Mrs. Lopez's car traveled 177.6 miles on 8 gallons of gas. Her car traveled an average of how many miles per gallon? Use a multiplication pattern. Write an equation and solve the problem. $8 \cdot a = 177.6$; 22.2 miles per gallon

18. *(29)* What number is $\frac{3}{8}$ of 6? What operation did you use to find your answer? $2\frac{1}{4}$; multiplication

▶* **19.** *(41)* **Justify** A shirt regularly priced at $40 is on sale for 25% off. Mentally calculate 25% of $40. Explain the method you used to arrive at your answer.

9. $10; 25% of 40 is $\frac{1}{4}$ of $40. ivide $40 by 4 o find 25% of 40.

* **20.** *(42)* Write a fraction equal to $\frac{5}{6}$ that has 12 as the denominator. Then subtract $\frac{7}{12}$ from the fraction. Reduce the answer. $\frac{10}{12} - \frac{7}{12} = \frac{3}{12} = \frac{1}{4}$

21. *(38)* **Analyze** The area of a square is 36 ft².

a. How long is each side of the square? 6 ft

b. What is the perimeter of the square? 24 ft

22. *(33, 35)* Write 27% as a fraction. Then write the fraction as a decimal number. $\frac{27}{100}$; 0.27

23. *(17)* Use a ruler to find the length of this rectangle to the nearest eighth of an inch. $1\frac{1}{8}$ inches

24. *(22, 33)* **Model** Seventy-five percent of the 20 answers were correct. Write 75% as a reduced fraction. Then find the number of answers that were correct. Draw a diagram to illustrate this fractional-parts problem. $\frac{3}{4}$; 15 correct answers

24. 20 answers: $\frac{3}{4}$ were correct: 5 answers, 5 answers, 5 answers; $\frac{1}{4}$ were not correct: 5 answers

25. *(29)* The product of $\frac{1}{2}$ and $\frac{2}{3}$ is $\frac{1}{3}$.

$$\frac{1}{2} \times \frac{2}{3} = \frac{1}{3}$$

Arrange these fractions to form another multiplication fact and two division facts. $\frac{2}{3} \times \frac{1}{2} = \frac{1}{3}$, $\frac{1}{3} \div \frac{1}{2} = \frac{2}{3}$, $\frac{1}{3} \div \frac{2}{3} = \frac{1}{2}$

▶ **26.** *(Inv. 2)* **Estimate** Which percent best describes the shaded portion of this circle? Explain why.

A 80% **C** 40%

B 60% **D** 20%

26. **B** Since a ittle more than nalf of the circle is shaded, a ittle more than 50% is shaded.

▶ See Math Conversations in the sidebar.

3 Written Practice (Continued)

Math Conversations

Discussion opportunities are provided below.

Problem 17 Formulate

Extend the Problem

"Suppose that last year Mrs. Lopez paid an average of $2.90 per gallon for gasoline and spent about $1500 for gasoline. Explain how to estimate the number of miles Mrs. Lopez drove last year, then name your estimate." Sample: Round $2.90 to $3.00 and round 22.2 miles per gallon to 20 miles per gallon; $1500 ÷ $3 = 500 gallons and 500 gallons × 20 miles per gallon = 10,000 miles.

Problem 19 Justify

Extend the Problem

"If the sales tax is 5%, how could you estimate the amount of tax using mental math?" Sample: Finding 10% of a number is the same as moving the decimal point in that number one place to the left. The sale price of the shirt is $30 ($40 − $10), and 10% of $30 is $3.00. Since the sales tax is 5%, find one-half of $3.00. The sales tax is about $1.50.

Problem 26 Estimate

To make a reasonable estimate, students must recognize that the whole circle represents 100%.

"What percent of the circle would be shaded if one-half of it was shaded?" 50%

"Is more than 50%, or less than 50%, of the circle shaded?" more than 50%

Errors and Misconceptions

Problem 15

Students may find the arithmetic easier to complete if they find the product 0.6 × 0.5 first. Whenever they multiply three factors, remind students that multiplication is associative, and the Associative Property gives them an opportunity to change the way the factors are grouped.

Problem 16

Ask students who write an answer of 0.782 to count the number of decimal places in the factors, and then remind them that the answer must contain the same number of decimal places.

(continued)

3 Written Practice (Continued)

Math Conversations

Discussion opportunities are provided below.

Problem 28 Analyze

Extend the Problem

"What other whole number or whole numbers could you use to form an equivalent division problem? Explain your answer." Sample: Any multiple of 3; using any multiple of 3 produces a fraction divisor that simplifies to a whole number.

Problem 30 Analyze

Explain that this problem is a multiple-step problem. One way for students to begin solving the problem is to first divide the number of feet in one mile by 2 to find the number of feet in one-half mile.

The problem can be solved a number of different ways. Encourage students to discuss the problem and share those different ways.

27. (35) Write nine hundredths

a. as a fraction. $\frac{9}{100}$

b. as a decimal number. 0.09

▶* **28.** (43) Form an equivalent division problem for $5 \div \frac{1}{3}$ by multiplying both the dividend and divisor by 3. Then find the quotient. $15 \div 1 = 15$

29. (18) The average number of students in three classrooms was 24. Altogether how many students were in the three classrooms? 72 students

▶* **30.** (27) Analyze Coach O'Rourke has a measuring wheel that records the distance the wheel is rolled along the ground. The circumference of the wheel is one yard. If the wheel is pushed half a mile, how many times will the wheel go around (1 mi = 5280 ft)? 880 times

Early Finishers
Real-World Application

Decide whether you can use an estimate to answer the question or if you need to compute an exact amount. Explain how you found your answer.

Emily and Jacob are equally sharing the \$13.65 cost of a lunch. Tax is 5% and they want to leave a 15% tip. What is each person's share of the cost? Sample: Estimate: 5% + 15% = 20%; Round the cost of the meal to \$14, and double 10% of \$14. Then divide the sum of those amounts by 2. \$14 + \$1.40 + \$1.40 = \$16.80; Each person's share is \$8.40.

238 Saxon Math Course 1

▶ See Math Conversations in the sidebar.

Looking Forward

Dividing a decimal number by a whole number prepares students for:

- **Lesson 49,** dividing a whole or decimal number by a decimal number.
- **Lesson 52,** dividing decimal numbers mentally by 10 and by 100.
- **Lesson 53,** using a decimal chart to keep track of the decimal point in division problems.
- **Lesson 74,** writing fractions as decimal numbers.
- **Lesson 76,** comparing fractions by converting them to decimal form.

Assessment

30–40 minutes *For use after Lesson 45*

Distribute **Cumulative Test 8** to each student. Two versions of the test are available in *Saxon Math Course 1 Course Assessments Book.* Have students complete the **Power-Up Test** first. Allow 10 minutes. Then have students work the 20 numbered items on the **Cumulative Test.** Students may use copies of the answer sheet to record their work. Track individual and class progress with the **Test Analysis** forms.

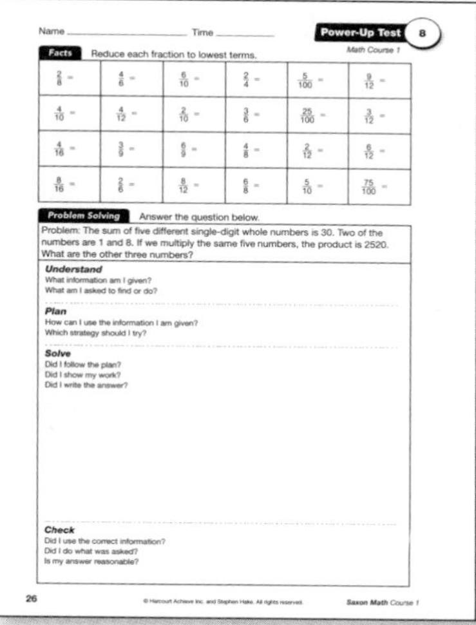

Power-Up Test 8

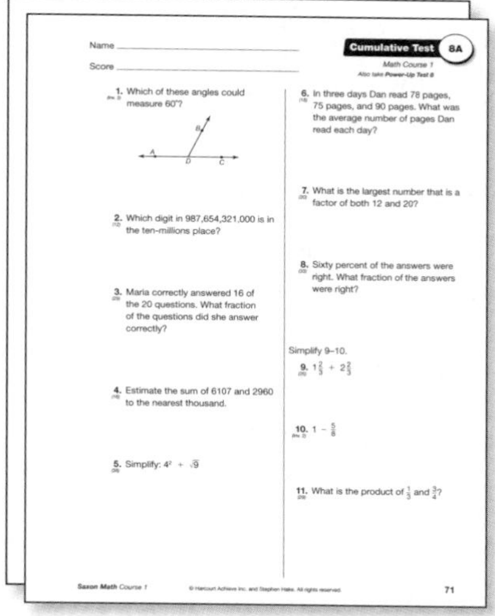

Cumulative Test 8A

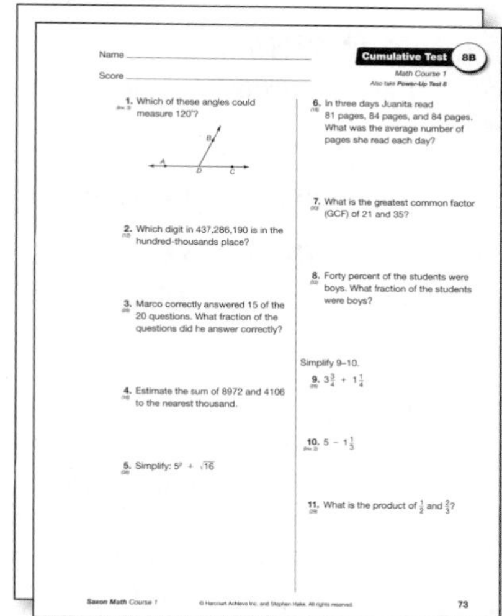

Alternative Cumulative Test 8B

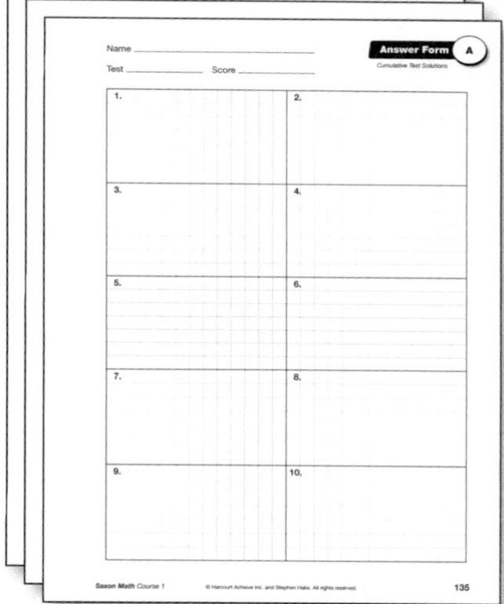

Optional Answer Forms

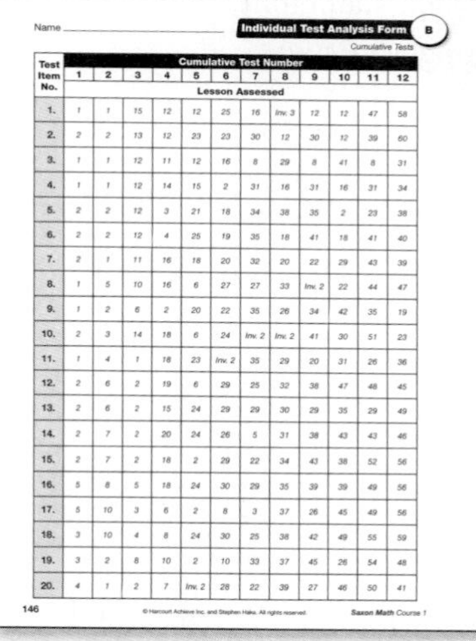

Individual Test Analysis Form

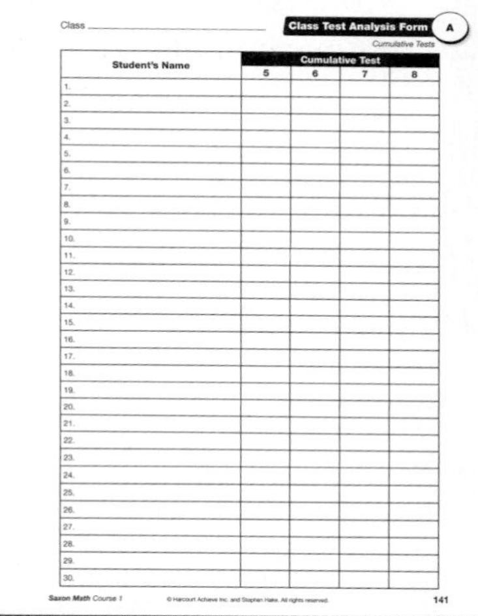

Class Test Analysis Form

Reteaching

Students who score below 80% on the assessment may be in need of reteaching. Look for the causes of student mistakes. If errors are conceptual, refer to the *Reteaching Masters* for reteaching.

Performance Activity 8

Representations

Assign after Lesson 45 and Test 8

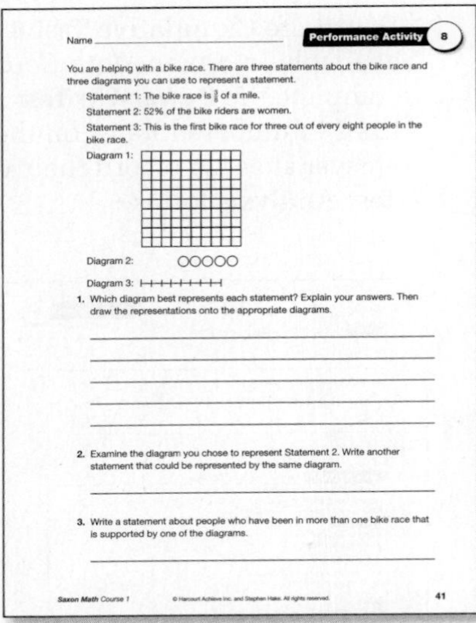

Name ____________ **Performance Activity 8**

You are helping with a bike race. There are three statements about the bike race and three diagrams you can use to represent a statement.

Statement 1: The bike race is $\frac{3}{8}$ of a mile.

Statement 2: 52% of the bike riders are women.

Statement 3: This is the first bike race for three out of every eight people in the bike race.

Diagram 1:

Diagram 2:

Diagram 3:

1. Which diagram best represents each statement? Explain your answers. Then draw the representations onto the appropriate diagrams.

2. Examine the diagram you chose to represent Statement 2. Write another statement that could be represented by the same diagram.

3. Write a statement about people who have been in more than one bike race that is supported by one of the diagrams.

Saxon Math Course 1 41

Performance Activity 8

Objectives

- Select the appropriate representation for a mathematical situation.
- Communicate ideas through writing.

Materials

Performance Activity 8

Preparation

Make copies of **Performance Activity 8.** (One each per student.)

Time Requirement

15–30 minutes; Begin in class and complete at home.

Activity

Explain to students that for this activity they will help with a bike race. There are three statements and three diagrams. The students will decide which diagram is best to use to create a representation of each statement and then explain their thinking. They will also create the representations. Explain that all of the information students need is on **Performance Activity 8.**

Criteria for Evidence of Learning

- Explains correctly why a diagram is a good representation of a given statement.
- Draws correct representation of each statement.
- Communicates ideas clearly through writing.

Meeting Standards

National Council of Teachers of Mathematics (NCTM)

Numbers and Operations

NO.1a Work flexibly with fractions, decimals, and percents to solve problems

Communication

CM.3a Organize and consolidate their mathematical thinking through communication

Representation

RE.5a Create and use representations to organize, record, and communicate mathematical ideas

RE.5b Select, apply, and translate among mathematical representations to solve problems

• Writing Decimal Numbers in Expanded Notation
• Mentally Multiplying Decimal Numbers by 10 and by 100

Objectives

- Write decimal numbers in expanded notation.
- Write a number written in expanded notation in decimal form.
- Mentally multiply whole numbers by 10 or by 100.
- Mentally multiply decimal numbers by 10 or by 100.

Lesson Preparation

Materials

- **Power Up G** (in *Instructional Masters*)
- **Manipulative Kit: inch rulers**

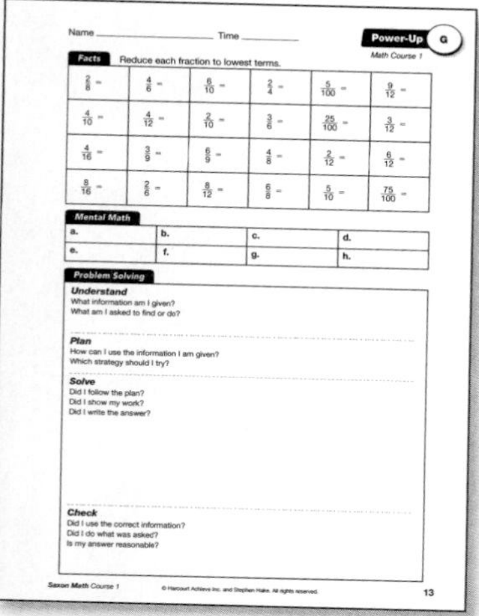

Power Up G

Math Language

Maintain	English Learners (ESL)
expanded notation	attach

Technology Resources

Student eBook Complete student textbook in electronic format.

Resources and Planner CD Assessment, reteaching, and instructional masters, plus a pacing calendar with standards.

Test and Practice Generator CD Create additional practice sheets and custom-made tests.

www.SaxonPublishers.com Visit for more student activities and planning materials.

Inclusion

Adaptations CD Adapted lessons, investigations, practice and assessments.

Meeting Standards

National Council of Teachers of Mathematics (NCTM)

Numbers and Operations

NO.1a Work flexibly with fractions, decimals, and percents to solve problems

NO.2a Understand the meaning and effects of arithmetic operations with fractions, decimals, and integers

NO.3a Select appropriate methods and tools for computing with fractions and decimals from among mental computation, estimation, calculators or computers, and paper and pencil, depending on the situation, and apply the selected methods

Power-Up Discussion

For use with Power Up, p. 239

Problem-Solving Strategy: Use Logical Reasoning

Copy this problem and fill in the missing digits:

```
    9_
9)_9_
  __
   __
   __
    0
```

Understand **Understand the problem.**

"What information are we given?"

We are shown a division problem with several missing digits.

"What are we asked to do?"

We are asked to fill in the missing digits.

Plan **Make a plan.**

"How can we use the information we know to do what we are asked to do?"

We think about the steps we take to solve long division problems. One of the steps is writing a digit in the quotient and then multiplying the digit by the divisor. Then we write the product underneath and subtract. We can start filling blanks in this problem by taking this step. We *use number sense and logical reasoning* as we continue looking for clues to help us fill in all the blanks.

Teacher Note: Students may find it helpful if you write each step on the board as you complete them.

Solve **Carry out the plan.**

"What two numbers do we write directly below the dividend?"

Nine (from the quotient) times 9 (the divisor) equals 81.

"What two-digit number with a 9 in the ones place minus 81 equals a one-digit number?"

The two-digit number is 89. We write an 8 in the hundreds place of the dividend.

"What number times 9 equals a number in the 80s?"

The number is 9. We write a 9 in the ones place of the quotient.

"Now we can continue finding the numbers that complete the problem."

```
    9_        9_        9_        99
9)_9_     9)89_     9)89_     9)891
  81        81        81        81
   __        8_        8_        81
   __        __        81        81
    0         0         0         0
```

Check **Look back.**

"How can we verify the solution is correct?"

We can use the inverse operation of division, multiplication, to check our answer: $99 \times 9 = 891$.

LESSON 46

• Writing Decimal Numbers in Expanded Notation
• Mentally Multiplying Decimal Numbers by 10 and by 100

Power Up — *Building Power*

facts Power Up G

mental math

a. **Calculation:** 4 × 525 2100

b. **Number Sense:** 567 − 120 447

c. **Number Sense:** 38 + 17 55

d. **Money:** \$5.75 + \$2.50 \$8.25

e. **Fractional Parts:** $\frac{1}{2}$ of 950 475

f. **Number Sense:** $\frac{2000}{100}$ 20

g. **Geometry:** The perimeter of a regular hexagon is 36 mm. What is the length of the sides of the hexagon? 6 mm

h. **Calculation:** 9 × 7, + 1, ÷ 8, × 3, + 1, × 2, − 1, ÷ 7 7

problem solving Copy this problem and fill in the missing digits:

```
   9_        99
9)_9_     9)891
  __        81
  __        81
  __        81
   0         0
```

New Concepts — *Increasing Knowledge*

writing decimal numbers in expanded notation

We may use **expanded notation** to write decimal numbers just as we have used expanded notation to write whole numbers. The values of some decimal places are shown in this table:

Decimal Place Values

1		$\frac{1}{10}$	$\frac{1}{100}$	$\frac{1}{1000}$
___	.	___	___	___
ones		tenths	hundredths	thousandths

We write 4.025 in expanded notation this way:

$$(4 \times 1) + \left(2 \times \frac{1}{100}\right) + \left(5 \times \frac{1}{1000}\right)$$

Facts Reduce each fraction to lowest terms.

$\frac{2}{8} = \frac{1}{4}$	$\frac{4}{6} = \frac{2}{3}$	$\frac{6}{10} = \frac{3}{5}$	$\frac{2}{4} = \frac{1}{2}$	$\frac{5}{100} = \frac{1}{20}$	$\frac{9}{12} = \frac{3}{4}$
$\frac{4}{10} = \frac{2}{5}$	$\frac{4}{12} = \frac{1}{3}$	$\frac{2}{10} = \frac{1}{5}$	$\frac{3}{6} = \frac{1}{2}$	$\frac{25}{100} = \frac{1}{4}$	$\frac{3}{12} = \frac{1}{4}$
$\frac{4}{16} = \frac{1}{4}$	$\frac{3}{9} = \frac{1}{3}$	$\frac{6}{9} = \frac{2}{3}$	$\frac{4}{8} = \frac{1}{2}$	$\frac{2}{12} = \frac{1}{6}$	$\frac{6}{12} = \frac{1}{2}$
$\frac{8}{16} = \frac{1}{2}$	$\frac{2}{6} = \frac{1}{3}$	$\frac{8}{12} = \frac{2}{3}$	$\frac{6}{8} = \frac{3}{4}$	$\frac{5}{10} = \frac{1}{2}$	$\frac{75}{100} = \frac{3}{4}$

1 Power Up

Facts

Distribute **Power Up G** to students. See answers below.

Mental Math

Before students begin the Mental Math exercise, do this counting exercise as a class.

Count by 12s from 12 to 108.

Encourage students to share different ways to mentally compute these exercises. Strategies for exercises **b** and **c** are listed below.

b. Subtract 100, then Subtract 20

567 − 100 = 467; 467 − 20 = 447

Subtract 20 from 567, then Subtract 100

567 − 20 = 547; 547 − 100 = 447

c. Change 38 to 40 and Change 17 to 15

38 + 2 = 40 and 17 − 2 = 15;

40 + 15 = 55

Add 2, then Subtract 2

38 + 2 = 40; 40 + 17 = 57; 57 − 2 = 55

Problem Solving

Refer to **Power-Up Discussion,** p. 239B.

2 New Concepts

Instruction

Have students recall that expanded notation is a way of writing a number as the sum of the products of the digits and the place values of the digits.

To introduce this lesson, you might choose to review Lesson 32 with students. In that lesson, students learned about the expanded notation of whole numbers.

(continued)

2 New Concepts (Continued)

Example 1

Instruction

Have students note that the zero in the tenths place of 5.06 is not included in the solution.

Example 2

Instruction

If students have difficulty changing numbers from expanded form to decimal form, suggest that they sketch a place value table and write the digits in the appropriate column, using a zero as a placeholder as needed. Invite students to reuse the table whenever necessary throughout this lesson.

10s	1s	.	$\frac{1}{10}$s	$\frac{1}{100}$s	$\frac{1}{1000}$s
		.	4	0	5

Instruction

Help students to remember how to shift the decimal point when mentally multiplying by 10 or by 100.

"When we multiply by 10 or by 100, we shift the decimal point the same number of places to the right as the number of zeros in 10 or 100. The number 10, for example, has one zero, so we shift the decimal point one place to the right when we multiply by 10. When we multiply by 100, which has two zeros, we shift the decimal point two places to the right."

Challenge students to use this information to help them mentally multiply 0.145 × 1000. 145

(continued)

The zero that serves as a placeholder is usually not included in expanded notation.

Example 1

Reading Math

We say the word *and* when we see a decimal point. Read 5.06 as "five and six hundredths."

Write 5.06 in expanded notation.

Solution

The 5 is in the ones place, and the 6 is in the hundredths place.

$$(5 \times 1) + \left(6 \times \frac{1}{100}\right)$$

Example 2

Write $(4 \times \frac{1}{10}) + (5 \times \frac{1}{1000})$ as a decimal number.

Solution

We write the decimal number with a 4 in the tenths place and a 5 in the thousandths place. No digits in the ones place or the hundredths place are indicated, so we write zeros in those places.

0.405

mentally multiplying decimal numbers by 10 and by 100

When we multiply whole numbers by 10 or by 100, we can find the product mentally by attaching zeros to the whole number we are multiplying.

24 × 10 = 240

24 × 100 = 2400

Thinking Skill

Predict

How many zeros are in the product of 600 × 400?

4 zeros

It may seem that we are just attaching zeros, but we are actually shifting the digits to the left. When we multiply 24 by 10, the digits shift one place to the left. When we multiply 24 by 100, the digits shift two places to the left. In each product zeros hold the 2 and the 4 in their proper places.

1000s	100s	10s	1s	
		2	4	24
	2	4	0	24 × 10 (one-place shift)
2	4	0	0	24 × 100 (two-place shift)

When we multiply a decimal number by 10, the digits shift one place to the left. When we multiply a decimal number by 100, the digits shift two places to the left. Here we show the products when 0.24 is multiplied by 10 and by 100.

10s	1s	.	$\frac{1}{10}$s	$\frac{1}{100}$s	
	0	.	2	4	0.24
	2	.	4		0.24 × 10 (one-place shift)
2	4	.			0.24 × 100 (two-place shift)

English Learners

To help students understand the concept of attaching zeros, write 24 on the board and say:

"Attach means to connect one thing to another. Watch while I attach a zero to the number 24."

Write a zero after the 4 in 24. Then write the number 24 again and ask a volunteer to attach 2 zeros to it. Repeat with other numbers always using the term *attach*.

Math Background

Writing decimal numbers in expanded notation differs from writing whole numbers in expanded notation because the digits in the decimal places of a decimal number represent fractions of a whole. Therefore, such digits are multiplied by fractions when written in expanded notation.

For example, the digit 9 in the tenths place in the decimal number 28.903 equals 9 tenths, $\frac{9}{10}$, or $9 \times \frac{1}{10}$. The digit 3 in the thousandths place equals 3 thousandths, $\frac{3}{1000}$, or $3 \times \frac{1}{1000}$. In the whole number part of 28.903, the digit 2 the tens place equals 2 tens, 20 or 2 × 10, and the 8 in the ones place equals 8 ones, 8 or 8 × 1.

In expanded notation, 28.903 is $(2 \times 10) + (8 \times 1) + (9 \times \frac{1}{10}) + (3 \times \frac{1}{1000})$.

Although it is the digits that are shifting one or two places to the left, we get the same effect by shifting the decimal point one or two places to the right.

0.24 × 10 = 2.4 (one-place shift)   0.24 × 100 = 24. = 24 (two-place shift)

Example 3

Multiply: 3.75 × 10

Solution

Since we are multiplying by 10, the product will have the same digits as 3.75, but the digits will be shifted one place. The product will be ten times as large, so we mentally shift the decimal point one place to the right.

3.75 × 10 = **37.5** (one-place shift)

We do not need to attach any zeros, because the decimal point serves to hold the digits in their proper places.

Example 4

Multiply: 3.75 × 100

Solution

When multiplying by 100, we mentally shift the decimal point two places to the right.

3.75 × 100 = 375. = **375** (two-place shift)

We do not need to attach zeros. Since there are no decimal places, we may leave off the decimal point.

Example 5

Multiply: $\frac{1.2}{0.4} \times \frac{10}{10}$

Solution

Multiplying both 1.2 and 0.4 by 10 shifts each decimal point one place.

$$\frac{1.2}{0.4} \times \frac{10}{10} = \frac{12}{4}$$

The expression $\frac{12}{4}$ means "12 divided by 4."

$$\frac{12}{4} = \mathbf{3}$$

Practice Set ▶ Write these numbers in expanded notation:

a. 2.05 $(2 \times 1) + (5 \times \frac{1}{100})$

b. 20.5 $(2 \times 10) + (5 \times \frac{1}{10})$

c. 0.205 $(2 \times \frac{1}{10}) + (5 \times \frac{1}{1000})$

▶ See Math Conversations in the sidebar.

2 New Concepts (Continued)

Example 4

Instruction

To give an example of when one or more zeros must be written in the product, write 24.9 × 100 on the board or overhead.

Ask students to name the product (2490) and explain why a zero needed to be included in the product.

Example 5

Instruction

In previous lessons, a fraction was reduced by dividing by the greatest common factor of the numerator and the denominator. You may choose to point out that the same method can be used to reduce $\frac{1.2}{0.4}$, the fraction in this example. However, students should recognize that dividing by the GCF is more complicated than multiplying by $\frac{10}{10}$, because the GCF of two decimal numbers can be difficult to identify, and the divisor for the division will be a decimal number.

Explain to students that the method shown in example 5 is a simple and useful way to clear the decimal points from the numerator and denominator of a fraction.

Practice Set

Problems a–e (Error Alert)

Ask students who have difficulty completing these problems to use the decimal place value chart they created earlier in this lesson.

(continued)

nclusion

Vhen multiplying a whole number by 10, 100, or 1000, simply add the same number of zeros to the number being multiplied. For example, if multiplying 37 by 100, add two zeros to 37 (for the two zeros in 100). When multiplying decimal number by 10, 100, or 1000, simply move the decimal point to the ight the same number of places as zeros. For example, if multiplying 1.23 by 00, move the decimal point two places to the right (for the two zeros in 100).

Ask students to complete the following table of equations and to describe the patterns that they observe.

65 × 1 = 65	10.32 × 1 = 10.32
65 × 10 = 650	10.32 × 10 = 103.2
65 × 100 = 6500	10.32 × 100 = 1032
65 × 1000 = 65,000	10.32 × 1000 = 10,320

2 New Concepts (Continued)

Practice Set

Problems f–k (Error Alert)

Before students write each product, ask them to answer the following question.

"How many places, and in which direction, do we move the decimal point?"

Problem i (Error Alert)

Students may give an incorrect answer of 25 because they forgot to write a zero in the ones place. Remind students that writing one or more zeros helps place the decimal point in the correct location.

Problems l and m (Conclude)

If necessary, remind students that whole numbers are members of the set {0, 1, 2, 3, 4, . . .}.

3 Written Practice

Math Conversations

Discussion opportunities are provided below.

Problem 5 (Analyze)

Extend the Problem

Challenge students to name the fraction and the percent of the earth's atmosphere that is *not* oxygen. $\frac{79}{100}$ and 79%

Errors and Misconceptions

Problem 1

Remind students who transpose the numerator and denominator of a fraction that the numerator of a fraction is its top number and the denominator of a fraction is its bottom number.

Invite students who make this error to suggest ways to remember what each term represents.

Problem 2

To complete the subtraction, students must regroup across two internal zeros.

If students regroup incorrectly, demonstrate on the board or overhead how to subtract 98.6 from 100.2. Then ask students to complete the subtractions shown below for extra practice.

200.5 − 134.7 65.8 800.1 − 526.2 273.9

(continued)

▶ Write these numbers in decimal form:

d. $(7 \times 10) + \left(8 \times \frac{1}{10}\right)$ 70.8

e. $\left(6 \times \frac{1}{10}\right) + \left(4 \times \frac{1}{100}\right)$ 0.64

▶ Mentally calculate each product:

f. 0.35 × 10 3.5 **g.** 0.35 × 100 35

h. 2.5 × 10 25 **i.** 2.5 × 100 250

j. 0.125 × 10 1.25 **k.** 0.125 × 100 12.5

▶ **Conclude** For the following statements, answer "true" or "false":

l. If 0.04 is multiplied by 10, the product is a whole number. false

m. If 0.04 is multiplied by 100, the product is a whole number. true

Multiply as shown. Then complete the division.

n. $\frac{1.5}{0.5} \times \frac{10}{10}$ 3 **o.** $\frac{2.5}{0.05} \times \frac{100}{100}$ 50

Written Practice — *Strengthening Concepts*

▶ **1.** (25) **Analyze** When a fraction with a numerator of 30 and a denominator of 8 is converted to a mixed number and reduced, what is the result? $3\frac{3}{4}$

▶ **2.** (13) **Formulate** Normal body temperature is 98.6° on the Fahrenheit scale. A person with a temperature of 100.2°F would have a temperature how many degrees above normal? Write an equation and solve the problem. 100.2 − 98.6 = *d*; 1.6°F

3. (15) Four and twenty is how many dozen? 2 dozen

4. (46) Write $(5 \times 10) + (6 \times \frac{1}{10}) + (7 \times \frac{1}{1000})$ in decimal form. 50.607

▶ **5.** (33, 35) Twenty-one percent of the earth's atmosphere is oxygen. Write 21% as a fraction. Then write the fraction as a decimal number. $\frac{21}{100}$; 0.21

6. (33) Twenty-one percent is slightly more than 20%. Twenty percent is equivalent to what reduced fraction? $\frac{1}{5}$

* **7.** (45) $5\overline{)6.35}$ 1.27 * **8.** (45) $4\overline{)0.5}$ 0.125 * **9.** (45) $8\overline{)1.0}$ 0.125

Find each unknown number:

* **10.** (43) $x + 3\frac{5}{8} = 9$ $5\frac{3}{8}$ * **11.** (43) $y - 16\frac{1}{4} = 4\frac{3}{4}$ 21

* **12.** (43) $1 - q = 0.235$ 0.765 * **13.** (43) $26.9 + 12 + w = 49.25$ 10.35

▶ See Math Conversations in the sidebar.

14. 5 cm^2; The area of the rectangle is 4 cm × 2.5 cm = 10 cm^2. Since 50% means $\frac{1}{2}$, the area of the shaded part is $\frac{1}{2}$ of 10 cm^2, which is 5 cm^2.

14. (31, 41) **Verify** Fifty percent of the area of this rectangle is shaded. What is the area of the shaded region? Explain your thinking.

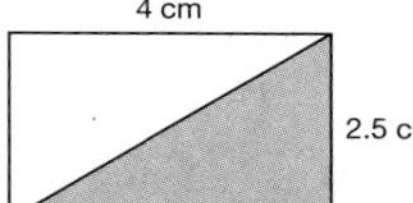

15. (23) **Connect** What is the ratio of the value of a dime to the value of a quarter? $\frac{10}{25} = \frac{2}{5}$

16. (39) 3.7 × 0.25 0.925

* **17.** (42) $\frac{3}{4} = \frac{?}{12}$ 9

18. (30) What is the least common multiple of 3, 4, and 8? 24

* **19.** (40, 44) Compare:

a. $\frac{1}{10}$ ⊜ 0.1

b. 0.1 ⊘ $(0.1)^2$

20. (34) Which digit is in the thousandths place in 1,234.5678? 7

21. (16) Estimate the quotient when 3967 is divided by 48. 80

22. (38) The area of a square is 100 cm^2. What is its perimeter? 40 cm

23. (14) John carried the football twice in the game. One play gained 6 yards. The other play lost 8 yards. Use a negative number to show John's total yardage for the game. −2

24. (29) $\frac{1}{2} \cdot \frac{4}{5}$ $\frac{2}{5}$

25. (29) $\left(\frac{3}{4}\right)\left(\frac{5}{3}\right)$ $1\frac{1}{4}$

▶ **26.** (27) **Connect** Laquesha bought a 24-inch-diameter wheel for her bicycle and measured it carefully. Arrange these measures in order from least to greatest: radius, diameter, circumference

circumference, radius, diameter

27. \$7.51; Round \$6.95 to \$7. 8% is a little less than 10%. 10% of \$7 is 70¢. Adding 70¢ to \$7 gives \$7.70. So \$7.51 is reasonable.

* **27.** (41) **Estimate** The chef's salad cost \$6.95. The sales-tax rate was 8%. What was the total cost including tax? Explain how to use estimation to check whether your answer is reasonable.

28. (17) Use a ruler to find the width of this rectangle to the nearest eighth of an inch. $\frac{6}{8}$ inch (or $\frac{3}{4}$ inch)

29. (30) **a.** How many $\frac{3}{8}$s are in 1? $\frac{8}{3}$

b. Use the answer to part **a** to find the number of $\frac{3}{8}$s in 3. 8

* **30.** (42) Rename $\frac{1}{2}$ and $\frac{1}{3}$ so that the denominators of the renamed fractions are 6. Then add the renamed fractions. $\frac{3}{6} + \frac{2}{6} = \frac{5}{6}$

▶ See Math Conversations in the sidebar.

3 Written Practice *(Continued)*

Math Conversations

Discussion opportunities are provided below.

Problem 26 Connect

If students are puzzled, suggest that they draw a picture of a circle to represent the bicycle wheel, and then label the circumference, a radius, and a diameter of the circle. Explain to students that they do not need to know the exact lengths of the circumference, the radius, and the diameter of any circle to be able to arrange those lengths in order from least to greatest or from greatest to least.

After completing the problem, ask,

"What is the exact relationship that is shared by the radius and the diameter of any circle?" For any circle, the length of a diameter is twice the length of a radius, and the length of a radius is one-half the length of a diameter.

Looking Forward

Multiplying a decimal number mentally by 10 or by 100 prepares students for:

- **Lesson 52,** dividing a decimal number mentally by 10 or by 100.

• Circumference
• Pi (π)

Objectives
- Determine the appropriate number of diameters in the circumference of a circle.
- Use 3.14 as an approximation of pi (π).
- Use the formula $C = \pi d$ to find the circumference of a circle.
- Use the formula $C = 2\pi r$ to find the circumference of a circle.

Lesson Preparation

Materials
- **Power Up E** (in *Instructional Masters*)
- **Lesson Activity 11** (in *Instructional Masters*)
- **Manipulative Kit: inch rulers**
- **Teacher-provided material: circular objects; string or masking tape; scissors; cloth tape measures; calculators**

Optional
- **Geometric Formulas poster**

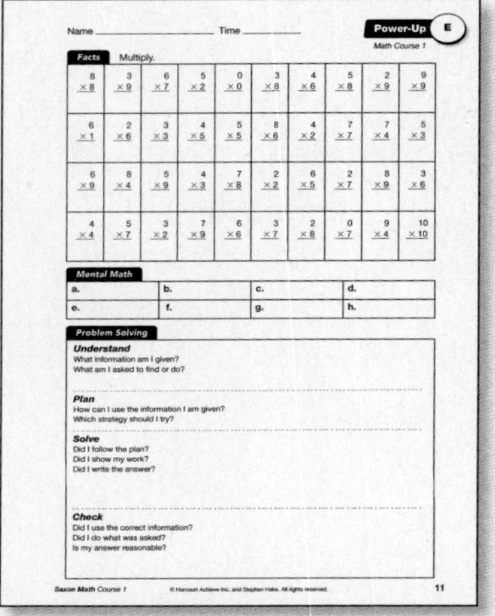

Power Up E

Math Language

New	English Learners (ESL)
pi (π)	approximation

Technology Resources

Student eBook Complete student textbook in electronic format.

Resources and Planner CD Assessment, reteaching, and instructional masters, plus a pacing calendar with standards.

Test and Practice Generator CD Create additional practice sheets and custom-made tests.

www.SaxonPublishers.com Visit for more student activities and planning materials.

Inclusion

Adaptations CD Adapted lessons, investigations, practice and assessments.

Meeting Standards

National Council of Teachers of Mathematics (NCTM)

Geometry

GM.1a Precisely describe, classify, and understand relationships among types of two- and three-dimensional objects using their defining properties

GM.4d Use geometric models to represent and explain numerical and algebraic relationships

Measurement

ME.2c Develop and use formulas to determine the circumference of circles and the area of triangles, parallelograms, trapezoids, and circles and develop strategies to find the area of more-complex shapes

Communication

CM.3d Use the language of mathematics to express mathematical ideas precisely

Power-Up Discussion *For use with Power Up, p. 244*

Problem-Solving Strategy: Use Logical Reasoning

Radley held a number cube so that he could see three adjoining faces. Radley said that he could see a total of 8 dots. Could he be correct? Explain your answer.

Understand — *Understand the problem.*

"What information are we given?"

Radley can see three adjoining faces on a number cube. He says he can see 8 dots.

"What are we asked to do?"

Determine if Radley is correct.

"What prior knowledge do we have?"

The dots on the opposite sides of a number cube add to seven. There are 21 dots total on a number cube.

Teacher Note: You may wish to have number cubes available for students.

Plan — *Make a plan.*

"What problem-solving strategy will we use?"

We will *use logical reasoning* and number sense to solve the problem.

Solve — *Carry out the plan.*

"What combinations of three different numbers total 8?"

$1 + 2 + 5$

$1 + 3 + 4$

"Are either of these combinations possible? Explain."

No, $1 + 2 + 5$ is not possible because $2 + 5 = 7$, so 2 and 5 are on opposite faces. Likewise, $1 + 3 + 4$ is not possible because 3 and 4 total 7 and are on opposite faces.

"Does Radley really see 8 dots?"

No. The combinations of dots that total 8 are not on adjoining faces.

Check — *Look back.*

"How can we verify our work?"

We can use a number cube and tilt it to different angles to see if we can see 8 dots.

Teacher Note: You may extend this lesson by differing the number of dots and adjoining faces Radley says he can see.

1 Power Up

Facts

Distribute **Power Up E** to students. See answers below.

Mental Math

Before students begin the Mental Math exercise, do this counting exercise as a class.

Count by 9s from 9 to 108.

Encourage students to share different ways to mentally compute these exercises. Strategies for exercises **a** and **c** are listed below.

a. Break Apart 925

$4(900) + 4(25) = 3600 + 100 = 3700$

Count On by 900, then by 25

Count: 900, 1800, 2700, 3600

Count: 3625, 3650, 3675, 3700

c. Change 56 to 57, and Change 19 to 20

$57 - 20 = 37$

Count Back by Tens, then Add 1

Count: 46, 36; $36 + 1 = 37$

Problem Solving

Refer to **Power-Up Discussion,** p. 244B.

Activity

Instruction

In order to complete this activity in one class period, the students' materials must be collected and organized ahead of time. On the day of this lesson, arrange students into groups of two to four, distribute the materials, and give each group a copy of **Lesson Activity 11** Finding the Number of Diameters in a Circumference.

(continued)

LESSON 47

• Circumference
• Pi (π)

Power Up *Building Power*

facts Power Up E

mental math

a. Calculation: 4×925 3700

b. Calculation: 3×87 261

c. Number Sense: $56 - 19$ 37

d. Money: $9.00 − $1.25 $7.75

e. Fractional Parts: $\frac{1}{2}$ of $12.50 $6.25

f. Money: $\frac{\$25.00}{10}$ $2.50

g. Probability: How many different outfits can be made with 3 shirts and 5 pairs of pants? 15

h. Calculation: $6 \times 8, + 2, \times 2, - 10, \div 9, + 5, \div 3, + 1, \div 6$ 1

problem solving Radley held a number cube so that he could see three adjoining faces. Radley said that he could see a total of 8 dots. Could he be correct? Explain your answer. No. See the problem-solving script for explanation.

New Concepts *Increasing Knowledge*

circumference Laquesha measured the diameter of her bicycle wheel with a yardstick and found that the diameter was 2 feet. She wondered whether she could find the circumference of the tire with only this information. In other words, she wondered how many diameters equal the circumference. In the following activity we will estimate and measure to find the number of diameters in a circumference.

Activity

Circumference

Materials needed:

- 2–4 different circular objects (e.g., paper plates, pie pans, flying disks, bicycle tires, plastic lids, trash cans)
- Lesson Activity 11
- string or masking tape
- scissors
- cloth tape measure(s)
- calculator(s)

Facts Multiply.

8 × 8 64	3 × 9 27	6 × 7 42	5 × 2 10	0 × 0 0	3 × 8 24	4 × 6 24	5 × 8 40	2 × 9 18	9 × 9 81
6 × 1 6	2 × 6 12	3 × 3 9	4 × 5 20	5 × 5 25	8 × 6 48	4 × 2 8	7 × 7 49	7 × 4 28	5 × 3 15
6 × 9 54	8 × 4 32	5 × 9 45	4 × 3 12	7 × 8 56	2 × 2 4	6 × 5 30	2 × 7 14	8 × 9 72	3 × 6 18
4 × 4 16	5 × 7 35	3 × 2 6	7 × 9 63	6 × 6 36	3 × 7 21	2 × 8 16	0 × 7 0	9 × 4 36	10 × 10 100

Model This activity has two parts. In the first part you and your group will cut a length of string as long as the diameter of each object you will measure. (A length of masking tape may be used in place of string.) Then you will wrap the string around the object and estimate the number of diameters needed to reach all the way around. To do this, first mark a starting point on the object. Wrap the string around the object, and mark the point where the string ends. Repeat this process until you reach the starting point, counting the whole lengths of string and estimating any fractional part. Do this for each object you selected.

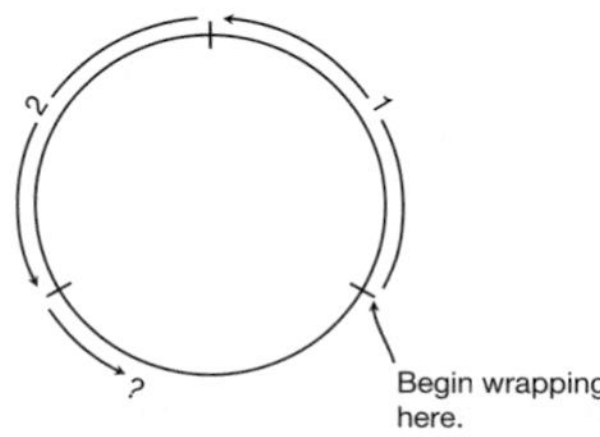

Thinking Skills

Connect

Remember that:

$\frac{1}{4} = 0.25$

$\frac{1}{2} = 0.5$

$\frac{3}{4} = 0.75$

Estimate In the second part of the activity, you will measure the circumference and diameter of the circular objects and record the measurements on a recording sheet. If you have a metric tape measure, record the measurements to the nearest centimeter. If you have a customary tape measure, record your answers to the nearest quarter inch in decimal form. Using a calculator, divide the circumference of each circle by its diameter to determine the number of diameters in the circumference. Round each quotient to the nearest hundredth.

Record your results on **Lesson Activity 11,** as shown below.

Part 1: Estimates

Object	Approximate number of diameters in the circumference
plate	$3\frac{1}{5}$
trash can	$3\frac{1}{4}$

Part 2: Measures

Object	Circumference	Diameter	$\frac{\text{Circumference}}{\text{Diameter}}$
plate	78 cm	25 cm	3.12
trash can	122 cm	38 cm	3.21

Activity *(Continued)*

Instruction

In part 1 of this activity, students will discover that the circumference of the circle is more than three times greater than the length of a diameter.

In part 2 of this activity, students will make and record measurements, and write ratios for those measurements that represent approximations of pi.

Encourage groups to compare the estimates they made in part 1 to the ratios of circumference divided by diameter that were recorded in part 2. To help make the comparisons, ask the members of each group to change the fractional parts of their estimates to decimals.

2 New Concepts

Instruction

You may wish to display the **Geometric Formulas** concept poster as you discuss the topic of pi (π) with students.

Emphasize that $C = 2\pi r$ and $C = \pi d$ are equivalent formulas for the circumference of a circle. Write $C = \pi d$ on the board. Then explain that the d for diameter can be replaced by $2r$ for two radii. Erase d and write $2r$ in its place, making $C = \pi 2r$. Then rearrange the factors to make $C = 2\pi r$.

Although the formula $C = 2\pi r$ can be written any number of ways (such as $C = \pi 2r$ or $C = \pi r 2$), it is usually written as $C = 2\pi r$.

Example

Instruction

Have students note that the problem gives the length of a radius, while the formula in the solution requires the length of a diameter.

Practice Set

Problem a Explain

The formulas are equivalent because for any circle, the value of d in $C = \pi d$ is the same as the value of $2r$ in $C = 2\pi r$.

(continued)

pi (π)

If we know the radius or diameter of a circle, we can calculate the approximate circumference of the circle. In the previous activity we found that for any given circle there are a little more than three diameters in the circumference. Some people use 3 as a very rough approximation of the number of diameters in a circumference. The actual number of diameters in a circumference is closer to $3\frac{1}{7}$, which is approximately 3.14. The exact number of diameters in a circumference cannot be expressed as a fraction or as a decimal number, so mathematicians use the Greek letter π **(pi)** to stand for this number.

Thinking Skill
Verify
Why can you use the formula $\pi 2r$ or $2\pi r$ and get the same answer? The Commutative Property of Multiplication

To find the circumference of a circle, we multiply the diameter of the circle by π. This relationship is shown in the formula below, where C stands for the circumference and d stands for the diameter.

$$C = \pi d$$

Since a diameter is equal to two radii ($2r$), we may replace d in the formula with $2r$. We usually arrange the factors this way:

$$C = 2\pi r$$

Reading Math
Symbols
We read $\approx$ as "is approximately equal to."

Unless otherwise noted, we will use 3.14 as an approximation for π. We may use a "wavy" equal sign to indicate that two numbers are approximately equal, as shown below.

$$\pi \approx 3.14$$

To use a formula such as $C = \pi d$, we **substitute** the measures or numbers we are given in place of the variables in the formula.

Example

Sidney drew a circle with a 2-inch radius. What is the circumference of the circle?

Solution

The radius of the circle is 2 inches, so the diameter is 4 inches. We multiply 4 inches by π (3.14) to find the circumference.

$$C = \pi d$$
$$C \approx (3.14)(4 \text{ in.})$$
$$C \approx 12.56 \text{ in.}$$

The circumference of the circle is about **12.56 inches.**

Justify Why is the answer about 12.56 inches reasonable for the circumference of the circle? Sample: It is reasonable because π is a little more than 3, and 3 times 4 is 12 inches.

Practice Set ▸ **a.** *Explain* In this lesson two formulas for the circumference of a circle are shown, $C = \pi d$ and $C = 2\pi r$. Why are these two formulas equivalent? The product of "2 times r" in the second formula is equivalent to d in the first formula because two radii equal one diameter. So two radii times π equals one diameter times π.

▸ See Math Conversations in the sidebar.

Math Background

Pi (π) is the ratio of the circumference of any circle to the length of its diameter. Pi is an irrational number that does not terminate and does not repeat. It contains an infinite number of digits, and its value, calculated to twenty decimal places, is 3.14159265358979323846.

English Learners

Explain that, in math, the terms **approximate** and **approximation** mean a value or an answer that is close to, but not, exact. Say, writing figures on the board to support the example:

"There were 51 sixth graders and 46 fifth graders in the park. The approximate number of students in the park was 100."

Explain that 3.14 is an approximation of the value of pi.

d. 2.36 inches; Sample: If the diameter were one inch, the circumference would be about 3.14 inches. Since the diameter is a little less than one inch, the circumference should be a little less than 3.14 inches.

f. C 90 ft; The radius is about 15 ft, so the diameter is about 30 ft. Using 3 as a rough approximation for π, we calculate that the circumference is about 3×30 ft, or about 90 ft.

▶ Find the circumference of each of these circles. (Use 3.14 for π.)

b. 6.28 in.

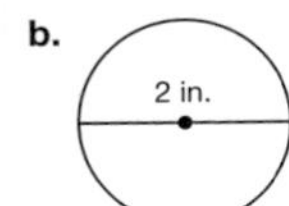

c. 18.84 cm

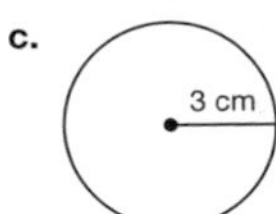

▶ **d.** Estimate The diameter of a penny is about $\frac{3}{4}$ of an inch (0.75 inch). Find the circumference of a penny. Round your answer to two decimal places. Explain why your answer is reasonable.

▶ **e.** Model Roll a penny through one rotation on a piece of paper. Mark the start and the end of the roll. How far did the penny roll in one rotation? Measure the distance to the nearest eighth of an inch. $2\frac{3}{8}$ inches

f. Justify The radius of the great wheel was $14\frac{7}{8}$ ft. Which of these numbers is the best rough estimate of the wheel's circumference? Explain how you decided on your answer.

A 15 ft **B** 60 ft **C** 90 ft **D** 120 ft

g. Use the formula $C = 2\pi r$ to find the circumference of a circle with a radius of 5 inches. (Use 3.14 for π.) 31.4 inches

Written Practice

Strengthening Concepts

1. (10) The first positive odd number is 1. The second is 3. What is the tenth positive odd number? 19

2. (15) Formulate A passenger jet can travel 600 miles per hour. How long would it take a jet traveling at that speed to cross 3000 miles of ocean? Write an equation and solve the problem. $600 \cdot h = 3000$; 5 hours

3. (15) José bought Carmen one dozen red roses, two for each month he had known her. How long had he known her? 6 months

▶ * **4.** (47) Conclude If $A = bh$, what is A when $b = 8$ and $h = 4$? 32

5. (2) The Commutative Property of Multiplication allows us to rearrange factors without changing the product. So $3 \cdot 5 \cdot 2$ may be arranged $2 \cdot 3 \cdot 5$. Use the commutative property of multiplication to rearrange these prime factors in order from least to greatest: $2 \cdot 2 \cdot 3 \cdot 3 \cdot 3 \cdot 5 \cdot 5 \cdot 7$

$3 \cdot 7 \cdot 2 \cdot 5 \cdot 2 \cdot 3 \cdot 3 \cdot 5$

6. (29) If $s = \frac{1}{2}$, what number does $4s$ equal? 2

▶ * **7.** (46) Generalize Write 6.25 in expanded notation. $(6 \times 1) + (2 \times \frac{1}{10}) + (5 \times \frac{1}{100})$

8. (33, 35) Write 99% as a fraction. Then write the fraction as a decimal number. $\frac{99}{100}$; 0.99

▶ * **9.** (45) $12\overline{)0.18}$ 0.015

* **10.** (45) $10\overline{)12.30}$ 1.23

▶ See Math Conversations in the sidebar.

2 New Concepts (Continued)

Practice Set

Problems b and c Error Alert

Students must recognize that in problem **b**, the diameter is given, and in problem **c**, the radius is given.

In both formulas, the value of pi is a factor in hundredths, and students should generalize that their answers must include at least two decimal places.

Problem d Estimate

"To round your answer to two decimal places, what is the least number of decimal places you must compute to?" three

Problem e Model

Ask students to compare their answer of the circumference of a penny to their estimate of the circumference of a penny which was made in problem **d.**

3 Written Practice

Math Conversations

Discussion opportunities are provided below.

Problem 4 Conclude

Point out that the formula $A = bh$ is commonly used to find the area of a parallelogram and sometimes used to find the area of a rectangle.

"Suppose this formula represents finding the area of a rectangle having a base (b) of 8 inches and a height (h) of 4 inches. What label should be included with our answer of 32?" square inches

Problem 7 Generalize

"When we write a decimal number in expanded notation, what fraction is used to represent the tenths place in the number?" $\frac{1}{10}$

"What fraction is used to represent the hundredths place in the number?" $\frac{1}{100}$

Errors and Misconceptions

Problem 9

Watch for students who do not recognize that the division must be continued by writing a zero in the thousandths place of the divisor.

(continued)

3 Written Practice (Continued)

Math Conversations

Discussion opportunities are provided below.

Problem 20 Explain

Extend the Problem

"What is the approximate circumference of one of Robert's bicycle wheels in feet?" about 5 feet

"Rounded to the nearest thousand, how many feet are in one mile?" 5000 feet

"Explain how to estimate the number of revolutions (or the number of times one of the wheels on Robert's bicycle will go completely around) if he rides one mile." Divide the number of feet in one mile by the circumference of a wheel.

"About how many revolutions does one of Robert's wheels make in one mile?" about 1000 revolutions

Errors and Misconceptions

Problem 11

Make sure students simplify $\sqrt{36}$ as 6 and 6^2 as 36.

(continued)

Find each missing number:

▶ **11.** (4, 38) $w \div \sqrt{36} = 6^2$ 216

* **12.** (43) $5y = 1.25$ 0.25

* **13.** (43) $n + 5\frac{11}{12} = 10$ $4\frac{1}{12}$

* **14.** (43) $m - 6\frac{2}{5} = 3\frac{3}{5}$ 10

15. (26) $8\frac{3}{4} + 5\frac{3}{4}$ $14\frac{1}{2}$

16. (29) $\frac{5}{3} \times \frac{5}{4}$ $2\frac{1}{12}$

* **17.** (42) $\frac{3}{4} = \frac{?}{20}$ 15

* **18.** (42) $\frac{3}{5} = \frac{?}{20}$ 12

19. (18) Bob's scores on his first five tests were 18, 20, 18, 20, and 20. His average score is closest to which of these numbers? C

A 17 **B** 18 **C** 19 **D** 20

▶* **20.** (47) Robert's bicycle tires are 20 inches in diameter. What is the circumference of a 20-inch circle? (Use 3.14 for π.) Explain why your answer is reasonable.

21. (19) Which factors of 20 are also factors of 30? 1, 2, 5, 10

* **22.** (46) Explain Mentally calculate the product of 6.25 and 10. Describe how you performed the mental calculation.

* **23.** (46) Multiply as shown. Then complete the division. 2.5

$$\frac{1.25}{0.5} \cdot \frac{10}{10}$$

* **24.** (41) Shelly answered 90% of the 40 questions correctly. What number is 90% of 40? 36

Refer to the chart shown below to answer problems **25** and **26.**

Planet	Number of Earth Days to Orbit Sun
Mercury	88
Venus	225
Earth	365
Mars	687

25. (13) Mars takes how many more days than Earth to orbit the Sun? 322 more days

26. (15) Estimate In the time it takes Mars to orbit the Sun once, Venus orbits the Sun about how many times? about 3 times

27. (17) Use an inch ruler to find the length and width of this rectangle. length = 1 inch, width = $\frac{3}{4}$ inch

20. 62.8 inches; The distance around a circle is a little more than three times the distance across the circle. The distance around a 20-inch diameter tire is a little more than 3 × 20 inches.

22. 62.5; Since the problem is to multiply by 10, simply shift the decimal point in 6.25 one place to the right.

▶ See Math Conversations in the sidebar.

28. Calculate the perimeter of the rectangle in problem 27. $3\frac{1}{2}$ inches
(8)

29. Rename $\frac{2}{5}$ so that the denominator of the renamed fraction is 10. Then subtract the renamed fraction from $\frac{9}{10}$. Reduce the answer. $\frac{4}{10}$; $\frac{9}{10} - \frac{4}{10} = \frac{5}{10} = \frac{1}{2}$
(42)

▶* **30.** Verify When we mentally multiply 15 by 10, we can simply attach a zero to 15 to make the product 150. When we multiply 1.5 by 10, why can't we attach a zero to make the product 1.50? (See below.)
(46)

Early Finishers
Real-World Application

Decide whether you can use an estimate to answer the question or if you need to compute an exact amount. Explain how you found your answer.

A music store is having a sale. Hassan wants to buy 3 CDs. One CD costs \$11.95. The other two CDs cost \$14.99 each. Hassan has \$50 but needs to use \$10 of it to repay a loan from his brother. Does Hassan have enough money to buy the CDs and repay his brother? Sample: Estimate: \$12 + 2(\$15) + \$10 = \$52; Hassan does not have enough money.

30. The numbers 1.5 and 1.50 are equivalent. Attaching a zero to a decimal number does not shift place values. To multiply 1.5 by 10, we can move the decimal point one place to the right, which shifts the place values and makes the product 15.

▶ See Math Conversations in the sidebar.

3 Written Practice (Continued)

Math Conversations

Discussion opportunities are provided below.

Problem 30 Verify

After completing the problem, ask,

"Using mental math, what is the product of twenty-five times ten?" 250

"What is the product of two and five tenths times ten?" 25

Looking Forward

Using pi to find the approximate circumference of a circle prepares students for:

- **Lesson 86,** finding the area of a circle.
- **Lesson 120,** finding the volume of a cylinder.

Subtracting Mixed Numbers with Regrouping, Part 1

Objectives

- Regroup to subtract mixed numbers with the same denominators.

Lesson Preparation

Materials

- **Power Up G** (in *Instructional Masters*)
- **Manipulative Kit: overhead fraction circles**

Optional

- **Teacher-provided material: fraction manipulatives** from Investigation 2

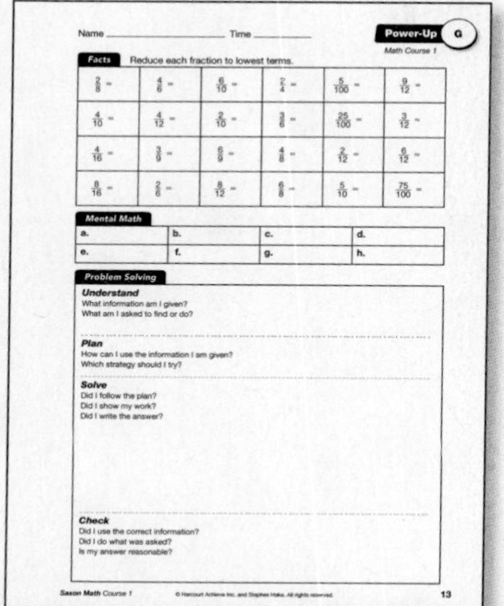

Power Up G

Math Language

English Learners (ESL)
per

Technology Resources

Student eBook Complete student textbook in electronic format.

Resources and Planner CD Assessment, reteaching, and instructional masters, plus a pacing calendar with standards.

Test and Practice Generator CD Create additional practice sheets and custom-made tests.

www.SaxonPublishers.com Visit for more student activities and planning materials.

Inclusion

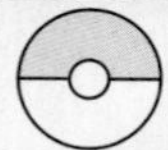

Adaptations CD Adapted lessons, investigations, practice and assessments.

Meeting Standards

National Council of Teachers of Mathematics (NCTM)

Numbers and Operations

NO.1a Work flexibly with fractions, decimals, and percents to solve problems

NO.2a Understand the meaning and effects of arithmetic operations with fractions, decimals, and integers

NO.3a Select appropriate methods and tools for computing with fractions and decimals from among mental computation, estimation, calculators or computers, and paper and pencil, depending on the situation, and apply the selected methods

NO.3b Develop and analyze algorithms for computing with fractions, decimals, and integers and develop fluency in their use

Power-Up Discussion *For use with Power Up, p. 250*

Problem-Solving Strategy: Draw a Diagram

Josepha is making sack lunches. She has two kinds of sandwiches, three kinds of fruit, and two kinds of juice. If each sack lunch contains one kind of sandwich, one kind of fruit, and one kind of juice, how many different sack-lunch combinations can Josepha make?

Understand ***Understand the problem.***

"What information are we given?"

Josepha has two types of sandwiches, three kinds of fruit, and two different juices to "build" sack lunches.

"Is this a combination or a permutation problem?"

It is a combination problem because different orders are not counted.

"What will a sack lunch contain?"

A sack lunch contains one sandwich, one piece of fruit, and one kind of juice.

"What are we asked to do?"

We are asked to determine how many choices of sack lunches are possible.

Plan ***Make a plan.***

"What problem-solving strategy will we use?"

We will *draw a* ***tree diagram*** to solve the problem.

Teacher Note: A tree diagram is a diagram that branches out from a single point. In our case, we will need two tree diagrams.

"How can we adapt the information to help us solve the problem?"

We should make up names for the types of sandwiches, fruits, and juices. We can use their initial letters as abbreviations in our tree diagram.

Solve ***Carry out the plan.***

"How do we begin?"

We will make one tree diagram for cheese sandwiches and one for peanut butter and jelly sandwiches. For each sandwich there are three different fruits. For each sandwich-fruit pair there are two kinds of juices. We will create a tree using each sandwich in different combinations with one fruit and one juice.

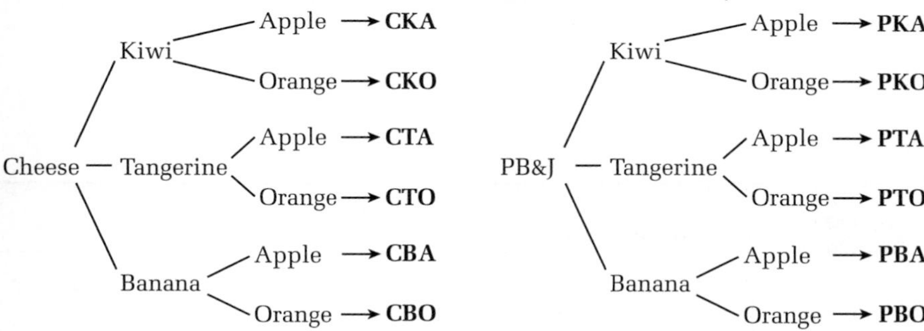

"How many sack-lunch choices are there for each type of sandwich?" 6

"How many different sack lunches are there in all?" 12

"How are the number of sandwiches (2), fruit (3), and juice (2) related to the number of combinations (12)?" $2 \times 3 \times 2 = 12$

"How does this relationship of number of items to combinations make sense in this problem?"

For each sandwich there are three fruits, so there are $2 \times 3 = 6$ sandwich-fruit combinations. For each of the six sandwich-fruit combinations there are two juice choices. So there are $6 \times 2 = 12$ combinations in all.

Check ***Look back.***

"Did we find the answer to the question that was asked?"

Yes, Josepha can make 12 different sack lunches.

1 Power Up

Facts

Distribute **Power Up G** to students. See answers below.

Mental Math

Before students begin the Mental Math exercise, do this counting exercise as a class.

Count up and down by $\frac{1}{8}$s between $\frac{1}{8}$ and 3.

Encourage students to share different ways to mentally compute these exercises. Strategies for exercises **d** and **e** are listed below.

d. Add $1.00, then Subtract 25¢

$4.50 + $1.00 = $5.50;
$5.50 − $0.25 = $5.25

Count On by Quarters

Start with $4.50. Count: $4.75, $5.00, $5.25

e. Use a Pattern

Since $\frac{1}{2}$ of $14 is $7 and $\frac{1}{2}$ of $16 is $8, $\frac{1}{2}$ of $15 is $7.50.

Break Apart $15.00

$\frac{1}{2}$ of $14 + $\frac{1}{2}$ of $1 = $7 + $0.50 = $7.50

Problem Solving

Refer to **Power-Up Discussion,** p. 250B.

2 New Concepts

Instruction

Have students note that the fractional part of the subtrahend is greater than the fractional part of the minuend.

(continued)

LESSON 48

• Subtracting Mixed Numbers with Regrouping, Part 1

Power Up *Building Power*

facts Power Up G

mental math

a. **Calculation:** 8 × 25 200

b. **Number Sense:** 630 − 50 580

c. **Number Sense:** 62 + 19 81

d. **Money:** $4.50 + 75¢ $5.25

e. **Fractional Parts:** $\frac{1}{2}$ of $15.00 $7.50

f. **Money:** $\frac{\$25.00}{100}$ $0.25

g. **Geometry:** What is the relationship between the radius and the diameter of a circle? the radius is half of the diameter

h. **Calculation:** 4 × 7, − 1, ÷ 3, × 4, ÷ 6, × 3, ÷ 2 9

problem solving

Josepha is making sack lunches. She has two kinds of sandwiches, three kinds of fruit, and two kinds of juice. If each sack lunch contains one kind of sandwich, one kind of fruit, and one kind of juice, how many different sack-lunch combinations can Josepha make? 12 sack lunches

New Concept *Increasing Knowledge*

Here is another "separating" problem about pies:

There were $4\frac{1}{6}$ pies on the restaurant shelf. The server sliced one of the whole pies into sixths. Then the server removed $1\frac{2}{6}$ pies. How many pies were left on the shelf?

Thinking Skill
Discuss
What words or phrases in the problem give clues about which operation we should use to answer the question? removed; were left

We may illustrate this problem with circles. There were $4\frac{1}{6}$ pies on the shelf.

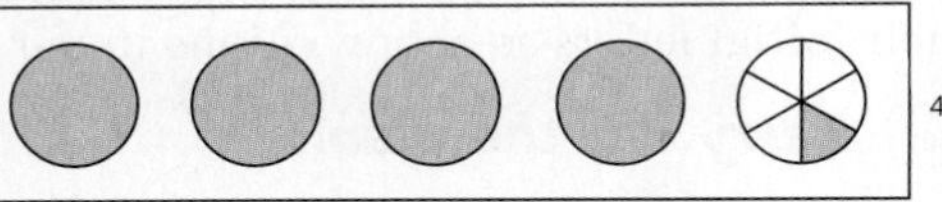

The server sliced one of the whole pies into sixths. This makes $3\frac{7}{6}$ pies, which equals $4\frac{1}{6}$ pies.

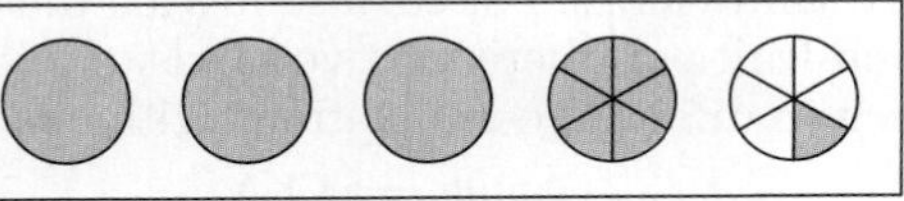

Facts Reduce each fraction to lowest terms.

$\frac{2}{8}=\frac{1}{4}$	$\frac{4}{6}=\frac{2}{3}$	$\frac{6}{10}=\frac{3}{5}$	$\frac{2}{4}=\frac{1}{2}$	$\frac{5}{100}=\frac{1}{20}$	$\frac{9}{12}=\frac{3}{4}$
$\frac{4}{10}=\frac{2}{5}$	$\frac{4}{12}=\frac{1}{3}$	$\frac{2}{10}=\frac{1}{5}$	$\frac{3}{6}=\frac{1}{2}$	$\frac{25}{100}=\frac{1}{4}$	$\frac{3}{12}=\frac{1}{4}$
$\frac{4}{16}=\frac{1}{4}$	$\frac{3}{9}=\frac{1}{3}$	$\frac{6}{9}=\frac{2}{3}$	$\frac{4}{8}=\frac{1}{2}$	$\frac{2}{12}=\frac{1}{6}$	$\frac{6}{12}=\frac{1}{2}$
$\frac{8}{16}=\frac{1}{2}$	$\frac{2}{6}=\frac{1}{3}$	$\frac{8}{12}=\frac{2}{3}$	$\frac{6}{8}=\frac{3}{4}$	$\frac{5}{10}=\frac{1}{2}$	$\frac{75}{100}=\frac{3}{4}$

Then the server removed $1\frac{2}{6}$ pies. So $2\frac{5}{6}$ pies were left on the shelf.

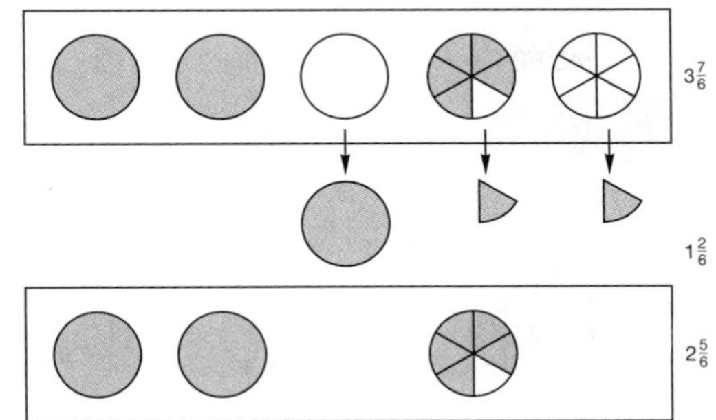

Now we show the arithmetic for subtracting $1\frac{2}{6}$ from $4\frac{1}{6}$.

$$\begin{array}{r} 4\frac{1}{6}\text{ pies} \\ -\,1\frac{2}{6}\text{ pies} \\ \hline \end{array}$$

Thinking Skill

Verify

How can you check the answer to the subtraction problem?

by adding: $2\frac{5}{6} + 1\frac{2}{6} = 3\frac{7}{6} = 4\frac{1}{6}$

We cannot subtract $\frac{2}{6}$ from $\frac{1}{6}$, so we rename $4\frac{1}{6}$. Just as the server sliced one of the pies into sixths, so we change one of the four wholes into $\frac{6}{6}$. This makes three whole pies plus $\frac{6}{6}$ plus $\frac{1}{6}$, which is $3\frac{7}{6}$. Now we can subtract.

$$\begin{array}{r} 4\frac{1}{6} \\ -\,1\frac{2}{6} \\ \hline \end{array} \xrightarrow{3 + \frac{6}{6} + \frac{1}{6}} \begin{array}{r} 3\frac{7}{6}\text{ pies} \\ -\,1\frac{2}{6}\text{ pies} \\ \hline 2\frac{5}{6}\text{ pies} \end{array}$$

Example

Subtract: $5\frac{1}{3} - 2\frac{2}{3}$

Solution

We cannot subtract $\frac{2}{3}$ from $\frac{1}{3}$, so we rename $5\frac{1}{3}$. We change one of the five wholes into $\frac{3}{3}$. Then we combine 4 and $\frac{3}{3} + \frac{1}{3}$ to get $4\frac{4}{3}$. Now we can subtract.

$$\begin{array}{r} 5\frac{1}{3} \\ -\,2\frac{2}{3} \\ \hline \end{array} \xrightarrow{4 + \frac{3}{3} + \frac{1}{3}} \begin{array}{r} 4\frac{4}{3} \\ -\,2\frac{2}{3} \\ \hline 2\frac{2}{3} \end{array}$$

Practice Set ▸ Subtract.

a. $4\frac{1}{3} - 1\frac{2}{3}$ $2\frac{2}{3}$

b. $3\frac{2}{5} - 2\frac{3}{5}$ $\frac{4}{5}$

c. $5\frac{2}{4} - 1\frac{3}{4}$ $3\frac{3}{4}$

d. $5\frac{1}{8} - 2\frac{4}{8}$ $2\frac{5}{8}$

e. $7\frac{3}{12} - 4\frac{10}{12}$ $2\frac{5}{12}$

f. $6\frac{1}{4} - 2\frac{3}{4}$ $3\frac{1}{2}$

▸ See Math Conversations in the sidebar.

2 New Concepts (Continued)

Instruction

Make sure students understand the connection between the second illustration on the previous page and the arithmetic $3 + \frac{6}{6} + \frac{1}{6}$. If students have difficulty understanding the connection, ask them to model the renaming and the subtraction using their fraction manipulatives.

Example

Instruction

Use the **Overhead Fraction Circles** to model this example.

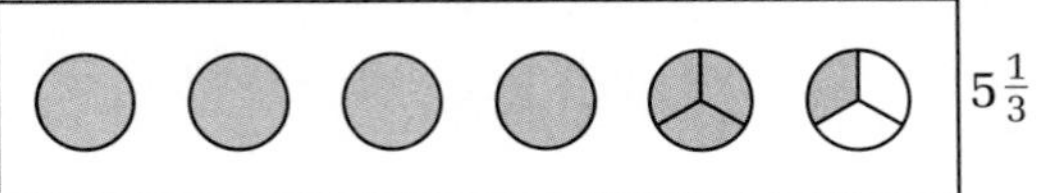

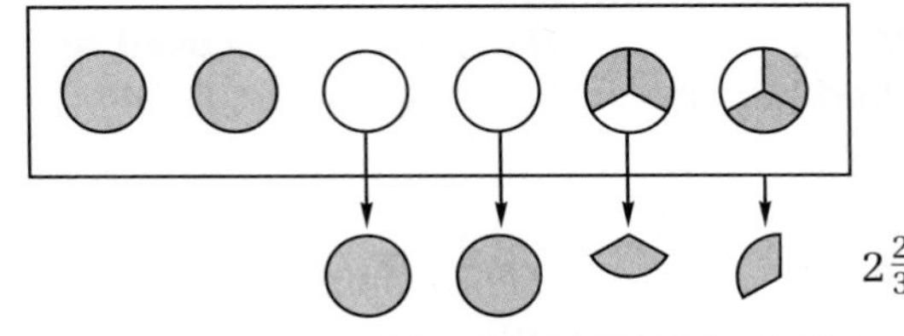

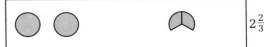

Practice Set

Problems a–f (Error Alert)

Students must rename once to complete each subtraction.

Before students begin problem **a,** ask:

"What fraction in thirds is another name for 1?" $\frac{3}{3}$

Before students begin problem **b,** ask:

"What fraction in fifths is another name for 1?" $\frac{5}{5}$

Ask a similar question before students begin each of the remaining problems.

Manipulative Use

Use **Overhead Fraction Circles** from the Manipulative Kit to model each of the text illustrations.

You will need two sets of $\frac{1}{6}$ and two sets of $\frac{1}{3}$ manipulatives. For additional full circles, photocopy the full circle manipulative or trace around it and cut out more full circles.

3 Written Practice

Math Conversations

Discussion opportunities are provided below.

Problem 2 Analyze

"How can you find the cost using mental math?" One of the factors is 10, and multiplying by 10 is the same as shifting the decimal point in the other factor one place to the right.

Problem 5 Analyze

"Explain how you can immediately know which of the numbers is least." Sample: −1 is least because it is the only number less than zero.

Problem 13 Analyze

"Explain how mental math can be used to find the cost." One of the factors is 100, and multiplying by 100 is the same as shifting the decimal point in the other factor two places to the right.

Problem 22 Justify

Explain that "one wind of the thread" means the same as winding the thread once around the spool.

Errors and Misconceptions

Problem 5

Watch for students who do not read carefully and incorrectly order the numbers from greatest to least.

Problem 10

Some students may omit the zero in the tenths place of the quotient and give an answer of 0.18. Remind these students that whenever they divide a decimal dividend, the quotient should include a decimal point, and a zero should be written in each empty place.

(continued)

---

g. Sample for exercise **a**:

$4\frac{1}{3} = 3\frac{4}{3}$

$-1\frac{2}{3}$

$2\frac{2}{3}$

g. Model Select one of the exercises to model with a drawing.

h. Formulate Select another exercise and write a word problem that is solved by the subtraction.

h. Sample for exercise **f**: From the trailhead to the summit is about $6\frac{1}{4}$ miles. After walking $2\frac{3}{4}$ miles, how much farther is it to the summit?

Written Practice *Strengthening Concepts*

1. (18) Analyze The average of two numbers is 10. What is the sum of the two numbers? 20

▶ * **2.** (46) What is the cost of 10.0 gallons of gasoline priced at \$2.279 per gallon? \$22.79

3. (32) The movie started at 11:45 a.m. and ended at 1:20 p.m. The movie was how many hours and minutes long? 1 hour 35 minutes

* **4.** (44) Classify Three of the numbers shown below are equal. Which number is not equal to the others? B

A $\frac{1}{2}$ **B** 0.2 **C** 0.5 **D** $\frac{10}{20}$

▶ * **5.** (44) Analyze Arrange these numbers in order from least to greatest:

1.02, 0.102, 0.12, 1.20, 0, −1

−1, 0, 0.102, 0.12, 1.02, 1.20

6. (37) 0.1 + 0.2 + 0.3 + 0.4 1 **7.** (39) (8)(0.125) 1

8. (11) Formulate Juan was hiking to a waterfall 3 miles away. After hiking 2.1 miles, how many more miles did he have to hike to reach the waterfall? Write an equation and solve the problem. $3 - 2.1 = r$; 0.9 mile

9. (16) Estimate the sum of 4967, 8142, and 6890. 20,000

▶* **10.** (45) $8\overline{)0.144}$ 0.018 * **11.** (45) $6\overline{)0.9}$ 0.15 * **12.** (45) $4\overline{)0.9}$ 0.225

▶* **13.** (46) What is the cost of 100 pens priced at 39¢ each? \$39

* **14.** (46) Write $(5 \times 10) + (6 \times \frac{1}{10}) + (4 \times \frac{1}{100})$ in standard form. 50.64

15. (30) What is the least common multiple of 6 and 8? 24

Find each unknown number:

* **16.** (43) $w - 7\frac{7}{12} = 5\frac{5}{12}$ 13 * **17.** (43) $12 - m = 5\frac{2}{3}$ $6\frac{1}{3}$

* **18.** (43) $n + 2\frac{3}{4} = 5\frac{1}{4}$ $2\frac{1}{2}$ * **19.** (43) $x + 3.21 = 4$ 0.79

20. (29) What fraction is $\frac{2}{3}$ of $\frac{3}{4}$? $\frac{1}{2}$

21. (14) Sam carried the football three times during the game. He had gains of 3 yards and 5 yards and a loss of 12 yards. Use a negative number to show Sam's overall yardage for the game. −4

▶* **22.** (47) Justify If a spool for thread is 2 cm in diameter, then one wind of thread is about how many centimeters long? (Use 3.14 for π.) Explain how to mentally check whether your answer is reasonable. about 6.28 cm; π is a little more than 3, and 3 × 2 cm is 6 cm. So 6.28 cm is a reasonable answer.

▶ See Math Conversations in the sidebar.

English Learners

Explain that **per** can mean different things, but in today's lesson it has a specific meaning that relates to real life. Say:

"Number two talks about the cost of gasoline. The cost is per gallon. Per, in this case, means 'for each' gallon."

Ask students to tell the class of other times they have seen or used the word "per."

23. If a rectangle is 12 inches long and 8 inches wide, what is the ratio of its length to its width? $\frac{3}{2}$
(23, 29)

24. The perimeter of this square is 4 feet. What is its perimeter in inches? 48 inches
(8)

12 in.
1 ft
12 in.
1 ft

25. The area of this square is one square foot. What is its area in square inches?
(31)
144 square inches

▶* 26. Evaluate If $d = rt$, and if $r = 60$ and $t = 4$, what does d equal? 240
(47)

27. Seventy-five percent of the 32 chairs in the room were occupied. Write 75% as a reduced fraction. Then find the number of chairs that were occupied. $\frac{3}{4}$; 24 chairs
(22, 33)

* 28. Rename $\frac{1}{3}$ and $\frac{1}{4}$ as fractions with denominators of 12. Then add the renamed fractions. $\frac{4}{12} + \frac{3}{12} = \frac{7}{12}$
(42)

▶* 29. Analyze Multiply as shown. Then simplify the answer. 5
(46)

$$\frac{3.5}{0.7} \cdot \frac{10}{10}$$

* 30. Explain There were $3\frac{1}{6}$ pies on the shelf. How can the server take $1\frac{5}{6}$ pies from the shelf?
(48)

30. The server can cut one of the whole pies into sixths. Then there will be $2\frac{7}{6}$ pies on the shelf. The server can remove $1\frac{5}{6}$ pies, leaving $1\frac{2}{6}$ pies ($1\frac{1}{3}$ pies) on the shelf.

Early Finishers
Real-World Application

Leonardo purchased 4 pounds of grapes. Leonardo gave his neighbor half a pound of grapes so he could make a fruit salad. Next, he gave his friend 0.09 lb of grapes for a snack. Lastly, Leonardo gave his brother 1.25 lb of grapes so his brother could make grape juice. What is the weight of the grapes Leonardo has left? Show your work.
4.0 − 0.5 − 0.09 − 1.25 = 2.16 pounds

▶ See Math Conversations in the sidebar.

3 Written Practice (Continued)

Math Conversations

Discussion opportunities are provided below.

Problem 26 Evaluate

"What operation does the expression rt **represent?"** multiplication

Problem 29 Analyze

"What happens to the decimal point in a number when you multiply the number by 10?" The decimal point in the number shifts one place to the right.

"Explain how to find the answer to this problem using only mental math." $3.5 \times 10 = 35$ and $0.7 \times 10 = 7$; $\frac{35}{7} = 35 \div 7 = 5$

Looking Forward

Regrouping to subtract mixed numbers with the same denominator prepares students for:

- **Lessons 55–57,** finding common denominators in order to add and subtract fractions.
- **Lesson 59,** adding mixed numbers.
- **Lesson 61,** adding three or more fractions.
- **Lesson 63,** subtracting mixed numbers with unlike denominators using regrouping.
- **Lesson 72,** using a fraction chart to recall steps for subtracting fractions.

• Dividing by a Decimal Number

Objectives

- Divide a decimal number or a whole number by a decimal number.

Lesson Preparation

Materials

- **Power Up H** (in *Instructional Masters*)
- **Manipulative Kit: inch rulers**

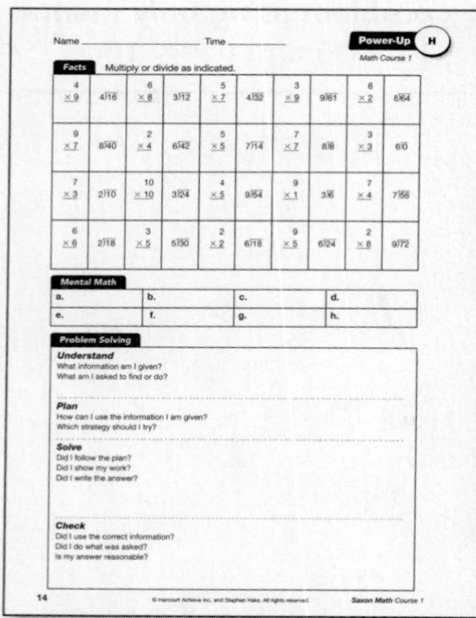

Power Up H

Math Language

English Learners (ESL)
jigsaw puzzle

Technology Resources

Student eBook Complete student textbook in electronic format.

Resources and Planner CD Assessment, reteaching, and instructional masters, plus a pacing calendar with standards.

Test and Practice Generator CD Create additional practice sheets and custom-made tests.

www.SaxonPublishers.com Visit for more student activities and planning materials.

Inclusion

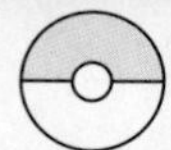

Adaptations CD Adapted lessons, investigations, practice and assessments.

Meeting Standards

National Council of Teachers of Mathematics (NCTM)

Numbers and Operations

NO.1a Work flexibly with fractions, decimals, and percents to solve problems

NO.3a Select appropriate methods and tools for computing with fractions and decimals from among mental computation, estimation, calculators or computers, and paper and pencil, depending on the situation, and apply the selected methods

NO.3b Develop and analyze algorithms for computing with fractions, decimals, and integers and develop fluency in their use

Power-Up Discussion *For use with Power Up, p. 254*

Problem-Solving Strategy: Use Logical Reasoning

Ned walked from his home to school following the path from H to I to J to K to L to M to S. After school he walked home from S to C to H. Compare the distance of Ned's walk to school to the distance of his walk home.

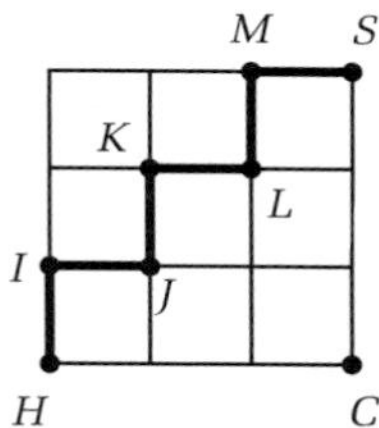

Understand — Understand the problem.

"What information are we given?"

We are given a diagram that shows the two different paths Ned walked. The diagram consists of one large square divided into nine equal-sized smaller squares.

"What are we asked to do?"

We are asked to compare the distance of Ned's walk to school to the distance of his walk home.

Plan — Make a plan.

"What problem-solving strategy will we use?"

We will *use logical reasoning* to analyze the diagram that has been provided to measure the distances of Ned's walks.

"How can we measure if the diagram is not labeled with specific units of measurement?"

We can count generic unit segments along each path that Ned walked.

Teacher Note: Explain the nature of generic units. Generic units include objects most people can identify (a pat of butter, a handful of berries, a pinch of salt) and also random markers we choose to use as markers because they are convenient to the situation (fifth house on the left, two tiles apart, two stop signs away).

Solve — Carry out the plan.

"What is the distance Ned walked from home to school?"

Ned's walk from home to school is traced in dark line segments. Each segment is one unit long, and we count 6 units along the path.

"The path Ned took home did not include as many turns. What is the distance of Ned's walk home?"

We count 3 units from point *S* to point *C* and 3 units from point *C* to point *H*, for a total of 6 units.

"How do the distances of Ned's walks compare?"

Each way is 6 units long as represented by the diagram. The lengths of Ned's walks are equal.

Check — Look back.

"How can we sensibly describe why our answer is correct?"

Even though Ned made more turns in his walk to school, each segment of his walk was shorter. We see that in both walks, Ned traversed the full length and the full width of the square without backtracking. Therefore, it makes sense that the distances of Ned's walks were equal.

Teacher Note: You may extend this lesson by having the students create other routes that measure the same distance.

1 Power Up

Facts

Distribute **Power Up H** to students. See answers below.

Mental Math

Before students begin the Mental Math exercise, do this counting exercise as a class.

Count by 12s from 12 to 120.

Encourage students to share different ways to mentally compute these exercises. Strategies for exercises **a** and **f** are listed below.

a. Count by 125

Count: 125, 250, 375, 500, 625, 750, 875, 1000

Break Apart 8 × 25

$(8 \times 100) + (4 \times 25 \times 2) = 800 + (100 \times 2) = 800 + 200 = 1000$

f. Cancel Zeros

$\frac{4000}{100} = \frac{40\cancel{00}}{1\cancel{00}} = \frac{40}{1} = 40$

Shift the Decimal Points

$\frac{4000}{100} = \frac{40.00}{1.00} = \frac{40}{1} = 40$

Problem Solving

Refer to **Power-Up Discussion**, p. 254B.

2 New Concepts

Instruction

Make sure students notice that multiplying a dividend and a divisor by 10:

- does not change the quotient, and
- is the same as shifting the decimal points in those numbers one place to the right.

(continued)

LESSON 49

• Dividing by a Decimal Number

Power Up *Building Power*

facts Power Up H

mental math

a. **Order of Operations:** $(8 \times 100) + (8 \times 25)$ 1000

b. **Number Sense:** $290 + 50$ 340

c. **Number Sense:** $58 - 19$ 39

d. **Money:** \$5.00 − \$3.25 \$1.75

e. **Fractional Parts:** $\frac{1}{2}$ of \$30.00 \$15.00

f. **Number Sense:** $\frac{4000}{100}$ 40

g. **Geometry:** A circle has a radius of 3 cm. Using 3.14 for π, what is the circumference of the circle? 18.84 cm

h. **Calculation:** 5×10, $\div 2$, $+ 5$, $\div 2$, $+ 5$, $\div 2$, $\div 2$ 5

problem solving Ned walked from his home to school following the path from H to I to J to K to L to M to S. After school he walked home from S to C to H. Compare the distance of Ned's walk to school to the distance of his walk home.
The distances are equal.

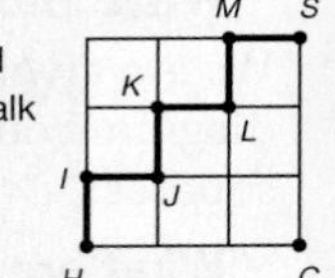

New Concept *Increasing Knowledge*

When the divisor of a division problem is a decimal number, we change the problem so that the divisor is a whole number.

$\frac{1.24}{0.4}$ $\quad 0.4\overline{)1.24}$

The divisor is a decimal number. We change the problem before we divide.

One way to change a division problem is to multiply the divisor and the dividend by 10. Notice in the whole-number division problem below that multiplying both numbers by 10 does not change the quotient.

$\begin{array}{r}2\\4\overline{)8}\end{array} \longrightarrow \begin{array}{r}2\\40\overline{)80}\end{array}$

Multiplying 4 and 8 by 10 does not change the quotient.

The quotient is not changed, because we formed an equivalent division problem just as we form equivalent fractions—by multiplying by a form of 1.

$$\frac{8}{4} \times \frac{10}{10} = \frac{80}{40}$$

Facts Multiply or divide as indicated.

$\begin{array}{r}4\\\times 9\\\hline 36\end{array}$	$\begin{array}{r}4\\4\overline{)16}\end{array}$	$\begin{array}{r}6\\\times 8\\\hline 48\end{array}$	$\begin{array}{r}4\\3\overline{)12}\end{array}$	$\begin{array}{r}5\\\times 7\\\hline 35\end{array}$	$\begin{array}{r}8\\4\overline{)32}\end{array}$	$\begin{array}{r}3\\\times 9\\\hline 27\end{array}$	$\begin{array}{r}9\\9\overline{)81}\end{array}$	$\begin{array}{r}6\\\times 2\\\hline 12\end{array}$	$\begin{array}{r}8\\8\overline{)64}\end{array}$
$\begin{array}{r}9\\\times 7\\\hline 63\end{array}$	$\begin{array}{r}5\\8\overline{)40}\end{array}$	$\begin{array}{r}2\\\times 4\\\hline 8\end{array}$	$\begin{array}{r}7\\6\overline{)42}\end{array}$	$\begin{array}{r}5\\\times 5\\\hline 25\end{array}$	$\begin{array}{r}2\\7\overline{)14}\end{array}$	$\begin{array}{r}7\\\times 7\\\hline 49\end{array}$	$\begin{array}{r}1\\8\overline{)8}\end{array}$	$\begin{array}{r}3\\\times 3\\\hline 9\end{array}$	$\begin{array}{r}0\\6\overline{)0}\end{array}$
$\begin{array}{r}7\\\times 3\\\hline 21\end{array}$	$\begin{array}{r}5\\2\overline{)10}\end{array}$	$\begin{array}{r}10\\\times 10\\\hline 100\end{array}$	$\begin{array}{r}8\\3\overline{)24}\end{array}$	$\begin{array}{r}4\\\times 5\\\hline 20\end{array}$	$\begin{array}{r}6\\9\overline{)54}\end{array}$	$\begin{array}{r}9\\\times 1\\\hline 9\end{array}$	$\begin{array}{r}2\\3\overline{)6}\end{array}$	$\begin{array}{r}7\\\times 4\\\hline 28\end{array}$	$\begin{array}{r}8\\7\overline{)56}\end{array}$
$\begin{array}{r}6\\\times 6\\\hline 36\end{array}$	$\begin{array}{r}9\\2\overline{)18}\end{array}$	$\begin{array}{r}3\\\times 5\\\hline 15\end{array}$	$\begin{array}{r}6\\5\overline{)30}\end{array}$	$\begin{array}{r}2\\\times 2\\\hline 4\end{array}$	$\begin{array}{r}3\\6\overline{)18}\end{array}$	$\begin{array}{r}9\\\times 5\\\hline 45\end{array}$	$\begin{array}{r}4\\6\overline{)24}\end{array}$	$\begin{array}{r}2\\\times 8\\\hline 16\end{array}$	$\begin{array}{r}8\\9\overline{)72}\end{array}$

We can also use this method to change a division by a decimal number to a division by a whole number.

Thinking Skill
Summarize
How can we mentally multiply a decimal number by 10 or 100? Move the decimal point either one place or two places to the right.

If we multiply the divisor and dividend in $\frac{1.24}{0.4}$ by 10, the new problem has a whole-number divisor.

$$\underset{\text{decimal divisor}}{\frac{1.24}{0.4}} \times \frac{10}{10} = \underset{\text{whole-number divisor}}{\frac{12.4}{4}}$$

We divide 12.4 by 4 to find the quotient.

$$4\overline{)12.4} = 3.1$$

Example 1

Divide: $\frac{1.24}{0.04}$

Solution

The divisor, 0.04, is a decimal number with two decimal places. To make the divisor a whole number, we will multiply $\frac{1.24}{0.4}$ by $\frac{100}{100}$, which shifts each decimal point two places to the right.

$$\frac{1.24}{0.04} \times \frac{100}{100} = \frac{124}{4}$$

This forms an equivalent division problem in which the divisor is a whole number. Now we perform the division.

```
   31
4)124
  12
   04
    4
    0
```

Example 2

Divide: $0.6\overline{)1.44}$

Solution

The divisor, 0.6, has one decimal place. If we multiply the divisor and dividend by 10, we will shift the decimal point one place to the right in both numbers.

$$06.\overline{)14.4}$$

This makes a new problem with a whole-number divisor, which we solve below.

```
   2.4
6)14.4
  12
   2 4
   2 4
     0
```


2 New Concepts (Continued)

Instruction

Explain that a decimal divisor must be changed to a whole number before division can begin. Help students generalize that multiplying a decimal dividend in tenths by 10 will change the dividend to a whole number, and multiplying a decimal dividend in hundredths by 100 will change the dividend to a whole number.

Emphasize the importance of multiplying both the dividend and the divisor by the same number.

Example 1

Instruction

Remind students that they can mentally multiply the dividend and the divisor by 100 simply by shifting the decimal point in each number two places to the right.

Example 2

Instruction

Have students note that shifting the decimal point in each number one place to the right is the same as multiplying each number by 10.

(continued)

Math Background

The concept of forming an equivalent division problem is not limited to multiplying a dividend and a divisor by 10 or 100. Other powers of 10 can also be used.

For example, to form an equivalent division for 6 ÷ 0.125, multiply the dividend and divisor by 1000.

$$\frac{6}{0.125} \times \frac{1000}{1000} = \frac{6000}{125} = 48$$

2 New Concepts (Continued)

Instruction

After discussing the arithmetic, invite a volunteer to explain how to check the answer. find the product of 2.4 and 6

Practice Set

Problems c–j (Error Alert)

Remind students that division cannot begin until each divisor is a whole number.

"What number can a divisor in tenths and its dividend be multiplied by to change the divisor to a whole number?" 10

"Multiplying a dividend and a divisor by 10 is the same as shifting the decimal points in those numbers how many places and in which direction?" one place to the right

"What number can a divisor in hundredths and its dividend be multiplied by to change the divisor to a whole number?" 100

"Multiplying a dividend and a divisor by 100 is the same as shifting the decimal points in those numbers how many places and in which direction?" two places to the right

3 Written Practice

Math Conversations

Discussion opportunities are provided below.

Problem 1 (Represent)

Extend the Problem

Ask students to write a symbolic expression to represent the problem, and then explain why parentheses must be a part of the expression. Sample: $0.2 + 0.3 - (0.2 \times 0.3)$; Without parentheses, the expression will not simplify to 0.44.

Problem 11 (Analyze)

Extend the Problem

"The factors in this problem have a total of four decimal places. Why don't we show four decimal places in the answer?" 0.018 is a simpler way to write 0.0180.

Errors and Misconceptions

Problem 9

When writing an equivalent division problem, a misconception students sometimes make is that a divisor in tenths and its dividend *must* be multiplied by 10. It is more appropriate to say that the divisor in tenths and its dividend *may* be multiplied by 10.

(continued)

Some people use the phrase "over, over, and up" to keep track of the decimal points when dividing by decimal numbers.

$06.\overline{)14.4}$ (over over, up)

Practice Set

a. We would multiply the divisor and dividend of $\frac{1.44}{1.2}$ by what number to make the divisor a whole number? 10

b. We would multiply the divisor and dividend of $0.12\overline{)0.144}$ by what number to make the divisor a whole number? 100

Thinking Skill (Discuss)

What do you notice about the answers in exercises a and b? The number of zeros in the answers is equal to the number of decimal places in the divisors.

▶ Change each problem so that the divisor is a whole number. Then divide.

c. $\frac{0.24}{0.4}$ $\frac{2.4}{4} = 0.6$

d. $\frac{9}{0.3}$ $\frac{90}{3} = 30$

e. $0.05\overline{)2.5}$ $5\overline{)250} = 50$

f. $0.3\overline{)12}$ $3\overline{)120} = 40$

g. $0.24 \div 0.8$ $2.4 \div 8 = 0.3$

h. $0.3 \div 0.03$ $30 \div 3 = 10$

i. $0.05\overline{)0.4}$ $5\overline{)40} = 8$

j. $0.2 \div 0.4$ $2 \div 4 = 0.5$

k. Find how many nickels are in \$3.25 by dividing 3.25 by 0.05. 65 nickels

Written Practice *Strengthening Concepts*

▶ * 1. (12, 39) When the product of 0.2 and 0.3 is subtracted from the sum of 0.2 and 0.3, what is the difference? 0.44

2. (22) (Model) Four fifths of a dollar is how many cents? Draw a diagram to illustrate the problem. 80¢

2. \$1.00: 20¢, 20¢, 20¢, 20¢ ($\frac{4}{5}$ of \$1.00); 20¢ ($\frac{1}{5}$ of \$1.00)

3. (31, 39) The rectangular, 99-piece "Nano" jigsaw puzzle is only 2.6 inches long and 2.2 inches wide. What is the area of the puzzle in square inches? 5.72 square inches

4. (39) Find the perimeter of the puzzle described in problem 3. 9.6 in.

* 5. (44) Compare:

a. 0.31 ⓪> 0.301 b. 31% ⓪> 30.1%

6. (38) $0.67 + 2 + 1.33$ 4

7. (39) $12(0.25)$ 3

* 8. (49) $0.07\overline{)3.5}$ 50

▶ * 9. (49) $0.5\overline{)12}$ 24

* 10. (45) $8\overline{)0.14}$ 0.0175

▶* 11. (39) $(0.012)(1.5)$ 0.018

Find each unknown number:

* 12. (43) $n - 6\frac{1}{8} = 4\frac{3}{8}$ $10\frac{1}{2}$

* 13. (42) $\frac{4}{5} = \frac{x}{100}$ 80

* 14. (43) $5 - m = 1.37$ 3.63

* 15. (43) $m + 7\frac{1}{4} = 15$ $7\frac{3}{4}$

▶ See Math Conversations in the sidebar.

English Learners

Explain **jigsaw puzzle.** Say:

"A jigsaw puzzle is a picture that has been cut into small odd shaped pieces. When all of the pieces are put back together, it makes a complete picture."

Ask students to tell about a jigsaw puzzle they put together. Ask what the completed picture was and how many pieces it had.

16. Write the decimal number one and twelve thousandths. 1.012
(35)

17. $5\frac{7}{10} + 4\frac{9}{10}$ $10\frac{3}{5}$
(26)

18. $\frac{5}{2} \cdot \frac{5}{3}$ $4\frac{1}{6}$
(29)

19. How much money is 40% of $25.00? $10.00
(41)

20. There are 24 hours in a day. James sleeps 8 hours each night.
(29)

a. Eight hours is what fraction of a day? $\frac{1}{3}$

b. What fraction of a day does James sleep? $\frac{1}{3}$

c. What fraction of a day does James not sleep? $\frac{2}{3}$

21. **List** What factors do 12 and 18 have in common (that is, the numbers that are factors of both 12 and 18). 1, 2, 3, 6
(19)

▶* 22. **Analyze** What is the average of 1.2, 1.3, and 1.7? 1.4
(18, 45)

23. **Estimate** Jan estimated that 49% of $19.58 is $10. She rounded 49% to 50% and rounded $19.58 to $20. Then she mentally calculated 50% of $20. Use Jan's method to estimate 51% of $49.78. Explain how to perform the estimate.
(41)

3. $25; Round ■% to 50% and ound $49.78 to 50. Since 50% quals $\frac{1}{2}$, find $\frac{1}{2}$ of 50.

24. a. How many $\frac{3}{4}$s are in 1? $\frac{4}{3}$
(30)

b. Use the answer to part **a** to find the number of $\frac{3}{4}$s in 4. $5\frac{1}{3}$

25. **Connect** Refer to the number line shown below to answer parts **a–c.**
(17)

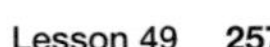

a. Which point is halfway between 1 and 2? *y*

b. Which point is closer to 1 than 2? *x*

c. Which point is closer to 2 than 1? *z*

26. Multiply and divide as indicated: $\frac{2 \cdot 3 \cdot 2 \cdot 5 \cdot 7}{2 \cdot 5 \cdot 7}$ 6
(5)

▶* 27. **Represent** We can find the number of quarters in three dollars by dividing $3.00 by $0.25. Show this division using the pencil-and-paper method taught in this lesson. $\frac{\$3.00}{\$0.25} \times \frac{100}{100} = \frac{\$300}{\$25} = 12$
(49)

28. **Connect** Use a ruler to find the length of each side of this square to the nearest eighth of an inch. Then calculate the perimeter of the square. side = $\frac{3}{4}$ inch; perimeter = 3 inches
(8)

▶ See Math Conversations in the sidebar.

3 Written Practice (Continued)

Math Conversations

Discussion opportunities are provided below.

Problem 22 Analyze

"Explain how to find the average of a group of numbers." Divide the sum of the numbers by the number of addends.

"What must we remember whenever we find the sum of two or more decimal numbers?" Sample: Align the decimal points in the numbers and write a decimal point in the sum.

Problem 27 Represent

Extend the Problem

Challenge students to describe different ways to solve the problem using mental math. Sample: Since there are 4 quarters in one dollar, there are 8 quarters in two dollars, and 12 quarters in three dollars.

(continued)

3 Written Practice (Continued)

Math Conversations

Discussion opportunities are provided below.

Problem 29 Estimate

Extend the Problem

"Suppose the tube is about 28 centimeters long. What is a reasonable estimate of the area of the tube? Explain your answer. Hint: Think about using scissors to cut the tube from top to bottom so it could be laid flat to form a rectangle." Sample: A reasonable estimate is 30 cm × 12 cm or 360 square cm. The length of the tube forms the longer dimension of the rectangle, and the circumference of the tube forms the shorter dimension of the rectangle. To estimate the area of the rectangle, round the length up and round the circumference down, then multiply.

▸* **29.** (47) A paper-towel tube is about 4 cm in diameter. The circumference of a paper-towel tube is about how many centimeters? (Use 3.14 for π.) about 12.56 cm

* **30.** (49) **Explain** Sam was given the following division problem:

$$\frac{2.5}{0.5}$$

Instead of multiplying the numerator and denominator by 10, he accidentally multiplied by 100, as shown below.

$$\frac{2.5}{0.5} \times \frac{100}{100} = \frac{250}{50}$$

Then he divided 250 by 50 and found that the quotient was 5. Did Sam find the correct answer to 2.5 ÷ 0.5? Why or why not?

30. Yes, Sam found the correct answer. Both $\frac{10}{10}$ and $\frac{100}{100}$ are equal to 1. When we multiply by different fraction names for 1, we get numbers that are equal even though they may look different. So $\frac{2.5}{0.5}$, $\frac{25}{5}$, and $\frac{250}{50}$ are three equivalent division problems with the same quotient.

Early Finishers
Real-World Application

After collecting tickets for three years, you are finally promoted to night manager of the local movie theater. You want to look good in your new job, so you try to increase profits.

The cost for a bucket of popcorn is as follows: the popcorn kernels and butter used in each bucket cost 5¢ and 2¢, and the bucket itself costs a quarter. Each bucket of popcorn sells for $3.00.

a. In one night you sold 115 buckets. What was your profit?

b. You really want to please your boss, so you decide to increase profits by charging more per bucket. How much must you charge for a bucket of popcorn to make a $365.70 profit from selling 115 buckets?

a. The total cost for each bucket of popcorn is 5¢ + 2¢ + 25¢ = 32¢. Since each bucket of popcorn sells for $3.00, the profit per bucket is $3.00 − $0.32 = $2.68. When $2.68 is multiplied by 115 buckets, the profit is $308.20.

b. $365.70 ÷ 115 = $3.18 profit on each bucket. Add the cost per bucket to find the amount you should charge for each bucket. $3.18 + $0.32 = $3.50 per bucket

▸ See Math Conversations in the sidebar.

Looking Forward

Dividing a decimal number or a whole number by a decimal number prepares students for:

- **Lesson 52,** dividing decimal numbers mentally by 10 and by 100.
- **Lesson 53,** using a decimals chart as a reminder of decimal division.
- **Lesson 84,** simplifying order-of-operations problems.
- **Lesson 119,** finding a whole when a percent is known.

• Decimal Number Line (Tenths)
• Dividing by a Fraction

Objectives

- Locate and identify decimal numbers on a number line divided into tenths.
- Divide a whole number by a fraction by multiplying the whole number by the fraction's reciprocal.

Lesson Preparation

Materials

- **Power Up G** (in *Instructional Masters*)

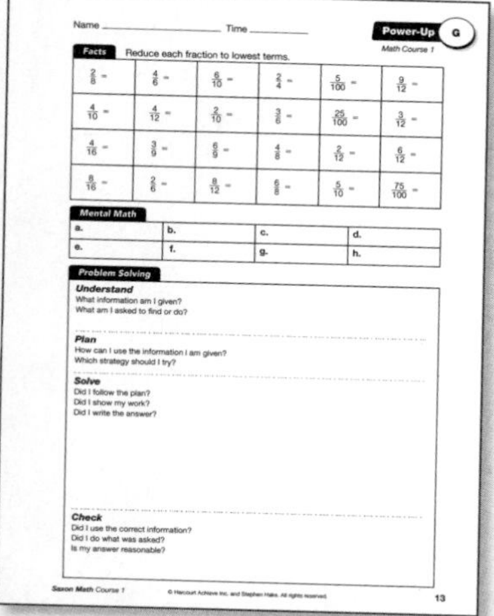

Power Up G

Math Language

	Maintain	English Learners (ESL)
	number line	**segment**
	reciprocals	

Technology Resources

Student eBook Complete student textbook in electronic format.

Resources and Planner CD Assessment, reteaching, and instructional masters, plus a pacing calendar with standards.

Test and Practice Generator CD Create additional practice sheets and custom-made tests.

www.SaxonPublishers.com Visit for more student activities and planning materials.

Inclusion

Adaptations CD Adapted lessons, investigations, practice and assessments.

Meeting Standards

National Council of Teachers of Mathematics (NCTM)

Numbers and Operations

NO.1a Work flexibly with fractions, decimals, and percents to solve problems

NO.1b Compare and order fractions, decimals, and percents efficiently and find their approximate locations on a number line

NO.3a Select appropriate methods and tools for computing with fractions and decimals from among mental computation, estimation, calculators or computers, and paper and pencil, depending on the situation, and apply the selected methods

NO.3b Develop and analyze algorithms for computing with fractions, decimals, and integers and develop fluency in their use

Power-Up Discussion

For use with Power Up, p. 259

Problem-Solving Strategy: Draw a Diagram/ Write an Equation

Half of a gallon is a half-gallon. Half of a half-gallon is a quart. Half of a quart is a pint. Half of a pint is a cup. Into an empty gallon container is poured a half-gallon of milk, plus a quart of milk, plus a pint of milk, plus a cup of milk. How much more milk is needed to fill the gallon container?

Understand Understand the problem.

"What information are we given?"

We are told that: half of a gallon = 1 half gallon, half of a half gallon = 1 quart, half of a quart = 1 pint, and half of a pint = 1 cup. We are also told that a half-gallon of milk, plus a quart of milk, plus a pint of milk, plus a cup of milk are poured into an empty gallon container.

"What are we asked to do?"

Determine how much more milk is needed to fill the gallon container.

Teacher Note: You may wish to have several empty containers on hand to help students visualize the differences in sizes.

Plan Make a plan.

"What problem-solving strategy will we use?"

We will *draw a diagram* to show how many cups are in a gallon, and we will *write equations* to convert each measurement of milk into cups. Then we will subtract the sum of the measurements from the number of cups in a gallon.

Solve Carry out the plan.

"Draw a diagram starting with the smallest unit, cups."

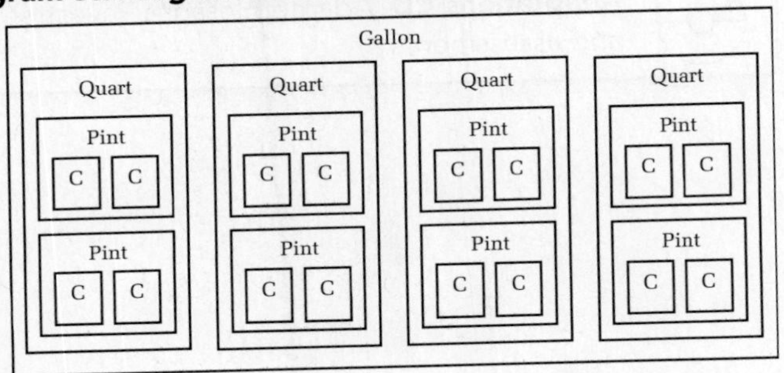

"According to our diagram, how many cups are in a gallon?"

sixteen

"Next, to determine how many cups of milk were poured into a gallon container, let's convert each measurement of milk into cups."

1 pint = 2 cups
1 quart = 2 pints = 4 cups
1 half gallon = 2 quarts = 4 pints = 8 cups

"Altogether, how many cups of milk were poured into the gallon container?"

8 cups + 4 cups + 2 cups + 1 cup = 15 cups

"How much more milk is needed to fill the gallon container?"

We subtract 16 − 15 to find that 1 more cup is needed.

Check Look back.

"Did we complete the task?"

Yes. We found how much more milk is needed to fill the gallon container (1 cup).

Teacher Note: You may wish to use empty containers to physically prove the solution.

LESSON

50

• Decimal Number Line (Tenths)
• Dividing by a Fraction

Power Up — *Building Power*

facts Power Up G

mental math

a. **Order of Operations:** $(8 \times 200) + (8 \times 25)$ 1800

b. **Number Sense:** $565 - 250$ 315

c. **Calculation:** $58 + 27$ 85

d. **Money:** \$1.45 + 99¢ \$2.44

e. **Fractional Parts:** $\frac{1}{2}$ of \$25.00 \$12.50

f. **Number Sense:** $\frac{5000}{10}$ 500

g. **Statistics:** Find the average of 134, 120, 96, and 98. 112

h. **Calculation:** 8×9, $+ 3$, $\div 3$, $- 1$, $\div 3$, $+ 1$, $\div 3$, $\div 3$ 1

problem solving Half of a gallon is a half gallon. Half of a half gallon is a quart. Half of a quart is a pint. Half of a pint is a cup. Into an empty gallon container is poured a half gallon of milk, plus a quart of milk, plus a pint of milk, plus a cup of milk. How much more milk is needed to fill the gallon container? 1 cup

New Concepts — *Increasing Knowledge*

decimal number line (tenths)

We can locate different kinds of numbers on the **number line.** We have learned to locate whole numbers, negative numbers, and fractions on the number line. We can also locate decimal numbers on the number line.

On the number line above, the distance between consecutive whole numbers has been divided into ten equal lengths. Each length is $\frac{1}{10}$ of the distance between consecutive whole numbers.

The arrow is pointing to a mark three spaces beyond the 1, so it is pointing to $1\frac{3}{10}$. We can rename $\frac{3}{10}$ as the decimal 0.3, so we can say that the arrow is pointing to the mark representing 1.3. When a unit has been divided into ten spaces, we normally use the decimal form instead of the fractional form to name the number represented by the mark.

Facts Reduce each fraction to lowest terms.

$\frac{2}{8} = \frac{1}{4}$	$\frac{4}{6} = \frac{2}{3}$	$\frac{6}{10} = \frac{3}{5}$	$\frac{2}{4} = \frac{1}{2}$	$\frac{5}{100} = \frac{1}{20}$	$\frac{9}{12} = \frac{3}{4}$
$\frac{4}{10} = \frac{2}{5}$	$\frac{4}{12} = \frac{1}{3}$	$\frac{2}{10} = \frac{1}{5}$	$\frac{3}{6} = \frac{1}{2}$	$\frac{25}{100} = \frac{1}{4}$	$\frac{3}{12} = \frac{1}{4}$
$\frac{4}{16} = \frac{1}{4}$	$\frac{3}{9} = \frac{1}{3}$	$\frac{6}{9} = \frac{2}{3}$	$\frac{4}{8} = \frac{1}{2}$	$\frac{2}{12} = \frac{1}{6}$	$\frac{6}{12} = \frac{1}{2}$
$\frac{8}{16} = \frac{1}{2}$	$\frac{2}{6} = \frac{1}{3}$	$\frac{8}{12} = \frac{2}{3}$	$\frac{6}{8} = \frac{3}{4}$	$\frac{5}{10} = \frac{1}{2}$	$\frac{75}{100} = \frac{3}{4}$

1 Power Up

Facts

Distribute **Power Up G** to students. See answers below.

Mental Math

Before students begin the Mental Math exercise, do this counting exercise as a class.

Count by 7s from 7 to 84.

Encourage students to share different ways to mentally compute these exercises. Strategies for exercises **b** and **d** are listed below.

b. Decompose 565

$550 - 250 + 15 = 300 + 15 = 315$

Subtract Hundreds

$500 - 200 = 300$ and $65 - 50 = 15$;
$300 + 15 = 315$

d. Change 99¢ to \$1, then Subtract 1¢

\$1.45 + \$1.00 = \$2.45;
\$2.45 − \$0.01 = \$2.44

Subtract 1¢ and add 1¢

\$1.45 − \$0.01 = \$1.44 and \$0.99 + \$0.01 = \$1.00; \$1.44 + \$1.00 = \$2.44

Problem Solving

Refer to **Power-Up Discussion**, p. 259B.

2 New Concepts

Instruction

A common error when working with number lines is to determine the interval of the number line by counting tick marks. For example, the number line at the right has nine tick marks between consecutive whole numbers, and some students may incorrectly conclude that the number line shows ninths.

Remind students to count equal lengths between consecutive numbers when determining the interval of a number line.

(continued)

2 New Concepts (Continued)

Example 1

Instruction

Before students name the location of the point, ask them to count the number of equal lengths between 6 and 7 or between 7 and 8. After students conclude that the number line shows tenths, ask them to name the decimal number that describes the location of the point.

Instruction

In the New Concept "dividing by a fraction," to help students understand why 3 is divided by $\frac{1}{4}$, ask them to explain how to solve this simpler problem.

"How many five dollar bills are equal to one ten dollar bill?" Divide the greater amount by the lesser amount; $\$10 \div \$5 = 2$

Example 2

Instruction

After learning that the answer is 8 pennies, ask students to discuss and share different ways to check the answer. Sample: Use repeated addition by adding $\frac{3}{4}$ eight different times. Since the denominators of the fractions are the same, the answer of the repeated addition is the sum of the numerators, or 3 times 8, written over 4. Because $\frac{24}{4} = 6$, the answer checks.

(continued)

Example 1

What decimal number is represented by point *y* on this number line?

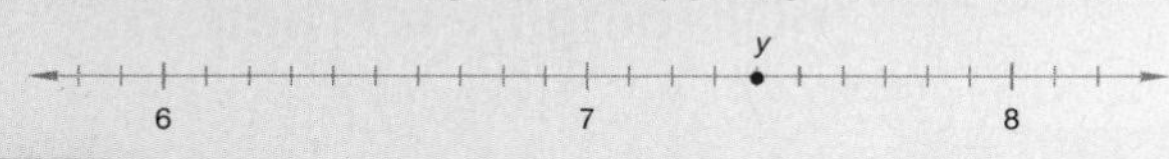

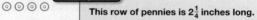

Solution

The distance from 7 to 8 has been divided into ten smaller segments. Point *y* is four segments to the right of the whole number 7. So point *y* represents $7\frac{4}{10}$. We write $7\frac{4}{10}$ as the decimal number **7.4**.

dividing by a fraction

The following question can be answered by dividing by a decimal number or by dividing by a fraction:

How many quarters are in three dollars?

If we think of a quarter as $\frac{1}{4}$ of a dollar, we have this division problem:

$$3 \div \frac{1}{4}$$

We solve this problem in two steps. First we answer the question, "How many quarters are in one dollar?" The answer is the reciprocal of $\frac{1}{4}$, which is $\frac{4}{1}$, which equals 4.

$$1 \div \frac{1}{4} = \frac{4}{1} = 4$$

Math Language

Two numbers whose product is 1 are **reciprocals.** $\frac{1}{4} \times \frac{4}{1} = 1$, so $\frac{1}{4}$ and $\frac{4}{1}$ are reciprocals.

For the second step, we use the answer to the question above to find the number of quarters in three dollars. There are four quarters in one dollar, and there are three times as many quarters in three dollars. We multiply 3 by 4 and find that there are 12 quarters in three dollars.

number of dollars → $3 \times 4 = 12$ ← number of quarters in one dollar; 12 ← number of quarters in three dollars

We will review the steps we took to solve the problem.

Original problem: How many quarters are in \$3? $\quad 3 \div \frac{1}{4}$

Step 1: Find the number of quarters in \$1. $\quad 1 \div \frac{1}{4} = 4$

Step 2: Use the number of quarters in \$1 to find the number in \$3. $\quad 3 \times 4 = 12$

Thinking Skill

Model

Draw a diagram to represent the number of quarters in \$3.

Example 2

This row of pennies is $2\frac{1}{4}$ inches long.

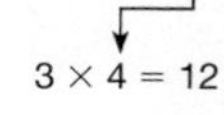

The diameter of a penny is $\frac{3}{4}$ of an inch. How many pennies are needed to make a row of pennies 6 inches long?

260 *Saxon Math Course 1*

Math Background

A number of different methods involving equivalent division problems can be used when dividing by a fraction. For example, three different methods can used to find $4 \div \frac{2}{3}$.

1. Multiply both 4 and $\frac{2}{3}$ by 3 (the denominator). The result is $12 \div 2$, which equals 6.
2. Divide both 4 and $\frac{2}{3}$ by 2 (the numerator). The result is $2 \div \frac{1}{3}$. Since there are three $\frac{1}{3}$s in 1, the number of $\frac{1}{3}$s in 2 is twice as many, which is 6.
3. Multiply both 4 and $\frac{2}{3}$ by $\frac{3}{2}$ (the reciprocal of $\frac{2}{3}$). The result is $6 \div 1$, which is

The third method is the most commonly used method to divide by a fraction. When that method is used, the quotient is immediately obvious once the dividend has been multiplied by the reciprocal of the divisor.

Solution

In effect, this problem asks, "How many $\frac{3}{4}$-inch segments are in 6 inches?" We can write the question this way:

$$6 \div \frac{3}{4}$$

We will take two steps. First we will find the number of pennies (the number of $\frac{3}{4}$-inch segments) in 1 inch. The number of $\frac{3}{4}$s in 1 is the reciprocal of $\frac{3}{4}$, which is $\frac{4}{3}$.

$$1 \div \frac{3}{4} = \frac{4}{3}$$

We will not convert $\frac{4}{3}$ to the mixed number $1\frac{1}{3}$. Instead, we will use $\frac{4}{3}$ in the second step of the solution. Since there are $\frac{4}{3}$ pennies in 1 inch, there are six times as many in 6 inches. So we multiply 6 by $\frac{4}{3}$.

$$6 \times \frac{4}{3} = \frac{24}{3} = 8$$

We find there are **8 pennies** in a 6-inch row. We will review the steps of the solution.

Thinking Skill

Connect

How many pennies are in a row that is 1 foot long?
16 pennies

Original problem: How many $\frac{3}{4}$s are in 6? $\quad 6 \div \frac{3}{4}$

Step 1: Find the number of $\frac{3}{4}$s in 1. $\quad 1 \div \frac{3}{4} = \frac{4}{3}$

Step 2: Use the number of $\frac{3}{4}$s in 1 to find the number of $\frac{3}{4}$s in 6. Then simplify the answer. $\quad 6 \times \frac{4}{3} = \frac{24}{3} = 8$

Practice Set

a. 0.1
b. 0.5
c. 0.9
d. 1.2
e. 1.6
f. 1.8

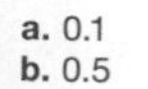

h. Sample:
Original Problem:
$12 \div \frac{3}{8}$
Step 1:
$1 \div \frac{3}{8} = \frac{8}{3}$
Step 2:
$12 \times \frac{8}{3} = 32$

▶ *Connect* To which decimal number is each arrow pointing?

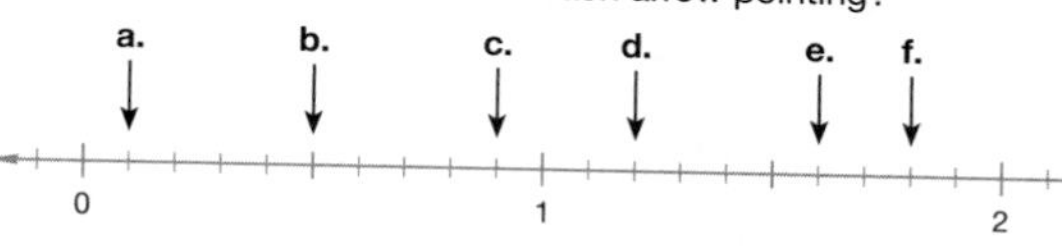

▶ **g.** *Formulate* Write and solve a division problem to find the number of quarters in four dollars. Use $\frac{1}{4}$ instead of 0.25 for a quarter. Follow this pattern:

Original Problem $4 \div \frac{1}{4}$
Step 1 $1 \div \frac{1}{4} = 4$
Step 2 $4 \times 4 = 16$

h. *Formulate* Write and solve a fraction division problem for this question:
Pads of writing paper were stacked 12 inches high on a shelf. The thickness of each pad was $\frac{3}{8}$ of an inch. How many pads were in a 12-inch stack? 32 pads

▶ See Math Conversations in the sidebar.

English Learners

Explain that a **segment** is a part of a line. Draw a triangle and a number line on the board and demonstrate each line segment. Say,

"A segment is a part or piece of a line. Look at the number line in Example 1. The line has been divided into ten small pieces between 7 and 8. Each of these pieces is a segment."

Ask a volunteer to explain how a line segment is different from a line.

2 New Concepts *(Continued)*

Practice Set

Problems a–f Error Alert

It is important for students to recognize the divisions into which the number line is divided.

"On the number line, how many equal units are between 0 and 1 and between 1 and 2?" ten

"What decimal part of 1 does each tick mark represent?" one tenth or 0.1

Problem g Formulate

"Explain how mental math can be used to check the answer." Sample: Since there are 4 quarters in one dollar, there are 8 quarters in two dollars, 12 quarters in three dollars, and 16 quarters in four dollars.

3 Written Practice

Math Conversations

Discussion opportunities are provided below.

Problem 1 Predict

Encourage students to make a table and look for a pattern to solve this problem.

Sample:

Number of Odd Numbers	1	2	3	4	5	6	
Sum	1	4	9	16	25	36	

Problem 2 Connect

Extend the Problem

"Describe a method we could use to check the answer." Sample: Multiply 6 by $\frac{8}{3}$, the reciprocal of the divisor; $6 \div \frac{3}{8} = 6 \times \frac{8}{3} = \frac{48}{3} = 16$.

Problem 11 Analyze

"The divisor is not a whole number. What number should we multiply the dividend and the divisor by to shift the decimal point two places to the right?" 100

Problem 12 Analyze

"How many places must we shift the decimal point, and in which direction, to make the divisor a whole number?" one place to the right

"What number should we multiply the dividend and the divisor by to shift both decimal points one place to the right?" 10

Errors and Misconceptions

Problems 4a and 4b

To help make the decimal numbers easier to compare, encourage students to attach extra zeros as needed so that both numbers have the same number of decimal places.

Problem 17

Point out to students that $1 \text{ m} \times 1 \text{ m} = 1 \text{ m}^2$ (one square meter). Students should infer from this fact that since 1 m = 100 cm, they can multiply 100 cm by 100 cm to find the number of square centimeters equal to one square meter.

(continued)

Written Practice *Strengthening Concepts*

▶ * **1.** (10) Predict The first three positive odd numbers are 1, 3, and 5. Their sum is 9. The first five positive odd numbers are 1, 3, 5, 7, and 9. Their sum is 25. What is the sum of the first ten positive odd numbers? What strategy did you use to solve this problem? 100; Find a pattern

▶ * **2.** (50) Connect Jack keeps his music CDs stacked in plastic boxes $\frac{3}{8}$ inch thick. Use the method taught in this lesson to find the number of boxes in a stack 6 inches tall. 16 boxes

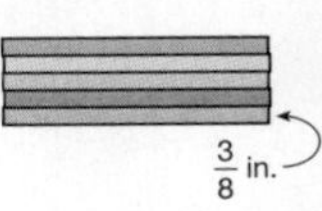

3. (15) The game has 12 three-minute rounds. If the players stop after two minutes of the twelfth round, for how many minutes did they play? 35 minutes

▶ **4.** (44) Compare:

a. 3.4 ⊘ 3.389 (>)   b. 0.60 ⊜ 0.600 (=)

Find each unknown number:

Math Language

Symbols

$\sqrt{\ }$ means *square root.* The **square root** of a number is one of two equal factors of the number.

5. (15) $7.25 + 2 + w = \sqrt{100}$ 0.75

6. (43) $6w = 0.144$ 0.024

7. (43) $w + \frac{5}{12} = 1^2$ $\frac{7}{12}$

* **8.** (43) $6\frac{1}{8} - x = 1\frac{7}{8}$ $4\frac{1}{4}$

9. (41) The book cost $20.00. The sales-tax rate was 7%. What was the total cost of the book including sales tax? $21.40

10. (38) $1 - 0.97$ 0.03

▶* **11.** (49) $0.12\overline{)7.2}$ 60

▶* **12.** (49) $0.4\overline{)7}$ 17.5

13. (45) $6\overline{)0.138}$ 0.023

14. (39) (3.75)(2.4) 9

15. (42) $\frac{3}{4} = \frac{?}{24}$ 18

16. (34) Which digit in 4.637 is in the same place as the 2 in 85.21? 6

▶ **17.** (31) One hundred centimeters equals one meter. How many square centimeters equal one square meter? 10,000 square centimeters

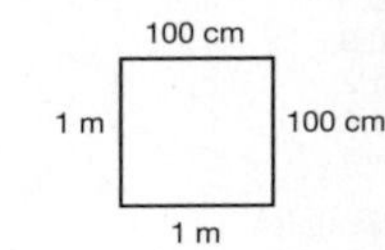

18. (30) What is the least common multiple of 6 and 9? 18

19. (26) $6\frac{5}{8} + 4\frac{5}{8}$ $11\frac{1}{4}$

20. (29) $\frac{8}{3} \cdot \frac{3}{1}$ 8

21. (29) $\frac{2}{3} \cdot \frac{3}{4}$ $\frac{1}{2}$

* **22.** (47) Justify The diameter of a soup can is about 7 cm. The label wraps around the can. About how many centimeters long must the label be to go all the way around the soup can? (Use $\frac{22}{7}$ for π.) Explain how to mentally check whether your answer is reasonable.

22. 22 cm; π is a little more than 3, and 3×7 cm is 21 cm. So 22 cm is reasonable.

* **23.** (18) Find the average of 2.4, 6.3, and 5.7. 4.8

* **24.** (49) Find the number of quarters in $8.75 by dividing 8.75 by 0.25. 35

▶ See Math Conversations in the sidebar.

▶ * 25. (50) **Connect** What decimal number corresponds to point A on this number line? 5.3

26. (no lesson ref) $\frac{2 \cdot 3 \cdot 5 \cdot 7}{2 \cdot 5}$ 21

27. (46) 0.375×100 37.5

* 28. (42) Rename $\frac{1}{3}$ as a fraction with 6 as the denominator. Then subtract the renamed fraction from $\frac{5}{6}$. Reduce the answer. $\frac{2}{6}$; $\frac{5}{6} - \frac{2}{6} = \frac{3}{6} = \frac{1}{2}$

* 29. (50) **Estimate** Points x, y, and z are three points on this number line. Refer to the number line to answer the questions that follow.

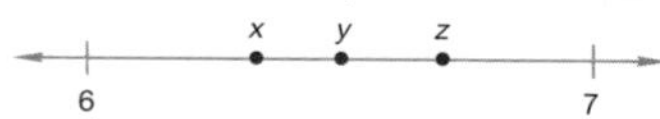

a. Which point is halfway between 6 and 7? *y*

b. Which point corresponds to $6\frac{7}{10}$? *z*

c. Of the points x, y, and z, which point corresponds to the number that is closest to 6? *x*

30. (21) **Clarify** Which of these numbers is divisible by both 2 and 5? C

A 552 **B** 255 **C** 250 **D** 525

Early Finishers
Real-World Application

Alex is planning a bicycle trip with his family. They want to ride a total of 195 miles through Texas seeing the sights. Alex and his family plan to ride five hours each day. They have been averaging 13 miles per hour on their training rides.

a. How many miles should they expect to ride in one day? $13 \times 5 =$ 65 miles

b. Should Alex's family be able to complete the ride in three days? Yes, $65 \times 3 = 195$ miles

Lesson 50 263

▶ See Math Conversations in the sidebar.

3 Written Practice (Continued)

Math Conversations

Discussion opportunities are provided below.

Problem 25 Connect

"On a number line, how do the numbers change as you move from left to right?" the numbers increase or become bigger

"How do the numbers change as you move from right to left?" the numbers decrease or become smaller

After completing the problem, ask,

"How can we check our answer?" Sample: If the location of the point was determined by counting up from 5 by tenths, we can count down from 6 by tenths to check the answer.

Looking Forward

Dividing a whole number by a fraction prepares students for:

Lesson 54, dividing fractions.

Lesson 68, dividing a mixed number by a whole number or a mixed number.

Lesson 70, reducing fractions before multiplying to simplify multiplication or division of fractions problems.

Lesson 72, using a fractions chart to recall division of fractions.

Lesson 115, writing fractional percents as fractions.

Assessment

30–40 minutes

For use after Lesson 50

Distribute **Cumulative Test 9** to each student. Two versions of the test are available in *Saxon Math Course 1 Course Assessments Book*. Have students complete the **Power-Up Test** first. Allow 10 minutes. Then have students work the 20 numbered items on the **Cumulative Test.** Students may use copies of the answer sheet to record their work. Track individual and class progress with the **Test Analysis** forms.

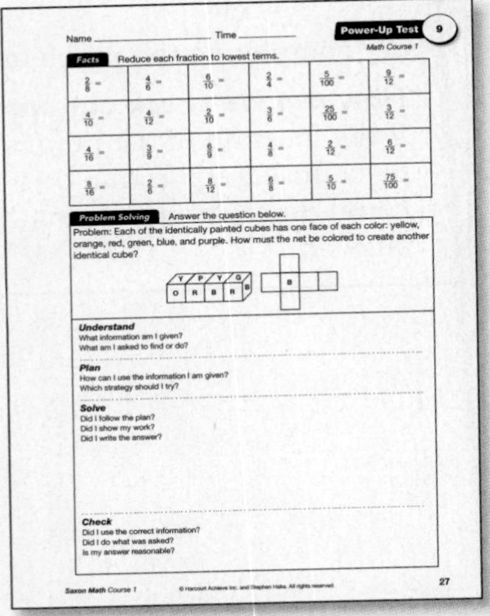

Name ____ Time ____

Power-Up Test 9

Math Course 1

Facts — Reduce each fraction to lowest terms.

Problem Solving — Answer the question below.

Problem: Each of the identically painted cubes has one face of each color: yellow, orange, red, green, blue, and purple. How must the net be colored to create another identical cube?

Understand
What information am I given?
What am I asked to find or do?

Plan
How can I use the information I am given?
Which strategy should I try?

Solve
Did I follow the plan?
Did I show my work?
Did I write the answer?

Check
Did I use the correct information?
Did I do what was asked?
Is my answer reasonable?

Saxon Math Course 1 — © Harcourt Achieve Inc. and Stephen Hake. All rights reserved. — 27

Power-Up Test 9

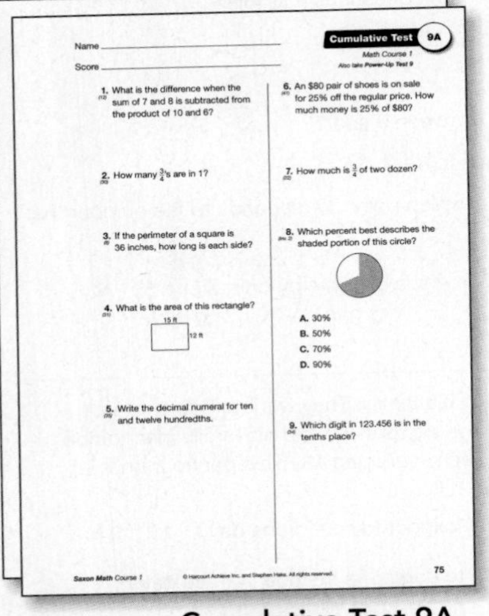

Name ____

Score ____

Cumulative Test 9A

Math Course 1

Also take Power-Up Test 9

1. What is the difference when the sum of 7 and 8 is subtracted from the product of 10 and 6?

2. How many $\frac{2}{3}$'s are in 1?

3. If the perimeter of a square is 36 inches, how long is each side?

4. What is the area of this rectangle?

5. Write the decimal numeral for ten and twelve hundredths.

6. An $80 pair of shoes is on sale for 25% off the regular price. How much money is 25% of $80?

7. How much is $\frac{2}{3}$ of two dozen?

8. Which percent best describes the shaded portion of this circle?

A. 30%
B. 50%
C. 70%
D. 90%

9. Which digit in 123.456 is in the tenths place?

Saxon Math Course 1 — © Harcourt Achieve Inc. and Stephen Hake. All rights reserved. — 75

Cumulative Test 9A

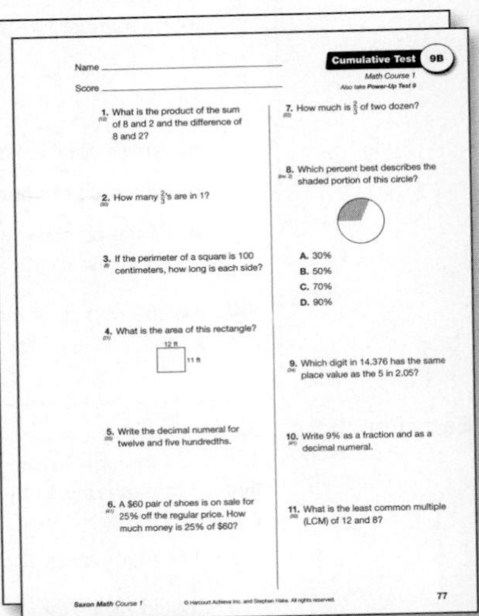

Name ____

Score ____

Cumulative Test 9B

Math Course 1

Also take Power-Up Test 9

1. What is the product of the sum of 8 and 2 and the difference of 8 and 2?

2. How many $\frac{2}{5}$'s are in 1?

3. If the perimeter of a square is 100 centimeters, how long is each side?

4. What is the area of this rectangle?

5. Write the decimal numeral for twelve and five hundredths.

6. A $60 pair of shoes is on sale for 25% off the regular price. How much money is 25% of $60?

7. How much is $\frac{2}{3}$ of two dozen?

8. Which percent best describes the shaded portion of this circle?

A. 30%
B. 50%
C. 70%
D. 90%

9. Which digit in 14.376 has the same place value as the 5 in 2.05?

10. Write 9% as a fraction and as a decimal numeral.

11. What is the least common multiple (LCM) of 12 and 8?

Saxon Math Course 1 — © Harcourt Achieve Inc. and Stephen Hake. All rights reserved. — 77

Alternative Cumulative Test 9B

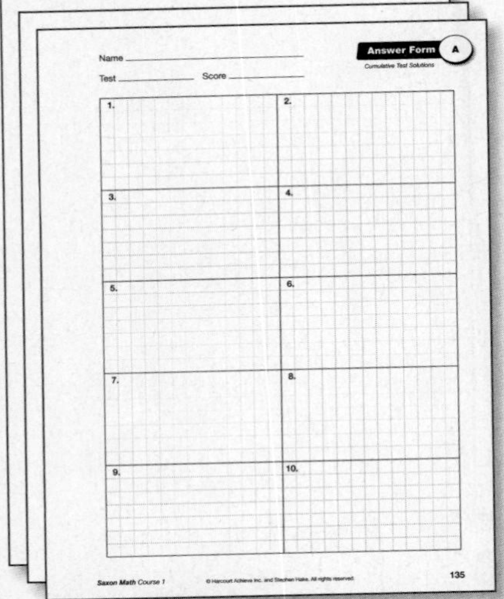

Name ____

Test ____ Score ____

Answer Form A

Cumulative Test Solutions

1. 2. 3. 4. 5. 6. 7. 8. 9. 10.

Saxon Math Course 1 — © Harcourt Achieve Inc. and Stephen Hake. All rights reserved. — 135

Optional Answer Forms

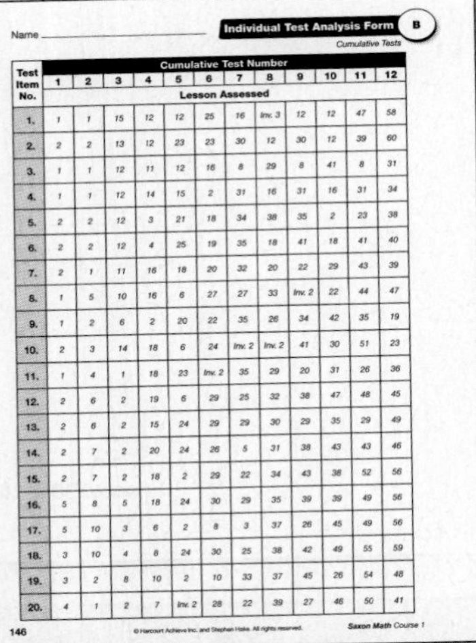

Name ____

Individual Test Analysis Form B

Cumulative Tests

Test Item No.	Cumulative Test Number 1	2	3	4	5	6	7	8	9	10	11	12
	Lesson Assessed											
1.	1	1	15	12	12	25	16	Inv. 3	12	12	47	58
2.	2	2	13	12	23	23	30	12	30	12	39	60
3.	1	1	12	11	12	16	8	29	8	41	8	31
4.	1	1	12	14	15	2	31	16	31	16	31	34
5.	2	2	12	3	21	18	34	38	35	2	23	38
6.	2	2	12	4	25	19	35	18	41	18	41	40
7.	2	1	11	16	18	20	32	20	22	29	43	39
8.	1	5	10	16	6	27	27	33	Inv. 2	22	44	47
9.	1	2	6	2	20	22	35	26	34	42	35	19
10.	2	3	14	18	6	24	Inv. 2	Inv. 2	41	30	51	23
11.	1	4	1	18	23	Inv. 2	35	29	20	31	26	36
12.	2	6	2	19	6	29	25	32	38	47	48	45
13.	2	6	2	15	24	29	29	30	29	35	29	49
14.	2	7	2	20	24	26	5	31	38	43	43	46
15.	2	7	2	18	2	29	22	34	43	38	52	56
16.	5	8	5	18	24	30	29	35	39	39	49	56
17.	5	10	3	6	2	8	3	37	26	45	49	56
18.	3	10	4	8	24	30	25	38	42	49	55	59
19.	3	2	8	10	2	10	33	37	45	26	54	48
20.	4	1	2	7	Inv. 2	28	22	39	27	46	50	41

146 — © Harcourt Achieve Inc. and Stephen Hake. All rights reserved. — Saxon Math Course 1

Individual Test Analysis Form

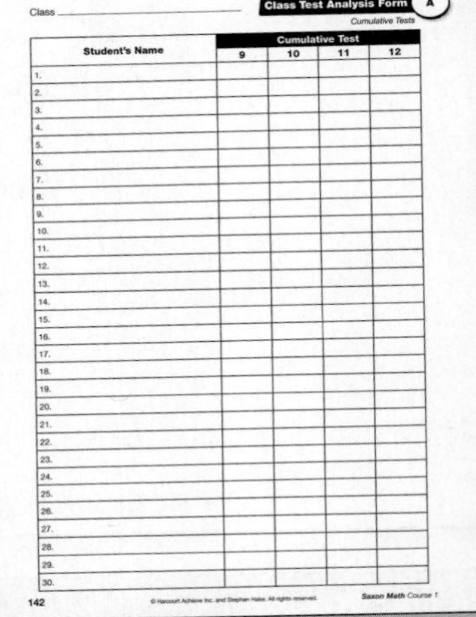

Class ____

Class Test Analysis Form A

Cumulative Tests

Student's Name	Cumulative Test 9	10	11	12
1.				
2.				
3.				
4.				
5.				
6.				
7.				
8.				
9.				
10.				
11.				
12.				
13.				
14.				
15.				
16.				
17.				
18.				
19.				
20.				
21.				
22.				
23.				
24.				
25.				
26.				
27.				
28.				
29.				
30.				

142 — © Harcourt Achieve Inc. and Stephen Hake. All rights reserved. — Saxon Math Course 1

Class Test Analysis Form

Reteaching

Students who score below 80% on the assessment may be in need of reteaching. Look for the causes of student mistakes. If errors are conceptual, refer to the *Reteaching Masters* for reteaching.

Customized Benchmark Assessment

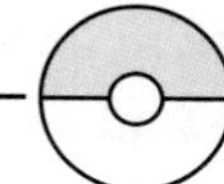

You can develop customized benchmark tests using the Test Generator located on the *Test & Practice Generator CD.*

This chart shows the lesson, the standard, and the test item question that can be found on the *Test & Practice Generator CD.*

LESSON	NEW CONCEPTS	LOCAL STANDARD	TEST ITEM ON CD
41	• Finding a Percent of a Number		5.41.1
42	• Renaming Fractions by Multiplying by 1		5.42.1
43	• Equivalent Division Problems		5.43.1
	• Finding Unknowns in Fraction and Decimal Problems		5.43.2
44	• Simplifying Decimal Numbers		5.44.1
	• Comparing Decimal Numbers		5.44.2
45	• Dividing a Decimal Number by a Whole Number		5.45.1
46	• Writing Decimal Numbers in Expanded Notation		5.46.1
	• Mentally Multiplying Decimals Numbers by 10 and 100		5.46.2
47	• Circumference		5.47.1
	• Pi (π)		5.47.2
48	• Subtracting Mixed Numbers with Regrouping, Part 1		5.48.1
49	• Dividing by a Decimal Number		5.49.1
50	• Decimal Number Line (Tenths)		5.50.1
	• Dividing by a Fraction		5.50.2

Using the Test Generator CD

- Develop tests in both English and Spanish.
- Choose from multiple-choice and free-response test items.
- Clone test items to create multiple versions of the same test.
- View and edit test items to make and save your own questions.
- Administer assessments through paper tests or over a school LAN.
- Monitor student progress through a variety of individual and class reports —for both diagnosing and assessing standards mastery.

Performance Task 9

The Veterinarian's Office

Assign after Lesson 50 and Test 9

Objectives

- Add and subtract fractions and mixed numbers.
- Communicate ideas through writing.

Materials

Performance Tasks 9A and **9B**

Preparation

Make copies of **Performance Tasks 9A** and **9B.** (One of each per student.)

Time Requirement

30–60 minutes; Begin in class and complete at home.

Task

Explain to students that for this task they will be learning about the work of a volunteer at a veterinarian's office. Students will answer questions about the weight of a puppy, the length of trails for dog walks, and the amount of food needed to feed the dogs. They will be required to use estimation and justify answers about the amount of food dogs eat. Point out that all of the information students need is on **Performance Tasks 9A** and **9B.**

Criteria for Evidence of Learning

- Completes table accurately.
- Adds and subtracts fractions and mixed numbers correctly.
- Communicates ideas clearly through writing.

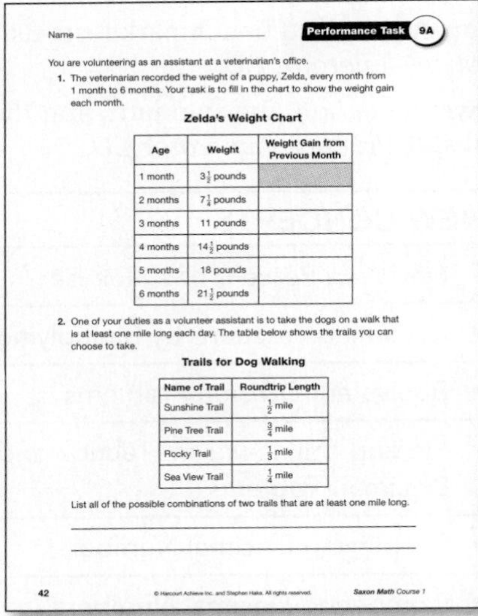

Name ____________________ **Performance Task 9A**

You are volunteering as an assistant at a veterinarian's office.

1. The veterinarian recorded the weight of a puppy, Zelda, every month from 1 month to 6 months. Your task is to fill in the chart to show the weight gain each month.

Zelda's Weight Chart

Age	Weight	Weight Gain from Previous Month
1 month	$3\frac{1}{2}$ pounds	
2 months	$7\frac{1}{4}$ pounds	
3 months	11 pounds	
4 months	$14\frac{1}{2}$ pounds	
5 months	18 pounds	
6 months	$21\frac{1}{2}$ pounds	

2. One of your duties as a volunteer assistant is to take the dogs on a walk that is at least one mile long each day. The table below shows the trails you can choose to take.

Trails for Dog Walking

Name of Trail	Roundtrip Length
Sunshine Trail	$\frac{1}{2}$ mile
Pine Tree Trail	$\frac{3}{4}$ mile
Rocky Trail	$\frac{1}{3}$ mile
Sea View Trail	$\frac{1}{4}$ mile

List all of the possible combinations of two trails that are at least one mile long.

____

____

42 © Harcourt Achieve Inc. and Stephen Hake. All rights reserved. *Saxon Math Course 1*

Performance Task 9A

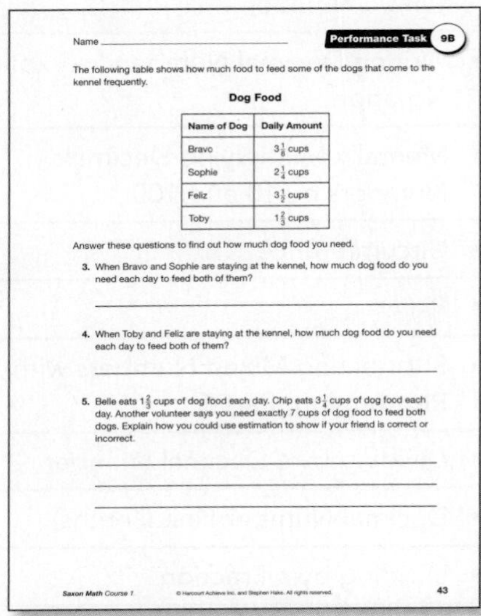

Name ____________________ **Performance Task 9B**

The following table shows how much food to feed some of the dogs that come to the kennel frequently.

Dog Food

Name of Dog	Daily Amount
Bravo	$3\frac{1}{8}$ cups
Sophie	$2\frac{1}{4}$ cups
Feliz	$3\frac{1}{2}$ cups
Toby	$1\frac{2}{3}$ cups

Answer these questions to find out how much dog food you need.

3. When Bravo and Sophie are staying at the kennel, how much dog food do you need each day to feed both of them?

____

4. When Toby and Feliz are staying at the kennel, how much dog food do you need each day to feed both of them?

____

5. Belle eats $1\frac{2}{3}$ cups of dog food each day. Chip eats $3\frac{1}{4}$ cups of dog food each day. Another volunteer says you need exactly 7 cups of dog food to feed both dogs. Explain how you could use estimation to show if your friend is correct or incorrect.

____

____

____

Saxon Math Course 1 © Harcourt Achieve Inc. and Stephen Hake. All rights reserved. 43

Performance Task 9B

Meeting Standards

National Council of Teachers of Mathematics (NCTM)

Numbers and Operations

NO.1a Work flexibly with fractions, decimals, and percents to solve problems

NO.2a Understand the meaning and effects of arithmetic operations with fractions, decimals, and integers

NO.3a Select appropriate methods and tools for computing with fractions and decimals from among mental computation, estimation, calculators or computers, and paper and pencil, depending on the situation, and apply the selected methods

Communication

CM.3a Organize and consolidate their mathematical thinking through communication

Representation

RE.5a Create and use representations to organize, record, and communicate mathematical ideas

Focus on
• Displaying Data

Objectives

- Create horizontal and vertical bar graphs, pictographs, and circle graphs to display qualitative data
- Create line plots and stem-and-leaf plots to display quantitative data.
- Find the mean, median, mode, and range for a set of data points.

Lesson Preparation

Materials

- **Manipulative kit: compasses, protractors**

Math Language

New	Maintain	English Learners (ESL)
bimodal	circle graph	assign
central angle	line plot	
mean		
median		
mode		
pictograph		
range		
sector		
stem-and-leaf plot		

Technology Resources

Student eBook Complete student textbook in electronic format.

Resources and Planner CD Assessment, reteaching, and instructional masters, plus a pacing calendar with standards.

Test and Practice Generator CD Create additional practice sheets and custom-made tests.

www.SaxonPublishers.com Visit for more student activities and planning materials.

Inclusion

Adaptations CD Adapted lessons, investigations, practice and assessments.

Meeting Standards

National Council of Teachers of Mathematics (NCTM)

Data Analysis and Probability

DP.1b Select, create, and use appropriate graphical representations of data, including histograms, box plots, and scatterplots

DP.2a Find, use, and interpret measures of center and spread, including mean and interquartile range

DP.2b Discuss and understand the correspondence between data sets and their graphical representations, especially histograms, stem-and-leaf plots, box plots, and scatterplots

Representation

RE.5a Create and use representations to organize, record, and communicate mathematical ideas

INVESTIGATION 5

In this investigation, students will compare various ways to display data.

Part 1: Displaying Qualitative Data

Instruction

Remind students that in Investigation 4, they learned that qualitative data often involves categories, such as the month of a person's birth or a person's favorite season of the year.

For any pictograph, it is essential for students to recognize the key and apply the relationship it describes.

"What is the key of a pictograph?" A key explains what each symbol of a pictograph represents.

"For this pictograph, what does each symbol represent?" one million cars or trucks

Math Conversations

Discussion opportunities are provided below.

Problem 1 **Conclude**

Before drawing the graph, ask students to describe how to make a horizontal bar graph and name the different components (such as a scale, axes labels and a title) that should be a part of every bar graph.

Problem 2 **Conclude**

Challenge students to decide if the fraction represents an actual number of vehicles, or an approximation, and explain why. An approximation; the data displayed by either graph are rounded to the nearest million.

Instruction

An important concept of circle graphs for students to remember is that the entire circle represents 1.

For example, if the sectors of a circle graph display percents, the sum of the percents should be 100% (unless the percents have been rounded) because 100% and 1 are equivalent—they are different names for the same number.

If the sectors of a circle graph display fractions, the sum of the fractions should be 1.

(continued)

(continued)

INVESTIGATION 5

Focus on

• Displaying Data

In this investigation we will compare various ways to display data.

part 1: displaying qualitative data

We have already displayed data with bar graphs and circle graphs. Now we will further investigate circle graphs and consider another graph called a **pictograph.**

There are four states that produce most of the cars and trucks made in the United States. One year's car and truck production from these states and others is displayed in the pictograph below.

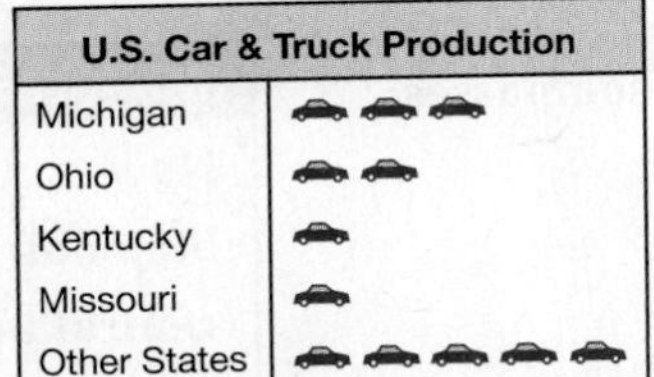

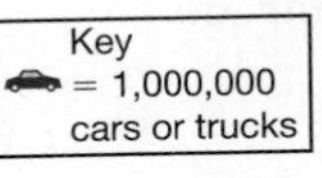

In a pictograph, pictured objects represent the data being counted. Each object represents a certain number of units of data, as indicated in the key. The two cars by Ohio, for example, indicate that 2,000,000 cars and trucks were produced in Ohio that year.

Conclude How many cars and trucks are produced in Michigan? In the four named states? In the nation? 3,000,000; 7,000,000; 12,000,000

▶ 1. **Conclude** Display the car and truck production data with a horizontal bar graph.

▶ 2. **Conclude** What fraction of U.S. car and truck production took place in Michigan? $\frac{1}{4}$ took place in Michigan

Another way to display qualitative data is in a **circle graph.** In a circle graph each category corresponds to a **sector** of the circle. Think of a circle as a pie; a sector is simply a slice of the pie. We use circle graphs when we are interested in the fraction of the group represented by each category and not so interested in the particular number of units in each category. Another name for a circle graph is a **pie chart.**

1. U.S. Car & Truck Production (in millions)

Michigan
Ohio
Kentucky
Missouri
Other States

1 2 3 4 5

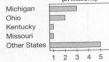

▶ See Math Conversations in the sidebar.

We have used a template with equal sectors to help us sketch a circle graph. We can also sketch circle graphs with the help of a compass and protractor. We can calculate the angle of each sector (section) of the circle if we know the fraction of the whole each part represents.

The sectors of a circle graph form central angles. A **central angle** has its vertex on the center of the circle and its rays are radii of the circle. Since the central angles of a full circle total 360°, the number of degrees in a fraction of a circle is the fraction times 360°. For example, if each sector is $\frac{1}{4}$ of the circle, then each central angle measures 90°.

$$\frac{1}{4} \times 360° = 90°$$

To construct a circle graph, we need to determine how many degrees to assign each category. Our bar graph shows that a total of 12 million cars and trucks were produced. First we find the fraction of cars and trucks produced in each state. Then we multiply by 360°.

Category	Count (millions)	Fraction
Michigan	3	$\frac{3}{12}$
Ohio	2	$\frac{2}{12}$
Kentucky	1	$\frac{1}{12}$
Missouri	1	$\frac{1}{12}$
Other States	5	$\frac{5}{12}$
Total	12	$\frac{12}{12}$

The sector of the circle graph representing Michigan will cover 90°.

$$\frac{3}{12} \times 360° = 90°$$

3. Determine the central angle measures of sectors for each category. Michigan 90°, Ohio 60°, Kentucky 30°, Missouri 30°, Other States 150°

▸ 4. Sketch the circle graph by following these instructions: Use a compass to draw a circle, then mark the center. Position the center of the protractor over the center of the circle and draw a 90° sector for Michigan. Continue around the circle drawing the appropriate angle measure for each category.

▸ 5. Compare the pictograph, bar graph, and circle graph. What are the benefits of each type of display? Sample: The pictograph shows the comparison between states using pictures. The bar graph also shows the comparison, but with bars instead of pictures. The circle graph shows production by a percent of the whole. We see that four states produce the majority of cars and trucks in the United States.

▸ See Math Conversations in the sidebar.

Part 1: Displaying Qualitative Data *(continued)*

Math Conversations

Discussion opportunities are provided below.

Instruction

"Explain how to multiply $\frac{3}{12}$ by 360°."

Sample: Write 360° as the numerator of a fraction that has a denominator of 1. Multiply the numerators and multiply the denominators, then use division and write the quotient in simplest form.

"Since $\frac{3}{12}$ of the circle represents 90°, how many degrees does $\frac{1}{12}$ of the circle represent? Use mental math." 30° (90° ÷ 3)

Problem 4

Students will need a compass and a protractor to complete the activity.

Problem 5

Invite volunteers to record the benefits of each type of graph in lists at the board.

English Learners

Tell students that the word **assign** means "to give to." Say:

"When a teacher assigns homework, he or she gives you homework."

Write the following on the board:

$$\frac{1}{4} \times 360° = 90°$$

Tell students that when they make a circle graph, they assign a number of degrees to each fraction of the circle. Write the following fractions on the board:

$$\frac{1}{2} \quad \frac{1}{5} \quad \frac{1}{12}$$

"If we are making a circle graph, what number of degrees would we assign to each of these fractions?"

Ask volunteers to assign degrees to each fraction.

$\frac{1}{2} \times 360° = 180°$, $\frac{1}{5} \times 360° = 72°$, $\frac{1}{12} \times 360° = 30°$

Part 2: Displaying Qualitative Data

Instruction

Remind students of their work in Investigation 4, in which they learned that numbers are often used to represent quantitative data, such as the number of students in a school, or the population of a city, state, or country.

Direct the students' attention to the test scores line plot and ask,

"Why does the line plot display 18 x's?"

The 18 x's represent 18 test scores.

Remind students that on a line plot such as this, the relationship of the number test scores to the number of x's is a 1 to 1 relationship. Point out that such a relationship is not true for all types of graphs. For example, each symbol on a pictograph often represents more than 1.

To remind students about the measures of central tendency, write the set of numbers {2, 3, 3, 8} on the board or overhead. Then ask students to use mental math to name each measure and explain how they found each measure.

mean: $(2 + 3 + 3 + 8) \div 4 = 4$
median: $(3 + 3) \div 2 = 3$
mode: 3
range: $8 - 2 = 6$

Make sure students understand that if a set of data, such as test scores, for example, consist of an even number of scores, the median is the mean or average of the two middle numbers.

(continued)

part 2: displaying quantitative data

We now turn to quantitative data. Quantitative data consists of individual measurements or numbers called **data points.** When there are many possible values for data points, we can group them in intervals and display the data in a histogram as we did in Investigation 1.

When we group data in intervals, however, the individual data points disappear. In order to display the individual data points, we can use a **line plot** as we did in Investigation 4.

Suppose 18 students take a test that has 20 possible points. Their scores, listed in increasing order, are

5, 8, 8, 10, 10, 11, 12, 12, 12, 12, 13, 13, 14, 16, 17, 17, 18, 19

We represent these data in the line plot below.

Reading Math
Each x in a line plot represents one individual data point.

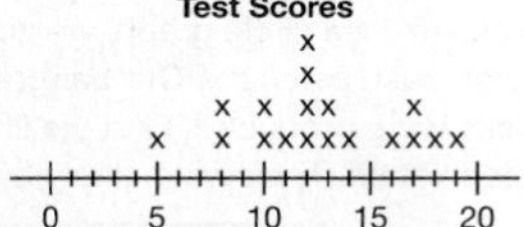

When describing numerical data, we often use terms such as **mean, median, mode,** and **range** which are defined below.

Mean: The average of the numbers.

Median: The middle number when the data are arranged in numerical order.

Mode: The most frequently occurring number.

Range: The difference between the greatest and least of the numbers.

To find the mean of the test scores above, we add the 18 scores and divide the sum by 18. The mean is about 12.6.

To find the median, we look for the middle score. If the number of scores were an odd number, we would simply select the middle score. But the number of scores is an even number, 18. Therefore, we use the average of the ninth and tenth scores for the median. We find that the ninth and tenth scores are both 12, so the median score is 12.

From the line plot we can easily see that the most common score is 12. So the mode of the test scores is 12.

We also see that the scores range from 5 to 19, so the range is 19–5, which is 14. That is, 14 points separate the lowest and highest score.

e student work.

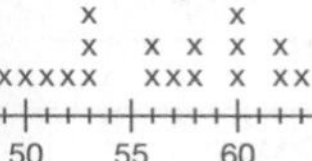

Leaf

| 789
| 0123336678
| 000223

6. **Explain** The daily high temperatures in degrees Fahrenheit for 20 days in a row are listed below. Organize the data by writing the temperatures in increasing order and display them in a line plot. Explain how you chose the values for the scale on your line plot.

60, 52, 49, 51, 47, 53, 62, 60, 57, 56,
58, 56, 63, 58, 53, 50, 48, 60, 62, 53

7. What is the median of the temperatures in problem **6?** 56°

8. The distribution of the temperatures in problem **6** is **bimodal** because there are two modes. What are the two modes? 53° and 60°

9. What is the range of the temperatures? (In this case, the range is the difference between the lowest temperature and the highest temperature.) 16 degrees

10. Quantitative data can be displayed in **stem-and-leaf plots.** The beginning of a stem-and-leaf plot for the data in problem **6** is shown below. The "stems" are the tens digits of the data points. The "leaves" for each stem are all the ones digits in the data points that begin with that stem.

We have plotted the data points for these heights: 47, 48, 49, 50, 51, 52, 53. Copy this plot. Then insert the rest of the temperatures from problem **6.**

Stem	Leaf
4	789
5	0123

11. Compare the stem-and-leaf plot from problem **10** to the line plot of the same data. Discuss the benefits of each type of display.
See student work.

extension Consider a problem to solve by gathering data. State the problem. Then conduct a study. Organize the collected data. Select two ways to display the data and explain your choices. Compare the two displays. Which would you use to present your study to your class? Interpret the data. Does the gathered data help to solve a problem or is it inconclusive?

▶ See Math Conversations in the sidebar.

Part 2: Displaying Qualitative Data *(continued)*

Math Conversations

Discussion opportunities are provided below.

Problem 6 Explain

"In the set of temperatures, what is the highest temperature?" 63°F

"What is the lowest temperature?" 47°F

"Why are the highest and lowest temperatures important when you choose a scale for your graph?" The scale must have sufficient range to display both the highest and the lowest temperatures.

When drawing and labeling the scale of a graph, a common error students make is forgetting to break the axis (in other words, making it jagged near the intersection of both axes) if the scale does not begin at zero. After students complete the scales of their graphs, ask

"Does your scale begin at zero degrees, or does it begin at some other number of degrees?"

For the benefit of those students who drew a scale that does not begin at zero degrees, sketch a possible scale on the board or overhead and demonstrate how to break the scale.

Extensions

In this activity, students are to design a survey question, conduct a survey using the question, and organize, display, and interpret the data that is collected.

After displaying the data two different ways, students should write a summary that describes how the displays are different. For example, does one display provide data or information that the other display does not provide? Is the data or information in one display easier to interpret? And so on.

Students should also indicate if the data they collected addressed the problem they were investigating or produced more questions than were answered.

Math Background

Mean, median, and *mode* are known as measures of central tendency. When working with these measures, a misconception students sometimes have is that for any given set of data, the measures must be different.

The idea that the measures must be different is a misconception because, for example, 2 represents the mean, the median, and the mode of the data set {1, 2, 2, 3}.

Looking Forward

Displaying data using graphs and finding mean, median, mode, and range of a set of data points prepares students for:

- **Investigation 9,** displaying data in a relative frequency table and finding experimental probability.
- **Investigation 10,** displaying outcomes from compound experiments and figuring the probability of the outcomes.

Section 6 Overview

Lessons 51–60, Investigation 6

Lesson Planner

LESSON	NEW CONCEPTS	MATERIALS	RESOURCES
51	• Rounding Decimal Numbers		Power Up H
52	• Mentally Dividing Decimal Numbers by 10 and by 100	Manipulative Kit: inch rulers	Power Up G
53	• Decimals Chart • Simplifying Fractions		Power Up D
54	• Reducing by Grouping Factors Equal to 1 • Dividing Fractions	Manipulative Kit: rulers, overhead fraction circles Fraction manipulatives from Investigation 2 3 by 5 cards	Power Up G
55	• Common Denominators, Part 1	Manipulative Kit: overhead fraction circles	Power Up I
56	• Common Denominators, Part 2	Manipulative Kit: metric rulers, overhead fraction circles Fraction manipulatives from Investigation 2	Power Up G
57	• Adding and Subtracting Fractions: Three Steps	Fraction manipulatives from Investigation 2	Power Up H
58	• Probability and Chance	Manipulative Kit: inch rulers, dot cubes, spinners	Power Up I
59	• Adding Mixed Numbers		Power Up G
60	• Polygons		Power Up I Common Polygons poster
Inv. 6	• Attributes of Geometric Solids	Manipulative Kit: color cubes, Relational GeoSolids Empty cereal box, scissors, tape	Investigation Activity 12 Investigation Activity 13

Lessons 51–60, Investigation 6

Lesson Highlights

Lessons 51–60, Investigation 6

Problem Solving

Strategies

- **Make an Organized List** Lessons 51, 58
- **Use a Chart** Lesson 59
- **Make It Simpler** Lessons 52, 57
- **Use Logical Reasoning** Lessons 53, 54, 55, 56, 60
- **Work Backwards** Lessons 55, 56
- **Write an Equation** Lessons 53, 57, 59

Real-World Applications

pp. 268–275, 278, 280, 283, 284, 289, 290, 292–299, 301, 304, 306–309, 312, 313, 316, 317

4-Step Process

Teacher Edition Lessons 51–60 (Power-Up Discussions)

Communications

Discuss

pp. 300, 307

Explain

pp. 270, 278, 287, 290, 305, 313

Formulate a Problem

pp. 293, 308

Connections

Math and Other Subjects

- **Math and History** pp. 270, 283, 296
- **Math and Geography** pp. 273, 287
- **Math and Science** pp. 275, 288, 297, 301, 306, 307, 308, 313
- **Math and Sports** pp. 280, 283, 298

Math to Math

- **Problem Solving and Measurement** Lessons 51, 52, 53, 54, 55, 56, 57, 58, 59, 60, Inv. 6
- **Algebra and Problem Solving** Lessons 57, 58, 59, 60
- **Fractions, Percents, Decimals, and Problem Solving** Lessons 51, 52, 53, 54, 55, 56, 57, 58, 59, 60
- **Fractions and Measurement** Lessons 51, 52, 53, 54, 55, 56, 57, 58, 60
- **Measurement and Geometry** Lessons 51, 52, 53, 54, 55, 56, 57, 58, 59, 60, Inv. 6
- **Probability and Statistics** Lessons 58, 59, 60

Representation

Manipulatives/Hands On

pp. 282, 286, 289, 291, 301, 302, 305, 315

Model

pp. 274, 275, 279, 284, 288, 294, 305, 312

Represent

pp. 271, 279, 284, 296, 304, 315, 318, 319

Formulate an Equation

pp. 270, 283, 296, 312

Technology

Student Resources

- **eBook**
- **Online Resources** at **www.SaxonPublishers.com/ActivitiesC1**
  - **Graphing Calculator Activity** Lesson 51
  - **Online Activities**
  - **Math Enrichment Problems**
  - **Math Stumpers**

Teacher Resources

- **Resources and Planner CD**
- **Adaptations CD** Lessons 51–60
- **Test & Practice Generator CD**
- **eGradebook**
- **Answer Key CD**

In this section, students continue to focus on concepts and skills involving fractions and decimals. Probability and chance are introduced and concepts involving lines and angles are applied to polygons.

Operation Sense

Equivalent forms are emphasized in these lessons.

Operations with decimal numbers are summarized in a chart in Lesson 53 that identifies the distinctions between operations with whole numbers and operations with decimal numbers. It is helpful for students to be able to draw this chart from memory. Students also round decimal numbers in Lesson 51 and mentally divide decimal numbers by powers of ten in Lesson 52.

Students simplify fractions in Lessons 53 and 54. They find common denominators to add and subtract fractions and mixed numbers in Lessons 55–57 and 59.

Probability

Fractions, decimals, and percents are connected to probability.

Students calculate probability and chance in Lesson 58. Subsequent instruction will distinguish between theoretical and experimental probability and explore ways to calculate compound events.

Spatial Thinking

Reasoning with two-dimensional figures is applied to three-dimensional figures.

The study of geometry continues with classifying polygons in Lesson 60 and identifying attributes of three-dimensional figures.

Assessment

A variety of weekly assessment tools are provided.

After Lesson 55:
- Power-Up Test 10
- Cumulative Test 10
- Performance Activity 10

After Lesson 60:
- Power-Up Test 11
- Cumulative Test 11
- Customized Benchmark Test
- Performance Task 11

Content Trace

Lessons 51–60, Investigation 6

LESSON	NEW CONCEPTS	PRACTICED	ASSESSED
51	• Rounding Decimal Numbers	Lessons 51, 52, 54, 55, 57, 60, 64, 78, 79, 80, 88, 90, 92, 93, 95, 107, 110, 111, 115, 117	Tests 11, 16, 21
52	• Mentally Dividing Decimal Numbers by 10 and by 100	Lessons 52, 53, 54, 55, 57, 58, 59, 60, 61, 68, 76, 84, 90, 94	Tests 11, 14, 15, 16
53	• Decimals Chart	Lessons 53, 54, 55, 56, 57, 58, 59, 60, 63, 64, 66, 67, 68, 82, 96	Tests 10, 11, 12, 13, 14, 15, 16, 17, 18, 19, 20, 21, 22, 23
	• Simplifying Fractions	Lessons 54, 55, 56, 57, 58, 59, 60, 63, 64, 66, 67, 68, 70, 81	Tests 13, 14, 15, 17, 18, 19, 21, 22, 23
54	• Reducing by Grouping Factors Equal to 1	Lessons 54, 55, 56, 57, 58, 62, 64, 65, 66, 67, 68, 69, 70, 71, 74, 75, 77, 79, 81, 83	Test 11
	• Dividing Fractions	Lessons 54, 55, 56, 57, 58, 59, 60, 61, 62, 63, 66, 68, 69, 70, 71, 72, 73, 74, 78, 81, 83	Tests 21, 22
55	• Common Denominators, Part 1	Lessons 55, 56, 57, 58, 61, 62, 63, 64, 66, 67, 68, 69, 70, 78, 100, 118	Tests 11, 16, 18
56	• Common Denominators, Part 2	Lessons 56, 57, 58, 59, 60, 62, 63, 65, 69, 70, 73, 88, 91, 94	Tests 12, 13, 15, 16
57	• Adding and Subtracting Fractions, Three Steps	Lessons 57, 58, 59, 60, 61, 62, 63, 64, 69, 70, 71, 73, 75, 77, 78, 79, 80, 81, 117	Tests 12, 13, 14, 15, 16, 17, 18, 19, 21, 22
58	• Probability and Chance	Lessons 58, 59, 60, 62, 65, 66, 67, 68, 72, 75, 77, 82, 85, 86, 92, 93, 94, 95, 96, 97, 98, 99, 100, 101, 102, 103, 104, 105, 106, 109, 111, 113, 116, 119, 120	Tests 12, 13, 14, 19
59	• Adding Mixed Numbers	Lessons 59, 60, 61, 64, 66, 67, 68, 70, 71, 72, 75, 85, 86, 90, 91, 92, 94, 96, 97, 100	Tests 12, 13, 15, 16, 17, 19, 21
60	• Polygons	Lessons 60, 61, 64, 65, 66, 67, 68, 69, 70, 71, 75, 77, 78, 82, 83, 92, 96, 101, 102, 107	Tests 12, 14, 15, 16
Inv. 6	• Attributes of Geometric Solids	Investigation 6, Lessons 61, 64, 65, 67, 68, 69, 70, 71, 73, 74, 75, 76, 81, 82, 83, 87, 90, 91, 92, 94, 95, 99, 101, 104	Tests 13, 14, 18, 19, 20

• Rounding Decimal Numbers

Objectives

- Round money amounts to the nearest cent.
- Round decimal numbers to the nearest hundredth, tenth, and whole number.

Lesson Preparation

Materials

- **Power Up H** (in *Instructional Masters*)

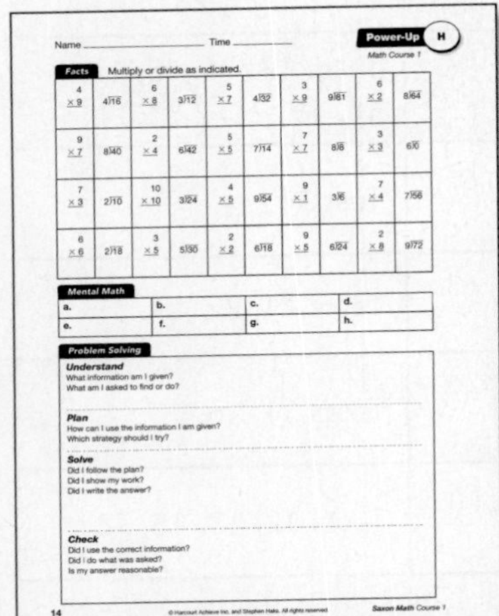

Power Up H

Math Language

	Maintain	English Learners (ESL)
	sales tax	collection

Technology Resources

Student eBook Complete student textbook in electronic format.

Resources and Planner CD Assessment, reteaching, and instructional masters, plus a pacing calendar with standards.

Test and Practice Generator CD Create additional practice sheets and custom-made tests.

www.SaxonPublishers.com Visit for more student activities and planning materials.

Inclusion

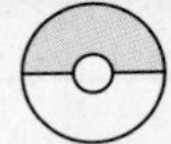

Adaptations CD Adapted lessons, investigations, practice and assessments.

Meeting Standards

National Council of Teachers of Mathematics (NCTM)

Numbers and Operations

NO.1a Work flexibly with fractions, decimals, and percents to solve problems

NO.3a Select appropriate methods and tools for computing with fractions and decimals from among mental computation, estimation, calculators or computers, and paper and pencil, depending on the situation, and apply the selected methods

NO.3c Develop and use strategies to estimate the results of rational-number computations and judge the reasonableness of the results

Problem Solving

PS.1c Apply and adapt a variety of appropriate strategies to solve problems

Power-Up Discussion *For use with Power Up, p. 268*

Problem-Solving Strategy: Make an Organized List

The smallest official set of dominos uses only the numbers 0 through 6. Each domino has two numbers on its face, and once a combination of numbers is used, it is not repeated. How many dominos are in the smallest official set of dominos? (*Note:* Combinations in which the two numbers are equal, called "doubles," are allowed. For example, the combination 3–3.)

Understand — Understand the problem.

"What information are we given?"

Each domino has two numbers, and the smallest official set of dominos uses only the numbers 0 through 6. Combinations of equal numbers are allowed.

"What are we asked to do?"

Determine the number of dominos in the smallest official set.

Teacher Note: If available, you may wish to have a set of dominos on hand for those students who may be unfamiliar with what they look like.

"Are we looking for combinations or permutations?"

Combinations. The two numbers 1 and 2 appear on only one domino.

Plan — Make a plan.

"What problem-solving strategy will we use?"

We will *make an organized* list of the pairs of numbers on each domino.

Solve — Carry out the plan.

"We will list the two numbers of each domino as an ordered pair:"

0, 0	0, 1	0, 2	0, 3	0, 4	0, 5	0, 6
	1, 1	1, 2	1, 3	1, 4	1, 5	1, 6
		2, 2	2, 3	2, 4	2, 5	2, 6
			3, 3	3, 4	3, 5	3, 6
				4, 4	4, 5	4, 6
					5, 5	5, 6
						6, 6

"How many dominos are in the smallest official set?"

Twenty-eight.

Check — Look back.

"Did we find the answer to the question that was asked?"

Yes. There are twenty-eight dominos in the smallest official set of dominos.

1 Power Up

Facts

Distribute **Power Up H** to students. See answers below.

Mental Math

Before students begin the Mental Math exercise, do this counting exercise as a class.

Count up and down by $\frac{1}{8}$s between $\frac{1}{8}$ and 3.

Encourage students to share different ways to mentally compute these exercises. Strategies for exercises **b** and **f** are listed below.

b. Count On by 70, then Count Back by 4

Start with 70. Count: 140, 210, 280

Start with 280. Count: 276, 272

Multiply Tens, then Multiply Ones

$(4 \times 60) + (4 \times 8) = 240 + 32 = 272$

f. Simplify the Numerator

$\frac{\$100.00}{100} = \frac{\$100}{100} = \frac{\$1}{1} = \$1$

Shift the Decimal Points

$\frac{\$100.00}{100} = \frac{\$1.0000}{1.00} = \frac{\$1}{1} = \$1$

Problem Solving

Refer to **Power-Up Discussion,** p. 268F.

2 New Concepts

Example 1

Instruction

Have students note that rounding a money amount to the nearest hundredth of a dollar is the same as rounding the amount to the nearest cent.

"Small amounts of money, such as sales tax amounts, are usually rounded to hundredths of a dollar. In our system of money, what coin has the same value as one hundredth of a dollar?" a penny

(continued)

LESSON 51

• Rounding Decimal Numbers

Power Up *Building Power*

facts Power Up H

mental math

a. Calculation: 8 × 125 1000

b. Calculation: 4 × 68 272

c. Number Sense: 64 − 29 35

d. Money: \$4.64 + 99¢ \$5.63

e. Fractional Parts: $\frac{1}{2}$ of \$150.00 \$75.00

f. Money: $\frac{\$100.00}{100}$ \$1.00

g. Measurement: Convert 36 hours to days. 1 day 12 hours

h. Calculation: 8 × 8, − 4, ÷ 2, + 2, ÷ 4, + 2, ÷ 5, × 10 20

problem solving

The smallest official set of dominos uses only the numbers 0 through 6. Each domino has two numbers on its face, and once a combination of numbers is used, it is not repeated. How many dominos are in the smallest official set of dominos? (*Note:* Combinations in which the two numbers are equal, called "doubles," are allowed. For example, the combination 3-3.) 28 dominoes

New Concept *Increasing Knowledge*

It is often necessary or helpful to round decimal numbers. For instance, money amounts are usually rounded to two places after the decimal point because we do not have a coin smaller than one hundredth of a dollar.

Example 1

Dan wanted to buy a book for \$6.89. The sales-tax rate was 8%. Dan calculated the sales tax. He knew that 8% equaled the fraction $\frac{8}{100}$ and the decimal 0.08. To figure the amount of tax, he multiplied the price (\$6.89) by the sales-tax rate (0.08).

$$\begin{array}{r} \$6.89 \\ \times\ 0.08 \\ \hline \$0.5512 \end{array}$$

How much tax would Dan pay if he purchased the book?

Solution

Sales tax is rounded to the nearest cent, which is two places to the right of the decimal point. We mark the places that will be included in the answer.

$0.55|12

Facts Multiply or divide as indicated.

4 × 9 36	4 4)16	6 × 8 48	4 3)12	5 × 7 35	8 4)32	3 × 9 27	9 9)81	6 × 2 12	8 8)64
9 × 7 63	5 8)40	2 × 4 8	7 6)42	5 × 5 25	2 7)14	7 × 7 49	1 8)8	3 × 3 9	0 6)0
7 × 3 21	5 2)10	10 × 10 100	8 3)24	4 × 5 20	6 9)54	9 × 1 9	2 3)6	7 × 4 28	8 7)56
6 × 6 36	9 2)18	3 × 5 15	6 5)30	2 × 2 4	3 6)18	9 × 5 45	4 6)24	2 × 8 16	8 9)72

Next we consider the possible answers. We see that $0.5512 is a little more than $0.55 but less than $0.56. We decide whether $0.5512 is closer to $0.55 or $0.56 by looking at the next digit (in this case, the digit in the third decimal place). If the next digit is 5 or more, we round up to $0.56. If it is less than 5, we round down to $0.55. Since the next digit is 1, we round $0.5512 down. If Dan buys the book, he will need to pay **$0.55** in sales tax.

Example 2

Sheila pulled into the gas station and filled the car's tank with 10.381 gallons of gasoline. Round the amount of gasoline she purchased to the nearest tenth of a gallon.

Solution

The tenths place is one place to the right of the decimal point. We mark the places that will be included in the answer.

$\underline{10.3}81$

Next we consider the possible answers. The number we are rounding is more than 10.3 but less than 10.4. We decide that 10.381 is closer to 10.4 because the digit in the next place is 8, and we round up when the next digit is 5 or more. Sheila bought about **10.4 gallons** of gasoline.

Visit www.SaxonPublishers.com/ActivitiesC1 *for a graphing calculator activity.*

Example 3

Estimate the product of 6.85 and 4.2 by rounding the numbers to the nearest whole number before multiplying.

Solution

We mark the whole-number places.

$\underline{6}.85 \qquad \underline{4}.2$

We see that 6.85 is more than 6 but less than 7. The next digit is 8, so we round 6.85 up to 7. The number 4.2 is more than 4 but less than 5. The next digit is 2, so we round 4.2 down to 4. We multiply the rounded numbers.

$7 \cdot 4 = 28$

We estimate that the product of 6.85 and 4.2 is about **28**.

Thinking Skill

Generalize

If you are rounding a whole number with two decimal places to the nearest whole number, what place do you look at to round?
the tenths place

Summarize Explain in your own words how to round a decimal number to the nearest whole number. See student work.

2 New Concepts (Continued)

Example 1 (Continued)

Instruction

Another way for students to round $0.5512 to the nearest cent is to identify the rounding place, then compare the digit immediately to its right to 5. If the digit to the right of the rounding place is less than 5, the digit in the rounding place does not change. If the digit to the right of the rounding place is 5 or more, the digit in the rounding place increases by 1. In either case, the rounding is completed by deleting all digits to the right of the rounding place.

Example 2

Instruction

A prerequisite skill for rounding is the ability to identify place values in a number. If necessary, ask students to name the place values from thousands to thousandths. thousands, hundreds, tens, ones, tenths, hundredths, thousandths

Then ask students to name the place values from thousandths to thousands. thousandths, hundredths, tenths, ones, tens, hundreds, thousands

Example 3

Instruction

Some students may find it awkward that one of the factors in this problem has two decimal places, while the other factor has only one.

Remind these students of the instruction to round each factor to the nearest whole number, and then point out that all of the decimal places in each factor will be eliminated after each factor has been rounded.

(continued)

Math Background

Example 3 shows one way to round two numbers before finding the product of the numbers. A different way to round numbers before finding their product is known as compensation.

Compensation is used when the factors are close to halves, such as 7.4×5.37. To estimate such a product, one factor is rounded up and the other factor is rounded down. Two very good estimates of the product 7.4×5.37 are shown below. Both estimates involve compensation.

- 7.4 rounds up to 8 and 5.37 rounds down to 5: $8 \times 5 = 40$
- 7.4 rounds down to 7 and 5.37 rounds up to 6: $7 \times 6 = 42$

2 New Concepts (Continued)

Practice Set

Problems a, b, and c Error Alert

When rounding to the nearest cent, students should infer that their answers must contain two decimal places.

Problems d, e, and f Error Alert

When rounding to the nearest tenth, students should infer that their answers must contain one decimal place.

Problems g, h, and i Error Alert

When rounding to the nearest whole number or whole dollar, students should infer that there will be no decimal places in their answers.

3 Written Practice

Math Conversations

Discussion opportunities are provided below.

Problem 4 Analyze

Extend the Problem

"Suppose that Shelly had $15 in her pocket, and while she was in the store, she wanted to know if she had enough money to pay for the CD before she took the CD to the cashier. How could Shelly have used mental math to estimate the cost of the CD, including tax?" Sample: Round $12.89 to $13 and round 8% to 10%; $13 + (10% of $13) is the same as $13 + $1.30 or $14.30. The estimated cost is $14.30.

Problem 5b Estimate

"In this problem, do we round the factor 3.14, or do we round the answer?" round the answer

(continued)

Practice Set

▶ Round to the nearest cent:

a. $6.6666 $6.67 **b.** $0.4625 $0.46 **c.** $0.08333 $0.08

▶ Round to the nearest tenth:

d. 0.12 0.1 **e.** 12.345 12.3 **f.** 2.375 2.4

▶ Round to the nearest whole number or whole dollar:

g. 16.75 17 **h.** 4.875 5 **i.** $73.29 $73

j. Estimate If the sales-tax rate is 6%, then how much sales tax is there on a $3.79 purchase? (Round the answer to the nearest cent.) 23¢

k. Estimate Describe how to estimate a 7.75% sales tax on a $7.89 item.

k. Round 7.75% to 8% and round $7.89 to $8. Find 8% of $8 (or 8¢ per dollar) is 64¢. Since both numbers were rounded up, the tax should be a little less than 64¢.

Written Practice *Strengthening Concepts*

1. (12, 25) Analyze When the third multiple of 8 is subtracted from the fourth multiple of 6, what is the difference? 0

2. (37) From Mona's home to school is 3.5 miles. How far does Mona travel riding from home to school and back home? 7 miles

3. (13) Formulate Napoleon I was born in 1769. How old was he when he was crowned emperor of France in 1804? Write an equation and solve the problem. 1804 − 1769 = *d*; 35 years old

▶ ***4.** (41, 51) Shelly purchased a music CD for $12.89. The sales-tax rate was 8%.

a. What was the tax on the purchase? $1.03

b. What was the total price including tax? $13.92

***5.** (47, 51) Malcom used a compass to draw a circle with a radius of 3 inches.

a. Find the diameter of the circle. 6 inches

▶ **b.** Estimate Find the circumference of the circle. Round the answer to the nearest inch. (Use 3.14 for π.) 19 inches

***6.** (51) Explain How can you round 12.75 to the nearest whole number?

6. The whole-number part of 12.75 is 12. The next digit, 7, is greater than 5, so round up to the next whole number, 13.

7. (37) 0.125 + 0.25 + 0.375 0.75

8. (43) 0.399 + *w* = 0.4 0.001

***9.** (49) $\frac{4}{0.25}$ 16

10. (45) $4\overline{)0.5}$ 0.125

11. (45) $3.25 \div \sqrt{100}$ 0.325

***12.** (48) $3\frac{5}{12} - 1\frac{7}{12}$ $1\frac{5}{6}$

13. (42) $\frac{5}{8} = \frac{?}{24}$ 15

***14.** (48) $5^2 - 17\frac{3}{4}$ $7\frac{1}{4}$

15. (39) (0.19)(0.21) 0.0399

16. (35) Write 0.01 as a fraction. $\frac{1}{100}$

17. (46) Write $(6 \times 10) + (7 \times \frac{1}{100})$ as a decimal number. 60.07

18. (38) Analyze The area of a square is 64 cm². What is the perimeter of the square? 32 cm

▶ See Math Conversations in the sidebar.

19. (30) What is the least common multiple of 2, 3, and 4? 12

20. (26) $5\frac{3}{10} + 6\frac{9}{10}$ $12\frac{1}{5}$

21. (29) $\frac{10}{3} \times \frac{1}{2}$ $1\frac{2}{3}$

▶* **22.** (50) **Connect** A collection of paperback books was stacked 12 inches high. Each book in the stack was $\frac{3}{4}$ inch thick. Use the method described in Lesson 50 to find the number of books in the stack. 16 books

23. (16) Estimate the quotient when 4876 is divided by 98. 50

24. (19) What factors do 16 and 24 have in common? 1, 2, 4, 8

25. 48; Rounded 11.8 to 12 and 3.89 to 4; then multiplied 12 by 4.

* **25.** (51) **Estimate** Find the product of 11.8 and 3.89 by rounding the factors to the nearest whole number before multiplying. Explain how you arrived at your answer.

▶* **26.** (50) **Analyze** Find the average of the decimal numbers that correspond to points x and y on this number line. 1

27. (5) $\frac{2 \cdot 2 \cdot 3 \cdot 3 \cdot 5}{2 \cdot 2 \cdot 3 \cdot 5}$ 3

28. $7.90; Since the problem is to multiply by 10, shift the decimal point in $0.79 one place to the right.

28. (46) **Justify** Mentally calculate the total price of ten pounds of bananas at $0.79 per pound. Explain how you performed the mental calculation.

29. (42) Rename $\frac{2}{3}$ and $\frac{3}{4}$ as fractions with 12 as the denominator. Then add the renamed fractions. Write the sum as a mixed number.
$\frac{8}{12} + \frac{9}{12} = \frac{17}{12} = 1\frac{5}{12}$

▶* **30.** (Inv. 5) **a.** **Represent** Jason's first nine test scores are shown below. Find the median and mode of the scores. median: 85; mode: 90

30. b. Sample:

85, 80, 90, 75, 85, 100, 90, 80, 90

b. Sketch a graph of Jason's scores. The heights of the bars should indicate the scores. Title the graph and label the two axes.

30. b. Sample:

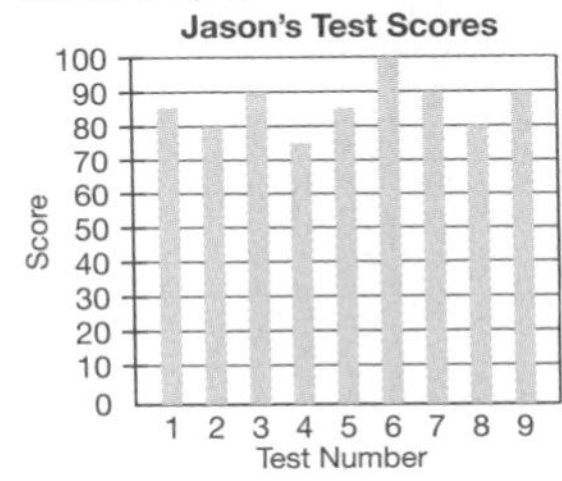

▶ See Math Conversations in the sidebar.

3 Written Practice (Continued)

Math Conversations

Discussion opportunities are provided below.

Problem 22 Connect

"Without solving the problem, explain how you know that the stack will contain more than 12 books." Sample: The height of the stack is divided by the thickness of each book. Since the divisor is less than 1, the quotient will be greater than the dividend.

Problem 30 Represent

"How is the median of a group of numbers different from the mode of those numbers?" The median is the middle number, or the mean of the two middle numbers, after the numbers have been ordered from least to greatest or from greatest to least. The mode is the number or numbers in the group that appear most often.

"Can the median of a set of data be the same as the mode of that data? Give an example to support your answer." Yes; for example, the median and the mode of the set {2, 3, 2} is 2.

Errors and Misconceptions

Problem 26 Analyze

To correctly identify the location of each point, students must first recognize that each whole number interval of the number line is divided into tenths.

Remind students to count equal lengths, not tick marks, when determining the interval of a number line.

English Learners

Explain the meaning of the term **collection.** Say,

"A collection is a group of objects to be seen, studied, or kept together. There is no specific number of objects in a collection."

Ask students to briefly share what they know about a collection.

Looking Forward

Rounding decimal numbers to the nearest whole number, tenth, or hundredth prepares students for:

- **Lesson 89,** using a calculator to estimate the square root of a number to two decimal places.
- **Lesson 111,** knowing how to write the answer to a division problem that has a remainder.
- **Lesson 116,** finding compound interest and rounding answers to the nearest cent.

• Mentally Dividing Decimal Numbers by 10 and by 100

Objectives

- Divide a decimal number by 10 mentally.
- Divide a decimal number by 100 mentally.

Lesson Preparation

Materials

- **Power Up G** (in *Instructional Masters*)
- **Manipulative kit: inch rulers**

Optional

- **Teacher-provided material: calculators**

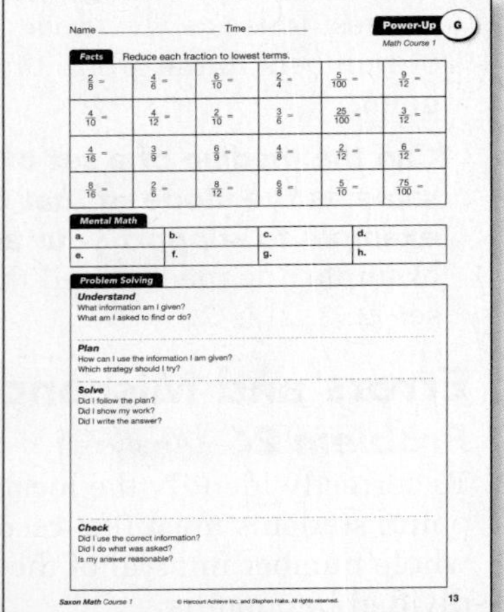

Power Up G

Math Language

English Learners (ESL)
unreduced

Technology Resources

Student eBook Complete student textbook in electronic format.

Resources and Planner CD Assessment, reteaching, and instructional masters, plus a pacing calendar with standards.

Test and Practice Generator CD Create additional practice sheets and custom-made tests.

www.SaxonPublishers.com Visit for more student activities and planning materials.

Inclusion

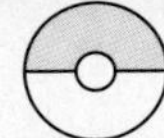

Adaptations CD Adapted lessons, investigations, practice and assessments.

Meeting Standards

National Council of Teachers of Mathematics (NCTM)

Numbers and Operations

NO.1a Work flexibly with fractions, decimals, and percents to solve problems

NO.2a Understand the meaning and effects of arithmetic operations with fractions, decimals, and integers

NO.3a Select appropriate methods and tools for computing with fractions and decimals from among mental computation, estimation, calculators or computers, and paper and pencil, depending on the situation, and apply the selected methods

Power-Up Discussion For use with Power Up, p. 272

Problem-Solving Strategy: Make it Simpler

The monetary systems in Australia and New Zealand have six coins: 5¢, 10¢, 20¢, 50¢, $1, and $2. The price of any item is rounded to the nearest 5 cents. At the end of Ellen's vacation in New Zealand she had two $2 coins. She wants to bring back at least one of each of the six coins. How many ways can she exchange one of the $2 coins for the remaining five coins?

Understand Understand the problem.

"What information are we given?"

The monetary systems in Australia and New Zealand have six coins: 5¢, 10¢, 20¢, 50¢, $1, and $2. The price of any item is rounded to the nearest 5 cents.

"What are we asked to do?"

Determine how many ways Ellen can exchange a $2 coin for the remaining five coins.

Plan Make a plan.

"What problem-solving strategy will we use?"

Since we know that she will need at least one of the five other coins, we can *make it simpler* by subtracting one of each coin from the $2, then determining how many ways she can receive the difference.

Solve Carry out the plan.

"What is the total worth of the 5 coins Ellen needs?"

$1 + 50¢ + 20¢ + 10¢ + 5¢ = $1.85

"What is the difference when we subtract the 5 coins from $2?"

15¢

"How many ways can Ellen receive 15¢?"

two ways (10¢ + 5¢ or 5¢ + 5¢ + 5¢)

"What combinations of coins total $2 and include at least one $1, 50¢, 20¢, 10¢, and 5¢ coin?"

1 $1 coin, 1 50¢ coin, 1 20¢ coin, 2 10¢ coins, 2 5¢ coins
1 $1 coin, 1 50¢ coin, 1 20¢ coin, 1 10¢ coin, 4 5¢ coins

Check Look back.

"Did we answer the question that was asked?"

Yes. There are only two ways Ellen can exchange one $2 coin and receive at least one of the remaining five coins.

1 Power Up

Facts

Distribute **Power Up G** to students. See answers below.

Mental Math

Before students begin the Mental Math exercise, do this counting exercise as a class.

Count by 12s from 12 to 132.

Encourage students to share different ways to mentally compute these exercises. Strategies for exercises **e** and **f** are listed below.

e. Use Known Halves

Since $\frac{1}{2}$ of 4 = 2 and $\frac{1}{2}$ of 6 = 3, $\frac{1}{2}$ of 5 = $2\frac{1}{2}$.

Use a Pattern

Since $\frac{1}{2}$ of 500 = 250 and $\frac{1}{2}$ of 50 = 25, $\frac{1}{2}$ of 5 = 2.5.

f. Use Place Value

2 tens × 4 tens = 8 hundreds = 800

Use a Pattern of Multiples

Since 2 × 4 = 8 and 2 × 40 = 80, 20 × 40 = 800.

Problem Solving

Refer to **Power-Up Discussion**, p. 272B.

2 New Concepts

Instruction

To help students remember how many places to the left to shift the decimal point when dividing by 10 or by 100, say

"When we divide by 10 or 100, we shift the decimal point the same number of places to the left as the number of zeros in 10 or in 100. The number 10 has one zero, so we shift the decimal point one place to the left when we divide by 10. When we divide by 100, which has two zeros, we shift the decimal point two places to the left."

(continued)

LESSON 52

• Mentally Dividing Decimal Numbers by 10 and by 100

Power Up *Building Power*

facts Power Up G

mental math

a. Number Sense: 4 × 250 1000

b. Number Sense: 368 − 150 218

c. Number Sense: 250 + 99 349

d. Money: \$15.00 + \$7.50 \$22.50

e. Fractional Parts: $\frac{1}{2}$ of 5 $2\frac{1}{2}$

f. Number Sense: 20 × 40 800

g. Geometry: A rectangle has a width of 4 in. and a perimeter of 18 in. What is the length of the rectangle? 5 in.

h. Calculation: 5 × 10, + 4, ÷ 6, × 8, + 3, ÷ 3 25

problem solving

The monetary systems in Australia and New Zealand have six coins: 5¢, 10¢, 20¢, 50¢, \$1, and \$2. The price of any item is rounded to the nearest 5 cents. At the end of Ellen's vacation in New Zealand she had two \$2 coins. She wants to bring back at least one of each of the six coins. How many ways can she exchange one of the \$2 coins for the remaining five coins? 2 ways (1 \$1 coin, 1 50¢ coin, 1 20¢ coin, 2 10¢ coins, and 2 5¢ coins or 1 \$1 coin, 1 50¢ coin, 1 20¢ coin, 1 10¢ coin, and 4 5¢ coins)

New Concept *Increasing Knowledge*

Thinking Skill
Verify
How can we check if the quotients are correct?
Multiply the quotient by the divisor.

When we divide a decimal number by 10 or by 100, the quotient has the same digits as the dividend. However, the position of the digits is shifted. Here we show 12.5 divided by 10 and by 100:

$$10\overline{)12.50} = 1.25 \qquad 100\overline{)12.500} = .125$$

When we divide by 10, the digits shift one place to the right. When we divide by 100, the digits shift two places to the right. Although it is the digits that are shifting places, we produce the shift by moving the decimal point. When we divide by 10, the decimal point moves one place to the left. When we divide by 100, the decimal point moves two places to the left.

Example 1

Divide: 37.5 ÷ 10

Facts Reduce each fraction to lowest terms.

$\frac{2}{8} = \frac{1}{4}$	$\frac{4}{6} = \frac{2}{3}$	$\frac{6}{10} = \frac{3}{5}$	$\frac{2}{4} = \frac{1}{2}$	$\frac{5}{100} = \frac{1}{20}$	$\frac{9}{12} = \frac{3}{4}$
$\frac{4}{10} = \frac{2}{5}$	$\frac{4}{12} = \frac{1}{3}$	$\frac{2}{10} = \frac{1}{5}$	$\frac{3}{6} = \frac{1}{2}$	$\frac{25}{100} = \frac{1}{4}$	$\frac{3}{12} = \frac{1}{4}$
$\frac{4}{16} = \frac{1}{4}$	$\frac{3}{9} = \frac{1}{3}$	$\frac{6}{9} = \frac{2}{3}$	$\frac{4}{8} = \frac{1}{2}$	$\frac{2}{12} = \frac{1}{6}$	$\frac{6}{12} = \frac{1}{2}$
$\frac{8}{16} = \frac{1}{2}$	$\frac{2}{6} = \frac{1}{3}$	$\frac{8}{12} = \frac{2}{3}$	$\frac{6}{8} = \frac{3}{4}$	$\frac{5}{10} = \frac{1}{2}$	$\frac{75}{100} = \frac{3}{4}$

Solution

Since we are dividing by 10, the answer will be less than 37.5. We mentally shift the decimal point one place to the left.

$$37.5 \div 10 = \mathbf{3.75}$$

Example 2

Divide: 3.75 ÷ 100

Solution

Since we are dividing by 100, we mentally shift the decimal point two places to the left. This creates an empty place between the decimal point and the 3, which we fill with a zero. We also write a zero in the ones place.

$$3.75 \div 100 = \mathbf{0.0375}$$

Practice Set Mentally calculate each quotient. Write each answer as a decimal number.

- ▶ **a.** 2.5 ÷ 10 0.25
- ▶ **b.** 2.5 ÷ 100 0.025
- ▶ **c.** 87.5 ÷ 10 8.75
- ▶ **d.** 87.5 ÷ 100 0.875
- ▶ **e.** 0.5 ÷ 10 0.05
- ▶ **f.** 0.5 ÷ 100 0.005
- ▶ **g.** 25 ÷ 10 2.5
- ▶ **h.** 25 ÷ 100 0.25

i. A stack of 10 pennies is 1.5 cm high. How thick is one penny in centimeters? In millimeters? 0.15 cm; 1.5 mm

Written Practice *Strengthening Concepts*

1. (29) What is the product of one half and two thirds? $\frac{1}{3}$

2. (13) A piano has 88 keys. Fifty-two of the keys are white. How many more white keys are there than black keys? 16 more white keys

3. (12) In the Puerto Rico Trench, the Atlantic Ocean reaches its greatest depth of twenty-eight thousand, two hundred thirty-two feet. Use digits to write that number of feet. 28,232 feet

▶ * **4.** (46, 52) *Justify* Mentally calculate each answer. Explain how you performed each mental calculation.

a. 3.75 × 10 **b.** 3.75 ÷ 10

4. **a.** 37.5; To multiply 3.75 by 10, shift the decimal point one place to the right. **b.** 0.375; To divide 3.75 by 10, shift the decimal point one place to the left.

▶ **5.** (23) At Carver School there are 320 students and 16 teachers. What is the student-teacher ratio at Carver? $\frac{20}{1}$

Simplify:

6. (5) $2 \cdot 2 \cdot 2 \cdot 2 \cdot 2$ 32

7. (39) (4)(0.125) 0.5

8. (29) $\frac{150}{12}$ $12\frac{1}{2}$

9. (49) $\frac{(1 + 0.2)}{(1 - 0.2)}$ 1.5

▶ See Math Conversations in the sidebar.

Math Background

Mentally dividing by 10 and by 100 differs from mentally multiplying by 10 and by 100 because multiplication and division are inverse operations.

When a number is divided by 10 or by 100, the decimal point in the number is shifted one or two places to the left. When a number is multiplied by 10 or by 100, the decimal point in the number is shifted one or two places to the right.

This pattern remains true when dividing or multiplying by other powers of ten, such as by 1000, by 10,000, by 100,000, and so on.

2 New Concepts (Continued)

Example 1

Instruction

If students need additional practice, write the numbers shown below on the board or overhead. Then ask students to mentally divide each number by 10 and then name the quotient.

0.49 0.049 297 29.7 15.9 1.59

Example 2

Instruction

If students need additional practice, write the numbers shown below on the board or overhead. Then ask students to mentally divide each number by 100 and then name the quotient.

315.7 3.157 86 0.86 0.1 0.001

Practice Set

Problems a–h

Before students write each quotient, ask them to answer the following question.

"How many places, and in which direction, do we shift the decimal point?"

Problems b and f (Error Alert)

Some students may forget to write one or more zeros in the quotient. Remind these students that shifting a decimal point sometimes creates empty spaces in the quotient, and a zero must be written in each empty place.

Offer the exercises shown below for additional practice.

4.3 ÷ 100 0.043 0.7 ÷ 100 0.007

3 Written Practice

Math Conversations

Discussion opportunities are provided below.

Problem 4 *Justify*

Extend the Problem

"In each problem, change 10 to 100. What are the new answers?" 375 and 0.0375

Errors and Misconceptions

Problem 5

Remind students who answer $\frac{320}{16}$ that a ratio should be expressed in simplest form whenever possible.

To help these students complete the division, point out that the common factors of 320 and 16 include 2, 4, 8, and 16.

(continued)

3 Written Practice (Continued)

Math Conversations

Discussion opportunities are provided below.

Problem 15 Estimate

"What two formulas can be used to find the circumference of any circle?" $C = 2\pi r$ and $C = \pi d$

"Which formula should we use to find the circumference of this circle?" Sample: Use $C = \pi d$ because the diameter of the circle is given.

Problem 16 Analyze

Suggest that students begin by listing the numbers, one above the other, with the decimal points lined up so that digits with the same place value are aligned for easy comparison.

Problem 21 Connect

Extend the Problem

"We learned that 16 pennies are needed to form a row 12 inches long. Twelve inches is the same as what number of feet?" 1

"How many feet are equal to one mile?" 5280

"How many pennies are needed to form a row 1 mile long? Use a calculator to help decide." 84,480

"What amount of money is that number of pennies? Use mental math." $844.80

Errors and Misconceptions

Problem 25

Before students attempt to identify the indicated number, make sure they notice that the number line is divided (between consecutive whole numbers) into 10 equal units. Because the number line shows tenths, a decimal form for the answer is appropriate.

(continued)

10. (29) $\frac{5}{2} \times \frac{4}{1}$ 10

Find each unknown number:

11. (43) $5\frac{1}{3} - m = 1\frac{2}{3}$ $3\frac{2}{3}$

12. (43) $m - 5\frac{1}{3} = 1\frac{2}{3}$ 7

13. (43) $\$10 - w = \$0.10$ $9.90

* **14.** (41, 51) **Estimate** At a 6% sales-tax rate, what is the tax on an $8.59 purchase? Round the answer to the nearest cent. 52¢

▶* **15.** (47, 51) **Estimate** The diameter of a tire on the car was 24 inches. Find the circumference of the tire to the nearest inch. (Use 3.14 for π.) 75 inches

▶* **16.** (44) **Analyze** Arrange these numbers in order from least to greatest:

1.02, 1.2, 0.21, 0.201 0.201, 0.21, 1.02, 1.2

17. (10) What is the missing number in this sequence?

1, 2, 4, 7, 11, __16__, 22, ...

18. (38) The perimeter of a square room is 80 feet. How many floor tiles 1 foot square would be needed to cover the area of the room? 400 tiles

19. (22) **Model** One foot is 12 inches. What fraction of a foot is 3 inches? Draw a diagram to illustrate the problem. $\frac{1}{4}$

19. 1 foot = 12 inches; $\frac{1}{4}$ of a foot: 3 inches; $\frac{3}{4}$ of a foot: 3 inches, 3 inches, 3 inches

20. (22) **Model** How many cents is $\frac{2}{5}$ of a dollar? Draw a diagram to illustrate the problem. 40¢

20. 1 dollar = 100 cents; $\frac{2}{5}$ of a dollar: 20 cents, 20 cents; $\frac{3}{5}$ of a dollar: 20 cents, 20 cents, 20 cents

▶* **21.** (50) **Connect** The diameter of a penny is $\frac{3}{4}$ inch. How many pennies are needed to form a row 12 inches long? Explain how you found your answer. 16 pennies; Sample: One method is to divide 12 by $\frac{3}{4}$.

22. (30) What is the least common multiple of 2, 4, and 6? 12

23. (29, 38) **a.** $\frac{4}{4} - \frac{2}{2}$ 0 **b.** $\sqrt{4} - 2^2$ −2

24. (7) **Estimate** About how many meters above the floor is the top of the chalkboard? about 2 meters in most classrooms

▶ **25.** (50) **Connect** To what decimal number is the arrow pointing on the number line below? 1.8

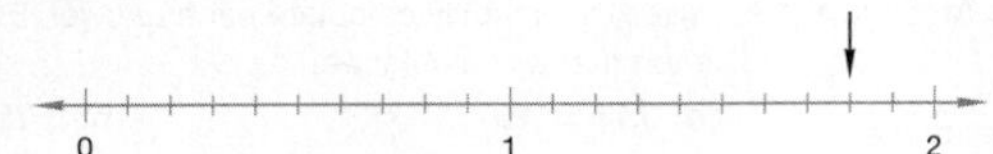

26. (42) Rename $\frac{1}{2}$ and $\frac{2}{3}$ as fractions with denominators of 6. Then add the renamed fractions. Write the sum as a mixed number. $\frac{3}{6} + \frac{4}{6} = \frac{7}{6} = 1\frac{1}{6}$

27. (8) **Model** Draw a square with a perimeter of 4 inches. Then shade 50% of the square.

27. Sample:
1 in.

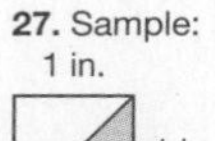

▶ See Math Conversations in the sidebar.

Use the data in the table to answer the problems **28–30.**

Gases in Earth's Atmosphere

Gas	Percent Composition
Nitrogen	78.08%
Oxygen	20.95%
Argon	0.93%
Other	0.04%

▶ **28.** (33, 35) **a.** Analyze Nitrogen makes up what percent of Earth's atmosphere? Round to the nearest whole-number percent. 78%

b. Write the answer to **a** as an unreduced fraction and as a decimal number. $\frac{78}{100}$; 0.78

29. (16, 35) **a.** About what percent of Earth's atmosphere consists of oxygen? Round to the nearest ten percent. 20%

b. Write the answer to **a** as a reduced fraction. $\frac{1}{5}$

30. (40, Inv. 5) Model Sketch a graph to display the data rounding to the nearest whole percent. Label the graph and explain why you chose that type of graph.

Sample:

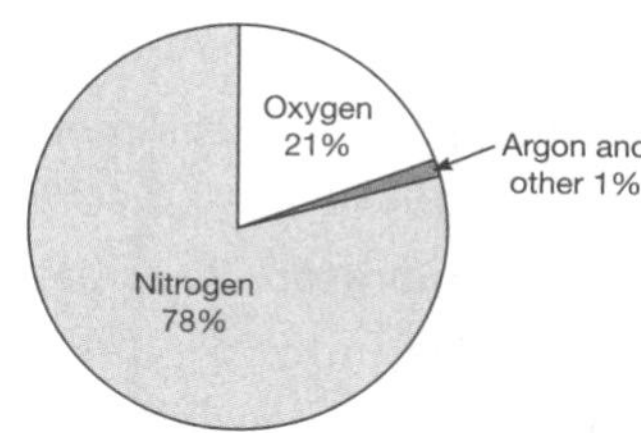

I used a circle graph because the data represents parts of a whole.

▶ See Math Conversations in the sidebar.

3 Written Practice (Continued)

Math Conversations

Discussion opportunities are provided below.

Problem 28 Analyze

"What percent of the Earth's atmosphere is nitrogen?" 78.08%

"When we round 78.08% to the nearest whole percent, what decimal place value in the number is not important? Explain why." The hundredths place. Sample explanation: Only the digit in the tenths place of a number is used to round the number to the ones place, so any digits to the right of the tenths place have no influence on how the number is rounded.

nglish Learners

/rite $\frac{4}{12}$ on the board. Say,

'The fraction $\frac{4}{12}$ is an unreduced fraction. 'Un' means 'not'. Therefore, unreduced means not reduced. What is the reduced fraction of $\frac{4}{12}$?" $\frac{1}{3}$

sk a volunteer to reduce the action $\frac{78}{100}$ from problem 28 on the oard.

Looking Forward

Mentally dividing decimal numbers by 10 and by 100 prepares students for:

- **Lesson 92,** writing numbers in expanded notation with exponents.
- **Lesson 113,** multiplying by powers of ten.

• Decimals Chart
• Simplifying Fractions

Objectives

- Recognize the rules involved in adding, subtracting, multiplying, and dividing decimal numbers.
- Simplify an improper fraction by first reducing it and then converting it to a mixed number.
- Simplify an improper fraction by first converting it to a mixed number and then reducing it.

Lesson Preparation

Materials

- **Power Up D** (*in Instructional Masters*)

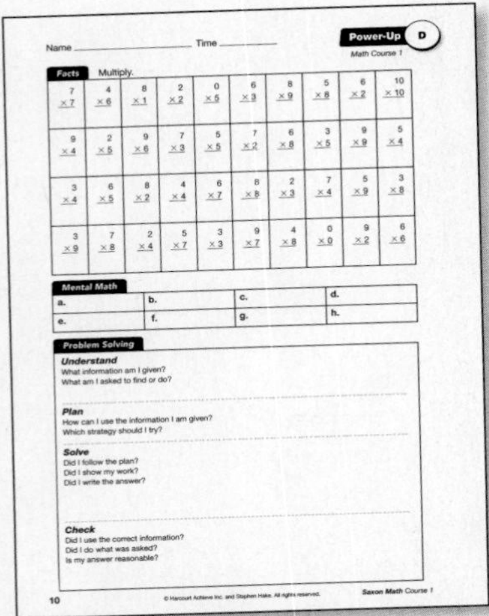

Name ____________ Time ________ **Power-Up D** *Math Course 1*

Facts Multiply.

7 × 7	4 × 6	8 × 1	2 × 2	0 × 5	6 × 3	8 × 9	5 × 8	6 × 2	10 × 10
9 × 4	2 × 5	9 × 6	7 × 3	5 × 5	7 × 2	6 × 8	3 × 5	9 × 9	5 × 4
3 × 4	6 × 5	8 × 2	4 × 4	6 × 7	8 × 8	2 × 3	7 × 4	5 × 9	3 × 8
3 × 9	7 × 8	2 × 4	5 × 7	3 × 3	9 × 7	4 × 8	0 × 0	9 × 2	6 × 6

Mental Math

a.	b.	c.	d.
e.	f.	g.	h.

Problem Solving

Understand
What information am I given?
What am I asked to find or do?

Plan
How can I use the information I am given?
Which strategy should I try?

Solve
Did I follow the plan?
Did I show my work?
Did I write the answer?

Check
Did I use the correct information?
Did I do what was asked?
Is my answer reasonable?

10 © Harcourt Achieve Inc. and Stephen Hake. All rights reserved. *Saxon Math* Course 1

Power Up D

Math Language

Maintain	English Learners (ESL)
reduce	corresponds

Technology Resources

Student eBook Complete student textbook in electronic format.

Resources and Planner CD Assessment, reteaching, and instructional masters, plus a pacing calendar with standards.

Test and Practice Generator CD Create additional practice sheets and custom-made tests.

www.SaxonPublishers.com Visit for more student activities and planning materials.

Inclusion

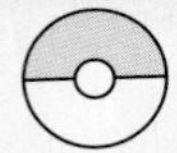

Adaptations CD Adapted lessons, investigations, practice and assessments.

Meeting Standards

National Council of Teachers of Mathematics (NCTM)

Numbers and Operations

NO.1a Work flexibly with fractions, decimals, and percents to solve problems

NO.2a Understand the meaning and effects of arithmetic operations with fractions, decimals, and integers

NO.3a Select appropriate methods and tools for computing with fractions and decimals from among mental computation, estimation, calculators or computers, and paper and pencil, depending on the situation, and apply the selected methods

Power-Up Discussion *For use with Power Up, p. 276*

Problem-Solving Strategy: Use Logical Reasoning/ Write an Equation

You can roll six different numbers with one toss of one number cube. You can roll eleven different numbers with one toss of two number cubes. How many different numbers can you roll with one toss of three number cubes?

Understand **Understand the problem.**

"What information are we given?"

We can roll six different numbers with one toss of a number cube (1–6) and eleven different numbers with one toss of two number cubes (2–12).

"What are we asked to do?"

We are asked to find how many different numbers we can roll with one toss of three number cubes.

Plan **Make a plan.**

"How can we use the information we know to do what we are asked to do?"

We will *use logical reasoning* to determine the greatest and least sums that can be rolled with three number cubes. Then we can find the total number of different sums possible. We will check our answer by *writing an equation.*

Solve **Carry out the plan.**

"What is the least number that can be rolled with three number cubes?"

The least number that can be rolled occurs if each number cube lands with 1 on top: $1 + 1 + 1 = 3$.

"What is the greatest number that can be rolled with three number cubes?"

The greatest number that can be rolled occurs if each number cube lands with 6 on top: $6 + 6 + 6 = 18$.

"Can we roll every whole number from 3 through 18 with three number cubes?"

Yes. We think of the lowest roll (three 1s). To make the cubes total 4, we could simply turn one of the cubes to show a 2. To make the cubes total 5, we could turn the same cube to show a 3. We can continue adding one to the total by turning cubes until all the cubes show a 6.

"How many different numbers can be rolled with three number cubes?"

Every whole number from 3 through 18 can be rolled, which is sixteen different numbers.

Check **Look back.**

"Did we complete the task?"

Yes, we determined how many different numbers can be rolled with three number cubes (16 numbers).

"How can we verify the solution is correct?"

We can write an equation. Eighteen is the largest number that can be rolled. There are two numbers that cannot be rolled, 1 and 2: $18 - 2 = 16$.

1 Power Up

Facts

Distribute **Power Up D** to students. See answers below.

Mental Math

Before students begin the Mental Math exercise, do this counting exercise as a class.

Count by 9s from 9 to 108.

Encourage students to share different ways to mentally compute these exercises. Strategies for exercises **b** and **e** are listed below.

b. Subtract 6 and Add 6

$256 - 6 = 250$ and $34 + 6 = 40$; $250 + 40 = 290$

Add Place Values

$200 + 50 + 30 + 6 + 4 = 200 + 80 + 10 = 290$

e. Use Doubles

Double 2 is 4 and double $\frac{1}{2}$ is 1; $4 + 1 = 5$

Use a Pattern

Since $250 + 250 = 500$ and $25 + 25 = 50$, $2.5 + 2.5 = 5.0$ or 5

Problem Solving

Refer to **Power-Up Discussion**, p. 276B.

2 New Concepts

Instruction

Invite students to discuss what they know about decimal arithmetic and develop generalizations about adding, subtracting, multiplying, and dividing decimal numbers. Sample generalizations are shown below.

- Decimal Addition: Align the decimal points, then add.
- Decimal Subtraction: Align the decimal points, then subtract.
- Decimal Multiplication: The total number of decimal places in the factors is the same as the number of decimal places in the product.
- Decimal Division: Place a decimal point in the quotient. Then divide.

(continued)

LESSON 53

• Decimals Chart
• Simplifying Fractions

Power Up *Building Power*

facts Power Up D

mental math

a. Calculation: 8×225 1800

b. Calculation: $256 + 34$ 290

c. Number Sense: $250 - 99$ 151

d. Money: $25.00 − $12.50 $12.50

e. Number Sense: Double $2\frac{1}{2}$. 5

f. Number Sense: $\frac{800}{20}$ 40

g. Geometry: A circle has a radius of 5 ft. What is the circumference of the circle? 31.4 ft

h. Calculation: 10×10, $- 20$, $+ 1$, $\div 9$, $\times 5$, $- 1$, $\div 4$ 11

problem solving You can roll six different numbers with one toss of one number cube. You can roll eleven different numbers with one toss of two number cubes. How many different numbers can you roll with one toss of three number cubes? 16

New Concepts *Increasing Knowledge*

decimals chart

For many lessons we have been developing our decimal arithmetic skills. We find that arithmetic with decimal numbers is similar to arithmetic with whole numbers. However, in decimal arithmetic, we need to keep track of the decimal point. The chart on the facing page summarizes the rules for decimal arithmetic by providing memory cues to help you keep track of the decimal point.

Across the top of the chart are the four operation signs (+, −, ×, ÷). Below each sign is the rule or memory cue to follow when performing that operation. (There are two kinds of division problems, each with a different cue.)

The bottom of the chart contains two reminders that apply to all of the operations.

Facts Multiply.

7 × 7 49	4 × 6 24	8 × 1 8	2 × 2 4	0 × 5 0	6 × 3 18	8 × 9 72	5 × 8 40	6 × 2 12	10 × 10 100
9 × 4 36	2 × 5 10	9 × 6 54	7 × 3 21	5 × 5 25	7 × 2 14	6 × 8 48	3 × 5 15	9 × 9 81	5 × 4 20
3 × 4 12	6 × 5 30	8 × 2 16	4 × 4 16	6 × 7 42	8 × 8 64	2 × 3 6	7 × 4 28	5 × 9 45	3 × 8 24
3 × 9 27	7 × 8 56	2 × 4 8	5 × 7 35	3 × 3 9	9 × 7 63	4 × 8 32	0 × 0 0	9 × 2 18	6 × 6 36

Decimal Arithmetic Reminders

Operation	+ or −	×	÷ by whole (*W*)	÷ by decimal (*D*)
Memory cue	line up	×; then count	up	over, over, up

You may need to …
- Place a decimal point to the right of a whole number.
- Fill empty places with zeros.

simplifying fractions

We simplify fractions in two ways. We **reduce** fractions to lowest terms, and we convert improper fractions to mixed numbers. Sometimes a fraction can be reduced and converted to a mixed number.

Example

Simplify: $\frac{4}{6} + \frac{5}{6}$

Solution

Math Language
A fraction is in **lowest terms** if the only common factor of the numerator and denominator is 1.

By adding the fractions $\frac{4}{6}$ and $\frac{5}{6}$, we get the improper fraction $\frac{9}{6}$. We can simplify this fraction. We may reduce first and then convert the fraction to a mixed number, or we may convert first and then reduce. We show both methods below.

$$\frac{4}{6} + \frac{5}{6} = \frac{9}{6}$$

Reduce First

1. Reduce: $\frac{9}{6} = \frac{3}{2}$
2. Convert: $\frac{3}{2} = 1\frac{1}{2}$

Convert First

1. Convert: $\frac{9}{6} = 1\frac{3}{6}$
2. Reduce: $1\frac{3}{6} = 1\frac{1}{2}$

Practice Set ▸

a. Connect Discuss how the rules in the decimals chart apply to each of these problems: See student work.

5 − 4.2   0.4 × 0.2   0.12 ÷ 3   5 ÷ 0.4

b. Draw the decimals chart on your paper. See student work.

Simplify:

c. $\frac{10}{12} + \frac{5}{12}$ $1\frac{1}{4}$ **d.** $\frac{9}{10} + \frac{6}{10}$ $1\frac{1}{2}$ **e.** $\frac{8}{12} + \frac{7}{12}$ $1\frac{1}{4}$

▸ See Math Conversations in the sidebar.

2 New Concepts (Continued)

Instruction

Until students have mastered addition, subtraction, multiplication, and division with decimal numbers, you may wish to post an enlarged version of the "Decimal Arithmetic Reminders" chart in the *Student Reference Guide* in the classroom for easy reference.

As a part of Power Up for several days you may wish to have students draw this chart or an abbreviated version of it from memory on the back of their Power Up page.

Example

Instruction

Make sure students understand that after they find the sum of the addends, they can choose to reduce that sum or convert that sum; both choices produce the same final answer.

Practice Set

Problem a Connect

Work through each of the four problems, asking students to cite a reference from the chart for each problem. Use the following questions to guide the discussion.

- What is the operation?
- What is the memory cue?
- What does the memory cue tell us to do?
- Are either of the two general cues (at the bottom of the chart) used in this problem?
- If so, how are they used?

clusion

fer students to the Decimal thmetic Reminders Chart in the udent Reference Guide. Help udents use it to predict how ny digits will follow the decimal int in each sum, difference, and oduct below. Then have students each calculation to check their edictions.

+ 4.1 7.2   42 − 0.21 41.79

× 4.1 12.71   31 × 0.41 12.71

k:

Which quotient is greater: 4.2 ÷ 2.1 or 42 ÷ 2.1?" 42 ÷ 2.1

Math Background

When the empty places in a number are filled with zeros, the zeros are called placeholders. Placeholder zeros do not increase or decrease a number. Their only function is to position the decimal point correctly.

3 Written Practice

Math Conversations

Discussion opportunities are provided below.

Problem 4 Analyze

Extend the Problem

"Suppose the team scored 62 points in its next game. How would that number of points affect the range?" The range would not change.

"How would that number of points affect the mean?" The mean would increase.

Invite students to work collectively or in groups to discuss the following question, and then share an answer and an explanation for it with the remainder of the class.

"By what number of points would the mean increase? Use mental math and explain your answer." The mean would increase by 1 point. The next game was the team's fifth game. During that game, the team scored 5 more points than its previous mean. Five extra points in five games increases the mean by 5 ÷ 5 or 1 point.

Problem 16 Analyze

Extend the Problem

"Explain how subtraction can be used to check your answer." Subtract each number from 1 or subtract 1 from each number, then compare the differences. The least difference is the number closest to 1.

Errors and Misconceptions

Problem 2

Instead of subtracting 4 hours and 45 minutes from 3:00 p.m., students may add that amount of time and conclude that the answer is 7:45 p.m. Point out that the turkey needs to have finished cooking by 3:00 p.m., so it must be put in the oven *before* that time.

(continued)

Written Practice *Strengthening Concepts*

1. We add or subtract only digits that have the same place value. When we line up the decimal points, digits with the same place value are automatically aligned.

* **1.** (53) **Explain** The decimals chart in this lesson shows that we line up the decimal points when we add or subtract decimal numbers. Why do we do that?

▶ **2.** (32) A turkey must cook for 4 hours 45 minutes. At what time must it be put into the oven in order to be done by 3:00 p.m.? 10:15 a.m.

* **3.** (50) Billy won the contest by eating $\frac{1}{4}$ of a berry pie in 7 seconds. At this rate how long would it take Billy to eat a whole berry pie? 28 seconds

▶ * **4.** (Inv. 5) In four games the basketball team scored 47, 52, 63, and 66 points. What is the mean of these scores? What is the range of these scores? 57 points; 19 points

Find each unknown number:

5. (43) $0.375x = 37.5$ 100

* **6.** (52) $\frac{m}{10} = 1.25$ 12.5

7. (33, 35) Write 1% as a fraction. Then write the fraction as a decimal number. $\frac{1}{100}$; 0.01

8. (38) $3.6 + 4 + 0.39$ 7.99

* **9.** (49) $\frac{36}{0.12}$ 300

10. (45) $\frac{0.15}{4}$ 0.0375

* **11.** (48) $6\frac{1}{4} - 3\frac{3}{4}$ $2\frac{1}{2}$

12. (28) $\frac{2}{3} \times \frac{3}{5}$ $\frac{2}{5}$

13. (26) $5\frac{5}{8} + 7\frac{7}{8}$ $13\frac{1}{2}$

14. (34) Which digit in 3456 has the same place value as the 2 in 28.7? 5

* **15.** (41, 51) The items Kameko ordered for lunch totaled $5.20. The sales-tax rate was 8%.

a. **Estimate** Find the sales tax to the nearest cent. 42¢

b. Find the total price for the lunch including sales tax. $5.62

▶* **16.** (50) Which number is closest to 1? B

A 1.2 **B** 0.9 **C** 0.1 **D** $\frac{1}{2}$

17. (47) **Estimate** The entire class held hands and formed a big circle. If the circle was 40 feet across the center, then it was how many feet around? Round the answer to the nearest foot. (Use 3.14 for π.) 126 feet

18. (8) What is the perimeter of this square? $1\frac{1}{2}$ in.

$\frac{3}{8}$ in.

19. (29) A yard is 36 inches. What fraction of a yard is 3 inches? $\frac{1}{12}$

20. (19) **a.** List the factors of 11. 1, 11

b. What is the name for a whole number that has exactly two factors? prime number

▶ See Math Conversations in the sidebar.

English Learners

On the board, write A = 10, 1 = KR, and Z = 50. Say:

"Corresponds means 'equal to' or 'matched with.' What does A correspond to? What does 1 correspond to? What does 50 correspond to?" 10; KR; Z

Refer to problem **29,** ask the students to identify the corresponding numbers to points A and B.

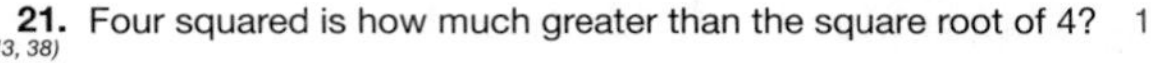

21. (13, 38) Four squared is how much greater than the square root of 4? 14

22. (30) What is the smallest number that is a multiple of both 6 and 9? 18

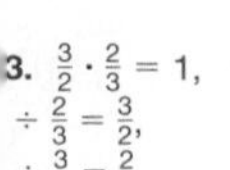

3. $\frac{3}{2} \cdot \frac{2}{3} = 1$, $\div \frac{2}{3} = \frac{3}{2}$, $\div \frac{3}{2} = \frac{2}{3}$

23. (30) The product of $\frac{2}{3}$ and $\frac{3}{2}$ is 1.

$$\frac{2}{3} \cdot \frac{3}{2} = 1$$

Use these numbers to form another multiplication fact and two division facts.

24. (5) $\dfrac{2 \cdot 3 \cdot 2 \cdot 5 \cdot 2 \cdot 5}{2 \cdot 5 \cdot 2 \cdot 5}$ 6

25. (42) $\frac{5}{6} = \frac{?}{24}$ 20

6.

26. (29) **Represent** Copy this rectangle on your paper, and shade two thirds of it.

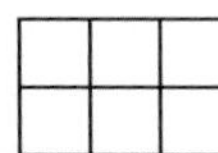

7. 350 students; 35 students, 35 students, 35 students (…% ride the bus); 35 students, 35 students, 35 students, 35 students, 35 students, 35 students, 35 students (…% do not ride the bus.)

27. (22, 33) **Model** Thirty percent of the 350 students ride the bus to Thompson School. Find the number of students who ride the bus. Draw a diagram to illustrate the problem. 105 students

28. (42) Rename $\frac{1}{4}$ and $\frac{1}{6}$ as fractions with denominators of 12. Then add the renamed fractions. $\frac{3}{12} + \frac{2}{12} = \frac{5}{12}$

▶* **29.** (50) **Connect** The number that corresponds to point *A* is how much less than the number that corresponds to point *B*? 1.3

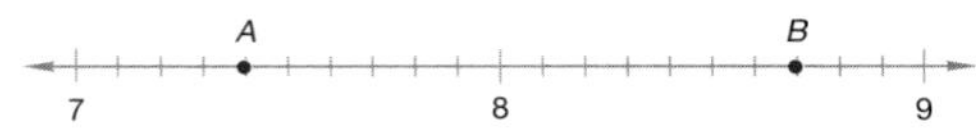

▶* **30.** (50) **Connect** The classroom encyclopedia set fills a shelf that is 24 inches long. Each book is $\frac{3}{4}$ inch thick. How many books are in the classroom set? (To answer this question, write and solve a fraction division problem using the method shown in Lesson 50.) 32 books

Early Finishers *Real-World Application*

At an online auction site, a model of a 1911 touring car was listed for sale. The twelve highest bids are shown below.

\$10 \$15 \$11 \$10 \$12 \$10 \$13 \$13 \$11 \$13 \$11 \$10

Which display—a stem-and-leaf plot or a line plot—is the most appropriate way to display this data? Draw the display and justify your choice. line plot; Sample: A line plot is the most appropriate display because it shows individual data points. Every bid begins with the digit 1, so a stem-and-leaf plot would not be a good choice as there would only be one stem. See student graphs.

▶ See Math Conversations in the sidebar.

Looking Forward

Simplifying fractions by changing improper fractions to mixed numbers in lowest terms prepares students for:

- **Lesson 54,** simplifying answers to division of fractions problems.
- **Lessons 55 and 57,** simplifying answers to problems with addition and subtraction of fractions with unlike denominators.
- **Lessons 59 and 61,** simplifying answers to problems with addition of mixed numbers.
- **Lessons 66 and 68,** simplifying answers to problems that involve multiplying and dividing mixed numbers.
- **Lesson 70,** reducing fractions before multiplying and then simplifying answers.

3 Written Practice *(Continued)*

Math Conversations

Discussion opportunities are provided below.

Problem 29 Connect

"One way to find this answer is to subtract. Explain how subtraction can be used to find the answer." Subtract the decimal number that represents Point *A* from the decimal number that represents Point *B*; $8.7 - 7.4 = 1.3$.

"Counting is another method that can be used to find the answer. Explain how counting can be used." Count the number of tenths from Point *A* to Point *B* or from Point *B* to Point *A*.

Problem 30 Connect

If students have difficulty recognizing that division is the operation that is used to solve the problem, ask them to solve a simpler problem first. For example:

"Suppose that the shelf is 24 inches long but each book is 6 inches thick. How many books would be on the shelf?" 4

"How did you find the answer?" divide 24 by 6

"How can you find the answer to problem 30?" divide 24 by $\frac{3}{4}$

• Reducing by Grouping Factors Equal to 1
• Dividing Fractions

Objectives

- Reduce a fraction by grouping factors in the numerator and denominator that are equal to 1.
- Use fraction manipulatives to show the division of a fraction by a fraction.
- Divide a fraction by a fraction.

Lesson Preparation

Materials

- **Power Up G** (in *Instructional Masters*)
- **Manipulative kit: rulers**
- **Manipulative kit: overhead fraction circles**
- **Teacher-provided material: fraction manipulatives** from Investigation 2

Optional

- **Teacher-provided material: 3 by 5 cards**

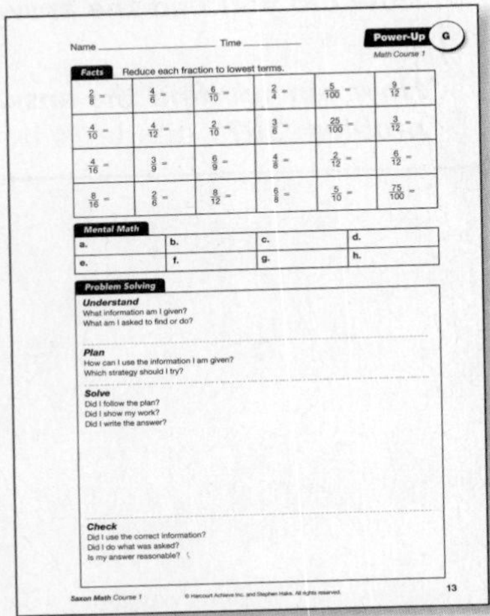

Power Up G

Math Language

Maintain	English Learners (ESL)
factors	combinations

Technology Resources

Student eBook Complete student textbook in electronic format.

Resources and Planner CD Assessment, reteaching, and instructional masters, plus a pacing calendar with standards.

Test and Practice Generator CD Create additional practice sheets and custom-made tests.

www.SaxonPublishers.com Visit for more student activities and planning materials.

Inclusion

Adaptations CD Adapted lessons, investigations, practice and assessments.

Meeting Standards

National Council of Teachers of Mathematics (NCTM)

Numbers and Operations

NO.1a Work flexibly with fractions, decimals, and percents to solve problems

NO.1f Use factors, multiples, prime factorization, and relatively prime numbers to solve problems

NO.2a Understand the meaning and effects of arithmetic operations with fractions, decimals, and integers

NO.3a Select appropriate methods and tools for computing with fractions and decimals from among mental computation, estimation, calculators or computers, and paper and pencil, depending on the situation, and apply the selected methods

Problem Solving

PS.1c Apply and adapt a variety of appropriate strategies to solve problems

Power-Up Discussion *For use with Power Up, p. 280*

roblem-Solving Strategy: Use Logical Reasoning

The PE class ran counterclockwise around the school block, starting and finishing at point A. Instead of running all the way around the block, Nimah took what she called her "shortcut," shown by the dotted line. How many meters did Nimah save with her "shortcut?"

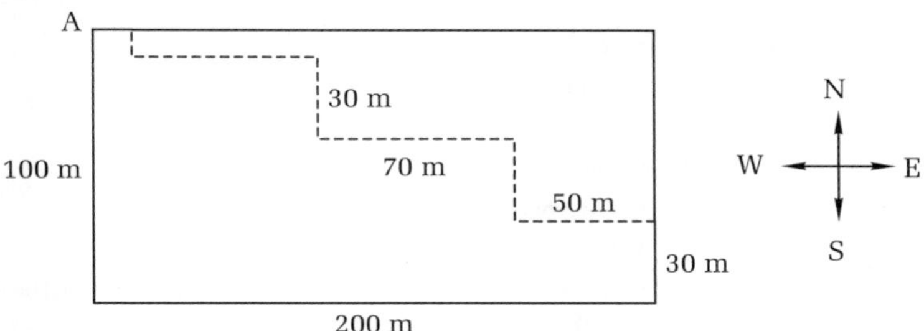

Understand **Understand the problem.**

"What information are we given?"

We are shown a labeled diagram of the route the P.E. class ran. A dotted line on the diagram represents the path Nimah took instead of following the regular route.

"What are we asked to do?

We are asked to find how many meters Nimah saved by using her own path instead of running all the way around the block.

Plan **Make a plan.**

"How can we use the information we know to do what we are asked to do?"

We see that for most of the run, Nimah followed the same route as her classmates. To find the distance Nimah saved, we will first *use logical reasoning* to find the length of her path. Then we will compare that distance to the distance she did not run with the rest of her class.

Solve **Carry out the plan.**

"How could we describe Nimah's "shortcut"?"

Nimah's path is a series of short jogs straight north and straight west.

"Add the lengths of each short run north from Nimah's path. What is the total length equal to?"

It is equal to the total length the class runs north.

"Add the lengths of each short run west from Nimah's path. What is the total length equal to?"

It is equal to the total length the class runs west.

"How many meters did Nimah save with her "shortcut"?"

Nimah's "shortcut" is not a shortcut at all. Each segment of Nimah's path is matched exactly by the length of a segment she did not run. Nimah saves 0 meters.

Check **Look back.**

"Did we answer the question that was asked?"

Yes. We found that Nimah did not save any distance with her "shortcut."

1 Power Up

Facts

Distribute **Power Up G** to students. See answers below.

Mental Math

Before students begin the Mental Math exercise, do this counting exercise as a class.

Count up and down by $\frac{1}{8}$s between $\frac{1}{8}$ and 3.

Encourage students to share different ways to mentally compute these exercises. Strategies for exercises **c** and **d** are listed below.

c. Add 100, then Subtract 1

$375 + 100 = 475$; $475 - 1 = 474$

Subtract 1 and Add 1

$375 - 1 = 374$ and $99 + 1 = 100$;
$374 + 100 = 474$

d. Add Dollars, then Add Cents

$\$8 + \$0.75 + \$5 = \$13 + \$0.75 = \$13.75$

Count On by Dollars

Start with \$8.75. Count: \$9.75, \$10.75, \$11.75, \$12.75, \$13.75

Problem Solving

Refer to **Power-Up Discussion**, p. 280B.

2 New Concepts

Instruction

Remind students that a fraction bar is a symbol that represents division. The dividend is above the bar and the divisor is below.

To introduce the lesson, you might choose to write the fraction on the board or overhead and invite a volunteer to simplify the fraction by multiplying the factors in the numerator and multiplying the factors in the denominator. Ask the volunteer to demonstrate how to reduce $\frac{60}{12}$. $\frac{60}{12} = 5$

Then use the lesson to show how the fraction can be simplified to 5 without having to multiply all of the factors in the numerator and in the denominator.

(continued)

LESSON 54

- **Reducing by Grouping Factors Equal to 1**
- **Dividing Fractions**

Power Up

Building Power

facts Power Up G

mental math

a. **Number Sense:** 6×250 1500

b. **Number Sense:** $736 - 400$ 336

c. **Number Sense:** $375 + 99$ 474

d. **Money:** $\$8.75 + \$5.00$ \$13.75

e. **Fractional Parts:** $\frac{1}{2}$ of 9 $4\frac{1}{2}$

f. **Number Sense:** 30×30 900

g. **Geometry:** Can you think of a time when a figure could have the same value for both its perimeter and its area? answers will vary

h. **Calculation:** 8×8, $- 1$, $\div 9$, $\times 7$, $+ 1$, $\div 5$, $\times 10$ 100

problem solving

The PE class ran counterclockwise around the school block, starting and finishing at point A. Instead of running all the way around the block, Nimah took what she called her "shortcut," shown by the dotted line. How many meters did Nimah save with her "shortcut?" 0 m (the paths are of equal distance)

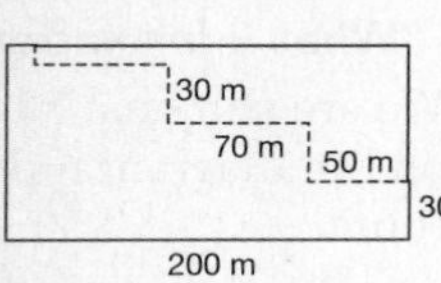

New Concepts

Increasing Knowledge

reducing by grouping factors equal to 1

The **factors** in the problem below are arranged in order from least to greatest. Notice that some factors appear in both the dividend and the divisor.

$$\frac{2 \cdot 2 \cdot 3 \cdot 5}{2 \cdot 2 \cdot 3}$$

Since $2 \div 2$ equals 1 and $3 \div 3$ equals 1, we will mark the combinations of factors equal to 1 in this problem.

$$\frac{\overset{1}{\cancel{2}} \cdot \overset{1}{\cancel{2}} \cdot \overset{1}{\cancel{3}} \cdot 5}{\cancel{2} \cdot \cancel{2} \cdot \cancel{3}}$$

Looking at the factors this way, the problem becomes $1 \cdot 1 \cdot 1 \cdot 5$, which is 5.

Verify Which property helps us know that $1 \cdot 5 = 5$? Identity Property of Multiplication

Facts Reduce each fraction to lowest terms.

$\frac{2}{8} = \frac{1}{4}$	$\frac{4}{6} = \frac{2}{3}$	$\frac{6}{10} = \frac{3}{5}$	$\frac{2}{4} = \frac{1}{2}$	$\frac{5}{100} = \frac{1}{20}$	$\frac{9}{12} = \frac{3}{4}$
$\frac{4}{10} = \frac{2}{5}$	$\frac{4}{12} = \frac{1}{3}$	$\frac{2}{10} = \frac{1}{5}$	$\frac{3}{6} = \frac{1}{2}$	$\frac{25}{100} = \frac{1}{4}$	$\frac{3}{12} = \frac{1}{4}$
$\frac{4}{16} = \frac{1}{4}$	$\frac{3}{9} = \frac{1}{3}$	$\frac{6}{9} = \frac{2}{3}$	$\frac{4}{8} = \frac{1}{2}$	$\frac{2}{12} = \frac{1}{6}$	$\frac{6}{12} = \frac{1}{2}$
$\frac{8}{16} = \frac{1}{2}$	$\frac{2}{6} = \frac{1}{3}$	$\frac{8}{12} = \frac{2}{3}$	$\frac{6}{8} = \frac{3}{4}$	$\frac{5}{10} = \frac{1}{2}$	$\frac{75}{100} = \frac{3}{4}$

Example 1

Reduce this fraction: $\dfrac{2 \cdot 2 \cdot 2 \cdot 5}{2 \cdot 2 \cdot 3 \cdot 5}$

Solution

We will mark combinations of factors equal to 1.

$$\frac{\overset{1}{2} \cdot \overset{1}{2} \cdot 2 \cdot \overset{1}{5}}{2 \cdot 2 \cdot 3 \cdot 5}$$

By grouping factors equal to 1, the problem becomes $1 \cdot 1 \cdot 1 \cdot \frac{2}{3}$, which is $\mathbf{\frac{2}{3}}$.

dividing fractions

When we divide 10 by 5, we are answering the question "How many 5s are in 10?" When we divide $\frac{3}{4}$ by $\frac{1}{2}$ we are answering the same type of question. In this case the question is "How many $\frac{1}{2}$s are in $\frac{3}{4}$?" While it is easy to see how many 5s are in 10, it is not as easy to see how many $\frac{1}{2}$s are in $\frac{3}{4}$. We remember from Lesson 50 that when the divisor is a fraction, we take two steps to find the answer. We first find how many of the divisors are in 1. This is the reciprocal of the divisor. Then we use the reciprocal to answer the original division problem by multiplying.

Example 2

How many $\frac{1}{2}$s are in $\frac{3}{4}$? $\left(\frac{3}{4} \div \frac{1}{2}\right)$

Solution

Before we show the two-step process, we will solve the problem with our fraction manipulatives. The question can be stated this way:

How many $\frac{1}{2}$s are needed to make $\frac{3}{4}$?

We see that the answer is more than one but less than two. If we take one $\frac{1}{2}$ and cut another $\frac{1}{2}$ into two equal parts, then we can fit the first $\frac{1}{2}$ and one of the smaller parts together to make three fourths.

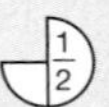

We see that we need $1\frac{1}{2}$ of the $\frac{1}{2}$ pieces to make $\frac{3}{4}$.

Now we will use arithmetic to show that $\frac{3}{4} \div \frac{1}{2}$ equals $1\frac{1}{2}$. The original problem asks, "How many $\frac{1}{2}$s are in $\frac{3}{4}$?"

$$\frac{3}{4} \div \frac{1}{2}$$

The first step is to find the number of $\frac{1}{2}$s in 1.

$$1 \div \frac{1}{2} = 2$$

The number of $\frac{1}{2}$s in 1 is 2, which is the reciprocal of $\frac{1}{2}$. So the number of $\frac{1}{2}$s in $\frac{3}{4}$ should be $\frac{3}{4}$ of 2. We find $\frac{3}{4}$ of 2 by multiplying.

$$\frac{3}{4} \times 2 = \frac{6}{4}, \text{ which equals } \mathbf{1\frac{1}{2}}$$

2 New Concepts (Continued)

Example 1

Instruction

To prove that the fraction is equal to $\frac{2}{3}$, ask students to find the product of the factors in the numerator and the product of the factors in the denominator, then reduce. $\frac{40}{60} \div \frac{20}{20} = \frac{2}{3}$

Example 2

Instruction

On an overhead projector, model $\frac{3}{4} \div \frac{1}{2}$ using Overhead Fraction Circles from the Manipulative Kit and ask students to duplicate your actions using their fraction manipulatives from Investigation 2. Begin by placing a $\frac{1}{2}$ piece next to three $\frac{1}{4}$ pieces on the projector.

"How many one halves are needed to make three fourths? Will it be more than one or less than one?" $1\frac{1}{2}$; more than 1

Show a second $\frac{1}{2}$ piece to students.

"We can cut another $\frac{1}{2}$ piece in half and fit it together with the first $\frac{1}{2}$ piece to make three fourths."

Cut the new $\frac{1}{2}$ piece in half, and cover the three $\frac{1}{4}$ pieces with one and a half $\frac{1}{2}$ pieces.

"One and a half $\frac{1}{2}$ pieces are in three fourths, so three fourths divided by one half equals one and a half."

(continued)

Math Background

Simplifying expressions by "removing" a factor of 1 is a skill students will frequently use in their study of algebra. In this lesson, students learn that expressions such as $\frac{5 \cdot 5}{5 \cdot 5}$ represent a combination of factors equal to 1.

In their future studies, students will learn about other expressions equal to 1, such as $\frac{x}{x}$, $\frac{n+2}{n+2}$, and $\frac{(a-b)}{(a-b)}$.

2 New Concepts (Continued)

Example 3

Instruction

On an overhead projector, model $\frac{1}{2} \div \frac{3}{4}$ using overhead fraction circles from the Manipulative Kit, and ask students to duplicate your actions using their fraction manipulatives from Investigation 2. Begin by placing three $\frac{1}{4}$ pieces next to a $\frac{1}{2}$ piece on the projector.

"How many three fourths are needed to make one half? As you can see, the answer will be less than 1. Three fourths is made of three parts. We can take away one of the three parts and see that two of the three parts equal $\frac{1}{2}$."

Move one $\frac{1}{4}$ piece away from the three $\frac{1}{4}$ pieces.

"Two out of three parts—or two thirds—of three fourths is needed to make one half. Therefore, one half divided by three fourths equals two thirds."

Practice Set

Problems a and b Error Alert

To reduce each fraction, encourage students to pair factors equal to 1. To help organize their work, students may want to draw a loop around paired factors.

(continued)

We simplified $\frac{6}{4}$ by reducing $\frac{6}{4}$ to $\frac{3}{2}$ and then converting $\frac{3}{2}$ to $1\frac{1}{2}$. We will review the steps we took to solve the problem.

Original problem:

How many $\frac{1}{2}$s are in $\frac{3}{4}$? $\qquad \frac{3}{4} \div \frac{1}{2}$

Step 1: Find the number of $\frac{1}{2}$s in 1. $\qquad 1 \div \frac{1}{2} = 2$

Step 2: Use the number of $\frac{1}{2}$s in 1 to find the number of $\frac{1}{2}$s in $\frac{3}{4}$. Then simplify the answer. $\qquad \frac{3}{4} \times 2 = \frac{6}{4} = 1\frac{1}{2}$

Example 3

How many $\frac{3}{4}$s are in $\frac{1}{2}$? $\left(\frac{1}{2} \div \frac{3}{4}\right)$

Solution

Using our fraction manipulatives, the question can be stated this way:

What fraction of is needed to make ?

The answer is less than 1. We need to cut off part of to make . If we cut off one of the three parts of three fourths (), we see that two of the three parts equal . So $\frac{2}{3}$ of $\frac{3}{4}$ is needed to make $\frac{1}{2}$.

Now we will show the arithmetic. The original problem asks, "How many $\frac{3}{4}$s are in $\frac{1}{2}$?"

$$\frac{1}{2} \div \frac{3}{4}$$

First we find the number of $\frac{3}{4}$s in 1. The number is the reciprocal of $\frac{3}{4}$.

$$1 \div \frac{3}{4} = \frac{4}{3}$$

The number of $\frac{3}{4}$s in 1 is $\frac{4}{3}$. So the number of $\frac{3}{4}$s in $\frac{1}{2}$ is $\frac{1}{2}$ of $\frac{4}{3}$. We find $\frac{1}{2}$ of $\frac{4}{3}$ by multiplying.

$$\frac{1}{2} \times \frac{4}{3} = \frac{4}{6}, \text{ which equals } \mathbf{\frac{2}{3}}$$

Again, we will review the steps we took to solve the problem.

Original problem:

How many $\frac{3}{4}$s are in $\frac{1}{2}$? $\qquad \frac{1}{2} \div \frac{3}{4}$

Step 1: Find the number of $\frac{3}{4}$s in 1. $\qquad 1 \div \frac{3}{4} = \frac{4}{3}$

Step 2: Use the number of $\frac{3}{4}$s in 1 to find the number of $\frac{3}{4}$s in $\frac{1}{2}$. Then simplify the answer. $\qquad \frac{1}{2} \times \frac{4}{3} = \frac{4}{6} = \frac{2}{3}$

Practice Set Reduce:

▸ **a.** $\frac{2 \cdot 2 \cdot 3 \cdot 5}{2 \cdot 2 \cdot 5}$ 3 $\qquad$ ▸ **b.** $\frac{2 \cdot 2 \cdot 3 \cdot 3 \cdot 5}{2 \cdot 2 \cdot 3 \cdot 5 \cdot 5}$ $\frac{3}{5}$

▸ See Math Conversations in the sidebar.

Inclusion

Canceling fractions makes the multiplication and division of fractions easier. Explain to students that the techniques they learned to reduce fractions to simplest terms can also be used when multiplying and dividing fractions. Demonstrate by using the examples below:

$$\frac{2}{\cancel{3}_1} \times \frac{\cancel{3}^1}{1} = 2 \qquad \frac{1}{4} \div \frac{3}{8} \longrightarrow \frac{1}{\cancel{4}_1} \times \frac{\cancel{8}^2}{3} = \frac{2}{3}$$

Emphasize that any numerator can be paired with any denominator to reduce fractions to lowest terms before multiplying. Refer students to the "Tests for Divisibility" in the Student Reference Guide if they need help in identifying pairs of numbers that have a common factor.

Have students use cancellation to find the product and quotient below:

$$\frac{24}{35} \times \frac{70}{8} \;\; 6 \qquad \frac{16}{18} \div \frac{32}{6} \;\; \frac{1}{6}$$

▶ **c.** How many $\frac{3}{8}$s are in $\frac{1}{2}$? $\left(\frac{1}{2} \div \frac{3}{8}\right)$ $1\frac{1}{3}$

▶ **d.** How many $\frac{1}{2}$s are in $\frac{3}{8}$? $\left(\frac{3}{8} \div \frac{1}{2}\right)$ $\frac{3}{4}$

Written Practice *Strengthening Concepts*

▶ * **1.** (53) **Summarize** Draw the decimals chart from Lesson 53. See student work.

2. (45) If 0.4 is the dividend and 4 is the divisor, what is the quotient? 0.1

3. (16) **Estimate** In 1900 the U.S. population was 76,212,168. In 1950 the population was 151,325,798. Estimate the increase in population between 1900 and 1950 to the nearest million. 75,000,000

4. (48) **Formulate** Marjani was $59\frac{3}{4}$ inches tall when she turned 11 and $61\frac{1}{4}$ inches tall when she turned 12. How many inches did Marjani grow during the year? Write an equation and solve the problem. $61\frac{1}{4} - 59\frac{3}{4} = d$; $1\frac{1}{2}$ inches

5. (5) $1000 - (100 - 1)$ 901

6. (25) $\dfrac{1000}{24}$ $41\frac{2}{3}$

▶ **7.** (18) What number is halfway between 37 and 143? 90

Find each unknown number:

8. (3) $\$3 - n = 24¢$ \$2.76

9. (43) $m + 3\frac{4}{5} = 6\frac{2}{5}$ $2\frac{3}{5}$

▶* **10.** (45) $4.2 \div 10^2$ 0.042

▶* **11.** (53) $(1.2 \div 0.12)(1.2)$ 12

12. (29, 38) $\left(\frac{4}{3}\right)^2$ $1\frac{7}{9}$

13. (38) $\sqrt{9} + \sqrt{16}$ 7

14. (12) Which digit is in the hundred-thousands place in 123,456,789? 4

▶ **15.** (41, 45) The television cost \$289.90. The sales-tax rate was 8%. How much was the sales tax on the television? \$23.19

▶* **16.** (9) **Connect** Use rulers to compare:

two centimeters (<) one inch

▶* **17.** (10) **Predict** Isadora found the sixth term of this sequence by doubling six and then subtracting one. She found the seventh term by doubling seven and subtracting one. What is the twelfth term of this sequence? 23

1, 3, 5, 7, 9, . . .

18. (31) How many square feet of tile would be needed to cover the area of a room 14 feet long and 12 feet wide? 168 square feet

19. (23) Nine of the 30 students played basketball on the school team.

a. What fraction of the students played on the team? $\frac{3}{10}$

b. What is the ratio of students who played basketball to students who did not play basketball? $\frac{3}{7}$

20. (42) **a.** $\frac{5}{6} = \frac{?}{24}$ 20 **b.** $\frac{5}{8} = \frac{?}{24}$ 15

▶ See Math Conversations in the sidebar.

2 New Concepts *(Continued)*

Practice Set

Problems c and d *Error Alert*

Remind students to simplify their answers.

3 Written Practice

Math Conversations

Discussion opportunities are provided below.

Problem 1 *Summarize*

You may choose to have students summarize the chart instead of drawing it. If students draw the chart, you may want to ask them to draw it in the front of their math notebooks or on 3 by 5 cards for convenient reference.

Problems 10 and 11 *Analyze*

Each problem includes more than one operation. For each problem, ask students to name the operation that should be completed first and to justify their choice.

Problem 16 *Connect*

"When we compare, we write a symbol of equality or a symbol of inequality. An equals sign is a symbol of equality. A greater than sign or a less than sign is a symbol of inequality."

"Which symbol is used to complete this comparison? Explain why." The less than symbol is used; 1 inch is about the same as $2\frac{1}{2}$ centimeters, so 2 centimeters must be less than 1 inch.

Problem 17 *Predict*

Extend the Problem

"Does this sequence have a one millionth term?" yes

"Using only mental math, name the one millionth term of this sequence." The term is 1 less than 2 million, or 1,999,999.

Errors and Misconceptions

Problem 7

Explain to students that the number halfway between 37 and 143 is the average of those numbers. To find the number that is halfway, ask students to divide the sum of the numbers by 2.

Problem 15

Remind students who compute the sales tax as \$23.192 that our system of money does not include a coin less than hundredths of a dollar so the amount must be rounded to the nearest cent.

(continued)

3 Written Practice (Continued)

Math Conversations

Discussion opportunities are provided below.

Problem 22 Represent

Encourage students to use their fraction manipulatives to model or check the solution.

Problems 25 and 26 Analyze

Each problem contains pairs of factors that can be grouped because the pairs are equal to 1. Before completing the problems, write each problem on the board or overhead and invite various students to each draw a loop around a factor pair that is equal to 1.

"Grouping these factor pairs removes them from the fraction. Why can we remove factor pairs from the fraction?" The factor pairs are equal to 1, and multiplying any non-zero number by 1 does not change the number.

---

21. What is the least common multiple of 3, 4, and 6? 12
(30)

▸* **22.** Represent How many $\frac{1}{2}$s are in $\frac{2}{3}$? $\left(\frac{2}{3} \div \frac{1}{2}\right)$ $1\frac{1}{3}$
(54)

23. Model Eighty percent of the 30 answers were correct. Write 80% as a reduced fraction. Then find the number of answers that were correct. Draw a diagram to illustrate the problem. $\frac{4}{5}$; 24 answers
(22, 23)

23. 30 answers
- $\frac{4}{5}$ were correct: 6 answers, 6 answers, 6 answers, 6 answers
- $\frac{1}{5}$ were not correct: 6 answers

24. Connect One inch equals 2.54 centimeters. A ribbon 100 inches long is how many centimeters long? 254 centimeters
(46)

Reduce:

▸* **25.** $\dfrac{2 \cdot 3 \cdot 5 \cdot 3 \cdot 2}{2 \cdot 3 \cdot 2 \cdot 5}$ 3
(54)

▸* **26.** $\dfrac{2 \cdot 3 \cdot 3 \cdot 5}{2 \cdot 2 \cdot 2 \cdot 3 \cdot 5}$ $\frac{3}{4}$
(54)

27. Rename $\frac{2}{3}$ and $\frac{1}{2}$ as fractions with denominators of 6. Then add the renamed fractions, and convert the answer to a mixed number. $\frac{4}{6} + \frac{3}{6} = \frac{7}{6} = 1\frac{1}{6}$
(42)

28. Justify The diameter of a wheel is 15 inches. How far would your hand move in one full turn of the wheel if you do not let go of the wheel? Round the answer to the nearest inch. (Use 3.14 for π.) Describe how to tell whether your answer is reasonable.
(47)

28. 47 inches; π is a little more than 3, and 3 × 15 inches is 45 inches. So 47 inches is reasonable.

29. Draw a rectangle that is $1\frac{1}{2}$ inches long and 1 inch wide.
(8, 31)

a. What is the perimeter of the rectangle? 5 inches

b. What is the area of the rectangle? $1\frac{1}{2}$ square inches

30. Analyze Instead of dividing $2\frac{1}{2}$ by $\frac{1}{2}$, Sandra formed an equivalent division problem with whole numbers by doubling the dividend and the divisor. What equivalent problem did she form, and what is the quotient? 5 ÷ 1 = 5
(43)

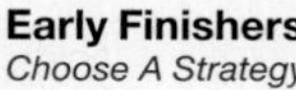

Early Finishers
Choose A Strategy

Brooke is planning to plant tulips around a circular flowerbed. The diameter of the flowerbed is about 4 feet. The tulips should be planted about 6 inches apart. She has 12 tulip bulbs. Her friend Jenna said she should buy 50% more. Is Jenna correct? Explain why or why not. You may use tiles to help you visualize the problem. Strategy: Act It Out

Sample: Jenna is not correct. 50% of 12 = 6 and 12 + 6 = 18, Brooke needs about 24 tulip bulbs, so she needs 100% percent more.

▸ See Math Conversations in the sidebar.

Looking Forward

Dividing fractions by fractions prepares students for:

- **Lesson 68,** dividing a mixed number by a whole number or another mixed number.
- **Lesson 70,** dividing fractions by reducing fraction terms before multiplying.
- **Lesson 72,** using a fraction chart to recall the steps for dividing fractions.
- **Lesson 115,** converting mixed-number percents to fractions.
- **Lesson 119,** solving an equation to find a whole when a percent is known.

Common Denominators, Part 1

Objectives

- Find the least common denominator of two fractions.
- Rename one fraction so that two fractions have common denominators.
- Add or subtract two fractions that do not have common denominators by renaming one of the fractions.

Lesson Preparation

Materials

- **Power Up I** (in *Instructional Masters*)
- **Manipulative kit: overhead fraction circles**

Power Up I

Math Language

New	Maintain	English Learners (ESL)
common denominator	least common multiple	exactly

Technology Resources

Student eBook Complete student textbook in electronic format.

Resources and Planner CD Assessment, reteaching, and instructional masters, plus a pacing calendar with standards.

Test and Practice Generator CD Create additional practice sheets and custom-made tests.

www.SaxonPublishers.com Visit for more student activities and planning materials.

Inclusion

Adaptations CD Adapted lessons, investigations, practice and assessments.

Meeting Standards

National Council of Teachers of Mathematics (NCTM)

Numbers and Operations

NO.1a Work flexibly with fractions, decimals, and percents to solve problems

NO.2a Understand the meaning and effects of arithmetic operations with fractions, decimals, and integers

NO.3a Select appropriate methods and tools for computing with fractions and decimals from among mental computation, estimation, calculators or computers, and paper and pencil, depending on the situation, and apply the selected methods

NO.3c Develop and use strategies to estimate the results of rational–number computations and judge the reasonableness of the results

Power-Up Discussion *For use with Power Up, p. 285*

Problem-Solving Strategies: Work Backwards/ Use Logical Reasoning

Copy this problem and fill in the missing digits:

```
   _4_
6)__6
  _
  __
   __
   __
   3_
    0
```

Understand **Understand the problem.**

"What information are we given?"

We are shown a division problem with missing digits in the quotient and the dividend.

"What are we asked to do?"

We are asked to complete the problem by filling in the missing digits.

Plan **Make a plan.**

"How can we use the information we know to do what we are asked to do?"

We will *work backwards* and use *number sense and logical reasoning* to fill in the blanks.

Solve **Carry out the plan.**

Teacher Note: Walk the students through filling in the blanks in the order shown.

_4_	_46	146	146	146	146
6)__6	6)__6	6)__6	6)__6	6)__6	6)876
_	_	6	6	6	6
__	__	__	__	27	27
__	__	__	24	24	24
_6	36	36	36	36	36
36	36	36	36	36	36
0	0	0	0	0	0

Check **Look back.**

"How can we verify the solution is correct/valid?"

We can work the original division problem; or we can use multiplication to check the division: $146 \times 6 = 876$.

Teacher Note: Remind students that multiplication and division are called "inverse operations." Ask students to name another pair of inverse operations.

LESSON 55

• Common Denominators, Part 1

Power Up

Building Power

facts Power Up I

mental math

a. **Calculation:** 8 × 325 2600

b. **Number Sense:** 329 + 50 379

c. **Number Sense:** 375 − 99 276

d. **Money:** \$12.50 − \$5.00 \$7.50

e. **Number Sense:** Double $3\frac{1}{2}$. 7

f. **Number Sense:** $\frac{600}{20}$ 30

g. **Measurement:** How many yards are in 60 inches? 1 yd. 2 ft

h. **Calculation:** 8 × 5, + 2, ÷ 6, × 7, + 7, ÷ 8, × 4, ÷ 7 4

problem solving Copy this problem and fill in the missing digits:

```
  _4_         146
6)__6       6)876
  _           6
  __          27
  __          24
   __          36
   3_          36
    0           0
```

New Concept

Increasing Knowledge

When the denominators of two or more fractions are equal, we say that the fractions have **common denominators.** The fractions $\frac{3}{5}$ and $\frac{2}{5}$ have common denominators.

The common denominator is 5.

The fractions $\frac{3}{4}$ and $\frac{1}{2}$ do not have common denominators because the denominators 4 and 2 are not equal.

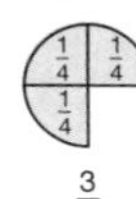

$\frac{1}{2}$

These fractions do not have common denominators.

Facts Write each improper fraction as a mixed number. Reduce fractions.

$\frac{5}{4} = 1\frac{1}{4}$	$\frac{6}{4} = 1\frac{1}{2}$	$\frac{15}{10} = 1\frac{1}{2}$	$\frac{8}{3} = 2\frac{2}{3}$	$\frac{15}{12} = 1\frac{1}{4}$
$\frac{12}{8} = 1\frac{1}{2}$	$\frac{10}{8} = 1\frac{1}{4}$	$\frac{3}{2} = 1\frac{1}{2}$	$\frac{15}{6} = 2\frac{1}{2}$	$\frac{10}{4} = 2\frac{1}{2}$
$\frac{8}{6} = 1\frac{1}{3}$	$\frac{25}{10} = 2\frac{1}{2}$	$\frac{9}{6} = 1\frac{1}{2}$	$\frac{10}{6} = 1\frac{2}{3}$	$\frac{15}{8} = 1\frac{7}{8}$
$\frac{12}{10} = 1\frac{1}{5}$	$\frac{10}{3} = 3\frac{1}{3}$	$\frac{18}{12} = 1\frac{1}{2}$	$\frac{5}{2} = 2\frac{1}{2}$	$\frac{4}{3} = 1\frac{1}{3}$

1 Power Up

Facts

Distribute **Power Up I** to students. See answers below.

Mental Math

Before students begin the Mental Math exercise, do this counting exercise as a class.

Count by 7s from 7 to 84.

Encourage students to share different ways to mentally compute these exercises. Strategies for exercises **b** and **f** are listed below.

b. Add Tens

$300 + 20 + 9 + 50 = 300 + 70 + 9 = 379$

Break Apart 329

$300 + 29 + 50 = 350 + 29 = 379$

f. Cancel Zeros

$\frac{600}{20} = \frac{60\not{0}}{2\not{0}} = \frac{60}{2} = 30$

Shift the Decimal Points

$\frac{600}{20} = \frac{60.0}{2.0} = \frac{60}{2} = 30$

Problem Solving

Refer to **Power-Up Discussion,** p. 285B.

2 New Concepts

Instruction

Have students recall that before two fractions can be added or subtracted, the fractions must have the same denominator.

"What is the sum of the fractions?" $\frac{5}{5}$ or 1

"What is the difference of the fractions?" $\frac{1}{5}$

"Why can we add and subtract these fractions?" they have a common denominator

(continued)

Manipulative Use

You may want to use the **Overhead Fraction Circles** from the Manipulative Kit to reinforce the concepts in the New Concepts and the example sections.

2 New Concepts (Continued)

Instruction

To reinforce the basic concept of adding fractions with unlike denominators, use the **Overhead Fraction Circles** to demonstrate each step of adding $\frac{3}{4}$ and $\frac{1}{2}$.

Place three $\frac{1}{4}$ pieces next to a $\frac{1}{2}$ piece. Then replace the $\frac{1}{2}$ piece with two $\frac{1}{4}$ pieces to rename $\frac{1}{2}$ as $\frac{2}{4}$. Lastly, combine the $\frac{1}{4}$ pieces to show that the sum of $\frac{3}{4}$ and $\frac{2}{4}$ is $\frac{5}{4}$.

Before students begin the example, invite them to compare and contrast the concepts of *least common multiples* and *greatest common factors*.

(continued)

Fractions that do not have common denominators can be renamed to form fractions that do have common denominators. Since $\frac{2}{4}$ equals $\frac{1}{2}$, we can rename $\frac{1}{2}$ as $\frac{2}{4}$. The fractions $\frac{3}{4}$ and $\frac{2}{4}$ have common denominators.

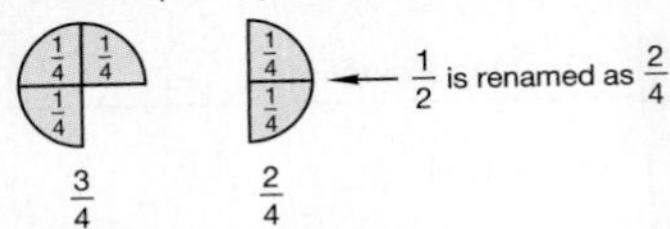

The common denominator is 4.

Fractions that have common denominators can be added by counting the number of parts, that is, by adding the numerators.

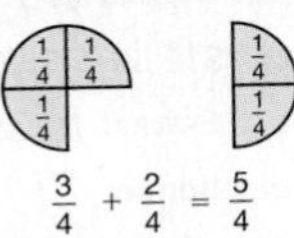

$$\frac{3}{4} + \frac{2}{4} = \frac{5}{4}$$

To add or subtract fractions that do not have common denominators, we rename one or more of them to form fractions that do have common denominators. Then we add or subtract. Recall that to rename a fraction, we multiply it by a fraction equal to 1. Here we rename $\frac{1}{2}$ by multiplying it by $\frac{2}{2}$. This forms the equivalent fraction $\frac{2}{4}$, which can be added to $\frac{3}{4}$.

Rename $\frac{1}{2}$.

$$\frac{1}{2} \times \frac{2}{2} = \frac{2}{4}$$

$$+\frac{3}{4} \qquad = \frac{3}{4}$$

Then add.

$$\frac{5}{4} = 1\frac{1}{4}$$

Simplify your answer, if possible.

Math Language

Review

The **least common multiple** is the smallest whole number that is a multiple of two given numbers.

To find the common denominator of two fractions, we find a common multiple of the denominators. The least common multiple of the denominators is the **least common denominator** of the fractions.

Example

Subtract: $\frac{1}{2} - \frac{1}{6}$

Solution

The denominators are 2 and 6. The least common multiple of 2 and 6 is 6. So 6 is the least common denominator of the two fractions. We do not need to rename $\frac{1}{6}$. We change halves to sixths by multiplying by $\frac{3}{3}$ and then we subtract.

Rename $\frac{1}{2}$.

$$\begin{array}{r} \frac{1}{2} \times \frac{3}{3} = \frac{3}{6} \\ -\frac{1}{6} \quad = \frac{1}{6} \\ \hline \frac{2}{6} = \frac{1}{3} \end{array}$$

Subtract $\frac{1}{6}$ from $\frac{3}{6}$.

Reduce.

Practice Set ▶ Find each sum or difference:

g. We can round to benchmark fractions such as $\frac{1}{2}$ and $\frac{1}{4}$ and add these fractions. Then we can check our written answers to see if the results are close.

a. $\frac{1}{2} + \frac{3}{8}$ $\frac{7}{8}$ **b.** $\frac{3}{8} + \frac{1}{4}$ $\frac{5}{8}$ **c.** $\frac{3}{4} + \frac{1}{8}$ $\frac{7}{8}$

d. $\frac{1}{2} - \frac{1}{4}$ $\frac{1}{4}$ **e.** $\frac{5}{8} - \frac{1}{4}$ $\frac{3}{8}$ **f.** $\frac{3}{4} - \frac{3}{8}$ $\frac{3}{8}$

g. Evaluate How can we use mental math to check our answers to **a–f?**

Written Practice *Strengthening Concepts*

1. When we divide a decimal number by a whole number using a division box, we place a decimal point in the quotient directly "up" from the decimal point in the dividend.

▶ * **1.** (53) Explain In the decimals chart, the memory cue for dividing by a whole number is "up." What does that mean?

▶ * **2.** (50) Connect How many $\frac{3}{8}$-inch-thick CD cases will fit on a 12-inch-long shelf? (To answer the question, write and solve a fraction division problem using the method shown in Lesson 50.) 32 CD cases

3. (15) The average pumpkin weighs 6 pounds. The prize-winning pumpkin weighs 324 pounds. The prize-winning pumpkin weighs as much as how many average pumpkins? 54 average pumpkins

* **4.** (55) $\frac{1}{8} + \frac{1}{2}$ $\frac{5}{8}$ * **5.** (55) $\frac{1}{2} - \frac{1}{8}$ $\frac{3}{8}$ * **6.** (55) $\frac{2}{3} - \frac{1}{6}$ $\frac{1}{2}$

7. (38) 6.28 + 4 + 0.13 10.41 **8.** (49) 81 ÷ 0.9 90

9. (52) 0.2 ÷ 10 0.02 **10.** (46) (0.17)(100) 17

11. (26) $\frac{3}{4} + 3\frac{1}{4}$ 4 **12.** (29) $\frac{5}{6} \cdot \frac{2}{3}$ $\frac{5}{9}$ **13.** (42) $\frac{5}{8} = \frac{?}{24}$ 15

14. (32) Mt. McKinley is the tallest mountain in North America. Its height in feet is shown in expanded notation below. Write the height of Mt. McKinley in standard form. 20,320 feet

(2 × 10,000) + (3 × 100) + (2 × 10)

▶ See Math Conversations in the sidebar.

Manipulative Use

You can use the **Overhead Fraction Circles** from the Manipulative Kit to model the example 2 solution.

Place a $\frac{1}{2}$ piece on the overhead projector. Point out that this piece must be renamed before a $\frac{1}{6}$ piece can be taken away from it. Replace the $\frac{1}{2}$ piece with three $\frac{1}{6}$ pieces, then take one $\frac{1}{6}$ piece away. Ask students to name the amount that remains. $\frac{2}{6}$

To show reducing $\frac{2}{6}$ to $\frac{1}{3}$, replace the two $\frac{2}{6}$ pieces with one $\frac{1}{3}$ piece.

2 New Concepts *(Continued)*

Example 2

Instruction

Make sure students recognize that subtraction does not occur until the denominators of the fractions are the same.

Practice Set

Problems a–f Error Alert

To add or subtract the fractions, students must rename one fraction in each problem. Before solving each problem, ask these questions.

"Are the denominators the same, or different?"

"If the denominators are different, we must rename one or both fractions. What is the least common multiple of the denominators?"

"Which fraction will we rename, and how will the least common multiple be used to rename that fraction?"

3 Written Practice

Math Conversations

Discussion opportunities are provided below.

Problem 1 Connect

Students may refer to the "Decimal Arithmetic Reminders" chart in Lesson 53 to answer this problem.

Problem 2 Connect

If students have difficulty recognizing how to solve the problem, ask them to solve a simpler problem first. For example:

"Suppose that the shelf is 12 inches long but each case is 2 inches thick. How many cases would fit on the shelf?" 6

"How did you find the answer?" divide 12 by 2

"How can you find the answer to Problem 2?" divide 12 by $\frac{3}{8}$

(continued)

3 Written Practice (Continued)

Math Conversations

Discussion opportunities are provided below.

Problem 18 Model

"How are the lengths of the sides of any square related?" the lengths are the same

"If you know the perimeter of a square, what operation can you use to find the length of each side?" divide the perimeter by 4

Problem 28 Analyze

The fraction contains pairs of factors that can be grouped because the pairs are equal to 1.

"Which pairs of factors in this fraction are equal to 1?"

Invite students to draw a loop around the factor pairs as the pairs are named.

"Once we have identified the factor pairs that are equal to 1, how do we complete the problem?" Write the product of the unpaired factors in the numerator over the product of the unpaired factors in the denominator, then reduce the fraction if possible.

Errors and Misconceptions

Problem 25

Students may misinterpret this problem and decide that there are two 12s in the number 1212. Tell students that they are to find the number of groups of 12 in 1212. To find the number of groups, students must divide 1212 by 12.

Problem 26

If students do not completely reduce the ratio $\frac{36}{48}$, and instead give an answer of $\frac{18}{24}$, $\frac{12}{16}$, or $\frac{9}{12}$, suggest that they inspect the numerator and the denominator to see if both can be divided by the prime numbers 2, 3, or 5.

---

15. (38, 51) Multiply 0.14 by 0.8 and round the product to the nearest hundredth. 0.11

16. (29) Compare: $\frac{2}{3} \ominus \frac{2}{3} \times \frac{2}{2}$

* **17.** (47) The Copernicus impact crater on the moon has a diameter of about 93 km. Assume the crater is round, and use 3.14 for π. What is the distance around the crater rounded to the nearest ten kilometers? 290 km

▶* **18.** (38) **Model** A 20-foot rope was used to make a square. How many square feet of area were enclosed by the rope? Draw a diagram to help you solve the problem.

18. 25 square feet; Sample:

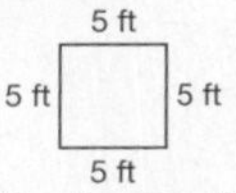

$5 + 5 + 5 + 5 = 20$

$A = s^2 = 5^2 = 25$

19. (29) What fraction of a dollar is six dimes? $\frac{3}{5}$

20. (30) What is the least common multiple (LCM) of 3 and 4? 12

21. (19) **a.** List the factors of 23. 1, 23

b. What is the name for a whole number that has exactly two factors? prime number

22. (30) By what fraction should $\frac{2}{5}$ be multiplied to form the product 1? $\frac{5}{2}$

23. (9, 38) Compare: $3^2 + 4^2 \ominus 5^2$

* **24.** (54) How many $\frac{2}{5}$s are in $\frac{1}{2}$? $(\frac{1}{2} \div \frac{2}{5})$ $1\frac{1}{4}$

▶ **25.** (15) How many 12s are in 1212? 101

▶ **26.** (23) The window was 48 inches wide and 36 inches tall. What was the ratio of the height to the width of the window? $\frac{3}{4}$

27. (29) What fraction of this group of circles is shaded? $\frac{1}{3}$

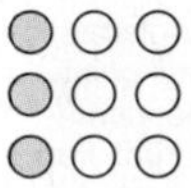

▶* **28.** (54) **Analyze** Reduce: $\frac{2 \cdot 3 \cdot 2 \cdot 5 \cdot 3 \cdot 7}{2 \cdot 2 \cdot 3 \cdot 5 \cdot 5 \cdot 5}$ $\frac{21}{25}$

29. (32) The performance began at 7:45 p.m. and concluded at 10:25 p.m. How long was the performance in hours and minutes? 2 hours 40 minutes

30. (28) **Conclude** Triangle *ABC* has three acute angles.

a. Which triangle has one right angle? triangle *GHI*

b. Which triangle has one obtuse angle? triangle *DEF*

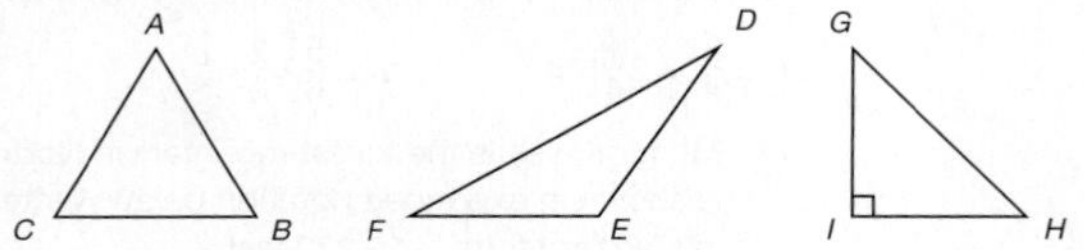

▶ See Math Conversations in the sidebar.

English Learners

Write the word **exactly** on the board. Say:

"Exactly is a word that means no more than or no less than. If a line segment measures exactly $\frac{1}{2}$ an inch, it cannot be written as $\frac{1}{4}$ or $\frac{3}{4}$ of an inch."

Ask the students to provide examples of other items and instances when it is necessary to be exact.

Looking Forward

Finding the least common denominator of two fractions, renaming fractions to form fractions with common denominators, and adding and subtracting fractions that do not have common denominators prepares students for:

- **Lesson 56,** renaming two fractions before adding, subtracting, or comparing fractions with common denominators.
- **Lesson 57,** adding and subtracting fractions in three steps (correct shape, perform operation, and simplify).
- **Lesson 61,** adding three or more fractions by renaming fractions so that they have common denominators.
- **Lesson 63,** subtracting mixed numbers with regrouping.

Assessment

30–40 minutes *For use after Lesson 55*

Distribute **Cumulative Test 10** to each student. Two versions of the test are available in *Saxon Math Course 1 Course Assessments Book.* Have students complete the **Power-Up Test** first. Allow 10 minutes. Then have students work the 20 numbered items on the **Cumulative Test.** Students may use copies of the answer sheet to record their work. Track individual and class progress with the **Test Analysis** forms.

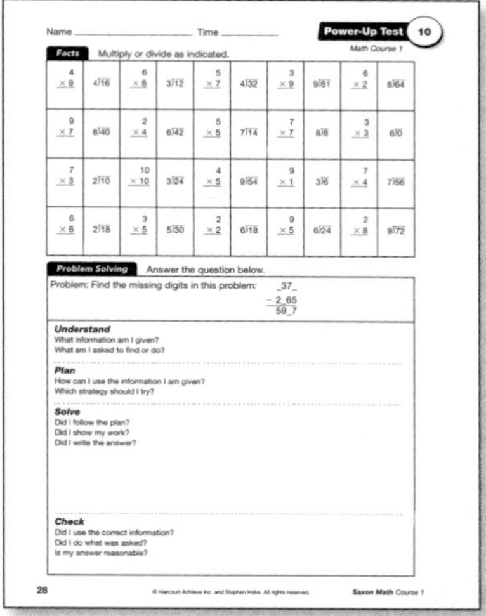

Name ______ Time ______ **Power-Up Test 10** *Math Course 1*

Facts Multiply or divide as indicated.

4×9	$4\overline{)16}$	6×8	$3\overline{)12}$	5×7	$4\overline{)32}$	3×9	$9\overline{)81}$	6×2	$8\overline{)64}$
9×7	$8\overline{)40}$	2×4	$6\overline{)42}$	5×5	$7\overline{)14}$	7×7	$8\overline{)8}$	3×3	$6\overline{)0}$
7×3	$2\overline{)10}$	10×10	$3\overline{)24}$	4×5	$9\overline{)54}$	9×1	$3\overline{)6}$	7×4	$7\overline{)56}$
6×6	$2\overline{)18}$	3×5	$5\overline{)30}$	2×2	$6\overline{)18}$	9×5	$6\overline{)24}$	2×8	$9\overline{)72}$

Problem Solving Answer the question below.

Problem: Find the missing digits in this problem: _37_ − 2_65 = 59_7

Understand
What information am I given?
What am I asked to find or do?

Plan
How can I use the information I am given?
Which strategy should I try?

Solve
Did I follow the plan?
Did I show my work?
Did I write the answer?

Check
Did I use the correct information?
Did I do what was asked?
Is my answer reasonable?

28 © Harcourt Achieve Inc. and Stephen Hake. All rights reserved. *Saxon Math Course 1*

Power-Up Test 10

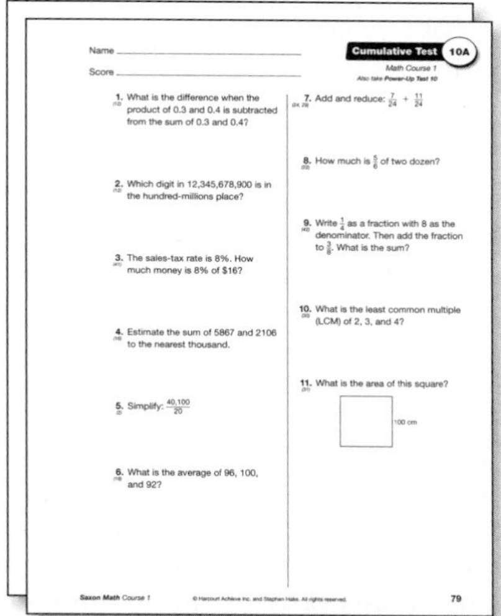

Name ______ Score ______ **Cumulative Test 10A** *Math Course 1* *Also take Power-Up Test 10*

1. What is the difference when the product of 0.3 and 0.4 is subtracted from the sum of 0.3 and 0.4?
2. Which digit in 12,345,678,900 is in the hundred-millions place?
3. The sales-tax rate is 8%. How much money is 8% of $16?
4. Estimate the sum of 5867 and 2106 to the nearest thousand.
5. Simplify: $\frac{40,100}{20}$
6. What is the average of 96, 100, and 92?
7. Add and reduce: $\frac{7}{24} + \frac{11}{24}$
8. How much is $\frac{5}{6}$ of two dozen?
9. Write $\frac{1}{4}$ as a fraction with 8 as the denominator. Then add the fraction to $\frac{3}{8}$. What is the sum?
10. What is the least common multiple (LCM) of 2, 3, and 4?
11. What is the area of this square? 100 cm

Saxon Math Course 1 © Harcourt Achieve Inc. and Stephen Hake. All rights reserved. 79

Cumulative Test 10A

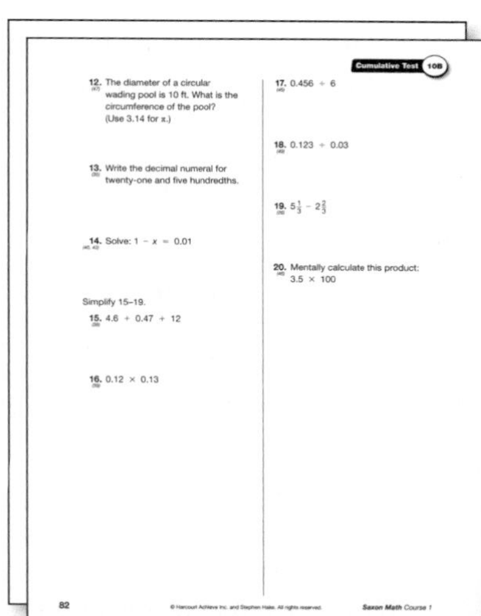

Cumulative Test 10B

12. The diameter of a circular wading pool is 10 ft. What is the circumference of the pool? (Use 3.14 for π.)
13. Write the decimal numeral for twenty-one and five hundredths.
14. Solve: $1 - x = 0.01$

Simplify 15–19.

15. $4.6 + 0.47 + 12$
16. 0.12×0.13
17. $0.456 \div 6$
18. $0.123 \div 0.03$
19. $5\frac{1}{3} - 2\frac{2}{3}$
20. Mentally calculate this product: 3.5×100

82 © Harcourt Achieve Inc. and Stephen Hake. All rights reserved. *Saxon Math Course 1*

Alternative Cumulative Test 10B

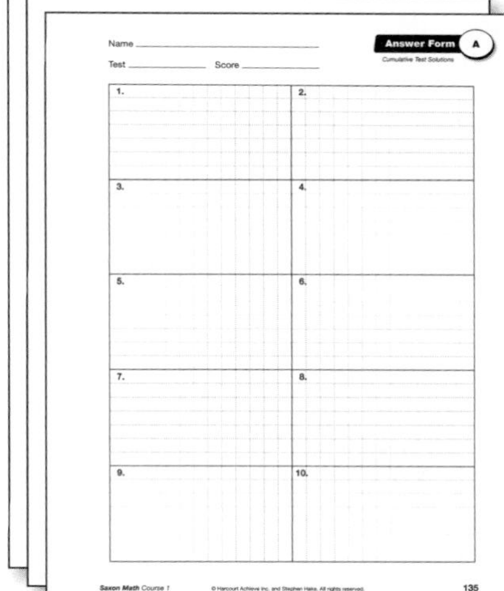

Name ______ Test ______ Score ______ **Answer Form A** *Cumulative Test Solutions*

1. 2. 3. 4. 5. 6. 7. 8. 9. 10.

Saxon Math Course 1 © Harcourt Achieve Inc. and Stephen Hake. All rights reserved. 135

Optional Answer Forms

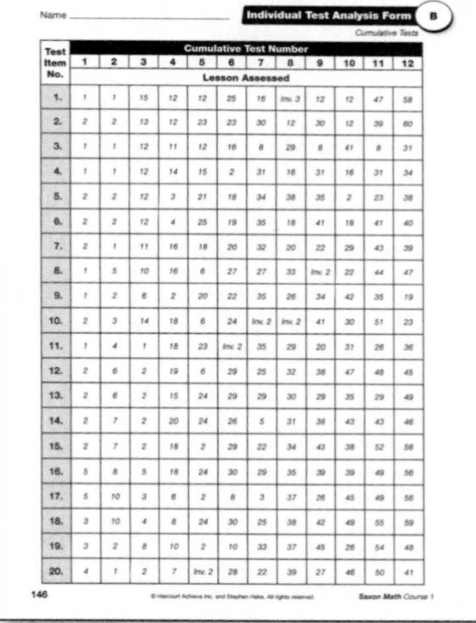

Name ______ **Individual Test Analysis Form B** *Cumulative Tests*

Test Item No.	Cumulative Test Number											
	1	2	3	4	5	6	7	8	9	10	11	12
	Lesson Assessed											
1.	1	1	15	12	12	25	16	Inv. 3	12	12	47	58
2.	2	2	13	12	23	23	30	12	30	12	39	60
3.	1	1	12	11	12	16	8	29	8	41	8	31
4.	1	1	12	14	15	2	31	16	31	16	31	34
5.	2	2	12	3	21	18	34	38	35	2	23	38
6.	2	2	12	4	25	19	35	18	41	18	41	40
7.	2	1	11	16	18	20	32	20	22	29	43	39
8.	1	5	10	16	6	27	27	33	Inv. 2	22	44	47
9.	1	2	6	2	20	22	35	26	34	42	35	19
10.	2	3	14	18	6	24	Inv. 2	Inv. 2	41	30	51	23
11.	1	4	1	18	23	Inv. 2	35	29	20	31	26	36
12.	2	6	2	19	6	29	25	32	38	47	48	45
13.	2	6	2	15	24	29	29	30	29	35	29	49
14.	2	7	2	20	24	26	5	31	38	43	43	46
15.	2	7	2	18	2	29	22	34	43	38	52	56
16.	5	8	5	18	24	30	29	35	39	39	49	56
17.	5	10	3	6	2	8	3	37	26	45	49	56
18.	3	10	4	8	24	30	25	38	42	49	55	59
19.	3	2	8	10	2	10	33	37	45	26	54	48
20.	4	1	2	7	Inv. 2	28	22	39	27	46	50	41

146 © Harcourt Achieve Inc. and Stephen Hake. All rights reserved. *Saxon Math Course 1*

Individual Test Analysis Form

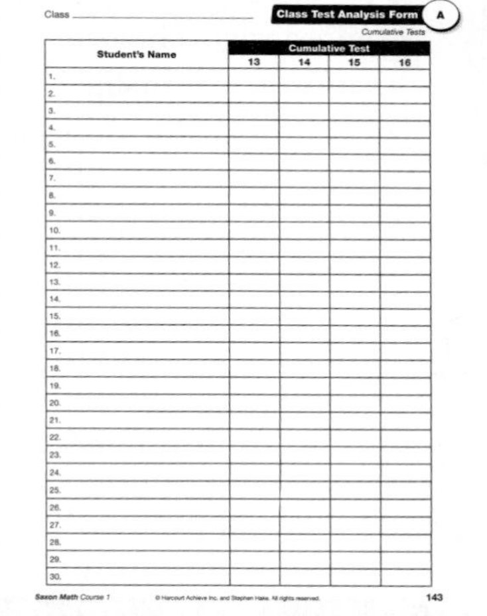

Class ______ **Class Test Analysis Form A** *Cumulative Tests*

Student's Name	Cumulative Test			
	13	14	15	16
1.				
2.				
3.				
4.				
5.				
6.				
7.				
8.				
9.				
10.				
11.				
12.				
13.				
14.				
15.				
16.				
17.				
18.				
19.				
20.				
21.				
22.				
23.				
24.				
25.				
26.				
27.				
28.				
29.				
30.				

Saxon Math Course 1 © Harcourt Achieve Inc. and Stephen Hake. All rights reserved. 143

Class Test Analysis Form

Reteaching

Students who score below 80% on the assessment may be in need of reteaching. Look for the causes of student mistakes. If errors are conceptual, refer to the *Reteaching Masters* for reteaching.

Performance Activity 10

Choosing Graphs and Interpreting Data

Assign after Lesson 55 and Test 10

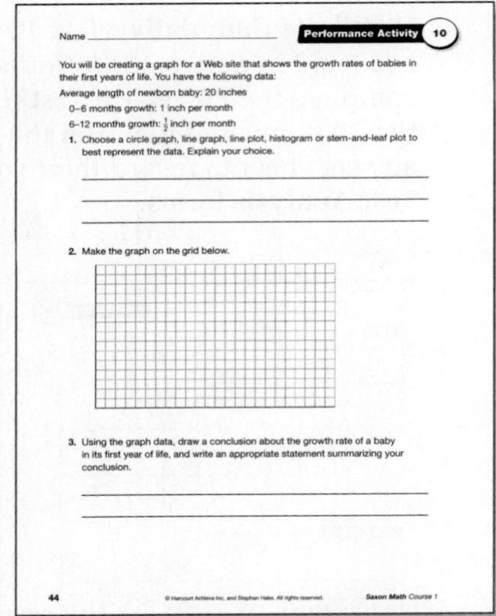

Name ____________ **Performance Activity 10**

You will be creating a graph for a Web site that shows the growth rates of babies in their first years of life. You have the following data:

Average length of newborn baby: 20 inches

0–6 months growth: 1 inch per month

6–12 months growth: $\frac{1}{2}$ inch per month

1. Choose a circle graph, line graph, line plot, histogram or stem-and-leaf plot to best represent the data. Explain your choice.

2. Make the graph on the grid below.

3. Using the graph data, draw a conclusion about the growth rate of a baby in its first year of life, and write an appropriate statement summarizing your conclusion.

44 *Saxon Math* Course 1

Performance Activity 10

Objectives

- Select the best kind of graph to use to represent a set of data.
- Draw a graph to represent a set of data.
- Draw conclusions from a set of data.
- Communicate ideas through writing.

Materials

Performance Activity 10

Preparation

Make copies of **Performance Activity 10.** (One each per student.)

Time Requirement

15–30 minutes; Begin in class and complete at home.

Activity

Explain to students that for this activity they are creating a graph for a Web site that shows the growth rates of babies in their first years of life. They will select the best kind of graph to use to represent the data and then make the graph. They will also draw a conclusion from the set of data. Explain that all of the information students need is on **Performance Activity 10.**

Criteria for Evidence of Learning

- Chooses a line graph to represent the data and explains why that is an appropriate choice.
- Draws a reasonable conclusion from the data.
- Communicates ideas clearly through writing.

Meeting Standards

National Council of Teachers of Mathematics (NCTM)

Data Analysis and Probability

DP.1b Select, create, and use appropriate graphical representations of data, including histograms, box plots, and scatterplots

DP.2b Discuss and understand the correspondence between data sets and their graphical representations, especially histograms, stem-and-leaf plots, box plots, and scatterplots

Reasoning and Proof

RP.2b Make and investigate mathematical conjectures

Communication

CM.3a Organize and consolidate their mathematical thinking through communication

Representation

RE.5a Create and use representations to organize, record, and communicate mathematical ideas

RE.5b Select, apply, and translate among mathematical representations to solve problems

• Common Denominators, Part 2

Objectives

- Rename two fractions so that they have common denominators.
- Add or subtract two fractions that do not have common denominators by renaming both fractions.
- Compare two fractions that do not have common denominators by renaming one or both fractions.

Lesson Preparation

Materials

- **Power Up G** (in *Instructional Masters*)
- **Manipulative Kit: metric rulers**
- **Manipulative Kit: overhead fraction circles**

Optional

- **Teacher-provided material: fraction manipulatives** from Investigation 2

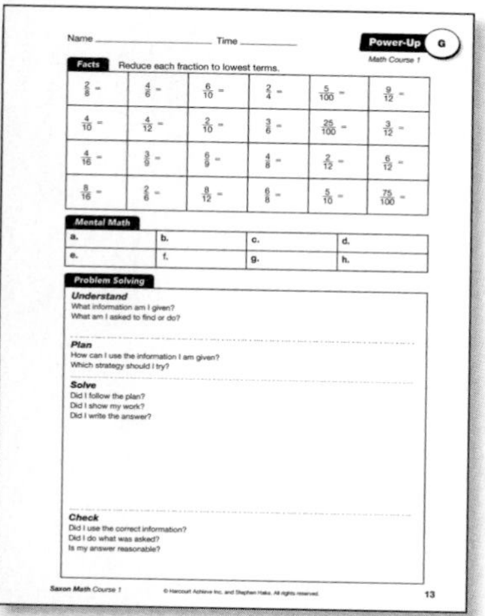

Power Up G

Math Language

English Learners (ESL)
estimate

Technology Resources

Student eBook Complete student textbook in electronic format.

Resources and Planner CD Assessment, reteaching, and instructional masters, plus a pacing calendar with standards.

Test and Practice Generator CD Create additional practice sheets and custom-made tests.

www.SaxonPublishers.com Visit for more student activities and planning materials.

Inclusion

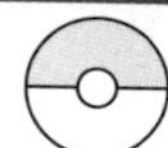

Adaptations CD Adapted lessons, investigations, practice and assessments.

Meeting Standards

National Council of Teachers of Mathematics (NCTM)

Numbers and Operations

NO.1a Work flexibly with fractions, decimals, and percents to solve problems

NO.2a Understand the meaning and effects of arithmetic operations with fractions, decimals, and integers

NO.3a Select appropriate methods and tools for computing with fractions and decimals from among mental computation, estimation, calculators or computers, and paper and pencil, depending on the situation, and apply the selected methods

NO.3c Develop and use strategies to estimate the results of rational-number computations and judge the reasonableness of the results

Power-Up Discussion

For use with Power Up, p. 289

Strategy: Work Backwards/Use Logical Reasoning

Terry folded a square piece of paper in half diagonally to form a triangle. Then he folded the triangle in half as shown, making a smaller triangle. With scissors Terry cut off the upper corner of the triangle. What will the paper look like when it is unfolded?

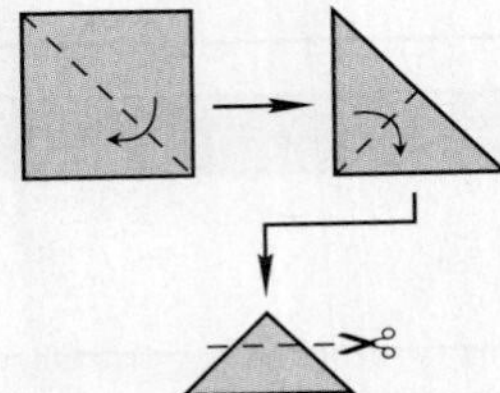

Understand **Understand the problem.**

"What information are we given?"

We are told how Terry folded and cut a square piece of paper.

"What are we asked to do?"

We are asked to determine what Terry's paper will look like when it is unfolded.

Plan **Make a plan.**

"What problem-solving strategy can we use?"

We can *work backwards* from the third step Terry followed to determine what part of the original paper will be affected by the cut. Then we can *use logical reasoning* to determine what that effect will be.

Solve **Carry out the plan.**

"What part of the paper is affected by the cut Terry makes?"

By focusing on the top vertex of the triangle and "working backwards" through the first two steps, we see that the middle of the paper will be affected by the cut and that the four edges of the paper are aligned at the bottom of the triangle.

"What is the effect of Terry's cut?"

Terry's cut makes a "hole" in the middle of the original square. Since all four edges are aligned at the bottom and Terry's cut is parallel to these edges, we can imagine that the resulting hole would be a square with sides parallel to the sides of the original square.

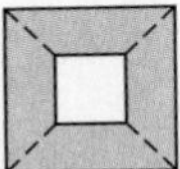

Check **Look back.**

"Did we find the answer to the question that was asked?"

Yes, we determined what Terry's square will look like when it is unfolded.

"How can we verify our answer?"

We can use a square piece of scrap paper as a model to act it out.

LESSON 56

• Common Denominators, Part 2

Power Up — *Building Power*

facts Power Up G

mental math

a. **Number Sense:** 8×250 2000

b. **Number Sense:** $462 - 350$ 112

c. **Number Sense:** $150 + 49$ 199

d. **Money:** $3.75 + $4.50 $8.25

e. **Fractional Parts:** $\frac{1}{2}$ of 15 $7\frac{1}{2}$

f. **Number Sense:** 30×40 1200

g. **Measurement:** How many centimeters are in 10 meters? 1000 cm

h. **Calculation:** 10×8, $+ 1$, $\div 9$, $\times 3$, $+ 1$, $\div 4$, $\times 6$, $- 2$, $\div 5$ 8

problem solving

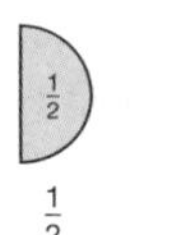

Terry folded a square piece of paper in half diagonally to form a triangle. Then he folded the triangle in half as shown, making a smaller triangle. With scissors Terry cut off the upper corner of the triangle. What will the paper look like when it is unfolded?

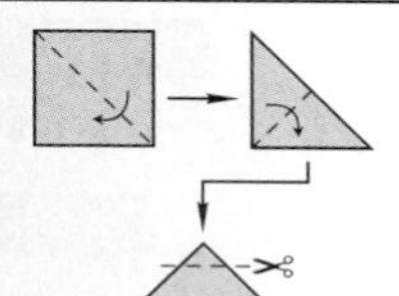

New Concept — *Increasing Knowledge*

In Lesson 55 we added and subtracted fractions that did not have common denominators. We renamed one of the fractions in order to add or subtract. In this lesson we will rename both fractions before we add or subtract. To see why this is sometimes necessary, consider the problem below.

Tony and Catherine ordered a pineapple pizza. Tony ate half and Catherine ate a third. What fraction of the pizza did Tony and Catherine eat?

We cannot add the fractions $\frac{1}{2}$ and $\frac{1}{3}$ by simply counting the number of parts, because the parts are not the same size (that is, the denominators are different).

$\frac{1}{2}$ $\frac{1}{3}$

These fractions do not have common denominators.

Facts — Reduce each fraction to lowest terms.

$\frac{2}{8} = \frac{1}{4}$	$\frac{4}{6} = \frac{2}{3}$	$\frac{6}{10} = \frac{3}{5}$	$\frac{2}{4} = \frac{1}{2}$	$\frac{5}{100} = \frac{1}{20}$	$\frac{9}{12} = \frac{3}{4}$
$\frac{4}{10} = \frac{2}{5}$	$\frac{4}{12} = \frac{1}{3}$	$\frac{2}{10} = \frac{1}{5}$	$\frac{3}{6} = \frac{1}{2}$	$\frac{25}{100} = \frac{1}{4}$	$\frac{3}{12} = \frac{1}{4}$
$\frac{4}{16} = \frac{1}{4}$	$\frac{3}{9} = \frac{1}{3}$	$\frac{6}{9} = \frac{2}{3}$	$\frac{4}{8} = \frac{1}{2}$	$\frac{2}{12} = \frac{1}{6}$	$\frac{6}{12} = \frac{1}{2}$
$\frac{8}{16} = \frac{1}{2}$	$\frac{2}{6} = \frac{1}{3}$	$\frac{8}{12} = \frac{2}{3}$	$\frac{6}{8} = \frac{3}{4}$	$\frac{5}{10} = \frac{1}{2}$	$\frac{75}{100} = \frac{3}{4}$

1 Power Up

Facts

Distribute **Power Up G** to students. See answers below.

Mental Math

Before students begin the Mental Math exercise, do this counting exercise as a class.

Count up and down by 25s between 25 and 300.

Encourage students to share different ways to mentally compute these exercises. Strategies for exercises **d** and **e** are listed below.

d. Add 25¢ and Subtract 25¢

$3.75 + $0.25 = $4.00 and $4.50 − $0.25 = $4.25; $4.00 + $4.25 = $8.25

Break Apart $4.50

$3.75 + $4.00 + $0.50 = $7.75 + $0.50 = $8.25

e. Use a Pattern

$\frac{1}{2}$ of $14 = 7$ and $\frac{1}{2}$ of $16 = 8$; $\frac{1}{2}$ of $15 = 7\frac{1}{2}$

Divide Place Values

$\frac{1}{2}$ of $10 = 5$ and $\frac{1}{2}$ of $5 = 2\frac{1}{2}$; $5 + 2\frac{1}{2} = 7\frac{1}{2}$

Problem Solving

Refer to **Power-Up Discussion,** p. 289B.

2 New Concepts

Instruction

Remind students they cannot find the sum or difference of two or more fractions until those fractions have common denominators.

(continued)

2 New Concepts (Continued)

Instruction

Point out that a least common denominator of two or more fractions is the least common multiple of those denominators.

Example 1

Instruction

To help students understand example 1, point out that the art above the example illustrates the addition. You might also choose to model the addition using the **Overhead Fraction Circles** from the Manipulative Kit.

Example 2

Instruction

Remind students that one way to find the least common multiple of two or more numbers is to list several multiples of each number, then identify the first (or least) multiple that is common to both lists.

(continued)

Renaming $\frac{1}{2}$ as $\frac{2}{4}$ does not help us either. In the fractions $\frac{2}{4}$ and $\frac{1}{3}$, the parts are still of different sizes.

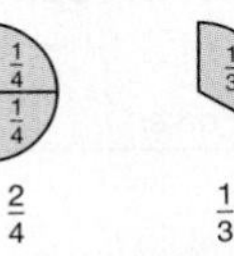

$\frac{2}{4}$ $\frac{1}{3}$

These fractions do not have common denominators.

We must rename both fractions in order to get parts that are the same size. The least common multiple of the denominators can be used as the common denominator of the renamed fractions. The least common multiple of 2 and 3 (the denominators of $\frac{1}{2}$ and $\frac{1}{3}$) is 6.

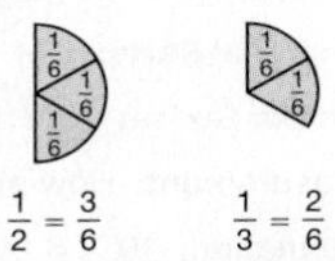

$\frac{1}{2} = \frac{3}{6}$ $\frac{1}{3} = \frac{2}{6}$

The common denominator is 6.

Example 1

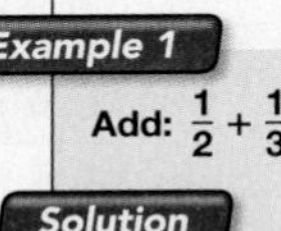

Add: $\frac{1}{2} + \frac{1}{3}$

Solution

The denominators are 2 and 3. The least common multiple of 2 and 3 is 6. We rename each fraction so that 6 is the common denominator. Then we add.

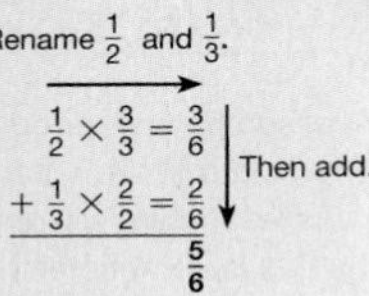

Rename $\frac{1}{2}$ and $\frac{1}{3}$.

$$\frac{1}{2} \times \frac{3}{3} = \frac{3}{6}$$
$$+\ \frac{1}{3} \times \frac{2}{2} = \frac{2}{6}$$
$$\frac{5}{6}$$

Then add.

Thinking Skill

Explain

How do you rename a fraction? Multiply the fraction by any fraction that is equal to 1.

Example 2

Risa saw that she had $\frac{3}{4}$ of a carton of 12 eggs. She used $\frac{2}{3}$ of a whole carton to make a batch of French toast for the family. What fraction of a carton of eggs was not used?

Solution

To find the fraction that remains, we subtract $\frac{2}{3}$ from $\frac{3}{4}$. The least common multiple of 4 and 3 is 12. We rename both fractions so that their denominators are 12 and then subtract.

Math Background

If students have difficulty identifying the least common denominator of two or more fractions, they can always use the product of the denominators as a common denominator.

For example, to add or subtract $\frac{5}{9}$ and $\frac{1}{6}$, each fraction can be renamed using 9×6 or 54 as the denominator.

However, this method will not always identify the *least* common denominator. For the fractions described above, the least common denominator is 18.

The method of using the product of the denominators as a common denominator can always be used to produce a correct answer, but it sometimes will require students to do much more arithmetic to complete the problem.

Rename $\frac{3}{4}$ and $\frac{2}{3}$. Then subtract.

$$\begin{array}{r} \frac{3}{4} \times \frac{3}{3} = \frac{9}{12} \\ -\frac{2}{3} \times \frac{4}{4} = \frac{8}{12} \\ \hline \frac{1}{12} \end{array}$$

We can check for reasonableness by thinking about the number of eggs. If the carton holds 12 eggs, then there were nine eggs in the carton because $\frac{3}{4}$ of 12 is 9. Risa used $\frac{2}{3}$ of 12 eggs, which is 8 eggs. Subtracting 8 from 9 leaves 1 egg in the carton, which is $\frac{1}{12}$ of a carton.

Renaming one or more fractions can also help us compare fractions. To compare fractions that have common denominators, we simply compare the numerators.

$$\frac{4}{6} < \frac{5}{6}$$

To compare fractions that do not have common denominators, we can rename one or both fractions so that they do have common denominators.

Example 3

Compare: $\frac{3}{8} \bigcirc \frac{1}{2}$

Solution

We rename $\frac{1}{2}$ so that the denominator is 8.

$$\frac{1}{2} \cdot \frac{4}{4} = \frac{4}{8}$$

We see that $\frac{3}{8}$ is less than $\frac{4}{8}$.

$$\frac{3}{8} < \frac{4}{8}$$

Therefore, $\frac{3}{8}$ is less than $\frac{1}{2}$.

$$\mathbf{\frac{3}{8} < \frac{1}{2}}$$

The answer is reasonable because the numerator of $\frac{3}{8}$, which is 3, is less than half of the denominator 8, indicating that the fraction is less than $\frac{1}{2}$.

Example 4

Compare: $\frac{2}{3} \bigcirc \frac{3}{4}$

Solution

The denominators are 3 and 4. We rename both fractions with a common denominator of 12.

$$\frac{2}{3} \cdot \frac{4}{4} = \frac{8}{12} \quad \frac{3}{4} \cdot \frac{3}{3} = \frac{9}{12}$$

We see that $\frac{8}{12}$ is less than $\frac{9}{12}$.

2 New Concepts *(Continued)*

Example 3

Instruction

Have students note that $\frac{1}{2}$ is renamed as eighths because 8 is the least common multiple of the denominators.

Then make sure students understand that once fractions have the same denominator, it is only necessary to compare the numerators.

"Since 3 is less than 4, $\frac{3}{8}$ is less than $\frac{4}{8}$."

Example 4

Instruction

It is important for students to generalize that fractions cannot be compared until the denominators of the fractions are the same.

"If two fractions have unlike denominators, what must we do to those fractions before we can compare them?" Rename them using a common denominator.

"Whenever we compare two fractions, what answers are possible?" One fraction is greater than, less than, or equal to, the other fraction.

(continued)

nclusion

\ simple shortcut will help students ompare two fractions with unlike lenominators. Tell students to cross nultiply and write the products bove the fractions. The greater raction is below the greater cross-product. Use the example below:

Compare: $\frac{1}{2} \bigcirc \frac{1}{3}$

Cross multiply: 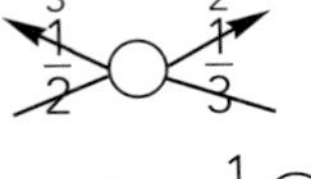

$3 > 2$, so $\frac{1}{2} \bigcirc\!\!\!\!> \frac{1}{3}$

Manipulative Use

Use the **Overhead Fraction Circles** from the Manipulative Kit to model example 3. Show students that $\frac{3}{8}$ is less than $\frac{1}{2}$ by placing three $\frac{1}{8}$ pieces together next to one $\frac{1}{2}$ piece and compare.

2 New Concepts (Continued)

Practice Set

Problems a–f Error Alert

For each problem, students need to identify a common denominator and rename both fractions. If students do not use the least common multiple of the denominators when renaming the fractions, they will need to reduce the sum or difference.

Problems g–i Error Alert

To make these comparisons, students may choose a common denominator that is not the least common denominator.

In problem h for example, the fractions $\frac{16}{24}$ and $\frac{18}{24}$ may be used to compare.

Although it may be more efficient for students to compare two fractions using the least common denominator, they should generalize that any common denominator may be used.

3 Written Practice

Math Conversations

Discussion opportunities are provided below.

Problem 1 Analyze

"Is 12 the least common denominator of 4 and 3?" yes

"The denominator 12 was chosen as a common denominator for us to use. What other common denominators could have been chosen for us to use?" any multiple of 12 that is greater than 12

Problem 7 Analyze

"Will this subtraction involve renaming? Explain why or why not." Yes; to subtract two fractions, the denominators must be the same.

"What is the least common denominator of 2 and 6?" 6

(continued)

$$\frac{8}{12} < \frac{9}{12}$$

Therefore, $\frac{2}{3}$ is less than $\frac{3}{4}$.

$$\frac{2}{3} < \frac{3}{4}$$

Generalize Use the answer to Example 4 to arrange these fractions in order from least to greatest. $\frac{3}{4}, \frac{1}{2}, \frac{2}{3}$ $\frac{1}{2}, \frac{2}{3}, \frac{3}{4}$

Practice Set ▸ Find each sum or difference:

a. $\frac{2}{3} - \frac{1}{2}$ $\frac{1}{6}$

b. $\frac{1}{4} + \frac{2}{5}$ $\frac{13}{20}$

c. $\frac{3}{4} - \frac{1}{3}$ $\frac{5}{12}$

d. $\frac{2}{3} + \frac{1}{4}$ $\frac{11}{12}$

e. $\frac{1}{3} - \frac{1}{4}$ $\frac{1}{12}$

f. $\frac{1}{2} - \frac{1}{10}$ $\frac{2}{5}$

▸ Before comparing, write each pair of fractions with common denominators:

g. $\frac{2}{3} \bigcirc \frac{1}{2}$ > $\frac{4}{6} > \frac{3}{6}$

h. $\frac{4}{6} \bigcirc \frac{3}{4}$ < $\frac{8}{12} < \frac{9}{12}$

i. $\frac{2}{3} \bigcirc \frac{3}{5}$ > $\frac{10}{15} > \frac{9}{15}$

Written Practice *Strengthening Concepts*

▸ * 1. (56) **Analyze** Add $\frac{1}{4}$ and $\frac{1}{3}$. Use 12 as the common denominator. $\frac{7}{12}$

* 2. (56) Subtract $\frac{1}{3}$ from $\frac{1}{2}$. Use 6 as the common denominator. $\frac{1}{6}$

3. (29) Of the 88 keys on a piano, 52 are white.
   a. What fraction of a piano's keys are white? $\frac{13}{22}$
   b. What is the ratio of black keys to white keys? $\frac{9}{13}$

4. (29) If $7\frac{1}{2}$ apples are needed to make an apple pie, how many apples would be needed to make two apple pies? 15 apples

* 5. (56) Subtract $\frac{1}{4}$ from $\frac{2}{3}$. Use 12 as the common denominator. $\frac{5}{12}$

6. (55) Add $\frac{1}{3}$ and $\frac{1}{6}$. Reduce your answer. $\frac{1}{2}$

▸ * 7. (55) **Analyze** Subtract $\frac{1}{2}$ from $\frac{5}{6}$. Reduce your answer. $\frac{1}{3}$

8. (1) \$3 + \$1.75 + 65¢   \$5.40

9. (39) (0.625)(0.4)   0.25

10. (49) $6^2 \div 0.08$ 450

11. (48) $3\frac{1}{8} - 1\frac{7}{8}$ $1\frac{1}{4}$

12. (29) $\frac{5}{8} \cdot \frac{2}{3}$ $\frac{5}{12}$

13. (22, 33) Forty percent of the 100 students in the World Language Club speak more than two languages.
   a. Write 40% as a reduced fraction. $\frac{2}{5}$
   b. How many students in the World Language Club speak more than two languages? 40 students

▸ See Math Conversations in the sidebar.

16. Yes. To estimate the distance the bike traveled, Molly found the circumference of the tire. She multiplied the diameter of the tire by 3, which is a very rough approximation for π. If Molly had used 3.14 for π, she would have calculated 6.28 ft for the circumference, which is about 6 ft 3 in.

14. (46) Write the following as a decimal number: 80.65

$$(8 \times 10) + \left(6 \times \frac{1}{10}\right) + \left(5 \times \frac{1}{100}\right)$$

15. (16) **Estimate** What is the sum of 3627 and 4187 to the nearest hundred? 7800

16. (47) **Justify** Molly measured the diameter of her bike tire and found that it was 2 feet across. She estimated that for every turn of the tire, the bike traveled about 6 feet. Was Molly's estimate reasonable? Why or why not?

▸* 17. (Inv. 5) **Analyze** What is the mean of 1.2, 1.3, 1.4, and 1.5? 1.35

18. (38) The perimeter of a square is 36 inches. What is its area? 81 square inches

19. (19) Here we show 24 written as a product of prime numbers:

$$2 \cdot 2 \cdot 2 \cdot 3$$

Show how 30 can be written as a product of prime numbers. $2 \cdot 3 \cdot 5$

Find each unknown number:

20. (43) $\frac{2}{3}w = 0$ 0

21. (30) $\frac{2}{3}m = 1$ $\frac{3}{2}$

22. (43) $\frac{2}{3} - n = 0$ $\frac{2}{3}$

Refer to this bar graph to answer problems **23–26.** Before you answer the questions, be sure you understand what the scale on the graph represents.

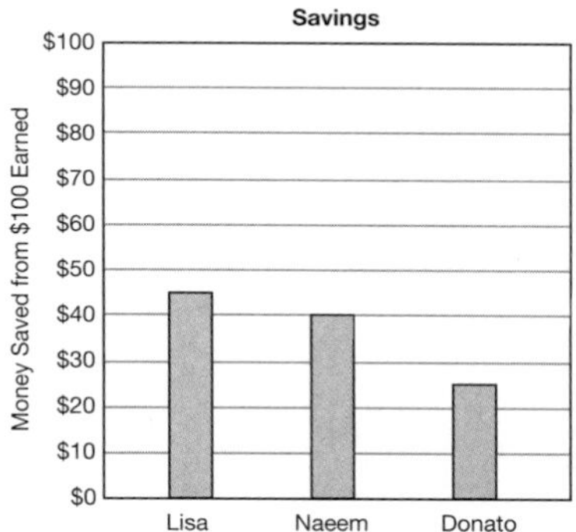

▸ 23. (Inv. 5) How much did Naeem spend? $60

24. (Inv. 4) How much more did Lisa save than Donato? $20 more

25. (29) What fraction of his earnings did Donato save? $\frac{1}{4}$

▸* 26. (40) **Formulate** Write a percent question that relates to the bar graph, and then answer the question. See student work.

▸* 27. (54) **Analyze** Reduce: $\frac{2 \cdot 3 \cdot 5}{2 \cdot 3 \cdot 5 \cdot 7}$ $\frac{1}{7}$

▸ See Math Conversations in the sidebar.

English Learners

On the board, write "Estimate the sum of 39 + 12 =." Say:

"Estimate means to calculate and come near in amount to an exact answer. For this problem, we can estimate the sum to be near, or about 50. Look at problem 15. Again, you are asked to estimate the sum of these two numbers, only this time to the nearest hundred. As you can see, the amount will not be exactly correct, but near the correct amount."

Ask a volunteer to round these numbers and get an estimate of the sum of the two numbers. Ask students when they would use estimating in every day life. Samples: walking about 3 blocks to school or having to complete about two hours of homework.

3 Written Practice *(Continued)*

Math Conversations

Discussion opportunities are provided below.

Problem 17 Analyze

"What is another word that means the same as mean?" average

"The first step in finding a mean or average is finding the sum of the numbers. What must you remember to do when you find the sum of the numbers in this problem?" align the decimal points in the numbers

Problem 26 Formulate

Extend the Problem

Invite students to exchange questions, then answer the questions and compare answers.

Problem 27 Analyze

Encourage students to use their fraction manipulatives to model or check the solution.

Errors and Misconceptions

Problem 23

Students must recognize that the graph describes the amount of money each person saved, but the question asks for the amount of money Naeem spent.

(continued)

3 Written Practice (Continued)

Errors and Misconceptions

Problem 29

Students may assume they must measure using a ruler or use centimeter grid paper to accurately divide each rectangle in half. Explain that measuring or using grid paper is not required because each diagonal of a rectangle divides a rectangle into two congruent parts.

* **28.** (54) How many $\frac{2}{3}$s are in $\frac{1}{2}$? $(\frac{1}{2} \div \frac{2}{3})$ $\frac{3}{4}$

▸ **29.** (7) **Model** Draw three rectangles that are 2 cm long and 1 cm wide. On each rectangle show a different way to divide the rectangle in half. Then shade half of each rectangle.

29. Sample:

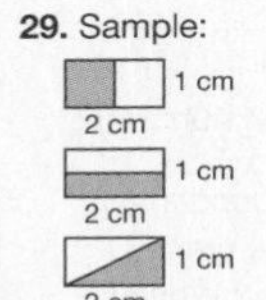

* **30.** (56) Compare: $\frac{2}{3}$ ⓒ $\frac{5}{6}$ (<)

Early Finishers
Real-World Application

Dalia and her three sisters make a pizza and decide to split it into four equal pieces (one for each person). Dalia finds out that her best friend is coming over, so she cuts her piece in half to share with her friend. What fraction of the whole pizza does Dalia have now? Show your work. $\frac{1}{2}$ of $\frac{1}{4} = \frac{1}{8}$ of the pizza

Looking Forward

Renaming two fractions before adding, subtracting, or comparing them prepares students for:

- **Lesson 57,** adding and subtracting fractions in three steps (correct shape, perform operation, and simplify).
- **Lesson 59,** adding mixed numbers by renaming fractions so that they have common denominators.
- **Lesson 61,** adding three or more fractions by renaming fractions so that they have common denominators.
- **Lesson 63,** subtracting mixed numbers with regrouping.
- **Lesson 76,** comparing fractions by converting them to decimal form.

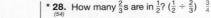

• Adding and Subtracting Fractions: Three Steps

Objectives

- Follow three steps—shape, operate, simplify—to add or subtract fractions.

Lesson Preparation

Materials

- **Power Up H** (in *Instructional Masters*)

Optional

- **Teacher-provided material: fraction manipulatives** from Investigation 2

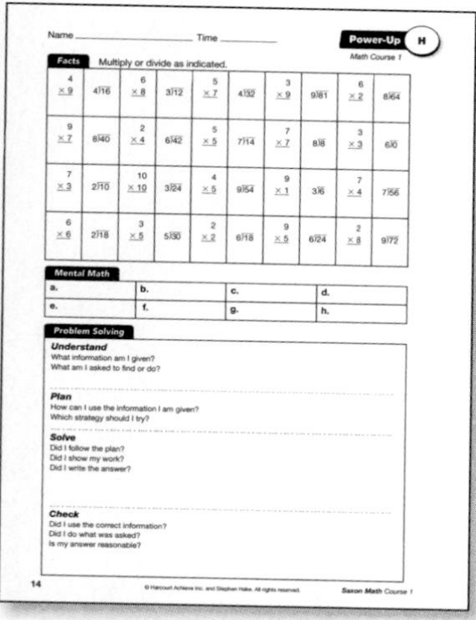

Power Up H

Math Language

English Learners (ESL)

rise

Technology Resources

Student eBook Complete student textbook in electronic format.

Resources and Planner CD Assessment, reteaching, and instructional masters, plus a pacing calendar with standards.

Test and Practice Generator CD Create additional practice sheets and custom-made tests.

www.SaxonPublishers.com Visit for more student activities and planning materials.

Inclusion

Adaptations CD Adapted lessons, investigations, practice and assessments.

Meeting Standards

National Council of Teachers of Mathematics (NCTM)

Numbers and Operations

NO.1a Work flexibly with fractions, decimals, and percents to solve problems

NO.2a Understand the meaning and effects of arithmetic operations with fractions, decimals, and integers

NO.3a Select appropriate methods and tools for computing with fractions and decimals from among mental computation, estimation, calculators or computers, and paper and pencil, depending on the situation, and apply the selected methods

NO.3b Develop and analyze algorithms for computing with fractions, decimals, and integers and develop fluency in their use

Problem Solving

PS.1c Apply and adapt a variety of appropriate strategies to solve problems

Power-Up Discussion *For use with Power Up, p. 295*

Problem-Solving Strategy: Make it Simpler/ Write an Equation

It takes ten hens one week to lay fifty eggs. How many eggs will sixty hens lay in four weeks?

Understand ***Understand the problem.***

"What information are we given?"

Ten hens can lay 50 eggs in one week.

"What makes this ratio problem different from ratio problems we have seen before? (Hint: How many different things are in proportion?)"

There are *three* values in proportion: hens, eggs, and weeks.

"What are we asked to do?"

Determine how many eggs 60 hens can lay in 4 weeks.

Plan ***Make a plan.***

"What problem-solving strategy will we use?"

We will *make it simpler* by only considering two values at a time and *write equations* to find the solution.

"How will we handle the three different values?"

We will compare two values at a time. First we will find how an increase in the number of hens affects the number of eggs. Then we will find how an increase in time affects the number of eggs.

Solve ***Carry out the plan.***

"If 10 hens lay 50 eggs in 1 week, how many eggs does 1 hen lay in 1 week?"

We divide the number of hens by 10, so we also divide the number of eggs by 10. One hen lays 5 eggs in a week.

"If 1 hen lays 5 eggs in 1 week, how many eggs can 60 hens lay in 1 week?"

We multiply to find the answer: 60×5 eggs per week $=$ 300 eggs per week.

"If 60 hens lay 300 eggs in one week, how many eggs can be laid in 4 weeks?"

We multiply again to find the answer: 300 eggs per week $\times$ 4 weeks $=$ 1200 eggs.

Check ***Look back.***

"Did we find the answer to the question that was asked?"

Yes. We found that 60 hens could lay 1200 eggs in 4 weeks.

LESSON 57

• Adding and Subtracting Fractions: Three Steps

Power Up — *Building Power*

facts Power Up H

mental math

a. **Calculation:** 8×425 3400

b. **Number Sense:** $465 + 250$ 715

c. **Number Sense:** $150 - 49$ 101

d. **Money:** $9.75 − $3.50 $6.25

e. **Number Sense:** Double $4\frac{1}{2}$. 9

f. **Number Sense:** $\frac{600}{30}$ 20

g. **Measurement:** Which is greater, a century or 5 decades? a century

h. **Calculation:** $2 \times 2, \times 2, \times 2, \times 2, \times 2, \div 8, \div 8$ 1

problem solving It takes ten hens one week to lay fifty eggs. How many eggs will sixty hens lay in four weeks? 1200 eggs

New Concept — *Increasing Knowledge*

We follow three steps to solve fraction problems:

Step 1: Put the problem into the correct **shape** or form if it is not already. (When adding or subtracting fractions, the correct form is with common denominators.)

Step 2: Perform the **operation** indicated. (Add, subtract, multiply, or divide.)

Step 3: **Simplify** the answer if possible. (Reduce the fraction or write an improper fraction as a mixed number.)

Example 1

Add: $\frac{1}{2} + \frac{2}{3}$

Solution

We follow the steps described above.

Step 1: Shape: write the fractions with common denominators.

Step 2: Operate: add the renamed fractions.

Step 3: Simplify: convert the improper fraction to a mixed number.

Facts Multiply or divide as indicated.

$4 \times 9 = 36$	4)16 → 4	$6 \times 8 = 48$	3)12 → 4	$5 \times 7 = 35$	4)32 → 8	$3 \times 9 = 27$	9)81 → 9	$6 \times 2 = 12$	8)64 → 8
$9 \times 7 = 63$	8)40 → 5	$2 \times 4 = 8$	6)42 → 7	$5 \times 5 = 25$	7)14 → 2	$7 \times 7 = 49$	8)8 → 1	$3 \times 3 = 9$	6)0 → 0
$7 \times 3 = 21$	2)10 → 5	$10 \times 10 = 100$	3)24 → 8	$4 \times 5 = 20$	9)54 → 6	$9 \times 1 = 9$	3)6 → 2	$7 \times 4 = 28$	7)56 → 8
$6 \times 6 = 36$	2)18 → 9	$3 \times 5 = 15$	5)30 → 6	$2 \times 2 = 4$	6)18 → 3	$9 \times 5 = 45$	6)24 → 4	$2 \times 8 = 16$	9)72 → 8

1 Power Up

Facts

Distribute **Power Up H** to students. See answers below.

Mental Math

Before students begin the Mental Math exercise, do this counting exercise as a class.

Count by 12s from 12 to 144.

Encourage students to share different ways to mentally compute these exercises. Strategies for exercises **a** and **c** are listed below.

a. Break Apart 425

$(8 \times 400) + (8 \times 25) = 3200 + 200 = 3400$

Multiply Place Values, then Add

$8 \times 400 = 3200$, $8 \times 20 = 160$, and $8 \times 5 = 40$; $3200 + 160 = 3360$; $3360 + 40 = 3400$

c. Subtract 50, then Add 1

$150 - 50 = 100$; $100 + 1 = 101$

Count Back by tens, Count On by 1

Start with 150. Count: 140, 130, 120, 110, 100; Start with 100. Count: 101

Problem Solving

Refer to **Power-Up Discussion,** p. 295B.

2 New Concepts

Instruction

Suggest that students use the mnemonic device SOS (Shape, Operation, Simplify) to help remember the three steps. Explain that the correct "shape" for fractions that are added or subtracted is common denominators. Students should notice the operation sign, then look at the denominators.

A. Notice the sign.

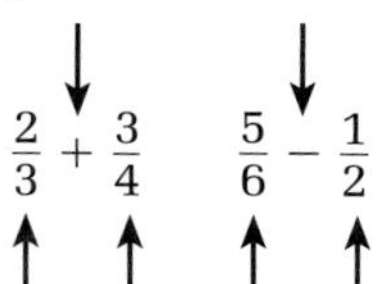

B. Look at the denominators.

If the denominators are the same, the fractions can be added or subtracted. If the denominators are not the same, then one or more of the fractions need to be renamed before adding or subtracting.

(continued)

2 New Concepts (Continued)

Example 1

Instruction

Point out that the term "operate" means "to complete the operation."

Example 2

Instruction

"A common denominator is needed to subtract two fractions. Name the least common denominator of 3 and 6, and explain why you named that number." 6; Sample: 6 is the first multiple of 3 that is greater than 3.

Practice Set

Problems a–f Error Alert

Students must rename one or both fractions in each problem before the operation can be completed. Encourage students to use the three steps presented earlier in this lesson to help complete each problem.

3 Written Practice

Math Conversations

Discussion opportunities are provided below.

Problem 3 Analyze

Extend the Problem

"Challenge volunteers to use 24 as the common denominator and mental math to rename the fractions." $2\frac{18}{4}$ and $2\frac{20}{4}$

Problem 7 Represent

Encourage students to use their fraction manipulatives to model or check the solution.

(continued)

---

1. Shape

$$\frac{1}{2} \times \frac{3}{3} = \frac{3}{6}$$
$$+\frac{2}{3} \times \frac{2}{2} = \frac{4}{6}$$
2. Operate
$$\frac{7}{6} = 1\frac{1}{6}$$
3. Simplify

Example 2

Subtract: $\frac{5}{6} - \frac{1}{3}$

Solution

Step 1: Shape: write the fractions with common denominators.

Step 2: Operate: subtract the renamed fractions.

Step 3: Simplify: reduce the fraction.

1. Shape

$$\frac{5}{6} \quad = \frac{5}{6}$$
$$-\frac{1}{3} \times \frac{2}{2} = \frac{2}{6}$$
2. Operate
$$\frac{3}{6} = \frac{1}{2}$$
3. Simplify

Practice Set ▶ Find each sum or difference:

a. $\frac{1}{2} + \frac{1}{6}$ $\frac{2}{3}$ **b.** $\frac{2}{3} + \frac{3}{4}$ $1\frac{5}{12}$ **c.** $\frac{1}{5} + \frac{3}{10}$ $\frac{1}{2}$

d. $\frac{5}{6} - \frac{1}{2}$ $\frac{1}{3}$ **e.** $\frac{7}{10} - \frac{1}{2}$ $\frac{1}{5}$ **f.** $\frac{5}{12} - \frac{1}{6}$ $\frac{1}{4}$

Written Practice *Strengthening Concepts*

1. (12, 29) **Analyze** What is the difference between the sum of $\frac{1}{2}$ and $\frac{1}{2}$ and the product of $\frac{1}{2}$ and $\frac{1}{2}$? $\frac{3}{4}$

2. (13) **Formulate** Thomas Jefferson was born in 1743. How old was he when he was elected president of the United States in 1800? Write an equation and solve the problem. 1800 − 1743 = *d*; 57 years old

▶ ***3.** (56) Subtract $\frac{3}{4}$ from $\frac{5}{6}$. Use 12 as the common denominator. $\frac{1}{12}$

***4.** (57) $\frac{1}{2} + \frac{2}{3}$ $1\frac{1}{6}$ ***5.** (57) $\frac{1}{2} + \frac{1}{6}$ $\frac{2}{3}$ ***6.** (57) $\frac{5}{6} + \frac{2}{3}$ $1\frac{1}{2}$

▶ ***7.** (54) **Represent** How many $\frac{3}{5}$s are in $\frac{3}{4}$? $\left(\frac{3}{4} \div \frac{3}{5}\right)$ $1\frac{1}{4}$

8. (52) $32.50 ÷ 10 $3.25 **9.** (5, 38) $\sqrt{4} - (1^2 - 0.2)$ 1.2

10. (49) 6 ÷ 0.12 50 **11.** (48) $5\frac{3}{8} - 2\frac{5}{8}$ $2\frac{3}{4}$ **12.** (29) $\frac{3}{4} \cdot \frac{5}{3}$ $1\frac{1}{4}$

▶ See Math Conversations in the sidebar.

13. (13, 33) Fifty percent of this rectangle is shaded. Write 50% as a reduced fraction. What is the area of the shaded part of the rectangle? $\frac{1}{2}$; 100 sq. mm

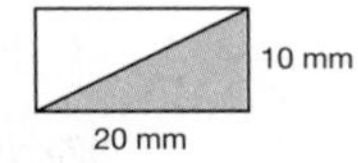

▶ 14. (34) What is the place value of the 7 in 3.567? thousandths

▶ 15. (45, 51) **Estimate** Divide 0.5 by 4 and round the quotient to the nearest tenth. 0.1

16. (44) Arrange these numbers in order from least to greatest: 0.03, 0.3, 3.0

0.3, 3.0, 0.03

17. (10) **Predict** In this sequence the first term is 2, the second term is 4, and the third term is 6. What is the twentieth term of the sequence? 40

2, 4, 6, 8, . . .

18. (23) In a deck of 52 cards there are four aces. What is the ratio of aces to all cards in a deck of cards? $\frac{4}{52} = \frac{1}{13}$

▶* 19. (31, 57) a. **Analyze** Calculate the perimeter of the rectangle shown. $1\frac{1}{2}$ in.

b. Multiply the length of the rectangle by its width to find the area of the rectangle in square inches. $\frac{1}{8}$ in.^{2}

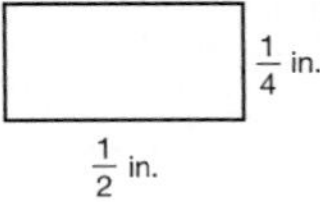

20. (29) What number is $\frac{5}{8}$ of 80? 50

▶ 21. (19) **Analyze** List the factors of 29. 1, 29

22. (30) What is the least common multiple of 12 and 18? 36

* 23. (56) Compare: $\frac{5}{8} < \frac{7}{10}$

24. (10) **Connect** What temperature is shown on this thermometer? -4°F

25. (14) If the temperature shown on this thermometer rose to 12°F, then how many degrees would the temperature have risen? 16°F

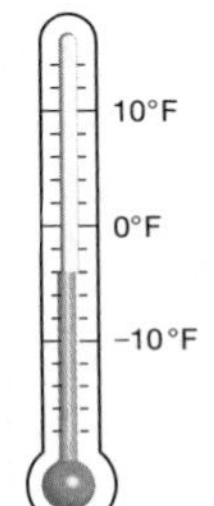

Lesson 57 297

▶ See Math Conversations in the sidebar.

3 Written Practice (Continued)

Math Conversations

Discussion opportunities are provided below.

Problem 15 Estimate

Extend the Problem

Invite a volunteer to change 0.5 to a fraction in simplest form and change 4 to an improper fraction, then demonstrate at the board or overhead how to complete a symbolic computation to find the fraction that represents the exact quotient.

$\frac{1}{2} \div \frac{4}{1} = \frac{1}{2} \times \frac{1}{4} = \frac{1}{8}$

Problem 19 Analyze

"To complete problem a, we must find the sum of the fractions. Explain how we can group the addends so that we don't need to use a common denominator to find the sum." Sample: Group $\frac{1}{2}$ and $\frac{1}{2}$ and group $\frac{1}{4}$ and $\frac{1}{4}$; the sum of $\frac{1}{2}$ and $\frac{1}{2}$ is 1 and the sum of $\frac{1}{4}$ and $\frac{1}{4}$ is $\frac{2}{4}$. So the sum of 1 and $\frac{2}{4}$ is $1\frac{2}{4}$ or $1\frac{1}{2}$.

Problem 21 Analyze

Remind students that the factors of all whole numbers greater than 1 always includes 1 and the number itself.

Errors and Misconceptions

Problem 14

Ask students who identify an incorrect place value to recite the place values from thousandths to hundred thousands or from hundred thousands to thousandths. If necessary, have students refer to the "Place Value" chart in the *Student Reference Guide* and work to commit the sequence of place values to memory.

Problem 15

Watch for students who give an answer of 8 or 8.0 because they transposed the dividend and the divisor.

(continued)

English Learners

Explain how "rose" and "risen" are forms of the word **rise.** Say:

"Rise means to 'go or get up'. In the morning we rise out of our bed. Rose and risen are tenses of rise. Look at problem 25. The temperature rose by 12F°. This means the temperature went up the number scale on the thermometer. It got hotter."

Ask a student volunteer to use any form of the word rise in a mathematical sentence.

Math Conversations

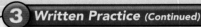

Discussion opportunities are provided below.

Problem 26 Analyze

"To reduce this fraction, what can we first do to reduce the amount of arithmetic we must complete?" Group factors that are equivalent to 1, then find the product of the ungrouped factors in the numerator and in the denominator.

▶* **26.** (54) Analyze Reduce: $\frac{2 \cdot 2 \cdot 3 \cdot 3 \cdot 5 \cdot 7}{2 \cdot 2 \cdot 5 \cdot 5 \cdot 7 \cdot 7}$ $\frac{9}{35}$

27. (29) What fraction of the group of circles is shaded? $\frac{1}{3}$

28. 24 CDs; Sample: $\frac{3}{8} \times 3 = \frac{9}{8}$, which is a little over 1 $(\frac{8}{8})$. So there are almost three $\frac{3}{8}$s in 1. Since $3 \times 9 = 27$, the actual answer will be a little less than 27. Twenty-four CDs is a reasonable answer.

* **28.** (50) Justify Ling has a 9-inch stack of CDs on the shelf. Each CD is in a $\frac{3}{8}$-inch-thick plastic case. How many CDs are in the 9-inch stack? Write and solve a fraction division problem to answer the question. Explain why your answer is reasonable.

* **29.** (55) Subtract $\frac{1}{2}$ from $\frac{4}{5}$. Use 10 as the common denominator. $\frac{3}{10}$

30. (47) The diameter of a regulation basketball hoop is 18 inches. What is the circumference of a regulation basketball hoop? (Use 3.14 for π.) 56.52 inches

Early Finishers
Real-World Application

Misty is going to bake a fruit cake for her sister. These are the ingredients:

$\frac{3}{4}$ cup butter
1 cup sugar
2 cups flour
3 cups golden raisins
$\frac{1}{2}$ cup cherries
1 cup crushed pineapple (with juice)

How many total cups of ingredients are needed for this recipe?
$1 + 2 + 3 + 1 + \frac{3}{4} + \frac{1}{2} = 7 + \frac{3}{4} + \frac{1}{2} = 7 + 1\frac{1}{4} = 8\frac{1}{4}$ cups

▶ See Math Conversations in the sidebar.

Looking Forward

Adding and subtracting fractions in three steps (correct shape, perform operation, and simplify) prepares students for:

- **Lesson 59,** adding mixed numbers by renaming fractions so that they have common denominators.
- **Lesson 61,** adding three or more fractions by renaming fractions so that they have common denominators.
- **Lesson 63,** subtracting mixed numbers with regrouping.
- **Lesson 72,** using a fractions chart to review the addition and subtraction of fractions.

Probability and Chance

Objectives

- Express the probability that an event will occur as a reduced fraction, a decimal, or a percent.
- Express the probability that an event will not occur as a reduced fraction, a decimal, or a percent.
- Find the probability of an event by dividing the number of outcomes in the event by the number of possible outcomes.

Lesson Preparation

Materials

- **Power Up I** (in *Instructional Masters*)
- **Manipulative Kit: inch rulers**

Optional

- **Manipulative Kit: dot cubes, spinners**

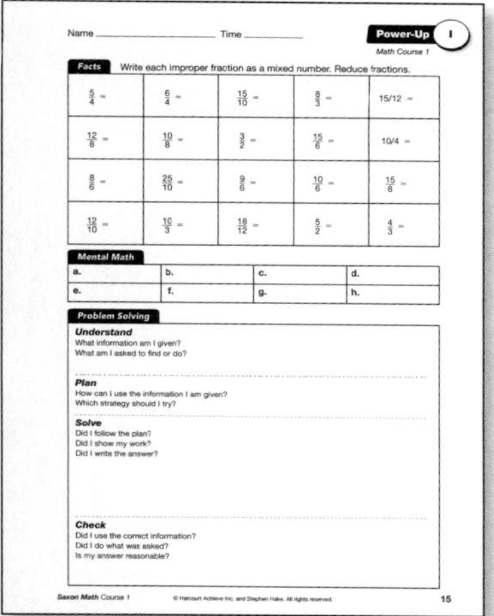

Name ______ Time ______ **Power-Up I** *Math Course 1*

Facts Write each improper fraction as a mixed number. Reduce fractions.

$\frac{5}{4}$ =	$\frac{6}{4}$ =	$\frac{15}{10}$ =	$\frac{8}{3}$ =	15/12 =
$\frac{12}{8}$ =	$\frac{10}{8}$ =	$\frac{3}{2}$ =	$\frac{15}{6}$ =	10/4 =
$\frac{8}{6}$ =	$\frac{25}{10}$ =	$\frac{9}{6}$ =	$\frac{10}{6}$ =	$\frac{15}{8}$ =
$\frac{12}{10}$ =	$\frac{10}{3}$ =	$\frac{18}{12}$ =	$\frac{5}{2}$ =	$\frac{4}{3}$ =

Mental Math

a.	b.	c.	d.
e.	f.	g.	h.

Problem Solving

Understand
What information am I given?
What am I asked to find or do?

Plan
How can I use the information I am given?
Which strategy should I try?

Solve
Did I follow the plan?
Did I show my work?
Did I write the answer?

Check
Did I use the correct information?
Did I do what was asked?
Is my answer reasonable?

Saxon Math Course 1 15

Power Up Test I

Math Language

New	English Learners (ESL)
chance	outcome
probability	
sample space	
complement of an event	

Technology Resources

Student eBook Complete student textbook in electronic format.

Resources and Planner CD Assessment, reteaching, and instructional masters, plus a pacing calendar with standards.

Test and Practice Generator CD Create additional practice sheets and custom-made tests.

www.SaxonPublishers.com Visit for more student activities and planning materials.

Inclusion

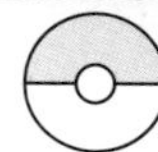

Adaptations CD Adapted lessons, investigations, practice and assessments.

Meeting Standards

National Council of Teachers of Mathematics (NCTM)

Data Analysis and Probability

DP.4a Understand and use appropriate terminology to describe complementary and mutually exclusive events

DP.4b Use proportionality and a basic understanding of probability to make and test conjectures about the results of experiments and simulations

DP.4c Compute probabilities for simple compound events, using such methods as organized lists, tree diagrams, and area models

Connections

CN.4c Recognize and apply mathematics in contexts outside of mathematics

Power-Up Discussion For use with Power Up, p. 299

Problem-Solving Strategy: Make an Organized List

When Erinn was 12 years old, she walked six dogs in her neighborhood every day to earn spending money. She preferred to walk two dogs at a time. How many different combinations of dogs could Erinn take for a walk?

Understand — Understand the problem.

"Which information from the problem do we need to use to find the solution?"

Erinn walked six dogs, and preferred to walk two at a time.

"What are we asked to do?"

Determine how many different pairs of dogs Erinn could take for a walk.

Plan — Make a plan.

"What problem-solving strategy will we use?"

We will *make an organized list* of the pairs of dogs Erinn could walk.

"Do we need to adapt any of the information?"

We will refer to the dogs as dog number 1, 2, 3, 4, 5, and 6. We will list the possible combinations of dogs as ordered pairs. Because we are only looking for *pairs* of dogs, we do not count different orders. Therefore, 1, 2 and 2, 1 represent the same pair of dogs. Once a pair is named, we will not repeat it in our list.

Solve — Carry out the plan.

"How do we begin?"

We begin by listing all the pairs containing 1, then all the pairs containing 2 (omitting any pairs already written in our table), then all the pairs containing 3, and so on:

1, 2	1, 3	1, 4	1, 5	1, 6
	2, 3	2, 4	2, 5	2, 6
		3, 4	3, 5	3, 6
			4, 5	4, 6
				5, 6

"What can we do with these ordered pairs to solve the problem?"

We count (or add) to find the total number of combinations:
$5 + 4 + 3 + 2 + 1 = 15$ different combinations of dogs Erinn could take for a walk.

Check — Look back.

"Did we find the answer to the question that was asked?"

Yes. We found that Erinn could walk 15 different pairs of dogs.

LESSON 58

• Probability and Chance

Power Up *Building Power*

facts Power Up I

mental math

a. **Calculation:** 2×75 150

b. **Number Sense:** $315 - 150$ 165

c. **Number Sense:** $250 + 199$ 449

d. **Money:** \$7.50 + \$12.50 \$20.00

e. **Fractional Parts:** $\frac{1}{2}$ of 25 $12\frac{1}{2}$

f. **Number Sense:** 20×50 1000

g. **Patterns:** Find the next number in the pattern: 4, 7, 10, 13

h. **Calculation:** 10×10, -1, $\div 11$, $\times 8$, $+3$, $\div 3$, $\div 5$ 5

problem solving When Erinn was 12 years old, she walked six dogs in her neighborhood every day to earn spending money. She preferred to walk two dogs at a time. How many different combinations of dogs could Erinn take for a walk? 15 combinations

New Concept *Increasing Knowledge*

We live in a world full of uncertainties.

What is the chance of rain on Saturday?
What are the odds of winning the big game?
What is the probability that I will roll the number needed to land on the winning space?

The study of **probability** helps us assign numbers to uncertain events and compare the likelihood that various events will occur.

Events that are certain to occur have a probability of one. Events that are certain not to occur have a probability of zero.

If I roll a number cube whose faces are numbered 1 through 6, the probability of rolling a 6 or less is one. The probability of rolling a number greater than 6 is zero.

Events that are uncertain have probabilities that fall anywhere between zero and one. The closer to zero the probability is, the less likely the event is to occur; the closer to one the probability is, the more likely the event is to occur. We typically express probabilities as fractions or as decimals.

Facts Write each improper fraction as a mixed number. Reduce fractions.

$\frac{5}{4} = 1\frac{1}{4}$	$\frac{6}{4} = 1\frac{1}{2}$	$\frac{15}{10} = 1\frac{1}{2}$	$\frac{8}{3} = 2\frac{2}{3}$	$\frac{15}{12} = 1\frac{1}{4}$
$\frac{12}{8} = 1\frac{1}{2}$	$\frac{10}{8} = 1\frac{1}{4}$	$\frac{3}{2} = 1\frac{1}{2}$	$\frac{15}{6} = 2\frac{1}{2}$	$\frac{10}{4} = 2\frac{1}{2}$
$\frac{8}{6} = 1\frac{1}{3}$	$\frac{25}{10} = 2\frac{1}{2}$	$\frac{9}{6} = 1\frac{1}{2}$	$\frac{10}{6} = 1\frac{2}{3}$	$\frac{15}{8} = 1\frac{7}{8}$
$\frac{12}{10} = 1\frac{1}{5}$	$\frac{10}{3} = 3\frac{1}{3}$	$\frac{18}{12} = 1\frac{1}{2}$	$\frac{5}{2} = 2\frac{1}{2}$	$\frac{4}{3} = 1\frac{1}{3}$

1 Power Up

Facts

Distribute **Power Up I** to students. See answers below.

Mental Math

Before students begin the Mental Math exercise, do this counting exercise as a class.

Count up and down by $\frac{1}{8}$s between $\frac{1}{8}$ and 2.

Encourage students to share different ways to mentally compute these exercises. Strategies for exercises **a** and **c** are listed below.

a. Multiply Tens and Multiply Ones
$2 \times 75 = 2 \times 70 + 2 \times 5 =$
$140 + 10 = 150$
Count On by 25
Start with 75. Count: 100, 125, 150

c. Subtract 1 and Add 1
$250 - 1 = 249$ and $199 + 1 = 200$;
$249 + 200 = 449$
Count On by 100, then Subtract 1
Start with 250. Count: 350, 450;
$450 - 1 = 449$

Problem Solving

Refer to **Power-Up Discussion,** p. 299B.

2 New Concepts

Instruction

Invite students to suggest a variety of other certain and uncertain events. After each event is named or described, ask the class to discuss the event and decide the probability of the event as zero, one, or greater than zero and less than one.

(continued)

2 New Concepts *(Continued)*

Instruction

"A number cube has faces labeled 1, 2, 3, 4, 5, and 6. What is the sample space for tossing the number cube once?" {1, 2, 3, 4, 5, 6}

Ask students to discuss the question below. Ask volunteers to record the answer on the board or overhead.

"What is the sample space for tossing two 1–6 number cubes at the same time?" {(1, 1), (1, 2), (1, 3), (1, 4), (1, 5), (1, 6), (2, 1), (2, 2), (2, 3), (2, 4), (2, 5), (2, 6), (3, 1), (3, 2), (3, 3), (3, 4), (3, 5), (3, 6), (4, 1), (4, 2), (4, 3), (4, 4), (4, 5), (4, 6), (5, 1), (5, 2), (5, 3), (5, 4), (5, 5), (5, 6), (6, 1), (6, 2), (6, 3), (6, 4), (6, 5), (6, 6)}

"How many outcomes altogether are in the sample space?" 36

On the board, draw a spinner like the one shown. Help students understand that the probabilities of the various spinner outcomes—$\frac{1}{2}$, $\frac{1}{4}$, $\frac{1}{4}$—are based on a large number of trials.

"Suppose you spin the spinner two times, and each time the spinner lands on A. Would it be correct for you to say that every time the spinner is spun two times, it will land on A both times? Why or why not?" No; Sample: Spin the spinner more times and sooner or later it will land on a different letter.

(continued)

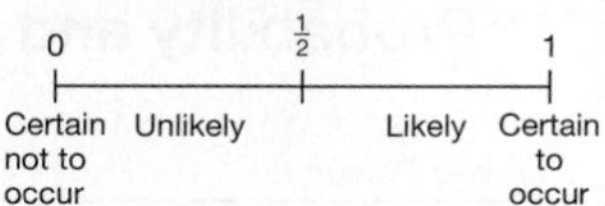

In this lesson we will practice assigning probabilities to specific events.

The set of possible outcomes for an event is called the **sample space.** If we flip a coin once, the possible outcomes are heads and tails, and the outcomes are equally likely.

Sample space = {heads, tails}

Using abbreviations, we might identify the sample space as {H, T}. If we flip a coin twice and list the results of each flip in order, then there are four equally likely possible outcomes.

Sample space = {HH, HT, TH, TT}

Imagine you spin the spinner below once. The spinner could land in sector A, in sector B, or in sector C. Since sector B and sector C have the same area, landing in either one is equally likely. Since sector A has the largest area, we can expect the spinner to land in sector A more often than in either sector B or sector C.

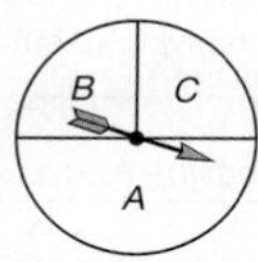

Sample space = {A, B, C}

No; The sectors are not the same size, so the outcomes are not equally likely.

Discuss What is the sample space for the experiment?

Conclude Are the three outcomes equally likely? Why or why not?

The probability of a particular outcome is the fraction of spins we expect to result in that outcome, if we spin the spinner many times. Since sector A takes up $\frac{1}{2}$ of the area, the probability that the spinner will land in A is $\frac{1}{2}$, or 0.5. In terms of area, sector B is half the size of sector A ($\frac{1}{2}$ of $\frac{1}{2}$). Sector B takes up $\frac{1}{4}$ of the area of the spinner. Therefore, the probability that the spinner will land in sector B is $\frac{1}{4}$, or 0.25.

This is also the probability that the spinner will land in sector C, since sectors B and C are equal in size. We know that the spinner is certain to land in one of the sectors, so the probabilities of the three outcomes must add up to 1.

$$\frac{1}{2} + \frac{1}{4} + \frac{1}{4} = 1 \quad \text{or} \quad 0.5 + 0.25 + 0.25 = 1$$

If we spin the spinner a large number of times, we would expect about $\frac{1}{2}$ of the spins to land in sector A, about $\frac{1}{4}$ of the spins to land in sector B, and about $\frac{1}{4}$ of the spins to land in sector C.

Math Background

The type of probability that is being presented in this lesson is theoretical probability. The theoretical probability of an event is different from the experimental probability of an event.

Theoretical probability describes what you can *expect* to happen in a great number of trials; experimental probability describes what *actually* happens.

In Investigation 8, students will learn more about experimental and theoretica probability.

Example 1

Meredith spins the spinner shown on the previous page 28 times. About how many times can she expect the spinner to land in sector A? In sector B? In sector C?

Solution

The spinner should land in sector A about $\frac{1}{2}$ of 28 times. Instead of multiplying by the fraction $\frac{1}{2}$, we can simply divide by 2.

$$28 \text{ times} \div 2 = 14 \text{ times}$$

The spinner should land in sector B about $\frac{1}{4}$ of 28 times. We divide the total number of spins by 4.

$$28 \text{ times} \div 4 = 7 \text{ times}$$

As we noted before, the probability that the spinner will land in sector B is equal to the probability that it will land in sector C. So Meredith can expect the spinner to land in sector A about **14 times,** in sector B about **7 times,** and in sector C about **7 times.**

It would be very unlikely for the spinner *never* to land in sector A in 28 spins. In 28 spins it also would be very unlikely for the spinner to *always* land in sector A. It would not be unusual, however, if the spinner were to land 12 times in sector A, 10 times in sector B, and 6 times in sector C. It is important to remember that probability indicates expectation; actual results may vary.

In the language of percent, we expect the spinner to land in sector A roughly 50% of the time, and we expect it to land in each of the other sectors roughly 25% of the time. When we express a probability as a percent, it is called a **chance.**

Example 2

A weather forecaster says that there is a 60% chance of rain tomorrow. Find the probability that it will rain tomorrow.

Solution

To find the probability that it will rain, we convert the chance, 60%, to a fraction and a decimal.

$$60\% = \frac{60}{100} = \frac{6}{10} = \mathbf{\frac{3}{5}}$$

$$60\% = \frac{60}{100} = 0.60 = \mathbf{0.6}$$

The probability of rain can be expressed as either $\frac{3}{5}$ or 0.6.

The **complement of an event** is the opposite of the event. The complement of event A is "not A." Consider the probability of rain for example. We are certain that it will either rain or not rain. The probabilities of these two possible outcomes must total 1. Subtracting the probability of rain from 1 gives us the probability that it will not rain.

2 New Concepts (Continued)

Example 1

Instruction

"Suppose that each day for one month, Meredith spins the spinner 28 times. Is it reasonable for her to expect that each day she spins the spinner, it will land on A exactly 14 times?" no

"Is it reasonable for her to expect that each day she spins the spinner, it will land on A about 14 times?" yes

Instruction

To help students understand the concept of the complement of an event, ask:

"Look at the spinner in example 1. What is the probability that the spinner will not land on C?" $\frac{1}{2} + \frac{1}{4} = \frac{3}{4}$

Point out that the probability of landing on C and not landing on C is equal to 1.

$$\frac{1}{4} + \frac{1}{2} + \frac{1}{4} = 1$$

Then ask students to express their answer as a decimal. 0.75

(continued)

anipulative Use

›nduct an experiment like the one described in example 1 using an ›erhead **Spinner** from the Manipulative Kit. Divide the spinner as shown.

y to students, "Let's see what happens if we try this experiment ourselves." in the spinner 28 times. Have students record the result of each spin. en discuss how the actual results differ from the theoretical (or expected) obability. Tell students that as the number of trials increases (for example, hey were to spin the spinner 500 times) the actual results will more closely atch the theoretical probability.

2 New Concepts (Continued)

Example 3

Instruction

Students should assume the cube has faces numbered 1, 2, 3, 4, 5, and 6.

Remind students that 1 is the sum of the probability of an event and the probability of the complement of that event.

Example 4

Instruction

Point out that the number of outcomes in any event are sometimes described as favorable outcomes.

(continued)

$$1 - \frac{6}{10} = \frac{4}{10} = \mathbf{\frac{2}{5}}$$

$$1 - 0.6 = \mathbf{0.4}$$

So the probability that it will not rain can be expressed as either $\frac{2}{5}$ or 0.4.

The probability of an event and the probability of its complement total 1.

In some experiments or games, all the outcomes have the same probability. This is true if we flip a coin. The probability of the coin landing heads up is $\frac{1}{2}$, and the probability of the coin landing tails up is also $\frac{1}{2}$. Similarly, if we roll a number cube, each number has a probability of $\frac{1}{6}$ of appearing on the cube's upturned side.

To find the probability of an event, we simply add the probabilities of the outcomes that make up the event. If all outcomes of an experiment or game have the *same* probability, then the probability of an event is:

$$\frac{\text{number of outcomes in the event}}{\text{number of possible outcomes}}$$

Example 3

Math Language
A *number cube* is a six-sided cube. Its sides are marked 1–6 with numbers or with dots.

A number cube is rolled. Find the probability that the upturned number is greater than 4. Then find the probability that the number is not greater than 4.

Solution

There are six possible, equally likely outcomes.

Sample space = {1, 2, 3, 4, 5, 6}

Two of the outcomes are greater than 4.

$$\frac{\text{number of outcomes in the event}}{\text{number of possible outcomes}} = \frac{2}{6} = \mathbf{\frac{1}{3}}$$

Thus the probability of greater than 4 is $\frac{1}{3}$. The complement of greater than 4 is not "less than 4." Rather, the complement of greater than 4 is "not greater than 4." Four of the six outcomes are not greater than 4.

$$\text{Probability of not greater than } 4 = \frac{4}{6} = \mathbf{\frac{2}{3}}$$

The calculation is reasonable because the probabilities of an event and its complement total 1, and $\frac{1}{3} + \frac{2}{3} = 1$.

Example 4

A bag contains 5 red marbles, 4 yellow marbles, 2 green marbles, and 1 orange marble. Without looking, Brendan draws a marble from the bag and notes its color.

What is the probability of drawing red?

What is the complement of this event?

What is the probability of the complement?

302 *Saxon Math Course 1*

Inclusion

Materials: number cube with numbers 1–6

Although the concepts are the same, probability is expressed using fractions or decimals, and chance is given as a percent. Use the following activity to reinforce this distinction. Begin by noting the distinction between probability and chance. Then show students a number cube and ask them to use percent to answer the following questions:

"What is the chance that this cube will land on a number less than 7?" 100%

"What is the chance that this cube will land on the number 8?" 0%

"What is the chance that this cube will land on an even number?" 50%

Ask the questions again and substitute the word *probability* for *chance*. Remind students to answer using a fraction or decimal. 1, 0, $\frac{1}{2}$

Solution

There are 12 possible outcomes in Brendan's experiment (each marble represents one outcome). The event we are considering is drawing a red marble. Since 5 of the possible outcomes are red, we see that the probability that the drawn marble is red is

$$\frac{\text{number of outcomes in the event}}{\text{number of possible outcomes}} = \mathbf{\frac{5}{12}}$$

The complement of drawing red is drawing **"not red."** Its probability can be found by subtracting $\frac{5}{12}$ from 1.

$$1 - \frac{5}{12} = \frac{7}{12}$$

So the probability of not red is $\mathbf{\frac{7}{12}}$.

Example 5

In the experiment in example 4, what is the probability that the marble Brendan draws is a primary color?

Solution

Red and yellow are primary colors. Green and orange are not. Since 5 possible outcomes are red and 4 are yellow, the probability that the drawn marble is a primary color is:

$$\frac{5+4}{12} = \frac{9}{12} = \mathbf{\frac{3}{4}}$$

Practice Set

Juan is waiting for the roller coaster at an amusement park. He has been told there is a 40% chance that he will have to wait more than 15 minutes.

a. Find the probability that Juan's wait will be more than 15 minutes. Write the probability both as a decimal and as a reduced fraction. 0.4; $\frac{2}{5}$

b. Find the probability that Juan's wait will not be more than 15 minutes. Express your answer as a decimal and as a fraction. 0.6; $\frac{3}{5}$

c. What word names the relationship between the events in **a** and **b?** complementary

A number cube is rolled. The faces of the cube are numbered 1 through 6.

d. What is the sample space? Sample space = {1, 2, 3, 4, 5, 6}

▸ **e.** What is the probability that the number rolled will be odd? Explain.

▸ **f.** What is the probability that the number rolled will be less than 6? $\frac{5}{6}$

▸ **g.** State the complement to the event in **f** and find its probability. The complement is "not less than 6." The probability of not less than 6 is $\frac{1}{6}$.

e. $\frac{1}{2}$; The possible odd numbers are 1, 3, and 5. So three of the six possible outcomes are odd, and $\frac{3}{6}$ reduces to $\frac{1}{2}$.

▸ See Math Conversations in the sidebar.

2 New Concepts (Continued)

Example 5

Instruction

Explain to students that the primary colors are red, yellow, and blue.

Practice Set

Problems e–i (Error Alert)

When finding the probability of an event and the probability of the complement of the event, a good way for students to check their work is to determine each probability independently.

For example, a student *incorrectly* names the probability of the event in problem **e** as $\frac{1}{3}$, and then subtracts $\frac{1}{3}$ from 1 to name $\frac{2}{3}$ as the probability of the complement of the event, the sum of the probabilities ($\frac{1}{3} + \frac{2}{3}$) will be 1. The student is likely to assume that the answers are correct. However, because the first answer is incorrect, the second answer is also incorrect.

A good way for students to work is to find the probability of the event, and then consider the scenario a second time to find the probability of the complement of the event. Students can then check their answers for reasonableness by comparing the sum of the probabilities to 1.

English Learners

Explain that **outcome** is the final consequence of an action. Say,

"An outcome is a result or an end product of doing something. This page discusses the possible outcomes of rolling a number cube, where the number on the cube is an example of an outcome—the result of rolling the cube."

Invite students to provide examples of outcomes, both from math and home.

3 Written Practice

Math Conversations

Discussion opportunities are provided below.

Problem 5 Analyze

"What number is the same as 6^2?" 36

"What number is the same as 8^2?" 64

"What number is the same as 10^2?" 100

"Does this problem represent an equation or an inequality? Tell why." Equation; $100 = 100$

Problem 16 Analyze

"100% represents the cost of the item or the items purchased, and 7% represents the cost of tax. How can the sum of those percents—100% plus 7% equals 107%—be used to find the total cost?" Change 107% to a decimal, then find the product of 1.07 and $9.79.

Invite a volunteer to demonstrate the arithmetic for 107% × $9.79 on the board or overhead.

Errors and Misconceptions

Problem 8

Students may assume that because subtraction is present in this equation, addition—the inverse operation—is used to find f, and its value is $3 + \frac{5}{6}$ or $3\frac{5}{6}$.

To help students recognize that this assumption is not correct, ask them to solve a simpler problem by changing $\frac{5}{6}$ to 1 and rewriting the equation. $3 - f = 1$

Students should conclude from the rewritten equation that the value of f is found by subtracting 1 from 3 $(f = 2)$ and conclude that the value of f in the given equation is found by subtracting $\frac{5}{6}$ from 3.

(continued)

Refer to the spinner at right for problems **h–k**.

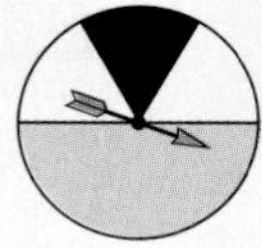

▸ **h.** What is the probability that the spinner will land in the blue sector? In the black sector? In either of the white sectors? (Note that $\frac{1}{3}$ of $\frac{1}{2}$ is $\frac{1}{6}$.) $\frac{1}{2}, \frac{1}{6}, \frac{1}{3}$

▸ **i.** Predict What is the probability that the spinner will not land on white? $\frac{2}{3}$

j. State the complement of the event in **i** and find its probability. The complement is "land on white." The probability of landing on white is $\frac{1}{3}$.

k. If you spin this spinner 30 times, roughly how many times would you expect it to land in each sector? blue: 15 times; white: 10 times; black: 5 times

l. Represent Roll a number cube 24 times and make a frequency table for the 6 possible outcomes. Which outcomes occurred more than you expected? See student work.

Written Practice — *Strengthening Concepts*

1. (12, 55) Analyze What is the difference between the sum of $\frac{1}{2}$ and $\frac{1}{3}$ and the product of $\frac{1}{2}$ and $\frac{1}{3}$? $\frac{2}{3}$

2. (29) The flat of eggs held $2\frac{1}{2}$ dozen eggs. How many eggs are in $2\frac{1}{2}$ dozen? 30 eggs

3. (18) In three nights Rumpelstiltskin spun $44,400 worth of gold thread. What was the average value of the thread he spun per night? $14,800

4. (56) Compare: $\frac{5}{8} \bigcirc \frac{1}{2}$ (>)

▸ **5.** (38) Analyze Compare: $6^2 + 8^2 \bigcirc 10^2$ (=)

Find each unknown number:

* **6.** (57) $m + \frac{3}{8} = \frac{1}{2}$ $\frac{1}{8}$ * **7.** (57) $n - \frac{2}{3} = \frac{3}{4}$ $1\frac{5}{12}$ ▸ * **8.** (43) $3 - f = \frac{5}{6}$ $2\frac{1}{6}$

9. (46) $32.50 × 10 $325.00 **10.** (39) (6.2)(0.48) 2.976 **11.** (49) 1.0 ÷ 0.8 1.25

12. (49) 120 ÷ 0.5 240 **13.** (30) $\frac{7}{8} \cdot \frac{8}{7}$ 1 **14.** (29) $\frac{5}{6} \cdot \frac{3}{4}$ $\frac{5}{8}$

15. (43) Connect Instead of dividing $7\frac{1}{2}$ by $1\frac{1}{2}$, Julie doubled both numbers and then divided mentally. What is the division problem Julie performed mentally, and what is the quotient? 15 ÷ 3 = 5

▸* **16.** (57) Analyze Find the total price including 7% tax on a $9.79 purchase. $10.48

17. (10) Predict What number is next in this sequence? 1 (or 1.0)

…, 0.6, 0.7, 0.8, 0.9, …

18. (38) Analyze The perimeter of this square is 4 cm. What is the area of the square? 1 cm²

▸ See Math Conversations in the sidebar.

* **19.** How many $\frac{3}{5}$s are in $\frac{3}{4}$? $(\frac{3}{4} \div \frac{3}{5})$ $1\frac{1}{4}$
(54)

Find each unknown number:

20. $0.32w = 32$ 100
(43)

21. $x + 3.4 = 5$ 1.6
(43)

* **22.** On one roll of a 1–6 number cube, what is the probability that the upturned face will show an even number of dots? $\frac{1}{2}$
(58)

23. Arrange these measurements in order from shortest to longest:
(7) 20 mm, 1 in., 3 cm
1 in., 3 cm, 20 mm

24. Larry correctly answered 45% of the questions.
(29, 33)

a. Explain Did Larry correctly answer more than or less than half the questions? How do you know?

b. Write 45% as a reduced fraction. $\frac{9}{20}$

25. Justify Describe how to mentally calculate $\frac{1}{10}$ of $12.50.
(52)

26. Reduce: $\frac{2 \cdot 5 \cdot 2 \cdot 3 \cdot 3 \cdot 7}{2 \cdot 2 \cdot 2 \cdot 5 \cdot 5 \cdot 7}$ $\frac{9}{10}$
(54)

▸* **27.** Analyze What is the sum of the decimal numbers represented by points x and y on this number line? 4
(50)

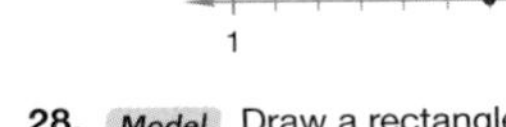

28. Model Draw a rectangle that is $1\frac{1}{2}$ inches long and $\frac{3}{4}$ inch wide. Then draw a segment that divides the rectangle into two triangles.
(7)

29. What is the perimeter of the rectangle drawn in problem 28? $4\frac{1}{2}$ inches
(8)

* **30.** If $A = lw$, and if $l = 1.5$ and $w = 0.75$, what does A equal? 1.125
(47)

24. a. less than half; 50% equals ½, and Larry answered less than 50% correctly.

25. Finding $\frac{1}{10}$ of $12.50 is the same as dividing $12.50 by 10. We shift the decimal point in $12.50 one place to the left, which makes $1.250. Then we remove the trailing zero. The answer is $1.25.

28. Sample:

$1\frac{1}{2}$ in.

$\frac{3}{4}$ in.

Early Finishers
Real-World Application

Millions of shares of stock are bought and sold each business day, and records are kept for stock prices for every trading day. Here are the closing prices, rounded to the nearest eighth, for one share of a corporation's stock during a week in 1978.

Mon.	Tu.	Wed.	Th.	Fri.
$\$14\frac{7}{8}$	$\$15\frac{1}{8}$	$\$15\frac{1}{4}$	$\$14\frac{3}{4}$	$\$14\frac{1}{2}$

Which display—a line graph or a bar graph—is the most appropriate way to display this data if you want to emphasize the changes in the daily closing prices? Draw the display and justify your choice. line graph; Sample: While a bar graph can be used to display comparisons, a line graph would be better because it clearly displays a change over time. See student graphs.

▸ See Math Conversations in the sidebar.

3 Written Practice (Continued)

Math Conversations

Discussion opportunities are provided below.

Problem 27 Analyze

"We are told that both x and y represent decimal numbers, and we are asked to find the sum of those numbers. What different things should we remember to do each time we add decimal numbers?" Sample: Align the addends by place value or align the decimal points, and place a decimal point in the answer.

Looking Forward

Finding the probability of an event and expressing it as a reduced fraction, a decimal, or a percent prepares students for:

- **Investigation 9,** finding experimental probability by performing experiments and by collecting data from surveys and presenting data in a relative frequency table.
- **Investigation 10,** performing compound experiments and creating tree diagrams and tables to display results.

• Adding Mixed Numbers

Objectives

- Use three steps—shape, operate, and simplify—to add mixed numbers with fractions that do not have common denominators.

Lesson Preparation

Materials

- **Power Up G** (in *Instructional Masters*)

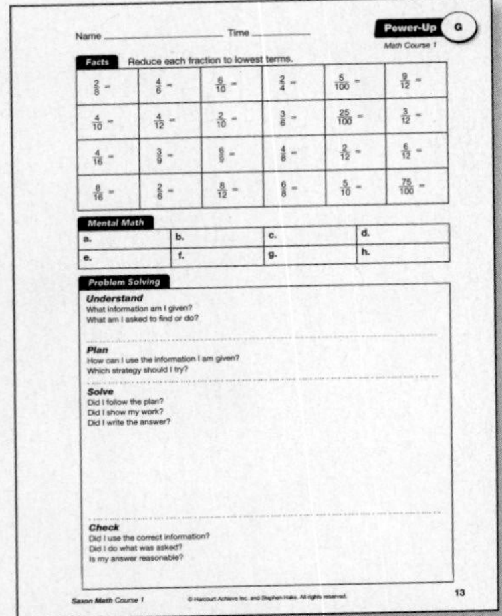

Power Up G

Math Language

English Learners (ESL)
relates

Technology Resources

Student eBook Complete student textbook in electronic format.

Resources and Planner CD Assessment, reteaching, and instructional masters, plus a pacing calendar with standards.

Test and Practice Generator CD Create additional practice sheets and custom-made tests.

www.SaxonPublishers.com Visit for more student activities and planning materials.

Inclusion

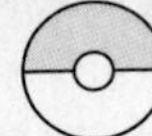

Adaptations CD Adapted lessons, investigations, practice and assessments.

Meeting Standards

National Council of Teachers of Mathematics (NCTM)

Numbers and Operations

NO.1a Work flexibly with fractions, decimals, and percents to solve problems

NO.2a Understand the meaning and effects of arithmetic operations with fractions, decimals, and integers

NO.3a Select appropriate methods and tools for computing with fractions and decimals from among mental computation, estimation, calculators or computers, and paper and pencil, depending on the situation, and apply the selected methods

NO.3b Develop and analyze algorithms for computing with fractions, decimals, and integers and develop fluency in their use

Power-Up Discussion *For use with Power Up, p. 306*

Problem-Solving Strategy: Use a Chart/ Write an Equation

Astronomers use the astronomical unit (AU) to measure distances in the solar system. One AU is equal to the average distance between Earth and the Sun, about 93,000,000 miles. On average, how many miles farther from the Sun is Saturn than Mars?

Planet	Distance from the Planet to the Sun (AU)
Mercury	0.39
Venus	0.72
Earth	1.00
Mars	1.52
Jupiter	5.20
Saturn	9.52

Understand — Understand the problem.

"What information are we given?"

We are given a chart of the distance from the planets to the Sun as measured in AU (astronomical units). We are told that one AU is about 93,000,000 miles.

"What are we asked to do?"

We are asked to determine how much farther from the Sun Saturn is than Mars.

Plan — Make a plan.

"What problem-solving strategy will we use?"

We will *use the chart* and *write an equation* to find the difference in distance between the two planets and the Sun.

Solve — Carry out the plan.

"Use the chart to find the difference in AU."

9.52 AU − 1.52 AU = 8 AU

"How many miles is 8 AU?"

We can multiply to find the number: 8 AU × 93,000,000 miles per AU = 744,000,000 miles.

"How do we answer the question?"

On average, Saturn is 744,000,000 miles farther from the Sun than Mars is.

Check — Look back.

"Did we find the answer to the question that was asked?"

Yes. We found how much farther Saturn is from the Sun than Mars.

"Does the answer also describe the distance from Mars to Saturn?"

No, the planets travel around the Sun at different rates, so the distance between planets is constantly changing. Our answer *does* mean that Mars and Saturn never are closer than about 744,000,000 miles.

"Estimate the greatest distance in miles Mars and Saturn ever are from each other."

When the planets are on opposite sides of the Sun they are about 9.5 + 1.5 = 11 AU apart or about 1,023,000,000 miles.

1 Power Up

Facts

Distribute **Power Up G** to students. See answers below.

Mental Math

Before students begin the Mental Math exercise, do this counting exercise as a class.

Count up and down by 3s between 3 and 36.

Encourage students to share different ways to mentally compute these exercises. Strategies for exercises **d** and **e** are listed below.

d. Subtract \$7, then Subtract \$0.75
\$15 − \$7 = \$8; \$8.00 − \$0.75 = \$7.25
Subtract \$8, then Add \$0.25
\$15 − \$8 = \$7; \$7.00 + \$0.25 = \$7.25

e. Double Dollars, then Double Cents
Double \$1 is \$2 and double \$0.50 is \$1.00; \$2 + \$1 = \$3
Use a Mixed Number
Since double $1\frac{1}{2}$ is 3, double \$1.50 is \$3.

Problem Solving

Refer to **Power-Up Discussion,** p. 306B.

2 New Concepts

Instruction

Remind students that whenever they need to choose a common denominator, choosing the least common denominator can reduce the amount of arithmetic that needs to be completed.

Example 1

Instruction

"In Step 1, the fraction part of $2\frac{1}{2}$ is multiplied by $\frac{3}{3}$. Does multiplying by $\frac{3}{3}$ change the value of $\frac{1}{2}$? Explain why or why not." No; $\frac{3}{3}$ is another name for 1, and the product of 1 and a non-zero number is that number; $\frac{3}{6}$ and $\frac{1}{2}$ are different names for the same number.

(continued)

LESSON 59

• Adding Mixed Numbers

Power Up *Building Power*

facts Power Up G

mental math

a. **Calculation:** 4 × 75 300
b. **Number Sense:** 279 + 350 629
c. **Number Sense:** 250 − 199 51
d. **Money:** \$15.00 − \$7.75 \$7.25
e. **Money:** Double \$1.50. \$3.00
f. **Number Sense:** $\frac{800}{40}$ 20
g. **Patterns:** Find the next number in the pattern: 12, 24, 36, 48
h. **Calculation:** 4 × 12, ÷ 6, × 8, − 4, ÷ 6, × 3, ÷ 2 15

problem solving

Astronomers use the astronomical unit (AU) to measure distances in the solar system. One AU is equal to the average distance between Earth and the Sun, about 93,000,000 miles. On average, how many miles farther from the Sun is Saturn than Mars? 744,000,000 miles

Planet	AU from the Planet to the Sun
Mercury	0.39
Venus	0.72
Earth	1.00
Mars	1.52
Jupiter	5.20
Saturn	9.52

New Concept *Increasing Knowledge*

We have been practicing adding mixed numbers since Lesson 26. In this lesson we will rename the fraction parts of the mixed numbers so that the fractions have common denominators. Then we will add.

Example 1

Add: $2\frac{1}{2} + 1\frac{1}{6}$

Solution

Step 1: Shape: write the fractions with common denominators.

Step 2: Operate: add the renamed fractions and add the whole numbers.

Facts Reduce each fraction to lowest terms.

$\frac{2}{8} = \frac{1}{4}$	$\frac{4}{6} = \frac{2}{3}$	$\frac{6}{10} = \frac{3}{5}$	$\frac{2}{4} = \frac{1}{2}$	$\frac{5}{100} = \frac{1}{20}$	$\frac{9}{12} = \frac{3}{4}$
$\frac{4}{10} = \frac{2}{5}$	$\frac{4}{12} = \frac{1}{3}$	$\frac{2}{10} = \frac{1}{5}$	$\frac{3}{6} = \frac{1}{2}$	$\frac{25}{100} = \frac{1}{4}$	$\frac{3}{12} = \frac{1}{4}$
$\frac{4}{16} = \frac{1}{4}$	$\frac{3}{9} = \frac{1}{3}$	$\frac{6}{9} = \frac{2}{3}$	$\frac{4}{8} = \frac{1}{2}$	$\frac{2}{12} = \frac{1}{6}$	$\frac{6}{12} = \frac{1}{2}$
$\frac{8}{16} = \frac{1}{2}$	$\frac{2}{6} = \frac{1}{3}$	$\frac{8}{12} = \frac{2}{3}$	$\frac{6}{8} = \frac{3}{4}$	$\frac{5}{10} = \frac{1}{2}$	$\frac{75}{100} = \frac{3}{4}$

Thinking Skill

Discuss

When should you reduce a fraction? when the fraction is not in lowest terms or it is an improper fraction

Step 3: Simplify: reduce the fraction.

1. Shape

$$2\frac{1}{2} \times \frac{3}{3} = 2\frac{3}{6}$$
$$+\ 1\frac{1}{6} \quad = 1\frac{1}{6}$$

2. Operate

$$3\frac{4}{6} = 3\frac{2}{3}$$

3. Simplify

Example 2

Add: $1\frac{1}{2} + 2\frac{2}{3}$

Solution

Thinking Skill

Verify

Why did we rename both fractions? Sample: We need a common denominator to add the fractions.

Step 1: Shape: write the fractions with common denominators.

Step 2: Operate: add the renamed fractions and add the whole numbers.

Step 3: Simplify: convert the improper fraction to a mixed number, and combine the mixed number with the whole number.

1. Shape

$$1\frac{1}{2} \times \frac{3}{3} = 1\frac{3}{6}$$
$$+\ 2\frac{2}{3} \times \frac{2}{2} = 2\frac{4}{6}$$

2. Operate

$$3\frac{7}{6} = 3 + 1\frac{1}{6} = 4\frac{1}{6}$$

3. Simplify

Practice Set ▶ Add:

a. $1\frac{1}{2} + 1\frac{1}{3}$ $2\frac{5}{6}$ **b.** $1\frac{1}{2} + 1\frac{2}{3}$ $3\frac{1}{6}$ **c.** $5\frac{1}{3} + 2\frac{1}{6}$ $7\frac{1}{2}$

d. $3\frac{3}{4} + 1\frac{1}{3}$ $5\frac{1}{12}$ **e.** $5\frac{1}{2} + 3\frac{1}{6}$ $8\frac{2}{3}$ **f.** $7\frac{1}{2} + 4\frac{5}{8}$ $12\frac{1}{8}$

Written Practice *Strengthening Concepts*

▶ **1.** (40) *Connect* What is the product of the decimal numbers four tenths and four hundredths? 0.016

2. (32) Larry looked at the clock. It was 9:45 p.m. The bus for his class trip leaves at 8:30 a.m. How many hours and minutes are there until the bus leaves? 10 hr 45 min

3. (12) Pluto orbits the sun at an average distance of about five billion, nine hundred million kilometers. Use digits to write that distance. 5,900,000,000 kilometers

*** 4.** (59) $2\frac{1}{2} + 1\frac{1}{6}$ $3\frac{2}{3}$ *** 5.** (59) $1\frac{1}{2} + 2\frac{2}{3}$ $4\frac{1}{6}$

6. (56) Compare: $\frac{1}{2} \ⓒ \frac{3}{5}$ (<) **7.** (56) Compare: $\frac{2}{3}$ ⓒ $\frac{6}{9}$ (=)

▶ See Math Conversations in the sidebar.

2 New Concepts (Continued)

Example 2

Instruction

To offer students a different way to practice the skill of adding mixed numbers, you might invite them to check the answer shown in the solution by changing each addend to an improper fraction, then finding and reducing the sum of those improper fractions.

The Math Background feature at the bottom of this page shows an example of this method.

Practice Set

Problems a–f (Error Alert)

To help students find the correct sums, encourage them to use the three steps—Shape, Operate, and Simplify—to solve these problems. Then ask volunteers to describe each step in each problem to the class.

3 Written Practice

Math Conversations

Discussion opportunities are provided below.

Problem 1 Connect

"What operation does the word 'product' represent?" multiplication

"How many decimal places should we expect to place in the product of these numbers? Explain your answer." Three; a factor in tenths has one decimal place and a factor in hundredths has two decimal places. The sum of the number of decimal places in the factors is three.

(continued)

Math Background

Students sometimes use an inverse operation to check an answer for reasonableness. When working with the sums of mixed numbers, a different way for students to check their work is to change the addends to improper fractions, then add and reduce the sum.

For example, the sum of the mixed numbers in example 2 is $4\frac{1}{6}$. To check the sum, change each addend to an improper fraction.

$$1\frac{1}{2} = \frac{3}{2} \text{ and } 2\frac{2}{3} = \frac{8}{3}$$

Rename one or both fractions using a common denominator.

$$\frac{3}{2} = \frac{9}{6} \text{ and } \frac{8}{3} = \frac{16}{6}$$

Add, then reduce if possible.

$$\frac{9}{6} + \frac{16}{6} = \frac{25}{6} \text{ and } \frac{25}{6} = 4\frac{1}{6}$$

3 Written Practice (Continued)

Math Conversations

Discussion opportunities are provided below.

Problem 15 Estimate

"Which digit in the number has a place value of millions? Tell how you know."
6; Sample explanation: The place values of the number, from right to left, are ones, tens, hundreds, thousands, ten thousands, hundred thousands, millions, and then ten millions.

Problem 25 Formulate

Extend the Problem

Invite students to exchange questions, then answer the questions and compare answers.

Problem 26 Connect

To help students understand why a division is used to represent the problem, share with them a simpler problem.

"Suppose Nefertiti could pronounce her name in 2 seconds. At that rate, how many times could she pronounce her name in 10 seconds? Explain how you found the answer." 5 times; divide 10 by 2

Remind students that dividing by a fraction is the same as multiplying by the reciprocal of that fraction.

Errors and Misconceptions

Problem 21

Students should assume, unless indicated otherwise, a cube that is simply described as a "number cube" has faces numbered 1, 2, 3, 4, 5, and 6.

In problem **a**, students should infer that the words "less than" suggest there may be more than one favorable outcome.

For problem **b**, it is helpful for students to recall that the sum of the probability of an event and the probability of the complement of that event is 1.

(continued)

8. *(48)* $8\frac{1}{5} - 3\frac{4}{5}$ $4\frac{2}{5}$

9. *(29)* $\frac{3}{4} \cdot \frac{5}{2}$ $1\frac{7}{8}$

* **10.** *(54)* How many $\frac{1}{2}$s are in $\frac{2}{5}$? $(\frac{2}{5} \div \frac{1}{2})$ $\frac{4}{5}$

11. *(39)* (0.875)(40) 35

12. *(45)* $0.07 \div 4$ 0.0175

13. *(49)* $30 \div d = 0.6$ 50

14. *(50)* **Analyze** What number is halfway between 0.1 and 0.24? 0.17

▶ **15.** *(16)* **Estimate** Round 36,428,591 to the nearest million. 36,000,000

16. *(14)* What temperature is 23° less than 8°F? −15°F

17. *(47)* **Estimate** Miguela wound a garden hose around a circular reel. If the diameter of the reel was 10 inches, how many inches of hose was wound on the first full turn of the reel? Round the answer to the nearest whole inch. (Use 3.14 for π.) 31 inches

* **18.** *(38)* How many square inches are needed to cover a square foot? 144 square inches

19. *(52)* One centimeter is what fraction of one meter? $\frac{1}{100}$

20. *(46, 52)* **Justify** Mentally calculate each answer. Describe how you performed each mental calculation.

a. 6.25×10

b. $6.25 \div 10$

20 a. 62.5; To multiply 6.25 by 10, shift the decimal point one place to the right. **b.** 0.625; To divide 6.25 by 10, shift the decimal point one place to the left.

▶* **21.** *(58)* **a.** With one toss of a single number cube, what is the probability of rolling a number less than three? $\frac{1}{3}$

b. Write the complement of the event in **a** and find its probability.

21. b. The complement is "rolling a number not less than three." The probability of rolling a number not less than three is $\frac{2}{3}$.

22. *(39, 44)* Compare: $(0.8)^2 < 0.8$

Refer to the line graph below to answer problems **23–25.**

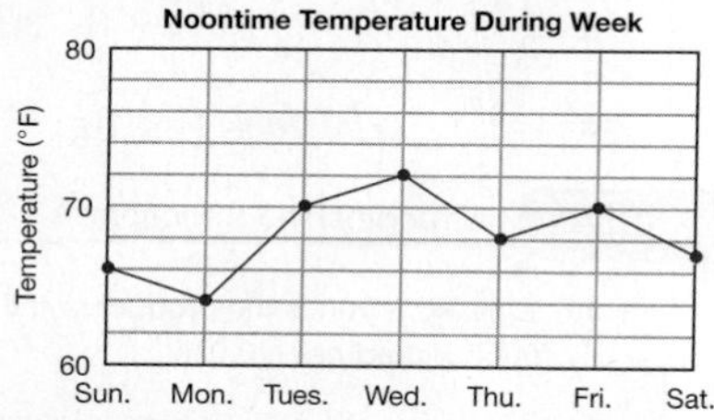

Math Language
Remember that **range** is the difference between the greatest and least numbers in a data set.

23. *(18, Inv. 5)* What was the range of the noontime temperatures during the week? 8°F

24. *(18)* What was the Saturday noontime temperature? 67°F

▶* **25.** *(18)* Write a question that relates to this line graph and answer the question. See student work.

▶* **26.** *(50)* **Connect** Nana can pack a bag of groceries in six tenths of a minute. At that rate, how many bags of groceries can she pack in 15 minutes? Write and solve a fraction division problem to answer the question. $15 \div \frac{6}{10}$; 25 bags of groceries

▶ See Math Conversations in the sidebar.

English Learners

Explain the meaning of the word **relates.** Show how a brother is related to a sister, or how subtraction relates to addition (inverse operation). Say,

"On this page, relates means to make a connection with or use something else. Problem 25 asks you to write a question that relates to the line graph. The problem is asking you to use the graph to create a question."

Ask a student volunteer to create a math question that relates to today's lesson to show understanding of term "relate."

27. One eighth is equivalent to $12\frac{1}{2}\%$. To what percent is three eighths equivalent? $37\frac{1}{2}\%$
(Inv. 2)

* 28. **Justify** Mentally calculate the total cost of 10 gallons of gas priced at $2.299 per gallon. Describe the process you used. $22.99; To multiply $2.299 by 10, shift the decimal point one place to the right.
(46)

* 29. **Analyze** Arrange these three numbers in order from least to greatest: $\frac{3}{4}$, the reciprocal of $\frac{3}{4}$, 1 $\frac{3}{4}$, 1, the reciprocal of $\frac{3}{4}$
(56)

30. **Evaluate** If $P = 2l + 2w$, and if $l = 4$ and $w = 3$, what does P equal? 14
(47)

Early Finishers
Real-World Application

The Estevez family has three children born in different years.

a. List all the possible birth orders by gender of the children. For example, boy, boy, boy is one possible order and boy, girl, boy is another. (Boy, Boy, Boy), (Boy, Boy, Girl), (Boy, Girl, Boy), (Boy, Girl, Girl), (Girl, Girl, Girl), (Girl, Girl, Boy), (Girl, Boy, Girl), (Girl, Boy, Boy)

b. Use the answer to **a** to find the probability that the Estevez family has two boys and one girl in any order. P(2 boys, 1 girl) $= \frac{3}{8}$

3 Written Practice (Continued)

Math Conversations

Discussion opportunities are provided below.

Problem 29 Analyze

"What is the reciprocal of $\frac{3}{4}$?" $\frac{4}{3}$

"How can you check to be sure that $\frac{4}{3}$ is the reciprocal of $\frac{3}{4}$?" Multiply $\frac{4}{3}$ and $\frac{3}{4}$; if the product is 1, $\frac{4}{3}$ is the reciprocal of $\frac{3}{4}$.

$\frac{4}{3} \times \frac{3}{4} = \frac{12}{12} = 1$

Looking Forward

Adding and subtracting fractions in three steps (correct shape, perform operation, and simplify) prepares students for:

- **Lesson 61,** adding three or more fractions by renaming fractions so that they have common denominators.
- **Lesson 63,** subtracting mixed numbers with regrouping.
- **Lesson 72,** using a fractions chart to review the addition and subtraction of fractions.

• Polygons

Objectives

- Identify a polygon by the number of sides it has.
- Identify different kinds of polygons.
- Find the length of a side of a regular polygon when given its perimeter.

Lesson Preparation

Materials

- **Power Up I** (in *Instructional Masters*)
- **Common Polygons poster**

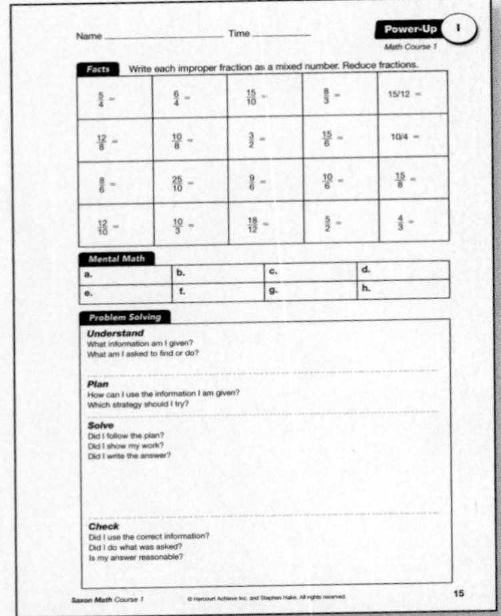

Name ______________ Time ________ **Power-Up I** *Math Course 1*

Facts Write each improper fraction as a mixed number. Reduce fractions.

$\frac{5}{4}$ =	$\frac{6}{4}$ =	$\frac{15}{10}$ =	$\frac{8}{3}$ =	15/12 =
$\frac{12}{8}$ =	$\frac{10}{8}$ =	$\frac{3}{2}$ =	$\frac{15}{6}$ =	10/4 =
$\frac{8}{6}$ =	$\frac{25}{10}$ =	$\frac{9}{6}$ =	$\frac{10}{6}$ =	$\frac{15}{8}$ =
$\frac{12}{10}$ =	$\frac{10}{3}$ =	$\frac{18}{12}$ =	$\frac{5}{2}$ =	$\frac{4}{3}$ =

Mental Math

a.	b.	c.	d.
e.	f.	g.	h.

Problem Solving

Understand
What information am I given?
What am I asked to find or do?

Plan
How can I use the information I am given?
Which strategy should I try?

Solve
Did I follow the plan?
Did I show my work?
Did I write the answer?

Check
Did I use the correct information?
Did I do what was asked?
Is my answer reasonable?

Saxon Math Course 1 © Harcourt Achieve Inc. and Stephen Hake. All rights reserved. 15

Power Up I

Math Language

New	Maintain	English Learners (ESL)
congruent	vertex	cover
quadrilateral		
regular polygon		

Technology Resources

Student eBook Complete student textbook in electronic format.

Resources and Planner CD Assessment, reteaching, and instructional masters, plus a pacing calendar with standards.

Test and Practice Generator CD Create additional practice sheets and custom-made tests.

www.SaxonPublishers.com Visit for more student activities and planning materials.

Inclusion

Adaptations CD Adapted lessons, investigations, practice and assessments.

Meeting Standards

National Council of Teachers of Mathematics (NCTM)

Geometry

GM.1a Precisely describe, classify, and understand relationships among types of two- and three-dimensional objects using their defining properties

GM.4d Use geometric models to represent and explain numerical and algebraic relationships

GM.4e Recognize and apply geometric ideas and relationships in areas outside the mathematics classroom, such as art, science, and everyday life

Power-Up Discussion *For use with Power Up, p. 310*

Problem-Solving Strategy: Use Logical Reasoning

Melina glued 27 small blocks together to make this cube. Then she painted each of the 6 faces of the cube a different color. Later the cube broke apart into the 27 small blocks it was made up of. How many of the smaller blocks had 3 painted faces? 2 painted faces? 1 painted face?

Understand ***Understand the problem.***

"What information are we given?"

Twenty-seven blocks were glued into a $3 \times 3 \times 3$ cube and then painted. Later, the cube broke apart.

"What are we asked to do?"

Determine how many of the 27 cubes have 1, 2, or 3 faces painted.

Plan ***Make a plan.***

"What problem-solving strategy will we use?"

We will *use logical reasoning* to visualize the location of the painted faces.

Solve ***Carry out the plan.***

"How many cubes will have no painted faces?"

Just one.

"What is its position in the cube?"

The cube in the very center.

"How many cubes will have 1 painted face?"

Six cubes will have 1 painted face.

"What is their position in the cube?"

The center block of each face of the original cube.

"How many cubes will have 3 painted faces?"

Eight cubes will have 3 painted faces.

"What is their position in the cube?"

The cubes at each vertex of the original cube.

"The remaining cubes will each have 2 painted faces. How many are there?"

We can subtract to find the number of cubes remaining: $27 - 1 - 6 - 8 = 12$. Twelve cubes will have 2 painted faces.

"What is their position in the cube?"

The center block of each edge of the original cube.

Check ***Look back.***

"How can we verify the solution is correct?"

We can sum our totals for each type of cube. If our answers are correct, the total should equal the number of smaller blocks in the original cube: $1 + 6 + 8 + 12 = 27$ blocks.

1 Power Up

Facts
Distribute **Power Up I** to students. See answers below.

Mental Math
Before students begin the Mental Math exercise, do this counting exercise as a class.

Count by 7s from 7 to 84.

Encourage students to share different ways to mentally compute these exercises. Strategies for exercises **e** and **f** are listed below.

e. Use a Pattern
Since $\frac{1}{2}$ of \$4 is \$2 and $\frac{1}{2}$ of \$6 is \$3, $\frac{1}{2}$ of \$5 is \$2.50.

Break Apart \$5
\$5 = \$4 + \$1; $\frac{1}{2}$ of \$4 is \$2 and $\frac{1}{2}$ of \$1 is \$0.50; \$2.00 + \$0.50 = \$2.50

f. Use a Pattern
$4 \times 5 = 20$; $4 \times 50 = 200$;
$40 \times 50 = 2000$

Use Facts
4 tens × 5 tens = 20 hundreds = 2000

Problem Solving
Refer to **Power-Up Discussion**, p. 310B.

2 New Concepts

Instruction
You may wish to display the **Common Polygons** concept poster as you discuss this topic with students.

(continued)

LESSON 60

• Polygons

Power Up *Building Power*

facts Power Up I

mental math

a. **Number Sense:** 2 × 750 1500

b. **Number Sense:** 429 − 250 179

c. **Number Sense:** 750 + 199 949

d. **Money:** \$9.50 + \$1.75 \$11.25

e. **Money:** $\frac{1}{2}$ of \$5 \$2.50

f. **Number Sense:** 40 × 50 2000

g. **Primes and Composites:** Name the prime numbers between 1 and 10. 2, 3, 5, 7

h. **Calculation:** 12 × 3, + 4, × 2, + 20, ÷ 10, × 5, ÷ 2 25

problem solving

Melina glued 27 small blocks together to make this cube. Then she painted each of the 6 faces of the cube a different color. Later the cube broke apart into the 27 small blocks it was made up of. How many of the smaller blocks had 3 painted faces? 2 painted faces? 1 painted face? 3 painted faces: 8 blocks; 2 painted faces: 12 blocks; 1 painted face: 6 blocks; no painted faces: 1 block

New Concept *Increasing Knowledge*

Polygons are closed, flat shapes with straight sides.

Example 1

Which of the following is a polygon?

A 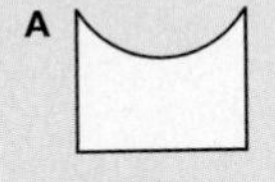

B 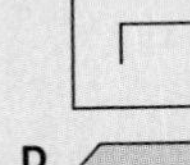

C 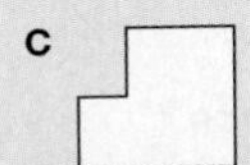

D

Solution

Only choice **C** is a polygon because it is the only closed, flat shape with straight sides.

Facts Write each improper fraction as a mixed number. Reduce fractions.

$\frac{5}{4} = 1\frac{1}{4}$	$\frac{6}{4} = 1\frac{1}{2}$	$\frac{15}{10} = 1\frac{1}{2}$	$\frac{8}{3} = 2\frac{2}{3}$	$\frac{15}{12} = 1\frac{1}{4}$
$\frac{12}{8} = 1\frac{1}{2}$	$\frac{10}{8} = 1\frac{1}{4}$	$\frac{3}{2} = 1\frac{1}{2}$	$\frac{15}{6} = 2\frac{1}{2}$	$\frac{10}{4} = 2\frac{1}{2}$
$\frac{8}{6} = 1\frac{1}{3}$	$\frac{25}{10} = 2\frac{1}{2}$	$\frac{9}{6} = 1\frac{1}{2}$	$\frac{10}{6} = 1\frac{2}{3}$	$\frac{15}{8} = 1\frac{7}{8}$
$\frac{12}{10} = 1\frac{1}{5}$	$\frac{10}{3} = 3\frac{1}{3}$	$\frac{18}{12} = 1\frac{1}{2}$	$\frac{5}{2} = 2\frac{1}{2}$	$\frac{4}{3} = 1\frac{1}{3}$

Math Language
The term *poly-* means "many," and *-gon* means "angles." The prefix of a polygon's name tells how many angles and sides the polygon has: *tri-* means 3, *quad-* means 4, and so on.

Polygons are named by the number of sides they have. The chart below names some common polygons.

Polygons

Shape	Number of Sides	Name of Polygon
△	3	triangle
▭	4	quadrilateral
⬠	5	pentagon
⬡	6	hexagon
⯃	8	octagon

Two sides of a polygon meet, or **intersect,** at a **vertex** (plural: **vertices**). A polygon has the same number of vertices as it has sides.

Example 2

What is the name of a polygon that has four sides?

Solution

The answer is not "square" or "rectangle." Squares and rectangles do have four sides, but not all four-sided polygons are squares or rectangles. The correct answer is **quadrilateral.** A rectangle is one kind of quadrilateral. A square is a rectangle with sides of equal length.

If all the sides of a polygon have the same length and if all the angles have the same measure, then the polygon is called a **regular polygon.** A square is a regular quadrilateral, but a rectangle that is longer than it is wide is not a regular quadrilateral.

We often use the word **congruent** when describing geometric figures. We say that polygons are congruent to each other if they have the same shape and size. We may also refer to segments or angles as congruent. Congruent segments have the same length; congruent angles have the same measure. In a regular polygon all the sides are congruent and all the angles are congruent.

Example 3

A regular octagon has a perimeter of 96 inches. How long is each side?

Solution

An octagon has eight sides. The sides of a regular octagon are the same length. Dividing the perimeter of 96 inches by 8, we find that each side is **12 inches.** Many of the red stop signs on our roads are regular octagons with sides 12 inches long.

2 New Concepts (Continued)

Instruction

Ask students to copy the chart into their notebooks for reference during this lesson.

On the **Common Polygons** concept poster, point out (or have students point out) the vertices of each polygon.

Refer to the section under example 2. On the board or overhead, ask one or more volunteers to draw and name a square, a rectangle that is not a square, and a rhombus that is not a square. Sample:

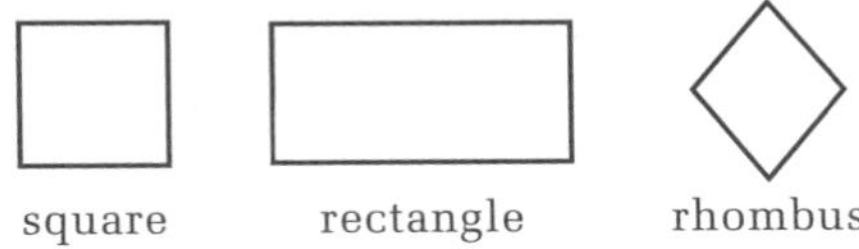

"What name describes all of these polygons? How do you know?" quadrilateral; all of the polygons have four sides

"Which of these figures are regular polygons? Why?" The square; all of its sides have the same length and all of its angles have the same measure.

Discuss with students why each of the other quadrilaterals is not a regular polygon. For example, although the rectangle has angles that are the same measure, it has sides that are not all the same length; and although the rhombus has sides that are the same length, it has angles that are not all the same measure.

(continued)

Math Background

A polygon is a simple closed curve that is composed of line segments. Each line segment is called a side of the polygon.

A polygon can have any number of sides, but it must have at least three sides.

2 New Concepts (Continued)

Practice Set

Problem c (Error Alert)

Even though students are not likely to know the name given to a 19-sided polygon, they should understand that a polygon can have any number of sides, as long as that number is three or more.

Problem e (Error Alert)

Because a polygon has the same number of vertices as it has sides, students can answer this question correctly by mistakenly thinking that the "vertices" of a polygon represent its "sides."

Make sure students understand that the vertices of a polygon are different from its sides.

3 Written Practice

Math Conversations

Discussion opportunities are provided below.

Problem 15 (Predict)

Extend the Problem

"Describe a way, that does not involve making a list or counting on, to predict the 100th term of this sequence." Sample: Except for the first two numbers in the sequence, the number in any term of the sequence seems to be one less than the product of the term and two; so I predict the 100th term to be $100 \times 2 - 1$ or 199.

Errors and Misconceptions

Problem 13

Watch for students who round the factors instead of the product. It can be difficult to catch this error because rounding 0.24 to 0.2 and rounding 0.26 to 0.3 produces the same answer as rounding the exact product to the nearest hundredth.

Remind students who make this error to read problems carefully and reread them a second time, whenever necessary.

(continued)

Practice Set

a. What is the name of this six-sided shape? hexagon

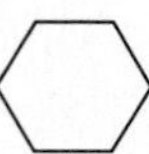

b. How many sides does a pentagon have? 5 sides

▶ c. Can a polygon have 19 sides? yes

d. What is the name for a corner of a polygon? vertex

▶ e. What is the name for a polygon with four vertices? quadrilateral

Written Practice *Strengthening Concepts*

1. (15) **Formulate** What is the cost per ounce of a 42-ounce box of oatmeal priced at \$1.26? Write an equation and solve the problem. $42 \cdot c = 1.26$; \$0.03 per ounce

* 2. (39, 51) **Estimate** Ling needs to purchase some gas so that she can mow her lawn. At the station she fills a container with 1.1 gallons of gas. The station charges $\$2.47\frac{9}{10}$ per gallon.

   a. How much will Ling spend on gas? Round your answer to the nearest cent. \$2.73

   b. Explain how to use estimation to check whether your answer is reasonable.

2. b. Ling bought only a little more than a gallon, so the cost should be only a little more than $\$2.47\frac{9}{10}$. The answer \$2.73 is reasonable.

3. (12) The smallest three-digit whole number is 100. What is the largest three-digit whole number? 999

* 4. (57) $\frac{3}{4} + \frac{5}{8}$ $1\frac{3}{8}$

* 5. (59) $1\frac{1}{2} + 3\frac{1}{6}$ $4\frac{2}{3}$

6. (29) $\frac{5}{5} \times \left(\frac{4}{4} - \frac{3}{3}\right)$ 0

7. (29) $\frac{3}{5} \cdot \frac{1}{3}$ $\frac{1}{5}$

* 8. (54) How many $\frac{1}{3}$s are in $\frac{3}{5}$? ($\frac{3}{5} \div \frac{1}{3}$) $1\frac{4}{5}$

9. (22) **Model** How much money is $\frac{5}{8}$ of \$24? Draw a diagram to illustrate the problem. \$15

9. \$24: $\frac{5}{8}$ of \$24 = \$3, \$3, \$3, \$3, \$3; $\frac{3}{8}$ of \$24 = \$3, \$3, \$3

10. (40) (0.65)(0.14) 0.091

11. (49) $65 \div 0.05$ 1300

12. (60) A quadrilateral has how many sides? 4 sides

▶* 13. (51) **Estimate** Round the product of 0.24 and 0.26 to the nearest hundredth. 0.06

14. (18) What is the average of 1.3, 2, and 0.81? 1.37

▶ 15. (10) **Predict** What is the sum of the first seven numbers in this sequence? 49

1, 3, 5, 7, . . .

16. (38) How many square feet are needed to cover a square yard? 9 square feet

17. (52) Ten centimeters is what fraction of one meter? $\frac{1}{10}$

▶ See Math Conversations in the sidebar.

English Learners

Draw a picture of a square, triangle and a rectangle on the board. Tape a piece of paper over each polygon as you explain and demonstrate the meaning of **cover.** Say,

"For problem 16, to cover an item means to put another surface on top of the space. For instance, to cover the square yard, the area inside the square yard has something over it."

Ask students to demonstrate their understanding of the word "cover" by asking them to cover a hand with a piece of paper, or describing what items can be used to cover a roof, a floor, or even a wall.

Find each unknown number:

18. (43) $3x = 1.2 + 1.2 + 1.2$ 1.2

19. (30) $\frac{4}{3}y = 1$ $\frac{3}{4}$

20. (49) $m + 1\frac{3}{5} = 5$ $3\frac{2}{5}$

* **21.** (58) $6\frac{1}{8} - w = 3\frac{5}{8}$ $2\frac{1}{2}$

22. (19) List What are the prime numbers between 40 and 50? 41, 43, 47

▸* **23.** (47) Analyze Pedro cut a lime into thin slices. The largest slice was about 4 cm in diameter. Then he removed the outer peel from the slice. About how long was the outer peel? Round the answer to the nearest centimeter. (Use 3.14 for π.) 13 cm

24. (50, 51) Connect **a.** To what decimal number is the arrow pointing? 5.4

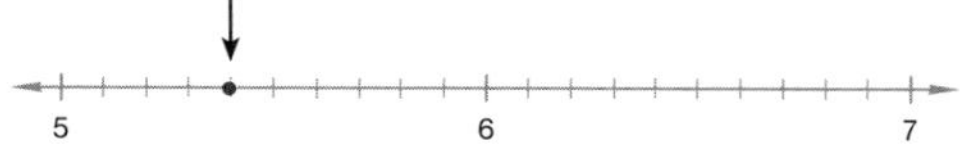

b. This decimal number rounds to what whole number? 5

▸* **25.** (58) Explain The face of this spinner is divided into 8 congruent sectors. What is the sample space? The spinner is spun once, what ratio expresses the probability that it will stop on a 3? Sample space = {1, 2, 3, 4} or {1, 1, 2, 2, 3, 3, 4, 4}; $\frac{1}{4}$

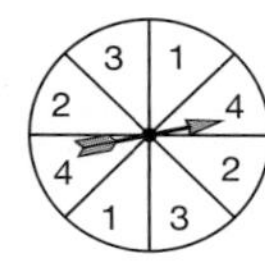

* **26.** (50) Estimate Mary found that the elm tree added about $\frac{3}{8}$ inch to the diameter of its trunk every year. If the diameter of the tree is about 12 inches, then the tree is about how many years old? Write and solve a fraction division problem to answer the question. $12 \div \frac{3}{8} = y$; about 32 years old

27. (29) Duncan's favorite TV show starts at 8 p.m. and ends at 9 p.m. Duncan timed the commercials and found that 12 minutes of commercials aired between 8 p.m. and 9 p.m. Commercials were shown for what fraction of the hour? $\frac{1}{5}$

* **28.** (43) Connect Instead of dividing 400 by 16, Fede thought of an equivalent division problem that was easier to perform. Write an equivalent division problem that has a one-digit divisor and find the quotient.

28. Samples: $200 \div 8 = 25$; $100 \div 4 = 25$; $50 \div 2 = 25$

29. (41) What is the total price of a $6.89 item plus 6% sales tax? $7.30

* **30.** (56) Compare:

a. $3\frac{1}{2} = \frac{6}{2} + \frac{1}{2}$ **b.** $\frac{5}{8} < \frac{3}{4}$

▸ See Math Conversations in the sidebar.

Looking Forward

Identifying polygons by the number of sides they have, using the term congruent to describe geometric figures, and finding the length of a side when given the perimeter of a regular polygon prepares students for:

- **Investigation 6,** naming and drawing geometric solids; counting faces, edges, and vertices; finding the surface area of a polyhedron; identifying the two-dimensional pattern of a solid; and counting cubes to find the volume of solids.
- **Lesson 64,** classifying and drawing quadrilaterals based on the characteristics of their sides and angles.
- **Lesson 98,** finding the sum of the angle measures of triangles and quadrilaterals.
- **Lesson 108,** using transformations (rotations, translations, and reflections) to position congruent triangles "on top of" each other.

3 Written Practice (Continued)

Math Conversations

Discussion opportunities are provided below.

Problem 23 Analyze

"When we are asked to find the length of the outer peel, what measurement of a circle are we being asked to find?" circumference

"Name the two formulas that can be used to find the circumference of a circle." $C = 2\pi r$; $C = \pi d$

Problem 25 Explain

"A ratio can be written as a fraction. Explain how to write the fraction that describes an outcome of 3." Sample: Write the number of favorable outcomes as the numerator of the fraction, and write the total number of possible outcomes as the denominator of the fraction.

Assessment

30–40 minutes *For use after Lesson 60*

Distribute **Cumulative Test 11** to each student. Two versions of the test are available in *Saxon Math Course 1 Course Assessments Book.* Have students complete the **Power-Up Test** first. Allow 10 minutes. Then have students work the 20 numbered items on the **Cumulative Test.** Students may use copies of the answer sheet to record their work. Track individual and class progress with the **Test Analysis** forms.

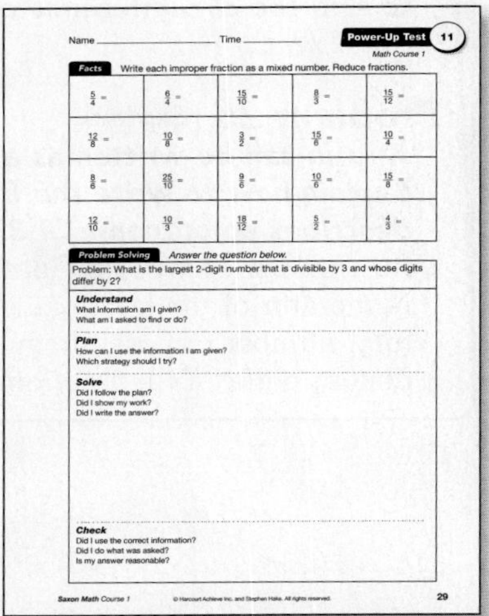

Name ______ Time ______

Power-Up Test 11
Math Course 1

Facts Write each improper fraction as a mixed number. Reduce fractions.

$\frac{5}{4}$ =	$\frac{6}{4}$ =	$\frac{15}{10}$ =	$\frac{8}{3}$ =	$\frac{15}{12}$ =
$\frac{12}{8}$ =	$\frac{10}{8}$ =	$\frac{3}{2}$ =	$\frac{15}{6}$ =	$\frac{10}{4}$ =
$\frac{8}{6}$ =	$\frac{25}{10}$ =	$\frac{9}{6}$ =	$\frac{10}{6}$ =	$\frac{15}{8}$ =
$\frac{12}{10}$ =	$\frac{10}{3}$ =	$\frac{18}{12}$ =	$\frac{5}{2}$ =	$\frac{4}{3}$ =

Problem Solving *Answer the question below.*

Problem: What is the largest 2-digit number that is divisible by 3 and whose digits differ by 2?

Understand
What information am I given?
What am I asked to find or do?

Plan
How can I use the information I am given?
Which strategy should I try?

Solve
Did I follow the plan?
Did I show my work?
Did I write the answer?

Check
Did I use the correct information?
Did I do what was asked?
Is my answer reasonable?

Saxon Math Course 1 © Harcourt Achieve Inc. and Stephen Hake. All rights reserved. 29

Power-Up Test 11

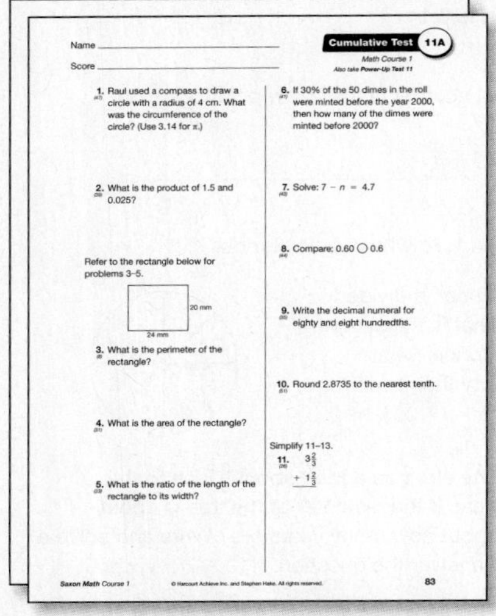

Name ______
Score ______

Cumulative Test 11A
Math Course 1
*Also take **Power-Up Test 11***

1. Raul used a compass to draw a circle with a radius of 4 cm. What was the circumference of the circle? (Use 3.14 for π.)

2. What is the product of 1.5 and 0.025?

Refer to the rectangle below for problems 3–5.

20 mm
24 mm

3. What is the perimeter of the rectangle?

4. What is the area of the rectangle?

5. What is the ratio of the length of the rectangle to its width?

6. If 30% of the 50 dimes in the roll were minted before the year 2000, then how many of the dimes were minted before 2000?

7. Solve: $7 - n = 4.7$

8. Compare: 0.60 ◯ 0.6

9. Write the decimal numeral for eighty and eight hundredths.

10. Round 2.8735 to the nearest tenth.

Simplify 11–13.

11. $3\frac{2}{3} + 1\frac{2}{3}$

Saxon Math Course 1 © Harcourt Achieve Inc. and Stephen Hake. All rights reserved. 83

Cumulative Test 11A

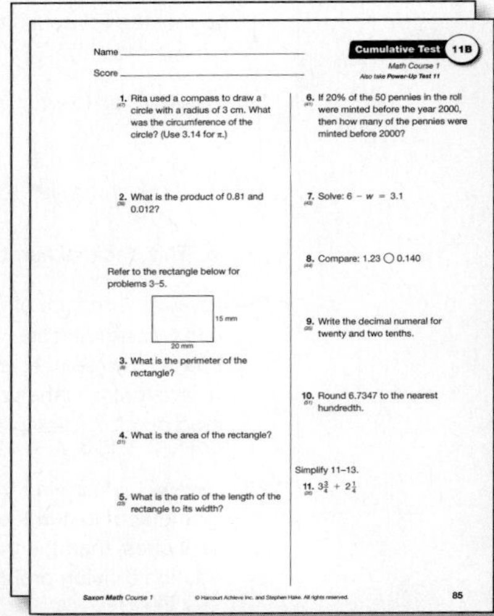

Name ______
Score ______

Cumulative Test 11B
Math Course 1
*Also take **Power-Up Test 11***

1. Rita used a compass to draw a circle with a radius of 3 cm. What was the circumference of the circle? (Use 3.14 for π.)

2. What is the product of 0.81 and 0.012?

Refer to the rectangle below for problems 3–5.

15 mm
20 mm

3. What is the perimeter of the rectangle?

4. What is the area of the rectangle?

5. What is the ratio of the length of the rectangle to its width?

6. If 20% of the 50 pennies in the roll were minted before the year 2000, then how many of the pennies were minted before 2000?

7. Solve: $6 - w = 3.1$

8. Compare: 1.23 ◯ 0.140

9. Write the decimal numeral for twenty and two tenths.

10. Round 6.7347 to the nearest hundredth.

Simplify 11–13.

11. $3\frac{3}{4} + 2\frac{1}{4}$

Saxon Math Course 1 © Harcourt Achieve Inc. and Stephen Hake. All rights reserved. 85

Alternative Cumulative Test 11B

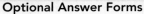

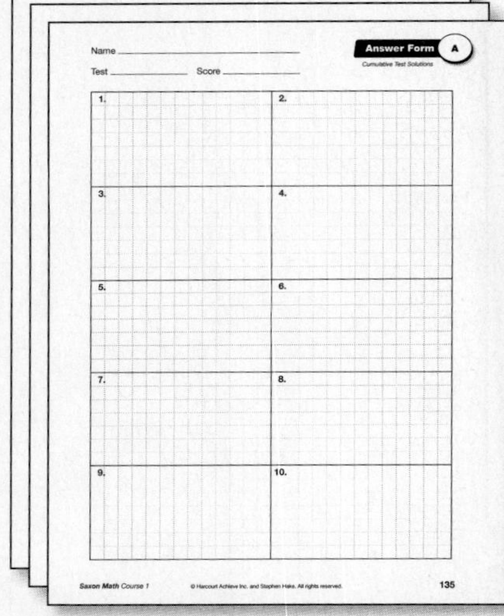

Name ______ Test ______ Score ______

Answer Form A
Cumulative Test Solutions

1. 2. 3. 4. 5. 6. 7. 8. 9. 10.

Saxon Math Course 1 © Harcourt Achieve Inc. and Stephen Hake. All rights reserved. 135

Optional Answer Forms

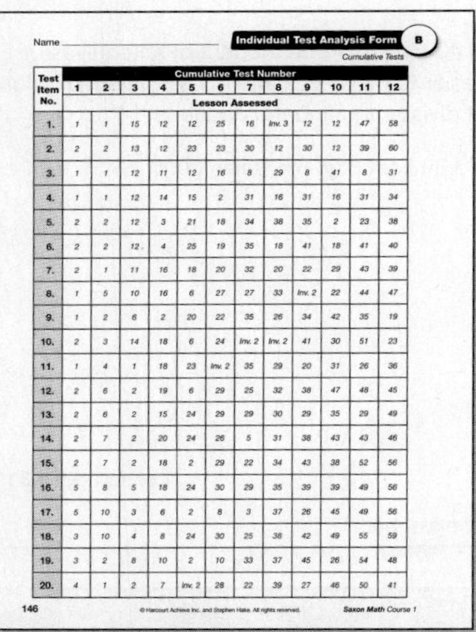

Name ______

Individual Test Analysis Form B
Cumulative Tests

Test Item No.	Cumulative Test Number 1	2	3	4	5	6	7	8	9	10	11	12
	Lesson Assessed											
1.	1	1	15	12	12	25	16	Inv. 3	12	12	47	58
2.	2	2	13	12	23	23	30	12	30	12	39	60
3.	1	1	12	11	12	16	8	29	8	41	8	31
4.	1	1	12	14	15	2	31	16	31	16	31	34
5.	2	2	12	3	21	18	34	38	35	2	23	38
6.	2	2	12	4	25	19	35	18	41	18	41	40
7.	2	1	11	16	18	20	32	20	22	29	43	39
8.	1	5	10	16	6	27	27	33	Inv. 2	22	44	47
9.	1	2	6	2	20	22	35	26	34	42	35	19
10.	2	3	14	18	6	24	Inv. 2	Inv. 2	41	30	51	23
11.	1	4	1	18	23	Inv. 2	35	29	20	31	26	36
12.	2	6	2	19	6	29	25	32	38	47	48	45
13.	2	6	2	15	24	29	29	30	29	35	29	49
14.	2	7	2	20	24	26	5	31	38	43	43	46
15.	2	7	2	18	2	29	22	34	43	38	52	56
16.	5	8	5	18	24	30	29	35	39	39	49	56
17.	5	10	3	6	2	8	3	37	26	45	49	56
18.	3	10	4	8	24	30	25	38	42	49	55	59
19.	3	2	8	10	2	10	33	37	45	26	54	48
20.	4	1	2	7	Inv. 2	28	22	39	27	46	50	41

146 © Harcourt Achieve Inc. and Stephen Hake. All rights reserved. *Saxon Math Course 1*

Individual Test Analysis Form

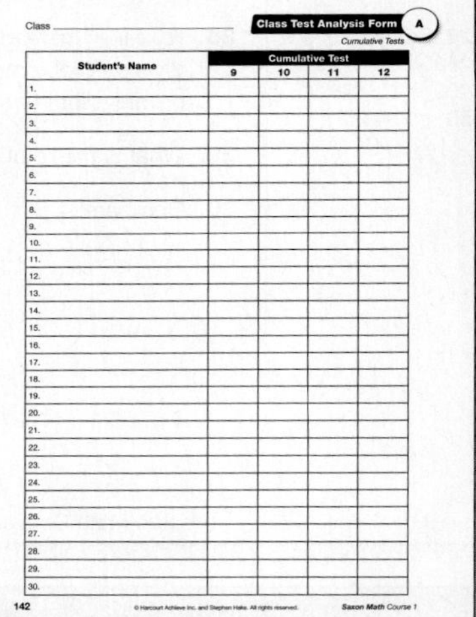

Class ______

Class Test Analysis Form A
Cumulative Tests

	Student's Name	Cumulative Test 9	10	11	12
1.					
2.					
3.					
4.					
5.					
6.					
7.					
8.					
9.					
10.					
11.					
12.					
13.					
14.					
15.					
16.					
17.					
18.					
19.					
20.					
21.					
22.					
23.					
24.					
25.					
26.					
27.					
28.					
29.					
30.					

142 © Harcourt Achieve Inc. and Stephen Hake. All rights reserved. *Saxon Math Course 1*

Class Test Analysis Form

Reteaching

Students who score below 80% on the assessment may be in need of reteaching. Look for the causes of student mistakes. If errors are conceptual, refer to the *Reteaching Masters* for reteaching.

Customized Benchmark Assessment

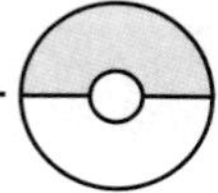

You can develop customized benchmark tests using the Test Generator located on the *Test & Practice Generator CD.*

This chart shows the lesson, the standard, and the test item question that can be found on the *Test & Practice Generator CD.*

LESSON	NEW CONCEPTS	LOCAL STANDARD	TEST ITEM ON CD
51	• Rounding Decimal Numbers		6.51.1
52	• Mentally Dividing Decimal Numbers by 10 and by 100		6.52.1
53	• Decimals Chart		6.53.1
	• Simplifying Fractions		6.53.2
54	• Reducing by Grouping Factors Equal to 1		6.54.1
	• Dividing Fractions		6.54.2
55	• Common Denominators, Part 1		6.55.1
56	• Common Denominators, Part 2		6.56.1
57	• Adding and Subtracting Fractions: Three Steps		6.57.1
58	• Probability and Chance		6.58.1
59	• Adding Mixed Numbers		6.59.1
60	• Polygons		6.60.1

Using the Test Generator CD

- Develop tests in both English and Spanish.
- Choose from multiple-choice and free-response test items.
- Clone test items to create multiple versions of the same test.
- View and edit test items to make and save your own questions.
- Administer assessments through paper tests or over a school LAN.
- Monitor student progress through a variety of individual and class reports —for both diagnosing and assessing standards mastery.

Performance Task 11

The Basketball Team

Assign after Lesson 60 and Test 13

Objectives

- Find the mean, median, mode and range of a set of data.
- Choose the best measure of central tendency to describe a set of data.
- Communicate ideas through writing.

Materials

Performance Tasks 11A and **11B**

Preparation

Make copies of **Performance Tasks 11A** and **11B.** (One each per student.)

Time Requirement

15–30 minutes; Begin in class and complete at home.

Task

Explain to students that for this task they will assist a basketball coach. Their task will be to analyze data about the team. They will find the mean, median, mode and range given several sets of data. They will decide whether to use the mean, median, or mode to describe a set of data and they will justify their choices. Point out that all of the information students need is on **Performance Tasks 11A** and **11B.**

Criteria for Evidence of Learning

- Finds the correct mean, median, mode, and range for a set of data.
- Chooses an appropriate measure of central tendency to describe a set of data and justifies the choice.
- Communicates ideas clearly through writing.

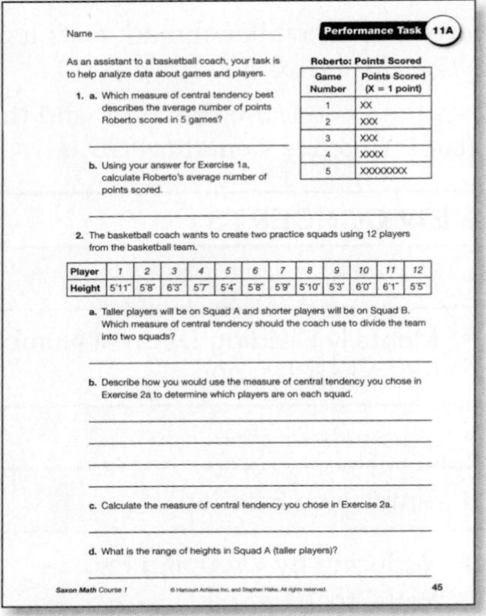

Name ____________ **Performance Task 11A**

As an assistant to a basketball coach, your task is to help analyze data about games and players.

Roberto: Points Scored

Game Number	Points Scored (X = 1 point)
1	XX
2	XXX
3	XXX
4	XXXX
5	XXXXXXXX

1. a. Which measure of central tendency best describes the average number of points Roberto scored in 5 games?

b. Using your answer for Exercise 1a, calculate Roberto's average number of points scored.

2. The basketball coach wants to create two practice squads using 12 players from the basketball team.

Player	1	2	3	4	5	6	7	8	9	10	11	12
Height	5′11″	5′8″	6′3″	5′7″	5′4″	5′8″	5′9″	5′10″	5′3″	6′0″	6′1″	5′5″

a. Taller players will be on Squad A and shorter players will be on Squad B. Which measure of central tendency should the coach use to divide the team into two squads?

b. Describe how you would use the measure of central tendency you chose in Exercise 2a to determine which players are on each squad.

c. Calculate the measure of central tendency you chose in Exercise 2a.

d. What is the range of heights in Squad A (taller players)?

Saxon Math Course 1 © Harcourt Achieve Inc. and Stephen Hake. All rights reserved. 45

Performance Task 11A

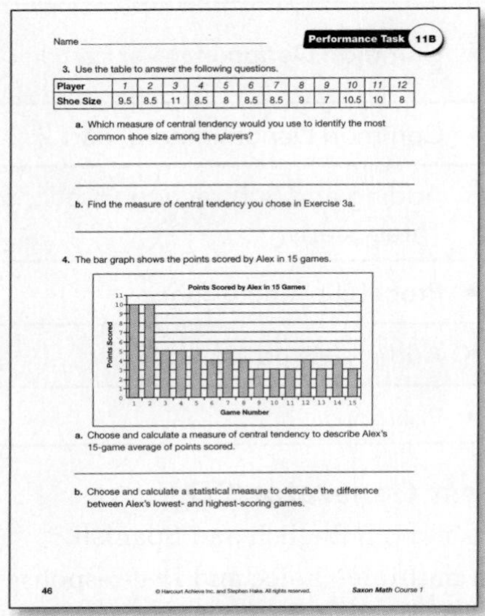

Name ____________ **Performance Task 11B**

3. Use the table to answer the following questions.

Player	1	2	3	4	5	6	7	8	9	10	11	12
Shoe Size	9.5	8.5	11	8.5	8	8.5	8.5	9	7	10.5	10	8

a. Which measure of central tendency would you use to identify the most common shoe size among the players?

b. Find the measure of central tendency you chose in Exercise 3a.

4. The bar graph shows the points scored by Alex in 15 games.

a. Choose and calculate a measure of central tendency to describe Alex's 15-game average of points scored.

b. Choose and calculate a statistical measure to describe the difference between Alex's lowest- and highest-scoring games.

46 © Harcourt Achieve Inc. and Stephen Hake. All rights reserved. *Saxon Math Course 1*

Performance Task 11B

Meeting Standards

National Council of Teachers of Mathematics (NCTM)

Data Analysis and Probability

DP.2a Find, use, and interpret measures of center and spread, including mean and interquartile range

Problem Solving

PS.1b Solve problems that arise in mathematics and in other contexts

Communication

CM.3d Use the language of mathematics to express mathematical ideas precisely

Connections

CN.4a Recognize and use connections among mathematical ideas

Focus on
• Attributes of Geometric Solids

Objectives

- Recognize, name, and draw common geometric solids.
- Identify the number of faces, edges, and vertices in various geometric solids.
- Find the surface area of a polyhedron.
- Identify patterns that can be folded into a specified three-dimensional figure.
- Determine the volume of a geometric solid by counting cubes.

Lesson Preparation

Materials

- **Investigation Activity 12** and **Investigation Activity 13** (in *Instructional Masters*)
- **Manipulative kit: Relational GeoSolids**

Optional

- **Manipulative kit: color cubes**
- **Teacher-provided material: empty cereal box, scissors, tape**

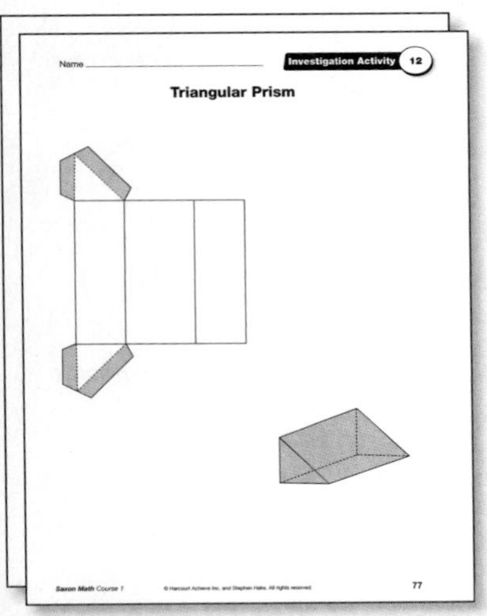

Investigation Activity 12, Investigation Activity 13

Math Language

New		English Learners (ESL)
cone	pyramid	dashes
cube	rectangular prism	
cylinder	sphere	
edge	triangular prism	
faces	vertices	
surface area	volume	
geometric solids		
polyhedron		

Technology Resources

Student eBook Complete student textbook in electronic format.

Resources and Planner CD Assessment, reteaching, and instructional masters, plus a pacing calendar with standards.

Test and Practice Generator CD Create additional practice sheets and custom-made tests.

www.SaxonPublishers.com Visit for more student activities and planning materials.

Inclusion

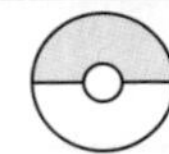

Adaptations CD Adapted lessons, investigations, practice and assessments.

Meeting Standards

National Council of Teachers of Mathematics (NCTM)

Geometry

GM.1a Precisely describe, classify, and understand relationships among types of two- and three-dimensional objects using their defining properties

GM.4d Use geometric models to represent and explain numerical and algebraic relationships

Communication

CM.3b Communicate their mathematical thinking coherently and clearly to peers, teachers, and others

CM.3d Use the language of mathematics to express mathematical ideas precisely

INVESTIGATION 6

In this investigation, students will explore characteristics of three-dimensional shapes.

Instruction

Display the models for the **Relational GeoSolids** from the Manipulative Kit. Ask students to name each geometric solid.

"In the real world, where might we find examples of each of these geometric solids?" Sample: triangular prism—the roof of a house; rectangular prism—a cereal box; cube—an ice cube; square pyramid—the pyramids of Egypt; cylinder—a can of soup; cone—a party hat; sphere—a basketball.

"In the real world, where might we find examples that are combinations of two or more geometric solids?" Sample: a gabled house is a rectangular prism and a triangular prism; a snow cone is a cone and a sphere.

Also encourage students to find examples of the solids in the classroom.

INVESTIGATION 6

Focus on

• Attributes of Geometric Solids

Polygons are two-dimensional shapes. They have length and width, but they do not have height (depth). The objects we encounter in the world around us are three-dimensional. These objects, called **geometric solids,** have length, width, and height; in other words, they take up space. The table below illustrates some three-dimensional shapes. You should learn to recognize, name, and draw each of these shapes.

Notice that if every face of a solid is a polygon, then the solid is called a **polyhedron.** Polyhedrons do not have any curved surfaces. So rectangular prisms and pyramids are polyhedrons, but spheres and cylinders are not.

Thinking Skill
Verify
Why is a cube also a rectangular prism? In a rectangular prism, all faces are rectangles. A square is a rectangle.

Geometric Solids

Shape	Name	Description
	Triangular Prism	Polyhedron
	Rectangular Prism	Polyhedron
	Cube	Polyhedron
	Pyramid	Polyhedron
	Cylinder	Not Polyhedron
	Cone	Not Polyhedron
	Sphere	Not Polyhedron

Name each shape using terms from the table above. Then name an object from the real world that has the same shape.

1. 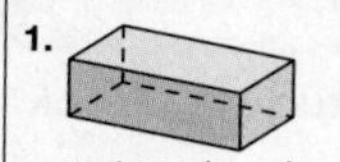
rectangular prism; box

2. cylinder; can

3. 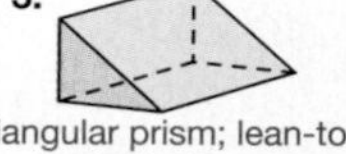
triangular prism; lean-to roof or half of a gable roof

4. 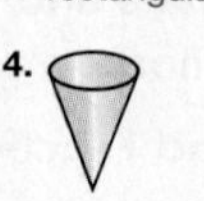
cone; cone

5. 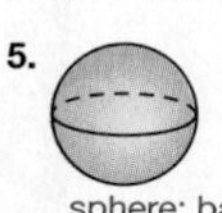
sphere; ball

6. 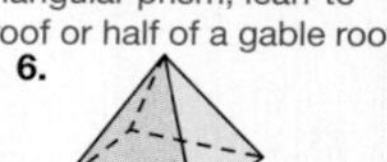
pyramid; pyramid

314 *Saxon* Math Course 1

Math Background

The shapes of the faces of a square pyramid differ from the shapes of the faces of a triangular prism.

square pyramid

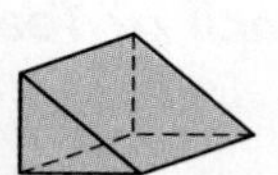
triangular prism

Four faces of a square pyramid are triangles, and the fifth face is a square. Two faces of a triangular prism are triangles, and the three other faces are rectangles or squares.

A square pyramid has one square base; a triangular prism has two triangular bases.

Solids can have **faces, edges,** and **vertices.** The illustration below points out a face, an edge, and a vertex of a cube.

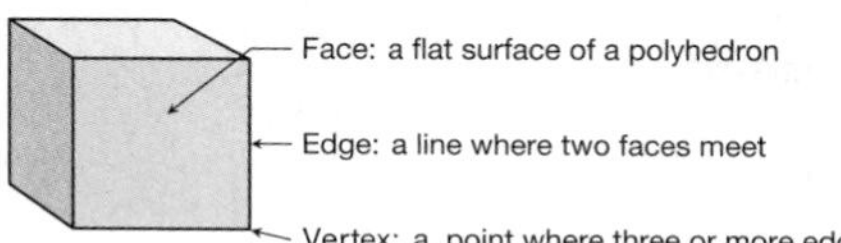
Face: a flat surface of a polyhedron
Edge: a line where two faces meet
Vertex: a point where three or more edges meet

7. A cube has how many faces? 6 faces

8. A cube has how many edges? 12 edges

9. A cube has how many vertices? 8 vertices

Activity

Comparing Geometric Solids

Materials: Relational GeoSolids

Using the solids, try identifying each shape by touch rather than by sight. Discuss the following questions.

- How can you tell if a solid is a polyhedron or not?
- How are a cone and a pyramid similar and different?
- How are a cone and a cylinder similar and different?
- How are cylinders and right prisms similar and different?

- If every face is flat, it is a polyhedron. If a surface is curved, it is not a polyhedron.
- A cone and pyramid both taper to a point (apex), but a cone has a curved surface tapering to a point and a pyramid has triangular faces tapering to the point.
- Both have a circular base. A cylinder has a second circular base while a cone tapers to a point (apex).
- Both cylinders and prisms have opposite ends that are congruent (congruent bases). However, a cylinder has a curved surface between the two ends while a right prism has rectangular faces between the two ends.

A pyramid with a square base is shown at right. One face is a square; the others are triangles.

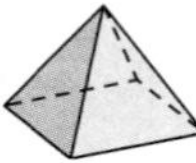

▸ 10. How many faces does this pyramid have? 5 faces

▸ 11. How many edges does this pyramid have? 8 edges

▸ 12. How many vertices does this pyramid have? 5 vertices

Represent When solids are drawn, the edges that are hidden from view can be indicated with dashes. To draw a cube, for example, we first draw two squares that overlap as shown.

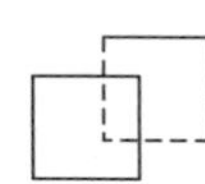

Then we connect the corresponding vertices of the two squares. In both steps we use dashes to represent the edges that are hidden from view. Practice drawing a cube.

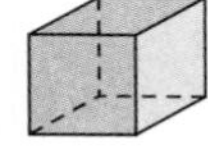

▸ 13. Draw a rectangular prism. Begin by drawing two rectangles as shown at right.

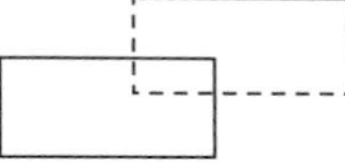

▸ See Math Conversations in the sidebar.

Instruction

If students have some difficulty visualizing the unseen faces, edges, and vertices of the cube, give them a cube to examine and use to help answer the questions.

Activity

The questions provide opportunities for students to compare and contrast attributes of the solids. All of the solids have a number of attributes which make them alike in some ways, and different in other ways. As students discuss the attributes, you might choose to record at the board or overhead various generalizations students make during the discussions. For example:

- Some geometric solids are polyhedrons; some are not.
- All solids of the same kind (such as cubes, for example) may not be the same size but have the same number of faces, vertices, and edges.
- Some solids have no faces and/or vertices and/or edges.

In addition to the questions that are provided, encourage students to display two different solids and ask their own questions to compare and contrast those solids.

Math Conversations

Discussion opportunities are provided below.

Problems 10–12 Analyze

After students identify the number of faces, edges, and vertices of the pyramid, give them an opportunity to learn that not all geometric solids have faces, edges, and vertices.

"Look at the Geometric Solids chart on the first page of the investigation. How many faces, edges, and vertices does a sphere have?" zero faces; zero edges; zero vertices.

English Learners

Have students look at the drawings of geometric solids on page 314. Say:

"When drawing a geometric solid, the edges that are hidden from view are often drawn with a broken line (or dashes) to indicate that they are unable to be seen in a real model.

Have students imagine a cube. The lines (edges) that cannot be seen are drawn as dashes. Ask them to try to draw a cube using dashes where appropriate.

Math Conversations

Discussion opportunities are provided below.

Problems 13–15 Model

Distribute models of rectangular prisms, triangular prisms, and cylinders to those students who may have difficulty drawing the solids. Holding the models and seeing them from different views can help students recognize the different segments and dashes that must be drawn to complete a drawing of each solid.

For each solid that students will draw, ask this question.

"How many faces, vertices, and edges does the solid have?"

Problem 17 Analyze

"When we know the area of one face of a cube, what operation or operations can we use to find the total surface area of the cube?" multiplication or addition

Instruction

"What solid is a cereal box an example of?" a rectangular prism

"What is true about the opposite faces of a rectangular prism?" The opposite faces are congruent.

Problem 21

To find the total surface area of the box, students must recognize that the computed areas of the faces in problems **18–20** must be doubled.

(continued)

▶ **14.** Draw a triangular prism. Begin by drawing two triangles as shown at right.

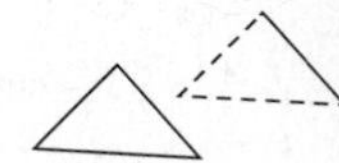

▶ **15.** Draw a cylinder. Begin by drawing a "flattened circle" as shown at right. This will be the "top" of the cylinder.

One way to measure a solid is to find the area of its surfaces. We can find how much surface a polyhedron has by adding the area of its faces. The sum of these areas is called the **surface area** of the solid.

Each edge of the cube at right is 5 inches long. So each face of the cube is a square with sides 5 inches long. Use this information to answer problems **16** and **17.**

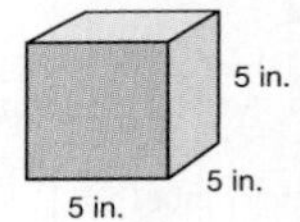

16. What is the area of each face of the cube? 25 in.^{2}

▶ **17.** Analyze What is the total surface area of the cube? 150 in.^{2}

A cereal box has six faces, but not all the faces have the same area. The front and back faces have the same area; the top and bottom faces have the same area; and the left and right faces have the same area. Here we show a cereal box that is 10 inches tall, 7 inches wide, and 2 inches deep.

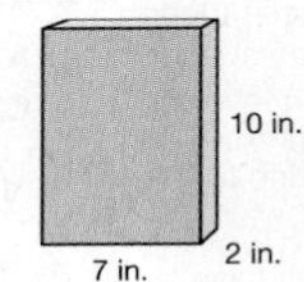

18. What is the area of the front of the box? 70 in.^{2}

19. What is the area of the top of the box? 14 in.^{2}

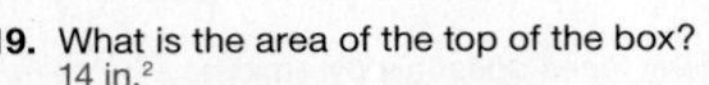

20. What is the area of the right panel of the box? 20 in.^{2}

▶ **21.** Combine the areas of all six faces to find the total surface area of the box. 208 in.^{2}

▶ See Math Conversations in the sidebar.

A container such as a cereal box is constructed out of a flat sheet of cardboard that is printed, cut, folded, and glued to create a colorful three-dimensional container. By cutting apart a cereal box, you can see the six faces of the box at one time. Here we show one way to cut apart a box, but many arrangements are possible.

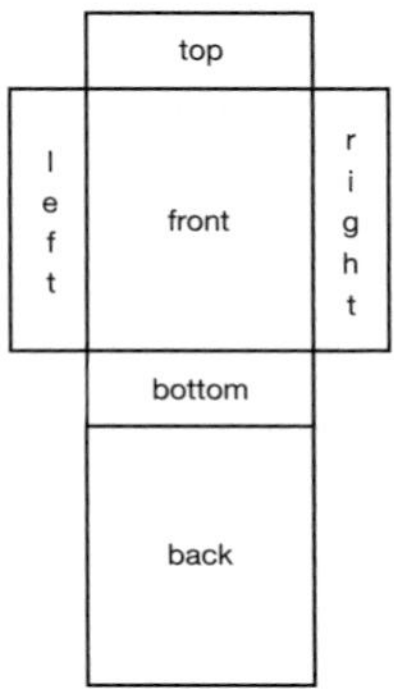

22. **Conclude** Here we show three ways to cut apart a box shaped like a cube. We have also shown an arrangement of six squares that does not fold into a cube. Which pattern below does not form a cube? **C**

A
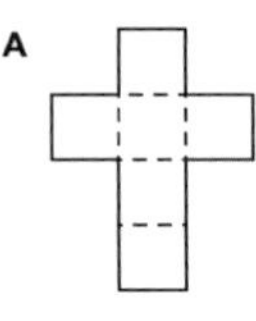

B
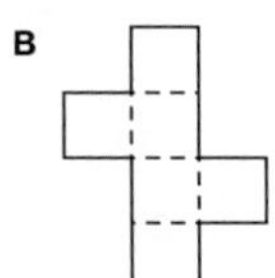

C
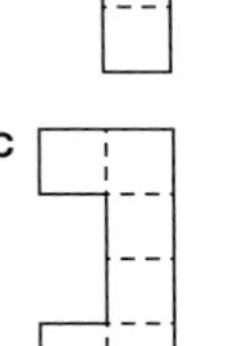

D
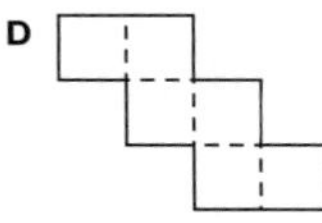

Instruction

Remind students that a cereal box is an example of a rectangular prism, and the opposite faces of a rectangular prism are congruent.

When a two- or three-dimensional drawing is broken out into a one-dimensional drawing, it is often called nets or maps.

Some students may have difficulty visualizing the three-dimensional shape into which each net can be folded. To help these students, encourage them to use a ruler and duplicate each net on grid paper. Then using a scissors, cut out each net and fold it along the dashes to learn what shape it forms.

You might challenge students to design other nets that can be cut and folded to form cubes or rectangular prisms. Opportunities for students to cut and form nets for triangular prisms and square pyramids are included in Extension b at the end of this investigation.

(continued)

Manipulative Use

To help prepare students for their work with **nets,** you might choose to bring an empty cereal box to class and demonstrate how to cut it apart, then have volunteers tape it together again.

Instruction

Invite students to use **Color Cubes** from the Manipulative Kit to make models of the solids shown in problems **23–25**. The models for problems **24** and **25** can be used a second time as students complete extension A at the end of the investigation.

After students complete problems **23–25**, you might choose to challenge them to name the number of cubes in each solid that are not visible. problem 23: two cubes are not visible; problem 24: eight cubes are not visible; problem 25: six cubes are not visible

In addition to measuring the surface area of a solid, we can also measure its **volume.** The volume of a solid is the amount of space it occupies. To measure volume, we use units that occupy space, such as cubic centimeters, cubic inches, or cubic feet. Here we show two-dimensional images of a cubic inch and a cubic centimeter:

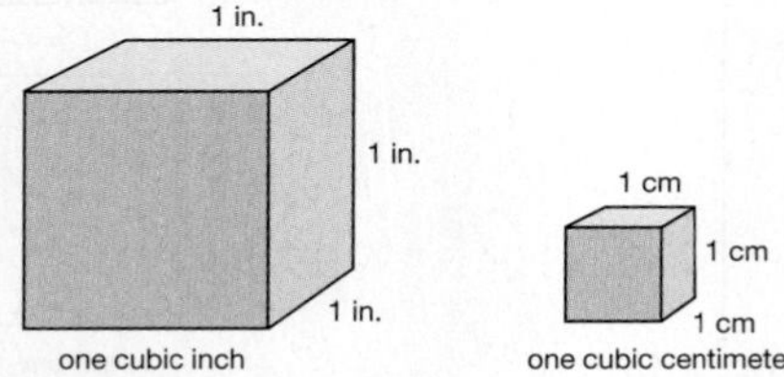

In problems **23–25** below, we will practice counting the number of cubes to determine the volume of a solid. In a later lesson we will expand our discussion of volume.

23. How many cubes are used to form this rectangular prism? 12 cubes

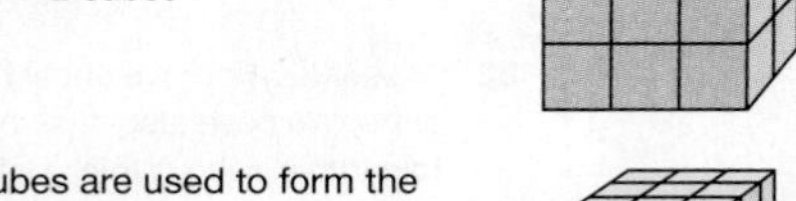

▶ **24.** How many small cubes are used to form the larger cube at right? 27 cubes

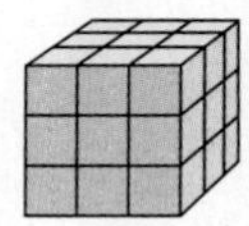

▶ **25.** How many cubes are used to build this solid? 18 cubes

Use the figures in problems **24** and **25** above to answer extension **a.**

extensions

▶ **a.** Represent Draw the front view, top view, side view, and bottom view of each figure. Explain how they are the same and how they are different.

a. See student work. The front, top, and bottom views are the same; the side views are different. The side view of the figure in problem 24 looks like the top, front, and bottom view of figures 24 and 25. Its side view shows a bottom layer with three cubes, a middle layer with two cubes, and a top layer with one cube.

▶ **b.** Estimate Bring an empty cereal container from home. Open the glue joints and unfold the box until it is flat. On the unprinted side of the box, label the front, back, side, top, and bottom faces. Identify the glue tabs or any overlapping areas.

Estimate the area of each of the six faces of the unfolded box. Do not include any glue tabs or overlapping areas in your estimate. Then estimate the amount of cardboard that was used to make the box.

Did you find the volume or the surface area of the cereal box? Explain your thinking. surface area; see student work

▶ See Math Conversations in the sidebar.

Extensions

a. ***Represent*** To help students visualize and sketch the different views, invite them to use the models they completed for problems **24** and **25.**

b. ***Estimate*** Encourage students to use some type of measurement "benchmark" to help estimate the dimensions of the faces. For example, the width of four fingers of one hand may be about 3 inches, or the length of an eraser may be about $1\frac{1}{2}$ inches.

An estimate of the different dimensions can then be made by multiplying the number of benchmarks by the length of the benchmark. For example, if an eraser is about $1\frac{1}{2}$ inches long, and a face has a length of about 4 erasers, the face is estimated to be about $4 \times 1\frac{1}{2}$ or 6 inches long.

Math Language
A two-dimensional pattern that folds to make a three-dimensional solid is called a **net.** Sometimes it is called a *map.*

d. 28 blocks; Sample: Each term increases by 3 blocks, so I added to find the tenth term: 6. 13 + 3 = 16 blocks; 7. 16 + 3 = 19; 8. 19 + 3 = 22; 9. 22 + 3 = 25; 10. 25 + 3 = 28 blocks.

e. See student work.

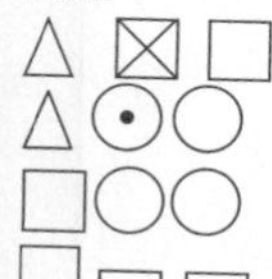

c. **Model** In problem **22,** we show three nets that will form a cube. **Investigation Activities 12 and 13** show nets for a triangular prism and a square pyramid. Cut out and fold these nets to form solids. Use tape to hold the shapes together. Describe how the solids are alike and different.

d. **Represent** How many blocks are in the tenth term of this pattern? Explain how you will represent the pattern to find the answer.

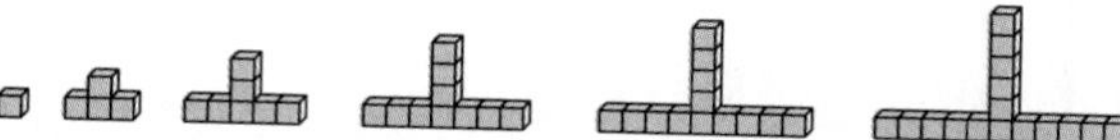

e. **Represent** Sketch the front, top, and bottom of each 3-dimensional figure.

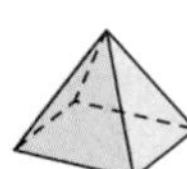
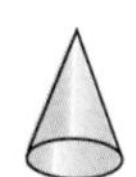

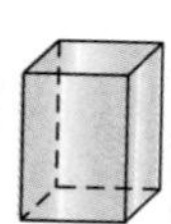

f. **Classify** Figures *A*, *B*, and *C* were sorted into a group based on one common attribute.

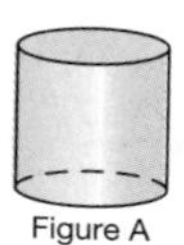
Figure A

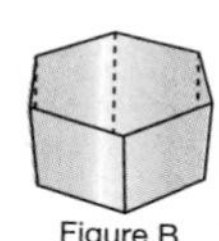
Figure B

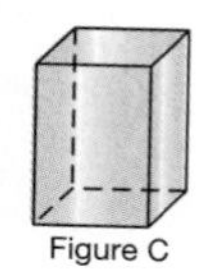
Figure C

Figures *D* and *E* do not belong in the group above.

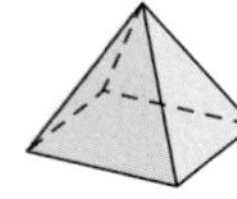
Figure D

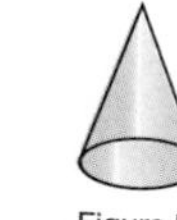
Figure E

What attribute is common to figures *A*, *B*, and *C* but not figures *D* and *E*? two bases

Sketch a figure that would belong in the group with figures *A*, *B*, and *C*. See student work.

c. Sample: Alike: Both figures have a base (or bases) that are polygons. The base of the triangular prism is a triangle; the base of the square pyramid is a square. Different: The sides of the prism are rectangles; the sides of the pyramid are triangles that taper to a point. The triangular prism has two bases, while the square pyramid has one.

▶ See Math Conversations in the sidebar.

c. Model Provide each student with a copy of **Investigation Activity 12** Triangular Prism and **Investigation Activity 13** Square Pyramid.

d. Represent Students should discover that it is difficult and tedious to draw the cubes to represent each term in the pattern. They should move to using numbers to represent each term. Each term increases by 3 cubes. The tenth term has 28 cubes. Some students may discover the formula $3n - 2$ to determine the blocks in the tenth term and use it to find the answer: $3(10) - 2 = 28$.

e. Represent If students are having difficulty, suggest that they use the Relational GeoSolids from the manipulative kit so they can view the solids from all sides as well as the top and bottom.

f. Classify Explain to students that they will need to compare the figures that do not belong to the group to the figures that do belong. Students may immediately say that figures *A, B,* and *C* are prisms and figures *E* and *F* are not. Ask them if the cylinder is a prism. Although the sorting characteristic is not "Prism", all three figures have two bases, which is also a characteristic of all prisms. Thus any prism will fit into the group.

Looking Forward

Naming and drawing geometric solids; counting faces, edges, and vertices; finding the surface area of polyhedrons; identifying a two-dimensional pattern of the faces of a solid; and counting cubes to find the volume of solids prepares students for:

- **Lesson 82,** finding the volume of rectangular prisms using a formula.
- **Lesson 120,** finding the volume of cylinders.
- **Investigation 12,** investigating polyhedrons and the Platonic solids by constructing models from patterns and drawing patterns.

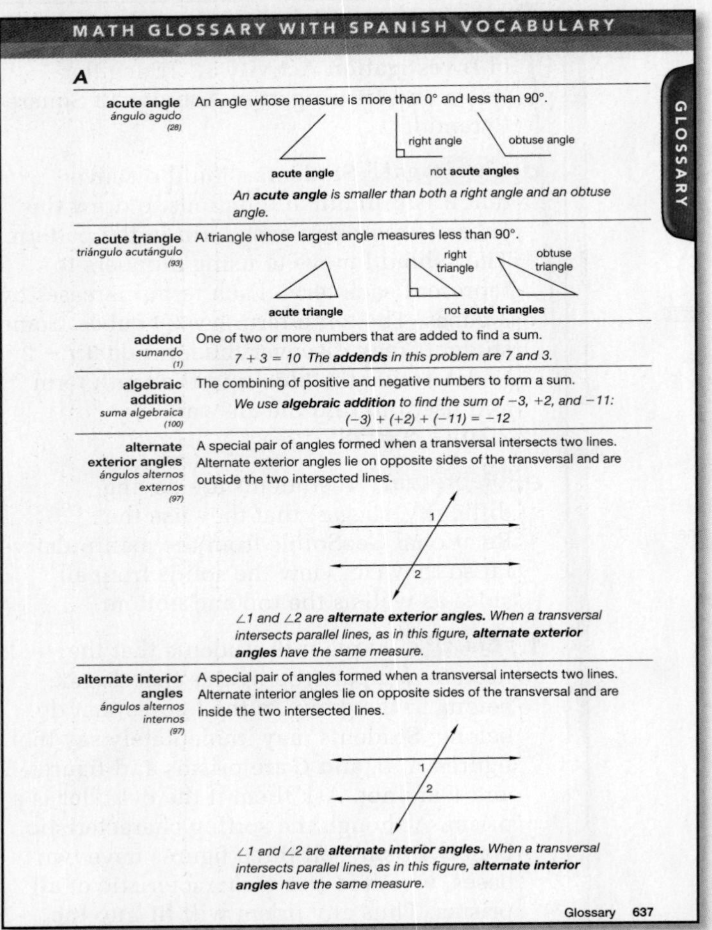

A

acute angle *ángulo agudo* (28) — An angle whose measure is more than 0° and less than 90°.

*An **acute angle** is smaller than both a right angle and an obtuse angle.*

acute triangle *triángulo acutángulo* (93) — A triangle whose largest angle measures less than 90°.

addend *sumando* (1) — One of two or more numbers that are added to find a sum.

*7 + 3 = 10 The **addends** in this problem are 7 and 3.*

algebraic addition *suma algebraica* (100) — The combining of positive and negative numbers to form a sum.

*We use **algebraic addition** to find the sum of −3, +2, and −11:*

$(-3) + (+2) + (-11) = -12$

alternate exterior angles *ángulos alternos externos* (97) — A special pair of angles formed when a transversal intersects two lines. Alternate exterior angles lie on opposite sides of the transversal and are outside the two intersected lines.

*∠1 and ∠2 are **alternate exterior angles.** When a transversal intersects parallel lines, as in this figure, **alternate exterior angles** have the same measure.*

alternate interior angles *ángulos alternos internos* (97) — A special pair of angles formed when a transversal intersects two lines. Alternate interior angles lie on opposite sides of the transversal and are inside the two intersected lines.

*∠1 and ∠2 are **alternate interior angles.** When a transversal intersects parallel lines, as in this figure, **alternate interior angles** have the same measure.*

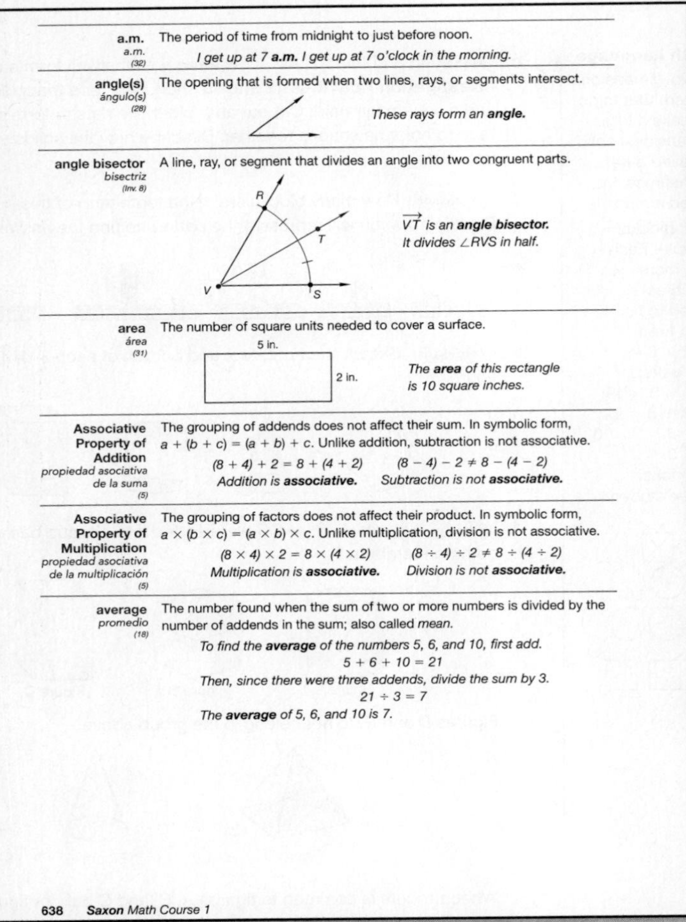

a.m. *a.m.* (32) — The period of time from midnight to just before noon.

*I get up at 7 **a.m.** I get up at 7 o'clock in the morning.*

angle(s) *ángulo(s)* (28) — The opening that is formed when two lines, rays, or segments intersect.

*These rays form an **angle.***

angle bisector *bisectriz* (Inv. 8) — A line, ray, or segment that divides an angle into two congruent parts.

*$\overrightarrow{VT}$ is an **angle bisector.** It divides ∠RVS in half.*

area *área* (31) — The number of square units needed to cover a surface.

*The **area** of this rectangle is 10 square inches.*

Associative Property of Addition *propiedad asociativa de la suma* (5) — The grouping of addends does not affect their sum. In symbolic form, a + (b + c) = (a + b) + c. Unlike addition, subtraction is not associative.

$(8 + 4) + 2 = 8 + (4 + 2)$ *Addition is **associative.***

$(8 - 4) - 2 \neq 8 - (4 - 2)$ *Subtraction is not **associative.***

Associative Property of Multiplication *propiedad asociativa de la multiplicación* (5) — The grouping of factors does not affect their product. In symbolic form, a × (b × c) = (a × b) × c. Unlike multiplication, division is not associative.

$(8 \times 4) \times 2 = 8 \times (4 \times 2)$ *Multiplication is **associative.***

$(8 \div 4) \div 2 \neq 8 \div (4 \div 2)$ *Division is not **associative.***

average *promedio* (18) — The number found when the sum of two or more numbers is divided by the number of addends in the sum; also called *mean.*

*To find the **average** of the numbers 5, 6, and 10, first add.*

$5 + 6 + 10 = 21$

Then, since there were three addends, divide the sum by 3.

$21 \div 3 = 7$

*The **average** of 5, 6, and 10 is 7.*

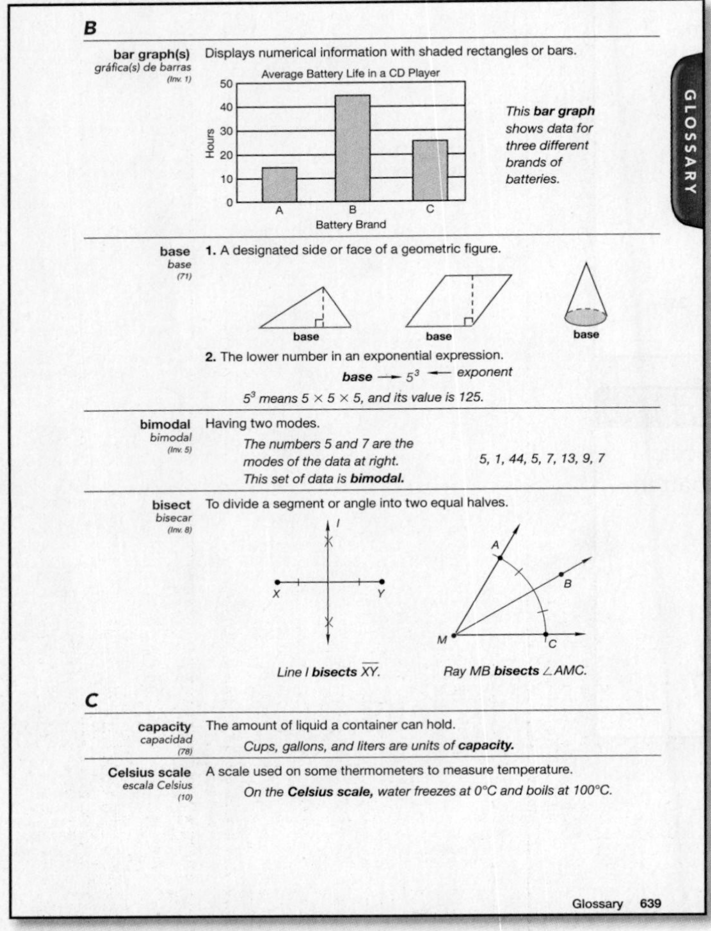

B

bar graph(s) *gráfica(s) de barras* (Inv. 1) — Displays numerical information with shaded rectangles or bars.

*This **bar graph** shows data for three different brands of batteries.*

base *base* (71) — 1. A designated side or face of a geometric figure.

2. The lower number in an exponential expression.

5^3

5^3 means 5 × 5 × 5, and its value is 125.

bimodal *bimodal* (Inv. 5) — Having two modes.

*The numbers 5 and 7 are the modes of the data at right. This set of data is **bimodal.***

5, 1, 44, 5, 7, 13, 9, 7

bisect *bisecar* (Inv. 8) — To divide a segment or angle into two equal halves.

*Line l **bisects** $\overline{XY}$.* *Ray MB **bisects** ∠AMC.*

C

capacity *capacidad* (78) — The amount of liquid a container can hold.

*Cups, gallons, and liters are units of **capacity.***

Celsius scale *escala Celsius* (10) — A scale used on some thermometers to measure temperature.

*On the **Celsius scale,** water freezes at 0°C and boils at 100°C.*

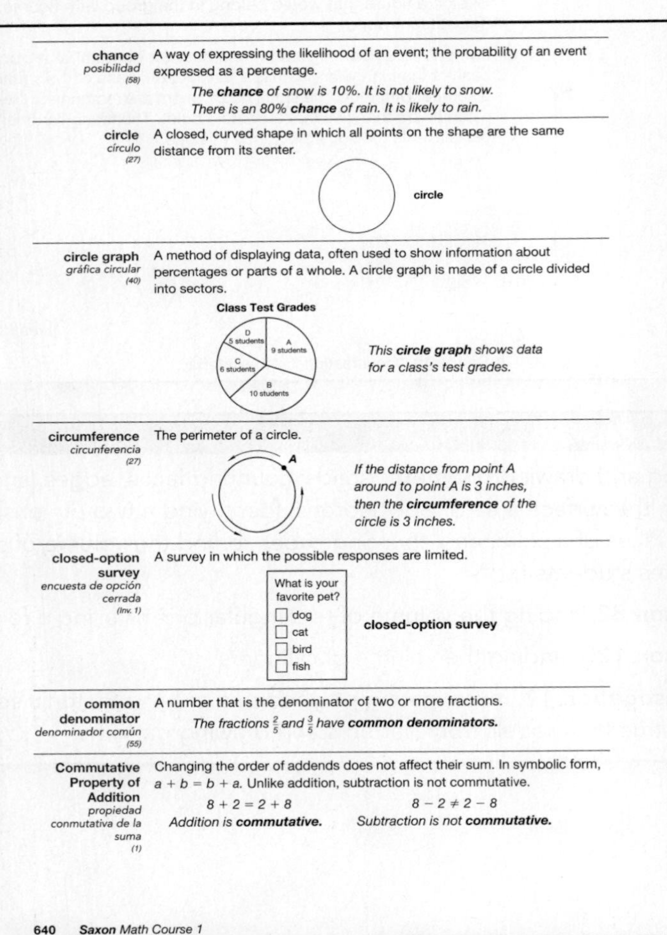

chance *posibilidad* (58) — A way of expressing the likelihood of an event; the probability of an event expressed as a percentage.

*The **chance** of snow is 10%. It is not likely to snow.*
*There is an 80% **chance** of rain. It is likely to rain.*

circle *círculo* (27) — A closed, curved shape in which all points on the shape are the same distance from its center.

circle graph *gráfica circular* (40) — A method of displaying data, often used to show information about percentages or parts of a whole. A circle graph is made of a circle divided into sectors.

*This **circle graph** shows data for a class's test grades.*

circumference *circunferencia* (27) — The perimeter of a circle.

*If the distance from point A around to point A is 3 inches, then the **circumference** of the circle is 3 inches.*

closed-option survey *encuesta de opción cerrada* (Inv. 1) — A survey in which the possible responses are limited.

common denominator *denominador común* (55) — A number that is the denominator of two or more fractions.

*The fractions $\frac{2}{5}$ and $\frac{3}{5}$ have **common denominators.***

Commutative Property of Addition *propiedad conmutativa de la suma* (1) — Changing the order of addends does not affect their sum. In symbolic form, a + b = b + a. Unlike addition, subtraction is not commutative.

$8 + 2 = 2 + 8$ *Addition is **commutative.***

$8 - 2 \neq 2 - 8$ *Subtraction is not **commutative.***

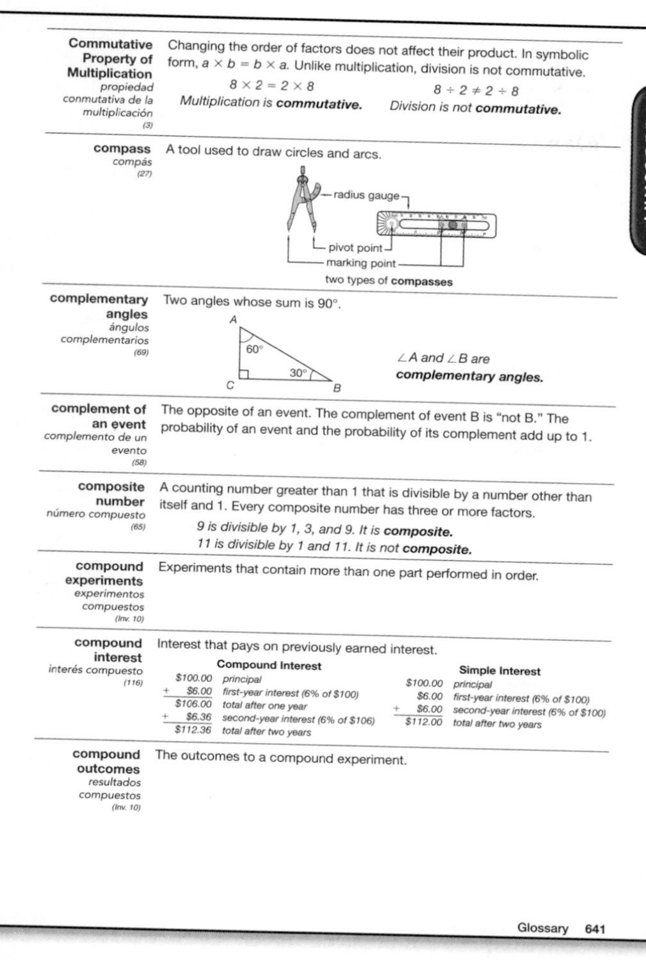

Commutative Property of Multiplication *propiedad conmutativa de la multiplicación* (3) — Changing the order of factors does not affect their product. In symbolic form, $a \times b = b \times a$. Unlike multiplication, division is not commutative.

$8 \times 2 = 2 \times 8$ — *Multiplication is **commutative.***

$8 \div 2 \neq 2 \div 8$ — *Division is not **commutative.***

compass *compás* (27) — A tool used to draw circles and arcs.

radius gauge; pivot point; marking point

two types of **compasses**

complementary angles *ángulos complementarios* (69) — Two angles whose sum is 90°.

A, 60°, 30°, C, B

*∠A and ∠B are **complementary angles.***

complement of an event *complemento de un evento* (58) — The opposite of an event. The complement of event B is "not B." The probability of an event and the probability of its complement add up to 1.

composite number *número compuesto* (65) — A counting number greater than 1 that is divisible by a number other than itself and 1. Every composite number has three or more factors.

*9 is divisible by 1, 3, and 9. It is **composite.***
*11 is divisible by 1 and 11. It is not **composite.***

compound experiments *experimentos compuestos* (Inv. 10) — Experiments that contain more than one part performed in order.

compound interest *interés compuesto* (116) — Interest that pays on previously earned interest.

Compound Interest

	$100.00	principal
+	$6.00	first-year interest (6% of $100)
	$106.00	total after one year
+	$6.36	second-year interest (6% of $106)
	$112.36	total after two years

Simple Interest

	$100.00	principal
	$6.00	first-year interest (6% of $100)
+	$6.00	second-year interest (6% of $100)
	$112.00	total after two years

compound outcomes *resultados compuestos* (Inv. 10) — The outcomes to a compound experiment.

GLOSSARY

Glossary 641

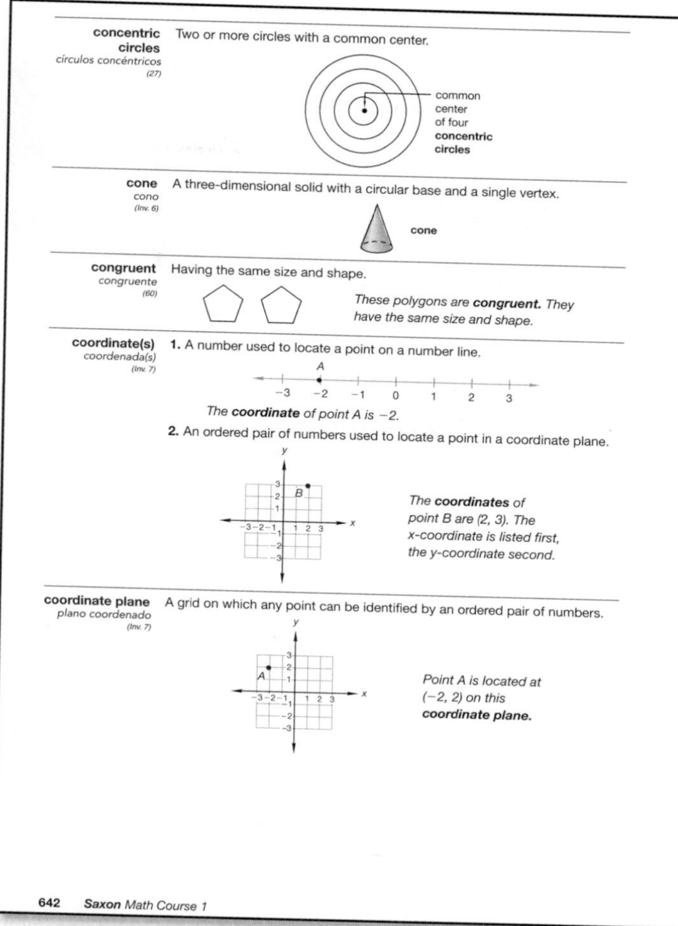

concentric circles *círculos concéntricos* (27) — Two or more circles with a common center.

common center of four **concentric circles**

cone *cono* (Inv. 6) — A three-dimensional solid with a circular base and a single vertex.

cone

congruent *congruente* (60) — Having the same size and shape.

*These polygons are **congruent.** They have the same size and shape.*

coordinate(s) *coordenada(s)* (Inv. 7) — **1.** A number used to locate a point on a number line.

A; −3 −2 −1 0 1 2 3

*The **coordinate** of point A is −2.*

2. An ordered pair of numbers used to locate a point in a coordinate plane.

*The **coordinates** of point B are (2, 3). The x-coordinate is listed first, the y-coordinate second.*

coordinate plane *plano coordenado* (Inv. 7) — A grid on which any point can be identified by an ordered pair of numbers.

*Point A is located at (−2, 2) on this **coordinate plane.***

642 *Saxon Math Course 1*

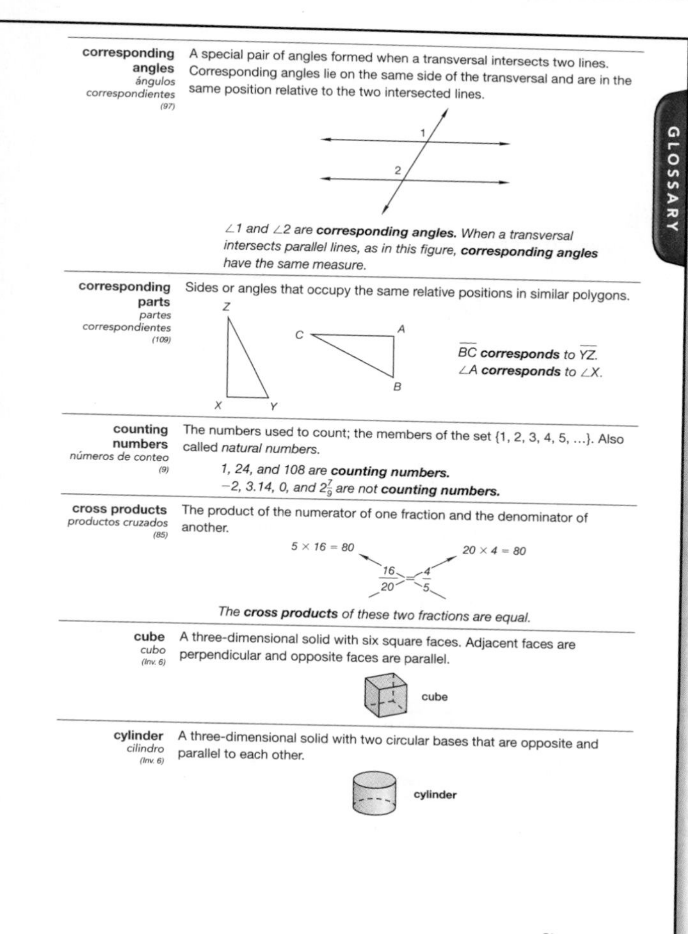

corresponding angles *ángulos correspondientes* (97) — A special pair of angles formed when a transversal intersects two lines. Corresponding angles lie on the same side of the transversal and are in the same position relative to the two intersected lines.

*∠1 and ∠2 are **corresponding angles.** When a transversal intersects parallel lines, as in this figure, **corresponding angles** have the same measure.*

corresponding parts *partes correspondientes* (109) — Sides or angles that occupy the same relative positions in similar polygons.

Z, X, Y, C, A, B

$\overline{BC}$ ***corresponds** to* $\overline{YZ}$.
*∠A **corresponds** to ∠X.*

counting numbers *números de conteo* (9) — The numbers used to count; the members of the set {1, 2, 3, 4, 5, …}. Also called *natural numbers.*

*1, 24, and 108 are **counting numbers.***
*−2, 3.14, 0, and $2\frac{7}{9}$ are not **counting numbers.***

cross products *productos cruzados* (85) — The product of the numerator of one fraction and the denominator of another.

$5 \times 16 = 80$ $\quad \frac{16}{20} = \frac{4}{5}$ $\quad 20 \times 4 = 80$

*The **cross products** of these two fractions are equal.*

cube *cubo* (Inv. 6) — A three-dimensional solid with six square faces. Adjacent faces are perpendicular and opposite faces are parallel.

cube

cylinder *cilindro* (Inv. 6) — A three-dimensional solid with two circular bases that are opposite and parallel to each other.

cylinder

GLOSSARY

Glossary 643

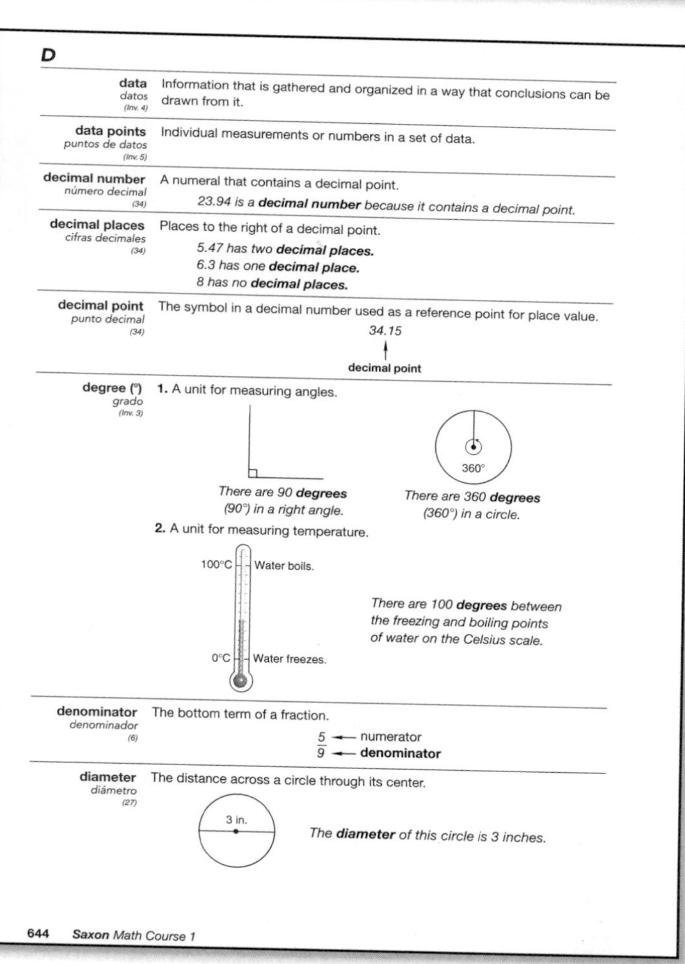

D

data *datos* (Inv. 4) — Information that is gathered and organized in a way that conclusions can be drawn from it.

data points *puntos de datos* (Inv. 5) — Individual measurements or numbers in a set of data.

decimal number *número decimal* (34) — A numeral that contains a decimal point.

*23.94 is a **decimal number** because it contains a decimal point.*

decimal places *cifras decimales* (34) — Places to the right of a decimal point.

*5.47 has two **decimal places.***
*6.3 has one **decimal place.***
*8 has no **decimal places.***

decimal point *punto decimal* (34) — The symbol in a decimal number used as a reference point for place value.

34.15

decimal point

degree (°) *grado* (Inv. 3) — **1.** A unit for measuring angles.

*There are 90 **degrees** (90°) in a right angle.*

360° — *There are 360 **degrees** (360°) in a circle.*

2. A unit for measuring temperature.

100°C Water boils. 0°C Water freezes.

*There are 100 **degrees** between the freezing and boiling points of water on the Celsius scale.*

denominator *denominador* (6) — The bottom term of a fraction.

5 ← numerator
9 ← **denominator**

diameter *diámetro* (27) — The distance across a circle through its center.

3 in.

*The **diameter** of this circle is 3 inches.*

644 *Saxon Math Course 1*

GLOSSARY

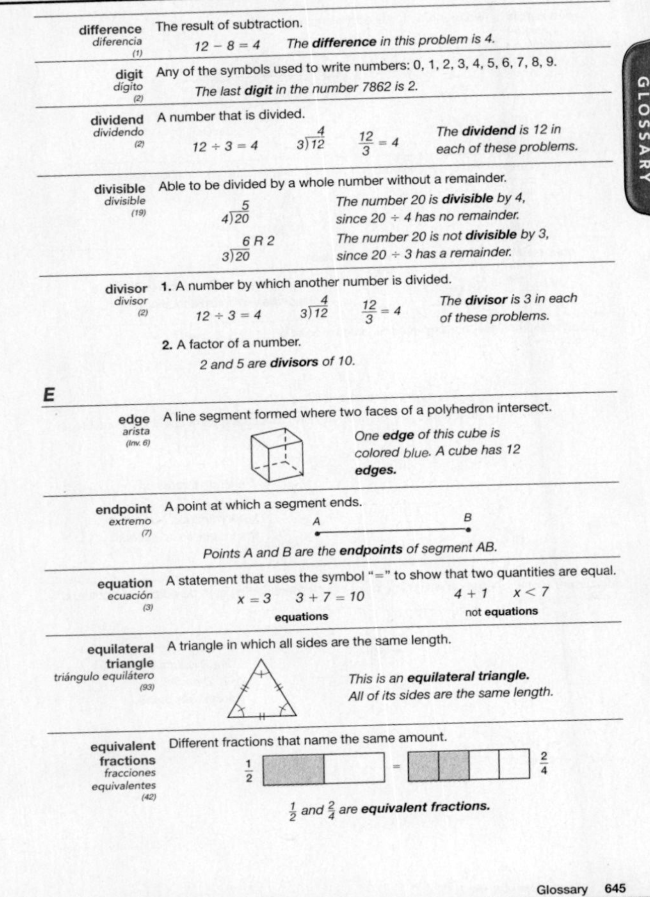

difference *diferencia* (1) The result of subtraction.

$12 - 8 = 4$ *The **difference** in this problem is 4.*

digit *dígito* (2) Any of the symbols used to write numbers: 0, 1, 2, 3, 4, 5, 6, 7, 8, 9.

*The last **digit** in the number 7862 is 2.*

dividend *dividendo* (2) A number that is divided.

$12 \div 3 = 4$ $\quad 3\overline{)12}$ (quotient 4) $\quad \frac{12}{3} = 4$ *The **dividend** is 12 in each of these problems.*

divisible *divisible* (19) Able to be divided by a whole number without a remainder.

$4\overline{)20}$ (quotient 5) *The number 20 is **divisible** by 4, since 20 ÷ 4 has no remainder.*

$3\overline{)20}$ (quotient 6 R 2) *The number 20 is not **divisible** by 3, since 20 ÷ 3 has a remainder.*

divisor *divisor* (2) 1. A number by which another number is divided.

$12 \div 3 = 4$ $\quad 3\overline{)12}$ (quotient 4) $\quad \frac{12}{3} = 4$ *The **divisor** is 3 in each of these problems.*

2. A factor of a number.

*2 and 5 are **divisors** of 10.*

E

edge *arista* (Inv. 6) A line segment formed where two faces of a polyhedron intersect.

*One **edge** of this cube is colored blue. A cube has 12 **edges**.*

endpoint *extremo* (7) A point at which a segment ends.

A B

*Points A and B are the **endpoints** of segment AB.*

equation *ecuación* (3) A statement that uses the symbol "=" to show that two quantities are equal.

$x = 3$ $\quad 3 + 7 = 10$ **equations** $\quad 4 + 1$ $\quad x < 7$ not **equations**

equilateral triangle *triángulo equilátero* (93) A triangle in which all sides are the same length.

*This is an **equilateral triangle**. All of its sides are the same length.*

equivalent fractions *fracciones equivalentes* (42) Different fractions that name the same amount.

$\frac{1}{2}$ = $\frac{2}{4}$

*$\frac{1}{2}$ and $\frac{2}{4}$ are **equivalent fractions**.*

GLOSSARY

Glossary 645

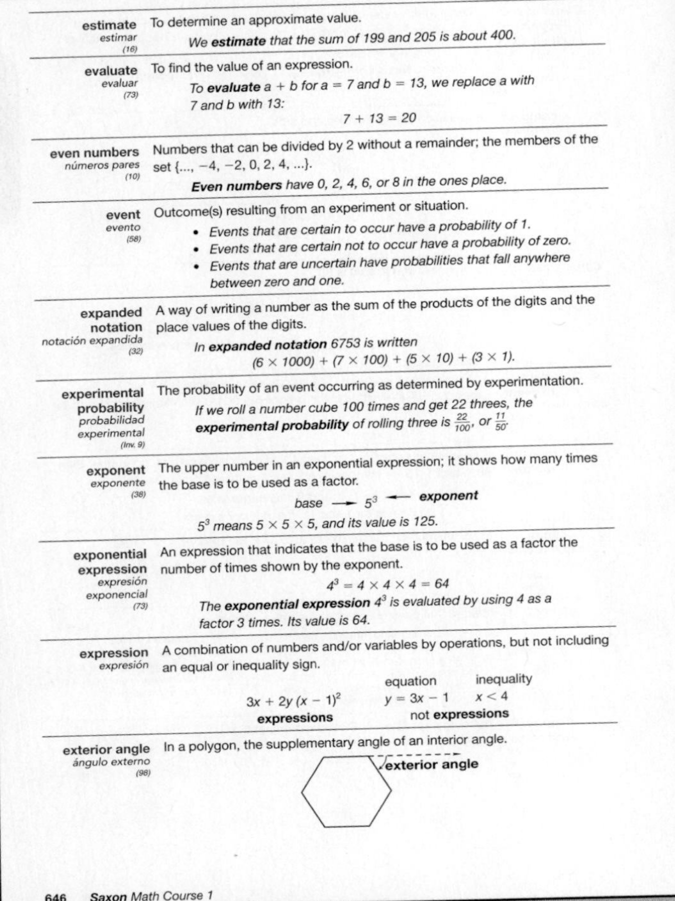

estimate *estimar* (16) To determine an approximate value.

*We **estimate** that the sum of 199 and 205 is about 400.*

evaluate *evaluar* (73) To find the value of an expression.

*To **evaluate** a + b for a = 7 and b = 13, we replace a with 7 and b with 13:*

$7 + 13 = 20$

even numbers *números pares* (10) Numbers that can be divided by 2 without a remainder; the members of the set {..., −4, −2, 0, 2, 4, ...}.

***Even numbers** have 0, 2, 4, 6, or 8 in the ones place.*

event *evento* (58) Outcome(s) resulting from an experiment or situation.

- *Events that are certain to occur have a probability of 1.*
- *Events that are certain not to occur have a probability of zero.*
- *Events that are uncertain have probabilities that fall anywhere between zero and one.*

expanded notation *notación expandida* (32) A way of writing a number as the sum of the products of the digits and the place values of the digits.

*In **expanded notation** 6753 is written* $(6 \times 1000) + (7 \times 100) + (5 \times 10) + (3 \times 1)$.

experimental probability *probabilidad experimental* (Inv. 9) The probability of an event occurring as determined by experimentation.

*If we roll a number cube 100 times and get 22 threes, the **experimental probability** of rolling three is $\frac{22}{100}$, or $\frac{11}{50}$.*

exponent *exponente* (38) The upper number in an exponential expression; it shows how many times the base is to be used as a factor.

base → 5^3 ← **exponent**

5^3 means $5 \times 5 \times 5$, and its value is 125.

exponential expression *expresión exponencial* (73) An expression that indicates that the base is to be used as a factor the number of times shown by the exponent.

$4^3 = 4 \times 4 \times 4 = 64$

*The **exponential expression** 4^3 is evaluated by using 4 as a factor 3 times. Its value is 64.*

expression *expresión* A combination of numbers and/or variables by operations, but not including an equal or inequality sign.

$3x + 2y(x - 1)^2$ **expressions** $\quad$ equation $y = 3x - 1$ $\quad$ inequality $x < 4$ not **expressions**

exterior angle *ángulo externo* (98) In a polygon, the supplementary angle of an interior angle.

exterior angle

646 Saxon Math Course 1

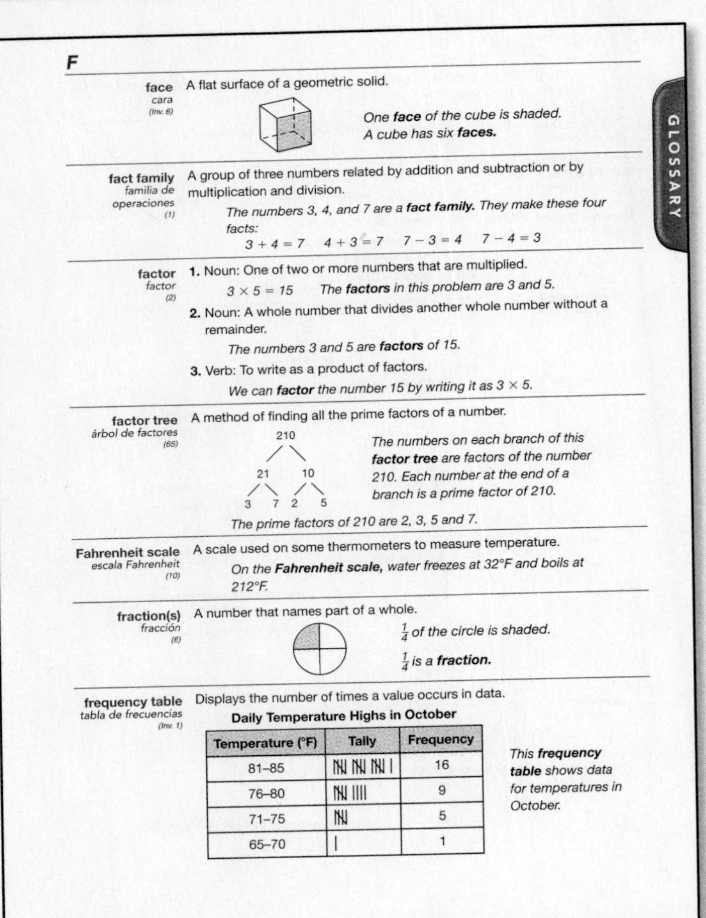

F

face *cara* (Inv. 6) A flat surface of a geometric solid.

*One **face** of the cube is shaded. A cube has six **faces**.*

fact family *familia de operaciones* (1) A group of three numbers related by addition and subtraction or by multiplication and division.

*The numbers 3, 4, and 7 are a **fact family**. They make these four facts:*

$3 + 4 = 7 \quad 4 + 3 = 7 \quad 7 - 3 = 4 \quad 7 - 4 = 3$

factor *factor* (2) 1. Noun: One of two or more numbers that are multiplied.

$3 \times 5 = 15$ *The **factors** in this problem are 3 and 5.*

2. Noun: A whole number that divides another whole number without a remainder.

*The numbers 3 and 5 are **factors** of 15.*

3. Verb: To write as a product of factors.

*We can **factor** the number 15 by writing it as 3 × 5.*

factor tree *árbol de factores* (65) A method of finding all the prime factors of a number.

210 → 21, 10; 21 → 3, 7; 10 → 2, 5

*The numbers on each branch of this **factor tree** are factors of the number 210. Each number at the end of a branch is a prime factor of 210.*

The prime factors of 210 are 2, 3, 5 and 7.

Fahrenheit scale *escala Fahrenheit* (10) A scale used on some thermometers to measure temperature.

*On the **Fahrenheit scale**, water freezes at 32°F and boils at 212°F.*

fraction(s) *fracción* (6) A number that names part of a whole.

$\frac{1}{4}$ of the circle is shaded.

*$\frac{1}{4}$ is a **fraction**.*

frequency table *tabla de frecuencias* (Inv. 1) Displays the number of times a value occurs in data.

Daily Temperature Highs in October

Temperature (°F)	Tally	Frequency
81–85	卌 卌 卌 I	16
76–80	卌 IIII	9
71–75	卌	5
65–70	I	1

*This **frequency table** shows data for temperatures in October.*

GLOSSARY

Glossary 647

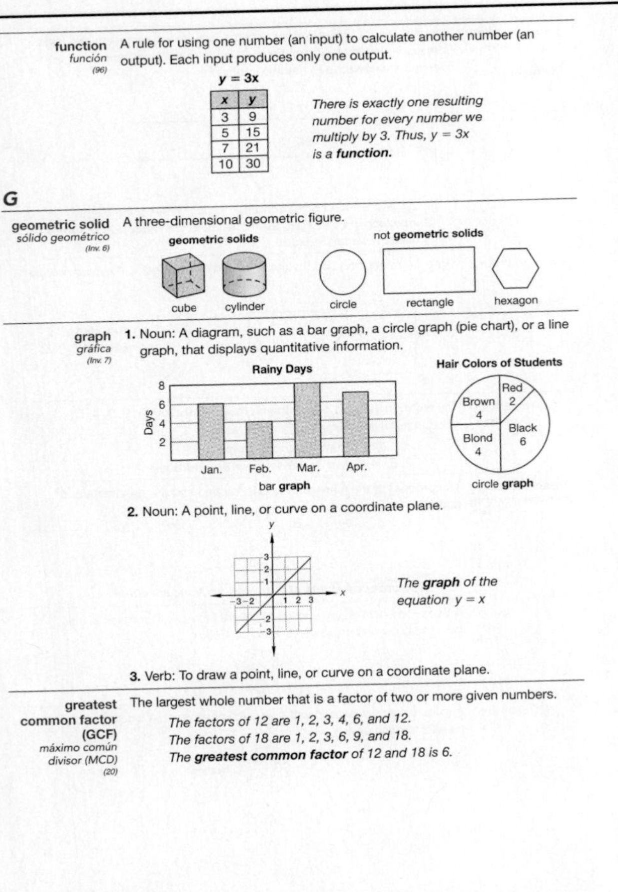

function *función* (96) A rule for using one number (an input) to calculate another number (an output). Each input produces only one output.

y = 3x

x	y
3	9
5	15
7	21
10	30

*There is exactly one resulting number for every number we multiply by 3. Thus, y = 3x is a **function**.*

G

geometric solid *sólido geométrico* (Inv. 6) A three-dimensional geometric figure.

geometric solids: cube, cylinder $\quad$ not **geometric solids**: circle, rectangle, hexagon

graph *gráfica* (Inv. 7) 1. Noun: A diagram, such as a bar graph, a circle graph (pie chart), or a line graph, that displays quantitative information.

bar **graph** $\quad$ circle **graph**

2. Noun: A point, line, or curve on a coordinate plane.

*The **graph** of the equation y = x*

3. Verb: To draw a point, line, or curve on a coordinate plane.

greatest common factor (GCF) *máximo común divisor (MCD)* (20) The largest whole number that is a factor of two or more given numbers.

The factors of 12 are 1, 2, 3, 4, 6, and 12.

The factors of 18 are 1, 2, 3, 6, 9, and 18.

*The **greatest common factor** of 12 and 18 is 6.*

648 Saxon Math Course 1

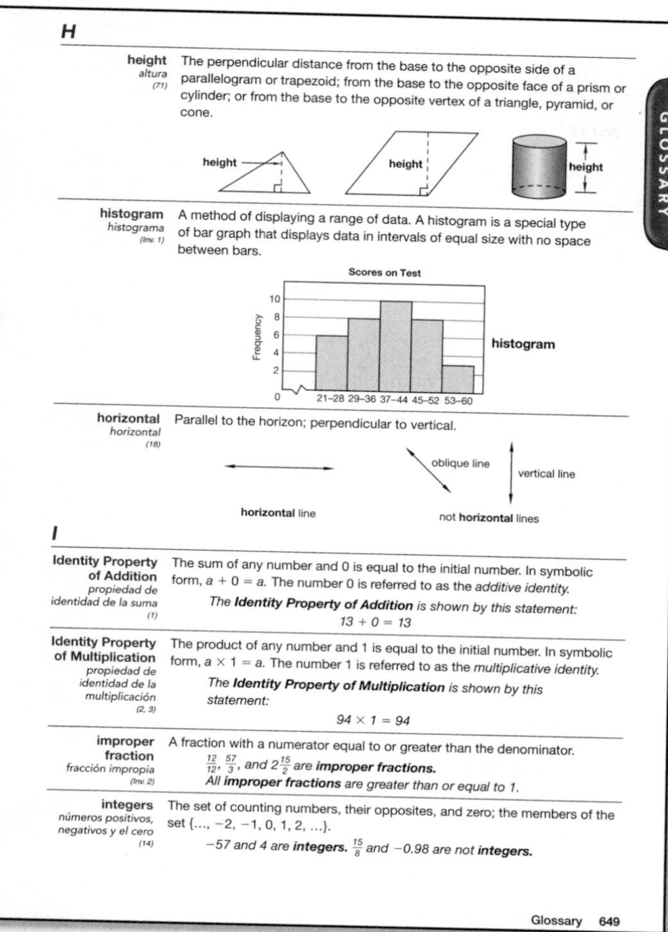

GLOSSARY

H

height *altura* (71) The perpendicular distance from the base to the opposite side of a parallelogram or trapezoid; from the base to the opposite face of a prism or cylinder; or from the base to the opposite vertex of a triangle, pyramid, or cone.

histogram *histograma* (Inv. 1) A method of displaying a range of data. A histogram is a special type of bar graph that displays data in intervals of equal size with no space between bars.

horizontal *horizontal* (18) Parallel to the horizon; perpendicular to vertical.

I

Identity Property of Addition *propiedad de identidad de la suma* (1) The sum of any number and 0 is equal to the initial number. In symbolic form, $a + 0 = a$. The number 0 is referred to as the *additive identity.*

*The **Identity Property of Addition** is shown by this statement:*
$13 + 0 = 13$

Identity Property of Multiplication *propiedad de identidad de la multiplicación* (2, 3) The product of any number and 1 is equal to the initial number. In symbolic form, $a \times 1 = a$. The number 1 is referred to as the *multiplicative identity.*

*The **Identity Property of Multiplication** is shown by this statement:*
$94 \times 1 = 94$

improper fraction *fracción impropia* (Inv. 2) A fraction with a numerator equal to or greater than the denominator.

*$\frac{12}{12}$, $\frac{57}{3}$, and $2\frac{15}{2}$ are **improper fractions.***
*All **improper fractions** are greater than or equal to 1.*

integers *números positivos, negativos y el cero* (14) The set of counting numbers, their opposites, and zero; the members of the set $\{\ldots, -2, -1, 0, 1, 2, \ldots\}$.

*-57 and 4 are **integers.** $\frac{15}{8}$ and -0.98 are not **integers.***

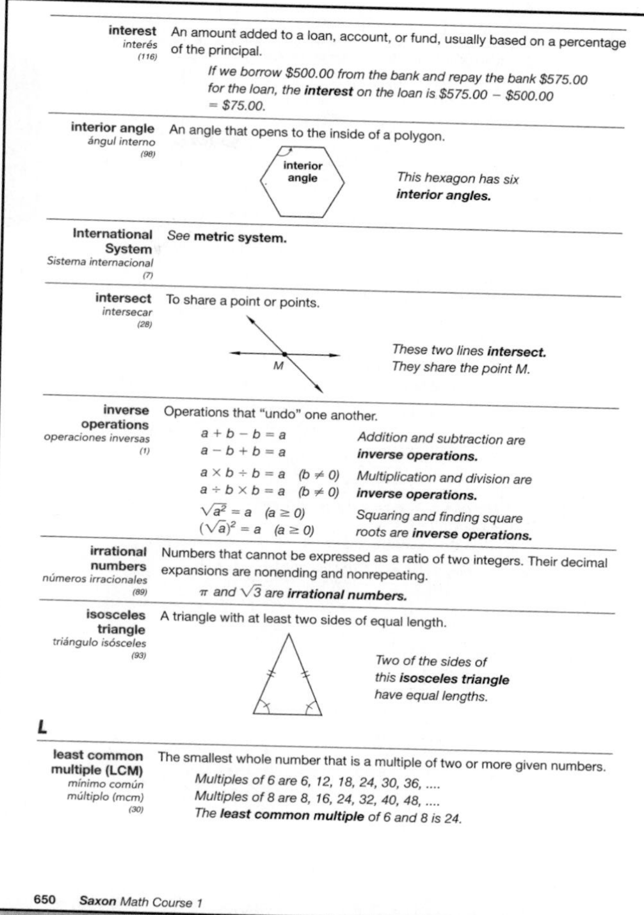

interest *interés* (116) An amount added to a loan, account, or fund, usually based on a percentage of the principal.

*If we borrow \$500.00 from the bank and repay the bank \$575.00 for the loan, the **interest** on the loan is \$575.00 − \$500.00 = \$75.00.*

interior angle *ángul interno* (98) An angle that opens to the inside of a polygon.

*This hexagon has six **interior angles.***

International System *Sistema internacional* (7) See **metric system.**

intersect *intersecar* (28) To share a point or points.

*These two lines **intersect.** They share the point M.*

inverse operations *operaciones inversas* (1) Operations that "undo" one another.

$a + b - b = a$
$a - b + b = a$
*Addition and subtraction are **inverse operations.***

$a \times b \div b = a \quad (b \neq 0)$
$a \div b \times b = a \quad (b \neq 0)$
*Multiplication and division are **inverse operations.***

$\sqrt{a^2} = a \quad (a \geq 0)$
$(\sqrt{a})^2 = a \quad (a \geq 0)$
*Squaring and finding square roots are **inverse operations.***

irrational numbers *números irracionales* (89) Numbers that cannot be expressed as a ratio of two integers. Their decimal expansions are nonending and nonrepeating.

*π and $\sqrt{3}$ are **irrational numbers.***

isosceles triangle *triángulo isósceles* (93) A triangle with at least two sides of equal length.

*Two of the sides of this **isosceles triangle** have equal lengths.*

L

least common multiple (LCM) *mínimo común múltiplo (mcm)* (30) The smallest whole number that is a multiple of two or more given numbers.

Multiples of 6 are 6, 12, 18, 24, 30, 36, ...
Multiples of 8 are 8, 16, 24, 32, 40, 48, ...
*The **least common multiple** of 6 and 8 is 24.*

GLOSSARY

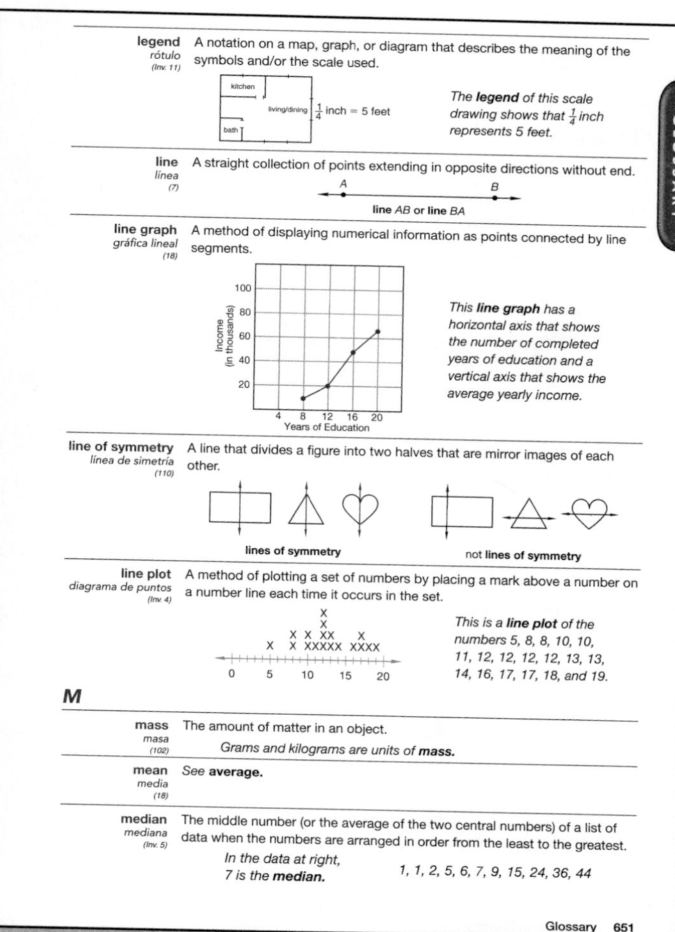

legend *rótulo* (Inv. 11) A notation on a map, graph, or diagram that describes the meaning of the symbols and/or the scale used.

*The **legend** of this scale drawing shows that $\frac{1}{4}$ inch represents 5 feet.*

line *línea* (7) A straight collection of points extending in opposite directions without end.

line AB or **line** BA

line graph *gráfica lineal* (18) A method of displaying numerical information as points connected by line segments.

*This **line graph** has a horizontal axis that shows the number of completed years of education and a vertical axis that shows the average yearly income.*

line of symmetry *línea de simetría* (110) A line that divides a figure into two halves that are mirror images of each other.

line plot *diagrama de puntos* (Inv. 4) A method of plotting a set of numbers by placing a mark above a number on a number line each time it occurs in the set.

*This is a **line plot** of the numbers 5, 8, 8, 10, 10, 11, 12, 12, 12, 12, 13, 13, 14, 16, 17, 17, 18, and 19.*

M

mass *masa* (102) The amount of matter in an object.

*Grams and kilograms are units of **mass.***

mean *media* (18) See **average.**

median *mediana* (Inv. 5) The middle number (or the average of the two central numbers) of a list of data when the numbers are arranged in order from the least to the greatest.

*In the data at right, 7 is the **median.***   1, 1, 2, 5, 6, 7, 9, 15, 24, 36, 44

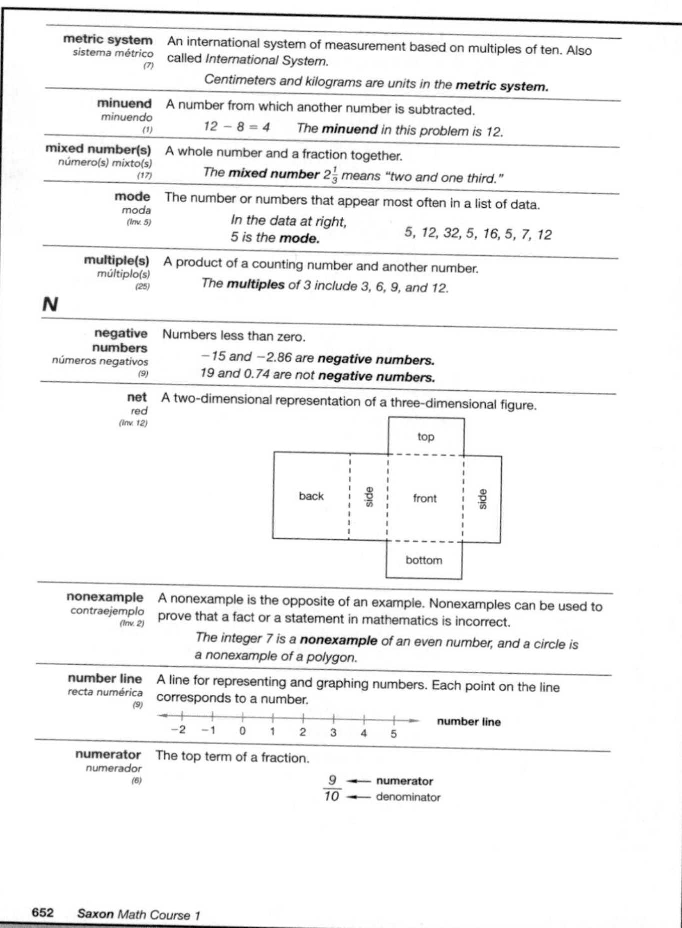

metric system *sistema métrico* (7) An international system of measurement based on multiples of ten. Also called *International System.*

*Centimeters and kilograms are units in the **metric system.***

minuend *minuendo* (1) A number from which another number is subtracted.

$12 - 8 = 4$ *The **minuend** in this problem is 12.*

mixed number(s) *número(s) mixto(s)* (17) A whole number and a fraction together.

*The **mixed number** $2\frac{1}{3}$ means "two and one third."*

mode *moda* (Inv. 5) The number or numbers that appear most often in a list of data.

*In the data at right, 5 is the **mode.***   5, 12, 32, 5, 16, 5, 7, 12

multiple(s) *múltiplo(s)* (25) A product of a counting number and another number.

*The **multiples** of 3 include 3, 6, 9, and 12.*

N

negative numbers *números negativos* (9) Numbers less than zero.

*-15 and -2.86 are **negative numbers.***
*19 and 0.74 are not **negative numbers.***

net *red* (Inv. 12) A two-dimensional representation of a three-dimensional figure.

nonexample *contraejemplo* (Inv. 2) A nonexample is the opposite of an example. Nonexamples can be used to prove that a fact or a statement in mathematics is incorrect.

*The integer 7 is a **nonexample** of an even number, and a circle is a nonexample of a polygon.*

number line *recta numérica* (9) A line for representing and graphing numbers. Each point on the line corresponds to a number.

numerator *numerador* (6) The top term of a fraction.

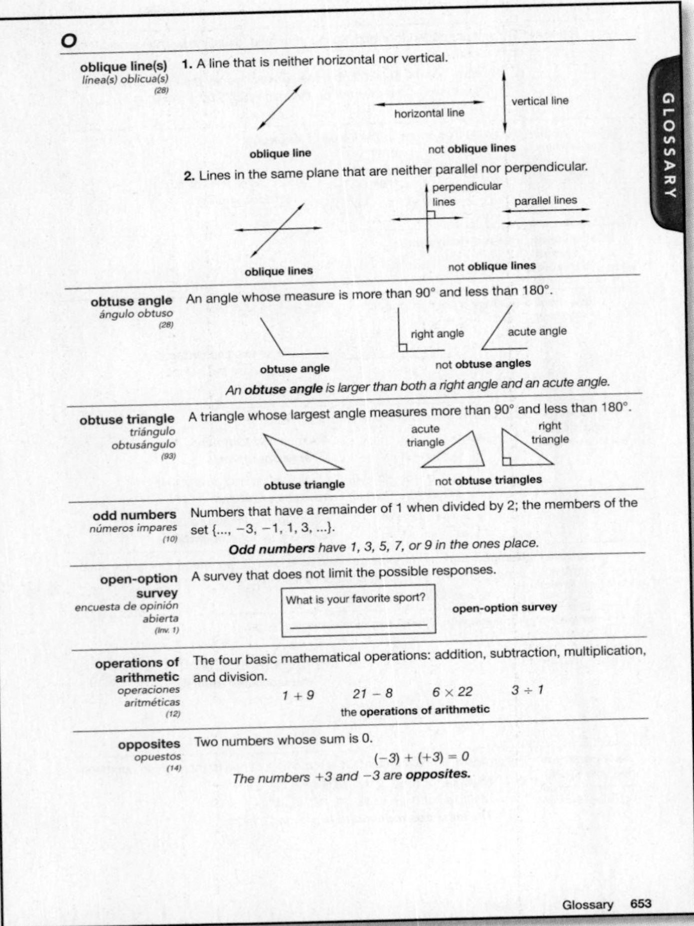

O

oblique line(s) *línea(s) oblicua(s)* (28) 1. A line that is neither horizontal nor vertical.

2. Lines in the same plane that are neither parallel nor perpendicular.

obtuse angle *ángulo obtuso* (28) An angle whose measure is more than 90° and less than 180°.

*An **obtuse angle** is larger than both a right angle and an acute angle.*

obtuse triangle *triángulo obtusángulo* (93) A triangle whose largest angle measures more than 90° and less than 180°.

odd numbers *números impares* (10) Numbers that have a remainder of 1 when divided by 2; the members of the set {..., −3, −1, 1, 3, ...}.

__Odd numbers__ have 1, 3, 5, 7, or 9 in the ones place.

open-option survey *encuesta de opinión abierta* (Inv. 1) A survey that does not limit the possible responses.

operations of arithmetic *operaciones aritméticas* (12) The four basic mathematical operations: addition, subtraction, multiplication, and division.

$1 + 9$ $21 - 8$ 6×22 $3 \div 1$

the operations of arithmetic

opposites *opuestos* (14) Two numbers whose sum is 0.

$(-3) + (+3) = 0$

*The numbers +3 and −3 are **opposites.***

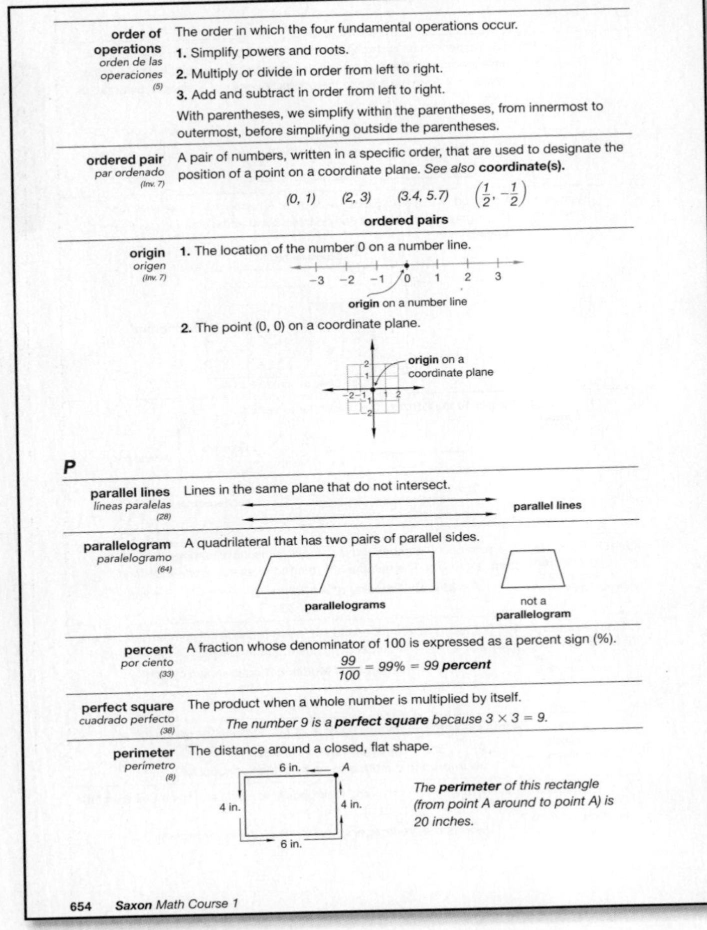

order of operations *orden de las operaciones* (5) The order in which the four fundamental operations occur.

1. Simplify powers and roots.
2. Multiply or divide in order from left to right.
3. Add and subtract in order from left to right.

With parentheses, we simplify within the parentheses, from innermost to outermost, before simplifying outside the parentheses.

ordered pair *par ordenado* (Inv. 7) A pair of numbers, written in a specific order, that are used to designate the position of a point on a coordinate plane. *See also* **coordinate(s).**

(0, 1) *(2, 3)* *(3.4, 5.7)* $\left(\frac{1}{2}, -\frac{1}{2}\right)$

ordered pairs

origin *origen* (Inv. 7) 1. The location of the number 0 on a number line.

2. The point (0, 0) on a coordinate plane.

P

parallel lines *líneas paralelas* (28) Lines in the same plane that do not intersect.

parallelogram *paralelogramo* (64) A quadrilateral that has two pairs of parallel sides.

percent *por ciento* (33) A fraction whose denominator of 100 is expressed as a percent sign (%).

$\frac{99}{100}$ = 99% = 99 ***percent***

perfect square *cuadrado perfecto* (38) The product when a whole number is multiplied by itself.

*The number 9 is a **perfect square** because 3 × 3 = 9.*

perimeter *perímetro* (8) The distance around a closed, flat shape.

*The **perimeter** of this rectangle (from point A around to point A) is 20 inches.*

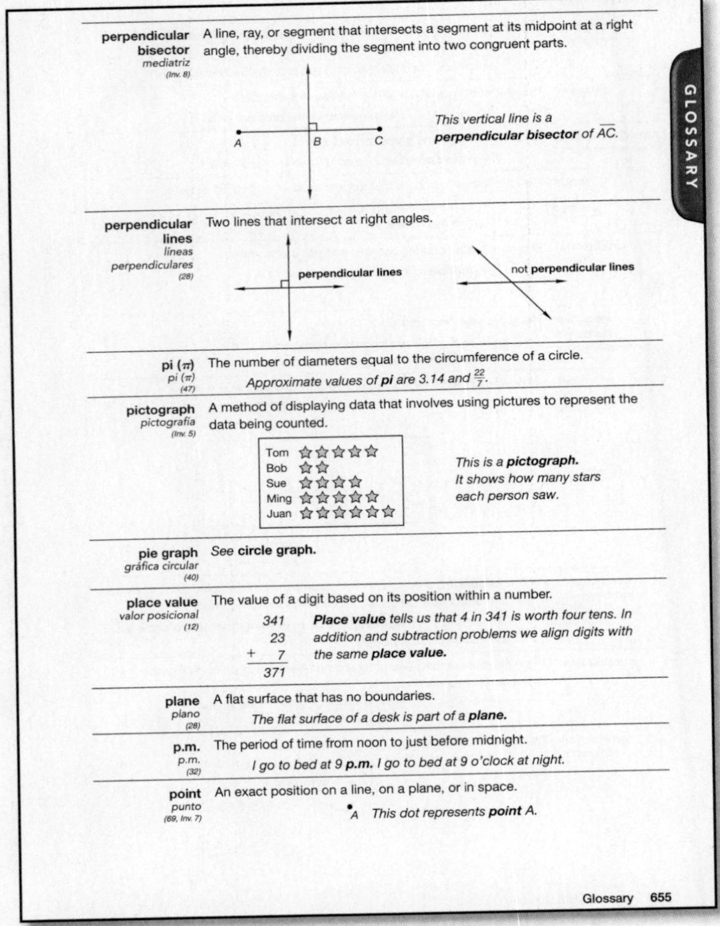

perpendicular bisector *mediatriz* (Inv. 8) A line, ray, or segment that intersects a segment at its midpoint at a right angle, thereby dividing the segment into two congruent parts.

*This vertical line is a **perpendicular bisector** of $\overline{AC}$.*

perpendicular lines *líneas perpendiculares* (28) Two lines that intersect at right angles.

pi (π) *pi (π)* (47) The number of diameters equal to the circumference of a circle.

*Approximate values of **pi** are 3.14 and $\frac{22}{7}$.*

pictograph *pictografía* (Inv. 5) A method of displaying data that involves using pictures to represent the data being counted.

*This is a **pictograph.** It shows how many stars each person saw.*

pie graph *gráfica circular* (40) See **circle graph.**

place value *valor posicional* (12) The value of a digit based on its position within a number.

$$\begin{array}{r} 341 \\ 23 \\ +\ \ 7 \\ \hline 371 \end{array}$$

Place value** tells us that 4 in 341 is worth four tens. In addition and subtraction problems we align digits with the same **place value.

plane *plano* (28) A flat surface that has no boundaries.

*The flat surface of a desk is part of a **plane.***

p.m. *p.m.* (32) The period of time from noon to just before midnight.

*I go to bed at 9 **p.m.** I go to bed at 9 o'clock at night.*

point *punto* (69, Inv. 7) An exact position on a line, on a plane, or in space.

*A This dot represents **point** A.*

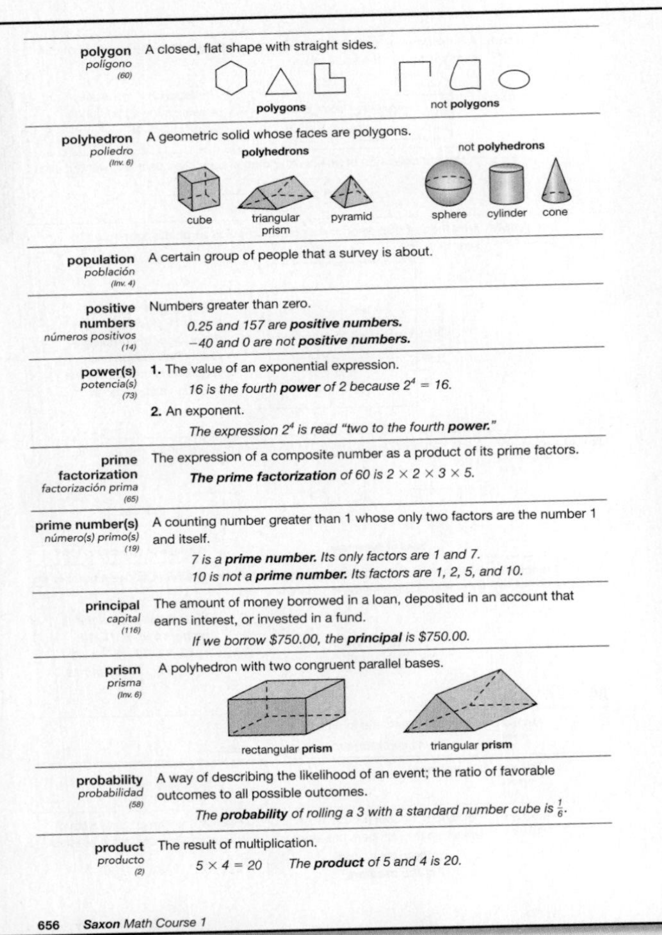

polygon *polígono* (60) A closed, flat shape with straight sides.

polyhedron *poliedro* (Inv. 6) A geometric solid whose faces are polygons.

population *población* (Inv. 4) A certain group of people that a survey is about.

positive numbers *números positivos* (14) Numbers greater than zero.

*0.25 and 157 are **positive numbers.***
*−40 and 0 are not **positive numbers.***

power(s) *potencia(s)* (73) 1. The value of an exponential expression.

*16 is the fourth **power** of 2 because $2^4 = 16$.*

2. An exponent.

*The expression 2^4 is read "two to the fourth **power.**"*

prime factorization *factorización prima* (65) The expression of a composite number as a product of its prime factors.

*The **prime factorization** of 60 is 2 × 2 × 3 × 5.*

prime number(s) *número(s) primo(s)* (19) A counting number greater than 1 whose only two factors are the number 1 and itself.

*7 is a **prime number.** Its only factors are 1 and 7.*
*10 is not a **prime number.** Its factors are 1, 2, 5, and 10.*

principal *capital* (116) The amount of money borrowed in a loan, deposited in an account that earns interest, or invested in a fund.

*If we borrow $750.00, the **principal** is $750.00.*

prism *prisma* (Inv. 6) A polyhedron with two congruent parallel bases.

probability *probabilidad* (58) A way of describing the likelihood of an event; the ratio of favorable outcomes to all possible outcomes.

*The **probability** of rolling a 3 with a standard number cube is $\frac{1}{6}$.*

product *producto* (2) The result of multiplication.

5 × 4 = 20 *The **product** of 5 and 4 is 20.*

proportion *proporción* (83) A statement that shows two ratios are equal.

$$\frac{6}{10} = \frac{9}{15}$$

These two ratios are equal, so this is a ***proportion.***

protractor *transportador* (Inv. 3) A tool used to measure and draw angles.

protractor

pyramid *pirámide* (Inv. 6) A three-dimensional solid with a polygon as its base and triangular faces that meet at a vertex.

pyramid

Q

quadrilateral *cuadrilátero* (60) Any four-sided polygon.

Each of these polygons has 4 sides. They are all ***quadrilaterals.***

qualitative *cualitativo* (Inv. 4) Expressed in or relating to categories rather than quantities or numbers.

Qualitative data *are categorical: Examples include the month in which someone is born and a person's favorite flavor of ice cream.*

quantitative *cuantitativo* (Inv. 4) Expressed in or relating to quantities or numbers.

Quantitative data *are numerical: Examples include the population of a city, the number of pairs of shoes someone owns, and the number of hours per week someone watches television.*

quotient *cociente* (2) The result of division.

$12 \div 3 = 4$ $\quad 3\overline{)12}$ = 4 $\quad \frac{12}{3} = 4$ *The* ***quotient*** *is 4 in each of these problems.*

R

radius *radio* (27) (Plural: *radii*) The distance from the center of a circle to a point on the circle.

A 2 in.

The ***radius*** *of circle A is 2 inches.*

range *intervalo* (Inv. 5) The difference between the largest number and smallest number in a list.

To calculate the ***range*** *of the data at right, we subtract the smallest number from the largest number. The* ***range*** *of this set of data is 29.* 5, 17, 12, 34, 29, 13

rate *tasa* (23) A ratio of measures.

ratio *razón* (23) A comparison of two numbers by division.

△△△
☆☆☆☆☆☆

There are 3 triangles and 6 stars. The ***ratio*** *of triangles to stars is* $\frac{3}{6}$ *(or* $\frac{1}{2}$*), which is read as "3 to 6" (or "1 to 2").*

rational numbers *números racionales* (23) Numbers that can be expressed as a ratio of two integers.

ray *rayo* (7) A part of a line that begins at a point and continues without end in one direction.

A B

ray *AB*

reciprocals *recíprocos* (30) Two numbers whose product is 1.

$\frac{3}{4} \times \frac{4}{3} = \frac{12}{12} = 1$ *Thus, the fractions* $\frac{3}{4}$ *and* $\frac{4}{3}$ *are* ***reciprocals.***

rectangle *rectángulo* (64) A quadrilateral that has four right angles.

rectangles not **rectangles**

rectangular prism *prisma rectangular* (Inv. 6) See **prism.**

reduce *reducir* (26) To rewrite a fraction in lowest terms.

If we ***reduce*** *the fraction* $\frac{9}{12}$*, we get* $\frac{3}{4}$*.*

reflection *reflexión* (108) Flipping a figure to produce a mirror image.

reflection

regular polygon *polígono regular* (60) A polygon in which all sides have equal lengths and all angles have equal measures.

regular polygons not **regular polygons**

rhombus *rombo* (64) A parallelogram with all four sides of equal length.

rhombuses not **rhombuses**

right angle *ángulo recto* (28) An angle that forms a square corner and measures 90°. It is often marked with a small square.

right angle obtuse angle acute angle not **right angles**

right triangle *triángulo rectángulo* (93) A triangle whose largest angle measures 90°.

right triangle acute triangle obtuse triangle not **right triangles**

rotation *rotación* (108) To rotate, or turn a figure about a specified point is called the *center of rotation.*

rotation

rotational symmetry *simetría rotacional* (110) A figure has rotational symmetry when it does not require a full rotation for the figure to look as if it re-appears in the same position as when it began the rotation, for example, a square or a triangle.

original position 45° turn **90° turn** 150° turn **180° turn** 210° turn **270° turn**

round *redondear* (16) A way of estimating a number by increasing or decreasing it to a certain place value. Example: 517 **rounds** to 520

S

sales tax *impuesto sobre la venta* (41) The tax charged on the sale of an item and based upon the item's purchase price.

If the ***sales-tax*** *rate is 7%, the* ***sales tax*** *on a $5.00 item will be $5.00 × 7% = $0.35.*

sample *muestra* (Inv. 1) A smaller group of a population that a survey focuses on.

sample space *espacio muestral* (58) Set of all possible outcomes of a particular event.

The ***sample space*** *of a 1–6 number cube is {1, 2, 3, 4, 5, 6}.*

scale *escala* (10) A ratio that shows the relationship between a scale drawing or model and the actual object.

If a drawing of the floor plan of a house has the legend 1 inch = 2 feet, the ***scale*** *of the drawing is* $\frac{1 \text{ in.}}{2 \text{ ft}} = \frac{1}{24}$*.*

scale drawing *dibujo a escala* (Inv. 11) A two-dimensional representation of a larger or smaller object.

Blueprints and maps are examples of ***scale drawings.***

scale factor *factor de escala* (Inv. 11) The number that relates corresponding sides of similar geometric figures.

25 mm 10 mm 10 mm 4 mm

The ***scale factor*** *from the smaller rectangle to the larger rectangle is 2.5.*

scale model *modelo a escala* (Inv. 11) A three-dimensional rendering of a larger or smaller object.

Globes and model airplanes are examples of ***scale models.***

scalene triangle *triángulo escaleno* (93) A triangle with three sides of different lengths.

All three sides of this ***scalene triangle*** *have different lengths.*

sector *sector* (Inv. 5) A region bordered by part of a circle and two radii.

This circle is divided into 3 ***sectors.***

segment *segmento* (7) A part of a line with two distinct endpoints.

A B

segment *AB* **or segment** *BA*

sequence *secuencia* (10) A list of numbers arranged according to a certain rule.

The numbers 2, 4, 6, 8, ... form a ***sequence.*** *The rule is "count up by twos."*

similar *semejante* (109) Having the same shape but not necessarily the same size. Corresponding angles of similar figures are congruent. Corresponding sides of similar figures are proportional.

A C B D E F

△ABC and △DEF are ***similar.*** *They have the same shape but not the same size.*

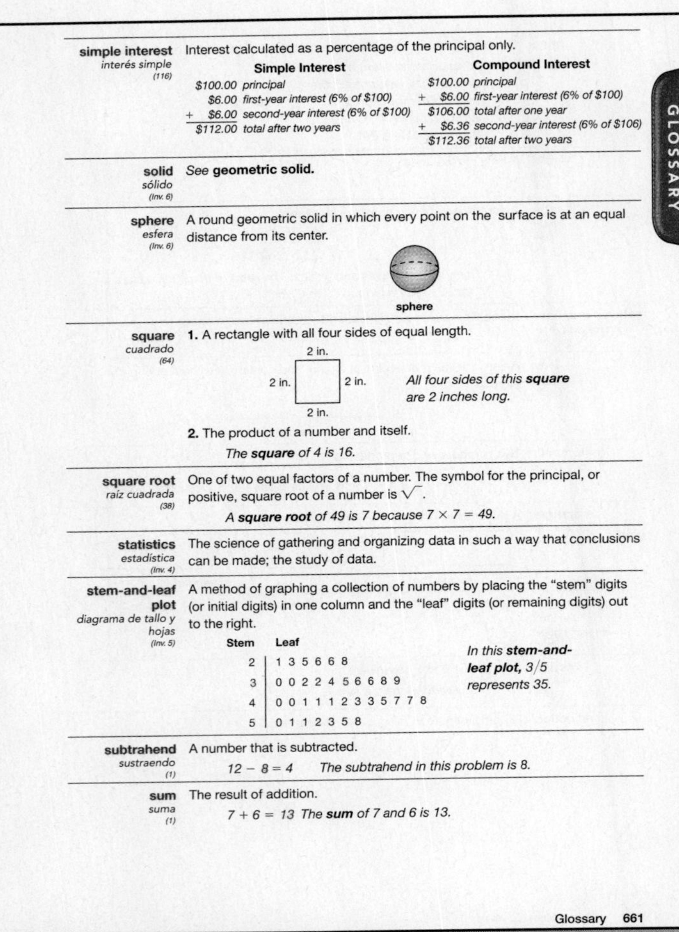

simple interest *interés simple* (116) Interest calculated as a percentage of the principal only.

Simple Interest		Compound Interest	
$100.00	principal	$100.00	principal
$6.00	first-year interest (6% of $100)	+ $6.00	first-year interest (6% of $100)
+ $6.00	second-year interest (6% of $100)	$106.00	total after one year
$112.00	total after two years	+ $6.36	second-year interest (6% of $106)
		$112.36	total after two years

solid *sólido* (Inv. 6) See **geometric solid.**

sphere *esfera* (Inv. 6) A round geometric solid in which every point on the surface is at an equal distance from its center.

sphere

square *cuadrado* (64) 1. A rectangle with all four sides of equal length.

*All four sides of this **square** are 2 inches long.*

2. The product of a number and itself.

*The **square** of 4 is 16.*

square root *raíz cuadrada* (38) One of two equal factors of a number. The symbol for the principal, or positive, square root of a number is $\sqrt{\ }$.

*A **square root** of 49 is 7 because $7 \times 7 = 49$.*

statistics *estadística* (Inv. 4) The science of gathering and organizing data in such a way that conclusions can be made; the study of data.

stem-and-leaf plot *diagrama de tallo y hojas* (Inv. 5) A method of graphing a collection of numbers by placing the "stem" digits (or initial digits) in one column and the "leaf" digits (or remaining digits) out to the right.

Stem	Leaf
2	1 3 5 6 6 8
3	0 0 2 2 4 5 6 6 8 9
4	0 0 1 1 1 2 3 3 5 7 7 8
5	0 1 1 2 3 5 8

*In this **stem-and-leaf plot,** 3|5 represents 35.*

subtrahend *sustraendo* (1) A number that is subtracted.

$12 - 8 = 4$ *The subtrahend in this problem is 8.*

sum *suma* (1) The result of addition.

$7 + 6 = 13$ *The **sum** of 7 and 6 is 13.*

GLOSSARY

Glossary 661

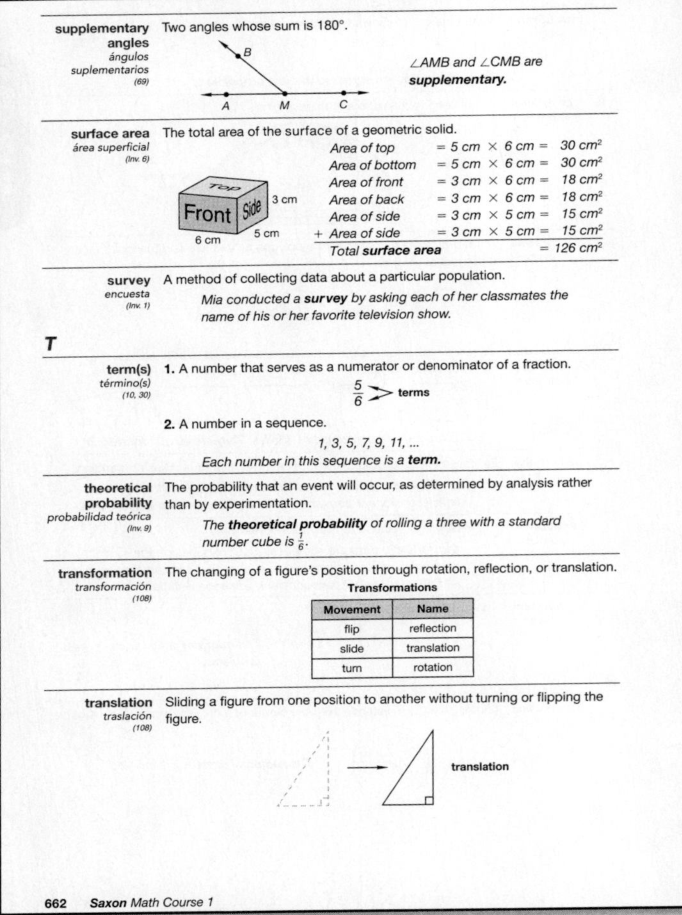

supplementary angles *ángulos suplementarios* (69) Two angles whose sum is 180°.

*∠AMB and ∠CMB are **supplementary.***

surface area *área superficial* (Inv. 6) The total area of the surface of a geometric solid.

Area of top	= 5 cm × 6 cm =	30 cm²
Area of bottom	= 5 cm × 6 cm =	30 cm²
Area of front	= 3 cm × 6 cm =	18 cm²
Area of back	= 3 cm × 6 cm =	18 cm²
Area of side	= 3 cm × 5 cm =	15 cm²
+ Area of side	= 3 cm × 5 cm =	15 cm²
Total **surface area**	=	126 cm²

survey *encuesta* (Inv. 1) A method of collecting data about a particular population.

*Mia conducted a **survey** by asking each of her classmates the name of his or her favorite television show.*

T

term(s) *término(s)* (10, 30) 1. A number that serves as a numerator or denominator of a fraction.

$\frac{5}{6}$ terms

2. A number in a sequence.

1, 3, 5, 7, 9, 11, ...

*Each number in this sequence is a **term.***

theoretical probability *probabilidad teórica* (Inv. 9) The probability that an event will occur, as determined by analysis rather than by experimentation.

*The **theoretical probability** of rolling a three with a standard number cube is $\frac{1}{6}$.*

transformation *transformación* (108) The changing of a figure's position through rotation, reflection, or translation.

Transformations

Movement	Name
flip	reflection
slide	translation
turn	rotation

translation *traslación* (108) Sliding a figure from one position to another without turning or flipping the figure.

translation

662 *Saxon Math Course 1*

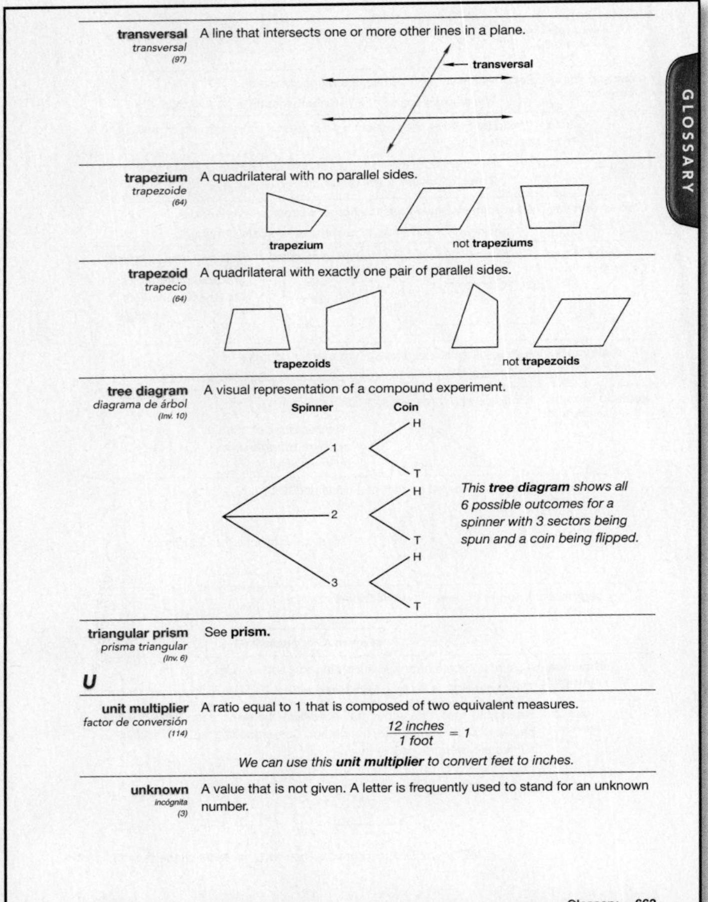

transversal *transversal* (97) A line that intersects one or more other lines in a plane.

transversal

trapezium *trapezoide* (64) A quadrilateral with no parallel sides.

trapezium — not trapeziums

trapezoid *trapecio* (64) A quadrilateral with exactly one pair of parallel sides.

trapezoids — not trapezoids

tree diagram *diagrama de árbol* (Inv. 10) A visual representation of a compound experiment.

Spinner — Coin

*This **tree diagram** shows all 6 possible outcomes for a spinner with 3 sectors being spun and a coin being flipped.*

triangular prism *prisma triangular* (Inv. 6) See **prism.**

U

unit multiplier *factor de conversión* (114) A ratio equal to 1 that is composed of two equivalent measures.

$\frac{12 \text{ inches}}{1 \text{ foot}} = 1$

*We can use this **unit multiplier** to convert feet to inches.*

unknown *incógnita* (3) A value that is not given. A letter is frequently used to stand for an unknown number.

GLOSSARY

Glossary 663

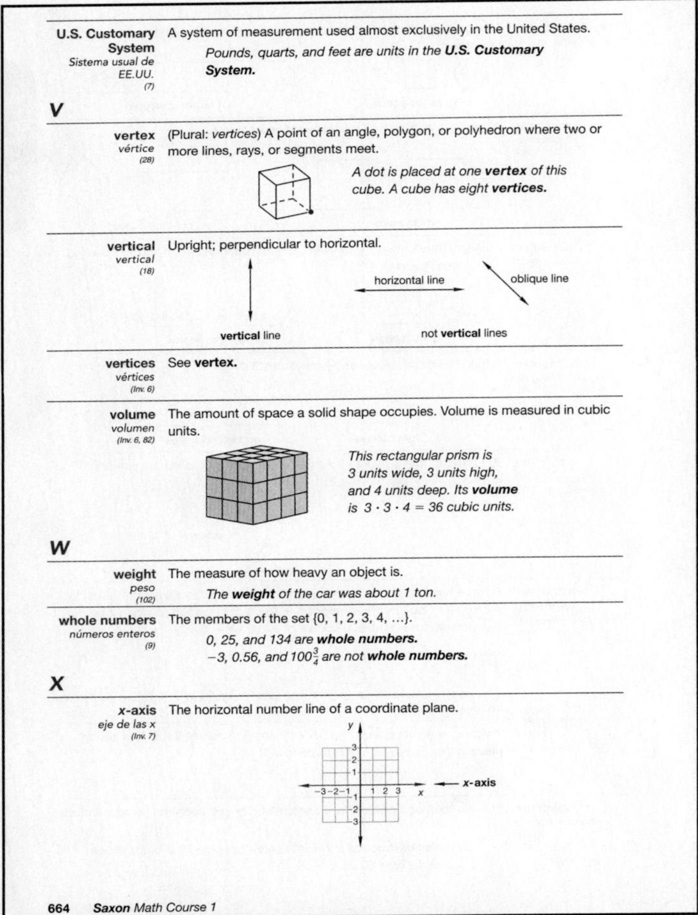

U.S. Customary System *Sistema usual de EE.UU.* (7) A system of measurement used almost exclusively in the United States.

*Pounds, quarts, and feet are units in the **U.S. Customary System.***

V

vertex *vértice* (28) (Plural: *vertices*) A point of an angle, polygon, or polyhedron where two or more lines, rays, or segments meet.

*A dot is placed at one **vertex** of this cube. A cube has eight **vertices.***

vertical *vertical* (18) Upright; perpendicular to horizontal.

vertical line — horizontal line — oblique line — not **vertical** lines

vertices *vértices* (Inv. 6) See **vertex.**

volume *volumen* (Inv. 6, 82) The amount of space a solid shape occupies. Volume is measured in cubic units.

*This rectangular prism is 3 units wide, 3 units high, and 4 units deep. Its **volume** is $3 \cdot 3 \cdot 4 = 36$ cubic units.*

W

weight *peso* (102) The measure of how heavy an object is.

*The **weight** of the car was about 1 ton.*

whole numbers *números enteros* (9) The members of the set {0, 1, 2, 3, 4, ...}.

*0, 25, and 134 are **whole numbers.***

*−3, 0.56, and $100\frac{3}{4}$ are not **whole numbers.***

X

x-axis *eje de las x* (Inv. 7) The horizontal number line of a coordinate plane.

x-axis

664 *Saxon Math Course 1*

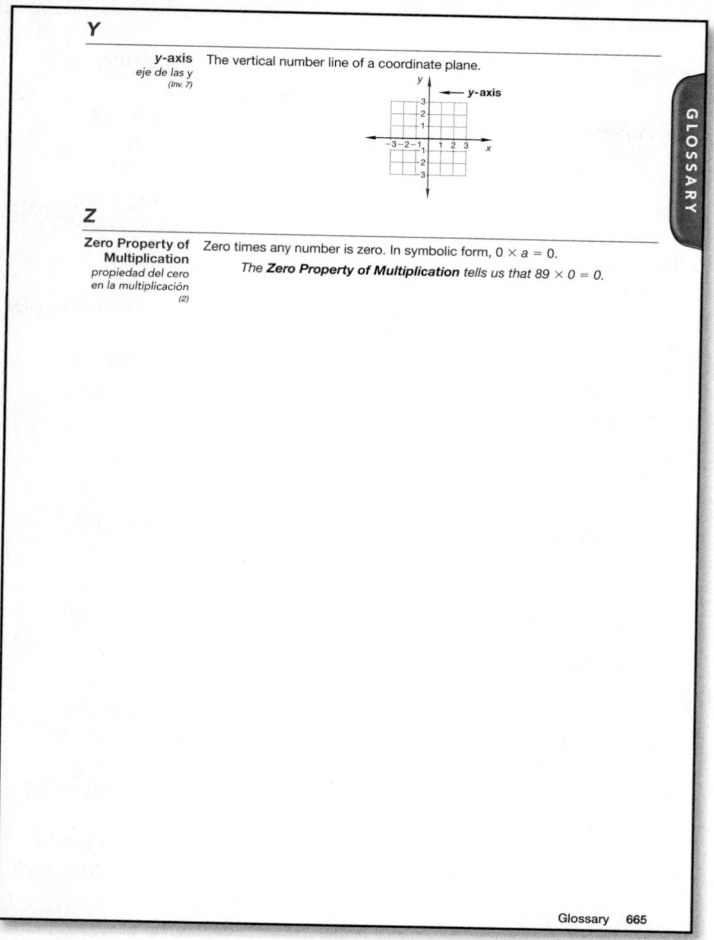

Y

y-axis
eje de las y
(Inv. 7)

The vertical number line of a coordinate plane.

Z

Zero Property of Multiplication
propiedad del cero en la multiplicación
(2)

Zero times any number is zero. In symbolic form, $0 \times a = 0$.

*The **Zero Property of Multiplication** tells us that $89 \times 0 = 0$.*

A

Abbreviations. *See also* Symbols and signs
a.m., 170
area (A), 475
base (b), 475
calculator memory keys, 608
Celsius (C), 80
centimeter (cm), 37
cup (c.), 404
Fahrenheit (F), 80
foot (ft), 37
gallon (gal), 404
Greatest Common Factor (GCF), 175
height (h), 475
inch (in.), 37, 38
kilometer (km), 37
kilowatt hours (kwh), 494
length (l), 475
lines, 353
liter (L), 37
meter (m), 37
mile (mi.), 37
millimeter (mm), 37
ounce (oz.), 404
perimeter (P), 475
pint (pt.), 404
p.m., 170
quart (qt.), 404
rays, 353
segments, 353
square (sq.), 165
square centimeters (cm^2), 197, 409
width (w), 475
yard (yd), 37
Act it out. *See* Problem-solving strategies
Activities
algebraic addition of integers, 543–544
angles
bisecting, 418–420
measurement, 162–163
area
of parallelograms, 370–371
of triangles, 408–409
bisectors
angle, 418–420
constructing, 420
perpendicular, 417–418
circles, drawing, 142
circumference, 244–246
comparing geometric solids, 315
compasses, 142
coordinate planes, 365–367
drawing
circles, 142
on the coordinate plane, 365–367
experimental probability, 470–473
fraction manipulatives, 109
parallelogram area, 370–371
perimeter, 42–43
perpendicular bisectors, 417–418
prime numbers, 102
probability experiment, 471–472
protractors, using, 162–163
rulers, inch, 37–38, 88–89
segments, bisecting, 417–418
Sign Game, 543–545
transformations, 562–563
Acute angles, 146–147, 161, 503–504
Acute triangles, 485
Addends, 8, 18–22, 59
Addition
addends in, 8, 18–22, 59. *See also* Sums
algebraic, 518–520, 543–547
associative property of, 30
checking answers by, 8
commutative property of, 8, 9, 10
of decimals, 8–9, 191–194, 276–277
and whole number, 195–199
even and odd numbers, 51
fact families, 7–11
of fractions
with common denominators, 127–131, 342
with different denominators, 285–294
SOS memory aid, 295–298
three or more, 320–323
three-step process, 295–298
identity property of, 8
of integers, 517–523, 543–547
of mixed measures, 534, 592–596
of mixed numbers, 136–140, 306–309
of money amounts, 7–11, 362, 379
of negative numbers, 518, 519
on number lines, 518
order of operations, 29
place value in, 8
of positive numbers, 518
in problems about combining, 58–62
of signed numbers, 542–547
subtraction as inverse of, 9, 10, 19
sums, 8, 83
of three numbers, 30
of units of measure, 421–425
unknown numbers in, 18–22
of whole numbers, 7–11
and decimals, 195–199
word problems, 58–62
Addition patterns, 58–62
Addition sequences (arithmetic sequences), 50
Advanced Learners. *See* Enrichment
Age, calculating, 69–70. *See also* Elapsed-time
Algebra, 123
adding integers, 517–523, 543–547
comparing integers, 47
graphing in the coordinate plane, 364
graphing on the coordinate plane, 363–367, 499–500, 581
multiplying integers, 587–591
ordering integers, 517–520
solving equations for unknown numbers
in addition, 18–22
in division and multiplication, 23–27, 123
in equal groups, 78–81
in fractions and decimals, 225–230
in proportions, 432, 442–443
in rate problems, 123
in sequences, 50
SOS method, 295–298, 306–309, 342, 349, 375–379
in subtraction, 18–22, 60–61
in word problems, 59, 60
subtracting integers, 517–523
writing algebraic equations, 543
Algebraic addition of integers, 517–521, 543–547
Algebraic logic calculators, 437
Alternate angles, exterior and interior, 504
a.m., 170
"and" in naming mixed numbers, 184
Angle bisectors, 418–420
Angle pairs, 504
Angles
activity with, 162–163
acute. *See* Acute angles
adjacent, in parallelograms, 369
alternate interior, 504
bisecting, 418–420
classifying, 163
complementary, 353–357
corresponding, 504, 567–569
degree measures of, 145
drawing with protractors, 161–163
exterior, 504, 508–509
interior, 146, 504, 508–512
measuring with protractors, 161–163
naming, 145–149
obtuse, 146–147, 161–163, 503, 504
opposite, in parallelograms, 368, 369
in parallelograms, 368, 369
in quadrilaterals, sum of measures, 508–512
right, 146–147
supplementary, 353–357, 369, 504, 508
symbol for, 145
of transversals, 503–507
in triangles
classification using, 485
sum of measures of, 508–512
vertex of, 147
Apex, 315
Approximately equal to (≈), 246, 462
Approximation. *See also* Estimation
Approximation, pi and, 246, 449, 627
Arcs, drawing with compasses, 418
Area
abbreviation for, 475
activity, 408–409
of bases, 427
of circles, estimating, 447–451
of complex shapes, 557–560
of cones, 630–636
of cubes, 497
of cylinders, 634–635
estimating, 447–451, 617–620
of geometric solids, 316, 630–636
of lateral surface, 634
of parallelograms, 369–371, 409, 474
perimeter compared to, 164
of prisms, 633
of rectangles, 164–168, 364–365, 474
of rectangular prisms, 497
of right triangles, 410
of squares, 165, 196–197, 474
of triangles, 408–412, 474
surface area, 316–318, 633–636
units of measure, 164, 197, 365, 422, 618

References in color indicate content exclusive to the Teacher's Manual.

"are in" as indicator of division, 135
Arithmetic mean. *See* Mean
Arithmetic operations. *See also* Addition; Division; Multiplication; Subtraction
  alignment in, 191
  answer terms of, 65
  with money, 7–18, 92, 258, 362, 379, 616
  rules for decimals, 276–277
  SOS memory aid, 295–298, 306–309
  terms for answers of, 65
  with units of measure, 421–425
  words that indicate, 250
Assessment. *See* Cumulative assessment; Customized benchmark assessment; Power-Up tests
Associative property, 30
Average, 93–98. *See also* Mean
Axis, horizontal and vertical, 95, 363

B

Bar graphs, 55, 84, 211, 265
Base(s)
  base ten, 64, 179
  exponents and, 196
Bases of geometric figures
  abbreviations for, 475
  cylinders, 634
  parallelograms, 370
  prisms, 630
  pyramids, 315, 630
  rectangular prism, 426
Base ten place value system, 64, 179
Benchmarks to estimate length, 37
Bimodal distribution, 267
Bias, in surveys, 214
Bisectors
  angle, 418–420
  geometric construction of, 417–420
  perpendicular, 417–418
Body temperature, 51
Boiling point, 51

C

Calculators. *See* also Graphing calculator, online activity references
  with algebraic logic, 437
  for checking answers, 608
  for compound interest, 608
  for converting fractions to decimals, 386
  finding square roots with, 462
  memory keys on, 608
  order of operations and, 74, 437
  simplifying with, 231–232
Canceling
  in reducing fractions, 358–362, 376
  in the Sign Game, 543
  unit multipliers and, 597–598
Capacity, 404–407
"Casting out nines," 533
Categories, explaining, 400
Celsius (C), 51, 80
Centimeter (cm), 37, 422
Centimeter cubed (cm^3), 318
Centimeter squared (cm^2), 164, 197, 409, 422
Chance, 299–305, 471. *See also* Probability
Checking answers. *See also* Inverse operations
  in addition problems, 8, 9
  calculators for, 608
  in division problems, 25, 272
  estimating for, 617
  guess-and-check method, 28, 460–464
  in mixed number problems, 329–332, 343
  in multiplication problems, 15, 43
  pairing technique, 63
  in subtraction problems, 9, 20, 61, 251
  in unknown-number problems, 19, 20, 25–26
Cipher to the rule of three, 452
Circle graphs, 205–215, 264–265
Circles
  activity, 142
  area of, 447–451, 626
  circumference of, 141–142, 244–246
  compasses for drawing, 142
  diameter of, 141–142, 190, 246
  fractional parts of, 115
  measures of, 141–144
  perimeter of. *See* Perimeter
  radius of, 141–142, 190
Circular cylinders. *See* Cylinders
Circumference, 141–142, 244–246. *See also* pi
Classification
  parallelograms, 334
  of polygons, 311
  of quadrilaterals, 333–337
  of triangles, 311, 484–487
Clock faces, fractional parts of, 111, 115
Clockwise/counterclockwise, 465
Closed curve, 23
Closed-option surveys, 57
Coins, problems using, 7
Coin toss experiments, 302
Combining, in word problems, 58–62
Commas in number systems, 64–65
Common denominators. *See also* Denominators
  in addition and subtraction of fractions, 127–131
    renaming both fractions, 289–294
    renaming one fraction, 285–288
  least common, 286, 320–321
  in multiplication and division of fractions, 342
  for subtraction of mixed numbers, 329–332
Common factors. *See* Factors; Greatest Common Factor (GCF)
Common multiples, 156, 157
Common polygons, 311
Communication
  Discuss, 13, 14, 15, 19, 20, 24, 43, 47, 75, 83, 112, 113, 123, 128, 139, 142, 151, 159, 218, 250, 256, 300, 307, 346, 359, 369, 404, 427, 448, 457, 467, 471, 488, 498, 543, 553, 588, 612, 623
  Formulate a problem, 26, 35, 57, 61, 62, 67, 79–80, 86, 97, 98, 140, 252, 261, 293, 308, 330, 344, 345, 361, 378, 459, 464, 550, 556, 585, 623
  Writing about mathematics, 11, 16, 17, 21, 22, 24, 27, 30, 31, 33, 34, 41, 44, 45, 49, 52, 67, 69, 71, 72, 79, 85, 91, 92, 97, 104, 107–108, 111, 125, 129, 143, 144, 148, 219, 223, 224, 246, 253, 258, 267, 270, 278, 287, 290, 305, 313, 323, 328, 330, 335, 340, 346, 356, 363, 373, 381, 384, 391, 392, 402, 405, 410, 433, 439, 444, 458, 459, 467, 481, 487, 515, 522, 530, 547, 552, 576, 595, 619, 622, 627
Commutative property
  of addition, 8, 9, 10
  of multiplication, 13, 246, 427, 428
  subtraction and the, 8, 10
Comparing
  decimals, 231–234
  defined, 173
  exponential expressions, 381
  fractions, 395–398, 441–446
  geometric solids, 315
  integers, 47
  number lines for, 46–49
  ratios and, 494
  symbols, for
    equal to (=), 47, 381
    greater than (>), 47, 110, 381
    less than (<), 47, 381
  word problems about, 68–72
Compasses
  activity, 142
  for bisecting angles, 418–420
  for bisecting segments, 417–418
  drawing with, 142, 418
  investigations, 417–420
  types of, 142
Complementary angles, 353–357
Complementary probability, 301–303, 400, 524–527
Complex shapes
  area of, 557–560
  defined, 538, 557
  drawing, 484, 538
  perimeter of, 538–542
Composite numbers, 102, 337
Compound interest, 606–611
Compound outcomes, 524–526
Cones, 314, 630–636
Congruence in geometric figures, 311, 408, 426, 561, 562, 566–567
Consecutive integers, 88
Construction, of bisectors in geometric figures, 417–420
Content highlights. *See* Section overviews
Content trace. *See* Section overviews
Conversion. *See also* Equivalent; Mixed measures
  of area, 618
  decimals
    fraction equivalents, 381–382, 385–389, 395–398
    by multiplication, 488–492
    percent equivalents, 216–217, 390–394, 488–492
    probabilities to, 387
    ratios to, 385–389
  defined, 152
  fractions
    decimal equivalents, 381–382
    decimals equivalents, 385–389, 395–398
    by division, 385–389
    percent equivalents, 216–217, 390–394, 488–492, 602–605
  improper fractions
    to mixed numbers, 133, 324–328, 342
    mixed numbers to, 324–328, 342
  of length
    centimeters to millimeters, 38, 39
    feet to yards, 598
    inches to centimeters, 38
    meters to centimeters, 38
  metric system, 404

- mixed numbers, 534
  - to improper fractions, 324–328, 342
  - by multiplication, 488–492
- percents
  - decimal equivalents, 216–217, 390–394, 488–492
  - fraction equivalents, 216–217, 390–394, 488–492, 602–605
  - by multiplication, 488–492
  - to probability, 301–302
- prefixes for, 533
- of ratios to decimals, 385–389
- unit multipliers for, 597–598
- units of measure, 323, 357, 404–405, 412, 534, 572
- U.S. Customary System, 404–405

Coordinate plane, 363–367, 499–500, 581
Corresponding angles, 504, 567–569
Corresponding parts, 566–572, 579
Counterclockwise/clockwise, 465
Counting exercises (Power-Up). *Counting exercises are found in the teacher wrap on the first page of every lesson.*
"Counting by twos," 51
Counting numbers
- defined, 46
- integers as, 74, 517
- multiples and, 156
- whole numbers and, 46

Cross products and proportions, 441–446
Cubed numbers, exponent indicating, 380
Cubes (geometric figures). *See also* Number cubes
- area of, 497
- attributes of, 314
- drawing, 314
- faces of, 315
- nets, 318, 319
- as rectangular prisms, 497
- as regular polyhedrons, 314
- volume of, 318, 428

Cubic centimeters (cm³), 318
Cubic units, 318, 426
Cumulative assessment, 53A, 81A, 108A, 135A, 160A, 186A, 210A, 238A, 263A, 288A, 313A, 341A, 362A, 394A, 416A, 446A, 469A, 496A, 523A, 552A, 577A, 605A, 629A
Cup (c.), 404–405
Customized benchmark assessment, 53B, 108B, 160B, 210B, 263B, 313B, 362B, 416B, 469B, 523B, 577B, 629B
Cylinders
- area of, 634–635
- attributes of, 314
- bases of, 634
- drawing, 314, 316
- height of, 626
- volume of, 626–629, 631–633

D

Data. *See also* Graphs
- collecting, 211–215
- displaying
  - bar graphs, 211, 213, 265
  - circle graphs, 264
  - histograms, 55
  - line graphs, 211, 305
  - line plots, 211, 213, 266, 279
  - pictographs, 264
  - qualitative, 211–213, 264–265
  - quantitative, 211–213, 266–267
  - stem-and-leaf plots, 264–267, 384, 487
- interpreting, 211–215
- mean, 95, 266
- median, 266
- mode, 266
- organizing, 211–215
- qualitative, 211–213, 264–265
- quantitative, 211–213, 266–267
- range, 266

Data point, 266
Decimal division, 236, 272–273, 385
Decimal numbers. *See* Decimals
Decimal place values, 8, 9, 178–181, 184, 239
Decimal points
- aligning by, 8, 9, 192
- "and" in reading or writing, 240
- in decimal division, 236, 272–273, 385
- money and, 8, 13, 15
- in multiplication by tens and hundreds, 240
- purpose of, 178, 184, 241
- shifting by division or multiplication, 240, 272–273
- whole numbers and, 195–199
- words that indicate, 240

Decimals
- adding, 8–9, 191–194, 276–277
  - to whole numbers, 195–199
- "and" in reading or writing, 184
- arithmetic operations rule, 276–277
- comparing, 231–234
- converting
  - by multiplication, 488–492
  - probabilities to, 387
  - ratios to, 385–389
- dividing
  - rules for, 276–277
  - by ten and by one hundred, 272–276
  - by whole numbers, 235–238
- dividing by, 254–258
- equivalent, 236
- expanded notation, 239–243
- fraction equivalents, 381–382, 385–389, 395–398, 513–516
- mixed, 183
- multiplying, 200–204, 232, 239–243, 276–277
- on number lines, 259–263
- percent equivalents, 216–217, 390–394, 488–492, 513–516
- reading, 182–186
- rounding, 268–271
- simplifying, 231–234
- subtracting, 191–194, 276–277
  - from whole numbers, 195–199
- unknown factors in, 452–455
- unknown numbers in, 225–230
- writing
  - alignment in, 8
  - in expanded notation, 239–243
  - fraction equivalents, 182–186, 380–384, 385–389, 513–516
  - as percents, 390–394, 488–492, 513–516
  - probabilities as, 387
  - ratios as, 385–389
  - and reading, 182–186

Decimals Chart, 276–279
Degrees, measuring turns by, 465
Denominators. *See also* Common denominators; Fractions
- decimals as, 182
- least common, 286, 320–321
- mixed numbers to improper fractions, 325
- multiplying, 150–151
- as term of a fraction, 32, 127, 343

Diagrams. *See also* Draw a picture or diagram
- graphs. *See* Graphs
- ratio boxes. *See* Ratio boxes

Diameter
- defined, 141, 190
- formula for, 246
- radius and, 141–142

Dice (dot cubes), 68, 174
Difference. *See also* Subtraction
- defined, 8, 11
- greater-lesser, 68
- later-earlier, 69, 170–171
- in operations of arithmetic, 8, 65

Digits
- place value of, 64
- shown in standard notation, 593
- summing for factors, 113

Discuss. *See* Communication
Distance. *See also* Length
- average, 263, 455
- estimating, 478
- measuring, 59, 478

Distribution, bimodal, 267
Dividends
- defined, 14, 103
- function of, 22
- missing, 25

Divisibility, 112–116
Division
- answers as mixed numbers, 132–135
- "are in" as indicator of, 135
- checking answers, 15, 25, 272
- converting fractions to decimals using, 385–389
- by decimals, 254–258
- of decimals
  - rules for, 276–277
  - by ten and by one hundred, 272–276
  - by whole numbers, 235–238
- dividends. *See* Dividends
- divisors. *See* Divisors
- equivalent, 225–230
- even numbers and, 51
- fact families, 8–12
- factors and, 99
- "for each" in, 123, 422
- by fractions, 33
- of fractions, 359
  - common denominators and, 152–153, 342
  - by fractions, 280–285
- of integers, 587–591
- long versus short method, 15
- mental math, 272–276
- of mixed numbers, 349–352
- of money, 12–18, 362, 379
- multiplication as inverse of, 15, 24, 452
- odd numbers and, 51
- order of operations, 29, 30, 47
- by primes, 337–341
- quotients. *See* Quotients
- remainders in, 15, 582
- short-division method, 15
- of signed numbers, 588
- symbols for, 14, 133, 385
- of units of measure, 421–425

unknown numbers in, 23–27, 123
of whole numbers, 12–18
by fractions, 259–263
word problems, 582–591
words that indicate, 123, 135, 423
Divisors
as decimals, 254–255
defined, 14
function of, 22
missing, 25
zero as, 14
dot-to-dot drawing, 365–367
Doubling, 51
Draw a picture or diagram. *See* Problem-solving strategies
Drawing. *See also* Diagrams; Graphs
activity, 142
compasses for, 142, 418
on coordinate planes, 581
cubes, 314
cylinders, 314, 316
geometric solids, 315–316
prisms, 314, 315
protractors for, 161–163
to scale, 52, 578–581

E

Early Finishers. *See* Enrichment
Edges, 315, 332, 497
Elapsed-time, 68–72, 169–173
Electrical-charge model in Sign Game, 543–545
Endpoints, 37
English learners. *English learner vocabulary is specified on applicable lesson opener and investigation opener pages.* 9, 19, 25, 30, 59, 75, 83, 94, 103, 113, 124, 130, 137, 152, 158, 163, 173, 179, 185, 194, 196, 214, 224, 228, 236, 240, 246, 252, 256, 261, 265, 271, 275, 278, 288, 293, 297, 303, 308, 312, 325, 343, 348, 355, 359, 363, 369, 387, 392, 396, 405, 414, 422, 432, 448, 458, 461, 466, 471, 482, 489, 501, 510, 536, 539, 543, 551, 555, 558, 562, 580 589, 594, 604, 615, 618
Enrichment
Early Finishers
Choose a strategy, 284, 352, 403, 523, 629
Math and architecture, 323
Math and geography, 483
Math and science 394, 451, 532
Math applications, 323, 435
Real-world applications, 17, 22, 31, 41, 77, 81, 92, 98, 104, 108, 116, 126, 131, 144, 155, 160, 177, 194, 204, 238, 249, 253, 258, 263, 279, 294, 298, 305, 309, 332, 357, 362, 379, 384, 412, 440, 446, 455, 469, 478, 487, 496, 516, 572, 591, 601, 605, 611, 616
Extend the Problem, 10, 30, 31, 34, 39, 40, 45, 49, 56, 61, 62, 72, 67, 72, 80, 85, 86, 91, 96, 103, 104, 106, 108, 110, 111, 115, 120, 125, 126, 129, 130, 131, 134, 135, 139, 140, 143, 147, 148, 154, 155, 159, 163, 167, 168, 172, 173, 175, 176, 177, 189, 198, 215, 220, 224, 229, 230, 234, 236, 237, 238, 242, 248, 256, 257, 258, 262, 270, 273, 274, 278, 283, 293, 296, 297, 308, 312, 323, 328, 332, 335, 340, 348, 352, 355, 361, 362, 373, 377, 378, 393, 397, 398, 402, 406, 407, 415, 416, 425, 429, 430, 440, 445, 446, 467, 450, 454, 458, 462, 464, 469, 478, 482, 486, 487, 492, 506, 511, 512, 516, 522, 527, 530, 531, 536, 547, 555, 556, 564, 565, 569, 571, 576, 577, 584, 586, 590, 591, 595, 600, 601, 603, 604, 605, 609, 619, 624, 625, 628
Investigation extensions
angles, drawing and measuring with protractors, 163
bar graphs, 57
bisectors, geometric construction of, 420
choose a method, 111
circle graphs, 214
compare fractions, 111
compound experiments, 527
cones, volume, 635
coordinate planes, 367
cubes, surface area of, 636
displaying data, 267
examples and non-examples, 111
experimental probability, 472–473
geometric solids, 319
histogram intervals, 57
prisms, volume, 635
scale factor, 581
surface area, 318, 636
surveys, 57
views of geometric figures, 318–319
volume, 635
Equal groups, 78–81, 117–121
Equalities. *See* Equivalent Forms
Equations. *See also* Representation
addition. *See* Addition
division. *See* Division
exponential. *See* Exponents
formulas. *See* Formulas
formulate an. *See* Representation
multiplication. *See* Multiplication
order of operations. *See* Order of Operations
with percents. *See* Percents
proportion. *See* Proportions
ratios. *See* Ratios
rewriting to simplify, 19
solving by inspection, 554
subtraction. *See* Subtraction
two-step, 13, 553–556
using inverse operations, 554
writing for problem-solving, 78–80, 151–153, 165–166, 169–171, 174, 175, 183–184, 192, 196–198, 217–218, 222, 226–228, 260, 268–269, 290–291, 342–343, 349–350, 409–410, 421–423, 427–428, 432–433, 474–475, 490, 509–510, 534, 539, 548–550, 553–554, 557–558, 592–594, 596, 607–608, 622–623, 627
Equilateral triangles, 484, 485
Equilibrium, 36
Equivalent forms
decimals, 236
defined, 137, 225
division problems, 225–230, 254–256
fractions
cross products for determining, 441–446
defined, 137
equal fractions as, 597
example of, 152
fraction-decimal-percent, 513–516
writing, 391
numbers, 225
ratios, 432, 442
Errors and misconceptions 11, 16, 21, 27, 31, 34, 35, 41, 45, 49, 53, 62, 67, 71, 76, 77, 80, 85, 91, 97, 104, 106, 108, 115, 121, 125, 134, 140, 143, 155, 159, 160, 167, 172, 176, 181, 185, 189, 190, 193, 198, 202, 208, 209, 220, 223, 229, 233, 237, 247, 252, 262, 271, 273, 274, 278, 283, 293, 294, 297, 304, 308, 312, 322, 323, 327, 330, 336, 340, 344, 348, 351, 355, 356, 360, 361, 373, 379, 383, 388, 392, 397, 402, 411, 416, 425, 430, 434, 435, 439, 444, 450, 454, 459, 464, 468, 476, 481, 483, 486, 491, 495, 496, 502, 506, 507, 512, 514, 521, 522, 530, 531, 535, 536, 541, 546, 547, 555, 559, 564, 569, 576, 577, 585, 589, 595, 599, 608, 615, 620, 624, 628
Estimation. *See also* Approximation
of area, 447–448, 617–620
benchmarks for, 37
checking answers with, 617
diameters in a circumference, 245–246
factors in, 30
grids for, 447–448, 617–618
guess-and-check method, 460–464
probability and, 472–473
products of factors that are mixed numbers, 343
in reading graphs, 84
reasonableness and, 83, 268–270, 460, 487, 582
by rounding, 83
of square roots, 460–464
of sums, 83
words that indicate, 84
Even numbers
"counting by twos," 51
factors of, 101
identifying, 112
Even number sequences, 51, 52
Examples and non-examples, 51, 52, 111, 163, 438
Expanded notation
with decimals, 239–243
with exponents, 479–484
place value and, 169
of whole numbers, 169–173
zero in, 169
Experimental probability, 470–473
Explain. *See* Communication
Exponents. *See also* Powers of ten
bases and, 196
correct form for, 380
expanded notation with, 479–484
finding values of, 381
fractions and, 479–484
function of, 380
order of operations with, 381, 479–484
powers of ten and, 381
reading and writing, 196, 380–381
Extend the problem. *See* Enrichment
Exterior angles, 504, 508–509

INDEX

F

Faces
  on number cubes, 18
  of rectangular prisms, 315
Fact families
  addition and subtraction, 7–11
  division and multiplication, 8–12
Facts Practice (Power-Up)
  Each lesson Power-Up presents a facts practice that builds fluency in basic math facts.
Factor pairs, 102
Factors. *See also* Prime factorization
  bases and, 196
  common factors, 105–106, 152, 175
  constant, 413–421
  defined, 12, 99, 105
  divisibility tests for, 112
  division and, 99
  equal to one, 280–285
  in estimation, 30
  of even numbers, 101, 112
  greatest common. *See* Greatest Common Factor (GCF)
  multiplying, 12, 99
  of positive integers, 99–100, 105–106, 114, 280–281, 441–442
  of prime numbers, 101, 106
  products and, 12, 99
  reducing fractions and, 150–155, 175
  strategy for finding, 100
  of ten, 100
  unknown
    in addition and subtraction, 18–22
    on both sides of an equation, 453
    calculating, 24
    decimal numbers, 452–455
    in division and multiplication, 23–27
    method of solving for, 452–453
    mixed numbers, 452–455
    in multiplication, 123
  whole numbers and, 102, 105
Factor trees, 337–341
Fahrenheit (F), 51, 80
Figures. *See* Geometric figures
Find a pattern. *See* Problem-solving strategies
Fluid ounces, 405
Foot (ft), 37
"for each"
  in division problems, 423
  in rate problems, 123
Formulas
  for area
    of bases, 427
    of circles, 448–449, 626
    of parallelograms, 369, 370, 371, 409, 474
    of rectangles, 200, 474
    of squares, 196, 474
    of triangles, 409, 474
  for bases, of prisms, 630
  common rates, 123
  for length
    circumference, 246
    diameter, 246
  for perimeter
    of octagons, 311
    of parallelograms, 474
    of rectangles, 474
    of squares, 474
    of triangles, 474
  for volume
    of cubes, 428
    of cylinders, 627
    of prisms, 630
    of pyramids, 630–631
Formulate a problem. *See* Communication
Four-step problem-solving process, 3, 7, 18, 23, 28, 36, 42, 59, 63, 69, 70, 87, 436
Fractional parts of the whole
  equal groups stories with, 117–121
  naming parts of, 32–35
Fractional-parts statements, 399–403
Fraction bar indicating division (—), 14, 133, 385
Fraction-decimal-percent equivalents, 513–516
Fraction-decimal-percent table, 514
Fraction manipulatives, 109–111
Fractions. *See also* Denominators; Mixed numbers
  adding
    with common denominators, 127–131, 342
    with different denominators, 285–294
    SOS memory aid, 295–298, 342
    three or more, 320–323
    three-step process, 295–298
  canceling terms, 358–362, 376
  common, 32
  with common denominators. *See* Common denominators
  comparing, 395–398, 441–446
  decimal equivalents, 381–382, 385–389, 395–398, 513–516
  denominator. *See* Denominators
  dividing
    by fractions, 280–285, 342, 359
    whole numbers by, 33, 259–263
  equal to one, 221–224, 290, 597–598
  equivalent
    cross products for determining, 441–446
    defined, 137
    equal fractions as, 597
    example of, 152
    fraction-decimal-percent, 513–516
    writing, 391
  exponents and, 479–484
  finding the whole using, 612–616
  improper, 138, 324–328, 342
  lowest terms, defined, 277
  multiplying
    common denominators for, 342
    cross product, 441–446
    process of, 150–155
    reducing before, 358–362
    three or more, 375–379
  on number lines, 87–92
  numerators. *See* Numerators
  percent equivalents, 216–217, 390–394, 488–492, 513–516, 602–605
  reciprocals. *See* Reciprocals
  reducing. *See* Reducing fractions
  renaming
    multiplying by one, 221–224, 290
    purpose of, 307
    without common denominators, 285–294
  simplifying, 276–279
  SOS memory aid for solving problems with, 295–298, 342, 349
  subtracting
    with common denominators, 127–131, 342
    with different denominators, 285–294
    three-step process, 295–298
    from whole numbers, 187–190
  terms of, 157
  unknown numbers, 225–230
  visualizing on clock faces, 111
  writing
    decimal equivalents, 182–186, 380–384, 385–389, 513–516
    percent equivalents, 174–177, 513–516, 602–605
    as percents, 390–394, 488–492
    whole numbers as, 151
Fractions chart, 375–379
Freedom 7 spacecraft, 581
Freezing point, 51
Frequency tables, 54–57, 470–473
Functions, 497–502, 552

G

Gallon (gal), 404–405
Gauss, Karl Friedrich, 63
GCF (Greatest common factor). *See* Greatest Common Factor (GCF)
Geometric figures
  bases of. *See* Bases of geometric figures
  bisectors, 417–420
  circles. *See* Circles
  congruence in, 311, 408, 426, 562, 566–567
  corresponding parts, 566–572, 579
  cubes. *See* Cubes (geometric figures)
  cylinders. *See* Cylinders
  perimeter of. *See* Perimeter
  polygons. *See* Polygons
  prisms. *See* Prisms
  quadrilaterals. *See* Quadrilaterals
  rectangles. *See* Rectangles
  similarity in, 566–572
  solids. *See* Solids
  squares. *See* Squares
  symmetry in, 573–578
  triangles. *See* Triangles
Geometric formulas, 474–478. *See also* Formulas
Graphing calculator, online activity references 74, 106, 157, 269, 364, 433, 480, 607
Graphing functions, 497–502
Graphs
  bar, 55, 84, 265
  circle, 205–215, 264–265
  on the coordinate plane, 363–367, 499–500, 581
  data on
    bar graphs, 211, 213, 265
    histograms, 55
    line graphs, 211, 305
    line plots, 211, 266, 305
    pictographs, 264
    stem-and-leaf plots, 264–267, 384, 487
  histograms, 55–57
  line, 93–98, 211
  on number lines. *See* Number lines
  pictographs, 264
  reading, 84
  stem-and-leaf plots, 267
Great Britain, 37

Greater-lesser subtraction pattern, 68
Greater than symbol (>), 47, 381
Greatest Common Factor (GCF), 106–111, 152–153, 175
Grids
the coordinate plane, 363–367
estimating using, 447–448, 617–618
Grouping property. *See* Associative property; Parentheses
Guess-and-check. *See* Problem-solving strategies

H

Halfway, 83, 95
Height
abbreviation for, 475
of cylinders, 626
of parallelograms, 370–371, 409
of prisms, 630
of pyramids, 630
of triangles, 409–410
Hexagons
characteristics of, 311
irregular, 557
Higher order thinking skills. *See* Thinking skills
Histograms, 54–57
Horizontal axis, 95, 363
Hundreds
in decimals, 182
mental math for
dividing, 272–276
multiplying by, 239–243
multiplying decimals by, 255–256
Hundredths, 179, 184

I

Identity property
of addition, 8
of multiplication, 14, 222, 280, 488
Improper fractions
converting mixed numbers to, 324–328, 342
defined, 138
Inch (in.), 37, 38, 39
Inches, cubic (in.^{3}), 318
Inclusion, 4, 15, 20, 38, 52, 64, 79, 84, 100, 114, 147, 153, 171, 175, 184. 197, 241, 277, 282, 291, 334, 339, 383, 406, 429, 467, 475, 498, 534, 588, 598, 619
Indirect information, 399–403
"in each" in equal groups, 79
Inequality symbols, 47, 110, 381
Infinity, 74
Information, finding unstated, 399–403
Integers
adding, 517–523
algebraic addition of, 520, 543–547
consecutive, 88
counting numbers as, 74, 517
defined, 74, 75, 88, 517
dividing, 587–591
multiplying, 587–591
on number lines, 517
ordering, 517–520
subtracting, 517–523
Interest, compound and simple, 606–611
Interior angles
forming, 146
sum of measures of, 508–512
of transversals, 504
International System of Units (SI), 37
Intersecting lines, angle pairs formed by, 145–149
Inverse operations
addition and subtraction, 9, 10, 19
division and multiplication, 15, 24, 452
squaring and square roots, 197
two-step equations, 554
Investigation extensions. *See* Enrichment
Investigations
angle bisectors, 418–420
angles, drawing and measuring with protractors, 161–163
bisectors, constructing, 417–420
compasses, 417–420
compound probability experiments, 524–527
cones, 630–636
coordinate planes, 363–367
cylinders, 630–636
data
collection, 211–215
displaying, 211–215, 264–267
interpreting, 211–215
organizing, 211–215
drawing
to scale, 578–581
using protractors, 161–163
experimental probability, 470–473
fraction manipulatives, 109–111
frequency tables, 54–57
geometric solids, 314–319
histograms, 54–57
models, to scale, 578–581
perpendicular bisectors, 417–418
prisms, volume of, 630–636
probability experiments, 470–473
protractors, 161–163
pyramids, volume of, 630–636
scale drawings and models, 578–581
scale factor, 578–581
surface area, 630–636
surveys, 54–57
volume
of cones, 630–636
of cylinders, 630–636
of prisms, 630–636
of pyramids, 630–636
Irrational numbers, 461–462
Irregular shapes, measuring, 618–619. *See also* Complex shapes
Isolation of the variable, 19
Isosceles triangles, 484, 485

J

Jordan curve, 23

K

Kilometer (km), 37
kilowatt hours (kwh), 494

L

Language, math, *See* Math language; Reading math; Vocabulary
Last-digit divisibility test, 112
Lateral surface area, 634
Later-earlier subtraction pattern, 69, 170–171
Least common denominator, 286, 320–321
Least common multiple (LCM), 156–163, 290
adding three or more fractions, 320–321
defined, 286
Legends, 578
Length. *See also* Circumference; Perimeter
abbreviation for, 475
activity, 37–38
benchmarks for, 37
conversion of units of measure, 38, 39, 598
estimating, 37
of segments, 37, 353–357
sides of a square, 43, 107
units of measure, 37, 43, 164, 422
Lesson highlights. *See* Section overviews
Lesson planner. *See* Section overviews
Less than
in subtraction, 75
Letters
points designated with, 353
used to represent numbers, 21
Lincoln, Abraham, 70, 452
Line graphs, 93–98, 211
Line plots, 211, 213, 266
Lines. *See also* Number lines; Segments
intersecting, 145–149
naming, 353
oblique, 145
parallel, 145, 503–507
perpendicular, 145, 369–371, 409, 417–418, 630
properties of, 37
segments and rays, 36–41
symbol for (↔), 37, 353
transversals, 503–507
Line segments. *See* Segments
Lines of symmetry, 573–574
Logical reasoning. *See* Problem-solving strategies
Long division versus short division, 15
Looking Forward, 11, 17, 31, 35, 41, 45, 48, 53, 62, 67, 77, 81, 86, 92, 98, 104, 108, 111, 116, 121, 126, 131, 135, 140, 144, 155, 160, 163, 168, 173, 176, 181, 186, 194, 199, 204, 209, 210, 215, 220, 224, 230, 234, 238, 243, 249, 253, 258, 263, 267, 271, 275, 279, 284, 288, 294, 298, 305, 309, 313, 319, 323, 328, 332, 336, 341, 345, 348, 352, 356, 362, 367, 374, 379, 384, 389, 394, 398, 403, 407, 412, 416, 420, 425, 430, 435, 440, 446, 455, 459, 464, 469, 473, 478, 483, 492, 496, 507, 516, 523, 532, 537, 542, 556, 565, 581, 604
Lowest terms of fractions, defined, 277

M

Make a model. *See* Problem-solving strategies
Make an organized list. *See* Problem-solving strategies
Make it simpler. *See* Problem-solving strategies
Manipulative Use, 8, 13 14, 109, 128, 161, 188, 251, 285, 287, 291, 301, 302, 317, 324, 369, 437, 462, 505, 558, 579, 585, 618
Manipulatives/Hands-on. *See* Representation

INDEX

Marbles, 302–303, 400, 471–473, 524–526
Mass versus weight, 533–537
Math and other subjects
and architecture 323, 512
and art 332, 347, 590
and geography 57, 75, 77, 84, 130, 131, 148, 233, 273, 287, 330, 483
history 52, 53, 63, 69, 70, 81, 85, 91, 103, 114, 119, 148, 154, 229, 270, 283, 296, 334, 360, 452, 560, 575, 577
music 327, 360, 624
other cultures 30, 37, 433
science 36, 52, 53, 62, 66, 71–73, 76, 77, 79, 80, 85, 97, 98, 103, 106, 108, 125, 130, 134, 154, 159, 223, 242, 248, 267, 275, 288, 297, 301, 306, 307, 308, 313, 361, 374, 377, 382, 401, 402, 403, 414, 444, 453, 491, 492, 505, 506, 531, 596
sports 26, 41, 44, 56, 61, 86, 91, 99, 107, 120, 122, 126, 134, 135, 154, 155, 216, 229, 236, 243, 252, 280, 283, 298, 323, 351, 395, 401, 415, 444, 445, 477–479, 507, 545, 563, 599, 601, 624
Math Background, 1, 9, 10, 15, 19, 24, 29, 33, 37, 43, 47, 51, 54, 65, 69, 74, 83, 88, 95, 100, 102, 106, 110, 113, 118, 133, 137, 142, 146, 151, 157, 162, 170, 176, 179, 183, 188, 196, 201, 207, 222, 226, 232, 240, 246, 255, 260, 267, 273, 278, 281, 290, 300, 307, 311, 314, 326, 327, 334, 338, 347, 350, 354, 359, 363, 381, 386, 400, 405, 409, 417, 422, 427, 432, 442, 453, 461, 466, 470, 481, 485, 494, 499, 509, 518, 524, 539, 554, 562, 567, 574, 578, 593, 627, 630
Math language, 21, 22, 64, 65, 74, 84, 88, 103, 105, 114, 122, 127, 135, 138, 146, 152, 156, 165, 190, 211, 216, 222, 225, 260, 262, 277, 286, 302, 308, 311, 319, 333, 350, 369, 376, 380, 405, 408, 417, 418, 426, 431, 432, 442, 461, 465, 494, 503, 529, 533, 548, 552, 561, 593, 596, 608
Math to math.
Algebra, Measurement, and Geometry, 320B
Algebra and Problem Solving, 7B, 58B, 112B, 164B, 216B, 268B, 320B, 368B, 474B, 528B, 582B
Fractions and Measurement, 7B, 58B, 112B, 164B, 216B, 320B, 368B, 474B, 528B, 582B
Fractions, Percents, Decimals, and Problem Solving, 7B, 58B, 164B, 216B, 268B, 320B, 368B, 474B, 528B, 582B
Measurement and Geometry, 7B, 58B, 112B, 164B, 216B, 268B, 320B, 474B, 528B, 582B
Probability and Statistics, 268B, 320B, 474B, 528B, 582B
Problem Solving and Measurement, 7B, 58B, 112B, 164B, 216B, 268B, 320B, 368B, 474B, 528B, 582B
Proportional Relationships and Geometry, 320B, 528B, 582B
Mean, 95, 266–267, 313. *See also* Average
Measurement. *See also* Units of measure
abbreviations of. *See* Abbreviations
of angles, 161–163
of area. *See* Area
benchmarks for, 37, 405, 534, 553
of capacity, 404–407
of circles. *See* Circles
common rates, 123
of height. *See* Height
of length. *See* Length
linear. *See* Length
parallax in, 50
of perimeters. *See* Perimeter
protractors for, 161–163
ratios of, 123–124
of rectangles. *See* Rectangles
of surface area. *See* Area
of temperature, 51, 52
of turns, 465–469
of volume. *See* Volume
Measures of central tendency. *See* Mean; Median; Mode
Median, 266–267, 313
Memory aids
calculator keys, 608
decimal number chart, 277
Please Excuse My Dear Aunt Sally, 480
SOS, 295–298, 306–309, 342, 349, 375–379
Mental Math Power-Up. *A variety of mental math skills and strategies are developed in the lesson Power Ups.*
Meter (m), 37
Metric system, 37, 38, 404–405. *See also* Units of measure
Mile (mi), 37
Miles per gallon (mpg), 123
Miles per hour (mph), 123, 422
Milliliter (mL), 404
Millimeter (mm), 37
Minuends, 8, 19
Minus sign. *See* Negative numbers; Signed numbers
Mirror images, 574
Missing numbers. *See* Unknown numbers
Mixed measures. *See also* Units of measure
adding and subtracting, 298, 534, 592–596
Mixed numbers. *See also* Improper fractions
adding, 136–140, 306–309
"and" in naming, 184
converting
to improper fractions, 324–328, 342
by multiplication, 488–492
defined, 88
dividing, 349–352
division answers as, 132–135
factor trees, 339
multiplying, 326, 342–345
on number lines, 87–92
ratios as, 122
subtracting
with common denominators, 329–332
and reducing answers, 136–140
with regrouping, 188, 250–253
unknown factors in, 452–455
Mode, 266–267, 313
Models. *See* also Make a model; Representation
of addition situations, 109, 127, 228, 285–287, 290, 295, 306–307, 320–321
of subtraction situations, 127–129, 187–188, 250–251, 290–291, 296
of parallelograms, 369
to scale, 578–581
Money
arithmetic operations with, 7–18, 92, 235, 258, 362, 379, 616
coin problems, 7
decimal places in, 8, 13, 179
interest, compound and simple, 606–611
rate in, 123
rounding with, 268–270
subtracting, 7–11
symbol for, 8, 13
writing, 79, 195
Multiples. *See also* Least common multiple (LCM)
calculating, 132–135
common, 156, 157, 286, 320
Multiplication. *See also* Exponents
associative property of, 30
checking answers, 15, 25, 43
commutative property of, 13, 246, 427, 428
of decimals, 200–204, 232, 239–243, 276–277
division as inverse of, 15, 24, 452
fact families, 8–12
factors and, 12, 24, 99
of fractions
common denominators and, 342
cross product, 441–446
process of, 150–155
three or more, 375–379
by fractions equal to one, 221–224
by hundreds, 239–243
identity property of, 14, 222, 280, 488
of integers, 587–591
mental math for, 239–243
of mixed numbers, 326, 342–345
of money, 12–18
"of" as term for, 150
"of" as term in, 350
order of operations, 29, 65
partial products, 13
by powers of ten, 592–596
reducing rates before, 493–496
of signed numbers, 587–589
symbols for, 12, 13, 31, 422
by tens, 13, 239–243
of three numbers, 30
two-digit numbers, 13
of units of measure, 421–425
unknown numbers in, 23–27, 123
of whole numbers, 12–18, 588
words that indicate, 150, 350
zero property of, 14
Multiplication sequences, 50
Multistep problems, 65–66

N

Naming. *See also* Renaming
"and" in mixed numbers, 184
angles, 145–149
complex shapes, 557
fractional parts, 32
lines, 353
polygons, 311
powers of ten, 594
rays, 353
segments, 353–354
Negative numbers. *See also* Signed numbers

addition of, 518, 519
algebraic addition of, 543–547
graphing, 363
integers as, 74
on number lines, 73–77
real-world uses of, 46
symbol for, 73, 543, 544
Negative signs (–), 73, 543, 544
Nets, 318, 319, 634
Non-examples. *See* Examples and non-examples
Nonprime numbers. *See* Composite numbers
Nonzero, meaning of, 217
Notation. *See* Expanded notation; Standard notation
Number cubes. *See also* Cubes
faces of, 18
probability with, 302, 387, 473
Number lines. *See also* Graphs
addition on, 518
comparing using, 46–49
counting numbers on, 46, 74
decimals on, 259–263
fractions on, 87–92
graphing on, 363–367
integers on, 74, 517
mixed numbers on, 87–92
negative numbers on, 73–77
opposite numbers on, 518, 520
ordering with, 46–49
origin of, 363
positive numbers of, 73
rounding with, 82
as rulers, 90
tick marks on, 46, 74, 88
whole numbers on, 46
Numbers. *See also* Digits; Integers
comparing. *See* Comparing
composite, 102, 337
counting. *See* Counting numbers
decimal. *See* Decimals
equal to one, 221–224, 280–285, 290, 597–598
equivalent, 225
even, 51, 101, 112
greater than one, 489
halfway, 95
large, reading and writing, 64–65
letters used to represent, 19, 21
missing. *See* Unknown numbers
mixed. *See* Mixed numbers
negative. *See* Negative numbers
nonprime. *See* Composite numbers
odd, 51, 52
percents of. *See* Percents
positive. *See* Positive numbers
prime. *See* Prime numbers
signed. *See* Signed numbers
whole. *See* Whole numbers
writing. *See* Expanded notation; Proportions; Standard notation
Number sentences. *See* Equations
Number systems
base ten, 64, 179
commas in, 64, 65
place value in, 169
Numerators. *See also* Fractions
adding, 128
mixed numbers to improper fractions, 326
multiplying, 150–151
subtracting, 128
as term of a fraction, 343
as term of fractions, 32

O

Oblique lines, 145
Obtuse angles
measuring, 161–163
naming, 146–147
of transversals, 503, 504
Obtuse triangles, 485
Octagons, 311, 364
Odd numbers, 51, 52
Odd number sequences, 51
Odometers, 59
"Of" as term for multiplication, 150, 350
One
as multiplicative identity, 13
numbers equal to, 221–224, 280–285, 290, 597–598
numbers greater than, 489
in numerator, 33
On-line resources. *See* Section overviews
Open-option surveys, 57
Operations
of arithmetic. *See* Arithmetic operations
inverse. *See* Inverse operations
order of. *See* Order of Operations
Opposite numbers
defined, 518
on number lines, 74, 520
symbol for (-), 544
of zero, 74
Ordered pairs, 363, 500
Ordering integers, 46–47
Order of Operations.
calculators for, 30, 74
division, 47
with exponents, 381, 479–484
memory aid. *See* Memory aids
parentheses in, 29, 30, 47, 381
Please Excuse My Dear Aunt Sally, 480
process, 28–31
rules for, 29, 47, 480
for simplification, 29, 436–440, 480
subtraction, 9
using calculators, 437
Organized lists for problem-solving, 42
Origin, 363
Ounce (oz.), 404–405

P

Pairing technique, 63
Pairs
corresponding angles, 504, 567–569
ordered, 363, 500
Parallax, 50
Parallel lines, 145, 503–507
Parallelograms
angles of, 368, 369
area of, 369–371, 409, 474
characteristics of, 333
height of, 370–371
model of, 369
perimeter of, 369, 474
properties of, 334, 368–374
as quadrilateral, 334
rectangles as, 334, 371
rhombus as, 596
sides of, 369
Parentheses
clarifying with, 481, 519
in order of operations, 29, 47, 381
symbol for multiplication, 12–13, 31
Partial products, 13
Patterns
equal groups, 117
for problem-solving, 7, 51, 59–61, 63, 68–70, 117, 138, 428
real world applications using, 319
in subtraction, 60, 68–70, 170–171
Pentagons, 311
Per, defined, 123, 423
Percents
converting
by multiplication, 488–492
to probability, 301–302
decimal equivalents, 216–217, 390–394, 488–492, 513–516
defined, 216, 548, 602
finding the whole using, 621–625
fraction equivalents, 216–217, 390–394, 488–492, 513–516, 602–605
greater than one hundred, 489
properties of, 216, 390
word problems, solving using proportions, 548–552
writing
decimals as, 390–394, 488–492, 513–516
fractional equivalents, 174–177, 602–605
fractions as, 390–394, 488–492, 513–516
symbol for, 174, 390
Perfect squares, 197, 460–464
Performance activities
Choosing Graphs and Interpreting Data, 288B
Difference Ways to Represent 1000, 186B
Examples and Nonexamples in Geometry, 394B
Formulas from Tables, 496B
Order of Operations, 446B
Planting a Garden, 552B
Proofs and Disproofs, 81B
Representations, 238B
Representing Fractions, Decimals, and Percents, 341B
Selecting Tools and Techniques, 135B
Similar Shapes, 605B
Performance tasks
The Basketball Team, 313C
Comparing Shapes with Different Bases, 469C
Creating Three-dimensional Figures from Nets, 523C
Drawing and Comparing Three-dimensional Shapes, 362C
Drawing by Scale, 629C
The Dog Kennel, 263C
Estimating Measurements, 160C
The Four Corners States, 108C
Inventory at a Grocery Store, 210C
Polygons on the Coordinate Plane, 416C
Symmetric Designs, 577C
Where the Green Grass Grows, 53C
Perimeter
abbreviation for, 475
activity about, 42–43
area vs., 164
of circles. *See* Circumference
of complex shapes, 538–542

INDEX

of octagons, 311
of parallelograms, 369, 474
of polygons, 44
of rectangles, 43, 364–365, 474
of squares, 43, 72, 474
of triangles, 474
units of measure, 43
Permutations, 42
Perpendicular bisectors, 417–418
Perpendicular lines
angles formed by, 145
in area of parallelograms, 369–371
bisectors, 417–418
for finding area, 409, 630
pi, 244–249, 448–449, 627
Pictographs, 264
Pie charts. *See* Circle graphs
Pie graphs. *See* Circle graphs
Pint (pt.), 404–405
Placeholder, zero as, 205–215, 277
Place value
in addition, 8
commas and, 64, 65
comparing numbers using, 47
in decimals, 8, 9, 178–181
and expanded notation, 169
powers of ten and, 64, 479, 593
in subtraction, 9
through trillions, 63–67
in whole numbers, 64
Place value chart, 64
Place value system, 65
Plane, the coordinate, 363–367, 499–500, 581
Platonic solids, 315
Please Excuse My Dear Aunt Sally, 480
Plots in word problems, 58–59
p.m., 170
Points
coordinates of, 363
decimal. *See* Decimal points
freezing and boiling, 51
on line graphs, 95
representing with letters, 353
Polygons. *See also* specific polygons
classifying, 311–312
common, 311
congruent, 408, 568
defined, 310–312
as faces of polyhedrons, 314
four-sided, 311
lines of symmetry, 574
naming, 311
perimeter of, 44
regular, 44, 311
sides to vertices relationship, 311
similar, 568
triangles as, 484
Polyhedrons, 314
Population, 55, 213
Positive numbers
algebraic addition of, 543–547
on number lines, 73
Sign Game, 543–545
symbol for, 543, 587
Powers. *See also* Exponents
and fractions, 479–484
reading correctly, 380–381
Powers of ten. *See also* Exponents
multiplying, 592–596
place value and, 64
whole number place values, 479
Power-Up. *See* Facts practice (Power-Up); Mental Math (Power-Up); Problem Solving problems (Power-Up)
Power-Up discussion. *See* Problem-solving strategies (Power-Up)
Power-Up tests, 53A, 81A, 108A, 135A, 160A, 186A, 210A, 238A, 263A, 288A, 313A, 341A, 362A, 394A, 416A, 446A, 469A, 496A, 523A, 552A, 577A, 605A, 629A
Prime factorization, 101, 337–341, 346–348, 381. *See also* Factors
Prime numbers
activity with, 102
composite numbers compared, 337
defined, 160
division by, 337–341
Erathosthenes' Sieve, 102
factors of, 101, 106
greatest common factor (GCF), 106
Principal, 606
Prisms
area of, 633
drawing, 314, 315
rectangular. *See* Rectangular prisms
triangular, 314, 316
volume of, 630–631
Probability
chance and, 299–305, 471
compound experiments, 524–527
converting to decimals, 387
of events, 471–473
events and their complement, 301–303, 400, 524–527
experimental, 470–473
range of, 300
theoretical, 470
Problem solving
cross-curricular. *See* Math and other subjects
four-step process. *See* Four-step problem-solving process
real world. *See* Real-world application problems
strategies. *See* Problem-solving strategies
overview. *See* Problem-solving overview
Problem-solving overview, 1–6
Problem Solving problems (Power-Up)
Each lesson Power-Up presents a strategy problem that is solved using the four-step problem-solving process.
Problem-solving strategies
Act it out or make a model, 50, 156, 178, 195,
Draw a picture or diagram 7, 73, 87, 105, 122, 127, 150, 156, 187, 200, 250, 259, 358, 385, 404, 408, 426, 460, 508, 553, 582, 592, 612
Find a pattern, 7, 23, 58, 63, 82, 368, 413, 488, 508, 528, 533, 543, 561, 566, 592
Guess and check, 28, 32, 132, 164, 169, 205, 390, 395, 441, 573, 602
Make an organized list, 12, 136, 169, 195, 221, 268, 299, 493, 380, 447
Make it simpler, 23, 63, 164, 187, 205, 272, 295, 329, 413, 431, 456, 465
Make or use a table, chart, or graph, 58, 73, 306, 320, 333, 421, 517, 548, 561
Use logical reasoning, 18, 28, 32, 36, 46, 68, 78, 99, 112, 122, 132, 136, 141, 145, 174, 178, 182, 191, 225, 231, 235, 239, 244, 254, 276, 285, 289, 310, 333, 337, 349, 353, 358, 375, 385, 390, 395, 431, 441, 452, 456, 460, 465, 479, 484, 493, 513, 517, 538, 548, 557, 573, 582, 597, 612, 626
Work backwards, 78, 285, 289, 342, 399, 404, 408, 413, 436, 497, 587
Write a number sentence or equation, 18, 87, 117, 191, 205, 216, 221, 259, 276, 280, 295, 306, 324, 329, 342, 346, 353, 452, 474, 503, 553, 557, 566, 597, 606, 617, 621
Problem-solving strategies (Power-Up discussion)
Act it out or make a model, 50B, 156B, 178B, 195B
Draw a picture or diagram 7F, 73B, 87B, 105B, 122B, 127B, 150B, 156B, 187B, 200B, 250B, 259B, 358B, 385B, 404B, 408B, 426B, 460B, 508B, 553B, 582F, 592B, 612B
Find a pattern, 7F, 23B, 58F, 63B, 82B, 368B, 413B, 488B, 508B, 528F, 533B, 543B, 561B, 566B, 592B
Guess and check, 28B, 32B, 132B, 164F, 169B, 205B, 390B, 395B, 441B, 573B, 602B
Make an organized list, 12B, 136B, 169B, 195B, 221B, 268F, 299B, 493B, 380B, 447B
Make it simpler, 23B, 63B, 164F, 187B, 205B, 272B, 295B, 329B, 413B, 431B, 456B, 465B, 566B
Make or use a table, chart, or graph, 58F, 73B, 306B, 320F, 333B, 421F, 517B, 548B, 561B
Use logical reasoning, 18B, 28B, 32B, 36B, 46B, 68B, 78B, 99B, 112F, 122B, 132B, 136B, 141B, 145B, 174B, 178B, 182B, 191B, 225B, 231B, 235B, 239B, 244B, 254B, 276B, 285B, 289B, 310B, 333B, 337B, 346B, 349B, 353B, 358B, 375B, 385B, 390B, 395B, 431B, 441B, 452B, 456B, 460B, 465B, 479B, 484B, 493B, 513B, 517B, 538B, 548B, 557B, 573B, 582F, 597B, 612B, 626B
Work backwards, 78B, 285B, 289B, 342B, 399B, 404B, 408B, 413B, 436B, 497B, 587B
Write a number sentence or equation, 18B, 87B, 117B, 191B, 205B, 216F, 221B, 259B, 276B, 280B, 295B, 306B, 324B, 329B, 342B, 353B, 452B, 474F, 503B, 553B, 557B, 566B, 597B, 606B, 617B, 621B
Products. *See also* Multiplication
defined, 12
factors and, 12, 99
multiples and, 156
partial, 13
of reciprocals, 157, 349
of signed numbers, 588
unknown numbers, 123
Proportions. *See also* Rates; Ratios
and cross products, 441–446
cipher to the rule of three, 452
defined, 431, 442, 443
in congruent figures, 568
in ratio word problems, 456–459
in scale drawings and models, 578–581

ratios relationship to, 431–432, 442–443, 529
solving
percent problems with, 548–552
using a constant factor, 457
using cross-products, 441–446
tables and, 39, 413–414, 497–501, 513–514, 548–550
unknown numbers in, 432, 442–443
writing, 432
Protractors, measuring and drawing angles, 161–163
Pyramids, 314, 315, 630–636

Q

Quadrilaterals
classifying, 311, 333–337
defined, 311, 333
parallelograms as. *See* Parallelograms
rectangles. *See* Rectangles
squares. *See* Squares
sum of angle measures in, 508–512
Qualitative data, 212–213, 264–265
Quantitative data, 212–213, 266–267
Quart (qt.), 404–405
Quotients. *See also* Division
calculating, 22
in decimal division, 235–236, 272–273
as decimals, 385
defined, 14
in equivalent division problems, 225
missing, 25
in operations of arithmetic, 65
of signed numbers, 588

R

Radius (radii), 141–142, 190
Range, 266–267, 300, 308, 313
Rates, 122–126
reducing before multiplying, 493–496
Ratio boxes, 456–458, 528–529, 548–550
Ratios
as comparisons, 494
converting to decimals, 385–389
defined, 122, 431, 494
equivalent, 432, 442
writing, 385–389
fractional form of, 122–126
problems involving totals, 528–532
proportions and, 431–432, 442–443, 529
reducing, 153
symbols for (:), 122
win-loss, 123
word problems
using constant factors, 413–421
using proportions, 456–459
using ratio boxes, 456–458
writing decimal equivalents, 385–389
Rays
defined, 146
lines and segments, 36–41
naming, 353
properties of, 37
symbol for, 37, 353
Reading
decimal points, 240
decimals, 182–186
exponents, 196, 380–381
graphs, 84
large numbers, commas in, 64–65
powers, 380–381
Reading math, 25, 31, 38, 47, 64, 65, 73, 79, 95, 110, 133, 147, 150, 161, 175, 196, 197, 240, 246, 266, 343, 353, 368, 409, 423, 427, 462, 494, 544, 567
Real-world application problems 9, 11–13, 16, 17, 20–22, 26, 27, 30, 31, 32, 34, 37, 39, 40–44, 46, 48, 51–62, 66, 67, 69–73, 75–77, 79, 80, 81, 83, 84, 86–88, 91–95, 98, 103, 104, 106–108, 114, 116, 117, 119–121, 124–131, 134, 135, 138–140, 143–145, 148–150, 153–155, 159, 160 163, 216, 218–220, 229, 230, 233, 234, 236–238, 242, 243, 247–250, 252–254, 256–264, 267, 268–275, 278, 280, 283, 284, 289, 290, 292–299, 301, 304, 306–309, 312, 313, 316, 317, 322, 323, 327, 330, 332, 334, 335, 336, 340–342, 344, 345, 347, 351, 355, 357, 360–362, 372, 374, 377–378, 382, 383, 387–389, 391–393, 395–397, 399, 401–403, 404, 406–408, 410, 413, 414, 416, 421, 424–425, 428–429, 431, 433–435, 438–440, 444–445, 449–451, 453–454, 456–459, 462, 466–469, 474, 476–483, 485–487, 491–495, 501, 502, 505–507, 510–512, 513–515, 522–523, 530–532, 535–537, 540–541, 543, 545, 546, 548–552, 555, 556, 558, 560, 563, 564, 566, 569, 570–572, 575–577, 582–587, 589–594, 596–597, 599–601, 603–605, 607–611, 613–615, 617–621, 624–625, 628–629, 634, 635
Reciprocals
calculating, 156–160
defined, 157, 260, 350
in division of fractions, 281, 359
product of, 349
Rectangles
area of, 164–168, 364–365, 474
formula for, 200
characteristics of, 333
drawing, 319
lines of symmetry, 574
as parallelograms, 334, 371
perimeter of, 364–365, 474
similar, 568–569
as squares, 334
vertices of, 365
Rectangular prisms
attributes of, 314
bases of, 426
cubes as, 497
drawing, 314, 315
faces of, 315
surface area of, 497
volume of, 426–430
Reducing fractions
by canceling, 358–362, 376
common factors in, 150–155, 175
by grouping factors equal to one, 280–285
manipulatives for, 136–140
before multiplying, 493–496
prime factorization for, 346–348
rules for, 307
and units of measure, 423
Reflections (flips) of geometric figures, 562–564
Regrouping in subtraction of mixed numbers, 188, 250–253, 329–332
Regular polygons, 44, 311
Relationships
of corresponding sides, 569
inverse operations. *See* Inverse operations
ratios and proportions, 431–432, 442–443, 529
remainders-divisors, 15
sides to angles in triangles, 484
sides to vertices in polygons, 311
spatial, in cube faces, 315
Relative frequency, 470
Remainder
in decimal division, 236
divisors and, 15
as mixed numbers, 132–135
writing, 582
of zero, 99
Reminders. *See* Memory aids
Renaming. *See also* Naming
fractions
multiplying by one, 221–224, 290
purpose of, 307
SOS memory aid, 295–298
without common denominators, 285–294
mixed measures, 593
mixed numbers, 306–309
Renderings, 580
Representation
Formulate an equation, 61, 66, 70, 71, 76, 79, 80, 85, 114, 134, 135, 143, 148, 159, 219, 229, 237, 242, 247, 252, 270, 283, 296, 312, 382, 387, 388, 396, 415, 416, 623
Manipulatives/Hands-On, 8, 13–15, 32, 33, 37, 38, 45, 48–50, 72, 76, 78, 82, 88–91, 94, 98, 104, 107, 109–111, 115, 121, 125–129, 136–138, 140, 142, 143, 148, 149, 151, 162, 163, 221, 230, 231, 245, 248, 251, 257, 265, 282, 286, 289, 291, 301, 302, 305, 315, 352, 364–366, 369–371, 379, 394, 398, 405, 408, 415, 425, 427, 429, 435, 459, 469, 483, 492, 500, 501, 504, 505, 509, 516, 518, 523, 530, 543, 544, 558, 560, 562, 563, 575, 577, 584–585, 596, 600, 605, 608, 614, 616, 618, 625–626
Model, 38, 42, 45, 94, 97, 98, 100, 104, 109, 110, 115, 119, 120, 121, 125, 126, 129, 135–138, 140, 143, 148, 149, 151, 159, 217, 223, 224, 230, 237, 245, 247, 252, 256, 260, 274, 275, 279, 284, 288, 294, 305, 312, 324, 334, 355, 367, 369, 370, 379, 394, 398, 401, 402, 406, 408, 414, 416, 425, 430, 440, 458–459, 462, 467, 469, 476, 478, 485, 492, 501–502, 510, 516, 521, 528, 530, 537, 550, 558, 560, 565, 576, 577, 603, 613, 615, 622, 629
Represent, 10, 11, 14, 16, 17, 31, 34, 35, 44, 45, 48, 49, 53, 54, 55, 57, 62, 76, 80–81, 86, 90, 91, 103, 106, 110, 115, 116, 121, 127, 131, 135, 142, 147, 155, 162, 163, 222, 224, 257, 271, 279, 284, 296, 304, 315, 318, 319, 323, 325, 339, 344, 348, 356, 357, 365-367, 370, 373, 388, 396, 415, 416, 435, 486, 487, 530, 560, 570, 610, 615, 624, 635
Representative samples, 214
Rhombus, 333–334, 596

INDEX

Right angles, naming, 146–147
Right triangles, 410, 485
Roosevelt, Franklin D., 81
Roots. *See* Square roots
Rotational symmetry, 575
Rotations (turns) of geometric figures, 562–563
Rounding. *See also* Estimation
decimals, 268–271
estimating by, 83
halfway rule, 83
money, 268–270
with number lines, 82
whole numbers, 82–86
Rounding up, 83
Rule of three, 452
Rules. *See also* Order of Operations
for decimal division, 276–277
of functions, 498–499
for reducing fractions, 307
of sequences, 50

S

Sample, 55
Samples, representative, 214
Sample space, 300
Scale
in drawings and models, 52, 578–581
drawing to, 578–581
models, 578–581
on rulers, 38
temperature, 51, 52
Scale factor, 432, 578–581
Scalene triangles, 484, 485
Scales, 50–57
Section overviews
Lesson planner, 7A, 58A, 112A, 164A, 261A, 268A, 320A, 368A, 421A, 474A, 528A, 582A
Lesson highlights and technology, 7B, 58B, 112B, 164B, 261B, 268B, 320B, 368B, 421B, 474B, 528B, 582B
Content highlights, 7C, 58C, 112C, 164C, 261C, 268C, 320C, 368C, 421C, 474C, 528C, 582C
Content trace, 7D, 58D, 112D, 164D, 261D, 268D, 320D, 368D, 421D, 474D, 528D, 582D
Segments. *See also* Lines
bisecting, 417–418
in creating complex shapes, 484
defined, 37
length of, 37, 353–357
on line graphs, 95
lines and rays, 36–41
measuring, 38, 39
naming, 353–354
properties of, 37
symbol for, 37, 353
Separating, word problems about, 58–62, 187, 188, 250
Sequences
addition, 50
even number, 51
multiplication, 50
odd number, 51
types of, 50–57
Shapes, complex. *See* Complex shapes
Short-division method, 15
SI (International System of Units), 37
Sides
corresponding, 567–569
of parallelograms, 369
and perimeter, 107
of polygons, 311
of quadrilaterals, 311
of regular octagons, 311
of regular polygons, 44, 311
of squares, 43, 107
of triangles, 484
Signs. *See* Symbols and signs
Signed numbers
adding, 543–547
defined, 543
electrical-charge model, 543–547
product of, 587–589
quotient of, 588
Sign Game, 543–545
Similar figures, 566–572
Simple interest, 606
Simplifying
calculators for, 231–232
decimals, 231–234
fractions, 276–279
order of operations for, 29, 436–440, 480
for problem-solving, 20, 23, 63, 295–298, 306–309, 342, 349, 375–379
SOS memory aid, 295–298
Solids
area of, 316–317, 630–636
edges of, 315, 497
faces of, 314–319
geometric, 314–319
investigations of, 314–319
vertices of, 315, 319, 631
volume of, 630–636
Solving equations. *See* Equations
SOS method
adding mixed numbers, 306–309
for fraction problems, 295–298, 342, 349
fractions chart from, 375–379
Spatial relationships, 315
Spheres, 314
Spinners, 300–301, 380
"Splitting the difference," 52
Square (sq.), 165
Square angles, 146
Square centimeters (cm^2), 164, 197, 409, 422
Squared numbers
exponents of, 195–199, 380–381
inverse of, 197
perfect squares of, 460–464
Square feet (ft^2), 164
Square inches ($in.^2$), 164
Square meters (m^2), 164
Square miles (mi^2), 164
Square roots
calculators for finding, 462
defined, 262
estimating, 460–464
exponents and, 195–199
inverse of, 197
of perfect squares, 460–464
symbol for ($\sqrt{\ }$), 197
Squares
area of, 165, 196–197, 474
as bases of pyramids, 315
characteristics of, 333
as faces of Platonic solids, 315
as parallelograms, 334
perimeter of, 43, 72, 474
as rectangles, 334
as rhombuses, 334
sides of, 43, 107
Square units, 164, 196–197, 365
Squaring a number, 196–197, 380
Stack, 338
Standard notation, 170, 593–594
Standard number cubes, 18
Statistical operations. *See also* Data
mean, 95, 266
median, 266
mode, 266
range, 266
Stem-and-leaf plots, 267
Substitution, 475
Subtraction. *See also* Difference
addition as inverse of, 9, 10
checking answers, 9, 20, 61, 251
commutative property in, 8, 10
of decimals, 9, 191–194, 276–277
from whole numbers, 195–199
elapsed-time, 68–72, 170–171
fact families, 7–11
of fractions
with common denominators, 127–131, 342
with different denominators, 285–294
SOS memory aid, 295–298
three-step process, 295–298
from whole numbers, 187–190
of integers, 517–523
later-earlier-difference, 170
"less than" in, 75
minuends role, 8, 19
of mixed measures, 592–596
of mixed numbers
process for, 136–140
with regrouping, 188, 250–253, 329–332
using common denominators, 329–332
from whole numbers, 187–190
of money, 7–11, 379
of negative numbers, 74
order of operations, 9, 29
place value in, 9
subtrahends role, 8, 19
of units of measure, 421–425
unknown numbers in, 18–22, 60–61
of whole numbers, 7–11
and decimals, 195–199
word problems
about comparing, 68–72
about separating, 58–62, 188
elapsed-time, 68–72
words that indicate, 75
Subtraction patterns, 60, 68–70, 171
Subtrahends, 8, 19
Sum-of-digits divisibility tests, 113
Sums, 8, 83. *See also* Addition
Sunbeam as metaphor, 37
Supplementary angles, 353–357, 369, 504, 508
Surface area. *See* Area
Surfaces, 145
Surveys. *See also* Qualitative data; Quantitative date
analyzing data from, 5–57, 211, 215
bias in, 214
closed-option, 57
conducting (collecting data), 55, 57, 211–215
displaying data from, 56–57, 212–215
open-option, 57

in probability experiments, 470–471
samples, 55–56, 213–214
Symbols and signs. *See also* Abbreviations
approximately equal to (≈), 246, 462
calculator memory keys, 608
of comparison
approximately equal to (≈), 246, 462
equal to (=), 47, 381
greater than (>), 47, 110, 381
less than (<), 47, 110, 381
degrees (°), 161
for division
(÷), 14
division box ($\overline{)\quad}$), 14
bar (—), 14, 133, 385
dollar sign ($), 8, 13
dots
for multiplication (•), 12–13, 422
on number cubes, 18, 68
as period in abbreviations (.), 38
equal to (=), 47, 110, 381, 453
fraction bar (—), 14, 133, 385
greater than (>), 47, 110, 381
of inequality
greater than (>), 47, 110, 381
less than (<), 47, 110, 381
less than (<), 47, 110, 381
lines (↔), 37, 353
in multiplication
dot (•), 12, 13, 422
parentheses (), 13, 31
×, 12, 441
negative numbers (–), 73, 543
parentheses ( ) for multiplication, 12, 13, 422
percent (%), 174, 390
points, 353
positive numbers (+), 543, 587
ratios (:), 122
rays (→↑), 37, 353
segments (—), 37, 353
square root ($\sqrt{\quad}$), 197, 262
Symmetry, 573–578

T

Teacher Tip, 109, 165, 192, 356, 371, 376, 412, 419, 443, 471, 476, 487, 501, 544, 545
Technology. *See* Section overviews
Temperature, 51. *See also* Thermometers
Tens
base ten number system, 64, 179
in decimals, 182
dividing using mental math, 272–276
factors of, 100
multiplying by, 13
with mental math, 239–243
multiplying decimals by, mentally, 255–256
Tenths, 179
Terms
of fractions, 157, 343
of sequences, 50
Theoretical probability, 470
Thermometers, 51, 52, 517
Thinking skills, 3, 4, 8, 9, 13, 14, 15, 20, 24, 29, 37, 51, 52, 59, 64, 69, 82, 90, 94, 102, 106, 112, 117, 128, 136, 141, 142, 146, 151, 161, 171, 175, 179, 188, 192, 201, 214, 218, 232, 236, 240, 246, 250, 251, 255, 269, 272, 290, 307, 326, 330, 332, 336, 337, 346, 349, 354, 358, 359, 363, 364, 381, 382, 391, 396, 409, 418, 427, 428, 448, 452, 457, 471, 472, 484, 485, 488, 504, 508, 517, 519, 525, 528, 528, 534, 543, 551, 553, 557, 558, 562, 574, 593, 612, 618, 622, 623, 626, 627
Thousands, 64, 183, 533
Thousandths, 533
Three-step method, 295–298
Tick marks on number lines, 46, 74, 88
Time, 170. *See also* Elapsed-time
Timekeeping systems, 170
Totals, ratio problems involving, 528–532
Trailing zeros, 14
Transformations of figures
reflections (flips), 562–564
rotations (turns), 562–563
translations (slides), 562–563
Translations (slides) of geometric figures, 562–563
Transversals, 503–507
Trapeziums, characteristics of, 333
Trapezoids, characteristics of, 333
Tree diagrams, 524
Triangles
activity, 408–409
acute, 485
angles, sum of measures, 508–512
area of, 408–412, 474
classifying, 311, 484–487
congruent, 562, 566–567
equilateral, 484, 485
as face of Platonic solid, 315
isosceles, 484, 485
lines of symmetry, 574
obtuse, 485
perimeter of, 474
as polygons, 484
right, 410, 485
scalene, 484, 485
sides of
for classification, 484
relationship to angles, 484
similar, 567–568
Triangular prisms, 314, 316
Trillions, 63–67
Turns, measuring, 465–469, 508–509
Two-step equations, 13, 553–556

U

Unit multipliers, 597–601. *See also* Conversion
Units of measure. *See also* Measurement; Mixed measures
for area, 164, 197, 365, 422, 618
arithmetic with, 421–425
capacity, 404–405
converting, 598
of length, 37–38, 43, 164, 422
mass and weight, 533–535
metric system, 37, 38, 404–405
reducing, 423
speed, 423
uniform, 43
U.S. Customary System, 37, 404–405, 534
for volume, 426, 627
Unknown numbers. *See also* Missing numbers
in addition, 18–22
checking answers, 19, 20, 25–26
defined, 20
in division and multiplication, 23–27
in equal groups, 78–81
in fractions and decimals, 225–230
missing products, 123
in proportions, 432, 442–443
in rate problems, 123
in sequences, 50
in subtraction, 18–22, 60–61
in word problems, 59, 60
Unknowns, 20
U.S. Customary System, 37, 404–405, 534. *See also* Units of measure
U.S. military system of timekeeping, 170
Use logical reasoning. *See* Problem-solving strategies

V

Variables, isolating, 19
Vertex (vertices)
of angles, 146, 147
of polygons, 311
of rectangles, 365
of solids, 315, 319, 631
Vertical axis, 95, 363
Vocabulary *See also* Math language; Reading math
Math vocabulary for each lesson and investigation is specified on the lesson opener and the investigation opener pages.
Volume
bases of solids and, 318
of cones, 631–633
of cubes, 318, 428
of cylinders, 626–629, 631–633
defined, 426
of prisms, 630–631
of pyramids, 630–631
of rectangular prisms, 426–430
units of measure, 426, 627

W

Water, freezing and boiling points of, 51
Weight versus mass, 533–537
Whole numbers
adding, 7–11
to decimals, 195–199
counting numbers and, 46
defined, 46
dividing, 12–18
decimals by, 235–238
doubling, 51
even and odd, 51
in expanded notation, 169–173
factors and, 102, 105
finding the
when fraction is known, 612–616
when percentage is known, 621–625
fractional parts of, 32–35, 117–121
multiplying, 12–18, 588
on number lines, 46
place value in, 64
rounding, 82–86
subtracting, 7–11
decimals, 195–199
fractions from, 187–190
mixed numbers from, 187–190
writing
with decimal points, 195–199
as fractions, 151, 342

Width, abbreviation for, 475
Win-loss ratio, 123
Work backwards. *See* Problem-solving strategies
Write a number sentence or equation. *See* Problem-solving strategies
Writing. *Also see* Communication
  decimals. *See* Decimals
  equations, 19, 543
  exponents, 196, 380–381
  fractions. *See* Fractions
  large numbers, 64–65
  money, 79, 195
  numbers. *See* Expanded notation; Proportions; Standard notation
  percents. *See* Percents
  proportions, 432
  ratios, 385–389
  remainders, 582
  whole numbers
    with decimal points, 195–199
    as fractions, 151, 342

X

x-axis, 363
x symbol for multiplication, 12, 441

Y

y-axis, 363
Years. *See* Age, calculating; Elapsed-time

Z

Zero
  in division, 14
  in expanded notation, 169
  exponents and, 381
  in multiplication, 14
  opposite of, 74
  as placeholder, 205–215, 277
  as power, 381
  properties of, 51, 73, 74, 101
  remainders of, 99
  in rounding, 82
  sign of, 73, 74
  trailing, 14
  in whole numbers, 46
Zero property of multiplication, 14

	COURSE 1	COURSE 2	COURSE 3
NUMBERS AND OPERATIONS			
Numeration			
digits	●		
read and write whole numbers and decimals	●	●	▲
place value to trillions	●	●	▲
place value to hundred trillions		●	▲
number line (integers, fractions)	●	●	▲
number line (rational and irrational numbers)		●	●
expanded notation	●	●	
comparison symbols (=, <, >)	●	●	▲
comparison symbols (=, <, >, ≤, ≥)		●	▲
compare and order rational numbers	●	●	▲
compare and order real numbers		●	●
scientific notation		●	●
Basic operations			
add, subtract, multiply, and divide integers	●	●	▲
add, subtract, multiply, and divide decimal numbers	●	●	▲
add, subtract, multiply, and divide fractions and mixed numbers	●	●	▲
add, subtract, multiply, and divide algebraic terms		●	●
add and subtract polynomials			●
add, subtract, multiply, and divide radical expressions			●
multiply binomials			●
mental math strategies	●	●	●
regrouping in addition, subtraction, and multiplication	●	●	▲
multiplication notations: $a \times b$, $a \cdot b$, $a(b)$	●	●	▲
division notations: division box, division sign, and division bar	●	●	▲
division with remainders	●	●	▲
Properties of numbers and operations			
even and odd integers	●	●	▲
factors, multiples, and divisibility	●	●	▲
prime and composite numbers	●	●	▲
greatest common factor (GCF)	●	●	▲
least common multiple (LCM)	●	●	▲
divisibility tests (2, 3, 5, 9, 10)	●	▲	▲
divisibility tests (4, 6, 8)		●	▲
prime factorization of whole numbers	●	▲	▲
positive exponents of whole numbers, decimals, fractions	●	●	▲
positive exponents of integers		●	▲
negative exponents of whole numbers		●	▲
negative exponents of rational numbers			●
square roots	●	●	●
cube roots		●	●
order of operations	●	●	▲
inverse operations	●	●	●

● Introduce and Develop
▲ Maintain and Apply

	COURSE 1	COURSE 2	COURSE 3
Estimation			
round whole numbers, decimals, mixed numbers	●	●	▲
estimate sums, differences, products, quotients	●	●	▲
estimate squares and square roots	●	●	●
determine reasonableness of solution	●	●	●
approximate irrational numbers		●	●
ALGEBRA			
Ratio and proportional reasoning			
fractional part of a whole, group, set, or number	●	●	▲
equivalent fractions	●	●	▲
convert between fractions, terminating decimals, and percents	●	●	▲
convert between fractions, repeating decimals, and percents		●	▲
reciprocals of numbers	●	●	▲
complex fractions involving one term in numerator/denominator		●	●
complex fractions involving two terms in numerator/denominator			●
identify/find percent of a whole, group, set, or number	●	●	▲
percents greater than 100%	●	●	▲
percent of change		●	●
solve proportions with unknown in one term	●	●	▲
find unit rates and ratios in proportional relationships	●	●	●
apply proportional relationships such as similarity, scaling, and rates	●	●	●
estimate and solve applications problems involving percent	●	●	●
estimate and solve applications problems involving proportional relationships such as similarity and rate		●	●
compare and contrast proportional and non-proportional linear relationships (direct and inverse variation)			●
Patterns, relations, and functions			
generate a different representation of data given another representation of data		●	●
use, describe, extend arithmetic sequence (with a constant rate of change)	●	●	●
input-output tables	●	●	●
analyze a pattern to verbalize a rule	●	●	▲
analyze a pattern to write an algebraic expression			●
evaluate an algebraic expression to extend a pattern		●	●
compare and contrast linear and nonlinear functions		●	●
Variables, expressions, equations, and inequalities			
solve equations using concrete and pictorial models	●	●	▲
formulate a problem situation for a given equation with one unknown variable		●	●
formulate an equation with one unknown variable given a problem situation	●	●	●
formulate an inequality with one unknown variable given a problem situation			●
solve one-step equations with whole numbers	●	▲	▲
solve one-step equations with fractions and decimals		●	▲
solve two-step equations with whole numbers	●	●	▲
solve two-step equations with fractions and decimals		●	●
solve equations with exponents			●

● Introduce and Develop
▲ Maintain and Apply

	COURSE 1	COURSE 2	COURSE 3
solve systems of equations with two unknowns by graphing			●
graph an inequality on a number line		●	●
graph pairs of inequalities on a number line			●
solve inequalities with one unknown		●	●
validate an equation solution using mathematical properties		●	●
GEOMETRY			
Describe basic terms			
point	●	●	▲
segment	●	●	▲
ray	●	●	▲
line	●	●	▲
angle	●	●	▲
plane	●	●	▲
Describe properties and relationships of lines			
parallel, perpendicular, and intersecting	●	●	●
horizontal, vertical, and oblique	●	●	●
slope		●	●
Describe properties and relationships of angles			
acute, obtuse, right	●	●	●
straight		●	●
complementary and supplementary	●	●	●
angles formed by transversals	●	●	●
angle bisector	●	●	
vertical angles		●	●
adjacent angles		●	●
calculate to find unknown angle measures	●	●	●
Describe properties and relationships of polygons			
regular	●	●	●
interior and exterior angles	●	●	
sum of angle measures	●	●	●
diagonals		●	●
effects of scaling on area		●	●
effects of scaling on volume		●	●
similarity and congruence	●	●	●
classify triangles	●	●	●
classify quadrilaterals	●	●	●
Use Pythagorean theorem to solve problems			
Pythagorean theorem involving whole numbers		●	●
Pythagorean theorem involving radicals			●
trigonometric ratios			●
3-Dimensional figures			
represent in 2-dimensional world using nets	●	●	●
draw 3-dimensional figures	●	●	●
Coordinate geometry			
name and graph ordered pairs	●	●	●
intercepts of a line		●	●
determine slope from the graph of line		●	●
formulate the equation of a line		●	●

● Introduce and Develop
▲ Maintain and Apply

	COURSE 1	COURSE 2	COURSE 3
identify reflections, translations, rotations, and symmetry	●	●	●
graph reflections across the horizontal or vertical axes	●	●	●
graph translations		●	●
graph rotations			●
graph dilations			●
graph linear equations		●	●
MEASUREMENT			
Measuring physical attributes			
use customary units of length, area, volume, weight, capacity	●	●	●
use metric units of length, area, volume, weight, capacity	●	●	●
use temperature scales: Fahrenheit, Celsius	●	●	●
use units of time	●	●	●
Systems of measurement			
convert units of measure	●	●	●
convert between systems	●	●	●
unit multipliers	●	●	●
Solving measurement problems			
perimeter of polygons, circles, complex figures	●	●	●
area of triangles, rectangles, and parallelograms	●	●	●
area of trapezoids		●	●
area of circles	●	●	●
area of semicircles and sectors		●	●
area of complex figures	●	●	●
surface area of right prisms and cylinders	●	●	●
surface area of spheres		●	●
surface area of cones and pyramids			●
estimate area	●	●	●
volume of right prisms, cylinders, pyramids, and cones	●	●	●
volume of spheres		●	●
estimate volume	●	●	●
Solving problems of similarity			
scale factor	●	●	●
similar triangles		●	●
indirect measurement		●	●
scale drawings: two-dimensional	●	●	●
scale drawings: three-dimensional			●
Use appropriate measurement instruments			
ruler (U.S. customary and metric)	●	●	▲
compass	●	●	●
protractor	●	●	●
thermometer	●	●	▲
DATA ANALYSIS AND PROBABILITY			
Data collection and representation			
collect and display data	●	●	●
tables and charts	●	●	▲

● Introduce and Develop
▲ Maintain and Apply

	COURSE 1	COURSE 2	COURSE 3
frequency tables	●	●	●
pictographs	●	●	
line graphs	●	●	▲
histograms	●	●	▲
bar graphs	●	●	▲
circle graphs	●	●	▲
Venn diagrams		●	●
scatter plots			●
line plots	●	●	▲
stem-and-leaf plots	●	●	▲
box-and-whisker plots		●	●
choose an appropriate graph	●	●	●
identify bias in data collection		●	▲
analyze bias in data collection			●
draw and compare different representations	●	●	●
Data set characteristics			
mean, median, mode, and range	●	●	▲
select the best measure of central tendency for a given situation		●	●
determine trends from data		●	●
predict from graphs		●	●
recognize misuses of graphical or numerical information		●	●
evaluate predictions and conclusions based on data analysis		●	●
Probability			
experimental probability	●	●	●
make predictions based on experiments	●	●	●
accuracy of predictions in experiments	●	●	●
theoretical probability	●	●	●
sample spaces	●	●	▲
simple probability	●	●	▲
probability of compound events	●	●	●
probability of the complement of an event	●	●	●
probability of independent events	●	●	●
probability of dependent events		●	●
select and use different models to simulate an event			●
PROBLEM SOLVING			
Connections			
identify and apply mathematics to everyday experiences	●	●	●
identify and apply mathematics to activities in and outside of school	●	●	●
identify and apply mathematics in other disciplines	●	●	●
identify and apply mathematics to other mathematical topics	●	●	●
Problem-solving skills and tools			
use a problem-solving plan	●	●	▲
evaluate for reasonableness	●	●	▲
use a proportion	●	●	▲
use a calculator	●	●	▲
use estimation	●	●	▲
use manipulatives	●	●	▲

● Introduce and Develop
▲ Maintain and Apply

SCOPE AND SEQUENCE

	COURSE 1	COURSE 2	COURSE 3
use mental math	●	●	▲
use number sense	●	●	▲
use formulas	●	●	▲
Problem-solving strategies			
choose a strategy	●	●	▲
draw a picture or diagram	●	●	▲
find a pattern	●	●	▲
guess and check	●	●	▲
act it out	●	●	▲
make a table, chart, or graph	●	●	▲
work a simpler problem	●	●	▲
work backwards	●	●	▲
use logical reasoning	●	●	▲
write a number sentence or equation	●	●	▲
Communication			
relate mathematical language to everyday language	●	●	●
communicate mathematical ideas using efficient tools	●	●	●
communicate mathematical ideas with appropriate units	●	●	●
communicate mathematical ideas using graphical, numerical, physical, or algebraic mathematical models	●	●	●
evaluate the effectiveness of different representations to communicate ideas	●	●	●
Reasoning and proof			
justify answers	●	●	●
make generalizations	●	●	●
make conjectures from patterns	●	●	●
make conjectures from sets of examples and nonexamples	●	●	●
validate conclusions using mathematical properties and relationships	●	●	●
ALGEBRA TOPICS APPENDIX			
graph sequences			●
formulate the equation of a line with given characteristics			●
formulate the equation of a line parallel/perpendicular to a given line			●
solve proportions with an unknown in two terms			●
graph linear inequalities			●
factor quadratics			●
solve quadratic equations			●
solve systems of linear equations using substitution			●
solve systems of linear equations using elimination			●
formulate an equation with two unknown variables given a problem situation			●
solve systems of linear inequalities with two unknowns			●
graph systems of linear inequalities			●

● Introduce and Develop
▲ Maintain and Apply